Handbook of Child Maltreatment

Child Maltreatment

Contemporary Issues in Research and Policy

Series Editors

Jill E. Korbin, Ph.D.
Professor of Anthropology
Associate Dean, College of Arts and Sciences
Director, Schubert Center for Child Studies
Crawford Hall, 7th Floor
10900 Euclid Avenue
Cleveland, OH 44106-7068, USA
jill.korbin@case.edu

Richard D. Krugman, MD
Distinguished Professor of Pediatrics and Dean
University of Colorado School of Medicine
Room C-1003 Bldg 500
Anschutz Medical Campus
13001 E. 17th Place
Aurora, CO 80045, USA
richard.krugman@ucdenver.edu

This series provides a high-quality, cutting edge, and comprehensive source offering the current best knowledge on child maltreatment from multidisciplinary and multicultural perspectives. It consists of a core handbook that is followed by two or three edited volumes of original contributions per year. The core handbook will present a comprehensive view of the field. Each chapter will summarize current knowledge and suggest future directions in a specific area. It will also highlight controversial and contested issues in that area, thus moving the field forward. The handbook will be updated every five years. The edited volumes will focus on critical issues in the field from basic biology and neuroscience to practice and policy. Both the handbook and edited volumes will involve creative thinking about moving the field forward and will not be a recitation of past research. Both will also take multidisciplinary, multicultural and mixed methods approaches.

For further volumes:
http://www.springer.com/series/8863

Jill E. Korbin • Richard D. Krugman
Editors

Sarah Miller-Fellows
Assistant Editor

Handbook of Child Maltreatment

 Springer

Editors
Jill E. Korbin
Office of the Dean
Case Western Reserve University
Cleveland, OH, USA

Richard D. Krugman
School of Medicine
University of Colorado
Aurora, CO, USA

Assistant Editor
Sarah Miller-Fellows
Case Western Reserve University
Cleveland, OH, USA

ISSN 2211-9701 ISSN 2211-971X (electronic)
ISBN 978-94-007-7207-6 ISBN 978-94-007-7208-3 (eBook)
DOI 10.1007/978-94-007-7208-3
Springer Dordrecht Heidelberg New York London

Library of Congress Control Number: 2013955305

Printed on acid-free paper

Springer is part of Springer Science+Business Media (www.springer.com)

Contents

Author Biographies

Jeanne L. Alhusen is currently the Morton and Jane Blaustein postdoctoral fellow in mental health and psychiatric nursing at Johns Hopkins University School of Nursing and a KL2 clinical research scholar at Johns Hopkins University School of Medicine. She has extensive clinical and research experience working with women and children impacted by intimate partner violence. Her doctoral studies were supported by a T32 training grant in interdisciplinary violence research, and an individual NRSA awarded by the National Institute of Nursing Research. Her current research is focused on the influence of poor maternal mental health, experiences of violence, and poor attachment on neonatal and early childhood developmental outcomes. Her BSN, MSN, and Ph.D. are from Villanova University, Duke University, and Johns Hopkins University. After completing her postdoctoral fellowship, she will be an Assistant Professor at the University of Virginia School of Nursing.

Lily Alpert is a Harold A. Richman Postdoctoral Research Fellow at Chapin Hall. Alpert's scholarly work focuses on research evidence use by public and private child welfare administrators. In this work, she draws on her prior experience bridging social science research and child welfare policy and practice as a Senior Policy Analyst at Children's Rights, and before that, as a SRCD/AAAS Congressional Fellow responsible for Senator Hillary Rodham Clinton's child welfare legislative portfolio.

Arlene Bowers Andrews social worker, community psychologist, and Carolina Distinguished Professor of Social Work at the University of South Carolina, has extensive experience in community-based practice and research about families affected by turbulence. She was a founder and director of the USC Institute for Families in Society, an interdisciplinary center that conducts research to enhance families through community partnerships. Dr. Andrews is author of *Social History Assessment* (Sage, 2007), *Victimization and Survivor Services* (Springer, 1992), *Send Me! The Story of Salkehatchie Summer Service* (Providence Publishing House, 2006), coeditor of *The UN Convention on the Rights of the Child: Implementing the Right to an Adequate Standard of Living* (Praeger, 1999), and coauthor of *In the Shadow of Death: Families of Loved Ones Who Face the Death Penalty* (Oxford University Press, 2006). Her work includes articles and book chapters regarding family strengthening, violence prevention, and community systems development.

Donald J. Baumann has a Ph.D. is in Social Psychology and over 30 years experience designing and managing large-scale research projects as both a Principal Investigator and as a Project Director. He has been on the faculties of the University of Texas, Trinity University, and Saint Edwards University. He has directed numerous national multi-year research and evaluation projects over the years. For the last 20 years, he has been housed in the Texas Department of Family and Protective Services where he was head of the Evaluation Section of Child Protective Services. He currently teaches at St. Edwards University and is a Senior Research Fellow at the American Humane Association. His areas of interest are decision-making, risk assessment, and disproportionality. He has written over 75 reports, articles, and book chapters.

William R. Beardslee is the Gardner-Monks Professor of Child Psychiatry at Harvard Medical School, and Director of Baer Prevention Initiatives and Chairman Emeritus, in the Department of Psychiatry at Boston Children's Hospital. Dr. Beardslee has led groundbreaking studies to develop and demonstrate effectiveness of early interventions for the prevention of mood disorders in high-risk children. The resulting interventions have been disseminated across many diverse U.S. communities and countrywide in Finland, Norway, and Costa Rica. The author of over 200 articles and chapters, as well as two books, Dr. Beardslee has written on topics from what enabled civil rights workers to endure and to change the southern USA, how resilience develops in children, to how families can overcome depression. Dr. Beardslee is the recipient of numerous prestigious awards and is on the Board of Children, Youth, and Families of the Institute of Medicine and the National Academy of Sciences.

Genevieve Benedetti is a project associate at Chapin Hall at the University of Chicago and currently serves as the Evaluation Coordinator for the Doris Duke Fellowships for the Promotion of Child Well-Being. In this capacity, she is responsible for conducting ongoing assessments of the progress fellows are achieving in the programs and coordinating with each fellow's academic and policy mentors. Her research interests include early childhood, systems development, and identifying new innovations in research across disciplines that will strengthen and move forward the child maltreatment field. Ms. Benedetti earned her master's in Public Policy from the Harris School of Public Policy at the University of Chicago, and she received her BA in Ethnic Studies and Gender and Women's Studies from the University of California at Berkeley.

Lucy Berliner is Director, Harborview Center for Sexual Assault and Traumatic Stress, and Clinical Associate Professor, University of Washington School of Social Work and Department of Psychiatry and Behavioral Sciences. Her activities include clinical practice with child and adult victims of trauma and crime; research on the impact of trauma and the effectiveness of clinical and societal interventions; and participation in local and national social policy initiatives to promote the interests of trauma and crime victims. Ms. Berliner is on the editorial boards of leading journals concerned with interpersonal violence, has authored numerous peer-reviewed articles and book chapters, and has served/serves on local and national boards of organizations, programs, and professional societies.

Kristin Bernard is a doctoral candidate in Clinical Science program in the Department of Psychology at the University of Delaware. She is interested in the effects of early adversity on children's development of behavioral and neurobiological regulation, as well as how optimal caregiving and preventative interventions may buffer at-risk children from problematic outcomes.

Sara R. Berzenski research investigates emotional development in the context of adversity, from a developmental psychopathology perspective. In particular, her research at the University of California, Riverside, has focused on the development of emotion competence, and more specifically, domains of self-regulation, including emotion, behavior, and physiology. Her research takes a systems-level approach to clarifying how these domains of functioning cohere to enable children to successfully meet the challenges of development in contexts of adversity and how these processes contribute to adult psychopathology and competence. Her research on child maltreatment seeks to clarify specific mechanisms by which adversity eventuates in negative adjustment (e.g., psychopathology) in some children, but resilience in others. Focusing on traditionally overlooked forms of maltreatment, her work in multiple samples has demonstrated pathways to adjustment as well as individual difference factors, emphasizing specific features (e.g., severity, chronicity) and subtypes (e.g., physical abuse, emotional abuse) of maltreatment.

Donald C. Bross is Professor of Pediatrics (Family Law) at the University of Colorado School of Medicine, and Director of Education and Legal Counsel for the Kempe Center for the Prevention and Treatment of Child Abuse and Neglect. Since being appointed to the faculty in 1976, he has represented maltreated children in court, drafted child protection legislation, and established the National Association of Counsel for Children (NACC), to advance the field of pediatric law. Awards include the Distinguished Service Award of the International Society for the Prevention of Child Abuse and Neglect (1994), Distinguished Service Award of the National Association of Counsel for Children (2000), University of Colorado School of Law Alumni Award for Distinguished Achievement in Education (2001), US Department of Health & Human Services Commissioner's Award (2003) for Leadership and Services in the Prevention of Child Abuse and Neglect, and the American Professional Society on the Abuse of Children Ronald C. Laney Distinguished Service Award (2011). He works clinically with The Children's Hospital Colorado Child Protection Team and the State and Regional Team against crimes on children. He has administered more than $6 million in research and services contracts and has more than 100 publications.

Jacquelyn C. Campbell is a national leader in research and advocacy in the field of intimate partner violence. Her studies paved the way for a growing body of interdisciplinary investigations by researchers in the disciplines of nursing, medicine, and public health. She is the Principal Investigator of an NIH-funded (T32) fellowship that provides funding for pre- and postdoctoral fellows in violence research. Elected to the Institute of Medicine in 2000, Dr. Campbell also was the Institute of Medicine/American Academy of Nursing/American Nurses' Foundation Senior Scholar in Residence and currently serves as Co-Chair of the IOM Forum on the Prevention of Global Violence. Other honors include the Pathfinder Distinguished Researcher by the Friends of the National Institute of Health and the National Institute for Nursing Research, Outstanding Alumna and Distinguished Contributions to Nursing Science Awards, Duke University School of Nursing, the American Society of Criminology Vollmer award, and being named one of the inaugural 17 Gilman Scholars at Johns Hopkins University.

Len I. Dalgleish was a psychologist who was instrumental in developing and testing approaches to understanding decision making in the context of service delivery. Dr. Dalgleish originated the General Assessment and Decision Making Model (GADM). In his many years working in applied clinical contexts, at the Department of Social Work (1981–1988) and the School of Psychology (1988–2005) at the University of Queensland, and at the Department of Nursing and Midwifery (2005–2010), University of Stirling, Scotland, he applied the psychology of judgment and decision making, to a variety of problems. These included the social worker's judgment of child safety and the decision to remove the child from the home. His international legacy in child welfare and other fields though his research, publications, presentations, and teaching remains highly influential.

Deborah Daro has played a key role in the development and assessment of evidence-based home visitation programs for the past 30 years and has worked with Federal administrators and Congressional leaders in crafting guidelines for Federal Maternal, Infant, and Early Childhood Program (MIECHV) passed as part of the Affordable Care Act of 2010. In June 2009, she testified before the House Ways and Means Committee in support of President Obama's original proposal outlining this legislation. Prior to joining Chapin Hall in January 1999, Dr. Daro contributed to the development of Healthy Families America (HFA), one of the nine evidence-based national home visiting models supported under MIECHV. She is considered one of the nation's leading experts in the area of child abuse prevention and was recently appointed to the Institute of Medicine's Committee on Child Maltreatment Research, Policy, and Practice for the Next Decade. Dr. Daro earned her Ph.D. in social welfare at the University of California at Berkeley.

Alan J. Dettlaff is Associate Professor in the Jane Addams College of Social Work, University of Illinois, Chicago. Dr. Dettlaff received his Ph.D. in Social Work from the University of Texas at Arlington in 2004. His practice background includes several years in public child welfare as a practitioner and administrator, where he specialized in investigations of child maltreatment. Dr. Dettlaff's research focuses on understanding and addressing racial disparities in the child welfare system and on understanding and addressing the unique needs of immigrant Latino children who come to the attention of this system. Dr. Dettlaff is also Principal Investigator of the Jane Addams Child Welfare Traineeship Project, which provides advanced training and financial assistance to students pursuing careers in child welfare.

Mary Dozier is the Amy E. DuPont Chair of Child Development in the Department of Psychology at the University of Delaware, where she directs the Infant Caregiver Project lab. She studies the development of infants and young children who have experienced maltreatment and disruptions in their relationships with caregivers. She developed the Attachment and Biobehavioral Catch-up (ABC) intervention for infants in foster care, infants living with their high-risk birth parents, and young children adopted internationally.

Brett Drake is Professor of School of Social Work at the George Warren Brown School of Social Work at Washington University in St. Louis. Drawing on his prior experience as a child abuse investigator in San Diego county, he has pursued research in early child welfare system response. Within the area of child maltreatment, Dr. Drake has focused particularly on the issue of substantiation, his work showing that substantiated and unsubstantiated families face similar risk of recurrence. He has also done considerable work in the areas of poverty and race as they relate to public child welfare, and has done longitudinal cross-sector work providing insight into life courses and cross-sector contacts among children and families who do and do not contact the child welfare system.

Howard Dubowitz is a Professor of Pediatrics and Director of the Center for Families at the University of Maryland School of Medicine, Baltimore. He is on the Council of the International Society for the Prevention of Child Abuse and Neglect and is President of the Helfer Society, an honorary international group of physicians working in the field of child maltreatment. He is also a board member of Prevent Child Abuse America. Dr. Dubowitz is a clinician, researcher, and educator, and he is active in the policy arena. His main interests are in child neglect and prevention. He edited Neglected Children: Research, Practice, and Policy and coedited the Handbook for Child Protection Practice as well as International Aspects of Child Abuse and Neglect and ISPCAN's World Perspectives on Child Abuse, 2012. Dr. Dubowitz has over 150 publications and has presented at many regional, national, and international conferences.

Byron Egeland is the Irving B. Harris Professor of Child Development at the University of Minnesota. He is a Co-Principal Investigator of the Minnesota Longitudinal Study of Risk and Adaptation, a 37-year longitudinal study of high-risk children and their families. He and his colleague Marti Erickson were the Principal Investigators of Project STEEP, an NIMH-funded prevention program for high-risk parents and their infants. Dr. Egeland is a fellow in the American Psychological Association, the American Psychological Society, and the American Association of Applied and Preventive Psychology. He coauthored *The Development of the Person*, which has won several awards, including the Eleanor Maccoby American Psychological Association Book of the Year in 2007. Dr. Egeland has served on numerous Boards, including Prevent Child Abuse America. He has published extensively in the areas of child maltreatment, child psychopathology, resilience, social and emotional development, and intervention/prevention with high-risk families.

Raquel T. Ellis is a Senior Study Director at Westat. She currently plays several key roles on the Permanency Innovations Initiative (PII), a national initiative to reduce long-term foster care. This includes leading an experimental evaluation of a trauma-focused practice model in Illinois. She has conducted research in the areas of adoption recruitment, relative search and engagement practices, informal kinship care, differential response, child welfare-juvenile court relations, contraceptive behaviors of community college students, clinical supervision of child welfare workers, and judicial decision-making during termination of parental rights proceedings. She also has 8 years of practice experience in the human service field, mainly in child welfare. She is the sole author of the Journal on Public Child Welfare article entitled, "Exploring the influence of juvenile court personnel on child welfare practice" and has coauthored several publications on vulnerable children and families.

Sara Wolf Feldman is a Researcher at Chapin Hall. Her work concentrates on the implementation and impact of child welfare reform efforts, both in the context of out-of-home care and preventive services. Dr. Feldman recently completed a study of the impact of a family-team conferencing model on child-level outcomes. She is currently overseeing the evaluation of Child Success New York City, an initiative designed to provide NYC's family foster care system with a formal, evidence-based foster care model.

As a part of her work, Dr. Feldman uses administrative data to understand private and public child welfare agency performance. Dr. Feldman has developed and measured performance outcomes in the areas of safety and risk assessments, maltreatment investigations, and the use of multiple response systems, foster care, and preventive services.

Dr. Feldman obtained her M.S.W. and Ph.D. degrees from Columbia University. Prior to joining Chapin Hall, Dr. Feldman worked as a clinical social worker and administrative supervisor within a large, New York City–based foster care agency.

Monica M. Fitzgerald is a licensed clinical psychologist and Assistant Professor at the Kempe Center for the Prevention and Treatment of Child Abuse and Neglect at the University of Colorado Medical School. Dr. Fitzgerald is the Director of Training and Evaluation in the Kempe Child Trauma Program and leads the "Evidence Based Practice Training Initiative" focusing on evaluating effective models to spread evidence-based, trauma-informed interventions. Dr. Fitzgerald is currently working as part of the SAMHSA-funded National Child Traumatic Stress Network, building the capacity to deliver evidence-based trauma-informed services for families involved in the military and child welfare. As Co-Principal Investigator on *Kempe Safe Start*, Dr. Fitzgerald is conducting a clinical trial evaluating strategic enhancement to Trauma-Focused Cognitive Behavioral Therapy. Dr. Fitzgerald is an expert trainer in evidence-based trauma-focused treatments and regularly conducts trainings, consultation, and evaluation. She is a Board member of the American Professional Society on the Abuse of Children.

John D. Fluke is an Associate Director for Systems Research and Evaluation and Associate Professor at the Kempe Center for the Prevention of Treatment of Child Abuse and Neglect in the Department of Pediatrics, University of Colorado School of Medicine. Dr. Fluke has over 32 years of experience in social service delivery system research in the area of Child Welfare and Mental Health Services for children including local, state, national, and international projects. He is internationally recognized as a researcher specializing in assessing and analyzing decision making in human services delivery systems. He is also known for his innovative and informative evaluation work in the areas of child maltreatment epidemiology, child welfare administrative data analysis, workload and costing, and performance and outcome measurement for children and family services. The author or coauthor of numerous scholarly publications, Dr. Fluke has presented papers at both national and international meetings and conferences.

Tamara Fuller is the Director of the Children and Family Research Center at the University of Illinois at Urbana-Champaign. Her research interests focus on the child protection system and the effectiveness of the services that are provided to families once they become involved in a maltreatment investigation. Her studies have examined the impact of safety assessment protocols on maltreatment recurrence, worker decision-making during child protection investigations, and predictors of maltreatment recurrence following reunification. Currently, Dr. Fuller serves as the evaluator of the statewide Differential Response randomized clinical trial in Illinois, which includes several studies that examine parent engagement in child protective services using both qualitative and quantitative methodologies.

Angelo P. Giardino received his medical degree from the University of Pennsylvania School of Medicine. He received his doctorate in education from Graduate School of Education at the University of Pennsylvania. Dr. Giardino currently serves as Vice President/Chief Medical Officer for Texas Children's Health Plan, which provides Medicaid and CHIP benefits to over 355,000 children in Southeast Texas. Dr. Giardino also serves as the Chief Quality Officer for Medicine at Texas Children's Hospital and is a Clinical Professor of Pediatrics at Baylor College of Medicine. He is board-certified by the American Board of Pediatrics in Pediatrics and Child Abuse.

Dr. Giardino has over 20 years experience as a pediatrician specializing in disease management and child maltreatment. His broad career goal is to raise awareness in the evaluation of child maltreatment, care for children with special needs, and to improve the health care delivery system for all. His academic accomplishments include publishing several textbooks on child abuse and neglect, presenting on a variety of pediatric topics at regional and national conferences.

Eileen R. Giardino is an Associate Professor at the School of Nursing at the University of Texas Health Science Center (UTHSC) at Houston. Dr. Giardino received her BSN and Ph.D. from the University of Pennsylvania, her MSN from Widener University, and her NP certification in adult and family from LaSalle University. Clinically, Dr. Giardino works as a nurse practitioner at a university student health service. Her academic accomplishments include coediting several text books in the areas of child maltreatment and intimate partner violence and she presents at professional meetings on issues related to physical assessment and conducting a differential diagnosis. Prior to moving to Houston, Dr. Giardino served on the board of directors for Bethany Christian Services in Fort Washington, PA; was on the advisory board for the LaSalle University Nursing Center in Philadelphia; and completed two terms on the board of directors for the Philadelphia Children's Alliance where she also chaired the Research Committee. Finally, Dr. Giardino teaches on a variety of topics in the adult and family nurse practitioner tracks at UTHSC at Houston and is involved in supervising a number of clinical preceptorships within the nurse practitioner training program.

Patricia Y. Hashima is a developmental psychologist with expertise in planning, implementing, and evaluating community-level approaches to promote the health and well-being of children, youth, and families. Most recently, Dr. Hashima was a behavioral scientist at the Centers for Disease Control and Prevention (CDC) where she collaborated with state and local public health officials and other federal and non-governmental agencies to create infrastructure at local, state, and national levels to further the application of science-based violence prevention strategies into everyday practice. Prior to her employment at CDC, she was a research associate at the Institute on Family and Neighborhood Life at Clemson University, where she was involved in a comprehensive child maltreatment prevention initiative to build systems of support for families of young children living in South Carolina. Dr. Hashima also was instrumental in bridging across disciplines while serving as the lead researcher on a project funded by the Administration of Children and Families of the US Department of Health and Human Services to build state-level research capacity at the South Carolina Department of Social Services. Additionally, she managed and directed the evaluation of South Carolina's Early Care and Education Technical Assistance System, a statewide coordinated system to facilitate the provision of high-quality support for educators of young children. Currently, Dr. Hashima is a private consultant in Decatur, Georgia.

Astrid Heppenstall Heger is the Executive Director of the Violence Intervention Program (VIP), located at the Los Angeles County (LAC) + University of Southern California (USC) Medical Center where she is a Professor of Clinical Pediatrics. Dr. Heger is the preeminent expert in the field of child sexual abuse and assault and the author of numerous articles in this field as well as the definitive textbook Evaluation of the Sexually Abused Child, now in its second edition. In 1984, Dr. Heger founded the Center for the Vulnerable Child (CVC), the first medically based child advocacy center in the world, annually evaluating over 15,000 child abuse and child sexual assault victims. In 1995, Dr. Heger established the first of its kind, "one stop shop" community Family Advocacy Center, offering medical, mental health, protective, legal, and social services to victims of family violence and sexual assault throughout Los Angeles County. Dr. Heger has received numerous honors and awards for her work with victims of abuse including the President's highest award for victim advocacy.

Grace W.K. Ho is currently a doctoral candidate at the Johns Hopkins University School of Nursing. She graduated with her BSN in 2009 and obtained a Post-Bachelor's Forensic Nursing Certificate, also from Johns Hopkins University School of Nursing. Her research interests include physical discipline, child physical abuse, and parenting perceptions and behaviors. Ms. Ho's dissertation study will use Q-methodology to examine how Chinese American mothers and pediatric nurses differentiate physical discipline from child physical abuse. Her doctoral studies are supported by the A.T. Mary Blades Foundation Scholarship, the Caylor Award, the Ellen Levi Zamoiski Fellowship, the Johns Hopkins University School of Nursing Scholarship, and the Jonas Center for Nursing Excellence. Her dissertation study is supported by the Sigma Theta Tau International (STTI)/American Nurses Foundation Research Award, the Southern Nursing Research Society Dissertation Award, and the STTI Nu Beta Chapter Research Award.

Sarah McCue Horwitz is a member of the faculty of the Department of Child and Adolescent Psychiatry at New York University. She has a Ph.D. in Epidemiology and Health Services from the Department of Epidemiology and Public Health, Yale University. Her areas of interest are children's mental health, children's mental health services and the implementation of evidenced practices in usual care. Dr. Horwitz has been a faculty member at Yale University, Case Western Reserve University, and Stanford University. She is currently involved in studies examining: the adoption of evidence-based practices by child serving mental health agencies; the use of learning collaboratives as a strategy to improve implementation of evidence-based practices; the physical health, and mental health, and mental health services use of children investigated by US child welfare agencies; and the effectiveness of a six session CBT-based intervention to alleviate symptoms of depression, anxiety, and trauma in women who have delivered an infant preterm.

Reena Isaac is a full-time forensic pediatrician in the Child Protection Program, section of the Emergency Medicine Service of Texas Children's Hospital. She was exposed to numerous cases of child abuse while completing her pediatric residency at Albert Einstein College of Medicine, Jacobi Medical Center, Bronx, New York. Inspired by learning that she could make a difference in a child's life, Dr. Isaac completed a forensic pediatric fellowship from Brown Medical School in Providence, Rhode Island. Her work brings education and research into communities to raise awareness, with the hope of reducing the rate of child abuse.

Melissa Jonson-Reid is Professor of Social Work and Director of the Brown Center for Violence and Injury Prevention at the George Warren Brown School of Social Work, Washington University. Her primary research interests include services and outcomes for abused and neglected children and child maltreatment prevention. She has received ongoing federal funding to explore how children reported for neglect and other reasons move through systems and experience various outcomes. Based on this work, she is currently evaluating a new intervention for mothers with young children in the child welfare system – "Early Childhood Connections." She currently directs the Centers for Disease Control and Prevention–funded Brown Center for Violence and Injury Prevention which focuses on child maltreatment, intimate partner violence, suicide, and sexual violence prevention and intervention. She is also an investigator and host for the current Translational Child Neglect Consortium annual meetings.

Homer D. Kern In 1980, Homer earned a Ph.D. degree in College Teaching and Political Science from the University of North Texas. His dissertation was "Burnout in Child Welfare Social Workers." He also has M.A. and B.A. degrees in Government and Political Science from Texas Tech University and the University of Southern California. He completed additional undergraduate work at the University of Vienna, and additional graduate work at several schools in Human Behavior, Law, Research, Statistics, Management, Social Work, and Computer Science.

After 2 years (1975–1977) as a generic Child Welfare caseworker, and 2 more years as a regional researcher/planner, he moved to a series of positions conducting statewide social services research for

Texas. In 1980, he also started providing part-time consulting and research for social service agencies around the nation. In 1996, he retired from what is now the Texas Department of Family and Protective Services and began full-time consulting nationally. He provided consultation and research for many social service agencies across the country for years. He is currently retired.

Robin Kimbrough-Melton is a Senior Instructor of Pediatrics in the University of Colorado School of Medicine and a faculty member in the Kempe Center for Prevention and Treatment of Child Abuse and Neglect. She teaches in *Health and Human Rights* in the Colorado School of Public Health. She holds adjunct appointment at Clemson University where she has taught courses on international law and human rights. As a lawyer, Professor Kimbrough-Melton has long been active in service system reform related to juvenile justice, criminal justice, education, social services and the courts. She is also the executive director of the American Orthopsychiatric Association. She has received awards for child advocacy from the American Psychological Association Division of Child, Youth, and Family Services and the South Carolina Professional Society on the Abuse of Children.

Stephanie C. Stronks Knapp is a Child/Adolescent Forensic Interviewer with the Federal Bureau of Investigations, Office for Victim Assistance, Denver, Colorado, and is an active member of the Innocence Lost Task Force for Colorado and Wyoming. She provides forensic interview training, case consultation and technical assistance to Tribal, Federal, State, and Local law enforcement agencies, as well as other members of the multidisciplinary team. Prior to her assignment with the FBI, Mrs. Knapp was Co-Director of the Kempe Child Protection Team at The Children's Hospital in Denver, Colorado.

Mrs. Knapp has provided expert witness testimony in both civil and criminal courts and has been qualified as an expert in Federal Court. Recently, Mrs. Knapp was honored by the US Attorney's Office at the District of Arizona's 2012 Victims of Crime ceremony and was recognized for "going above and beyond" in serving victims of crime.

Mrs. Knapp is a graduate from the University of St. Catherine in St. Paul, Minnesota, with a bachelor's degree in Social Work and a minor in Spanish, and the University of Denver's Graduate School of Social Work with a dual concentration in Health and Child and Family Welfare.

Brandon A. Kohrt is a medical anthropologist and psychiatrist at the Duke Global Health Institute. He conducts global mental health research focusing on populations affected by war-related trauma and chronic stressors of poverty, discrimination, and lack of access to healthcare and education. He has worked in Nepal for 16 years using a biocultural developmental perspective integrating epidemiology, cultural anthropology, ethnopsychology, and neuroendocrinology. With Transcultural Psychosocial Organization (TPO), Nepal, he designed and evaluated psychosocial reintegration packages for child soldiers in Nepal. He currently works with The Carter Center Mental Health Liberia Program developing anti-stigma campaigns and family psychoeducation programs. He was a Laughlin Fellow of the American College of Psychiatrists and a John Spiegel Fellow of the Society for the Study of Psychiatry and Culture (SSPC). Dr. Kohrt has contributed to numerous documentary films including *Returned: Child Soldiers of Nepal's Maoist Army*.

Jill E. Korbin is Associate Dean, Professor of Anthropology, Director of the Schubert Center for Child Studies, and Co-Director of the Childhood Studies Program in the College of Arts and Sciences at Case Western Reserve University. Korbin earned her Ph.D. in 1978 from the University of California at Los Angeles. Her awards include the Margaret Mead Award (1986) from the American Anthropological Association and the Society for Applied Anthropology; a Congressional Science Fellowship (1985–1986 in the Office of Senator Bill Bradley) through the American Association for the Advancement of Science and the Society for Research in Child Development; the Wittke Award for Excellence in Undergraduate Teaching at Case Western Reserve University (1992); and a Fulbright Senior Specialist Award (2005). Korbin served on the National Research Council's Panel on Research on Child Abuse and Neglect, and the Institute of Medicine's Panel on Pathophysiology and Prevention of Adolescent and Adult Suicide. Korbin served for multiple years on the Executive Committee of the International Society for Prevention of Child Abuse and Neglect (ISPCAN), and as an Associate Editor, Book Review Editor, or Editorial Board Member for Child Abuse and Neglect: The International Journal. Korbin has published numerous articles on child maltreatment in relationship to culture and context, and edited the first volume on culture and child maltreatment, Child Abuse and Neglect: Cross-Cultural Perspectives (1981, University of California Press). Korbin's research interests include culture and human development; cultural, medical and psychological anthropology; neighborhood, community, and contextual influences on children and families; child maltreatment; and child and adolescent well-being.

Richard D. Krugman is Distinguished Professor of Pediatrics, Vice Chancellor for Health Affairs, and Dean of the University of Colorado (CU) School of Medicine. He served as Director of the C. Henry Kempe National Center for the Prevention and Treatment of Child Abuse and Neglect from 1981 to 1992 and has gained international prominence in the field of child abuse. Dr. Krugman is a graduate of Princeton University and earned his medical degree at New York University School of Medicine. A board-certified pediatrician, he did his internship and residency in pediatrics at the University of Colorado School of Medicine. Following a two-year appointment in the early 1970s with the Public Health Service at the National Institute of Health and the Food and Drug Administration, Dr. Krugman joined the CU faculty in 1973. He went back to the Washington area in 1980 as a Robert Wood Johnson Health Policy Fellow and served for a year as a legislative assistant in the office of U.S. Senator Dave Durenberger of Minnesota. He has earned many honors in the field of child abuse and neglect and headed the U.S. Advisory Board of Child Abuse and Neglect from 1988 to 1991. Dr. Krugman is a member of the Institute of Medicine (IOM) and has authored over 100 original papers, chapters, editorials, and four books and stepped down after 15 years as Editor-in-Chief of Child Abuse and Neglect: The International Journal in 2001.

Scott D. Krugman is Chairman, Department of Pediatrics, and Director, Community Medicine and Wellness Service Line at MedStar Franklin Square Medical Center, and Clinical Professor, Pediatrics and Epidemiology, at the University of Maryland School of Medicine. He is board-certified in General Pediatrics and Child Abuse Pediatrics and is the founder and medical director of MedStar Franklin Square's Child Protection Team. In addition to child abuse evaluations, he initiated child abuse prevention services at the hospital. Dr. Krugman is also a member of the Child Abuse Medical Providers (CHAMP) faculty, the Baltimore County Child Fatality Review Team, the Baltimore County Child Protection Review Panel, and a past member of the State Council on Child Abuse and Neglect and the board of The Family Tree. He is past-chair of the Child Maltreatment Committee of the Maryland Chapter of the American Academy of Pediatrics and current president of the chapter.

Wendy G. Lane is an Assistant Professor in the Department of Epidemiology and Public Health and the Department of Pediatrics at the University of Maryland School of Medicine. She is board-certified in General Pediatrics, Child Abuse Pediatrics, and Preventive Medicine, and conducts medical evaluations for children with suspected abuse and neglect at the University of Maryland Medical Center and the Howard County Child Advocacy Center. Her research focuses on the epidemiology and prevention of child maltreatment and disparities in identification and reporting of maltreatment. Dr. Lane serves as Co-Chair of the Child Abuse Special Interest Group of the Academic Pediatric Association and Chair of the Child Maltreatment and Foster Care Committee for the Maryland Chapter of the American Academy of Pediatrics.

Teresa Lind is a graduate student in the Clinical Science program in the Department of Psychology at the University of Delaware. She previously earned an A.B. in History and Slavic Languages & Literatures from Harvard College and an M.A. in Psychology from Boston University. She is interested in the influence of early adverse childhood experiences, such as institutionalization, foster care, and maltreatment, on child behavior and development.

Ben Mathews is an Associate Professor in the School of Law at Queensland University of Technology in Brisbane, Australia. He is also Director of Research in the School of Law and is a member of QUT's Health Law Research Centre and QUT's Children and Youth Research Centre. His major area of research expertise is in children and the law, with a focus on issues concerning law and child maltreatment, civil damages for child abuse, children and educational systems, medico-legal issues, children's rights, cultural violence against children, and children's criminal responsibility. He has conducted large multidisciplinary studies of laws regarding the reporting of child maltreatment and has published extensively in Australia and internationally, with over 50 publications. His research and knowledge translation has led to changes in law, policy, and practice.

Gary B. Melton is Professor of Pediatrics in the University of Colorado School of Medicine, Professor of Community and Behavioral Health in the Colorado School of Public Health, and associate director for community engagement and prevention in the Kempe Center for Prevention and Treatment of Child Abuse and Neglect. He holds adjunct appointments at Clemson University and the University of the Free State (South Africa). Professor Melton has served as president of Childwatch International, the American Orthopsychiatric Association, the American Psychology-Law Society, and the Society for Child and Family Policy and Practice. He has received awards for distinguished contributions for scholarship and public service from the American Psychological Association (three times), the American Psychological Foundation, the American Orthopsychiatric Association, the American Professional Society on Abuse of Children, and Prevent Child Abuse America. He is coeditor of *American Journal of Orthopsychiatry* and *Child Abuse and Neglect*.

Nancy Miller is the Director of Policy and Government Affairs for the National Council of Juvenile and Family Court Judges. Nancy previously served as the Director of the Permanency Planning for Children Department of NCJFCJ. Prior to this, Nancy served as the Oregon Judicial Department's Deputy State Court Administrator for Program Operations, where she worked on court improvement in juvenile, civil, family, and criminal law; legislative efforts; and directed judicial and employee education and strategic planning efforts. Nancy has worked in the child welfare and juvenile justice fields for 30 years, including work as a juvenile court probation officer, a child welfare agency protective services caseworker, and as a residential treatment center program coordinator.

Sarah Miller-Fellows is a graduate student in the Department of Anthropology and the Department of Public Health and a research associate at the Schubert Center for Child Studies at Case Western Reserve University. She previously received a B.A. in anthropology and French studies from Smith College and an M.A. in medical anthropology from Case Western Reserve University. Her research interests include reproduction, early childcare, genetic disorders, infectious disease, and religious identity. Her M.P.H. thesis examines the relationship between childhood infection with schistosomiasis and adult subfertility among women in coastal Kenya. Her dissertation research will explore how Amish parents experience pregnancy and caring for young children in the context of a high rate of genetic disorders.

Beth E. Molnar is a social and psychiatric epidemiologist. She is an Associate Professor of Health Sciences and an Associate Director of the Institute on Urban Health Research at Northeastern University. Dr. Molnar's research is grounded in three public health domains: social epidemiology, prevention science, and psychiatric epidemiology. Studies focus on three major areas: (1) violent, traumatic experiences (including child maltreatment, sexual violence, community violence) and ways they affect children and adolescents; (2) the social context of high-risk behaviors such as youth violence (the latter often being sequelae of the first), and development and evaluation of violence prevention interventions. Areas of Dr. Molnar's expertise include multilevel methods, community-based participatory research, and survey research. Using both qualitative and quantitative methods, strongly influenced by Bronfenbrenner's Bioecological Theory of Human Development,

Dr. Molnar has focused on identifying neighborhood-level social resources that can be mobilized to decrease violence in both families and communities.

Michael Nash received his undergraduate degree from UCLA and his law degree from Loyola Law School in Los Angeles. Prior to being appointed as a Municipal Court Judge in 1985, Judge Nash served as Deputy Attorney General in the criminal division of the California Attorney General's Office where he handled criminal appeals and trials for over 10 years. Judge Nash was elevated to the Superior court in 1989 and has served in the Juvenile Court since 1990. Since 1995, he has served as either Presiding Judge of the Juvenile Court or Supervising Judge of the Juvenile Dependency Court in Los Angeles. He is President of the National Council of Juvenile and Family Court Judges.

Vincent J. Palusci is Professor of Pediatrics at New York University School of Medicine in New York City where he is a board-certified general and child abuse pediatrician at the Bellevue Hospital Frances L. Loeb Child Protection and Development Center. He received his medical degree from the University of Medicine and Dentistry of New Jersey and completed his internship and residency in pediatrics at New York University/Bellevue Hospital Center. He entered private practice and later joined the faculty of the College of Human Medicine at Michigan State University where he was a TRECOS fellow and earned a master's degree in epidemiology. Dr. Palusci is a member of the International Society for the Prevention of Child Abuse and Neglect, the board of directors of the American Professional Society on the Abuse of Children, the Ray E. Helfer Society, and is Fellow of the American Academy of Pediatrics. He serves as Editor-in-Chief of the APSAC Advisor and as an appointee of the American Board of Pediatrics Child Abuse Subboard. Dr. Palusci edited Shaken Baby Syndrome: A Multidisciplinary Response with Dr. Steven Lazoritz (2002) and Child Abuse and Neglect—A Diagnostic Guide (2010) and received the Ray E. Helfer Award for child abuse prevention in 2004 from the American Academy of Pediatrics and the National Alliance for Children's Trust and Prevention Funds.

Laura J. Proctor is a research scientist at Judge Baker Children's Center, Harvard Medical School. She studies the short- and long-term impact of maltreatment and other adverse childhood experiences on children's socioemotional and behavioral development. Dr. Proctor's current research is conducted with data from the Consortium for Longitudinal Studies of Child Abuse and Neglect (LONGSCAN), a 20-year multi-site study of the antecedents and consequences of child maltreatment. Dr. Proctor received her doctoral degree in clinical psychology from the University of Southern California. Before obtaining her doctoral degree, Dr. Proctor worked as a journalist in San Francisco, Los Angeles, and Guatemala City, and directed the program development office of the Mexican Institute for Family and Policy Research in Mexico City.

Tali Raviv received her BA degree from Emory University, and both a master's degree and Ph.D. in Child Clinical Psychology from University of Denver. Her work has focused on the areas of program development and evaluation for at-risk youth and families, including families exposed to poverty and maltreated children. She is also interested in studying risk and resilience processes in these at-risk populations and improving access to high-quality mental health services. Dr. Raviv is a current member of the Trauma Treatment Service and the Community-Linked Mental Health Services Program at Ann and Robert H. Lurie Children's Hospital of Chicago and an Assistant Professor of Clinical Psychiatry and Behavioral Sciences at Northwestern University's Feinberg School of Medicine.

Jesse R. Russell is a Director of Research – Midwest with the National Council on Crime and Delinquency. Previously, he was Senior Research Associate with the National Council of Juvenile and Family Court Judges. From 2006–2010, he held the position of Assistant Professor at the John Whitehead School of Diplomacy and International Relations at Seton Hall University. At Seton Hall, Dr. Russell taught undergraduate and graduate courses in research methods and oversaw master's thesis projects. Dr. Russell facilitates research efforts relating to a broad array of local, statewide, and national projects in juvenile justice and child welfare.

Andrea J. Sedlak, Westat Vice President and social psychologist, specializes in research on victimized, vulnerable, and troubled children, youth, and families. She designed and directed the last three cycles of the National Incidence Study of Child Abuse and Neglect (NIS-2, NIS-3, and NIS-4) and national surveys on youth in juvenile justice custody for the US Department of Justice. Currently, she directs the national evaluation of the Permanency Innovations Initiative (PII), which builds evidence for interventions that reduce the risk of children remaining in long-term foster care, and the Third National Incidence Studies of Missing, Abducted, Runaway, and Thrownaway Children (NISMART-3), which will provide updated estimates of the numbers of these children and describe their characteristics and experiences. She is also Principal Investigator on the second National Survey of Youth in Custody (NSYC-2), the Survey of Juveniles Charged in Adult Criminal Courts, and the National Juvenile Probation Census Project.

Kamala F. Smith currently serves as Research Analyst at Abt Associates, carrying a broad portfolio of work in behavioral health policy analysis and program evaluation, including study of families with high social and health risks and service members and veterans with post-traumatic stress disorder. She pursues her interest in both intimate partner violence (IPV) and family violence, which emerged while working as a parental stress line counselor and an emergency room victim advocate. Ms. Smith has coauthored numerous posters and publications on different forms of violence including IPV, rape, and torture. She spent 2 years working in the Women's Division of the National Center for PTSD as a member of the research teams examining the psychological impacts of IPV on women and the use of cognitive behavioral therapies to treat PTSD. Additionally, Ms. Smith has worked internationally to expand mental health services for victims of sex trafficking. She has a BA in psychology from Boston University and an MPH from Johns Hopkins Bloomberg School of Public Health.

Heather N. Taussig is a clinical psychologist and an Associate Professor of Pediatrics and Psychiatry at the Kempe Center for the Prevention of Child Abuse and Neglect and the University of Colorado School of Medicine. She obtained her undergraduate training from Harvard University, her graduate training from the SDSU/UCSD Joint Doctoral program in Clinical Psychology, and completed her clinical internship at Stanford University. Dr. Taussig developed and directs the Fostering Healthy Futures program, an NIH-funded randomized controlled trial of an intervention for youth in foster care. She was named *Outstanding Young Professional* for her work on child abuse and neglect by the International Society for the Prevention of Child Abuse and Neglect and was appointed by Governor Ritter to serve on the Foster Care and Permanence Task Force (Senate Bill 07-64).

Susan G. Timmer is a research scientist at the CAARE Diagnostic and Treatment Center, UC Davis Children's Hospital, a faculty member of the Human Development Graduate Group, and Clinical Assistant Professor in the School of Medicine. Her research focuses on evaluating the effectiveness of PCIT and its core components, and investigating parent-child relationship processes in the context of children's experience of maltreatment.

Anthony J. Urquiza is a clinical psychologist and Director of Mental Health Services and Clinical Research at the CAARE Center, Department of Pediatrics, UC Davis Children's Hospital. He is a faculty member of the Human Development Graduate Group and clinical faculty in the School of Medicine. His primary clinical research interests and publications address all types of child maltreatment and family violence, with an emphasis on interventions for high-risk families. Dr. Urquiza is director of the PCIT Training Center.

Viola Vaughan-Eden PhD, LCSW is a clinical and forensic social worker providing mental health services to children and families in Southeastern Virginia for more than 25 years. She serves as a consultant, evaluator and expert witness in child maltreatment cases throughout Virginia and the United States. Dr. Vaughan-Eden lectures to multidisciplinary groups of professionals on the psycho-social needs of child abuse victims and their families all over the US and abroad including Japan, Russia, Spain and Turkey. She is President of the American Professional Society on the Abuse of Children (APSAC) and Co-Editor of the Journal of Forensic Social Work. Dr. Vaughan-Eden is the recipient of the 2011 National Children's Advocacy Center's Outstanding Service Award in Mental Health and the 2012 National Association of Social Workers - Virginia Chapter Lifetime Achievement Award. Her chapter on *Nonoffending Mothers of Sexually Abused Children* is based on her clinical experience and dissertation research. www.violavaughaneden.com

Michael S. Wald is the Jackson Eli Reynolds Professor of Law at Stanford University. He joined the faculty in 1967. His teaching and research focuses on children and public policy, especially with respect to child maltreatment. He was Director of the Stanford Center on Child, Youth, and their Families from 1984–1987.

Professor Wald served as the reporter for the American Association's Standards Related to Child Abuse and Neglect and has helped author legislation related to child welfare at the federal and state levels.

Professor Wald has held a number of nonacademic positions related to child welfare. He was Director of the San Francisco Human Services Agency in 1996–1997, Deputy General Counsel of the US Department of Health and Human Services from 1993–1995, and has sat as a juvenile court judge in California. He also has been a member of the US Advisory Committee on Child Abuse and Neglect, was chair of the California State Advisory Committee on Child Abuse, and the Carnegie Foundation Commission on Children 0–3.

Cathy Spatz Widom is a Distinguished Professor in the Psychology Department at John Jay College of Criminal Justice and a member of the Graduate Faculty at City University of New York. Professor Widom has served on the faculties of Harvard, Indiana, University at Albany, and New Jersey Medical School. She is currently on the Committee on Law and Justice at the National Research Council (NRC) and a member of the Institute of Medicine study panel on child abuse and neglect. She has been elected a fellow of the American Psychological Association, American Psychopatho-logical Association, and American Society of Criminology. Professor Widom is coeditor of the *Journal of Quantitative Criminology* and on the editorial boards of psychology, criminology, and child maltreatment journals. Widom has published extensively on the long-term consequences of child abuse and neglect and has received numerous awards for her research.

Fred H. Wulczyn is a Senior Research Fellow at and founding staff member of Chapin Hall at the University of Chicago. His public sector experience includes a decade long post with the New York State Department of Social Services. Today, he splits his time between Chapin Hall and the United States Department of Health and Human Services where he is a special advisor to Commissioner Bryan Samuels, who oversees the US child welfare system.

Dr. Wulczyn's principal areas of expertise focus on child welfare broadly defined, with an emphasis on child maltreatment and foster care. He is the founding director of the Center for State Child Welfare Data, a collaborative effort involving Chapin Hall, the National Association of Public Child Welfare Administrators and the University of California at Berkeley. As Special Assistant to Commissioner Samuels, Dr. Wulczyn is also leading a redesign of the methods used by the federal government to monitor the performance of state child welfare agencies. In recognition of his work, Dr. Wulczyn has received the 2005 Peter Forsythe Award, the 2011 Flynn Prize, and an honorary Doctorate of Humane Letters by Marywood University.

Tuppett M. Yates earned her Ph.D. in developmental psychopathology and clinical science from the Institute of Child Development at the University of Minnesota in 2005. She is an Associate Professor at the University of California, Riverside (UCR), where she directs the Adversity and Adaptation Laboratory (www.adlab.ucr.edu). Dr. Yates' research focuses on how childhood adversity influences developmental pathways toward psychopathology and competence with particular emphases on social and regulatory developmental processes. Her current research activities center on longitudinal studies of risk and resilience, including an investigation of formal school transition among 250 preschooler-caregiver dyads, and a study of young adult transitions among 200 youth as they "age out" of the foster care system. Dr. Yates has extensive clinical experience with high-risk youth. She is also the founder and director of the UCR Guardian Scholars (www.guardianscholars.ucr.edu), which provides a comprehensive network of support to emancipated foster youth as they pursue higher education.

Introduction

Jill E. Korbin and Richard D. Krugman

One of the early pioneers in the field of Child Maltreatment was Brandt Steele. He was the psychiatrist on the original "Battered Child" paper with C. Henry Kempe in 1962 (Kempe et al. 1962). Brandt saw his first case in 1956 and spent nearly a half century listening to abused children and abusive adults before his death in 2005 at the age of 97. One of his favorite sayings was "If you don't understand someone's behavior, you don't have enough history." He always took time to pause and to listen, to ask questions and to try to understand what it was that led to the behaviors – and the consequences of those behaviors.

With that in mind, you may wonder what it was that led us to start this new *Handbook of Child Maltreatment* and the series, *Child Maltreatment: Contemporary Issues in Research and Policy* of which it is a part. There are many books and journals now that regularly report on what is new or what is going on in the field of child maltreatment. Substantial progress has been made in addressing child maltreatment, as will be seen in the chapters in this volume. Nevertheless, many of the core questions of the field remain, and the chapters point us in the direction both of what is known, and, perhaps even more importantly, what remains to be known to make progress in helping abused children, their families, and their communities.

The complexity of child abuse and neglect has posed many challenges. We asked our colleagues in the field if they would contribute to a volume whose aim is to review what we know and what we don't know at this stage of the development of the field of child maltreatment with an emphasis on what we need to be doing from here. We asked for "executive summaries" of the decades of work that have gone on in specific areas, with the additional aim of having future volumes of the series be specific monographs that build on these chapters and update them as time goes on. Other chapters could have been and will be included in future versions of the *Handbook*, which we intend to update approximately every 5 years.

We initially planned to have the *Handbook* be the first volume in the series, followed by monographs taking up the issues presented in the *Handbook*. Along the way, we realized that last year (2012) was the 50th anniversary of the Battered Child paper (Kempe et al. 1962). We then decided to take a different path, and Volume 1 of this series was published to commemorate that event (Krugman and Korbin 2013). We invited professionals who had worked with or been influenced by Henry Kempe and his work to comment specifically on four of Kempe's key papers with an eye towards where this work had led the field.

J.E. Korbin (*)
College of Arts and Sciences, Case Western Reserve University, Cleveland, OH, USA
e-mail: Jill.Korbin@case.edu

R.D. Krugman
School of Medicine, University of Colorado, Aurora, CO, USA

Thirty years ago, there was a saying in Washington, DC: "where you stand depends on where you sit." If you search that phrase now, it is attributed to Nelson Mandela – and the truth of who said it first is not as important as the truth of the phrase. The field of child abuse and neglect is one that is a sub-set of some very large fields: anthropology, criminology, law, medicine, pediatrics, psychiatry, psychology, social work, and sociology, to name just some. Not surprisingly, those scholars and practitioners who come from each of these fields (and others) tend to see the problem from that perspective.

The organization of the *Handbook* is along reportorial lines: What is child maltreatment? Why does it occur? What are the consequences? What can and should we do about it? How does child maltreatment look in a more global perspective?

The first section of the *Handbook* addresses one of the major challenges in child maltreatment work: What are we talking about? What *is* child abuse and neglect? At its most basic, since the beginning of the "field," we have questioned whether child maltreatment can be measured in behaviors of caregivers or by the identified injuries and consequences to children that result in agency reports. Most research on child maltreatment relies on cases reported to child protective services. Chapter 1 by Sedlak and Ellis helps us to understand "what it is" by examining national incidence studies and trends in reporting. The next three chapters examine the major forms of maltreatment that are identified by mandatory reporting statutes: child neglect by Proctor and Dubowitz in Chapter 2; physical abuse by Palusci in Chapter 3; and sexual abuse by Heger in Chapter 4. A final chapter in this section, Chapter 5 by Krugman and Lane, tackles one of the most disturbing forms of child maltreatment, when a child dies as the result of abuse and/or neglect.

A second challenge, and the second section of this book, addresses the basic question of why child maltreatment occurs. An early and persisting explanation for the existence of child maltreatment is that it is passed from generation to generation, and that the abused children of today become the abusive parents of tomorrow. In Chapter 6, Bezenski, Yates and Egeland assess the evidence for intergenerational transmission of abusive parenting. Another explanation asks whether child maltreatment is most powerfully related to poverty. Drake and Jonson-Reid in Chapter 7 tackle this issue. Related to poverty, in Chapter 8, Dettlaff brings to bear the evidence and arguments for and against disproportionality in child maltreatment report rates, asking if disproportionality exists and how the answer to this question has shaped our understandings of why child maltreatment occurs. Another line of thinking about the etiology of child maltreatment is that there are certain children who are more susceptible to being maltreated. In Chapter 9, Giardino, Giardino and Issac consider the evidence related to the maltreatment of children with disabilities. Child maltreatment also has been explained by asking whether some families (including parents) are simply more violent than others. In Chapter 10, Alhusen and colleagues review the challenges of understanding the dynamics and overlap of intimate partner violence and child maltreatment.

A third challenge in child maltreatment work is assessing the consequences of maltreatment. One might argue that the very experience of an abused or neglected child is sufficient in and of itself to demand a concerted response, both to help the child and family and to prevent future abuse to that child or any other child. It has been very difficult to sort out the consequences of child maltreatment from other difficult circumstances in which children live, such as poverty and disadvantage. Increasing evidence, however, has pointed to the long-term consequences of early adverse experiences, including maltreatment. Yet, the pathways from child maltreatment to difficulties later in life remain less clear. Are abused children compromised neurologically, leading to later difficulties? Are abused children set on a path leading them to risky behaviors, including substance abuse, dating violence, early sexuality? At the core of these questions is the concern to determine the balance of risk and resilience, why some abused children have dire consequences from the experience, some seem to function well in some areas and not others, and some go on to lead lives indistinguishable from their non-maltreated peers. This section of the book examines two of these issues. In Chapter 11, Bernard, Lind and Dozier examine the consequences to the developing brain and neurological development among maltreated children, as well as the evidence for whether these early consequences can be mitigated. In Chapter 12, Widom brings together evidence about the life course of abused children taking a prospective rather than the usual retrospective approach. The reader is also referred to the earlier Chapter 6 that considers one of the most persistent beliefs about child maltreatment and its consequences – intergenerational transmission of abusive parenting such that the abused child of today becomes the abusive parent of tomorrow.

The fourth, and largest section, considers what we should do about child maltreatment. These chapters address such efforts despite the challenges examined in the earlier sections including lack of definitional clarity and questions about etiologies and outcomes. Wald begins this section in Chapter 13 with a broad view of what the goals of ensuring child well-being should be and how child protection fits into this framework. He considers options, expanded upon in several subsequent chapters about how we might move forward towards those goals.

While there has sometimes been a tension between prevention and treatment in the field, particularly as to where resources should be devoted, both are represented in this section. The first subsection deals with prevention issues, beginning with an overview by Daro and Benedetti in Chapter 14. This overview of where we have been and need to go is followed by Chapter 15 by Molnar and Beardslee who argue for a community approach to prevention and Chapter 16 by Hashima also suggesting a broader public health approach to prevention. An example of one community-based prevention program, Strong Communities, is the focus of Chapter 17 by Melton. The subsection concludes with Wulczyn and colleagues' questions in Chapter 18 about the match, or mismatch, between resources and needs.

The next subsection turns to treatment approaches, beginning with Timmer and Urquiza's Chapter 19 that brings together issues in child development with empirically based programs. The three chapters that follow emphasize different approaches to intervention. Fitzgerald and Berliner in Chapter 20 examine psychosocial interventions for abused and neglected children; Taussig and Raviv foster care in Chapter 21; and Andrews mutual support and self-help for maltreating parents in Chapter 22. Vaughan-Eden's Chapter 23 asks that the field consider non-offending mothers of sexually abused children. Fuller's Chapter 24 then examines what we know about the successes of differential or alternative response approaches to working with maltreating families. The subsection concludes with Fluke and colleagues' Chapter 25 that brings us back to the basics of how child protective services make decisions that bring maltreatment cases to the attention of intervenors in the first place.

In the last subsection on legal issues, in Chapter 26, Mathews and Bross consider legal approaches, including mandatory reporting. Russell and colleagues in Chapter 27 offer a perspective on the judicial process. Knapp's Chapter 28 brings the perspective of law enforcement, which is responsible for the initial investigations.

Finally, we end with Section V that calls us back to thinking about the broader international and cross-cultural human experience. In Chapter 29, Kimbrough-Melton considers how international law and conventions have shaped our views of, and responses to, child maltreatment. Kimbrough-Melton includes a consideration of how international law has addressed the balance between the universal rights and needs of children with cultural diversity in behaviors and beliefs about what is regarded as abusive to children around the world. Kohrt concludes the volume in Chapter 30 by bringing a biocultural perspective to the consideration of child maltreatment.

We are grateful to those who contributed to this volume and to our colleagues at Springer for affording us the opportunity to bring this *Handbook*, and this new series, forward to the field. We look forward to the work of our colleagues that will be reflected in regular updates to the *Handbook* and new books to expand our knowledge and contribute to the well-being of children, their families, and their communities. Because *Child Maltreatment: Contemporary Issues in Research and Policy* will be a dynamic and ongoing series, we value reader's comments about what was helpful or other directions we could explore in future volumes, both in updates of the *Handbook* and future monographs. To the reader, this series is for you.

References

Kempe, C. H., Silverman, F. N., Steele, B. F., Droegmueller, W., & Silver, H. K. (1962). The battered child syndrome. *Journal of the American Medical Association, 181*, 17–24.

Krugman, R. D., & Korbin, J. E. (2013). *C. Henry Kempe: A 50 year legacy to the field of child abuse and neglect.* Dordrecht: Springer.

Part I
Child Maltreatment:
What Is It?

Chapter 1
Trends in Child Abuse Reporting

Andrea J. Sedlak and Raquel T. Ellis

Introduction

Organized public efforts to protect children from abuse and neglect began in the late 1800s with the rise of private organizations that took public stances against cruelty to children (Schene 1998). Although the 1935 Social Security Act provided funding to states for child welfare services to vulnerable children, mandated reporting laws were enacted only after Dr. Henry Kempe's 1962 article on the "battered child syndrome" raised widespread concern and brought national attention to child physical abuse inflicted by parents and caregivers (Kempe et al. 1962; Melton 2005).

In the same year that Kempe and his colleagues published their seminal article, 1962, the Children's Bureau held two meetings to explore strategies for addressing the problem. These culminated in a model child abuse reporting law, which the Children's Bureau disseminated widely to child welfare organizations and state legislatures (Nelson 1984). The model state child protection act authorized state departments of social services and/or child protective services to receive suspected child maltreatment reports and authorized the reporting of child maltreatment by any person, while requiring certain professionals who have frequent interactions with children (such as law enforcement and medical professionals) to report suspected maltreatment (Kalichman 1993).

By 1967, all states and the District of Columbia had enacted mandatory child maltreatment reporting laws, incorporating some or all of the provisions of the Model Act (Nelson 1984). Federal legislation was enacted in 1974, when Congress passed the Child Abuse Prevention and Treatment Act (CAPTA, P.L. 93-247). CAPTA established the National Center on Child Abuse and Neglect (NCCAN) to provide policy and standard guidelines for handling the reports, and offered limited grants to states to develop child protective services. CAPTA also established requirements for state reporting laws, which states had to meet in order to be eligible for state service grants (Nelson 1984; Schene 1998).

Mandatory reporting requirements. Section 1.5 of this volume discusses the legal issues surrounding mandatory reporting requirements. For purposes here it is important to recognize that these vary from state to state, both in terms of who must report and the types of maltreatment they must report. Only about 18 states require *any individual* who suspects child maltreatment to report.[1] In most states, specific professionals who have frequent interactions with children are mandated reporters, whereas other professionals and members of the general public are simply encouraged to voluntarily report. The professionals most commonly identified as mandated reporters in State statutes include medical,

---

[1] States frequently amend their laws (Child Welfare Information Gateway 2009a).

A.J. Sedlak (✉) • R.T. Ellis
Westat, Rockville, MD, USA

J.E. Korbin and R.D. Krugman (eds.), *Handbook of Child Maltreatment*, Child Maltreatment 2, DOI 10.1007/978-94-007-7208-3_1, © Springer Science+Business Media Dordrecht 2014

mental health, social work, educational and legal professionals (Child Welfare Information Gateway 2011a). State laws also mention judges, attorneys, court-appointed special advocates, Christian Science practitioners, and the staff and volunteers of various social service or community agencies including health and human services, public housing, public assistance, domestic violence, and victim and rape centers. Some state statutes also identify public or private agency staff who provide recreational or sports activities, animal protection or control, veterinarians, and computer and internet providers' installation or repair staff.

States' statutes vary substantially in the degree of detail in their descriptions of the malctreatment that must be reported and in whether they include or exclude a given type of maltreatment from the requirement. An extensive review of states' reporting statutes (Sedlak et al. 2003) considered the number of specific acts mentioned in states' statutes and found that most states provided highly differentiated definitions of sexual abuse and of physical neglect. Less than one-third of states gave a moderately differentiated definition of mandated physical abuse, whereas only one-tenth of states did so for emotional abuse. Only about one-half of states even mentioned emotional neglect or educational neglect, with extremely little differentiation of the acts or omissions defined in these categories.

Recent information on current state statutes indicates the situation is unchanged for educational neglect, with just a slight majority of states' statutes mentioning it at all (Child Welfare Information Gateway 2011a). Recently, child protective service agencies have increasingly considered a child's exposure to domestic violence to be a form of maltreatment, but states that mention it vary in their treatment of it, with some states including it in their definition of physical abuse, others considering it to be a form of neglect. However, most states still omit any mention of it and one state specifically excludes it from maltreatment that must be reported. Only about one-fourth of states include in utero exposure to drugs in their definitions of abuse or neglect (Child Welfare Information Gateway 2011b).

CPS responses. Some cases of child maltreatment never reach CPS because the individual who noticed the situation and suspected maltreatment did not contact CPS to report it. Once an individual reports the maltreatment of a child to a local CPS agency or state or regional hotline, the referral undergoes a screening process to determine whether the situation meets the agency's criteria for a CPS investigation. Referrals are screened-out with no investigation when there is insufficient information to contact the family for follow-up and when the situation described in the report does not meet a state's legal definition of child maltreatment. The agency will not provide any direct response to screened-out cases although they may tell the reporter to contact another agency or service.

Some CPS agencies can offer a non-investigative response to selected low risk cases that do not meet their standards for investigation. These non-investigative responses go by a variety of labels, including "differential response," "alternative response," "multi-track response," and "dual-track" response. Whatever their label, these responses involve offering services to meet various needs of the child and family in order to prevent the family from becoming a high-risk case. The CPS agency does not focus on gathering evidence to confirm the occurrence of abuse or neglect and the family is not legally mandated to accept the agency's intervention (as they may be with a CPS investigation response). Differential response systems began to emerge in the early 1990s a result of dissatisfaction with the inflexible and limited capacity of the CPS response, the adversarial orientation of CPS (which can discourage family engagement and compliance), and the inability of traditional child welfare services to address the underlying causes of the safety issues that bring families to the attention of CPS (Child Welfare Information Gateway 2008; Daro et al. 2005; Farrow 1997; Schene 2005; Zielewski et al. 2006).

Challenges of studying mandated reporting. The fact that reporting of child abuse and neglect is mandated by law makes it difficult to study reporting directly. Researchers cannot explicitly ask respondents to describe child abuse cases they have encountered and then ask whether they have reported these specific cases. To do so is to ask respondents whether they have complied with the law. Moreover, present-day human subjects protection standards would require a researcher to forewarn respondents that they risk acknowledging illegal behavior in answering these questions. With or without this explicit warning, researchers do not expect that respondents would truthfully answer direct questions about whether they reported specific cases they have observed.

As a result, researchers have studied reporting behaviors indirectly. The evidence reviewed in this chapter reflects three main strategies. First, an important source of evidence comes from examining the reports that CPS agencies receive. This research can describe trends in what comes to CPS and how CPS responds. Thus, it can quantify the reports that are screened out as well as the percentage of screened-in cases that receive investigations or other agency responses. However, this approach can describe only those children who come to CPS attention. A second tactic has been to observe the overlap of different data sources—to ask mandated reporters to describe the maltreated children they encounter and then to see whether these children are among the children who received CPS investigations in the jurisdiction during the same timeframe. This approach identifies the maltreated children who *should* come to CPS attention and reveals how many receive a CPS investigation. However, as discussed below, other strategies are needed to understand whether the children who did not receive CPS investigation were not reported or were not screened-in for an investigation. Finally, a third perspective on reporting child abuse and neglect comes from studies that have asked mandated reporters about the factors that generally affect their decisions to report or have asked participants whether they would report the situations described in hypothetical vignettes, varying the vignette situations to see how different factors affect their reporting decisions.

The first two approaches are the methods used in the only studies that provide national-level information on mandated reporters and CPS agency processes: the National Child Abuse and Neglect Data System (NCANDS) and the National Incidence Study on Child Abuse and Neglect (NIS). Congress mandated both studies in the CAPTA legislation and both are sponsored by the Children's Bureau in the U.S. Department of Health and Human Services. NCANDS provides data annually on all cases referred to CPS, showing whether CPS screened the referral in for an agency response and, if so, whether the case was investigated or received an alternative response other than investigation. NIS, which is conducted periodically, represents all children recognized as maltreated by a wide array of community professionals who are generally mandated reporters. NIS determines whether CPS investigated these children by obtaining CPS data independently and comparing the children the professionals identify with those who received CPS investigation. Both NCANDS and NIS reveal trends over time. NCANDS shows year-to-year changes in CPS referrals and responses; NIS shows changes across its periodic cycles in recognized maltreatment and investigation rates.

Referrals to CPS and CPS Responses: Evidence from NCANDS

NCANDS examines only those cases referred to CPS and describes the national patterns of reports, screen-outs, investigations, and alternative responses. It also indicates trends over time both in the number of maltreated children reported and in the sources of reports to CPS. NCANDS cannot determine whether trends over time reflect changes in the occurrence of maltreatment or changes in the behaviors of the reporters to CPS. Established in 1988 by CAPTA, NCANDS has evolved from a system based on aggregate data to one based almost exclusively on case-level data from participating states.

Referrals. Some researchers refer to these as "reports," but NCANDS calls them "referrals." Referrals are contacts with CPS concerning the welfare of a child who is suspected to be abused or neglected. Over the 2001–2010 decade, referrals to CPS agencies consistently increased from about 2.7 million referrals involving about five million children in 2001 to an estimated 3.3 million referrals concerning about 5.9 million children in 2010 (US. DHHS 2003a, 2011). Taking account of the increased size of the U.S. child population over this interval, these statistics reflect a 14 % rise in the rate at which children are referred to CPS. Over the same period, the percentage of referrals that CPS agencies screened in for an agency response decreased from 67.3 % to 60.7 %.

CPS responses to reports. NCANDS reserves the term "report" for those referrals that CPS screens in for an agency response. The response can either be a formal investigation or an alternative, non-investigative response. In an investigation, the agency seeks to determine whether the maltreatment allegations are founded and to assign a disposition. If the allegations are founded (the child has been harmed or is at risk of harm), the agency seeks to reduce risk and protect the child. If necessary, CPS investigators may petition the court to order the family to participate in services and safety plans or to remove the child from the home into foster care. Agencies that can provide a non-investigative response (called an "alternative response" or "differential response") generally do so for cases deemed as low to moderate risk. Such non-investigative pathways focus on assessment and on engaging the family in services to improve the child's safety, without determining whether maltreatment occurred, identifying perpetrators, or resorting to court orders to mandate service participation (National Quality Improvement Center on Differential Response in Child Protective Services 2011).

NCANDS first provided data on CPS use of alternative responses in *Child Maltreatment 2000* (US DHHS 2002), when eight states assigned alternative response dispositions for their screened-in reports. Over the subsequent decade, the number of states submitting alternative response dispositions to NCANDS gradually increased, with 14 states doing so in 2010 (US DHHS 2011). NCANDS information on the number of children that receive an alternative response is incomplete because CAPTA only recently required states to submit NCANDS data on their alternative response cases.[2] What is clear, however, is that the use and stage of implementation of alternative/differential response systems varies across states over the years. Summarizing the available literature since 1993, researchers at the National Quality Improvement Center on Differential Response in Child Protective Services (QIC-DR) show steady growth in the number of states that are piloting differential response or using it statewide (2011). Their current map shows that 17 states operate differential response statewide; five states have implemented it regionally or in selected counties; 12 say they are planning or considering it; five are using an approach for cases that screen-out of investigation that do not meet the QIC-DR differential response definition; and three states report that they tried but discontinued it.

However, this general trend of increased usage of alternative/differential responses may mask a notable degree of year-to-year "churn" in their use, with different states starting and stopping. The QIC-DR does not provide state-level information about the growth pattern, but NCANDS reports suggest that, since 2000, 21 states have used alternative response at one time or another; only four states have used it throughout all 11 years. Thirteen states adopted alternative response at some point and used it consistently since then. Another eight states used it at some time during the period but not consistently thereafter; (from NCANDS dispositions, it appears that five of these states tried it, abandoned it, and then reinstituted it). The "churn" at the state level is perhaps even greater at the local level, where individual county CPS agencies may pilot-test the approach for a delimited period. Sedlak and Li (2009) reported results from two nationally representative surveys of local CPS agencies and found that significantly fewer local county CPS agencies offered alternative responses in 2005–2006 than had just 4 years earlier in 2002.

To date, only three evaluations of differential response have used random assignment designs. Overall, results indicate that, compared to investigation, families and program staff are more satisfied with the process, families are more engaged, and cooperation between CPS and partner agencies is better. Although, there appears to be no negative effect on child safety, findings on measures of improved safety (re-reports, removals to foster care) have shown slight or no benefit (National Quality Improvement Center on Differential Response in Child Protective Services 2011). Long-term CPS costs show contradictory results (Loman et al. 2010; Siegel and Loman 2006).

---

[2] Required in the CAPTA reauthorization act of 2010.

Sources of CPS reports. Professional sources are responsible for the majority of reports, 59 % in 2010, up from 56 % in 2005 and 53 % in 1995. The greatest professional contributors have consistently been education, law enforcement, and social services and mental health—each of these groups contributed more than 16 % of reports in 2010. Over the years, the contributions of law enforcement and social services/mental health have increased by about 4 percentage points each, whereas educational sources have remained relatively consistent since 2000. Medical sources rank fourth among professionals. Since 2005, medical sources have provided just over 8 % of reports, down from 11 % in 1995.

Report dispositions. NCANDS distinguishes nine CPS report dispositions. The majority of reports are *unsubstantiated*, which means that the agency's investigation determined there was insufficient evidence to conclude or suspect maltreatment under state law. Between 2000 and 2010, the percentage of unsubstantiated reports increased from 58 % to 64 %. In 2010, 22 % of reports were *substantiated*, meaning that the allegation of maltreatment or risk was supported or founded according to state law or policy. This reflects a decrease since 2000, when 28 % of reports were substantiated. Only a small minority of states distinguish *indicated* reports to signify that, although the evidence is not sufficient to substantiate maltreatment or risk, there is reason to suspect that the allegation is true. Both the number of states using the indicated disposition and the percentage of reports assigned this disposition decreased over the 2000–2010 period, from ten to six states and from 3 % to 1 % of reports. In line with the gradual increase in the number of states offering an alternative response (noted above), the percentage of reports receiving some type of *alternative response* disposition has risen as well: from 6 % of reports in 2000 to 10 % in 2010. Most states that offer an alternative response classify all reports they assign to this response as *alternative response nonvictim* reports. In 2010, 12 of the 14 states that provided alternative response dispositions adopted this practice; only two states distinguished some of their reports with the disposition *alternative response victim* to convey that their agency had determined that at least one child in the report was a victim of maltreatment. Since 2000, less than 1 % of reports receive this disposition.[3] Only small percentages of reports receive other dispositions (such as intentionally false, closed without a finding, missing, or not classified in NCANDS). Taken together, these comprised less than 4 % of reports that received a CPS response in 2010.

Victimization rates. Considering all dispositions that indicate victimization (substantiated, indicated, and alternative response victim), the percentage of reports with one or more identified victims has decreased substantially in the past decade, from nearly one-third (32 %) in 2001 to less than one-fourth (24 %) in 2010. Victimization rates at the child level also reveal substantial declines, as Fig. 1.1 illustrates.

During the past two decades, the overall rate of maltreatment was at its highest in 1993, with 153 victims per 10,000.[4] Over the intervening years, it declined 38 % to its most recent level of 93 victims per 10,000 in 2011 (US DHHS 2006, 2010a, b, 2011, 2012).

Figure 1.1 also shows that the component categories of physical abuse and sexual abuse declined dramatically over this period. The rate of physical abuse declined 56 % from an all-time high of 36.5 children per 10,000 in 1992 to 16.0 children per 10,000 in 2011. Sexual abuse was at its highest rate

---

[3] Nearly all States that use the disposition of "alternative response victim" also use the "alternative response nonvictim" classification. During a few years in the past decade, one or two States have used only the disposition of "alternative response victim" for their alternative response cases.

[4] NCANDS defines a victim as a child for whom maltreatment was substantiated, indicated, or alternative response victim. Most victims (93 % in 2010) have substantiated maltreatment (US DHHS 2011). The rates given here for overall maltreatment, and for the component categories through 2008, are duplicated rates, meaning that a child is counted in every report where he or she is found to be a victim. The unduplicated rates, which count each child victim just once, are available in NCANDS publications for 2005 and later (US DHHS 2010b, 2011, 2012). These also evidence declining trend lines, but below the duplicated rates depicted in the graph. For instance, the rate of overall unduplicated maltreatment drops from 109 per 10,000 in 2005 to 91 per 10,000 in 2011.

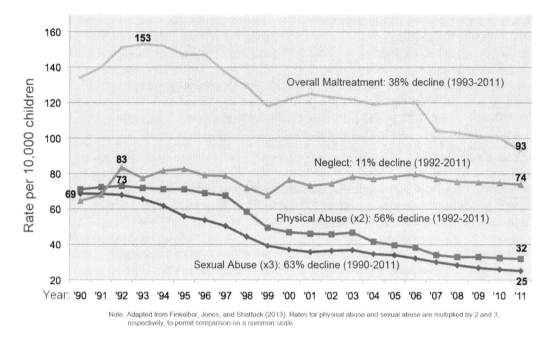

Fig. 1.1 Child victimization rates in CPS reports, based on NCANDS data through 2011

in 1990, when CPS substantiated 22.9 children per 10,000 as sexually abused. By 2011, the sexual abuse rate had declined 63 % to a rate of 8.4 children per 10,000. Neglect, the most prevalent category of maltreatment, showed a much smaller decline of 11 % over the long-term, from 83.4 to 73.9 children in 10,000 between 1992 and 2010.

Summary of NCANDS findings and trends. Over the past decade, referrals to CPS have increased, but CPS has screened in proportionally fewer for an agency response and states appear to be gradually moving toward use of alternative or differential responses for a sector of their screened-in referrals. Greater percentages of reports come from professional sources. Lower percentages are substantiated or indicated and more are unsubstantiated or receive an alternative response disposition. Since the early 1990s, NCANDS data show decreasing rates of child victimization, especially in the maltreatment categories of physical and sexual abuse.

Incidence of Maltreatment and CPS Investigation Rates: Evidence from NIS

The NIS (Sedlak et al. 2010a) provides estimates of the incidence of child abuse and neglect in the United States, as recognized by mandated reporters.[5] It is the only national study that goes beyond CPS data to obtain information about the occurrence of maltreatment that is recognized by a broad spectrum of community professionals. Using samples to provide nationally representative estimates, NIS gathers data on all maltreated children investigated by CPS agencies in the study sample and on children recognized as maltreated by professionals in the same communities. Most of these community professionals, termed "sentinels," are mandated reporters in their jurisdictions. They

---

[5] The NIS follows the usage of CAPTA in referring to its findings as "incidence estimates." In the epidemiological literature, however, they would be more appropriately termed "annual prevalence estimates." Technically, they are period prevalence estimates, where the focal period is a year.

Table 1.1 National incidence of endangerment standard maltreatment in the NIS–3 and NIS–4 (rates per 1,000 children)

Maltreatment category	NIS-3 (1993)	NIS–4 (2005–2006)
All maltreatment	41.9	39.5
All abuse[a]	18.2	11.3
Physical abuse[a]	9.1	6.5
Sexual abuse[a]	4.5	2.4
Emotional abuse[a]	7.9	4.1
All neglect	29.2	30.6
Physical neglect	19.9	16.2
Emotional neglect[a]	8.7	15.9
Educational neglect	5.9	4.9

[a]The difference between the NIS–3 and NIS–4 incidence rates is significant at $p \leq 0.05$

remain on the lookout for maltreated children in the course of their work in schools; day care centers; hospitals; law enforcement agencies; departments of juvenile probation, public health, and public housing; shelters for domestic violence victims and for runaway or homeless youth; and community mental health and social service agencies. The four NIS cycles conducted since 1979 used similar methods and applied standardized definitions to classify maltreatment. The endangerment standard definitions, the most inclusive standard, were used in the last three NIS cycles.[6]

Table 1.1 lists the major categories of endangerment standard maltreatment, indicating those categories where rates in the NIS–4 (2005–2006) significantly differed from NIS-3 rates (1993).

The rate of abuse overall decreased significantly, as did the rates of physical, sexual, and emotional abuse. The rate of abuse overall decreased 38 %, from 18.2 children per 1,000 in the NIS-3 to 11.3 children per 1,000 in the NIS–4. Physical abuse decreased 29 % from 9.1 to 6.5 per 1,000; sexual abuse decreased 47 % from 4.5 to 2.4 per 1,000; and emotional abuse decreased 48 % from 7.9 to 4.1 per 1,000. The physical and sexual abuse findings corroborate the NCANDS trends described above, but in broader context. The NCANDS trends reflect only cases reported to and substantiated by CPS, whereas the NIS trends apply to all children recognized as maltreated, including those not referred to CPS and those referred to CPS but not screened in.

The NIS data also reveal more differentiated trends: Subsequent analyses of the NIS[7] indicate that, whereas the rate of sexual abuse decreased at all levels of severity, the rates of physical and emotional abuse significantly decreased only for children who were moderately harmed or endangered—but not for those seriously harmed—by this maltreatment.

While the NIS–4 found that rate of emotional abuse decreased, it also revealed that the rate of emotional neglect *increased* significantly.[8] NIS classifies a number of acts and omissions as emotional neglect, including exposure to domestic violence. Subsequent analyses indicated that the number of children per 1,000 who were exposed to domestic violence more than tripled since the time of the NIS-3, which likely indicates increased recognition that such exposure can endanger the child (Child Welfare Information Gateway 2009a). Not only do domestic violence and child abuse frequently co-occur in the same households, but children's exposure to domestic violence has harmful consequences in itself (Edelson 1999) and may warrant coordinated responses from child protective services and services for domestic violence victims (Bragg 2003).

Since NIS obtains data independently from both CPS and community professionals, it can indicate whether the maltreated children that sentinels identify are among the maltreated children that CPS investigated in their jurisdictions. Table 1.2 shows the CPS investigation rates for the major categories

---

[6] The NIS–4 findings report and technical reports provide further details (Sedlak et al. 2010a, b, c; Hartge et al. 2010).

[7] The authors conducted these analyses to further characterize the NIS trends. To date, they are not published elsewhere.

[8] NCANDS does not distinguish between emotional abuse and emotional neglect.

Table 1.2 Changes in rates
of CPS investigation of
children with endangerment
standard maltreatment,
overall and by maltreatment
category

Maltreatment category	NIS-3 (1993)	NIS–4 (2005–2006)
All maltreatment[a]	33 %	43 %
All abuse[b]	39 %	49 %
Physical abuse	45 %	52 %
Sexual abuse[b]	44 %	56 %
Emotional abuse[a]	28 %	40 %
All neglect[a]	28 %	41 %
Physical neglect	35 %	41 %
Emotional neglect[a]	22 %	50 %
Educational neglect	7 %	9 %

[a]The difference between the NIS–3 and NIS–4 investigation
rates is significant at $p \leq 0.05$
[b]The difference between the NIS–3 and the NIS–4 investigation rates is statistically marginal (i.e., $0.10 > p > 0.05$)

of Endangerment Standard maltreatment in the NIS-3 and NIS–4. Overall, only a minority of maltreated children NIS identifies are among those in CPS investigations (43 % of all maltreated children). However, investigation rates did improve in the NIS–4, with CPS investigating one-half or
more of the children in several categories (52 % of physically abused children; 56 % of sexually
abused children; and 50 % of those emotionally neglected). The NIS–4 rates of CPS investigation
were significantly higher than NIS-3 rates for overall maltreatment and for emotional abuse and emotional neglect. Investigation rates were marginally higher for overall abuse and sexual abuse.

Given that many maltreated children do not receive CPS investigation, one would at least hope that
the more serious cases would be likely to receive CPS investigation.[9] This true for children who die as
a result of their maltreatment (81 % investigated), for those who suffer extreme or such traumatic
maltreatment that harm can be inferred (53 % investigated), and for those seriously endangered by
their maltreatment (60 % investigated). However, only minorities of children who experienced serious
injury or harm are investigated (31 %), at a rate similar to the investigation rate for moderately harmed
children (29 %). The investigation rate for seriously endangered children was significantly higher in
the NIS-4 (60 %) than in the NIS-3 (where it was just 40 %).

Sentinels in different community agencies recognize maltreated children at different rates. School
sentinels have always recognized the most children. In the NIS–4, they submitted data on 39 % of the
children whose maltreatment fit the Endangerment Standard definitions. Sentinels in law enforcement
agencies ranked second, identifying 19 % of the maltreated children; sentinels in hospitals ranked
third, contributing 13 % of the children. Other sentinel groups each identified 4 % or less of the maltreated children (day care and mental health 4 % each, juvenile probation 3 %, public health and social
services 2 % each, shelters 1 %, public housing <1 %). Other, nonsentinel sources[10] also contribute to
the NIS–4 estimates of maltreated children through their investigated reports to CPS, accounting for
13 % of all maltreated children.

---

[9]The NIS classifies children on the basis of the most severe injury or harm they suffered from maltreatment.: fatal
(maltreatment caused the child's death), serious (child needed professional treatment to alleviate current suffering or
prevent significant long-term impairment), moderate (observable symptoms lasting at least 48 h), inferred (no
observable harm recorded, but the extreme or traumatic nature of maltreatment makes it probable the child sustained
significant injury or impairment), or endangered (the maltreatment acts or omissions seriously endangered the child but
the child appears not to have been harmed).

[10]These include other governmental social service agencies, other (non-sentinel) professionals or agencies (e.g., community health clinics not affiliated with a hospital, private practice pediatricians, physicians, therapists) and all other
sources (primarily the general public, such as neighbors, friends, family, anonymous callers, and the victims
themselves).

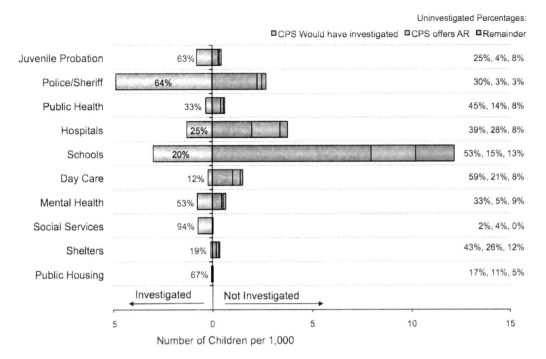

Fig. 1.2 Children with endangerment standard maltreatment in the NIS–4, by sentinel sources, CPS investigation rates, and uninvestigated classifications

Figure 1.2 displays this pattern for the sentinel sources,[11] indicating the number of maltreated children per 1,000 a source contributed by the absolute length of the bar. The figure also shows that CPS investigation rates are different for children recognized as maltreated by different sources.

The left side of the figure indicates the percentage of the children from that source who received CPS investigation. (The right side of the figure, representing the uninvestigated children, is discussed below.) Sentinel groups with the highest CPS investigation rates are social services (94 %), public housing (67 %), law enforcement (64 %), juvenile probation (63 %), and mental health agencies (53 %). CPS investigation rates are lower for maltreated children who were identified by sentinels in day care centers (12 %), shelters (19 %), schools (20 %), and hospitals (25 %).

The predominance of school personnel in recognizing maltreated children in this figure is in sharp contrast to the relatively low rate of CPS investigation of the maltreated children schools identify. The contribution of school sentinels to the right-hand side of the figure, which represents Endangerment Standard children who are not investigated, outweighs the contribution of all the other sentinel groups combined.

The NIS data indicate whether CPS investigated maltreatment of a child, but do not explain why maltreated children are not investigated. Until the most recent NIS cycle, the NIS–4, uninvestigated children had represented an enigma to the study. The NIS could not determine whether the sentinels who recognized maltreatment did not report it to CPS or whether they did report it to CPS but CPS did not investigate the child because the circumstances did not fit the agency's criteria for screening the case in for investigation. These alternatives have quite different policy implications.

---

[11] This figure excludes the 13 % of all maltreated children who enter the NIS data *only* through the CPS-investigated reports—from nonsentinel sources (previous footnote). NIS has no information about maltreated children these sources encounter who are not investigated.

To understand why maltreated children are not investigated, the NIS–4 included several supplementary studies. The *CPS Screening Policies Study* (*SPS*) obtained detailed information about CPS screening criteria (Greene et al. 2013). The *CPS Structure and Practices Mail Survey* (*SPM*) obtained information about the CPS agencies' organization and operations (Sedlak et al. 2013).

Maltreated children living in jurisdictions where a state or regional hotline conducted screening were less likely to receive a CPS investigation than children in jurisdictions where the local CPS agency conducted all screening. This was especially true for children who were already harmed by maltreatment and those who were physically abused. Also, physically and emotionally maltreated children, whether abused or neglected, were less likely to receive investigation if they lived in jurisdictions where CPS could offer an alternative, noninvestigative response.

In the SPS, project staff interviewed the intake supervisors in NIS–4 CPS agencies about their agencies' screening criteria. The supervisors indicated how their agency would respond to situations described in 60 vignettes, representing maltreatment that met the study definitions in all NIS–4 classification codes. Would their agency screen the described situation in for investigation, screen it out, or would they need to know more before making that decision? If they would need to know more, what information would they need and how would it affect their decision? Using the criteria the supervisors described, NIS–4 coders re-examined the details on the uninvestigated maltreated children in the main study data and decided whether the CPS agency with jurisdiction would have screened the children in for CPS investigation.

Figure 1.2 shows the percentage of maltreated children that CPS did not but would have investigated on the right side of each bar. It is reasonable to assume that these children were not reported to CPS. If sentinels had contacted CPS with the information that they gave to the NIS about these children, and if CPS applied the criteria the screening supervisors described, then CPS would have investigated another 53 % of the children recognized as maltreated by school sentinels and another 59 % of those submitted to NIS by day care staff. In fact, combining the children CPS would have investigated with those who actually did receive CPS investigation accounts for more than 80 % of the maltreated children identified by sentinels in juvenile probation, police/sheriff, mental health, social services, and public housing, more than 70 % of those recognized in public health, schools, and day care, and more than 60 % of those recognized in hospitals and shelters.

The remaining uninvestigated children, those whom CPS screening criteria would have screened out of investigation, may or may not have been reported to CPS. If they were reported, some may have been assigned for an alternative (noninvestigative) agency response if the CPS agency in question offered it. Both the SPS and the SPM asked whether the CPS agencies offered an alternative response during the time of the NIS–4. The NIS found significantly lower investigation rates in CPS jurisdictions that could provide an alternative, noninvestigative agency response, suggesting that some cases that might have received investigation in the past are diverted to the alternative response track in these agencies (Sedlak et al. 2010a).

The second section of the bars on the right side of Fig. 1.2 shows the uninvestigated children who resided in jurisdictions where they could have received an alternative agency response.[12] These are substantial minorities of the children recognized as maltreated in hospitals (28 %), shelters (26 %), and day care (21 %), and they represent 15 % of the maltreated children identified by school sentinels, 14 % of those identified in public health agencies, and 11 % of the children submitted to NIS by public housing personnel.

The balance of uninvestigated children in Fig. 1.2 are those whom CPS would definitely have screened out with no agency response and those for whom the agency's screening criteria did not indicate a clear decision.

---

[12] The percentages shown in Fig. 1.2 display a best-case scenario in that they assume that all the children in these jurisdictions would have met the agency's criteria for assignment to the alternative response track.

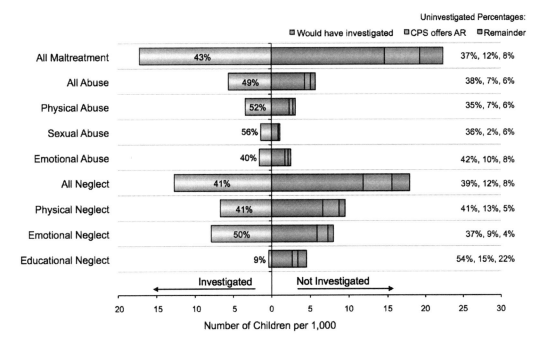

Fig. 1.3 Children with endangerment standard maltreatment in the NIS–4, by maltreatment category, CPS investigation rate, and uninvestigated classifications

Figure 1.3 applies this same classification to children with different types of maltreatment. Children who experienced multiple types of maltreatment are depicted in each applicable category. Combining the children CPS would have investigated if they were reported with the children who actually were investigated accounts for over 80 % of children in every maltreatment category except educational neglect, where the combined total represents 63 % of the children. As noted earlier, many CPS agencies do not investigate educational neglect per se. The educationally neglected children submitted to NIS commonly experienced other types of maltreatment as well. Their other maltreatment may explain why CPS investigated or would have investigated their circumstances. After considering the percentage of maltreated children who lived in jurisdictions where CPS offered an alternative response, only 8 % of all maltreated children remain without investigation and with no potential for some type of CPS agency response.

Using the same approach when classifying maltreated children by the severity of their outcomes from maltreatment indicated that the combined total of children who actually received and children who would have received CPS investigation accounted for 99 % of those fatally injured, 85 % of those seriously injured and of those whose injury could be inferred from the severity of their maltreatment, and 82 % of those deemed to have been seriously endangered by their maltreatment. The children with the lowest combined percentage (76 %) were those moderately harmed by their maltreatment.

Summary of NIS findings and trends. The NIS offers a broad view of the scope of child maltreatment. It identifies maltreated children beyond those that receive CPS investigation by collecting independent data on children recognized as maltreated by a variety of community professionals, most of whom are mandated reporters. Consistent with the NCANDS results, the NIS found that rates of physical abuse and sexual abuse decreased significantly between 1993 and 2005–2006. NIS also found that the rate of emotional abuse decreased whereas the rate of emotional neglect increased significantly.

The NIS shows that CPS investigates only a minority of maltreated children, both overall and in most specific categories of abuse and neglect. Additional data on the criteria CPS uses to screen cases in for investigation indicated that 37 % of maltreated children were not reported to CPS—they fit the agency's criteria for investigation, but were not among the children who received investigation. If these uninvestigated children had been reported to CPS, 80 % of all maltreated children would have received CPS investigation. Considering whether the uninvestigated children lived in jurisdictions where CPS offered alternative responses, NIS also determined that another 12 % of maltreated children could have received an alternative response. Thus, a combined total of 92 % of maltreated children either were investigated, would have been investigated if they had been reported, or might have received an alternative agency response if they were reported. The remaining 8 % of maltreated children include both those who would have been screened out of CPS investigations by agency screening criteria and those for whom it was not clear how the CPS screening criteria would apply to their cases. Thus, the NIS–4 findings imply that CPS screening activities should exclude only a small percentage of maltreated children from receiving CPS attention. The primary reason maltreated children are not investigated is that community professionals who recognize their maltreatment do not report them to CPS.

Nonreporting by Mandated Reporters

It is clear that many maltreated children never receive CPS attention because no one reports them. Besides the NIS findings, discretionary reporting is well-documented by other researchers (Conti 2011; Dixon and Dixon 2007; Flaherty et al. 2006; Zellman 1990). As noted in the introduction, a third perspective on reporting of child abuse and neglect comes from studies that have asked mandated reporters about the factors that generally affect their decisions to report or have asked participants whether they would report the situations described in hypothetical vignettes. The findings in this section indicate that reporting decisions are affected by the characteristics of the reporters, their agencies, the maltreatment situation, and the expected consequences of reporting.

Who Does and Does Not Report Child Maltreatment

Whether professionals report suspected child maltreatment to CPS depends on many factors, both individual and agency-level, including their professional identity, personal history, culture and views, training, and the policy in their workplace.

Professional identity. The NCANDS shows that professionals contribute most of the referrals that CPS screens in for some type of agency response, while the NIS results corroborate the importance of professionals in recognizing the majority of maltreated children, but also show considerable variation across professional groups in the numbers of maltreated children they identify and in the extent to which they report these children to CPS.

The NIS–4 included another supplemental study, the *Sentinel Definitions Survey (SDS)*, that offers additional insight into the relationship between professional identity and reporting behaviors (McPherson and Sedlak 2013). After the main NIS–4 data collection, a sample of 2,455 professionals who had served as NIS sentinels participated in a survey about their general experiences reporting cases to CPS. Among sentinels whose employers permitted them to report directly to CPS, only 62 % said they personally had done so. More sentinels in law enforcement (87 %) and health agencies (77 %) said they had reported a case, compared to 54 % of school personnel and 50 % of other sentinels.[13]

---

[13] In NIS, "other" sentinels were employees with direct service responsibilities at day care centers, shelters, public housing, social services, and mental health services.

The SDS participants also reviewed a series of vignettes representing maltreatment situations that fit the NIS definitions. On average, nearly one-fourth (23 %) of sentinels said they would *not* report these situations to CPS. Professional sentinel groups differed on this. More school professionals (33 %) said they would not report the maltreatment situations, compared to 23 % of sentinels in health professions, 24 % in law enforcement, and 27 % in other professions.

Workplace policy. In the SDS, 14 % of all sentinels said their agencies did not allow them to report child maltreatment directly to CPS. Gatekeeping was most frequently reported in schools: one-fifth of school sentinels (20 %) said their agencies did not allow direct reporting, compared to just 4 % of sentinels in health agencies and 2 % of those in law enforcement (McPherson and Sedlak 2013).

Organizational position also influences reporting behavior. O'Toole and Webster (1999) surveyed a sample of 480 public school teachers in Ohio using case vignettes and found that teachers who held administrative positions were less likely to say they would report the described cases than those not in administrative positions. These findings may reflect administrators' closer adherence to any school policies restricting direct reporting or governing reporting procedures.

Having a procedure for reporting child maltreatment does not necessarily mean prohibiting staff from reporting directly; it may instead reflect the agency's emphasis on the importance of mandatory reporting responsibilities. This may explain why Greytak (2009) found that having a standard procedure for reporting abuse was a component of school environments that fostered reporting. Teachers in schools with standard reporting procedures were more than six times as likely to be exposed to information about child abuse or mandatory reporting, were more knowledgeable about indicators of maltreatment and reporting procedures, and more confident in their abilities to identify maltreatment and make a report.

Training. It is not surprising that training on their responsibilities as mandated reporters correlates with professionals' reporting behaviors. Swartz (1995), cited by Gretak (2009), found that teachers who had more training were more likely to report abuse, but at least 3–4 h of training were required for the effect to be detectable. In the NIS–4 SDS (McPherson and Sedlak 2013), nearly one-fourth (24 %) of sentinels had neither received written instructions nor attended a workshop about their state's reporting requirements while working in their current agency. More sentinels who received training on mandated reporting at their current agency said they had reported suspected child maltreatment during their job tenure (67 %) compared to those who with no training (53 %).

Personal history, culture, and attitudes. Reporters' ethnicity and their views on the acceptability of corporal punishment can also influence reporting decisions, but the literature reveals complex interactions and mixed results. Ibanez and colleagues (2006) surveyed an ethnically diverse sample of 378 students at a southwestern university, assessing their acceptance of corporal punishment and level of ethnic identity, and asking whether they would report cases in vignettes that varied the child's ethnicity and described a parent using physical punishment. Level of ethnic identity and acceptance of corporal punishment predicted reporting decisions only for African Americans; those with high ethnic identity were less likely to indicate they would report the cases that featured an African American child and those accepting of corporal punishment were less likely to say they would report any cases, regardless of the child's ethnicity. The authors suggested that the findings reflect differences in ethnic cultures of in-group protectiveness and attitudes toward corporal punishment.

Ashton (2004) also found that reporter ethnicity, approval of corporal punishment, and immigration status all affected decisions to report child maltreatment in vignettes among 262 undergraduate students in a northeast metropolitan area. Students were more likely to say they would report maltreatment described in vignettes if they were White, born in the U.S., or disapproved of corporal punishment.

Lane and colleagues (2002) reviewed charts of 388 children at an urban children's hospital who were hospitalized for skull or long bone fractures. Reviewers classified injuries as accidental, abusive, or indeterminate. More minority children (28 %) experienced abuse compared to White children (12 %). Controlling for independent judgments of the likelihood of abuse and the appropriateness of performing a skeletal survey to detect occult fractures, minority children ages 12 months–3 years were more likely to receive a skeletal survey and to be reported to CPS.

Nevertheless, ethnicity has not consistently emerged as influential in child maltreatment reporting. Ashton (2010) administered a vignette survey to 808 social workers in New York and found that, although social workers of different ethnicities differed in their approval of corporal punishment and perception of maltreatment, they did not differ in their decisions about reporting maltreatment. Egu and Weiss (2003) studied 540 ethnically diverse elementary school teachers in California and found that neither child nor teacher ethnicity affected judgments about whether a vignette described abuse or should be reported.

Bluestone (2005) used several standardized scales to examine the personal histories of physical punishment and the perceived fairness of the discipline they received during childhood among 80 nursing and education students enrolled at an urban community college in New York. Respondents who reported histories of more severe physical punishment and who perceived their experience with discipline during childhood as fair tended to perceive more physical punishment behaviors as appropriate.

Why Mandated Reporters Fail to Report

Factors that contribute to discretionary reporting include reporters' concerns about compromising their rapport with the child and family, uncertainty as to whether a particular case warrants a report, and concerns about the ramifications of filing a report (Conti 2011; Dixon and Dixon 2007; Flaherty et al. 2004, 2006; Schultz 1990).

Lack of definitive evidence of maltreatment. Flaherty and colleagues (2006) conducted a mail-survey using a random sample of members of the American Academy of Pediatrics. The survey asked about their reporting of actual cases of child maltreatment as well as decisions about reporting based on a case vignette. A total of 851 members responded to the survey, an overall response rate of 53 %. Those who said they did not always report suspected child maltreatment said they based their decision on a lack of evidence of maltreatment and their belief that they could intervene with the family more effectively than CPS. Zellman (1990) found similar results in a cross-disciplinary study of 1,196 mandated reporters in 15 states (including medical and mental health professionals, social workers, child care professionals, and school administrators). Of the 40 % who said they did not always report suspected child maltreatment, most (60 %) cited lack of evidence as the main reason.

Level of severity of child maltreatment. The severity of the child maltreatment also influences decisions about reporting (Egu and Weiss 2003; Jones et al. 2008; Zellman 1990). Ashton (1999) surveyed 86 first-year social work graduate students in New York State using a series of vignettes that described problematic parent behaviors. Individual respondents were more likely to say they would report situations that they regarded as serious, but a given scenario required an extremely serious rating before the majority of respondents said they would report it to CPS. Participants were much more likely to report abuse that involved physical violence with imminent harm to young children. Similarly, O'Toole and Webster (1999) used case vignettes with a sample of 480 Ohio-based public school teachers and found that type of abuse (sexual abuse) and seriousness of the behavior in the vignette were the strongest predictors of decisions about reporting, with between five and eight times the impact of other case characteristics. Carleton (2006) surveyed 157 parents, day care providers, elementary and high school teachers, and undergraduate students in Ohio about whether they would report the emotional abuse described in a series of case vignettes. The perceived seriousness of the situation was most predictive of expected reporting behavior for both mandated and non-mandated reporters.

Family history and reporter familiarity with the child and family. Some studies demonstrate that reporting decisions relate to the professional's familiarity with the family and the family's history.

Examining data from a national survey of mandated reporters that used vignettes, Zellman (1992) found that reporters are more likely to intend to report when the family has a previous history of child maltreatment. Jones and colleagues (2008) found similar results when examining actual reporting behaviors among a sample of primary care clinicians. They conducted qualitative phone interviews with 75 pediatric primary care clinicians about their actual reporting behavior and found that their familiarity with the family, feedback from consultants, and the case history all affected their decisions to report suspicious injuries to CPS. Clinicians who said they had reported a child's injury to CPS also said they had little familiarity with the family or that they had previous child maltreatment suspicions about the family. Other case-specific factors that influenced CPS reporting were the inconsistencies between the family's explanation as to the cause of the injury and the characteristics of the injury itself, the clinician's inability to determine the cause of the injury after ruling out other medical diagnoses, and the family's delay in seeking treatment for the injury. Clinicians also weighed input from consulting with a colleague or other specialist in their decision to report.[14]

Experience with and perceptions of CPS. In understanding why mandated reporters do not report, it is important to recognize that reporting is an interactive system, with reporters' behavior shaped by their knowledge and expectations of CPS responses. Concerns about the quality of the services CPS provides and the expected outcomes from reporting, including the potential trauma the child might experience, have led some reporters to view the costs to the family as outweighing the benefits. Tilden and colleagues (1994) reported that only about one-half of the 755 social workers, psychologists, and physicians and less than two-fifths of 766 dental professionals and nurses believed mandated reporting of child abuse to be helpful in addressing the problem of abuse. Zellman (1990) found that 19 % of her sample of 1,196 mandated reporters identified the poor quality of CPS services as a key reason for their failure to consistently report suspected child maltreatment, while a similar percentage thought that they could do a better job of helping the child. Jones and colleagues (2008) found very similar results. In their study, the anticipated outcomes of reporting to CPS were a main factor influencing clinicians' decisions on reporting suspicious injuries they had treated. If reporters expected a negative outcome on the basis of their previous experiences with CPS, they did not report. Also, many who did not report felt they could monitor the situation and watch for additional injuries through follow-up sessions with the family. Carleton (2006) also found that belief in the efficacy of CPS predicted whether the 94 non-mandated reporters they surveyed said they would report the maltreatment described in the vignettes.

Studies also document professionals' concerns about the lack of CPS feedback about the case status and outcome after they make a report and their dissatisfaction with CPS intervention in child case reports they made in the past (Flaherty et al. 2000, 2004, 2006; Zellman 1990). Corroborating these results, the NIS supplementary study on CPS structures and practices (SPM) found that CPS agencies vary in whether they inform mandated reporters of the outcome of an investigation. Nearly one-half of local county CPS agencies (46 %) always notify the reporter, 42 % only sometimes notify the reporter, and 12 % never do so (Sedlak et al. 2013).

Summary of studies of mandated reporters. Studies of mandated reporters provide insight into a number of factors that influence decisions about reporting child maltreatment. Professional identity has a strong influence, with staff in law enforcement and health agencies more likely to report than school personnel or professionals in other agencies. Agency policies and training have an impact as well. Agencies differ in whether they allow direct reporting to CPS, with policies that bar direct reporting more common in schools. At the same time, professionals are more likely to report maltreatment when they receive adequate training on identifying symptoms of maltreatment and on their mandatory

---

[14] This study also demonstrated how the legal implications of failing to report can affect responses; some clinicians changed their original opinion that an injury was caused by abuse when explaining why they did not report the case to CPS.

reporting responsibilities. Professionals also report more when their workplace establishes clear procedures for reporting child maltreatment reporting, highlighting the importance of their responsibility. Interestingly, the inconsistent results related to reporters' personal characteristics, such as their culture and views on corporal punishment, suggest that other factors can override or modulate the influence of personal backgrounds and dispositions on professionals' reporting decisions.

The context and characteristics of the maltreatment also affect discretionary reporting. Reporters are more likely to decide to report cases that have a CPS history or when they regard the maltreatment as severe. In contrast, they are less likely to decide to report when the evidence of maltreatment is weak or unclear, when they are familiar with the family, and when they have concerns about the quality of services CPS will provide and the consequences of reporting.

These findings are illuminating, but caution in generalizing some of these conclusions is warranted, since most studies of mandated reporters are limited in scope, type of respondents, and geographical area. Professionals' statements about their reporting intentions in relation to vignettes may not correspond to their reporting behaviors when they encounter real cases in their workplace. Study designs have been disproportionately exploratory, providing descriptive results. Universally, they have been one-time efforts, which are not informative about trends or changes over time.

Conclusions

Federal and state legislation around child maltreatment reporting has been in effect for the better part of four decades. To ensure that maltreated children come to the attention of CPS, most states' mandatory reporting statutes identify categories of professionals who often come into contact with children and describe the types of maltreatment they must report.

National trends in rates of child abuse and neglect. Two sources indicate national trends: the NCANDS in referrals to CPS and CPS responses, and the NIS in both the maltreated children that professionals recognize and the percentage of maltreated children who receive CPS investigation. Both sources indicate that rates of sexual abuse and physical abuse have declined since the early 1990s. The NIS, which distinguishes emotional abuse and emotional neglect, also found that, since 1993, the rate of emotional abuse decreased, but the rate of emotional neglect increased.

If only NCANDS had observed declines in CPS substantiations of sexual and physical abuse, they could be discounted as reflecting changes in reporting or screening practices rather than true declines in prevalence. However, the fact that the NIS documents similar declines in the broader context of all children recognized by professionals (sentinels) argues against discounting them as reporting or screening artifacts. These declines are clearly not the result of CPS agencies' increasing use of alternative or differential response. Since the 2010 CAPTA reauthorization, which requires states to submit NCANDS data on their alternative response cases, NCANDS rates of sexual and physical abuse have continued to decline. Also note that the NIS includes all children who receive CPS investigation and uninvestigated children that sentinels recognize as maltreated, those who were screened out of CPS investigation (who could have received an alternative response) and those never reported to CPS.

The fact that findings from other studies of violence against juveniles also show declines implies that the actual occurrence of sexual and physical maltreatment events may have decreased (Finkelhor and Jones 2006). This is clearest for the decrease in sexual violence, for which the evidence is quite consistent and widespread, pervading victim self-report surveys and reported crime statistics.

The trend in physical abuse is less consistent across sources. As reported above, both NIS and NCANDS indicate declines in this category. However, other sources, such as hospitalization data, do not (Finkelhor and Jones 2012; Leventhal and Gaither 2012; Wood et al. 2012). Further analyses of the NIS, reported here, examined subcategories of physical abuse and found that the decline only applied for children moderately harmed or endangered by this maltreatment—the rate of children who were seriously or fatally injured by physical abuse did not decline. Perhaps sources that primarily encounter serious cases, such as hospitals, fail to see a decline in physical abuse rates. It could be that moderate and severe physical abuse trend differently. Trocme and Lindsey (1996) noted a number of studies showing that parents who severely injure or kill their children are more likely to have serious psychiatric problems than other physically abusive parents. If the incidence of these psychiatric problems in the parent population has remained fairly stable, one would expect rates of serious abuse to show little change over time, while for moderate physical abuse, more affected by other causal factors, rates may exhibit notable changes over time.

To advance our understanding of these issues, future research should look beyond trends in overall rates, examining different severities of abuse and their correlated problems (such as parental mental health problems) to determine how these relate to different trend results. Also note that trends in rates at the county, state, and regional levels have received scant research attention. Analyses that relate findings to differences in policies, service availability, or agency organization and procedures could help guide future decisions about policy, practice, and resource allocation.

Mandated reporting does not work as many might expect it should. Historically, the NIS has found that majorities of children in most maltreatment categories have gone uninvestigated. Although the NIS–4 found that the overall rate of investigation had increased significantly (to 43 %, up from 33 % in 1993), with higher percentages of emotionally abused, emotionally neglected, and sexually abused children receiving CPS investigation, the majority of maltreated children are still uninvestigated. Additional NIS findings indicate that this is largely due to the failure of mandated reporters to report these cases to CPS. If the NIS sentinels had reported these children to CPS, giving CPS the information they gave to the NIS, and if the CPS agencies applied the screening criteria that they said they use, then CPS would have investigated 80 % of the maltreated children NIS identified (Sedlak et al. 2010a). Another 12 % of the maltreated children were uninvestigated but living in CPS jurisdictions where they could have been assigned to an alternative response track if they had been reported to CPS. Thus, if all maltreated children NIS identified had been reported to CPS, only 8 % would not have received any CPS attention.

Given that the CPS system is the principal means of protecting children in the U.S., it relies on all mandated professionals reporting the maltreated children they see to CPS. The findings here indicate that this system is not working as many assume it does: professionals, especially those in hospitals, schools, day care, and shelters, report only a minority of the maltreated children they encounter. A number of studies document some of the barriers to reporting, such as lack of training, policies restricting or barring direct reporting, doubts about the quality of the evidence they observed, and concerns about the consequences of reporting.

How much of a problem is mandated reporting noncompliance? The mandatory reporting system is a work in progress. Despite the observed levels of noncompliance, findings also offer reasons for optimism. First, the rate of investigation has increased, as shown in Table 1.2, which implies that the rate of reporting has improved. Second, both NIS and NCANDS indicate that maltreatment has been declining in the categories of sexual abuse and physical abuse. Reduced rates of maltreatment occurrence indicate successful prevention—the ultimate goal of child protection. Finally, as described above, professionals sometimes decide not to report because they believe they can have a more positive impact on the situation in the context of their ongoing relationship with the family. It is not clear how many of the unreported maltreated children receive attention outside the traditional system and nothing is known about how their outcomes compare to the outcomes of similar children who are reported.

What can improve the current CPS system? Assuming that the preferred solution would be for the child protection system to work as originally envisioned, the findings reported in this chapter suggest several strategies that could raise rates of investigation and reporting. One avenue would improve CPS screening practices, identifying and altering those protocols that lower investigation rates by screening out cases that should receive attention. NIS found that CPS agencies that use state or regional hotlines investigate lower percentages of the maltreated children in their jurisdictions. This indicates that screening protocols have important effects that are not well understood. What procedures do state or regional hotlines employ that can influence the final clinical judgment about whether an investigation is warranted? Are there critical differences in their methods of inquiry, documentation, staff training and experience, or quality assurance checks that could be improved? Exactly what efficiencies are gained by centralizing the screening process? What measures are needed to ensure equivalent attention for the maltreated children they screen?

Another avenue would explore how CPS practices can improve reporting by addressing the lack of trust in CPS. Do media campaigns to enhance the public's perception of CPS have any impact on improving reporting behaviors? Several organizations, including Annie E. Casey Foundation (Bonk et al. 2001), the University of North Carolina at Chapel Hill School of Social Work (Jaudon and McMahon 2005), and American Public Human Services Association (APHSA) (APHSA 2010), have developed strategic communication resources for child welfare agencies to aid them in proactively shaping the public view of the agency. Better understanding of how to maximize the effectiveness of these communication strategies would help to guide CPS agencies' efforts to improve their relationships with their service communities.

How does policy affect compliance with mandatory reporting? The field should also continue to examine ways to improve child maltreatment reporting. One area that warrants particular attention is the impact of policy on nonreporting.

States' statutes are mute on required training for professionals who are mandated reporters, despite the evidence that this makes a difference, nor do the laws address workplace policies that may prohibit individual employees from reporting. How much could legislation that focused on these issues affect compliance with mandatory reporting requirements?

Additionally, the prevalence of nonreporting may in part derive from the fact that failure to report has no consequences for the mandated reporter in most states. According to 2011 information on states' mandated reporting statutes (Price 2012, updated from Child Welfare Information Gateway 2009b), the laws of 33 states do not specify any penalty for failure to report, while only 15 states' statutes indicate a fine, prison time, or both. The laws in just five states described conditions that would make nonreporting a felony; most of the remaining states considered nonreporting a misdemeanor or named it as an offense but did not classify it. Three states had no statute that explicitly mentioned nonreporting as an offense.

In the wake of recent, highly publicized cases of failures to report abuse (e.g., the Jerry Sandusky sex abuse scandal in Pennsylvania), state and federal attention has focused on legislative changes to increase penalties for nonreporting and/or expand the range of mandated reporters (Wolfe 2012). A number of states have recently considered or passed revisions to their laws on penalties for nonreporting, including Florida, Virginia, Kansas, and Maryland (Francilus 2012; Jackson 2012; Associated Press 2012; Sears 2012). However, even in states that specify penalties, prosecutions for nonreporting are rare. To inform future policy and legislation, it would help to know whether and how penalties for not reporting affect reporting behaviors.

What interventions with mandatory reporters can help? Research that documents systemic interventions to improve mandated reporting and evaluates their effectiveness is conspicuously lacking. The field could benefit by identifying efficient ways to enhance training and on identifying the most effective training approaches. Researchers could explore the type (pre-service or continuing education), content, approach, and amount of training that improves reporting among different types of professionals. For example, how effective is training on indicators of maltreatment or on the responsibilities of mandated reporters? Does training that incorporates information about CPS protocols, including the criteria for case substantiation, the reasons behind protective custody decisions, and the alternative services available (i.e. differential response) improve reporting? Does training that is led by CPS staff improve reporting? Is there something about the training that reporters with high investigation rates (e.g., law enforcement) receive that could benefit reporters that have lower investigation rates (e.g., school personnel)?

In order to substantially influence rates of reporting, the findings described in this chapter point to schools as the most promising place to begin. Because school professionals identify such large numbers of maltreated children, their low rate of reporting has a disproportionate impact on the overall low rate of CPS investigation (or other response). Future research should examine ways to address the specific barriers that reduce reporting by schools. How much of an influence do gatekeeping policies have on whether school personnel report cases and can these policies be modified? How can CPS involvement respect and support the school reporter's ongoing relationship with the child and family? Can CPS forge ongoing partnerships with schools to enhance school involvement in protecting children? A number of agencies have implemented variety of school-based prevention and family support programs, some of which include direct individual services (Crosson-Tower 2003; U.S. Department of Health and Human Services, Administration for Children and Families, Children's Bureau 2003b). Future efforts could benefit from a comprehensive inventory of the different school-based programs that are currently operating and a detailed assessment of their impact.

The foregoing synopsis of ways to improve rates of mandatory reporting begs the question of whether the current CPS is equipped to handle the influx of additional reports. The scenario in 1999 in Minnesota, when state legislators amended the definition of child neglect to include a child's exposure to domestic violence, is a cautionary tale of the disruption that can ensue when changes elicit an unexpected volume of new referrals (Edelson et al. 2006). Initially considered a simple change, it resulted in what Edelson and colleagues termed "great turmoil" throughout the state's county CPS agencies. The only additional funding appropriated was for newly instituted alternative response efforts in pilot counties, but with the new mandate, maltreatment referrals began to rise rapidly, with dramatic increases in caseloads—potentially more than 50 % statewide. With significantly more identification and screening, the strained system could provide fewer services to children. In response to pressure from an unlikely coalition of county social services administrators and the battered women's advocacy community, the state legislature essentially repealed the changed definition in 2000, and the system stabilized. However, thousands of children who were found under the expanded reporting guidelines to be in need of services are now no longer visible to the system. If improved compliance with mandatory reporting brings additional children to the attention of CPS, the system must be ready to serve them. Even simple changes can have dramatic, unintended negative consequences, and added resources must keep pace with expanded demand for them.

Can changes in the system better serve the children and families who need intervention? In his commentary, "Mandated reporting: A policy without reason," Melton (2005) offered a poignant scenario to illustrate the inherent problems with the current system: A neighbor observes that the children next door are poorly dressed and fed and are often left unsupervised. Realizing that their mother has multiple problems (financial and job insecurity, lack of child care resources or family support, chronic health problems, and depression), the neighbor calls CPS to get help for the family. She expects that her call will quickly trigger some basic services. However, the call is considered an allegation of wrongdoing and the agency investigates to determine if neglect occurred. If service is offered, it is likely to be a required parent education class—which will not address the family's immediate problems. The neighbor is not involved further, assuming she has fulfilled her legal and moral obligations. Moreover, when her call brings no relief, she may be less likely to turn to CPS in the future. The findings presented earlier in this chapter indicate the alternative scenario, in which even many professionals fail to report cases of maltreatment for various reasons, including not wanting to jeopardize their relationship with the family and not believing that CPS intervention will benefit the child or family.

An alternative or differential response system is an attempt to address the service needs of families referred to CPS who may benefit from interventions to enhance child safety and avoid the need for CPS involvement in the future. These innovations, which send lower risk families into an "assessment" rather than an "investigation" track, avoid applying punitive, blame-assignment procedures to these families and instead link them to services to prevent future maltreatment. As reported earlier, the NIS found that CPS agencies that can offer a differential, or alternative response track also investigate lower percentages of maltreated children in their jurisdictions, implying that these agencies divert some cases that might otherwise have received investigation to their alternative response track. Over the past decade, increasing numbers of states and local agencies have adopted or expressed interest in adopting a differential response option, despite the lack of standard criteria for screening cases in, variability in protocols for serving the families, and the fact that the jury is still out on evidence for a beneficial impact on children's safety and on the relative costs of the alternative response compared to traditional investigation.

Despite the popularity of alternative response, little is known about compliance with mandatory reporting laws in jurisdictions that provide an alternative response track. Initial reports on differential response efforts offer some preliminary indications that the effect on mandatory reporters is not entirely positive. In Colorado, Winokur and colleagues (2012) noted that, although most caseworkers felt the community responses were positive, some perceived the agency's move to a differential response option had strained the relationship between CPS and schools, law enforcement, and therapists. Also, in Colorado, school staff complained about the increased time it took to answer the agency's questions in their new screening practice, and in Colorado and Ohio county prosecutors, law enforcement officials, and guardians ad litem have had concerns about the safety of the children (Brown et al. 2012). In sum, although these programs are well-regarded by families and caseworkers, they may frustrate mandated reporters who have come to expect that their referrals will trigger investigation and more assertive intervention. At the same time, since the assessment option is entirely at the CPS agency's discretion, and since potential reporters may still regard CPS as primarily an investigative agency, they may not consider referring cases to CPS in order to obtain services for the families.

To date, most research attention has focused on alternative or differential systems that are administered within the CPS agency, with the agency deciding to assign the case to an assessment or investigation track during the screening process. In fact, the availability of multiple tracks for screened-in referrals was a core element of the differential response systems that American Humane and the Child Welfare League of America included in their national study (Kaplan and Merkel-Holguin 2008). However, other models, with response options not constrained within the CPS agency, also exist. For example, the California differential response model offers three pathways, the first of which applies to screened-out cases, which are formally referred to voluntary community service agencies (Bagdasaryan et al. 2008). Minnesota's Parent Support Outreach program began as service provision to screened-out cases but expanded to include self-referred families and families referred by community professionals or by the Temporary Assistance to Needy Families (TANF) program. Participating counties provided services either through community-based social service providers or, in counties with insufficient community providers, through the county child welfare agency (Thompson et al. 2008).

Little is known about how other approaches for dealing with families in need of services may affect mandated reporters. Are mandated reporters more likely to submit their concerns about the welfare of a child if they can refer the family for assessment and services without having to make an allegation of wrongdoing? Delaronde and colleagues (2000) asked professionals for their opinions of the existing reporting mandate and an alternative policy, whereby the reporter could report a suspected case to CPS or consult an independent Critical Intervention Specialist. Their alternative policy required that the reporter contact CPS about sexual abuse, serious physical abuse, and maltreatment that posed imminent danger for a child, but allowed the reporter to consult a Critical Intervention Specialist for other cases to determine how to deal with the case (including deciding whether to report it to CPS). Professionals who had not complied with the mandatory reporting law in the past were more likely to favor this alternative policy than were professionals who had been consistent reporters. Perhaps professionals who do not currently comply with mandatory reporting would improve if they could submit their concerns about a child who is not in imminent danger to an independent gateway to services. Of course, as they learn more about a family, the workers in this service gateway would report the case to CPS for an investigation if necessary, and as noted above, sufficient community services would have to be available to meet the increased demand for them. Future reform initiatives could consider approaches that allow the reporters to submit referrals through a gateway to social services that does not necessarily engage the traditional (investigatory) CPS agency functions. Future evaluations of reforms should attempt to assess their impact on mandatory reporting.

Acknowledgements   The authors thank the many colleagues who read, discussed, and critiqued earlier drafts of this chapter. George Gabel, Ronna Cook, and David Finkelhor provided especially helpful feedback, questions, and recommendations.

References

American Public Human Services Association (APHSA). (2010). *Positioning public child welfare guidance: Communications guidance*. Washington, DC: American Public Human Services Association. Available at: http://www.ppcwg.org/images/files/Communications%20Guidance(2).pdf.

Ashton, V. (1999). Worker judgments of seriousness about and reporting of suspected child maltreatment. *Child Abuse & Neglect, 23*(6), 539–548.

Ashton, V. (2004). The effects of personal characteristics on reporting of maltreatment. *Child Abuse & Neglect, 28*, 985–997.

Ashton, V. (2010). Does ethnicity matter? Social workers' personal attitudes and professional behaviors in responding to child maltreatment. *Advances in Social Work, 11*(2), 129–143.

Associated Press. (2012). *House approves Kansas child abuse reporting changes*. Wichita: The Wichita Eagle. February 23. Available at: http://www.kansas.com/2012/02/23/2227424/house-approves-kansas-child-abuse.html.

Bagdasaryan, S., Furman, W., & Franke, T. (2008). Implementation of California's differential response model in small counties, in Exploring Differential Response: One Pathway Toward Reforming Child Welfare. *Protecting Children, 23*(1&2), 40–56.

Bluestone, C. (2005). Personal disciplinary history and views of physical punishment: Implications for training mandated reporters. *Child Abuse Review, 14*, 240–258.

Bonk, K., Monihan, K., Combs, C., Omang, J., Mattingly, J., Goodhand, J., Good, M., Knipp, M., & Vincent, P. (2001). *Strategic communications: Media relations for child welfare*. Baltimore: Annie E. Casey Foundation, Family to Family Tools for Rebuilding Foster Care. Available at: http://www.aecf.org/upload/publicationfiles/strategic%20communications.pdf.

Bragg, H. L. (2003). *Child protection in families experiencing domestic violence*. Washington, DC: U.S. Department of Health and Human Services. Child abuse and neglect user manual series.

Brown, B., Merkel-Holguin, L., & Hahn, A. (2012). *Differential response: Early implementation and fidelity*. Cross-site report of the National Quality Improvement Center on Differential Response in Child Protective Services.

Carleton, R. A. (2006). Does the mandate make a difference? Reporting decisions in emotional abuse. *Child Abuse Review, 15*, 19–37.

Child Welfare Information Gateway. (2008). *Differential response to reports of child abuse and neglect*. Washington, DC: U.S. Department of Health and Human Services, Administration for Children and Families. Available at http://www.childwelfare.gov/pubs/issue_briefs/differential_response/.

Child Welfare Information Gateway. (2009a). *Child witnesses to domestic violence: Summary of state laws*. Washington, DC: U.S. Department of Health and Human Services, Administration for Children and Families. Available at http://www.childwelfare.gov/systemwide/laws_policies/statutes/witnessdv.cfm - _ftn3.

Child Welfare Information Gateway. (2009b). *Penalties for failure to report and false reporting of child abuse and neglect: Summary of state laws*. Washington, DC: U.S. Department of Health and Human Services, Administration for Children and Families. Available at http://www.childwelfare.gov/systemwide/laws_policies/statutes/reportall.pdf.

Child Welfare Information Gateway. (2011a). *Mandatory reports of child abuse and neglect: Summary of state laws.* Washington, DC: U.S. Department of Health and Human Services, Administration for Children and Families. Available at http://www.childwelfare.gov/systemwide/laws_policies/statutes/manda.cfm.

Child Welfare Information Gateway. (2011b). *Definitions of child abuse and neglect.* Washington, DC: U.S. Department of Health and Human Services, Administration for Children and Families. Available at http://www.childwelfare.gov/systemwide/laws_policies/statutes/define.cfm.

Conti, S. (2011). Lawyers and mental health professionals working together: Reconciling the duties of confidentiality and mandatory child abuse reporting. *Family Court Review, 49*(2), 388–399.

Crosson-Tower, C. (2003). *The role of educators in preventing and responding to child abuse and neglect.* Washington, DC: U.S. Department of Health and Human Services.

Daro, D., Budde, S., Baker, S., Nesmith, A., & Harden, A. (2005). *Creating community responsibility for child protection: Findings and implications from the evaluation of the Community Partnerships for Protecting Children Initiative.* Chicago: Chapin Hall at the University of Chicago. Available at http://www.chapinhall.org/research/report/creating-community-responsibility-child-protection-findings-and-implications-evaluat.

Delaronde, S., King, G., Bendel, R., & Reece, R. (2000). Opinions among mandated reporters toward child maltreatment reporting policies. *Child Abuse & Neglect, 24*(7), 901–910.

Dixon, J. W., & Dixon, K. E. (2007). Attorney-client privilege versus mandatory reporting by psychologists: Dilemma, conflict, and solution. *Journal of Forensic Psychology Practice, 6*, 69–78.

Edelson, J. L. (1999). Children's witnessing of adult domestic violence. *Journal of Interpersonal Violence, 14*(8), 839–870.

Edelson, J. L., Gassman-Pines, J., & Hill, M. B. (2006). Defining child exposure to domestic violence as neglect: Minnesota's difficult experience. *Social Work, 51*(2), 167–174.

Egu, C. L., & Weiss, D. J. (2003). The role of race and severity of abuse in teachers' recognition or reporting of child abuse. *Journal of Child and Family Studies, 12*(4), 465–474.

Farrow, F. (1997). *Child protection: Building community partnerships.* Cambridge, MA: Harvard University.

Finkelhor, D., & Jones, L. (2006). Why have child maltreatment and child victimization declined? *Journal of Social Issues, 62*(4), 685–716.

Finkelhor, D., & Jones, L. (2012). *Have sexual abuse and physical abuse declined since the 1990s?* Durham, NH: Crimes Against Children Research Center, University of New Hampshire.

Finkelhor, D., Jones, L., & Shattuck, A. (2013). *Updated trends in child maltreatment, 2011.* Durham, NH: Crimes Against Children Research Center.

Flaherty, E. G., Sege, R., Binns, H. J., Mattson, C. L., & Christoffel, K. K. (2000). Health care providers' experience reporting child abuse in the primary care setting. *Archives of Pediatrics & Adolescent Medicine, 154*, 489–493.

Flaherty, E. G., Jones, R., & Sege, R. (2004). Telling their stories; primary care practitioners' experience evaluating and reporting injuries caused by child abuse. *Child Abuse & Neglect, 28*, 939–945.

Flaherty, E. G., Sege, R., Price, L. L., Christoffel, K. K., Norton, D. P., & O'Connor, K. G. (2006). Pediatrician characteristics associated with child abuse identification and reporting: Results from a national survey of pediatricians. *Child Maltreatment, 11*(4), 361–369.

Francilus, J. (2012). '*Protection of vulnerable persons' act criminalizes failure to report child abuse in Florida.* New York, NY: The Huffington Post, October 1, 2012. Available at http://www.huffingtonpost.com/2012/10/01/new-florida-child-abuse-law_n_1929053.html

Greene, A.D., McPherson, K., & Sedlak, A.J. (2013). *Fourth national incidence study of child abuse and neglect (NIS–4): CPS Screening Policies Study (SPS).* OPRE Report. Washington, DC: Office of Planning, Research, and Evaluation, Administration for Children and Families, U.S. Department of Health and Human Services.

Greytak, E. (2009). *Are teachers prepared? Predictors of teachers' readiness to serve as mandated reporters of child abuse.* University of Pennsylvania. Publicly accessible Penn Dissertations. Paper 57. Available at http://repository.upenn.edu/edissertations/57

Hartge, J., Basena, M., Cober, C., Klein, S., & Sedlak, A. J. (2010). *Fourth national incidence study of child abuse and neglect (NIS–4) technical report II: Data collection report.* Rockville: Westat, Inc.. Prepared under contract to the U.S. Department of Health and Human Services.

Ibanez, E. S., Borrego, J., Pemberton, J. R., & Terao, S. (2006). Cultural factors in decision-making about child physical abuse: Identifying reporter characteristics influencing reporting tendencies. *Child Abuse & Neglect, 30*, 1365–1379.

Jackson, A. (2012). *Reports of suspected abuse now required: New state law now in effect.* Martinsville, VA: Martinsville Bulletin. August 19. Available at: http://www.martinsvillebulletin.com/article.cfm?ID=34340.

Jaudon, B., & McMahon, J. (2005). *Media outreach guide for rural child welfare agencies.* Chapel Hill: University of North Carolina. Available at: http://www.ruralsuccess.org/RSP_mediaguide.pdf.

Jones, R., Flaherty, E. G., Binns, H. J., Price, L. L., Slora, E., Abney, D., Harris, D. L., Christoffel, K. K., & Sege, R. D. (2008). Clinicians' description of factors influencing their reporting of suspected child abuse: Report of the child abuse reporting experience study research group. *Pediatrics, 122*(2), 259–266.

Kalichman, S. C. (1993). *Mandated reporting of suspected child abuse: Ethics, law, & policy.* Washington, DC: American Psychological Association.

Kaplan, C., & Merkel-Holguin, L. (2008). Another look at the national study on differential response in child welfare, in Exploring Differential Response: One Pathway Toward Reforming Child Welfare. *Protecting Children, 23*(1&2), 5–21.

Kempe, C. H., Silverman, F. N., Steele, B. F., Droegemueller, W., & Silver, H. K. (1962). The battered-child syndrome. *Journal of the American Medical Association, 181*(1), 17–24.

Lane, W. G., Rubin, D. M., Monteith, R., & Christian, C. W. (2002). Racial differences in the evaluation of pediatric fractures for physical abuse. *Journal of the American Medical Association, 288*(13), 1603–1609.

Leventhal, J. M., & Gaither, J. R. (2012). Incidence of serious injuries due to physical abuse in the United States: 1997–2009. *Pediatrics, 130*(5), 1–6.

Loman, L. A., Filonow, C. S., & Siegel, G. (2010). *Ohio alternative response pilot project evaluation: Final report.* St. Louis: Institute of Applied Research. Available at http://www.iarstl.org/papers/OhioAREvaluation.pdf.

McPherson, K., & Sedlak, A.J. (2013). *Fourth national incidence study of child abuse and neglect (NIS–4): Sentinel Definitions Survey (SDS).* OPRE Report. Washington, DC: Office of Planning, Research, and Evaluation, Administration for Children and Families, U.S. Department of Health and Human Services.

Melton, G. B. (2005). Mandated reporting: A policy without reason. *Child Abuse & Neglect, 29,* 9–18.

National Quality Improvement Center on Differential Response in Child Protective Services. (2011). *Differential response in child protective services: A literature review, version 2.* Aurora, CO: Kempe Center, University of Colorado. Available at http://www.ucdenver.edu/academics/colleges/medicalschool/departments/pediatrics/subs/can/DR/qicdr/Pages/Resources.aspx.

Nelson, B. J. (1984). *Making an issue of child abuse: Political agenda setting for social problems.* Chicago: University of Chicago Press.

O'Toole, R., & Webster, S. W. (1999). Teachers' recognition and reporting of child abuse: A factorial survey. *Child Abuse & Neglect, 23*(11), 1083–1101.

Price, S. (2012). *Penalities for failing to report suspected child abuse.* OLR Research Report. Hartford, CT: Connecticut General Assembly, Office of Legislative Research. Available at http://www.cga.ct.gov/2012/rpt/2012-R-0058.htm.

Schene, P. A. (1998). Past, present and future roles of child protective services. *The Future of Children, 8*(1), 23–27.

Schene, P. (2005). The emergence of differential response, in Differential Response in Child Welfare. *Protecting Children, 20*(2 and 3), 4–7.

Schultz, L. G. (1990). Confidentiality, privilege, and child abuse reporting. *Issues in Child Abuse Accusations, 2*(4). Northfield, MN: Institute for Psychological Therapies. Available at http://www.ipt-forensics.com/journal/volume2/j2_4_5.htm.

Sears, B. (2012). *Jacobs calls for penalty for failing to report child abuse.* Towson, MD: The Towson Patch, February 8, 2012. Available at http://towson.patch.com/articles/jacobs-calls-for-penalty-for-failing-to-report-child-abuse.

Sedlak, A. & Li, S. (2009). *Recent trends in local child protective services practices.* Washington, DC: U.S. Department of Health and Human Services. Office of the Assistant Secretary for Planning and Evaluation. Available at http://aspe.hhs.gov/hsp/09/TrendsinCPS/index.shtml.

Sedlak, A.J., Mettenburg, J., Schultz, D., & Cook, D. (2003). *Planning for NIS-4. Task 9B—enhancement option 2: NIS definitions review.* Report under contract No. 282-98-0015, Delivery Order No. 40 for the Children's Bureau, Administration on Children, Youth, and Families, U.S. Department of Health and Human Services. Rockville, MD: Westat.

Sedlak, A. J., Mettenburg, J., Basena, M., Petta, I., McPherson, K., Greene, A., & Li, S. (2010a). *Fourth national incidence study of child abuse and neglect (NIS–4): Report to Congress.* Washington, DC: U.S. Department of Health and Human Services, Administration for Children and Families. Available at http://www.acf.hhs.gov/programs/opre/research/project/national-incidence-study-of-child-abuse-and-neglect-nis-4-2004-2009.

Sedlak, A. J., Gragg, F., Mettenburg, J., Ciarico, J., Winglee, M., Shapiro, G., Hartge, J., Li, S., Greene, A., & McPherson, K. (2010b). *Fourth national incidence study of child abuse and neglect (NIS–4) technical report I: Design and methods summary.* Rockville: Westat, Inc. Prepared under contract to the U.S. Department of Health and Human Services.

Sedlak, A. J., Mettenburg, J., Winglee, M., Ciarico, J., Basena, M., Rust, K., Shapiro, G., Goksel, H., Hartge, J., Park, I., & Clark, J. (2010c). *Fourth national incidence study of child abuse and neglect (NIS–4) technical report III: Analysis report.* Rockville: Westat, Inc.. Prepared under contract to the U.S. Department of Health and Human Services.

Sedlak, A.J., McPherson, K., Shusterman, G., & Li, S. (2013). *Fourth national incidence study of child abuse and neglect (NIS–4): CPS structure and practices mail survey (SPM).* OPRE Report. Washington, DC: Office of Planning, Research, and Evaluation, Administration for Children and Families, U.S. Department of Health and Human Services.

Siegel, G., & Loman, L. (2006). *Extended follow-up study of Minnesota's family assessment response: Final report.* St. Louis: Institute of Applied Research. Retrieved from http://www.iarstl.org/papers/FinalMNFARReport.pdf.

Swartz, D. D. (1995). *Teachers' awareness of and willingness to report suspected child abuse*. Unpublished Dissertation. Bloomington, IN: Indiana University.

Thompson, D., Siegel, G. L., & Loman, A. (2008). The parent support outreach program: Minnesota's early intervention track, in Exploring Differential Response: One Pathway Toward Reforming Child Welfare. *Protecting Children, 23*(1&2), 23–29.

Tilden, V. P., Schmidt, T. A., Limandri, B. J., Chiodo, G. T., Garland, M. J., & Loveless, P. A. (1994). Factors that influence clinicians' assessment and management of family violence. *American Journal of Public Health, 84*(4), 628–633.

Trocmé, N., & Lindsey, D. (1996). What can child homicide rates tell us about the effectiveness of child welfare services? *Child Abuse & Neglect, 20*(3), 171–184.

U.S. Department of Health and Human Services, Administration on Children, Youth and Families. (2002). *Child maltreatment 2000*. Available at http://www.acf.hhs.gov/programs/cb/research-data-technology/statistics-research/child-maltreatment.

U.S. Department of Health and Human Services, Administration on Children, Youth and Families. (2003a). *Child maltreatment 2001*. Available at http://www.acf.hhs.gov/programs/cb/research-data-technology/statistics-research/child-maltreatment.

U.S. Department of Health and Human Services, Administration for Children and Families, Children's Bureau. (2003b). School-based child maltreatment programs: Synthesis of lessons learned. Available at https://www.childwelfare.gov/pubs/focus/schoolbased/index.cfm.

U.S. Department of Health and Human Services, Administration for Children and Families, Administration on Children, Youth and Families, Children's Bureau. (2006). *Child maltreatment 2004*. Available at http://www.acf.hhs.gov/programs/cb/research-data-technology/statistics-research/child-maltreatment.

U.S. Department of Health and Human Services, Administration for Children and Families, Administration on Children, Youth and Families, Children's Bureau. (2010a). *Child maltreatment 2008*. Available at http://www.acf.hhs.gov/programs/cb/research-data-technology/statistics-research/child-maltreatment.

U.S. Department of Health and Human Services, Administration for Children and Families, Administration on Children, Youth and Families, Children's Bureau. (2010b). *Child maltreatment 2009*. Available at http://www.acf.hhs.gov/programs/cb/research-data-technology/statistics-research/child-maltreatment.

U.S. Department of Health and Human Services, Administration for Children and Families, Administration on Children, Youth and Families, Children's Bureau. (2011). *Child maltreatment 2010*. Available from http://www.acf.hhs.gov/programs/cb/research-data-technology/statistics-research/child-maltreatment.

U.S. Department of Health and Human Services, Administration for Children and Families, Administration on Children, Youth and Families, Children's Bureau. (2012). *Child maltreatment 2011*. Available from http://www.acf.hhs.gov/programs/cb/research-data-technology/statistics-research/child-maltreatment.

Winokur, M., Drury, I., Batchelder, K., Mace, S., Amell, J., Bundy-Fazioli, K., & Tungate, S. (2012). *Colorado year 1 site visit final report*. Fort Collins: Social Work Research Center, Colorado State University. Available at http://www.colorado.gov/cs/Satellite?blobcol=urldata&blobheadername1=Content-Disposition&blobheadername2=Content-Type&blobheadervalue1=inline%3B+filename%3D%22Colorado+Year+One+Site+Visit.pdf%22&blobheadervalue2=application%2Fpdf&blobkey=id&blobtable=MungoBlobs&blobwhere=1251779502829&ssbinary=true.

Wolfe, D. S. (2012). Revisiting child abuse reporting laws. *Social Work Today, 12*(2), 14.

Wood, J. H., Medina, S. P., Feudtner, C., Luan, X., Localio, R., Fieldston, E. S., & Rubin, D. M. (2012). *Pediatrics, 130*(2), e358–e364.

Zellman, G. (1990). Child abuse reporting and failure to report among mandated reporters. *Journal of Interpersonal Violence, 5*(1), 3–22.

Zellman, G. L. (1992). The impact of case characteristics on child abuse reporting decisions. *Child Abuse & Neglect, 14*(3), 325–336.

Zielewski, E. H., Macomber, J., Bess, R., & Murray, J. (2006). *Families' connections to services in an alternative response system*. Washington, DC: Urban Institute.

Chapter 2
Child Neglect: Challenges and Controversies

Laura J. Proctor and Howard Dubowitz

Neglect is the most common and most frequently fatal form of child maltreatment, yet it continues to garner less attention than abuse in terms of research, financial allocation, policy initiatives, and public awareness. Child neglect poses unique challenges to researchers and policymakers, due in part to the inherent difficulties in reaching consensus on how best to define, understand, and respond to a heterogeneous, multiply-determined phenomenon that typically occurs not as a result of what adults do, but what they fail to do. Even more so than physical, sexual, and emotional abuse, child neglect disproportionately affects the poorest families and occurs on a continuum with no clear cut points. It tends to be chronic rather than episodic, frequently does not result in immediate harm to the child, and mostly lacks evidence of malicious intent. Three decades have passed since researchers first raised the alarm regarding the "neglect of neglect" (Wolock and Horowitz 1984), which referred to the lack of attention paid to neglect relative to abuse, despite evidence that it is far more common and just as harmful. In the intervening years, the importance of child neglect has been acknowledged both by researchers, who have produced a small but growing body of evidence on causes, consequences, and interventions (Kotch et al. 2008; Mills et al. 2011; Dubowitz et al. 2002; Chaffin et al. 2012; Slack et al. 2011), and by advocates and policy makers, who have made important advances in how we conceptualize and respond to this problem (Kaplan et al. 2009). There is no question that research, policy, and advocacy focusing specifically on child neglect have led to advances in recent years. However, it is still disproportionately understudied relative to physical and sexual abuse, given its high prevalence and deleterious impact on the child (Dubowitz 1994; Chaffin 2006). Furthermore, key areas of disagreement continue to hamper our knowledge and practice regarding child neglect.

L.J. Proctor, Ph.D. (✉)
Judge Baker Children's Center, Harvard Medical School, 53 Parker Hill Avenue, Boston, MA 02120, USA
e-mail: lproctor@jbcc.harvard.edu

H. Dubowitz, MB.Ch.B, MS, FAAP
Division of Child Protection Department of Pediatrics, University of Maryland School of Medicine, University of Maryland Medical Center, 520 W. Lombard Street, Baltimore, MD 21201, USA
e-mail: hdubowitz@peds.umaryland.edu

J.E. Korbin and R.D. Krugman (eds.), *Handbook of Child Maltreatment*, Child Maltreatment 2, DOI 10.1007/978-94-007-7208-3_2, © Springer Science+Business Media Dordrecht 2014

Defining Child Neglect

Challenges to Definitional Consensus

A first and necessary step for synthesizing research findings across studies and developing evidence-based policies is to reach consensus on what constitutes child neglect. This continues to pose a challenge for several reasons. Neglect is unique in that, unlike other forms of maltreatment, defining it does not typically involve an abusive act, but rather omissions in parental care. As with abuse, child neglect involves identifying a threshold that distinguishes neglectful parenting from non-neglectful parenting. Even physical abuse, which by comparison to neglect may seem straightforward to identify, has posed definitional challenges. When does corporal punishment cross the line into physical abuse? Does it depend on how old the child is? Whether an implement is used? How frequently it is applied?

In the case of neglect, defining the threshold at which less-than-optimal parenting crosses the line into child neglect has proven particularly elusive. Certain types of extreme situations, such a severely ill child who is not brought to medical attention or a toddler left unsupervised for hours, are more easily identified as neglect. Other omissions, such as not providing clean clothing, adequate food, or access to education, may only be recognized as neglect if an ongoing pattern is observed. Some forms of chronic under-stimulation, such as leaving young children in front of a television for hours each day, or providing them with few opportunities for interacting with responsive adults, may exert pernicious effects on the developing child without crossing the legal threshold into neglect (Center on the Developing Child at Harvard University 2012). Even in extreme incidents resulting in child fatalities, consensus can be difficult to reach regarding whether or not the parent or caregiver's behavior constituted neglect (Schnitzer et al. 2011). And because definitions of neglect typically include not only actual harm to the child, but also potential harm, it can be difficult to quantify how risky a situation must be before we consider it neglectful. Finally, different types of professionals may need to define neglect differently as a result of their differing mandates and roles. For example, a pediatrician focused on optimizing children's health may have a relatively low threshold for viewing a situation as neglect, whereas a child protective services (CPS) worker, guided by state law, usually has a higher threshold. A prosecutor is likely to have the highest threshold, pursuing only the most egregious cases of neglect.

Ideally, a definition of neglect would be based on empirical data demonstrating the actual or probable harm associated with particular circumstances. In practice, judgments regarding neglect tend to depend on multiple factors, including the immediate circumstances; characteristics of the parent, family, and home; the history of parental behavior; the age, abilities, and behavior of the individual child; and societal norms (Schnitzer et al. 2011; DePanfilis 2006). Nearly two decades after the National Academy of Sciences called for more stringent definitions of neglect (National Research Council 1993), no standard exists for operationalizing and measuring neglect during infancy, childhood and adolescence (Straus and Kantor 2005; Dubowitz et al. 1998, 2005; Coohey 2003; Burke et al. 1998; Sternberg and Lamb 1991; Zuravin 1999).

Parent-Focused (Omissions) Versus Child-Focused (Meeting Needs)

One fundamental tension that continues to thwart a consensus regarding what constitutes child neglect is whether definitions should focus on the behavioral omissions of parents or on the unmet needs of children. A focus on unmet needs suggests that neglect should be viewed as occurring when a child's basic needs are not adequately met, resulting in actual or potential harm (Dubowitz et al. 1993, 2005b). This child-focused perspective is in contrast to prevailing CPS definitions of neglect, based on parental omissions in care. Laws and policies at the State and Federal level typically define neglect in terms of parental failures to provide adequate care which result in actual harm or risk of harm to the child. At the federal level, the Child Abuse Prevention and Treatment Act (CAPTA) Reauthorization Act of 2010 offers states a minimal definition of abuse and neglect as a "recent act or failure to act on the part of a parent or caretaker, which results in death, serious physical or emotional harm, sexual abuse or exploitation, or an act or failure to act which presents an imminent risk of serious harm." At the state level, neglect is frequently defined as the failure or inability of a parent or other person responsible for the child to provide needed food, clothing, shelter, medical care, supervision, or education, causing actual or potential harm to the child's health, safety, and well-being (Ansell et al. 2012).

There are several advantages to the child-focused approach. It fits with a primary goal of helping ensure children's safety, health, and development. It is also less blaming and more constructive, a key issue as practitioners try to work with families (Dubowitz 2009). Child-focused definitions can draw attention to other potential contributors to the neglect that are frequently present, in addition to parents. This approach, in turn, encourages a broader policy response to the problems underpinning neglect.

Parents are primarily responsible for meeting their children's needs. However, ecological frameworks (Bronfenbrenner 1977, 1979; Belsky 1993) for understanding child neglect recognize that there are usually multiple and interacting contributors to how children's material, medical, emotional and educational needs are met. Some contributing factors are largely beyond parental control, such as flaws or failures in our economic, social, healthcare and educational systems. For example, children who experience food insecurity, a lack of health insurance, or homelessness can be construed as experiencing forms of societal failure, or neglect. There are ample data demonstrating that poverty jeopardizes children's health, development, and safety (Lempinen 2012; Yoshikawa et al. 2012; Leventhal and Brooks-Gunn 2011; Evans 2004; McLoyd 1998). Poverty can thus be construed as a form of societal neglect, particularly in a country with enormous resources. In a recent study comparing 20 Western countries based upon financial inputs and child mortality, UNICEF concluded that "the USA health care system appears the least efficient and effective in meeting the needs of its children" (Pritchard and Williams 2011). Some of the largest public health crises affecting youth are largely acknowledged as societal problems with structural causes. Infant mortality, childhood obesity, juvenile diabetes, asthma, poor dental health, lead poisoning, and preventable injuries have all been linked to extrafamilial environment, public policy, or system-level factors. The child protection system, however, focuses narrowly on parental or caregiver omissions in care (i.e., fault or accountability), although 12 state laws explicitly exclude circumstances attributable to poverty in their neglect definitions (Ansell et al. 2012).

A child-focused approach also has the potential for increasing consensus regarding what constitutes neglect. Over time and across societies, views have evolved of what are considered "basic" needs of children. The United Nations Convention on the Rights of the Child attests to a remarkable degree of agreement, as does research in the US comparing views of whites and African Americans, low and middle income groups (Dubowitz et al. 1998). "Basic" refers to a critical need that if not met would likely result in significant harm (e.g., inadequate food). Empirical evidence supports several needs as basic, including having adequate food, health care, shelter, education, supervision/protection, and emotional support and nurturance (Dubowitz et al. 2005; Prince and Howard 2002; Newman et al. 2010). Other concerns may emerge from a broad societal consensus, such as inadequate hygiene or sanitation, and inadequate clothing, which are typically considered neglect when persistent.

We advocate defining child neglect as any situation in which a child's basic needs are not adequately met, resulting in actual or potential harm (Dubowitz et al. 1993, 2005). This broad definition of neglect necessarily includes neglect resulting from conditions associated with poverty, rather than parental omissions. When unmet needs are determined to be largely a result of parental omissions, CPS involvement is appropriate. Alternative strategies, other than CPS, may be more appropriate for some types of unmet needs (e.g., food insecurity, homelessness). There is a challenge in the many situations of neglect with multiple and interacting contributors. The burdens of poverty are, for example, linked to parental mental health and substance abuse problems, impeding the care children receive.

Actual Versus Potential Harm

In theory, the importance of recognizing and responding to potential harm is widely accepted. Most state definitions of neglect now include circumstances of potential harm, in addition to actual harm. However, many of those laws further specify that the harm must be imminent. And in practice, the issue of potential harm is largely ignored, with families typically receiving attention only after harm has occurred. The issue of whether neglect definitions should require actual, potential, or imminent harm is of special concern because the impact of neglectful circumstances may only be apparent years later. While serious immediate harm can and frequently does result from child neglect, longer-term effects associated with the cumulative effects of chronic neglect are much more prevalent, if less visible (Nelson et al. 1993; Wilson and Homer 2005). Requiring that harm must be imminent is not consistent with the evidence regarding the consequences of child neglect, and creates an unnecessary barrier to intervention in situations where the harm, though serious and long-lasting, may be gradual and cumulative. From a research perspective, measuring the occurrence of neglect separately from harm to the child is critical in order to study the short- and long-term effects of child neglect (Straus and Kantor 2005).

In some instances, epidemiological data permit reasonable predictions of both the likelihood and severity of harm. For example, we can estimate the increased risk of a serious head injury from a fall off a bicycle when not wearing a helmet compared to being protected (Wesson et al. 2008). In contrast, predicting the likelihood of harm when an 8-year old is left home alone for a few hours is difficult. Such circumstances often only come to light when actual harm ensues. However, in many more instances, neglect occurs via the accumulation over time of multiple episodes that do not per se appear to qualify as neglect. Many parental lapses, such as not providing needed medication, lack of supervision, or inadequate hygiene, do not constitute child neglect when they occur once or sporadically. But as these sub-threshold episodes accumulate, they can result in a child's needs being chronically unmet. This non-episodic, chronic, and cumulative neglect is increasingly recognized by child welfare agencies, with more than 30 states adopting alternative response systems (DePanfilis 2006; Child Welfare Information Gateway 2012). However, substantial systemic and organizational barriers remain to be addressed before widespread changes in traditional CPS responses can occur (Steib and Blome 2009).

Heterogeneity of Neglect

Clearly, the different types of unmet needs children may experience represent a wide range of circumstances. In general, researchers, policymakers, and professionals describe several broad types of neglect (Sedlak et al. 2010). *Physical neglect* refers to the failure to meet a child's basic physical needs, such as food, clothing, shelter, personal hygiene, or medical care. Physical neglect also includes abandonment, refusal of custody, illegal transfer of custody, and unstable custody arrangements. *Medical neglect* occurs when a health care need is not met, due to either denial or delay of care. *Inadequate supervision* refers to not meeting a child's age-appropriate need for supervision and protection, either by a lack of supervision, supervision by inappropriate or unsafe caregivers, or exposure to hazards inside or outside of the home (e.g., weapons, drugs, poisons). *Emotional neglect* refers to not meeting the child's developmental or emotional needs, including inadequate nurturance or affection, chronic or domestic violence in the child's presence, ignoring the child's need for stimulation, isolating the child from others, involving the child in illegal activities, knowingly permitting drug or alcohol abuse or other maladaptive behavior, failure or refusal to seek needed treatment for a behavioral problem, inadequate structure, inappropriate expectations, or exposure to maladaptive behaviors and environments (e.g., drug trafficking). *Educational neglect* can refer to not enrolling a school-age child in school or providing appropriate homeschooling, refusing efforts to address a diagnosed special education need, knowingly permitting chronic truancy, or a pattern of keeping the child home without legitimate reason.

In addition to different types of neglect, it is useful to characterize other dimensions of the neglect – the severity, number of incidents (frequency), developmental timing, duration (or chronicity), and co-occurrence with abuse and other adversities. *Severity* is viewed in terms of the likelihood and seriousness of harm. A severe form of neglect is one where a child's inadequate care results in serious harm, actual or potential. And, the greater the likelihood of such harm, the more severe is the neglect. *Frequency*, or number of incidents, can be helpful in documenting an ongoing pattern. This dimension can be difficult to assess; the number of CPS reports offers a very crude proxy. *Developmental timing* is important to consider because the age and developmental stage of the child are closely linked to what a child's basic needs are, as well as the potential consequences of the neglect. *Chronicity*, a pattern of needs not being met over time, is a particularly salient dimension in the case of neglect. Some experiences of neglect are usually only worrisome when they occur repeatedly (e.g., poor hygiene or sanitation). Thus, assessing signs of chronicity is important when determining whether a particular experience constitutes neglect (Kaplan et al. 2009). Duration of CPS involvement, or the time between the first and most recent reports, may serve as a proxy for chronicity.

Importance of Chronicity

Although there are no longitudinal studies tracking temporal patterns of neglect from childhood to adolescence, there is evidence of the chronic nature of neglect compared to other types of maltreatment. In comparison to children who experience physical or sexual abuse, children who are neglected are more likely to experience re-reporting or recurrence (Fluke et al. 2005; DePanfilis and Zuravin 1998, 1999). Children who are re-reported to CPS are typically re-reported for multiple types of maltreatment, both within and across time (Jonson-Reid et al. 2003, 2010; Proctor et al. 2012). Regardless of the type of maltreatment reported initially (i.e., physical abuse, sexual abuse or neglect), re-reports are most likely to be for neglect (Jonson-Reid et al. 2003). These findings regarding the chronicity of neglect are consistent with evidence that parenting practices and family interaction dimensions in general are relatively stable over time (Forehand and Jones 2002; Loeber et al. 2000; Pettit et al. 2001). At the same time, there is also evidence of contextually-based variability and change over time in parenting (Holden and Miller 1999). Increased knowledge about temporal patterns of neglect and the correlates of stability and change is important, given the links between temporal patterns of maltreatment and youth outcomes (English et al. 2005; Thornberry et al. 2001; Ireland et al. 2002) (Smith et al. 2005; Kaplow and Widom 2007; Thornberry et al. 2010). There is strong evidence that the multiple victimizations and adversities reflected by re-reports exert a cumulative influence on children's short- and long-term health and behavior (Turner et al. 2010; Chapman et al. 2007; Dube et al. 2003a; Whitfield et al. 2003; English et al. 2005), especially if they persist across developmental periods (English et al. 2005; Jaffee and Maikovich-Fong 2011). Repeated reports also place a tremendous burden on CPS resources. It has been estimated that cases with multiple referrals cost CPS seven times that of other cases (Loman 2006). For these reasons, learning how to best serve families who are at high risk for recidivism is critical for promoting child safety, permanency, and well-being and has important implications for effective, sustainable practice and policy.

Developmentally Appropriate Definitions

Children's needs change dramatically over the course of development. Although there is broad consensus that definitions of neglect should be developmentally sensitive (National Research Council 1993; Straus and Kantor 2005; Black and Dubowitz 1999; Slack et al. 2003), research and practice to date have focused almost exclusively on infants and young children. In contrast, very little work has been done on the neglect of adolescents' basic needs (Clark et al. 2004; Williamson et al. 1991; Rees et al. 2011). A focus on unmet needs can be useful for informing developmentally sensitive definitions of neglect during middle childhood and adolescence. During adolescence, youth clearly depend less on their parents for immediate physical supervision, protection, and fulfillment of physical needs. Nonetheless, there are compelling reasons to identify and respond to neglect in adolescence. Adolescence is second only to infancy in terms of physical, cognitive, behavioral, and social changes (Feldman and Elliott 1990; Eccles 1999). The many transitions of adolescence offer both opportunity and risk (Graber and Brooks-Gunn 1996). Positive developmental pathways may be disrupted, and earlier negative patterns may be reversed. As adolescents negotiate these transitions, they continue to depend on their parents in a number of important ways. Adolescents demonstrate greater risk taking and susceptibility to peer influence (Gardner and Steinberg 2005), and poorer judgment (Cauffman and Steinberg 2000) than adults. As a result, current biopsychosocial perspectives consider the entire adolescent period to be a uniquely vulnerable period. Child needs shift from direct supervision and assistance with immediate physical needs to a combination of monitoring and emotional support. Parents play a critical role in protecting adolescents from risks and promoting their successful negotiation of developmental tasks and adjustment to new transitions (Fergus and Zimmerman 2005; Masten et al. 1999).

Cultural Context

Another issue is the cultural context in which neglect is defined. For example, in many cultures, young children help care for their younger siblings. This is both a necessity and considered important in learning to be responsible. Yet, others may view the practice as unreasonably burdensome for the child caregiver and too risky an arrangement. There is no easy resolution to such a debate. Clearly, the risks and supports in the United States might be very different from those in the country of origin. There is a need to recognize the importance of the cultural context and how it influences child rearing practices and the meaning and consequences of experiences for children. It is, however, also important to recognize that just because a certain practice is normative within a culture, does not necessarily mean that it does not harm children (Korbin and Spilsbury 1999).

Incidence/Prevalence

Attempts to estimate the true incidence of child neglect are sharply limited by definitional issues and by the fact that its effects can be less immediately visible than those of physical or sexual abuse. Despite these limitations, federal and other statistics provide evidence that neglect is far more common than other types of maltreatment, tends to co-occur with other types of maltreatment, and – in contrast with observed trends for abuse – does not appear to be declining.

The annual *Child Maltreatment* report provides incidence statistics based on CPS data collected through the Children's Bureau's National Child Abuse and Neglect Data System (NCANDS). In 2010, as in prior years, neglect was the type of maltreatment most frequently substantiated by CPS

(Kumsta et al. 2010). Four-fifths (78.3 %) of substantiated CPS reports were for neglect and an additional 2.4 % were for medical neglect, compared to 17.6 % for physical abuse, 9.2 % for sexual abuse, and 8.1 % for psychological maltreatment, (another 10.3 % of substantiations were for "other" types of maltreatment that may be conceptually linked to neglect, including abandonment and newborn drug exposure). This translates to a rate of 80 per 1,000 children identified as neglected. Additionally, 68.1 % of reported maltreatment fatalities involved neglect either alone or in combination with another maltreatment type. Most of these were due to lapses in supervision contributing to deaths by drowning or in fires. While rates for substantiated physical and sexual abuse declined by 55 % and 65 % respectively between 1992 and 2009 (Jones and Finkelhor 2009), rates for substantiated CPS reports of neglect have remained fairly stable since the early 1990s (Kumsta et al. 2010).

Because child maltreatment is often not observed, detected, or reported to CPS, the National Incidence Studies of Child Abuse and Neglect (NIS) offer a preferable estimate of maltreatment incidence. The NIS includes children identified as maltreated by professionals trained to act as sentinels in a representative sample of US counties. The NIS-4 gathered data for 2005–2006. Including children who were either harmed or endangered, neglect was identified in 30.6 per 1,000 children, compared to 6.5 for physical abuse, 4.1 for emotional abuse, and 2.4 for sexual abuse. Incidence rates for specific types of neglect were 16.2 per 1,000 for physical neglect, 15.9 for emotional neglect, and 4.9 for educational neglect (Sedlak et al. 2010). One important limitation of the NIS is that it does not include laypersons as sentinels, even though they are typically the source of almost half of all CPS reports. Thus, it provides a gross underestimate of actual neglect.

The first and second National Surveys of Child and Adolescent Well-Being (NSCAW I and II) (Administration on Children, & Youth and Families 2010; Casanueva et al. 2011) also provide nationally representative data on rates of neglect among children and families in the child welfare system. NSCAW I (Administration on Children, & Youth and Families 2010) studied more than 5,000 children (ages 0-14) who entered the child welfare system between October 1999 and December 2000. Focusing on the most serious of the forms of maltreatment children experienced, neglect was the primary cause for placement for 60 % of the children. Of these children, equal percentages had experienced "failure to provide" and "failure to supervise." Ten percent of the children experienced physical abuse, and 8 % suffered sexual abuse. Among the four most common types of maltreatment (physical abuse, sexual abuse, failure to provide, and failure to supervise), 41 % of children experienced more than one of type of maltreatment. For example, nearly two-thirds of those experiencing sexual abuse were not adequately supervised. NSCAW II (Casanueva et al. 2011) used a similar sampling strategy to NSCAW I, and includes 5,873 children (ages 0-17.5 years) who entered the child welfare system between February 2008 and April 2009. Overall, neglect was the most prevalent (51.8 %) and often considered by caseworkers the most serious type of maltreatment for an individual child (32.5 %).

In addition to federal incidence studies, the Adverse Childhood Experiences (ACE) and National Comorbidity Survey Replication (NCS-R) also collected retrospective prevalence data with adults as part of the larger effort to study the health impact of childhood adversities. Differences in measurement and sampling, as well as the limitations of retrospective data, complicate the interpretation of differing prevalence rates. The ACE Study, conducted by the Centers for Disease Control and Prevention and Kaiser Permanente in San Diego, found that among more than 17,000 adult patients assessed in face-to-face interviews between 1995 and 1997, 14.8 % reported experiencing emotional neglect and 9.9 % reported experiencing physical neglect prior to age 18 (Dong et al. 2004). Rates of co-occurrence among the multiple adversities assessed was high (Dong et al. 2004). The NCS-R found that among a nationally representative sample of more than 9,000 adults assessed in face-to-face interviews during 2001–2003, 5.6 % reported neglect (Green et al. 2010).

Additionally, data exist from a variety of other sources on what may be termed societal neglect – circumstances where children's material, medical, or educational needs are not adequately met largely because of gaps in services and inadequate policies and programs. In the United States, more than 16 million children, or one in five, live in poverty (Dobrova-Krol et al. 2010) or in a household experiencing food insecurity, meaning that access to adequate food is limited by a lack of money and other resources (Roth and Sweatt 2011). Over seven million children lack health insurance (Cohen and Martinez 2012). Some 1.6 million children annually experience homelessness (Roth et al. 2006). Two-thirds of U.S. eighth graders score below the proficient level on the National Assessment of Educational Progress (NAEP) in reading (66 %) or mathematics (65 %) (Ethier and Milot 2009; Martínez 2008). Approximately 24,000 youth workers are injured on the job annually (Bureau of Labor Statistics et al. 2011), and in 2011, 82 youth workers age 19 and under suffered a fatal work-related injury (Bureau of Labor Statistics and U.S. Department of Labor 2011).

Risk Factors

There is no single cause of child neglect. On the contrary, a child whose basic needs are not being met typically represents a complex breakdown involving multiple levels of the child's environment. Contributing factors include societal, community, and familial contexts, as well as individual (parent and child) factors. For example, although maternal factors such as depression and substance use are often associated with child neglect, they do not necessarily lead to neglect. The likelihood of neglect increases when such individual problems occur within the context of societal and community risks such as poverty, a lack of neighborhood resources, and social isolation. Understanding the failure to meet a child's basic needs is not difficult when we consider, for example, the situation of a low-income single mother living in a dangerous neighborhood with two young children – one with ADHD, the other with severe asthma – who is being evicted and has little social or material support.

Ecological-developmental theories (Bronfenbrenner 1977, 1979; Belsky 1993), which emphasize the dynamic nature of relations among individuals, the immediate settings in which they live, and the larger context in which both individuals and settings are embedded, provide a helpful framework for discussing and studying factors that contribute to child neglect. Most parents whose children's needs are not being met are struggling with the accumulation of multiple stressors. Research has identified many factors that are correlated with neglect, but we still know very little about why some families exposed to these factors go on to experience child neglect, and others do not. A primary limitation regarding our knowledge of risk factors for child neglect is the paucity of prospective research. This makes it exceedingly difficult to distinguish between predictors, consequences, and correlates of neglect. Another key limitation is that most research has focused on parental problems, with much less attention to community and societal problems such as food insecurity and lack of health insurance. A more nuanced understanding of the factors that contribute to child neglect will necessarily involve increased attention not just to risk factors but to risk processes (Luthar 2006; Rutter 2006). More theory-based research is needed on mediator and moderator processes associated with neglect, as well as interactions between factors at multiple levels of the environment. While research has contributed knowledge to each of these areas, longitudinal studies that follow families over time and examine multiple levels of the environment are scarce.

Societal Context

Poverty

Neglect is the type of maltreatment most strongly linked to poverty. In NIS-4, the rate of neglect for children in low socioeconomic status households was nearly seven times higher than for other children (46.5 vs. 6.7 per 1,000) (Sedlak et al. 2010). However, most low-income families do not neglect their children. The direct effects of poverty on children and the co-occurrence of poverty and neglect make it difficult to disentangle their effects. In addition to its influence on family functioning, poverty directly threatens and harms children's health, development, and safety in a multitude of ways. It increases children's exposure to environmental hazards (e.g., lead, violence), hunger, a lack of recreational opportunities, low quality schools, and inferior health and health care (Evans 2004; McLoyd et al. 2006; Blair et al. 2011; Lipina and Colombo 2009), and jeopardizes their health status (Dobrova-Krol et al. 2010; Lipina et al. 2009), adaptive behavior (Slopen et al. 2010), and academic and professional attainment (Lipina et al. 2009; Howard et al. 2009b; McLoyd et al. 2009) not only during childhood, but into adulthood (Lipina and Colombo 2009; Luthar 1999; Duncan and Brooks-Gunn 1997). Poverty can also contribute to other risk factors for neglect, such as food insecurity, poor maternal nutrition, maternal depression, and stressful life events (Weill 2012; Belle 1990). Poverty, of course, is not distributed randomly. Children who are African American or Hispanic, live in single-mother families, or are under age five are most likely to be poor (Dobrova-Krol et al. 2010).

Countries differ in their provision of a social safety net, or social services, aiming to reduce poverty and poverty-related suffering. The US has one of the highest child poverty rates among high income nations, yet one of the smallest safety nets (Mishel et al. 2012). Programs designed to provide income (e.g., Earned Income Tax Credit, unemployment insurance, Temporary Assistance to Needy Families, or federal housing subsidies) or meet the needs of families with children (e.g., Medicaid, Supplemental Nutrition Assistance Program [SNAP] or Food Stamps, Head Start, WIC, public housing) have an impact both on maltreatment rates (Lee and Mackey-Bilaver 2007) and on the health and development of children living in poverty (Hinrichs 2010; Currie 2006).

Child Welfare and Health Professions

In addition to policies affecting poverty, society also influences the risk of child neglect via the social work and health care professions that serve children. The child welfare system (Child Welfare Information Gateway 2011), the very system intended to assist children in need of care and protection, can contribute to neglect. As painfully articulated in 1991 by the National Commission on Children, "If the nation had deliberately designed a system that would frustrate the professionals who staff it, anger the public who finance it, and abandon the children who depend on it, it could not have done a better job than the present child welfare system" (National Commission on Children 1991). Inadequately financed, with staff who are generally undertrained and overwhelmed, and with poorly coordinated services, CPS are often unable to fulfill their mandate of protecting children. In the case of health professionals, problematic communication with parents not understanding their child's condition or treatment plan is pervasive (Farrell and Kuruvilla 2008), and at times health professionals themselves fail to comply with recommended procedures and treatments, thereby compromising children's health (Lam et al. 2004). They may also fail to detect children's medical or psychosocial needs, perhaps contributing to their neglect.

Community/Neighborhood Context

Social Capital

The community context and its resources influence parent–child relationships and are strongly associated with child maltreatment (Garbarino and Crouter 1978; Garbarino 1991; Garbarino and Kostelny 1992; Garbarino and Barry 1997). A community rich in social capital, such as family-centered activities, quality and affordable child care, and a good transportation system, enhances the ability of families to nurture and protect their children. Informal support networks, safety, and recreational facilities also support healthy family functioning. Garbarino and Crouter (1978) described the feedback process whereby neighbors may monitor each other's behavior, recognize difficulties, and intervene. This feedback can be supportive, diminish social isolation, and help families obtain services. On the other hand, families in neighborhoods characterized by few social services may be less able to give and share, and may be mistrustful of neighborly exchanges (Garbarino and Sherman 1980). In this way, a family's problems may be compounded rather than ameliorated by the neighborhood context, increasing the risk that families' and children's needs will not be met.

Family Context

Parent–Child Relationship

Numerous studies on dyadic interactions have found evidence of disturbances in parent–child relationships among families of neglected children, including less mutual engagement by both mother and child (Dietrich et al. 1983) and disturbances in attachment between mother and infant (Crittenden 1985; Egeland and Vaughn 1981). Parents of neglected children interact less with their children (Bousha and Twentyman 1984) and have more negative interactions with their children (Burgess and Conger 1978), compared to parents of both abused and non-maltreated children. In one observational study, neglectful mothers, compared with non-neglectful mothers, provided less support in response to their children's emotional cues, were less likely to discuss feelings with the children, and reported more negative emotion (Edwards et al. 2005).

Stressful Life Experiences

The cumulative stress experienced by families has been strongly associated with child maltreatment. Among caregivers reported for maltreatment in NSCAW II, more than half were experiencing high levels of stress; almost half did not have another supportive adult in the household, and about a quarter were having trouble paying for basic necessities (Casanueva et al. 2011). Among maltreatment types, neglect, in particular, has been associated with high levels of stress. In one study, the highest level of stress, reflecting concerns about unemployment, illness, eviction, and arrest, was noted among families of neglected children compared with abusive and control families (Gaines et al. 1978).

Family Chaos and Violence

Family chaos and the parent characteristics that are associated with it have been linked to child neglect. Observed family interactions have suggested that families with child neglect are less organized, more chaotic, less verbally expressive, and showed less positive and more negative affect than comparison families (Gaudin et al. 1996). Based on 25 years of research on child neglect, Polansky observed that neglectful families tended to differ markedly from other families with regard to composition, stability, and caregiver's global level of functioning (Polansky et al. 1992). He noted that families of neglected children tend to be fragmented and characterized by constant change, with the caregiver and children moving in and out of living situations with others. Similarly, in his work with neglected children, Kadushin (1988) described chaotic families with impulsive mothers who repeatedly demonstrated poor planning and judgment, coupled with either father absence or negative mother-father relationships. Intimate partner violence has also been linked to an increased risk of child neglect (Dixon et al. 2007; McGuigan and Pratt 2001).

Individual Parent Factors

Caregiver Depression

Maternal depression has consistently been identified as a predictor of neglect (Kotch et al. 1995; Chaffin et al. 1996). Depression can interfere with mothers' ability to provide consistent affectionate, stimulating contact to their infants, and in extreme cases, mothers may be unable to respond to their children's needs at all (Crittenden 1999). A meta-analysis by Lovejoy and colleagues (Lovejoy et al. 2000) found that the relation between maternal depression and negative maternal parenting behavior was moderated by timing of the depression, with the strongest effects for current, as opposed to past, depression. In addition, effects were strongest for low-income women and mothers of infants, highlighting the vulnerability early in life when women are transitioning to a new role and may have limited support and confidence, particularly in low-income communities. There is also preliminary evidence that paternal depression predicts neglect in father-involved families (Lee et al. 2012).

Substance Use

Parental substance abuse has long been associated with child neglect (Chaffin et al. 1996; Kelleher et al. 1994; Kirisci et al. 2001; Ondersma 2002; Stewart et al. 2006) and with maltreatment re-referral and recurrence, which typically involve neglect (Laslett et al. 2012; Brook and McDonald 2009; Fuller and Wells 2003; Connell et al. 2007; Wolock et al. 2001). Using prospective data from the National Institute of Mental Health's landmark Epidemiologic Catchment Area survey, Chaffin and colleagues (Chaffin et al. 1996) found that among non-maltreating parents, substance abuse tripled the risk of subsequent child neglect. When studied together, substance abuse appears to be a relatively stronger predictor of neglect compared with other parent risk factors such as depression, social support, and negative life events (Chaffin et al. 1996; Ondersma 2002; Laslett et al. 2012; Brook and McDonald 2009; Fuller and Wells 2003; Connell et al. 2007; Wolock et al. 2001). It also predicts severity of neglect (Kirisci et al. 2001). Substance abuse also predicts maltreatment re-referral when the child remains with the reported parent (Connell et al. 2007), as well as reentry to care following reunification for children who are placed in foster care (Brook and McDonald 2009). There is evidence that both alcohol and drug abuse confer similar risk for recurrence (Laslett et al. 2012).

Isolation and Lack of Social Support

Neglect has been associated with social isolation (Berlin et al. 2011; Polansky et al. 1985b). Single parenthood without support from a spouse, family, or friends poses a risk for neglect. Neglectful parents report greater loneliness and weaker informal social supports than non-neglectful controls (Gaudin et al. 1993). In one study, mothers of neglected children perceived themselves as isolated and as living in unfriendly neighborhoods (Polansky et al. 1985a). Their neighbors saw them as deviant and avoided social contact with them. Mothers of neglected children may have less help with child care and fewer enjoyable social contacts compared with those where neglect was not a concern (Jones and McNeely 1980). Another study found that maltreating parents showed lower levels of community integration, participation in community social activities, and use of formal and informal organizations than did parents providing adequate care (Gracia and Musitu 2003). Seagull (1987) asked whether social isolation is a contributory factor to neglect or a symptom of underlying dysfunction. In any case, social isolation appears to be strongly associated with child maltreatment, and particularly with neglect.

Developmental History, Personality, and Level of Functioning

A wide body of evidence suggests that mothers who were maltreated as children are at much higher risk of neglecting or abusing their own children than other mothers. There is some evidence of specificity for maltreatment type, with mothers who were neglected as children being more than twice as likely as other mothers to neglect their own children (Kim 2009). In the case of neglect, the notion of intergenerational transmission rests generally on the observation that a neglectful childhood diminishes the psychological resources available to a parent (Belsky 1993). In his work with families in Appalachia and Philadelphia, Polansky focused heavily on parental personality and level of functioning as contributors to child neglect (Polansky et al. 1981, 1985). He described low-functioning mothers with pervasive coping deficits who tended to fit one of two profile types: "apathetic-futile" or "impulse-ridden" (Polansky et al. 1981). Deficient parental problem-solving skills, poor parenting skills, and inadequate knowledge of children's developmental needs have also been associated with neglect (Polansky et al. 1985a, b; Herrenkohl et al. 1983).

Information Processing

Researchers have begun examining the ways in which parental deficits in social information processing (i.e., encoding and interpretation of cues, goal selection, access to possible responses, and response decision) may contribute to child neglect by impairing accurate recognition of, and response to, children's emotions and needs (Crittenden 1993, 1999; Hildyard and Wolfe 2007; Azar et al. 2012). Crittenden (1993, 1999) described three types of neglect patterns associated with deficits in cognitive processing, affective processing, or both. The first type, "disorganized," describes families who respond impulsively and emotionally. The family operates in a crisis mode and appears chaotic and disorganized, overlooking the child's needs. The second type, "emotionally neglecting," includes families who may handle the demands of daily living (e.g., ensuring food and clothing), but are minimally attentive to their child's emotional needs. The third type, "depressed," describes families with depressed caregivers who are unable to process either cognitive or affective information, leaving children to fend for themselves emotionally and physically (Crittenden 1999). Consistent with these findings, one study of event-related potentials (ERPs) recorded from neglectful and control mothers as they viewed and categorized pictures of infant cries, laughs, and neutral faces found that neglectful mothers displayed an overall attenuated brain response in late positive potentials that was related to their higher scores in social anhedonia (Rodrigo et al. 2011). This finding suggest that the brain's failures in the early differentiation of cry stimuli and in the sustained processing of infant expressions related to social anhedonia may underlie the insensitive responding in neglectful mothers.

Child Factors

There is evidence that children with developmental disabilities are at heightened risk of maltreatment, yet are underreported and underserved compared to the general population of children (Fudge Schormans and Sobsey 2007; Bruhn 2004; Hibbard and Desch 2007). However, children with substantiated maltreatment who have disabilities may be more likely to be placed in out of home placement than those without disabilities (Lightfoot et al. 2011). More research is needed in order to provide more accurate population-based statistics both on incidence and on service needs and provision with this population of vulnerable youth (Horner-Johnson and Drum 2006; Kendall-Tackett et al. 2005).

There is also evidence that behavioral or mental health problems increase risk of maltreatment for young children (Jaudes and Mackey-Bilaver 2008), as do maternal perceptions of child temperament. In one study, maternal reports of more difficult child temperament predicted emotional, but not physical neglect (Harrington et al. 1998). Another study reported that physical victimization by an intimate partner and the mother's own childhood history of maltreatment were significantly associated with the mother's perception of difficult temperament (Casanueva et al. 2010).

Protective Factors

Very little research has been conducted specifically on protective factors for child neglect. Knowledge regarding protective factors that may prevent the occurrence of neglect is urgently needed to support and inform strength-based and health-promotion approaches for preventing child neglect.

General Factors

Ecological-developmental theories (Bronfenbrenner 1977, 1979; Belsky 1993) suggest that protective factors may occur at multiple levels of the environment. These may be individual caregiver characteristics (e.g., parental sense of competence) or environmental (e.g., social support, neighborhood resources). For example, there is longstanding support for the protective effect of a strong social network. Higher levels of social support are, for example, associated with lower rates of physical neglect, and increased use of nonphysical disciplinary methods (McCurdy 2005). Another potential protective factor is a parent's sense of competence or efficacy regarding their parenting; it may offset the challenges of child rearing and help prevent neglect (Coleman and Karraker 1998).

Context-Specific Factors

Resilience (Luthar 2006) perspectives stress that risk and protective factors do not exert the same influence across settings, but are instead specific to the particular context of each high-risk setting (Luthar 2006; O'Connell et al. 2009.) The high-risk setting for most child neglect is one characterized by poverty and multiple stressors in combination with individual parent risk factors. At the same time, children's basic needs are met in many families who share similar characteristics. A handful of studies have identified protective or promotive factors that may distinguish between these high-risk families and families in which child neglect occurs. These studies have homed in on hypothesized protective factors with high salience to the specific context of child neglect. For example, child neglect occurs disproportionately, but not exclusively, in single parent families (Connell-Carrick 2003). One study found that while presence of a father or father figure was not enough to protect against neglect, fathers who had been involved for a longer period of time, who felt more efficacious in their parenting, and who were more involved in household tasks were less likely to have neglected children (Dubowitz et al. 2000). Father presence has also been associated with better cognitive development and greater perceived competence and social acceptance by children in high-risk settings. Among children in the multisite Longitudinal Studies of Child Abuse and Neglect (LONGSCAN) consortium, child reports of father support were linked to child self-perceptions of competence including social competence, and fewer depressive symptoms (Dubowitz et al. 2001). Neglect is also associated with food insecurity (Duva and Metzger 2010). Another study found that financial management skills may buffer the effects of poverty on household food security (Gundersen and Garasky 2012). There is also neurobiological evidence suggesting that early physical contact between mothers and infants contributes to maternal caregiving behavior (Strathearn 2011). One recent study examined the relationship between breastfeeding duration and subsequent child maltreatment in a large birth cohort monitored prospectively over 15 years. This study found that children who were breastfed for 4 or more months were nearly four times less likely to be neglected compared with non-breastfed children (Strathearn et al. 2009).

These studies, which focused on single protective factors with high salience to the context of child neglect, represent a promising approach. It is also the case that, like risk factors, protective factors can exert a cumulative effect. In one study, a combination of higher maternal education, positive family affect, more supportive services, and fewer stressful life events predicted the provision of adequate physical care among low-income families (Casady and Lee 2002). Like research on risk factors, more longitudinal studies examining processes or mechanisms that underlie observed associations with neglect are needed (Luthar 2006; Rutter 2006).

Consequences

Child neglect can and frequently does result in serious physical, neurological, and socioemotional harm, including serious injury, lifelong impairments and sometimes death. The type and extent of harm depends on many factors, including dimensions of the neglect (type, severity, frequency, developmental timing, chronicity, and co-occurrence with abuse and other adversities) and the presence or absence of other risk and protective factors within children, their caregivers, and their environments.

Although neglect is involved in 80 % of child welfare cases, relatively few maltreatment studies have focused on the consequences of neglect. In any study using a non-experimental research design, it is difficult to disentangle the effects of child neglect from the effects of co-occurring adversities such as child abuse, violence exposure, residential instability, and family dysfunction such as substance abuse, psychopathology, and conflict. It is also difficult to link particular dimensions of neglect (e.g., type, timing) to particular child outcomes, since most neglected children experience multiple unmet needs over more than one developmental period, and also experience multiple deleterious outcomes.

Neurobiological (Center on the Developing Child at Harvard University 2012; Shonkoff et al. 2012; De Bellis 2005; Shonkoff 2010), developmental psychopathology (Sroufe and Rutter 1984), and ecological (Bronfenbrenner 1977, 1979) frameworks are useful for conceptualizing the consequences of child neglect. Neurobiological perspectives (Center on the Developing Child at Harvard University 2012; Shonkoff et al. 2012; De Bellis 2005; Shonkoff 2010) shed light on the underlying mechanisms by which neglect exerts a deleterious and lasting influence on children's physical, cognitive, and socioemotional health and development (Lempinen 2012; Blair and Raver 2012). Developmental psychopathology (Sroufe and Rutter 1984) describes the processes by which neglect disrupts a child's successful negotiation of stage-salient developmental tasks, producing skills deficits in the child that increase the probability of subsequent maladjustment.(Cicchetti and Toth 1995) For example, neglect in early childhood may disrupt a child's development of healthy attachment relationships and the ability to regulate emotion, leaving the child with emotional and social behavior deficits that increase the likelihood of subsequent maladjustment. Ecological theory (Bronfenbrenner 1977, 1979) underlines the importance of recognizing and addressing the influence of multiple environmental influences both on parenting and on children's development. Together, these frameworks provide a useful heuristic for understanding how the effects of childhood neglect may cascade over time into multiple levels and domains of child, adolescent, and adult functioning (Shonkoff et al. 2012; Masten and Cicchetti 2010).

Most child neglect research has been limited to child welfare samples in which children with reported or substantiated neglect are compared with nonneglected or nonmaltreated controls.

A handful of studies have examined retrospective youth or adult reports of childhood neglect. This research has found evidence of pervasive effects on children's physical, cognitive, and socioemotional development.

Complementing these findings are results from a wide body of research on early deprivation and stress in animals and humans. Animal models have long supported the notion that frequent physical contact with a maternal caregiver is a biological necessity for both physical and psychological development. Studies with infant rodents and primates suggest that maternal deprivation is associated with impaired physical, social, behavioral, and cognitive development, including deficits in executive functioning, biological stress response systems, and social behavior (Harlow et al. 1971; Sanchez and Pollak 2009). Research with children who have experienced early neglect and deprivation in institutional settings has also provided strong evidence of serious and lasting neurobiological effects. Children who have experienced early deprivation in an institutional context demonstrate diminished electrical activity in the brain (Tarullo et al. 2011; Marshall and Fox 2004), decreased brain metabolism and connectivity (Eluvathingal et al. 2006; Sheridan et al. 2012), and smaller than typical prefrontal cortex volumes (Frodl et al. 2010; Edmiston et al. 2011). They also evidence alterations in the two main biological stress response systems, the sympathetic-adrenal-medullary (SAM) system (Gunnar et al. 2009) and the hypothalamic-pituitary-adrenal (HPA) axis (Carlson and Earls 1997). Consistent with these effects, they also experience pervasive growth problems and poor physical health (Johnson and Gunnar 2011). Studies of post-adoption or foster placement outcomes for institutionalized children suggest that early intervention can reduce some of the pernicious effects of early deprivation (Rutter et al. 2010). However, these studies also suggest that deprivation that is severe, early, and lasts for longer periods can result in more pervasive deficits that are less responsive to intervention (Gunnar et al. 2001; van Ijzendoorn and Juffer 2006; Colvert et al. 2008; Marshall et al. 2008). Taken together, findings from these areas of research strongly support unique, biologically-based effects of neglect on the developing child, independent of the many stressors and adversities with which child neglect typically co-occurs.

Physical Development

Consistent with findings from research on early maternal deprivation, infants and children whose basic needs are not met are at risk for a wide range of physical consequences in the short- and long-term, including malnutrition, chronic or acute infections, failure to thrive, compromised brain development, unintentional injury and death, self-injury and suicidality, and lifelong health problems (Sfoggia et al. 2008; Block and Krebs 2005). In one study, neglect chronicity predicted lower body mass index in middle childhood compared with nonneglected controls (Bennett et al. 2010). Additionally, medical and dental neglect exert direct effects on child health, increasing risk for chronic conditions such as asthma and diabetes, and dental caries and periodontal disease (American Academy of Pediatric Dentistry, American Academy of Pediatrics 2011). All of these problems, in turn, can affect both the cognitive and socioemotional development of the child. In 2010, two-thirds of an estimated 1,560 maltreatment fatalities were due to neglect. Many more neglect fatalities go unrecognized due to the difficulty of identifying and investigating neglect following "accidental" deaths that may have been caused by child neglect (e.g., lapses in supervision contributing to deaths by drowning or in fires) (Schnitzer et al. 2011).

Neuroimaging studies have provided general support regarding the short- and long-term impact of both abuse and neglect on brain volume and function (van Harmelen et al. 2010; Nelson et al. 2011; White et al. 2012). However, given the heterogeneity of neglect, the high co-occurrence of neglect with other forms of maltreatment, and the multitude of risk factors associated with neglect, it is difficult to draw precise conclusions regarding observed effects from extant studies. Poverty itself has been associated with disruption of early brain development (Lempinen 2012). Consistent with prior research indicating that early deprivation disrupts development and functioning of the HPA system, there is also preliminary evidence of such disruptions for children in foster care, and evidence that neglect may play a unique role. In particular, foster children with histories of severe physical neglect were more likely than other foster children to have low morning cortisol levels (Bruce et al. 2009). With regard to longer-term health outcomes, the Adverse Childhood Experiences study has found that childhood neglect and co-occurring adversities increase an individual's risk for many of the nation's leading preventable health problems through adulthood (Newman et al. 2010; Nelson et al. 1993; Wilson and Homer 2005; Straus and Kantor 2005; Wesson et al. 2008; Child Welfare Information Gateway 2012; Steib and Blome 2009; Sedlak et al. 2010; Fluke et al. 2005), including smoking (Anda et al. 1999; Topitzes et al. 2010; Edwards et al. 2007; Ford et al. 2011), smoking-related lung disease (Anda et al. 2008; Brown et al. 2010), drug use and abuse (Moran et al. 2004; Kilpatrick et al. 2000; Kilpatrick et al. 2003; Clark et al. 1997; Hussey et al. 2006; Shin et al. 2009; Lansford et al. 2010; Duncan et al. 1996; Sheridan 1995; Ireland and Widom 1994; Widom et al. 1995; Dube et al. 2002, 2003b, 2006), obesity (Bennett et al. 2010; Knutson et al. 2010; Schneiderman et al. 2012; Shin and Miller 2012; Williamson et al. 2002; Grilo et al. 2005; Rohde et al. 2008; Bentley and Widom 2009), HIV/AIDS-related sexual risk behaviors (Oberlander et al. 2011; Jones et al. 2010; Elliott et al. 2002; Merrick et al. 2008; Voisin 2005; Wilson and Widom 2008, 2009; Hillis et al. 2004; Ramiro et al. 2010), and suicidality (Dube et al. 2001; Stein et al. 2010; Bruffaerts et al. 2010; Thompson et al. 2012a, b; Duke et al. 2011).

Cognitive Development

Child neglect is associated with impaired cognition and academic functioning in childhood and adolescence independent of abuse (Mills et al. 2011; Wodarski et al. 1990). Both neglect and the circumstances of poverty in which it is typically embedded have been linked to poor academic performance (Nikulina et al. 2011; Chapple and Vaske 2010). In one study, neglected children evidenced lower scores for IQ, reading, mathematics, and multiple neurocognitive domains compared with nonmaltreated controls, and neglected children who were experiencing symptoms of PTSD performed more poorly than those who were not (De Bellis et al. 2009). In another study, child neglect was associated with lower reading ability and perceptual reasoning at age 14. There is some evidence that neglect is associated with poorer school outcomes than physical abuse (Fantuzzo et al. 2011), and that youth who have experienced both abuse and neglect may experience more school-based disciplinary problems and grade repetitions than youth who have only experienced one form of maltreatment (Kendall-Tackett and Eckenrode 1996). In a longitudinal study of extremely low birth weight infants, those who were referred to CPS for suspected neglect had poorer general cognitive functioning at age 4, and those whose neglect was substantiated experienced a progressive decline in cognitive function over time (at 1, 2, and 4 years), compared with the nonneglected infants. They had a significantly smaller head circumference at 2 and 4 years, but not at birth (Strathearn et al. 2001.) Among a sample of severely neglect children, specific factors such as cognitive development, the mother's own physical and emotional abuse experience as a child, and the mother's low acceptability level towards her child predicted language delay more parsimoniously than did a cumulative risk factors index (Sylvestre and Mérette 2010).

Socioemotional Development

Consistent with its physical and cognitive effects, neglect exerts a wide range of effects on behavioral, emotional, and social adjustment in both the short and long term.

Neglect has been associated with symptoms of internalizing behavior problems, PTSD, dissociation, shame-proneness, depression, and withdrawn social behavior (Nikulina et al. 2011; Hoffman-Plotkin and Twentyman 1984; Bennett et al. 2010b; Milot 2010). Compared with non-neglected controls, neglected children experience poorer quality mother-child interactions (Milot 2010; Wilson et al. 2008), expect less emotional support and more conflict from their mothers (Shipman et al. 2005), and exhibit more avoidant and disorganized attachment (Venet et al. 2007). A meta-analysis of 33 observational studies found that three categories of parental behaviors (positivity, aversiveness, and involvement) distinguished neglectful parents from non-maltreating parents, with the largest mean effect sizes for involvement (Wilson et al. 2008). During interaction tasks with their mothers, neglected children demonstrate poorer emotional understanding than non-maltreated controls (Edwards et al. 2005; Shipman et al. 2005). In emotion recognition experiments, neglected children have more difficulty discriminating emotional expressions, and see fewer distinctions between emotions, compared with non-neglected controls (Pollak et al. 2000), and these differences persist even when controlling for IQ and conducting a follow-up assessment 1 year later (Sullivan et al. 2008).

Neglect has also been associated with externalizing behavior problems, aggression, and substance use (Kotch et al. 2008; Hoffman-Plotkin and Twentyman 1984; Straus and Savage 2005; Shin et al. 2012; Chen 2011). Specifically, neglect during early childhood may be a more powerful predictor of aggression than physical abuse at any age. Using data from LONGSCAN consortium, Kotch and colleagues examined the association between early childhood neglect (birth to age 2 years) and later childhood aggression at ages 4, 6, and 8 years, compared with aggression's associations with early childhood abuse and later abuse and neglect. They found that only early neglect significantly predicted aggression. Early abuse, later abuse, and later neglect were not significantly predictive in a controlled model with all four predictors (Kotch et al. 2008). The link with aggression may persist as children grow older. A prospective study with a community sample found that neglected children were more likely to be rejected by their peers in early adolescence and were more likely to be violent later in adolescence (Chapple et al. 2005). And in a study of university students in 17 nations, Straus and colleagues found that a self-reported childhood history of neglect was associated with having assaulted or injured a dating partner (Straus and Savage 2005). Parents who report having been neglected in their childhood are 2.6 times as likely to report their own neglectful parenting behavior and twice as likely to report physically abusive parenting than those who do not (Kim 2009). A history of neglect also increases risk of being arrested for juvenile drug and alcohol offenses (Chen 2011). The frequency of neglect and physical abuse, individually and in conjunction, have also been associated with trajectories of binge drinking during adolescence and higher rates of peak drinking during young adulthood (Shin et al. 2012).

Neglect During Adolescence

Most research has been conducted with samples who experienced neglect during infancy or childhood. In a rare study of neglect that occurred during adolescence, youth who reported neglect were more likely to be influenced by social pressure to drink alcohol and more likely to develop alcohol use disorders than nonneglected youth (Clark et al. 2004). These results are consistent with evidence from diverse traditions outside maltreatment research on the importance of adequate parental monitoring (Li et al. 2000a, b; Crouter et al. 1990, 1993; Dornbusch 1985; Crouter and Head 2002; Hartos et al. 2002) and emotional support and warmth (Marta 1997; Stice et al. 1993; Holahan et al. 1995; Barrera and Stice 1998; Wills and Cleary 1996; Helsen et al. 2000) during adolescence. Additionally, child neglect is associated with a constellation of environmental and individual caregiver factors that may persist as children enter adolescence, such as poverty, residential instability, relatively young caregiver age, number of people in the home, single parenthood, chaotic family functioning, low parental warmth, caregiver's history of abuse, caregiver depression, caregiver substance abuse, and lack of parenting and problem solving skills (Connell-Carrick 2003; Dunn et al. 2002; Dubowitz 1999).

Measurement

Identifying and assessing neglect poses challenges to both professionals and researchers. Professionals face numerous practical obstacles, including time constraints, narrow legal definitions of neglect, and a lack of training and resources. In general, only the most serious cases of neglect, in which the child is at risk of imminent harm, are screened in and investigated by CPS agencies. Many families who are experiencing neglect and would benefit from intervention are screened out because they have not yet met the CPS threshold for neglect (DePanfilis 2006). Because a clear understanding of the nature and context of neglect is key to intervention, a comprehensive assessment is needed. At a minimum, an assessment should determine whether or not neglect has occurred, the nature and severity of the neglect, whether the child will be safe, what factors are contributing to the neglect, what protective factors are present, and what interventions have been tried, with what results.

The paucity of valid and reliable measures of neglect has been an important contributor to the so-called "neglect of neglect" (Straus and Kantor 2005). No standard currently exists for operationalizing and measuring neglect in childhood and adolescence (Straus and Kantor 2005; Dubowitz et al. 1998, 2005; Coohey 2003; Burke et al. 1998; Sternberg and Lamb 1991; Zuravin 1999). Neglect is typically measured via CPS or caseworker reports, child or parent reports, or – less frequently – direct observation. The choice of data source is driven by cost, convenience, the conceptualization of neglect, and the purpose of the assessment. Direct observation of children's home environments and family interactions can minimize reporting biases. However, in addition to the cost and effort, there are problems with the representativeness of the situation and the ability to capture neglect when parents know they are being observed. While not designed specifically for neglect, self-report measures that have been used to assess neglect include the Family Functioning Style Scale (Deal et al. 1988), Family Needs Scale (Dunst et al. 1988), and Support Functions Scale. Observational measures include the Family Assessment Form (McCroskey et al. 1991), Child Well-being Scales (CWBS) (Magura and Moses 1986), and the Home Observation for Measure of the Environment (HOME) (Caldwell and Bradley 1979). In addition to these clinical assessment measures, researchers working with CPS data have developed ways to quantify the severity of reported neglect. For example, the widely used Maltreatment Classification System (MCS) (Barnett et al. 1993) contains codes for severity based on the authors' perspectives of how harmful different scenarios are. However, using CPS data excludes children with less severe, although potentially harmful, neglect, due to the relatively high thresholds for CPS reports and investigations.

While not widely adopted, a handful of survey instruments have been developed that focus specifically on neglect. Survey measures of neglect include self- and interviewer-administered questions, with data obtained from children/youth, retrospectively reporting adults, and/or caregivers. In an attempt to overcome the limitations of CPS data on neglect and permit a more nuanced assessment with a broader population, Straus and colleagues have developed a series of measures that aim to measure the neglect of children's physical, emotional, supervision, and cognitive needs. Based on Straus's original Neglect Scale (Harrington et al. 2002; Straus et al. 1995a), versions of the Multidimensional Neglect Behavior Scale (MNBS) have been developed for use with adolescents and retrospectively reporting adults (Straus et al. 1995b; Straus 2006), children 6-9 years and 10-15 years (Kaufman Kantor et al. 2004a) and parents of children 0-15 years (Kaufman Kantor et al. 2004b; Holt et al. 2004). The measures have demonstrated good internal consistency for the overall scale. Findings regarding the specific subscales and the factor structure of the measures when used with different study populations have been somewhat mixed (Harrington et al. 2002; Straus et al. 1995; Kaufman Kantor et al. 2004a).

Building on the work of Straus and colleagues, LONGSCAN (Runyan et al. 1998) investigators modified the MNBS-A for adolescents and adults for use with their high-risk, ethnically diverse, multi-site sample during adolescence. The resulting scale (Knight et al. 2008) measures youth's perception of their interactions with parents or primary caregivers. LONGSCAN investigators found evidence for a theoretically defined, empirically validated self-report measure of neglectful behavior by parents that yielded three factors: provision of physical needs, emotional support, and parental monitoring (Dubowitz et al. 2011). The LONGSCAN findings fit generally with those of prior factor analytic studies to support a multidimensional conceptualization of neglect. Straus et al. (1995), using a sample of primarily white college students found two factors: emotional/cognitive and supervision/physical. Harrington et al. (2002) found four factors in a low income sample of mothers: emotional, supervisory, physical, and cognitive. And a preliminary test of the MNBS-CR for children also found initial support for the same four core domains as Harrington et al. did (Kaufman Kantor et al. 2004a).

In addition to Straus's measures, the recently developed ISPCAN (International Society for Prevention of Child Abuse and Neglect) Child Abuse Screening Tool Children's Version (ICAST-C) contains a 6-item neglect scale that demonstrated good internal consistency in a four-country pilot test (Zolotor et al. 2009). The parent version, ICAST-P, includes only three neglect items, with poor internal consistency, and the retrospective version, ICAST-R (Dunne et al. 2009), does not contain neglect items. The measure was developed as a multi-national, consensus-based survey instrument with input from scientists in 40 countries, and is available in six languages.

Directly asking children and youth to report on their experiences has advantages over reports by caregivers (Widom et al. 2004, 2005). Children's perceptions of their own possible neglect are important and may influence outcomes. Obtaining information directly from youth rather than from caregivers may be more accurate (Dubowitz et al. 2011), involving a shorter recall period with less bias, and less stigma attached to reporting whether their needs have been met. Social desirability may be diminished by using a self-administered computerized approach and focusing on children's needs, rather than on caregiver behavior (Kim et al. 2008; Knight et al. 2000; Black and Ponirakis 2000). One clear challenge to interpreting survey measures of neglect is that the resulting data are continuous; the issue of a potential threshold effect remains to be studied (i.e., an empirical basis for when parental behavior or a child's unmet needs cross the line into neglect). We can develop theoretically based thresholds, but the challenge is in determining whether they correspond to meaningful outcomes such as short- and long-term adjustment, functioning, and health; recidivism and chronicity; and response to different types of preventive and treatment interventions.

Treatment

There has been very little empirical work to evaluate treatment interventions for neglect. This paucity of research is compounded by the tremendous heterogeneity that characterizes neglect in term of its clinical presentation, the proximal risk factors that contribute to its occurrence, and its impact on the child. Because of these issues, it is often more appropriate to think about core treatment principles rather than specific treatment approaches. Core principles for addressing neglect include thorough and ongoing assessment of the needs and functioning of the individual child and family and provision of services tailored to meet those needs. Implicit in these principles are the importance of tailoring treatment to individual families, targeting the child's needs directly rather than assuming that the indirect effects of services provided to parents will be adequate, and recognizing that many children and families with repeatedly referred to CPS will need longer-term intervention. It has long been recognized that there is no single way to promote growth-fostering parenting (Belsky 1993). In the case of neglect, tailoring treatment is important because the factors influencing a family's ability to meet a child's needs may vary so widely. Some mothers may need treatment for depression, while others may need services related to domestic violence. The issue of direct attention for the child is critical given the pernicious short- and long-effects of neglect on multiple domains of child functioning. Evidence-based treatments are available for many of the risk factors and child outcomes associated with neglect.

Among the handful of parenting programs that specifically target child neglect, SafeCare stands out as a widely implemented program with a growing evidence base. SafeCare is a home-based behavioral skills parent training model that focuses on child behavior management and activity planning, home safety and household management, and child health and development. In the largest and most recent trial of the program in a child welfare system, Chaffin and colleagues (2012) conducted a randomized comparative outcome trial of SafeCare in a scaled-up, statewide implementation in Oklahoma. Maltreatment recidivism was examined over the course of 6 years. Adding SafeCare to the usual in-home service program reduced child welfare reports for neglect and abuse by about 26 % compared to the same in-home services without SafeCare among parents of children age five or younger. A few characteristics of this trial make the findings particularly striking. Ninety percent of participating parents had been reported for neglect, and the average number of prior encounters with child protective services was five. This type of chronic neglect has historically been considered especially difficult to treat. And the trial was conducted within the context of a scaled-up, statewide implementation. Even for interventions with strong experimental evidence, trials at this scale can suffer from fidelity issues and program drift, which can diminish treatment effects.

Historically, CPS systems have treated the parents, with the assumption that the treatment will benefit the child indirectly. However, the importance of intervening directly with children who have experienced neglect is gaining increasing recognition. There is growing evidence that treatment models that include direct attention to the child, such as Attachment and Biobehavioral Catch-Up Intervention (Dozier et al. 2006, 2008), Child-Parent Psychotherapy (Lieberman et al. 1991, 2006), and Multidimensional Treatment Foster Care for Preschoolers (Fisher et al. 2000, 2007; Fisher and Kim 2007), can improve maltreated children's stress regulation, behavior, and parent–child attachment (Dozier et al. 2006, 2008; Lieberman et al. 1991, 2006; Fisher et al. 2000, 2007; Fisher and Kim 2007). Child-based intervention in the form of early childhood education can also play a critical role in promoting the positive development of children in families affected by poverty and multiple stressors (Duncan and Magnuson 2006).

The notion that new treatment approaches are needed to tackle chronic neglect is also gaining increasing attention. Whether focusing on chronic neglect specifically (Kaplan et al. 2009) or chronic maltreatment (Jonson-Reid et al. 2010; Proctor et al. 2012; Chaffin et al. 2011), this attention effectively includes chronic neglect, since nearly 80 % of CPS cases involve neglect and families with neglect tend to experience multiple referrals for multiple types of maltreatment. Differential response approaches, which are less adversarial, more family-centered, and more individually tailored than traditional CPS investigations, are gaining increased acceptance and empirical support (Loman and Siegel 2012). This approach holds particular value for families experiencing chronic child neglect, because it goes beyond immediate safety issues in an attempt to address the multiple underlying stressors and needs that contribute to them. Additionally, new evidence is emerging that is shaping the way we think about intervening with chronically maltreating families. Chaffin and colleagues tested whether patterns of risk factor improvement predicted lower recidivism risk even among chronic CPS cases (Chaffin et al. 2011). They identified heterogeneous classes of risk factor trajectories based on changes in parental depression, concrete resources, social support, and child abuse potential. They found that although chronic cases did experience high problem levels and typically only modest improvement, chronicity also was associated with a greater probability of falling into a trajectory class that experienced sustained improvement in risk factors. Cases in this trajectory class had high problem levels that improved over the course of services, showed sustained improvement at a 6-month follow-up assessment, and experienced less recidivism over a 3-year period than cases in the other classes. While these findings are consistent with the popular perception that chronic maltreatment cases show limited improvement with services, they also suggest that in the cases where improvement does occur, recidivism risk can be reduced even among the most chronic cases. This is consistent with other recent findings from a study that used cross-sector, longitudinal administrative data, indicating that services may be associated with reduced recurrence even after multiple re-reports (Loman 2006).

Taken together, the evidence from these studies belies the notion that neglect, including chronic neglect, is untreatable. They support the importance of intervening directly with children, in addition to parents. They also suggest that while such chronic cases may respond to episodic service delivery, alternative models that are tailored to the longer-term needs of such families warrant increased attention.

Prevention

Preventing the occurrence of neglect and its wide-ranging consequences is a considerably less costly and more effective approach than treating them after they occur. By the time a family comes to the attention of CPS for suspected child neglect, the family is likely already in crisis, as a result of multiple problems, unmet needs, and stressors that have not been adequately addressed for some time. Unfortunately, prevention has not been prioritized. Dissemination of effective preventive approaches has been hampered by several factors including underlying systemic issues that favor a reactive, episodic, investigation-focused response (Steib and Blome 2009) and a lack of funding for preventive policies and programs.

Ideally, prevention begins before the earliest point at which a child can experience unmet needs. The lasting harm that can be done to the developing fetus has been well documented (i.e., via inadequate prenatal care and nutrition, and exposure to teratogens). However, the impact of preventive interventions for individual families at risk will be sharply limited unless those interventions occur within a larger context of policies that promote healthy environments and make resources available for families who need them. A broad approach is needed to provide a strong safety net for our poorest families. A recent National Research Council and Institute of Medicine report on preventing mental, emotional, and behavioral disorders among youth (National Research Council et al. 2009) stressed the urgency of shifting the field of prevention from a paradigm that focuses on risk factors to one that emphasizes the broad promotion of supportive family, school, and community environments as well as individual traits and skills.

The extreme heterogeneity of child neglect, the many interacting contributors to neglect, and the high co-occurrence of neglect with other childhood adversities such as abuse and violence exposure demand a broad approach to prevention. Some families are most at risk due to a shortage of food, and others due to maternal depression or domestic violence. The list of potential risk factors is long, and varies from family to family. Yet underlying these diverse etiologies and clinical manifestations is a common environmental substrate. Nearly all families in which neglect occurs share the uniting feature of an accumulation of multiple major stressors and adversities. Targeting the larger environment in which families raise children will pay far richer dividends than limiting our interventions to individual families who appear at risk. An ecological framework (Bronfenbrenner 1977, 1979; Belsky 1993) supports the importance of preventive efforts that target multiple levels of a child's environment, including the underlying systemic issues that frequently impede parents' abilities to meet their children's needs, such as poverty, mental health resources, and substance abuse treatment, as well as the particular needs of individual families and caregivers. Given that the U.S. has one of the highest child poverty rates compared to other developed countries, yet also has one of the lowest levels of social spending (Pritchard and Williams 2011; Mishel et al. 2012), we cannot ignore the systemic contributors to child neglect. Programs such as the Special Supplemental Nutrition Program for Women, Infants and Children (WIC), Supplemental Nutrition Assistance Program (SNAP), Medicaid and The State Children's Health Insurance Program (SCHIP), and Head Start are a critical and integral component of preventing child neglect by providing poor families with access to adequate resources for meeting their children's needs (Lee and Mackey-Bilaver 2007; Currie 2006; Howell and Kenney 2012).

At the same time, society is comprised of individuals and families, many of whom could benefit substantially from preventive interventions that target them directly. Although it wasn't designed to prevent child maltreatment, the pioneering Nurse-Family Partnership (NFP) is one of the most well-researched and widely-implemented programs for preventing child maltreatment (Olds et al. 1983, 1986, 1994; Eckenrode et al. 2010; Kitzman et al. 1997). In this program, registered nurses visit low-income, first-time mothers, beginning during pregnancy and continuing until the child is two. In a randomized trial and several follow-up studies, the program has been associated with a decreased risk of child maltreatment (Olds et al. 1983, 1986) and several other positive outcomes related to maternal and child health and well-being (Olds et al. 1983, 1986, 1994; Eckenrode et al. 2010; Kitzman et al. 1997). In addition to NFP, several other home-visiting programs have been tested, with widely varying results (Howard and Brooks-Gunn 2009). Healthy Families America (HFA) is a common approach using paraprofessionals as home visitors. There have been encouraging findings particularly from the New York program (Duggan et al. 2007; DuMont et al. 2008). We still have much to learn regarding the optimal features of such programs (e.g., frequency of visits, curriculum, training and discipline of visitors), especially as related specifically to neglect. Evidence-based parent training programs such as PCIT, Triple-P, and Incredible Years are also increasingly being used for maltreatment prevention, though more work remains to be done studying their effect on risk for neglect.

The increased development and dissemination of evidence-based prevention programs, and their continued evaluation with rigorous research, is also a key goal. NPF reaches only 20,000 families with newborns a year, compared to four million births in the US each year. We have policies and programs that are promising, but we need more, and further evaluation. We also need investment in finding better strategies. There is also considerable opportunity for recognizing and creating new domains and mechanisms of influence at different points in the family life cycle, and involving different child- and family- focused professions. For example, there is evidence that center-based preschools, especially those that include parental involvement and family support services, can decrease the incidence of neglect (Mersky et al. 2009). There is also evidence that primary care pediatricians can contribute to the prevention of neglect. In a randomized trial of the Safe Environment for Every Kid (SEEK) model of pediatric primary care, the program resulted in significantly lower rates of child maltreatment as assessed via several indicators, including fewer CPS reports, fewer instances of possible medical neglect documented as treatment nonadherence, fewer children with delayed immunizations, and less harsh punishment reported by parents (Dubowitz et al. 2009). A second trial in a relatively low risk sample, demonstrated less harsh discipline and psychological aggression in families exposed to the *SEEK* model of primary care (Dubowitz et al. 2012).

What is needed is a broad approach that includes multiple levels, from policies that provide a healthy environment in which families can meet their children's needs to programs targeting individual caregivers early in the family life cycle, and continuing as long as they are effective. As the 2009 NRC and IOM report concludes, "The gap between what is known and what is being done is far too large. It can be addressed only by continuing to refine the science and by a strong commitment to develop the infrastructure and put in place systems that allow for equitable delivery of preventive interventions on a population based, large-scale basis" (National Research Council and Institute of Medicine 2009). The continued poor status of the U.S. in terms of infant mortality, child poverty, and social expenditures is evidence of the considerable work needed at a policy level. There is also a tremendous need to improve existing systems (e.g., access to healthcare) and institutions (e.g., public schools) to enhance children's health, development and safety, and prevent their neglect. A shift in our policy and practice paradigm is needed, to one that acknowledges the importance of primary and secondary prevention, but also explicitly emphasizes the promotion and support of healthy, nurturing environments that are conducive to childrearing.

References

Administration on Children, & Youth and Families. (2010). U.S. Department of Health and Human Services. National Survey of Child and Adolescent Well-Being (NSCAW): CPS sample component wave 1 data analysis report.

American Academy of Pediatric Dentistry, American Academy of Pediatrics. (2011). Oral and dental aspects of child abuse and neglect. *Pediatric Dentistry, 31*(6), 147–150.

Anda, R. F., Croft, J. B., Felitti, V. J., et al. (1999). Adverse childhood experiences and smoking during adolescence and adulthood. *JAMA: The Journal of the American Medical Association, 282*(17), 1652–1658.

Anda, R. F., Brown, D. W., Dube, S. R., Bremner, J. D., Felitti, V. J., & Giles, W. H. (2008). Adverse childhood experiences and chronic obstructive pulmonary disease in adults. *American Journal of Preventive Medicine, 34*(5), 396–403.

Ansell, E. B., Gu, P., Tuit, K., & Sinha, R. (2012). Effects of cumulative stress and impulsivity on smoking status. *Human Psychopharmacology: Clinical and Experimental, 27*(2), 200–208.

Azar, S. T., Stevenson, M. T., & Johnson, D. R. (2012). Intellectual disabilities and neglectful parenting: Preliminary findings on the role of cognition in parenting risk. *Journal of Mental Health Research in Intellectual Disabilities, 5*(2), 94–129.

Barnett, D., Manly, J. T., & Cicchetti, D. (1993). Defining child maltreatment: The interface between policy and research. In D. Cicchetti & S. L. Toth (Eds.), *Advances in applied developmental psychology: Child abuse, child development and social policy* (pp. 7–73). Norwood: Ablex.

Barrera, M., & Stice, E. (1998). Parent-adolescent conflict in the context of parental support: Families with alcoholic and nonalcoholic fathers. *Journal of Family Psychology, 12*(2), 195–208.

Belle, D. (1990). Poverty and women's mental health. *The American Psychologist, 45*(3), 385–389.

Belsky, J. (1993). Etiology of child maltreatment: A developmental-ecological analysis. *Psychological Bulletin, 114*(3), 413–434.

Bennett, D. S., Sullivan, M. W., Thompson, S. M., & Lewis, M. (2010a). Early child neglect: Does it predict obesity or underweight in later childhood? *Child Maltreatment, 15*(3), 250–254.

Bennett, D. S., Sullivan, M. W., & Lewis, M. (2010b). Neglected children, shame-proneness, and depressive symptoms. *Child Maltreatment, 15*(4), 305–314.

Bentley, T., & Widom, C. S. (2009). A 30-year follow-up of the effects of child abuse and neglect on obesity in adulthood. *Obesity, 17*(10), 1900–1905.

Berlin, L. J., Appleyard, K., & Dodge, K. A. (2011). Intergenerational continuity in child maltreatment: Mediating mechanisms and implications for prevention. *Child Development, 82*(1), 162–176.

Black, M. M., & Dubowitz, H. (1999). Child neglect: Research recommendations and future directions. In H. Dubowitz (Ed.), *Neglected children: Research, practice, and policy* (pp. 261–277). Thousand Oaks: Sage.

Black, M. M., & Ponirakis, A. (2000). Computer-administered interviews with children about maltreatment. *Journal of Interpersonal Violence, 15*(7), 682–695.

Blair, C., & Raver, C. C. (2012). Child development in the context of adversity: Experiential canalization of brain and behavior. *The American Psychologist, 67*(4), 309–318.

Blair, C., Raver, C. C., Granger, D., Mills-Koonce, R., & Hibel, L. (2011). Allostasis and allostatic load in the context of poverty in early childhood. *Development and Psychopathology. Special Issue: Allostatic Load Part 1, 23*(3), 845–857.

Block, R. W., & Krebs, N. F. (2005). Failure to thrive as a manifestation of child neglect. *Pediatrics, 116*(5), 1234–1237.

Bousha, D. M., & Twentyman, C. T. (1984). Mother-child interactional style in abuse, neglect, and control groups: Naturalistic observations in the home. *Journal of Abnormal Psychology, 93*(1), 106–114.

Bronfenbrenner, U. (1977). Toward an experimental ecology of human development. *The American Psychologist, 32*(7), 513–531.

Bronfenbrenner, U. (1979). *The ecology of human development: Experiments by nature and design.* Cambridge, MA: Harvard University Press.

Brook, J., & McDonald, T. (2009). The impact of parental substance abuse on the stability of family reunifications from foster care. *Children and Youth Services Review, 31*(2), 193–198.

Brown, D. W., Anda, R. F., Felitti, V. J., et al. (2010). Adverse childhood experiences are associated with the risk of lung cancer: A prospective cohort study. *BMC Public Health, 10*, 20.

Bruce, J., Fisher, P. A., Pears, K. C., & Levine, S. (2009). *Morning cortisol levels in preschool-aged foster children: Differential effects of maltreatment type*. New Jersey: Wiley.

Bruffaerts, R., Demyttenaere, K., Borges, G., et al. (2010). Childhood adversities as risk factors for onset and persistence of suicidal behaviour. *The British Journal of Psychiatry, 197*(1), 20–27.

Bruhn, C. M. (2004). Children with disabilities: Abuse, neglect, and the child welfare system. *Journal of Aggression Maltreatment & Trauma, 8*(1–2), 173–203.

Bureau of Labor statistics, & U.S. Department of Labor. (2011). Census of fatal occupational injuries (preliminary data).

Bureau of Labor Statistics, U.S. Department of Labor, & Survey of Occupational Injuries and Illnesses in Cooperation with Participating State Agencies. (2011). Nonfatal occupational injuries and illnesses requiring days away from work, 2010.

Burgess, R. L., & Conger, R. D. (1978). Family interaction in abusive, neglectful, and normal families. *Child Development, 49*(4), 1163–1173.

Burke, J., Chandy, J., Dannerbeck, A., & Watt, J. W. (1998). The parental environment cluster model of child neglect: An integrative conceptual model. *Child Welfare, 77*(4), 389–405.

Caldwell, B. M., & Bradley, R. H. (1979). *Home observation for measurement of the environment: Administration manual*. Little Rock: University of Arkansas.

Carlson, M., & Earls, F. (1997). Psychological and neuroendocrinological sequelae of early social deprivation in institutionalized children in romania. In C. S. Carter, I. I. Lederhendler, & B. Kirkpatrick (Eds.), *The integrative neurobiology of affiliation* (pp. 419–428). New York: New York Academy of Sciences.

Casady, M. A., & Lee, R. E. (2002). Environments of physically neglected children. *Psychological Reports, 91*(3), 711–721.

Casanueva, C., Goldman-Fraser, J., Ringeisen, H., Lederman, C., Katz, L., & Osofsky, J. D. (2010). Maternal perceptions of temperament among infants and toddlers investigated for maltreatment: Implications for services need and referral. *Journal of Family Violence, 25*(6), 557–574.

Casanueva, C., Smith, K., Dolan, M., & Ringeisen, H. (2011). *NSCAW II baseline report: Maltreatment*. OPRE Report #2011-27c, Washington, DC: Office of Planning, Research and Evaluation, Administration for Children and Families, U.S. Department of Health and Human Services.

Cauffman, E., & Steinberg, L. (2000). (Im)maturity of judgment in adolescence: Why adolescents may be less culpable than adults. *Behavioral Sciences & the Law, 18*(6), 741–760.

Center on the Developing Child at Harvard University. (2012). *The science of neglect: The persistent absence of responsive care disrupts the developing brain: Working Paper 12*. www.developingchild.harvard.edu

Chaffin, M. (2006). The changing focus of child maltreatment research and practice within psychology. *Journal of Social Issues, 62*(4), 663–684.

Chaffin, M., Kelleher, K., & Hollenberg, J. (1996). Onset of physical abuse and neglect: Psychiatric, substance abuse, and social risk factors from prospective community data. *Child Abuse & Neglect, 20*(3), 191–203.

Chaffin, M., Bard, D., Hecht, D., & Silovsky, J. (2011). Change trajectories during home-based services with chronic child welfare cases. *Child Maltreatment, 16*(2), 114–125.

Chaffin, M., Hecht, D., Bard, D., Silovsky, J. F., & Beasley, W. H. (2012). A statewide trial of the SafeCare home-based services model with parents in child protective services. *Pediatrics, 129*(3), 509–515.

Chapman, D. P., Dube, S. R., & Anda, R. F. (2007). Adverse childhood events as risk factors for negative mental health outcomes. *Psychiatric Annals, 37*(5), 359–364.

Chapple, C. L., & Vaske, J. (2010). Child neglect, social context, and educational outcomes: Examining the moderating effects of school and neighborhood context. *Violence and Victims, 25*(4), 470–485.

Chapple, C. L., Tyler, K. A., & Bersani, B. E. (2005). Child neglect and adolescent violence: Examining the effects of self-control and peer rejection. *Violence and Victims, 20*(1), 39–53.

Chen, W.-Y., Propp, J., deLara, E., & Corvo, K. (2011). Child neglect and its association with subsequent juvenile drug and alcohol offense. *Child & Adolescent Social Work Journal, 28*(4), 273–290.

Child Welfare Information Gateway. (2011). *How the child welfare system works*. Washington, DC: U.S. Department of Health and Human Services, Children's Bureau.

Child Welfare Information Gateway. (2012). *Acts of omission: An overview of child neglect*. Washington, DC: Department of Health and Human Services, Children's Bureau.

Cicchetti, D., & Toth, S. L. (1995). A developmental psychopathology perspective on child abuse and neglect. *Journal of the American Academy of Child and Adolescent Psychiatry, 34*(5), 541–565.

Clark, D. B., Lesnick, L., & Hegedus, A. M. (1997). Traumas and other adverse life events in adolescents with alcohol abuse and dependence. *Journal of the American Academy of Child & Adolescent Psychiatry, 36*(12), 1744–1751.

Clark, D. B., Thatcher, D. L., & Maisto, S. A. (2004). Adolescent neglect and alcohol use disorders in two-parent families. *Child Maltreatment, 9*(4), 357–370.

Cohen, R. A., & Martinez, M. E. (2012). Health insurance coverage: Early release of estimates from the national health interview survey, 2011. National Center for Health Statistics. June 2012. Available from http://www.cdc.gov/nchs/nhis/releases.htm

Coleman, P. K., & Karraker, K. H. (1998). Self-efficacy and parenting quality: Findings and future applications. *Developmental Review, 18*(1), 47–85.

Colvert, E., Rutter, M., Kreppner, J., et al. (2008). Do theory of mind and executive function deficits underlie the adverse outcomes associated with profound early deprivation? Findings from the English and Romanian adoptees study. *Journal of Abnormal Child Psychology, 36*(7), 1057–1068.

Connell, C. M., Bergeron, N., Katz, K. H., Saunders, L., & Tebes, J. K. (2007). Re-referral to child protective services: The influence of child, family, and case characteristics on risk status. *Child Abuse & Neglect, 31*(5), 573–588.

Connell-Carrick, K. (2003). A critical review of the empirical literature: Identifying correlates of child neglect. *Child and Adolescent Social Work Journal, 20*(5), 389.

Coohey, C. (2003). Defining and classifying supervisory neglect. *Child Maltreatment, 8*(2), 145–156.

Crittenden, P. M. (1985). Maltreated infants: Vulnerability and resilience. *Journal of Child Psychology and Psychiatry, 26*(1), 85–96.

Crittenden, P. M. (1993). An information-processing perspective on the behavior of neglectful parents. *Criminal Justice and Behavior Special Issue Child Neglect, 20*(1), 27–48.

Crittenden, P. M. (1999). Child neglect: Causes and contributors. In H. Dubowitz (Ed.), *Neglected children: Research, practice and policy* (pp. 47–68). Thousand Oaks: Sage.

Crouter, A. C., & Head, M. R. (2002). Parental monitoring and knowledge of children. In M. H. Bornstein (Ed.), *Handbook of parenting: Vol. 3: Being and becoming a parent* (2nd ed., pp. 461–483). Mahwah: Lawrence Erlbaum Associates.

Crouter, A. C., MacDermid, S. M., McHale, S. M., & Perry-Jenkins, M. (1990). Parental monitoring and perceptions of children's school performance and conduct in dual- and single-earner families. *Developmental Psychology, 26*(4), 649–657.

Crouter, A. C., McHale, S. M., & Bartko, W. T. (1993). Gender as an organizing feature in parent–child relationships. In R. A. Pierce & M. A. Black (Eds.), *Life-span development: A diversity reader* (pp. 3–15). Dubuque: Kendall-Hunt.

Currie, J. M. (2006). *The invisible safety net: Protecting the nation's poor children and families.* Princeton: Princeton University Press.

De Bellis, M. D. (2005). The psychobiology of neglect. *Child Maltreatment, 10*(2), 150–172.

De Bellis, M. D., Hooper, S. R., Spratt, E. G., & Woolley, D. P. (2009). Neuropsychological findings in childhood neglect and their relationships to pediatric PTSD. *Journal of the International Neuropsychological Society, 15*(6), 868–878.

Deal, A. G., Trivette, C. M., & Dunst, C. J. (1988). Family Functioning Style Scale. In C. J. Dunst, C. M. Trivette, & A. G. Deal (Eds.), *Enabling and empowering families: Principles and guidelines for practice* (pp. 179–184). Cambridge, MA: Brookline Books.

DePanfilis, D. (2006). *Child neglect: A guide for prevention, assessment, and intervention.* Washington, DC: Department of Health and Human Services, Administration on Children and Families, Administration for Children, Youth, and Families, Children's Bureau, Office on Child Abuse and Neglect.

DePanfilis, D., & Zuravin, S. J. (1998). Rates, patterns, and frequency of child maltreatment recurrences among families known to CPS. *Child Maltreatment, 3*(1), 27–42.

DePanfilis, D., & Zuravin, S. J. (1999). Epidemiology of child maltreatment recurrences. *The Social Service Review, 73*(2), 218–239.

Dietrich, K. N., Starr, R. H., & Weisfeld, G. E. (1983). Infant maltreatment: Caretaker-infant interaction and developmental consequences at different levels of parenting failure. *Pediatrics, 72*(4), 532–540.

Dixon, L., Hamilton-Giachritsis, C., Browne, K., & Ostapuik, E. (2007). The co-occurrence of child and intimate partner maltreatment in the family: Characteristics of the violent perpetrators. *Journal of Family Violence, 22*(8), 675–689.

Dobrova-Krol, N. A., van Ijzendoorn, M. H., Bakermans-Kranenburg, M. J., & Juffer, F. (2010). Effects of perinatal HIV infection and early institutional rearing on physical and cognitive development of children in Ukraine. *Child Development, 81*(1), 237–251.

Dong, M., Anda, R. F., Felitti, V. J., et al. (2004). The interrelatedness of multiple forms of childhood abuse, neglect, and household dysfunction. *Child Abuse & Neglect, 28*(7), 771–784.

Dornbusch, S. M., et al. (1985). Single parents, extended households, and the control of adolescents. *Child Development, 56*(2), 326–341.

Dozier, M., Peloso, E., Lindhiem, O., et al. (2006). Developing evidence-based interventions for foster children: An example of a randomized clinical trial with infants and toddlers. *Journal of Social Issues, 62*(4), 767–785.

Dozier, M., Peloso, E., Lewis, E., Laurenceau, J.-P., & Levine, S. (2008). Effects of an attachment-based intervention of the cortisol production of infants and toddlers in foster care. *Development and Psychopathology. Special Issue: Integrating Biological Measures into the Design and Evaluation of Preventive Interventions, 20*(3), 845–859.

Dube, S. R., Anda, R. F., Felitti, V. J., Chapman, D. P., Williamson, D. F., & Giles, W. H. (2001). Childhood abuse, household dysfunction, and the risk of attempted suicide throughout the life span: Findings from the adverse childhood experiences study. *JAMA: The Journal of the American Medical Association, 286*(24), 3089–3096.

Dube, S. R., Anda, R. F., Felitti, V. J., Edwards, V. J., & Croft, J. B. (2002). Adverse childhood experiences and personal alcohol abuse as an adult. *Addictive Behaviors, 27*(5), 713–725.

Dube, S. R., Felitti, V. J., Dong, M., Giles, W. H., & Anda, R. F. (2003a). The impact of adverse childhood experiences on health problems: Evidence from four birth cohorts dating back to 1900. *Preventive Medicine: An International Journal Devoted to Practice and Theory, 37*(3), 268–277.

Dube, S. R., Felitti, V. J., Dong, M., Chapman, D. P., Giles, W. H., & Anda, R. F. (2003b). Childhood abuse, neglect, and household dysfunction and the risk of illicit drug use: The adverse childhood experiences study. *Pediatrics, 111*(3), 564–572.

Dube, S. R., Miller, J. W., Brown, D. W., et al. (2006). Adverse childhood experiences and the association with ever using alcohol and initiating alcohol use during adolescence. *The Journal of Adolescent Health, 38*(4), e1–e10.

Dubowitz, H. (1994). Neglecting the neglect of neglect. *Journal of Interpersonal Violence, 9*, 556–560.

Dubowitz, H. (1999). *Neglected children: Research, practice, and policy*. Thousand Oaks: Sage.

Dubowitz, H. (2009). Tackling child neglect: A role for pediatricians. *Pediatric Clinics of North America, 56*(2), 363–378.

Dubowitz, H., Black, M., Starr, R. H., & Zuravin, S. (1993). A conceptual definition of child neglect. *Criminal Justice & Behavior, 20*(1), 8–26.

Dubowitz, H., Klockner, A., Starr, R. H., & Black, M. M. (1998). Community and professional definitions of child neglect. *Child Maltreatment, 3*(3), 235–243.

Dubowitz, H., Black, M. M., Kerr, M. A., Starr, R. H., Jr., & Harrington, D. (2000). Fathers and child neglect. *Archives of Pediatrics & Adolescent Medicine, 154*(2), 135–141.

Dubowitz, H., Black, M. M., Cox, C. E., et al. (2001). Father involvement and children's functioning at age 6 years: A multisite study. *Child Maltreatment, 6*(4), 300–309.

Dubowitz, H., Papas, M. A., Black, M. M., & Starr, R. H. (2002). Child neglect: Outcomes in high-risk urban preschoolers. *Pediatrics, 109*(6), 1100–1107.

Dubowitz, H., Newton, R. R., Litrownik, A. J., et al. (2005). Examination of a conceptual model of child neglect. *Child Maltreatment, 10*(2), 173–189.

Dubowitz, H., Feigelman, S., Lane, W., & Kim, J. (2009). Pediatric primary care to help prevent child maltreatment: The Safe Environment for Every Kid (SEEK) model. *Pediatrics, 123*(3), 858–864.

Dubowitz, H., Villodas, M. T., Litrownik, A. J., et al. (2011). Psychometric properties of a youth self-report measure of neglectful behavior by parents. *Child Abuse & Neglect, 35*(6), 414–424.

Dubowitz, H., Lane, W. G., Semiatin, J. N., & Magder, L. S. (2012). The SEEK model of pediatric primary care: Can child maltreatment be prevented in a low-risk population? *Academic Pediatrics, 12*(4), 259–268.

Duggan, A., Caldera, D., Rodriguez, K., Burrell, L., Rohde, C., & Crowne, S. S. (2007). Impact of a statewide home visiting program to prevent child abuse. *Child Abuse & Neglect: The International Journal, 31*(8), 801–827.

Duke, N. N., Pettingell, S. L., McMorris, B. J., & Borowsky, I. W. (2011). Adolescent violence perpetration: Associations with multiple types of adverse childhood experiences. *Pediatrics, 125*(4), e778–e786.

DuMont, K., Mitchell-Herzfeld, S., Greene, R., et al. (2008). Healthy Families New York (HFNY) randomized trial: Effects on early child abuse and neglect. *Child Abuse & Neglect: The International Journal, 32*(3), 295–315.

Duncan, G. J., & Brooks-Gunn, J. (1997). *Consequences of growing up poor*. New York: Russell Sage.

Duncan, G. J., & Magnuson, K. (2006). Costs and benefits from early investments to promote human capital and positive behavior. In N. F. Watt, C. Ayoub, R. H. Bradley, J. E. Puma, & W. A. LeBoeuf (Eds.), *The crisis in youth mental health: Critical issues and effective programs, Vol. 4: Early intervention programs and policies* (pp. 27–51). Westport: Praeger Publishers/Greenwood Publishing Group.

Duncan, R. D., Saunders, B. E., Kilpatrick, D. G., Hanson, R. F., & Resnick, H. S. (1996). Childhood physical assault as a risk factor for PTSD, depression, and substance abuse: Findings from a national survey. *The American Journal of Orthopsychiatry, 66*(3), 437–448.

Dunn, M. G., Tarter, R. E., Mezzich, A. C., Vanyukov, M., Kirisci, L., & Kirillova, G. (2002). Origins and consequences of child neglect in substance abuse families. *Clinical Psychology Review, 22*(7), 1063–1090.

Dunne, M. P., Zolotor, A. J., Runyan, D. K., et al. (2009). ISPCAN child abuse screening tools retrospective version (ICAST-R): Delphi study and field testing in seven countries. *Child Abuse & Neglect, 33*(11), 815–825.

Dunst, C. J., Cooper, C. S., Weeldreyer, J. C., Synder, K. D., & Chase, J. H. (1988). Family needs scale. In C. J. Dunst, C. M. Trivette, & A. G. Deal (Eds.), *Enabling and empowering families: Principles and guidelines for practice* (pp. 149–151). Cambridge, MA: Brookline Books.

Duva, J., & Metzger, S. (2010). Addressing poverty as a major risk factor in child neglect: Promising policy and practice. *Protecting Children, 25*(1), 63–74.

Eccles, J. S. (1999). The development of children ages 6 to 14. *The Future of Children, 9*(2), 30–44.

Eckenrode, J., Campa, M., Luckey, D. W., et al. (2010). Long-term effects of prenatal and infancy nurse home visitation on the life course of youths: 19-Year follow-up of a randomized trial. *Archives of Pediatrics & Adolescent Medicine, 164*(1), 9–15.

Edmiston, E. E., Wang, F., Mazure, C. M., et al. (2011). Corticostriatal-limbic gray matter morphology in adolescents with self-reported exposure to childhood maltreatment. *Archives of Pediatrics & Adolescent Medicine, 165*(12), 1069–1077.

Edwards, A., Shipman, K., & Brown, A. (2005). The socialization of emotional understanding: A comparison of neglectful and nonneglectful mothers and their children. *Child Maltreatment, 10*(3), 293–304.

Edwards, V. J., Anda, R. F., Gu, D., Dube, S. R., & Felitti, V. J. (2007). Adverse childhood experiences and smoking persistence in adults with smoking-related symptoms and illness. *Permanente Journal, 11*(2), 5–13.

Egeland, B., & Vaughn, B. E. (1981). Failure of "bond formation" as a cause of abuse, neglect, and maltreatment. *The American Journal of Orthopsychiatry, 51*(1), 78–84.

Elliott, G. C., Avery, R., Fishman, E., & Hoshiko, B. (2002). The encounter with family violence and risky sexual activity among young adolescent females. *Violence and Victims, 17*(5), 569–592.

Eluvathingal, T. J., Chugani, H. T., Behen, M. E., et al. (2006). Abnormal brain connectivity in children after early severe socioemotional deprivation: A diffusion tensor imaging study. *Pediatrics, 117*(6), 2093–2100.

English, D. J., Graham, J. C., Litrownik, A. J., Everson, M., & Bangdiwala, S. I. (2005). Defining maltreatment chronicity: Are there differences in child outcomes? *Child Abuse & Neglect. Special Issue: Longitudinal Studies of Child Abuse and Neglect (LONGSCAN), 29*(5), 575–595.

Ethier, L. S., & Milot, T. (2009). Effet de la durée, de l'âge d'exposition à la négligence parentale et de la comorbidité sur le développement socioémotionnel à l'adolescence. *Neuropsychiatrie de l'Enfance et de l'Adolescence, 57*(2), 136–145.

Evans, G. W. (2004). The environment of childhood poverty. *The American Psychologist, 59*(2), 77–92.

Fantuzzo, J. W., Perlman, S. M., & Dobbins, E. K. (2011). Types and timing of child maltreatment and early school success: A population-based investigation. *Children and Youth Services Review, 33*(8), 1404–1411.

Farrell, M. H., & Kuruvilla, P. (2008). Assessment of parental understanding by pediatric residents during counseling after newborn genetic screening. *Arch Pediatr Adolesc Med, 162*(3), 199–204.

Feldman, S. S., & Elliott, G. R. (Eds.). (1990). *At the threshold: The developing adolescent.* Cambridge: Harvard University Press.

Fergus, S., & Zimmerman, M. A. (2005). Adolescent resilience: A framework for understanding healthy development in the face of risk. *Annual Review of Public Health, 26*, 399–419.

Fisher, P. A., & Kim, H. K. (2007). Intervention effects on foster preschoolers' attachment-related behaviors from a randomized trial. *Prevention Science, 8*(2), 161–170.

Fisher, P. A., Gunnar, M. R., Chamberlain, P., & Reid, J. B. (2000). Preventive intervention for maltreated preschool children: Impact on children's behavior, neuroendocrine activity, and foster parent functioning. *Journal of the American Academy of Child and Adolescent Psychiatry, 39*(11), 1356–1364.

Fisher, P. A., Stoolmiller, M., Gunnar, M. R., & Burraston, B. O. (2007). Effects of a therapeutic intervention for foster preschoolers on diurnal cortisol activity. *Psychoneuroendocrinology, 32*(8–10), 892–905.

Fluke, J. D., Shusterman, G. R., Hollinshead, D. M., & Yuan, Y.-Y. T. (2005). *Rereporting and recurrence of child maltreatment: Findings from NCANDS.* Washington, DC: Department of Health and Human Services, Office of the Assistant Secretary for Planning and Evaluation.

Ford, E. S., Anda, R. F., Edwards, V. J., et al. (2011). Adverse childhood experiences and smoking status in five states. *Preventive Medicine, 53*(3), 188–193.

Forehand, R., & Jones, D. J. (2002). The stability of parenting: A longitudinal analysis of inner-city african-american mothers. *Journal of Child & Family Studies, 11*(4), 469–483.

Frodl, T., Reinhold, E., Koutsouleris, N., Reiser, M., & Meisenzahl, E. M. (2010). Interaction of childhood stress with hippocampus and prefrontal cortex volume reduction in major depression. *Journal of Psychiatric Research, 44*(13), 799–807.

Fudge Schormans, A., & Sobsey, D. (2007). *Maltreatment of children with developmental disabilities. A comprehensive guide to intellectual and developmental disabilities* (pp. 467–487). Baltimore: Paul H Brookes Publishing.

Fuller, T. L., & Wells, S. J. (2003). Predicting maltreatment recurrence among CPS cases with alcohol and other drug involvement. *Children and Youth Services Review, 25*(7), 553–569.

Gaines, R., Sangrund, A., Green, A. H., & Power, E. (1978). Etiological factor in child maltreatment: A multivariate study of abusing, neglecting, and normal mothers. *Journal of Abnormal Psychology, 87*(5), 531–540.

Garbarino, J. (1991). The context of child abuse and neglect assessment. In J. C. Westman (Ed.), *Who speaks for the children? The handbook of individual and class child advocacy* (pp. 183–203). Sarasota: Professional Resource Exchange.

Garbarino, J., & Barry, F. (1997). The community context of child abuse and neglect. In J. Garbarino & J. Eckenrode (Eds.), *Understanding abusive families: An ecological approach to theory and practice* (pp. 56–85). San Francisco: Jossey-Bass.

Garbarino, J., & Crouter, A. (1978). Defining the comminity context for parent–child relations: The correlates of child maltreatment. *Child Development, 49*(3), 604–616.

Garbarino, J., & Kostelny, K. (1992). Child maltreatment as a community problem. *Child Abuse & Neglect, 16*(4), 455–464.

Garbarino, J., & Sherman, D. (1980). High-risk neighborhoods and high-risk families: The human ecology of child maltreatment. *Child Development, 51*(1), 188–198.

Gardner, M., & Steinberg, L. (2005). Peer influence on risk taking, risk preference, and risky decision making in adolescence and adulthood: An experimental study. *Developmental Psychology, 41*(4), 625–635.

Gaudin, J. M., Jr., Polansky, N. A., Kilpatrick, A. C., & Shilton, P. (1993). Loneliness, depression, stress, and social supports in neglectful families. *The American Journal of Orthopsychiatry, 63*(4), 597–605.

Gaudin, J. M., Polansky, N. A., Kilpatrick, A. C., & Shilton, P. (1996). Family functioning in neglectful families. *Child Abuse & Neglect, 20*(4), 363–377.

Graber, J. A., & Brooks-Gunn, J. (1996). Transitions and turning points: Navigating the passage from childhood through adolescence. *Developmental Psychology, 32*(4), 768–776.

Gracia, E., & Musitu, G. (2003). Social isolation from communities and child maltreatment: A cross-cultural comparison. *Child Abuse & Neglect, 27*(2), 153–168.

Green, J. G., McLaughlin, K. A., Berglund, P. A., et al. (2010). Childhood adversities and adult psychiatric disorders in the national comorbidity survey replication I: Associations with first onset of DSM-IV disorders. *Archives of General Psychiatry, 67*(2), 113–123.

Grilo, C. M., Masheb, R. M., Brody, M., Toth, C., Burke-Martindale, C. H., & Rothschild, B. S. (2005). Childhood maltreatment in extremely obese male and female bariatric surgery candidates. *Obesity Research, 13*(1), 123–130.

Gundersen, C. G., & Garasky, S. B. (2012). Financial management skills are associated with food insecurity in a sample of households with children in the United States. *The Journal of Nutrition, 142*(10), 1865–1870.

Gunnar, M. R., Morison, S. J., Chisholm, K., & Schuder, M. (2001). Salivary cortisol levels in children adopted from Romanian orphanages. *Development and Psychopathology, 13*(3), 611–628.

Gunnar, M. R., Frenn, K., Wewerka, S. S., & Van Ryzin, M. J. (2009). Moderate versus severe early life stress: Associations with stress reactivity and regulation in 10-12-year-old children. *Psychoneuroendocrinology, 34*(1), 62–75.

Harlow, H. F., Harlow, M. K., & Suomi, S. J. (1971). From thought to therapy: Lessons from a primate laboratory. *American Scientist, 59*(5), 538–549.

Harrington, D., Black, M. M., Starr, R. H., Jr., & Dubowitz, H. (1998). Child neglect: Relation to child temperament and family context. *The American Journal of Orthopsychiatry, 68*(1), 108–116.

Harrington, D., Zuravin, S., DePanfilis, D., Ting, L., & Dubowitz, H. (2002). The neglect scale: Confirmatory factor analyses in a low-income sample. *Child Maltreatment, 7*(4), 359–368.

Hartos, J., Eitel, P., & Simons-Morton, B. (2002). Parenting practices and adolescent risky driving: A three-month prospective study. *Health Education & Behavior, 29*(2), 194–206.

Helsen, M., Vollebergh, W., & Meeus, W. (2000). Social support from parents and friends and emotional problems in adolescence. *Journal of Youth and Adolescence, 29*(3), 319–335.

Herrenkohl, R. C., Herrenkohl, E. C., & Egolf, B. P. (1983). Circumstances surrounding the occurrence of child maltreatment. *Journal of Consulting and Clinical Psychology, 51*(3), 424–431.

Hibbard, R. A., & Desch, L. W. (2007). Maltreatment of children with disabilities. *Pediatrics, 119*(5), 1018–1025.

Hildyard, K., & Wolfe, D. (2007). Cognitive processes associated with child neglect. *Child Abuse & Neglect, 31*(8), 895–907.

Hillis, S. D., Anda, R. F., Dube, S. R., Felitti, V. J., Marchbanks, P. A., & Marks, J. S. (2004). The association between adverse childhood experiences and adolescent pregnancy, long-term psychosocial consequences, and fetal death. *Pediatrics, 113*(2), 320–327.

Hinrichs, P. (2010). The effects of the national school lunch program on education and health. *Journal of Policy Analysis and Management, 29*(3), 479–505.

Hoffman-Plotkin, D., & Twentyman, C. T. (1984). A multimodal assessment of behavioral and cognitive deficits in abused and neglected preschoolers. *Child Development, 55*(3), 794–802.

Holahan, C. J., Valentiner, D. P., & Moos, R. H. (1995). Parental support, coping strategies, and psychological adjustment: An integrative model with late adolescents. *Journal of Youth and Adolescence, 24*(6), 633–648.

Holden, G. W., & Miller, P. C. (1999). Enduring and different: A meta-analysis of the similarity in parents' child rearing. *Psychological Bulletin, 125*(2), 223–254.

Holt, M. K., Straus, M. A., & Kaufman Kantor, G. (2004). A short-form of the parent-report multidimensional neglectful behavior scale. Paper presented at the conference on victimization of children and youth: An International Research Conference, Portsmouth, NH, 12 July 2004.

Horner-Johnson, W., & Drum, C. E. (2006). *Prevalence of maltreatment of people with intellectual disabilities: A review of recently published research.* New Jersey: Wiley.

Howard, K. S., & Brooks-Gunn J. (2009). *The role of home-visiting programs in preventing child abuse and neglect.* David and Lucile Packard Foundation.

Howard, T., Dresser, S. G., & Dunklee, D. R. (2009b). *Poverty is not a learning disability: Equalizing opportunities for low SES students* (p. 140). Thousand Oaks: Corwin Press.

Howell, E. M., & Kenney, G. M. (2012). The impact of the Medicaid/CHIP expansions on children: A synthesis of the evidence. *Medical Care Research & Review, 69*(4), 372–396.

Hussey, J. M., Chang, J. J., & Kotch, J. B. (2006). Child maltreatment in the United States: Prevalence, risk factors, and adolescent health consequences. *Pediatrics, 118*(3), 933–942.

Ireland, T., & Widom, C. S. (1994). Childhood victimization and risk for alcohol and drug arrests. *The International Journal of the Addictions, 29*(2), 235–274.

Ireland, T. O., Smith, C. A., & Thornberry, T. P. (2002). Developmental issues in the impact of child maltreatment on later delinquency and drug use. *Criminology, 40*(2), 359–396.

Jaffee, S. R., & Maikovich-Fong, A. K. (2011). Effects of chronic maltreatment and maltreatment timing on children's behavior and cognitive abilities. *Journal of Child Psychology and Psychiatry, 52*(2), 184–194.

Jaudes, P. K., & Mackey-Bilaver, L. (2008). *Do chronic conditions increase young children's risk of being maltreated?* *Child Abuse & Neglect, 32*(7), 671–681.

Johnson, D. E., & Gunnar, M. R., IV. (2011). Growth failure in institutionalized children. *Monographs of the Society for Research in Child Development, 76*(4), 92–126.

Jones, L., & Finkelhor, D. (2009). *Updated trends in child maltreatment, 2007.* Durham: Crimes against Children Research Center.

Jones, J., & McNeely, R. L. (1980). Mothers who neglect and those who do not: A comparative study. *Social Casework, 61*, 559–567.

Jones, D. J., Runyan, D. K., Lewis, T., et al. (2010). Trajectories of childhood sexual abuse and early adolescent HIV/AIDS risk behaviors: The role of other maltreatment, witnessed violence, and child gender. *Journal of Clinical Child and Adolescent Psychology, 39*(5), 667–680.

Jonson-Reid, M., Drake, B., Chung, S., & Way, I. (2003). Cross-type recidivism among child maltreatment victims and perpetrators. *Child Abuse & Neglect, 27*(8), 899–917.

Jonson-Reid, M., Emery, C. R., Drake, B., & Stahlschmidt, M. J. (2010). Understanding chronically reported families. *Child Maltreatment, 15*(4), 271–281.

Kadushin, A. (1988). Neglect in families. In E. W. Nunnally & C. S. Chilman (Eds.), *Mental illness, delinquency, addictions, and neglect* (pp. 147–166). Thousand Oaks: Sage.

Kaplan, C., Schene, P., DePanfilis, D., & Gilmore, D. (2009). Introduction: Shining light on chronic neglect. *Protecting Children, 24*(1), 2–8.

Kaplow, J. B., & Widom, C. S. (2007). Age of onset of child maltreatment predicts long-term mental health outcomes. *Journal of Abnormal Psychology, 116*(1), 176–187.

Kaufman Kantor, G., Holt, M. K., Mebert, C. J., et al. (2004a). Development and preliminary psychometric properties of the multidimensional neglectful behavior scale-child report. *Child Maltreatment, 9*(4), 409–428.

Kaufman Kantor, G., Holt, M., & Straus, M. A. (2004b). *The parent-report multidimensional neglectful behavior scale.* Durham: Family Research Laboratory.

Kelleher, K., Chaffin, M., Hollenberg, J., & Fischer, E. (1994). Alcohol and drug disorders among physically abusive and neglectful parents in a community-based sample. *American Journal of Public Health, 84*(10), 1586–1590.

Kendall-Tackett, K. A., & Eckenrode, J. (1996). The effects of neglect on academic achievement and disciplinary problems: A developmental perspective. *Child Abuse & Neglect, 20*(3), 161–169.

Kendall-Tackett, K., Lyon, T., Taliaferro, G., & Little, L. (2005). Why child maltreatment researchers should include children's disability status in their maltreatment studies. *Child Abuse & Neglect, 29*(2), 147–151.

Kilpatrick, D. G., Acierno, R., Saunders, B., Resnick, H. S., Best, C. L., & Schnurr, P. P. (2000). Risk factors for adolescent substance abuse and dependence: Data from a national sample. *Journal of Consulting and Clinical Psychology, 68*(1), 19–30.

Kilpatrick, D. G., Ruggiero, K. J., Acierno, R., Saunders, B. E., Resnick, H. S., & Best, C. L. (2003). Violence and risk of PTSD, major depression, substance abuse/dependence, and comorbidity: Results from the national survey of adolescents. *Journal of Consulting and Clinical Psychology, 71*(4), 692–700.

Kim, J. (2009). Type-specific intergenerational transmission of neglectful and physically abusive parenting behaviors among young parents. *Children and Youth Services Review, 31*(7), 761–767.

Kim, J., Dubowitz, H., Hudson-Martin, E., & Lane, W. (2008). Comparison of 3 data collection methods for gathering sensitive and less sensitive information. *Ambulatory Pediatrics, 8*(4), 255–260.

Kirisci, L., Dunn, M. G., Mezzich, A. C., & Tarter, R. E. (2001). Impact of parental substance use disorder and child neglect severity on substance use involvement in male offspring. *Prevention Science, 2*(4), 241–255.

Kitzman, H., Olds, D. L., Henderson, C. R., et al. (1997). Effect of prenatal and infancy home visitation by nurses on pregnancy outcomes, childhood injuries, and repeated childbearing. A randomized controlled trial. *Journal of the American Medical Association, 278*(8), 644–652.

Knight, E. D., Runyan, D. K., Dubowitz, H., et al. (2000). Methodological and ethical challenges associated with child self-report of maltreatment: Solutions implemented by the LongSCAN consortium. *Journal of Interpersonal Violence, 15*(7), 760–775.

Knight, E. D., Smith, J. S., Martin, L., Lewis, T., & the LONGSCAN Investigators. (2008). Measures for assessment of functioning and outcomes in longitudinal research on child abuse Vol 3: Adolescence. Accessible at the LONGSCAN web site (http://www.iprc.unc.edu/longscan/).

Knutson, J. F., Taber, S. M., Murray, A. J., Valles, N.-L., & Koeppl, G. (2010). The role of care neglect and supervisory neglect in childhood obesity in a disadvantaged sample. *Journal of Pediatric Psychology, 35*(5), 523–532.

Korbin, J. E., & Spilsbury, J. C. (1999). Cultural competence and child neglect. In H. Dubowitz (Ed.), *Neglected children: Research, practice, and policy* (pp. 69–88). Thousand Oaks: Sage.

Kotch, J. B., Browne, D. C., Ringwalt, C. L., Stewart, P. W., et al. (1995). Risk of child abuse or neglect in a cohort of low-income children. *Child Abuse & Neglect, 19*(9), 1115–1130.

Kotch, J. B., Lewis, T., Hussey, J. M., et al. (2008). Importance of early neglect for childhood aggression. *Pediatrics, 121*(4), 725–731.

Kumsta, R., Rutter, M., Stevens, S., & Sonuga-Barke, E. J. (2010). IX. Risk, causation, mediation, and moderation. *Monographs of the Society for Research in Child Development, 75*(1), 187–211.

Lam, B. C. C., Lee, J., & Lau, Y. L. (2004). Hand hygiene practices in a neonatal intensive care unit: A multimodal intervention and impact on nosocomial infection. *Pediatrics, 114*(5), e565–e571.

Lansford, J. E., Dodge, K. A., Pettit, G. S., & Bates, J. E. (2010). Does physical abuse in early childhood predict substance use in adolescence and early adulthood? *Child Maltreatment, 15*(2), 190–194.

Laslett, A.-M., Room, R., Dietze, P., & Ferris, J. (2012). Alcohol's involvement in recurrent child abuse and neglect cases. *Addiction, 107*(10), 1786–1793.

Lee, B. J., & Mackey-Bilaver, L. (2007). Effects of WIC and food stamp program participation on child outcomes. *Children and Youth Services Review, 29*, 501–517.

Lee, S. J., Taylor, C. A., & Bellamy, J. L. (2012). Paternal depression and risk for child neglect in father-involved families of young children. *Child Abuse & Neglect: International Journal, 36*(5), 461–469.

Lempinen, E. W. (2012). Poverty can harm early brain development, researchers say. *Science, 337*(6093), 428.

Leventhal, T., & Brooks-Gunn, J. (2011). Changes in neighborhood poverty from 1990 to 2000 and youth's problem behaviors. *Developmental Psychology, 47*(6), 1680–1698.

Li, X., Stanton, B., & Feigelman, S. (2000a). Impact of perceived parental monitoring on adolescent risk behavior over 4 years. *The Journal of Adolescent Health, 27*(1), 49–56.

Li, X., Feigelman, S., & Stanton, B. (2000b). Perceived parental monitoring and health risk behaviors among urban low-income african-american children and adolescents. *The Journal of Adolescent Health, 27*(1), 43–48.

Lieberman, A. F., Weston, D. R., & Pawl, J. H. (1991). Preventive intervention and outcome with anxiously attached dyads. *Child Development, 62*(1), 199–209.

Lieberman, A. F., Ippen, C. G., & Van Horn, P. (2006). Child-parent psychotherapy: 6-month follow-up of a randomized controlled trial. *Journal of the American Academy of Child & Adolescent Psychiatry, 45*(8), 913–918.

Lightfoot, E., Hill, K., & LaLiberte, T. (2011). Prevalence of children with disabilities in the child welfare system and out of home placement: An examination of administrative records. *Children and Youth Services Review, 33*(11), 2069–2075.

Lipina, S. J., & Colombo, J. A. (2009). *Poverty and brain development during childhood: An approach from cognitive psychology and neuroscience.* Washington, DC: American Psychological Association.

Loeber, R., Drinkwater, M., Yin, Y., Anderson, S. J., Schmidt, L. C., & Crawford, A. (2000). Stability of family interaction from ages 6 to 18. *Journal of Abnormal Child Psychology, 28*(4), 353–369.

Loman, L. A. (2006). *Families frequently encountered by child protection services: A report on chronic abuse and neglect.* St. Louis: Institute of Applied Research.

Loman, L. A., & Siegel, G. L. (2012). Effects of anti-poverty services under the differential response approach to child welfare. *Children and Youth Services Review, 34*(9), 1659–1666.

Lovejoy, M. C., Graczyk, P. A., O'Hare, E., & Neuman, G. (2000). Maternal depression and parenting behavior: A meta-analytic review. *Clinical Psychology Review, 20*(5), 561–592.

Luthar, S. S. (1999). *Poverty and children's adjustment.* Thousand Oaks, CA: Sage.

Luthar, S. S. (2006). Resilience in development: A synthesis of research across five decades. In D. Cicchetti & D. J. Cohen (Eds.), *Developmental psychopathology: Risk, disorder, and adaptation* (pp. 740–795). New York: Wiley.

Magura, S., & Moses, B. S. (1986). *Outcome measures for child welfare services.* Washington, DC: Child Welfare League of America.

Marshall, P. J., & Fox, N. A. (2004). A comparison of the electroencephalogram between institutionalized and community children in Romania. *Journal of Cognitive Neuroscience, 16*(8), 1327–1338.

Marshall, P. J., Reeb, B. C., Fox, N. A., Nelson, C. A., & Zeanah, C. H. (2008). Effects of early intervention on EEG power and coherence in previously institutionalized children in Romania. *Development and Psychopathology, 20*(3), 861–880.

Marta, E. (1997). Parent-adolescent interactions and psychosocial risk in adolescents: An analysis of communication, support and gender. *Journal of Adolescence, 20*(5), 473–487.

Martínez, G. S. (2008). El maltrato infantil: Mecanismos subyacentes. *Avances en Psicología Latinoamericana, 26*(2), 171–179.

Masten, A. S., & Cicchetti, D. (2010). Developmental cascades. *Development and Psychopathology, 22*(3), 491–495.

Masten, A. S., Hubbard, J. J., Gest, S. D., Tellegen, A., Garmezy, N., & Ramirez, M. (1999). Competence in the context of adversity: Pathways to resilience and maladaptation from childhood to late adolescence. *Development and Psychopathology, 11*(1), 143–169.

McCroskey, J., Nishimoto, R., & Subramanian, K. (1991). Assessment in family support programs: Initial reliability and validity testing of the family assessment form. *Child Welfare, 70*(1), 19–33.

McCurdy, K. (2005). The influence of support and stress on maternal attitudes. *Child Abuse & Neglect, 29*(3), 251–268.

McGuigan, W. M., & Pratt, C. C. (2001). The predictive impact of domestic violence on three types of child maltreatment. *Child Abuse & Neglect, 25*(7), 869–883.

McLoyd, V. C. (1998). Socioeconomic disadvantage and child development. *The American Psychologist, 53*(2), 185–204.

McLoyd, V. C., Aikens, N. L., & Burton, L. M. (2006). Childhood poverty, policy, and practice. In E. Sigel Irving, W. Damon, & M. Lerner Richard (Eds.), *Handbook of child psychology* (Child psychology in practice 6th ed., pp. 2700–2775). Hoboken: Wiley.

McLoyd, V. C., Kaplan, R., Purtell, K. M., Bagley, E., Hardaway, C. R., & Smalls, C. (2009). Poverty and socioeconomic disadvantage in adolescence. In R. M. Lerner & L. Steinberg (Eds.), *Handbook of adolescent psychology, Vol 2: Contextual influences on adolescent development* (3rd ed., pp. 444–491). Hoboken: Wiley.

Merrick, M. T., Litrownik, A. J., Everson, M. D., & Cox, C. E. (2008). Beyond sexual abuse: The impact of other maltreatment experiences on sexualized behaviors. *Child Maltreatment Special Issue: Children with Sexual Behavior Problems, 13*(2), 122–132.

Mersky, J. P., Topitzes, J., & Reynolds, A. J. (2009). Chronic neglect: Prediction and prevention. *Protecting Children, 24*(1), 67–77.

Mills, R., Alati, R., O'Callaghan, M., et al. (2011). Child abuse and neglect and cognitive function at 14 years of Age: Findings from a birth cohort. *Pediatrics, 127*(1), 4–10.

Milot, T., St-Laurent, D., Ethier, L. S., & Provost, M. A. (2010). Trauma-related symptoms in neglected preschoolers and affective quality of mother-child communication. *Child Maltreatment, 15*(4), 293–304.

Mishel, L., Bivens, J., GouLd, E., & Shierholz, H. (2012). *The state of working America* (12th ed.). Ithaca: Cornell University Press.

Moran, P. B., Vuchinich, S., & Hall, N. K. (2004). Associations between types of maltreatment and substance use during adolescence. *Child Abuse & Neglect, 28*(5), 565–574.

National Commission on Children. (1991). *Beyond rhetoric: A new American agenda for children and families.* Washington, DC: GPO. Quote on p. 293.

National Research Council. (1993). *Panel on high-risk youth, losing generations: Adolescents in high-risk settings.* Washington, DC: Academic.

National Research Council and Institute of Medicine. (2009). Preventing mental, emotional, and behavioral disorders among young people: Progress and possibilities. Committee on the prevention of mental disorders and substance abuse among children, youth, and young adults: Research advances and promising interventions. In M. E. O'Connell, T. Boat & K. E. Warner (Eds). *Board on children, youth, and families, division of behavioral and social sciences and education.* Washington, DC: The National Academies Press.

Nelson, K. E., Saunders, E. J., & Landsman, M. J. (1993). Chronic child neglect in perspective. *Social Work, 38*(6), 661.

Nelson, C. A., Bos, K., Gunnar, M. R., & Sonuga-Barke, E. J. S. (2011). The neurobiological toll of early human deprivation. *Monographs of the Society for Research in Child Development, 76*(4), 127–146.

Newman, S., Leventhal, T., & Gennetian, L. A. (2010). Meeting children's basic needs: Introduction. *Children and Youth Services Review, 32*(9), 1133–1137.

Nikulina, V., Widom, C., & Czaja, S. (2011). The role of childhood neglect and childhood poverty in predicting mental health, academic achievement and crime in adulthood. *American Journal of Community Psychology, 48*(3/4), 309–321.

O'Connell, M. E., Boat, T., & Warner, K. E. (2009). *Preventing mental, emotional, and behavioral disorders among young people: Progress and possibilities.* Washington, DC: National Academies Press.

Oberlander, S. E., Wang, Y., Thompson, R., et al. (2011). Childhood maltreatment, emotional distress, and early adolescent sexual intercourse: Multi-informant perspectives on parental monitoring. *Journal of Family Psychology, 25*(6), 885–894.

Olds, D., Edkenrode, J., Henderson, C., & Kitzman, H. (1983). Long-term effects of home visitation on maternal life course and child abuse and neglect: Fifteen-year follow-up of a randomized trail. *Journal of the American Medical Association, 278*(8), 637–643.

Olds, D. L., Henderson, C. R., Chamberlin, R., & Tatelbaum, R. (1986). Preventing child abuse and neglect: A randomized trial of nurse home visitation. *Pediatrics, 78*(1), 65.

Olds, D. L., Henderson, C. R., Jr., & Kitzman, H. (1994). Does prenatal and infancy nurse home visitation have enduring effects on qualities of parental caregiving and child health at 25 to 50 months of life? *Pediatrics, 93*(1), 89–98.

Ondersma, S. J. (2002). Predictors of neglect within low-SES families: The importance of substance abuse. *The American Journal of Orthopsychiatry, 72*(3), 383–391.

Pettit, G. S., Laird, R. D., Dodge, K. A., Bates, J. E., & Criss, M. M. (2001). Antecedents and behavior-problem outcomes of parental monitoring and psychological control in early adolescence. *Child Development, 72*(2), 583–598.

Polansky, N. A., Chalmers, M. A., Buttenwieser, E. W., & Williams, D. P. (1981). *Damaged parents: An anatomy of child neglect.* Chicago: University of Chicago Press.

Polansky, N. A., Gaudin, J. M., Ammons, P. W., & Davis, K. B. (1985a). The psychological ecology of the neglectful mother. *Child Abuse & Neglect, 9*(2), 265–275.

Polansky, N. A., Ammons, P. W., & Gaudin, J. M. (1985b). Loneliness and isolation in child neglect. *Social Casework, 66*(1), 38–47.

Polansky, N. A., Gaudin, J. M., & Kilpatrick, A. C. (1992). Family radicals. *Children and Youth Services Review. Special Issue: Reforming Child Welfare Through Demonstration and Evaluation, 14*(1–2), 19–26.

Pollak, S. D., Cicchetti, D., Hornung, K., & Reed, A. (2000). Recognizing emotion in faces: Developmental effects of child abuse and neglect. *Developmental Psychology, 36*(5), 679–688.

Prince, D. L., & Howard, E. M. (2002). Children and their basic needs. *Early Childhood Education Journal, 30*(1), 27–31.

Pritchard, C., & Williams, R. (2011). Poverty and child mortality in the USA and other western countries as an indicator of 'how well a country meets the needs of its children' (UNICEF). *International Journal of Adolescent Medicine and Health, 23*(3), 251–255.

Proctor, L. J., Aarons, G. A., Dubowitz, H., et al. (2012). Trajectories of maltreatment re-reports from ages 4 to 12: Evidence for persistent risk after early exposure. *Child Maltreatment, 17*(3), 207–217.

Ramiro, L. S., Madrid, B. J., & Brown, D. W. (2010). Adverse childhood experiences (ACE) and health-risk behaviors among adults in a developing country setting. *Child Abuse & Neglect, 34*(11), 842–855.

Rees, G., Stein, M., & Hicks, L. (2011). *Adolescent neglect: Research, policy and practice.* London: Jessica Kingsley.

Rodrigo, M. J., León, I., Quiñones, I., Lage, A., Byrne, S., & Bobes, M. A. (2011). Brain and personality bases of insensitivity to infant cues in neglectful mothers: An event-related potential study. *Development and Psychopathology, 23*(1), 163–176.

Rohde, P., Ichikawa, L., Simon, G. E., et al. (2008). Associations of child sexual and physical abuse with obesity and depression in middle-aged women. *Child Abuse & Neglect, 32*, 878–887.

Roth, T. L., & Sweatt, J. D. (2011). Epigenetic marking of the BDNF gene by early-life adverse experiences. *Hormones and Behavior, 59*(3), 315–320.

Roth, T. L., Levenson, J. M., Sullivan, R. M., & Sweatt, J. D. (2006). Epigenetic marking of the genome by early experiences: Implications for long-lasting effects of early maltreatment on adult cognitive and emotional health. In S. M. Sturt (Ed.), *Child abuse: New research* (pp. 79–114). Hauppauge: Nova.

Runyan, D. K., Curtis, P. A., Hunter, W. M., et al. (1998). LONGSCAN: A consortium for longitudinal studies of maltreatment and the life course of children. *Aggression & Violent Behavior, 3*(3), 275–285.

Rutter, M. (2006). Implications of resilience concepts for scientific understanding. In B. M. Lester, A. Masten, & B. McEwen (Eds.), *Resilience in children* (pp. 1–12). Malden: Blackwell Publishing.

Rutter, M., Sonuga-Barke, E. J., Beckett, C., et al. (2010). Deprivation-specific psychological patterns: Effects of institutional deprivation. *Monographs of the Society for Research in Child Development, 75*(1).

Sanchez, M. M., & Pollak, S. D. (2009). Socioemotional development following early abuse and neglect: Challenges and insights from translational research. In M. de Haan & M. R. Gunnar (Eds.), *Handbook of developmental social neuroscience* (pp. 497–520). New York: Guilford Press.

Schneiderman, J. U., Mennen, F. E., Negriff, S., & Trickett, P. K. (2012). Overweight and obesity among maltreated young adolescents. *Child Abuse & Neglect, 36*(4), 370–378.

Schnitzer, P. G., Covington, T. M., & Kruse, R. L. (2011). Assessment of caregiver responsibility in unintentional child injury deaths: Challenges for injury prevention. *Injury Prevention, 17*, 45–54.

Seagull, E. A. (1987). Social support and child maltreatment: A review of the evidence. *Child Abuse & Neglect, 11*(1), 41–52.

Sedlak, A. J., Mettenburg, J., Basena, M., Petta, I., McPherson, K., Greene, A., & Li, S. (2010). *Fourth national incidence study of child abuse and neglect (NIS-4): Report to Congress.* Washington, DC: Department of Health and Human Services, Administration for Children and Families.

Sfoggia, A., Pacheco, M. A., & Grassi-Oliveira, R. (2008). History of childhood abuse and neglect and suicidal behavior at hospital admission. *Crisis: The Journal of Crisis Intervention and Suicide Prevention, 29*(3), 154–158.

Sheridan, M. J. (1995). A proposed intergenerational model of substance abuse, family functioning, and abuse/neglect. *Child Abuse & Neglect, 19*(5), 519–530.

Sheridan, M. A., Fox, N. A., Zeanah, C. H., McLaughlin, K. A., & Nelson, C. A., III. (2012). Variation in neural development as a result of exposure to institutionalization early in childhood. *PNAS Proceedings of the National Academy of Sciences of the United States of America, 109*(32), 12927–12932.

Shin, S. H., & Miller, D. P. (2012). A longitudinal examination of childhood maltreatment and adolescent obesity: Results from the National Longitudinal Study of Adolescent Health (AddHealth) study. *Child Abuse & Neglect, 36*(2), 84–94.

Shin, S. H., Edwards, E., Heeren, T., & Amodeo, M. (2009). Relationship between multiple forms of maltreatment by a parent or guardian and adolescent alcohol use. *The American Journal on Addictions, 18*(3), 226–234.

Shin, S. H., Miller, D. P., & Teicher, M. H. (2012). Exposure to childhood neglect and physical abuse and developmental trajectories of heavy episodic drinking from early adolescence into young adulthood. *Drug and Alcohol Dependence, 127*(1–3), 31–38.

Shipman, K., Edwards, A., Brown, A., Swisher, L., & Jennings, E. (2005). Managing emotion in a maltreating context: A pilot study examining child neglect. *Child Abuse & Neglect, 29*(9), 1015–1029.

Shonkoff, J. P. (2010). Building a new biodevelopmental framework to guide the future of early childhood policy: The effects of early experience on development. *Child Development, 81*(1), 357–367.

Shonkoff, J. P., Garner, A. S., Siegel, B. S., et al. (2012). The lifelong effects of early childhood adversity and toxic stress. *Pediatrics, 129*(1), e232–e246.

Slack, K. S., Holl, J., Altenbernd, L., McDaniel, M., & Stevens, A. B. (2003). Improving the measurement of child neglect for survey research: Issues and recommendations. *Child Maltreatment, 8*(2), 98–111.

Slack, K. S., Berger, L. M., DuMont, K., et al. (2011). Risk and protective factors for child neglect during early childhood: A cross-study comparison. *Children and Youth Services Review, 33*(8), 1354–1363.

Slopen, N., Fitzmaurice, G., Williams, D. R., & Gilman, S. E. (2010). Poverty, food insecurity, and the behavior for childhood internalizing and externalizing disorders. *Journal of the American Academy of Child and Adolescent Psychiatry, 49*(5), 444–452.

Smith, C. A., Ireland, T. O., & Thornberry, T. P. (2005). Adolescent maltreatment and its impact on young adult antisocial behavior. *Child Abuse & Neglect, 29*(10), 1099–1119.

Sroufe, L. A., & Rutter, M. (1984). The domain of developmental psychopathology. *Child Development, 55*(1), 17–29.

Steib, S., & Blome, W. W. (2009). How can neglected organizations serve neglected children? *Protecting Children, 24*(1), 9–19.

Stein, D. J., Chiu, W. T., Hwang, I., et al. (2010). Cross-national analysis of the associations between traumatic events and suicidal behavior: Findings from the WHO world mental health surveys. *PloS One, 5*(5), 2010.

Sternberg, K. J., & Lamb, M. E. (1991). Can we ignore context in the definition of child maltreatment? *Development and Psychopathology, 3*(1), 87–92.

Stewart, C., Mezzich, A. C., & Bang-Shiuh, D. (2006). Parental psychopathology and paternal child neglect in late childhood. *Journal of Child and Family Studies, 15*(5), 542–553.

Stice, E., Barrera, M., & Chassin, L. (1993). Relation of parental support and control to adolescents' externalizing symptomatology and substance use: A longitudinal examination of curvilinear effects. *Journal of Abnormal Child Psychology, 21*(6), 609–629.

Strathearn, L. (2011). Maternal neglect: Oxytocin, dopamine and the neurobiology of attachment. *Journal of Neuroendocrinology, 23*(11), 1054–1065.

Strathearn, L., Gray, P. H., O'Callaghan, M. J., & Wood, D. O. (2001). Childhood neglect and cognitive development in extremely low birth weight infants: A prospective study. *Pediatrics, 108*(1), 142–151.

Strathearn, L., Mamun, A. A., Najman, J. M., & O'Callaghan, M. J. (2009). Does breastfeeding protect against substantiated child abuse and neglect? A 15-year cohort study. *Pediatrics, 123*(2), 483–493.

Straus, M. A. (2006). Cross-cultural reliability and validity of the multidimensional neglectful behavior scale adult recall short form. *Child Abuse & Neglect, 30*(11), 1257–1279.

Straus, M. A., & Kantor, G. K. (2005). Definition and measurement of neglectful behavior: Some principles and guidelines. *Child Abuse & Neglect, 29*(1), 19–29.

Straus, M. A., & Savage, S. A. (2005). Neglectful behavior by parents in the life history of university students in 17 countries and its relation to violence against dating partners. *Child Maltreatment, 10*(2), 124–135.

Straus, M. A., Kinard, M. E., & Williams, L. M. (1995a). *The neglect scale*. Durham, NH: University of New Hampshire, Family research laboratory. Available in: http://pubpages.unh.edu/~mas2/

Straus, M. A., Kinard, M. E., & Williams, L. M. (1995b). *The multidimensional neglectful behavior scale, Form A: Adolescent and adult-recall version*. Durham, NH: University of New Hampshire: Family Research Laboratory. Available in: http://pubpages.unh.edu/~mas2/

Sullivan, M. W., Bennett, D. S., Carpenter, K., & Lewis, M. (2008). Emotion knowledge in young neglected children. *Child Maltreatment, 13*(3), 301–306.

Sylvestre, A., & Mérette, C. (2010). Language delay in severely neglected children: A cumulative or specific effect of risk factors? *Child Abuse & Neglect, 34*(6), 414–428.

Tarullo, A. R., Garvin, M. C., & Gunnar, M. R. (2011). Atypical EEG power correlates with indiscriminately friendly behavior in internationally adopted children. *Developmental Psychology, 47*(2), 417–431.

Thompson, R., Litrownik, A. J., Isbell, P., et al. (2012a). Adverse experiences and suicidal ideation in adolescence: Exploring the link using the LONGSCAN samples. *Psychology of Violence, 2*(2), 211–225.

Thompson, R., Proctor, L. J., English, D. J., Dubowitz, H., Narasimhan, S., & Everson, M. D. (2012b). Suicidal ideation in adolescence: Examining the role of recent adverse experiences. *Journal of Adolescence, 35*(1), 175–186.

Thornberry, T. P., Ireland, T. O., & Smith, C. A. (2001). The importance of timing: The varying impact of childhood and adolescent maltreatment on multiple problem outcomes. *Development and Psychopathology, 13*(4), 957–979.

Thornberry, T. P., Henry, K. L., Ireland, T. O., & Smith, C. A. (2010). The causal impact of childhood-limited maltreatment and adolescent maltreatment on early adult adjustment. *The Journal of Adolescent Health, 46*(4), 359–365.

Topitzes, J., Mersky, J. P., & Reynolds, A. J. (2010). Child maltreatment and adult cigarette smoking: A long-term developmental model. *Journal of Pediatric Psychology, 35*(5), 484–498.

Turner, H. A., Finkelhor, D., & Ormrod, R. (2010). Poly-victimization in a national sample of children and youth. *American Journal of Preventive Medicine, 38*(3), 323–330.

van Harmelen, A.-L., van Tol, M.-J., van der Wee, N. J. A., et al. (2010). Reduced medial prefrontal cortex volume in adults reporting childhood emotional maltreatment. *Biological Psychiatry, 68*(9), 832–838.

van Ijzendoorn, M. H., & Juffer, F. (2006). The Emanuel Miller Memorial Lecture 2006: Adoption as intervention. Meta-analytic evidence for massive catch-up and plasticity in physical, socio-emotional, and cognitive development. *Journal of Child Psychology and Psychiatry, 47*(12), 1228–1245.

Venet, M., Bureau, J.-F., Gosselin, C., & Capuano, F. (2007). Attachment representations in a sample of neglected preschool-age children. *School Psychology International, 28*(3), 264–293.

Voisin, D. R. (2005). The relationship between violence exposure and HIV sexual risk behavior: Does gender matter? *The American Journal of Orthopsychiatry, 75*(4), 497–506.

Weill, J. D. (2012). Hunger in America. *Clearinghouse Review, 46*(5/6), 189–201.

Wesson, D. E., Stephens, D., Lam, K., Parsons, D., Spence, L., & Parkin, P. C. (2008). Trends in pediatric and adult bicycling deaths before and after passage of a bicycle helmet law. *Pediatrics, 122*(3), 605–610.

White, M. G., Bogdan, R., Fisher, P. M., Muñoz, K. E., Williamson, D. E., & Hariri, A. R. (2012). FKBP5 and emotional neglect interact to predict individual differences in amygdala reactivity. *Genes, Brain, and Behavior, 11*(7), 869–878.

Whitfield, C. L., Anda, R. F., Dube, S. R., & Felitti, V. J. (2003). Violent childhood experiences and the risk of intimate partner violence in adults: Assessment in a large health maintenance organization. *Journal of Interpersonal Violence, 18*(2), 166–185.

Widom, C. S., Ireland, T., & Glynn, P. J. (1995). Alcohol abuse in abused and neglected children followed-up: Are they at increased risk? *Journal of Studies on Alcohol, 56*(2), 207–217.

Widom, C. S., Raphael, K. G., & DuMont, K. A. (2004). The case for prospective longitudinal studies in child maltreatment research: Commentary on Dube, Williamson, Thompson, Felitti, and Anda. *Child Abuse & Neglect, 28*(7), 715–722.

Widom, C. S., Dutton, M. A., Czaja, S. J., & DuMont, K. A. (2005). Development and validation of a new instrument to assess lifetime trauma and victimization history. *Journal of Traumatic Stress, 18*(5), 519–531.

Williamson, J. M., Borduin, C. M., & Howe, B. A. (1991). The ecology of adolescent maltreatment: A multilevel examination of adolescent physical abuse, sexual abuse, and neglect. *Journal of Consulting and Clinical Psychology, 59*(3), 449–457.

Williamson, D. F., Thompson, T. J., Anda, R. F., Dietz, W. H., & Felitti, V. (2002). Body weight and obesity in adults and self-reported abuse in childhood. *International Journal of Obesity and Related Metabolic Disorders, 26*(8), 1075–1082.

Wills, T. A., & Cleary, S. D. (1996). How are social support effects mediated? A test with parental support and adolescent substance use. *Journal of Personality and Social Psychology, 71*(5), 937–952.

Wilson, D., & Homer, W. (2005). Chronic child neglect: Needed developments in theory and research. *Families in Society, 86*(4), 471–481.

Wilson, H. W., & Widom, C. S. (2008). An examination of risky sexual behavior and HIV in victims of child abuse and neglect: A 30-year follow-up. *Health Psychology, 27*(2), 149–158.

Wilson, H. W., & Widom, C. S. (2009). Sexually transmitted diseases among adults who had been abused and neglected as children: A 30-year prospective study. *American Journal of Public Health, 99*, S197–S203.

Wilson, S. R., Rack, J. J., Shi, X., & Norris, A. M. (2008). Comparing physically abusive, neglectful, and non-maltreating parents during interactions with their children: A meta-analysis of observational studies. *Child Abuse & Neglect, 32*(9), 897–911.

Wodarski JS, Kurtz PD, Gaudin Jr JM, Howing PT. (1990). Maltreatment and the School-Age Child: Major Academic, Socioemotional, and Adaptive Outcomes. *Social Work, 35*(6), 506–513.

Wolock, I., & Horowitz, B. (1984). Child maltreatment as a social problem: The neglect of neglect. *The American Journal of Orthopsychiatry, 54*(4), 530–543.

Wolock, I., Sherman, P., Feldman, L. H., & Metzger, B. (2001). Child abuse and neglect referral patterns: A longitudinal study. *Children and Youth Services Review. Special Issue: Assessing and Managing Risk in Child Protective Services, 23*(1), 21–47.

Yoshikawa, H., Aber, J. L., & Beardslee, W. R. (2012). The effects of poverty on the mental, emotional, and behavioral health of children and youth: Implications for prevention. *The American Psychologist, 67*(4), 272–284.

Zolotor, A. J., Runyan, D. K., Dunne, M. P., et al. (2009). ISPCAN child abuse screening tool Children's version (ICAST-C): Instrument development and multi-national pilot testing. *Child Abuse & Neglect, 33*(11), 833–841.

Zuravin, S. (1999). Child neglect: A review of definitions and measurement research. In H. Dubowitz (Ed.), *Neglected children: Research, practice and policy* (pp. 24–46). Thousand Oaks: Sage.

Chapter 3
Current Issues in Physical Abuse

Vincent J. Palusci

Current Issues in Physical Abuse

The victimization of children by physical abuse remains an all-too-common occurrence around the globe (Akmatov 2011; Gray 2010). Violence against children exists in every country of the world, cutting across culture, class, education, income and ethnic origin (United Nations 2006). While international estimates vary and likely underestimate the extent of the problem, over 100,000 children were found to be physically abused in the U.S. in 2011, at a rate of almost two children per 1,000 with an estimated 1,570 fatalities in the US alone (U.S. Department of Health and Human Services 2012). Child maltreatment is the reported cause of death in almost 3,500 children under the age of 15 annually in the industrialized world, with the highest risk in infants less than 1 years of age (UNICEF 2003). In addition to death and physical injury, growing evidence further links child maltreatment to physical and emotional disease and disability during adulthood (Widom et al. 2012).

Definitions

While a variety of definitions have been used, child maltreatment generally includes one or more of these five types: physical abuse, sexual abuse, neglect, psychological maltreatment, and other exploitation. The World Health Organization (1999) broadly defines these types of maltreatment for data collection and intervention, with physical abuse defined as that which results in actual or potential physical harm from an interaction or lack of an interaction, which is reasonably within the control of a parent or person in a position of responsibility, power or trust. There may be a single or repeated incidents. The United Nations Convention on the Rights of the Child (1989) states that a child is "[e]very human being below the age of 18 years unless, under the law applicable to the child, majority is attained earlier" and that child maltreatment consists of "all forms of physical or mental violence, injury and abuse, neglect or negligent treatment, maltreatment or exploitation, including sexual abuse." It also includes "intentional use of physical force or power, threatened or actual, against a child, by an individual or group that either results in or has a high likelihood of resulting in actual or potential harm to the child's health, survival, development or dignity."

V.J. Palusci, M.D., M.S. (✉)
New York University School of Medicine, New York, NY, USA
e-mail: Vincent.palusci@nyumc.org

J.E. Korbin and R.D. Krugman (eds.), *Handbook of Child Maltreatment*, Child Maltreatment 2,
DOI 10.1007/978-94-007-7208-3_3, © Springer Science+Business Media Dordrecht 2014

In the U.S., the Institute of Medicine (IOM 2012) notes that the U.S. federal code defines child physical abuse as: "non-accidental physical injury (ranging from minor bruises to severe fractures and or death) as a result of punching, beating, kicking, biting, shaking, throwing, stabbing, choking, hitting (with a hand, stick, strap, or other object), burning, or otherwise harming a child, that is inflicted by a parent, caregiver, or other person who has responsibility for the child." Children who are harmed in armed conflict generally fall outside these child maltreatment regulations but are covered under other local and international statutes and the mandate of the Office of the Special Representative of the UN Secretary-General for Children and Armed Conflict.

History

Physicians have noted specific injuries that stem from child maltreatment, with early identification of physical abuse as a diagnosis in the medical literature by John Caffey and others (Caffey 1946, 1972, 1974). In the 1950s, Paul Woolley and William Evans (1955) in Detroit noted the presence of significant injuries that were inconsistent with parental explanations. Much of what we know about maltreatment stems from this early work in physical abuse. Discussions began with Silverman's identification of fractures (1953, 1972) and Henry Kempe's landmark article naming the battered child syndrome (Kempe et al. 1962). Since that time, articles in the medical literature on maltreatment have escalated in number, having first concentrated on physical abuse in the 1960s and 1970s, and later sexual abuse, domestic violence, neglect, and Munchausen by proxy (American Academy of Pediatrics 1966). In the 45 years since, the subject of child maltreatment has become a universal topic, not restricted to one professional community or to one type of professional for its identification. The "Battered Child Syndrome" has influenced laws, social policies and social practices in several helpful (and not so helpful) ways (Bross and Mathews 2013). As the field has grown, professionals have had to broaden their intellectual and personal perspectives not only to identify, report and prosecute physical abuse, but also to provide interventions to protect children and prevent further abuse.

Epidemiology

The victimization of children through abuse and neglect remains an all too common occurrence. In the United States, 1–2 per 1,000 children are victimized by physical abuse each year, and young children and infants have the highest rates. Maltreated children suffer from a variety of behavior problems and mental disorders in addition to physical injuries (Kaplan et al. 1999). The Adverse Childhood Experiences study has noted the powerful relationship between adverse childhood experiences and several conditions of adulthood, including risk of suicide, alcoholism, depression, illicit drug use, and other lifestyle changes (Felitti et al. 1998). While the exact pathways are still being explored, childhood abuse is thought to affect adult health by putting people at risk for depression and post-traumatic stress disorders, difficulties in relationships, and negative beliefs and attitudes towards others (Kendall-Tackett 2002).

Two large administrative sources provide information about the U.S. annual incidence of child maltreatment, the National Child Abuse and Neglect Data System (NCANDS) and the National Incidence Studies of child abuse and neglect (NIS). NCANDS contains aggregate and case-level data on child abuse reports received by state Child Protective Service (CPS) agencies, and almost all U.S. states and territories provide information annually about the outcomes of child abuse reports, types of maltreatment, child and family factors and services being provided (IOM 2012).

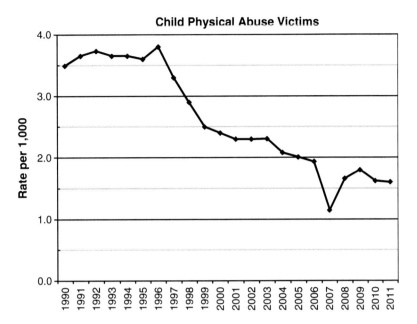

Fig. 3.1 U.S. child physical abuse rates, per 1,000 child population, 1990–2011

National estimates of the overall numbers of victims (substantiated or indicated CPS reports) as well as victims identified with physical abuse show decline over the 20+ years of nationally collected data in the U.S. (Fig. 3.1). This represents a decrease from a high of 261,605 cases in 1996, following similar trends in other national crime statistics (IOM 2012). In contrast, NIS samples sentinel counties to identify under two standards: the harm standard (relatively stringent in that it generally requires that an act or omission result in demonstrable harm in order to be classified as abuse or neglect) and the endangerment standard (which allows children who were not yet harmed by maltreatment to be counted if the CM was confirmed by CPS or identified as endangerment by professionals outside CPS, either by their parents or other adults) (Sedlak et al. 2010). The Fourth National Incidence Study of Child Abuse and Neglect (NIS–4) also shows an overall decrease in the incidence of maltreatment since the NIS–3, as well as decreases in some specific maltreatment categories and increases in others. Using the stringent Harm Standard definition, more than 1.25 million children (an estimated 1,256,600 children) experienced maltreatment during the NIS–4 study year (2005–2006). A large percentage (44 %) or an estimated total of 553,300 were abused, and most of these abused children experienced physical abuse (58 %). "Harm Standard" physical abuse cases decreased from an estimated 381,700 at the time of the NIS–3 to an estimated 323,000 in the NIS–4 (a 15 % decrease in number and a 23 % decline in the rate). Under "Endangerment," the estimated number of physically abused children decreased from an estimated 614,100 children to 476,600 (22 % decrease in number, 29 % decline in the rate) (Sedlak et al. 2010).

Smaller independent samples offer additional information. In the Carolinas, the incidence of harsh physical discipline was found to be 4.3 % of respondents (with 2.4 % shaking infants), and a retrospective prevalence survey, 24 % of adolescents reported being physically assaulted (Hussey et al. 2006; Theodore et al. 2005). The range of incidence rates of abusive head trauma (AHT) has been found to be 27.5–32.2 per 100,000 in a large U.S. inpatient database with 6.6 to 7.4 million discharges annually during 1997–2009 (Leventhal and Gaither 2012). Lane and colleagues (2012) noted hospital discharge rates of 1.8 per 100 k, with 25 % of head trauma in infants being AHT.

While the overall reported numbers of child physical abuse are declining in national statistics, a number of smaller samples have suggested a rise in more serious child physical abuse associated with the U.S. economic recession. Berger and colleagues (2011) noted that the abusive head trauma rate increased from 8.9 to 14.7 per 100,000, and Huang and colleagues (2011) noted a doubling from 0.7 to 1.4 per month during the recession. Wood and colleagues (2012) noted increasing rates of children admitted to hospitals for physical abuse over 10 years 2000–2009, rising from 0.8 % to 3 % annually. Rates of physical abuse reportedly also fell in the UK during 1974–2008 (Sidebotham et al. 2012).

Several factors have been associated with physical abuse. Unlike previous NIS cycles, NIS–4 found strong and pervasive race differences in the incidence of maltreatment with rates of maltreatment for Black children significantly higher than those for White and Hispanic children. Under the Harm Standard, children with confirmed disabilities had significantly lower rates of physical abuse and of moderate harm from maltreatment, but they had significantly higher rates of emotional neglect and of serious injury or harm. NIS-4 also confirmed findings from other studies which associated increased physical abuse in poor, larger, unemployed families, with one parent and an unrelated caregiver present. Zhou and colleagues (2006) found that infant maltreatment can best be predicted when there are young mothers less than 20 years, who are unmarried, with inadequate prenatal care, are poor, who smoke during the pregnancy, or when there are three or more siblings. In a NCANDS sample, parent emotional problems, alcohol abuse and other family violence were found to be associated with the recurrence of physical abuse before age 3 years (Palusci et al. 2005).

Studies in the United Kingdom have shown similar rates and risk factors. In a population-based study in Wales in the late 1990s, severe physical abuse, defined as death, traumatic brain injury, intracranial hemorrhage, Munchausen by proxy, internal injuries, fractures, burns, and bites, was seen in 54 per 100,000 infants annually. When data from both child protection registers and a pediatrician surveillance system were combined, the incidence rose to 114 per 100,000 (Sibert et al. 2002). A random survey of 2,869 young adults throughout the United Kingdom noted that the prevalence of maltreatment during their childhood was 16 % of the sample (May-Chatal and Cawson 2005). Of these, 7 % had serious physical abuse, 6 % had emotional abuse, 11 % had sexual abuse with contact, 6 % had absence of care, and 5 % had absence of supervision. Using a cohort from the Avon Longitudinal Study of Parents and Children (ALSPAC), risk factors noted to be associated with abuse were parental unemployment, public housing, overcrowding, lack of car ownership, and a poor social network (Sidebotham et al. 2002). In a later analysis, the strongest risks were found to be socioeconomic deprivation and from other factors in the parents' own background (Sidebotham et al. 2006).

It has been consistently estimated that 1–2 per 100,000 U.S. children annually are fatally maltreated (U.S. Advisory Board 1995; US DHHS 2012). More than three-quarters (78 %) of these deaths were in children under 4 years of age, and 44 % were among infants. Physical abuse, alone or in combination with neglect, causes most of these deaths, but there have been persistent concerns about a systematic underascertainment of these fatalities (Crume et al. 2002; Tursz et al. 2010; U.S. Government Accountability Office 2011). Using an inpatient hospital database, there were 6.2 per 100,000 children, with 300 deaths, with higher rates for infants and children receiving Medicaid (Leventhal et al. 2012). Separating abuse from deaths due to neglect is problematic (Knight and Collins, 2005). Family configuration, child gender, social isolation, lack of support, maternal youth, marital status, poverty, and parenting practices contribute to increased risk (Jenny and Isaac 2006; Rangel et al. 2010). Children residing in households with unrelated adults were significantly more likely to die from inflicted injuries than were children residing with two biologic parents, and increased risk was also elevated with step, foster and adoptive parents (Schnitzer and Ewigman 2005; Stiffman et al. 2002). Among newborns, 2.1 per 100,000 in North Carolina were killed or left to die each year, usually by their mothers, many of whom were poor, had no prenatal care, or were adolescents (Herman-Giddens et al. 2003). There were more boys than girls, and infant boys had the highest rate (18.5 per 100,000). Higher mortality from all causes of injuries has been noted in African American, Native American and Alaskan Native children (Pressley 2007). A review in the U.K. identified child age less than 5 years, non-organic failure to thrive, prior abuse or unexplained injuries, caregiver youth, inexperience, mental illness, drug and alcohol abuse, stress and poverty as risk factors (Browne and Lynch 1995). Independent of these factors, a prior CPS report of maltreatment has been associated with almost six times the risk for death from later injury (Putnam-Hornstein 2011).

Unlike the reported incidence of sexual abuse, in which it has been suggested that at least some of the decrease is real, it is not clear if or why physical abuse rates have actually declined (Finkelhor and Jones 2006; Finkelhor et al. 2013). While economic indicators improved in the 1990s, the number of cases continued to fall in NCANDS during 2008–2011 during an economic recession in the U.S. This may indicate that states are changing how they count child maltreatment fatalities and how they are delivering that information to NCANDS as could occur with differential response systems (IOM 2012). Further studies are needed to ascertain whether the number of physical cases is continuing to decline and the causes why this is occurring.

In response to the estimated undercount of child abuse fatalities, a Congressional Commission will investigate how and why children die in the U.S. and how child death review and other systems can best respond (Protect Our Kids Act 2013). Additionally, further analyses are also needed to illuminate the implications of NIS–4 findings and the interrelationships among the different factors associated with the incidence of maltreatment. Do households with more children have higher incidence rates even when household socioeconomic status is taken into account? Are differences based on race truly independent of socioeconomic or minority status or do they reflect biases in reporting or investigation? Why do the majority of maltreated children identified by NIS not receive CPS investigation? Have prevention programs in hospitals or the community contributed to a real decline in physical abuse cases and fatalities?

International initiatives are underway to expand knowledge about the epidemiology of child maltreatment beyond currently available statistics. The ISPCAN Child Abuse Screening Tool (ICAST) children's instrument is one of three tools designed by a panel of child maltreatment experts from 40 countries to study the prevalence of childhood victimization. Other tools have been designed to study child victimization from parents' perspectives on their child rearing and from the young adult on childhood experiences (Zolotor et al. 2009). Using the parent version, approximately 15 % of children were shaken, 24 % were hit on the buttocks with an object, and 37 % were spanked. Two percent of parents reported choking and smothering their child (Runyan et al. 2009). A retrospective version was also tested (Dunne et al. 2009). Further assessment and wider implementation are planned.

Impact and Costs

A variety of long-term harms beyond acute physical injury have been linked to physical abuse. Physical abuse is usually (if not always) accompanied by psychological maltreatment with its attendant belittling, spurning and other emotional damage to the child's ego, emotional health and development. A variety of ailments have been identified in over 60 papers since 1998 by internist Vincent Felitti, pediatrician Robert Anda and their colleagues studied the relationship of childhood adversity and a variety of lifelong physical and emotional outcomes (CDC 2012; Felitti et al. 1998). These ten adverse childhood experiences, or "ACEs" as they have come to be called, include exposure to emotional abuse, physical abuse, contact sexual abuse, alcohol/substance abuse, mental illness, criminal behavior, parental separation/divorce and domestic violence. Using a retrospective study design, they surveyed 17,337 adult HMO members (average age 57 years) and linked events during childhood in a dose–response fashion with cardiovascular disease, cancer, AIDS and other sexually transmitted diseases, unwanted often-high-risk pregnancies, chronic obstructive pulmonary disease, and a legacy of self-perpetuating child abuse. While it is hard to believe now, many medical and child welfare professionals did not see the linkages among child abuse and other common "social problems" with poor health and premature death in adulthood. While there have been questions about the validity of the study design, studies using ACEs have moved to less affluent samples to fit within an accepted universal ecobiodevelopmental framework for understanding health promotion and disease prevention across the lifespan, supported by recent additional advances in neuroscience, molecular biology and the social sciences (Palusci 2013).

Longitudinal follow-up, such as that offered by Widom and colleagues (2012), would be helpful to prospectively validate the harms of physical abuse during childhood. Widom and colleagues noted increased malnutrition, glycemic control and kidney and liver disease up to 30 years after physical abuse; additional studies of this nature would significantly add to our national healthcare discussion regarding the value of physical abuse prevention.

Costs related to serious physical abuse are heavily influenced by the long-term medical burden associated with injury and lost productivity. Abusive head trauma has been noted to account for 10–15 % of all child maltreatment-related deaths, and neurologic complications effect at least as many as 60 % of those survivors with motor deficits, seizures, developmental delays and blindness. Several studies have demonstrated that abused children have longer hospital stays, more severe injuries, worse medical outcomes, and higher hospital charges and are more likely to die. Deborah Daro (1988) projected that the national cost and future productivity loss of severely abused and neglected children is between $658 million and $1.3 billion each year in the U.S., assuming that their impairments would reduce their future earnings by as little as from 5 % to 10 %. However, drawing from Maxfield and Widom's work (1996), Fight Crime: Invest in Kids (Alexander et al. 2003) noted that child abuse and neglect costs Americans at least $80 billion annually. Prevent Child Abuse America (Wang and Holton 2008) used "conservative" estimates to calculate direct and indirect costs as $103.8 billion in 2007. The seemingly large costs of child abuse and neglect pale in comparison with the economic and human burden of adult poor health and premature death. Fang and colleagues (2012) noted that the average abused child cost $210,012 in 2010 dollars, generalizing to $124 million annually in the U.S. in total and future costs. It is clear that despite these varying calculations and projected financial costs, physical abuse significantly affects the physical and mental health of our entire population.

International Issues and Cultural Practices

Cultural competence, the ability to understand and work with communities other than one's own, is needed if we are to address the roles of international issues and cultural practices (Korbin 2002). In addition to lower quality of care and preventable morbidity and mortality, failure to appreciate the importance of culture and language can result in unnecessary child abuse evaluations and clinician bias (Flores et al. 2002). Cultural competency is being increasingly incorporated into training for health care professionals, who should be able to accurately distinguish different cultural parenting discipline practices from child maltreatment (Terao et al. 2001) and should also distinguish cultural practices that may mimic those findings of child abuse (e.g. coining) which may resemble bruises (Look and Look 1997). If children are in danger, interventions necessary to protect them are indicated even if the parents think they are doing the right thing. All the components of the care continuum should work together towards culturally competent care, including healthcare workers, professional bodies, organizations, and systems within which all this occurs (Raman and Hodes 2012).

Cultural practices, complementary and alternative medicines, and variations in parenting across the world potentially cross over into child physical abuse, including the use of physical discipline and corporal punishment, FGM, cupping, moxibustion, therapeutic burning, and coining. Spanking and other forms of corporal punishment are widely accepted and used throughout the world. Using a modified parent–child Conflict Tactics Scale to assess parental discipline in Brazil, Chile, Egypt, India, Philippines, and the United States, nearly all 14,239 mothers surveyed used nonviolent discipline and verbal or psychological punishment (Runyan et al. 2010). Physical punishment was used in at least 55 % of the families. Spanking rates (open hand on buttocks) ranged from a low of 15 % in an educated community in India to a high of 76 % in a Philippine community. Similarly, there was a wide range in the rates of children who were hit with objects (9–74 % [median: 39 %]) or beaten by their parents (0.1–28.5 %). Spanking and less traumatic forms of physical discipline have been found to increase the chance of physical injury, and the child may not understand the connection between the behavior and the punishment (Straus 1994). Although the child may react with shock from being spanked and stop the undesired behavior, repeated spanking may cause agitated, aggressive behavior in the child that may lead to physical altercations between the child and parent. Spanking is associated with higher rates of physical aggression, more substance abuse, and increased risk of crime and violence when used with older children and adolescents (Straus 1994).

There is consensus against using extremely harsh methods of physical punishment, such as burning or smothering, which are rare in all countries. Shaking continues to be used; 20 % of parents in nine communities admitted shaking children younger than 2 years (Runyan et al. 2010). In a larger survey of discipline practices by Gray (2010), 33–94 % of children reported receiving violent punishment in countries ranging from Bosnia and Herzegovina (33 %) to Yemen (94 %); 1–44 % experienced severe physical discipline. Similar parental acceptance of physical punishment was reported in children as young as 2 years. More violent discipline is used in countries where more domestic violence, polygamy, and child labor is reported, and more education and more books in the home were associated with a greater use of nonviolent discipline strategies. Corporal punishment in schools has been prohibited in at least 108 countries worldwide, but 78 of these did not prohibit corporal punishment as a disciplinary measure in penal institutions for children in conflict with the law, and 43 did not prohibit it as a judicial sentence of the courts for young people convicted of an offense (Global Initiative 2010). While some steps have been taken, more global adoption of corporal punishment bans has the potential to further decrease injuries when harsh punishment crosses the line to become child physical abuse.

In addition to child welfare systems in the U.S. and other countries, the United Nations Convention on the Rights of the Child (UNCRC) has taken a broader approach to establishing societal recognition of children's rights. The UNCRC was adopted and opened for signature, ratification and accession by General Assembly resolution 44/25 of 20 November, 1989. It entered into force in 1990 and was ratified by all countries except the United States and Somalia (Doek 2009). Specific provisions deal with a child's right to protection from all forms of violence, abuse, and exploitation; this applies to all children with their families, refugees, and those in armed conflict. The UNCRC brought fundamental change to the international community despite ongoing discussion about its limitations (Mulinge 2010; Svevo-Cianci 2010). According to the UNCRC, violence against children is not only morally and socially unacceptable but it now violates a fundamental right to respect for and protection of inherent human dignity, physical and mental integrity, and equal protection under the law. By ratification, 193 countries committed themselves and are legally bound to respect, protect, and fulfill the rights of children. These countries also undertook many legislative, social, and other measures to bring their laws and practices into compliance with the UNCRC. While much of the legal framework required by the UNCRC is in place, U.S. ratification and full implementation of the UNCRC would accelerate the social changes needed to fully recognize children's rights in the U.S. and would elevate the U.S. position as a world leader in this area.

Skin Lesions

The most common injury from physical abuse affects the skin by bruising or burning. Any skin lesion beyond temporary reddening should be considered as potential physical abuse when (1) the injury is inflicted and nonaccidental, (2) the pattern of injury fits biomechanical models of abusive trauma, (3) the pattern corresponds to infliction with an instrument that would not occur through play or in the environment, (4) the history provided is not in keeping with the child's development, or (5) the history does not explain the injury (Kellogg et al. 2007). The aging of bruises in children has received considerable attention and current guidelines are severely limited in their ability to precisely time when an injury occurred. Pattern, depth (degree), and healing of burns helps in determining their specificity for maltreatment. Developmental and other considerations need to be entertained as there are a host of potential confounders or 'mimics' which need to be reviewed when coming to a diagnosis. Some children as young as 10 months of age, for example, have been shown to have the developmental capability to climb into the bath, suggesting that nonspecific burn patterns could be attributed to actions by the child rather than the parent in some cases (Allasio and Fischer 2005).

The distribution of lesions can be a critical factor in determining if a child has been abused. Certain sites are highly correlated with abuse, such as buttocks, the lower back, the posterior aspects of the extremities and the ears (Maguire et al. 2005). Bruising at other sites, such as the bony prominences of the forehead, the elbows and lower legs, are consistent with the normal childhood trauma seen in mobile children. Sugar and colleagues (1999) noted "those who don't cruise rarely bruise," signaling we should be concerned when non-walking infants or motor delayed children have bruising. Inflicted bruising may have clear patterns or may be non-specific. When an object is used, the pattern of the injury may clearly show the outline of the object. Another form of patterned bruising comes from biting. A careful inspection and measurement of the lesion can determine if a bite is human or animal, adult or child, or self-inflicted. Since the most common skin manifestation of physical abuse is multiple bruises in different stages of healing, it is imperative to use a diagram and appropriate imaging to document the color, distribution and pattern of these injuries.

A burn is the destruction of skin and underlying tissue caused by the application of a physical agent. These agents may be chemicals, heat, cold, or electrical in nature. Since the spectrum of burns can range from a simple isolated injury to the involvement of major portions of the child's body, the clinician should assess the type of agent, the distribution and extent of the burn, and the history given of how the burn occurred (Toon et al. 2011). Many burns in childhood are accidental but are also the result of poor judgment or the failure of the caretaker to provide adequate supervision. Here, as in other forms of abuse, the developmental age and the size of the child are very important. Inflicted burns often have very specific patterns such as those seen with immersion or dunking. Burns may result from splash, immersion, or contact with a heated instrument or utensil, a flame, a chemical/caustic agent or an electrical source.

Accidental burns/scalds commonly involve hot liquids in contact with a child's face, neck, and upper chest (Drago 2005). If a child pulls down a cup of hot water, this will produce a different pattern than if he had pulled a cup of thick liquid. The action may be modified by the height from which the hot liquid fell, the vehicle that contained the hot substance, and the child's size. Immersion burns present with distinctive patterns that result from placing the child in hot water. The patterns include stocking/glove burns that are symmetrical burns of the extremities. Forced immersion of the child in a tub can produce a burn pattern with well-demarcated lesions and little or no evidence of splash.

Contact burns can present with identifiable object patterns such as an iron or a cigarette lighter. A child can easily have contact an the iron left on the floor or by pulling the cord. Other sources of contact burns are room heaters, hair curling irons, electric cooking utensils, and radiators which can each produce distinctive lesions. Lit cigarettes can produce lesions that can be difficult to distinguish from chicken pox or impetigo given the similarity of the size and distribution.

A variety of diagnostic issues await further study. As the Institute of Medicine points out, there is a great deal of additional data needed by clinicians on the frontlines to assist in determining which children need evaluation for abuse, when subspecialists should be called and what tests should be done (IOM 2012). There are still issues on how to fund training for physicians to recognize and report abusive bruises and how to best train case workers, social workers and other investigators about medical issues. More research is needed to study innovative systems-level changes that may address challenges associated with decision making on medical issues by frontline workers.

Fractures

Acute fractures may be clinically apparent as soft tissue swelling over a fracture site, a deformity of the involved limb, or as a decrease in movement with or without external bruising. Infants may present with irritability and/or not using an affected limb. Healing fractures may be identified as palpable lesions consistent with callus formation, especially over the ribs (Jenny and the Committee on Child Abuse and Neglect 2006). The absence of swelling or bruises near a fracture site is not uncommon in fractures of the extremities and ribs. A case series of 703 consecutive skeletal series reported 11 % fractures, with higher rates in infants less than 6 months old, apparent life threatening events, seizures and abusive head trauma. 79 % had healing fractures seen (Duffy et al. 2011). One study reported that when skeletal surveys were done, 23 % identified additional fractures, 10 % in the hands, feet or spine (Lindberg et al. 2013). Follow up x-rays in 1–2 weeks have been found to identify additional fractures in 8.5 % of children (Bennett et al. 2011a).

There is no fracture type that is pathognomonic for abuse, and all fracture types can potentially result from inflicted injury. The diagnosis of inflicted fracture must be made through careful correlation of the history provided by the caregiver with the child's developmental level and physical and radiographic findings. Classic metaphyseal lesions, rib fractures (particularly posteriorly), scapular fractures, vertebral spinous process fractures, and sternal fractures all have a high specificity for abuse (Kleinman 1998). Common, nonspecific injuries include subperiosteal new bone formation, clavicular fractures, diaphyseal fractures of long bones, and linear skull fractures. There are some fracture types and findings of intermediate specificity that are concerning but may be accidental if a clearly plausible mechanism is provided. This group includes multiple fractures (particularly when bilateral), fractures of different ages, epiphyseal separation, digital fractures, vertebral body fractures and subluxations, and complex skull fractures.

The age of fractures can be helpful in assessing the plausibility of the history, and multiple fractures of different ages raise the suspicion of abuse. Fracture healing manifests as periosteal reaction, also called callus, which is radiographically apparent after 10–14 days, and can be earlier in infants (Halliday et al. 2011; Prosser et al. 2012). Subperiosteal new bone formation can be a normal finding in infants under 6 months of age when it is found along the shafts of long bones and is symmetrical on both sides of the body. Skull fractures cannot be dated with accuracy, however, when non-accidental trauma is suspected, appropriate skeletal studies should be done as outlined by the American College of Radiology (1997). Skeletal survey is the standard diagnostic investigation when there is concern for physical abuse of infants and toddlers under 2 years old. It includes anteroposterior (AP) views of the extremities including feet, with the exception of the hands which are imaged in the posterioaterior view; AP and lateral skull; AP and lateral views of the thorax and oblique ribs; AP pelvis; and lateral views of the spine. Radiologic evaluation is necessary to assess both the fracture itself and overall status of the bony skeleton to identify any metabolic/genetic process that might produce bone fragility. A discussion of the various metabolic bones diseases associated with fractures is beyond the scope of this chapter, and a pediatric radiologist should be utilized since familiarity with the presentation of growth variables in the pediatric patient is very important in determining if the findings are consistent with non-accidental trauma or other explanations.

Several areas of continuing medical research include the delineation of the diagnosis, pathophysiology and injury mechanics of fractures, head trauma and other abuse injuries. Further research is indicated, and physicians should appropriately search and test for alternate explanations while appropriately weighting the strong available evidence to ensure that a child remains protected from harm. CT, for example has been suggested to be a more sensitive test for rib fractures, yet the increased radiation exposure may not warrant it for screening (Berdon 2012). While it has been noted that vitamin D deficiency does not predispose to fracture in the absence of clinical rickets (British Paediatric and Adolescent Bone Group 2012; Slovis 2012), additional studies regarding the quantitative effects of such deficiencies could be helpful. Newer imaging modalities, such as diffusion tensor imaging, offer valuable ways to detect the effects of AHT, but further studies are needed to help us integrate them into clinical practice (Hart and Rubia 2012; Xu et al. 2013; Yoshida et al. 2013).

Head Trauma

The leading cause of abusive mortality and morbidity is inflicted traumatic brain injury (American Academy of Pediatrics 2009). With mortality rates of 10–50 % and more than 90 % of survivors having significant developmental sequelae, physical abuse to the head has been noted to have patterns of injuries that are distinct from accidental or medical causes. At least 1,400 cases of fatal abusive head trauma occur annually in the United States, and there is growing sophistication in our ability to differentiate these fatalities from those from nonabusive causes. Prior to 1974, the presence of subdural hematomas in infants who had no apparent history or evidence of trauma was given the diagnosis of "idiopathic subdural hematoma of infancy". With the publication of the article by Caffey in 1974 based on interviews of caretakers, this entity became known as the "Shaken Baby Syndrome" and later the "Shaken Baby/Impact Syndrome" as the awareness of this clinical entity grew and applied to related clinical situations (Caffey 1974). New diagnostic technologies developed in the last century, from radiographs to sophisticated computer-assisted imaging techniques, have proved invaluable in visualizing internal bleeding and injury.

The mechanism for the injury has been described as the violent shaking of an infant resulting in the movement of the brain within the skull and related hemorrhage within the eye and optic nerve. Subdural bleeding is thought to be caused by the disruption of the bridging veins within the subdural space. Rib fractures are attributed to the compression of the chest by the caretaker as the infant was shaken. This mechanism of injury is consistent with the histories given by providers over the years in which the caretaker sought to silence the crying infant by grabbing the child around the thorax and shaking the child until the child stopped crying. Alternative terms for this clinical entity are now being used, including Abusive Head Trauma or Non-Accidental Head Injury. Such terms can be used to indicate head trauma without reference to the mode of injury other than its being non-accidental in nature. Pierce and Bertocci (2008) noted that infants and children under 3 years with interhemispheric subdural hemorrhage were found to have a greater than 99 % probability of intentional trauma, and predictive values of a variety of injuries have been calculated (Kemp 2011). However, a pattern of head crush injuries increasingly seen after TV falls reminds us that these findings are not always pathognomonic for abusive head trauma (Deisch et al. 2011). Whether external hydrocephalus or "benign extra-axial fluid of infancy" predisposes to subdural bleeding is still not clear. The potential contribution of birth and other factors such as maternal anti-Ro antibodies is also provocative (Edwards et al. 2012).

Approximately 4–6 % of abused children have ocular findings. Any ocular injury can be the result of abuse, and all forms of abuse may have ophthalmic manifestations (Levin 2010). The incidence of retinal hemorrhages (RH) in shaken-baby syndrome (SBS) is 85 %, but higher in children who have died versus unimpaired survivors. There is an association between severity of brain injury and RH severity, and RH can rarely occur without intracranial hemorrhage or cerebral edema (Levin 1991). Approximately two-thirds of victims have RHs that are too numerous to count and are multilayered. These RHs extend out to the retinal periphery, with no particular anatomic pattern, and cover the majority of the retinal surface. Macular retinoschisis also indicates trauma. RH cannot be dated with precision. Massive numbers of superficial or small-dot hemorrhages can resolve within 24 h. There is some evidence that mild increases of hemorrhage, or appearance of hemorrhage not previously present, can occur early during hospitalization in very ill children, which underscores the need for prompt ophthalmology consultation and retinal evaluation (Gilles et al. 2003). A small number of infants have been noted to have RH after birth which resolve within 2 weeks. It is also known that RHs in the posterior pole are associated with non-abusive causes. The overwhelming body of literature supports a conclusion that severe hemorrhagic retinopathy in otherwise previously well children without obvious history to the contrary (e.g., head crush or high velocity impact) suggests that the child has been submitted to abusive repetitive acceleration-deceleration trauma with or without head impact (Levin 2010).

Other Injuries

While the genitals and anus can be physically abused, these injuries will be discussed with sexual abuse (Heger this volume, Chap. 4). There is a growing body of knowledge about abusive abdominal and chest trauma which are often 'silent' injuries with potentially devastating consequences. Abdominal injuries are the second leading cause of death after abusive head trauma but are difficult to assess given their occult nature, relative lack of bruising, and potential for significant delay in symptoms. Even with a history of a severe blow to the abdomen, bruising of the skin is often not seen. Examination may reveal guarding and change/loss of bowel sounds. Lab studies must address injuries to all the abdominal organs including the kidneys. CT scans of the abdomen are very useful in determining the extent of these injuries when the physical findings are diffuse and non-specific. Direct blows to the abdomen such as a punch, kick or use of an object can injure both solid and hollow viscus organs which are both impacted and compressed against the vertebral column (Herr and Fallat 2006). One study demonstrated that solid organ injuries were most common in both accidental and inflicted trauma. Hollow viscus alone or in combination with solid organ damage was more common in cases of inflicted injuries (Wood et al. 2005). Recent studies suggest that abdominal CT imaging and liver function and pancreatic testing should be carried out in all abusive head trauma victims to identify occult abdominal trauma given that 25 % or more of even fatal abdominal trauma cases can have few or no visible external bruises (Herr and Fallat 2006). Inflicted chest injuries in children are uncommon as a single episode of trauma but are often seen in conjunction with other non-accidental injuries such as inflicted head trauma with compression fractures of the ribs. Direct blows to the chest wall rarely present with damage to the heart or the thoracic duct (Guleserian et al. 1996). Many of these injuries are fatal and only identified at post mortem exam. Cardiac troponins have been found to be increased after abuse chest trauma, and the time course and screening evaluation of serologic markers for abusive abdominal trauma need further study (Bennett et al. 2011b).

Preventing Physical Abuse

Preventing child abuse and neglect spares children physical and psychological pain and improves their long-term health. Dubowitz (2002) noted that prevention "is intuitively and morally preferable to intervening after the fact." There is increasing evidence supporting the effectiveness of several universal and selective prevention interventions, but the effectiveness of most programs is still not known (MacMillan et al. 2009; Mikton and Butchart 2009; Palusci and Haney). Robert Caldwell (1992) estimated that the costs of a home visitor program in Michigan would be 3.5 % of the $823 million estimated cost of child abuse, and small reductions in the rate of child maltreatment were thought to make prevention cost effective. Home visiting programs are not uniformly effective, parenting programs appear to improve parenting but not necessarily reduce child maltreatment, and some family programs are successful in reducing physical abuse but not neglect.

Ray Helfer (1987) noted the "window of opportunity" that is present in the perinatal period to enhance parent–child interactions and prevent physical abuse. Several program models have shown promise based upon key periods, including prepregnancy planning, early conception, late pregnancy, prelabor and labor, immediately following delivery, and at home with the child. Opportunities for prevention include teaching parents and caregivers to cope with infant crying and how to provide a safe sleep environment for their infant. A meta-analysis of several early childhood interventions concluded that the evidence for their preventing child maltreatment is weak, but longer-term studies may show reductions in child maltreatment similar to other programs such as home visiting, when longer follow-up can be achieved (Reynolds et al. 2009).

Several parent education programs have been evaluated for their association with decreases in physical abuse and neglect. Family Connections, a multifaceted, home visiting community-based child neglect prevention program, showed "cost effective" improvements in risk and protective factors and behavioral outcomes (DePanfilis et al. 2008). To address a specific form of physical abuse, Mark Dias and colleagues (2005) devised a hospital-based parent education program implemented immediately after birth that has been shown to decrease the incidence of shaken baby syndrome. Barr and colleagues (2009) have devised a program of parent education in late pregnancy, delivery, and early infancy phases to change maternal knowledge and behaviors relevant to infant shaking. Using a randomized controlled trial, they were able to demonstrate how "The Period of Purple Crying" was able to increase maternal knowledge scores, knowledge about the dangers of shaking, and sharing that information with other caretakers.

A recent randomized trial in an inner-city clinic with high-risk families was able to show lower rates of maltreatment, CPS reports, harsh punishment, and improved health services after an intervention of pediatric resident education (Dubowitz et al. 2009). Several barriers (time, training, culture, sensitive issues) to widespread implementation can be addressed by identifying potential strategies, such as the use of handouts and local news stories, to begin a dialogue during routine pediatric visits (Sege et al. 2006).

With the generosity of the Doris Duke Charitable Foundation, the American Academy of Pediatrics launched a program called *Practicing Safety: Connected Kids* aimed at decreasing child abuse and neglect by enhancing anticipatory guidance and increasing screening provided by pediatric practices to children ages 0–3 years, focusing on helping parents and families to raise resilient children. Each counseling topic discusses the child's development, the parent's feelings and reactions in response to the child's development and behavior, and specific practical suggestions on how to encourage healthy social, emotional, and physical growth in an environment of support and open communication. Practices screened for maternal depression and improved in discussing the issues of coping with crying, maternal bonding, toilet training and discipline (American Academy of Pediatrics 2005).

Beyond the traditional medical model, multidisciplinary teams have been formed to address the training, education, research, and clinical needs at specialized institutions such as children's hospitals and universities (Krugman 2013). In the community, multidisciplinary reviews of child deaths have been identified as a key source of information for enhanced case ascertainment and response (American Academy of Pediatrics 2010; Durfee and Tilton-Durfee 2013; Jenny and Isaac 2006). Child death review teams have had some success in better classifying deaths and in developing policies and programs to reduce further deaths and injuries (Douglas and Cunningham 2008; Hochstadt 2006; Johnston et al. 2011; Rimsza et al. 2002; Schnitzer et al. 2008). Child death reviews have expanded to other countries and to reviews of unintentional deaths, fetal-infant mortality and for children within the child welfare system (Palusci 2010; Schnitzer et al. 2011; Sidebotham et al. 2011). In one study (Palusci et al. 2010), a 9 % decrease in deaths related to child welfare system deficiencies was noted over a 6-year period after implementing team recommendations.

Questions exist regarding the appropriate level of health-based services for victimized children, whether their treatment is best provided by primary care physicians or nonphysician specialists, and the long-term outcomes from different levels of services (Makoroff et al. 2002). Do advanced practice nurses, sexual assault nurse examiners, generalists, emergency physicians or child abuse subspecialists, for example, offer better care or promise better outcomes after examination, or are there really no differences in outcome for the child? Many medical services occur in what are now called child advocacy centers (CACs) in the U.S., which began in the 1980s to provide specialized services for children, usually for concerns of sexual abuse. The CAC model utilizes professionals from a variety of disciplines, including police, child protective services agencies, social services, counselors, and physicians and nurses to provide "a coordinated response" to child abuse (National Children's Alliance 2011). These centers have developed both within and separate from hospitals. Many CACs have expanded beyond sexual abuse evaluations, but less is known about whether this model results in improved medical outcomes (Faller and Palusci 2007). Children's hospitals have also recognized and supported this work as well, with refinement of services and funding streams within the medical model (National Association of Children's Hospitals and Related Institutions [NACHRI] 2005).

While mandated reporting and investigation of suspected child abuse is believed to result in the early identification and provision of a variety of services to help families and prevent further harm to children, some studies have not shown the benefits of post-investigation services (Palusci et al. 2005). Unfortunately, other than rehabilitation and effective services for families, the only options appear to be criminal investigation and prosecution. The outcomes of programs could be strengthened through an intentional focus on the contexts of intervention programs and individual families (IOM 2012). Additional research is necessary on the sustainability of reform and population-level change. The system also could benefit from a greater understanding of the critical elements necessary for high-quality interventions and a sense of how much programs can adapt while retaining those ingredients.

Differential response, also referred to as dual track, multiple track or alternative response, is a system reform that enables U.S. child protective service agencies to respond differently to accepted reports of child abuse and neglect based on factors such as the type and severity of the alleged maltreatment, the number and sources of previous reports, and the willingness of the family to participate in services (USDHHS 2012). It is not known how this is being applied to child physical abuse cases or whether this will result in improved services for children and families (Hughes et al. 2013). Additional research is needed to study how investigation and service models and their implementation will affect outcomes for children and families – in particular, safety, permanency and well-being.

Summary

Beginning with medical recognition of abusive injuries and expanding throughout the community, the history of child physical abuse serves as an example of sweeping social change in the U.S. and the development of systems and services for children and families which can improve their health and development and maximize their potential contribution to society. There is a solid knowledge base explaining the patterns of injuries and epidemiologic risk factors for child physical abuse, and there continues to be biomedical advances in our understanding and approach to its identification, evaluation, treatment and services. The public health harms and costs of child physical abuse demand a continuing examination of cultural practices, discipline, and societal responses. Continued research and policy development both within medicine and within society as a whole provide an evidence base to determine what is needed to address and prevent this devastating form of child maltreatment.

References

Akmatov, K. S. (2011). Child abuse in 28 developing and transitional countries – results from the multiple indicator cluster surveys. *International Journal of Epidemiology, 40*(1), 219–227.

Alexander, R., Baca, L., Fox, J. A., Frantz, M., Huffman, L., et al. (2003). *New hope for preventing child abuse and neglect: Proven solutions to save lives and prevent future crime.* Washington, DC: Fight Crime: Invest in Kids. Retrieved 26 Sept 2008, from http://www.fightcrime.org/reportlist.php.

Allasio, D., & Fischer, H. (2005). Immersion scald burns and the ability of young children to climb into a bath tub. *Pediatrics, 115,* 1419–1421.

American Academy of Pediatrics. (1966). Maltreatment of children: The physically abused child. *Pediatrics, 37,* 377–381.

American Academy of Pediatrics. (2005). *Connected kids: Safe strong secure, a new violence prevention program from the American Academy of Pediatrics.* Elk Grove Village: Author.

American Academy of Pediatrics Committee on Child Abuse and Neglect. (2009). Abusive head trauma in infants and children. *Pediatrics, 123,* 1409–1411.

American Academy of Pediatrics Committee on Child Abuse and Neglect, Committee on Injury, Violence, and Poison Prevention, Council on Community Pediatrics, American Academy of Pediatrics. (2010). Policy statement–child fatality review. *Pediatrics, 126,* 592–596.

American College of Radiology. (1997). *ACR standards, standard for skeletal surveys in children* (Vol. 23, pp. 1–4). Reston: ACR.

Barr, R. G., Rivara, F. P., Barr, M., Cummings, P., Taylor, J., Lengua, L. J., & Meredith-Benitez, E. (2009). Effectiveness of educational materials designed to change knowledge and behaviors regarding crying and shaken baby syndrome in mothers of newborns: A randomized, controlled trial. *Pediatrics, 123*(6), 972–980.

Bennett, B. L., Chua, M. S., Care, M., Kachelmeyer, A., & Mahabee-Gittens, M. (2011a). Retrospective review to determine the utility of follow-up skeletal surveys in child abuse evaluations when the initial skeletal survey is normal. *BMC Research Notes, 4,* 354.

Bennett, B. L., Macabee-Gittens, M. S., Chua, M., & Hirsch, R. (2011b). Elevated cardiac troponin I level in cases of thoracic nonaccidental trauma. *Pediatric Emergency Care, 10,* 941–944.

Berdon, W. E. (2012). A modest proposal: Thoracic CT for rib fracture diagnosis in child abuse (letter). *Child Abuse & Neglect, 36,* 200–201.

Berger, R. P., Fromkin, J. B., Stutz, H., Makoroff, K., Scribano, P. V., Feldman, K., Tu, L. C., & Fabio, A. (2011). Abusive head trauma during a time of increased unemployment: A multicenter analysis. *Pediatrics, 128,* 637–643.

British Paediatric and Adolescent Bone Group. (2012). British paediatric and adolescent bone group's position statement on vitamin D deficiency. *British Medical Journal, 345,* e8182.

Bross, D. C., & Mathews, B. (2013). The battered child syndrome: Changes in the law and child advocacy. In R. D. Krugman & J. E. Korbin (Eds.), *C. Henry Kempe: A fifty year legacy to the field of child abuse and neglect* (pp. 39–50). New York: Springer.

Browne, K. D., & Lynch, M. A. (1995). The nature and extent of child homicide and fatal abuse. *Child Abuse Review, 4,* 309–316.

Caffey, J. (1946). Multiple fractures of the long bones of infants suffering from chronic subdural hematoma. *American Journal of Roentgenology, 56,* 163–173.

Caffey, J. (1972). On the theory and practice of shaking infants. Its potential residual effects of permanent brain damage and mental retardation. *American Journal of Diseases of Children, 124,* 161–169.

Caffey, J. (1974). The whiplash shaken baby syndrome: A manual shaking by the extremities with whiplash-induced intracranial and intraocular bleeding, linked with residual permanent brain damage and mental retardation. *Pediatrics, 54,* 396–403.

Caldwell, R. A. (1992). The costs of child abuse vs. child abuse prevention: Michigan's experience. Accessed 26 Sept 2008, at: https://www.msu.edu/~bob/cost1992.pdf.

Centers for Disease Control and Prevention. Adverse Childhood Experiences (ACE) study: Major findings by publication year. Available at: http://www.cdc.gov/ace/year.htm. Accessed 15 June 2012.

Crume, T. L., DiGuiseppi, C., Byers, T., Sirotnak, A. P., & Garrett, C. J. (2002). Underascertainment of child maltreatment fatalities by death certificates, 1990–1998. *Pediatrics, 110*(2 Pt 1), e18.

Daro, D. (1988). *Confronting child abuse: Research for effective program design.* Washington, DC: National Academy Press.

Deisch, J., Quinton, R., & Gruszecki, A. C. (2011). Craniocerebral trauma inflicted by television falls. *Journal of Forensic Science, 56*(4), 1049–1053.

DePanfilis, D., Dubowitz, H., & Kunz, J. (2008). Assessing the cost effectiveness of family connections. *Child Abuse & Neglect, 32*(3), 335–351.

Dias, M. S., Smith, K., deGuehery, K., Mazur, P., Li, V., & Shaffer, M. I. (2005). Preventing abusive head trauma among infant and young children: A hospital-based, parent education program. *Pediatrics, 115*(4), 470–477.

Doek, J. E. (2009). The CRC 20 years: An overview of some of the major achievements and remaining challenges. *Child Abuse & Neglect, 33*(11), 771–782.

Douglas, E. M., & Cunningham, J. M. (2008). Recommendations from child fatality review teams: Results of a US nationwide exploratory study concerning maltreatment fatalities and social service delivery. *Child Abuse Review, 17*, 331–351.

Drago, D. A. (2005). Kitchen scalds and thermal burns in children five years and younger. *Pediatrics, 115*, 10–16.

Dubowitz, H. (2002). Preventing child neglect and physical abuse: A role for pediatricians. *Pediatrics in Review, 23*(6), 191–196.

Dubowitz, H., Feigelman, S., Lane, W., & Kim, J. (2009). Pediatric primary care to help prevent child maltreatment: The Safe Environment for Every Kid (SEEK) model. *Pediatrics, 123*(3), 858–864.

Duffy, S. O., Squires, J., Fromkin, J. B., & Berger, R. P. (2011). Use of skeletal surveys to evaluate for physical abuse: Analysis of 703 consecutive skeletal surveys. *Pediatrics, 127*, e47–e52.

Dunne, M. P., Zolotor, A. J., Runyan, D. K., Andreva-Miller, I., Choo, W. Y., Dunne, S. K., Gerbaka, B., Isaeva, O., Jain, D., Kasim, M. S., Macfarlane, B., Mamyrova, N., Ramirez, C., Volkova, E., & Youssef, R. (2009). ISPCAN child abuse screening tools retrospective version (ICAST-R): Delphi study and field testing in seven countries. *Child Abuse & Neglect, 33*(11), 815–825.

Durfee, M., & Tilton-Durfee, D. (2013). Fatal child abuse neglect. In R. D. Krugman & J. E. Korbin (Eds.), *C. Henry Kempe: A fifty year legacy to the field of child abuse and neglect* (pp. 79–88). New York: Springer.

Edwards, R. J., Allport, R. J., Stoodley, N. G., O'Callaghan, F. O., Lock, R. J., Carter, M. R., & Ramanan, A. V. (2012). External hydrocephalus and subdural bleeding in infancy associated with transplacental anti-Ro antibodies. *Archives of Diseases in Children, 97*, 316–319.

Faller, K. C., & Palusci, V. J. (2007). Children's advocacy centers: Do they lead to positive case outcomes? *Child Abuse & Neglect, 31*, 1021–1029.

Fang, X., Brown, D. S., Florence, C. S., & Mercy, J. A. (2012). The economic burden of child maltreatment in the United States and implications for prevention. *Child Abuse & Neglect, 36*, 156–165.

Felitti, V. J., Anda, R. F., Nordenberg, D., Williamson, D. F., Spitz, A. M., Edwards, V., Koss, M. P., & Marks, J. S. (1998). The relationship of adult health status to childhood abuse and household dysfunction. *American Journal of Preventive Medicine, 14*, 245–258.

Finkelhor, D., & Jones, L. (2006). Why have child maltreatment and child victimization declined? *Journal of Social Issues, 62*, 685–716.

Finkelhor, D., Jones, L., & Shattuck, A. (2013). Updated trends in child maltreatment, 2011. Durham: University of New Hampshire Crimes Against Children Research Center. Available at: http://www.unh.edu/ccrc/pdf/CV203_Updated%20Trends%20in%20Child%20Maltreatment%202008_8-6-10.pdf. Accessed 5 Feb 2013.

Flores, G., Rabke-Verani, J., Pine, W., & Sabharwal, A. (2002). The importance of cultural and linguistic issues in the emergency care of children. *Pediatric Emergency Care, 18*, 271–284.

Gilles, E., McGregor, M., & Levy-Clarke, G. (2003). Retinal hemorrhage asymmetry in inflicted head injury: A clue to pathogenesis? *Journal of Pediatrics, 143*(4), 494–499.

Global Initiative to End Corporal Punishment (2010). End all corporal punishment of children. http:/www.endcorporal-punishment.org. Accessed 21 Nov 2010.

Gray, J. (Ed.). (2010). *World perspectives on child abuse* (9th ed.). Aurora: International Society for Prevention of Child Abuse and Neglect.

Guleserian, K. J., Gilchrist, B. F., Luks, F. L., et al. (1996). Child abuse as a cause of traumatic chylothorax. *Journal of Pediatric Surgery, 31*, 1696–1697.

Halliday, K. E., Broderick, N. J., Somers, J. M., & Hawkes, R. (2011). Dating fractures in infants. *Clinical Radiology, 66*, 1049–1054.

Hart, H., & Rubia, K. (2012). Neuroimaging of child abuse: A critical review. *Frontiers in Human Neuroscience, 52*(6), 1–24. doi:10.3389/fnhum.2012.00052.

Helfer, R. E. (1987). The perinatal period, a window of opportunity for enhancing parent-infant communication: An approach to prevention. *Child Abuse & Neglect, 11*(4), 565–579.

Herman-Giddens, M. E., Smith, J. B., Manjoo Mittal, M., Carlson, M., & Butts, J. D. (2003). Newborns killed or left to die by a parent: A population-based study. *Journal of the American Medical Association, 289*(11), 1425–1429.

Herr, S., & Fallat, M. E. (2006). Abusive abdominal and thoracic trauma. *Clinical Pediatric Emergency Medicine, 7*, 149–152.

Hochstadt, N. J. (2006). Child death review teams: A vital component of child protection. *Child Welfare, 85*(4), 653–670.

Huang, M. I., O'Riordan, M. A., Fitzenrider, E., McDavid, L., Cohen, A. R., & Robinson, S. (2011). Increased incidence of nonaccidental head trauma in infants associated with the economic recession. *Journal of Neurosurgery. Pediatrics, 8*, 171–176.

Hughes, R. C., Rycus, J. S., Saunders-Adams, S. M., Hughes, L. E., & Hughes, K. N. (2013). Issues in differential response. *Research on social work practice,* published online 9 January 2013. doi: 10.1177/1049731512466312.

Hussey, J. M., Chang, J. J., & Kotch, J. B. (2006). Child maltreatment in the United States: Prevalence, risk factors and adolescent health consequences. *Pediatrics, 118,* 933–942.

Institute of Medicine and National Research Council. (2012). *Child maltreatment research, policy, and practice for the next decade: Workshop summary.* Washington, DC: The National Academies Press.

Jenny, C., & Isaac, R. (2006). The relation between child death and child maltreatment. *Archives of Diseases of Children, 91*(3), 265–269.

Jenny, C. J., & The Committee on Child Abuse and Neglect. (2006). Evaluating infants and young children with multiple fractures. *Pediatrics, 118,* 1299–1303.

Johnston, B. D., Bennett, E., Pilkey, D., Wirtz, S. J., & Quan, L. (2011). Collaborative process improvement to enhance injury prevention in child death review. *Injury Prevention, 17*(Suppl 1), i71–i76.

Kaplan, S. J., Labruna, V., Pelcovitz, D., et al. (1999). Physically abuse adolescents: Behavior problems, functional impairment, and comparison of informants' reports. *Pediatrics, 104,* 430–449.

Kellogg, N. D., & The Committee on Child Abuse and Neglect. (2007). The evaluation of suspected child physical abuse. *Pediatrics, 119,* 1232–1241.

Kemp, A. M. (2011). Abusive head trauma: Recognition and the essential investigation. *Archives of Diseases in Children–Education and Practice Edition.* doi: 10.1136/adc.2009.170449

Kempe, C. H., Silverman, F. N., Steele, B. F., Droegemueller, W., & Silver, H. K. (1962). The battered child syndrome. *Journal of the American Medical Association, 181,* 17–24.

Kendall-Tackett, K. (2002). The health effects of childhood abuse: Four pathways by which abuse can influence health. *Child Abuse & Neglect, 26,* 715–719.

Kleinman, P. K. (1998). *Diagnostic imaging of child abuse* (2nd ed.). St. Louis: Mosby.

Knight, L. D., & Collins, K. A. (2005). A 25-year retrospective review of deaths due to pediatric neglect. *The American Journal of Forensic Medicine and Pathology, 26*(3), 221–228.

Korbin, J. E. (2002). Culture and child maltreatment: Cultural competence and beyond. *Child Abuse & Neglect, 26,* 637–644.

Krugman, S. D. (2013). Multidisciplinary teams. In R. D. Krugman & J. E. Korbin (Eds.), *C. Henry Kempe: A fifty year legacy to the field of child abuse and neglect* (pp. 71–78). New York: Springer.

Lane, W. G., Dubowitz, H., Langenberg, P., & Dischinger, P. (2012). Epidemiology of abusive abdominal trauma hospitalizations in United States children. *Child Abuse & Neglect, 36,* 142–148.

Leventhal, J. M., & Gaither, J. R. (2012). Incidence of serious injuries due to physical abuse in the United States: 1997 to 2009. *Pediatrics, 130*(5), e847–e852. doi:10.1542/peds.2012-0922.

Leventhal, J. M., Martin, K. D., & Gaither, J. R. (2012). Using U.S. data to estimate the incidence of serious physical abuse in children. *Pediatrics, 129*(3), 458–464.

Levin, A. V. (1991). Ocular complications of head trauma in children. *Pediatric Emergency Care, 7,* 129–130.

Levin, A. V. (2010). Retinal hemorrhage in abusive head trauma. *Pediatrics, 126,* 961–970.

Lindberg, D. M., Harper, N. S., Laskey, A. L., Berger, R. P., & The ExSTRA Investigators. (2013). Prevalence of abusive fractures of the hands, feet, spine, or pelvis on skeletal survey: Perhaps "uncommon" is more common than suggested. *Pediatric Emergency Care, 29*(1), 26–29.

Look, K. M., & Look, R. M. (1997). Skin scraping, cupping, and moxibustion that may mimic physical abuse. *Journal of Forensic Science, 42,* 103–105.

MacMillan, H. L., Wathen, C. N., Fergusson, D. M., Leventhal, J. M., & Taussig, H. N. (2009). Interventions to prevent child maltreatment and associated impairment. *Lancet, 373,* 250–266.

Maguire, S., Mann, M. K., Siebert, J., & Kemp, A. (2005). Can you age bruises accurately in children? A systematic review. *Archives of Diseases of Childhood, 90,* 187–189.

Makoroff, K. L., Brauley, J. L., Brandner, A. M., Myers, P. A., & Shapiro, R. A. (2002). Genital examinations for alleged sexual abuse of prepubertal girls: Findings by pediatric emergency medicine physicians compared with child abuse trained physicians. *Child Abuse & Neglect, 26*(12), 1235–1242.

Maxfield, M. G., & Widom, C. S. (1996). The cycle of violence: Revisited six years later. *Archives of Pediatric and Adolescent Medicine, 150*(4), 390–395.

May-Chatal, C., & Cawson, P. (2005). Measuring child maltreatment in the United Kingdom: A study of the prevalence of child abuse and neglect. *Child Abuse & Neglect, 29,* 969–984.

Mikton, C., & Butchart, A. (2009). Child maltreatment prevention: A systematic review of reviews. *Bulletin of the World Health Organization, 87,* 353–361.

Mulinge, M. M. (2010). Persistent socioeconomic and political dilemmas to the implementation of the 1989 United Nations' convention on the rights of the child in sub-Saharan Africa. *Child Abuse & Neglect, 34*(1), 10–17.

National Association of Children's Hospitals and Related Institutions. (2005). *Defining the children's hospital role in child maltreatment.* Alexandria: Author.

National Children's Alliance (2011). About us. Retrieved 14 Feb 2011, from http://www.nca-online.org/welcome.html.

Palusci, V. J. (2010). Using citizen review panels to assess child maltreatment fatalities. *APSAC Advisor, 22*(4), 9–12.

Palusci, V. J. (2013). Adverse childhood experiences and lifelong health. *Journal of the American Medical Association Pediatrics, 167*(1), 95–96.

Palusci, V. J., & Haney, M. L. (2010). Strategies to prevent child maltreatment and integration into practice. *APSAC Advisor, 22*(1), 8–17.

Palusci, V. J., Smith, E. G., & Paneth, N. (2005). Predicting recurrence of child maltreatment in young children using NCANDS. *Children and Youth Services Review, 27*(6), 667–682.

Palusci, V. J., Yager, S., & Covington, T. M. (2010). Effects of a citizen's review panel in preventing child maltreatment fatalities. *Child Abuse & Neglect, 34*(5), 324–331.

Pierce, M. C., & Bertocci, G. (2008). Injury biomechanics and child abuse. *Annual Review of Biomedical Engineering, 10*, 85–106.

Pressley, J. C., Barlow, B., Kendig, T., & Paneth-Pollak, R. (2007). Twenty year trends in fatal injuries to very young children: The persistence of racial disparities. *Pediatrics, 119*(4), e875–e884.

Prosser, I., Lawson, Z., Evans, A., Harrison, S., Maguire, S., & Kemp, A. M. (2012). A timetable for the radiologic features of fracture healing in young children. *American Journal of Radiology, 198*, 1014–1020.

Protect Our Kids Act (2013). www.govtrack.us/congress/bills/112/hr6655. Accessed 3 Aug 2013.

Putnam-Hornstein, E. (2011). Report of maltreatment as a risk factor for injury death: A prospective birth cohort study. *Child Maltreatment, 16*, 163–174.

Raman, S., & Hodes, D. (2012). Cultural issues in child maltreatment. *Journal of Paediatrics and Child Health, 48*, 30–37.

Rangel, E. L., Burd, R. S., Falcone, R. A., Jr., & The Multicenter Child Abuse Disparity Group. (2010). Socioeconomic disparities in infant mortality after nonaccidental trauma: A multicenter study. *Journal of Trauma, 69*(1), 20–25.

Reynolds, A. J., Mathieson, L. C., & Topitzes, J. W. (2009). Do early childhood interventions prevent child maltreatment? *Child Maltreatment, 14*(5), 182–206.

Rimsza, M. E., Schackner, R. A., Bowen, K. A., & Marshall, W. (2002). Can child deaths be prevented? The Arizona child fatality review program experience. *Pediatrics, 110*(1 Pt 1), e11.

Runyan, D. K., Dunne, M. P., Zolotor, A. J., Madrid, B., Jain, D., Gerbaka, B., Menick, D. M., Andreva-Miller, I., Kasim, M. S., Choo, W. Y., Isaeva, O., Macfarlane, B., Ramirez, C., Volkova, E., & Youssef, R. M. (2009). The development and piloting of the ISPCAN child abuse screening tool-parent version (ICAST-P). *Child Abuse & Neglect, 33*(11), 826–832.

Runyan, D. K., Shankar, V., Hassan, F., Hunter, W. M., Jain, D., Paula, C. S., Bangdiwala, S. I., Ramiro, L. S., Muñoz, S. R., Vizcarra, B., & Bordin, I. A. (2010). International variations in harsh child discipline. *Pediatrics, 126*(3), e701–e711.

Schnitzer, P. G., & Ewigman, B. G. (2005). Child deaths resulting from inflicted injuries: Household risk factors and perpetrator characteristics. *Pediatrics, 116*(5), e687–e693.

Schnitzer, P. G., Covington, T. M., Wirtz, S. J., Verhoek-Oftedahl, W., & Palusci, V. J. (2008). Public health surveillance of fatal child maltreatment: Analysis of three state programs. *American Journal of Public Health, 98*(2), 296–303.

Schnitzer, P. G., Covington, T. M., & Kruse, R. L. (2011). Assessment of caregiver responsibility in unintentional child injury deaths: Challenges for injury prevention. *Injury Prevention, 17*(Suppl 1), i45–i54.

Sedlak, A. J., Mettenburg, J., Basena, M., Petta, I., McPherson, K., Greene, A., & Li, S. (2010). *Fourth national incidence study of child abuse and neglect (NIS–4): Report to Congress.* U.S. Washington, DC: Department of Health and Human Services, Administration for Children and Families.

Sege, R. D., Hatmaker-Flanigan, E., De Vos, E., Levin-Goodman, R., & Spivak, H. (2006). Anticipatory guidance and violence prevention: Results from family and pediatrician focus groups. *Pediatrics, 117*, 455–463.

Sidebotham, P., Heron, J., Golding, J., & The ALSPAC Study Team. (2002). Child maltreatment in the 'children of the nineties': Deprivation, class and social networks. *Child Abuse & Neglect, 26*, 1243–1259.

Sidebotham, P., Heron, J., & The ALSPAC Study Team of Bristol. (2006). Child maltreatment in the 'children of the nineties': A cohort study of risk factors. *Child Abuse & Neglect, 30*, 497–522.

Sidebotham, P., Bailey, S., Belderson, P., & Brandon, M. (2011). Fatal child maltreatment in England, 2005–2009. *Child Abuse & Neglect, 35*(4), 299–306.

Sidebotham, P., Atkins, B., & Hutton, J. L. (2012). Changes in rates of violent child deaths in England and Wales between 1974 and 2008: An analysis of national mortality data. *Archives of Diseases in Children, 97*, 193–199.

Siebert, J. R., Payne, E. H., Kemp, A. M., et al. (2002). The incidence of severe physical abuse in Wales. *Child Abuse & Neglect, 26*, 267–276.

Silverman, F. M. (1953). The roentgen manifestations of unrecognized skeletal trauma in infants. *American Journal of Radiology, 69*, 413–426.

Silverman, F. M. (1972). Unrecognized trauma in infants, the battered child syndrome, and the syndrome of Ambroise Tardieu. *Radiology, 104*, 347–353.

Slovis, T. L., Strouse, P. J., Coley, B. D., & Rigsby, C. K. (2012). The creation of non-disease: An assault on the diagnosis of child abuse. *Pediatric Radiology, 42*(8), 903–905.

Stiffman, M. N., Schnitzer, P. G., Adam, P., Kruse, R. L., & Ewigman, B. G. (2002). Household composition and risk of fatal child maltreatment. *Pediatrics, 109*(4), 615–621.

Straus, M. A. (1994). *Beating the devil out of them: Corporal punishment in American families.* San Francisco: Lexington Books.

Sugar, N. F., Taylor, J. A., & Feldman, K. W. (1999). Bruises in infant and toddlers: those who don't cruise rarely bruise. Puget Sound Pediatric Network. *Archives of Pediatric and Adolescent Medicine, 153*, 399–403.

Svevo-Cianci, K., & Lee, Y. (2010). Twenty years of the convention on the rights of the child: Achievements in and challenges for child protection implementation, measurement and evaluation around the world. *Child Abuse & Neglect, 34*(1), 1–4.

Terao, S. Y., Borrego, J., & Urquiza, A. J. (2001). A reporting and response model for culture and child maltreatment. *Child Maltreatment, 6*, 158–168.

Theodore, A. D., Chang, J. J., Runyan, D. K., Hunter, W. M., Bangdiwala, S. I., & Agans, R. (2005). Epidemiologic features of the physical and sexual maltreatment of children in the Carolinas. *Pediatrics, 115*, e331–e337.

Toon, M. H., Maybauer, D. M., Arceneoux, L. L., Fraser, J. F., Meyer, W., Runge, A., & Maybauer, M. O. (2011). Children with burn injuries-assessment of trauma, neglect, violence and abuse. *Journal of Injury and Violence Research, 3*(2), 98–110.

Tursz, A., Crost, M., Gerbouin-Rérolle, P., & Cook, J. M. (2010). Underascertainment of child abuse fatalities in France: Retrospective analysis of judicial data to assess underreporting of infant homicides in mortality statistics. *Child Abuse & Neglect, 34*(7), 534–544.

U.S. Advisory Board on Child Abuse and Neglect (1995). *A nation's shame: Fatal child abuse and neglect in the United States.* Washington, DC: U.S. Department of Health and Human Services, Administration for Children and Families.

U.S. Department of Health and Human Services. (2012). *Child maltreatment 2011: Reports from the states to the national child abuse and neglect data system.* Washington, DC: U.S. Government Printing Office.

U.S. Government Accountability Office (2011). *Child maltreatment: Strengthening national data on child fatalities could aid in prevention* (GAO-11-599). Washington, DC: U.S. Government Printing Office. Retrieved 4 Apr 2012, from: http://www.gao.gov/assets/330/320774.pdf.

UNICEF (2003). *A league table of child maltreatment deaths in rich nations. Innocenti Report Card No.5,* Florence Italy: UNICEF Innocenti Research Center.

United Nations (1989). *Convention on the Rights of the Child* (CRC).

United Nations (2006). *United Nations Secretary-General's report on violence against children.* Retrieved 15 Jan 2013, from: http://www.unviolencestudy.org/.

Wang, C. T., & Holton, J. (2008). *Total estimated cost of child abuse and neglect in the United States.* Chicago: Prevent Child Abuse America.

Widom, C. S., Czaja, S. J., Bentley, T., & Johnson, M. S. (2012). A prospective investigation of physical health outcomes in abused and neglected children: New findings from a 30-year follow-up. *American Journal of Public Health, 102*(6), 1135–1144.

Wood, J., Rubin, D. M., Nance, M. L., & Christian, C. W. (2005). Distinguishing inflicted versus accidental abdominal injuries in young children. *The Journal of Trauma, 59*, 1203–1208.

Wood, J. N., Medina, S. P., Feundtner, C., Luan, X., Localio, R., Fieldston, E. S., & Rubin, D. M. (2012). Local macro-economic trends and hospital admissions for child abuse, 2000–2009. *Pediatrics, 130*, e358–e364.

Woolley, P. V., & Evans, W. A. (1955). Significance of skeletal lesions in infants resembling those of traumatic origin. *Journal of the American Medical Association, 158*, 539–547.

World Health Organization (1999). *Report of the consultation on child abuse prevention.* World Health Organization, Geneva. Retrieved 15 Jan 2013, from: http://whqlibdoc.who.int/hq/1999/WHO_HSC_PVI_99.1.pdf.

Xu, D., Mukherjee, P., & Barkovich, J. (2013). Pediatric brain injury: Can DTI scalars predict functional outcome? *Pediatric Radiology, 43*, 55–59.

Yoshida, S., Oishi, K., Faria, A. V., & Mori, S. (2013). Diffusion tensor imaging of normal brain development. *Pediatric Radiology, 43*, 15–27.

Zhou, Y., Hallisey, E. J., & Freymann, G. R. (2006). Identifying perinatal risk factors for infant maltreatment: An ecological approach. *International Journal of Health Geography, 5*, 53–63.

Zolotor, A. J., Runyan, D. K., Dunne, M. P., Jain, D., Péturs, H. R., Ramirez, C., Volkova, E., Deb, S., Lidchi, V., Muhammad, T., & Isaeva, O. (2009). ISPCAN child abuse screening tool children's version (ICAST-C): Instrument development and multi-national pilot testing. *Child Abuse & Neglect, 33*(11), 833–841.

Chapter 4
Child Sexual Abuse: The History, Current State of the Art and the Challenges for the Future: A Pediatric Perspective

Astrid Heppenstall Heger

After 30 years, the sexual abuse of children has finally been accepted by both the public and the medical professionals as a reality for many children. Three decades ago one of the major challenges was to persuade the public and also practicing medical professionals, that child sexual abuse was a real problem. Acceptance has not come quickly or without debate and backlash! The public is watching stories emerging from the Catholic Church, Boy Scouts, elementary schools and programs focused on children's sports activities. Despite acceptance by professionals and public, child sexual abuse remains a major problem in the field of child abuse and neglect and in a recent meta-analysis based on almost ten million participants, the overall estimated global prevalence was 127/1,000 in self reports and 4/1,000 in informant studies (Stoltenborgh et al. 2011). With heightened awareness and media coverage, prevention programs began to sprout up across the country, children began to disclose in a variety of settings.

The first to recognize the need for the identification, diagnosis and treatment of children who have been sexually abused were the child abuse pediatricians. However, there were few expert physicians who had sufficient knowledge to assess normal pre-pubertal anatomy and identify appropriately those findings that were diagnostic of prior trauma associated with sexual abuse/assault. Therefore, children who disclosed sexual abuse were evaluated in a wide range of settings by medical professionals with various levels of expertise and training.

The role of the medical professional is critical. Most parents, social workers and law enforcement look to us to provide them with the answer to the question "Has anything happened to my child?" In addition, the testimony from the medical professional is the single most important part of the evidence presented in court that results in convictions (Berliner and Barbieri 1984; Palusci et al. 1999; Runyan et al. 1988).

Over the years, the primary medical professional continued to play an important role in the identification and assessment of children impacted by sexual abuse. However, because of the evolution of regional centers of excellence (child advocacy centers, hospital based child abuse teams and research centers in university hospitals) most primary providers now refer children on to multidisciplinary centers staffed with experts in both the interviewing of children and the medical assessment. The evolution of centers of excellence based in research and reason in both interview strategies and medical diagnosis of child sexual abuse has provided a dramatic improvement in advocacy for children. This has been a major stabilizing factor in creating a standard of care essential for the well-being of the child victim and the family.

A.H. Heger, M.D. (✉)
Keck School of Medicine, University of Southern California, Los Angeles, USA

Violence Intervention Program, S. Mark Taper Family Advocacy Center, 1721 Griffin Avenue, Los Angeles, CA 90031, USA
e-mail: heger@usc.edu

J.E. Korbin and R.D. Krugman (eds.), *Handbook of Child Maltreatment*, Child Maltreatment 2, DOI 10.1007/978-94-007-7208-3_4, © Springer Science+Business Media Dordrecht 2014

Unlike any other clinical diagnosis, a report of sexual abuse usually results in a criminal investigation, possible arrest of the alleged perpetrator and the potential for trial, conviction and long prison sentences (Cross et al. 1994). This legal response has significant outcomes for the victim (Landwirth 1987), the alleged perpetrator and the family. Additional challenges to maintaining the highest standard of assessment, diagnosis and treatment have come from the commercialization of the forensic assessments to such a degree that individuals with minimal training and little if any peer review and oversight, can create a forensic assessment site that caters to the diagnostic needs of law enforcement. Any diagnosis driven by money and the legal system can become diverted from staying true to the science and the neutrality of a medical conclusion. This is of course true of professionals who find themselves hired by either the defense bar or the prosecution. It is therefore critical that the assessment and diagnosis is done with the highest degree of integrity and expertise based in research and reason by individuals with experience and who remain involved in ongoing peer review.

The medical assessment is difficult and when done poorly can cause potential harm to the child and the family. Both ends of the spectrum are dangerous; missing the fact that abuse is occurring can create the situation where the child continues to be abused and quickly learns that he/she cannot find help. When normal medical findings are misinterpreted as abnormal, the impact is equally damaging. Children may be taken away from a protective family environment and sent into foster care where additional abuse and neglect may occur (Paradise et al. 1999).

Now 35 years after Kempe (1978) and Sgroi (1982) described child sexual abuse as "a hidden problem in pediatrics" we have board certification in child abuse pediatrics; child sexual abuse is routinely taught in medical schools and included in pediatric training curriculae around the world. There is an established scientific protocol that relies on photodocumentation, common terminology and a cohesive peer review process. Professional groups have developed written guidelines outlining the significance or insignificance of various anatomical findings and have come to a degree of consensus on findings that are diagnostic of prior trauma.

A consistent theme through all of the research and reason is that medical professionals must play an independent and conservative role (Krugman 1988), questioning the sole reliance on medical findings when coming to a diagnosis of sexual abuse. This is particularly true when the legal system comes into the picture. This relationship of medicine and the criminal justice system creates a difficult interface between medical professionals, who as scientists are always looking to improve their knowledge and move towards a thorough, evidence-based diagnosis, and the legal system that seeks a definitive diagnosis, chiseled in stone in a brief moment in time. This conflict makes it difficult for professionals to grow in their knowledge, provide testimony that reflects these changes and review cases from the past, where convictions were made based on clinical concepts that are no longer held as the standard. Changing a position on what is clinical evidence of sexual abuse is difficult for many practitioners. The public media attention (Cheit et al. 2010) afforded these cases as well as the contentious nature of the legal system create an environment unique for medical professionals. The attention afforded any change of opinion can result in the medical professional becoming the story rather than focusing on the scientific assessment of the entirety of the case.

Perhaps the most important impact of both the increasing professionalism of medical examiners and the public acceptance of child sexual abuse as a reality is prevention. By providing children with an opportunity to disclose, children are seen earlier, interventions are more efficient and appropriate, investigations accurate, prosecutions effective and the actual rates of sexual abuse seem to be declining (Finkelhor et al. 2005; Finkelhor and Jones 2011). Obviously there is a wide range (both quality and quantity) of prevention programs provided children in school settings or implemented through primary care providers. Testing the impact of these programs (Wurtele 2009) shows that, like the programs themselves, there is a variable impact on the child and that the ongoing reliance on children disclosing, i.e. "Why didn't you tell?", places the burden on the victim rather than the adults charged with their protection. However, there is an important side benefit and impact from the implementation of prevention programs; parents are more likely to begin the conversation and communication with their own child about appropriate behaviors between adults and children and hopefully begin to listen to children all the way to the end of their sentences. Some professionals in working with parents of children who have been sexually abused ask the parent, regardless of the circumstances, to assume the responsibility for the child's abuse. "It is my responsibility to keep you safe....I failed you." Taking the guilt and blame off the victim promotes healing and impacts the long-term negative effects of child sexual abuse.

History from the child remains the single most important factor in making the diagnosis of sexual abuse (Berliner and Barbieri 1984; Frasier 1997). Other than the perpetrator, the child is the only witness to the crime. Over the past 30 years there has been an increasing volume of research on the reliability of a child's report of sexual abuse. Initially much of the research was focused on how to undermine the accuracy of the child's report of abuse. More recently research has progressed towards developing evidence-based methods to interview children effectively and in such a way that the information from the interview can withstand the vigorous challenges of the legal system. These tools have been incorporated into the National Institutes of Child Health and Human Development (NICHD) structured interview protocol. This protocol has been reviewed and tested and found to provide useful and usable set of guidelines that allow trained interviewers to conduct more consistent and replicable investigative interviews (Lamb et al. 2007). The current reliance on non-leading, research supported evaluation techniques lead to more accurate interviews and assessments which validate the disclosures from the child and should be the basis for moving forward with investigations and prosecutions. Most child advocacy centers have revamped their approach to interviewing children who have disclosed abuse and now rely on approaches that have been researched and tested (Lyon 2005) (see Table 4.1).

Prior to assessing the child, the medical professional has an obligation to review all available information provided by both the system, i.e. social services and law enforcement, and from the parents. Parents and guardians can provide essential past behavioral and medical history that should be taken into consideration when assessing for possible sexual abuse. The social and legal systems may provide us with significant past history of their involvement with the family which can help in planning for safety. After gathering as much information as possible from parents, guardians, social workers and police, the medical professional should review important aspects of the episode(s) of abuse with the disclosing child (Table 4.2).

Most children are reluctant to discuss with a stranger an event that was been both traumatic and potentially produced a sense of guilt and responsibility. The fact that the child has presented for interview and examination may well mean that law enforcement is involved and that a parent or someone close to them has been arrested. This enhances the stress and trauma to the child, and it is essential that the examining medical professional takes the time to reassure the child, reducing the fear and stress and remembering that the process of performing a medical examination of a child who has been sexually abused can be the one part of the intervention and evaluation that recreates the abuse in the mind of the child. The medical professional must therefore participate in reassuring the child, talking with the child, explaining the examination and proceeding only when the child understands and agrees to the examination.

The Medical History: The role of the medical professional in the history taking is not to pry out of the child more information than the child is willing to provide at that time, but rather to establish before and during the examination if the child can report what happened, where they were touched, was there pain or ejaculation, and the identity of the offender. This information can then be used to direct the examination and if and where forensic evidence may be found. The documentation of any statements made by the child in the course of the evaluation can then be included in the testimony by the examining professional. Often in the young child there are spontaneous utterances which are admissible in any court. The medical professional is most interested in the nature of the assault or abuse, while the location and details about the perpetrator, e.g. what was the alleged perpetrator wearing, what was the color of the wallpaper, may be more important to the investigator who is attempting to identify the "where" and the "who" of the allegations.

Table 4.1 Ten step investigative interview (Printed with permission from Lyon 2005)

---

1. **Don't know instruction**

If I ask you a question and you don't know the answer, then just say, "I don't know."

So if I ask you "What is my dog's name?", what do you say?

OK because you don't know

But what if I ask you "Do you have a dog?"

OK because you do know

2. **Don't understand instruction**

If I ask you a question and you don't know what I mean or what I'm saying, you can say, "I don't know what you mean." I will ask it a different way

So if I ask you "what is your gender?", what do you say?

That's because "gender" is a hard word. So I would say, "Are you a boy or a girl?"

3. **You're wrong instruction**

Sometimes I make mistakes or say the wrong thing. When I do, you can tell me that I am wrong

So, if I say, "you are 30 years old," what do you say?

OK, so how old are you?

4. **Ignorant interviewer instruction**

I don't know what's happened to you

I won't be able to tell you the answers to my questions

5. **Promise to tell the truth**

It is really important that you tell me the truth

Do you promise that you will tell me the truth?

Will you tell me any lies?

6. **Practice narratives**

(a) **Like to do/don't like to do**

First, I'd like you to tell me about things you LIKE to do

Follow up with "tell me more" questions

e.g. "You said you like to play soccer. Tell me more about soccer."

Now tell me about the things you don't like to do

Follow up with "tell me more" questions

(b) **Last birthday**

Now tell me about your last birthday. Tell me everything that happened

Follow up with "what happened next" questions, e.g. "You said you played in the bouncy. What did you do next?"

7. **Allegation**

(If child discloses abuse, go directly to Allegation Follow up. Determine in advance which allegation questions you will ask.)

(a) **Tell me why I came to talk to you**

Or, tell me why you came to talk to me

e.g. "It's really important for me to know why I came to talk to you/you came to talk to me."

(b) **I heard you saw**

e.g. "I heard you saw a policeman last week. Tell me what you talked about."

(c) **Someone's worried**

e.g. "Is your mom worried that something may have happened to you? Tell me what she is worried about."

(d) **Someone bothered you**

e.g. "I heard that someone might have bothered you. Tell me everything about that."

(e) **Something wasn't right**

e.g. "I heard that someone may have done something to you that wasn't right. Tell me everything about that."

8. **Allegation follow up**

You said that (repeat allegation). Tell me everything that happened. e.g. "You said that Uncle Bill hurt your pee-pee. Tell me everything that happened."

(continued)

Table 4.1   (continued)

9. Follow up with "tell me more" and "what happened next" questions
Avoid yes/no and forced-choice questions

10. Multiple incidents
Did (repeat allegation) happen one time or more than one time?
Tell me everything that happened the time you remember the most…
Tell me everything that happened the first time…
Tell me everything that happened the last time…
Was there another time?

Table 4.2   APSAC definitions (Myers 2010)

General terms
Erythema: A redness of the skin or mucous membranes produced by congestion of the capillaries
Periurethral bands: Small bands, lateral to the urethra that connect the periurethral tissues to the wall of the vestibule
Perihymenal bands: Small bands of tissue lateral to the hymen, that form a connection between the perihymenal structures and the wall of the vestibule
Midline sparing (linea vestibularis): A vertical pale/avascular line across the PF
Median raphe: A ridge or furrow that marks the line of union of the two halves of the perineum
Longitudinal intravaginal ridges: Narrow mucosa-covered ridges of tissue on the vaginal wall that may be found in all four quadrants
Labial adhesions: Adherence of the outer-most mucosal surfaces of the vestibular walls
Asymmetry of the fossa: The asymmetrical attachment of the labia minora to the fossa (normal variant)

Changes in the hymenal edge
Angularity of Hymen: Relatively sharp angles in the contour of the hymenal inner edge. (May be evidence of prior trauma.)
Cleft/notch: An angular or v-shaped indentation on the edge of the hymenal membrane. May extend to the muscular attachment of the hymen. (May be evidence of prior trauma.)
Fimbriated/Denticular: Hymen with multiple projections or indentations along the edge, creating a ruffled appearance (a congenital variant)
Concavity: A curved or hollowed u-shaped depression the edge of the hymenal membrane
Key-hole configuration: The appearance of the hymenal orifice when the posterior lateral portions of the hymenal membrane project into the orifice creating a concavity inferiorly – (descriptive term that may be misinterpreted)
Irregular hymenal edge: A disruption in the smooth contour of the hymen
Narrow hymenal rim: Term used to describe the wide of the hymenal membrane in the coronal plane (an abnormally narrowed membrane may be evidence of prior trauma)

Now we have established the value of disclosure and history taking from the child, we can move into the arena of the value of the medical evaluation, the interpretation of the clinical findings and the value of the laboratory and forensic evidence.

The Medical Examination: The actual examination is the single encounter during the evaluation/ investigation process that most closely resembles the actual abuse. Since there has been the creation of wonderful, child-friendly centers of excellence, hopefully every child has the opportunity to be evaluated by the experts practicing in this environment. Since so many children once seen by primary care medical professionals are now referred to these centers of excellence, the order of the evaluation may vary depending on the reason for the referral.

For example, if a primary provider believes that there is something "wrong" with the child's genitalia, the first step in the evaluation may be to explain the examination (honesty is the best policy) i.e. "Dr. Jones saw something on your vagina that he was worried about, and I need to take a quick look." And then proceed to do just that. If the primary care professional was just flat out wrong in their assessment of the anatomy, there is little if any reason, and in fact it may be counterproductive, to engage in a lengthy forensic interview prior to doing an examination and photodocumentation. However if the child/adolescent has disclosed sexual abuse, a thorough forensic and therapeutic interview with a mental health professional would be helpful to the professional when coming to the conclusion that abuse had occurred.

This is the most difficult aspect of the assessment of any child or adolescent for possible sexual abuse. The examiner must approach the child with care and honesty, explaining the process and establishing rapport with both the child and the accompanying adult. Giving the child control and power may be critical in limiting the amount of emotional trauma the child experiences from the examination. Most examinations are performed in the supine position with gentle traction on the labia or buttocks in order to gain better visualization of the genital area. Labial traction, in girls allows the examiner to visual internal structures and photograph evidence of prior trauma (if present). The clear standard is photodocumentation. If there is trauma present it is the responsibility of the examiner to document the trauma rather than assuming the stance in court of "Well you had to be there!" The purpose of the photos is to document abnormal findings to prevent the need for re-examination. Unfortunately, the legal system can put enormous pressure on examiners to have abnormal examinations in support of the prosecution and without the substantiation of good photos, the examiner may feel the need to make excuses for why the photos do not represent what was reported to the police, rather than taking a position, that it is "normal to be normal" (Heger and Emans 1992; Heger et al. 2000).

After the examination is completed it is important to reassure both the child and the parents and provide them with an honest assessment of your findings.

Medical evidence: There are primarily two types of medical evidence: (1) laboratory and (2) clinical. The laboratory evidence includes those cases of acute assault of either the child or adolescent looking for ejaculate or trace evidence that will help identify the assailant. The other laboratory evidence is evaluation for possible sexually transmitted infections.

There is a low prevalence rate of sexually transmitted infections in children. Therefore, because of the forensic importance, caution must be taken to assess appropriately and exclude any false-positives (CDC 2010; Shapiro and Makoroff 2006). When evaluating the significance of a substantiated case of an STI, the medical professional must be thorough to exclude any nonsexual transmission. At the time of the examination cultures and other laboratory means for assessing the presence of STI's may be used, treatment is usually withheld until infection is proven. HIV is the one exception to this rule, since quick treatment is essential in preventing the transmission.

Sexually Transmitted Infections: Confirmed (laboratory) diagnosis of gonorrhea, syphilis, trichomonas, chlamydia and HIV, outside of the neonatal period fall under the category of mandated reporting and in most cases are considered to be diagnostic of sexual contact if the clinician has excluded any possible non-sexual transmission (CDC 2010; Shapiro and Makoroff 2006).

Forensic Evidence: The advances in the ability of the forensic laboratories to analyze minute quantities of DNA from a range of sources not just spermatozoa, has greatly enhanced the ability of the legal system to identify offenders and successfully prosecute them. In cases of children under the age of 14 the DNA is enough; in children 14 and older the question of consent is always an issue. Although traditionally, society has looked at 18 as the age of consent, the legal system no longer applies this rule in many cases in which they determine are consensual. Now the varied application of the law reflects a societal change as teenagers are becoming consensually sexual active at earlier and earlier ages. This has impacted the application of the laws and in some states impacted the laws requiring the reporting of sexual activity, consensual and non-consensual.

In the pre-verbal child, the presence of DNA material may be the only evidence that can be used in court to protect the child and prosecute the accused. Therefore it is critical that in acute cases (traditionally under 72 h) that the examiner pay close attention to examining for forensic evidence. This includes meticulous examination of the skin and clothing of the child, and coordination with law enforcement to access any possible evidence left behind at the site of the assault. Most assaults of pre-adolescent children involve acts that do not involve actual penetration and ejaculation into the vaginal, anus or mouth of the child but the forensic evidence may be found on the unwashed clothing the child was wearing or on bedding, towels, rugs, etc. from the crime scene. Working with law enforcement it is important to remind them that research results indicate that there is a better chance of recovering forensic evidence of ejaculation when police investigating the report evaluate the geography of the abuse rather than relying solely on the evidence obtained at the time of the examination i.e. forensic evidence is most likely found at the site of the assault, not on the child (Christian et al. 2000).

If the identity of the perpetrator is known, careful forensic analysis is warranted of his/her person and clothing. The advances of forensic analysis have been able to identify victim cells on the penis, finger, etc. of the offender. In adolescents where the defense is usually that all sexual activity was consensual, the clinical documentation of any trauma, genital and extra-genital, becomes equally important with the forensic evidence. In sexual assault centers, the most important "rape" kits to process would be those from unidentified assailants and from cases involving young children where this documentation goes a long way towards substantiating the history from the child. Centers should form alliances with local crime laboratories to focus attention on stranger rape cases and cases involving the very young child.

Another area of forensic oversight that medical professionals should be involved in is the "forensic" therapeutic termination of a pregnancy that resulted from an assault. Trained forensic professionals should attend all procedures that produce fetal tissue in order to maintain the chain of evidence and provide the crime laboratory with the ability to determine forensic evidence of paternity.

Clinical Evidence: Research and Reason: 30 years ago the successful investigation and prosecution of child sexual abuse was a rarity and relied most commonly on forensic evidence that supported a report of ejaculation. In addition the child had to be of an age to be found credible in a court of law. Clinical evidence of sexual assault or abuse was rare and documentation of an injury was completely reliant on the medical professional's memory of what was seen at the time of the genital examination. These drawings from memory then became the significant forensic evidence in the investigation of these cases. In 1982 there were at most 3–4 physicians in the United States who were examining preadolescent girls for evidence of sexual abuse; none were taking photographs.

Early research into the medical diagnosis of the sexual abuse of children focused on reporting on the medical evaluation/findings of children referred for possible sexual abuse. These children were referred after disclosure of abuse, exposure to an abusive environment or because a genital examination by a primary care medical professional needed further clarification. The earliest articles reported on rates of abnormal genital findings in the child that were as high as 80 % (Cantwell 1981; Emans et al. 1987; Hobbs and Wynne 1987). Many of these reports based their results on a higher rate of acute trauma, sexually transmitted diseases and positive forensic findings (Orr and Prietto 1979; Rimsza and Niggermann 1982). Two of the articles (Cantwell 1981; Pugno 1999) focused solely on hymenal diameters as a significant indicator. Other studies included erythema and swelling along with changes in anal tone on their list of positive findings (Hobbs and Wynne 1987).

Since then there has been an explosion of research and clinical reports on the medical evaluation of the sexually abused child. The first decade of research on child sexual abuse, covered a wide range of clinical findings but lacked a consistency in terminology, methods and results. Furthermore there were no "normal" controls in these cases and thus the research came to dangerous conclusions of what was considered to be diagnostic of abuse. Equally important, without a strong scientific research foundation of what constituted normal pre-adolescent anatomy, many non-specific findings were reported as being post-traumatic. Since 1989 most of the published research has relied on photodocumentation first described in 1986 (Teixeira 1982; Woodling and Heger 1986). Photodocumentation enhanced the potential for consistency and peer review.

With photodocumentation, peer review and standard terminology in place as a means to review and standardization, the next research step was understanding normal anatomy. Once normal anatomy was established, this research could be used as a standard to compare with the vast number of cases that were in the literature that had reported on findings in children who had reported abuse. Without this comparison and foundation, any variation, say in hymeneal anatomy, might be interpreted as post-traumatic and regardless of the history from the child, catapult the case into the criminal arena or at the very least into the child protection process. Research into hymeneal morphology and non-specific changes, both vaginal and anal, was a good starting point (Gardner 1992; Heger and Emans 1992; McCann et al. 1989, 1990; Pokorny 1987). However, research into normal anatomy was fraught with challenges. Questions were always raised about whether the children really abused and just not report-ing. In other words, how does one recruit children from a general pediatric population where parents are willing to have them interviewed and then have their genitals examined and photographed? It was because of these questions that research was undertaken to study the anatomy of newborn girls (Berenson et al. 1991). Researchers decided that (1) children in the nursery are highly unlikely to be abused and (2) parents were less likely to balk at having a newborn's genitalia examined and photo-graphed. Thereby the selection process was neither complicated with questions about whether the child was abused or not nor with the serious objections from parents. After this study it became clear that there was a wide range of normal hymeneal shapes, non-specific anatomical variations of the hymen and peri-hymeneal anatomy that could not be attributed to post-traumatic changes. Other nor-mal studies, of both vaginal and peri-anal findings, were then undertaken recruiting subjects from general pediatric practices, and when photographs were taken and could be reviewed these studies substantiated each other and were consistent with what one would predict to see based on the normal newborn study (Berenson et al. 1992, 1993; Heger and Emans 1992; Heger et al. 2002a; Myhre et al. 2001, 2003). Photodocumentation also produced a series of references that included photographic atlases that illustrated what was being described in the literature and became teaching tools and refer-ence guides (Heger and Emans 1992; Heger et al. 2000). With the reliance on photodocumentation, peer review and standardized terminology starting in the late 1980s the rates of abnormal examina-tions decreased to <3 % by 2000 (Berenson et al. 2000; Heger et al. 2002b). By 2010 most centers were reporting standardized abnormal findings under 5–8 % (Adams 2011; Berenson et al. 2002; Berkoff et al. 2008; Bowen and Aldous 1999; DeLago et al. 2008; Dubowitz et al. 1992; Kellogg et al. 1998; Leder et al. 1999; Muram 1989).

This progression towards recognizing that normal is the norm was grounded by the use of photod-ocumentation that provided the means for standard methods and terminology and most importantly for peer review and research replication. The important concept was that researchers and reviewers could see and agree on what they were describing and even reach agreement on the significance of each finding. This ability to replicate and review pushed the field towards a consistency of what was reported as abnormal or diagnostic of abuse and/or penetrating trauma. Understanding the diagnosis of child sexual abuse is a dynamic discipline and the research continues to provide necessary data and should support a more accurate and consistent diagnosis of child sexual abuse.

The proliferation of research and peer review improved the understanding of normal anatomy and non-specific findings and many of the anatomical findings that were reported as abnormal in the early studies are now considered by many researchers to be non-specific genital variations. These non-specific anatomical variations include enlarged hymeneal diameter, narrowing of the hymeneal edge, partial notching or clefts of the posterior hymeneal rim, erythema or swelling, bumps or irregularities and changes in tone or rugal patterns of the anus (Heger 1996; Heger and Emans 1990, 1992; McCann and Voris 1991; McCann et al. 1990; Myhre et al. 2003; Myhre et al. 2001).

With the improved access to emergency evaluations of sexual assault a better understanding of the importance of acute injuries developed. Following these injuries to healing was the basis for longitu-dinal studies that identified the more significant findings to be acute trauma, hymeneal transections and genital scarring. Sexually transmitted diseases and positive forensics continued to provide critical diagnostic evidence.

Photodocumentation, peer review and consensus on terminology also contributed to the development of standards of practice and classification schemes as well as consensus papers (AAP 2001, 2005; Adams et al. 1992; APSAC 1990, 1995, 1998; Muram 1989; RCPCH 2008). Acceptance of standardization was furthered by the adoption of state protocols for interviewing children and documenting medical findings.

Based in research and standardization of clinical diagnosis medical experts in this field have come to agree that in most cases of sexual abuse there will be no definitive clinical evidence of trauma (Adams et al. 1994; Berenson et al. 2000; Heger et al. 2002b; Kellogg and Parra 1991). Working in multidisciplinary teams such as advocacy centers, medical professionals play an important role in advocating for clear, concise histories from children, conservative, careful medical and laboratory evaluations and supportive follow-up and treatment, both medical and psychological. The absence of definitive medical findings or forensic evidence that sexual abuse/assault as occurred should not preclude a case from moving appropriately through the legal system. The inappropriate reliance on medical evidence as the only standard for prosecution can ultimately lead to "over diagnosis" by eager examiners hoping to help a case through to prosecution. These can then create a pattern for "abnormal" examinations that does not meet national standards based on research and experience. When "over-diagnosis" occurs and statements are made that normal findings are diagnostic of abuse, children who are not abused may be placed in dangerous foster homes and sustain real abuse or neglect. We have longed supported the notion that children should be listened to and believed; but when they deny abuse shouldn't we also be listening.

Why are the examinations so often normal? First let's examine the reasons behind the lack of clinical evidence in most cases of child sexual abuse or assault. Most cases of child sexual abuse are normal because of the nature of the abuse and the delay in disclosure. It has been shown that in most cases of child sexual abuse involving the pre-adolescent child, there is no penetration of the vagina which could result in diagnostic post-traumatic anatomical changes in the hymen and/or posterior fourchette. Most often children are involved in fondling, manipulation, oral and anal intercourse. At the same time, any anal penetration, unless evaluated quickly, heals without evidence of trauma. Mucous membranes heal quickly and without significant scarring. Thereby, even when there is penetration of the vagina or anus, if there is any delay in the evaluation, evidence of acute trauma will heal quickly and by the time an expert medical examiner sees the child the trauma has healed and the examination may be normal. In other cases, the child has not disclosed immediately, creating the same delay in examination and again all possible trauma can heal and the examination is again normal.

Once a girl has started the process of estrogenization of her external genitalia and hymen the assessment for possible trauma associated with penetration becomes even more complicated. Estrogen causes the mucosa of the vaginal introitus and hymen to thickened and become more resistant to trauma. The hymen becomes elastic and can be easily stretched with penetration occurring without acute trauma. When there is tearing or trauma to the hymen it heals quickly and often times completely unless the damage is so egregious that it results in a complete transaction of the hymen to the base. Small tears, hematomas, petechiae, unless documented acutely within hours to several days of the assault, leave no diagnostic evidence that trauma occurred. The healing of a small tear will at most leave only a notch on the edge of the hymen that is indistinguishable from the normal fimbriated hymen of the adolescent. Even pregnant teens have been shown to have normal introital and hymeneal anatomy (AAP 2001; Adams and Knudson 1996; Adams et al. 1994, 2004; Emans et al. 1994; Jones et al. 2003; Kellogg and Parra 1991; Pierce 2004).

Evaluating pornography cases referred to child abuse pediatricians we have gained insight into the nature of abuse perpetrated (and photographed) by those preying on children. Clearly there is rarely an attempt to engage in penile-vaginal penetration before puberty. Oral sex, anal penetration, simulated intercourse and masturbation are the chosen sexual activities with young children.

In addition, any delay in the evaluation of the child or adolescent results in a loss of both clinical and forensic evidence. Forensic evidence is easily lost through delays, both from the process of normal bathing and washing of clothes, but also in the deterioration of any forensic material that would be helpful in validating a history of ejaculation. A potential solution to the challenge of capturing any and all of the evidence that is present in cases of child sexual abuse is in building assessment centers that are available 24/7 staffed with medical experts. In addition when evaluation programs are integrated with aggressive community and school-based projects that promote early, accurate disclosures by children, appropriate evaluations can be undertaken quickly and effectively (Palusci et al. 2006).

Since historically, the mistakes that were made in the reporting of genital and anal findings as abnormal when the examining medical professional was seeing only those children referred for sexual abuse and/or did not have a basic understanding of the normal variations and non-specific changes of the hymen or anus. Because there is such a wide range of non-specific findings, it was critical that the standard of what was abnormal was not based just on what the examiner was recording or photographing in cases where the child reported abuse. The absolute diagnosis of post-traumatic anatomical changes is dependent on following acute injures to complete healing. Therefore, once research had established what was normal and that there was a high degree of normal variation as well as the presence of non-specific findings in the appearance of both vaginal and anal anatomy, research then turned to an understanding of how to interpret findings as they healed..

Studies were undertaken to document acute trauma and follow trauma to healing (Bond et al. 1995; Boos 1999; Boos et al. 2003; Dowd et al. 1994; Finkel 1989; Heppenstall-Heger et al. 2003; McCann et al. 1992, 2007a, b). These studies were seeing children and adolescents with acute injuries and then following to healing looking for those signs that were different from what had been documented in the studies of normal anatomy or established non-specific findings. Results of this research indicated that trauma heals quickly and in most cases completely. Anal trauma usually heals without any residual.

Clearly **acute injuries** to either the genital area or to the anus are evidence of trauma. They are easy to see and are completely consistent with trauma regardless of location (Bond et al. 1995; Boos 1999; Boos et al. 2003; Dowd et al. 1994; Herrmann and Crawford 2002). The only question remaining is whether it was accidental or non-accidental. The acute injuries occur anywhere on the 360° of the vaginal introitus and hymen and to the anal and peri-anal area. By documenting the acute injuries and then following to complete healing, the injuries provide the researcher important information on how the genital and anal tissues heal and what findings remain that can be differentiated from normal variations and non-specific changes.

Evaluation of post-traumatic changes that are diagnostic of sexual abuse focused attention on the posterior (180°) hymen and fourchette. Research into normal anatomy and non-specific findings had reported that most of the non-specific hymeneal changes (i.e. crescentic hymen, no hymen in a portion of the ventral 180°, support bands, deep notches between 9 and 3 clockwise) are normally present in the ventral 180° of the hymen. Even when acute injuries were present in the ventral 180°, it was impossible to come to the conclusion that after healing these injuries resulted in changes to the hymen or perihymeneal tissues that were diagnostic of prior trauma. Any hymeneal variations in the ventral 180° of the hymen could be a range of non-specific findings such as the persistence of a posterior rim hymen/crescentic hymen, or congenital notches.

However, these studies did show that In trauma to the hymen, the one finding (unless surgically repaired) that was never found in the normal population and in fact persisted into puberty was a complete transection of the posterior rim of the hymen or a significant deep tear to the hymen and posterior fourchette as well as egregious anal tears or burns. Partial hymeneal tears and acute trauma to the peri-hymeneal tissues or anal verge usually healed without findings that could be distinguished from non-specific findings documented in children selected for non-abuse.

Questions about anal tone and changes in anal relaxation during examination remain unanswered and since tone is hard to document with photographs and thereby come under peer review and scrutiny, it remains primarily a subjective finding (Heger et al. 2002b; McCann et al. 1989).

Finally with the acceleration of knowledge, photo-documentation, peer review groups, and national professional organizations; a system of classification of language and findings emerged (Adams 2011; Royal College of Paediatrics and Child Health RCPCH 2008). The process of classification and professional clinical agreements has the ability to evolve over time with access to more research. This standardization of research, language and classification schemes supported a more consistent level of diagnosis over the past 10–15 years (Adams et al. 2004; Berenson et al. 2000; Berkoff et al. 2008; Heger et al. 2002b).

Current consensus of the significance of anatomical findings in the United States was collected and published by Joyce Adams in collaboration with members of the Helfer Society. The collective agreement in the significance of the findings included centers of excellence, staffed by the pre-eminent child abuse pediatricians in the United States and their positions on various findings are:

Non-Specific Findings: congenital variations of the hymenal morphology i.e. annular, crescentic (posterior rim) redundant, septate or cribiform, micro perforate and imperforate; periurethral or vestibular bans; intravaginal ridges or columns; hymenal bumps or mounds; hymenal tags or septal remnants, midline avascular area; hymenal notch/cleft in the ventral half of the hymenal rim between 9 and 3 o'clock supine clockwise; shallow notches/clefts in the posterior rim, external hymenal ridge, the smooth area adjacent to the anal verge (anteriorly or posteriorly) i.e. diastasis ani; perianal skin tag, changes in pigmentation of either the peri vaginal or peri anal areas; changes in the thickness of the hymen (from translucent to thickened); and partial anal dilatation with traction on the buttocks.

Medical Conditions: Changes in vascularity surrounding the hymen, erythema of either the genital or anal areas; labial adhesions/fusion (which may break down with minor trauma or during the examination); transient fragility of the posterior fourchette that may break down during the examination; non-specific vaginal discharge (culture should be considered); anal fissures (superficial splits in the skin); venous congestion surrounding the anus usually occurring during prolonged position in knee-chest position (either prone or supine) during examination.

Other Medical/Congenital Findings More Often Misdiagnosed as Abuse: Urethral prolapse (more common in African-American girls); lichen sclerosus (may be present in both girls and boys and present as an atropic area surrounding both the vaginal introitus and the anus can break down and present as bleeding); non-STI ulcers that may be cause by a wide range of viruses; failure of midline fusion (vaginal, perineal, anal), rectal prolapsed; complete dilation of the anal sphincters to less than 2 cm; changes in the appearance of the anal folds or exposure of the pectinate line that appears to resemble trauma because of the red irregularity of this line; other acute findings such as erythema due to beta hemolytic streptococci; and of course accidental acute trauma such as a straddle injury that may be misinterpreted as due to sexual abuse (see below; accidental trauma).

Findings More Concerning for Abuse: In this category one would need to rely heavily on the history from the child and parent. As discussed in the paragraph on the research into the healing patterns of acute injury; these signs discussed are those which are found after healing trauma, but are also documented in research reports from children who selected for non-abuse and examined. They include: deep notches or clefts in the posterior 180° of the hymen that extend beyond 50 % of the estimated width of the hymen; deep/complete notches or clefts in adolescent girls at the 3 or 9 o'clock positions (any deep or complete notches above these landmarks would be impossible to differentiate from non-specific findings or hymeneal variations); marked anal dilatation to greater than 2 cm or more in the absence of constipation or other conditions that would impact the ability of the child to maintain control of the anal sphincters (note: measuring of the degree of dilatation requires photodocumentation with an accurate measuring device visible in the photo); and finally those infections that can be sexually transmitted, but also have a high prevalence rate through (1) transmission at birth (2) autoinoculation or (3) transmission from family members in a non-sexual manner (herpes, condyloma accuminata are those most frequently questioned).

Diagnostic of Trauma: It is important to differentiate between accidental and non-accidental trauma based on the history from the caretakers; child and other witnesses.

Any acute genital or anal injury **should be evaluated as a possible indicator of non-accidental trauma**. However, injury to the penis, labia minor and majora, posterior fourchette, perineum, and anal verge are all consistent with the straddle injury (as well as sexual assault). Penetrating injuries to either the hymen or to the anal verge can also be accidental injury if the child falls on an object than can penetrate. Findings such as bruising of the hymen, a complete or partial tear of the hymen are more likely to be evidence of penetrating trauma as is a perianal laceration (not fissure) that extends to the anal sphincter. In addition, in girls it is important to remember that the vagina is a potential space; the hymen is tissue that is then stretched across the potential space through labial traction applied by the examiner, and when traction is released the hymen becomes redundant and may actually protrude through the labia minor (particularly in thin girls) and be subject to injury to the edges if there is a straddle injury to that area. Additionally, acute trauma to a pre-existing condition such as lichen sclerosis or a labial fusion/adhesion can result in a break in the skin or adhesion resulting in "blood in the underwear" Finally in adolescent girls, consensual sexual activity can result in trauma to the hymen as well as the posterior fourchette. History again plays an enormously important role in coming to the diagnosis of non-accidental injuries.

Non-acute findings that may be diagnosed as caused by non-accidental trauma: Any scarring of the peri-anal area is highly unusual, and previous infections or diseases such as Crohn's; medical/ surgical interventions or accidental injuries must be ruled out. Changes in the posterior fourchette such as labial fusions, linea vestibularis or prior accidental trauma, such as seen in significant straddle injuries, must be ruled out before coming to the conclusion that the findings are due to a sexual assault.

Findings that are indicative of prior penetrating trauma: The most concerning finding of past penetrating trauma is a healed complete transection of the hymen between 3 and 9 o'clock (clockwise) which is found in either the pre-adolescent or adolescent girl. There is growing consensus (Berkoff et al. 2008) that this defect in the hymen does not necessarily need to be complete but the presence of a deep cleft/notch or defect is equally concerning and not found in girls selected for non-abuse. This cleft may be "knife like" and narrow or present with what appears to be a missing segment of the hymen that extends to the base and will persist as "missing hymen" from an early age through puberty if not repaired at the time of the injury.

Follow-up and treatment: The medical professional is responsible not only for treating the injuries and infections, but to guarantee that any medical prophylaxis is made available to the child. This is particularly important in teenagers when our responsibility extends to verifying immunization status for hepatitis B and condyloma accuminata and providing pregnancy prophylaxis. For any victim of high risk sexual assault, the medical professional must also provide the appropriate information for HIV prophylaxis as well as hepatitis B. It is the usual policy to treat the adolescent and adult victim of assault with appropriate antibiotics and screening for any other STIs with a planned timeline for follow-up and reassessment. For children, if it is a high risk assault, not only should HIV prophylaxis be offered, but baseline values for possible exposures to STI should be taken and then retaken at follow up within 3 months. Routine antibiotics for the young child have not been the standard of care, but follow-up with cultures or NAATs has been recommended with treatment when appropriate.

Access to mental health support for both the child and the non-offending family members makes this passage through disclosure, evaluation and examination and often involvement with social workers and the police less onerous and has been shown to positively impact the long-term emotional outcomes (Bernier et al. 1994).

Where Do We Go from Here?

Over the past two decades the interest in the field of child sexual abuse has shifted from the medical diagnosis, assessing normal anatomy, STIs in children and conditions misdiagnosed as abuse to prevalence and incidence, prevention, outcomes, mental health interventions and treatment. It is interesting to read recent reports that the estimate of the incidence of CSA is actually declining (Finkelhor and Jones 2011; Jones et al. 2001).

1. Is sexual abuse declining or have we (professionals and society) become immune to the volume of cases; are we more tolerant because of the amount of sexual material we are exposed to in the media, the amount of internet sexual contacts and interface? Has the internet increased the likelihood that a child may be sexually abused or has the easy access to child pornography on line made abuse less likely? Are children less vulnerable because they are more electronically savvy, carry phones, and spend hours and hours on electronic devices, making the act of sexually assaulting the child less likely and children who are home on their iPads less available? Does the access to sexually explicit materials on the internet make children more vulnerable because their normal defenses are lowered? These are all questions that need to be addressed by both professionals and parents.
2. Have new official reporting guidelines impacted the reality of the statistics? I.e. are we reporting sexual abuse by strangers as sexual abuse or as negligence and failure to protect on the part of the parents?
3. If we were challenged to review all of our cases from 15 to 20 years ago how would we stack up against the current state of knowledge in child sexual abuse cases? If there are those languishing in jail because of a report or testimony that was provided by the medical professional, should we be revisiting this issue with the district attorney and the courts? In some states there are draconian sentences for any sexual act against a child, and if the *only* evidence is that provided by the medical professional, should these cases be re-evaluated?
4. The evaluation of the genitalia of all children should be routine in all pediatric evaluations. If medical professional hold a line against overdiagnosis then no family should be afraid to have their child's genitalia examined or even photographed. It is when there is routine disregard for the diagnostic standards established through peer review and national published guidelines, that a child's and thus the parent's rights to stay together may be impacted.
5. Evaluating research: because it is so difficult to access clinical data and document findings in children who have not been abused, researchers may be tempted to turn to review articles based on "evidence-based research" or meta-analysis of all published research on a particular topic. Unfortunately, if the researcher has a particular bent in his/her opinion of what is normal or abnormal, they will tend to review and include in the review or meta-analysis article only those research products that agree with their hard-held ideas of what is normal and abnormal. For example in most of the recent large reviews of children referred for possible sexual abuse (Berenson et al. 2000; Heger et al. 2002b) a positive rate for diagnostic findings was under 5 %.

   Therefore the question is do we include outliers in our case reviews or meta-analysis? Should we exclude the outliers such as studies with a positive rate of greater than 80 % of children evaluated for possible sexual abuse. Without some extraordinary circumstances in the researcher's center, it is highly unlikely that this rate is consistent with what is currently known about the medical/forensic diagnosis of sexual abuse.

   Common sense should prevail? When reading and reviewing such a difference in the rates of positive examination in one small, but homogenous, population, a reasonable reviewer would have to question the validity of a report of greater that 80 % positive findings, when the international trend has been drastically lower and most research in this area indicate a rate that is always under 10 %. Research into why studies in different parts of the world vary so greatly would be important and in fact, since photodocumentation has become the standard of care it would be important, prior to publishing these articles with the astronomically high positive rates, that all of the clinical material be reviewed by a panel of experts who should validate this anomalous data. Without a critical analysis of research we will continue to have "junk in –junk out."

6. We obviously need more data on the normal anatomy of girls and boys. I would recommend that these studies should be prospective, and when this is done, that ALL of the clinical data, the photographs, etc. be gathered and reviewed by experts in the field. This would allow the field to be more comfortable with the reliability of the data and make it more likely to be acceptable for publication.

7. There needs to be access 24/7 to immediate, appropriate and expert evaluations of children who report sexual abuse or of children who present with genital complaints consistent with injury which may be accidental or non-accidental. Clearly the ability of the examiner to document injuries is dependent on timing. Genital injuries heal quickly and completely, and good assessments and diagnosis appear to be dependent on expeditious evaluations.

8. Independent evaluation of cases involving child pornography would be helpful in understanding why examinations are predicted to be less than 5 % abnormal in children who report being sexually abused. The field needs a research project by a group of specialists in a federal court house who would review cases of child pornography and (1) assign ages to the children and (2) identify the various acts perpetrated on the children based on the level of sexual maturation. Results of this study would answer that long-standing questions of what sexual acts are performed on children at various sexual maturation stages, and since most perpetrators have ongoing access to their victims, does it make sense that they would not engage in acts that would result in trauma and exposure in the preadolescent child?

9. Impact studies would provide important insight into how we evaluate children, our availability and what we do after we have come to the conclusion that a child needs intervention and protection, if we were to assess the impact of our interventions and involvement in the lives of our patients over the years. Were we in fact therapeutic in the lives of children or did we only provide further stress and trauma?

10. Finally, I suggest that we all could get involved with Innocence Projects across the country and apply our considerable growth in knowledge and research in reviewing and promoting the review of these cases. This of course is a study in courage, but I believe that it would elevate what we do today to a new level of science and honesty in the eyes of those who should be willing to identify and protect children from those who would do them harm. We should never participate in the potential harm of removing a child from protective parents and family, based on bad or outdated science.

References

Adams, J. (2011). Medical evaluation of suspected child sexual abuse; 2011 update. *Journal of Child Sexual Abuse, 20*, 588–605.

Adams, J., & Knudson, S. (1996). Genital findings in adolescent girls referred for suspected abuse. *Archives of Pediatrics & Adolescent Medicine, 150*, 850.

Adams, J., Harper, K., & Knudson, S. (1992). A proposed system for the classification of anogenital findings in children with suspected sexual abuse. *Journal of Pediatric and Adolescent Gynecology, 5*, 73–75.

Adams, J., Harper, K., Knudson, S., & Revilla, J. (1994). Examination findings in legally confirmed child sexual abuse; It's normal to be normal. *Pediatrics, 94*(3), 310–317.

Adams, J., Botash, A., & Kellogg, N. (2004). Differences in hymenal morphology between adolescent girls with and without a history of consensual sexual intercourse. *Archives of Pediatrics & Adolescent Medicine, 158*(3), 280–285.

American Academy of Pediatrics (AAP), & Committee on Adolescence. (2001). Care of the adolescent sexual assault victim. *Pediatrics, 107*, 1476.

American Academy of Pediatrics (AAP), Committee on Child Abuse and Neglect, & Kellogg, N. (2005). Clinical report: The evaluation of sexual abuse of children. *Pediatrics, 116*(2), 506–512.

American Professional Society on the Abuse of Children (APSCA). (1990). *Guidelines for the psychosocial evaluation of suspected sexual abuse in children.* Chicago: APSAC.

American Professional Society on the Abuse of Children (APSCA). (1995). *Practice guidelines: Photographic documentation of child abuse.* Chicago: APSAC.

American Professional Society on the Abuse of Children (APSCA). (1998). *Glossary of terms and the interpretations of findings for child sexual abuse evidentiary examinations.* Chicago: APSAC.

Berenson, A., Heger, A., & Andrews, S. (1991). Appearance of the hymen in newborns. *Pediatrics, 87*(4), 458–465.

Berenson, A., Heger, A., Hayes, J., Bailey, R., & Emans, S. (1992). Appearance of the hymen in prepubertal girls. *Pediatrics, 89*(3), 387–394.

Berenson, A., Somma-Garcia, A., & Barnett, S. (1993). Perianal findings in infants 18 months of age or younger. *Pediatrics, 91*(4), 838–840.

Berenson, A., Chacko, M., Wiemann, C., Mishaw, C., Friedrich, W., & Grady, J. (2000). A case–control study of anatomic changes resulting from sexual abuse. *American Journal of Obstetrics and Gynecology, 182*(4), 820–834.

Berenson, A. B., Chacko, M. R., Wiemann, C. M., Mishaw, C. O., Friedrich, W. N., & Grady, J. J. (2002). Use of hymenal measurements in the diagnosis of previous penetration. *Pediatrics, 109*(2), 228–235.

Berkoff, M., Zolotar, A., Makoroff, K., Thackeray, J., Shapiro, R., & Runyan, D. (2008). Has this prepubertal girl been sexually abused? *Journal of the American Medical Association, 300*(23), 2779–2792. Retrieved from http://jama.amaassn.org/cgi/content/full/300/23/2779.

Berliner, L., & Barbieri, M. (1984). The testimony of the child victim of sexual assault. *Journal of Social Issues, 1984*(40), 125.

Bernier, L., Williams, R., & Zetzer, H. (1994). Efficacy of treatment for victims of child sexual abuse. *The Future of Children, 1994*(4), 156.

Bond, G., Dowd, M., Landsman, I., & Rimsza, M. (1995). Unintentional perineal injury in prepubescent girls: a multicenter, prospective report of 56 girls. *Pediatrics, 1995*(95), 628.

Boos, S. C. (1999). Accidental hymenal injury mimicking sexual trauma. *Pediatrics, 103*(6), 1287–1289.

Boos, S. C., Rosas, A. J., Boyle, C., & McCann, J. (2003). Anogenital injuries in child pedestrians run over by low-speed motor vehicles: Four cases with findings that mimic child sexual abuse. *Pediatrics, 112*(1), e77–e84. [Electronic Version], http://www.pediatrics.org/cgi/content/full/112/1/e77.

Bowen, K., & Aldous, M. (1999). Medical evaluation of sexual abuse in children without disclosed or witnessed abuse. *Archives of Pediatrics & Adolescent Medicine, 153*, 1160–1164.

Cantwell, H. (1981). Vaginal inspection as it relates to child sexual abuse in girls under thirteen. *Child Abuse & Neglect, 7*, 171–176.

Centers for Disease Control and Prevention (CDC) (2010). Sexually transmitted diseases treatment guidelines, 2010. *MMWR, 59*, 1–110.

Cheit, R., Shavit, Y., & Reiss-Davis, Z. (2010). Magazine coverage of child sexual abuse, 1992–2004. *Journal of Child Sexual Abuse, 19*, 99–117.

Christian, C., Lavelle, J., DeJong, A., et al. (2000). Forensic evidence findings in prepubertal victims of sexual assault. *Pediatrics, 106*, 100.

Cross, T. P., De Vos, E., & Whitcomb, D. (1994). Prosecution of child sexual abuse: Which cases are accepted. *Child Abuse & Neglect, 19*, 1431–1442.

DeLago, C., Deblinger, E., Schroeder, C., & Finkel, M. (2008). Girls who disclose sexual abuse; Urogenital symptoms and signs after genital contact. *Pediatrics, 122*(2), 281–286. Retrieved from http://www.pediatrics.org/cgi/content/full./122/e281.

Dowd, M., Fitzmaurice, L., Knapp, J., et al. (1994). The interpretation of urogenital findings in children with straddle injuries. *Journal of Pediatric Surgery, 29*, 7.

Dubowitz, H., Black, M., & Harrington, D. (1992). The diagnosis of child sexual abuse. *American Journal of Diseases of Children, 146*, 688–693.

Emans, S., Woods, E., Flagg, N., et al. (1987). Genital findings in sexually abused, symptomatic and asymptomatic girls. *Pediatrics, 79*, 778.

Emans, S. J., Woods, E. R., Allred, E. N., & Grace, E. (1994). Hymenal findings in adolescent women: Impact of tampon use and consensual sexual activity. *Journal of Pediatrics, 125*(1), 153–160.

Finkel, M. (1989). Anogenital trauma in sexually abused children. *Pediatrics, 84*(92), 317–322.

Finkelhor, D., & Jones, L. (2011). *Updated trends in child maltreatment, 2010.* Durham: Crimes Against Children Research Center.

Finkelhor, D., Ormrod, R., Turner, H., & Hamby, S. (2005). The victimization of children and youth: a comprehensive, national survey. *Child Maltreatment, 10*, 5–25.

Frasier, L. (1997). The pediatrician's role in child abuse interviewing. *Pediatric Annals, 26*, 306.

Gardner, J. J. (1992). Descriptive study of genital variation in healthy, nonabused premenarchal girls. *Journal of Pediatrics, 120*(2, Pt. 1), 258–260.

Heger, A. (1996). Twenty years in the evaluation of the sexually abused child: Has medicine helped or hurt the child and the family? *Child Abuse & Neglect, 20*(10), 893–897.

Heger, A., & Emans, S. (1990). Introital diameter as the criterion for sexual abuse. *Pediatrics, 85*, 222.

Heger, A., & Emans, S. J. (1992). *Evaluation of the sexually abused child: A medical textbook and photographic atlas.* New York: Oxford University Press.

Heger, A., Emans, S. J., & Muram, D. (Eds.). (2000). *Evaluation of the sexually abused child: A medical textbook and photographic atlas* (2nd ed.). New York: Oxford University Press.

Heger, A. H., Ticson, L., Guerra, L., Lister, J., Zaragoza, T., McConnell, G., et al. (2002a). Appearance of the genitalia in girls selected for nonabuse: review of hymenal morphology and non-specific findings. *Journal of Pediatric and Adolescent Gynecology, 15*(1), 27–35.

Heger, A., Ticson, L., Velasquez, O., & Bernier, R. (2002b). Children referred for possible sexual abuse: Medical findings in 2384 children. *Child Abuse & Neglect, 26*(6–7), 645–659.

Heppenstall-Heger, A., McConnell, G., Ticson, L., Guerra, L., Lister, J., & Zaragoza, T. (2003). Healing patterns in anogenital injuries: A longitudinal study of injuries associated with sexual abuse, accidental injuries, or genital surgery in the preadolescent child. *Pediatrics, 112*(4), 829–837.

Herrmann, B., & Crawford, J. (2002). Genital injuries in prepubertal girls from inline skating accidents. *Pediatrics, 110*(2), 16. Retrieved from http://w2ww.pediatrics.org/cgi/content/full/110/2/e16.

Hobbs, C. J., & Wynne, J. M. (1987). Child sexual abuse; an increasing rate of diagnosis. *Lancet, 1*, 837–841.

Jones, L., Finkelhor, D., & Kopiec, K. (2001). Why is sexual abuse declining? A survey of state child protection administrators. *Child Abuse & Neglect, 25*, 1139.

Jones, J. S., Rossman, L., Hartman, M., & Alexander, C. C. (2003). Anogenital injuries in adolescents after consensual sexual intercourse. *Academic Emergency Medicine, 10*(12), 1378–1383.

Kellogg, N., & Parra, J. (1991). Genital anatomy in pregnant adolescents, "Normal" doesn't mean "nothing happened". *Pediatrics, 113*(1), 67–69. Retrieved from http://www.pediatrics.org/cgi/content/full/113/1/e67.

Kellogg, N. D., Parra, J. M., & Menard, S. (1998). Children with anogenital symptoms and signs referred for sexual abuse evaluations. *Archives of Pediatrics & Adolescent Medicine, 152*(7), 634–641.

Kempe, C. H. (1978). Sexual abuse, another hidden pediatric problem; the 1977 C. Anderson Aldrich lecture. *Pediatrics, 62*, 382–389.

Krugman, R. (1988). It's time to wave the yellow flag: Editorial. *Child Abuse & Neglect, 12*, 293–294.

Lamb, M., Orbach, Y., Hershkowitz, I., Esplin, P., & Horowitz, D. (2007). Structured forensic interview protocols improve the quality and informativeness of investigative interviews with children. *Child Abuse & Neglect, 31*, 1201–1231.

Landwirth, J. (1987). Children as witnesses in child sexual abuse trials. *Pediatrics, 60*, 585.

Leder, M., Emans, S., Hafler, J., et al. (1999). Addressing sexual abuse in the primary care setting. *Pediatrics, 104*, 270.

Lyon, T. (2005). Selected writings, The Author, University of Southern California.

McCann, J., & Voris, J. (1991). Perianal injuries resulting from sexual abuse; A longitudinal study. *Pediatrics, 91*(2), 390–397.

McCann, J., Voris, J., Simon, M., & Wells, R. (1989). Perianal findings in prepubertal children selected for non-abuse: A descriptive study. *Child Abuse & Neglect, 13*(2), 179–193.

McCann, J., Voris, J., Simon, M., & Wells, R. (1990). Genital findings in prepubertal girls selected for non-abuse: A descriptive study. *Pediatrics, 86*(3), 428–439.

McCann, J., Voris, J., & Simon, M. (1992). Genital injuries resulting from sexual abuse; A longitudinal study. *Pediatrics, 89*(2), 307–317.

McCann, J., Miyamoto, S., Boyle, C., & Rogers, K. (2007a). Healing of hymenal injuries in prepubertal and adolescent girls; A descriptive study. *Pediatrics, 119*(5), 1094–1106.

McCann, J., Miyamoto, S., Boyle, C., & Rogers, K. (2007b). Healing of nonhymenal genital injuries in prepubertal and adolescent girls; A descriptive study. *Pediatrics, 120*(5), 1000–1011. Retrieved from http://www.pediatrics.org/cgi/content/full/120/5/e77.

Muram, D. (1989). Child sexual abuse: Relationship between sexual acts and genital findings. *Child Abuse & Neglect, 13*, 211–216.

Myers, J. E. B. (2010). *The ASPAC handbook on child maltreatment.* (3rd Ed.) Sage: Los Angeles.

Myhre, A., Berntzen, K., & Bratlid, D. (2001). Perianal anatomy in non-abused preschool children. *Acta Paediatrica, 90*(11), 1321–1328.

Myhre, A., Berntzen, K., & Bratlid, D. (2003). Genital anatomy in non-abused preschool girls. *Acta Pediatrica, 92*(123), 1453–1462.

Orr, D. P., & Prietto, S. V. (1979). Emergency management of sexually abused children. *American Journal of Diseases of Children, 133*, 628–631.

Palusci, V. J., Cox, E. O., Cyrus, T. A., Heartwell, S. W., Vandervort, F. E., & Potts, E. S. (1999). Medical assessment and legal outcome in child sexual abuse. *Archives of Pediatrics & Adolescent Medicine, 153*(4), 388–392.

Palusci, V., Cox, E., Shatz, E., & Schultze, J. (2006). Urgent medical assessment after child sexual abuse. *Child Abuse & Neglect, 30*(4), 367–380.

Paradise, J., Winter, M., & Finkel, M. (1999). Influence of the history on physicians' interpretations of girls' genital findings. *Pediatrics, 103*, 980.

Pierce, A. M. (2004). Anal fissures and anal scars in anal abuse – are they significant? *Pediatric Surgery International, 20*(5), 334–338.

Pokorny, S. F. (1987). Configuration of the prepubertal hymen. *American Journal of Obstetrics and Gynecology, 157*, 950.

Pugno, P. (1999). Genital findings in prepubertal girls evaluated for sexual abuse; a different perspective on hymenal measurements. *Archives of Family Medicine, 8*(5), 403–406.

Rimsza, M. E., & Niggermann, E. H. (1982). Medical evaluation of sexually abused children: a review of 311 cases. *Pediatrics, 69*, 8–14.

Royal College of Paediatrics and Child Health (RCPCH. (2008). *The physical signs of child sexual abuse* (An evidence-based review and guidance for best practice). London: RCPCH.

Runyan, D., Everson, M., Edelsohn, G., Hunter, W., & Coulter, M. (1988). Impact of legal intervention on sexually abused children. *Journal of Pediatrics, 113*, 647–653.

Sgroi, S. M. (1982). *Handbook of clinical intervention in child sexual abuse*. Lexington: DC Heath. 1982.

Shapiro, R., & Makoroff, K. (2006). Sexually transmitted diseases in sexually abused girls and adolescents. *Current Opinion in Obstetrics & Gynecology, 18*, 492–497.

Stoltenborgh, M., van Ljzenbdoorn, M. H., Euser, E. M., & Bakermans-Kranenburg, M. J. (2011). A global perspective on child sexual abuse; meta-analysis of prevalence around world. *Child Maltreatment, 16*(2), 79–101.

Teixeira, W. R. (1982). Hymenal colposcopic examination in sexual offenses. *The American Journal of Forensic Medicine and Pathology, 2*, 209–214.

Woodling, B. A., & Heger, A. (1986). The use of the colposcope in the diagnosis of sexual abuse in the pediatric age group. *Child Abuse & Neglect, 10*, 111–114.

Wurtele, S. (2009). Preventing sexual abuse of children in the twenty-first century; preparing for challenges and opportunities. *Journal of Child Sexual Abuse, 18*, 1–18.

Chapter 5
Fatal Child Abuse

Scott D. Krugman and Wendy G. Lane

Background and History

From early Greek mythology (Stavrianos et al. 2008) to recent sensational headlines (Auburn and Grady 2012), child abuse fatalities have persisted through ages and cultures. For over 150 years, the medical literature has described child abuse fatalities. One of the earliest discussions of fatal child abuse was published in 1860 by Ambroise Tardieu, a French Professor of Legal Medicine in Paris. His classic paper, reprinted in 2005 (Roche et al. 2005) described the autopsy findings of 32 child fatalities of Parisian children – 19 of whom were killed by their parents.

Coupled with the descriptions in the literature of child abuse fatalities are calls for prevention. Just as Tardieu's calls for French physicians and society to address child fatalities were ignored, so have been recent efforts. In 1995, Donna Shalala, then Secretary of the Department of Health and Human Services, called Child Abuse Fatalities "the Nation's shame" (U.S. Advisory Board 1995). Not much has been done by our federal government to address the problem in the almost 20 years since that publication, except for a recent GAO report recommending improvements in data collection (United States GAO 2011). Few events challenge our child protection system as much as the death of infants and children – whether by violent beatings or shakings, suffocation, deliberate or incidental poisoning, or as a result of neglect (either supervisional or emotional).

The first challenge in trying to address child abuse fatalities arises from a lack of data on the exact number of child abuse deaths in this country. Under ascertainment of child abuse fatalities has been recognized since the 1990s (Herman-Giddens et al. 1999; Crume et al. 2002). Current fatality rates are estimates and child death investigations vary from community to community. Without accurate data and clear risk factors, prevention remains elusive. This chapter will review the current literature on the epidemiology of fatal child abuse, the role of child death investigations in ascertaining the cause of death, the causes of child abuse fatalities, and current prevention efforts.

S.D. Krugman, M.D. (✉)
Department of Pediatrics, MedStar Franklin Square Medical Center,
9000 Franklin Square Dr, Baltimore, MD 21237, USA
e-mail: scott.krugman@medstar.net

W.G. Lane, M.D., MPH
Department of Epidemiology and Public Health & Department of Pediatrics, University of Maryland
School of Medicine, 660 West Redwood St, Baltimore, MD 21201, USA
e-mail: wlane@epi.umaryland.edu

Epidemiology of Fatal Child Maltreatment

U.S. data from NCANDS (National Child Abuse and Neglect Data System) report 1,770 cases of fatal child maltreatment in 2009 and 1,560 in 2010. These numbers represent 2.3 cases per 100,000 in 2009 and 2.07 cases per 100,000 in 2010. It is likely that these numbers underestimate the true number of child maltreatment fatalities, because not all fatalities are identified as maltreatment, and not all identified cases of fatal maltreatment are reported to state child welfare agencies (U.S. GAO 2011). As many as 50–60 % of child maltreatment deaths may be missed in official reports (Crume et al. 2002; Herman-Giddens et al. 1999). The challenges in identifying all child maltreatment fatalities make it difficult to determine trends in maltreatment fatalities over time. While data from NCANDS indicate a 46 % increase in fatalities between 1993 and 2007, data from the FBI and national vital statistics show an approximate 40 % decline in fatal maltreatment during the same time period (Finkelhor and Jones 2012).

The largest percentage of fatalities occurs among the youngest children. Nearly half (47.7 %) of child maltreatment fatalities in the U.S. in 2010 were among infants (<1 year of age), 14 % were among 1 year olds, 17 % were among 2–3 year olds, and 11 % were among 4–7 year olds. Neglect accounted for the largest proportion of deaths, with 68.1 % of deaths attributable to neglect alone, or neglect and another form of maltreatment. Forty-five percent of deaths involved physical abuse, with or without another form of maltreatment.

Boys are at higher risk of fatal maltreatment than girls (2.5 vs. 1.7 cases per 100,000 in 2010). White children make up the largest percentage of maltreatment fatalities (43.6 %); however rates of fatal maltreatment are higher among African-American (3.9/100,000), Native American/Alaskan Native (1.9/100,000), and Hispanic children (1.9/100,000) compared to whites (1.7/100,000).

A number of studies have identified abusive head trauma as the most common cause of fatal maltreatment, accounting for 42–45 % of deaths (Collins and Nichols 1999; Kajese et al. 2011). Asphyxia, including drowning, accounts for an additional 22–25 %, and abdomino-throacic trauma accounts for approximately 12 % of deaths. Identified triggers include crying, toileting, and general noncompliance (Kajese et al. 2011).

When examining all maltreatment deaths, mothers are the most frequently identified perpetrator. Mothers were solely responsible for 29 % of child maltreatment fatalities in 2010, mother and father were jointly responsible for 22 %, and mother and "other" were responsible for 9 %. Fathers were solely responsible for 17 % of deaths. Non-parent perpetrators accounted for only 12 % of fatalities. One major difference has been noted when looking specifically at deaths from physical abuse compared to those from all forms of maltreatment. While females, mostly mothers, are the most common perpetrator when all forms of fatal maltreatment are considered, males are the primary perpetrators of physical abuse fatalities, accounting for about two-third of these deaths (Stiffman et al. 2002; Schnitzer and Ewigman 2005).

A number of factors may increase the risk for fatal maltreatment. Data from Missouri child fatalities showed an eightfold increased likelihood of death from maltreatment when an unrelated adult was living in the home, and a 4.7-fold increased likelihood of death from maltreatment if the child lived with step, foster, or adoptive parents (Stiffman et al. 2002). Additional risk factors include teenage pregnancy and maternal failure to complete high school (Kajese et al. 2011; Schnitzer and Ewigman 2005), caregiver substance abuse and intimate partner violence in the home (US DHHS 2011), late prenatal care, poverty, and prior CPS reports (Schnitzer and Ewigman 2005). A large number of children in the home may be a specific risk factor for fatal neglect. In one study comparing deaths from neglect to those from abuse, 41 % of families with fatal neglect had five or more members. Families with neglect deaths had more children living in the home than those with deaths from abuse (mean of 3.3 vs. 1.8 children, p <0.001) (Margolin 1990).

At least three studies have specifically examined fatal maltreatment during the first year of life (Paulozzi and Sells 2002; Overpeck et al. 1998; Herman-Giddens et al. 2003). Each of these studies identified the first week of life as a particularly high risk period for homicide, with a second peak at 2–3 months. About 9 % of infant homicides took place during the first week of life; mothers were responsible for the vast majority of these first week deaths (Overpeck et al. 1998; Herman-Giddens et al. 2003). Risk factors for infant homicide include mother's age <15 years, a second child to a teenage mother, lack of prenatal care, and less than 12 years of education.

Child Death Evaluation

As noted above, the actual number of child abuse fatalities in the United States is an estimate, and not an exact number. Often death certificates do not reflect the fact that a child died as a result of abuse (Herman-Giddens et al. 1999; Crume et al. 2002). To understand why child abuse fatality determination is so difficult, it is important to first understand the status of cause of death determination in the United States. No uniform system for death determination exists in this country as some states have a coroner system, others have a medical examiner system, and others have a mixture of both (Fig. 5.1). In general, medical examiners are forensic pathologists trained in the autopsy and forensic investigations, while coroners are elected or appointed officials who may or may not be physicians. Currently, there are 2,000 distinct jurisdictions for death investigation in the United States, ranging in size from a small county to an entire state. Unfortunately, there are only 1,000 forensic pathologists in the United States and even fewer with specialized training in pediatric pathology. The subsequent variability that exists in investigation technique and quality is one reason for a significant underestimate in the 2,000 child abuse fatalities annually in the United States.

Two major efforts have tried to address the issue of inadequate death investigations. The first was the development of a standardized child fatality review process (Covington et al. 2005). The second and

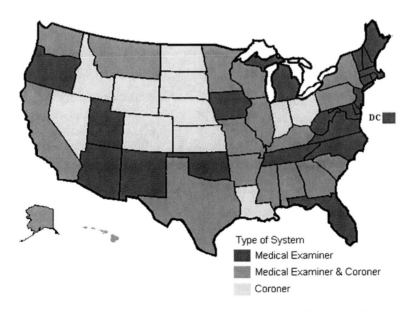

Fig. 5.1 System of death investigation by state (Reproduced from Krugman and Krugman 2007)

more recent was the creation of standardized protocols for child death investigation and corresponding database through the Centers for Disease Control. Examples of these protocols for infant death scene investigation and autopsy can be found at: http://www.childdeathreview.org/investigation.htm and http://www.cdc.gov/SIDS/PDF/SUIDIforms.pdf.

Ideal Process for Child Death Investigation

A thorough and complete death investigation of any sudden and unexpected death in a child has three stages: scene investigation, autopsy, and collateral history from involved professionals. The scene investigation has been made popular recently by television crime shows such as CSI, but it is the stage of the investigation that is most likely overlooked or inadequately completed. Many jurisdictions will utilize specific protocols for infant or childhood scene investigation and use trained homicide detectives to respond to the home or location of death immediately after the child dies. In the ideal situation, trained police officers will respond immediately to the scene of every sudden and unexplained child death and conduct a thorough scene investigation, often in conjunction with investigators from the medical examiner's office. The scene investigation should assess where the child was found, who the child was with, and what the child was doing at the time of death. In the case of a child found dead in a bed or crib, the position in which the child was put to sleep, the position in which the child was found, and the presence of other objects in the bed should be documented. The presence of cigarette smoke, toxic or illegal substances, or any other evidence should be collected and documented. Blood and other body fluids should be collected for forensic analysis, and photos of the entire scene should be taken.

The autopsy of a dead child also must be done by a pathologist familiar with causes of childhood death. A complete autopsy includes an external examination, internal examination, histological examination, toxicological studies, microbiological tests, and metabolic screening for genetic conditions. Most infant deaths should include a skeletal survey or CT scan to evaluate for occult or healing fractures. Often, crucial organs such as the brain, eyes, or heart need to be sent to pathological specialists for evaluation.

Finally, before determining a cause of death, the coroner or medical examiner should evaluate the past medical and social history of the child. The past medical history can help elucidate the cause of death in circumstances such as children with seizure disorders or cardiac conditions. A high risk social situation may lead the examiner to list the cause of death as undermined when a definitive cause cannot be identified. The term SUDI (Sudden Unexplained Death of Infancy) is often used in this situation. Unfortunately, there is not universal agreement on use of the term and it varies from locale to locale. In many states, however, this term is used to describe the cause of death in infants who died suddenly and unexpectedly, but do not meet the criteria for SIDS because of potential social or environmental risk factors. Over the past decade, the rate of SIDS has decreased significantly, but the SUDI rate has increased, likely because of the re-classification into the latter group of children who used to be called SIDS before thorough investigations were routine (American Academy of Pediatrics 2005).

Child Fatality Review Teams

The child fatality review process completes the second part of the cause of death determination for children. Child fatality review (CFR) began in the late 1970s. Local teams were founded in Los Angeles, Oregon and North Carolina with the goal of better identifying child abuse fatalities

(Michigan Public Health Institute 2005a). In the 1990s, studies from Missouri (Ewigman et al. 1993), New York (Herman-Giddens et al. 1999), and Colorado (Crume et al. 2002) demonstrated that up to 61 % fatalities due to child abuse were not coded as such on death certificates, which artificially lowered the true rate of child abuse fatalities in vital statistics records. The CFR process was able to better classify the deaths. In 1993, the federal Child Abuse Prevention and Treatment Act (CAPTA) required states to include information on child death review in their state program plans. In the past decade, CFR teams have been formed in all 50 states and the District of Columbia, and many teams focus on determining the cause of all child deaths, not just those secondary to child abuse. Many teams will consist of medical, forensic, law enforcement, social services, school, and citizen representatives who meet regularly to review all sudden and unexpected child deaths.

The CFR process is best understood as a quality control/process improvement system. While there is some variation in focus among teams, the majority of teams are a multidisciplinary group that conducts reviews of all unexpected childhood deaths in a community with the purpose of better understanding why the child died in order to prevent future deaths. This goal is broader than the original teams which only sought to identify fatal child abuse, but the broader goal has helped create process improvements in the identification of fatal child abuse. One of the primary objectives of CFR teams is to "ensure the accurate identification and uniform, consistent reporting of the cause and manner of every child death" (Michigan Public Health Institute 2005b). By reviewing every unexpected death in a locale, each community can ensure that their death investigators are conducting appropriate scene investigations and autopsies which are crucial in cause of death determination. Other objectives of CFR include improving agency responses to evaluating deaths in general, homicides in particular, and protecting other siblings in a family (Michigan Public Health Institute 2005b). Each of these efforts in a community will lead to improved case ascertainment as well as prevention of future deaths from fatal child abuse.

More information on local and state CFR teams, a "how-to" manual, and further information can be accessed at the National MCH Center for Child Death Review's website at http://www.childdeathreview.org.

Causes of Fatal Child Abuse Deaths

Abusive Head Trauma

Abusive head trauma (AHT) describes a constellation of abusive head injuries to children including shaking, shaking with an impact, and direct blows to the head (Christian et al. 2009). While some controversy exists regarding the exact mechanism of "Shaken Baby Syndrome" multiple publications of perpetrator confessions (Starling et al. 2004) and comparative studies to accidental injuries (Vinchon et al. 2010; Bechtel et al. 2004) implicate shaking as a mechanism of traumatic brain injury in young children. A thorough analysis of the biomechanical controversies of the entity "Shaken Baby Syndrome" is beyond the focus of this chapter. AHT as an entity is the most frequent cause of fatal child abuse in infants under 1 year old.

Estimates for the incidence of AHT vary from 5/100,000 to 41.5/100,000 depending on the definition and methodology (Wirtz and Trent 2008; Dias et al. 2005). In general, a broader definition of AHT and younger ages will lead to higher estimates as compared to narrow definitions using passive surveillance methods, like hospital discharges (Wirtz and Trent 2008). Recent publications using active prospective surveillance in North Carolina (Keenan 2008) and Edinburgh, Scotland (Minns et al. 2008), and analysis of national inpatient databases (Ellingson et al. 2008) place the incidence around 20/100,000 births.

Risk factors for AHT can be categorized according to the child, the family and the adult perpetrator. Male children are at higher risk than females. Premature infants and those with disabilities are also at higher risk (Herman et al. 2011; Starling et al. 1995, 2004). Young parents, military parents, unstable family situations, and lower socioeconomic status are family-related risk factors for AHT (Herman et al. 2011) while substance abuse, psychiatric disorders or an unreasonable expectation of child behavior are adult risk factors (Herman et al. 2011; Schnitzer and Ewigman 2005). Most often, the perpetrator is the baby's father or mother's boyfriend, while female babysitters and mothers follow (Herman et al. 2011; Starling et al. 1995).

The majority of the cases of AHT occur in young infants between 2 and 6 months of age. The age-specific incidence overlaps with a slight lag to the peak months of infant crying (Barr et al. 2006; Lee et al. 2007). Coping with a crying infant can be difficult, especially for men. Shaking an infant appears to be a response to disciplining a child under 2 years of age across many cultures. Parents worldwide report using shaking as discipline, with a rate of 2.6 % in North Carolina to 25 % in Chile, and over 40 % in India slums (Runyan 2008). Shaking an infant may provide a positive-feedback loop for caregivers (Barr and Runyan 2008): as shaking quiets the infant and leaves no external marks that could be perceived as an unacceptable cultural practice.

Infants who die from AHT often present to the hospital in extremis. Recent research has demonstrated that children who present for medical care with initial Glasgow Coma Scores (GCS) of 5 or below had a 58 times greater odds of dying than children with a GCS of 12 or higher (Shein et al. 2012). The initial presentation of fatal AHT often includes seizures, apnea or coma, while mild AHT cases can present with fussiness or vomiting (Herman et al. 2011). The intracranial findings most often include subdural hemorrhages and subarachnoid hemorrhages, while contusions and other parenchymal injuries such as axonal injury can also occur (Herman et al. 2011). Secondary injuries from hypoxia can lead to cerebral edema or hypoxic-ischemic injuries (Herman et al. 2011). The overall mortality rate for AHT victims ranges from 11 % to 35.7 % (Shein et al. 2012; Chiesa and Duhaime 2009; Keenan et al. 2003) while almost two thirds of victims will have some neurologic sequelae (Chiesa and Duhaime 2009).

Fatal Munchausen's Syndrome by Proxy

Munchausen's Syndrome by Proxy (MSBP), also referred to as pediatric condition falsification, and medical child abuse is a cluster of symptoms that include illness in a child that is either fabricated or produced by a caregiver leading to frequent physician or hospital visits for medical treatment. The etiology of the symptoms is denied by the perpetrator, and symptoms resolve once the child is removed from the perpetrator's care (Rosenberg 1987).

Estimates of the incidence of MSBP are difficult to ascertain, as the diagnosis can be challenging, many cases go undiagnosed, and many are not reported. The best studies have used either prospective or retrospective surveillance to identify cases and national census data for population estimates. McClure and colleagues calculated a rate of 0.5/100,000 for children <16 years of age, and 2.8/100,000 for children <1 year of age in the UK and Ireland. These estimates included cases of non-accidental poisoning and suffocation (McClure et al. 1996). Denny and colleagues (2001) estimated an incidence of 2/100,000 in New Zealand using a survey of all pediatricians in the country.

Data on MSBP fatality rates have also been variable. None of the cases in Denny's study were fatal, possibly because he only requested information from pediatricians (Denny et al. 2001). Rosenberg reported a 9 % fatality rate (Rosenberg 1987), and two separate studies found rates of approximately 6 % (McClure et al. 1996; Sheridan 2003). Alexander and colleagues (1990) calculated a mortality rate of 31 %. However, their sample included five index cases and eight siblings of the index cases.

Fatal MSBP is most often due to poisoning or suffocation. Poisoning or suffocation was identified as the cause of death in all cases in the Alexander and McClure series (Alexander et al. 1990; McClure et al. 1996). Two articles examining only cases of smothering both demonstrated high mortality rates; 18 % in one and 33 % in the other (Rosen et al. 1986; Meadow 1999). Sheridan's study did not provide data on the cause of death, bud did list patient symptoms. Among the 27 deaths in her series, approximately half had symptoms of apnea, 22 % had a history of cyanosis, 22 % had vomiting, and 18 % had anorexia or feeding problems (Sheridan 2003). Case reports of fatal MSBP have typically cited poisoning or suffocation as the cause of death (Vennemann et al. 2005; Valentine et al. 1997; Meadow 1993; Bartsch et al. 2003; Schneider et al. 1996). Causes of poisoning have included barbiturates, benzodiazepines, ipecac, tricyclic antidepressants, and salt (Vennemann et al. 2005; Valentine et al. 1997; Meadow 1993; Bartsch et al. 2003; Schneider et al. 1996).

Suffocation Versus SIDS

The determination of an infant suffocation death can be extremely difficult to differentiate from Sudden Infant Death Syndrome (SIDS). SIDS was first defined in the 1970s by consensus statement as a diagnosis of exclusion in which a child under the age of 1 year dies with no known cause. The vast majority of children who die from SIDS are under 6 months and found in an unsafe sleep position, such as prone sleeping. In order to assign SIDS as the cause of death of an infant, a complete and thorough death investigation must occur as described above. Unfortunately, because of poor death investigations and because suffocating an infant with a pillow can occur despite a completely unremarkable scene investigation and no findings on autopsy, it is estimated between 1 % and 5 % of SIDS cases are actually due to infanticide (American Academy of Pediatrics 2006).

The confusion and debate among professionals between SIDS and suffocation became an issue at the first description of SIDS. The "apnea hypothesis," in which infants who have recurrent episodes of apnea later die of SIDS, was one of the first hypotheses for the etiology of SIDS. For decades, researchers in a few areas of the country believed that perinatal pneumograms (sleep studies monitoring heart rates and oxygen levels) could predict future risk of SIDS by identifying infants with apnea. Additionally, siblings of SIDS victims were placed on monitors to prevent SIDS as there was general acceptance that siblings carried a higher risk of dying from SIDS (Kelly et al. 1982). Unfortunately, the hypothesis was based primarily on the deaths of infants whose mothers were repeatedly suffocating them (Steinschneider 1972; Firstman and Talan 1997) and the likelihood of infanticide increases as the number of infants in the same family die of SIDS. Many studies at the time additionally disproved the apnea hypothesis and risk of sibling deaths (Meadow 1990; Southall et al. 1982; Schechtman et al. 1991).

Only a thorough death investigation will have the possibility of discriminating death by suffocation from SIDS (American Academy of Pediatrics 2006). Findings that may suggest suffocation include pulmonary intraavleolar hemorrhages on autopsy and a history of oropharyngeal blood (Southall et al. 1997), but neither is specific enough to conclusively diagnose suffocation (Krous et al. 2007). The majority of suffocation deaths have no forensic findings in either the scene investigation or autopsy, making it challenging to ascertain the cause of death and the exact number of suffocation deaths each year.

Fatal Poisoning

Poisoning can occur when a child ingests, inhales, or aspirates a toxic substance, or when a toxin is injected or absorbed through the skin. Several different types of child maltreatment can lead to death by poisoning. These include neglect, MSBP, severe punishment gone awry, and manslaughter/homicide. Poisoning in the context of MSBP has already been discussed. This section will therefore focus on neglect, severe punishment, and homicide.

Fatal poisoning can be due to neglect in situations where the caregivers' lack of supervision leads to the ingestion of a toxic substance. In the context of poisoning from illegal drugs, the caregivers' possession and use of illegal substances inherently places the child at risk of harm, and these cases should routinely be reported to child protective services. When a mobile child ingests, inhales, or aspirates a household product or medication, it may be challenging to determine whether neglect was involved, and whether the case should be reported to child protective services. However, fatal poisoning from several common household products should raise concern for exposure to illegal drug production (Farst et al. 2007). For example, pseudophedrine and ephedrine are precursors for methamphetamine production. Solvents (e.g. acetone, paint thinner, kerosene), reducing agents (e.g. red phosphorus from match strike plates, iodine, ammonia, and lithium), bases (e.g. sodium hydroxide from drain opener, and ammonium hydroxide from household cleaners), and acids (e.g. hydrochloric or sulfuric acid) are used in the production of methamphetamine (Farst et al. 2007).

The most frequently reported toxins implicated in fatal poisoning as punishment include pepper, salt, and water. Death has been reported in a number of children who were force fed black pepper. The cause of death in all cases was aspiration (Henretig et al. 2009; Cohle et al. 1988). Punishment by forced water ingestion may cause hyponatremia, seizures, and cerebral edema (Tilelli and Ophoven 1986; Dine and McGovern 1982; Keating et al. 1991), which can be fatal. Force feeding of salt, often in conjunction with fluid restriction may be used as punishment, frequently for enuresis (Baugh et al. 1983; Dockery 1992; Feldman and Robertson 1979).

Poisoning of children with sedatives to stop crying or keep them quiet may be considered a subset of poisoning as punishment. Case reports have included a 3-year old poisoned with diphenhydramine for sedation and emesis cessation (Pragst et al. 2006) and a 4-year old given haloperidol to punish his bad behavior and make him sleep (Satar et al. 2001). In other cases, a 10-month old was injected with heroin by mother's boyfriend to keep the infant quiet, and a 1-year old was fed rum and coke to keep him quiet (Henretig et al. 2009).

Parents who choose to commit suicide may decide to kill their children at the same time through poisoning or other means. Two case series from Hong Kong described instances of suicide/homicide. Of the 15 total families, there were three child deaths from poisoning. Two of the 14 were poisoned, one by coal gas, and another two by carbon monoxide from burning charcoal (Hon 2011; Lee et al. 2002). In these cases, the majority of perpetrators were mothers, who committed suicide by jumping from buildings (Hon 2011). These cases differ from the poisonings seen in MSBP because there is no history of frequent medical visits or unusual or inexplicable illness symptoms. A final form of homicide involves the use of children as drug mules – having them ingest drugs for surreptitious transport (Beno et al. 2005; Traub et al. 2004).

Fatal Neglect

Fatal neglect can encompass a broad range of causes of death. Many involve a lack of supervision, as with drowning, falls, leaving a child unattended in a hot vehicle, or burns and suffocation from residential fires. Fatal neglect may also occur from poor parental decision making, such as placement of an infant in an unsafe sleeping environment, driving with a child while intoxicated, or failure to use a car seat or seat belt for the child. A third category of fatal neglect includes medical neglect, in which the death could have been prevented with medical intervention. Fatal medical neglect may be the result of parental religious beliefs or use of unproven, non-traditional forms of treatment. Finally, nutritional neglect may lead to fatal starvation.

Determining whether an unintentional injury death involves neglect can be challenging, particularly in instances of lack of supervision and failure to protect. Professionals may be reluctant in these situations to report to child protective services, believing that the family has already suffered enough, and that they don't want to blame the family for an "accident" (Ewigman et al. 1993). Even child fatality review teams may have difficulty labeling a lapse of supervision or failure to protect as neglect because of differing definitions, lack of standards regarding supervision, and changing norms (Schnitzer et al. 2011). Therefore, the number and percentage of child deaths involving some degree of neglect are probably vastly underestimated.

NCANDS data from 2010 indicate about two-thirds of child maltreatment fatalities involve some component of neglect (US DHHS 2011). About half of these deaths are the result of neglect alone, and another half involve neglect and at least one other form of maltreatment. In a 25 year retrospective review of fatal neglect in South Carolina, 16 cases of definite neglect were identified. Six (24 %) of these involved nutritional neglect, with malnutrition, starvation, or dehydration, and four (16 %) involved drowning. There were also several cases of toxic ingestions, hyperthermia, hypothermia, electrocution, and lack of medical care (Knight and Collins 2005). Because this review excluded "gray zone" cases, it underestimates the proportion of fatal neglect cases from lack of supervision, unsafe sleep environments, and motor vehicle crashes in which children were not properly restrained.

Neglect Deaths from Drowning – Drowning deaths may involve neglect in both infants and older children. One example is a parent who is bathing an infant or toddler and leaves briefly to answer the telephone, leaving the child unattended. In addition, mobile toddlers and young children have drowned from falling into buckets filled with water or cleaning solution. Toddlers or preschoolers may drown in home swimming pools when safety gates are absent or unsecured. Lapses in supervision, including supervision while intoxicated may contribute to drowning in swimming pools as well as natural bodies of water. A 2011 review of 5 years of pediatric drowning deaths in Washington State indicated that 68 % (21 of 31) of the drowning fatalities in children under 5 years of age involved some degree of neglect. While the authors noted that most of the 21 were due to isolated acts of inadequate supervision, they also indicated that ten of these families had prior CPS referrals (Quan et al. 2011).

Neglect Deaths from Household Fires – There are a number of different ways in which neglect may contribute to child deaths in household fires. Parents may leave children unattended in a home where a fire starts, leaving the child unable to escape because he is sleeping, is overcome by smoke inhalation, and/or does not know how to escape. An intoxicated adult may be present and unable to help the children escape. The fire may be started by a child with inadequate supervision who has easy access to matches or a lighter. In one study of residential fires in North Carolina, 48 children <18 years died in the course of a year – 14 of these died in nine fires without adult supervision, and seven died in four fires in which one or more surviving adults was impaired by alcohol or other drugs (Marshall et al. 1998). An epidemiologic study of house fires in Scotland had similar findings; parental intoxication was present in 30 % of 168 fires with child deaths, and 30 % involved some lapse in supervision (Squires and Busuttil 1995).

Heat Related Deaths – Death from hyperthermia may occur when children are left unattended in cars, or when unattended children climb into unlocked cars. There are few studies in the literature examining these deaths, in part because there is no specific ICD codes to identify these cases (Guard and Gallagher 2005). One study used news reports to identify 171 deaths over 8 years in children ≤5 years. The majority of these deaths (125, or 73 %) occurred when parents left children unattended in the car, while the remaining cases were instances in which an unsupervised child climbed into an unlocked car. Among the 125 cases where children were left in cars, caregivers in about half forgot or were unaware of the child in the car. In another 27 % the caregiver deliberately left a child in the car, either because he did not want to wake a sleeping child, or because he wanted to restrain a child while participating in another activity (Guard and Gallagher 2005).

Fatal Medical Neglect – Fatal medical neglect may occur when parents deny their children access to needed medical care because of religious or cultural beliefs. They may instead opt for prayer, laying on of hands, faith healing, or other techniques. Asser and Swan (1997) published a review of religion-motivated medical neglect in which they retrospectively identified 172 child and perinatal fatalities over a 20 year period. Child deaths were primarily from infections, diabetes, malignancies, congenital heart disease, abdominal surgical disorders, and dehydration. The authors determined that 140 of the 172 children had at least a 90 % chance of survival, and all but three of the children could have benefitted from medical treatment.

The American Academy of Pediatrics has strongly objected to religious treatment in lieu of standard medical care, stating that children, "have the right to appropriate medical evaluation when it is likely that a serious illness, injury, or other medical condition endangers their lives or threatens substantial harm or suffering. Under such circumstances, parents and other guardians have a responsibility to seek medical treatment, regardless of their religious beliefs" (AAP 1997). Federal laws in the United States regarding religious exemptions for medical care have changed several times over the past four decades. In 1974, the U.S. Department of Health, Education and Welfare required religious exemption laws for states receiving federal child abuse prevention and treatment (CAPTA) funding. While this requirement was removed in 1983, many states have opted to maintain their religious exemption laws (Sinal et al. 2008).

Fatal Malnutrition/Starvation – Failure to thrive and malnutrition may occur for a number of reasons, including lack of knowledge of nutritional needs or formula preparation, parental mental health or substance abuse, breastfeeding difficulties, medical problems causing difficulty feeding, increased caloric needs, and/or vomiting and diarrhea. Purposeful withholding of food is uncommon, but may occur as a form of punishment or parental rejection (Kellogg and Lukefar 2005). Given the nutritional and health care resources in developed countries, neglect is likely a contributor to all fatalities with malnutrition as the sole cause of death.

Children who die from starvation are most often infants and toddlers (Kellogg and Lukefar 2005; Knight and Collins 2005; Berkowitz 2001). Published cases provide caretaker histories of minor complaints, sudden onset of symptoms, and lack of recognition or acknowledgement of child's severe symptoms (Kellogg and Lukefar 2005; Knight and Collins 2005). Yet these children all had a lack of subcutaneous fat and signs of dehydration at presentation. Autopsy findings included skin tenting, prominent ribs, loss of adipose tissue and poor muscle tone (Knight and Collins 2005). Parents in several cases reported that the child had just recently eaten, though the children's stomachs were empty on autopsy. Lack of medical care beyond the newborn period was common (Kellogg and Lukefar 2005).

Determination of the cause of death will naturally rely on autopsy findings, but growth data may be helpful in supporting placement decisions for siblings and criminal court proceedings. Growth charts will typically show a cessation of weight gain before linear growth and head circumference growth stops (Berkowitz 2001). If prior growth parameters are available, it may be possible to estimate the length of time without adequate nutrition (Berkowitz 2001).

Prevention

Child abuse fatality prevention uses two general strategies: parent education and home visitation. Approaches to parent education (e.g. Parents As Teachers (PAT) and Healthy Families America) provide new parents with knowledge about parenting and child development with the intention that it will reduce the likelihood that a child will be abused in that family (for a review of parent education programs see the Packard Foundation *Future of Children* report, 1999). These programs are not specific for child fatality prevention and have mixed success in preventing non-fatal child abuse (Duggan et al. 2007; Donelan-McCall et al. 2009).

Thirty five years ago, Gray and colleagues (1979) identified children at risk of physical abuse and neglect by observing the parents' interaction with their infants prenatally and perinatally. The provision of a lay home visitor to these families reduced the level and severity of physical abuse and neglect. These were not controlled studies, but indicated that providing stressed, at-risk parents someone to contact could potentially prevent abusive and neglectful situations. While not specifically shown to reduce childhood mortality, Olds' home visiting studies using public health nurses intervening with high-risk mothers pre- and post-natally have demonstrated significant reductions in rates of child abuse reports, subsequent alcohol abuse, criminal behavior and other childhood negative well-being outcomes in a variety of settings (Olds et al. 1997; Donelan-McCall et al. 2009).

More recent primary preventive strategies that show promise provide education to parents of newborns about AHT. Dias in 2005 published an effective strategy that includes providing all parents of newborns a pamphlet about AHT and crying, showing parents a video, and having them sign a "commitment statement" to warn any caregiver about the dangers of shaking babies (Dias et al. 2005). This relatively simple nursery intervention reduced the incidence of AHT in Western NY 61 % compared to historical and geographical controls. More recent studies have questioned the effectiveness of the video as an intervention (Keenan and Leventhal 2010).

The CFR process itself may lead to a reduction in child deaths, though these results are not specific for maltreatment-related fatalities. Work from Georgia (Luallen et al. 1998) and Arizona (Rimsza et al. 2002) have shown a reduction in unintentional deaths. While a decrease in fatal abuse has not been demonstrated, the same process of identifying and modifying risk factors may help. Alternatively, proper review and well functioning death investigation systems may initially increase the measured incidence due to improved classification.

Unfortunately, there is no single effective strategy to prevent fatal child abuse deaths. The low overall incidence of childhood abuse fatalities coupled with the high prevalence of risk factors for fatal child abuse leads to a low predictive value for any individual or combination of risk factors. Any intervention needs to reach a large number of individuals in order to prevent one death. It is likely that a variety of approaches are needed to prevent child fatalities. Increased provision of effective strategies such as education in the newborn period, new parent support via home visitation, and community involvement in assuring healthy families will be the only way to significantly reduce the rates of fatal child abuse.

References

Alexander, R., Smith, W., & Stevenson, R. (1990). Serial Munchausen syndrome by proxy. *Pediatrics, 86*, 581–585.

American Academy of Pediatrics Committee on Bioethics. (1997). Religious objections to medical care. *Pediatrics, 99*, 279–281.

American Academy of Pediatrics, Task Force on Sudden Infant Death Syndrome. (2005). The changing concept of sudden infant death syndrome: Diagnostic coding shifts, controversies regarding the sleeping environment, and new variables to consider in reducing risk. *Pediatrics, 116*, 1245–1255.

American Academy of Pediatrics, Hymel, K. P., & The Committee on Child Abuse and Neglect and National Association of Medical Examiners. (2006). Distinguishing sudden infant death syndrome from child abuse fatalities. *Pediatrics, 118*, 421–427.

Asser, S. M., & Swan, R. (1997). Child fatalities from religion-motivated neglect. *Pediatrics, 101*, 625–629.

Auburn, A., & Grady, J. (2012). How the news frames child maltreatment: Unintended consequences. http://www.preventchildabuse.org/canp/resources/pdf/HowTheNewsFramesChildAbuse.pdf. Accessed 13 Aug 2012.

Barr, R. G., & Runyan, D. K. (2008). Inflicted childhood neurotrauma: The problem set and challenges to measuring incidence. *American Journal of Preventive Medicine, 34*(4S), S106–S111.

Barr, R. G., Trent, R. B., & Cross, J. (2006). Age-related incidence curve of hospitalized shaken baby syndrome cases: Convergent evidence for crying as a trigger to shaking. *Child Abuse & Neglect, 30*(1), 7–16.

Bartsch, C., Ribe, M., Schutz, H., Weigand, N., & Weiler, G. (2003). Munchausen syndrome by proxy (MSBP): An extreme form of child abuse with a special forensic challenge. *Forensic Science International, 137*, 147–151.

Baugh, J. R., Krug, E. F., & Weir, M. R. (1983). Punishment by salt poisoning. *Southern Medical Journal, 76*, 540–541.

Bechtel, K., Stoessel, K., Leventhal, J. M., Ogle, E., Teague, B., Lavietes, S., Banyas, B., Allen, K., Dziura, J., & Duncan, C. (2004). Characteristics that distinguish accidental from abusive injury in hospitalized young children with head trauma. *Pediatrics, 114*(1), 165–168. Jul.

Beno, S., Calello, D., Baluffi, A., & Henretig, F. M. (2005). Pediatric body packing: Drug smuggling reaches a new low. *Pediatric Emergency Care, 21*, 744–746.

Berkowitz, C. D. (2001). Fatal child neglect. *Advances in Pediatrics, 48*, 331–361.

Chiesa, A., & Duhaime, A. C. (2009). Abusive head trauma. *Pediatric Clinics of North America, 56*, 317–331.

Christian, C., Block, B., & The Committee on Child Abuse and Neglect. (2009). Abusive head trauma in infants and children. *Pediatrics, 123*, 1409–1411.

Cohle, S. D., Trestrail, J. D., Graham, M. A., Oxley, D. W., Walp, B., & Jachimczyk, J. (1988). Fatal pepper aspiration. *American Journal of Disease of Children, 42*, 633–636.

Collins, K. A., & Nichols, C. A. (1999). A decade of pediatric homicide: A retrospective study at the medical university of South Carolina. *American Journal Forensic Medicine and Pathololology, 20*, 169–172.

Covington, C. M., Foster, V., & Rich, S. K. (2005). The child death review case reporting system: Systems manual. *National MCH Center for Child Death Review*. Retrieved 24 Aug 2010, from http://www.childdeathreview.org/reports/CDR%20Systems%20Manual.pdf.

Crume, T. L., DiGuiseppi, C., Byers, T., Sirotnak, A. P., & Garrett, C. J. (2002). Underascertainment of child maltreatment fatalities by death certificates, 1990–1998. *Pediatrics, 110*, e18.

Denny, S. J., Grant, C. C., & Pinnock, R. (2001). Epidemiology of Munchausen syndrome by proxy in New Zealand. *Journal of Paediatric and Child Health, 37*, 240–243.

Dias, M. S., Smith, K., DeGuehery, K., Mazur, P., Li, V., & Shaffer, M. L. (2005). Preventing abusive head trauma among infants and young children: A hospital-based, parent education program. *Pediatrics, 115*(4), e470–e477.

Dine, M. S., & McGovern, M. E. (1982). Intentional poisoning of children—an overlooked category of child abuse: Report of seven cases and review of the literature. *Pediatrics, 70*, 32–35.

Dockery, W. G. (1992). Fatal intentional salt poisoning associated with a radiopaque mass. *Pediatrics, 89*, 964–965.

Donelan-McCall, N., Eckenrode, J., & Olds, D. L. (2009). Home visiting for the prevention of child maltreatment: Lessons learned during the past 20 years. *Pediatric Clinic of North America, 56*(2), 389–403.

Duggan, A., Caldera, D., Rodriguez, K., Burrell, L., Rohde, C., & Crowne, S. S. (2007). Impact of a statewide home visiting program to prevent child abuse. *Child Abuse & Neglect, 31*(8), 801–827. Epub 2007 Sep 5.

Ellingson, K. D., Leventhal, J. M., & Weiss, H. B. (2008). Using hospital discharge data to track inflicted traumatic brain injury. *American Journal of Preventive Medicine, 34*(4S), S157–S162.

Ewigman, B., Kivlahan, C., & Land, G. (1993). The Missouri child fatality study: Underreporting of maltreatment fatalities among children younger than five years of age, 1983 through 1986. *Pediatrics, 91*, 330–337.

Farst, K., Duncan, J. M., Moss, M., Ray, R. M., Kokoska, E., & James, L. P. (2007). Methamphetamine exposure presenting as caustic ingestions in children. *Annals of Emergency Medicine, 49*, 341–343.

Feldman, K., & Robertson, W. O. (1979). Salt poisoning: Presenting symptom of child abuse. *Veterinary and Human Toxicology, 21*, 341–343.

Finkelhor, D., & Jones, L. (2012). Have sexual abuse and physical abuse declined since the 1990s? Crimes Against Children Research Center Bulletin. CV267: P 1–6. Online at: www.unh.edu/ccrc. Accessed 9 Nov 2012.

Firstman, R., & Talan, J. (1997). *The death of innocents*. New York: Bantam Books.

Gray, J. D., Cutler, C. A., Dean, J. G., & Kempe, C. H. (1979). Prediction and prevention of child abuse and neglect. *Journal of Social Issues, 35*, 127–139.

Guard, A., & Gallagher, S. S. (2005). Heat related deaths to young children in parked cars: An analysis of 171 fatalities in the United States, 1995–2002. *Injury Prevention, 11*, 33–37.

Henretig, F. M., Paschall, R. T., & Donaruma-Kwoh, M. M. (2009). Child abuse by poisoning. In R. M. Reece & C. W. Christian (Eds.), *Child abuse: Medical diagnosis and management* (3rd ed., pp. 549–599). Oak Grove Village: American Academy of Pediatrics.

Herman, B. E., Makoroff, K. L., & Corneli, H. M. (2011). Abusive head trauma. *The New England Journal of Medicine, 27*, 65–69.

Herman-Giddens, M. E., Brown, G., Verbeist, S., Carlson, P. J., Hooten, E. J., Howell, E., & Butts, J. D. (1999). Underascertainment of child abuse mortality in the United States. *Journal of the American Medical Association, 282*, 463–467.

Herman-Giddens, M. E., Smith, J. B., Mittal, M., Carlson, M., & Butts, J. D. (2003). Newborns killed or left to die by a parent: A population-based study. *Journal of the American Medical Association, 289*, 1425–1429.

Hon, K. L. (2011). Dying with parents: An extreme form of child abuse. *World Journal of Pediatrics, 7*, 266–268.

Kajese, T. M., Nguyen, L. T., Pham, G. Q., Melhorn, K., & Kallail, K. J. (2011). Characteristics of child abuse homicides in the state of Kansas from 1994 to 2007. *Child Abuse & Neglect, 35*, 147–154.

Keating, J. P., Schears, G. J., & Dodge, P. R. (1991). Oral water intoxication in infants. An American epidemic. *The American Journal of Disease of Children, 145*, 985–990.

Keenan, H. T. (2008). Practical asptects of conducting a prospective statewide incidence study: The incidence of serious inflicted traumatic brain injury in North Carolina. *American Journal of Preventive Medicine, 34*(4S), S120–S125.

Keenan, H. T., & Leventhal, J. M. (2010). A case–control study to evaluate Utah's shaken baby prevention program. *Academic Pediatrics, 10*(6), 389–394.

Keenan, H. T., Runyan, D. K., Marshall, S. W., Nocera, M. A., Merten, D. F., & Sinal, S. H. (2003). A population based study of inflicted traumatic brain injury in young children. *Journal of the American Medical Association, 290,* 621–626. 922–9.

Kellogg, N. D., & Lukefar, J. L. (2005). Criminally prosecuted cases of child starvation. *Pediatrics, 116,* 1309–1316.

Kelly, D. H., Twanmoh, J., & Shannon, D. C. (1982). Incidence of apnea in siblings of sudden infant death syndrome victims studied at home. *Pediatrics, 70*(1), 128–131.

Knight, L. D., & Collins, K. A. (2005). A 25-year retrospective review of deaths due to pediatric neglect. *The American Journal of Forensic Medical and Pathology, 26,* 221–228.

Krous, H. F., Haas, E. A., Masoumi, H., Chadwick, A. E., & Stanley, C. (2007). A comparison of pulmonary intra-alveolar hemorrhage in cases of sudden infant death due to SIDS in a safe sleep environment or to suffocation. *Forensic Science International, 172*(1), 56–62. Epub 2007 Jan 12.

Krugman, S. D., & Krugman, R. D. (2007). Evaluating risk factors for fatal child abuse. In J. C. Campbell (Ed.), *Assessing dangerousness: Violence by batterers and child abusers.* New York: Springer.

Lee, A. C., Ou, Y., Lam, S. Y., & Kam, C. W. (2002). Non-accidental carbon monoxide poisoning from burning charcoal in attempted combined homicide-suicide. *Journal of Pediatrics and Child Health, 38,* 465–468.

Lee, C., Barr, R. G., Catherine, N., & Wicks, A. (2007). Age-related incidence of publicly-reported shaken baby syndrome cases: Is a crying a trigger for shaking? *Journal of Development and Behavioral Pediatrics, 30,* 7–16.

Luallen, J. J., Rochat, R. W., Smith, S. M., O'Neil, J., Rogers, M. Y., & Bolen, J. C. (1998). Child fatality review in Georgia: A young system demonstrates its potential for identifying preventable deaths. *Southern Medical Journal, 91,* 414–419.

Margolin, L. (1990). Fatal child neglect. *Child Welfare, 49,* 309–320.

Marshall, S. W., Runyan, C. W., Bangdiwala, S. I., Linzer, M. A., Sacks, J. J., & Butts, J. D. (1998). Fatal residential fires: Who dies and who survives? *Journal of the American Medical Association, 279,* 1633–1637.

McClure, R. J., Davis, P. M., Meadow, S. R., & Sibert, J. R. (1996). Epidemiology of Munchausen syndrome by proxy, non-accidental poisoning, and non-accidental suffocation. *Archives of Disease in Childhood, 75,* 57–61.

Meadow, R. (1990). Suffocation, recurrent apnea, and sudden infant death. *Journal of Pediatrics, 117,* 351–357.

Meadow, R. (1993). Non-accidental salt poisoning. *Archives of Disease in Childhood, 68,* 448–452.

Meadow, R. (1999). Unnatural sudden infant death. *Archives of Disease in Childhood, 80,* 7–14.

Michigan Public Health Institute (2005a). History of child death review in the United States. Retrieved 25 Aug 2012, from http://www.childdeathreview.org/Promo/history.pdf.

Michigan Public Health Institute (2005b). The child death review process. Retrieved 25 Aug 2012, from http://www.childdeathreview.org/cdrprocess.htm.

Minns, R. A., Jones, P. A., & Mok, J. Y. K. (2008). Incidence and demography of non-accidental head injury in southeast Scotland from a national database. *American Journal of Preventive Medicine, 34*(4S), S126–33.

Olds, D. L., Eckenrode, J., Henderson, C. R., Kitzman, H., Powers, J., Cole, R., Sidora, K., Morris, P., Pettitt, L. M., & Luckey, D. (1997). Long-term effects of home visitation on maternal life course and child abuse and neglect. Fifteen-year follow-up of a randomized trial. *JAMA, 278,* 637–643.

Overpeck, M. D., Brenner, R. A., Trumble, A. C., Trifiletti, L. B., & Berendes, H. W. (1998). Risk factors for infant homicide in the U.S. *The New England Journal of Medicine, 339,* 1211–1216.

Paulozzi, L., & Sells, M. (2002). Variation in homicide risk during infancy – United States, 1989–1998. *Morbility and Morality Weekly Report, 51*(9), 187–189.

Pragst, F., Herre, S., & Bakdash, A. (2006). Poisonings with diphenhydramine – a survey of 68 clinical and 55 death cases. *Forensic Science International, 161,* 189–197.

Quan, L., Pilkey, D., Gomez, A., & Bennett, E. (2011). Analysis of paediatric drowning deaths in Washington State using the child death review (CDR) for surveillance: What CDR does and does not tell us about lethal drowning injury. *Injury Prevention, 17,* i28–i33.

Rimsza, M. E., Schackner, R. A., Bowen, K. A., & Marshall, W. (2002). Can child deaths be prevented? The Arizona child fatality review program experience. *Pediatrics, 110,* e11.

Roche, J. A., Fortin, G., Labbe, J., Brown, J., & Chadwick, D. (2005). The work of Ambroise Tardieu: The first definitive description of child abuse. *Child Abuse & Neglect, 29,* 325–334.

Rosen, C. L., Frost, J. D., Jr., & Glaze, D. G. (1986). Child abuse and recurrent infant apnea. *Journal of Pediatrics, 109,* 1065–1067.

Rosenberg, D. A. (1987). Web of deceit: A literature review of Munchausen's syndrome by proxy. *Child Abuse & Neglect, 11,* 547–563.

Runyan, D. K. (2008). The challenges of assessing the incidence of inflicted traumatic brain injury: A world perspective. *American Journal of Preventive Medicine, 34*(4S), S112–S115.

Satar, S., Yilmaz, H. L., Gokel, Y., & Toprak, N. (2001). A case of child abuse: Haloperidol poisoning of a child caused by his mother. *European Journal of Emergency Medicine, 8*, 317–319.

Schechtman, V. L., Harper, R. M., Wilson, A. J., & Southall, D. P. (1991). Sleep apnea in infants who succumb to sudden infant death syndrome. *Pediatrics, 87*, 841–886.

Schneider, D. J., Perez, A., Knilans, T. E., Daniels, S. R., Bove, K. E., & Bonnell, H. (1996). Clinical and pathologic aspects of cardiomyopathy from ipecac administration in Munchausen's syndrome by proxy. *Pediatrics, 97*, 902–906.

Schnitzer, P. G., & Ewigman, B. G. (2005). Child deaths resulting from inflicted injuries: Household risk factors and perpetrator characteristics. *Pediatrics, 116*, e687–e693.

Schnitzer, P. G., Covington, T. M., & Kruse, R. L. (2011). Assessment of caregiver responsibility in unintentional injury deaths: Challenges for injury prevention. *Injury Prevention, 17*, i45–i54.

Shein, S. L., Bell, M. J., Kochanek, P. M., Tyler-Kabara, E. C., Wisniewski, S. R., Feldman, K., Makoroff, K., Scribano, P. V., & Berger, R. P. (2012). Risk factors for mortality in children with abusive head trauma. *Journal of Pediatrics, 161*(4), 716–722.e1. doi:10.1016/j.jpeds.2012.03.046. Epub 2012 May 11.

Sheridan, M. S. (2003). The deceit continues: An updated literature review of Munchausen syndrome by proxy. *Child Abuse & Neglect, 27*, 431–451.

Sinal, S. H., Cabinum-Foeller, E., & Socolar, R. (2008). Religion and medical neglect. *Southern Medical Journal, 101*, 703–706.

Southall, D. P., Richards, J. M., Rhoden, K. J., et al. (1982). Prolonged apnea and cardiac arrhythmias in infants discharged from neonatal intensive care units: Failure to predict an increased risk for sudden infant death syndrome. *Pediatrics, 70*, 844–851.

Southall, D. P., Plunkett, M. C., Banks, M. W., Falkov, A. F., & Samuels, M. P. (1997). Covert video recordings of life-threatening child abuse: Lessons for child protection. *Pediatrics, 100*(5), 735–760.

Squires, T., & Busuttil, A. (1995). Child fatalities in Scottish house fires 1980–1990: A case of child neglect? *Child Abuse & Neglect, 19*, 865–873.

Starling, S. P., Holden, J. R., & Jenny, C. (1995). Abusive head trauma: The relationship of perpetrators to their victims. *Pediatrics, 95*, 259–262.

Starling, S. P., Patel, S., Burke, B. L., Sirotnak, A. P., Stronks, S., & Rosquist, P. (2004). Analysis of perpetrator admissions to inflicted traumatic brain injury in children. *Archives of Pediatrics & Adolescent Medicine, 158*(5), 454–458.

Stavrianos, C., Stavrianou, I., & Kafas, P. (2008). Child abuse in greek mythology: A review. *The Internet Journal of Forensic Science, 3*(1). doi: 10.5580/19ef. http://www.ispub.com/journal/the-internet-journal-of-forensic-science/volume-3-number-1/child-abuse-in-greek-mythology-a-review.html. Accessed 13 Aug 2012.

Steinschneider, A. (1972). Prolonged apnea and the sudden infant death syndrome: Clinical and laboratory observations. *Pediatrics, 50*, 646–654.

Stiffman, M. N., Schnitzer, P. G., Adam, P., Kruse, R. L., & Ewigman, B. G. (2002). Household composition and risk of fatal child maltreatment. *Pediatrics, 109*, 615–621.

Tilelli, J. A., & Ophoven, J. P. (1986). Hyponatremic seizures as a presenting symptom of child abuse. *Forensic Science International, 30*, 213–217.

Traub, S., Hoffman, R. S., & Neelson, L. S. (2004). Pediatric "body packing". *Archives of Pediatrics & Adolescent Medicine, 57*, 174–177.

U.S. Advisory Board on Child Abuse and Neglect (1995). *A Nation's shame: Fatal child abuse and neglect in the United States.* Fifth Report, Washington, DC.

U.S. Department of Health and Human Services, Administration for Children, & Families, Administration on Children, Youth and Families, Children's Bureau (2011). *Child maltreatment 2010.* Available from http://www.acf.hhs.gov/programs/cb/stats_research/index.htm#can.

United States Government Accountability Office (2011). Child maltreatment: Strengthening national data on child fatalities could aid in prevention. Report #GAO-11-599. Washington, DC.

Valentine, J. L., Schexnayder, S., Jones, J. G., & Sturner, W. Q. (1997). Clinical and toxicological findings in two young siblings and autopsy findings in one sibling with multiple hospital admissions resulting in death. Evidence suggesting Munchausen syndrome by proxy. *The American Journal of Forensic and Medical Patholology, 18*, 276–281.

Vennemann, B., Bajanowski, T., Karger, B., Pfeiffer, H., Kohler, H., & Brinkmann, B. (2005). Suffocation and poisoning: The hard-hitting side of Munchausen syndrome by proxy. *International Journal of Legal Medicine, 119*, 98–102.

Vinchon, M., de Foort-Dhellemmes, S., Desurmont, M., & Delestret, I. (2010). Confessed abuse versus witnessed accidents in infants: comparison of clinical, radiological, and ophthalmological data in corroborated cases. *Child's Nervous System, 26*(5), 637–645.

Wirtz, S. J., & Trent, R. B. (2008). Passive surveillance of shaken baby syndrome using hospital inpatient data. *American Journal of Preventive Medicine, 34*(4S), S134–S139.

Part II
Child Maltreatment:
Why Does It Occur?

Chapter 6
A Multidimensional View of Continuity in Intergenerational Transmission of Child Maltreatment

Sara R. Berzenski, Tuppett M. Yates, and Byron Egeland

A Multidimensional View of Continuity in Intergenerational Transmission of Child Maltreatment

Over the past several decades, researchers have reached a relative consensus that while experiencing maltreatment in childhood is a risk factor for maltreating one's own children, this consequence is far from an inevitability. Rates of intergenerational transmission of maltreatment (IGTM) range from 6.7 % to 70 % in the literature. The variability in estimated rates of IGTM mirrors the methodological heterogeneity in maltreatment research (e.g., retrospective vs. prospective designs, inconsistent maltreatment definitions, differing concordance calculation techniques) (see Dixon et al. 2005; Ertem et al. 2000, for review; Kaufman and Zigler 1989). In the absence of fully prospective investigations of IGTM (i.e., where both parent and child experiences are assessed longitudinally), the most comprehensive estimate of the "true" rate of IGTM is ~30 % (Kaufman and Zigler 1989). However, the marked variability across published estimates remains concerning and suggests the need to critically evaluate extant approaches to the conceptualization and investigation of IGTM.

In addition to varying estimates of IGTM, research points to an array of mechanisms underlying maltreatment continuity and discontinuity across generations. For example, younger parenting and parental psychopathology have been implicated in IGTM, whereas, factors supporting desistance of maltreatment across generations include supportive relationships, psychotherapy, and capacities for meaning making and experiential integration (see Dixon et al. 2005; Egeland 1993; Egeland et al. 2002 for more detailed reviews of risk and protective factors; Egeland et al. 1988; Egeland and Susman-Stillman 1996; Kaufman and Zigler 1993). Yet even these risk and protective factors may be qualified by individual and contextual characteristics. Indeed, the most consistent finding across the sizable literature on the manifestations and mechanisms of IGTM is its inconsistency.

In this chapter, we apply key concepts from the integrative paradigm of developmental psychopathology to inform a new approach to IGTM research that will simultaneously facilitate greater sensitivity and specificity in our understanding of patterns of maltreatment continuity and discontinuity across generations. First, we review key models of continuity and discontinuity within the broader framework

S.R. Berzenski (✉)
California State University, Northridge, CA, USA
e-mail: sara.berzenski@csun.edu

T.M. Yates
University of California, Riverside, CA, USA

B. Egeland
University of Minnesota, Minneapolis, MN, USA

J.E. Korbin and R.D. Krugman (eds.), *Handbook of Child Maltreatment*, Child Maltreatment 2, DOI 10.1007/978-94-007-7208-3_6, © Springer Science+Business Media Dordrecht 2014

of developmental psychopathology and highlight the added value of extending this framework to IGTM research. Second, we revisit the phenomenology of IGTM with particular emphasis on the information provided by instances of persistence and desistence across different forms of maltreatment. Third, we suggest a new approach to understanding and investigating mechanisms underlying the etiology of IGTM within a developmental psychopathology framework. Fourth, we offer specific recommendations for future research on IGTM and discuss implications for ongoing efforts to prevent it.

A Multidimensional View of Continuity

Developmental psychopathology adopts an organizational view of development, which emphasizes the coherence of adaption over time (Rutter and Sroufe 2000; Sroufe 1990; Sroufe and Rutter 1984; Werner 1957). In this perspective, both continuity and discontinuity in adaptive organization reflect and follow from a fundamentally coherent course of development (Rutter et al. 2006; Sroufe 1979; Sroufe and Jacobvitz 1989). As such, both continuous and discontinuous patterns of adaptation are worthy of study, and both further our understanding of development broadly. In this chapter, we outline a new, multidimensional model of IGTM that is informed by central tenets of organizational theory and developmental psychopathology.

First, given the reciprocally informative relations between studies of continuity and discontinuity, we encourage research focused on processes by which maltreatment persists across generations, as well as on those that precipitate discontinuities and "break the cycle." Patterns of persistence and desistence occur within individual development, as well as across individuals and generations (Rutter 1989). For example, research on parenting practices reveals meaningful continuity and discontinuity across the developmental continuum (Pianta et al. 1989a). Although maternal sensitivity is largely stable across development, parenting behavior cannot be explained fully by this continuity. Pianta and colleagues (1989a) found that discontinuities in maternal sensitivity were equally important for understanding development because they revealed the salience of child and situational factors (e.g., marital relationship quality, child gender). As applied to the study of IGTM, we suggest that principles of continuity and discontinuity operate across generations, and research must attend not only to examples in which the cycle is perpetuated, but also to instances of "lawful discontinuity" (Belsky 1993, p. 416) that break the cycle.

Second, the fundamental coherence of development rests at the level of function, despite potential variations in form (Rutter 1989; Sameroff and Chandler 1975; Waddington 1940). For example, the ability to seek care when distressed in early childhood engenders a capacity to manage distress independently in later development such that an apparent transition in form (i.e., dependence to independence) belies a fundamental continuity in function (i.e., the capacity to self-regulate in accordance with developmentally salient challenges and resources). Similarly, children with histories of avoidant attachment can display anger in early development and passivity in later development (Sroufe and Jacobvitz 1989), yet this is not an example of inconsistency, but rather reflects changes in the form or expression of continuous maladaptation.

A central premise of this chapter is that, as with development broadly, we may best understand IGTM by attending to the multidimensional nature of continuity in terms of form *and* function. In homotypic continuity, both adaptive form and function are continuous, as when a history of child physical abuse predicts perpetration of child physical abuse on the next generation. In heterotypic continuity, the adaptive form may change while the function remains constant, as when a history of child physical abuse predicts perpetration of child emotional abuse on the next generation. This integrated view of IGTM offers a framework within which both types of continuity are appreciated and acknowledged, but appropriately distinguished such that information can be gained about persistence of form and/or function.

A Multidimensional View of Child Maltreatment

It is important to consider possible differences in the form of IGTM continuity because child maltreatment represents a constellation of related, yet distinct, experiences. Most forms of maltreatment involve acts of commission that inflict direct harm on a child (i.e., child physical abuse, CPA; child sexual abuse, CSA; child emotional abuse, CEA), but others involve acts of omission that deny a child basic developmental needs (i.e., child neglect, CN). Even within the broader category of abuse, there are important distinctions with respect to the target of injury (e.g., physical injury; attack on sense of self; Socolar et al. 1995; Toth et al. 1997) and developmental effects on particular domains of adaptive functioning (e.g., CPA and aggression; CN and impaired social relationships; Briere and Runtz 1990; Hildyard and Wolfe 2002). Individual maltreatment experiences also differ with respect to the severity of the event, the identity of the perpetrator, and ages of onset and offset. Despite robust differences across individuals' experiences of child maltreatment, however, researchers often proceed as though any childhood adversity at the hands of a caregiver is equivalent. As attention to each of these features is appropriately increasing in the maltreatment literature broadly, we believe the study of IGTM will particularly benefit from greater attention to the specific implications of maltreatment subtype.

Consideration of subtypes remains a challenge in broader maltreatment research as well. Given considerable comorbidity across maltreatment experiences (Claussen and Crittenden 1991; Higgins and McCabe 1999; Ney et al. 1994), it is often difficult to identify unique effects associated with each type of exposure. Should one attempt the difficult task of obtaining a sample that has experienced a single type of maltreatment, the sample would likely differ from typically maltreated children, who generally experience multiple subtypes in combination (Claussen and Crittenden 1991). Moreover, there are statistical challenges to obtaining information about individual subtypes in samples that have experienced multiple forms of maltreatment. The dominant homogenized maltreatment model, which was largely born out of necessity, has generated useful information about overall patterns of child maltreatment. However, a shift toward greater specificity has begun to establish a new paradigm, one in which consideration of individual differences in maltreatment experience is paramount. Studies increasingly emphasize the importance of unique effects of single maltreatment types, and, more recently, this work has been extended to successfully reveal unique effects of different combinations of multiple maltreatment subtypes (Berzenski and Yates 2011; Pears et al. 2008). As applied to the study of IGTM, we suggest that a focus on subtype specificity will reveal that, just as the experiences of subtypes of maltreatment have different correlates and consequences, the continuity of these experiences across generations may vary as well.

A Multidimensional View of IGTM Phenomenology

Adopting a nuanced appreciation for meaningful distinctions across forms of continuity (Rutter 1989), as well as forms of maltreatment (Briere and Runtz 1990), we offer a sensitive and specific framework to guide future research on IGTM. Thus far, studies of IGTM have classified caregivers as maltreated if they experienced one or more of any subtype of abuse or neglect, even when some participants experienced one type of maltreatment and other participants experienced different or multiple types. Likewise, researchers typically define maltreatment as continuous across generations if the children of these caregivers experience one or more subtypes of abuse or neglect. While aggregated studies have been the norm, and were perhaps necessary to establish broad parameter estimates of IGTM, the failure of extant research to converge on a coherent model of IGTM suggests that it is time to refine our focus.

Kaufman and Zigler (1989) argued that it was *not* important to separately examine subtypes (specifically CPA, CSA, and CN) in research on IGTM "because the intervention implications of these three forms of maltreatment are quite similar" (p. 130). Nearly 25 years ago, this assertion may have been both useful and appropriate. However, in light of new information regarding the specificity of maltreatment experiences, effects, and intervention efforts (e.g., MacMillan et al. 2009), the utility of this unitary framework has been realized and may, in fact, inhibit progress toward a complete understanding of IGTM. We argue that a more precise paradigm will clarify extant research findings and reveal previously obscured patterns of continuity and discontinuity.

First, greater attention to maltreatment subtypes will contribute to increased clarity in the communication of research findings. Until recently, the majority of studies on IGTM have been done with participants who experienced CPA alone or in combination with other maltreatment subtypes. In fact, there are no known studies with aggregated samples of maltreatment that exclude CPA. Indeed, the entire literature on rates and mechanisms of IGTM might be more accurately described as a compendium on the intergenerational transmission of CPA. At times, even studies exclusively measuring CPA have referred to it simply as 'abuse,' with cursory acknowledgment of the specific content of the experience restricted to the method section (e.g., Pears and Capaldi 2001). In other studies, distinct types of child maltreatment (e.g., CPA and CEA; CPA and CN) are combined into a homogenous construct (i.e., "maltreatment"), even when the heterogeneity of these experiences is acknowledged (Berlin et al. 2011; Cort et al. 2011; Dixon et al. 2005; Egeland and Susman-Stillman 1996; Hunter and Kilstrom 1979). Although some studies have investigated the continuity of particular subtypes of maltreatment, certain types have been investigated more than others (i.e., CPA and CSA more than CEA or CN). Moreover, the field suffers from a lack of integration with respect to information learned from these individual studies. Therefore, it is essential to distinguish research studies that represent findings specific to one type of maltreatment (usually CPA) from those that can be generalized across multiple types of maltreatment, and it is equally important to integrate research on other individual subtypes into this corpus of work.

Second, greater specificity may clarify the meaning of variability in published rates of IGTM across studies and samples. Confounding single and multiple maltreatment experiences may contribute to confusion when trying to compare transmission rates across studies. In addition, attempting to compare separate studies in which different experiences of maltreatment are treated as equivalent (e.g., one study in which participants experienced CPA and CN, and one in which they experienced CPA and CEA) may cause findings to appear inconsistent due to methodological, rather than actual, differences. Parsing experiences of multiple versus unitary maltreatment, and of different types of maltreatment, may uncover previously undiscernable information about each experience and clarify rates of IGTM.

Third, type-specific investigations may reveal important information about mechanisms by which specific maltreatment experiences are transmitted. Certain types of maltreatment may be more vulnerable to particular mechanisms of transmission than others and/or specific mechanisms may operate differently in the context of particular maltreatment subtypes. Although it is less common to experience one type of maltreatment than multiple types, findings regarding independent subtypes may nevertheless shed light on basic developmental processes that underlie the phenomenon of IGTM as a whole. Eventually, this understanding may inform discussions of IGTM patterns and suggest how various mechanisms may interact in the context of each individual's unique experiences. Therefore, we will both review literature that has homogenized the experience of IGTM and integrate studies of individual subtypes of IGTM to elucidate differences and commonalities in the phenomenology and etiology of IGTM.[1]

---

[1] We examine CPA, CSA, CEA, and CN in this chapter. While exposure to domestic violence (DV) is a pernicious form of child maltreatment, a vast literature exists on the IGT of DV, the exploration of which is beyond the scope of this review. Indeed the entirely separate literature on DV illustrates our concern that research on IGTM has been constrained by a lack of integration of research on unitary experiences, and the exclusion of multiply embedded contexts. Moreover, we specifically examine IGTM in mothers and exclude fathers from this discussion. While there is some research on fathers as perpetrators of maltreatment, this extra dimension is ancillary to our main focus on subtypes of maltreatment in our current discussion. Therefore, when we discuss type-specific transmission of CSA, for example, we will be referring to mothers who experienced CSA and their children who have experienced CSA, even though mothers do not typically perpetrate this type of maltreatment.

As discussed previously, *homotypic IGTM* occurs when a mother who experienced a particular type of maltreatment has a child who experiences the same type of maltreatment (e.g., CPA for the mother and for the child). *Heterotypic IGTM* occurs when a mother who experienced a particular type of maltreatment has a child who experiences a different type of maltreatment (e.g., CPA for the mother and CEA for the child). Despite variation in form, heterotypic IGTM is functionally continuous in that both mother and child are maltreated, albeit in different ways. Of note, studies that aggregate different subtypes of maltreatment experienced by the mother, the child, or both, preclude identification of the specific form of continuity and thus constitute instances of *undifferentiated IGTM*.

Homotypic and Heterotypic IGTM

Adopting a multidimensional view of continuity when studying IGTM opens several promising questions: First, is homotypic continuity more prevalent than heterotypic continuity? A few studies have examined type-specific IGTM to evaluate the hypothesis that homotypic continuity is more common than heterotypic continuity. However, these studies have had mixed results, which may be due to their varying methodological approaches. For example, some comparisons used control groups or otherwise accounted for base rates of maltreatment subtypes (Kim 2009; Ney 1988), yet others did not include these directed comparisons, and subsequently reported less evidence for type-specific IGTM (Pianta et al. 1989b). While second generation maltreatment is often measured as a composite of multiple subtypes, the studies mentioned above, as well as key examples of single subtype investigations, can begin to shed light on the extent of type-specific IGTM for each of the four subtypes of child maltreatment examined here. In so doing, we will address a second question about whether particular types of maltreatment are more vulnerable to homotypic continuity than others.

Child physical abuse. Studies of CPA reveal moderate consistency of transmission rates. Pears and Capaldi (2001) investigated CPA in a sample of at-risk boys and found that 23 % of mothers who had experienced CPA had physically abused their sons, while 10 % of mothers who had not experienced CPA had physically abused their sons. They concluded that CPA increased the odds of second generation CPA by a factor of 2. Even more strikingly, Kim (2009) found that CPA in the first generation increased the odds of CPA in the second generation by a factor of 5, with 15.7 % of CPA mothers' children experiencing CPA, compared to 3.6 % of non-CPA mothers. Moreover, Kim was one of only a few investigators to compare rates of homotypic CPA transmission to those of heterotypic CPA transmission while taking base rates into account. In this sample, 17.6 % of CPA mothers had children with histories of CN, which was similar to the 15.7 % rate of homotypic CPA transmission; however, when compared to the base rate incidence of CN among *non-CPA* mothers, which was 13 %, CPA in the first generation did not significantly increase the likelihood of second generation CN. Taken together, these findings suggest that homotypic continuity for CPA is greater than heterotypic continuity, once base rates are taken into account. Pianta and colleagues (1989b) found a very similar 17 % homotypic transmission rate of CPA by age 6, but this number was not compared to rates among non-CPA mothers. Although Pianta and colleagues (1989b) suggest that their findings did not support type-specific continuity because the same percentage (17 %) of CPA mothers had children with CN, their percentages mirror Kim's (2009) findings, and cannot be interpreted fully in the absence of a base rate comparison. Additionally, Ney (1988) found that the correlations between mothers' CPA and CPA in the next generation were comparable to correlations between CPA and CEA in the next generation, and higher than those between CPA and CN or CSA, which were not significant. However, the absence of base rate comparisons limited the author's ability to interpret these findings with regard to the relative magnitude of homotypic versus heterotypic IGTM. On the whole, research suggests that there is significant homotypic continuity of CPA (see Ertem et al. 2000, for review), but variability in both methodology (e.g., base rate comparisons) and sampling (e.g., documented vs. reported maltreatment; clinical vs. community samples) precludes any firm conclusions regarding specific rates of IGTM of CPA at this time.

Child sexual abuse. Most studies examining the IGTM of CSA do not compare CSA to other forms of abuse. Although several studies have published rates of homotypic CSA transmission, findings are complicated by the notable discontinuity between victims and perpetrators across generations. While male victims of CSA are often studied as potential perpetrators of CSA in the next generation, female CSA victims may not perpetrate CSA, but still may have children who experience CSA at the hands of their partners or other adults who have access to their children (Glasser et al. 2001). Maternal behaviors that contribute to CSA in the next generation may be better classified as neglect due to failure to protect the child, which makes it difficult to talk about type-specific CSA transmission in consistent terms. As discussed earlier, however, this review focuses on specific maltreatment experiences of mothers and their children irrespective of perpetrator identity. Thus, we define instances when mothers with a history of CSA have children who experience CSA as homotypic IGTM of CSA. This nuanced approach to understanding the IGTM of CSA highlights another advantage of differentiating among subtypes of IGTM, as mechanisms underlying homotypic CSA transmission may differ from instances when a formerly victimized parent becomes the direct perpetrator of the same type of abuse in the second generation.

In general, studies of homotypic CSA transmission put rates between 20 % and 30 % (Beltran 2010), but it is difficult to compare these studies methodologically. Many studies on CSA in particular are retrospective, drawing on samples of sexually abused children and inquiring about the maltreatment history of their parents (see Collin-Vezina and Cyr 2003, for review). This method of IGTM estimation provides inflated rates compared to prospective or quasi-prospective studies. Moreover, as noted previously, these studies often do not include control groups with which to look at odds ratios or make base rate comparisons. Two studies on samples of sexually abused children have included control groups, and both find increased rates of CSA among the children of CSA mothers (57 % compared to 44.7 % of controls, Leifer et al. 2004; 74 % compared to 25.8 % of controls, Oates et al. 1998). Still, even with the inclusion of a control group, these studies are not comparable to those adopting quasi-prospective designs to investigate other types of maltreatment, as sampling may be inherently biased in retrospective studies. One study that recruited families for domestic violence, rather than CSA, found an increased risk of CSA of 3.6 times for girls whose mothers had experienced CSA (McCloskey and Bailey 2000). Biased sampling approaches, such as patients who are currently in therapy (Glasser et al. 2001), and the absence of prospective designs limit our understanding of CSA transmission. Indeed, some research suggests that, though moderate homotypic continuity of CSA may exist, rates may be lower than heterotypic relations between CSA and physical CN (Ney 1988), which may be consistent with the categorization of second generation sexual abuse as a "failure to protect" the child on the part of the mother. In sum, relative to the literature on the IGTM of CPA, less is known about transmission patterns of CSA.

Child emotional abuse. There is a very small literature on the IGTM of CEA. This dearth of information is particularly concerning amidst increasing evidence that CEA may be the most pernicious form of maltreatment (Berzenski and Yates 2010, 2011; Kent et al. 1999; McGee et al. 1997; Spertus et al. 2003; Yates and Wekerle 2009). Ney (1988) found that CEA correlated most strongly with CEA in the next generation, with smaller but significant relations with CPA and a non-significant relation with emotional CN in the next generation. Perhaps more than any other subtype, research on CEA is complicated by a lack of definitional clarity, and an underrepresentation of CEA reports in documented maltreatment cases. Therefore, it may be useful to begin studying the IGTM of CEA by examining relations between CEA in the first generation and rejecting or verbally hostile parenting in the second generation. Studies of this nature provide some support for homotypic transmission of CEA (Whitbeck et al. 1992), but there is insufficient research to determine both whether or not CEA evidences higher rates of homotypic continuity, relative to heterotypic transmission patterns (i.e., type-specific transmission), and the specific IGTM rates of each.

Child neglect. As discussed previously, CN differs from other maltreatment types, in that it consists of acts of omission, rather than commission. Therefore, the IGTM of CN may differ from other types of maltreatment. Failure to protect a child by exposing her/him to other types of maltreatment is one area in which CN overlaps with other reported instances of maltreatment, but several other forms of neglect exist. CN may take on physical, supervisory, and/or emotional forms, but the field has not yet parsed the IGTM of CN across those specific categories. Kim (2009) found that 21.1 % of parents who experienced CN had children with CN histories, compared to 9.3 % of parents who did not experience CN (an odds ratio of 2.61). Among parents with a history of CN, 9.9 % physically abused their children, compared to 5.1 % without such histories (an odds ratio of 2.03). However, although both homotypic and heterotypic transmission rates were significant, only mothers' CN (and not mothers' CPA history) predicted CN in the second generation when other factors (e.g., ethnicity, number of children in the household) were controlled. Although they did not report specific IGTM rates for CN, Pianta and colleagues (1989b) observed that the maltreatment of children whose mothers had a history of CN "primarily took the form of neglect" (p. 244). Ney (1988) found that mothers' own physical CN was most strongly related to physical CN of their own children, and, secondarily, to CSA in the next generation. Although these relations are consistent with a model of failure to protect, the obtained correlations were not significant. In contrast, Ney (1988) found that mothers' own history of emotional CN was significantly correlated with their child's emotional CN, as well as with CEA and, to a lesser extent, CPA in the next generation.

Summary. Taken together, these findings suggest that type-specific transmission of child maltreatment does exist, such that homotypic continuity of IGTM is more prevalent than heterotypic continuity of IGTM, although the extent and details of this phenomenon remain unclear. In most studies that used odds ratios and base rates, the experience of a type of maltreatment was more likely to relate to that same type of maltreatment in the second generation (i.e., homotypic IGTM) than to other types (i.e., heterotypic IGTM), though other types of maltreatment remain more likely to occur than no maltreatment at all. Such instances of type-specificity (i.e., higher rates of homotypic IGTM relative to heterotypic IGTM) were most pronounced in studies of CPA, however, this is also the area in which the most studies have been conducted. That said, in cases where CPA and CN were examined in the same sample, CPA seemed to evidence more type-specific transmission than CN. More studies of particular subtypes of maltreatment transmission, within sample comparisons of type-specific transmission, and continued comparison and integration of these findings, are essential next steps toward a comprehensive and necessarily multidimensional understanding of IGTM.

Undifferentiated IGTM

Beyond the form of continuity and the relative prevalence of type-specific transmission, a third question informed by this new framework for understanding IGTM asks whether certain subtypes of maternal maltreatment are more vulnerable to IGTM in general than others. Studies measuring undifferentiated IGTM, in which experiences in the second generation are aggregated across type, are best suited to address this third question. In one sample of maltreated mothers, for example, mothers who had specifically experienced CPA had children who had been maltreated 68.1 % of the time, compared to 61.7 % of non-CPA mothers, while mothers who had experienced CSA had maltreated children 71.6 % of the time compared to 59.1 % of non-CSA mothers, and mothers who had experienced CN had maltreated children 63.7 % of the time, compared to 64.2 % of non-CN mothers (Zuravin et al. 1996). Although these rates of undifferentiated IGTM are fairly comparable, the authors note that there was a trend for CSA to increase the risk of second generation maltreatment marginally more than the other two types of maltreatment. Similarly, Pianta and colleagues (1989b) found a rate of

60 % transmission from mothers with a history of CPA to any type of maltreatment by age 6, a 69.2 % rate in mothers with a history of CSA, and a 44.4 % rate in mothers with a history of CN. Spieker and colleagues (1996) compared odds ratios in a logistic regression predicting aggregated child maltreatment and found that CPA and CSA had similar weights, with CSA yielding an odds ratio of 2.6 for second generation maltreatment, while CPA was slightly lower at 2.3. Lastly, Berlin and colleagues (2011) found that 16.7 % of mothers who had experienced CPA had maltreated children, compared with 7.1 % of controls, whereas 9.4 % of mothers who had experienced CN had maltreated children, which was a non-significant difference compared to 7.7 % of controls with maltreated children. Additionally, although Ney (1988) analyzed subtypes of maltreatment independently, he found higher correlations between mothers' own CPA, CEA, and emotional CN experience and maltreatment of their own children, than between mothers' own history of physical CN or CSA in and maltreatment of their children.

Summary. Evidence as to whether specific types of maltreatment in one generation differ in their likelihood of predicting any maltreatment in the next generation remains equivocal. There seems to be trend suggesting that CSA may evidence slightly higher rates of undifferentiated continuity, followed by CPA, and then CN. This lack of clarity may follow from the varied methodological and definitional challenges researchers face when studying any particular maltreatment type. Moreover, other aspects of the maltreatment experience may affect IGTM rates, and may differ systematically between subtypes. For example, severity of maltreatment is associated with higher rates of IGTM (Collin-Vezina and Cyr 2003; Crouch et al. 2001; Leifer et al. 2004; Spieker et al. 1996; Zuravin et al. 1996), and certain types of maltreatment may average higher severity rates than others. Alternately, certain forms of maltreatment may evidence greater comorbidity with other maltreatment types, which, in turn, is associated with higher rates of IGTM (Kim 2009). Albeit mixed, the extant evidence base highlights the need for ongoing research efforts, and illustrates how a multidimensional model of continuity in research on IGTM can further these efforts.

A Multidimensional View of IGTM Etiology

As with rates of transmission, the mechanisms by which maltreatment in the first generation influences the prevalence and form of maltreatment in the second generation may vary by subtype. In studies that have examined specific types of maltreatment, it is possible to examine the mechanisms associated with each type to inform an integrated view of if and how these mechanisms may vary across different forms of maltreatment. Given the lack of clarity in aggregated research studies, we focus our discussion of IGTM etiology on studies of specific maltreatment subtypes. Mechanisms of IGTM fall into three categories when viewed from the multidimensional perspective: those that are specific to particular subtypes (e.g., only explain transmission of CPA but not other types of maltreatment), those that appear to be common to all subtypes, and those that are present across multiple types of maltreatment but operate differently depending on the subtype.

IGTM Mechanisms Specific to Subtypes

Several mechanisms for IGTM have been identified specifically in studies of CPA, including parents' use of and attitudes toward discipline, and the depth of parents' social networks. Consistency of parental discipline in the second generation has been supported as an explanatory mechanism underlying the IGTM of CPA, with research suggesting that lower levels of disciplinary consistency are associated with higher rates of homotypic IGTM (Pears and Capaldi 2001). Similarly, social learning theory and mechanisms suggest that parents' aggressive behavior toward their children may be a learned behavior stemming from observing their own parents' aggressive disciplinary styles, particularly for understanding IGTM in the related domain of corporal punishment (Muller et al. 1995). Crouch and colleagues (2001) suggest that social support may influence CPA transmission. By assessing mothers' retrospective perceptions of early social support in their own childhood, they determined that mothers' own CPA experiences were associated with less perceived early support, less current social support, and increased risk of CPA for their own children. These findings illustrate the power of social relationships and are consistent with well supported models of undifferentiated IGTM, which indicate that social isolation contributes to IGTM (Berlin et al. 2011), whereas stable adult relationships are a key factor in breaking the abuse cycle (Egeland et al. 1988).

Mechanisms that have been specifically noted in studies of other types of maltreatment include a high rate of substance abuse with homotypic CSA transmission (Leifer et al. 2004; McCloskey and Bailey 2000) and low marital quality with rejecting parenting behaviors in parents who experienced CEA (Belsky et al. 1989). However, given the dearth of studies examining transmission of specific maltreatment types apart from CPA and CSA, it is premature to draw conclusions about IGTM mechanisms that are specific to particular maltreatment subtypes. These mediators may need to be tested in studies focused on other types of IGTM. For example, research on the sequelae of CN suggests that it predicts social withdrawal (Hildyard and Wolfe 2002) and that social withdrawal in turn is a risk for perpetrating CN (Coohey 1996). Based on these associations, it stands to reason that social isolation may be a mediator of CN transmission, but this link has yet to be tested directly. Additionally, there may be other as yet unexplored mechanisms of transmission that are subtype-specific.

IGTM Mechanisms Common Across Subtypes

Insecure attachment has been implicated in the IGTM of several maltreatment subtypes, including CPA and CSA, as well as in studies of undifferentiated continuity (Collin-Vezina and Cyr 2003; Egeland et al. 2002, 1988; Leifer et al. 2004; Rodriguez and Tucker 2011; Zuravin et al. 1996). Difficulty forming healthy attachments has been identified as a consequence of multiple types of child maltreatment, as each type interferes in some way with the perception of caregivers as reliable sources of security. Attachment theory proposes that the nature of the early relationship between the primary caregiver and the child influences and shapes the child's construction of beliefs and expectations about how s/he will be treated by significant others (Bowlby 1982). At an early age, the child constructs a cognitive model that best fits the reality of her/his experience. This model is maintained largely outside of awareness and greatly influences how an individual perceives and interprets the behavior of others (Weinfield et al. 1999). A young child who is exposed to sensitive, emotionally responsive, and consistent care develops beliefs that others will be available, supportive, and can be counted on in times of distress. Physically abused children develop beliefs and expectations that others are likely to reject them, will respond in a hostile fashion, and cannot be trusted or counted on for support. Neglected children expect others to be unresponsive, unavailable, and/or unwilling to meet their needs. Given the pernicious impact of malevolent caregiving on attachment, it is not unexpected that insecure and/or disorganized attachment organizations are a shared mechanism underlying IGTM across multiple maltreatment types. Difficulties forming and maintaining positive relationships are also implicated in undifferentiated IGTM research (Egeland et al. 1988; Leifer et al. 2004; Lunkenheimer et al. 2006) and further support the salience of attachment organization as a subtype-general mechanism of IGTM.

IGTM Mechanisms That Operate Differently Depending on Subtype

Lastly, common factors have been implicated in the IGTM of multiple types of maltreatment, but these same factors may operate in unique ways to foster or hinder the transmission of a particular maltreatment type. For example, parental psychopathology consistently emerges as a probable mechanism of transmission in a variety IGTM studies, yet the specific influence of particular forms of psychopathology on the transmission of specific maltreatment subtypes may vary. In the case of CPA, both depression and posttraumatic stress disorder (PTSD) have been shown to *reduce* the likelihood of IGTM (Pears and Capaldi 2001). However, regarding CSA, depression and PTSD have been shown to *increase* the likelihood of IGTM (Leifer et al. 2004). Evaluating yet another type of psychopathology, research has shown that dissociation predicts increased IGTM of *both* CPA and CSA (Collin-Vezina and Cyr 2003; Leifer et al. 2004; Narang and Contreras 2000), as well as undifferentiated IGTM (Egeland and Susman-Stillman 1996). Indeed in one instance, when aggregating experiences of CPA and CN in the same study, psychopathology did not emerge as a significant mediator of IGTM (Berlin et al. 2011). This may reflect effects in opposite directions for CPA and CN simply cancelling each other out. This study is yet another indicator that aggregation may obscure important findings specific to individual subtypes, and that mediation analyses should be specific to both types of maltreatment and types of psychopathology.

One possible explanation for this particular discrepancy is that CPA involves a direct act against a child, which may be less likely to be carried out if highly symptomatic mothers disengage with the parenting task. In contrast, CSA may become more likely in the context of maternal disengagement, which may follow from high levels of internalizing problems and is consistent with the previously described "failure to protect" model of CSA transmission. This would leave the child vulnerable to CSA by other perpetrators, while actually acting as a protective factor against active CPA by the parent. However, it is also worth acknowledging that depending on the nature of the analysis it could be that parents who perpetuate the CSA cycle experience more psychopathology in the aftermath of this occurrence rather than before it, due to the difficulty in dealing with their child having gone through the same experience as they had (Oates et al. 1998). Furthermore, dissociation, which mediates both types of abuse continuity, may be the exception to this disengagement model because it may be indicative of more severe disturbances in coherent understanding of the abuse experience and ability to integrate it. This finding is consistent with research demonstrating both integration of experience, and the related factor of extended experience in therapy, are predictors of breaking the abuse cycle (Egeland et al. 2002, 1988).

In addition to factors that differentially increase or decrease the likelihood of IGTM, other factors may be universally protective, but differ in the mechanism by which they operate. For example, awareness and coherent understanding of one's childhood experiences, which has been implicated in many types of IGTM (Egeland et al. 1988), may protect children against maltreatment transmission for different reasons depending on the subtype. For CPA transmission, it may be important in helping a mother with a history of CPA in her childhood to be more forgiving of her child's missteps and less prone to CPA in disciplinary contexts. Alternatively, for CSA transmission, awareness of one's own past may help a mother identify with her child's vulnerability and recognize a need for protection from potential CSA perpetrators. Once again, more detailed investigations of IGTM pathways, focusing on particular subtypes, are indicated in further understanding these mechanisms. Furthermore, no known studies of IGTM of CEA or CN exclusively have been identified. Therefore, discussions of mechanisms of transmission in these particular subtypes at this point would be purely speculative.

Future Directions and Recommendations

Growing evidence suggests there is a significant degree of homotypic IGTM. However, there is a need for substantially more evidence from comparative studies, as well as from independent studies of specific types of maltreatment, to solidify the interpretations offered here. Particularly in the case of

CPA, where the most work has been done, a maternal history of CPA appears to be associated with an increased risk of CPA in the next generation (i.e., homotypic IGTM), though it is also less robustly linked with other types of maltreatment (i.e., heterotypic IGTM). Definitional and methodological issues pervade all maltreatment research, but the lack of evidence is particularly troublesome in the case of CEA and CN. Although we do not propose that IGTM is by any means exclusively homotypic, the preponderance of evidence suggests that there is at least a modicum of type-specific IGTM such that, by and large, rates of homotypic IGTM exceed those of heterotypic IGTM across maltreatment subtypes.

In terms of undifferentiated IGTM, studies that aggregate maltreatment subtypes in the second generation suggest that each subtype of parent's own maltreatment is more likely to lead to some form of maltreatment in the second generation as compared to not being maltreated. Although modest, the extant evidence suggests that these rates of undifferentiated IGTM may be most pronounced in the wake of parent's own histories of CPA or CSA, relative to histories of CEA or CN. As discussed previously, however, it is possible that this evidentiary base reflects the relatively greater corpus of research on CPA and CSA, relative to that on CEA and CN.

Regarding the etiology of IGTM, select mechanisms may be specific to particular types of maltreatment transmission, such as disciplinary actions and attitudes being uniquely related to CPA transmission. Other mechanisms seem common to all types of maltreatment, such as social and attachment difficulties. Finally, it's very intriguing that certain mechanisms appear to be universally involved in IGTM, but operate differently depending on the specific subtype of maltreatment. In particular, some forms of psychopathology, such as depression, may be implicated in the transmission of both CPA and CSA, but operate very differently in the context of each, with depression *decreasing* rates of CPA transmission and *increasing* CSA transmission. The clarity afforded by a multidimensional approach to understanding IGTM may counter or clarify the null or inconsistent findings that have been obtained in undifferentiated studies of maltreatment (e.g., Berlin et al. 2011; Dixon et al. 2005).

Given the variation in mechanisms of transmission across subtypes, feasibly implementing targeted clinical interventions may prove difficult. Therefore, attachment, as a mechanism that appears universal, is potentially the most promising area in which to efficiently intervene. Empirical data support an association between parents' cognitive representations of their own childhood relationships and the quality of attachment they form with their infants (Zeanah et al. 1993). Yet Collins (1996) and others have shown that cognitive models formed based on early relationship experiences may change as the individual encounters new relationship experiences. Using relationship-based intervention techniques and strategies, a number of promising programs exist that are designed to promote a secure attachment and enhance the quality of the parent-child relationship (for a review, see Sameroff et al. 2004 and Egeland et al. 2000). However, very few attachment-based programs have been implemented and evaluated with maltreating parents. One exception is the work of Cicchetti et al. (2006) at Mt. Hope Family Center, where infants and preschoolers were randomly assigned to Psychoeducational Parent Training or Child Parent Psychotherapy, and were compared to a group of mothers and infants who were receiving treatment-as-usual services in the community. Post-intervention findings indicated that the two interventions were equally successful in increasing attachment security, whereas the community sample continued to display high rates of attachment insecurity and disorganization (Cicchetti et al. 2006). Using a new sample of preschool children with histories of maltreatment, these researchers evaluated the effects of the two interventions on the child's cognitive model. The children in the Child Parent Psychotherapy condition evidenced a greater decline in maladaptive representations of self and mother relative to children in the Psychoeducational intervention and community samples. These results differ from those with infants in that only the relationship-based intervention resulted in more positive representations of self *and* mother compared to the intervention that focused on parenting skills (Toth et al. 2002). These findings point to the malleability of representations of self and caregiver using a relationship-based intervention derived from attachment theory. This broad approach to intervention with maltreated children has tremendous implications for preventing maltreatment in the next generation.

Although we believe the field is ripe for the adoption of this new multidimensional perspective on IGTM, we recognize that this process will be accompanied by many challenges. First and foremost, the noted comorbidity of maltreatment types makes subtype-specific investigations important, but also makes it difficult to draw conclusions about specific types of maltreatment in isolation. In addition, the other features of maltreatment that make individual experiences distinct (e.g., severity, perpetrator, chronicity) also deserve attention in this new specificity-oriented framework. We suggest that a paradigm shift toward an emphasis on maltreatment subtype will pave the way for increasingly specified investigations and foster our ability to address each and every feature of an individual's experience of IGTM. Similarly, the environmental characteristics that covary with maltreatment (e.g., risky neighborhoods, poverty) often persist across generations and contribute to IGTM. As such, broader contextual influences of risk (and protection) should be integrated into a fully specified model of IGTM. Our focus here is on subtypes of maltreatment because they represent the broadest level at which we can begin to examine specific experiences. However, we support and encourage a more basic evolution in how we think about IGTM, as well as greater attention to specificity wherever appropriate and whenever possible. In light of these limitations, we offer recommendations that detail the successive increments by which this paradigm can be practically applied in research and practice.

The multidimensional model of IGTM detailed in this chapter points to several recommendations to advance future research on IGTM. First, more work needs to be done on independent subtypes of maltreatment, their potential for type-specific IGTM, their transmission to composite measures of child maltreatment (i.e., undifferentiated IGTM), and mechanisms of transmission that may be specific to each subtype, general across types, or operate in different ways across types. In particular, CEA and CN are virtually untouched areas of study. Despite the difficulties inherent in measuring these types of maltreatment, it is imperative that we attempt to focus more attention on these areas, even if only by directing increased attention to related constructs, such as parental rejection (e.g., Belsky et al. 1989), for the time being. Just as the overall maltreatment literature has acknowledged an increased need for research on CEA and CN, so, too, does the literature on IGTM call for their due consideration.

Second, studies that already measure several types of maltreatment must put forth greater effort to compare them explicitly, rather than simply aggregating or ignoring the existence of subtypes. Although aggregation may be appropriate and informative for some analyses, as well as a necessity given statistical power considerations, it would be helpful to also include comparative analyses, or at least descriptive results, along with more traditional, main-effect models. Providing descriptive information when a given study lacks the power to appropriately test differences would nevertheless provide invaluable information to future meta-analysts who could eventually combine the information from several small studies of this type. As these types of comparisons begin to converge on common rates of transmission and estimates of homotypic continuity, intervention and prevention efforts can be more appropriately allocated and structured.

Third, as more evidence becomes available in these areas, it will be necessary to do a more comprehensive analysis in which evidence from various studies can be compared and integrated through a conceptual review or, ideally, a meta-analysis. The available evidence already provides fertile ground for this type of investigation, however, once certain areas (e.g., CEA and CN) are enhanced, a meta-analysis of rates and mechanisms of transmission of subtypes will be extraordinarily helpful.

Finally, in the absence of one's ability to do more research in this area, to change one's methodology, and/or to modify the types of maltreatment sampled or measured, we offer a universal recommendation to be more careful about how we discuss these constructs and how we frame our interpretations. Part of the danger in extant research approaches rests in their lack of clarity about definitions of maltreatment. In addition to definitional clarity, interpretations must be approached carefully. If aggregated maltreatment groups are used, conclusions should not be drawn about single subtypes (e.g., abuse, if abuse and neglect are included concurrently). Similarly, in examinations of single subtypes, generalizations about mechanisms of transmission of maltreatment broadly should not be made. To the extent that we fail to adopt greater specificity in our dissemination efforts, we risk overlooking important implications for practice at best or misinforming prevention and intervention efforts at worst.

Despite gaps in extant research on IGTM, and the need for clarity and explication in several areas, we believe the field is ready for a more focused and considered program of research on IGTM. Indeed, the variability of extant research findings points to the need for a change in perspective and approach. In order for the field to progress beyond adding generalized studies with similarly variable findings, we need to change our framework, and move towards greater specificity. From this shift in paradigm we will be able to more effectively target intervention and preventive efforts toward appropriate avenues and more fully understand the developmental pathways from unique experience to adaptation.

References

Belsky, J. (1993). Etiology of child maltreatment: A developmental ecological analysis. *Psychological Bulletin, 114*(3), 413–434. doi:10.1037/0033-2909.114.3.413.

Belsky, J., Youngblade, L., & Pensky, E. (1989). Childrearing history, marital quality, and maternal affect: Intergenerational transmission in a low-risk sample. *Development and Psychopathology, 1*(04), 291–304. doi:10.1017/S0954579400000481.

Beltran, N. P. (2010). Long-term psychological consequences of child sexual abuse. *Papeles del Psicologo, 31*(2), 191–201.

Berlin, L. J., Appleyard, K., & Dodge, K. A. (2011). Intergenerational continuity in child maltreatment: Mediating mechanisms and implications for prevention. *Child Development, 82*(1), 162–176. doi:10.1111/j.1467-8624.2010.01547.x.

Berzenski, S. R., & Yates, T. M. (2010). A developmental process analysis of the contribution of childhood emotional abuse to relationship violence. *Journal of Aggression, Maltreatment & Trauma, 19*(2), 180–203. doi:10.1080/10926770903539474.

Berzenski, S. R., & Yates, T. M. (2011). Classes and consequences of multiple maltreatment: A person-centered analysis. *Child Maltreatment, 16*(4), 250–261. doi:10.1177/1077559511428353.

Bowlby, J. (1982). *Attachment and loss: Vol. 1. Attachment* (2nd ed.). New York: Basic Books.

Briere, J., & Runtz, M. (1990). Differential adult symptomatology associated with three types of child abuse histories. *Child Abuse & Neglect, 14*(3), 357–364. doi:10.1016/0145-2134(90)90007-G.

Cicchetti, D., Rogosch, F. A., & Toth, S. L. (2006). Fostering secure attachment in infants in maltreating families through preventive interventions. *Development and Psychopathology, 18*(3), 623–650. doi:10.1017/S0954579406060329.

Claussen, A. H., & Crittenden, P. M. (1991). Physical and psychological maltreatment: Relations among types of maltreatment. *Child Abuse & Neglect, 15*(1–2), 5–18. doi:10.1016/0145-2134(91)90085-R.

Collins, N. L. (1996). Working models of attachment: Implications for explanation, emotion, and behavior. *Journal of Personality and Social Psychology, 71*, 810–832. doi:10.1037/0022-3514.71.4.810.

Collin-Vezina, D., & Cyr, M. (2003). Current understanding about intergenerational transmission of child sexual abuse. *Child Abuse & Neglect, 27*(5), 489–507.

Coohey, C. (1996). Child maltreatment: Testing the social isolation hypothesis. *Child Abuse & Neglect, 20*(3), 241–254. doi:10.1016/S0145-2134(95)00143-3.

Cort, N. A., Toth, S. L., Cerulli, C., & Rogosch, F. (2011). Maternal intergenerational transmission of childhood multitype maltreatment. *Journal of Aggression, Maltreatment & Trauma, 20*(1), 20–39. doi:10.1080/10926771.2011.537740.

Crouch, J. L., Milner, J. S., & Thomsen, C. (2001). Childhood physical abuse, early social support, and risk for maltreatment: Current social support as a mediator of risk for child physical abuse. *Child Abuse & Neglect, 25*(1), 93–107. doi:10.1016/S0145-2134(00)00230-1.

Dixon, L., Browne, K., & Hamilton-Giachritsis, C. (2005). Risk factors of parents abused as children: A mediational analysis of the intergenerational continuity of child maltreatment (part I). *Journal of Child Psychology and Psychiatry, 46*(1), 47–57. doi:10.1111/j.1469-7610.2004.00339.x.

Egeland, B. (1993). A history of abuse is a major risk factor for abusing the next generation. In R. Gelles & D. R. Loseke (Eds.), *Current controversies on family violence* (pp. 197–208). Newbury Park: Sage.

Egeland, B., & Susman-Stillman, A. (1996). Dissociation as a mediator of child abuse across generations. *Child Abuse & Neglect, 20*(11), 1123–1132. doi:10.1016/0145-2134(96)00102-0.

Egeland, B., Jacobvitz, D., & Sroufe, L. A. (1988). Breaking the cycle of abuse. *Child Development, 59*(4), 1080–1088. doi:10.2307/1130274.

Egeland, B., Weinfield, N. S., Bosquet, M., & Cheng, V. K. (2000). Remembering, repeating and working through: Lessons from attachment-based interventions. In J. D. Osofsky & H. E. Fitzgerald (Eds.), *Infant mental health in groups at high risk* (WAIMH handbook of infant mental health, Vol. 4, pp. 35–89). New York: Wiley.

Egeland, B., Bosquet, M., & Chung, A. L. (2002). Continuities and discontinuities in the intergenerational transmission of child maltreatment: Implications for breaking the cycle of abuse. In K. Browne, H. Hanks, P. Stratton, & C. E. Hamilton (Eds.), *Early prediction and prevention of child abuse: A handbook* (pp. 217–232). Chichester: Wiley.

Ertem, I. O., Leventhal, J. M., & Dobbs, S. (2000). Intergenerational continuity of child physical abuse: How good is the evidence? *The Lancet, 356*, 814–819.

Glasser, M., Kolvin, I., Campbell, D., Glasser, A., Leitch, I., & Farrelly, S. (2001). Cycle of child sexual abuse: Links between being a victim and becoming a perpetrator. *The British Journal of Psychiatry, 179*(6), 482–494. doi:10.1192/bjp.179.6.482.

Higgins, D. J., & McCabe, M. P. (1999). Multiple forms of child abuse and neglect: Adult retrospective reports. *Aggression and Violent Behavior, 6*(6), 547–578. doi:10.1016/S1359-1789(00)00030-6. DOI:10.1016/S1359-1789%2800%2900030-6#doilink.

Hildyard, K. L., & Wolfe, D. A. (2002). Child neglect: Developmental issues and outcomes. *Child Abuse & Neglect, 26*(6–7), 679–695. doi:10.1016/S0145-2134(02)00341-1.

Hunter, R., & Kilstrom, N. (1979). Breaking the cycle in abusive families. *The American Journal of Psychiatry, 136*(10), 1320–1322.

Kaufman, J., & Zigler, E. F. (1989). The intergenerational transmission of child abuse. In D. Cicchetti & V. Carlson (Eds.), *Child maltreatment: Theory and research on the causes and consequences of child abuse and neglect* (pp. 129–150). New York: Cambridge University Press.

Kaufman, J., & Zigler, E. F. (1993). The intergenerational transmission of abuse is overstated. In R. Gelles & D. R. Loseke (Eds.), *Current controversies on family violence* (pp. 209–221). Newbury Park: Sage.

Kent, A., Waller, G., & Dagnan, D. (1999). A greater role of emotional than physical or sexual abuse in predicting disordered eating attitudes: The role of mediating variables. *International Journal of Eating Disorders, 25*(2), 159–167. doi:10.1002/(SICI)1098-108X(199903)25:2<159::AID-EAT5>3.3.CO;2-6.

Kim, J. (2009). Type-specific intergenerational transmission of neglectful and physically abusive parenting behaviors among young parents. *Children and Youth Services Review, 31*(7), 761–767. doi:10.1016/j.childyouth.2009.02.002. DOI:10.1016/j.childyouth.2009.02.002#doilink.

Leifer, M., Kilbane, T., & Kalick, S. (2004). Vulnerability or resilience to intergenerational sexual abuse: The role of maternal factors. *Child Maltreatment, 9*(1), 78–91. doi:10.1177/1077559503261181.

Lunkenheimer, E., Kittler, J., Olson, S., & Kleinberg, F. (2006). The intergenerational transmission of physical punishment: Differing mechanisms in mothers' and fathers' endorsement? *Journal of Family Violence, 21*(8), 509–519. doi:10.1007/s10896-006-9050-2.

MacMillan, H. L., Wathen, C. N., Barlow, J., Fergusson, D. M., Leventhal, J. M., & Taussig, H. N. (2009). Interventions to prevent child maltreatment and associated impairment. *The Lancet, 373*(9659), 250–266. doi:10.1016/s0140-6736(08)61708-0.

McCloskey, L. A., & Bailey, J. A. (2000). The intergenerational transmission of risk for child sexual abuse. *Journal of Interpersonal Violence, 15*(10), 1019–1035. doi:10.1177/088626000015010001.

McGee, R. A., Wolfe, D. A., & Wilson, S. K. (1997). Multiple maltreatment experiences and adolescent behavior problems: Adolescents' perspectives. *Development and Psychopathology, 9*(1), 131–149. doi:10.1017/S0954579497001107.

Muller, R. T., Hunter, J. E., & Stollak, G. (1995). The intergenerational transmission of corporal punishment: A comparison of social learning and temperament models. *Child Abuse & Neglect, 19*(11), 1323–1335. doi:10.1016/0145-2134(95)00103-F.

Narang, D. S., & Contreras, J. M. (2000). Dissociation as a mediator between child abuse history and adult abuse potential. *Child Abuse & Neglect, 24*(5), 653–665. doi:10.1016/S0145-2134(00)00132-0.

Ney, P. G. (1988). Transgenerational child abuse. *Child Psychiatry and Human Development, 18*(3), 151–168. doi:10.1007/BF00709728.

Ney, P. G., Fung, T., & Wickett, A. R. (1994). The worst combinations of child abuse and neglect. *Child Abuse & Neglect, 18*(9), 705–714. doi:10.1016/0145-2134(94)00037-9.

Oates, R. K., Tebbutt, J., Swanston, H., Lynch, D. L., & O'Toole, B. I. (1998). Prior childhood sexual abuse in mothers of sexually abused children. *Child Abuse & Neglect, 22*(11), 1113–1118. doi:10.1016/S0145-2134(98)00091-X.

Pears, K. C., & Capaldi, D. M. (2001). Intergenerational transmission of abuse: A two-generational prospective study of an at-risk sample. *Child Abuse & Neglect, 25*(11), 1439–1461. doi:10.1016/S0145-2134(01)00286-1.

Pears, K. C., Kim, H. K., & Fisher, P. A. (2008). Psychosocial and cognitive functioning of children with specific profiles of maltreatment. *Child Abuse & Neglect, 32*(10), 958–971. doi:10.1016/j.chiabu.2007.12.009.

Pianta, R. C., Sroufe, L. A., & Egeland, B. (1989a). Continuity and discontinuity in maternal sensitivity at 6, 24, and 42 months in a high-risk sample. *Child Development, 60*(2), 481–487. doi:10.2307/1130992.

Pianta, R. C., Egeland, B., & Erickson, M. F. (1989b). The antecedents of maltreatment: Results of the mother-child interaction research project. In D. Cicchetti & V. Carlson (Eds.), *Child maltreatment: Theory and research on the causes and consequences of child abuse and neglect* (pp. 203–253). New York: Cambridge University Press.

Rodriguez, C. M., & Tucker, M. C. (2011). Behind the cycle of violence, beyond abuse history: A brief report on the association of parental attachment to physical child abuse potential. *Violence and Victims, 26*(2), 246–256.

Rutter, M. (1989). Pathways from childhood to adult life. *Journal of Child Psychology and Psychiatry, 30*(1), 23–51. doi:10.1111/j.1469-7610.1989.tb00768.x.

Rutter, M., & Sroufe, L. A. (2000). Developmental psychopathology: Concepts and challenges. *Development and Psychopathology, 12*, 265–296. doi:10.1017/S0954579400003023.

Rutter, M., Kim-Cohen, J., & Maughan, B. (2006). Continuities and discontinuities in psychopathology between childhood and adult life. *Journal of Child Psychology and Psychiatry, 47*(3–4), 276–295. doi:10.1111/j.1469-7610.2006.01614.x.

Sameroff, A. J., & Chandler, M. J. (1975). Reproductive risk and the continuum of caretaking casualty. In F. D. Horowitz, M. Hetherington, S. Scarr-Salapatek, & G. Siegel (Eds.), *Review of child development research* (Vol. 4, pp. 187–243). Chicago: Chicago University Press.

Sameroff, A. J., McDonough, S. C., & Rosenblum, K. L. (Eds.) (2004). *Treating parent-infant relationship problems: Strategies for intervention.* New York: Guilford Press.

Socolar, R. R. S., Runyan, D. K., & Amaya-Jackson, L. (1995). Methodological and ethical issues related to studying child maltreatment. *Journal of Family Issues, 16*(5), 565–586. doi:10.1177/019251395016005004.

Spertus, I. L., Yehuda, R., Wong, C. M., Halligan, S., & Seremetis, S. V. (2003). Childhood emotional abuse and neglect as predictors of psychological and physical symptoms in women presenting to a primary care practice. *Child Abuse & Neglect, 27*(11), 1247–1258. doi:10.1016/j.chiabu.2003.05.001.

Spieker, S. J., Bensley, L., McMahon, R. J., Fung, H., & Ossiander, E. (1996). Sexual abuse as a factor in child maltreatment by adolescent mothers of preschool aged children. *Development and Psychopathology, 8*(03), 497–509. doi:10.1017/S0954579400007239.

Sroufe, L. A. (1979). The coherence of individual development: Early care, attachment, and subsequent developmental issues. *American Psychologist, 34*(10), 834–841. doi:10.1037/0003-066X.34.10.834.

Sroufe, L. A. (1990). An organizational perspective on the self. In D. Cicchetti & M. Beeghly (Eds.), *The self in transition: Infancy to childhood* (pp. 281–307). Chicago: The University of Chicago.

Sroufe, L. A., & Jacobvitz, D. (1989). Diverging pathways, developmental transformations, multiple etiologies and the problem of continuity in development. *Human Development, 32*(3–4), 196–203. doi:10.1159/000276468.

Sroufe, L. A., & Rutter, M. (1984). The domain of developmental psychopathology. *Child Development, 55*, 17–29. doi:10.2307/1129832.

Toth, S. L., Cicchetti, D., Macfie, J., & Emde, R. N. (1997). Representations of self and other in the narratives of neglected, physically abused, and sexually abused preschoolers. *Development and Psychopathology, 9*(4), 781–796. doi:10.1017/S0954579497001430.

Toth, S. L., Maughan, A., Manly, J. T., Spagnola, M., & Cicchetti, D. (2002). The relative efficacy of two interventions in altering maltreated preschool children's representational models: Implications for attachment theory. *Development and Psychopathology, 14*, 877–908. doi:10.1017/S095457940200411X.

Waddington, C. H. (1940). *Organizers and genes.* Cambridge: Cambridge University Press.

Weinfield, N. S., Sroufe, L. A., Egeland, B., & Carlson, E. (1999). The nature of individual differences in infant-caregiver attachment. In J. Cassidy & P. Shaver (Eds.), *Handbook of attachment: Theory, research, and clinical application* (pp. 68–88). New York: Guilford Press.

Werner, H. (1957). The concept of development from a comparative and organismic point of view. In D. B. Harris (Ed.), *The concept of development* (pp. 125–148). Minneapolis: University of Minnesota Press.

Whitbeck, L. B., Hoyt, D. R., Simons, R. L., Conger, R. D., Elder, G. H., Lorenz, F. O., et al. (1992). Intergenerational continuity of parental rejection and depressed affect. *Journal of Personality and Social Psychology, 63*(6), 1036–1045. doi:10.1037/0022-3514.63.6.1036.

Yates, T. M., & Wekerle, C. (2009). The long-term consequences of childhood emotional maltreatment on development: (Mal)adaptation in adolescence and young adulthood [Special issue]. *Child Abuse & Neglect, 33*.

Zeanah, C. H., Benoit, D., Barton, M., Regan, C., Hirshberg, L., & Lipsitt, L. (1993). Representations of attachment in mothers and their one-year-old infants. *Journal of the American Academy of Child and Adolescent Psychiatry, 32*, 278–286. doi:10.1097/00004583-199303000-00007.

Zuravin, S., McMillen, C., DePanfilis, D., & Risley-Curtiss, C. (1996). The intergenerational cycle of child maltreatment. *Journal of Interpersonal Violence, 11*(3), 315–334. doi:10.1177/088626096011003001.

Chapter 7
Poverty and Child Maltreatment

Brett Drake and Melissa Jonson-Reid

Child maltreatment and poverty are strongly associated with each other, but we lack a comprehensive understanding of why and how they are associated. This chapter will overview theories and empirical findings relating to poverty and child maltreatment in an attempt to show various ways in which poverty and child maltreatment may be related. It is our central premise that no single explanatory model of this relationship exists. There is no "one size fits all" way of understanding how poverty and child maltreatment relate to each other. Most prominent in its absence is a satisfying and empirically robust theory of the causal relationships between poverty and child maltreatment. Causation is an important question because understanding causality can provide guidance relating to practice and policy. For example, if we had confidence that the bulk of shared variance between maltreatment and poverty was because poverty caused maltreatment, then this would suggest that child welfare intervention and policy should focus either on poverty directly (e.g. through poverty alleviation programs) or indirectly (e.g. through programs designed to buffer the impact of poverty upon maltreatment risk). On the other hand, if individual level factors (such as inability to tolerate stress) or structural factors (such as availability of key resources) are important in causing both poverty and child maltreatment independently, then a logical place to start would be a reduction of those underlying factors, with gains to be expected in both poverty and maltreatment.

The explicit acknowledgement of the strong relationship between poverty and child maltreatment dates back at least a generation, to Leroy Pelton's seminal 1978 work "Child Abuse and Neglect: The Myth of Classlessness." At that time, there were many reasons for scholars to avoid acknowledging that child maltreatment and poverty were related, including a preoccupation with psychodynamic causality, an unwillingness to frame child maltreatment as a problem specific to the "underclass", and a desire not to engage in socioeconomic victim-blaming (Pelton 1978; Drake and Pandey 1996). It was widely believed at that time that known socioeconomic disparities in official child maltreatment rates stemmed from the increased visibility of the poor (Jason 1984) or reporting bias (Zellman 1992) rather than from a higher incidence of actual child maltreatment among the poor. In the past 30 years these views have changed substantially, partly due to several large federally funded research programs which have addressed the issue, most notably the National Incidence Studies on Child Abuse and Neglect (NIS). These data have been supported by a range of cross-sectional studies (Berger 2004; Drake and Pandey 1996), some longitudinal work (e.g. Nikulina et al. 2011; Jonson-Reid et al. 2009) and the increasing availability and quality of administrative child welfare and child well-being data.

B. Drake, Ph.D. (✉) • M. Jonson-Reid, Ph.D.
Brown School of Social Work, Washington University in St. Louis, Campus Box 1196,
One Brookings Drive, St. Louis, MO 63119, USA
e-mail: brettd@wustl.edu; jonsonrd@wustl.edu

J.E. Korbin and R.D. Krugman (eds.), *Handbook of Child Maltreatment*, Child Maltreatment 2,
DOI 10.1007/978-94-007-7208-3_7, © Springer Science+Business Media Dordrecht 2014

Poverty

Defining Poverty. Poverty can be variously described. Sometimes people will define poverty at the individual or family level. This can be done as a continuous measure (e.g. income per year in dollars) or as a dichotomous (yes/no) measure, such as if the family or individual is below the federal poverty line or is receiving public assistance or publically funded medical care. Researchers have also examined individual and family poverty in relation to the level of difficulty securing material resources (Slack et al. 2004) and the presence or absence of assets independent of income (Shanks 2011).

Poverty can also be discussed as a neighborhood variable. Neighborhood poverty is most usefully measured at the tract or zipcode level (Aron et al. 2010; Lery 2009) and may represent the percentage of residents (or families, or children) below the poverty line (e.g. 42 % of families below poverty) or may describe their median income (e.g. $23,098 per family per year). Each measure of poverty (individual/family or neighborhood) has advantages and disadvantages. For example, if you are interested in understanding a family's ability to afford quality day care, the family level variable may be more important. If you are interested in understanding a family's exposure to environmental risks associated with poverty (e.g. limited local resource availability) then the neighborhood measure variable may be of more interest.

Poverty is not a stand-alone construct. It is closely associated with a number of other factors, including age, education, and family structure. In addition, poverty is not static; people move in and out of poverty. This section will briefly cover some of the key relationships between poverty and other factors which bear on child maltreatment.

Poverty, Time and Age. Poverty is a burden carried mainly by the young. 20.7 % of all American children are below the poverty level. Similarly, 20.7 % of Americans aged 18–24 are below the poverty level, with 14.9 % of people aged 25–34 being below the poverty level. Only 10 % or less of all age groups over 45 are in poverty (U.S. Census Bureau 2012 Table 713). From a historical perspective, rates of child poverty have formed something of a shallow "U" over the past two decades. The lowest rate in the last 30 years was 15.6 % in 2000, while rates in the early 1990s and currently are about 20 %.

At the individual level, poverty changes over time. One way to think about the dimension of time is to ask the question "how likely is a person to be poor at any time in their lives?" By age 65, more than half of all Americans will have spent a year below the poverty line (Rank and Hirschl 1999). This number is far worse for Blacks, with 84 % spending at least a year in poverty by age 65. While we tend to think of "the poor" as a stable group, this is simply not the case, with people moving in and out of poverty over time.

Poverty and Family Structure. Family structure is also strongly related to poverty. Among married-couple families in 2009, the median income was $71,627. For male householders with no spouse present, this drops to $41,501 and the corresponding number for female householders is $29,770, only 42 % that of married couple families (U.S. Census Bureau 2012).

All of the above relationships interact with the issue of child maltreatment. In almost every respect, those families most at risk for child maltreatment are also disfavored by the demographics of poverty.

Poverty and Race. When considering poverty, there are important complexities attendant to race which should be mentioned. Income or below poverty measures will almost always understate financial stresses on racial minorities, particularly Blacks. When comparing Black and White families of equal income or poverty status, the White families will tend to have much higher assets (Shanks 2011; Oliver and Shapiro 2006) and will generally live in areas with lower neighborhood poverty. For example, in the year 2000, 14.6 % of poor white children lived in high poverty neighborhoods – neighborhoods with 40 % childhood poverty or higher. The corresponding figures for Blacks and Hispanics are 43.5 % and 33.1 %, respectively (Drake and Rank 2009). In short, poor minority children commonly live in poor areas, while poor white children are far more likely to live in middle-class neighborhoods.

Are We Really Sure Poverty and Child Maltreatment Are Associated?

Research is consistent in findings that poor children are overrepresented among maltreated children at a ratio of 3:1 or higher. There are two major recent efforts to better understand child maltreatment using nationally representative samples, the National Incidence Studies (NIS) and the National Study on Child and Adolescent Well Being (NSCAW).

The fourth National Incidence Study on Child Abuse and Neglect (NIS-4: Sedlak et al. 2010) is the largest epidemiological study to date designed to measure actual child maltreatment in the United States. The NIS identifies maltreatment both through the use of official reports and also through contacting "sentinels" in the community – individuals such as doctors and teachers who should be aware of maltreatment if present. Using the "endangerment" standard, which is not dissimilar from "substantiated" in child welfare parlance, they found that parents not in the labor force were about three times as likely to maltreat their children compared to employed parents (Sedlak et al. 2010, pp. 5–7). Parents categorized as "Low SES" were about five times as likely to maltreat their children as other parents (Sedlak et al. 2010, pp. 5–15). These differences were most pronounced for neglect (a difference of about seven to one) and less pronounced for physical and sexual abuse (differences of about three to one). This finding of neglect having more sensitivity to poverty is consistent with other work (Coulton et al. 1995; Drake and Pandey 1996).

Unlike the NIS, The National Study on Child and Adolescent Well-Being II (NSCAW II) includes only officially reported children. Baseline data show that 58.1 % of officially reported families with in-home biological parents live below the poverty level (Dolan et al. 2011, p. 10). This is a rate about three times as great as the national child poverty rate of about 20 %, consistent with the NIS findings.

The findings from NIS and NSCAW findings are representative of the general literature. We now have access to a wide range of studies using very different methods from very different parts of the country, and they are quite consistent in showing a similar maltreatment differential associated with poverty. For example, full-population studies using administrative data consistently show about a three to one increased risk for poor children compared to nonpoor children (Sabol et al. 2004; Putnam-Hornstein and Needell 2011), and often with higher ratios for neglect than for other kinds of maltreatment (Drake and Pandey 1996). Recently, birth records have been linked to child abuse reporting data with similar findings across several different states. In Alaska, California, Florida and Georgia a set of between 5 and 8 perinatal risk factors predicted later maltreatment in early childhood. Some of the common factors across sites are highly associated with poverty such as maternal age less than 20 years, births to unmarried mothers, being a Medicaid beneficiary, and a history of inadequate prenatal care (Putnam-Hornstein and Needell 2011; Wu et al. 2004; Zhou et al. 2006). These effects have been shown to hold within Black, Hispanic and White racial groups (Freisthler et al. 2007).

Greater debate exists as to the relative difference income makes within a disadvantaged population. Some studies of families exiting Temporary Assistance for Needy Families (TANF) have found somewhat conflicting relationships between income and maltreatment for certain subgroups. For example, Nam and colleagues (2006) found that for women without a prior work history, getting a job after TANF actually increased the risk of CPS investigation. Another study found that increased earnings through employment after TANF was associated with a decreased likelihood of a report of maltreatment controlling for whether or not the exit from TANF was voluntary (Beimers 2009). A study of TANF applicants found little relationship of income per se to maltreatment, but did find an association between hardships experienced due to poverty and maltreatment (Dworsky et al. 2007). Finally, a study of TANF recipients using an experimental design found that small increases in income over a given year were associated with a decrease in likelihood of a screened in report of maltreatment (Cancian et al. 2010).

The Question of Anti-Poor Bias in Identifying Child Maltreatment

Do poor people get reported or investigated more just because they're poor? While this sounds reasonable, and undoubtedly does happen, research suggests that bias is not the key factor driving the overrepresentation of the poor in child welfare caseloads. There is a long history of vignette studies which have been consistent in showing no associations or low associations between SES and stated intention to report (Turbett and O'Toole 1983; Benson et al. 1991; Zellman 1992). Recent work (Laskey et al. 2011) has continued this trend, with a randomized large scale vignette study (N = 2,109) showing that low SES only slightly increased likelihood of an abuse diagnosis (48 % vs. 43 %) among physicians. Among the more powerful associations reported was a one-third higher rate of skeletal surveys being ordered by physicians among poor infants with traumatic brain injury, compared to nonpoor infants (Wood et al. 2010). Increased rates of skeletal surveys could uncover more evidence of injury and therefore lead to higher reporting rates.

Another way to evaluate the degree to which the SES association with maltreatment may be a biased or non-biased measurement is to observe other child well-being indicators which are not subject to bias in reporting. Chief among these is infant mortality. While national data on infant mortality relative to poverty are unavailable, state level data can be located. In Milwaukee, zipcode level analysis suggests that infant mortality rates are about three times higher (18 per 1,000 live births compared to 6 per 1,000 live births) when comparing zip codes with median incomes below $30,000 per year to zip codes with incomes in the $40,000 per year or higher range (City of Milwaukee Health Department 2010). In Michigan, infant death rates were about two and a half times higher for children in census tracts with 20 % or greater poverty when compared to children in tracts with less than 5 % poverty (Michigan Department of Community Health 2010).

One recent study used a wide range of data sources to address the issue of poverty bias directly (Jonson-Reid et al. 2009). This study attempted to determine if poor children reported to child welfare looked the same across a wide range of characteristics and outcomes as other poor children. If poverty alone were sufficient to cause child welfare system involvement, if poor people were commonly reported without valid reason, then one might expect poor children who are reported to child welfare and poor children who are not reported to look fairly similar to each other. On the other hand, if the child welfare reporting system is capturing families with different levels of need than those who are low income but not reported, then you would expect those poor children who are reported to show evidence of much higher risk factors and higher numbers of negative outcomes compared to children who are never reported. Jonson-Reid and colleagues (2009) followed three groups of children using cross-sector administrative data, with children followed for at least 12 years. The first group (n = 3,337) included children who had received Aid to Families with Dependent Children ("AFDC") or Temporary Assistance to Needy Families ("TANF") and had also had a child abuse or neglect ("CAN") report, the "CAN/AFDC" group. The second group – "AFDC Only" (n = 2,389) included children with a history of AFDC or TANF but no history of a CAN report. The final group included children with a CAN report but no AFDC or TANF history, the "CAN only group" (n = 1,587). Compared to other poor children who did not have a CAN report, poor children with CAN reports were more than three times more likely to have a status offense, more than twice as likely to have a record of juvenile delinquency, almost twice as likely to have emergency room or hospital care for a violent injury, were about one and a half times as likely to have emergency room or hospital care for an unintentional head injury or fracture, were more than twice as likely to have a record of teen pregnancy and were more than four times as likely to receive mental health services. Compared to the CAN only group, the CAN/AFDC group was generally at about twice the risk for the above mentioned indicators. These ratios occurred after controlling for child gender, age, disability status, parental age at birth of child, parental substance abuse history, parental mental health history, and neighborhood income. We believe this study shows several things. First, and most importantly, the segment of the impoverished population which is formally identified by child protective services is at dramatically higher risk across a broad range of domains than other poor children who are not brought to the attention of CPS. Second, the higher risks and worse outcomes found in the CAN/AFDC group compared to the CAN only group demonstrates that among maltreated children, poor children seem to be at particularly high risk and to be more likely to experience negative outcomes.

In interpreting these findings, we are left with a fairly simple question – "can the much higher rates of child abuse reporting and identification among the poor be largely explained by bias?" The answer appears to be that while some limited bias may exist, there is no evidence suggesting that bias explains a large proportion of the observed 3:1 or higher differential between the poor and the non-poor in observed or reported child maltreatment. In summary, child maltreatment is clearly associated with poverty. The strength of this relationship is well established and remarkable in magnitude. What is not well understood at all are the dynamics of this relationship. There are any number of theoretical positions which could be postulated in explanation of this observed association. The next section will overview some of those models and frameworks.

Poverty and Child Maltreatment: Frameworks and Theories

Poverty: In the broadest sense, we might break theories of poverty into two classifications; the individual and the structural. These are sometimes linked with conservative and liberal political positions. Individual perspectives emphasize psychological constructs such as values, work ethics and other personal or family characteristics which support economic success, such as the ability to delay gratification and the development of pro-social skills. The structural perspective emphasizes social forces which directly impact the individual's capacity to earn. These include the availability of the necessary tools to procure a job, especially education. Even given that individuals can gain the skills necessary for employment, they also require that an open opportunity structure be in place so that qualified individuals can find work. As examples, the failure of many inner-city schools and the decline in manufacturing jobs in the United States are suggested as structural factors resulting in increased levels of poverty (Rank et al. 2003). The current mismatch between skill sets held by the unemployed and the large number of unfilled Science, Technology, Engineering and Mathematics (STEM) jobs is another example.

Child Maltreatment: There have been a number of grand theories and a number of specific models forwarded to explain why child maltreatment occurs. If one looks at theoretical models which have historically been used to attempt to understand child maltreatment they are striking in their focus on the individual and the family. Stress and coping theories, family systems theories, attachment theories and neurobiological explanations are quite common and may be presented with or without much emphasis on ecological levels beyond the immediate family. Explanations of maltreatment rooted in learning theory or psychodynamic approaches also tend to restrict key constructs to the parent, child and that immediate environment, even when acknowledging the importance of poverty (Polansky et al. 1972). It was, in part, a preoccupation with such theoretical positions which Pelton (1978) suggested may have caused the earlier tendency to view maltreatment and poverty as unrelated. An optimistic reader might note that these kinds of models are increasingly being embedded in an ecological context (e.g. Cicchetti and Valentino 2006), and a move towards more comprehensive and environmentally informed understandings of child maltreatment seems to be in progress. While theoretical enlightenment may have occurred in this respect, some who conduct research are still struggling with this issue "on the ground," as a few key studies still do not include environmental, or even income variables as controls.

Neighborhoods, Poverty and Child Maltreatment: It is well established that a range of social problems (crime, infant mortality, school dropout, child maltreatment, etc....) are "bundled"

(Sampson 2004, p. 107) at the neighborhood level, particularly in areas of concentrated poverty. The "why" of this bundling has been approached from a number of different perspectives. Frameworks direct us towards which domains should be considered and what perspectives we should take when we are attempting to understand child maltreatment in the neighborhood context. Coulton and colleagues (2007) have identified two distinct traditions used to understand neighborhood effects on child maltreatment, the first involves a sociological emphasis on poverty and problems in areas of concentrated poverty, while the second begins with individuals and families and focuses on child and family development and functioning within the broader environment. One could supplement Coulton and colleagues' two ways of understanding neighborhoods relative to child maltreatment by adding an additional general framework for considering poverty and child maltreatment structure per se – a more purely economic perspective (Becker 1978) emphasizing resource availability (services, quality education, good day care, employment opportunities, etc....).

The first set of perspectives look at neighborhood *context* and emphasize social disorganization, collective efficacy and other mechanisms by which neighborhood structures, norms and behaviors may influence their members. This is primarily a sociological approach, in which the initial focus is on the troubled community. Collective efficacy and social disorganization theories suggest that some communities have fewer social bonds, less ability to effectively meet challenges and little ability to exercise social control over members (Sampson 1992). Under such models, parents are seen as living up to (or down to) local expectations. Values, guidelines and expectations are seen as rooted in the community and having general impacts across a range of domains. In addition to values, a community with low collective efficacy lacks practical means to meet needs of its members. These can be formal, such as local community support programs which are effective and well integrated into the community, or informal, such as the willingness of neighbors to help others in times of need. The idea of social capital is similar and related. This idea incorporates aspects of community like collective efficacy but may also include individual factors like norms and values (Uphoff 1999). Hypothetically one could be poor but have high levels of social capital and have lower risk of untoward outcomes like maltreatment. One large cross-sectional study found a protective effect of social capital for neglect and psychologically harsh parenting, although the effect of effects associated with receipt of public assistance in models of neglect were not fully offset by social capital (Zolotor and Runyan 2006). Another study linked survey data with national child maltreatment report data and found that both poverty at the family and community level as well as social supports were important in explaining risk of child maltreatment (Merritt 2009).

The developmental/ecological perspective begins with a focus on children, families and parents and then moves outwards and asks how larger-level structures may impact them. These positions often trace back through Belsky (1990) or Bronfenbrenner (1979). At their core, these frameworks remind us to incorporate multiple levels of environmental influences while attempting to understand individuals and families. For example, Belsky encourages us to consider individual factors, family factors, community factors and cultural factors when attempting to understand child maltreatment. While historically important, these distinctions are largely in emphasis and accent. No matter how these frameworks are parsed, the subject matter remains the same – we are merely gazing into the same jewel through different facets. More complex models of how the community environment influences the family and subsequent outcomes are now being proposed (Shanks 2011) but remain largely untested.

In addition, it is possible that there are regional or cultural variations in how these factors influence the development of maltreating behavior. For example, a multilevel study examining how neighborhood characteristics affect parental corporal punishment and physical abuse in Chicago neighborhoods found that immigrant concentration (mostly Latino) at the neighborhood level was associated with lower risk for parent-child physical aggression controlling for child gender and age, family's SES, race, age, gender, unemployment, and family composition (Molnar et al. 2003). On the other hand, Hussey and colleagues (2005) using the National Longitudinal Study of Adolescent Health found that first generation youth were 1.55 times more likely to experience lack of supervision as children compared to native children after controlling for other factors like income and region of residence. Finally it appears that the intersection of poverty and race with maltreatment may vary according to whether a family resides in an urban or rural area (Schuck 2005).

Poverty and Parenting: Poverty is associated with a range of negative parental and family characteristics (Leventhal 2000) including hostile parenting (Afifi 2007) harsh discipline (Smith and Brooks Gunn 1997) and lower parental warmth (Brown et al. 1998). Poverty and fewer positive parenting practices have been shown to be associated with worse executive functioning and lower IQ, an outcome possibly mediated by child stress as measured by cortisol levels (Blair et al. 2011; Zalewski et al. 2012). There is some evidence that the relationship between poverty and maltreatment may be mediated (transmitted through) or moderated (changed by) parental and family characteristics. Slack and colleagues (2004) found evidence that good parenting characteristics can reduce the degree to which a history of infrequent employment may be associated with neglect. There is some recent longitudinally derived evidence that even within poor populations, negative parenting tends to recur within families intergenerationally (Kovan et al. 2009).

Emerging Theoretical Complexity: There is emerging consensus that the possible pathways between poverty and maltreatment may be both very complex and highly individualistic on a case-by-case basis. For example, the above cited work (Zalewski et al. 2012) suggests that poverty may cause parental stress, which may result in neglect or harsh parenting, which may result in stress in a child, which may result in specific physical reactions, particularly relative to the Hypothalamic-Pituitary-Adrenal (HPA) axis, which may result in long term negative cognitive and behavioral effects, which could easily feed back into higher risk of maltreatment. Such emerging models have multiple mediating constructs (parenting, child physiological response) and also multiple moderating constructs (social support, parental impulse control, child vulnerability to stress). The degree to which individuals vary in each of these constructs will substantially limit the explanatory power of any simple model. While not specific to maltreatment, Shanks (2011) postulates a similarly complex model that focuses on how community effects interact with family and individual effects to influence child well-being. While the empirical linkage between poverty and maltreatment is both robust and remarkable for the ease in which it can be scientifically determined through a number of different means, the unpacking of how that relationship manifests causally will be a daunting scientific challenge and is unlikely to result in a simple and satisfying "one size fits all" set of answers.

Poverty, Immigrants and Child Maltreatment

Hispanics are an increasingly large proportion of the United States population and are going to remain a population comprised largely of recent immigrants for the foreseeable future. As of 2005, the child population was 59 % White, 20 % Hispanic, 16 % Black and 5 % Asian. By 2050, it is projected that 35 % of children in the United States will be Hispanic, only slightly lower than the number of Whites (40 %). The percentage of Asians is expected to double, to 10 %, while the proportion of Blacks will drop slightly to 14 %. One might expect that this expansion in the Hispanic population will occur simultaneously with a higher rate of Hispanics who are not recent immigrants (a generational "aging" of the Hispanic population). This effect is not so strong as might be expected, however. The percentage of all Hispanics who are first-generation immigrants is currently 40 %, and is anticipated to drop only to 33 % by 2050. The percentage of Hispanics who are third generation or higher is expected to remain quite stable, moving from 32 % in 2005 to 33 % in 2050 (above figures from Passel and Cohn 2008). In simple terms, while the proportion of children who are Hispanics will continue to increase, they will continue to be largely first and second generation. This has implications for the rates of maltreatment we might expect in the future.

Currently, Hispanic families are about three times as likely to below the poverty level as White families, a ratio not dissimilar from Blacks. Despite this, their official child maltreatment rates are roughly the same as Whites, and considerably lower than that of Blacks (USDHHS 2011). It is unlikely that this is a result of reporting bias, as the roughly 1:1 correspondence between reported maltreatment between Hispanics and Whites is mirrored by similarities in infant mortality, low birth weight and prematurity (Drake et al. 2011), as well as being consistent with NIS-4 estimates (Sedlak et al. 2010). This has been referred to variously as the "Hispanic Paradox" or the "Healthy Immigrant Effect", sometimes simply as the "epidemiological paradox". It is has been comprehensively studied in the medical literature, especially with respect to perinatal issues, and holds even when controlling for a wide range of known risk factors (e.g. Romero et al. 2012). Recognition of this paradox is now emerging in the child welfare literature (Dettlaff 2012). It appears that parental behaviors at least partly mediate the relationship between immigration status and lower child maltreatment risk. "At the time of their infants' births, the Spanish-speaking Latina mothers demonstrated higher SES risk, whereas the English-speaking Latina and non-Latina Caucasian mothers demonstrated higher psychosocial risk. Three years later, the English-speaking Latina and non-Latina Caucasian mothers reported harsher parenting behaviors than the Spanish-speaking Latina mothers" (Martin et al. 2011, p. 64). This is supported by an analysis of data from the National Study of Child and Adolescent Wellbeing (NSCAW) which found higher levels of risk among native-born Hispanic mothers compared to foreign born Latino mothers in a child welfare sample (Dettlaff et al. 2009). The above findings also suggest a decay of the protection afforded by the healthy immigrant effect the longer a family remains in the United States

Child Welfare Services and Poverty

Modern child protective services were born in the wake of the groundbreaking article "the battered child syndrome", published in the Journal of the American Medical Association in 1962 (Kempe et al. 1962). It may be worth recalling how the authors of that work conceptualized the etiology of maltreatment:

> Psychiatric factors are probably of prime importance in the pathogenesis of the disorder, but our knowledge of these factors is limited. Parents who inflict abuse on their children do not necessarily have psychopathic or socio-pathic personalities or come from borderline socioeconomic groups, although most published cases have been in these categories. In most cases some defect in character structure is probably present; often parents may be repeating the type of child care practiced on them in their childhood. (Kempe et al. 1962)

We see that while the linkage with poverty existed from the beginning of the modern literature, the emphasis was squarely on psychological aspects of the perpetrator. One recent commentator notes that "The assumption early in the history of the modern child protection system was that the problem of child maltreatment was reducible to "syndromes" – in effect, that abusive and neglecting parents were either very sick or very evil" (Melton 2005, p. 11). The early avoidance of a more sociological or ecological shading of the issue makes sense as the pioneering works casting child welfare in eco-logical terms were still over a decade distant. It is with this background that any attempt to understand the role of child welfare services relative to poverty must begin. This primary focus on the individual continues to the present day, as modern characterizations of child maltreatment treatment or preven-tion (e.g. USDHHS 2008) still cast an overwhelming emphasis on parental factors and interventions directly bearing on parental behavior, such as child maltreatment awareness and parenting education. Only limited attention is paid to poverty-related issues such as the provision of concrete services.

As another example, one of the best online resources, the California Evidence Based Clearinghouse For Child Welfare (n.d.) cites 35 different topic areas (e.g. parent training, post-permanency services, youth transitioning into adulthood) without specific mention of socioeconomic factors and their role in maltreatment etiology or treatment. The Clearinghouse lists 21 programs relevant to child maltreatment which have been classified as having the highest scientific rating of "1," meaning the intervention is "well supported by research evidence." Of these programs, more than half are responses to specified mental health disorders (e.g. depression, substance abuse) and only two programs, both home visiting programs (Healthy Families America, Nurse Family Partnership) feature an emphasis on low income families. While other interventions can be applied to poverty-related issues (e.g. Multisystemic Therapy) the home visiting programs seem to be the current interventions most directly relevant to poverty.

Several studies have highlighted the degree to which families that come to the attention of child welfare are "multi-problem" families facing many additional barriers beyond poverty (Dworsky et al. 2007; Small and Kohl 2012; Walsh and Mattingly 2012). Even among families reported for the first time to child protective services, it is clear that many families not only need services but have already encountered other service systems for child or caregiver issues (Jonson-Reid et al. 2010). Unfortunately, in most cases the child protection staff are unaware of these pre-existing services and or needs, leading to some calling for greater connectivity between data systems to improve response to high risk families (Jonson-Reid and Drake 2008). It is not known how this might improve the capacity to complete effective case plans for families coming to the attention of child welfare for the first time.

Public child welfare is not typically charged with primary prevention, meaning that we do not usually consider child welfare intervention in terms of preventing initial maltreatment. Public child welfare is also generally not charged with secondary prevention; the provision of services to at-risk children. It is most commonly administered as tertiary prevention in expectation of reducing or preventing continued or subsequent maltreatment. A potential exception to this can be found in differential response (or "alternative response") systems which may provide services to high risk families that may or may not already be engaged in maltreating behaviors (e.g., Loman and Siegel 2012). Yet another exception can be found in the rare instances in which families who were "screened out" at the time of report due to not meeting criteria for abuse or neglect are connected to support services (Jonson-Reid et al. 2010; Loman et al. 2009; Waldfogel 2009). There is some indication that services directly addressing poverty for families where this is risk, reduce the later risk of maltreatment (Loman et al. 2009). In a school-based family support program, there was indication that the provision of case management and in-home family services reduced later reports of maltreatment (Jonson-Reid et al. 2010).

For families facing other barriers in addition to poverty such as adult mental health needs (Small and Kohl 2012), it seems likely that services would only be effective for those families where there is fit between the need and services. Lower income families may face significant barriers to accessing such services which may in turn result in reduction in the apparent effect of child welfare services since these services are dependent upon services provided by other organizations. Findings regarding the impact of family support child welfare services (the lowest intensity provided to families considered at lower risk) are at an early stage, although there are some studies suggesting positive effects of low intensity child welfare involvement (Jonson-Reid et al. 2010).

Child Welfare Policy and Poverty

Should poverty per se, manifesting in inability to provide children with basic necessities, be considered maltreatment? A number of states (e.g. Missouri, North Carolina) have legislated that situations due to poverty alone cannot be sufficient grounds for a finding of child maltreatment. From a different perspective, it has been posited that children living in conditions in which their basic needs are not met in a country with significant resources could be considered neglect at the societal level (Dubowitz et al. 1993). Certainly, not all poor children are at risk of maltreatment. As Jonson-Reid and colleagues (2009) point out, low income children reported for maltreatment appear to face worse challenges than similarly poor children who never come to the attention of CPS. A range of other known relationships, such as the Hispanic Paradox discussed earlier, also support the view that poverty in and of itself, is not the sole driver of maltreating behavior.

On the other hand, poverty is certainly not a desirable state for families at best and appears to be one of the prime factors in the development of abusive or neglecting behaviors at worst. With some exceptions (Duva and Metzger 2010) relatively little attention has been paid to understanding economic intervention as compared to parenting, mental health or other family functioning approaches, and much of that attention has been in governmental websites or the grey literature, forums aimed more squarely at practitioners and policy makers. A few researchers have directly called for improved provision of material supports to prevent maltreatment. For example, Courtney and colleagues (2005) found that after welfare reform there was an increased overlap between 1999 TANF applicants and child welfare as compared to 1996 AFDC applicants and child welfare, raising concerns that more concrete supports for persons newly entering the workforce were needed. To our knowledge no studies specific to employment support and maltreatment prevention exist. There are interesting emerging findings suggesting that the provision of concrete supports can have preventive impacts. A study of TANF recipients found that small increases in income over a given year were associated with a decrease in likelihood of a screened in report of maltreatment (Cancian et al. 2010). Some evidence from an evaluation of differential response in Minnesota suggests a positive impact on the provision of material assistance for lower risk families (Loman and Siegel, 2004).

Outside child welfare, home visitation has been widely supported as a means to prevent child abuse and neglect. Despite recent federal funding initiatives promoting home visitation, many promising home visitation programs and many key client populations have not been well studied (Daro and Dodge 2010; Paulsell et al. 2011). While nurse home visiting has been described as a well-researched intervention (California Evidence Based Clearinghouse For Child Welfare n.d.) most research has focused on models that target first-time mothers or programs that begin during the prenatal period. This makes it difficult to translate them directly to public child welfare settings, which are not primary prevention agencies. Results of past evaluations of nurse home visitation programs' efficacy in preventing child abuse range include positive, negative and inconclusive results (Duggan et al. 2000, 2007; LeCroy and Krysik 2011). While nurse home visiting models have typically targeted low income populations (Olds et al. 1999) the common restriction to first-time mothers or prenatal enrollment may exclude some of the highest risk populations that do not seek prenatal care within a given time frame (Katz et al. 2011) or experience depression after a significant duration of poverty and subsequent births (Abrams and Curran 2009). Few to scale versions of nurse home visiting target the level of risk faced by child welfare. An exception to this is the Nurses for Newborns model in Missouri. While not yet supported by randomized trial, a recent evaluation suggested that in rural areas the rates of child abuse and neglect reports were higher for families with screened out reports without NFN than families with screened out reports with NFN (Lanier et al. 2012).

A shift toward addressing the relationship between poverty and child maltreatment will require a shift toward thinking about the creation of a universal safety net sufficient to promote genuine child well-being. As many authors point out, services to low income families are siloed despite vast overlaps in the populations served, systems often provide only cursory services, and concerted efforts to monitor how the various systems do or do not interact to produce outcomes is non-existent in most areas (Courtney et al. 2008; Jonson-Reid and Drake 2008; Jonson-Reid 2011). MacMillan and colleagues (2009) point out that despite the promise and theoretical appeal of prevention programs at the community level that include a safety net for families, rigorous evaluations to help guide policy in this regard do not exist. There are two avenues for supporting improved policy in this regard. One is to build the infrastructure that rewards collaboration and tracks outcomes for multi-system families. This would allow for more accurate assessment of costs and savings for various policy and large scale program initiatives. Second, we could build on the small number of studies that address the promise of material supports. While there have been recent calls for studies on the impact of supportive housing

(Administration for Children and Families 2012), these are generally directed towards families already engaged in child welfare and are arguably too narrow and not sufficiently preventative. Perhaps a similar approach could be used to encourage large scale, rigorously evaluated approaches to addressing poverty at the family and/or community levels as maltreatment prevention. Further existing well-supported longitudinal studies like the Panel Study of Income Dynamics could be augmented so that links to community variables and child maltreatment outcomes (for example, child maltreatment reporting data) are included.

Macroeconomic Factors and Child Maltreatment

Scholars have long sought to understand to understand the association between macroeconomic factors, particularly unemployment, and child maltreatment. At the cross-sectional level, it is well established that neighborhood unemployment predicts child maltreatment reports (Freistler et al. 2004; Krishnan and Morrison 1995). This effect has been found separately both for male unemployment (Gillham et al. 1998) and for female labor force participation (Ernst 2000). What is less clear are temporal relationships between macroeconomic factors and child maltreatment rates over time. Finkelhor and Jones (2006) suggested that economic improvement in the 1990s may have contributed to the decline of abuse during that period. Early work from Colorado used longitudinal tracking of unemployment rates and child physical abuse reports, finding a strong link between unemployment and physical abuse, but not sexual abuse reports (Krugman et al. 1986). There has recently been a renewed interest in this area attendant to an unfortunate but scientifically useful natural experiment; the great recession.

Child Maltreatment Rates Over Time: General Findings. Our understanding of child maltreatment and poverty is strongly influenced by our understanding of child maltreatment as it fluctuates over time. By comparing changes in observed rates to known macroeconomic conditions, we can gain insight about possible relationships between the two. Unfortunately, this is not a straightforward exercise. Finkelhor and Jones (2006, 2009) have compared rates of physical and sexual abuse from national report (NCANDS) data to crime data from the National Crime Victimization Survey and found similar levels of decline in child abuse and juvenile criminal victimization (e.g. assault, robbery) during the 1992–2004 period, with most of these indicators dropping by about half. They did not note a corresponding drop in child neglect over the same period. They discuss a number of possible mechanisms for this decline, but favor three in particular; economic improvements during the 1990s, larger numbers of available change agents (helping professionals) and improved psychopharmacology. Their findings were recently supported by findings from the third and fourth waves of the National Incidence Studies, which also showed that maltreatment rates had declined between 1993 and 2006 (Sedlak et al. 2010). In summary, Finkelhor and Jones's work (2012) strongly indicates a drop in child sexual abuse, may indicate a drop in child physical abuse and does not provide evidence supporting a drop in child neglect.

When looking at national data, using substantiated cases or "victims" rather than raw report numbers may be problematic. According to national report data, in 1995, 36.7 % of the 2,723,001 investigated children were classed as "Substantiated" or "Indicated". In 2010, that number, including the new category of "Alternative Response Victim" had dropped to 23.7 % (USDHHS 1996; USDHHS 2011) of the 3,604,100 children who received a response. This probably reflects a tightening of criteria for substantiation and the increase in Alternative Response services, in which a substantiation decision is generally not made. Individual state substantiation levels (e.g. Missouri) clearly show how substantiation rates can drop dramatically after implementation of an Alternative Response track. In any case, the likelihood that substantiation criteria change over time makes comparison of substantiated or "victim" level data somewhat questionable. Other sources, such as raw reporting rates, or medical diagnostic data can also be subject to variability over time, as public awareness changes or medical professionals become more aware of or likely to provide a given diagnosis. Even given these weaknesses, we feel that reporting rates do provide a useful touchstone for understanding maltreatment rates over time.

The Great Recession and National Data. The National Child Abuse Data System (NCANDS) provides information on official child maltreatment reports. The simplest metric, reports with a disposition, has remained flat during the great recession so far. In 2010, there were 3.3 million referrals made, involving about 5.9 million children (USDHHS 2011). In 2006, there were 3.3 million referrals made, involving approximately 6.0 million children. Given the slight increase in child population during this timeframe, this may represent a slight decline in total reports. NCANDS also shows a decrease in child abuse victimization (essentially reports which are screened in and officially determined to be maltreatment) from 11.0 per 1,000 to 9.2 per 1,000 during the 2006–2010 timeframe (USDHHS 2011). The number of officially reported unique child fatalities during the immediate pre-recession period was 2.00/100,000 children in 2006, and 2.28 in 2007. The recession period numbers are similar, moving from 2.28 in 2007 to 2.32 in 2009 and down again to 2.07 in 2010.

It is possible, however, that the above numbers may mask larger changes in specific forms of abuse. Given the findings in the area of nonaccidental head trauma, we might expect that physical abuse would be increasing. This, however, is not the case. In 2006, 16.0 % of victims were found to suffer physical abuse, compared to 8.8 % for sexual abuse and 64.1 % for neglect in 2006 (USDHHS 2007). In 2010, 17.6 % of victims classified as suffering from physical abuse, 9.2 % for sexual abuse, while 78.3 % were reported for neglect (USDHHS 2011). The victimization type measure is overlapping, and the number of victimization types per victim increased from 1.14 in 2006 to 1.26 in 2010, reflecting a general trend for cases to be classified under more than one category. Despite this, it is evident that no large changes have occurred in the proportionalities of the different kinds of maltreatment among official victims.

Another possibility is that younger children may be more at risk during times of economic downturn. This might explain how findings of increased trauma among young children may be occurring in the face of stable overall maltreatment reporting rates. In 2006, 38.6 % of all victims were between the ages of 0 and 3. In 2010, this number dropped slightly to 34.0 % of all victims, contrary to what might be expected.

Some state level analyses are also available. Millett and colleagues (2011) tracked all seven states for which recent economic and child maltreatment data were available covering the period of the great recession; Arizona, California, Massachusetts, Missouri, North Carolina, Oregon and Wisconsin. Unemployment rates, labor force participation, and food stamp usage were compared to child maltreatment reports. In all cases, unemployment and food stamp use increased markedly during the period of the recession. In no state, however, did child abuse rates show an appreciable increase. Neither bivariate analyses, empirical growth plots nor regression analyses showed any relationship between these economic indicators and maltreatment reports in any state.

The Great Recession and Hospital Data. Several very recent studies have looked at rates of various kinds of brain injury relative to the great recession. Huang and colleagues (2011) looked at all traumas to children 0–2 years old in a single Level I pediatric trauma center. They tracked rates of "all traumas," "accidental head traumas" and "nonaccidental head traumas" during pre-recession (12/2001–11/2007) and recession (12/07 -6/10) periods. They found slight nonsignificant declines in monthly overall trauma rates when comparing pre-recession and recession periods (6.4 vs. 5.8 per month). They also found a slight reduction in accidental head trauma (2.0 vs. 1.9 per month). Conversely, they found a statistically significant doubling of nonaccidental head traumas when comparing the pre-recession and recession periods (0.7 vs. 1.4).

Berger and colleagues (2011) tracked rates of Abusive Head Trauma (formerly "Shaken Baby Syndrome") which was verified by hospital child protection teams in children under 5 years of age.

They split their data into pre-recession (1/2004 through 11/2007) and recession (12/2007 through 6/2009) periods. They studied three geographical areas, including a Pennsylvania region, an Ohio region and a region based around Seattle. This study found no association between rates of Abusive Head Trauma and unemployment rates, even when those rates were lagged. Rates of Abusive Head Trauma were between 25 % higher (Ohio region) and 140 % higher (Pennsylvania region). The Seattle region showed a 108 % increase in Abusive Head Trauma, despite three being virtually no change in the unemployment rates in that region (5.4 % vs. 5.6 %). If accurate, these findings suggest that one devastating but numerically small subset of physical abuse, Abusive Head Trauma, may be increasing, but that that increase is not linked to unemployment rates.

Wood and colleagues (2012) looked at data from 38 hospitals, linking them to macroeconomic indicators for the Metropolitan Statistical Areas in which each hospital was located. Interpretation of their findings is complicated, as they did not report physical abuse rates based on population, but reported physical abuse rates as a percentage of all hospital admissions, during a time in which total hospital admissions declined. They reported small increases in child physical abuse admission rates (as a proportion of all hospital admissions) and high risk TBI rates (as a proportion of all hospital admissions) in hospitals located in Metropolitan Statistical Areas with high foreclosure rates (Wood et al. 2012, pp. e360–e361). Counterintuitively, a "clear relationship between unemployment and physical abuse was not found" (Wood et al. 2012, p. 362). Of even greater interest, an examination of their data (figure 2, page e361) shows that rates of child abuse admissions and high risk TBI actually declined since the beginning of the great recession.

Another team (Leventhal and Gaither 2012) used data from the Kids Inpatient Database, most recently sampled from 44 states and 4,121 hospitals, tracking serious injuries due to physical abuse. They found that measured incidence estimates for 1997, 2000, 2003, 2006 and 2009 were generally flat, with a small increase in reports for children 0–18 years (6.1 per 100,000 vs. 6.4 per 100,000) from 2006 to 2009. The rate for children less than 1 year of age moved from 57.5 per 100,000 in 2006 to 62.3 in 2009. This last statistic is somewhat misleading, however, as the less than 1 year of age rate for 2002 was 62.1, virtually identical to the 2009 figure, the trend in the 2003–2009 period being essentially a shallow "v".

Summary of Differences in Magnitude of Macroeconomic Effects in Hospital Data. Huang and colleagues (2011) found a doubling of nonaccidental head trauma (but not of other kinds of trauma) at a single site, a very large difference when comparing the 6 years prior to and two and a half years following the great recession. Berger and colleagues (2011) looked at three hospitals, finding increases in Abusive Head Trauma ("Shaken Baby Syndrome") ranging from low (+25 %) to very large (+140 %) when comparing the 3 years prior to and following the onset of the great recession. Wood and colleagues (2012), using data from 38 hospitals, found very small increases (<10 %) in child physical abuse and high risk TBI rates associated with mortgage delinquency and foreclosure rates and, contrary to the other studies, found declines in child abuse admission rates between the start of the great recession and the end of 2009. Finally, as stated above, Leventhal and Gaither (2012), with by far the largest sample, found no large changes in serious physical abuse injuries in the 1997–2009 timeframe. Overall, the hospital-based data for severe injuries caused by physical child abuse do not yet show a consistent pattern of escalation during the great recession.

Summary

There are things we know for certain about poverty and child maltreatment. We know that actual (i.e. not simply officially reported) child maltreatment and poverty are related. We know that officially reported child maltreatment and poverty are related. We know that this relationship is not largely due to an anti-poor bias in reporting or identification. We know that the relationship between poverty and maltreatment occurs within all racial and ethnic groups, but we know that immigrants do far better than non-immigrants across child well-being measures, probably including child maltreatment. We know that Black children are not only more likely to be poor compared to Whites, but look even worse off when financial assets and chances of living in areas of concentrated poverty are considered. We are reasonably sure that poverty is more strongly related to neglect than to abuse, particularly sexual abuse.

There are things we know we need to understand better. Many of these are critically important. Chief among these is the matter of causality. The general domains of poverty, community, individual characteristics, parenting and maltreatment are clearly related, but we have yet to develop a convincing, comprehensive and generally useful causal model. Frameworks, such as provided by Bronfenbrenner and Belsky, are a step in the right direction, as they guide us toward relevant constructs. We still lack an understanding of the order, magnitude and valence of relationships between elements of these domains. For example, it has been commonly suggested that that poverty may cause stress which may cause maltreatment (Drake and Pandey 1996). Poverty may also degrade collective efficacy (Sampson and Morenoff 2004), resulting in a range of negative outcomes, including maltreatment. The mechanisms of intergenerational effects are not well understood, with recent work suggesting that epigenetic effects may play a far more powerful role than previously imagined (Roth et al. 2008). In the absence of a sound causal understanding, it is difficult to generate services which will fit the needs of maltreating families in poverty. To date, the only serious attempts to deal directly with poverty and maltreatment in combination seem to be from states and counties which offer concrete child welfare services and through home visiting programs. This is terribly inadequate.

Finally, there are undoubtedly key parts of the poverty/maltreatment puzzle that we remain ignorant of. For example, the whole perspective of epigenetics, that environment can cause lasting changes to how genes are expressed is very new. Researchers who attempted to understand, for example, intergenerational effects within low income communities simply did not have this perspective available to them. There are undoubtedly important discoveries to be made and perspectives to be found which will be useful to future researchers, practitioners and policy makers. More direct attention paid to the issue of poverty and maltreatment is needed to hasten this.

Policy and practice are now lagging science in this area. While we have acknowledged that child maltreatment and poverty are co-occurring and interrelated, the majority of evidence-based practices remain narrowly psychological, generally skill-based in nature. Modification of existing programs to acknowledge the problems faced by the poor is warranted. Generation of new programs specifically addressing the poverty-related problems encountered by these families may be useful.

We do not mean the tone of this concluding section to be negative or unhopeful. Looking back two or three decades, we see that most child welfare researchers, practitioners and policy makers were in a state of denial regarding the increased risk of maltreatment among poor children. There has been a powerful and positive historical shift in recognition of the problem. This has been accompanied by an explosion of frameworks and theoretical perspectives relating to neighborhood and other environmental conditions and dynamics. Increasingly, empirical research in the area of child welfare incorporates socioeconomic controls, something long overdue. Given this clear and marked progress, we may have reason to hope that a chapter such as this, written 10 or 20 years from now, will be able to provide more certain science and more guidance for poverty and policy.

References

Abrams, L. S., & Curran, L. (2009). "And you're telling me not to stress?" A grounded theory study of postpartum depression symptoms among low-income mothers. *Psychology of Women Quarterly, 33*(2009), 351–362.

Administration for Children and Families. (2012). Partnerships to demonstrate the effectiveness of supportive housing for families in the child welfare system. Available online at http://www.acf.hhs.gov/grants/open/foa/view/HHS-2012-ACF-ACYF-CA-0538.

Afifi, T. O. (2007). Child abuse and adolescent parenting: Developing a theoretical model from an ecological perspective. *Journal of Aggression Maltreatment & Trauma, 14*(3), 89–105.

Aron, S., McCrowel, J., Moon, A., Yamano, R., Roark, D., Simmons, M., Tatanashvili, Z., & Drake, B. (2010). Analyzing child welfare data across four levels of geographic aggregation: Which is best? *Social Work Research, 13*(4), 392–399.

Becker, G. (1978). *The economic approach to human behavior*. Chicago: University of Chicago Press.

Beimers, D. (2009). *Factors influencing child maltreatment among families leaving temporary assistance to needy families*. Dissertation. Case Western Reserve University.

Belsky, J. (1990). Child maltreatment: An ecological integration. *American Psychologist, 35*(4), 320–355.

Benson, D., Swann, A., O'Toole, R., & Turbett, J. (1991). Physician's recognition and response to child abuse: Northern Ireland and the USA. *Child Abuse & Neglect, 15*, 57–67.

Berger, L. (2004). Income, family structure, and child maltreatment risk. *Children and Youth Services Review, 26*(8), 725–748.

Berger, R. P., Fromkin, J. B., Stutz, H., et al. (2011). Abusive head trauma during a time of increased unemployment: A multicenter analysis. *Pediatrics, 128*(4), 637–643.

Blair, C et al. (2011). Salivary cortisol mediates effects of poverty and poverty and parenting on executive functions in early childhood. *Child Development, 82*(6), 1970–1984.

Bronfenbrenner, U. (1979). *The ecology of human development: Experiments by nature and design*. Cambridge, MA: Harvard University Press. ISBN 0-674-22457-4.

Brown, J., Cohen, P., Johnson, J., & Salzinger, S. (1998). A longitudinal analysis of risk factors for child maltreatement: Findings of a 17-year prospective study of officially recorded and self-reported child abuse and neglect. *Child Abuse & Neglect, 22*(11), 1065–1078.

California Evidence Based Clearinghouse for Child Welfare (n.d.). Available online at http://www.cebc4cw.org/.

Cancian, M., Slack, KS, Yan, M. (2010). The effect of family income on risk of maltreatment. Institute for Research on Poverty Discussion paper 1385-10.

Cicchetti, D., & Valentino, K. (2006). An ecological transactional perspective on child maltreatment: Failure of the average expectable environment and its influence upon child development. In D. Cicchetti & D. J. Cohen (Eds.), *Developmental psychopathology* (Risk, disorder, and adaptation 2nd ed., Vol. 3, pp. 129–201). New York: Wiley.

City of Milwaukee Health Department. (2010). 2010 City of Milwaukee Fetal Infant Mortality Review (FIMR) Report. Available online at www.milwaukee.gov/2010_FIMR_Report.pdf.

Coulton, C., Korbin, J., Su, S., & Chow, J. (1995). Community level factors and child maltreatment rates. *Child Development, 66*(5), 1262–1276.

Coulton, C., Crampton, D., Irwin, M., Spilbury, J., & Korbin, J. (2007). How neighborhoods influence child maltreatment: A review of the literature and alternative pathways. *Child Abuse & Neglect, 31*, 117–1142.

Courtney, M., Dworsky, A., Piliavin, I., & Zinn, A. (2005). Involvement of TANF applicant families with child welfare services. *The Social Service Review, 79*(1), 119–157.

Courtney, M. E., Dworsky, A., Piliavin, I., & McMurtry, S. (2008). Comparing welfare and child welfare populations: An argument for rethinking the safety net. In D. Lindsey & A. Shlonsky (Eds.), *Child welfare research: Advances for practice and policy*. New York: Oxford University Press.

Daro, D., & Dodge, K. (2010). Strengthening home-visiting intervention policy: Expanding re-search, building knowledge. In R. Haskins & W. S. Barnett (Eds.), *New directions for America's preschool policies* (pp. 79–86). Washington, DC: NIERR and Brookings.

Dettlaff, A. (2012). Immigrant children and families and the public child welfare system: Considerations for legal systems. *Juvenile and Family Court Journal, 63*(1), 19–30.

Dettlaff, A., Earner, I., & Phillips, S. (2009). Latino children of immigrants in the child welfare system: Prevalence, characteristics and risk. *Children and Youth Services Review, 31*(7), 775–783.

Dolan, M., Smith, K., Casanueva, C., & Ringensen, H. (2011). NSCAW II baseline report: introduction to NSCAW II. OPRE Report #2011-27a, Washington, DC: Office of Planning, Research and Evaluation, Administration for Children and Families, U.S. Department of Health and Human Services.

Drake, B., & Pandey, S. (1996). Understanding the relationship between neighborhood poverty and child maltreatment. *Child Abuse & Neglect, 20*(11), 1003–1018.

Drake, B., & Rank, M. (2009). The racial divide among American children in poverty: Assessing the importance of neighborhoods. *Children and Youth Services Review, 31*(12), 1264–1271.

Drake, B., Jolley, J., Lanier, P., Fluke, J., Barth, R., & Jonson-Reid, M. (2011). Racial bias in child protection? A comparison of competing explanations using national data. *Pediatrics, 127*(3), 471–478. doi:10.1542/peds.2010-1710.

Dubowitz, H., Black, M., Starr, R., & Zuravin, S. (1993). A conceptual definition of child neglect. *Criminal Justice and Behavior, 20*(1), 8–26.

Duggan, A., Wyndham, A., MacFarlane, E., Fuddy, L., Rhode, C., Buchbinder, S., & Sia, C. (2000). Hawaii's healthy start program of home visiting for high-risk families: Evaluation of family identification, family engagement and service delivery. *Pediatrics, 105*, 250–259.

Duggan, A., Caldera, D., Rodriguez, K., Burrell, L., Rohde, C., & Crowne, S. S. (2007). Impact of a statewide home visiting program to prevent child abuse. *Child Abuse & Neglect, 31*(8), 801–827.

Duva, J., & Metzger, S. (2010). Addressing poverty as a major risk factor in child neglect: Promising policy and practice. *Protecting Children, 25*(1), 63–74.

Dworsky, A., Courtney, M., & Zinn, A. (2007). Child, parent, and family predictors of child welfare services involvement among TANF applicant families. *Children and Youth Services Review, 29*(6), 802–820.

Ernst, J. (2000). Mapping child maltreatment: Looking at neighborhoods in a suburban county. *Child Welfare League of America, 79*(5), 555–572.

Finkelhor, D., & Jones, L. (2006). Why have child maltreatment and child victimization declined? *Journal of Social Issues, 62*(4), 685–716. Available online at http://www.unh.edu/ccrc/Trends/papers.html.

Finkelhor, D., & Jones, L. (2009). *Updated trends in child maltreatment.* Crimes Against Children Research Center, University of New Hampshire. Available online at www.unh.edu/ccrc/Trends/papers.html.

Finkelhor, D., & Jones, L. (2012). *Have sexual abuse and physical abuse declined since the 1990s?* Durham, NH: Crimes against Children Research Center (CV267).

Freisthler, B., Bruce, E., & Needell, B. (2007). Understanding the geospatial relationship of neighborhood characteristics and rates of maltreatment for black, Hispanic and white children. *Social Work, 52*(1), 7–16.

Freistler, B., Midanik, L., & Gruenewald, P. (2004). Alcohol outlets and child physical abuse and neglect: Applying routine activities theory to the study of child maltreatment. *Journal of Studies on Alcohol, 65*(5), 586–592.

Gillham, B., Tanner, G., & Cheyne, B. (1998). Unemployment rates, single parent density, and indices of child poverty: Their relationship to different categories of child abuse and neglect. *Child Abuse & Neglect, 22*(2), 79–90.

Huang, M. I., O'Riordan, M. A., Fitzenrider, E., McDavid, L., Cohen, A. R., & Robinson, S. (2011). Increased incidence of nonaccidental head trauma in infants associated with the economic recession. *Journal of Neurosurgery. Pediatrics, 8*(2), 171–176.

Hussey, J., Marshall, J., English, D., Knight, E., Lau, A., Dubowitz, H., & Kotch, J. (2005). Defining maltreatment according to substantiation: Distinction without a difference? *Child Abuse & Neglect, 29*(5), 479–492.

Jason, J. (1984). Centers for Disease Control and the epidemiology of violence. *Child Abuse & Neglect, 8,* 279–283.

Jonson-Reid, M. (2011). Disentangling system contact and services: A key pathway to evidence – based children's policy. *Children and Youth Services Review, 33*(5), 598–604.

Jonson-Reid, M., & Drake, B. (2008). Multi-sector longitudinal administrative databases: An indispensable tool for evidence-based policy for maltreated children and their families. *Child Maltreatment, 13*(4), 392–399.

Jonson-Reid, M., Drake, B., & Kohl, P. (2009). Is the overrepresentation of the poor in child welfare caseloads due to bias or need? *Children and Youth Services Review, 31,* 422–427.

Jonson-Reid, M., Emery, C., Drake, B., & Stahlschmidt, M. (2010). Understanding chronically re-reported cases: Implications for services and research. *Child Maltreatment, 15,* 271–281.

Katz, K. S., Jarrett, M. H., El-Mohandes, A. A., Schneider, S., McNeely-Johnson, D., & Kiely, M. (2011). Effectiveness of a combined home visiting and group intervention for low income African American mothers: The pride in parenting program. *Journal for Maternal Child, Health, 15*(1), 75–84.

Kempe, C. H., Silverman, F., Steele, B., Droegemueller, W., & Silver, H. (1962). The battered child syndrome. *Journal of theAmerican Medical Association, 181,* 4–11.

Kovan, N., Chung, A., & Sroufe, A. (2009). The intergenerational continuity of observed early parenting: A prospective, longitudinal study. *Developmental Psychology, 45*(5), 1205–1213.

Krishnan, V., & Morrison, K. (1995). An ecological model of child maltreatment in a Canadian province. *Child Abuse & Neglect, 19*(1), 101–113.

Krugman, R., Lenherr, M., Betz, L., & Fryer, E. (1986). The relationship between unemployment and physical abuse of children. *Child Abuse & Neglect, 10*(3), 415–418.

Lanier, P., Jonson-Reid, M., Stahlschmidt, M., Cooper, B., Recktenwald, A., & Ohlemiller, M. (2012). Maltreatment prevention for high-risk families with newborns served by a nurse home-visiting program. Presented at the 20th Annual Colloquium of the American Professional Society on the Abuse of Children (APSAC), Chicago.

Laskey, A., Stump, T., Perkins, S., Zimet, G., Sherman, S., & Downs, S. (2011). Influence of race and socioeconomic status on the diagnosis of child abuse: A randomized study. *Pediatrics, 160*(6), 1003–1008.

LeCroy, C., & Krysik, J. (2011). Randomized trial of the healthy families Arizona home visiting program. *Children and Youth Services Review, 33*(10), 1761–1766.

Lery, B. (2009). Neighborhood structure and foster care entry risk: The role of spatial scale in defining neighborhoods. *Children and Youth Services Review, 31*(3), 331–337.

Leventhal, T. (2000). The neighborhoods they live in: The effects of neighborhood residence on child and adolescent outcomes. *Psychological Bulletin, 126*(2), 309–337.

Leventhal, J., & Gaither, J. (2012). Incidence of serious injuries due to physical abuse in the United States: 1997–2009. *Pediatrics, 130*(5), e847–e852.

Loman, A., & Siegel, G. (2004). *Minnesota alternative response evaluation: Final report.* St. Louis: Institute of Applied Research. Retrieved August 24, 2012, from www.iarstl.org/papers/ ARFinalEvaluationReport.pdf.

Loman, A., & Siegel, G. (2012). Effects of anti-poverty services under the differential response approach to child welfare. *Children and Youth Services Review, 34*(9), 1659–1666.

Loman, T., Shannon, C., Sapokaite, L., & Siegel, G. (2009). *Minnesota parent support outreach program evaluation*. Missouri: Institute of Applied Research.

MacMillan, H., Wathen, C., Barlow, J., Fergusson, D., Leventhal, J., & Taussig, H. (2009). Interventions to prevent child maltreatment and associated impairment. *Lancet, 373*, 250–266.

Martin, C., Fisher, P., & Kim, H. (2011). Risk for maternal harsh parenting in high-risk families from birth to age three: Does ethnicity matter? *Preventative Science, 13*, 64–74.

Melton, G. (2005). Mandated reporting: A policy without reason. *Child Abuse & Neglect, 29*(1), 9–18.

Merritt, D. (2009). Child abuse potential: Correlates with child maltreatment rates and structural measures of neighborhoods. *Children and Youth Services Review, 31*(8), 927–934.

Michigan Department of Community Health. (2010). Table 26: Infant death and infant death rates and live births by Census Tract Poverty. Michigan Residents, 2007–2009. Available onine at http://www.mdch.state.mi.us/pha/osr/InDxMain/InfPovertyTableObject.asp.

Millet, L., Lanier, P., & Drake, B. (2011). Are economic trends associated with child maltreatment? Preliminary results from the recent recession using state level data. *Children and Youth Services Review, 33*(7), 1280–1287.

Molnar, B., Buka, S., Brennan, R., Holton, J., & Earls, F. (2003). A multilevel study of neighborhoods and parent-to-parent child physical aggression: Results from the project on human development in Chicago neighborhoods. *Child Maltreatment, 8*(2), 84–97.

Nam, Y., Meezan, W., & Danziger, S. (2006). Welfare recipients involvement with child protective services after welfare reform. *Child Abuse & Neglect, 30*, 1181–1199.

Nikulina, V., Widom, C., & Czaja, S. (2011). The role of childhood neglect and childhood poverty in predicting mental health, academic achievement and crime in adulthood. *American Journal of Community Psychology, 48*, 309–321.

Olds, D. L., Henderson, C. R., Kitzman, H. J., Eckenrode, J. J., Cole, R. E., & Tatelbaum, R. C. (1999). Prenatal and infancy home visitation by nurses: Recent findings. *The Future of Children, 9*, 44–65.

Oliver, M., & Shapiro, T. (2006). *Black wealth, white wealth* (2nd ed.). New York: Routledge.

Passel, J., & Cohn, D. (2008). U.S. population projections. Pew Research Center. Available online at www.pewhispanic.org/files/reports/85.pdf.

Paulsell, D., Avellar, S., Sama Martin, E., & Del Grosso, P. (2011). *Home visiting evidence of effectiveness review: Executive summary*. Washington, DC: Office of Planning, Research and Evaluation, Administration for Children and Families, U.S. Department of Health and Human Services.

Pelton, L. (1978). Child abuse and neglect: The myth of classlessness. *The American Journal of Orthopsychiatry, 48*, 608–617.

Polansky, N., Borgman, R., & DeSaix, C. (1972). *The roots of futility*. San Francisco: Jossey Bass.

Putnam-Hornstein, E., & Needell, B. (2011). Predictors of child protective service contact between birth and age five: An examination of California's 2002 birth cohort. *Children and Youth Services Review, 33*(11), 2400–2407.

Rank, M., & Hirschl, T. (1999). The likelihood of poverty across the American life span. *Social Work, 44*(3), 201–206.

Rank, M. R., Yoon, H. S., & Hirschl, T. A. (2003). American poverty as a structural failing: Evidence and arguments. *Journal of Sociology & Social Welfare, 30*(4), 3–29.

Romero, C., Duke, J., Dabelea, D., Romero, T., & Ogden, L. (2012). Does the epidemiologic paradox hold in the presence of risk factors for low birth weight infants among Mexican-born women in Colorado? *Journal of Health Care for the Poor and Underserved, 23*(2), 604–614.

Roth, T., Lubin, F., Funk, A., & Sweatt, J. (2008). Lasting epigenetic influence of early-life adversity on the BDNF gene. *Biological Psychiatry, 65*(9), 760–769.

Sabol, W., Coulton, C., & Polusky, E. (2004). Measuring child maltreatment risk in communities: A life table approach. *Child Abuse & Neglect, 26*(9), 967–983.

Sampson, R. (1992). Family management and child development: Insights from social disorganization theory. In J. McCord (Ed.), *Advances in criminological theory* (Vol. 3). New Brunswick: Transaction Publishers. Chapter 4.

Sampson, R. (2004). Neighbourhood and community. *New Economy, 11*(2), 106–113.

Sampson, R. J., & Morenoff, J. D. (2004). Spatial (dis)advantage and homicide in Chicago neighborhoods. In M. F. Goodchild & D. G. Janelle (Eds.), *Spatially integrated social science*. Oxford: Oxford University Press.

Schuck, A. (2005). Explaining black-white disparity in maltreatment: Poverty, female-headed families, and urbanization. *Journal of Marriage and the Family, 67*, 543–551.

Sedlak, A. J., Mettenburg, J., Basena, M., Petta, I., McPherson, K., Greene, A., & Li, S. (2010). *Fourth national incidence study of child abuse and neglect (NIS–4): Report to Congress*. Washington, DC: U.S. Department of Health and Human Services, Administration for Children and Families.

Shanks, T. (2011). Examining the dynamic pathways through which economic security interacts with households to mitigate stress and shape child outcomes. The Annie E. Casey Foundation. http://www.caseyfoundation.org/~/media/Pubs/Topics/Economic%20Security/Family%20Economic%20Supports/Examiningthedynamicpathwaysthroughwhicheconomicsecurityinteractswithhouseholds/FamilyOutcomesFullPaperwithreferences10%2019%2011.pdf.

Slack, K., Holl, J., McDaniel, M., Yoo, J., & Bolger, K. (2004). Understanding the risks of child neglect: An exploration of poverty and parenting characteristics. *Child Maltreatment, 9*(4), 395–408.

Small, E., & Kohl, P. (2012). African American caregivers and substance abuse in child welfare: Identification of multiple risk profiles. *Journal of Family Violence, 27*, 415–426.

Smith, J., & Brooks-Gunn, J. (1997). Correlates and consequences of harsh discipline for young children. *Archives of Pediatrics & Adolescent Medicine, 151*(8), 777–786.

Turbett, J., & O'Toole, R. (1983). Teacher's recognition and reporting of child abuse. *Journal of School Heatlh, 53*, 605–608.

United States Department of Health and Human Services. (1996). *Child maltreatment 1995*. Washington, DC: US Government Printing Office.

United States Department of Health and Human Services. (2007). *Child maltreatment 2006*. Washington, DC: US Government Printing Office.

U.S. Department of Health and Human Services. (2008). Factsheet: Preventing child abuse and neglect. Child Welfare Information Gateway. Available online at http://www.childwelfare.gov/pubs/factsheets/preventingcan.pdf.

United States Department of Health and Human Services. (2011). *Child maltreatment 2010*. Washington, DC: US Government Printing Office.

United States Census Bureau. (2012). Statistical abstract of the United States. Available Online at http://www.census.gov/compendia/statab/.

Uphoff, C. (1999). Understanding social capital: Learning from the analysis and experiences of participation. In I. Dasgupta & P. Seregeldin (Eds.), *Social capital: A multifaceted perspective*. Washington, DC: World Bank.

Waldfogel, J. (2009). Prevention and the child protection system. *The Future of Children, 19*(2), 195–210. Preventing Child Maltreatment.

Walsh, W., & Mattingly, M. (2012). *Understanding child abuse in rural and urban America: Risk factors and maltreatment substantiation*. Durham, NH: Carsey Institute.

Wood, J., Hall, M., Schilling, S., Keren, R., Mitra, N., & Rubin, D. (2010). Disparities in the evaluation and diagnosis of abuse among infants with traumatic brain injury. *Pediatrics, 126*(3), 408–411.

Wood, J., Medina, S., Feudtner, C., Luan, X., Localio, R., Fieldston, E., & Localio, R. (2012). Local macroeconomic trends and hospital admissions for child abuse, 2000–2009. *Pediatrics, 130*(2), 358–364.

Wu, S., Ma, C., Carter, R., Ariet, M., Feaver, E., Resnick, M., & Roth, J. (2004). Risk factors for infant maltreatment: A population-based study. *Child Abuse & Neglect, 28*, 1253–1254.

Zalewski, M., Lengua, L. J., Fisher, P. A., Trancik, A., Bush, N. R., & Meltzoff, A. N. (2012). Poverty and single parenting: Relations with preschoolers' cortisol and effortful control. *Infant Child Development*. doi:10.1002/icd.1759.

Zellman, G. (1992). The impact of case characteristics on child abuse reporting decisions. *Child Abuse and Nelgect, 15*, 57–74.

Zhou, Y., Hallisey, E., & Freymann, G. (2006). Identifying perinatal risk factors for infant maltreatment: An ecological approach. *International Journal of Health Geographics, 5*, 53. doi:10.1186/1476-072X-5-53.

Zolotor, A., & Runyan, D. (2006). Social capital, family violence, and neglect. *Pediatrics, 117*, e1124–e1131.

Chapter 8
The Evolving Understanding of Disproportionality and Disparities in Child Welfare

Alan J. Dettlaff

The overrepresentation of children of color in the child welfare system has long represented a prominent concern in the field of child welfare. Commonly referred to as *disproportionality,* this phenomenon has most significantly affected Black children, with data from 2010 indicating that Black children represented 29 % of children in foster care, although they represented only 14.5 % of children in the general population (United States Department of Health and Human Services 2011; United States Census Bureau 2012).[1] This overrepresentation of Black children has been observed in the child welfare system for more than 40 years (Billingsley and Giovannoni 1972), yet persists as a national concern, and has led to questions regarding the fairness of child welfare policies and practices and whether those policies and practices unfairly disadvantage children of color.

Although the presence of racial disproportionality in the child welfare system has been well documented, research has been less successful in identifying the explanatory factors associated with this phenomenon. At issue is whether the observed levels of overrepresentation result from a form of racial bias within child welfare systems or from differing levels of need among children and families of color. Recent critiques of efforts to address disproportionality have brought increased attention to this issue, particularly concerning observed disparities in the incidence of maltreatment and the subsequent need for intervention. Bartholet (2009), in her paper *The Racial Disproportionality Movement in Child Welfare: False Facts and Dangerous Directions,* contended that the observed differences in the representation of Black children in the child welfare system occur because Black children are in fact maltreated at higher rates than children of other races, and thus should be placed into foster care at higher rates than other children. She contended that higher rates of maltreatment in Black families are to be expected because Black children are more likely to be exposed to many of the risk factors associated with maltreatment, including poverty, substance abuse, and single parenting.

These claims were initially met with resistance, as prior research, most notably the federally funded National Incidence Studies of Child Abuse and Neglect (NIS), conducted in 1980 (NIS-1), 1986 (NIS-2), and 1993 (NIS-3), had consistently shown no significant differences in the actual incidence of maltreatment across children of different racial groups (Sedlak 1991; Sedlak and Broadhurst 1996; Sedlak and Schultz 2005). However, findings from the recently released NIS-4 (Sedlak et al. 2010b)

---

[1] Disproportionality has also been observed among Native American/Alaska Native children at the national level. As of 2010, Native American/Alaska Native children represented 1.9 % of children in foster care and 0.9 % of children in the general population (Summers et al. 2012). However, the body of research on disproportionality, as well as the current debate concerning the appropriate response to disproportionality, has focused primarily on Black children.

A.J. Dettlaff, Ph.D., MSW (✉)
Jane Addams College of Social Work (MC 309), University of Illinois at Chicago, 1040 W. Harrison, Chicago, IL 60607, USA
e-mail: aland@uic.edu

J.E. Korbin and R.D. Krugman (eds.), *Handbook of Child Maltreatment*, Child Maltreatment 2, DOI 10.1007/978-94-007-7208-3_8, © Springer Science+Business Media Dordrecht 2014

found for the first time that rates of maltreatment for Black children were significantly higher than those for White or Hispanic children. In supplemental analyses of these race differences, the authors concluded that these observed differences were the result of greater precision of the NIS-4 estimates, as well as an increased disparity in income between Black and White families since the NIS-3 (Sedlak et al. 2010a).

The discussion raised by Bartholet and the subsequent findings of the NIS-4 have led to calls to reevaluate efforts to address disproportionality, particularly those efforts that have focused on reducing bias within child welfare systems, with critics suggesting that it is not bias, but rather disproportionate need, that results in disproportionality (e.g., Drake et al. 2011). Yet others contend that racial bias still plays a role in contributing to disproportionality, despite differences in rates of maltreatment (e.g., Dettlaff et al. 2011; Rivaux et al. 2008).

The body of research that has emerged over the past several years and the resulting critiques of efforts to address disproportionality have ignited a debate within the child welfare field that has elicited strong feelings from many involved, with most scholars aligning themselves with one side or the other, while those in child welfare agencies and educational environments are left questioning the meaning of these new research findings and how to proceed with efforts to address this issue. This chapter will address this debate and discuss how the understanding of disproportionality has evolved over time. The chapter will propose recommendations for addressing disproportionality and disparities in child welfare systems based on current evidence that allows for the acknowledgement of differing risk and rates of maltreatment, while also acknowledging the potential for racial bias to exacerbate these differences, resulting in further harm and disparate outcomes for Black children.

Defining and Identifying Disproportionality and Disparities

The terms disproportionality and disparities have held numerous definitions in the child welfare literature devoted to this topic. The concept of disproportionality in child welfare grew from efforts in the juvenile justice system to measure and understand disproportionate minority contact and arose out of growing awareness and acknowledgement that children of different races were represented in the child welfare system at different rates (Derezotes and Poertner 2005). The initial identification and use of the term disproportionality was intended to document this phenomenon and to acknowledge the need to better understand why this was occurring (Derezotes and Poertner 2005). However, as the use of the terms disproportionality and disparities have evolved over time, they have taken on connotations that denote a problem resulting from racial bias or differential treatment of children of color. Yet the presence of disproportionality and disparities in the child welfare system is not indicative of either a problem or of racial bias in the absence of evidence to support this. Understanding the meaning of these terms and what they mean for child welfare systems is an important component in developing an appropriate response to address them.

Disproportionality

The term disproportionality refers to the state of being out of proportion. It describes a condition that exists when the proportion of people of a certain race or ethnicity in a target population differs from the proportion of people of the same group in a reference population. In the context of the child welfare system, disproportionality is most commonly used to describe a condition when the proportion of one group in the child welfare population (i.e., children in foster care) is either proportionately larger (overrepresented) or smaller (underrepresented) than the proportion of the same group in the general child population. Although this comparison of children in foster care to children in the general population is the most common use of the term, disproportionality can also exist at other decision points (e.g., substantiated maltreatment investigations).[2] In and of itself, overrepresentation in the child welfare system is not a problem, as representation in this system should be based on need. Thus, the presence of disproportionality is not indicative of either a problem or of bias, in the absence of data that addresses its causes. A caveat to this is whether what is perceived as need is influenced by bias. This will be addressed later in the chapter.

As stated previously, data from 2010 show that Black children represented 29 % of children in foster care, although they represented only 14.5 % of children in the general population, indicating a disproportionality ratio of 2.0.[3] This represents a decrease in disproportionality since 2000 when Black children represented 38 % of children in foster care and 16 % of the child population, a ratio of 2.5 (Summers et al. 2012). In addition to overrepresentation at the national level, Black children have historically been overrepresented at the state level. In 2000, Black children were overrepresented in all 50 states with disproportionality ratios ranging from 1.1 (Massachusetts) to 8.3 (Wisconsin). Disproportionality ratios were greater than 2.0 in 41 states. As of 2010, Black children were overrepresented in 46 states, with ratios ranging from 1.1 (Mississippi) to 5.3 (Wyoming). Ratios exceeded 2.0 in only 30 states, a decrease of 11 states. Disproportionality ratios decreased in all but five states, while four states (Alaska, Hawaii, Maine, and Oregon) showed no evidence of disproportionality for Black children (Summers et al. 2012). These data indicate that disproportionality has largely declined at both the national level and the state level over the past decade.

Disparity

While disproportionality refers to the state of being out of proportion, disparity refers to a state of being unequal. In the child welfare system, disparity is typically used to describe unequal outcomes experienced by one racial or ethnic group when compared to *another* racial or ethnic group (in contrast, disproportionality compares the proportion of one racial/ethnic group in the child welfare system to the *same* racial/ethnic group in the population). Disparities can occur at every decision-making point in the child welfare system, including the initial report that brings children to the attention of the system, acceptance of reports for investigation, substantiation of maltreatment, entries into substitute care, and exits from substitute care. For example, if the rate of Black children being reported to the child welfare system in a state differed considerably when compared to the rate of White children being reported to the same system, this would denote a disparity. Ultimately, disparities that occur in both entries to the system and exits from the system produce disproportionality. Thus, understanding where disparities exist and why they are occurring is essential to understanding disproportionality. However, similar to disproportionality, the presence of a disparity at a given decision-making point is not an indicator of bias or of disparate treatment in the absence of data that identifies the explanatory factors contributing to the disparity. However, even these data may be subject to caution depending on which alternative factors are included in the analyses.

Over the past two decades, a considerable number of studies have identified disparities at various decision-making points along the child welfare service delivery pathway. These include the initial report of alleged maltreatment (Fluke et al. 2003; Lu et al. 2004), acceptance for investigation (Gryzlak et al. 2005; Zuravin et al. 1995), substantiation of alleged maltreatment (Ards et al. 2003; Rolock and

---

[2] Additionally, the reference population can be either the general child population or the population of children that experience a particular event (e.g., investigated reports of maltreatment).

[3] The disproportionality ratio for Black children is calculated by dividing the percentage of Black children in substitute care for a given year by the percentage of Black children in the child population (under 18) in the same year.

Testa 2005), placement into out-of-home care (Rivaux et al. 2008; Wulczyn and Lery 2007), and exits from care (Hill 2005; Lu et al. 2004). Several studies have examined factors that may explain these disparities and findings have been mixed regarding the role of race. Some studies have found that race is a significant factor at various decision-making points (e.g., Hill 2005; Lu et al. 2004; Rivaux et al. 2008), while others have found no significant effect for race when controlling for other factors (e.g., Goerge and Lee 2005; Harris et al. 2005). Still others have found that it is a combination of race with other factors that results in observed disparities (e.g., type of abuse by race – Gryzlak et al. 2005; severity of injury by race – Sedlak and Schultz 2005; family structure by race – Harris and Courtney 2003).

While the existence of racial disproportionality and disparities in the child welfare system has been well established, of concern to the field are the explanatory factors that underlie them, as these are the issues that must be understood in order to develop appropriate responses, as well as shape policy. The remainder of this chapter will consider the evolving understanding of disproportionality from its early identification in the child welfare system to the shifting dialogue that has occurred in recent years to shape the current understanding of this phenomenon.

Early Understandings of Disproportionality

The overrepresentation of Black children in the child welfare system was first brought to national attention by Billingsley and Giovannoni (1972) in their seminal publication, *Children of the Storm: Black Children and American Child Welfare.* Prior to the 1950s, Black children were largely excluded from child welfare systems, as the bulk of agencies providing child welfare services were created to serve poor White immigrants (Hogan and Siu 1988). Yet as changes in migration patterns occurred among Blacks during the 1950s and 1960s, both from rural to urban areas and from the South to the North, along with an increased focus on integration and decreasing poverty rates among White children, the involvement of Black children in the child welfare system grew steadily (Billingsley and Giovannoni 1972; Hogan and Siu 1988). By the end of the 1970s, a number of studies had identified that Black children had emerged as the most overrepresented group in this system (e.g., Close 1983; Magura 1979; Shyne and Schroeder 1978). As awareness of this overrepresentation grew throughout the 1980s and 1990s, this led to increasing calls for states to develop responses to address this issue, leading to several states passing legislation mandating system responses in the mid-2000s (e.g., Michigan Department of Human Services and Skillman Foundation 2006; Texas Health and Human Services Commission 2006), as well as national efforts to assist in these responses (e.g., Casey Family Programs 2009).

Among most scholars, there has always been acknowledgment that different levels of representation in the child welfare system can be driven by different levels of need and that Black families may be particularly vulnerable to many of the risk factors associated with child welfare system involvement. Yet regardless of the reasons disproportionality exists, it is a concern for a number of reasons, primary among these being the consequences to children and families that can result from placement in out-of-home care. Multiple studies have documented that children who are removed from their homes experience not only significant trauma but also are more likely than other children to experience negative outcomes as adults, including low educational attainment, homelessness, poverty, unemployment, unplanned pregnancies, mental health disorders, and involvement in the criminal justice system (Courtney et al. 2010, 2001; Pecora et al. 2003). Although it is unclear whether these negative outcomes can be attributed to children's placement in foster care or to their abusive family backgrounds, recent research by Doyle (2007) suggests that outcomes for children at the margin of placement (i.e., cases where child protection investigators may disagree about the recommendation for removal) are better for children who remain in their homes, with children removed from their homes experiencing higher delinquency rates, higher teen birth rates, and lower earnings.

But in addition, for Black families, overrepresentation in the child welfare system not only separates parents from children, but also contributes to feelings of anger, hostility, and distrust of governmental systems (Roberts 2008). In addition to individual and family consequences, the disproportionate involvement of Blacks in the child welfare system and the resulting negative outcomes can serve to perpetuate many of the oppressive conditions and negative stereotypes that have historically affected the Black population (Roberts 2002). When combined with the disproportionate involvement of Black children in other systems, the persistent overrepresentation of Black children in the child welfare system was viewed by many as a concern that warranted further investigation and understanding.

However, as awareness of disproportionality increased, findings from the National Incidence Studies of Child Abuse and Neglect (NIS) were increasingly used to frame the issue as a problem resulting from racism and/or discrimination against Black children. The NIS is a mandated effort of the U.S. Department of Health and Human Services and has been conducted at varying intervals since 1978. The goal of the NIS is to provide estimates of the incidence of child abuse and neglect in the United States and to report changes in incidence over time. In contrast to *official* rates of maltreatment, which are determined by substantiated investigations of abuse or neglect conducted by child protective services (CPS) agencies, the NIS attempts to estimate the *actual* incidence of maltreatment in the United States by collecting data from community professionals in sentinel agencies, in addition to data from CPS. Thus, the NIS estimates include children in the official CPS statistics and those who are not. The NIS employs two standards in identifying maltreatment – the Harm Standard, which requires that an incident resulted in demonstrable harm to a child, and the Endangerment Standard, which includes children who have not yet been harmed but were believed to be endangered as a result of maltreatment. This latter category includes cases that were substantiated by a CPS agency (Sedlak et al. 2010b).

Prior to the release of NIS-4 in 2010, the NIS had been conducted on three occasions – NIS-1 in 1979 and 1980, NIS-2 in 1986, and NIS-3 in 1993. These prior studies had consistently found no significant differences in *actual* rates of maltreatment between Black children and children of other races. Specifically, NIS-3 reported:

> No significant or marginal racial differences in the incidence of maltreatment were found either within the NIS-3 data or in the comparison of changes since the NIS-2. This was true for both the Harm Standard and the Endangerment Standard findings. It is interesting to note that this is also the case in the NIS-2. That is, there were no significant race differences in any category for either standard, and none of the changes between the NIS-1 and the NIS-2 were modified by child's race. (Sedlak and Broadhurst 1996, pp. 4.28–4.29)

The report went on to state:

> The NIS findings suggest that the different races receive differential attention somewhere during the process of referral, investigation, and service allocation, and that the differential representation of minorities in the child welfare population does not derive from inherent differences in the rates at which they are abused or neglected (pp. 8–7).

Thus, both the findings from the NIS data and the conclusions drawn in the NIS-3 final report suggest rather unequivocally that there are no racial differences in the incidence of maltreatment and that any differential rates of representation for children of color are not the result of differences in rates of maltreatment. The report even raises the issue of "differential attention" as a factor that can explain the overrepresentation of minority children.

Following the release of the NIS-3 report in 1996, these findings began to be used by some as evidence of racial bias within the child welfare system. For example, using data from the National Data Archive on Child Abuse and Neglect (NCANDS), Morton (1999) found that Black children were involved in substantiated cases of maltreatment at a rate that was disproportionate to their percentage in the population in 40 states for which data were available. In his discussion of these findings, Morton cited the NIS-3, stating, "This…directly contradicts the apparent higher incidence rate suggested by founded allegations of child maltreatment. How could the reported incidence based on founded allegations be so significantly out of proportion, given the NIS-3 findings?" (p. 25). Given the lack of racial differences found in the NIS-3, he later states, "As a result, one could argue that there should be proportional racial representation throughout the system. If proportional representation does not exist, a strong argument is created for the existence of differential treatment by race" (p. 26). Similarly, in a paper published the same year, Yegidis and Morton (1999) wrote:

> All three National Incidence Studies (NIS) conducted by the Department of Health and Human Services concluded that there are no significant or marginal differences in the incidence of child maltreatment based on race. Since incidence is measured in rates per thousand, this means that all groups should be represented in the child welfare system consistent with their proportion of the population as a whole. If not, then a basis for the presumption of bias exists (p. 1).

This use of the NIS-3 findings persisted throughout the next decade, with many additional studies comparing the lack of racial differences in rates of maltreatment as found in the NIS-3 with the consistent overrepresentation of Black children in the child welfare system as evidence of a growing problem.

Responses Associated with the NIS Findings

One of the first studies to examine the apparent contradiction of the NIS findings with the observed overrepresentation of Black children in the child welfare system was an examination of NIS-1 data by Ards et al. (1998) to determine the extent to which sample selection bias contributed to the finding that no racial differences were present in the incidence of maltreatment. Their analyses concluded that this apparent contradiction may exist due to four factors: (1) reporting rates differed by race, (2) reporting rates differed by type of maltreatment, (3) the NIS design excluded certain categories of reporters, and (4) the cases most likely to be addressed by CPS agencies may have differed from the maltreatment categories used by the NIS. A major finding from this study was the determination that sample selection bias resulting from the exclusion of family, friends, and neighbors as report sources altered the interpretation of findings regarding maltreatment reports for Black children, but not for White children. Thus, the authors cautioned the interpretation of the NIS findings, stating "before the finding of no racial difference in child maltreatment is accepted unequivocally in the child maltreatment literature, additional attention must be paid to the design features of the NIS study that leave ambiguous the question of racial disparities in child maltreatment" (p. 113).

Additionally, in response to Morton's (1999) article suggesting that the overrepresentation of Black children was related to higher rates of substantiation in cases involving Black children, Ards et al. (1999) analyzed data from the 1993, 1994, and 1995 NCANDS to test the hypothesis that substantiation rates would be higher in states with larger percentages of Black victims, if the premise was true that cases involving Black children were more likely to be substantiated than cases involving White children. However, they did not find a positive relationship between the two, rejecting the hypothesis that race influenced substantiation. Additionally, Ards et al. (1999) re-examined data from NIS-1 to determine whether racial differences existed in substantiation rates among CPS cases and whether differences existed in substantiated and unsubstantiated cases in reviewer ratings of whether cases were "very probable" or whether there was "insufficient evidence." Their results found no racial differences in either comparison, concluding that these findings may "rule out Morton's hypothesis that black child maltreatment cases are disproportionately substantiated" (p. 1212). In addressing the importance of this issue and the factors contributing to disproportionality, the authors concluded:

> The policy implications of this debate are profound. If we are to believe the NIS data, we should focus our resources on combating racial bias in reporting, substantiation, and case openings. And, there is every reason to believe that the potential exists for racial bias in the child protective services. However, if this racial bias is not the cause of the overrepresentation of black children among abused children, then we should look elsewhere to confront the disparities that we observe. We are concerned that too little attention has been paid to the structural factors that may contribute to underlying racial differences in abuse (pp. 1212–1214).

Further critiques emerged concerning the validity of the NIS-3 findings concerning the lack of racial differences in the incidence of maltreatment. Specifically, Barth (2005) raised additional concerns regarding the potential for sample selection bias due to the exclusion of friends and kin among the community sentinels trained to identify maltreatment, as was previously identified by Ards et al. (1998). Barth also expressed concern regarding an oversampling of referrals from suburban communities due to flawed procedures in urban communities that were present in the NIS design. While some acknowledged the validity of these concerns (e.g., Chibnall et al. 2003; Wulczyn 2003), others challenged these critiques, contending that these concerns would not substantively change the findings produced by the NIS (Hill 2006). Ultimately, despite these critiques, most contended that the NIS-3 data were the most reliable and definitive source of data on the national incidence of maltreatment that were available (Barth 2005; Hill 2006).

Subsequent Prevailing Theories Regarding Disproportionality

Despite being acknowledged since the 1970s, significant national attention concerning racial disproportionality did not occur until the early 2000s, following the publication of the NIS-3, which resulted in several prominent calls for action due to the suggestion of racial bias given the inconsistency between the NIS-3 findings and Black children's involvement in child welfare systems. This led to a considerable increase in studies examining disproportionality and in attempts to explain this phenomenon. By the mid-2000s, several scholars had proposed theories, based on available evidence, explaining the existence of racial disproportionality. Hines et al. (2004) reviewed the existing literature and proposed four potential factors that were likely interrelated: (1) parent and family risk factors, (2) social factors including poverty and community risks, (3) race and class biases in the child welfare system, and (4) the impact of child welfare policies such as the Multi-Ethnic Placement Act (MEPA) and the Adoption and Safe Families Act (ASFA) on children of color. Barth (2005) also proposed four models for explaining disproportionality: (1) differential need resulting from differential risk (although it was acknowledged that this did not fit well with the NIS-3), (2) racial bias that affects decision-making in child welfare agencies, (3) placement dynamics, including the increasing use of kinship care, which may result in longer lengths of stay, and (4) the multiplicative model, which suggests that the three prior factors are all at play and interact to produce disproportionality. Similarly, findings from a Government Accountability Office (GAO) (2007) study examining disproportionality concluded that there were three major contributing factors to this phenomenon: (1) higher rates of poverty among Black families and the resulting risks, (2) bias and cultural misunderstandings in child welfare systems, and (3) longer stays in foster care due to difficulty in recruiting adoptive parents and the greater reliance on kinship care in cases with Black children. Thus, in much of the literature, there was consistent awareness that disproportionality was a complex phenomenon that likely resulted from multiple factors, including those within families, within communities, and within the system.

Yet, the notion of racial bias as the primary contributor to disproportionality, particularly in light of the NIS-3 findings, propelled much of the dialogue, to the point where the two phenomena – racial bias and disproportionality – appeared synonymous. For example, a policy brief published by Casey Family Programs (n.d.) in the mid-2000s stated that the existence of racial disproportionality, defined as the overrepresentation of children of color in the foster care system, is "an indicator that the child welfare system is not functioning fairly or equitably" (p. 1). No acknowledgement of any other potential explanations was provided. This prevailing notion was also apparent in many of the scholarly publications written prior to 2010. For example, in the introductory article of a special issue on racial disproportionality published by the Child Welfare League of America, Cross (2008) states,

> The real culprit appears to be our own desire to do good and to protect children from perceived threats and our unwillingness to come to terms with our own fears, deeply ingrained prejudices, and dangerous ignorance of those who are different from us. These factors cumulatively add up to an unintended race or culture bias that pervades the field and exponentially compounds the problem of disproportionality at every decision point in the system (p. 12).

Emergence of Disparity as a More Useful Indicator

By the mid-2000s, concerns had been raised regarding the ways in which disproportionality was being measured and the subsequent interpretations of those measures. Ards et al. (2003) used data from Minnesota in 2000 to examine rates of substantiation within the state. First, the authors found that statewide rates of disproportionality were inflated due to a failure to disaggregate counties with large populations of children of color from counties with small populations, suggesting caution when using statewide rates of disproportionality to drive policy considerations when those statistics included data from widely dispersed geographical areas. But secondly, the study highlighted the value of using a conditional population as the denominator to calculate disproportionality by showing the difference between substantiation-to-population disproportionality (i.e., the percentage of Black children in substantiated cases compared to the percentage of Black children in the child population) and substantiation-to-report disproportionality (i.e., the percentage of Black children in substantiated cases compared to the percentage of Black children in reports of alleged maltreatment). While rates of substantiation-to-population disproportionality for Blacks revealed some of the highest disproportionality rates in the nation, the substantiation-to-report statistic showed virtually no presence of disproportionality. The logic of using a conditional population as the reference population was that not all children in the general population are at risk of the occurrence under examination – in this example, a substantiated investigation. Only children who are involved in a report of alleged maltreatment can be involved in a substantiated case of maltreatment, thus selecting reports of alleged maltreatment as the base population eliminates bias that may have occurred in prior events or decisions. While there may be scenarios where the use of the population denominator is more appropriate, this marked one of the first studies to document a potential limitation in calculating disproportionality statistics using the general population as the reference group, particularly when those statistics are used to drive policy considerations.

Along with growing awareness of the limitations of the general population as a reference group, the concept of *disparity* began to emerge as a potentially useful indicator in identifying and understanding racial differences in the child welfare system. Despite considerable use in other fields including juvenile justice and public health, the measurement of disparity in child welfare was not commonly used prior to the last decade. Fluke et al. (2003) were among the first to calculate a measure of disparity in investigated and substantiated reports and to discuss how this measure differed from disproportionality. Using NDCANS data from five states, Fluke et al. calculated a disparity index for Black, Asian, Hispanic, and Native American children to represent the odds of those children being involved in investigated or substantiated reports *in comparison to* White children (the reference group). This differed considerably from the disproportionality measure, which compared children of each racial category to that same group's representation in the general population.

Others have since addressed the limitations of the disproportionality measure as a means of identifying and understanding racial differences (Myers 2011; Shaw et al. 2008). These include challenges in assessing changes over time, as disproportionality is dependent on the size of a given population as a proportion of the total population, which may also increase or decrease over time, as well as a bias toward showing no effect when the racial group of interest is a large proportion of the population. These methodological limitations, combined with increased awareness of the limitations of the general population as a reference category, have largely shifted focus from the identification of disproportionality to the identification of disparity and the use of decision-point analyses, which calculate disparity at various decision-points along the child welfare pathway by using a prior decision point (rather than the general population) as the reference category.[4]

---

[4]A more thorough description of the utility of decision-point analyses and the differences between population-based and decision-based denominators can be found in Fluke et al. (2011).

Shifting Dialogue

While advances were being made in ways to understand and measure disproportionality and disparity among researchers and scholars, the prevailing notion of disproportionality and disparities as problems resulting from racial bias remained among most within the field. This was evident in many of the state-level initiatives designed to respond to disproportionality in their child welfare systems. For example, following a legislative mandate to address disproportionality in the Texas child welfare system, a priority in the state's response was the provision of a training entitled *Undoing Racism* for administrators, front-line staff, and community stakeholders (James et al. 2008). *Undoing Racism* is a two-and-a-half-day workshop conducted by the People's Institute for Survival and Beyond that is designed to educate and empower participants to "undo" the structures of racism that hinder racial equality and to become effective organizers for change. The philosophy of the People's Institute states that racism is "the single most critical barrier to building effective coalitions for social change," and that racism "can be undone only if people understand what it is, where it comes from, how it functions, and why it is perpetuated" (PISAB 2006). As of 2010, over 2,000 staff and external stakeholders had participated in the *Undoing Racism* workshop (Baumann et al. 2010). According to a policy report released by the Alliance for Racial Equity in Child Welfare (2009), at least 7 other states – including California, Florida, Illinois, Indiana, Massachusetts, Minnesota, and Washington – have used either *Undoing Racism* or *Knowing Who You Are,* a curriculum developed by Casey Family Programs highlighting the importance of understanding and addressing racial identity, as key elements in their overall strategies to address disproportionality.

Yet the dialogue concerning disproportionality shifted considerably following the publication of Bartholet's paper in 2009. In this paper, Bartholet critiqued the assertion that disproportionality was caused by racial discrimination or systemic biases in decision-making, stating that those making this assertion were overly relying on statistics from the NIS to justify their position, and ignoring evidence to the contrary. She presented multiple critiques of the NIS data, and stated that the commonly cited assertion that these data showed no evidence of racial differences in maltreatment had been effectively debunked. The paper then drew upon multiple studies that documented the increased exposure among Black families to predictors of child maltreatment, including poverty, unemployment, single-parenting, substance abuse, and disadvantaged neighborhoods, to make the claim that Black children were overrepresented in the child welfare system not because of racial bias, but because maltreatment rates were higher among Black families. Thus, overrepresentation was not only to be expected but also appropriate.

But in addition to presenting an argument that overrepresentation was the result of a higher incidence of maltreatment rather than bias or discrimination, Bartholet (2009) directly criticized the emphasis among child welfare systems that focused almost exclusively on addressing racial bias while ignoring other potential causes, stating, "Focus on the claimed racism of child welfare workers puts attention on a non-problem, while ignoring the real problems of the black community – the societal legacy of racial injustice and the miserable socio-economic conditions that characterize too many black lives" (p. 878). Of greatest concern, she further contended that this emphasis on racial bias and the goal of reducing the number of removals of Black children would ultimately result in harm to those children, stating,

> If black children are in fact subject to serious maltreatment by their parents at higher rates than white children, it is in their interest to be removed at higher rates than white children. If the child welfare system is wrongfully found discriminatory, and, as a result, stops removing black children at serious risk for ongoing maltreatment, the children will suffer immediate and dangerous consequences (p. 874).

Rather than focusing their efforts on addressing racial bias, Bartholet suggested that child welfare systems' efforts should be directed toward reducing maltreatment rates among Black children by expanding prevention programs, and through greater attention, both among child welfare systems and the larger society, to reducing the underlying social problems experienced by many Black families that increase their risk exposure.

For many in the child welfare field, the attention that this paper drew led to their first exposure to the critiques of the NIS data, which had persisted as the driving force behind claims of racial bias, along with the possibility of those claims not being true. But although this paper served to raise the dialogue and challenge some previously held beliefs, many continued to hold the belief that there were no racial differences in maltreatment, in the absence of solid evidence documenting those differences. This changed in 2010, following the long-awaited publication of the NIS-4 (Sedlak et al. 2010b). NIS-4 collected data in 2005 and 2006, and sampled considerably more counties, as well as more CPS and sentinel agencies, than in previous versions of the study, which resulted in more precise estimates (i.e., smaller standard errors) than in prior versions. Specifically, NIS-4 sampled 122 counties, in contrast to 42 counties sampled in NIS-3, and 29 counties sampled in NIS-2 (Sedlak 1991; Sedlak and Broadhurst 1996; Sedlak et al. 2010). And for the first time, findings from the NIS-4 showed that rates of maltreatment for Black children were significantly higher than those for White or Hispanic children in several maltreatment categories. While there were differences according to maltreatment type, results of the NIS-4 found that Black children experienced significantly higher rates of overall maltreatment, overall abuse, physical abuse, and serious harm from their maltreatment (Sedlak et al. 2010b). This was found under both the Harm Standard and the Endangerment Standard used by the NIS-4. The authors also noted that although the NIS-4 found a general decline in rates of maltreatment since the NIS-3, that decline was not consistent across racial groups. Rather, maltreatment rates for White children decreased more or increased less than maltreatment rates for Black children across several maltreatment categories (Sedlak et al. 2010b).

In supplemental analyses of these observed race differences, the authors concluded that these differences were partly the result of the greater precision of the NIS-4 estimates, as well as an increased gap in income between Black and White families since the NIS-3 (Sedlak et al. 2010a). While the percentage of Black children living in the lowest income households increased, some interesting patterns also emerged among certain abuse types concerning the relationship between maltreatment, race, and socioeconomic status that may also explain some of the observed differences in maltreatment rates. While Black children were found to be at significantly greater risk of experiencing physical abuse than White children, this difference was not present among low-income households. Rather, the racial difference was present among non-low income households. This same pattern was observed in the overall maltreatment and emotional maltreatment categories under the Endangerment Standard (Sedlak et al. 2010a).

While these findings were initially a surprise to some, Drake and Jonson-Reid (2011) pointed out that racial differences in maltreatment were in fact present in both the NIS-2 and NIS-3. In their review of the prior findings, they stated, "Although not significantly different, the NIS-2 and NIS-3 race point estimates were consistent with each other and with the NIS-4, both in general magnitude and valence. Black children were 87 % more likely than White children to be victims of maltreatment in the NIS-2, 51 % more likely in the NIS-3, and 73 % more likely in the NIS-4" (p. 17). They point out that the failure to achieve statistical significance in the prior versions of the NIS was not evidence of a lack of racial differences. Rather, large confidence intervals in both the NIS-2 and NIS-3 prevented the differences that were present in the race estimates from achieving statistical significance.

The combination of the Bartholet paper, which rejected the claims of the prior NIS findings, along with data from the NIS-4 which documented significant racial differences in rates of child maltreatment (and the likelihood of misinterpretations of the prior NIS data), substantively changed the discourse concerning racial disproportionality and disparities in the United States. The logic that had previously been used to support the notion that the overrepresentation of Black children was an indicator of bias in the child welfare system could no longer be applied, as the best and most current evidence now indicated that Black children experienced maltreatment at rates greater than children of other races. The Bartholet paper and the NIS-4 also brought renewed focus to the relationship between poverty and maltreatment, and the likelihood that greater exposure to poverty among Black families was a significant contributor to their overrepresentation in the child welfare system. This was further demonstrated in a study conducted by Drake et al. (2011) that received considerable attention upon release. Entitled, *Racial Bias in Child Protection? A Comparison of Competing Explanations Using National Data,* Drake and colleagues used national data to compare disproportionality ratios of child maltreatment from child welfare agencies to disproportionality ratios of other public health outcomes, including infant mortality, low birth weight, and premature birth. This comparison was based on the assertion that these outcomes are sensitive to the same risk factors, particularly poverty. Yet, while child maltreatment as measured by child welfare agencies may be subject to bias, the latter public health outcomes are not. Thus, if disproportionality ratios of maltreatment were considerably higher than disproportionality ratios of the other public health outcomes, that would indicate the presence of bias in the measurement of maltreatment. However, if the disproportionality ratios were similar, this would indicate that it is risk, rather than bias, that drives the disproportionality observed among all of the outcomes. Results indicated that the disproportionality ratios for negative outcomes for Black children compared to White children ranged from 1.79 to 2.97. The disproportionality ratio for overall maltreatment was 1.84, while the disproportionality ratio for poverty was 2.87. As the disproportionality ratio for child maltreatment was consistent with other negative outcomes, the authors concluded that risk, rather than bias, contributes to those negative outcomes across categories. While the authors did not dismiss the possibility of bias entering into the measurement of maltreatment, they concluded that their findings demonstrated that the disproportionately higher rates of poverty among Black families was the primary factor contributing to disproportionately higher rates of negative health outcomes, including maltreatment, among Black children.

Since the publication of the Drake et al. (2011) study, several additional studies have shown a relationship between poverty and maltreatment among Black families, and have found that when controlling for the effects of poverty, race is not a significant factor in the observed racial differences (e.g., Laskey et al. 2012; Needell and Putnam-Hornstein 2012). Combined with the NIS-4 findings on racial differences in maltreatment, as well as the role of poverty, many have called for a fundamental shift in both the discourse on disproportionality and in the ways in which child welfare systems respond to disproportionality (e.g., Bartholet 2011; Bartholet et al. 2011; Drake et al. 2011). These calls have advocated for responses that emphasize the role of poverty in contributing to disproportionality and a focus on prevention programs targeted to disadvantaged Black communities as well as broader responses that address the underlying social conditions that contribute to disproportionately negative outcomes among Black families. Simultaneously, these authors have called for the reevaluation of responses that have focused solely on anti-racism or cultural competence training, particularly when evidence does not warrant its continued focus.

Poverty and Emerging Evidence of Racial Bias

Although poverty does not cause maltreatment, a large body of research developed over the past two decades has documented that maltreatment occurs disproportionately among poor families (e.g., Drake et al. 2009; Drake and Pandey 1996; Freisthler et al. 2007). This was confirmed in the most recent NIS-4, which found that children in low socioeconomic status households experienced some form of maltreatment at a rate more than five times the rate of other children (Sedlak et al. 2010b). However, because of the absence of racial differences in maltreatment in prior versions of the NIS, the relationship between poverty and the overrepresentation of Black children in the child welfare system had often been rejected (e.g., Morton 1999; Yegidis and Morton 1999).

Yet while findings from the NIS-4, as well as subsequent studies, have supported the initial arguments made by Bartholet (2009), they do not completely explain the presence of disproportionality and disparities in the child welfare system, nor do they sufficiently explain away the possibility of racial bias playing a role in their existence. The bulk of studies that have examined disproportionality and disparities over the past two decades have not included measures of income in their attempts to identify the factors contributing to those disparities. A small number of studies have included measures of community poverty in their analyses (e.g., Ards et al. 2003; Goerge and Lee 2005), while others have included measures such as employment status of parents (e.g., Drake 1996; Hill 2005) or receipt of public benefits (e.g., Goerge and Lee 2005; Needell and Putnam-Hornstein 2012) as proxies for poverty. However, few previous studies have attempted to control for the effects of family income on observed disproportionality and disparities. Given the strong relationship between poverty and maltreatment, this has limited the conclusions that can be drawn regarding the role of race as a contributing factor. However, a recently emerging body of research has begun to examine various child welfare decision points, while controlling for family income as well as risk of maltreatment, in attempts to isolate the effects of race and its contribution to racial disparities.

Using data from the Texas child welfare system, Rivaux et al. (2008) examined two related decision points –the decision to provide services to families, and among those in need of services, the decision to remove a child from home in lieu of providing in-home services. To control for poverty, the authors used measures of family household income gathered by caseworkers as part of the maltreatment investigation, and to control for risk of maltreatment, the authors used a risk score constructed by summing the scores of risk scales completed by caseworkers as part of their assessment. Additional covariates included family and child characteristics, region of the state, type of reporter, and type of maltreatment. After controlling for both poverty and risk, the results indicated that race was a significant predictor of both the decision to provide services and the decision to remove children from the home. Specifically, Black children were 20 % more likely to be involved in cases in which services were provided compared to White children. Among those in need of services, Black children were 77 % more likely to be removed and placed into foster care in lieu of receiving services in their home when compared to White children.

The inclusion of risk in this study, in addition to family income, allowed for an important interpretation to be made regarding the role of race as a factor contributing to these outcomes. In the child welfare system, decisions to remove children and place them in foster care are primarily based on the assessment of risk of future maltreatment. When risk is too great to warrant the provision of services within the home, removal is deemed necessary. Thus by holding both risk and income constant, the emergence of race as a significant predictor of removal indicates that the race of the child influenced the decisions made regarding that child, suggesting that racial bias in decision-making remains an important factor in contributing to racial disparities.

The authors of this study also identified an interesting relationship between race, income, and risk. As would be expected, results of this study found that lower income was associated with higher perceptions of risk. However, among cases opened for services and in which children were removed, Blacks were assessed as having *lower* risk than White families. The authors suggested that rather than race directly influencing the assessment of risk, the observed disparities may be better explained by differences in the *decision threshold* caseworkers use when making decisions to remove a child or provide services, with the threshold higher for Whites than for Blacks. Building from the prior work of Dalgleish (2003, 2006), who used a signal detection framework (Tanner and Swets 1954) to develop a model of assessment and decision-making, the authors argued that while individuals' assessments of risk can be similar, their decision thresholds might differ. Factors influencing the assessment are those associated with the current situation or case (e.g., income), while factors influencing the decision threshold are those from the decision makers' history or experience. In other words, the authors suggested that although income is a factor that influences risk assessment, it is not a factor that influences the decision threshold. Rather, the threshold is influenced by factors associated with the decision-maker, such as their perceptions of race. Thus, their findings suggested that although Black families were assessed as having lower risk, there was a different threshold for taking action (i.e., removal or service provision) for Blacks than for Whites, with Black children removed at a lower risk threshold than White children.

Following this study, Dettlaff et al. (2011) used the same data to examine the substantiation decision. However, to further examine the relationship between race, risk, and income, two separate logistic regression models were analyzed. The first model controlled for income in testing the relationship between race and substantiation, while the second model controlled for both income and risk. In the first model, controlling for income and other covariates, race was not a significant predictor of the substantiation decision. Rather, income was the stronger explanatory factor with the lowest income category (less than $10,150) nearly twice as likely as the highest income category ($40,550 and greater) to predict substantiation. This finding added support to the theory that it is the disproportionately high number of Black children living in poverty and the associated risks, rather than their race itself, which contributes to the observed disparities. However, when caseworkers' assessment of risk was included in the second model, the role of income and race as explanatory factors changed considerably. When controlling for both income and risk, race significantly predicted the substantiation decision, with Black children 15 % more likely to be involved in a substantiated report compared to White children.

These results provided further support to the theory developed by Rivaux et al. (2008) of differences in decision-making thresholds. Similar to the prior study, lower income was associated with higher risk, while Black families in both substantiated and unsubstantiated cases were assessed by caseworkers as having lower risk than White families. Yet when controlling for risk, it was not poverty that significantly predicted substantiation, but rather race that emerged as the significant predictor. Again, this suggested that although income may influence the assessment of risk, it is not a factor that influences their decision to act. Rather, the findings suggested that there are racial differences in the threshold used by caseworkers in making the substantiation decision. Specifically, the decision threshold for substantiation is higher for Whites than it is for Blacks.

While the results of these studies have provided important evidence concerning the potential for race and racial bias to impact decision-making in child welfare, and thus the overrepresentation of Black children, it is important to note that other studies using different sources of data have not found a relationship between race and observed disparities after controlling for measures of poverty (e.g., Laskey et al. 2012; Needell and Putnam-Hornstein 2012). However, this emerging line of research has highlighted the need for continued research that includes measures of income and risk in attempts to understand the explanatory factors contributing to disproportionality and disparities.

Current and Emerging Understandings of Disproportionality and Disparities

In their extensive recent review and analysis of the body of research on racial disproportionality and disparities in child welfare, Fluke et al. (2011) provided four explanations of these phenomena based on the most current available evidence: (1) disproportionate need resulting from differential risk that exists due to the disproportionate number of children and families of color living in poverty, as well as other risk factors associated with child maltreatment; (2) racial bias and discrimination, which may be present at the individual level among child welfare staff and community and mandated reporters, as well as institutional racism which may be inherent in the policies and practices of child welfare agencies; (3) child welfare system factors, including a lack of resources to adequately address the needs of children and families of color, as well as the characteristics of child welfare agency staff, and (4) geographical context, including neighborhood effects such as concentrated poverty on maltreatment rates, as well as other community contextual factors that may contribute to differential rates of maltreatment or placement outcomes.

The similarity of these explanatory factors to those that had been posited prior to the shifting dialogue resulting from the Bartholet article and the findings of the NIS-4 suggests that, despite new research findings on racial differences in maltreatment and the role of poverty, racial disproportionality and disparities are complex phenomena that are likely caused by multiple factors that each warrant attention and consideration by child welfare systems. Although current evidence strongly indicates that poverty and associated risk factors are significant contributors to the disproportionality and disparities that exist in child welfare, they are not the sole explanatory factors. While it can be debated which factors contribute *most* to the resulting disproportionality and disparities, a more holistic approach may be to acknowledge the relative contribution of each and to support the continued exploration and understanding of these phenomena.

As stated at the beginning of this chapter, the existence of racial disproportionality and disparities in the child welfare system is not under debate. Yet, over the past two decades, disproportionality and disparities have become value-laden terms that are synonymous with racial bias and/or racial discrimination. As a result, disproportionality has come to be viewed as a problem that is unjust and needs to be rectified. However, by describing disproportionality as a problem, with no consideration for the multiple factors that may be involved, it is inferred that the solution to disproportionality is proportionate representation. Yet, there is no empirical argument or evidence to suggest that proportional representation is an appropriate goal. This is not to suggest that disproportionality should not continue to be studied and addressed by child welfare systems. However, it is important to distinguish between disproportionality that results from racial bias and disproportionality that results from differential risk and need. While the former is a problem, the latter is an appropriate system response. Thus, a simplistic policy goal of reducing or eliminating disproportionality is neither suitable nor justifiable. Rather, a goal should be to reduce and eliminate disproportionality that is caused by racial bias. This should be accompanied by research that documents where and to what extent bias exists in the decision-making process in order to develop appropriate strategies to address it.

Similarly, it is clear that a general strategy by child welfare systems that focuses solely on efforts to reduce racial bias or improve cultural competence neglects many of the important issues that contribute to this problem. However, at the other end of this debate, critiques that contend that efforts to address racial bias should be abandoned are similarly misguided. Failure to acknowledge the potential for racial bias to influence decision-making in child welfare simply creates an environment in which bias, prejudice, and stereotypes remain unchecked. Multiple studies from the field of neuroscience have confirmed the pervasiveness of implicit racial biases that can impact decision-making (e.g., Amodio and Devine 2006; Maroney 2009; Navarrete et al. 2009). Additional studies have documented that unconscious or implicit biases can impact both decision-making and memory retention (e.g., Blair et al. 2004; Eberhardt et al. 2006; Pittinsky et al. 2006). Until evidence exists that child welfare practitioners are somehow immune to the effects of this bias, efforts to address racial bias remain warranted.

At the same time, this does not mean that disproportionality that results from disproportionate need is not also a problem that warrants concern. First, interventions to address disproportionality should focus on the prevention of maltreatment and the reduction of maltreatment-related risk factors. But beyond this, addressing the underlying social conditions that contribute to disproportionate need should be a priority not only for the child welfare system, but also for the communities in which disadvantaged children of color reside, and the broader society that is concerned about racial inequities. Yet, this is a problem that requires vastly different strategies and collaboration with external systems and stakeholders to produce an effective response. In addition to prevention programs, child welfare systems need to engage with community partners in the development of programs that provide support for poor families who struggle to meet the needs of their children in impoverished and disadvantaged communities. Families living in these communities struggle to provide care for their children and have few, if any, community resources available. A concentrated effort by child welfare agencies and other community stakeholders to address these issues may facilitate children being maintained in their homes and reducing disproportionality.

In considering this type of response, it is important to emphasize that disproportionality and disparities cannot be addressed without substantive changes within children welfare systems and in how they have historically responded to children and families. Few successful models for engaging in community partnerships exist and barriers are immense; yet, child welfare systems must recognize that disproportionality is not a problem that can be addressed in isolation. The safety, permanency, and well-being of children are community responsibilities. This includes community members, community service providers, law enforcement, the courts, schools, local government, and other community stakeholders. To be successful, a strategic plan for community engagement must be developed through a coalition of child welfare administrators and community stakeholders that emphasizes developing and utilizing support systems within the community to monitor the safety of children and providing services to reduce risk while maintaining children in their homes. Where resources do not exist in communities for strengthening families and protecting children, child welfare agencies need to work with community leaders to develop them.

Beyond the commitment of child welfare agencies, communities must be willing to not only partner with child welfare agencies but also acknowledge their own role in contributing to the problem. Many communities lack the resources necessary to safely maintain children in their homes and will need to work in partnership with child welfare agencies to develop those resources. Yet, the burden is on the child welfare system to begin the process of engagement to facilitate these partnerships. In doing so, child welfare agencies need to recognize the barriers that exist to community engagement. These include fear, distrust, and a perception of child welfare agencies as harmful within many communities of color. Overcoming these barriers will require a longstanding commitment that begins with efforts to promote healing and a change in those perceptions.

Finally, the current debate concerning the appropriate response to disproportionality has called increased attention to the need to use data appropriately to identify the presence of disproportionality and disparities and to understand the explanatory factors behind them. Inaccurate or inappropriate use of indicators can not only create misleading information but also undermine efforts to address these phenomena. Much additional research is needed that examines the extent to which observed disparities result from differential need and the extent to which they result from bias. Yet, given the strong relationship between poverty and maltreatment, any effort to understand the source of observed disparities must include an examination of poverty as an explanatory factor, as well as other sociodemographic characteristics, before conclusions regarding the role of bias can be made. Studies that are unable to include measures of income need to acknowledge the considerable limitation this creates and express caution in the interpretation of findings. Similarly, researchers and child welfare administrators need to be cautious in their interpretation of prior studies that did not include measures of poverty, particularly when they are used in the development of policy and programs designed to address disproportionality.

Disproportionality and Latino Children

While the large body of research examining disproportionality and disparities has focused on Black children, there is growing awareness of the need to better understand these issues as they affect Latino children. At the national level, Latino children have historically been underrepresented in the child welfare system. As of 2010, Latino children represented 18.3 % of children in foster care, while they represented 20.1 % of children in the general population, a disproportionality ratio of 0.9 (Summers et al. 2012). However, this emphasis on national statistics has obscured significant statewide differences in which Latino children are overrepresented in some states while underrepresented in others. In 2010, Latino children were overrepresented in six states, with the greatest overrepresentation occurring in Maine, where they were represented in foster care at a proportion more than double their share of the general population. It is also important to note that within certain states that have proportional representation at the state level, there can be considerable overrepresentation at the regional level. For example, in California, Latino children are slightly underrepresented at the state level, yet in Santa Clara county, one of the largest counties in the state, they are significantly over-represented, with Latino children comprising 64.5 % of children in care, although they represent only 39 % of the child population (Needell et al. 2012).

At the same time that overrepresentation is a concern in certain states and jurisdictions, there is growing concern regarding the underrepresentation of Latino children in others. Of the 42 states in which Latino children were underrepresented in 2010, 17 states had considerably high rates of under-representation, where Latino children were represented at a proportion less than half their percentage in the general population. Although underrepresentation may be viewed positively, it may also indi-cate that Latino children in need of intervention are not being properly identified. This is a particular concern for children in immigrant families, where more than 80 % of young children live with at least one non-citizen parent (Capps et al. 2004). These parents are likely to be particularly fearful of contact with the child welfare system, and are likely to avoid contact with other social service systems due to concerns over their immigration status (Capps et al. 2004). Thus, children in immigrant families may be less likely to come into contact with many of the social service systems that serve as mandated reporters to child welfare agencies.

This issue is complicated by the lack of information available on the number of Latino children in immigrant families who enter the child welfare system, as this data is not collected at the state or national levels. Thus, their representation in the system and how their involvement differs from children in U.S. born families is unknown. However, data from the Texas child welfare system in 2005 found that although Latino children were slightly underrepresented at the state level, Latino children of U.S. born parents were overrepresented, while immigrant children and U.S.-born children of immi-grants were both considerably underrepresented, resulting in an overall appearance of underrepresen-tation (Vericker et al. 2007). Specifically, immigrant Latino children represented 7 % of children in Texas, yet they represented only 1 % of children in care. Children of immigrants represented nearly 20 % of all children in Texas, yet they represented only 8 % of children in care. Conversely, Latino children of U.S.-born parents represented only 22 % of all children in Texas, but made up 33 % of children in substitute care. Recent data from California has produced similar findings, with Latino children of U.S. born parents considerably more likely to enter foster care than children of Latino immigrants (Needell and Putnam-Hornstein 2012).

Although these data suggest that Latino children in immigrant families are less likely to enter sub-stitute care, and thus may contribute to overall rates of underrepresentation, the reasons for this are unclear. While the previously mentioned concerns due to immigration status may be a factor, data from the National Survey of Child and Adolescent Well-being (NSCAW) suggest that there may be differences in the presence of risk factors in immigrant Latino families that may account for some of these differences. These data show that children of Latino immigrants are significantly less likely than children of U.S. born Latinos to live in homes with many of the risk factors associated with child maltreatment including active drug abuse, poor parenting skills, recent histories of arrest, and high family stress (Dettlaff et al. 2009). These data also identified a number of protective factors that are more likely to be present in immigrant families than in U.S. born Latino families. Thus, underrepre-sentation among Latino immigrant children may be the result of strengths that mitigate risk that are less likely to be present in U.S.-born families.

Ultimately, both overrepresentation and underrepresentation have implications for the safety and well-being of Latino children. Research concerning the factors contributing to both overrepresenta-tion and underrepresentation is very limited, although some studies have documented disparities at certain entry and exit points that may contribute to disproportionality (Ards et al. 2003; Church et al. 2005; Osterling and Han 2011). However, much additional research is needed to enhance the under-standing of disproportionality and disparities affecting Latino children. Although research has begun to address some of these issues, the body of research addressing Latino children's experiences in this system is in its infancy.

Conclusion

Racial disproportionality and disparities in the child welfare system are not caused by a single factor. As a result, efforts to address disproportionality and disparities need to address the complexity of factors that contribute to these phenomena, including racial bias, poverty, and disproportionate need. Future research, as well as efforts by child welfare systems, should continue to examine the impact of racial bias on decision-making and to identify strategies to reduce and eliminate this effect. At the same time, child welfare systems need to work collaboratively with communities affected by disproportionality to develop programs that respond to the underlying social conditions within communities that contribute to disproportionate need. Further research documenting these partnerships and their outcomes is needed to facilitate broader systems change that improves outcomes for children of color, their families, and communities.

References

Alliance for Racial Equity in Child Welfare. (2009). *Policy actions to reduce racial disproportionality and disparities in child welfare: A scan of eleven states*. Washington, DC: Author.

Amodio, D. M., & Devine, P. G. (2006). Stereotyping and evaluation in implicit race bias: Evidence for independent constructs and unique effects on behavior. *Journal of Personality and Social Psychology, 91*, 652–661.

Ards, S., Chung, C., & Myers, S. (1998). The effects of sample selection bias on racial differences in child abuse reporting. *Child Abuse & Neglect, 22*, 103–115.

Ards, S. D., Chung, C., & Myers, S. L. (1999). Letter to the editor. *Child Abuse & Neglect, 23*, 1211–1215.

Ards, S. D., Myers, S. L., Malkis, A., Sugrue, E., & Zhou, L. (2003). Racial disproportionality in reported and substantiated child abuse and neglect: An examination of systemic bias. *Children and Youth Services Review, 25*, 375–392.

Barth, R. (2005). Child welfare and race: Models of disproportionality. In D. Derezotes, J. Poertner, & M. Testa (Eds.), *Race matters in child welfare: The overrepresentation of black children in the system* (pp. 25–46). Washington, DC: CWLA Press.

Bartholet, E. (2009). The racial disproportionality movement in child welfare: False facts and dangerous directions. *Arizona Law Review, 51*, 871–932.

Bartholet, E. (2011). *Race and child welfare: Disproportionality, disparity, discrimination: Re-assessing the facts, re-thinking the policy options*. Retrieved from http://www.law.harvard.edu/programs/about/cap/cap-conferences/rd-conference/rd-conference-papers/rdconceptpaper---final.pdf

Bartholet, E., Wulczyn, F., Barth, R. P., & Lederman, C. (2011). *Race and child welfare*. Chicago: Chapin Hall at the University of Chicago.

Baumann, D. J., Fluke, J., Graham, J. C., Wittenstrom, K., Hedderson, J., Rivaux, S., Dettlaff, A. J., … Brown, N. (2010). *Disproportionality in Child Protective Services: The preliminary results of statewide reform efforts in Texas*. Austin: Texas Department of Family and Protective Services.

Billingsley, A., & Giovannoni, J. M. (1972). *Children of the storm: Black children and American child welfare*. New York: Harcourt Brace Jovanivich.

Blair, I. V., Judd, C. M., & Chapleau, K. M. (2004). The influence of afrocentric facial features in criminal sentencing. *Psychological Science, 15*, 674–679.

Capps, R., Fix, M., Ost, J., Reardon-Anderson, J., & Passel, J. (2004). *The health and well-being of young children of immigrants*. Retrieved from Urban Institute website: http://www.urban.org/publications/311139.html

Casey family programs. (n.d.). *Disproportionality: The overrepresentation of children of color in the child welfare system* [Policy brief]. Retrieved from http://www.casey.org/Resources/Publications/pdf/DisproportionalityPolicyBrief.pdf

Chibnall, S., Dutch, N. M., Jones-Harden, B., Brown, A., Gourdine, R., Smith, J., Boone, A., & Snyder, S. (2003). *Children of color in the child welfare system: Perspectives from the child welfare community*. Washington, DC: Department of Health and Human Services.

Church, W. T., Gross, E. R., & Baldwin, J. (2005). Maybe ignorance is not always bliss: The disparate treatment of Hispanics within the child welfare system. *Children and Youth Services Review, 27,* 1279–1292.

Close, M. M. (1983). Child welfare and people of color: Denial of equal access. *Social Work Research & Abstracts, 19*(4), 13–20.

Courtney, M., Piliavin, I., Grogan-Kaylor, A., & Nesmith, A. (2001). Foster care transitions to adulthood: A longitudinal view of youth leaving care. *Child Welfare, 80,* 685–717.

Courtney, M. E., Dworsky, A., Lee, J. S., & Rapp, M. (2010). *Midwest evaluation of the adult functioning of former foster youth: Outcomes at ages 23 and 24.* Chicago: Chapin Hall at the University of Chicago.

Cross, T. L. (2008). Disproportionality in child welfare. *Child Welfare, 87*(2), 11–20.

Dalgleish, L. I. (2003). Risk, needs and consequences. In M. C. Calder (Ed.), *Assessments in child care: A comprehensive guide to frameworks and their use* (pp. 86–99). Dorset: Russell House Publishing.

Dalgleish, L. I. (2006, September). *Testing for the effects of decision bias on overrepresentation: Applying the GADM model.* Paper presented at the 16th ISPCAN International Congress on child abuse and neglect, York, United Kingdom.

Derezotes, D., & Poertner, J. (2005). Factors contributing to the overrepresentation of black children in the child welfare system. In D. Derezotes et al. (Eds.), *Race matters in child welfare: The overrepresentation of black children in the system* (pp. 1–23). Washington, DC: CWLA Press.

Dettlaff, A. J., Earner, I., & Phillips, S. D. (2009). Latino children of immigrants in the child welfare system: Prevalence, characteristics, and risk. *Children and Youth Services Review, 31,* 775–783.

Dettlaff, A. J., Rivaux, S. R., Baumann, D. J., Fluke, J. D., Rycraft, J. R., & James, J. (2011). Disentangling substantiation: The influence of race, income, and risk on the substantiation decision in child welfare. *Children and Youth Services Review, 33,* 1630–1637.

Doyle, J. J. (2007). Child protection and child outcomes: Measuring the effects of foster care. *The American Economic Review, 97,* 1583–1610.

Drake, B. (1996). Predictors of preventive services provision among unsubstantiated cases. *Child Maltreatment, 1,* 168–175.

Drake, B., & Jonson-Reid, M. (2011). NIS interpretations: Race and national incidence studies of child abuse and neglect. *Children and Youth Services Review, 33,* 16–20.

Drake, B., & Pandey, S. (1996). Understanding the relationship between neighborhood poverty and specific types of child maltreatment. *Child Abuse and Neglect, 20,* 1003–1018.

Drake, B., Lee, S. M., & Jonson-Reid, M. (2009). Race and child maltreatment reporting: Are blacks overrepresented? *Children and Youth Services Review, 31,* 309–316.

Drake, B., Jolley, J. M., Lanier, P., Fluke, J., Barth, R. P., & Jonson-Reid, M. (2011). Racial bias in child protection? a comparison of competing explanations using national data. *Pediatrics, 127,* 471–478.

Eberhardt, J. L., Davies, P. G., Purdie-Vaughns, B. J., & Johnson, S. L. (2006). Looking deathworthy: Perceived stereotypicality of black defendants predicts capital-sentencing outcomes. *Psychological Science, 17,* 383–386.

Fluke, J. D., Yuan, Y. T., Hedderson, J., & Curtis, P. A. (2003). Disproportionate representation of race and ethnicity in child maltreatment: Investigation and victimization. *Children and Youth Services Review, 25,* 359–373.

Fluke, J. D., Harden, B. J., Jenkins, M., & Ruehrdanz, A. (2011). A research synthesis on child welfare disproportionality and disparities. In *Disparities and disproportionality in child welfare: Analysis of the research* (pp. 1–93). Washington, DC: Center for the Study of Social Policy.

Freisthler, B., Bruce, E., & Needell, B. (2007). Understanding the geospatial relationship of neighborhood characteristics and rates of maltreatment for black, Hispanic, and white children. *Social Work, 52,* 7–16.

Goerge, R. M., & Lee, B. J. (2005). The entry of children from the welfare system into foster care: Differences by race. In D. Derezotes, J. Poertner, & M. Testa (Eds.), *Race matters in child welfare: The overrepresentation of black children in the system* (pp. 173–185). Washington, DC: CWLA Press.

Gryzlak, B. M., Wells, S. J., & Johnson, M. A. (2005). The role of race in child protective services screening decisions. In D. Derezotes, J. Poertner, & M. Testa (Eds.), *Race matters in child welfare: The overrepresentation of African American children in the system* (pp. 63–96). Washington, DC: CWLA Press.

Harris, M. S., & Courtney, M. E. (2003). The interaction of race, ethnicity, and family structure with respect to the timing of family reunification. *Children and Youth Services Review, 25,* 409–429.

Harris, G., Tittle, G., & Poertner, J. (2005). Factors that predict the decision to place a child in substitute care. In D. Derezotes, J. Poertner, & M. Testa (Eds.), *Race matters in child welfare: The overrepresentation of African American children in the system* (pp. 163–172). Washington, DC: CWLA Press.

Texas Health and Human Services Commission. (2006). *Disproportionality in child protective services: Statewide reform effort begins with examination of the problem.* Austin: Author.

Hill, R. B. (2005). The role of race in parental reunification. In D. Derezotes, J. Poertner, & M. Testa (Eds.), *Race matters in child welfare: The overrepresentation of black children in the system* (pp. 215–230). Washington, DC: CWLA Press.

Hill, R. B. (2006). *Synthesis of research on disproportionality in child welfare: An update.* Washington DC: Casey-CSSP Alliance for Racial Equity in the Child Welfare System.

Hines, A. M., Lemon, K., Wyatt, P., & Merdinger, J. (2004). Factors related to the disproportionate involvement of children of color in the child welfare system: A review and emerging themes. *Children and Youth Services Review, 26,* 507–527.

Hogan, P. T., & Siu, S. (1988). Minority children and the child welfare system: An historical perspective. *Social Work, 33,* 493–498.

James, J., Green, D., Rodriguez, C., & Fong, R. (2008). Addressing disproportionality through undoing racism, leadership development, and community engagement. *Child Welfare, 87,* 279–296.

Laskey, A. L., Stump, T. E., Perkins, S. M., Zimet, G. D., Sherman, S. J., & Downs, S. M. (2012). Influence of race and socioeconomic status on the diagnosis of child abuse: A randomized study. *The Journal of Pediatrics, 160,* 1003–1008.

Lu, Y., Landsverk, J., Ellis-MacLeod, E., Newton, R., Ganger, W., & Johnson, I. (2004). Race, ethnicity, and case outcomes in child protective services. *Children and Youth Services Review, 26,* 447–461.

Magura, S. (1979). Trend analysis in foster care. *Social Work Research & Abstracts, 15*(4), 29–36.

Maroney, T. A. (2009). Unlearning fear of out-group others. *Law and Contemporary Problems, 72,* 83–88.

Michigan Department of Human Services & Skillman Foundation. (2006). *Equity: Moving toward better outcomes for all of Michigan's children.* Lansing: Michigan Department of Human Services.

Morton, T. D. (1999). The increasing colorization of America's child welfare system: The overrepresentation of black children. *Policy and Practice, 57*(4), 23–30.

Myers, S. L. (2011). Response to a research synthesis on child welfare disproportionality and disparities. In *Disparities and disproportionality in child welfare: Analysis of the research* (pp. 107–112). Washington, DC: Center for the Study of Social Policy.

Navarrete, C. D., Olsson, A., Ho, A. K., Mendes, W. B., Thomsen, L., & Sidanius, J. (2009). Fear extinction to an outgroup face: The role of target gender. *Psychological Science, 20,* 155–158.

Needell, B., & Putnam-Hornstein, E. (2012, January). *A population-based analysis of race and poverty as risk factors for maltreatment.* Paper presented at the Annual Conference of the Society for Social Work Research, Washington, DC.

Needell, B., Webster, D., Armijo, M., Lee, S., Dawson, W., Magruder, J.., … Nuttbrock, A. (2012). *Child welfare services reports for California.* Retrieved from University of California at Berkeley Center for Social Services Research website: http://cssr.berkeley.edu/CWSCMSreports/

Osterling, K. L., & Han, M. (2011). Reunification outcomes among Mexican immigrant families in the child welfare system. *Children and Youth Services Review, 33,* 1658–1666.

Pecora, P., Williams, J., Kessler, R., Downs, C., O'Brien, K., Hiripi, E., & Morello, S. (2003). *Assessing the effects of foster care: Early results from the Casey National Alumni Study.* Seattle: Casey Family Programs.

People's Institute for Survival and Beyond. (2006). *Anti-racist principles for effective organizing and social change.* Retrieved from http://www.pisab.org

Pittinsky, T. L., Shih, M. J., & Trahan, A. (2006). Identity cues: Evidence from and for intra-individual perspectives on positive and negative stereotyping. *Journal of Applied Social Psychology, 36,* 2215–2239.

Casey Family Programs. (2009). *Breakthrough series collaborative: Reducing racial disproportionality and disparate outcomes for children and families of color in the child welfare system.* Washington, DC: Author.

Rivaux, S. L., James, J., Wittenstrom, K., Baumann, D., Sheets, J., Henry, J., & Jeffries, V. (2008). The intersection of race, poverty, and risk: Understanding the decision to provide services to clients and to remove children. *Child Welfare, 87,* 151–168.

Roberts, D. (2002). *Shattered bonds: The color of child welfare.* New York: Civitas.

Roberts, D. (2008). The racial geography of child welfare: Toward a new research paradigm. *Child Welfare, 87*(2), 125–150.

Rolock, N., & Testa, M. (2005). Indicated child abuse and neglect reports: Is the investigation process racially biased? In D. Derezotes et al. (Eds.), *Race matters in child welfare: The overrepresentation of African American children in the system* (pp. 119–130). Washington, DC: CWLA Press.

Sedlak, A. (1991). *National incidence and prevalence of child abuse and neglect 1988: Revised report.* Washington, DC: Department of Health and Human Services.

Sedlak, A. J., & Broadhurst, D. (1996). *Third national incidence study of child abuse and neglect: Final report.* Washington, DC: Department of Health and Human Services.

Sedlak, A. J., & Schultz, D. (2005). Racial differences in child protective services investigation of abused and neglected children. In D. Derezotes et al. (Eds.), *Race matters in child welfare: The overrepresentation of black children in the system* (pp. 97–118). Washington, DC: CWLA Press.

Sedlak, A. J., McPherson, K., & Das, B. (2010a). *Supplementary analyses of race differences in child maltreatment rates in the NIS-4.* Washington, DC: Department of Health and Human Services, Administration for Children and Families.

Sedlak, A. J., Mettenburg, J., Basena, M., Petta, I., McPherson, K., Greene, A., & Li, S. (2010b). *Fourth national incidence study of child abuse and neglect (NIS–4): Report to Congress.* Washington, DC: Department of Health and Human Services, Administration for Children and Families.

Shaw, T. V., Putnam-Hornstein, E., Magruder, J., & Needell, B. (2008). Measuring racial disparity in child welfare. *Child Welfare, 87*(2), 23–36.

Shyne, A. W., & Schroeder, A. G. (1978). *National study of social services to children and their families: An overview.* Rockville: Westat.

Summers, A., Wood, S., & Russell, J. (2012). *Disproportionality rates for children of color in foster care.* Reno: National Council of Juvenile and Family Court Judges.

Tanner, W. P., & Swets, J. A. (1954). A decision-making theory of visual detection. *Psychological Review, 61*, 401–409.

U.S. Census Bureau. (2012). *2010 census data* [Data file]. Retrieved from http://2010.census.gov/2010census/data/

U.S. Department of Health and Human Services, Administration for Children and Families, Administration on Children, Youth and Families, Children's Bureau. (2011). *The AFCARS report: Preliminary FY 2010 estimates as of June 2011.* Retrieved from http://www.acf.hhs.gov/programs/cb/stats_research/afcars/tar/report18.pdf

U.S. Government Accountability Office. (2007). *Black children in foster care: Additional HHS assistance needed to help states reduce the proportion in care* (GAO Publication No. GAO-07-816). Washington, DC: Author

Vericker, T., Kuehn, D., & Capps, R. (2007). Latino children of immigrants in the Texas child welfare system. *Protecting Children, 22*(2), 20–40.

Wulczyn, F. (2003). Closing the gap: Are changing exit patterns reducing the time black children spend in foster care relative to Caucasian children? *Children and Youth Services Review, 25*, 431–462.

Wulczyn, F., & Lery, B. (2007). *Racial disparity in foster care admissions.* Chicago: Chapin Hall Center for Children, University of Chicago.

Yegidis, B., & Morton, T. D. (1999). *Ideas in action: Item bias and CPS assessments.* Atlanta: Child Welfare Institute.

Zuravin, S., Orme, J., & Hegar, R. (1995). Disposition of child physical abuse reports: Review of the literature and test of a predictive model. *Children and Youth Services Review, 17*, 547–566.

Chapter 9
Child Maltreatment and Disabilities: Increased Risk?

Angelo P. Giardino, Eileen R. Giardino, and Reena Isaac

Introduction

Children with disabilities or special health care needs are at increased risk for child maltreatment. There are multifaceted sets of factors that place these children at an increased risk for maltreatment. First, the very existence of a disability or special need in a child that diminishes his or her ability to communicate, react, and meet parental or societal expectations can make some children more vulnerable. Second, the unexpected realization of new parents that a child of theirs may never reach the full potential of their nondisabled peers may be particularly devastating to some. Finally, the increased care giving needs that a health condition or a disability may require is likely to add stress to a family setting which may also increase risk for maltreatment (Garbarino et al. 1987).

The Federal Maternal and Child Health Bureau (MCHB) defines children with special health care needs as *"those who have or are at increased risk for a chronic physical, developmental, behavioral, or emotional condition and who also require health and related services of at type or amount beyond that required by children generally* (McPherson et al. 1998, p. 18)." The definition broadly includes children who have a chronic physical, developmental, behavioral or emotional condition and who also require services and supports beyond what is needed by routinely developing children (McPherson et al. 1998). The definition also includes children with a variety of needs beyond typical physical health care, including early intervention services, special education and related services, mental health and substance abuse services, as well as some community based social supports. A conservative estimate of children with chronic conditions of varying severity in the US is 10–13 million (Newacheck et al. 1998). Most recently, the 2005–6 National Survey of Children with Special Health Care Needs (NS-CSHCN) shows that an estimated 14 % of US children and adolescents (birth through age 17 years) who have special health care needs and an estimated 22 % of US households that include at least one child or adolescent with such a need (USDHHS 2007).

A.P. Giardino, M.D., Ph.D., MPH (✉)
Texas Children's Health Plan, Houston, TX, USA

Academic General Pediatrics, Texas Children's Hospital, Houston, TX, USA

Department of Pediatrics, Baylor College of Medicine, Houston, TX, USA
e-mail: apgiardi@texaschildrens.org

E.R. Giardino, Ph.D., RN, FNP-BC, ANP-BC
The University of Texas School of Nursing at Houston, Houston, TX, USA

R. Isaac, M.D.
Department of Pediatric Emergency Medicine, Texas Children's Hospital, Houston, TX, USA

Department of Pediatrics, Baylor College of Medicine, Houston, TX, USA

J.E. Korbin and R.D. Krugman (eds.), *Handbook of Child Maltreatment*, Child Maltreatment 2,
DOI 10.1007/978-94-007-7208-3_9, © Springer Science+Business Media Dordrecht 2014

Child maltreatment along with its synonym, child abuse and neglect has diverse medical, developmental, psychosocial, and legal consequences. There are a wide range of situations such as caregiver acts of commission or omission that have injurious effects on the child's physical, developmental, and psychosocial well-being. Clinicians are aware that the presence of disabilities in a child could be (1) a *risk factor* for child maltreatment to occur, or (2) a *result* of child maltreatment that has occurred. The broad categories of child maltreatment are physical abuse, sexual abuse, emotional/psychological abuse, and neglect, while neglect is subcategorized into the areas of physical, supervisional, educational, and emotional/psychological abuse (see Chaps. 2–5).

It is important that professionals who care for children with special health care needs also work with families and supporting community agencies to help ensure the health and safety of the children. Clinicians should anticipate possible abuse, mitigate risk factors, promote protective factors, and address any treatment needs that arise. A key guiding principle in the area of disabilities and special health care needs is collaboration across disciplines and agencies to meet the essential needs of children and their families. Collaborative decision making remains an ideal way to assure the safety and health of all children, regardless of their developmental path.

This chapter explores factors that place children with special health care needs at risk for child maltreatment and addresses the emerging epidemiologic research that characterizes the extent of this risk. The chapter concludes with practical clinical applications for this information.

Background

Early clinical studies suggesting the association between children with special health care needs and the risk for and incidence of child maltreatment were the start of an evolving body of literature on the topic. Several subsequent large scale epidemiological studies carefully explored the association of child maltreatment among children with special health care needs. See Table 9.1.

Hershkowitz and colleagues (2007) studied abuse characteristics reported by a large sample of children with disabilities. They found there were more children with disabilities who were alleged victims of sexual abuse than who were typically developing children and that disabled children were more likely to delay disclosure of abuse than their typically developing counterparts. The study sample children reported more serious offences and more repeated sexual abuse incidents than the typically developing children. The authors recommended that criminal justice agencies and social welfare professionals should have an increased awareness of the possibility of the occurrence of child abuse when dealing with children with disabilities.

Jaudes and Mackey-Bilaverb (2008) examined the relationship between young children with chronic health conditions and the risk of maltreatment by studying claims of Medicaid enrollment data. The study found that in their study sample of children ages birth to 3 years old, 11.7 % were maltreated (abused or neglected). Of that group, children diagnosed with behavioral or mental health conditions were 1.95 times more likely to be victims of child abuse or neglect than normally developing children. The study found that children who both experienced abuse or neglect before age 3 and had a behavioral health condition were 10 times more likely to be maltreated again. Study findings suggest that professionals who work with children with chronic health conditions be aware of the increased incidence of abuse in this population be better able to identify abuse, and then intervene to protect of these children.

A review of studies published between 1996 and 2009 on the relationship of disabled children to child abuse and child protection found that disabled children are significantly more likely than their normally developed peers to experience child abuse (Stalker and McArthur 2012). Studies also found that there may be an under-reporting of the true extent of maltreatment, as well as a highly disproportionate relationship between children with disabilities, and especially child neglect. The authors suggest a compromised response of professionals to the abuse of disabled children (Stalker and McArthur 2012).

Table 9.1 Early clinical studies and topical reviews

Source	Description	Findings
Hunter et al. (1978)	255 infants discharged to their parents from UNC NICU between May 1975 and June, 1976	3.9 % were reported for maltreatment during the ensuing year (0.5 % expected)
		Maltreated Infants:
		Were less mature at birth
		Had more congenital defects
Glaser and Bentovim (1979)	175 children discussed at Hospital for Sick Children (London) weekly maltreatment meeting between 1973 and 1977	38 % had pre-existing disability
		Acts of omission – most frequent form of maltreatment in disability group
		Rate of abuse increases with child's age
Diamond and Jaudes (1983)	86 children with cerebral palsy seen at LaRabida Children's Hospital (Chicago) between September 1979 and August 1980	11 % suffered maltreatment following diagnosis
		22 % viewed as at risk for maltreatment.
Hergenroeder et al. (1985)	40 children discharged from Children's Hospital of Pittsburgh between July, 1976 and June, 1978 and diagnosed as having been maltreated	Compared to 40 controls from ambulatory clinics
		Incidence of prematurity 2.5 times higher in study group
		Higher number of second or later births.
Ammerman et al. (1989)	150 children with disabilities admitted for neuropsychiatric treatment at Western Psychiatric Institute (Pittsburgh)	39 % exhibited past or current evidence for maltreatment with 28 % being rated as definite or probable.
		Higher rate of institutional care, more siblings in family and less likely to be profoundly mentally retarded.
Sullivan et al. (1991)	482 (274 male and 208 female) children with disabilities and documented maltreatment who were evaluated at Boys Town National Research Hospital (Omaha)	Over half of the children had communication related disability
		Boys in residential setting had a high rate of sexual abuse compared to girls and the general population.
White et al. (1987)	Review which explores theoretical, definitional, and methodologic issues	Focus on:
		Family and situational factors
		Child factors
		Focus on:
		Studies support but do not confirm linkages between children with disabilities and risk of maltreatment.
Tharinger et al. (1990)	Review explores issue of vulnerability to sexual abuse in children (and adults) who are intellectually impaired	Focus on professional response
		Better training needed in identification, evaluation and treatment
		Reasons for vulnerability
		Lifelong caregivers
		Institutional
		Judgement
		Sexual

Conceptual Models

Conceptual models provide a framework for people to understand factors and dynamics that cause certain phenomena to occur. Children with disabilities or special health care needs may be at greater risk for maltreatment due to reasons that include difficult behaviors and social inabilities that can

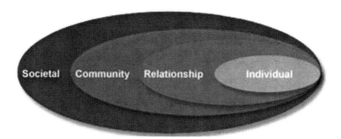

Fig. 9.1 Ecological Model for Understanding Violence: The Socio-Ecological Model considers the complex interplay between an individual, his/her caregiving relationships, the community in which the individual and caregivers live, and their societal values and priorities (CDC 2009)

cause increased stress in their caregiving environment. The human ecology or socio-ecological model developed by Urie Bronfenbrenner (1977) is a paradigm that outlines factors that place people at risk for child abuse and neglect (See Fig. 9.1). The model defines child development in the context of an interacting, dynamic system that includes individual child development, caregivers, the child's family and relationships within the care giving environment (micro system), the community in which the child and family exist, external forces applied to the system (exosystem), and sociocultural values that overlay the community and its families (macro system) (Bronfenbrenner 1977). Garbarino (1977) showed how the nature of the roles of the parent and child, family relationships, social stress, and social and cultural values interact related to child abuse and neglect (Belsky 1980; Justice et al. 1985).

From a practical perspective, the prevention of violence and child maltreatment requires that people first understand what causes or influences dysfunctional interactions that may, in turn, result in violence within families and caregiving environments. The four system levels of the social-ecological model (individual, relationship, community, and society) consider how factors may interact in the system levels to then put individuals and families at higher risk for violence and child maltreatment (Dahlberg and Krug 2002). The Centers for Disease Control (CDC) (2009) uses the social-ecological model as a prevention strategy to identify risk factors that may cause violence in a family or human environment. Prevention strategies in the form of developmentally appropriate interventions to address each level of the model are more likely to sustain prevention efforts over time than any single intervention (CDC 2009).

Ray Helfer (1973, 1987), a pediatrician and luminary in the early field of child maltreatment, described a clinical and developmental perspective based on the principles of the ecological model as a way to understand the etiology of child maltreatment. The Helfer approach identifies factors that describe the child and caregiver events, triggers and stressors that may occur in the child's environment that can result in risk for injury, actual injury, or neglect. Although, there are no justifications to inflict injury on a child, the Helfer model identifies factors that may underlie the risk for injury including characteristics of a child that may predispose the occurrence of child maltreatment (Helfer 1973, 1987).

Table 9.2 shows caregiver factors, child factors, and environmental factors associated with potential child abuse or neglect. Specific factors associated with risk for abuse or neglect include prematurity and disabilities (Breslau et al. 1982; White et al. 1987; Garbarino et al. 1987). For example, a premature infant may be at higher risk for maltreatment due to medical fragility, increased stress associated from the level of medical care that prematurity requires, or decreased bonding between child and parent (Sameroff and Abbe 1978). Caregiver factors suggest that physically, developmentally, and mentally challenged children are at increased risk due to the high demand that their special needs place on the caregiver (Frisch and Rhodes 1982; Gabarino et al. 1987). The special needs of

Table 9.2 Factors associated with potential abuse or neglect (Helfer 1973)

Component	Examples
Caregiver factors	Personal history
	Personality style
	Psychological functioning
	Expectations of the child
	Ability to nurture and assist the child's developmental progress
	Rearing practices modeled during the parents' own upbringing
	Degree of social isolation characteristic of the parent (i.e. his or her ability to ask for and receive help from other individuals in the social network)
	Support of the caregiver's partner in assisting with the parenting role
	Ability to deal with internal and external difficulty and coping strategies
Child factors	Prematurity and disability
	Poor bonding with caregiver
	Medical fragility
	Level of medical care of premature children
	Special needs of physically and mentally disabled children
	Child perceived as "difficult"
Environmental factors	Poverty
	Significant life events
	Caregiver-child interaction patterns
	Caregiver role conflicts

children cause increased stress, fewer satisfactory interactions between child and caregivers, and fewer support systems from family and non-family members.

The special health care needs of a child may be an essential factor in the complicated set of circumstances that predisposes a child to maltreatment. Physical limitations that impair the child's functioning at an independent or expected level may place the child at risk, while behavioral or cognitive limitations that affect a child's capacity for emotional restraint or appropriate development further place the child at risk (Sullivan and Knutson 1998). Children with special health care needs typically have a heightened dependence upon caregivers, while their difficulties in communication and comprehension make them less able to seek protection from maltreatment when it does occur.

Children with disabilities and special health care needs may be at higher risk for possible sexual abuse and exploitation. It is easier for a perpetrator to disguise sexual maltreatment, and the child may be less likely to verbalize abuse or be believed by caregivers if abusive interactions are disclosed. Children with disabilities and special health care needs are often helped by multiple caregivers (whether familial, therapeutic, or educational), which in turn further increases the number of people with access to the child. Increased access of caregivers offers increased opportunities for potential harm to these children (Sobsey 1994).

Child maltreatment may also result in the development of permanent or temporary disabilities, which can then precipitate further abuse (Jaudes and Diamond 1985). A previously normally developing child with abusive head trauma (AHT) is an example of how child abuse creates a long term disability (Frasier 2008). AHT is one of the most devastating forms of physical child abuse and is a preventable major public health problem. The outcomes for maltreatment inflicted neurotrauma are often more devastating than other causes of childhood head injuries such as accidental trauma or falls. Approximately 7–30 % of infants who are victims of AHT die, 30–50 % have significant cognitive or neurologic deficits, while 30 % have a chance of recovery with continued risk of long-term neurologic sequela (Frasier 2008). Ongoing neurologic problems include cognitive and behavioral disturbances, developmental delay, motor and visual deficits, and/or learning deficits.

Stress

Stress is a subjective phenomenon that varies from one person to another. Situations that cause stress to one individual may or may not be stressful to another. The internal anxiety and stressors related to the perception of an inability to meet external demands is often a factor in the occurrence of abusive interactions (Selye 1956; Gabarino et al. 1987). Caregiver stress and frustration are often factors in child maltreatment (Straus and Kantor 1987). Individual or collective coping strategies may mitigate the amount of stress experienced in a given situation. Environmental factors that may increase the incidence of maltreatment include inadequate economic resources, limited community and social supports, and stressful interactions between the child and the caregiver(s).

The most common stressors related to child maltreatment are associated with poverty. Poverty-related stressors include significant life events, caregiver-child interaction patterns, and caregiver role conflicts (Justice and Justice 1976; Straus and Kantor 1987). The health care provider can identify child specific and environmental factors that may place the child at increased risk for injury, provide the caregiver with ongoing anticipatory guidance related to these stressors, and make appropriate referrals to needed support and resources for the caregivers.

Discipline and Corporal Punishment

Caregiver use of corporal punishment is a risk factor for physical abuse among children with special health care needs, as well as routinely developing children. Corporal punishment is allowed in public schools of 21 states in the United States, and can include examples such as physical striking a child, making the child do humiliating activities such as cleaning or repetitive tasks, or physical exercise inconsistent with the child's abilities, to name a few (Sullivan 2009). Though, consistent limit setting and developmentally appropriate discipline is a normal aspect of child rearing (Berger et al. 1988; Straus 1987), discipline becomes maltreatment when the correction causes bodily or psychological harm. Uncontrolled punishment that results in clinical findings such as ecchymosis, muscle injury, hematomas, fractures, intracranial bleeds, and death is grounds for the health care provider to report such findings to child protective services and law enforcement agencies (Straus et al. 1980). The American Academy of Pediatrics' (AAP) Committee on Psychosocial Aspects of Child and Family Health (1998) states the potential deleterious side effects and the "limited effectiveness" and recommends offering guidance to families on effective discipline that includes "consideration of the parent–child relationship, reinforcement of desired behaviors, and the consequences for negative behaviors" (p. 723). Despite little support for the effectiveness of corporal punishment over non-physical forms of discipline (Gershoff 2008; McCormick 1992) it remains a socially acceptable form of punishment among many caregivers, despite the known negative outcomes (Socolar and Stein 1995).

The behavioral challenges of children with disabilities may add higher levels of concern and frustration to the caregiver, and increase the possibility of physical abuse or corporal punishment. Caregivers may find that the child's challenging behavioral characteristics of noncompliance, aggressive behaviors, or communication problems do not respond well to more traditional means of correction or discipline (Hibbard et al. 2007). Knutson and colleagues (2004) found that mothers of children with profound hearing impairments were more likely to use physical discipline for concerning behaviors than those with children having normal hearing. The increased frustration of caregivers of children with communication problems may be due to a perception that the child intentionally fails to respond to verbal guidance (Hibbard et al 2007).

The use of restraints and aversive interventions are still practiced in homes and institutions, and considered by some as necessary to modify a child's behavior, and even beneficial to the wellbeing of children with disabilities (Sullivan 2009). Aversive techniques may involve unpleasant or painful stimuli as the means to change an unacceptable or inappropriate behavior that usual disciplinary input does not affect (Hibbard et al. 2007). Restraint measures include practices such as prolonged seclusion, tie downs, or therapeutic holding. The Autism National Committee condemns the widespread use of restraints and supports the belief that using restraints restricts the civil and human rights of people with disabilities. There are a number of restraint-related deaths of children and adults and incidents of Post-traumatic stress disorder among persons subjected to the systematic use of restraints [from: Autism National Committee. Position on Restraints. Web site http://www.autcom.org/articles/Position4.html; accessed 8/12/12]. The Autism National Committee called for legislative changes to limit the use of restraints on children and adults with disabilities to brief, emergency situations involving serious threat of injury to the person with disabilities or to others.

The socio-ecological model helps explain factors that put children with special health care needs at increased risk for experiencing child maltreatment in the context of interactions among and between family members, and within the community and society in which they live. Garbarino and colleagues (1987) explored the ecological view as to why children with disabilities and special health care needs would be at increased risk for child maltreatment and found that the following circumstances may contribute to the increased risk:

- Characteristics that make a child unacceptable or difficult to care for,
- Increased caregiver stress,
- Caregiver vulnerabilities and lack of coping strategies,
- A deteriorating pattern of interaction between caregiver and child, and
- Cultural beliefs, such as reliance upon corporal punishment, that foster attitudes or actions conducive to abuse.

Epidemiology

With information drawn from clinical studies and reviews, and insights drawn from the socio-ecological model related to the risk of child maltreatment among children with special health care needs, we now turn attention to larger population based studies examining the quantitative data available to characterize that risk.

The epidemiologic exploration of the connection between the presence of special health care needs and the risk for experiencing child maltreatment depends largely on the definitions used and the study samples (Sullivan 2009). This is true for many public health issues and is particularly challenging for studies involving children with special health care needs and/or disabilities since definitions vary widely and not all researchers use the highly inclusive Federal MCHB definition. Estimates of risk for abuse and prevalence and incidence of child maltreatment among children with special health care needs may vary depending on the definition of special needs and the construction of the study sample. Five pivotal data sources help frame the epidemiology of child maltreatment among children with special health care needs and/or disabilities. The five sources which use population level data include: (1) the annual reports of counted cases reported to child protective services that are compiled and reported nationally, (2) the congressionally mandated 1993 NCAAN report (Crosse et al. 1993), (3) two large scale studies conducted in Nebraska by Sullivan and Knutson, (4) the 2008 National Survey of Children's Exposure to Violence, and (5) The Fourth National Incidence Study (NIS-4) (Sedak et al. 2010).

1. NCANDS: Counting (National Child Abuse and Neglect Data System)
   NCANDS compiles yearly statistics of the child maltreatment reports to child protective services across the nation. Since 2003, the NCANDS reports include information on the presence of disabilities, although not all states reliably provide that level of data. For example, of the 754,000 victims of substantiated child maltreatment in 2010, 35 states provided data on the presence or absence of a disability in the 355,435 cases in those 35 states. 56,238 children among the 355,435 victims of child maltreatment had at least one disability (which represents 15.8 % of the case in those 35 disability reporting states). Specific disabilities reported included global cognitive problems, emotional disturbances, visual or hearing difficulties, a variety of learning disabilities, physical challenges, behavioral problems, or some other disabling condition (USDHHS 2010a). Table 9.3 lists 5 years of available data from NCANDS on child maltreatment among children with disabilities:

2. NCCAN 1993 Report (Crosse et al. 1993)
   The US Congress through the Child Abuse and Prevention, Adoption, and Family Services Act of 1988 mandated that the National Center on Child Abuse and Neglect (NCCAN) conduct a study of the incidence of child maltreatment among children with disabilities. Crosse and colleagues (1993) completed the NCCAN study that provided data on the incidence of abuse among children with disabilities using a nationally representative sample of US children. The study determined that the estimated incidence of maltreatment among children with disabilities was approximately 1.7 times greater than the estimated incidence in children without disabilities. The increased risk included all forms of maltreatment. The 1993 NCCAN study support the notion that there is a link between disabilities and maltreatment. The study found:

   - The incidence of maltreatment (number of children maltreated annually per 1,000 children) among children with disabilities was 1.7 times higher than the incidence of maltreatment for children without disabilities.
   - Child Protective Service (CPS) caseworkers reported that disabilities led to or contributed to child maltreatment in 47 % of the maltreated children with disabilities.
   - CPS caseworkers reported that a disability led to or contributed to maltreatment in 67 % of the children with a serious emotional disturbance, 76 % of those with a physical health problem, and 59 % of hyperactive children.
   - The incidence of physical abuse among maltreated children with disabilities was 9 per 1,000, a rate 2.1 times the rate for maltreated children without disabilities.
   - Among maltreated children with disabilities, the incidence of physical neglect was 12 per 1,000, a rate 1.6 times the rate for maltreated children without disabilities.
   - The incidence of emotional neglect among maltreated children with disabilities was 2.8 times as great as for maltreated children without disabilities.
   - The study's foremost methodologic limitation was its reliance on child protective services (CPS) workers to assess the presence or absence of disabilities among the children. Most CPS determinations were based on opinion rather than data derived from physicians or other professionals trained to diagnose disabilities. Also, the study was limited to cases of intrafamilial abuse identified through CPS agencies. Abuse perpetrated by extrafamilial entities such as residential facilities are underrepresented which could of significant importance considering that children with special health care needs are likely served in these extrafamilial settings (See Table 9.4).

3. Nebraska Studies (Sullivan and Knutson 1998, 2000)
   The first Sullivan and Knutson (1998) study electronically merged the databases of hospitals (or Boys Town National Research Hospital), Nebraska central registry, and law enforcement records of children who were patients of Boys Town National Research Hospital. They compared data of children with no records of maltreatment in any of those agencies to determine associations

Table 9.3 NCANDS data 2006 to 2009 (USDHHS 2008, 2009, 2010a, b, 2011)

Report	2010	2009	2008	2007	2006
Estimated overall number of child maltreatment victims (with and without disabilities)	754,000	762,000	772,000	794,000	905,000
Number of states reporting on child's disability status	35	42	22	42	44
Number of child victims in reporting states (with and without disabilities)	355,435	484,076	218,165	567,614	678,558
Number of child victims with disability in reporting states	56,238	53,514	32,712	45,836	52,194
Percent of child victims with disability in reporting states	15.8	11.1	15.0	8.1	7.7
Disability sub groups (see Appendix 1)					
Behavior problem					
Total	14,023	14,202	11,586	17,494	20,500
Percent	3.9	2.9	5.3	3.1	3.0
States reporting	31	36	22	37	38
Emotionally disturbed					
Total	11,201	9,928	8,126	10,547	12,898
Percent	3.2	2.1	3.7	1.9	1.9
States reporting	35	42	22	42	44
Learning disability					
Total	5,213	5,011	3,244	4,951	5,683
Percent	1.5	1.0	1.5	0.9	0.8
States reporting	32	38	20	39	39
Mental retardation					
Total	2,036	2,100	1,708	2,587	3,194
Percent	0.6	0.4	0.8	0.5	0.5
States reporting	34	41	22	40	43
Other medical condition					
Total	18,603	17,062	13,513	17,315	18,093
Percent	5.2	3.5	6.2	3.1	2.7
States reporting	34	41	22	41	41
Physically disabled					
Total	2,893	3,273	1,230	1,937	2,532
Percent	0.8	0.7	0.6	0.3	0.4
States reporting	32	37	21	41	42
Visually or hearing impaired					
Total	2,269	1,938	1,368	1,969	2,367
Percent	0.6	0.4	0.6	0.3	0.3
States reporting	32	37	22	39	41

between disabilities and maltreatment. The study, which used professionally based diagnoses of disabilities and evidence of substantiated maltreatment from CPS and law enforcement records, found a twofold disability rate among maltreated children (Sullivan and Knuston 1998). Study findings showed neglect as the most prevalent form of maltreatment, followed by physical and sexual abuse. A little more than half of the maltreated study sample endured multiple forms of maltreatment. More girls than boys were victims of sexual abuse, but no gender relationship was determined for neglect or physical abuse. The study provided a more comprehensive and inclusive breadth of data that offers evidence for the association between child maltreatment and disabilities.

Demographic perpetrator data from the Sullivan and Knuston (1998) study is noteworthy. Approximately 98.8 % of children were neglected by family members, with less than 1 % of neglect cases perpetrated by nonfamily members. Stepparents were the most frequent perpetrators of the intrafamilial neglect. Female parents, whether biological or stepparents, were involved in

Table 9.4 Summary NCCAN study (Crosse et al. 1993)

Data collection February-April, 1991 (initial) June-August, 1991 (follow-up)	Results	Limitations
Nationally representative sample	14 % of children whose maltreatment was substantiated had a suspected disability	Relied on "suspected" assessment of disability by CPS case worker
1,249 cases of maltreatment (substantiated)	9 % of children in general population have a disability (7–10 %)	Disability designation not as certain as those made by a health care professional
1,834 children who were maltreated	Ratio = 1.57	Case worker is best source of information on disability in maltreatment cases
257 children with disabilities		

Recommendations
CPS risk assessment should include disabilities
CPS case workers should be educated on:
Disability/maltreatment relationship, and
Identifying disabilities and appropriate referrals in these cases
Professional education needed
State and federal data systems should include information on disabilities
Prevention efforts needed
More research needed

From: Crosse et al. (1993)

69 % of the cases. Family members accounted for the vast majority of perpetrators of physical abuse, with the proportion of male and female approximately equal in both samples. Study findings showed that extra familial perpetrators of physical abuse included most often baby sitters, parental paramours (live-in), and peers, with less than 1 % committed by school personnel. Approximately 53–55 % of sexual abuse was committed by intrafamilial perpetrators. Parents committed 71 % of the intrafamilial sexual abuse, with siblings committing the remaining 29 %. Approximately 92.4 % of sexual abuse perpetrators were known to the child victim prior to the abuse, and 82 % of the sexual abuse perpetrators were male (Sullivan and Knuston 1998).

Sullivan and Knutson (2000) later studied a school-based population and reported that children with disabilities were 3.4 times more likely to be maltreated than their nondisabled peers. The findings showed the risk for physical abuse among children with a physical disability was approximately 1.2 times that of nondisabled children, while the risk for physical abuse among children with disabilities such as mental retardation or speech and language impairments ranged from 2 to 7.3 times that of nondisabled children (Sullivan and Knuston 2000). The study suggests that professionals working with children with disabilities in school based populations should increase their vigilance of the possibility of the increased incidence of abuse in this population. See Table 9.5 below:

4. 2008 National Survey of Children's Exposure Violence (Turner et al. 2011)

This study used a nationally representative sample of 4,046 children aged 2–17 years of age to examine the association between several different types of disability and exposure to several forms of victimization. (Turner et al. 2011). The types of violence/victimization included child maltreatment, sexual victimization, peer assault and bullying and property crimes and the four types of disabilities were included, namely, physical disability, internalizing disorders, attention related disorders, and developmental/learning disorders. The authors addressed at the "macro level" the risk for these forms of violence among those children and adolescents with disabilities and then drilled down to the "micro level" to explore the associations among specific disabilities and specific types of violence. Overall, children with any disability reported significantly higher rates

Table 9.5 Nebraska Studies Data (Sullivan and Knutson 1998, 2000)

Data collection	Results	Limitations
1998 Hospital-based study (Sullivan and Knutson 1998)	Maltreatment among children with disabilities was 2× greater than maltreatment among those without disabilities (p. 281)	
Electronic merger of data- bases of children who had been hospitalized	Disabilities associated with longer durations of maltreatment (p. 283 & 285)	
	Intrafamilial sexual abuse more likely in children with communication disabilities (p. 283)	
2000 School-based study (Sullivan and Knutson 2000)	Children with disabilities: 31 % maltreatment rate	Analyses under represent young children and severely disabled children (p. 1267)
Electronic merger of data-bases of school records with central registry, foster care review board and police databases.	Children without disabilities: 9 % maltreatment rate (p. 1268)	
	Child with disability is 3.4 times more likely to be maltreated than child without disability (p. 1265 & 68)	
	Children who were both maltreated and disabled missed more school days than children who were neither (p. 1267)	
	Children with disabilities 3.88 times more likely to be emotionally abused than children without disabilties (p. 1266)	
	Lowest academic achievement scores found in children both maltreated and disabled (p. 1267)	

of all forms of victimization compared to children without a disability. However, children with specific disabilities displayed varying patterns of the victimization for which they were most at risk. Regarding child maltreatment, children with physical disabilities, internalizing disorders, and attentional disorders reported elevated levels of maltreatment while children with developmental and learning disorders did not report significantly higher rates of child maltreatment. Statistical analysis looked at a number of other factors such as living in a single- or two-parent household, presence or absence of mother or father having psychological disorders, and socio economic status which further refined the risk for child maltreatment. The most notable limitation to the was that children with severe disabilities were likely underrepresented because children aged 10 through 17 years of age were likely to be excluded because they were unable to complete the required interview. Nonetheless, the authors bring an increased awareness of the complexity inherent in trying to assess the level of increased risk for child maltreatment among children with disabilities and special health care needs and call attention to the value in exploring specific types of disabilities as we seek to assess the risks (Turner et al. 2011).

5. The Fourth National Incidence Study of Child Abuse and Neglect (NIS-4) Report to Congress

The Fourth National Incidence Study of Child Abuse and Neglect (NIS-4) Report to Congress is the most recent national incidence study of child maltreatment mandated by the US Congress in the Keeping Children and Families Safe Act of 2003 (P.L. 108-36). NIS-4 is the first report in this series to collect information on confirmed disabilities and used data from the Office of Special Education for the incidence of disabilities among children. The report states that readers should view the initial results in the NIS series with caution as the relationship of disability status with risk for maltreatment were minimum estimates.

The NIS used a different methodology than that used by the yearly counting of cases reported to CPS, and instead viewed maltreated children investigated by CPS agencies as representing only the "tip of the iceberg" (U.S. Department of Health and Human Services 2009). Children investigated by CPS are included along with maltreated children who are identified by professionals in a wide range of agencies in representative communities, and gathered from a nationally representative sample of 122 counties. CPS agencies in these counties provided data about all children in cases they accepted for investigation during 1 of 2 reference periods (September 4, 2005 through December 3, 2005, or February 4, 2006 through May 3, 2006). Additionally, professionals in these same counties served as NIS-4 sentinels and reported data about maltreated children identified by the following organizations: elementary and secondary public schools; public health departments; public housing authorities; short-stay general and children's hospitals; state, county, and municipal police/sheriff departments; licensed daycare centers; juvenile probation departments; voluntary social services and mental health agencies; shelters for runaway and homeless youth; and shelters for victims of domestic violence.

The results of the 2010 NIS-4 report were challenging to interpret with regard to the risk of disabilities for child maltreatment (Sedlak et al. 2010). Contrary to the findings of the 1993 NCAAN study and the Sullivan and Knutson (1998, 2000) epidemiologic studies, the NIS-4 did not show a consistent overall increased risk posed by disability. The harm standard in the NIS-4 was more clear cut set of definitions for child maltreatment than used in previous studies. The NIS-4 found: (1) a significantly lower incidence of physical abuse among children with disabilities compared to those without disabilities; (2) no significant difference in incidence comparing children with disability to those without for sexual abuse, physical neglect, educational neglect, emotional abuse and the other category of maltreatment; (3) a significantly higher incidence of emotional neglect for children with disabilities compared to those without; and (4) a significantly higher risk for serious harm for children with disabilities compared to those without disabilities (See Table 9.6).

In summary, there is an emerging and more detailed understanding of the risk of child maltreatment among children with special health care needs. This shows that the overall increased risk suggested by clinical studies needs to be further refined to factor in specific categories of disabilities and types of abuse in order to be more fully understood. The initial conclusion that children with disabilities are at increased risk for child maltreatment appears to be true, but specific forms of abuse may be more likely among children with specific categories of disabilities or special needs. Over time, we can expect to further characterize this risk in a more targeted and accurate manner as more research is done on these more nuanced associations.

Policy and Research Issues

Children with disabilities and special health care needs are at risk for exposure to violence including child maltreatment. An adequate response requires services including medical intervention, special education, appropriate communication, sensitive law enforcement interactions, and tailored mental health interventions for this special population. Furthermore, professionals across all of these disciplines and agencies must know about prevention approaches as well.

In order to further enhance the evidence and our understanding surrounding the risk for child maltreatment among children and adolescents with disabilities and special health care needs, additional attention will need to be given to some very basic health services research fundamentals. As the literature cited above demonstrates, definitions of who is in the population need to be agreed upon and standardized so that the data collected will be comparable from study to study and across serving agencies. In addition, provisions must be made within our various agencies and across systems to actually collect data on the presence of a disability or special health care need among victims of violence, including child maltreatment, if we are to more fully understand the risk faced by these children and adolescents. Once rigorous data is collected and analyzed, this information can be shared

Table 9.6 The Fourth National Incidence Study of Child Abuse and Neglect (NIS-4) Report to Congress (Sedlak et al. 2010)

	Results (statistically significant)	Limitations
Data collection: 9/4/2005 to 12/3/2005 and 2/4/2006 to 5/3/2006	*Physical abuse* Children with confirmed disability had lower rate (3.1/1,000) vs. children without disability (4.2/1,000) *Emotional neglect* Children with confirmed disability had a higher rate (4.7/1,000) vs. children without a disability (2.3/1,000) *Risk for serious injury* Children with a confirmed disability were more likely (8.8/1,000) to experience serious harm/injury vs. children without a disability (5.8/1,000) (See Tables 9.5 and 9.6.)	The NIS-4 incidence rates for children with disabilities are minimum estimates since this study only pertains to children living in household settings where as the population statistics upon which the denominator is calculated comes from the Office of Special Education and Rehabilitation services which uses a larger population of children living in both household and outside of household settings. (See footnote 51.)

broadly with researchers, clinicians and ultimately policy makers to educate professionals about how best to serve this population and to continuously improve service provision to them at the point of care.

From a research and policy making perspective, what becomes clear when one examines and then tries to apply the findings from several decades of academic literature in the areas of disabilities and child maltreatment is that the initial generic clinical impression of an overarching increased risk for maltreatment among those children with disabilities and special health care needs must be further refined and become more specific to account for various forms of disabilities and different types of violence. In the words of Turner and colleagues (2011):

> "Not all forms of disability are associated with equivalent levels of risk. Similarly, it is beneficial to consider many different forms of victimizations since the level of risk will also differ by the type of victimization. This kind of more differentiated analysis provides a clearer understanding of the nature of the problem. Thus, finding variations in the effects of disability on different types of victimization more accurately delineates the risk for disabled children and can provide clues concerning mechanisms that place disabled children at risk." (p. 281)

Sullivan (2009) calls our attention to a number of research issues in her comprehensive review of 50 papers related to studying children with disabilities who are exposed to a broad range of types of violence (including child maltreatment). First, she reminds us that children and youth with disabilities were included as a specific subpopulation in Healthy People 2010 for the first time since the 1979 inception of this important national health promotion and disease prevention agenda. This is important since having children with disabilities and special health care needs identified in this authoritative process will open up opportunities to encourage inclusion of this population in sample development and data collection efforts across a wide number of research projects and health services evaluation efforts. Second, she counsels investigators to move past the concern over multiple definitional frameworks which has become a barrier to research and instead, while working to standardize definitions, to continue doing valid and reliable studies by adopting and consistently adhering to an appropriate paradigm through a given research protocol. Third, she challenges disability and violence researchers to move beyond an overreliance on telephone surveys for incidence data since that introduces confounders into methodology (e.g., people with hearing impairments or cognitive disabilities may not be able to fully participate). Instead, researchers working with policy makers and regulatory agencies need to develop creative opportunities to link data sets while respecting privacy rights in order to have precise and accurate data bases come together upon which health services research can be conducted. Finally, fourth, Sullivan (2009) plainly states that researchers in this area "need to do more than count and categorize the number of children with disabilities (p. 212)" and move to developing more robust insights into what this counting and categorizing actually means when it comes to exposure to violence and how can this evidence be used to enhance knowledge and guide future practice.

In summary, there is growing recognition for the need for researchers, clinicians and policy makers to embrace a more refined approach towards examining the relationships between and among forms of disability and types of violence. Ideally, this recognition should position investigators across disciplines to move to evermore useful levels of specificity in their research questions going from the simple, "does a disability place a child at risk for maltreatment" to the more nuanced but more informative, "what disabilities place children at risk for different types of violence." The literature discussed thus far provides a window into how rich and informative this more refined approach will likely be as we all work together to understand the risks that children with disabilities and special health care needs may face in their environments and as we seek to best serve them from both a prevention and treatment standpoint.

Appendix I

Definitions

Behavior Problem, Child
A child's behavior in the school or community that adversely affects socialization, learning, growth, and moral development. May include adjudicated or nonadjudicated behavior problems. Includes running away from home or a placement.

Disability
A child is considered to have a disability if one of more of the following risk factors has been identified: mentally retarded child, emotionally disturbed child, visually impaired child, child is learning disabled, child is physically disabled, child has behavioral problems, or child has some other medical problem. In general, children with such conditions are undercounted as not every child receives a clinical diagnostic assessment.

Emotionally Disturbed
A clinically diagnosed condition exhibiting one or more of the following characteristics over a long period of time and to a marked degree: an inability to build or maintain satisfactory interpersonal relationships inappropriate types of behavior or feelings under normal circumstances a general pervasive mood of unhappiness or depression or a tendency to develop physical symptoms or fears associated with personal problems. The diagnosis is based on the Diagnostic and Statistical Manual of Mental Disorders (the most recent edition of DSM). The term includes schizophrenia and autism. This term can be applied to a child or a caregiver.

Learning Disability
A clinically diagnosed disorder in basic psychological processes involved with understanding or using language, spoken or written, that may manifest itself in an imperfect ability to listen, think, speak, read, write, spell or use mathematical calculations. The term includes conditions such as perceptual disability, brain injury, minimal brain dysfunction, dyslexia, and developmental aphasia. This term can be applied to a caregiver or a child.

Mental Retardation

A clinically diagnosed condition of significantly less-than-average general cognitive and motor functioning existing concurrently with deficits in adaptive behavior that adversely affect socialization and learning. This term can be applied to a caregiver or a child.

Other Medical Condition

A medical condition other than mental retardation, visual or hearing impairment, physical disability, or emotionally disturbed, that significantly affects functioning or development or requires special medical care such as chronic illnesses. Includes HIV positive or AIDS diagnoses. This term can be applied to a caregiver or a child.

Physically Disabled

A clinically diagnosed physical condition that adversely affects day-to-day motor functioning, such as cerebral palsy, spina bifida, multiple sclerosis, orthopedic impairments, and other physical disabilities. This term can be applied to a caregiver or a child.

Visually or Hearing Impaired

A clinically diagnosed condition related to a visual impairment or permanent or fluctuating hearing or speech impairment that may significantly affect functioning or development. This term can be applied to a caregiver or a child.

USDHHS (2008, 2009, 2010a, b, 2011)

References

American Academy of Pediatrics. (1998). Committee on psychosocial aspects of child and family health. *Guidance for Effective Discipline Pediatrics, 101*(4), 723–728.

Ammerman, R. T., Van Hasselt, V. B., Hersen, M., McGonigle, J., Lubetsky J., & Martin J. (1989). Abuse and neglect in psychiatrically hospitalized multihandicapped children. *Child Abuse & Neglect, 13*, 335–343. doi:10.1016/0145-2134(89)90073-2.

Belsky, J. (1980). Child maltreatment: An ecological integration. *American Psychologist, 35*(4), 320–335. doi:10.1037/0003-066X.35.4.320.

Berger, A. M., Knutson, J. F., Mehm, J. G., & Perkins, K. A. (1988). The self-report of punitive childhood experiences of young adults and adolescents. *Child Abuse & Neglect, 12*, 251–262.

Breslau, N., Staruch, K. S., & Mortimer, E. A. (1982). Psychological distress in mothers of disabled children. *American Journal of Disabilities of Children, 136*, 682–686.

Bronfenbrenner, U. (1977). Toward an experimental ecology of human development. *American Psychology, 32*, 515–531.

Center for Disease Control and Prevention. (2009). *The social-ecological model: A framework for prevention.* http://www.cdc.gov/violenceprevention/overview/social-ecologicalmodel.html. Accessed 11 Aug 2012.

Crosse, S., Kaye, E., & Ratnofsky, A. (1993). *A report on the maltreatment of children with disabilities.* Washington, DC: National Center on Child Abuse and Neglect.

Dahlberg, L. L., & Krug, E. G. (2002). Violence-a global public health problem. In E. Krug, L. L. Dahlberg, J. A. Mercy, A. B. Zwi, & R. Lozano (Eds.), *World report on violence and health* (pp. 1–56). Geneva: World Health Organization.

Diamond, L. J., & Jaudes, P. K. (1983). Child abuse in a cerebral palsied population. *Developmental Medicine and Child Neurology, 25*, 169–174.

Frasier, L. D. (2008). Abusive head trauma in infants and young children: A unique contributor to developmental disabilities. *Pediatric Clinics of North America, 55*, 1269–1285.

Frisch, L., & Rhodes, F. (1982). Child abuse and neglect in children referred for learning evaluations. *Journal of Learning Disabilities, 15*, 583–586.

Garbarino, J. (1977). *The human ecology of child maltreatment.* Washington, DC: Distributed by ERIC Clearinghouse. http://www.eric.ed.gov/contentdelivery/servlet/ERICServlet?accno=ED138356

Gabarino, J., Brookhouser, P. E., & Authier, K. J. (1987). *Special children – special risks. The maltreatment of children with disabilities.* New York: Aldine De Gruyter.

Gershoff, E. T. (2008). *Report on physical punishment in the United States: What research tells us about its effects on children*. Columbus: Center for Effective Discipline.

Glaser, D., & Bentovim, A. (1979). Abuse and risk to handicapped and chronically ill children. *Child Abuse and Neglect, 3*,565–575. doi:10.1016/0145-2134(79)90082-6.

Helfer, R. E. (1973). The etiology of child abuse. *Pediatrics, 51*, 777–779.

Helfer, R. E. (1987). The developmental basis of child abuse and neglect: An epidemiological approach. In R. E. Helfer & R. S. Kempe (Eds.), *The battered child* (4th ed., pp. 60–80). Chicago: University of Chicago Press.

Hergenroeder, A. C., Taylor, P. M., Rogers, K. D., & Taylor. F. H. (1985) Neonatal characteristics of maltreated infants and children, *Archives of Pediatrics & Adolescent Medicine, 139*(3):295–298. doi:10.1001/archpedi.1985.02140050089032.

Hershkowitz, I., Lamb, M. E., & Horowitz, D. (2007). Victimization of children with disabilities. *American Journal of Orthopsychiatry, 77*(4), 629–635.

Hibbard, R. A., Desch, L. D., & AAP Committee on Child Abuse and Neglect, & Council on Children with Disabilities. (2007). Clinical report: Maltreatment of children with disabilities. *Pediatrics, 119*(5), 1018–1025.

Hunter, R. S., Kilstrom, N., Kraybill, E. N., & Loda, F. (1978). Antecedents of child abuse and neglect in premature infants. *Pediatrics, 61*, 629–635.

Jaudes, P. K., & Diamond, L. J. (1985). The handicapped child and child abuse. *Child Abuse and Neglect, 9*(3), 341–347.

Jaudes, P. K., & Mackey-Bilaverb, L. (2008). Do chronic conditions increase young children's risk of being maltreated? *Child Abuse & Neglect, 32*(7), 671–681.

Justice, B., & Justice, R. (1976). *The abusing family*. New York: Human Sciences Press.

Justice, B., Calvert, A., & Justice, R. (1985). Factors mediating child abuse as a response to stress. *Child Abuse & Neglect, 9*, 359–363.

Knutson, J. F., Johnson, C., & Sullivan, P. M. (2004). Disciplinary choices of mothers of deaf children and mothers of normally hearing children. *Child Abuse & Neglect, 28*, 925–937.

McCormick, K. F. (1992). Attitudes of primary care physicians toward corporal punishment. *Journal of the American Medical Association, 267*, 3161–3165.

McPherson, M., Arango, P., Fox, H., Lauver, C., McManue, M., Newachedk, P. W., Perrin, J. M., Shonkoff, H. P., & Strickland, B. (1998). A new definition of children with special health care needs. *Pediatrics, 102*, 137–139. doi:10.1542/peds.102.1.137.

Newacheck, P. W., Strickland, B., Shonkoff, J. P., Perrin, J. M., McPherson, M., McManus, M., Lauver, C., Fox, H., & Arango, P. (1998). An epidemiologic profile of children with special health care needs. *Pediatrics, 102*(1 Pt 1), 117–123.

Sameroff, A., & Abbe, L. (1978). The consequences of prematurity: Understanding and therapy. In H. Pick (Ed.), *Psychology: From research to practice*. New York: Plenum.

Sedlak, A. J., Mettenburg, J., Basena, M., Petta, I., McPherson, K., Greene, A., & Li, S. (2010). *Fourth national incidence study of child abuse and neglect (NIS–4): Report to Congress, Executive summary*. Washington, DC: U.S. Department of Health and Human Services, Administration for Children and Families.

Selye, H. (1956). *The stress of life*. New York: McGraw-Hill.

Sobsey, D. (1994). *Violence and abuse in the lives of people with disabilities: The end of silent acceptance?* Baltimore: Paul H. Brookes Publishing Co.

Socolar, R. R. S., & Stein, R. E. K. (1995). Spanking infants and toddlers: Maternal belief and practice. *Pediatrics, 95*, 105–111.

Stalker, K., & McArthur, K. (2012). Child abuse, child protection and disabled children: a review of recent research. *Child Abuse Review, 21*, 24–40.

Straus, M. A. (1987). Is violence toward children increasing? A comparison of 1975 and 1985 national survey rates. In R. J. Gelles (Ed.), *Family violence* (2nd ed., pp. 78–88). Newbury Park: Sage.

Straus, M. A., & Kantor, G. K. (1987). Stress & child abuse. In R. E. Helfer & R. S. Kempe (Eds.), *The battered child*. Chicago: University of Chicago Press.

Straus, M. A., Gelles, R. J., & Steinmetz, S. (1980). *Behind closed doors: Violence in the American family*. Newbury Park: Sage Publications (originally published by Doubleday/Anchor).

Sullivan, P. M. (2009). Violence exposure among children with disabilities. *Clinical Child and Family Psychology Review, 12*(2), 196–216.

Sullivan, P. M., & Knutson, J. F. (1998). The association between child maltreatment and disabilities in a hospital-based pediatric sample. *Child Abuse & Neglect, 22*(4), 271–288.

Sullivan, P. M., & Knutson, J. F. (2000). Maltreatment & disabilities: A population-based epidemiological study. *Child Abuse & Neglect, 24*, 1257–1274.

Sullivan, P. M., Brookhauser, P. E., Scanlan, J. M., Knutson, J. F., & Schulte, L. E. (1991). Patterns of physical and sexual abuse of communicatively handicapped children. *Annals of Otology Rhinology and Laryngology, 100*(3), 188–194.

Tharinger, D., Burrows Horton, C., & Millea, S. (1990). Sexual abuse and exploitation of children and adults with mental retardation and other handicaps. *Child Abuse & Neglect, 14*, 301–312.

Turner, H. A., Vanderminden, J., Finkelhor, D., Hamby, S., & Shattuck, A. (2011). Disability and victimization in a national sample of children and youth. *Child Maltreatment, 16*(4), 275–286.

U.S. Department of Health and Human Services, Administration on Children, Youth and Families. (2008). *Child maltreatment 2006*. Washington, DC: U.S. Government Printing Offce.

U.S. Department of Health and Human Services, Administration on Children, Youth and Families. (2009). *Child maltreatment 2007*. Washington, DC: U.S. Government Printing Office.

U.S. Department of Health and Human Services, Administration for Children and Families, Administration on Children, Youth and Families, Children's Bureau. (2010a). *Child maltreatment 2008*. Available from http://www.acf.hhs.gov/programs/cb/stats_research/index.htm#can

U.S. Department of Health and Human Services, Administration for Children and Families, Administration on Children, Youth and Families, Children's Bureau. (2010b). *Child maltreatment 2009*. Available from http://www.acf.hhs.gov/programs/cb/stats_research/index.htm#can

U.S. Department of Health and Human Services, Administration for Children and Families, Administration on Children, Youth and Families, Children's Bureau. (2011). *Child maltreatment 2010*. Available from http://www.acf.hhs.gov/programs/cb/stats_research/index.htm#can

U.S. Department of Health and Human Services, Health Resources and Services Administration, Maternal and Child Health Bureau. (2007). *The National Survey of Children with Special Health Care Needs Chartbook 2005–2006*. Rockville: U.S. Department of Health and Human Services. Retrieved from http://mchb.hrsa.gov/cshcn05/MI/NSCSHCN.pdf

White, R., Benedict, M. I., Wulff, L., & Kelly, M. (1987). Physical disabilities as risk factors for child maltreatment: A selected review. *Physical Disabilities, 57*, 93–101.

Chapter 10
Addressing Intimate Partner Violence and Child Maltreatment: Challenges and Opportunities

Jeanne L. Alhusen, Grace W.K. Ho, Kamala F. Smith, and Jacquelyn C. Campbell

Intimate partner violence (IPV) is a public health issue existing in most countries, occurring across all demographic, ethnic, cultural and socio-economic lines. Women of child-bearing age are at the highest risk of IPV, and the prevalence of IPV is disproportionately high in families with children younger than 5 years of age (Bair-Merritt 2010). The 2010 United States' Centers for Disease Control National Intimate Partner and Sexual Assault Survey (NISVS) population based study found that nearly half (47.1 %) of respondents were between 18 and 24 years of age when they first experienced violence by an intimate partner. More than one in five women (22.4 %) experienced some form of IPV for the first time between the ages of 11 and 17 years.

Research has documented a pervasive link between intimate partner violence and child maltreatment (CM) (Connelly et al. 2006; Holt et al. 2008). The complex nature of such overlap requires understanding, and this chapter provides a foundation for understanding the relation between IPV and childhood maltreatment. Specifically, an overview of related epidemiology will be discussed, and a discussion of the comorbidity of IPV and CM will be presented at length with attention to cultural considerations. The chapter will conclude with recommendations for further avenues of research as well as policy implications.

We use the term intimate partner violence (IPV), although other terms have been used interchangeably in the literature, such as domestic violence, domestic abuse, spousal abuse, and battering. Our definition of IPV is condensed from the US Centers for Disease Control and Prevention (CDC): physical and/or sexual assault or threats of assault against a married, cohabitating, or dating current or estranged intimate partner by the other partner, including emotional abuse and controlling behaviors in a relationship where there has been prior physical and/or sexual assault (Saltzman et al. 2002).

An estimated one in three women globally has experienced some form of sexual, physical, or psychological violence, most often inflicted by an intimate partner (Watts and Zimmerman 2002). In a recent, multi-country population-based survey, women representing ten different countries reported their experiences of violence. The lifetime prevalence of physical IPV ranged from 13 % in Japan to 61 % in rural Peru, with the majority of women reporting prevalence estimates between 23% and 49 %. In the US, the NISVS population-based study found a weighted lifetime prevalence for IPV as: 32.9 % for physical assault, 9.4 % for intimate partner rape, and 35.6 % for intimate partner physical assault, rape and/or stalking, with past year prevalence of physical assault at 4 % (Black et al. 2011).

J.L. Alhusen, Ph.D., CRNP (✉) • G.W.K. Ho, BSN • J.C. Campbell, Ph.D., RN, FAAN
Johns Hopkins University School of Nursing, Baltimore, MD, USA
e-mail: jalhuse1@jhu.edu; gho4@jhu.edu; jcampbe1@jhu.edu

K.F. Smith, MPH
Abt Associates, Cambridge, MA, USA
e-mail: kamala_smith@abtassoc.com

J.E. Korbin and R.D. Krugman (eds.), *Handbook of Child Maltreatment*, Child Maltreatment 2,
DOI 10.1007/978-94-007-7208-3_10, © Springer Science+Business Media Dordrecht 2014

Another recent population-based study investigating IPV among women in 12 major US cities found a prevalence of 9.8 % in the past 2 years (Walton-Moss et al. 2005). Although accurate incident estimates of IPV are difficult to obtain, research estimates that nearly 5.3 million incidents of IPV occur each year in the US, affecting three million women annually (Black et al. 2011; Chang et al. 2005).

Pregnancy may represent a period of unique vulnerability to IPV due to changes in women's physical, social, emotional, and financial needs. Previous research has reported a wide range of prevalence of abuse during pregnancy (0.9–20.1 %; Gazmararian et al. 1996), though the majority of studies have found prevalence ranging from 3.9 % to 8.3 % (Gazmararian et al. 1996; Helton et al. 1987; Martin et al. 2001; Saltzman et al. 2003). While an accurate prevalence of IPV during pregnancy is unclear, research demonstrates that a substantial minority of women experience violence during pregnancy. IPV during pregnancy is associated with considerable risk to the health of the woman and her unborn child. Low pregnancy weight gain, anemia, infections, bleeding in the first and second trimester, preterm labor, high blood pressure or edema, severe nausea, vomiting or dehydration, kidney infection, urinary tract infection, as well as hospital visits related to such morbidity are positively correlated with IPV (Cokkinides et al. 1999; Silverman et al. 2006). Premature birth, uterine rupture, hemorrhage, an infant requiring intensive care unit care, and maternal or fetal death are also associated with exposure to IPV during pregnancy (El Kady et al. 2005). The majority of recent studies have demonstrated a significant relationship between IPV during pregnancy and an elevated risk of delivering a low birth weight neonate (e.g. Silverman et al. 2006). A meta-analysis of eight studies, across the US and Canada, used a fixed-effects model and found women who reported experiencing IPV during pregnancy were 40 % more likely to give birth to a low birth weight baby (Murphy et al. 2001).

The numerous mental health sequelae among abused women include depression, posttraumatic stress disorder (PTSD), phobias, anxiety, panic disorders, and substance abuse disorders (Carbone-Lopez et al. 2006; Pico-Alfonso et al. 2006). A comprehensive meta-analysis by Golding (1999) showed that abused women were three to five times more likely to experience depression, suicidality, PTSD, alcohol abuse, and drug abuse than the general population. Depression in abused women has been associated with daily stressors, childhood abuse, forced sex in the relationship, marital separations, change in residence, increased number of children, and child behavior problems (Campbell and Lewandowski 1997; Cascardi et al. 1999). Factors influencing the development of PTSD in abused women include dominant partners, social isolation, severity and number of violent episodes, presence of forced sex, a past history of child sexual abuse, trauma-related guilt, and avoidant coping strategies (Astin et al. 1995; Vitanza et al. 1995; Street et al. 2005).

Co-occurrence of IPV and Child Maltreatment

There is considerable agreement that the presence of IPV in a household is a risk factor for CM (Kerker et al. 2000; Tajima 2000). Early research examining the relation between IPV and CM was primarily focused on specific populations, namely, families of children reported to child protective services (CPS) for maltreatment and women residing in battered women's shelters. Edleson (1999) reviewed seven local and state CPS studies and found IPV occurred in 26–73 % of families reported to CPS. Appel and Holden (1998) conducted an integrative review of 17 studies of battered women and found a median co-occurrence rate of 41 %, although the rates of overlap were even higher in some of the studies included in the review. Correlations between child and spouse abuse were moderate to strong ($r = .28–.56$). However, the selection bias in these studies preclude an enhanced understanding of how these findings reflect the relation of IPV and CM in community-based and population-based settings. This is evidenced by a more recent review of four representative community samples that found a co-occurrence rate between 5.6 % and 11 % (Edleson et al. 2003).

Recent research examining the co-occurrence of IPV and CM found the rates of IPV are higher among couples living with children compared to couples without children (McDonald et al. 2006), suggesting the presence of children in violent homes is a risk factor. However, data on the prevalence of children witnessing IPV varies considerably (Herrenkohl et al. 2008). It was previously estimated that between 3 and 10 million children witness IPV or parental violence each year (Carlson 1984; Straus and Gelles 1990), but research suggests these numbers are increasing. Based on a nationally representative sample, McDonald and colleagues (2006) estimated that IPV occurs within approximately 30 % of homes that include youth living with two parents, indicating that in the U.S., approximately 15.5 million children live in homes where IPV has occurred within the last year, and approximately seven million children live in households where severe partner violence has occurred within the last year. However, these estimates are considered to be underestimates due to underreporting that occurs in these national surveys (McDonald et al. 2006). In the National Survey of Child and Adolescent Well-Being, a national probability study of 5,501 children ages 0–14 randomly selected among families entering the U.S. child welfare system between 1999 and 2000, Hazen and colleagues (2004) reported a lifetime prevalence of physical IPV of 45 % for mothers of children reported to CPS, with a past year incidence rate of 29 %. Similar findings were reported by English and colleagues (2005) in the state of Washington, where IPV was reported in nearly half (47 %) of CPS cases investigated and assigned a moderate to high level of risk. A reanalysis of data collected from the 1985 National Family Violence Surveys reported that 19.4 % of families reported some type of violence, with 78 % reporting IPV directed only toward the woman, 15 % reporting CM alone, and 7 % reporting both IPV and CM (Tajima 2004). These findings are limited by the failure to consider psychological abuse, sexual abuse, and neglect.

The majority of empirical studies conducted suggest that the presence of IPV in a home increases the risk of CM, with some variance attributable to the perpetrator, type of violence, and type of maltreatment. Rumm and colleagues (2000) analyzed data collected from families on active duty in the U.S. army using an established database of IPV and CM reports. They found that reported IPV increased the risk of CM twofold after adjusting for age and rank (proxy for socioeconomic status) of the military parent (Rumm et al. 2000). In another study, researchers utilized a large high-risk cohort (n = 2,544) participating in a CM prevention program to examine both IPV risk as well as CM through age 5. Results indicated that IPV increased the odds of child physical abuse (OR 3.38), psychological abuse (OR 2.20), and neglect (OR 2.18) (McGuigan and Pratt 2001).

Prevalence Among Racial and Ethnic Minority Groups

IPV and CM exist across all demographic strata, but their prevalence is unevenly distributed across racial and ethnic groups. For example, according to the NISVS study (Black et al. 2011), multiracial women reported the highest lifetime prevalence of physical IPV (50.4 %), followed by American Indian/ Alaska Native women (40.9 %); Black women reported higher rates of IPV (40.9 %) than their Hispanic (35.2 %) and White counterparts (31.7 %), and Asian/Pacific Islander women reported the lowest rate (<19 %) as compared to all racial groups. However, in the Walton-Moss and colleagues (2005) analysis, the racial/ethnic differences between African-American, White, and Hispanic women disappeared when income, education, and employment of victims and perpetrators were controlled. In terms of racial/ethnic differences, the 2010 National Child Abuse and Neglect Data System (NCANDS) also showed that children of African-American, American Indian/ Alaska Native, and multiple racial descent had the highest rates of CM victimization (14.6, 11.0, and 12.7 per 1,000 children in the same race or ethnicity respectively), while reports of CM victimization were lowest among Asian and Pacific Islanders (Children's Bureau 2011). Although IPV and CM are disproportionately high among American Indian, Alaska Native, African-American, and mixed racial groups, the prevalence of IPV and CM co-occurrence in these groups remain unclear because no known study has parsed out the prevalence of IPV and CM co-occurrence based on race and ethnicity. However, it is likely that racial and ethnic groups with high rates of IPV are also more vulnerable to CM. According to NCANDS data, over a fourth (25.7 %) of reported CM victims were also exposed to IPV, either against or perpetrated by a caregiver (Children's Bureau 2011). This is likely an underestimation of IPV and CM co-occurrence, particularly if child witnessing of IPV is also considered a form of CM.

Shared Risk Factors

The relation between IPV and CM may best be understood by examining the risk factors commonly associated with them. These include family-related factors such as poverty, neighborhood violence, parental history of severe punishment, marital conflict, social isolation, and life stressors, such as unemployment and financial strain (Gerwirtz and Edleson 2007; Herrenkohl et al. 2008; Kessler et al. 2001; Tajima 2004). Perpetrator-related risk factors for both IPV and CM include poor mental health, low educational achievement, criminal history, unemployment, and substance use (Dube et al. 2001; Hartley 2002; Herrenkohl et al. 2008; Kessler et al. 2001; Tajima 2004).

More specifically, in a multisite study of misdemeanor IPV cases, Fantuzzo and colleagues (1997) found that in homes in which IPV was present, there was a higher prevalence of substance use, mental illness, and crime in the family. Similarly, Dong and colleagues (2004) found that individuals reporting one or more forms of CM or prior IPV exposure had higher family prevalence of prior substance use, mental illness, and criminal acts. Hartley (2002) concluded that the co-occurrence of IPV and physical child abuse was related to fathers' use of illicit substances and history of arrest for criminal offenses involving infractions other than IPV. Tajima (2004) also reported an overlap in IPV and CM, where lower educational attainment and poor physical and mental health were related to their co-occurrence.

Poverty has been perhaps the most well documented risk factor for co-occurring forms of family violence (Gewirtz and Edleson 2007; Herrenkohl et al. 1991; Lee et al. 2004). With respect to IPV, low income or unemployment among women has been found to be a risk factor for IPV victimization, although more so for recent IPV than lifetime IPV (e.g. BJS 2012; Tjaden and Thoennes 2000; Vest et al. 2002). There is also a demonstrated relation between family violence and related contextual factors, including neighborhood disadvantage (e.g., low income, lack of home conveniences, physical remoteness, crime, neighborhood instability) and violence within the community (Margolin and Gordis 2000).

Maternal stress (Crouch and Behl 2001; Margolin et al. 2003), maternal depression (Hazen et al. 2004), and unwanted or unintended pregnancy (Pallitto et al. 2005) are also associated with CM and IPV victimization (Taylor et al. 2009). Research findings suggest that women who experience IPV during pregnancy have a higher potential for CM perpetration compared to women who do not experience such abuse (Casanueva and Martin 2007; Margolin and Gordis 2000; Margolin et al. 2003). Increased CM perpetration risk among women exposed to IPV may be explained by the increased levels of stress, higher rates of depression, or unintended pregnancy resulting from IPV (Taylor et al. 2009).

Cultural Considerations

A large body of literature suggests that culture and social norms play a prominent role in the differential nature and distribution of IPV and CM. For example, in cultures where premarital sexual relationships are restricted, IPV is closely linked to marriage, whereas in cultures where premarital or extramarital sexual relationships are norm, IPV is no longer associated with marital status (Jewkes 2002). In the US, marriage dissolution presents the greatest risk factor for IPV victimization. According to the Bureau of Justice Statistics (2012), nonfatal IPV victimization is almost two times higher for divorced women and over seven times higher for separated women compared to their never married counterparts, while rates of nonfatal IPV victimization are lowest for women who were married or widowed. As a result, children residing in households undergoing marriage dissolution have an increased risk of witnessing IPV.

In cultures with high rates of nonmarital childbirth, separation, divorce, cohabitation, or remarriage, children are more likely to live in households with adults who are not biologically related to them. For example, in 2009, 53 % of Hispanic births, 65 % of American Indian/ Alaska Native births, and 73 % of non-Hispanic black births were nonmarital, while rates of births to unmarried Asian/ Pacific Islander and non-Hispanic white women were substantially lower (17 % and 29 % respectively; National Vital Statistics System 2011). Marriage and cohabitation rates also vary by race and ethnicity. According to the 2002 National Survey of Family Growth (National Center for Health Statistics 2010), non-Hispanic black women were least likely to be ever married (39 %) compared to their non-Hispanic white and Hispanic counterparts (63 % and 58 % respectively). However, non-Hispanic black women were just as likely to have ever cohabitated as non-Hispanic white and Hispanic women (approximately 50 %), and cohabitating men and women were more likely to report that their partners had children prior to the current relationship (National Center for Health Statistics 2010).

As a result, the prevalence of having a non-biological parent surrogate in the home may vary by race and ethnicity based on the uneven distribution of nonmarital childbirth, marriage, and cohabitation rates across these groups, and some evidence suggests having a non-biological parent surrogate may be a CM risk factor. In a longitudinal study that followed 644 mother-infant dyads, Radhakrishna and colleagues (2001) found that the risk of CM in homes with a non-biological father figure was over two times higher than in families with only the biological mother or with both biological parents in the home, even after adjusting for high risk variables (e.g. maternal depression, number of siblings, and maternal education). Recent research also suggest that families with non-biological father figures tend to have decreased caregiving quality (Berger 2004), while families with stepfathers showed an elevated risk of CM in the home (Van Ijzendoorn et al. 2009).

Similarly, some literature suggests that women with children who are not biologically related to the abuser have an elevated risk for IPV victimization, and this elevated risk persists even if they have biological children with their current partner (Daly et al. 1993; Miner et al. 2012). In addition, some evidence suggests that living in stepfamily households place women at higher risk for more severe forms of physical violence (Brownridge 2004). Although having a non-biological child of the male partner in the home substantially increases the risk of femicide over and above prior domestic violence (Campbell et al. 2003) and was associated with intimate partner violence on bivariate association, it was not an independent risk factor for IPV in the 11 city study by Walton-Moss and colleagues (2005). This is in contrast to an earlier study by Daly, Wiseman and Wilson (1997) who did find such a relationship. Children are also significantly more likely to intervene in an IPV episode if they are not biologically related to the abuser and if the adult couple is not married (Edleson et al. 2003). Taken together, cultural differences in family structure, formation, and stability may be one factor that contributes to the differential distribution of IPV and CM across racial and ethnic groups in the US.

Specific cultural values, beliefs, and ideals may serve as risk factors of IPV and CM. For example, much research has examined Latino cultural values that may help explain IPV and CM in the Latino community. Many propose that the Latino concept of *machismo,* or values and behaviors associated with masculinity, invulnerability, and bravery (Whitaker and Reese 2007), may enforce controlling and aggressive behaviors among Latino men (Chan 2011). On the other hand, the concept of *marianismo*, or positive feminine traits such as submissiveness and self-sacrificing behaviors, may promote Latina women to defer their own needs to in order to be good wives and mothers (Edelson et al. 2007). Similarly, the concept of *respeto,* or respect, is taught to Latino children, which emphasizes the unchallenged power of the father (Perilla 1999), and the notion that husbands and fathers possess the ultimate authority in the family is deeply engrained in the Latino culture (Edelson et al. 2007). As a result, these cultural values may increase the risk of IPV and CM. Importantly, *familismo*, a fundamental Latino value that emphasizes family harmony and loyalty, and *simpatia,* an emphasis on being socially uncon-frontational, may discourage IPV and CM reporting among Latinos (Caetano et al. 2002).

The underrepresentation of certain racial and ethnic groups in IPV and CM reports may be attribut-able to their cultural tendencies to underreport. For example, Asian American and Pacific Islanders report the lowest rates of IPV and CM in national representative surveys, but community-based and culture-specific studies continue to find significantly higher rates of family violence (including use and endorsement of harsh physical discipline) in these groups (Raj and Silverman 2003; Rhee 1997; Yoshioka and Dang 2000). Many studies found that Asian Americans possess rigid traditional atti-tudes on gender roles, patriarchal norms, male dominance, and female subordination, which are linked to higher acceptance and justification of marital violence (e.g. Bui and Morash 1999; Dasgupta 2000; Kim and Sung 2000; Lee 2007; Xu et al. 2001; Yick and Agbayani-Siewert 1997). Similarly, cultural values in male dominance, beliefs in absolute parental authority and child obedience, and normative acceptance of physical discipline may explain why Asian American CM victims are more likely to be maltreated by a man in the family as compared to other ethnic groups (Zhai and Gao 2009), and why Asian American children are less likely to label physical discipline as abuse, despite higher physical discipline use by parents (Lau et al. 2006). Taken together, these cultural values and beliefs on the acceptance, justification, and normative use of violence in the home may explain the low reports of IPV and CM among Asian Americans. Importantly, other cultural values, such as family cohesion, privacy, fear of shame, and domestic harmony may further impede Asian Americans from seeking formal support and reporting to authorities (Lee and Hadeed 2009; Zhai and Gao 2009).

The cultural implications of IPV and CM in the US increase in complexity as the ethnic constitu-tion of the American population continues to change. As of January 1, 2010, an estimated 12.6 million legal permanent residents (i.e. foreign-born immigrants) reside in the US (Department of Homeland Security 2011). However, the rates and risks of IPV and CM among immigrants remain unclear. For example, while some research suggests that immigrant status is associated with higher rates of CM (Hussey et al. 2006), other research found that rates of parent-to-child physical aggression are lower in neighborhoods with higher immigrant concentration (Molnar et al. 2003). Similarly, the reported lifetime prevalence of IPV among immigrant women varies widely, ranging from 12 % to 50 %, and may be as high as 77 % (Menjivar and Salcido 2002).

Understanding IPV and CM co-occurrence in the immigrant population is particularly challenging because traditional cultural values and beliefs change as immigrants acculturate and adopt values and beliefs from the host culture. Studies examining the relationship between acculturation and IPV and CM have produced mixed results. While higher levels of acculturation may decrease IPV risk due to better education, higher standard of employment, and more financial independence, it may conversely confer higher IPV risk due to loss of social control and alienation from traditional culture (Kasturirangan et al. 2004). Similarly, acculturation influences parenting perceptions and behaviors (Elliott and Urquiza 2006), which may affect CM risk in immigrant children. For example, some evidence sug-gests that less acculturated parents and parents in families with greater parent–child acculturation discrepancy (i.e. children more acculturated than their parents) are more likely to endorse physical discipline use (Acevedo 2000; Park 2001). However, these findings are not uniform across different minority groups, and the influence of acculturation on parenting perceptions and behaviors may be vastly different, even among racially similar but culturally diverse groups (Tajima and Harachi 2010).

To date, only one study has examined the risk of IPV and CM co-occurrence among immigrants. In a national longitudinal cohort study, Taylor and colleagues (2009) found that despite lower reports of CM among foreign-born mothers, IPV conferred greater relative risk of CM perpetration on foreign-born mothers than it did on US-born mothers. However, our knowledge in the link between IPV and CM among immigrants remains limited. These findings support the need to further examine IPV and CM risks, co-occurrence, and its association with acculturation in the immigrant population, with particular attention to the differential influence of acculturation on ethnically diverse groups.

Consequences of IPV Exposure

A recent meta-analysis conducted by Kitzmann and colleagues (2003) revealed that children who witness IPV have significantly worse psychosocial outcomes than non-witnesses ($d = -0.40$). However there were no significant differences in psychosocial outcomes between IPV witnesses and physically abused children ($d = 0.15$), demonstrating that the psychological impacts of witnessing IPV can be just as devastating as physical abuse itself. Long-term developmental problems, including low self-esteem, depression, anxiety, and school failure, are also more common in children who witness IPV in their home (Lichter and McCloskey 2004; Litrownik et al. 2003; Moffitt and Caspi 2003). Children exposed to IPV are also at risk for a variety of adjustment difficulties, including aggressive and oppositional behavior, anxiety and depressive symptoms, social problems, and cognitive difficulties (Jouriles et al. 2008).

Some research suggests that there may be a dose–response relationship between witnessing violence as a child and developing adjustment problems as an adult. For example, violence severity, i.e. the amount of violence that the child is exposed to, has been shown to be associated with children's maladjustment (Grych et al. 2002; Howell 2011; Kilpatrick and Williams 1998; Wolfe et al. 2003). However, there are family attributes that are associated with positive adaptation, and may act as protective factors against the deleterious outcomes of witnessing IPV. For example, Howell (2011) found that having at least one warm, loving parent or surrogate caregiver who provides firm limits and boundaries, socioeconomic advantage, and more parental involvement were associated with higher resiliency in children exposed to violence.

Intergenerational Transmission

Much research has focused on understanding the mechanisms by which intergenerational transmission (IGT) of violence occurs (Black et al. 2010). Witnessing IPV as a child has been found in the literature to help explain the etiology of IPV, and social learning theory provided the initial theoretical underpinnings for the IGT of violence (Black et al. 2010; Egeland 1993; Hotaling and Sugarman 1986.) The theory surrounding the IGT of violence posits that children who experience violence from their parents and/or witness violence between their parents learn that violence is an acceptable method for dealing with conflict in interpersonal relationships and, therefore, are more likely to use violence in their adult relationships (Egeland 1993). Albert Bandura's early studies on childhood aggression (Bandura 1971, 1973, 1986) provided the foundation for social learning theory and demonstrated how observational learning might be the link between witnessing violence between parents and using violence in relationships as an adult (Black et al. 2010).

Empirical Evidence of IGT

There is a substantial body of literature providing empirical evidence for the IGT of violence (Kerley et al. 2010; Kwong et al. 2003; Renner and Slack 2006). However, different associations have been reported depending on the type of violence being examined and the gender of the victim/perpetrator (Black et al. 2010; Franklin and Kercher 2012; Stith et al. 2004.) For example, Franklin and Kercher (2012) found a significant association between family-of-origin violence and psychological violence victimization and perpetration. In addition, the acceptance of violence significantly correlated with physical violence perpetration, indicating there might be an additional link between experiencing and/or witnessing violence as a child and accepting violence in relationships as an adult. Black and colleagues (2010) examined the impact of witnessing interparental violence on the physical and psychological IPV experienced in emerging adult relationships in a sample of 223 undergraduate students and found evidence for specific modeling of violence with both physical and psychological violence. Witnessing either type of violence as a child appeared to be significantly associated with experiencing that same type of violence in emerging adult relationships.

The literature examining gender differences in IGT demonstrates that both boys and girls who are exposed to IPV are at an increased risk of accepting violence in their future relationships (Fantuzzo et al. 1991; Grych et al. 2000), but boys from violent families are at a greater risk of perpetrating violence in their teenage and young adult relationships (Pelcovitz et al. 1994) whereas girls are more likely to exhibit internalizing behaviors (Cummings et al. 1999; Sternberg et al. 1998). The existing literature on the IGT of violence presents a complex picture of risk factors and mechanisms that warrant further study.

ACE Study

The Adverse Childhood Experiences (ACE) Study was a large collaborative study designed to examine the long-term relationship between ACEs and a variety of health behaviors and health outcomes in adulthood (Felitti et al. 1998). Many reports stemming from the ACE study found strong associations between different types of abuse and household dysfunction and numerous health and social outcomes (Anda et al. 1999; Dube et al. 2001; Felitti et al. 1998; Hillis et al. 2000, 2001). Whitfield and colleagues (2003) examined the association between violent childhood experiences and the risk of IPV in adults and found that witnessing domestic violence increased women's risk of experiencing IPV twofold (adjusted OR=2.3; 95 % CI=1.6, 3.1). Additionally, women who reported multiple forms of adverse childhood events, i.e. physical abuse, sexual abuse, and witnessed IPV, were 3.5 times more likely to report IPV victimization.

Adverse childhood events (ACE) occur concurrently and not independently, so it is important to assess different forms of ACEs rather than examining them individually. If witnessing IPV is to be considered an ACE, then it should also be assessed for in children (Dong et al. 2004). Prevention efforts should address the negative effects of childhood exposure to violence in order to prevent IPV. Furthermore, an assessment of all women for both past histories of abuse as well as current abuse is necessary to best address these issues before IPV becomes a problem.

Limitations of Existing Research

The substantial differences in prevalence rates of the co-occurrence of IPV and CM are in part due to the failure to distinguish between types of family violence, the reliance on investigating prevalence and incidence rates in clinical samples of abused women and of physically abused children, lack of standardized measures for assessment, small sample sizes, and limitations of administrative data stemming from separate social service systems. Despite the considerable overlap of IPV and childhood maltreatment, researchers often approach these two forms of violence as separate entities, which impedes our progress in addressing the occurrence and co-occurrence of both forms.

The differences in prevalence of co-occurring IPV and CM extend to minority populations as well. First, population-based studies on IPV and CM seldom include a representative sample across all racial and ethnic groups and often combine ethnically similar but culturally diverse populations into monolithic groups, thereby precluding a detailed understanding of IPV and CM prevalence in different minority groups. In addition, no known study has examined IPV and CM co-occurrence based on race and ethnicity. Second, the majority of our research efforts in IPV and CM focus on non-Hispanic whites, while few studies have examined IPV and CM in minority groups, especially those with the highest victimization rates (i.e. American Indian and Alaska Natives). Also, despite Asian Americans and Pacific Islanders having the lowest reported rates of IPV and CM, one must be cognizant of their cultural values, or even their existing language barriers (Weil and Lee 2004), that may preclude reporting. Therefore, more IPV and CM research in minority groups is warranted to better understand the etiology of differential IPV and CM distribution across racial and ethnic groups, with particular attention to the role of acculturation. Lastly, many researchers have noted the intersectionality between race/ethnicity and other political, socioeconomic, and environmental factors that influence IPV and CM outcomes across these groups (e.g. Elliott and Urquiza 2006; Euser et al. 2011; Kasturirangan et al. 2004; Menjivar and Salcido 2002). Therefore, more longitudinal, culture-specific research that accounts for these variables is warranted to enhance our understanding of the cultural implications of IPV and CM risk and co-occurrence.

Policy Implications

The overlap and intersections between IPV and CM have been established for a number of years, and although the nature of the overlap has been studied to some extent, the dynamics are not entirely understood. The major controversies in the field have centered around issues of official reporting of child abuse in cases of domestic violence and how best to address prevention and treatment issues.

Just knowing the large extent of overlap suggests the need for regular, systematic cross training between domestic violence advocates and child protective service workers on the local level. This collaborative training could assist workers to routinely consult with each other on cases with high potential for either dynamic to occur as well as in cases where both are already occurring. The consultations need to be collaborative and focused on helping families to provide the best environment for children rather than investigatory and punitive in nature. One aspect that is frightening for mothers who are victims of IPV, as well domestic violence professionals, is that women will feel like they are being made to choose between their children and their equally loved spouse. Women must be assisted in finding ways to end violence in their children's lives as well as in their own lives; the goal is to work toward maintaining and enhancing her relationship with her spouse if that is what she wants. One way that research can help foster this need is to develop and test culturally appropriate collaborative interventions that have these options in mind.

Other policy implications are to enhance, sustain, and rigorously evaluate parenting components of domestic violence abuser intervention programs and to develop and test parallel programs in child abuse family interventions that address the relationships among adult caregivers. Similarly, child abuse prevention programs such as the Nurse Family Partnership and other home visitation programs need to systematically, routinely, and periodically assess for domestic violence and provide domestic violence prevention and/or intervention components within the home visitation program, such as the DOVE intervention (Eddy et al. 2008). State and federal funding for increasing and enhancing home visitation as well as Healthy Start programs need to mandate the same kind of systematic, routine, and periodic IPV assessment and interventions with rigorous funded evaluations. Child custody assessments, mediation, and decisions should routinely take into account actual and potential domestic violence with in depth domestic violence training for mediators, assessors, and judges and magistrates provided by domestic violence experts. In parallel, there needs to be evidence- based child abuse prevention interventions provided within domestic violence advocacy and along with interventions for children who have witnessed domestic violence. Our knowledge, although incomplete, of racial, ethnic, and cultural influences on the overlap of IPV and CM as well as on parenting and partnering practices indicates that policies and interventions need to be culturally appropriate at the least and culturally specific where such interventions have been developed and tested.

In addition, there have been a few tested IPV prevention initiatives for dating violence and the evidence for effectiveness is still premature. While dating violence prevention programs are a promising strategy, to date the evidence supported interventions have been school-based interventions, and were delivered universally (i.e., were not targeted to an at risk group) (Whitaker et al. 2006). Further research is needed on how the various programs work, their specific components, and their generalizability to other populations. With the evidence we have synthesized, it is clear that children and youth who have experienced the overlap of IPV and CM are at increased risk for both victimization and perpetration. Thus, a research and funding priority should include the development and testing of targeted prevention interventions. These intervention programs must account for the cultural context in which partner violence develops. In a field with so much overlap, with the well documented "double whammy" effect for children when they witness both, as well as the high potential for children experiencing both to perpetuate the cycle of IPV and child abuse, there is no excuse for our policies to not take into account what is known and to include mandates for research on what directions will be most effective.

References

Acevedo, M. C. (2000). The role of acculturation in explaining the differences in prenatal health-risk behaviors, mental health, and parenting beliefs of Mexican American and Euro-American at-risk women. *Child Abuse & Neglect, 24*, 111–127.

Anda, R. F., Croft, J. B., Felitti, V. J., Nordenberg, D., Giles, W. H., Williamson, D. F., & Giovino, G. A. (1999). Adverse childhood experiences and smoking during adolescence and adulthood. *Journal of the American Medical Association, 282*, 1652–1658.

Appel, A., & Holden, G. (1998). The co-occurrence of spouse and physical child abuse: A review and appraisal. *Journal of Family Psychology, 12*(4), 578–599.

Astin, M. C., Ogland-Hand, S. M., Coleman, E. M., & Foy, D. S. (1995). Posttraumatic stress disorder and childhood abuse in battered women: Comparisons with maritally distressed women. *Journal of Consulting and Clinical Psychology, 63*(2), 308–312.

Bair-Merritt, M. H. (2010). Intimate partner violence. *Pediatrics in Review/American Academy of Pediatrics, 31*(4), 145–150.

Bandura, A. (1971). Social learning theory of aggression. In J. F. Knutson (Ed.), *Control of aggression: Implications from basic research* (pp. 201–250). Chicago: Aldine-Atherton.

Bandura, A. (1973). *Aggression: A social learning analysis*. Englewood Cliffs: Prentice-Hall.

Bandura, A. (1986). The social learning perspective: Mechanisms of aggression. In H. Toch (Ed.), *Psychology of crime and criminal justice* (pp. 198–236). Prospect Heights: Waveland Press.

Berger, L. M. (2004). Income, family structure, and child maltreatment risk. *Children and Youth Services Review, 26*(8), 725–748.

Black, D. S., Sussman, S., & Unger, J. B. (2010). A further look at the intergenerational transmission of violence: Witnessing interparental violence in emerging adulthood. *Journal of Interpersonal Violence, 25*(6), 1022–1042.

Black, M. C., Basile, K. C., Breiding, M. J., Smith, S. G., Walters, M. L., Merrick, M. T., … Stevens, M. R. (2011). *The National Intimate Partner and Sexual Violence Survey (NISVS): 2010 summary report*. Atlanta: National Center for Injury Prevention and Control, Centers for Disease Control and Prevention.

Brownridge, D. A. (2004). Male partner violence against women in stepfamilies: An analysis of risk and explanations in the Canadian milieu. *Violence and Victims, 19*, 17–36.

Bui, H. N., & Morash, M. (1999). Domestic violence in the Vietnamese immigrant community: An exploratory study. *Violence Against Women, 5*, 769–795.

Bureau of Justice Statistics. (2012). *Intimate partner violence in the U.S.: Victim characteristics*. Retrieved on 2 July 2012, from http://bjs.ojp.usdoj.gov/content/intimate/victims.cfm

Caetano, R., Schafer, J., Field, C., & Nelson, S. M. (2002). Agreement on reports of intimate partner violence among White, Black, and Hispanic couples in the United States. *Journal of Interpersonal Violence, 17*(12), 1308–1322.

Campbell, J. C., & Lewandowski, L. A. (1997). Mental and physical health effects of intimate partner violence on women and children. *The Psychiatric Clinics of North America, 20*(2), 353–374.

Campbell, J. C., Webster, D., Koziol-McLain, J., Block, C., Campbell, D., Curry, M. A., ... Laughon, K. (2003). Risk factors for femicide in abuse relationships: Results from a multisite case control study. *American Journal of Public Health, 93*(7), 1089–1097.

Carbone-Lopez, K., Kruttschnitt, C., & Macmillan, R. (2006). Patterns of intimate partner violence and their associations with physical health, psychological distress, and substance use. *Public Health Reports (Washington, DC: 1974), 121*(4), 382–392.

Carlson, B. E. (1984). Children's observations of interpersonal violence. In A. Roberts (Ed.), *Battered women and their families* (pp. 147–167). New York: Springer.

Casanueva, C. E., & Martin, S. L. (2007). Intimate partner violence during pregnancy and mothers' child abuse potential. *Journal of Interpersonal Violence, 22*(5), 603–622.

Cascardi, M., O'Leary, D. K., & Schlee, K. A. (1999). Co-occurence and correlates of posttraumatic stress disorder and major depression in physically abused women. *Journal of Family Violence, 14*, 227–248.

Chan, K. L. (2011). Children exposed to child maltreatment and intimate partner violence: A study of co-occurrence among Hong Kong Chinese families. *Child Abuse & Neglect, 35*, 532–542.

Chang, J., Berg, C. J., Saltzman, L. E., & Herndon, J. (2005). Homicide: A leading cause of injury deaths among pregnant and postpartum women in the United States, 1991–1999. *American Journal of Public Health, 95*(3), 471–477.

Children's Bureau. (2011). *Child maltreatment 2010*. Retrieved on 2 July 2012, from http://www.acf.hhs.gov/programs/cb/pubs/cm10/cm10.pdf

Cokkinides, V. E., Coker, A. L., Sanderson, M., Addy, C., & Bethea, L. (1999). Physical violence during pregnancy: Maternal complications and birth outcomes. *Obstetrics and Gynecology, 93*, 661–666.

Connelly, C. D., Hazen, A. L., Coben, J. H., Kelleher, K. J., Barth, R. P., & Landsverk, J. A. (2006). Persistence of intimate partner violence among families referred to child welfare. *Journal of Interpersonal Violence, 21*(6), 774–797.

Crouch, J. L., & Behl, L. E. (2001). Relationship among parental beliefs in corporal punishment, reported stress, and physical child abuse potential. *Child Abuse & Neglect, 25*, 413–419.

Cummings, E. M., Pepler, D. J., & Moore, T. E. (1999). Behavior problems in children exposed to wife abuse: Gender differences. *Journal of Family Violence, 14*, 133–156.

Daly, M., Singh, L. S., & Wilson, M. (1993). Children fathered by previous partners: A risk factor for violence against women. *Canadian Journal of Public Health, 84*(3), 209–210.

Daly, M., Wiseman, K. A., & Wilson, M. I. (1997). Women with children sired by previous partners incur excess risk of uxoricide. *Homicide Studies, 1*, 61–71.

Dasgupta, S. D. (2000). Changing the course: An overview of domestic violence in the South Asian community in the United States. *Journal of Social Distress and the Homeless, 9*, 173–185.

Department of Homeland Security. (2011). *Estimates of the legal permanent resident population in 2010*. Retrieved on 10 Nov 2011, from http://www.dhs.gov/xlibrary/assets/statistics/publications/ois_lpr_pe_2010.pdf

Dong, M., Anda, R. F., Felitti, V. J., Dube, S. R., Williamson, D. F., Thompson, T. J., ... Giles, W. H. (2004). The interrelatedness of multiple forms of childhood abuse, neglect, and household dysfunction. *Child Abuse & Neglect, 28*(7), 771–784.

Dube, S. R., Anda, R. F., Felitti, V. J., Croft, J. B., Edwards, V. J., & Giles, W. H. (2001). Growing up with parental alcohol abuse: Exposure to childhood abuse, neglect, and household dysfunction. *Child Abuse & Neglect, 25*(12), 1627–1640.

Eddy, T., Kilburn, E., Chang, C., Bullock, L., & Sharps, P. (2008). Facilitators and barriers for implementing home visit interventions to address intimate partner violence: Town and gown partnerships. *The Nursing Clinics of North America, 43*, 419–435.

Edelson, M. G., Hokoda, A., & Ramos-Lira, L. (2007). Differences in effects of domestic violence between Latina and non-Latina women. *Journal of Family Violence, 22*, 1–10.

Edleson, J. L. (1999). The overlap between child maltreatment and woman battering. *Violence Against Women, 5*(2), 134–154.

Edleson, J. L., Mbilinyi, L. F., Beeman, S. K., & Hagemeister, A. K. (2003). How children are involved in adult domestic violence: Results from a four-city telephone survey. *Journal of Interpersonal Violence, 18*(1), 18–32.

Egeland, B. (1993). A history of abuse is a major risk factor for abusing the next generation. In R. J. Gelles & D. R. Loseke (Eds.), *Current controversies on family violence* (pp. 197–208). Newbury Park: Sage.

El Kady, D., Gilbert, W. M., Xing, G., & Smith, L. H. (2005). Maternal and neonatal outcomes of assaults during pregnancy. *Obstetrics and Gynecology, 105*(2), 357–363.

Elliott, K., & Urquiza, A. (2006). Ethnicity, culture, and child maltreatment. *Journal of Social Issues, 62*(4), 787–809.

English, D. J., Upadhyaya, M. P., Litrownik, A. J., Marshall, J. M., Runyan, D. K., Graham, J. C., & Dubowitz, H. (2005). Maltreatment's wake: The relationship of maltreatment dimensions to child outcomes. *Child Abuse & Neglect, 29*(5), 597–619.

Euser, E. M., van Ijzendoorn, M. H., Prinzie, P., & Bakermans-Kranenburg, M. J. (2011). Elevated child maltreatment rates in immigrant families and the role of socioeconomic differences. *Child Maltreatment, 16*(1), 63–73.

Fantuzzo, J. W., DePaola, L. M., Lambert, L., Martino, T., Anderson, G., & Sutton, S. (1991). Effects of interparental violence on the psychological adjustment and competencies of young children. *Journal of Consulting and Clinical Psychology, 59*, 258–265.

Fantuzzo, J., Boruch, R., Beriama, A., Atkins, M., & Marcus, S. (1997). Domestic violence and children: Prevalence and risk in five major U.S. cities. *Journal of the American Academy of Child and Adolescent Psychiatry, 36*(1), 116–122.

Felitti, V. J., Anda, R. F., Nordenberg, D., Williamson, D. F., Spitz, A. M., Edwards, V., Koss, M. P., & Marks, J. S. (1998). Relationship of childhood abuse and household dysfunction to many of the leading causes of death in adults: The adverse childhood experiences (ACE) study. *American Journal of Preventative Medicine, 14*, 245–258.

Franklin, C. A., & Kercher, G. A. (2012). The intergenerational transmission of intimate partner violence: Differentiating correlates in a random community sample. *Journal of Family Violence, 27*(3), 187–199.

Gazmararian, J. A., Lazorick, S., Spitz, A. M., Ballard, T. J., Saltzman, L. E., & Marks, J. S. (1996). Prevalence of violence against pregnant women. *JAMA : The Journal of the American Medical Association, 275*(24), 1915–1920.

Gewirtz, A. H., & Edleson, J. L. (2007). Young children's exposure to intimate partner violence: Towards a developmental risk and resilience framework for research and intervention. *Journal of Family Violence, 22*(3), 151–164.

Golding, J. M. (1999). Intimate partner violence as a risk factor for mental disorders: A meta-analysis. *Journal of Family Violence, 14*, 99–132.

Grych, J. H., Fincham, F. D., Jouriles, E. N., & McDonald, R. (2000). Interparental conflict and child adjustment: Testing the mediational role of appraisals in the cognitive contextual framework. *Child Development, 71*(6), 1648–1661.

Grych, J. H., Wachsmuth-Schlaefer, T., & Klockow, L. L. (2002). Interparental aggression and young children's representations of family relationships. *Journal of Family Violence, 16*(2), 259–272.

Hartley, C. C. (2002). The co-occurrence of child maltreatment and domestic violence: Examining both neglect and child physical abuse. *Child Maltreatment, 7*(4), 349–358.

Hazen, A. L., Connelly, C. D., Kelleher, K., Landsverk, J., & Barth, R. (2004). Intimate partner violence among female caregivers of children reported for child maltreatment. *Child Abuse & Neglect, 28*(3), 301–319.

Helton, A. S., McFarlane, J., & Anderson, E. T. (1987). Battered and pregnant: A prevalence study. *American Journal of Public Health, 77*(10), 1337–1339.

Herrenkohl, R. C., Herrenkohl, E. C., Egolf, B. P., & Wu, P. (1991). The developmental consequences of child abuse: The Lehigh longitudinal study. In R. H. J. Starr & D. A. Wolfe (Eds.), *The effects of child abuse and neglect: Issues and research* (pp. 57–81). New York: Guilford.

Herrenkohl, T. I., Sousa, C., Tajima, E. A., Herrenkohl, R. C., & Moylan, C. A. (2008). Intersection of child abuse and children's exposure to domestic violence. *Trauma, Violence & Abuse, 9*(2), 84–99.

Hillis, S. D., Anda, R. F., Felitti, V. J., Nordenberg, D., & Marchbanks, P. A. (2000). Adverse childhood experiences and sexually transmitted diseases in men and women: A retrospective study. *Pediatrics, 106*, E11.

Hillis, S. D., Anda, R. F., Felitti, V. J., & Marchbanks, P. A. (2001). Adverse childhood experiences and sexual risk behaviors in women: A retrospective cohort study. *Family Planning Perspectives, 33*, 206–211.

Holt, S., Buckley, H., & Whelan, S. (2008). The impact of exposure to domestic violence on children and young people: A review of the literature. *Child Abuse & Neglect, 32*(8), 797–810.

Hotaling, G. T., & Sugarman, D. B. (1986). An analysis of risk markers in husband to wife violence: The current state of knowledge. *Violence and Victims, 1*(2), 101–124.

Howell, K. H. (2011). Resilience and psychopathology in children exposed to family violence. *Aggression and Violent Behavior, 16*(6), 562–569.

Hussey, J. M., Chang, J. J., & Kotch, J. B. (2006). Child maltreatment in the United States prevalence, risk factors, and adolescent health consequences. *Pediatrics, 118*(3), 933–942.

Jewkes, R. (2002). Intimate partner violence: Causes and prevention. *The Lancet, 359*, 1423–1429.

Jouriles, E., McDonald, R., Slep, A., Heyman, R., & Garrido, E. (2008). Child abuse in the context of domestic violence: Prevalence, explanations, and practice implications. *Violence and Victims, 23*, 221–235.

Kasturirangan, A., Krishnan, S., & Riger, S. (2004). The impact of culture and minority status on women's experience of domestic violence. *Trauma, Violence & Abuse, 5*(4), 318–332.

Kerker, B. D., Horwitz, S. M., Leventhal, J. M., Plichta, S., & Leaf, P. J. (2000). Identification of violence in the home: Pediatric and parental reports. *Archives of Pediatrics & Adolescent Medicine, 154*(5), 457–462.

Kerley, K. R., Xiaohe, X., Bangon, S., & Alley, J. M. (2010). Exposure to family violence in childhood and intimate partner perpetration or victimization in adulthood: Exploring intergenerational transmission in urban Thailand. *Journal of Family Violence, 25*, 337–347.

Kessler, R. C., Molnar, B. E., Feurer, I. D., & Appelbaum, M. (2001). Patterns and mental health predictors of domestic violence in the United States: Results from the national comorbidity survey. *International Journal of Law and Psychiatry, 24*(4–5), 487–508.

Kilpatrick, K. L., & Williams, L. M. (1998). Potential mediators of post-traumatic stress disorder in child witnesses to domestic violence. *Child Abuse & Neglect, 22*(4), 319–330.

Kim, J. Y., & Sung, K. (2000). Conjugal violence in Korean American families: A residue of the cultural tradition. *Journal of Family Violence, 15*, 331–345.

Kitzmann, K. M., Gaylord, N. K., Holt, A. R., & Kenny, E. D. (2003). Child witnesses to domestic violence: A meta-analytic review. *Journal of Consulting and Clinical Psychology, 71*(2), 339–352.

Kwong, M. J., Bartholomew, K., Henderson, A. J. Z., & Trinke, S. J. (2003). The intergenerational transmission of relationship violence. *Journal of Family Psychology, 17*, 288–301.

Lau, A. S., Huang, M. M., Garland, A. F., McCabe, K. M., Yeh, M., & Hough, R. L. (2006). Racial variation in self-labeled child abuse and associated internalizing symptoms among adolescents who are high risk. *Child Maltreatment, 11*(2), 168–181.

Lee, E. (2007). Domestic violence and risk factors among Korean immigrant women in the United States. *Journal of Family Violence, 22*, 141–149.

Lee, Y. S., & Hadeed, L. (2009). Intimate partner violence among Asian immigrant communities: Health/mental health consequences, help-seeking behaviors, and service utilization. *Trauma, Violence & Abuse, 10*(2), 143–170.

Lee, L. C., Kotch, J. B., & Cox, C. E. (2004). Child maltreatment in families experiencing domestic violence. *Violence and Victims, 19*(5), 573–591.

Lichter, E. L., & McCloskey, L. A. (2004). The effects of childhood exposure to marital violence on adolescent gender-role beliefs and dating violence. *Psychology of Women Quarterly, 28*(4), 344–357.

Litrownik, A. J., Newton, R., Hunter, W. M., English, D., & Everson, M. D. (2003). Exposure to family violence in young at-risk children: A longitudinal look at the effects of victimization and witnessed physical and psychological aggression. *Journal of Family Violence, 18*(1), 59–73.

Margolin, G., & Gordis, E. B. (2000). The effects of family and community violence on children. *Annual Review of Psychology, 51*, 445–479.

Margolin, G., Gordis, E. B., Medina, A. M., & Oliver, P. (2003). The co-occurrence of husband-to-wife aggression, family of origin aggression, and child abuse potential in a community sample: Implications for parenting. *Journal of Interpersonal Violence, 18*, 413–440.

Martin, S. L., Mackie, L., Kupper, L. L., Buescher, P. A., & Moracco, K. E. (2001). Physical abuse of women before, during, and after pregnancy. *JAMA : The Journal of the American Medical Association, 285*(12), 1581–1584.

McDonald, R., Jouriles, E. N., Ramisetty-Mikler, S., Caetano, R., & Green, C. E. (2006). Estimating the number of American children living in partner-violent families. *Journal of Family Psychology, 20*(1), 137–142.

McGuigan, W. M., & Pratt, C. C. (2001). The predictive impact of domestic violence on three types of child maltreatment. *Child Abuse & Neglect, 25*(7), 869–883.

Menjivar, C., & Salcido, O. (2002). Immigrant women and domestic violence: Common experiences in different countries. *Gender and Society, 16*(6), 898–920.

Miner, E. J., Shackelford, T. K., Block, C. R., Starratt, V. G., & Weekes-Shackelford, V. A. (2012). Risk for death for life-threatening injury for women with children not sired by the abuse. *Human Nature, 23*(1), 89–97.

Moffitt, T. E., & Caspi, A. (2003). Preventing the intergenerational continuity of antisocial behaviour: Implications of partner violence. In D. P. Farrington & J. W. Coid (Eds.), *Early prevention of adult antisocial behaviour* (pp. 109–129). Cambridge, UK: Cambridge University Press.

Molnar, B. E., Buka, S. L., Brennan, R. T., Holton, J. K., & Earls, F. A. (2003). A multilevel study of neighborhoods and parent-to-child physical aggression: Results from the project on human development in Chicago neighborhoods. *Child Maltreatment, 8*(2), 84.

Murphy, C. C., Schei, B., Myhr, T. L., & Du Mont, J. (2001). Abuse: A risk factor for low birth weight? A systematic review and meta-analysis. *Canadian Medical Association Journal, 164*(11), 1567–1572.

National Center for Health Statistics. (2010). Marriage and cohabitation in the United States: A statistical portrait based on cycle 6 (2002) of the National Survey of Family Growth. *Vital and Health Statistics, 23*(28). Retrieved on 3 July 2012, from http://www.cdc.gov/nchs/data/series/sr_23/sr23_028.pdf

National Vital Statistics System. (2011). Births: Final data for 2009. *National Vital Statistics Reports, 60*(1). Retrieved on 1 July 2012, from http://www.cdc.gov/nchs/data/nvsr/nvsr60/nvsr60_01.pdf#table15

Pallitto, C. C., Campbell, J. C., & O'Campo, P. (2005). Is intimate partner violence associated with unintended pregnancy? A review of the literature. *Trauma, Violence & Abuse, 6*(3), 217–235.

Park, M. S. (2001). The factors of child physical abuse in Korean immigrant families. *Child Abuse & Neglect, 25*, 945–958.

Pelcovitz, D., Kaplan, S., Goldenberg, B., Mandel, F., Lehane, J., & Guarrera, J. V. (1994). Post-traumatic stress disorder in physically abused adolescents. *Journal of the American Academy of Child and Adolescent Psychiatry, 33*(3), 305–312.

Perilla, J. L. (1999). Domestic violence as a human rights issue: The case of immigrant Latinos. *Hispanic Journal of Behavioral Sciences, 21*, 107–133.

Pico-Alfonso, M. A., Garcia-Linares, M. I., Celda-Navarro, N., Blasco-Ros, C., Echeburua, E., & Martinez, M. (2006). The impact of physical, psychological, and sexual intimate male partner violence on women's mental health: Depressive symptoms, posttraumatic stress disorder, state anxiety, and suicide. *Journal of Women's Health (2002), 15*(5), 599–611.

Radhakrishna, A., Bou-Saada, I. E., Hunter, W. M., Catellier, D. M., & Kotch, J. B. (2001). Are father surrogates a risk factor for child maltreatment? *Child Maltreatment, 6*(4), 281–289.

Raj, A., & Silverman, J. (2003). Intimate partner violence against South Asian women in Greater Boston. *Journal of the American Medical Women's Association, 2*(57), 111–114.

Renner, L. M., & Slack, K. S. (2006). Intimate partner violence and child maltreatment: Understanding intra- and inter-generational connections. *Child Abuse & Neglect, 30*(6), 599–617.

Rhee, S. (1997). Domestic violence in the Korean immigrant family. *Journal of Sociology and Social Welfare, 24*, 63–77.

Rumm, P. D., Cummings, P., Krauss, M. R., Bell, M. A., & Rivara, F. P. (2000). Identified spouse abuse as a risk factor for child abuse. *Child Abuse & Neglect, 24*(11), 1375–1381.

Saltzman, L. E., Fanslow, J. L., McMahon, P. M., & Shelly, G. A. (2002). *Intimate partner violence surveillance: Uniform definitions and recommended data elements.* (No. version 1.0). Atlanta: Centers for Disease Control and Prevention.

Saltzman, L. E., Johnson, C. H., Gilbert, B. C., & Goodwin, M. M. (2003). Physical abuse around the time of pregnancy: An examination of prevalence and risk factors in 16 states. *Maternal and Child Health Journal, 7*(1), 31–43.

Silverman, J., Decker, M., Reed, E., & Raj, A. (2006). Intimate partner violence victimization prior to and during pregnancy among women residing in 26 U.S. states: Associations with maternal and neonatal health. *American Journal of Obstetrics and Gynecology, 195*, 140–148.

Sternberg, K. J., Lamb, M. E., & Dawud-Noursi, S. (1998). Understanding domestic violence and its effects: Making sense of divergent reports and perspectives. In G. W. Holden, R. Geffner, & E. W. Jouriles (Eds.), *Children exposed to family violence* (pp. 121–156). Washington, DC: American Psychological Association.

Stith, S. M., Smith, D. B., Penn, C. E., Ward, D. B., & Tritt, D. (2004). Intimate partner physical abuse perpetration and victimization risk factors: A meta-analytic review. *Aggression and Violent Behavior, 10*, 65–98.

Straus, M. A., & Gelles, R. J. (1990). *Physical violence in American families: Risk factors and adaptations to violence in 8,145 families.* New Brunswick: Transaction Publishers.

Street, A. E., Gibson, L. E., & Holohan, D. R. (2005). Impact of childhood traumatic events, trauma-related guilt, and avoidant coping strategies on PTSD symptoms in female survivors of domestic violence. *Journal of Traumatic Stress, 18*(3), 245–252.

Tajima, E. A. (2000). The relative importance of wife abuse as a risk factor for violence against children. *Child Abuse & Neglect, 24*(11), 1383–1398.

Tajima, E. A. (2004). Correlates of the co-occurrence of wife abuse and child abuse among a representative sample. *Journal of Family Violence, 19*, 399–410.

Tajima, E. A., & Harachi, T. W. (2010). Parenting beliefs and physical discipline practices among Southeast Asian immigrants: Parenting in the context of cultural adaptation to the United States. *Journal of Cross-Cultural Psychology, 41*(2), 212–235.

Taylor, C. A., Guterman, N. B., Lee, S. J., & Rathouz, P. J. (2009). Intimate partner violence, maternal stress, nativity, and risk for maternal maltreatment of young children. *American Journal of Public Health, 99*(1), 175–183.

Tjaden, P., & Thoennes, N. (2000). *Full report of the prevelance, incidence, and consequences of violence against women: Findings from the national violence against women survey* (Vol. No. 181867). Washington, DC: US Department of Justice.

Van IJzendoorn, M. H., Euser, E. M., Prinzie, P., Juffer, F., & Bakermans-Kranenburg, M. J. (2009). Elevated risk of child maltreatment in families with stepparents but not with adoptive parents. *Child Maltreatment, 14*(4), 369–375.

Vest, J. R., Catlin, T. K., Chen, J. J., & Brownson, R. C. (2002). Multistate analysis of factors associated with intimate partner violence. *American Journal of Preventive Medicine, 22*(3), 156–164.

Vitanza, S., Vogel, L. C., & Marshall, L. L. (1995). Distress and symptoms of posttraumatic stress disorder in abused women. *Violence and Victims, 10*(1), 23–34.

Walton-Moss, B. J., Manganello, J., Frye, V., & Campbell, J. C. (2005). Risk factors for intimate partner violence and associated injury among urban women. *Journal of Community Health, 30*(5), 377–389.

Watts, C., & Zimmerman, C. (2002). Violence against women: Global scope and magnitude. *Lancet, 359*(9313), 1232–1237.

Weil, J. M., & Lee, H. H. (2004). Cultural considerations in understanding family violence among Asian American pacific islander families. *Journal of Community Health Nursing, 21*(4), 217–227.

Whitaker, D. J., & Reese, L. (2007). *Preventing intimate partner violence and sexual violence in racial/ethnic minority communities: CDC's demonstration projects.* Atlanta: National Center for Injury Prevention and Control, Centers for Disease Control and Prevention.

Whitaker, D. J., Morrison, S., Lindquist, S., Hawkins, S. R., O'Neil, J. A., Nesius, A. M., Mathew, A., & Reese, L. (2006). A critical review of interventions for the primary prevention of perpetration of partner violence. *Aggression and Violent Behavior, 11*, 151–166.

Whitfield, C. L., Anda, R. F., Dube, S. R., & Felitti, V. J. (2003). Violent childhood experiences and the risk of intimate partner violence in adults: Assessment in a large health maintenance organization. *Journal of Interpersonal Violence, 18*(2), 166–185.

Wolfe, D. A., Crooks, C. V., Lee, V., McIntyre-Smith, A., & Jaffe, P. G. (2003). The effects of children's exposure to domestic violence: A meta-analysis and critique. *Clinical Child and Family Psychology Review, 6*, 171–187.

Xu, X., Campbell, J. C., & Zhu, F. C. (2001). Intimate partner violence against Chinese women: The past, present, and future. *Trauma, Violence & Abuse, 4*, 196–315.

Yick, A. G., & Agbayani-Siewert, P. (1997). Perceptions of domestic violence in a Chinese American community. *Journal of Interpersonal Violence, 12*, 832–846.

Yoshioka, M. R., & Dang, Q. (2000). *Asian family violence report: A study of Chinese, Cambodian, Korean, South Asian and Vietnamese communities in Massachusetts.* Retrieved on 24 July 2012, from http://www.atask.org/site/images/pdf/asianfamilyviolencereport.pdf

Zhai, F., & Gao, Q. (2009). Child maltreatment among Asian Americans: Characteristics and explanatory framework. *Child Maltreatment, 14*(2), 207–224.

Part III
Child Maltreatment:
What Are the Consequences?

Chapter 11
Neurobiological Consequences of Neglect and Abuse

Kristin Bernard, Teresa Lind, and Mary Dozier

As an altricial species, human infants depend on caregivers for even the most basic regulatory functions (Hofer 1994, 2006; Winberg 2005). Because infants are so dependent on their caregivers for help with regulation, neglect and abuse pose serious threats to development. Indeed, maltreatment can undermine children's biological regulation and interfere with brain development. In this chapter, we will review evidence with respect to the key neurobiological systems that are altered as a result of maltreatment: the hypothalamic-pituitary-adrenal (HPA) axis of the stress response system; the amygdala, which is involved in emotion processing and emotion regulation; the hippocampus, which facilitates learning and memory; the corpus callosum, which integrates functions between hemispheres; and the prefrontal cortex, which is involved in higher order cognitive functioning. Additionally, we will discuss a number of methodological and conceptual issues relevant to understanding the neurobiological effects of maltreatment, implications for intervention, and critical directions for future research.

Characterizing Maltreatment

Young children come into the world biologically prepared to depend on their caregivers, and "expect" a caregiver who will provide protection from danger and serve co-regulatory functions. In general, the quality of care that children receive varies along a normal continuum, and children are prepared to adapt to this range of caregiver behaviors. Maltreatment, however, falls far outside the range of species-expectant care. Abuse (i.e., physical abuse, sexual abuse, emotional abuse) consists of frightening, hurtful, and/or threatening input from the caregiver to the child. Neglect, on the other hand, represents the lack of necessary and expected input by the caregiver, and can take several forms. In some cases, caregivers neglect their children by failing to meet basic needs for food, supervision, or medical care. These physical and health needs are often the issues that catch the attention of Child Protective Services. In addition to these forms of physical and medical neglect, neglecting caregivers may be emotionally unresponsive or unavailable. The most extreme form of neglect is institutional care, which is characterized by both psychosocial and sensory deprivation (Nelson 2007). In institutional settings, there are often low staff-to-child ratios and high staff turn-over, leading to few opportunities for interactions with consistent caregivers.

Despite recent advances, researchers face many challenges in attempting to understand the short- and long-term impacts of the range of maltreatment types (i.e., abuse, neglect from caregivers, extreme

K. Bernard (✉) • T. Lind • M. Dozier
University of Delaware, Newark, USA
e-mail: kbernard@psych.udel.edu; tlind@psych.udel.edu; mdozier@psych.udel.edu

J.E. Korbin and R.D. Krugman (eds.), *Handbook of Child Maltreatment*, Child Maltreatment 2, DOI 10.1007/978-94-007-7208-3_11, © Springer Science+Business Media Dordrecht 2014

neglect/privation of institutional care) on child functioning and development. One of these challenges is teasing apart the impact of child maltreatment from other co-occurring factors. For example, children involved with Child Protective Services due to neglect or abuse often face a multitude of inherently overlapping and concurrent risk factors, including poverty, prenatal substance exposure, and parent psychopathology (Dubowitz et al. 1987; Lyons et al. 2005; McCurdy 2005). These concurrent risk factors can make it particularly difficult to identify the specific consequences of maltreatment on children's neurobiology. Although some researchers have pointed to these many confounding factors as a limitation of maltreatment research (e.g., Hart and Rubia 2012), it is also important to consider that controlling for confounding variables might lead to unrepresentative samples of children and findings that lack generalizability. Instead, it is important that researchers characterize children's experiences of maltreatment, measure concurrent risk factors, and report comorbid psychopathology. This will allow for the examination of factors that contribute to specific neurobiological effects and profiles, such as the timing, type, and severity of maltreatment.

HPA Axis and Biological Regulation

A key biological system that is impacted by maltreatment is the hypothalamic-pituitary-adrenocortial (HPA) axis. Glucocorticoids (cortisol in humans, corticosterone in rodents) are steroid hormones produced as an end product of the HPA system. The HPA axis serves two orthogonal functions: mounting a stress response and maintaining a diurnal rhythm. Following exposure to a stressor, corticotrophin-releasing hormone (CRH) is released by the paraventricular nuclei of the hypothalamus. The CRH travels through the bloodstream to the anterior pituitary and releases adrenocorticotropic hormone (ACTH), which signals the production and release of glucocorticoids (i.e., cortisol in humans) by the adrenal gland (Gunnar and Quevedo 2007). This cascade of biochemical reactions is designed to promote immediate survival by directing energy away from processes that are less critical to immediate survival, such as immune functioning, growth, digestion, and reproduction (Gunnar and Cheatham 2003).

In addition to mounting a stress response, glucocorticoids serve a major role in maintaining circadian patterns of daily activity, such as waking and sleeping (Gunnar and Cheatham 2003). Basal, or diurnal, levels of cortisol vary across the day. In humans, diurnal cortisol levels peak about 30 min after wake-up, decrease sharply by mid-morning, and continue to decrease gradually until bedtime (Gunnar and Donzella 2002). This diurnal pattern remains relatively consistent from around 3 months of age through adulthood (Larson et al. 1998; Price et al. 1983), although the gradual decline from mid-morning to afternoon is less reliably observed in children under 4-years-old (Bruce et al. 2002; Watamura et al. 2003).

The HPA axis is highly sensitive to the effects of early experiences, with consequences most often observed on diurnal regulation. The most consistent findings have shown that children who have experienced maltreatment display flatter, more blunted, patterns of diurnal regulation, relative to non-maltreated children (Bernard et al. 2010; Bruce et al. 2009a; Dozier et al. 2006; Fisher et al 2006; Gunnar and Vasquez 2001). For example, Bernard and colleagues (2010) compared patterns of diurnal (i.e., wake-up to bedtime) cortisol production among three groups of children: children involved with Child Protective Services who were placed in foster care, children involved with Child Protective Services who remained with their high-risk birth parents, and low-risk comparison children. Children who remained with their high-risk birth parents displayed the most perturbed patterns of diurnal cortisol regulation, marked by a blunted slope. These children had wake-up cortisol levels that were significantly lower and bedtime levels that were significantly higher than cortisol levels of both foster children and low-risk children. Foster children also had blunted slopes, but less marked than children who remained in high-risk environments. Similar flattened diurnal rhythms have been found in institutionalized children (Bruce et al. 2000; Carlson and Earls 1997). Flattened diurnal cortisol patterns may reflect down-regulation of HPA axis activity following earlier hyperactivation (Carpenter et al. 2009; Fries et al. 2005). Notably, some studies have reported elevated levels of basal cortisol, but typically in the presence of a concurrent psychological disorder, such as depression (Hart et al. 1996; Kaufman 1991; Tarullo and Gunnar 2006).

Disrupted HPA axis regulation may exert negative effects on a number of other biological systems. For example, the HPA axis is closely connected with the immune system, with cortisol thought to terminate inflammatory responses after stressors (Miller et al. 2002; Sapolsky et al. 2000). Emerging evidence shows that children and adults who experience abuse or neglect show increased markers of inflammation, such as C-reactive protein (Danese et al. 2007, 2009), and impaired immune competence, measured as elevated HSV-1 antibody levels (Shirtcliff et al. 2009). Additionally, excessive exposure to cortisol via early life stress may cause damage to developing brain regions (Teicher et al. 2003; Twardosz and Lutzker 2010). Several brain regions that we describe below, including limbic regions, such as the amygdala and hippocampus, and frontal regions may be particularly susceptible to the effects of dysregulated cortisol, due to the high number of glucocorticoid receptors in these areas (Brake et al. 2000; Schatzberg and Lindley 2008; Wellman 2001).

Amygdala, Emotion Processing, and Anxiety

Fronto-limbic networks, including structures of the medial prefrontal cortex, anterior cingulate cortex, amygdala, and hippocampus, are implicated in the regulation of emotion. The amygdala, in particular, plays a critical role in the processing of emotional information, including perceiving emotion in faces, evaluating threatening information, and fear conditioning (Davis and Whalen 2001). The amygdala goes through rapid development within the first several years of life (Tottenham et al. 2009), and is particularly susceptible to early adversity. Indeed, maltreated children show difficulties that could be linked to amygdala dysfunction, such as more internalizing problems, heightened anxiety, and emotional reactivity (Ellis et al. 2004; Juffer and van IJzendoorn 2005; Kaplow and Widom 2007; Tottenham et al. 2009; Zeanah et al. 2009), and deficits in emotional processing, including difficulty discriminating emotions and perceptual biases for threatening information (Dalgleish et al. 2001; Pollak et al. 2000; Vorria et al. 2006), relative to non-maltreated children.

Although the structure of the amygdala does not appear to be affected by abuse or neglect occurring with biological parents (De Bellis et al. 2001; Tottenham and Sheridan 2010; Woon and Hedges 2008), extreme deprivation associated with institutional care causes significant changes to amygdala volume. Tottenham and colleagues (2010) found that amygdala volume was enlarged in children adopted from institutional care. Importantly, these effects were observed years after adoption, suggesting that the amygdala may fail to recover from the effects of early adversity, similar to what has been found in animal models (Vyas and Pillai 2004). The length of time spent in institutional care was positively associated with amygdala volume, suggesting a dose–response relationship between early adversity and amygdala volume (Tottenham et al. 2010). Additionally, larger amygdala volume was associated with parent-reported child anxiety and internalizing behavior problems. Mehta and colleagues (2009) similarly found that children adopted from Romanian institutions showed larger relative right amygdala volume than never institutionalized children. These structural changes to amygdala volume are especially informative, given that larger amygdala volume is associated with greater likelihood of anxiety disorders in non-maltreated samples (De Bellis et al. 2000; Etkin and Wager 2007; Thomas et al. 2001).

Functional MRI (fMRI) studies have also shown that early adversity leads to a sensitized amygdala. In a study by Tottenham and colleagues (2011), previously institutionalized children completed an Emotional Face Go/No-Go task, for which they were required to press a button to target emotional expressions that were presented frequently ('Go' trials) and inhibit pressing the button to non-target distracter emotional expressions that were presented infrequently ('No-Go' trials). Children completed two conditions: fear faces as the target with neutral faces as the distracter, and neutral faces as the target with fear faces as the distracter. Relative to comparison children, previously institutionalized children showed heightened amygdala activity to fearful faces compared to neutral faces. Comparison children did not show differential amygdala response between emotional expressions, similar to findings of typically developing children in other studies (Thomas et al. 2001). The heightened activity to fearful faces shown in previously institutionalized children is similar to adult-like amygdala processing of emotional information (Stein et al. 2007), suggesting precocial development. Additionally, previously institutionalized children showed heightened amygdala activation to distracter stimuli relative to comparison children, suggesting that previously institutionalized children struggled to ignore the emotional content of the distracter stimuli (Tottenham et al. 2011). Greater amygdala activation was associated with poorer social competence, and less eye contact (Tottenham et al. 2011).

In another fMRI study of amygdala response in children who experienced early adversity, Maheu and colleagues (2010) examined children in US foster care and children adopted from institutional care. Children viewed pictures of angry, fearful, happy, and neutral faces across a series of tasks designed to manipulate the focus of attention (i.e., attend to fear cues, anger cues, or physical attributes, or passive viewing). Across conditions, children with a history of neglect showed greater activation of the left amygdala to fearful and angry faces, relative to neutral faces. Heightened amygdala activation in the angry vs. neutral contrast was associated with more placement changes and less time with the adoptive family. With regard to behavioral task differences, neglected children showed faster reaction times than comparison children to rating angry faces, similar to what has been observed in other studies of maltreated children (Pollak and Tolley-Schell 2003). Thus, this study also suggests heightened sensitivity of the amygdala to threatening information.

Studies of neglected and physically abused children tell a similar story of disturbed emotion processing. In a series of studies, Pollak and colleagues showed that post-institutionalized and neglected children demonstrated a general deficit in discriminating emotional expressions, whereas physically abused children showed enhanced attention to and processing of negative emotional cues (Pollak et al. 2000; Pollak and Sinha 2002; Pollak and Tolley-Schell 2003; Vorria et al. 2006; Wismer-Fries and Pollak 2004). For example, Pollak and Sinha (2002) found that physically abused children detected facial cues of anger with less sensory information than non-maltreated controls.

Physiological measures also suggest disrupted processing of emotional information in neglected and physically abused children. Event-related potentials (ERPs) measure changes in the brain's electrical activity in response to an internal or external stimulus or event. ERPs can be extracted from the ongoing electroencephalogram (EEG) by averaging activity across a large number of trials, causing random activity to be canceled out and stimulus-related responses to remain. Given that ERP "components" (i.e., positive and negative peaks) can be quantified in terms of latency, amplitude, and location/distribution on the scalp, inferences can be drawn regarding the time course, degree of engagement, and functional significance of processing specific events or stimuli (Picton et al. 2000). The P300 (i.e., positive deflection occurring approximately 300 ms after a stimulus) is associated with attention to emotionally evocative visual stimuli, such as emotional faces; larger P300 activity reflects greater activation or attention to a particular stimulus (Eimer and Holmes 2007; Olofsson et al. 2008). Whereas non-maltreated children show similar P300 activity across emotional expressions, maltreated children show larger P300s to angry target faces (Pollak et al. 1997, 2001). Additionally, physically abused children demonstrate increased P300 activity when required to disengage from angry faces, possibly reflecting increased allocation of attention to cues of threat (Pollak and Tolley-Schell 2003).

Taken together, these findings suggest potential mechanisms for the heightened risk of anxiety disorders among maltreated children. Larger amygdala volume, heightened amygdala sensitivity, and differential neurological processing of emotional stimuli are all associated with the development of anxiety disorders (Barros-Loscertales et al. 2006; De Bellis et al. 2000; Derryberry and Reed 2002; Vasey et al. 1996).

Hippocampus, Learning, and Memory

The hippocampus plays an important role in episodic and declarative memory and spatial learning (Andersen et al. 2007; Eichenbaum and Otto 1992; Ghetti et al. 2010). Similar to the amygdala, the hippocampus is part of the limbic system. Given its high density of glucocorticoid receptors and prolonged development (Benes et al. 1994; Giedd et al. 1996b; Patel et al. 2000), the hippocampus appears to be particularly susceptible to stress early in life (Gould and Tanapat 1999; Sapolsky et al. 1990). The hippocampus also plays a major role in modulating the HPA axis response to stressors (Kim and Yoon 1998). Specifically, binding of cortisol to hippocampal receptors signals a negative feedback loop, turning off the HPA axis response. Damage to the hippocampus due to maltreatment can have negative functional consequences for its roles in regulating the stress response system, as well as cognitive functions such as memory formulation (de Quervain et al. 1998; McLaughlin et al. 2013).

The majority of studies examining the effects on maltreatment on hippocampal structure have been conducted with children diagnosed with maltreatment-related PTSD and have found no evidence of hippocampal volume deficits compared to healthy, non-maltreated controls (Carrion et al. 2001; De Bellis et al. 1999, 2001, 2002a). One exception was a study conducted by Tupler and De Bellis (2006), which found that children with maltreatment-related PTSD had significantly larger hippocampal volume compared to healthy controls, and that hippocampal volume positively related to age of trauma onset and level of psychopathology. Structural MRI studies of children adopted from institutional care have generally found no difference in hippocampal volume compared to never institutionalized controls (Mehta et al. 2009; Tottenham and Sheridan 2010).

In contrast to the studies of maltreatment-related structural changes during childhood, studies have consistently found decreased hippocampal volume among adults who experienced childhood maltreatment compared to adults who did not experience childhood maltreatment (For a review, see Woon and Hedges 2008; Andersen et al. 2008; Andersen and Teicher 2004; Schmahl et al. 2003). For example, Bremner and colleagues (1997) reported a smaller left hippocampal volume among adults with PTSD who had experienced childhood maltreatment compared to adults without PTSD who did not report histories of childhood maltreatment. Reductions in left hippocampal volume were also found in adults with histories of childhood maltreatment and other psychopathology, including dissociative identity disorder (Stein et al. 1997), borderline personality disorder (Driessen et al. 2000), and major depressive disorder (Vythilingam et al. 2002). A recent structural MRI study comparing participants from the general community with high and low scores on self-report measures of childhood maltreatment found that volume reduction in left hippocampal areas was linked to childhood maltreatment (Teicher et al. 2012). However, Pederson and colleagues (2004) found no differences in hippocampal volume or associated memory deficits between adults with PTSD who reported childhood maltreatment, adults without PTSD who reported childhood maltreatment, and non-maltreated, healthy controls. Results from a meta-analysis of hippocampal volumes in adults with trauma-related PTSD suggest that smaller hippocampal volumes in maltreated adults may be specific to PTSD rather than maltreatment itself (Kitayama et al. 2005).

Functional MRI studies have found evidence of disrupted hippocampal functioning in maltreated children. Carrion and colleagues (2010) used fMRI to examine children with maltreatment-related posttraumatic stress symptoms during the encoding and retrieval of visually presented nouns. Compared to healthy control children, the maltreated children with posttraumatic stress symptoms demonstrated reduced activation of the right hippocampus during the retrieval component of the task. In addition, greater severity of avoidance and numbing symptoms was associated with reduced left hippocampal activation during retrieval (Carrion et al. 2010). Bremner and colleagues (2003) utilized PET imaging to examine hippocampal function during a verbal declarative memory task among adult survivors of sexual abuse with and without PTSD. In addition to showing reduced hippocampal volume, the women with abuse and PTSD showed a failure of left hippocampal activation during a verbal memory task. These changes to the structure and function of the hippocampus, among other neural structures (e.g., striatum, dorsolateral prefrontal cortex), may explain, at least in part, impairments in short-term and long-term memory functioning in maltreated children (Beers and DeBellis 2002; Bremner et al. 1995; Navalta et al. 2006).

Prefrontal Cortex, Executive Functions, and ADHD

The prefrontal cortex is responsible for a variety of executive functions in the brain, including higher order cognitive functions such as planning, memory, inhibitory control, and allocation of attention (Miller and Cohen 2001). Relative to some other brain structures, the development of the prefrontal cortex is protracted, extending from birth through adulthood (Gogtay et al. 2004; Rubia et al. 2006; Sowell et al. 2003). Frontal systems are very sensitive to early experience, which may interfere with its structural and functional development (Hart and Rubia 2012; McLaughlin et al. 2013). Maltreated children and institutionalized children show higher rates of ADHD and problems with executive functions than comparison children, problems that are frontally mediated (Kreppner et al. 2001; Nolin and Ethier 2007; Pechtel and Pizzagalli 2010; Stevens et al. 2008).

Evidence is mixed with regard to structural changes in the prefrontal cortex following maltreatment. Hanson and colleagues (2010) found that physically abused children showed volumetric differences in several areas in the prefrontal cortex, relative to comparison children, including smaller volumes of the right orbitofrontal cortex, right ventral-medial prefrontal cortex, and dorsolateral prefrontal cortex. Carrion and colleagues (2008) also found decreased grey matter volume in the prefrontal cortex in children with interpersonal trauma and PTSD symptoms. Similar patterns have been observed in children with ADHD, with ADHD linked to reductions in cortical grey matter volume, often in regions of the prefrontal cortex (Ellison-Wright et al. 2008; Shaw et al. 2006). Studies of adults who experienced maltreatment in childhood have demonstrated decreased grey matter volume in the prefrontal cortex (Andersen et al. 2008; Tomoda et al. 2009). In contrast, some studies examining children with PTSD following maltreatment relative to control children have shown the opposite effect, with larger grey matter volume in prefrontal cortex areas (Carrion et al. 2009; Richert et al. 2006) or no effect when controlling for total brain volume (De Bellis et al. 2002b).

Despite mixed evidence regarding structural changes in the prefrontal cortex, a number of studies suggest that maltreatment is associated with functional changes in the prefrontal cortex and associated brain regions. In particular, there is evidence that maltreated children show patterns of neural activation during tasks requiring executive function that are similar to patterns observed in children with ADHD. For example, Carrion and colleagues (2008) examined neural activation using fMRI in a sample of maltreated children with PTSD and non-maltreated comparison children. Children completed a Go/No-Go task during which they were required to inhibit a prepotent response (i.e., press a button to every letter except X). During No-Go trials, non-maltreated children showed increased activation in the middle frontal gyrus, a region implicated in response inhibition. Contrarily, maltreated children did not show increased activation in this region and instead displayed greater activation in the anterior cingulate cortex and the medial frontal gyrus. This pattern of differential neural activation, including both the deficit in middle frontal gyrus' activity and increased activation of the anterior cingulate and medial frontal gyrus, are similar to patterns observed in children with ADHD (Booth et al. 2005; Schulz et al. 2004).

Parallel to these findings in maltreated children, previously institutionalized adolescents have been found to demonstrate disruptions in the prefrontal network during response inhibition tasks. Specifically, Mueller and colleagues (2010) found that neglected children (including both previously institutionalized and domestically adopted children) expended more cognitive resources, evidenced by greater activation in several regions of the prefrontal cortex (e.g., left inferior frontal cortex, anterior cingulate cortex) during response inhibition trials of a Go/No-Go task, compared to children without a history of maltreatment. Findings from these studies mark disruptions in prefrontal networks, which are associated with behavioral problems of inhibitory control, impulsivity, and attentional control.

Corpus Callosum, White Matter Tracts, and Cortical Differentiation

The corpus callosum is the largest white matter structure in the brain, and consists of around 200 million white matter fibers connecting the cortical areas of the two hemispheres (Aboitiz et al. 1992; van der Knaap and van der Ham 2011). It facilitates interhemispheric communication for processes such as emotion, arousal, higher cognition, and motor and sensory functions (Giedd et al. 1996a; Kitterle 1995). Although the white matter fibers composing the corpus callosum are fully formed before birth, myelination continues throughout childhood and adulthood (Giedd et al. 1996a; Teicher et al. 2004). Myelination refers to the production of myelin sheath, the fatty tissue insulating axons. In normal childhood development, the volume of the corpus callosum increases with age as a result of this myelination process (Giedd et al. 1999; Luders et al. 2010). In general, thick myelinated fibers with large diameters provide a faster transmission of sensory-motor information, whereas the thin fibers with a small diameter provide a slower transmission between associated areas (Bloom and Hynd 2005). Myelinated regions such as the corpus callosum are susceptible to the impacts of early exposure to high levels of stress hormones, which suppress the glial cell division that is critical for myelination (Lauder 1983).

The corpus callosum's continuing development throughout childhood and its composition of major myelinated fiber tracts makes it particularly susceptible to the effects of maltreatment. Maltreatment has been found to be associated with structural changes to the corpus callosum, particularly in middle and posterior regions. Teicher and colleagues (2004) compared corpus callosum volume in three groups of children: abused/neglected children with psychiatric disorders, children with psychiatric disorders but no abuse/neglect, and healthy children with no abuse/neglect (control). Results from structural magnetic resonance imaging showed that the total corpus callosum area of the abused/neglected children was smaller than both healthy control children and children with psychiatric disorders and no abuse/neglect. In addition, total corpus callosum area did not differ between healthy control children and children with psychiatric disorders and no abuse/neglect. These results suggest that it may be exposure to maltreatment itself, and not a diagnosis of psychopathology, that is associated with decreased corpus callosum volume.

Results from other studies that have examined maltreatment-related PTSD suggest that it may be more difficult to tease apart the relative contribution of maltreatment versus psychopathology on observed differences in corpus callosum structure. In a group of hospitalized children with psychiatric illness, Teicher and colleagues (1997) compared maltreated children with psychiatric diagnoses to maltreated children without psychiatric diagnoses (controls). They found that the midsaggital area of the corpus callosum was significantly smaller in maltreated children with psychiatric disorders compared to maltreated children without psychiatric disorders, particularly among males (Teicher et al. 1997). A number of studies have similarly found that children and adolescents with maltreatment-related PTSD have smaller areas of the corpus callosum than comparison children, with observed differences more pronounced in males (De Bellis et al. 1999, 2002a; De Bellis and Keshavan 2003). Notably, these findings parallel those seen in animal studies with early life stress predicting smaller corpus callosum size and gender-dependent effects (Berrebi et al. 1988; Juraska and Kopcik 1988; Sanchez et al. 1998). Despite overlapping findings across studies, there have been non-significant findings as well. In post-institutionalized adolescents, for example, Mehta and colleagues (2009) found reduced total grey and white matter volumes, but no differences in corpus callosum size, relative to controls.

Although studies utilizing structural MRI have generally revealed a relationship between early adversity and disruptions in the macrostructural integrity of the brain, few studies have examined the impact of early adversity on the microstructural integrity of the brain's white matter. Diffusion tensor imaging (DTI) is a functional neuroimaging model that measures the rate and directionality of water diffusion in the brain and allows for multidimensional scans of axon networks (Neil et al. 2002). DTI utilizes the metric of fractional anisotropy, which is the ratio of directional to non-directional water movement in a single imaging voxel. Fractional anisotropy provides information about axon size, myelination, axonal connections and orientation, with lower fractional anisotropy reflecting reduced integrity of white matter structures (Mooshagian 2008). Two DTI studies examined the association of institutional care with the structural connectivity of the white matter pathways. Eluvathingal and colleagues (2006) examined children in middle childhood who had been adopted into the US from Eastern European institutions. Children had spent between 17 and 60 months in the institutions before adoption. Results showed that fractional anisotropy values in the left uncinate fasciculus (which connects the orbitofrontal cortex to the anterior temporal lobe) were significantly decreased in the internationally adopted children compared with non-adopted children. In addition, a neuropsychological assessment found that the internationally adopted group of children had relatively mild specific cognitive impairment and impulsivity. A second DTI study found reduced fractional anisotropy among previously institutionalized children from orphanages in Eastern Europe and Central Asia in the uncinate fasciculus and the superior longitudinal fasciculus (Govindan et al. 2010). These white matter abnormalities were associated with duration of time in the orphanage and with symptoms of inattention and hyperactivity.

Structural differences of reduced white matter may be associated with less efficient cognitive functioning among children to experience early adversity, as examined by recording EEG activity. Electroencephalogram (EEG) reflects spontaneous fluctuations in electrical activity in the brain from electrodes placed on the scalp. The fluctuations, or rhythmic activity, of the electrical signals is divided into different frequency bands, including theta (4–6 Hz), alpha (7–12 Hz), and beta (13–20 Hz). The Bucharest Early Intervention Project (BEIP) is a rare experimental study of human neglect, in that institutionalized children in Romania were randomly assigned to high quality foster care or care as usual in the institutions (Zeanah et al. 2003). At a baseline assessment, children with histories of institutionalization showed different patterns of EEG activity relative to comparison children. Specifically, when children were enrolled in the BEIP study (between 6 and 30 months of age) and before random assignment, institutionalized children had higher levels of theta power (low-frequency brain activity) and lower levels of alpha and beta power (high-frequency activity) compared with children who were not institutionalized (Marshall et al. 2004). Given that the proportion of alpha and beta power relative to theta power should increase as the brain matures (Marshall et al. 2002), the pattern of activity observed in institutionalized children suggests a maturational delay or deficit in cortical development (Marshall et al. 2004). Notably, these patterns of reduced high-frequency activity and increased low-frequency activity in institutionalized children remain similar at 42 months of age (Marshall et al. 2008). The profiles of resting EEG characterized by reduced high-frequency activity and increased low-frequency activity are similar to patterns found among children with ADHD (Barry et al. 2003; Harmony et al. 1990). Baseline EEG activity among BEIP children, specifically lower alpha power and higher theta power, was predictive of elevated symptoms of hyperactivity and impulsivity several years later (McLaughlin et al. 2010). Children living in poverty also demonstrate increased low-frequency and decreased high-frequency activity, and associated symptoms of ADHD (Harmony et al. 1990; Johnson et al. 1999; Otero 1997).

Changes to the structure and connectivity of white matter tracks may be associated with patterns of cortical differentiation (McLaughlin et al. 2013). EEG coherence is considered a marker of synchrony in activity across scalp regions (Thatcher et al. 1986). EEG coherence is inversely related to cognitive ability, with reduced coherence associated with higher IQ, improved cognitive performance, and advanced language development (Gasser et al. 1988; Marosi et al. 1995; Mundy et al. 2003). Essentially, decreased coherence is thought to reflect greater differentiation, complexity, and specialization of brain regions (Thatcher et al. 2008; Marshall et al. 2008). Two studies found that maltreated children showed increased EEG coherence in the left hemisphere of the brain, relative to non-maltreated children (Ito et al. 1998; Miskovic and Schmidt 2010). Both studies found no group differences in right hemisphere coherence. Thus, maltreated children show *asymmetry* in intrahemispheric coherence, marked by greater EEG coherence in the left hemisphere relative to the right hemisphere, whereas non-maltreated children do not have this pattern of asymmetry across hemispheres. Further, Miskovic and Schmidt (2010) found that higher left hemisphere coherence mediated the association between maltreatment and general psychiatric impairment (i.e., composite of symptoms across psychiatric disorders).

Changes to the corpus callosum and other white matter tracks, along with patterns of cortical differentiation such as reduced EEG coherence, may be associated with cognitive impairments, including academic under-performance and lower IQ reported in some studies of abused or neglected children (Carrey et al. 1995; De Bellis et al. 2009; Loman et al. 2009), as well as language and emotion regulation difficulties (Choi et al. 2009). However, more research is needed to examine the behavior sequalae of changes in white matter structure and connectivity.

Effects of Maltreatment on Broader Neural Networks

Although we have organized our review around specific brain regions and their associated functions, it is important to note these systems are structurally and functionally interconnected. In their review of neuroimaging studies on child abuse, Hart and Rubia (2012) summarize two key circuits that are impacted by childhood maltreatment: fronto-limbic circuits and frontostriatal circuits. The fronto-limbic circuits comprise frontal cortical regions (i.e., medial prefrontal cortex, orbitofrontal cortex, and rostral anterior cingulate cortex) and limbic structures (i.e., hippocampus and amygdala). As described above, maltreatment affects these regions in a number of ways, such as in reduced hippocampal volume, and increased activation in the hippocampus and amydala to negative facial expressions. Disruptions in fronto-limbic circuits may be associated with problems in emotion regulation, reward processing, motivation, and aggression observed among individuals who experience maltreatment (Adolphs 2002). The key regions that communicate within the fronto-striatal circuits include frontal regions (i.e., dorsal anterior cingulate cortex, dorsolateral prefrontal cortex, and inferior frontal cortex), the basal ganglia, parieto-temporal cortex, and cerebellum. Structural and functional changes across these areas likely contribute to performance difficulty in tasks requiring executive functions such as working memory and attentional control (Christakou et al. 2009; Rubia et al. 2006).

Neurobiological Plasticity and Interventions

An exciting recent course of maltreatment research involves the examination of interventions that influence maltreated children's neurobiology, a direction that has implications for both policy and care. Interventions that change the child's social environment, through parenting behavior or family structure, can at least partially reverse or prevent the effects of early adverse experiences on biological regulation and brain development.

Diurnal cortisol regulation. Parenting interventions can help to normalize maltreated children's diurnal regulation of cortisol levels. In a randomized trial of a family-based therapeutic intervention, Fisher and colleagues (2007) examined diurnal patterns of cortisol regulation across 12 months. Foster children were randomly assigned to receive regular foster care or Multidimensional Treatment Foster Care for Preschoolers. This family-based therapeutic intervention involved intensive parent training and ongoing support and supervision to foster parents, designed to enhance responsive and consistent caregiving. Foster children in the control condition showed increasingly blunted wake-up to bedtime cortisol patterns across the study, reflecting the disrupted diurnal regulation typically found among maltreated children (Bernard et al. 2010; Bruce et al. 2009a). The family-based therapeutic intervention appeared to prevent this flattening over time, with foster children who received the intervention showing stable patterns of cortisol production over time similar to non-maltreated children. Cicchetti and colleagues (2011) also found that maltreated children who received early preventative interventions (e.g., child-parent psychotherapy) maintained morning cortisol levels that were similar to non-maltreated peers. In contrast, maltreated children who received routine community care progressively showed lower levels of morning cortisol. Thus, in these studies, rather than normalizing diurnal cortisol regulation, the interventions served to prevent disruptions in HPA axis functioning.

Similarly, the Attachment and Biobehavioral Catch-up intervention (ABC; Dozier and the Infant Caregiver Project Lab 2012) has been shown to enhance cortisol regulation among maltreated children. The ABC intervention is a 10-session manualized intervention delivered in families' homes, which aims to enhance caregivers' sensitivity to child distress, increase synchrony and responsiveness to child cues, and decrease intrusive and frightening behavior. In a recent study, children identified as at-risk for maltreatment were randomly assigned to receive the ABC intervention or a control intervention. Relative to children whose parents received the control intervention, ABC children showed more normative cortisol production, marked by a higher wake-up level and steeper morning to bedtime slope (Dozier et al. 2012).

Taken together, these studies of parenting interventions offer evidence of preventative and normalizing effects on children's biological regulation. The findings of these very different interventions conducted at different developmental periods are remarkably similar. The ABC intervention is implemented during infancy, a time when children are highly dependent on their parents for co-regulation. It helps parents to function more effectively as co-regulators by interacting with their children in more synchronous and nurturing ways. Multidimensional Treatment Foster Care is implemented during the preschool period, a time when children are expected to have developed the ability to regulate somewhat independently. Multidimensional Treatment Foster Care helps foster parents establish reliable contingencies, leading children to experience a predictable interpersonal world. Thus, Multidimensional Treatment Foster Care helps caregivers set up an environment that supports children's regulation, whereas ABC helps parents function as co-regulators themselves.

EEG activity and coherence. The Bucharest Early Intervention Project (BEIP) offers incredible opportunities to observe causal effects of institutionalization on brain and behavioral development because it used a randomized control trial design (Zeanah et al. 2003). Institutionalized children showed more low-frequency (i.e., theta) and less high-frequency (i.e., alpha and beta) EEF activity than non-institutionalized children when assessed at baseline and in early childhood following randomization (Marshall et al. 2004, 2008). By 8 years of age, however, previously institutionalized children who were randomly assigned to receive foster care showed EEG activity that was similar to non-institutionalized children (Vanderwert et al. 2010). Furthermore, this remediation of brain activity was most evident for children placed in foster care before 24 months, suggesting a better chance of recovery with early intervention than for children placed at older ages. With regard to EEG coherence, Marshall and colleagues (2008) found minimal differences between children randomized to foster care versus children randomized to care as usual in the institution. However, within the foster care group, earlier age of foster care placement was associated with reduced short-distance EEG coherence. As described above, decreased EEG coherence is associated with improved language outcomes and cognitive functioning (Gasser et al. 1988; Mundy et al. 2003). These studies highlight that, although patterns of brain activity are affected by early adversity, an enriched environment can remediate this damage.

White matter volume. In a follow-up study of 8- to 11-year-old children in the Bucharest Early Intervention Project, Sheridan and colleagues (2012) found structural brain changes between children who were randomly assigned to receive care as usual in the institution versus children who were randomly assigned to receive foster care. Consistent with findings from Mehta and colleagues (2009), institutionalized children who received care as usual had smaller total white matter volume and smaller posterior corpus callosum volume than children who were never institutionalized. Notably, by middle childhood, there were no significant differences in total white matter volume or posterior corpus callosum volume between the group of previously institutionalized children that were randomized into foster care and children who had never been institutionalized. This study highlights the neuroplasticity of white matter following severe environmental deprivation.

Physiological markers of pre-frontal cortex function. In a randomized trial of Multidimensional Treatment Foster Care for Preschoolers (MTFC-P), foster children who received the family-based intervention showed enhanced psychophysiological processing during a task tapping executive functioning, relative to children in regular foster care (Bruce et al. 2009b). Specifically, children completed a flanker task, for which children had to identify the color of the middle circle in a row of five circles. The task included congruent trials, in which all five circles were the same color, and incongruent trials, in which different colored circles flanked the center circle. The task requires executive processes of attention allocation and response monitoring, involving regions of the prefrontal cortex and anterior cingulate cortex (Botvinick et al. 1999). Performance feedback followed the child's response. Intervention group assignment (treatment foster care vs. regular foster care) had significant effects on children's ERP responses to feedback. Specifically, foster children who received the intervention showed differential responses to negative feedback compared to positive feedback, as evidenced by greater feedback-related negativity. This psychophysiological responsiveness to external feedback was similar to that observed in non-maltreated children. Contrarily, children in regular foster care did not show ERP differences according to feedback type. Thus, these findings suggest that a family-based intervention for foster children can enhance brain activity associated with response monitoring, a critical process for behavioral control (Bruce et al. 2009a).

Policy Implications

Research supporting the effectiveness of intervention programs on enhancing biological regulation and brain development carries important implications for policy. A critical step for preventing the neurobiological consequences of childhood maltreatment lies in the dissemination of these models of early intervention. Effective dissemination, in which interventions are delivered to the intended population, implemented as designed, and tested through ongoing research efforts, can be challenging for many reasons. Funding to support collaborative networks of basic researchers (i.e., studying neurobiological effects of maltreatment), prevention scientists, policy makers, child welfare agencies, and service providers is needed to push these dissemination efforts forward.

Directions for Future Research

A greater understanding of the neurobiological consequences of child abuse and neglect has developed within the last decade, offering significant insights into how disturbances of biological regulation and brain development may contribute to impairment across socioemotional, behavioral, and physical health domains. Here, we highlight several important directions for future research.

Within the maltreatment literature, there are substantial differences with regard to the nature of maltreatment experiences. Children often vary in the type of maltreatment experienced (e.g., sexual abuse, physical abuse, neglect), as well as the severity and chronicity of the maltreatment. Additionally, children from high-risk environments often face a host of co-occurring risk factors that may play a role in the development of regulation and brain regions. These risk factors include psychosocial stressors that impact the family (e.g., poverty, community violence) as well as non-optimal characteristics of the caregivers (e.g., psychopathology, low education), and prenatal risk factors (e.g., exposure to substances, preterm birth). Studies examining children who experience severe deprivation of institutional care have refined the unique effects of extreme neglect on brain development. In future studies, it will be important to better measure and characterize the nature of children's maltreatment experiences. Examining the timing of maltreatment, in particular, may help identify sensitive periods of brain development, contributing to developmentally informed approaches for intervention.

We have reviewed findings from studies that utilize a number of different methodological approaches (e.g., fMRI, EEG, neuroendocrine markers) to examine the neurobiological consequences following abuse and neglect. Because these methods are often used in isolation, it can be difficult to understand connections across systems. Therefore, questions remain regarding the influence of structural brain changes on cognitive functioning, the connection between functional changes in the brain and expressions of behavior, and so on. Another direction for future research is the integration of different methodologies in order to better understand associations across the implicated neurobiological systems.

Additionally, research to date has focused on neurobiological changes that occur following childhood maltreatment. Given increasing interest in understanding the factors that contribute to maltreatment recurrence (Helie and Bouchard 2010), a critical direction for future research is examining whether neurobiological changes place children at risk for re-abuse. Changes to brain development and biological regulation are associated with increased behavioral and psychological problems (e.g., ADHD, deficits of executive function). Presumably, these changes may make children harder to parent, particularly for parents that are highly stressed, lacking in social support, and living under impoverished conditions. Longitudinal studies that incorporate neurobiological markers as possible predictors of maltreatment recurrence could further inform prevention and intervention efforts.

Summary

Experiences of childhood maltreatment, including abuse and neglect, lead to changes in biological regulation and brain development. The brain appears to demonstrate great plasticity early in development. As a result, problematic environments, whether characterized by unexpected threatening input in the case of abuse or lack of input in the case of neglect, result in changes to developing biological systems, including the HPA axis and a number of brain regions. Brain systems remain somewhat plastic throughout much of childhood, with different systems developing at different rates. Thus, when children experience enriched environments following maltreatment, some systems can demonstrate remarkable recovery. Over time, the brain appears to become somewhat less plastic, supporting the need for intervention programs that are implemented early and aim to enhance key aspects of children's early caregiving environments.

References

Aboitiz, F., Scheibel, A. B., Fisher, R. S., & Zaidel, E. (1992). Fiber composition of the human corpus callosum. *Brain Research, 598*, 143–153.

Adolphs, R. (2002). Neural systems for recognizing emotions. *Current Opinion in Neurobiology, 12*, 169–177.

Andersen, S. L., & Teicher, M. H. (2004). Delayed effects of early stress on hippocampal development. *Neuropsychopharmacology, 29*, 1988–1993.

Andersen, P., Morris, R., Amaral, D., Bliss, T., & O'Keefe, J. (2007). *The hippocampus book*. Oxford: Oxford University Press.

Andersen, S. L., Tomoda, A., Vincow, E. S., Valente, E., Polcari, A., & Teicher, M. H. (2008). Preliminary evidence for sensitive periods in the effect of childhood sexual abuse on regional brain development. *The Journal of Neuropsychiatry and Clinical Neurosciences, 20*, 292–301.

Barrós-Loscertales, A., Meseguer, V., Sanjuán, A., Belloch, V., Parcet, M. A., ... Ávila, C. (2006). Striatum gray matter reduction in males with an overactive behavioral activation system. *European Journal of Neuroscience, 24*, 2071–2074.

Barry, R. J., Clarke, A. R., & Johnstone, S. J. (2003). A review of electrophysiology in attention-deficit/hyperactivity disorder: I. Qualitative and quantitative electroencephalography. *Clinical Neurophysiology, 114*, 171–183.

Beers, S. R., & De Bellis, M. D. (2002). Neuropsychological function in children with maltreatment-related posttraumatic stress disorder. *The American Journal of Psychiatry, 159*, 483–486.

Benes, F. M., Turtle, M., Khan, Y., & Farol, P. (1994). Myelination of a key relay zone in the hippocampal formation occurs in the human brain during childhood, adolescence, and adulthood. *Archives of General Psychiatry, 51*, 477–484.

Bernard, K., Butzin-Dozier, Z., Rittenhouse, J., & Dozier, M. (2010). Young children living with neglecting birth parents show more blunted daytime patterns of cortisol production than children in foster care and comparison children. *Archives of Pediatrics & Adolescent Medicine, 164*, 438–443.

Berrebi, A. S., Fitch, R. H., Ralphe, D. L., Denenberg, J. O., Friedrich, V. L., & Denenberg, V. H. (1988). Corpus callosum: Region-specific effects of sex, early experience and age. *Brain Research, 438*, 216–224.

Bloom, J. S., & Hynd, G. W. (2005). The role of the corpus callosum in interhemispheric transfer of information: Excitation or inhibition? *Neuropsychology Review, 15*, 59–71.

Booth, J. R., Burman, D. D., Meyer, J. R., Lei, Z., Trommer, B. L., ... Mesulam, M. M. (2005). Larger deficits in brain networks for response inhibition than for visual selective attention in ADHD. *Journal of Child Psychology and Psychiatry, 46*, 94–111.

Botvinick, M., Nystrom, L., Fissell, K., Carter, C., & Cohen, J. (1999). Conflict monitoring vs. selection-for-action in anterior cingulate cortex. *Nature, 402*, 179–181.

Brake, W. G., Sullivan, R. M., & Gratton, A. (2000). Perinatal distress leads to lateralized medial prefrontal cortical dopamine hypofunction in adult rats. *Journal of Neuroscience, 20*, 5538–5543.

Bremner, J. D., Randall, P., Scott, T. W., Capelli, S., Delaney, R., ... Charney, D. S. (1995). Deficits in short-term memory in adult survivors of childhood abuse. *Psychiatry Research, 59*, 97–107.

Bremner, J. D., Randall, P., Vermetten, E., Staib, L. W., Bronen, R. A., ... Charney, D. S. (1997). Magnetic resonance imaging-based measurement of hippocampal volume in posttraumatic stress disorder related to childhood physical and sexual abuse: A preliminary report. *Society of Biological Psychiatry, 41*, 23–42.

Bremner, J. D., Vythilingam, M., Vermetten, E., Southwick, S. M., McGlashan, T., ... Khan, S., et al. (2003). MRI and PET study of deficits in hippocampal structure and function in women with childhood sexual abuse and posttraumatic stress disorder. *American Journal of Psychiatry, 160*, 924–932.

Bruce, J., Kroupina, M., Parker, S., & Gunnar, M. R. (2000). *The relationships between cortisol patterns, growth retardation, and developmental delay in post-institutionalized children*. Paper presented at the International Conference on Infant Studies. Brighton.

Bruce, J., Davis, E. P., & Gunnar, M. R. (2002). Individual differences in children's cortisol response to the beginning of the new school year. *Psychoneuroendocrinology, 27*, 635–650.

Bruce, J., Fisher, P. A., Pears, K. C., & Levine, S. (2009a). Morning cortisol levels in preschool-aged foster children: Differential effects of maltreatment type. *Developmental Psychobiology, 51*, 14–23.

Bruce, J., McDermott, J. M., Fisher, P. A., & Fox, N. (2009b). Using behavioral and electrophysiological measures to assess the effects of a preventative intervention: A preliminary study with preschool-aged foster children. *Prevention Science, 10*, 129–140.

Carlson, M., & Earls, F. (1997). Psychological and neuroendocrinological sequelae of early social deprivation in institutionalized children in Romania. In C. S. Carter, I. I. Lederhendler, & B. Kirkpatrick (Eds.), *The integrative neurobiology of affiliation* (pp. 419–428). New York: New York Academy of Sciences.

Carpenter, L. L., Tyrka, A. R., Ross, N. S., Khoury, L., Anderson, G. M., & Price, L. H. (2009). Effect of childhood emotional abuse and age on cortisol responsivity in adulthood. *Biological Psychiatry, 66*, 69–75.

Carrey, N. J., Butter, H. J., Persinger, M. A., & Bialik, R. J. (1995). Physiological and cognitive correlates of child abuse. *Journal of the American Academy of Child and Adolescent Psychiatry, 34*, 1067–1075.

Carrion, V. G., Weems, C. F., Eliez, S., Patwardhan, A., Brown, W., ... Reiss, A. L. (2001). Attenuation of frontal asymmetry in pediatric posttraumatic stress disorder. *Society of Biological Psychiatry, 50*, 943–951.

Carrion, V. G., Garrett, A., Menon, V., Weems, C. F., & Reiss, A. L. (2008). Posttraumatic stress symptoms and brain function during a response-inhibition task: An fMRI study in youth. *Depression and Anxiety, 25*, 514–526.

Carrion, V. G., Weems, C. F., Watson, C., Eliez, S., Menon, V., & Reiss, A. L. (2009). Converging evidence for abnormalities of the prefrontal cortex and evaluation of midsagital structures in pediatric posttraumatic stress disorder: An MRI study. *Psychiatry Research, 172*, 226–234.

Carrion, V. G., Haas, B. W., Garrett, A., Song, S., & Reiss, A. L. (2010). Reduced hippocampal activity in youth with posttraumatic stress symptoms: An fMRI study. *Journal of Pediatric Psychology, 35*, 559–569.

Choi, J., Jeong, B., Rohan, M. L., Polcari, A. M., & Teicher, M. H. (2009). Preliminary evidence for white matter tract abnormalities in young adults exposed to parental verbal abuse. *Biological Psychiatry, 65*, 227–234.

Christakou, A., Brammer, M., Giampetro, V., & Rubia, K. (2009). Right ventromedial and dorsolateral prefrontal cortices mediate adaptive decisions under ambiguity by integrating choice utility and outcome evaluation. *Journal of Neuroscience, 29*, 11020–11028.

Cicchetti, D., Rogosch, F., Toth, S. L., & Sturge-Apple, M. L. (2011). Normalizing the development of cortisol regulation in maltreated infants through preventive interventions. *Development and Psychopathology, 23*, 789–800.

Dalgleish, T., Moradi, A. R., Taghavi, M. R., Neshat-Doost, H. T., & Yule, W. (2001). An experimental investigation of hypervigilance for threat in children and adolescents with post-traumatic stress disorder. *Psychological Medicine, 31*, 541–547.

Danese, A., Pariante, C. M., Caspi, A., Taylor, A., & Poulton, R. (2007). Childhood maltreatment predicts adult inflammation in a life-course study. *Proceedings of the National Academy of Sciences, 104*, 1319–1324.

Danese, A., Moffitt, T. E., Harrington, H. Milne, B. J., Polanszyk, G., … Caspi, A. (2009). Adverse childhood experiences and adult risk factors for age-related disease: Depression, inflammation, and clustering of metabolic risk markers. *Archives of Pediatrics and Adolescent Medicine, 163*, 1135–1143.

Davis, M., & Whalen, P. J. (2001). The amygdala: Vigilance and emotion. *Molecular Psychiatry, 6*, 13–34.

De Bellis, M. D., & Keshavan, M. S. (2003). Sex differences in brain maturation in maltreatment-related pediatric posttraumatic stress disorder. *Neuroscience and Biobehavioral Reviews, 27*, 103–117.

De Bellis, M. D., Keshavan, M. S., Clark, D. B., Casey, B. J., Giedd, J. N., … Ryan, N. D. (1999). Developmental traumatology part II: Brain development. *Biological Psychiatry, 45*, 1271–1284.

De Bellis, M. D., Casey, B. J., Dahl, R. E., Birmaher, B., Williamson, D. E., … Ryan, N. D. (2000). A pilot study of amygdala volumes in pediatric generalized anxiety disorder. *Biological Psychiatry, 48*, 51–57.

De Bellis, M. D., Hall, J., Boring, A. M., Frustaci, K., & Moritz, G. (2001). A pilot longitudinal study of hippocampal volumes in pediatric maltreatment-related posttraumatic stress disorder. *Biological Psychiatry, 50*, 305–309.

De Bellis, M. D., Keshavan, M. S., Shifflett, H., Iyengar, S., Beers, … Moritz, G. (2002a). Brain structures in pediatric maltreatment-related posttraumatic stress disorder: A sociodemographically matched study. *Biological Psychiatry, 52*, 1066–1078.

De Bellis, M. D., Keshavan, M. S., Frustaci, K., Shifflett, H., Iyengar, S., & Hall, J. (2002b). Superior temporal gyrus volumes in maltreated children and adolescents with PTSD. *Biological Psychiatry, 51*, 544–552.

De Bellis, M. D., Hooper, S. R., Spratt, E. G., & Woolley, D. (2009). Neuropsychological findings in childhood neglect and their relationships to pediatric PTSD. *Journal of the International Neuropsychological Society, 15*, 868–878.

de Quervain, D. J. F., Roozendaal, B., & McGaugh, J. L. (1998). Stress and glucocorticoids impair retrieval of long-term spatial memory. *Nature, 394*, 787–790.

Derryberry, D., & Reed, M. A. (2002). Anxiety-related attentional biases and their regulation by attentional control. *Journal of Abnormal Psychology, 111*, 225–236.

Dozier, M., & The Infant Caregiver Project Lab. (2012). *Attachment and biobehavioral catch-up*. University of Delaware: Unpublished document.

Dozier, M., Manni, M., Gordon, M. K., Peloso, E., Gunnar, M. R., … Levine, S. (2006). Foster children's diurnal production of cortisol: An exploratory study. *Child Maltreatment, 11*, 189–197.

Dozier, M., Bernard, K., Bick, J., & Gordon, M. K. (2012). *Normalizing the diurnal production of cortisol: The effects of an early intervention for high-risk children*. Unpublished manuscript, University of Delaware, Newark.

Driessen, M., Herrmann, J., Stahl, K., Zwaan, M., Meier, S., … Petersen, D. (2000). Magnetic resonance imaging volumes of the hippocampus and the amygdala in women with borderline personality disorder and early traumatization. *Archives of General Psychiatry, 57*, 1115–1122.

Dubowitz, H., Hampton, R. L., Bithoney, W. G., & Newberger, E. H. (1987). Inflicted and noninflicted injuries: Differences in child and familial characteristics. *The American Journal of Orthopsychiatry, 57*, 525–535.

Eichenbaum, H., & Otto, T. (1992). The hippocampus: What does it do? *Behavioral and Neural Biology, 57*, 2–36.

Eimer, M., & Holmes, A. (2007). Event-related brain potential correlates of emotional face processing. *Neuropsychologia, 45*, 15–31.

Ellis, B. H., Fisher, P. A., & Zaharie, S. (2004). Predictors of disruptive behavior, developmental delays, anxiety, and affective symptomatology among institutionally reared Romanian children. *Journal of the American Academy of Child and Adolescent Psychiatry, 43*, 1283–1292.

Ellison-Wright, I., Ellison-Wright, Z., & Bullmore, E. (2008). Structural brain change in attention deficit hyperactivity disorder identified by meta-analysis. *BMC Psychiatry, 8*, 51–57.

Eluvathingal, T. J., Chugani, H. T., Behen, M. E., Juhász, C., Muzik, O., … Makki. M. (2006). Abnormal brain connectivity in children after early severe socioemotional deprivation: A diffusion tensor imaging study. *Pediatrics, 117*, 2093–2100.

Etkin, A., & Wager, T. D. (2007). Functional neuroimaging of anxiety: A meta-analysis of emotional processing in PTSD, social anxiety disorder, and specific phobia. *The American Journal of Psychiatry, 164*, 1476–1488.

Fisher, P. A., Gunnar, M. R., Dozier, M., Bruce, J., & Pears, K. C. (2006). Effects of therapeutic interventions for foster children on behavioral problems, caregiver attachment, and stress regulatory neural systems. *Annals of the New York Academy of Sciences, 1094*, 215–225.

Fisher, P. A., Stoolmiller, M., Gunnar, M. R., & Burraston, B. O. (2007). Effects of a therapeutic intervention for foster preschoolers on diurnal cortisol activity. *Psychoneuroendocrinolgy, 32*, 892–905.

Fries, E., Hesse, J., Hellhammer, J., & Hellhammer, D. (2005). A new view on hypocortisolism. *Psychoneuroendocrinology, 30*, 1010–1016.

Gasser, T., Jennen-Steinmetz, C., Sroka, L., Verteger, R., & Mocks, J. (1988). Development of the EEG of school-age children and adolescents. II. Topography. *Electroencephalography and Clinical Neurophysiology, 69*, 100–109.

Ghetti, S., DeMaster, D. M., Yonelinas, A. P., & Bunge, S. A. (2010). Developmental differences in medial temporal lobe function during memory encoding. *The Journal of Neuroscience, 30*, 9548–9556.

Giedd, J. N., Rumsey, J. M., Castellanos, F. X., Rajapakse, J. C., Kaysen, D., … Rapoport, J. L. (1996a). A quantitative MRI study of the corpus callosum in children and adolescents. *Developmental Brain Research, 91*, 274–280.

Giedd, J. N., Vaituzis, A. C., Hamburger, S. D., Lange, N., Rajapakse, J. C., … Rapoport, J. L. (1996b). Quantitative MRI of the temporal lobe, amygdala, and hippocampus in normal human development: Ages 4–18 years. *Journal of Comparative Neurology, 366*, 223–230.

Giedd, J. N., Blumenthal, J., Jefferies, N. O., Rajapakse, J. C., Vaituzis, A. C., … Castellanos, F. X. (1999). Development of the human corpus callosum during childhood and adolescence: A longitudinal MRI study. *Progressive Neuropsychopharmacological and Biological Psychiatry, 23*, 571–588.

Gogtay, N., Sporn, A., Clasen, L. S., Nugent, T. F., Greenstein, D., … Rapoport, J. L. (2004). Comparison of progressive cortical gray matter loss in childhood-onset schizophrenia with that in childhood-onset atypical psychoses. *Archives of General Psychiatry, 61*, 17–22.

Gould, E., & Tanapat, P. (1999). Stress and hippocampal neurogenesis. *Biological Psychiatry, 46*, 1472–1479.

Govindan, R. M., Behen, M. E., Helder, E., Makki, M. I., & Chugani, H. T. (2010). Altered water diffusivity in cortical association tracts in children with early deprivation identified with tract-based spatial statistics (TBSS). *Cerebral Cortex, 20*, 561–569.

Gunnar, M. R., & Cheatham, C. L. (2003). Brain and behavior interfaces: Stress and the developing brain. *Infant Mental Health Journal, 24*, 195–211.

Gunnar, M. R., & Donzella, B. (2002). Social regulation of the cortisol levels in early human development. *Psychoneuroendocrinology, 27*, 199–220.

Gunnar, M. R., & Quevedo, K. (2007). The neurobiology of stress and development. *Annual Review of Psychology, 58*, 145–173.

Gunnar, M. R., & Vazquez, D. M. (2001). Low cortisol and a flattening of expected daytime rhythm: Potential indices of risk in human development. *Development and Psychopathology, 13*, 515–538.

Hanson, J. L., Chung, M. K., Avants, B. B., Shirtcliff, E. A., Gee, J. C., … Pollak, S. D. (2010). Early stress is associated with alterations in the orbitofrontal cortex: A tensor-based morphometry investigation of brain structure and behavioral risk. *Journal of Neuroscience, 30*, 7466–7472.

Harmony, T., Marosi, E., Díaz de León, A. E., Becker, J., & Fernández, T. (1990). Effect of sex, psychosocial disadvantages and biological risk factors on EEG maturation. *Electroencephalography and Clinical Neurophysiology, 75*, 482–491.

Hart, H., & Rubia, K. (2012). Neuroimaging of child abuse: A critical review. *Frontiers in Human Neuroscience, 6*, 1–24.

Hart, J., Gunnar, M., & Cicchetti, D. (1996). Altered neuroendocrine activity in maltreated children related to symptoms of depression. *Development and Psychopathology, 8*, 201–214.

Helie, S., & Bouchard, C. (2010). Recurrent reporting of child maltreatment: State of knowledge and avenues for research. *Children and Youth Services Review, 32*, 416–422.

Hofer, M. (1994). Hidden regulators in attachment, separation, and loss. *Monographs of the Society for Research in Child Development, 59*, 192–207.

Hofer, M. (2006). Psychobiological roots of early attachment. *Current Directions in Psychological Science, 15*, 84–88.

Ito, Y., Teicher, M. H., Glod, C. A., & Ackerman, E. (1998). Preliminary evidence for aberrant cortical development in abused children: A quantitative EEG study. *The Journal of Neuropsychiatry and Clinical Neurosciences, 10*, 298–307.

Johnson, J. G., Cohen, P., Dohrenwend, B. P., Link, B. G., & Brook, J. S. (1999). A longitudinal investigation of social causation and social selection processes involved in the association between socioeconomic status and psychiatric disorders. *Journal of Abnormal Psychology, 108*, 490–499.

Juffer, F., & van IJzendoorn, M. H. (2005). Behavior problems and mental health referrals of international adoptees: A meta-analysis. *Journal of the American Medical Association, 293*, 2501–2515.

Juraska, J. M., & Kopcik, J. R. (1988). Sex and environmental influences on the size and ultrastructure of the rat corpus callosum. *Brain Research, 450,* 1–8.

Kaplow, J. B., & Widom, C. S. (2007). Age of onset of child maltreatment predicts long-term mental health outcomes. *Journal of Abnormal Psychology, 116,* 176–187.

Kaufman, J. (1991). Depressive disorders in maltreated children. *Journal of the American Academy of Child and Adolescent Psychiatry, 30,* 257–265.

Kim, J. J., & Yoon, K. S. (1998). Stress: Metaplastic effects in the hippocampus. *Trends in Neurosciences, 21,* 505–509.

Kitayama, N., Vaccarino, L. V., Kutner, M., Weiss, P., & Bremner, J. D. (2005). Magnetic resonance imaging (MRI) measurement of hippocampal volume in posttraumatic stress disorder: A meta-analysis. *Journal of Affective Disorders, 88,* 79–86.

Kitterle, F. L. (Ed.). (1995). *Hemispheric communication: Mechanisms and models.* Hillsdale: Lawrence Erlbaum.

Kreppner, J. M., O'Connor, T. G., Rutter, M., Beckett, C., Castle, J., … Groothues, C. (2001). Can inattention/overactivity be an institutional deprivation syndrome? *Journal of Abnormal Child Psychology, 29,* 513–528.

Larson, M. C., White, B. P., Cochran, A., Donzella, B., & Gunnar, M. (1998). Dampening of the cortisol response to handling at 3 months in human infants and its relation to sleep, circadian cortisol activity, and behavioral distress. *Developmental Psychobiology, 33,* 327–337.

Lauder, J. M. (1983). Hormonal and humoral influences on brain development. *Psychoneuroendocrinology, 8,* 121–155.

Loman, M. M., Wiik, K. L., Frenn, K. A., Pollak, S. D., & Gunnar, M. R. (2009). Postinstitutionalized children's development: Growth, cognitive, and language outcomes. *Journal of Developmental and Behavioral Pediatrics, 30,* 426–434.

Luders, E., Thompson, P. M., & Toga, A. W. (2010). The development of the corpus callosum in the healthy human brain. *Journal of Neuroscience, 30,* 10985–10990.

Lyons, S. J., Henly, J. R., & Schuerman, J. R. (2005). Informal support in maltreating families: Its effect on parenting practices. *Children and Youth Services Review, 27,* 21–38.

Maheu, F. S., Dozier, M., Guyer, A. E., Mandell, D., Peloso, E., … Ernst, M. (2010). A preliminary study of medial temporal lobe function in youths with a history of caregiver deprivation and emotional neglect. *Cognitive, Affective, & Behavioral Neuroscience, 10,* 34–49.

Marosi, E., Harmony, T., Becker, J., Reyes, A., Bernal, J., … Guerrero, V. (1995). Electroencephalographic coherences discriminate between children with different pedagogical evaluation. *International Journal of Psychophysiology, 19,* 23–32.

Marshall, P. J., Bar-Haim, Y., & Fox, N. A. (2002). Development of the EEG from 5 months to 4 years of age. *Clinical Neurophysiology, 113,* 1199–1208.

Marshall, P. J., Fox, N. A., & BEIP Core Group. (2004). A comparison of the electroencephalogram between institutionalized and community children in Romania. *Journal of Cognitive Neuroscience, 16,* 1327–1338.

Marshall, P. J., Reeb, B. C., Fox, N. A., Nelson, C. A., & Zeanah, C. H. (2008). Effects of early intervention on EEG power and coherence in previously institutionalized children in Romania. *Development and Psychopathology, 20,* 861–880.

McCurdy, K. (2005). The influence of support and stress on maternal attitudes. *Child Abuse & Neglect, 29,* 251–268.

McLaughlin, K. A., Fox, N. A., Zeanah, C. H., Sheridan, M. A., Marshall, P., & Nelson, C. A. (2010). Delayed maturation in brain electrical activity partially explains the association between early environmental deprivation and symptoms of attention-deficit/hyperactivity disorder. *Biological Psychiatry, 68,* 329–336.

McLaughlin, K. A., Sheridan, M. A., & Nelson, C. A. (2013). Adverse childhood experiences and brain development: Neurobiological mechanisms linking the social environment to psychiatric disorders. In K. Koenen, S. Rudenstine, & S. Galea (Eds.), *Life course epidemiology of mental health disorders.* Oxford: Oxford University Press.

Mehta, M. A., Golembo, N. I., Nosarti, C., Colvert, E., Mota, A., … Sonuga-Barke, E. J. S. (2009). Amygdala, hippocampal, and corpus callosum size following severe early institutional deprivation: The English and Romanian Adoptees study pilot. *Journal of Child Psychology and Psychiatry, 50,* 943–951.

Miller, E. K., & Cohen, J. D. (2001). An integrative theory of prefrontal cortex function. *Annual Review of Neuroscience, 24,* 167–202.

Miller, G. E., Cohen, S., & Ritchey, A. K. (2002). Chronic psychological stress and the regulation of pro-inflammatory cytokines: A glucocorticoid-resistance model. *Health Psychology, 21,* 531–541.

Miskovic, V., & Schmidt, L. A. (2010). Cross-regional cortical synchronization during affective image viewing. *Brain Research, 1362,* 102–111.

Mooshagian, E. (2008). Anatomy of the corpus callosum reveals its function. *Journal of Neuroscience, 28,* 1535–1536.

Mueller, S. C., Maheu, F. S., Dozier, M., Peloso, E., Mandell, D., … Ernsta, M. (2010). Early-life stress is associated with impairment in cognitive control in adolescence: An fMRI study. *Neuropsychologia, 48,* 3037–3044.

Mundy, P., Fox, N., & Card, J. (2003). EEG coherence, joint attention and language development in the second year. *Developmental Science, 6*, 48–54.

Navalta, C. P., Polcari, A., Webster, D. M., Boghossian, A., & Teicher, M. H. (2006). Effects of childhood sexual abuse on neuropsychological and cognitive function in college women. *The Journal of Neuropsychiatry and Clinical Neurosciences, 18*, 45–53.

Neil, J., Miller, J., Mukherjee, P., & Hüppi, P. S. (2002). Diffusion tensor imaging of normal and injured developing human brain: A technical review. *NMR in Biomedicine, 15*, 543–552.

Nelson, C. (2007). A neurobiological perspective on early human deprivation. *Child Development Perspectives, 1*, 13–18.

Nolin, P., & Ethier, L. (2007). Using neuropsychological profiles to classify neglected children with or without physical abuse. *Child Abuse & Neglect, 31*, 631–643.

Olofsson, J. K., Nordin, S., Sequeria, H., & Polich, J. (2008). Affective picture processing: An integrative review of ERP findings. *Biological Psychology, 77*, 247–265.

Otero, G. A. (1997). Poverty, cultural disadvantage and brain development: A study of pre-school children in Mexico. *Electroencephalography and Clinical Neurophysiology, 102*, 512–516.

Patel, P. D., Lopez, J. F., Lyons, D. M., Burke, S., Wallace, M., & Schatzberg, A. F. (2000). Glucocorticoid and mineralocorticoid receptor mRNA expression in squirrel monkey brain. *Journal of Psychiatric Research, 34*, 383–392.

Pechtel, P., & Pizzagalli, D. A. (2010). Effects of early life stress on cognitive and affective function: An integrated review of human literature. *Psychopharmacology, 214*, 55–70.

Pederson, C. L., Maurer, S. H., Kaminski, P. L., Zander, K. A., Peters, C. M., … Osborn, R. E. (2004). Hippocampal volume and memory performance in a community-based sample of women with posttraumatic stress disorder secondary to child abuse. *Journal of Traumatic Stress, 17*, 37–40.

Picton, T. W., Bentin, S., Berg, P., Donchin, E., Hillyard, S. A., … Taylor, M. J. (2000). Guidelines for using human event-related potentials to study cognition: Recording standards and publication criteria. *Psychophysiology, 37*, 127–152.

Pollak, S. D., & Sinha, P. (2002). Effects of early experience on children's recognition of facial displays of emotion. *Developmental Psychology, 38*, 784–791.

Pollak, S. D., & Tolley-Schell, S. A. (2003). Selective attention to facial emotion in physically abused children. *Journal of Abnormal Psychology, 112*, 323–338.

Pollak, S. D., Cicchetti, D., Klorman, R., & Brumaghin, J. T. (1997). Cognitive brain event-related potentials and emotion processing in maltreated children. *Child Development, 68*, 773–787.

Pollak, S. D., Cicchetti, D., Hornuny, K., & Reed, A. (2000). Recognizing emotion in faces: Developmental effects of child abuse and neglect. *Developmental Psychology, 36*, 679–688.

Pollak, S. D., Klorman, R., Thatcher, J. E., & Cicchetti, D. (2001). P3b reflects maltreated children's reactions to facial displays of emotion. *Psychophysiology, 38*, 267–274.

Price, D. A., Close, D. C., & Fielding, B. A. (1983). Age of appearance of circadian rhythm in salivary cortisol values in infancy. *Archives of Disease in Childhood, 58*, 454–456.

Richert, K. A., Carrion, V. G., Karchemskiy, A., & Reiss, A. I. (2006). Regional differences of the prefrontal cortex in pediatric PTSD: An MRI study. *Depression and Anxiety, 23*, 17–25.

Rubia, K., Smith, A. B., Wooley, J., Nosarti, C., Heyman, I., … Brammer, M. (2006). Progressive increase of fronto-striatal brain activation from childhood to adulthood during event-related tasks of cognitive control. *Human Brain Mapping, 27*, 973–993.

Sanchez, M. M., Hearn, E. F., Do, D., Rilling, J. K., & Herndon, J. G. (1998). Differential rearing affects corpus callosum size and cognitive function of rhesus monkeys. *Brain Research, 812*, 38–49.

Sapolsky, R. M., Uno, H., Rebert, C. S., & Finch, C. E. (1990). Hippocampal damage associated with prolonged glucocorticoid exposure in primates. *Journal of Neuroscience, 10*, 2897–2902.

Sapolsky, R. M., Romero, L. M., & Munch, A. U. (2000). How do glucocorticoids influence stress responses? Integrating permissive, suppressive, stimulatory, and preparative actions. *Endocrine Reviews, 21*, 55–89.

Schatzberg, A. F., & Lindley, S. E. (2008). Glucocorticoid antagonists in neuropsychiatric disorders. *European Journal of Pharmacology, 583*, 358–364.

Schmahl, C. G., Vermetten, E., Elzinga, B. M., & Bremner, J. D. (2003). Magnetic resonance imaging of hippocampal and amygdala volume in women with childhood abuse and borderline personality disorder. *Psychiatry Research: Neuroimaging, 122*(3), 193–198.

Schulz, K. P., Fan, J., Tang, C. Y., Newcorn, J. H., Buchsbaum, M. S., … Halperin, J. M. (2004). Response inhibition in adolescents diagnosed with attention deficit hyperactivity disorder during childhood: An event-related fMRI study. *The American Journal of Psychiatry, 161*, 1650–1657.

Shaw, P., Lerch, J., Greenstein, D., Sharp, W., Clasen, L., … Rapoport, J. (2006). Longitudinal mapping of cortical thickness and clinical outcome in children and adolescents with Attention-Deficit/Hyperactivity Disorder. *Archives of General Psychiatry, 63*, 540–549.

Sheridan, M. A., Fox, N. A., Zeanah, C. H., McLaughlin, K. A., & Nelson, C. A. (2012). Variation in neural development as a result of exposure to institutionalization early in childhood. *Proceedings of the National Academy of Sciences of the United States of America, 109*, 12927–12932.

Shirtcliff, E. A., Coe, C. L., & Pollak, S. D. (2009). Early childhood stress is associated with elevated antibody levels to herpes simplex virus type 1. *Proceedings of the National Academy of Sciences of the United States of America, 106*, 2963–2967.

Sowell, E. R., Peterson, B. S., Thompson, P. M., Welcome, S. E., Henkenius, A. L., & Toga, A. W. (2003). Mapping cortical change across the human life span. *Nature Neuroscience, 6*, 309–315.

Stein, M. B., Koverola, C., Hanna, C., Torchia, M. G., & McClarty, B. (1997). Hippocampal volume in women victimized by childhood sexual abuse. *Psychological Medicine, 27*, 951–959.

Stein, M. D., Simmons, A. N., Feinstein, J. S., & Paulus, M. P. (2007). Increased amygdala and insula activation during emotion processing in anxiety-prone subjects. *The American Journal of Psychiatry, 164*, 318–327.

Stevens, S. E., Sonuga-Barke, E. J. S., Kreppner, J. M., Beckett, C., Castle, J., … Rutter, M. (2008). Inattention/overactivity following early severe institutional deprivation: Presentation and associations in early adolescence. *Journal of Abnormal Child Psychology, 36*, 385–398.

Tarullo, A. R., & Gunnar, M. R. (2006). Child maltreatment and the developing HPA axis. *Hormones and Behavior, 50*, 632–639.

Teicher, M. H., Ito, Y., Glod, C. A., Andersen, S. L., Dumont, N. L., & Ackerman, E. (1997). Preliminary evidence for abnormal cortical development in physically and sexually abused children using EEG coherence and MRI. *Annals of the New York Academy of Sciences, 821*, 160–175.

Teicher, M. H., Andersen, S. L., Polcari, A., Anderson, C. M., Navalta, C. P., & Kim, D. M. (2003). The neurobiological consequences of early stress and childhood maltreatment. *Neuroscience and Biobehavioral Reviews, 27*, 33–44.

Teicher, M. H., Dumont, N. L., Ito, Y., Vaituzis, C., Giedd, J. N., & Andersen, S. L. (2004). Childhood neglect is associated with reduced corpus callosum area. *Biological Psychiatry, 56*, 80–85.

Teicher, M. H., Anderson, C. M., & Polcari, A. (2012). Childhood maltreatment is associated with reduced volume in the hippocampal subfields CA3, dentate gyrus, and subiculum. *Proceedings of the National Academy of Sciences, 109*, E562–E572.

Thatcher, R. W., Krause, P. J., & Hrybyk, M. (1986). Cortico-cortical associations and EEG coherence: A two-compartmental model. *Electroencephalography and Clinical Neurophysiology, 64*, 123–143.

Thatcher, R. W., North, D. M., & Biver, C. J. (2008). Development of cortical connections as measured by EEG coherence and phase delays. *Human Brain Mapping, 29*, 1400–1415.

Thomas, K. M., Drevets, W. C., Dahl, R. E., Ryan, N. D., Birmaher, B., … Casey, B. J. (2001). Amygdala response to fearful faces in anxious and depressed children. *Archives of General Psychiatry, 58*, 1057–1063.

Tomoda, A., Suzuki, H., Rabi, K., Sheu, Y., Polcari, A., & Teicher, M. H. (2009). Reduced prefrontal cortical gray matter volume in young adults exposed to harsh corporal punishment. *NeuroImage, 47*, T66–T71.

Tottenham, N., & Sheridan, M. A. (2010). A review of adversity, the amygdala and the hippocampus: A consideration of developmental timing. *Frontiers in Human Neuroscience, 3*, 1–18.

Tottenham, N., Hare, T. A., & Casey, B. J. (2009). A developmental perspective on human amygdala function. In P. J. Whalen & E. A. Phelps (Eds.), *The Human Amygdala* (pp. 107–117). New York: Guilford Press.

Tottenham, N., Hare, T. A., Quinn, B. T., McCarry, T. W., Nurse, M., … Casey, B. J. (2010). Prolonged institutional rearing is associated with atypically large amygdala volume and difficulty in emotion regulation. *Developmental Science, 13*, 46–61.

Tottenham, N., Hare, T. A., Millner, A., Gilhooly, T., Zevin, J. D., & Casey, B. J. (2011). Elevated amygdala response to faces following early deprivation. *Developmental Science, 14*, 190–204.

Tupler, L. A., & De Bellis, M. D. (2006). Segmented hippocampal volume in children and adolescents with posttraumatic stress disorder. *Biological Psychiatry, 59*, 523–529.

Twardosz, S., & Lutzker, J. R. (2010). Child maltreatment and the developing brain: A review of neuroscience perspectives. *Aggression and Violent Behavior, 15*, 59–68.

van der Knaap, L. J., & van der Ham, I. J. M. (2011). How does the corpus callosum mediate interhemispheric transfer? A review. *Behavioural Brain Research, 223*, 211–221.

Vanderwert, R. E., Marshall, P. J., Nelson, C. A., Zeanah, C. H., & Fox, N. A. (2010). Timing of intervention affects brain electrical activity in children exposed to severe psychosocial neglect. *PLoS One, 5*, e11415.

Vasey, M. W., el-Hag, N. D., & Daleiden, E. L. (1996). Anxiety and the processing of emotionally threatening stimuli: Distinctive patterns of selective attention among high- and low-test-anxious children. *Child Development, 67*, 1173–1185.

Vorria, P., Papaligoura, Z., Sarafidou, J., Kopakaki, M., Dunn, J., … Kontaopoulou, A. (2006). The development of adopted children after institutional care: A follow-up study. *Journal of Child Psychology and Psychiatry, 47*, 1246–1253.

Vyas, A., & Pillai, A. G. (2004). Recovery after chronic stress fails to reverse amygdaloid neuronal hypertrophy and enhanced anxiety-life behavior. *Neuroscience, 128*, 667–673.

Vythilingam, M., Heim, C., Newport, J., Miller, A. H., Anderson, E., … Bremner, J. D. (2002). Childhood trauma associated with smaller hippocampal volume in women with major depression. *American Journal of Psychiatry, 159*, 2072–2080.

Watamura, S. E., Donzella, B., Alwin, J., & Gunnar, M. R. (2003). Morning-to-afternoon increases in cortisol concentrations for infants and toddlers at child care: Age differences and behavioral correlates. *Child Development, 74*, 1006–1020.

Wellman, C. L. (2001). Dendritic reorganization in pyramidal neurons in medial prefrontal cortex after chronic corticosterone administration. *Journal of Neurobiology, 49*, 245–253.

Winberg, J. (2005). Mother and newborn baby: Mutual regulation of physiology and behavior- a selective review. *Developmental Psychobiology, 47*, 217–229.

Wismer-Fries, A. B., & Pollak, S. D. (2004). Emotion understanding in post institutionalized Eastern European children. *Development and Psychopathology, 16*, 355–369.

Woon, F. L., & Hedges, D. W. (2008). Hippocampal and amygdala volumes in children and adults with childhood maltreatment-related posttraumatic stress disorder: A meta-analysis. *Hippocampus, 18*, 729–736.

Zeanah, C. H., Nelson, C. A., Fox, N. A., Smyke, A. T., Marshall, P. J., … Koga, S. F. (2003). Designing research to study the effects of institutionalization on brain and behavioral development: The Bucharest early intervention project. *Development and Psychopathology, 15*, 885–907.

Zeanah, C. H., Egger, H. L., Smyke, A. T., Nelson, C. A., Fox, N. A., … Guthrie, D. (2009). Institutional rearing and psychiatric disorders in Romanian preschool children. *American Journal of Psychiatry, 166*, 777–785.

Chapter 12
Longterm Consequences of Child Maltreatment

Cathy Spatz Widom

Introduction

Over the past three decades, considerable progress has been made in understanding the long-term consequences of childhood victimization. As part of these developments, etiological models of child maltreatment have evolved to include ecological (Belsky 1980; Garbarino 1977), transitional (Wolfe 1991), and transactional (Cicchetti and Carlson 1989) perspectives among them. One of the most common models is referred to as a "transactional-bioecological model" that attempts to conceptualize the relative contributions of risk and protective factors in children's development outcomes (Bronfenbrenner 1979; Cicchetti et al. 1993). The conceptual model underlying the organization of this chapter is a modified ecological one that considers the individual in the context of the broader social environment in which he or she functions (see Fig. 12.1). The child is viewed within the context of a family, and in turn, children and families are embedded in a larger social system that includes communities, neighborhoods and cultures.

The assumption underlying the model is that behavior is complex and development is multiply determined by characteristics of the individual, parents and family, and neighborhood and/or community and interactions. "Risk and protective factors include individual child characteristics such as genetic and constitutional propensities and cognitive strengths and vulnerabilities; parent characteristics such as mental health, education lee, sense of efficacy, and resourcefulness; family factors such as quality of the parent-child relationship, emotional climate, and marital quality; community connectedness factors such as parental social support, social resources, and children's peer relationship; and neighborhood factors such as availability of resources, adequacy of housing, and levels of crime and violence" (Sameroff and Fiese 2000, p. 121).

The model also emphasizes the need to consider how certain factors may interact with characteristics of the person to buffer the individual from negative long-term consequences and to increase the likelihood of positive outcomes. That is, the model explicitly acknowledges the contribution of contextual variables (neighborhood and community level factors) to the consequences of child maltreatment.

Figure 12.1 represents a schematic model that guides the organization of this chapter and the discussion of the cascade of consequences that may develop after childhood experiences of abuse and neglect. Using a series of concentric circles, the child is depicted as embedded or existing within the context of a family, and in turn, children and families are embedded in a larger social system that

C.S. Widom (✉)
Psychology Department, John Jay College and Graduate Center, City University of New York,
524 West 59th Street, Suite 10.63.03, New York, NY 10019, USA
e-mail: cwidom@jjay.cuny.edu

J.E. Korbin and R.D. Krugman (eds.), *Handbook of Child Maltreatment*, Child Maltreatment 2,
DOI 10.1007/978-94-007-7208-3_12, © Springer Science+Business Media Dordrecht 2014

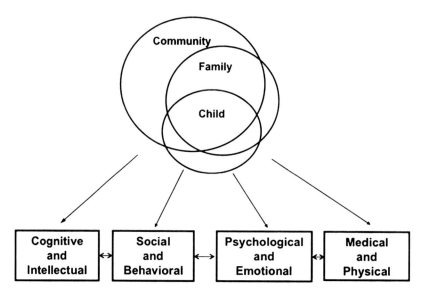

Fig. 12.1 Cascade of consequences

includes communities, neighborhoods and cultures. In contrast to the traditional ecological model, the circles representing the child, family, and larger community (which includes neighborhood and culture) are *not* totally embedded in one another and represent important areas of *non-overlap*. Specifically, although the child lives largely within the context of a family, Fig. 12.1 recognizes that the child also spends time outside and independent from the family unit and in the larger community. Areas of non-overlap of the child within the family will change with the age of the child, so that as the child gets older, he or she will typically spend more time out of the family and in the community and in the context of peers. For some children, there may be increasing amounts of unsupervised time, spent in ways of which parents may be unaware. Figure 12.1 also calls attention to aspects of the developing child that may occur and exist outside both the family and community. That is, there may be experiences unique to the child, independent of family and/or community context. These areas of non-shared experience (areas of non-overlap) may be particularly important in terms of subsequent development for severely abused or neglected children. This model also recognizes that families live within the context of neighborhoods and communities and that families are influenced in major ways by the surrounding environment or context. The label "community" is used here to refer to the broader social context in which families exist. However, "community" can represent small block groups, local neighborhoods, census tracts, or larger contexts such as cities, states, and countries. Figure 12.1 shows that experiences of families may lie outside the neighborhood or community, that is, that families are often isolated from the larger community. Finally, the model recognizes that behavior is complex and multiply determined, that certain risk factors predispose an individual to a variety of maladaptive and/or problem behaviors, and that protective factors or interventions may act to mitigate ultimate outcomes.

Using this schematic model to organize the material in this chapter, the second part of this chapter reviews the literature on the "cascade of consequences of childhood maltreatment" across multiple domains of functioning, including cognitive and academic, social and behavioral, psychiatric and emotional, and physical health and neurobiological. The chapter does not pretend to be comprehensive or exhaustive, but illustrative and representative. There is a focus on longitudinal studies, because the strengths of prospective studies is that they include the clear and unambiguous temporal order of maltreatment and subsequent outcomes, avoidance of recall bias, minimization of selection inclusion of participants on the basis of the outcome, and the opportunity to adjust for social and individual confounding factors a they occur (Gilbert et al. 2009). Where possible, consequences for specific types of childhood maltreatment (physical abuse, sexual abuse, neglect, and emotional maltreatment) are described, but limitations of the existing literature make this quite difficult. Because negative effects of childhood maltreatment are not inevitable, the third section of this chapter describes research on resilience and protective factors that may buffer maltreated children from succumbing to negative consequences. The fourth section of the chapter describes some research on the role of contextual factors and the important role that they play in influencing the development of the child. Finally, there is a discussion of the challenges to the field and a brief section on gaps in knowledge and suggestions for future research.

Cascade of Consequences of Childhood Maltreatment

Cognitive and Academic Performance Outcomes

Deficiencies in reading ability and academic performance have been documented in physically abused children followed up into adolescence and young adulthood. Several prospective studies have established that poor school performance (e.g. poor grades, poor scores on standardized achievement tests, grade retention, placement in special education) is often an outcome of childhood abuse and neglect (Eckenrode et al. 2001; Egeland 1997; Jonson-Reid 2004; Kinard 1999; Leiter 2007; Perez and Widom 1994). There is fairly consistent evidence that child maltreatment often has negative consequences for cognitive functioning and academic performance, beginning in early childhood and extending into adulthood. These consequences are not exclusively found in physically abused children, but have been reported in neglected children as well (Eckenrode et al. 1993; Erickson et al. 1989; Wodarski et al. 1990). Compared to adults without maltreatment histories, adults with a documented history of child abuse or neglect were found to have lower scores on tests of intelligence, reading ability, and academic achievement (42 % of maltreated children completed high school compared with two-thirds of the matched comparison group)(Perez and Widom 1994). Jonson-Reid and colleagues (2004) found that maltreatment predicted entry into special education after controlling for early medical conditions.

Social and Behavioral Consequences

Maltreated children have also been found to manifest behavioral and social problems, including reports of being physically assaultive toward peers and aggressive in school settings at young ages and at risk for conduct disorder, school problems, delinquency, crime and violence in adolescence and young adulthood. Maltreated children show higher levels of aggression and withdrawal than non-maltreated children (Herrenkohl and Herrenkohl 2007; Sternberg et al. 2006; Rogosch and Cicchetti 1994). Kim and Cicchetti (2010) found that when maltreated children have trouble regulating emotions they are at increased risk for problematic peer relations. Dodge and colleagues (1995) found that physical abuse was associated with major increase in risk of parent-reported externalizing problems among children in third and fourth grades compared to children who did not have histories of abuse. Research has also shown that neglected children appear more socially withdrawn in preschool years (Crittendon and Ainsworth 1989) and are more isolated during free play and engage in fewer social interactions with other children (Hildyard and Wolfe 2002). Longitudinal studies suggest that neglected children experience significant internalizing problems and that they may have more emotional problems than physically abused children (Manly et al. 2001). Neglected children have been described as more aggressive, disruptive and non-cooperative in comparison to non-maltreated children, but less aggressive than their physically abused peers (Manly et al. 2001). Maltreated children are also at increased risk of running away from home (Kaufman and Widom 1999).

One of the most common consequences of child maltreatment is based on the notion of a "cycle of violence" (Widom 1989a), in which physically abused children were believed to go on to become perpetrators of violence in adolescence and adulthood. This theory was based on the early observations that maltreated children were at increased risk for delinquency and crime and particularly violence and, until the late 1980s, this body of research relied primarily on cross-sectional studies. However, in a paper in *Science* on the "cycle of violence", Widom (1989b) described the results of a prospective cohort design study in which children with documented cases of physical and sexual abuse and neglect were matched with children without maltreatment histories and the criminal histories for both groups were assessed. She reported that that being abused and neglected as a child increased the likelihood of arrest as a juvenile by 53 %, as an adult by 38 %, and for a violent crime by 38 %. In addition, although physically abused children were at elevated risk for violence, she found that neglected children were at increased risk as well.

Since that time, several large prospective investigations in different parts of the United States have documented a relationship between childhood abuse and neglect and juvenile and/or young adult crime (English et al. 2001; Lansford et al. 2007; Maxfield and Widom 1996; Smith and Thornberry 1995; Stouthamer-Loeber et al. 2001; Widom 1989b; Zingraff et al. 1993). Despite differences in geographic region, time period, youths' ages, sex of the children, definition of child maltreatment, and assessment technique, these six prospective investigations provide evidence that childhood maltreatment increases later risk for delinquency and violence. Replication of this relationship across a number of well-designed studies supports the generalizability of results and increases confidence in them. Indeed, conclusions from research are strengthened through replication, since the limitations of any one study may impact the interpretation of findings (Taubes 2007). One recent meta-analysis showed that childhood physical abuse was strongly related to violence in girls (Hubbard and Pratt 2002). Maxfield and Widom (1996) also reported an increase in risk for arrest for a juvenile, adult, and violent crime in abused and neglected girls, compared to matched control girls.

Prospective studies have reported that child maltreatment increases a person's risk for *prostitution*. Widom and Kuhns (1996) reported that child abuse and neglect increased a person' risk for prostitution by almost threefold (odds ratio of 2.96) and this was particularly true for sexually abused females (OR = 2.58). In one study, Tamang (2005) found that 1 % of the sample of 268 childhood sexual abuse victims reported having engaged in prostitution, compared to 0 % of the sample of 2,625 non-victims. Abuse has also been associated with early onset of consensual sexual activity and with subsequent disrupted home life characterized by events such as running away (Fergusson et al. 1997; Noll et al. 2003). More recent research (Wilson and Widom 2009a) has examined pathways from child abuse and neglect to prostitution, looking at several potential mediators (early sexual initiation, running away, juvenile crime, school problems, and early drug use). Wilson and Widom (2009a) found that early sexual initiation was the strongest mediator in the pathway from child abuse and neglect to prostitution, although these youth problem behaviors cumulatively increased risk for prostitution.

Maltreated children have also been found to be at increased risk for *revictimization*, or the increased risk for subsequent victimization at some point in their lives. Most of this work has focused on victims of sexual abuse (Cloitre et al. 1996; Coid et al. 2001; Maker et al. 2001; Merrill et al. 1999; Messman and Long 1996; Sappington et al. 1997; Schaaf and McCanne 1998). According to Arata (2002), about one-third of child sexual abuse victims reported experiencing repeated victimization and sexual abuse victims had a two to three times greater risk of adult revictimization than women without a history of child sexual abuse. Relatively few studies have examined whether victims of childhood physical abuse are at risk for revictimization (Cloitre et al. 1996; Coid et al. 2001; Desai et al. 2002; Schaaf and McCanne 1998). Even fewer have focused on childhood neglect. However, in one paper describing the results of a prospective follow-up study of individuals with documented cases of childhood physical and sexual abuse and neglect and matched controls (Widom et al. 2008), abused and neglected individuals reported a higher number of traumas and victimization experiences than controls and all types of childhood victimization (physical abuse, sexual abuse, and neglect) were associated with increased risk for lifetime revictimization. Childhood victimization increased risk for physical and sexual assault/abuse, kidnapping/stalking, and having a family friend murdered or commit suicide, but not for general traumas, witnessing trauma, or crime victimization.

Although a large cross-sectional literature reports a relationship between child abuse (primarily sexual abuse) and *teenage pregnancy*, the findings from longitudinal studies are not consistent. One longitudinal study (Herrenkohl et al. 1998) found that preschool and school-aged physical abuse, occurring alone or in combination with neglect, was associated with teenage parenthood. However, two other longitudinal studies did not find an increase in risk for teenage parenthood (Widom and Kuhns 1996) or early pregnancy (Lansford et al. 2002) associated with child abuse.

Much has been written about a possible connection between childhood abuse and adult sexual orientation. Cross-sectional studies comparing self-reports of gay, lesbian, and bisexual individuals with those of heterosexual comparison samples (Balsam et al. 2005; Cameron and Cameron 1995; Corliss et al. 2002; Eskin et al. 2005; Garcia et al. 2002; Hughes et al. 2000, 2001; Saewyc et al. 1999; Tjaden et al. 1999; Tomeo et al. 2001) have generally found that adolescents and adults with same-sex sexual orientations retrospectively report high rates of childhood physical, sexual, and/or emotional abuse in their backgrounds, although not all studies have found this pattern of results (Bell et al. 1981; Meston et al. 1999). In a recent paper, using a prospective cohort design with documented cases of childhood physical and sexual abuse and neglect, Wilson and Widom (2010) found that childhood physical abuse and neglect were *not* associated with increased likelihood of same-sex cohabitation or sexual partners. However, individuals with documented histories of childhood sexual abuse were more likely than controls to report ever having had same-sex sexual partners and this finding was primarily for men in the sample. It should be acknowledged, however, that this outcome remained relatively rare among sexually abused men.

Relatively little is known about the consequences of child abuse and neglect for adult *economic outcomes*. Currie and Widom (2010) studied a sample of court substantiated cases of childhood physical and sexual abuse and neglect during 1967–1971 who were matched with non-abused and non-neglected children and followed into adulthood. Outcome measures of economic status and productivity were assessed when the participants were approximately 41 years old. Currie and Widom (2010) found that adults with documented histories of childhood abuse and/or neglect have lower levels of education, employment, earnings, and fewer assets as adults, compared to matched control children. There is a 14 % gap between individuals with histories of abuse/neglect and controls in the probability of employment in middle age, controlling for background characteristics, demonstrating that abused and neglected children experience large and enduring economic consequences. In addition, these authors concluded that maltreatment appears to affect men and women differently, with larger effects for women than men.

Mental Health Outcomes

Numerous cross-sectional studies have reported associations between child maltreatment and some form of psychiatric disorder or mental health problem, including depression, anxiety, substance abuse, and post-traumatic stress disorder. However, because information about both the independent variable (child maltreatment) and dependent variable (the outcome or particular set of problems) is obtained at the same point in time, determining the temporal ordering of the child maltreatment and outcomes is difficult to reliably establish. For this reason, we focus on the results of longitudinal or cohort studies in evaluating outcomes, although not to the exclusion of cross-sectional studies.

One longitudinal study followed a large sample of children who had documented cases of physical and sexual abuse and neglect and a matched control group into young adulthood and assessed their risk of *posttraumatic stress disorder* (PTSD). Widom (1999) reported that childhood victimization was associated with increased risk for lifetime and current PTSD, present in 38 % of the sexually abused individuals, 33 % of those physically abused, and 31 % of those neglected, compared to 20 % of the controls. Recognizing that other factors need to be taken into account in understanding a child's risk for certain outcomes (earlier Fig. 12.1), Widom (1999) found that the relationship between child-hood abuse and neglect and the number of PTSD symptoms persisted, despite the introduction of covariates associated with risk for both. Thus, she concluded that child abuse and neglect contributed to increased risk for PTSD; however, family, individual and lifestyle variables also place individuals at risk and contributed to symptoms of PTSD.

In another longitudinal study that followed a group of children in Columbia County (New York) from childhood to adulthood, individuals who had experienced childhood abuse or neglect were four times more likely to be diagnosed with *personality disorders* than those without such a history (Johnson et al. 1999). Using the same sample, childhood emotional, physical, and supervision neglect were also associated with increased risk of personality disorders and elevated symptoms of *anxiety and depression*, especially during early adolescence, even after childhood physical or sexual abuse were controlled statistically (Johnson et al. 2000). By adulthood, these problems were in remission among the adults with known neglect backgrounds, whereas those with physical abuse backgrounds showed increasing antisocial and problem behaviors (Cohen et al. 2001).

Maltreatment places children at increased risk for experiencing *depression* in adolescence (Thornberry et al. 2001) and adulthood (Widom et al. 2007a). Brown and colleagues (1999) found that maltreatment was associated with a nearly threefold increase in the rate of depression in adolescence, but this risk was diminished when controlling for other adverse conditions. In contrast, in adulthood the increased risk of depression associated with maltreatment remained when other factors were con-trolled, illustrating the complexity of understanding development and the need to study development over the life course.

Using a prospective cohort design study, Widom and colleagues (2007a) found that individuals with documented cases of childhood physical abuse and those who experienced multiple types of abuse were at increased risk for a lifetime diagnosis of major depressive disorder. Neglected children were at increased risk for depression (approximately one quarter of the neglected children met the criteria for lifetime MDD and 15 % for current MDD). Sexual abuse did not predict a depression diagnosis in adulthood, but rather those adults with a history of childhood sexual abuse reported more depression symptoms than people who did not experience such childhood trauma.

Child abuse has been associated with increased risk of *alcohol problems*. Numerous studies have reported higher rates of physical and sexual abuse among alcohol abusers than in general population samples (e.g. Brems et al. 2004; Clark et al. 1997; Langeland and Hartgers 1998). Individuals who report having been abused as children generally report higher rates of problematic alcohol use (Dube et al. 2002; Fergusson and Lynskey 1997; Galaif et al. 2001; Miller and Downs 1993; Nelson et al. 2002; Wilsnack et al. 1997). However, the most consistent and strongest findings have shown a rela-tionship between child abuse and alcohol problems in women, but not for men (Miller and Mancuso 2004; Miller et al. 1997; Simpson and Miller 2002; Widom and Hiller-Strumhofel 2001). Girls with a history of physical abuse tend to start using substances (including alcohol, marijuana, tobacco, etc.) at younger ages than youth without such histories (Lansford et al. 2010). Girls with documented histories of childhood abuse and neglect were at increased risk for a diagnosis of alcohol abuse and/ or dependence in young adulthood (approximate age 29), compared to matched controls, whereas this increase in risk was not found for maltreated men (Widom et al. 1995). A similar pattern of results emerged in a later follow-up with these participants about 10 years later when they were approximately 40 years old. Women with documented histories of child abuse and/or neglect were more likely to be drinking excessively in middle adulthood than those without documented histories of child maltreatment (Widom et al. 2007b), and again, there was no difference between maltreated men and control men in terms of excessive drinking.

Hundreds of papers have been published describing a relationship between child maltreatment and *substance abuse*, primarily based on cross-sectional designs. Few longitudinal studies have followed abused and/or neglected children into adulthood and, based on these few studies (Gilbert et al. 2009; Widom et al. 1999), the evidence linking child abuse and substance abuse is mixed. Widom and colleagues (1999) studied a large group of abused and neglected children and matched controls and assessed them at approximate age 29. Followed prospectively, these abused and neglected individuals were *not* at increased risk for a DSM-III-R drug abuse diagnosis in young adulthood, despite the fact that both groups had high rates of drug abuse problems. Interestingly, this same sample was followed up again in middle adulthood (approximate age 40) and the results differed. Although a different measure was used to assess drug use, abused and/neglected individuals were at increased risk for current illicit drug use at this later age (Widom et al. 2006), again, illustrating the importance of longitudinal studies that can capture developmental changes over time.

In two different reports (Luntz and Widom 1994; Weiler and Widom 1996) abused and neglected children were followed up into adulthood and assessed in terms of their risk for *antisocial personality disorder* (ASPD) and *psychopathy*. In both cases, based on findings from a prospective design study, childhood victimization was found to increase risk for ASPD and psychopathy. Victims of child abuse and/or neglect had significantly higher scores on the Psychopathy Checklist (PCL-R) than matched controls, despite controls for demographic characteristics and criminal history. It is noteworthy that the Luntz and Widom (1994) paper was based on preliminary findings from a larger study of the consequences of child maltreatment (699 subjects). These early findings showed an increase in risk for antisocial personality disorder for abused and neglected males only, compared to control males, not for females. These preliminary findings were clearly consistent with expectations and gender stereotypes, and particularly supported the assumption that maltreated males externalize their pain and suffering. However, in subsequent analyses based on the complete sample (N= 1,196), the findings showed significant increases in risk for antisocial personality disorder for abused and neglected males *and* females, compared to same sex controls. This second, more complete, set of findings (Widom 1998) is often overlooked, but is important in terms of understanding the consequences of childhood victimization.

Childhood maltreatment also an effect on *suicide attempts* in adolescence and adulthood (Brown et al. 1999; Fergusson et al. 2008; Gilbert et al. 2009; Widom 1998). Among adults in their late 20s, Widom (1998) found that 19 % of those with abuse or neglect histories had made at least one suicide attempt, as compared with 8 % from a matched community sample. Ferguson and colleagues (2008) found high rates among a New Zealand sample as well. These effects are seen for physical and sexual abuse even when accounting for other associated risk factors (Fergusson et al. 2008; Widom 1998). Using a prospective design, Trickett and colleagues (2011) also found that women who had been severely sexually abused had more incidents of self-harm and suicidal behaviors than a control group of women who had not been sexually abused.

Intergenerational Transmission of Abuse and Neglect

Another pervasive assumption in the field of child maltreatment is that there is an "intergenerational transmission of abuse and neglect", or the notion that abused children grow up to become abusive parents (Kempe and Kempe 1978; Steele and Pollock 1968). In an early review of this literature,

Kaufman and Zigler (1987) estimated that about one-third of individuals who were abused or neglected will maltreat their own children, compared to about 5 % of parents without histories of maltreatment, suggesting an increase in risk, but also noting that the majority of parents with histories of maltreatment do not go on to maltreat their own children. Since that time, there have been several reviews of the literature on the intergenerational transmission of abuse and neglect that attempt to evaluate the strength of the growing body research.

Ertem and colleagues (2000) systematically reviewed studies of the intergeneration transmission of child physical abuse and included (1) studies that provided information about physical abuse in two consecutive generations and (2) a comparison group or non-abused group. They developed a scale of eight methodological standards derived from a hypothetical experimental design to examine the validity of the studies they included. Among the ten studies they reviewed, only one study met all eight standards, three met more than four, and two met only one standard.

Stith and colleagues (2009) conducted a meta-analysis of 15 studies published between 1975 and 2000 that examined risk factors for child physical abuse and neglect that included information about parents' history of abuse. Analyzing these studies in the aggregate, these authors found that parents' experience of childhood abuse had a moderate effect in predicting subsequent acts of physical abuse and also reported a small, but significant, effect for predicting subsequent acts of neglect.

A recent paper by Thornberry and colleagues (2012) examined the strength of the evidence base for the intergenerational transmission of child maltreatment as well, but these authors expanded their criterion to include studies of neglect and sexual abuse in addition to physical abuse. They included 47 studies and evaluated them against 11 methodological criteria that they established to indicate the strength of the evidence. Most of the studies they reviewed supported the conclusion that a parental history of child maltreatment is a risk factor for maltreatment perpetration; however, they also expressed concern about the predictive value of many of these studies due to methodological limitations. Most of those studies met less than half of the authors' methodological criteria. Nine studies were identified as the most methodologically sound of the group and results from those studies were mixed in regard to support for the intergenerational transmission hypothesis. Four of those studies generally supported the theory (Dixon et al. 2005; Egeland et al. 1988; Pears and Capaldi 2001; Thompson 2006); three found only limited support for only one type of maltreatment (Berlin et al. 2011; Renner and Slack 2006; Sidebotham et al. 2001), and one found no evidence of transmission of maltreating behavior (Altemeier et al. 1986). Based on their review, Thornberry and his colleagues concluded that the generally broad acceptance of the assumption of an intergenerational transmission of maltreatment is based on results from studies with substantial methodological limitations.

Medical and Physical Health Consequences

Research has been increasingly concerned with the physical and health effects of childhood abuse or neglect. Early studies with physically abused children documented significant neuropsychological handicaps, including growth retardation, central nervous system damage, mental retardation, learning and speech disorders, and poor school performance. Although numerous cross-sectional studies have described relationships between some form of child adversity, including abuse, and some health outcomes (Felitti et al. 1998), few longitudinal studies exist and those which do exist have generally focused on selected outcomes, particularly obesity. Different forms of maltreatment have been linked with increased body mass index and increased rates of obesity in childhood, adolescence, and adulthood. Some studies link neglect but not abuse to obesity (e.g., Johnson et al. 2002; Lissau and Sorensen 1994; Noll et al. 2007), and some link abuse but not neglect to obesity (Bentley and Widom 2009). Knutson and colleagues (2010) found that specific types of neglect (supervisory vs. care) predicted obesity at different ages. Care neglect, defined as inattention to such things as provision of adequate food and clothing, predicted body mass index at younger ages, whereas supervisory neglect, defined as parental lack of availability, predicted body mass index at older ages.

In the first study to directly assess physical health consequences in a large sample of children with documented cases of physical and sexual abuse and neglect and matched controls, Widom and colleagues (2012a) reported on their assessment involving a medical status exam (measured health outcomes and blood tests) and interview when the participants were about 41 years old. After adjusting for age, sex, and race, child maltreatment predicted above normal hemoglobin A1C (HbA1c), lower albumin levels, poor peak air flow, and vision problems in adulthood. These results indicate that maltreated children are at increased risk for poor glycemic control (diabetes), liver and kidney disease, poor lung functioning, and vision problems, respectively. In addition, these authors also found evidence that different types of child abuse and neglect are associated with different physical health outcomes 30 years later. Physical abuse predicted malnutrition, albumin (kidney and liver disease), blood urea nitrogen (kidney disease), and HbA1c (diabetes). Neglect predicted HbA1c, albumin, poor peak air flow, and oral health and vision problems. Sexual abuse predicted Hepatitis C and oral health problems. Recognizing the importance of the social context, these researchers also found that additional controls for childhood socio-economic status (SES), adult SES, unhealthy behaviors, smoking, and mental health problems played varying roles in attenuating or intensifying these relationships. Nonetheless, these findings provide clear evidence that child abuse and neglect affects long-term health status, increasing risk for diabetes, lung disease, malnutrition, and vision problems.

Numerous cross-sectional studies have described associations between self-reports of childhood abuse and a history of sexually transmitted diseases (STDs) among adolescents or adults (Fergusson et al. 1997; Koenig and Clark 2004: Senn et al. 2006). Two additional studies have found that individuals reporting childhood sexual abuse were more likely than those without such histories to have positive results on biological tests for STDs (Bartholow et al. 1994; Ohene et al. 2005). Using data from a prospective cohort design study with documented cases of child physical and sexual abuse and neglect who were followed up into adulthood (approximate age 41), Wilson and Widom (2009b) analyzed data from participants who completed a medical examination and questions about whether they had had STDs in the past. Childhood sexual abuse increased risk of any STD and sexual and physical abuse increased risk for more than one type of STD. These results applied primarily to women and Whites, but for syphilis, sexual abuse increased risk only among women and Blacks.

There has also been work to suggest that the stress associated with child abuse and neglect may give rise to abnormal brain chemistry, which in turn may lead to problem behaviors at later points in life. This research calls attention to the interactions among early experiences, the neurobiology of stress, and brain development. These studies rely largely on animal models (primarily rodents) that allow experimental manipulation of adverse experiences during selected developmental stages, including prenatal and early infancy. These studies have shown that "early parental care profoundly influences brain development, regulates gene expression, and shapes the neural systems that in humans are involved in vulnerability to affective disorders in response to later stressful life events" (Gunnar et al. 2006, p. 653).

An expanding animal and human literature has documented the effects of poor caregiving and early trauma on emotion regulation and related neuroendocrine systems, including the HPA and its central nervous system regulation (DeBellis 2001; Gunnar 2000; Heim et al. 2002; Liu et al. 1997; Meaney et al. 1996). These effects are thought to mediate alterations in social behavior, behavior regulation, and mental and physical health risk (Heim and Nemeroff 2001; Perry and Pollard 1998; Vythilingam et al. 2002). Research with adults who report being victims of maltreatment or chronic stress show increased vigilance and novelty aversion (Boyce et al. 2001; Lupien and McEwen 1997; Lupien et al. 2002) and impaired resilience and reduced social competence (Kiecolt-Glaser et al. 2003), along with altered HPA activity (Lupien et al. 2001; Tout et al. 1998). In animal models, such effects appear to be organizational, enduring and linked to subsequent parenting behavior (Champagne and Meaney 2001; Suomi 1991, 1999).

Other recent developments in animal research have been made in studying the neurodevelopmental impact of maternal abuse, separation, and neglect on long-term biobehavioral outcomes, primarily with animal models. For example, because of their ability to manipulate, randomly assign, and conduct cross-fostering analyses, these animal studies have begun to provide important tools for studying epigenetic mechanisms. This body of new work suggests that changes in the activity of genes, established through epigenetic mechanisms such as DNA methylation and histone modifications, may be observed as a consequence of early- and later-life adversity (Roth and Champagne 2012). Though this new research is based primarily on animal models to simulate neglect, abuse, chronic stress, and trauma, Roth and Champagne suggest that these epigenetic effects may serve as an important biological mechanism linking these experiences of the organism to long-term changes in physiology, neurobiology, and behavior there may be lasting epigenetic impact that may be manifest not only in individuals with direct exposure but also may be passed on to the next generation.

Resilience and Protective Factors

Not all maltreated children succumb to their early adverse childhood experiences or develop problem behaviors. Researchers have speculated on potential factors that might buffer or protect maltreated children from developing negative consequences, focusing primarily on characteristic of the child or the environment. Garmezy (1981) has called these *protective factors* – those dispositional attributes, environmental conditions, biological predispositions and positive events that can act to mitigate against early negative experiences. For example, in one early study, Frodi and Smetana (1984) found that, if one controls for IQ, differences between maltreated and non-maltreated children in their ability to discriminate emotions disappeared. Farber and Egeland (1987) found few competent "survivors" among physically or emotionally neglected children. Children who were more likely to be competent were those children whose mothers showed some interest in them and were able to respond to them emotionally. For sexually abused children, one positive mediating variable appears to be the presence of a supportive, positive relationship with a non-abusive parent or sibling (Conte and Schuerman 1988). Herrenkohl and colleagues (1994) found that having a stable caretaker and a high intellectual capacity were associated with resilience in the adolescents in their sample.

McGloin and Widom (2001) examined resilience in children with documented histories of physical, sexual abuse or neglect and a matched control group who were followed up into adulthood. Criteria for resilience involved meeting thresholds for success within at least six of the eight domains of employment, education, homelessness, social activity, psychiatric disorders, substance abuse, self-reported violence and official arrest records. At approximate age 29, less than a quarter of the abused or neglected group met the criteria for overall resilience (that is, resilient in at least six domains) compared to 41 % of the controls. Interestingly, females were more likely to be resilient in general. In further work with this sample, DuMont and colleagues (2007) examined whether individual, family, and neighborhood level characteristics would predict resilience in maltreated children in adolescence and young adulthood. DuMont and colleagues found that almost half (48 %) of the abused and neglected children in adolescence and nearly one-third in young adulthood were resilient. Over half of those who were resilient in adolescence remained resilient in young adulthood, whereas 11 % of the non-resilient adolescents were resilient in young adulthood. Females were more likely to be resilient during both time periods. Being white, non-Hispanic decreased and growing up in a stable living situation increased the likelihood of resilience in adolescence, but not in young adulthood. Stressful life events and a supportive partner promoted resilience in young adulthood. Neighborhood advantage did not exert a direct effect on resilience, but moderated the relationship between household stability and resilience in adolescence and between cognitive ability and resilience in young adulthood.

Using data from the Environmental Risk Longitudinal Study, a nationally representative sample of 1,116 twin pairs and their families in England, Jaffee and colleagues (2007) found that maltreated boys who had above-average intelligence and were temperamentally well adjusted were more likely to be resilient; however, these characteristics did not predict resilience in maltreated girls. Maltreated children who were exposed to domestic violence and whose parents had substantial depression or substance use problems were less likely to be resilient. In contrast, maltreated children who lived in low-crime, cohesive, proactive neighborhoods were more likely to be resilient. A maltreated child's individual strengths predicted resilience in the context of a family or neighbourhood characterized by low levels of stressors, but not in the context of high levels of stressors. Again, this longitudinal analysis showed the importance of contextual factors that appeared to promote or interfere with the emergence and stability of resilience following childhood maltreatment.

Mersky and Topitzes (2010) used prospective data from the Chicago Longitudinal Study to explore the relationship between childhood maltreatment and outcomes in early adulthood (ages 18–24). Resilience was defined as meeting criteria across several domains, including high school completion, college attendance, income level, incarceration, substance abuse, depressive symptomatology and life satisfaction. Participants were considered resilient overall if they met the criteria for resilience in at least five of the seven domains. Only 15.7 % of the maltreated participants were resilience overall, compared to nearly 40 % of the non-maltreated sample and females were more likely to be resilient than males.

Taking a different approach to understanding how maltreated children develop and either succumb or survive and assuming that the achievement of important developmental roles may represent "turning points" for at risk children, Allwood and Widom (2013) examined whether attainment of three developmental roles (high school graduation, employment, and marriage) mediate the relationship between childhood abuse and neglect and adult arrest. Although childhood abuse and neglect predicted decreased likelihood of graduating from high school, current employment, and current marriage, successful achievement of these developmental roles was associated with a significant *decrease* in risk for adult arrest, controlling for age, sex, and race. The introduction of each developmental role reduced the magnitude of the association between child maltreatment and adult arrest, even though child abuse and neglect remained significant.

Researchers have also been studying the ways in which *genetic factors* may buffer children who experience such adverse and stressful environments so as to minimize negative consequences. Some of recent research has moved away from searching for simple main effects of maltreatment on outcomes and instead has focused on the interactions between childhood maltreatment and certain genotypes relating to psychological and behavioral outcomes, including antisocial behavior, alcoholism, anxiety disorders, posttraumatic stress disorder (PTSD), depression, and suicidality. Caspi and colleagues (2002) were the first to hypothesize that behavioral heterogeneity in outcomes associated with childhood maltreatment may be a consequence of behaviorally relevant functional differences in underlying genetic risk factors. Since then, other studies and a meta-analysis (Taylor and Kim-Cohen 2007) have found that a genetic variation associated with high transcription of MAOA, an enzyme that regulates neurotransmitter systems that are related to emotion regulation and stress response, acts as a protective factor and appears to weaken the relationship between childhood maltreatment and antisocial behavior (Aslund et al. 2011; Caspi et al. 2002; Foley et al. 2004). However, other researchers have failed to replicate this pattern (Huizinga et al. 2006) or have only partially replicated these results (Widom and Brzustowicz 2006). The MAOA genotype also appears to influence risk for depression among victims of childhood maltreatment (Cicchetti et al. 2007). In a review of the literature, Jaffee (2012) concluded that there is "substantial evidence that maltreatment has environmentally mediated effects on psychopathology. Notably, the results of quantitative genetic studies confirm findings from prospective, epidemiological studies in showing that (a) characteristics of parents and families rather than characteristics of children better explain why some children are more likely to be maltreated than others and (b) maltreatment has direct effects on youth psychopathology, even controlling for genes common to parents and children." Although she also noted that the results from these types of gene by environment studies must be considered with caution, in part because of the lack of comparable measures of the independent variable (maltreatment) and the dependent or outcome variable across studies.

Importance of Contextual Factors

There is increasing recognition that it is necessary to consider how contextual factors influence the consequences of child maltreatment, as suggested in Fig. 12.1. Schuck and Widom (2005) directly examined the importance of contextual factors in their study of the impact of neighborhood conditions on the relationship between child maltreatment and criminal behavior. Using multilevel data that incorporated information about the person (the child), families, and neighborhoods and hierarchical generalized linear modeling, these authors found that neighborhood disadvantage and stability moderated the relationship between early child maltreatment and offending. Specifically, the effect of early child maltreatment on later juvenile and adult criminal behavior was strongest for those individuals from the most disadvantaged and most stable neighborhoods. As described earlier in this chapter, Jaffee and colleagues (2007) and Dumont and colleagues (2007) also found that ecological factors (characteristics of neighborhoods or families) moderated the impact of childhood maltreatment and, in particular, influencing the likelihood of resilience for maltreated children. In the Lansford and colleagues (2002) study, the results showed that maltreated adolescents performed significantly worse than others on a variety of indicators when analyses were not adjusted (controls for appropriate confounding factors); however, the results of adjusted analyses revealed that, with the exception of school absences, all effects were accounted for by risk factors associated with maltreatment rather than maltreatment per se. In a recent paper using multi-level modeling to examine the roles of neighborhood, family and individual factors in predicting a person's risk for mental health and psychosocial outcomes, Nikulina and colleagues (2011) found that childhood family poverty played an important role in predicting subsequent risk for PTSD, crime, and academic achievement. Finally, there is also recent evidence of the importance of contextual factors on physical health outcomes. Widom and colleagues (2012a) found that controlling for childhood socio-economic status (SES), adult SES, unhealthy behaviors, smoking, and mental health problems played varying roles in attenuating or intensifying relationships between child abuse and neglect and subsequent physical health outcomes.

Another developing area of research focuses on the extent to which cultural factors, race, and ethnic background may have an impact on the development of maltreated children. For example, a few studies have reported a race differential in the extent to which maltreated children are at increased risk for being arrested for a violent crime compared to non-maltreated children (Maxfield and Widom 1996; Zingraff et al. 1993), although others did not find such differences (Grogan-Kaylor 2005). One study found that sexually abused non-Hispanic girls reported greater posttraumatic stress symptoms than both sexually abused Hispanic girls and non-sexually abused non-Hispanic girls (Canez 2000). In contrast, Lau and colleagues (2006) did not find race or ethnic differences in emotional correlates of punitive parenting and, in another study, race/ethnicity did not moderate the relationship between documented cases of maltreatment and internalizing and externalizing symptoms in youths (Hatcher et al. 2009). In married cohabiting couples who reported abuse as a child, Caetano and colleagues (2003) found that for White males and females, childhood physical abuse was associated with alcohol problems in adulthood. In contrast, among Black males, observing parental violence was associated with alcohol problems in adulthood, but physical abuse was not. Roberts and colleagues (2011) reported that among those exposed to trauma, PTSD risk was slightly higher among Blacks and lower among Asians compared with Whites, after adjustment for characteristics of the trauma exposure (including child maltreatment).

Widom and colleagues (2012b) examined the extent to which children of different races and ethnic backgrounds manifest the consequences of childhood neglect in similar or different ways, focusing on multiple domains of functioning (academic/intellectual, social/behavioral, and psychiatric). They found that Black and White neglected children showed negative consequences for IQ, reading ability and occupational status compared to controls. Compared to same race/ethnic group controls, neglected White children showed extensive mental health consequences, Black children showed more anxiety and dysthymia, and Hispanic children showed increased risk for alcohol problems (although their sample of Hispanic children was quite small and they urged caution in interpreting these findings). Black and White neglected children differed in risk for violence compared to same race controls: neglected Black children were arrested for violence two times more often than Black controls, whereas neglected White children were more likely than White controls to report engaging in violence. Widom and her colleagues interpreted these findings as providing some support for theories hypothesizing no differences in the impact of child neglect based on race or ethnicity (racial invariance), differences in outcomes with neglected minority children being twice stigmatized (double jeopardy), and neglected minority children showing fewer consequences (resilience) than White neglected children. However, these authors noted that there is sparse research examining these issues and that their findings represent only a first step in examining whether there are race and ethnicity similarities and differences in consequences of childhood maltreatment, particularly since this analysis was confined to neglect children only.

Challenges and Controversies

The validity of various methods of assessing and studying maltreatment remain a source of ongoing debate. Research on the reliability and validity of retrospective reports of childhood victimization experiences is fairly rare. Empirical evidence of the validity of reports of earlier childhood experiences indicates only weak relationships with documented childhood events. Henry and colleagues (1994) compared the extent of agreement between prospective and retrospective measures across multiple content domains in a large sample of 18-year old youth who had been studied prospectively from birth. These authors found no evidence to support the validity of retrospective measures of subjective psychological states and processes (such as recollections of childhood experiences. Using a very different design, Offer and colleagues (2000) examined autobiographical memory in a longitudinal study of a group of 73 mentally healthy 14-year old males (studied initially in 1962) and re-interviewed at approximately age 48. Offer and his colleagues found significant differences between adult memories of adolescence and what was actually reported during adolescence, including questions about parental discipline. "If the accurate memory of one's past is not better than chance in the mentally healthy individual, even more care should probably be taken in obtaining accurate historical information in the medical, psychological, or otherwise health-compromised individual" (Offer et al. 2000, p. 735).

There continues to be a heavy reliance on cross-sectional designs, where participants are asked simultaneously about whether they have experienced abuse in their lifetimes, often many years in the past, and about their current psychological problems or functioning. With this design, there is little possibility of examining causal relationships and there remains considerable ambiguity in the meaning of the relationships or associations described in the literature. For example, depression may be a direct or indirect consequence of child maltreatment. Depressed children may be more likely to be targeted for maltreatment or depression may be a function of other characteristics of the environment in which the maltreated child lives (e.g., having a depressed mother). Understanding whether associations are a direct or indirect function of child maltreatment has implications for whether and how secondary prevention interventions are designed and implemented.

There is a related problem with recall bias that affects our ability to make inferences about the association between retrospectively assessed childhood maltreatment and later outcomes (Raphael 1987). For example, White and colleagues (2007) found that current life status, including depression, drug problems, and life dissatisfaction, were related to adult retrospective reports of physical abuse for both men and women. There are also studies that have directly compared findings based on retrospective reports with a particular sample and findings from the same sample using prospective longitudinal data. In research on the consequences of child abuse for pain (McBeth et al. 2001) and drug abuse (Widom et al. 1999), retrospective self-reports of child abuse showed strong relationships to these outcomes (pain, drug abuse). In contrast, when abused and neglected children were followed up into adulthood (prospectively), they did not differ from control children on these outcomes. Together, these findings suggest that recall bias in the report of childhood abuse can artifactually cause an association between self-reported child abuse and neglect and later outcomes.

In one longitudinal birth cohort study of youth who were part of the Christchurch (New Zealand) Health and Development Study, young people at ages 18 and 21 years were questioned about their childhood exposure to physical punishment and sexual abuse. Fergusson and colleagues (2000) found that reports of childhood sexual abuse and physical punishment were relatively unstable and that the values of kappa for test-retests of abuse reporting were in the region of 0.45. In another longitudinal study of the congruence between adolescent's self-reports and their adult retrospective reports of parental discipline practices and physical abuse in adolescence, using a representative sample of adolescent in New Jersey who were followed up into young adulthood, men and women who were interviewed five times between the ages of about 12 and 30 years were asked to recall parenting behaviors and these reports were compared against what these individuals reported at the time. In the study mentioned earlier, White and colleagues (2007) found only fair agreement on reports of discipline practices and physical abuse (most kappas between 0.20 and 0.40).

Also, frequently forgotten in the debate about the accuracy of reporting is that it is virtually impossible to determine the extent of false positives, that is, whether there is "over-reporting". For example, some individuals who report a given form of abuse in childhood misrepresent some or all of their childhood experiences (Rich 1990). Short of following an individual child throughout the course of every day of his or her entire life, no one has yet been able to determine a way to make this assessment accurately. Though the presumption is that retrospective self-reports are accurate, from a scientific perspective, attempts to systematically assess the possible existence and extent of over-reporting would be worthwhile.

Studies of child abuse often utilize convenience samples, specialized samples (inpatients, clients in therapy groups, incarcerated individuals), college students, or members of HMOs that may limit the generalizability of the findings. Although statistical controls for appropriate variables are important, cross-sectional snapshots of these samples may not represent the larger victimized population. This is one of the advantages of prospective longitudinal studies, since they permit the researcher to follow large groups of children into the future, regardless of their successes, failures, or deaths along the way and provide an opportunity to determine whether there is a downward social drift that occurs to some individuals as a result of their childhood victimization experiences.

Another controversy in the field is reflected in the position that some researchers have taken with regard to whether child maltreatment per se causes subsequent problems or whether adverse environments in which maltreated children typically exist influence negative adult outcomes. For example, researchers have argued that the associations between child maltreatment and later adjustment problems can be accounted for by confounding factors, such as poverty and family stress (Fergusson et al. 2000; Smith and Thornberry 1995). In the Lansford and colleagues (2002) study described earlier, the results showed that most of the effects were accounted for by other risk factors associated with maltreatment rather than maltreatment per se. On the other hand, in a recent paper using multi-level modeling to examine the roles of neighborhood, family and individual factors in predicting a person's risk for mental health and psychosocial outcomes, Nikulina and colleagues (2011) directly tested the predictive power of childhood poverty compare to childhood neglect. These researchers found that the three childhood characteristics they examined – neglect, family poverty, and neighborhood poverty – each had different effects on long-term development. Childhood neglect and childhood family poverty were important independent contributors to risk for PTSD, crime, and academic achievement, whereas childhood neighborhood poverty was not. However, these findings clearly showed that childhood neglect has consequences of its own, distinct from poverty.

What Are the Gaps?

There continues to be a critical need to improve the construct validity of measures to assess child maltreatment and to assess elements of the maltreatment experience, including type, chronicity frequency, and perpetrator identity (McCrory et al. 2010). There is also a tendency to assume that the effects of sexual or physical abuse or neglect are similar and that we can treat maltreatment as a "bundle" (Damashek and Chaffin 2012). However, some of the newer research reviewed here demonstrates that there are differences in psychological, behavioral, and physical health consequences of physical and sexual abuse and neglect. These findings lead to the recommendation for more future research with sensitive designs with adequate power to detect differences in consequences of child maltreatment. Relatedly, there is evidence that some maltreated children go on to experience other forms of maltreatment (revictimization) over the life span (Jonson-Reid et al. 2012; Widom et al. 2008). Does it make a difference in outcomes for the child which form of abuse/neglect occurred first and the age at which the abuse/neglect first occurred? Recent research on the age of onset of abuse/neglect suggests that there are different consequences depending on age of onset (Kaplow and Widom 2007). However, few longitudinal studies have addressed these questions.

Prospective longitudinal designs are needed, ideally beginning before the birth of the child, to assess the consequences of child maltreatment, while providing an opportunity to adjust for social and individual confounding factors as they occur, and to minimize the reliance on recall and the selection of participants on the basis of the outcome (Gilbert et al. 2009). Animal analogue studies are also needed, because they provide an opportunity to systematically examine these relationships and to exert tight control over relevant variables. Questions will always remain about the extent to which findings can be generalized and the extent to which the animal analogue "maltreatment" studies are representative of maltreatment in humans.

Important questions remain that challenge investigators and clinicians in the field. What are the mechanisms whereby childhood abuse and neglect leads to short and long-term consequences? What other factors account for the fact that not all abused and neglected children manifest negative consequences and, according to some studies, appear rather resilient? To what extent does child maltreatment represent the extreme end of a continuum of parenting or is it a totally separate phenomenon with different etiology and consequences? How do sub-cultural differences in normative standards of child abuse and neglect affect consequences for children? Are there gender and race/ethnicity differences in the consequences of childhood maltreatment and what might explain these differences? Given that much research and clinical practice is based on a person's (client's) report of his or her childhood experiences, to what extent does the person's cognitive appraisal of the child's experience or experience with the events influence outcomes? To what extent does the long-term impact of childhood abuse and neglect depend on characteristics of the community or practices of the community and justice and social service systems in which the child lived at the time of the abuse? What is the role of these "extra-individual" factors in understanding the developmental trajectories of maltreated children? How do changes in family poverty or neighborhood poverty over the life course alter trajectories for maltreated children? Although maltreating families are thought to be socially isolated, does the social isolation occur prior to the maltreatment (and perhaps be a cause of the maltreatment) or is it a consequence of the maltreatment and withdrawal from the community?

Conclusions

This chapter has demonstrated that child maltreatment has consequences that have the potential to cascade across multiple domains of functioning across the life span and affect the child's ability to become a productive member of society. It is hoped that the findings presented here reinforce recommendations for the importance of early health care prevention for abused and neglected children. At the same time, it is critical to remember that not all children succumb to the negative effects of child maltreatment and that these outcomes are not inevitable. It is also important to recognize that the long-term consequences of childhood neglect are at least as damaging as physical or sexual abuse, despite the fact that neglect has received the least scientific and public attention. There are numerous myths about the consequences of child maltreatment that continue to be passed on, but it is hoped that the findings presented here will encourage scholars and practitioners to recognize that some of these beliefs have not been empirically supported (e.g., that only abused boys go on to perpetrate violence, where the empirical evidence shows that maltreated boys and girls are at increased risk to engage in violence) or have not been adequately tested. Finally, using complex multi-level modeling, research is beginning to examine in differences in consequences based on characteristics of the abuse or neglect experience, the child, the family, and the community in recognition that these are complex social issues that need more complex models to progress in understanding.

References

Allwood, M., & Widom, C. S. (2013) Child abuse and neglect, developmental role attainment, and adult arrests. *Journal of Research in Crime and Delinquency*. First published January 21, 2013. doi: 10.1177/0022427812471177.

Altemeier, W. A., O'Connor, S., Sherrod, K. B., Tucker, D., & Vietz, P. (1986). Outcome of abuse during childhood among pregnant low income women. *Child Abuse & Neglect, 10*, 319–330.

Arata, C. M. (2002). Child sexual abuse and sexual revictimization. *Clinical Psychology: Science and Practice, 9*(2), 135–164.

Aslund, C., Nordquist, N., Comasco, E., Leppert, J., Oreland, L., & Nilsson, K.W. (2011). Maltreatment, MAOA, and delinquency: Sex differences in gene-environment interaction in a large population-based cohort of adolescents. *Behavioral Genetics, 41*, 262–272.

Balsam, K. F., Rothblum, E. D., & Beauchaine, T. P. (2005). Victimization over the life span: A comparison of lesbian, gay, bisexual, and heterosexual siblings. *Journal of Consulting and Clinical Psychology, 73*, 477–487.

Bartholow, B. N., Doll, L. S., Joy, D., Bolan, G., Harrison, J. S., Moss, P. M., & McKiman, D. (1994). Emotional, behavioral, and HIV risks associated with sexual abuse among homosexual and bisexual men. *Child Abuse and Neglect, 18*(9), 745–761.

Bell, A. P., Weinberg, M. S., & Hammersmith, S. K. (1981). *Sexual preference: Its development in men and women*. Bloomington: Indiana University Press.

Belsky, J. (1980). Child maltreatment: An ecological integration. *The American Psychologist, 35*, 320–335.

Bentley, T., & Widom, C. S. (2009). A 30-year follow-up of the effects of child abuse and neglect on obesity in adulthood. *Obesity, 17*(10), 1900–1905.

Berlin, L. J., Appleyard, K., & Dodge, K. A. (2011). Intergenerational continuity in child maltreatment: Mediating mechanisms and implications for prevention. *Child Development, 82*(1), 162–176.

Boyce, W. T., Quas, J., Alkon, A., Smider, N. A., Essex, M. J., & Kupfer, D. J. (2001). Autonomic reactivity and risk for psychopathology in middle childhood. *The British Journal of Psychiatry, 179*, 144–150.

Brems, C., Johnson, M. E., Neal, D., & Freemon, M. (2004). Childhood abuse history and substance use among men and women receiving detoxification services. *The American Journal of Drug and Alcohol Abuse, 30*(4), 799–821.

Bronfenbrenner, U. (1979). *The ecology of human development: Experiments by nature and design*. Cambridge, MA: Harvard University Press.

Brown, J., Cohen, P., Johnson, J., & Smailes, E. (1999). Childhood abuse and neglect: Specificity of effects on adolescent and young adult depression and suicidality. *Journal of the American Academy of Child and Adolescent Psychiatry, 38*(12), 1490–1496.

Caetano, R., Field, C. A., & Scott, N. (2003). Association between childhood physical abuse, exposure to parental violence, and alcohol problems in adulthood. *Journal of Interpersonal Violence, 18*(3), 240–257.

Cameron, P., & Cameron, K. (1995). Does incest cause homosexuality? *Family Research Institute, 76*, 611–621.

Canez, I. E. (2000). *Predictions of posttraumatic stress symptomatology in Hispanic versus non-Hispanic maltreated children.* Doctoral dissertation, University of California, San Diego.

Caspi, A., McClay, J., Moffit, T. E., Mill, J., Martin, J., & Craig, I. A. (2002). Role of genotype in cycle of violence in maltreated children. *Science, 297*, 851–854.

Champagne, F., & Meaney, M. J. (2001). Like mother, like daughter: Evidence for non-genomic transmission of parental behavior and stress responsivity. *Progress in Brain Research, 133*, 287–302.

Cicchetti, D., & Carlson, V. (1989). *Child maltreatment: Theory and research on the causes and consequences of child abuse and neglect.* New York: Cambridge University Press.

Cicchetti, D., Toth, S. L., & Lynch, M. (1993). The developmental sequelae of child maltreatment: Implications for war-related trauma. In L. A. Leavitt & N. A. Fox (Eds.), *The psychological effects of war and violence on children* (pp. 41–71). Hillsdale: Lawrence Erlbaum Associates.

Cicchetti, D., Rogosch, F. A., & Sturge-Apple, M. L. (2007). Interactions of child maltreatment and serotonin transporter and monoamine oxidase A polymorphisms: Depressive symptomatology among adolescents from low socio-economic status backgrounds. *Development and Psychopathology, 19*, 1161–1180.

Clark, D. B., Lesnick, L., & Hegedus, A. M. (1997). Traumas with other adverse life events in adolescents with alcohol abuse and dependence. *Journal of the American Academy of Child and Adolescent Psychiatry, 36*(12), 1744–1751.

Cloitre, M., Tardiff, K., Marzuk, P. M., & Leon, A. C. (1996). Childhood abuse and subsequent sexual assault among female inpatients. *Journal of Traumatic Stress, 9*, 473–482.

Cohen, P., Brown, J., & Smailes, E. (2001). Child abuse and neglect and the development of mental disorders in the general population. *Development and Psychopathology, 13*, 981–999.

Coid, J., Petruckevitch, A., Feder, G., Chung, W., Richardson, J., & Moorey, S. (2001). Relation between childhood sexual and physical abuse and risk of revictimisation in women: A cross-sectional survey. *Lancet, 358*, 450–454.

Conte, J. R., & Schuerman, J. R. (1988). The effects of sexual abuse on children: A multidimensional view. *Journal of Interpersonal Violence, 2*, 380–390.

Corliss, H. L., Cochran, S. D., & Mays, V. M. (2002). Reports of parental maltreatment during childhood in the United States population-based survey of homosexual, bisexual, and heterosexual adults. *Child Abuse & Neglect, 26*, 165–1178.

Crittendon, P. M., & Ainsworth, M. D. S. (1989). Child maltreatment and attachment theory. In D. Cicchetti & V. Carlson (Eds.), *Child maltreatment* (pp. 432–463). New York: Cambridge University Press.

Currie, J., & Widom, C. S. (2010). Long-term consequences of child abuse and neglect on adult economic well-being. *Child Maltreatment, 15*(2), 111–120.

Damashek, A. L., & Chaffin, M. J. (2012). Child abuse and neglect. In P. Sturmey & M. Hersen (Eds.), *Handbook of evidence-based practice in clinical psychology* (pp. 647–678). New York: Wiley.

De Bellis, M. D. (2001). Developmental traumatology: The psychobiological development of maltreated children and its implications for research, treatment, and policy. *Development and Psychopathology, 13*(3), 539–564.

Desai, S., Arias, I., Thompson, M. P., & Basile, K. C. (2002). Childhood victimization and subsequent adult revictimization assessed in a nationally representative sample of women and men. *Violence and Victims, 17*(6), 639–653.

Dixon, L., Browne, K., & Hamilton-Giachritsis, C. (2005). Risk factors of parents abused as children: A mediational analysis of the intergenerational continuity of child maltreatment (part 1). *Journal of Child Psychology and Psychiatry, and Allied Disciplines, 46*(1), 47–57.

Dodge, K. A., Pettit, G. S., Bates, J. E., & Valente, E. (1995). Social information-processing patterns partially mediate the effect of early physical abuse on later conduct problems. *Journal of Abnormal Psychology, 104*(4), 632–643.

Dube, S. R., Anda, R. F., Felitti, V. J., Edwards, V. J., & Croft, J. B. (2002). Adverse childhood experiences and personal alcohol abuse as an adult. *Addictive Behaviors, 27*, 713–725.

DuMont, K. A., Widom, C. S., & Czaja, S. J. (2007). Predictors of resilience in abused and neglected children grown-up: The role of individual and neighborhood characteristics. *Child Abuse & Neglect, 31*(3), 255–274.

Eckenrode, J., Laird, M., & John, D. (1993). School performance and disciplinary problems among abused and neglected children. *Developmental Psychology, 29*, 53–62.

Eckenrode, J., Zielinski, D., Smith, E., Marcynyszyn, L. A., Henderson, C. R., Kitzman, H., … Olds, D. L. (2001). Child maltreatment and the early onset of problem behaviors: Can a program of nurse home visitation break the link? *Development and Psychopathology, 13*, 873–890.

Egeland, B. (1997). Mediators of the effects of child maltreatment on developmental adaptation in adolescence. In D. Cicchetti & S. L. Toth (Eds.), *Rochester symposium on developmental psychology: Developmental perspectives on trauma: Theory, research, and intervention* (Vol. 8, pp. 403–434). Rochester: University of Rochester Press.

Egeland, B., Jacobvitz, D., & Sroufe, L. A. (1988). Breaking the cycle of abuse. *Child Development, 59*, 1080–1088.

English, D. J., Widom, C. S., & Brandford, C. (2001). *Childhood victimization and delinquency, adult criminality, and violent criminal behavior: A replication and extension, final report (NCJ192291).* Rockville: National Institute of Justice.

Erickson, M. F., Egeland, B., & Pianta, R. (1989). The effects of maltreatment on the development of young children. In D. Cicchetti & V. Carlson (Eds.), *Child maltreatment: Theory and research on the causes and consequences of child abuse and neglect* (pp. 647–684). New York: Cambridge University Press.

Ertem, I. O., Leventhal, J. M., & Dobbs, S. (2000). Intergenerational continuity of childhood physical abuse: How good is the evidence? *Lancet, 356*(9232), 814–819.

Eskin, M., Kaynak-Demir, H., & Demir, S. (2005). Same-sex sexual orientation, childhood sexual abuse, and suicidal behavior in university students in Turkey. *Archives of Sexual Behavior, 31,* 185–195.

Farber, E. A., & Egeland, B. E. (1987). Invulnerability among abused and neglected children. In E. J. Anthony & B. Cohler (Eds.), *The invulnerable child* (pp. 253–288). New York: Guilford Press.

Felitti, V. J., Anda, R. F., Nordenberg, D., Williamson, D. F., Spitz, A. M., Edwards, V., … Marks, J. S. (1998). Relationship of childhood abuse and household dysfunction to many of the leading causes of death in adults: The Adverse Childhood Experiences (ACE) study. *American Journal of Preventive Medicine, 14*(4), 245–258.

Fergusson, D. M., & Lynskey, M. T. (1997). Physical punishment/maltreatment during childhood and adjustment in young adulthood. *Child Abuse & Neglect, 21*(7), 617–630.

Fergusson, D. M., Horwood, L. J., & Lynskey, M. T. (1997). Childhood sexual abuse, adolescent sexual behaviors and sexual revictimization. *Child Abuse & Neglect, 21*(8), 789–803.

Fergusson, D. M., Horwood, J. L., & Woodward, L. J. (2000). The stability of child abuse reports: A longitudinal study of the reporting behaviour of young adults. *Psychological Medicine, 30,* 529–544.

Fergusson, D. M., Boden, J. M., & Horwood, L. J. (2008). Exposure to childhood sexual and physical abuse and adjustment in early adulthood. *Child Abuse & Neglect, 32,* 607–619.

Foley, D. L., Eaves, L. J., Wormley, B., et al. (2004). Childhood adversity, monoamine oxidase A genotype, and risk for conduct disorder. *Archives of General Psychiatry, 61,* 738–744.

Frodi, A., & Smetana, J. (1984). Abused, neglected, and nonmaltreated preschoolers' ability to discriminate emotions in others: The effects of IQ. *Child Abuse & Neglect, 8,* 459–465.

Galaif, E. R., Stein, J. A., Newcomb, M. D., & Bernstein, D. P. (2001). Gender differences in the prediction of problem alcohol use in adulthood: Exploring the influence of family factors and childhood maltreatment. *Journal of Studies on Alcohol, 62*(4), 486–493.

Garbarino, J. (1977). The human ecology of child maltreatment: A conceptual model for research. *Journal of Marriage and the Family, 39*(4), 721–735.

Garcia, J., Adams, J., Friedman, L., & East, P. (2002). Links between past abuse, suicide ideation, and sexual orientation among San Diego college students. *Journal of American College Health, 51,* 9–14.

Garmezy, N. (1981). Children under stress: Perspectives on antecedents and correlates of vulnerability and resistance to psychopathology. In A. I. Rabin, J. Arnoff, A. M. Barclay, & R. A. Zucker (Eds.), *Further explorations in personality* (pp. 196–269). New York: Wiley.

Gilbert, R., Widom, C. S., Browne, K., Fergusson, D. M., Elspeth, W., & Janson, S. (2009). Child Maltreatment 1 Burden and consequences of child maltreatment in high-income countries. *Lancet, 373*(9657), 68–81.

Grogan-Kaylor, A. (2005). Corporal punishment and the growth trajectory of children's antisocial behavior. *Child Maltreatment, 10*(3), 283–292.

Gunnar, M. R. (2000). Early adversity and the development of stress regulation. In C. E. Nelson (Ed.), *The Minnesota symposia on child psychology, Vol 31: The effects of early adversity on neurobehavioral development. Minnesota symposia on child psychology* (pp. 163–200). Mahwah: Lawrence Erlbaum Associates.

Gunnar, M. R., Fisher, P. A., & The Early Experience, Stress, and Prevention Network. (2006). Bringing basic research on early experience and stress neurobiology to bear on preventive interventions for neglected and maltreated children. *Development and Psychopathology, 18,* 651–677.

Hatcher, S. S., Maschi, T., Morgen, K., & Toldson, I. A. (2009). Exploring the impact of racial and ethnic differences in the emotional and behavioral responses of maltreated youth: Implications for culturally competent services. *Children and Youth Services Review, 31*(9), 1042–1048.

Heim, C., & Nemeroff, C. B. (2001). The role of childhood trauma in the neurobiology of mood and anxiety disorders: Preclinical and clinical studies. *Biological Psychiatry, 49,* 1023–1039.

Heim, C., Newport, D. J., Wagner, D., Wilcox, M. M., Miller, A. H., & Nemeroff, C. B. (2002). The role of early adverse experience and adulthood stress in the prediction of neuroendocrine stress reactivity in women: A multiple regression analysis. *Depression and Anxiety, 15,* 117–125.

Henry, B., Moffitt, T. E., Caspi, A., Langley, J., & Silva, P. A. (1994). On the "remembrance of things past": A longitudinal evaluation of the retrospective method. *Psychological Assessment, 6*(2), 92–101.

Herrenkohl, T. I., & Herrenkohl, R. C. (2007). Examining the overlap and prediction of muliple forms of child maltreatment, stressors, and socioeconomic status: A longitudinal analysis of youth outcomes. *Journal of Family Violence, 22,* 553–562.

Herrenkohl, E. C., Herronkohl, R. C., & Egolf, B. (1994). Resilient early school-age children from maltreating homes: Outcomes in late adolescence. *The American Journal of Orthopsychiatry, 64*(2), 301–309.

Herrenkohl, E. C., Herrenkohl, R. C., Egolf, B. P., & Russo, M. J. (1998). The relationship between early maltreatment and teenage parenthood. *Journal of Adolescence, 21*(3), 291–303.

Hildyard, K. L., & Wolfe, D. A. (2002). Child neglect: Developmental issues and outcomes. *Child Abuse & Neglect, 26*(6–7), 679–695.

Hubbard, D. J., & Pratt, T. C. (2002). A meta-analysis of the predictors of delinquency among girls. *Journal of Offender Rehabilitation, 34*, 1–13.

Hughes, T. L., Haas, A. P., Razzando, L., Cassidy, R., & Matthews, A. (2000). Comparing lesbians' and heterosexual women's mental health: A multi-site survey. *Journal of Gay & Lesbian Social Services, 11*, 57–76.

Hughes, T. L., Johnson, T., & Wilsnack, S. C. (2001). Sexual assault and alcohol abuse: A comparison of lesbians and heterosexual women. *Journal of Substance Abuse, 13*, 515–532.

Huizinga, D., Haberstick, B. C., Smolen, A., et al. (2006). Childhood maltreatment, subsequent antisocial behavior, and the role of monoamine oxidase A genotype. *Biolgical Psychiatry, 60*(7), 677–683.

Jaffee, S. R. (2012). Teasing out the role of genotype in the development of psychopathology in maltreated children. In C. S. Widom (Ed.), *Trauma psychopathology and violence: Causes, consequences or correlates?* (pp. 49–75). New York: Oxford University Press.

Jaffee, S. R., Caspi, A., Moffitt, T. E., Polo-Thomas, M., & Taylor, A. (2007). Individual, family and neighborhood factors distinguish resilient from non-resilient maltreated children: A cumulative stressors model. *Child Abuse & Neglect, 31*(3), 231–253.

Johnson, J. G., Cohen, P., Brown, J., Smailes, E. M., & Bernstein, D. P. (1999). Childhood maltreatment increases risk for personality disorders during early adulthood. *Archives of General Psychiatry, 56*, 600–606.

Johnson, J. G., Smailes, E. M., Cohen, P., Brown, J., & Bernstein, D. P. (2000). Associations between four types of childhood neglect and personality disorder symptoms during adolescents and early adulthood: Findings of a community-based longitudinal study. *Journal of Personality Disorders, 14*(2), 171–187.

Johnson, J. G., Cohen, P., Kasen, S., & Brook, J. S. (2002). Childhood adversities associated with risk for eating disorders or weight problems during adolescence or early adulthood. *The American Journal of Psychiatry, 159*, 394–400.

Jonson-Reid, M. (2004). Child welfare services and delinquency: The need to know more. *Child Welfare, LXXXIII*(2), 157–173.

Jonson-Reid, M., Drake, B., Kim, J., Porterfield, S., & Han, L. (2004). A prospective analysis of the relationship between reported child maltreatment and special education eligibility among poor children. *Child Maltreatment, 9*, 382–394.

Jonson-Reid, M., Kohl, P. L., & Drake, B. (2012). Child and adult outcomes of chronic maltreatment. *Pediatrics, 129*, 839–845.

Kaplow, J. B., & Widom, C. S. (2007). Age of onset of child maltreatment predicts long-term mental health outcomes. *Journal of Abnormal Psychology, 116*, 176–187.

Kaufman, J. G., & Widom, C. S. (1999). Childhood victimization, running away, and delinquency. *Journal of Research in Crime and Delinquency, 36*(4), 347–381.

Kaufman, J., & Zigler, E. (1987). Do abused children become abusive parents? *The American Journal of Orthopsychiatry, 57*, 186–192.

Kempe, R. S., & Kempe, C. H. (1978). *Child abuse*. Cambridge, MA: Harvard University Press.

Kiecolt-Glaser, J. K., Bane, C., Glaser, R., & Malarkey, W. B. (2003). Love, marriage, and divorce: Newlyweds' stress hormones foreshadow relations changes. *Journal of Consulting and Clinical Psychology, 71*, 176–188.

Kim, J., & Cicchetti, D. (2010). Longitudinal pathways linking child maltreatment, emotion regulation, peer relations, and psychopathology. *Journal of Child Psychology and Psychiatry, 51*, 706–716.

Kinard, E. M. (1999). Psychosocial resources and academic performance in abused children. *Children and Youth Services Review, 21*, 351–376.

Knutson, J. F., Taber, S. M., Murray, A. J., Valles, N., & Knoeppl, G. (2010). The role of care neglect and supervisory neglect in childhood obesity in a disadvantaged sample. *Journal of Pediatric Psychology, 35*, 523–530.

Koenig, L. J., & Clark, H. (2004). Sexual abuse of girls and HIV infection among women: Are they related? In L. J. Koenig, L. S. Doll, A. O'Leary, & W. Pequegnat (Eds.), *From child sexual abuse to adult sexual risk: Trauma, revictimization, and intervention* (pp. 69–92). Washington, DC: American Psychological Association.

Langeland, W., & Hartgers, C. (1998). Child sexual and physical abuse and alcoholism: A review. *Journal of Studies on Alcohol, Supplement 59*(3), 336–348.

Lansford, J. E., Dodge, K. A., Pettit, G. S., Bates, J. E., Crozier, J., & Kaplow, J. (2002). A 12-year prospective study of the long-term effects of early child physical maltreatment on psychological, behavioral, and academic problems in adolescence. *Archives of Pediatrics & Adolescent Medicine, 156*, 824–830.

Lansford, J. E., Miller-Johnson, S., Berlin, L. J., Dodge, K. A., Bates, J. E., & Pettit, G. S. (2007). Early physical abuse and later violent delinquency: A prospective longitudinal study. *Child Maltreatment, 12*, 233–245.

Lansford, J. E., Dodge, K. A., Pettit, G. S., & Bates, J. E. (2010). Does physical abuse in early childhood predict substance use in adolescence and early adulthood? *Child Maltreatment, 15*(2), 190–194.

Lau, A. S., Litrownik, A. J., Newton, R. R., Black, M. M., & Everson, M. D. (2006). Factors affecting the link between physical discipline and child externalizing problems in black and white families. *Journal of Community Psychology, 34*(1), 89–103.

Leiter, J. (2007). School performance trajectories after the advent of reported maltreatment. *Children and Youth Services Review, 29*, 363–382.

Lissau, I., & Sorensen, T. I. A. (1994). Parental neglect during childhood and increased risk of obesity in young adulthood. *Lancet, 343*, 324–330.

Liu, D., Diorio, J., Tannenbaum, B., Caldji, C., Francis, D., Freedman, A., … Meaney, M. J. (1997). Maternal care, hippocampal glucocorticoid receptors, and hypothalamic-pituitary-adrenal responses to stress. *Science, 277*(5332), 1659–1662.

Luntz, B. K., & Widom, C. S. (1994). Antisocial personality disorder in abused and neglected children grown up. *The American Journal of Psychiatry, 151*(5), 670–674.

Lupien, S. J., & McEwen, B. S. (1997). The acute effects of corticosteroids on cognition: Integration of animal and human model studies. *Brain Research Reviews, 24*, 1–27.

Lupien, S. J., King, S., Meaney, M. J., & McEwen, B. S. (2001). Can poverty get under your skin? Basal cortisol levels and cognitive function in children from low and high socioeconomic status. *Development and Psychopathology, 13*, 653–676.

Lupien, S. J., Wilkinson, C. W., Brière, S., Ménard, C., Kin, N. Y., & Nair, N. P. V. (2002). The modulatory effects of corticosteroids on cognition: Studies in young human populations. *Psychoneuroendocrinology, 27*, 401–416.

Maker, A. H., Kemmelmeir, M., & Peterson, C. (2001). Child sexual abuse, peer sexual abuse, and sexual assault in adulthood: A multi-risk model of revictimization. *Journal of Traumatic Stress, 14*(2), 351–368.

Manly, J. T., Kim, J. E., Rogosch, F. A., & Cicchetti, D. (2001). Dimensions of child maltreatment and children's adjustment: Contributions of developmental timing and subtype. *Development and Psychopathology, 13*, 759–782.

Maxfield, M. G., & Widom, C. S. (1996). The cycle of violence: Revisited six years later. *Archives of Pediatric and Adolescent Medicine, 150*(4), 390–395.

McBeth, J., Morris, S., Benjamin, S., Silman, A. J., & Macfarlane, G. J. (2001). Associations between adverse events in childhood and chronic widespread pain in adulthood: Are they explained by differential recall? *Journal of Rheumatology, 28*(10), 2305–2309.

McCrory, E., De Brito, S. A., & Viding, E. (2010). Research Review: The neurobiology and genetics of maltreatment and adversity. *Journal of Child Psychology and Psychiatry, 51*(10), 1079–1095.

McGloin, J. M., & Widom, C. S. (2001). Resilience among abused and neglected children grown up. *Development and Psychopathology, 13*(4), 1021–1038.

Meaney, M. J., Bhatnagar, S., Larocque, S., McCormick, C. M., Shanks, N., Sharma, S., … Plotsky, P. M. (1996). Early environment and the development of individual differences in the hypothalamic-pituitary-adrenal stress response. In C. R. Pfeffer (Ed.), *Severe stress and mental disturbance in children* (pp. 85–127). Washington, DC: American Psychiatric Press.

Merrill, L. L., Newell, C. E., Thomsen, C. J., Gold, S. R., Milner, J. S., Koss, M. P., & Rosswork, S. G. (1999). Childhood abuse and sexual revictimization in a female Navy recruit sample. *Journal of Traumatic Stress, 12*, 211–225.

Mersky, J. P., & Topitzes, J. (2010). Comparing early adult outcomes of maltreated and non-maltreated children: A prospective longitudinal investigation. *Children and Youth Services Review, 32*(8), 1086–1096.

Messman, T. L., & Long, P. J. (1996). Child sexual abuse and its relationship to revictimization in adult women: A review. *Clinical Psychology Review, 16*(5), 397–420.

Meston, C. M., Heiman, J. R., & Trapnell, P. D. (1999). The relation between early abuse and adult sexuality. *Journal of Sex Research, 36*, 385–395.

Miller, B. A., & Downs, W. R. (1993). The impact of family violence on the use of alcohol by women. *Alcohol Health and Research World, 17*(2), 137–143.

Miller, B. A., & Mancuso, R. F. (2004). Connecting childhood victimization to later alcohol/drug problems: Implications for prevention. *The Journal of Primary Prevention, 25*(2), 149–169.

Miller, B. A., Maguin, E., & Downs, W. R. (1997). Alcohol, drugs, and violence in children's lives. In M. Galanter (Ed.), *Recent developments in alcoholism* (Alcohol and violence: Epidemiology, neurobiology, psychology, family issues, Vol. 13, pp. 357–385). New York: Plenum Press.

Nelson, E., Heath, A. C., Madden, P. A., et al. (2002). Association between self-reported childhood sexual abuse and adverse psychosocial outcomes: Results from a twin study. *Archives of General Psychiatry, 59*(2), 139–145.

Nikulina, V., Widom, C. S., & Czaja, S. (2011). The role of childhood neglect and childhood poverty in predicting mental health, academic achievement and crime in adulthood. *American Journal of Community Psychology, 48*(3–4), 309–321.

Noll, J. G., Trickett, P. K., & Putnam, F. W. (2003). A prospective investigation of the impact of childhood sexual abuse on the development of sexuality. *Journal of Consulting and Clinical Psychology, 71*, 575–586.

Noll, J. G., Zeller, M. H., Trickett, P. K., & Putnam, F. W. (2007). Obesity risk for female victims of childhood sexual abuse: A prospective study. *Pediatrics, 120*, e61–e67.

Offer, D., Kaiz, M., Howard, K. I., & Bennett, E. S. (2000). The altering of reported experiences. *Journal of the American Academy of Child and Adolescent Psychiatry, 39*, 735–742.

Ohene, S., Halcon, L., Ireland, M., Carr, P., & McNeely, C. (2005). Sexual abuse history, risk behavior, and sexually transmitted diseases: The impact of age at abuse. *Sexually Transmitted Diseases, 32*, 358–363.

Pears, K. C., & Capaldi, D. M. (2001). Intergenerational transmission of abuse: A two-generational prospective study of an at-risk sample. *Child Abuse & Neglect, 25*(11), 1439–1461.

Perez, C. M., & Widom, C. S. (1994). Childhood victimization and longterm intellectual and academic outcomes. *Child Abuse & Neglect, 18*(8), 617–633.

Perry, B. D., & Pollard, R. (1998). Homeostasis, stress, trauma, and adaptation: A neurodevelopmental view of childhood trauma. *Child and Adolescent Psychiatric Clinics of North America, 7*, 33–51.

Raphael, K. G. (1987). Recall bias: A proposal for assessment and control. *International Journal of Epidemiology, 16*(2), 167–169.

Renner, L. M., & Slack, K. S. (2006). Intimate partner violence and child maltreatment: Understanding intra-and intergenerational connections. *Child Abuse & Neglect, 30*, 599–617.

Rich, C. L. (1990). Accuracy of adults' reports of abuse in childhood. *The American Journal of Psychiatry, 147*(10), 1389–1390.

Roberts, A. L., Gilman, S. E., Breslau, J. B., & Koenen, K. C. (2011). Race/ethnic differences in exposure to traumatic events, development of post-traumatic stress disorder, and treatment-seeking for post-traumatic stress disorder in the United States. *Psychological Medicine: A Journal of Research in Psychiatry and the Allied Sciences, 41*(1), 71–83.

Rogosch, F. A., & Cicchetti, D. (1994). Illustrating the interface of family and peer relations through the study of child maltreatment. *Social Development, 3*, 291–308.

Roth, T. L., & Champagne, F. A. (Eds.). (2012). Epigenetic pathways and the consequences of adversity and trauma. (pp. 23–48) In Widom, C. S. (Ed.), *Trauma, psychopathology, and violence: Causes, consequences or correlates?* New York: Oxford University Press.

Saewyc, E. M., Bearinger, L. H., Blum, R. W., & Resnick, M. D. (1999). Sexual intercourse, abuse, and pregnancy among adolescent women: Does sexual orientation make a difference. *Family Planning Perspective, 31*, 127–131.

Sameroff, A. J., & Fiese, B. H. (2000). Transactional regulation: The developmental ecology of early intervention. In J. P. Shonkoff & S. J. Meisels (Eds.), *Handbook of early childhood interventions* (pp. 138–159). New York: Cambridge University Press.

Sappington, A. A., Pharr, R., Tunstall, A., & Rickert, E. (1997). Relationships among child abuse, date abuse, and psychological problems. *Journal of Clinical Psychology, 53*(4), 319–329.

Schaaf, K. K., & McCanne, T. R. (1998). Relationship of childhood sexual, physical, and combined sexual and physical abuse to adult victimization and posttraumatic stress disorder. *Child Abuse & Neglect, 22*(11), 1119–1133.

Schuck, A. M., & Widom, C. S. (2005). Understanding the role of neighborhood context in the long-term criminal consequences of child maltreatment. *American Journal of Community Psychology, 36*(3/4), 207–222.

Senn, T. E., Carey, M. P., Vanable, P. A., Coury-Doniger, P., & Urban, M. A. (2006). Childhood sexual abuse and sexual risk behavior among men and women attending a sexually transmitted disease clinic. *Journal of Consulting and Clinical Psychology, 74*, 720–731.

Sidebotham, P., Golding, J., & Team, A. S. (2001). Child maltreatment in the "children of the nineties". A longitudinal study of parental risk factors. *Child Abuse & Neglect, 25*(9), 1177–1200.

Simpson, T. L., & Miller, W. R. (2002). Concomitance between childhood sexual and physical abuse and substance use problems: A review. *Clinical Psychology Review, 22*, 27–77.

Smith, C., & Thornberry, T. P. (1995). The relationship between childhood maltreatment and adolescent involvement in delinquency. *Criminology, 33*(4), 451–481.

Steele, B. F., & Pollock, C. D. (1968). A psychiatric study of parents who abuse infants and small children. In C. H. Kempe & R. E. Helfer (Eds.), *The battered child* (pp. 103–147). Chicago: The University of Chicago Press.

Sternberg, K. J., Lamb, M. E., Guterman, E., & Abbott, C. B. (2006). Effects of early and later family violence on children's behavior problems and depression: A longitudinal, multi-informant perspective. *Child Abuse & Neglect, 30*, 283–306.

Stith, S. M., Liu, T., Davies, L. C., Boykin, E. L., Alder, M. C., Harris, J. M., Som, A., McPherson, M., & Dees, J. E. M. E. G. (2009). Risk factors in child maltreatment: A meta-analytic review of the literature. *Aggression and Violent Behavior, 14*, 13–29.

Stouthamer-Loeber, M., Loeber, R., Homish, D. L., & Wei, E. (2001). Maltreatment of boys and the development of disruptive and delinquent behavior. *Development and Psychopathology, 13*, 941–955.

Suomi, S. J. (1991). Early stress and adult emotional reactivity in rhesus monkeys. In G. Bock & J. Whelan (Eds.), *Childhood environment and adult disease* (pp. 171–188). Chichester: Wiley.

Suomi, S. J. (1999). Early stress and adult emotional reactivity in rhesus monkeys. In J. S. P. R. Cassidy (Ed.), *Handbook of attachment: Theory, research, and clinical applications* (pp. 181–197). New York: Guilford Press.

Tamang, A. (2005). *A study of trafficked Nepalese girls and women in Mumbai and Kolkata, India.* Kathmandu: Terre des homes Foundation.

Taubes, G. (2007, September 16). Do we really know what makes us healthy? *New York Times Magazine,* Retrieved from http://www.nytimes.com

Taylor, A., & Kim-Cohen, J. (2007). Meta-analysis of gene-environment interactions in developmental psychopathology. *Development and Psychopathology, 19,* 1029–1037.

Thompson, R. (2006). Exploring the link between maternal history of childhood victimization and child risk of maltreatment. *Journal of Trauma Practice, 5,* 57–72.

Thornberry, T. P., Ireland, T. O., & Smith, C. A. (2001). The importance of timing: The varying impact of childhood and adolescent maltreatment on multiple problem outcomes. *Development and Psychopathology, 13,* 957–979.

Thornberry, T. P., Knight, K. E., & Lovegrove, P. J. (2012). Does maltreatment beget maltreatment? A systematic review of the intergenerational literature. *Trauma, Violence & Abuse, 13*(3), 135–152.

Tjaden, P., Thoennes, N., & Allison, C. J. (1999). Brief report: Comparing violence over the life span in samples of same-sex and opposite-sex cohabitants. *Violence and Victims, 14,* 413–425.

Tomeo, M. E., Templer, D. L., Anderson, S., & Kotler, D. (2001). Comparative data of childhood adolescence molestation in heterosexual and homosexual persons. *Archives of Sexual Behavior, 30,* 535–541.

Tout, K., de Haan, M., Campbell, E. K., & Gunnar, M. R. (1998). Social behavior correlates of cortisol activity in child care: Gender differences and time-of-day effects. *Child Development, 69*(5), 1247–1262.

Trickett, P. K., Noll, J. G., & Putnam, F. W. (2011). The impact of sexual abuse on female development: Lessons from a multigenerational, longitudinal research study. *Development and Psychopathology, 23,* 453–476.

Vythilingam, M., Heim, C., Newport, J., Miller, A. H., Anderson, E., Bronen, R., … Bremner, J. D. (2002). Childhood trauma associated with smaller hippocampal volume in women with major depression. *The American Journal of Psychiatry, 159,* 2072–2080.

Weiler, B. L., & Widom, C. S. (1996). Psychopathy and violent behaviour in abused and neglected young adults. *Criminal Behavior and Mental Health, 6,* 253–271.

White, H. R., Widom, C. S., & Chen, P.-H. (2007). Congruence between adolescents' self-reports and their adult retrospective reports regarding parental discipline practices during their adolescence. *Psychological Reports, 101,* 1079–1094.

Widom, C. S. (1989a). Does violence beget violence? A critical examination of the literature. *Psychological Bulletin, 106*(1), 3–28.

Widom, C. S. (1989b). The cycle of violence. *Science, 244,* 160–166.

Widom, C. S. (1998). Childhood victimization: Early adversity and subsequent psychopathology. In B. P. Dohrenwend (Ed.), *Adversity, stress, and psychopathology* (pp. 81–95). New York: Oxford University Press.

Widom, C. S. (1999). Posttraumatic stress disorder in abused and neglected children grown up. *The American Journal of Psychiatry, 156*(8), 1223–1229.

Widom, C. S., & Brzustowicz, L. M. (2006). MAOA and the "cycle of violence": Childhood abuse and neglect, MAOA genotype, and risk for violent and antisocial behavior. *Biological Psychiatry, 60*(7), 684–689.

Widom, C. S., & Hiller-Strumhofel, S. (2001). Alcohol abuse as a risk factor for and consequence of child abuse. *Alcohol Research & Health, 25*(1), 52–57.

Widom, C. S., & Kuhns, J. B. (1996). Childhood victimization and subsequent risk for promiscuity, prostitution, and teenage pregnancy: A prospective study. *American Journal of Public Health, 86,* 1607–1612.

Widom, C. S., Ireland, T., & Glynn, P. J. (1995). Alcohol abuse in abused and neglected children followed-up: Are they at increased risk? *Journal of Studies on Alcohol, 56,* 207–217.

Widom, C. S., Weiler, B. L., & Cottler, L. B. (1999). Childhood victimization and drug abuse: A comparison of prospective and retrospective findings. *Journal of Consulting and Clinical Psychology, 67*(6), 867–880.

Widom, C. S., Marmorstein, N. R., & White, H. R. (2006). Childhood victimization and illicit drug use in middle adulthood. *Psychology of Addictive Behaviors, 20*(4), 394–403.

Widom, C. S., DuMont, K., & Czaja, S. J. (2007a). A prospective investigation of major depressive disorder and comorbidity in abused and neglected children grown up. *Archives of General Psychiatry, 64*(1), 49–56.

Widom, C. S., White, H. R., Czaja, S. J., & Marmorstein, N. R. (2007b). Long-term effects of child abuse and neglect on alcohol use and excessive drinking in middle adulthood. *Journal of Studies on Alcohol and Drugs, 68*(3), 317–326.

Widom, C. S., Czaja, S. J., & Dutton, M. A. (2008). Childhood victimization and lifetime revictimization. *Child Abuse & Neglect, 32,* 785–796.

Widom, C. S., Czaja, S., Bentley, T., & Johnson, M. S. (2012a). A prospective investigation of physical health outcomes in abused and neglected children: New findings from a 30-year follow-up. *American Journal of Public Health, 102*(6), 1135–1144.

Widom, C. S., Czaja, S., Wilson, H. W., Allwood, M., & Chauhan, P. (2012b). Do the long-term consequences of neglect differ for children of different races and ethnic backgrounds? *Child Maltreatment.* doi:10.1177/1077559512460728. published online 16 October 2012.

Wilsnack, S. C., Vogeltanz, N. D., Klassen, A. D., & Harris, T. R. (1997). Childhood sexual abuse and women's substance abuse: National survey findings. *Journal of Studies on Alcohol, 58*(3), 264–271.

Wilson, H. W., & Widom, C. S. (2009a). The role of youth problem behaviors in the path from child abuse and neglect to prostitution: A prospective examination. *Journal of Research on Adolescence, 20*(1), 210–236.

Wilson, H. W., & Widom, C. S. (2009b). Sexually transmitted diseases among abused and neglected children grown up: A 30-year prospective study. *American Journal of Public Health, 99*(S1), S197–203.

Wilson, H. W., & Widom, C. S. (2010). Does physical abuse, sexual abuse, or neglect in childhood increase the likelihood of same-sex sexual relationships and cohabitation? A prospective 30-year follow-up. *Archives of Sexual Behavior, 39*(1), 63–74.

Wodarski, J. S., Kurtz, P. D., Gaudin, J. M., & Howing, P. T. (1990). Maltreatment and the school-age child: Major academic, socioemotional and adaptive outcomes. *Social Work Research & Abstracts, 35*(6), 506–513.

Wolfe, D. A. (1991). *Preventing physical and emotional abuse of children.* New York: Guilford Press.

Zingraff, M. T., Leiter, J., Myers, K. A., & Johnsen, M. (1993). Child maltreatment and youthful problem behavior. *Criminology, 31*, 173–202.

Part IV
Child Maltreatment:
What Can and Should We Do About It?

Chapter 13
Beyond Maltreatment: Developing Support for Children in Multiproblem Families

Michael S. Wald

Introduction

The proper role of the state with respect to regulating parenting has long been a source of controversy in the United States,[1] where many people believe that there generally should be a separation of government and family. This has led to a very limited role of government in regulating and monitoring child rearing. Unless a parent's behavior falls below a standard that is considered abuse or neglect (maltreatment) there is no government oversight of parenting. In essence, parenting is divided into two categories for purposes of most public policy – acceptable and maltreatment. The child protection system (CPS) is charged with responding to parenting that is considered maltreatment, which is defined primarily in terms of physical harms (actual or potential) to, or sexual conduct with, a child.[2] The focus of the CPS system is on children who have already suffered, or are in imminent danger of suffering, such harms. The primary goal of intervention is to prevent reoccurrence of these harms (Wald 1975; Wulczyn et al. 2005).

While it is recognized that children may need better parental care than is provided by many "acceptable" parents, no system has *responsibility* for trying to help children whose development is adversely affected by problematic parenting that does not involve harms that fall within the definition of maltreatment (NRC-IOM 2009a). There are a variety of parenting programs and support services available to parents who seek them out, but these services do not reach a significant proportion of the parents and children that need them the most, either due to lack of availability or the failure of the parent to seek or accept the services.

Yet, as discussed below, there is good reason to believe that 15–20 % of children live in homes where the quality of parenting puts them at risk of very poor outcomes during childhood and into adulthood. Only about a third of these families are brought under the supervision of the CPS system. Some commentators have called for expanding the definition of maltreatment and/or the

---

[1] This chapter focuses primarily on U.S. policy since issues related to regulating parenting must be viewed in light of a range of particular cultural and economic factors. However, many of the issues discussed here are similar to those facing policy makers in other in economically developed countries (Lonne et al. 2009).

[2] While definitions vary by state, all statutes include parental conduct that results in physical injury (actual or threatened) to the child or engaging in sexual relations with the child or failing to protect a child from sexual relations with an adult. Most cases labeled "neglect" also involve the threat of physical harm due to inadequate supervision, unsafe home conditions, etc. Failure to send a child to school and some forms of parental conduct that lead to mental harms also are included in many states' definitions.

M.S. Wald (✉)
Stanford University, Stanford, CA, USA
e-mail: mwald@stanford.edu

J.E. Korbin and R.D. Krugman (eds.), *Handbook of Child Maltreatment*, Child Maltreatment 2,
DOI 10.1007/978-94-007-7208-3_13, © Springer Science+Business Media Dordrecht 2014

level of CPS intervention because they believe that the current system leaves too many children at-risk of substantial developmental problems (Bartholet 1999, 2012; Dwyer 2008; Garbarino 1977; Polansky et al. 1972). Others have resisted using the concept of maltreatment and the child protection system as a central way to promote outcomes other than safety (Wald 1975; Goldstein et al. 1979; Lindsey 2004; Weithorn 2012). There is consensus, however, that current policies are not meeting the needs of many children. Over the past 20 years, a number of commentators, including the US Advisory Board on Child Abuse and Neglect, have called for new approaches to helping parents other than through CPS (US Advisory Board 1991). But there has been only limited response.

A new discussion is needed with respect to state policies towards parenting. Rather than focusing primarily on defining maltreatment,[3] this discussion should start by focusing on what **outcomes** for children society wants to try attain through public policies and programs. After deciding on outcomes, it would be necessary to examine the effect of parenting on the likelihood that a child attains the desired outcomes. When the quality of parenting appears to be a central component in whether a child is likely to attain a particular outcome, it would then be necessary to examine what policies, including use of the child protection system, are appropriate in trying to address the impact of such parenting.

In this chapter, I use an outcomes-focused framework to examine the policy issues regarding state oversight of parenting, including maltreatment. I begin by identifying four outcomes that generally are the goals of public policy regarding children (although legislatures often do not identify specific outcomes in enacting legislation). I suggest that the major focus of state activity regulating and monitoring parenting should be on parenting that negatively impacts two of these outcomes:(a) children's safety during childhood and (b) their capacity to become *self-sufficient* adults. For purposes of this discussion, I label such parenting as "inadequate parenting," although I recognize that it is important to avoid stigmatizing labels when developing public policies.[4]

I then examine what types of state actions might help all parents provide minimally adequate care. With respect to this question, I divide parenting behaviors into two categories: (a) parental behaviors that should be labeled maltreatment *because* they require intervention through the child protection system (in essence, the purpose of labeling parental behavior as maltreatment is to allow the state to require reporting of the parent's behavior, to investigate the child's home environment, to require parental participation in services, and in some instance to terminate parental rights Wald 1975, 1976) and (b) other forms of highly inadequate parenting which, I will argue, should be addressed by systems other than CPS.

Finally, I examine some of the issues in designing a system of services that truly helps parents and children. Over the past 50 years a great deal of attention has been given to the rules that govern the child protection system. Unfortunately, too much of the debate has been about policy and not enough about how to implement a system of services, including deciding what system, or combination of systems – CPS, health, education, social services – should be charged with responsibility for helping parents function in a manner that meets their children's needs and assessing how those systems could be improved. Policy debates that do not consider implementation issues are not likely to generate useful approaches.

---

[3] There is still no agreed upon definition of maltreatment. In the U.S., each state uses its own definition of maltreatment for both mandatory-reporting laws and in establishing the bases for court involvement in child protection; definitions vary among countries as well (Waldfogel 1998; Lonne et al. 2009). There are widely varying rates of reported and substantiated maltreatment among the states (Appendix). It is highly unlikely that these variations reflect underlying differences in the levels of actual parental behaviors in each state.

[4] I find the terms maltreatment or child abuse/neglect even more problematic, since they imply a willfulness that is often not present with respect to the parental behavior and certainly do not support a strengths-based approach.

Choosing Outcomes for Parenting Policies

Everyone knows that parenting powerfully influences a child's well-being. (Brooks-Gunn and Markham 2005, p. 140)

Almost all experts would agree with this statement by two leading researchers on child development. However, determining how much focus there should be on trying to alter parenting as a *primary* means of promoting children's well-being is complex. The influence of the quality of parenting on a child's well-being varies with respect to the specific outcomes (or aspects of well-being) that are the goals of a particular policy. In addition, it may be more effective to focus primarily on other factors that influence a child's development, for example school quality, rather than on parental behavior, in trying to help children achieve some outcomes.

There are at least four different outcomes that underlie different policies. One of these relates to a child's well-being during childhood, while the others focus on how a child fares in adulthood. While these outcomes are inter-related, they raise very different policy issues and choices.

1. Protection from Harms During Childhood

   One clear goal of public policy is to protect children from factors that substantially impair their physical (and mental)[5] health and safety during childhood. The focus in this regard is protecting a child's current well-being (as well as their future prospects). This is the core goal of child maltreatment laws, which try to protect children from parental actions that are likely to cause current physical injury or severe emotional harms. There is little disagreement about this goal, although there is disagreement over the types of harms that should be included in the definition of maltreatment.

2. Economic Success in Adulthood

   Most government policies regarding children, including those focused on parenting, are designed more to provide children with an opportunity to acquire the academic and social/emotional skills that are seen as necessary to succeed in adulthood, rather than to promote the quality of their lives during childhood.[6] A critical issue for policy development is how success is conceptualized, since the relationship of parenting to the desired level of success is likely quite dependent on the definition of success. Most commonly, success is defined in economic terms. Policy-makers, advocates, and researchers generally focus on two different levels of economic success when promoting various policies for children.

   (a) Achieving Basic Economic Well-being as Adults

   One outcome is being capable of self-support during adulthood. This outcome is usually operationalized as trying to minimize the number of children who will live in poverty as adults (Levine and Zimmerman 2010; Duncan et al. 2010a). This is a minimal goal for public policy, but at least 10 % of adults in the U.S. are poor over an extended period of time during adulthood (Ratcliffe and McKernan 2012).

   (b) Attaining "Middle-Class" Income

   A second possible goal for public policy would be to try to provide children with the skills needed to achieve a comfortable level of economic well-being during adulthood; for example

---

[5] The commitment to protecting mental health appears to be less strong than to physical health in terms of funding and legislative attention.

[6] The separation is not as stark as I am drawing. There is considerable spending on other aspects of children's current well-being other than safety, such as subsidizing health care expenses for children, trying to improve the quality of child care, and providing recreation and after-school care. But public expenditures on these services usually are justified and assessed in terms of preparation for adulthood, not in improving the quality of life for children.

some commentators focus on whether children attain the skills needed to have a "middle-class" income, which economist Isabel Sawhill defines as income three times the poverty level (Sawhill et al. 2012). Achieving middle-class status generally requires obtaining a post-secondary credential or marrying someone with these qualifications. In recent years, about 60 % of children born in the United States have middle-class incomes by age 40 (Sawhill et al. 2012).

3. Healthy, Happy Lives

While most advocacy and research focuses on economic outcomes in adulthood, some advocates push for a broader set of "well-being" outcomes. For example, some commentators propose that basic well-being in adulthood should include having a minimal level of physical and mental health (Felitti et al. 1998; NRC-IOM 2009a). A committee of the National Academy of Sciences recently proposed that public policy be designed "to create a society in which young people arrive at adulthood with the skills, interests, assets, and health habits needed to live healthy, happy, and productive lives in caring relationships with others" (NRC-IOM 2009a, p. 387). Others talk of helping children achieve "optimal" development.

4. Equal Opportunity

A fourth outcome that many policy-makers, academics, and advocates consider central in developing public policies for children is to eliminate unequal economic outcomes in childhood and adulthood that are highly correlated with the income, race, or ethnicity of a child's parents (Duncan and Murname 2011; Future of Children 2006). This goal is often discussed as closing the "achievement gap." This outcome differs from the other three in that it does not require any particular level of well-being or economic attainment; it is the inequality of opportunity that is the target of these policies, although the hope is to help children from low-income families achieve the levels of success being achieved by those from higher income families.

Each of these outcomes (other than "optimal" development which is indefinable and is not measurable) has merit as a goal for public policies. But they may not all be appropriate as the goal for policies that focus on influencing parenting as a primary means of achieving the outcome. In choosing the outcomes that should be the focus of parenting policy, policy-makers should be guided by both the importance of enabling children to attain the outcome and the evidence regarding the relationship of parenting to the achievement of the outcome. While research finds that it matters a great deal who a child's parents **are** in predicting whether a child achieves any of the long-term developmental goals just identified (Brooks-Gunn and Markham 2005), it is far less clear why this is so. Child development research clearly shows that styles of parent–child interactions can influence a child's academic and social development. However, for the most part, these differences have relatively small effects on most outcomes. This is not surprising given that the quality of parenting falls along a continuum and is not static. It is only when the quality of parenting falls significantly below the levels generally found in most households that the evidence indicates a strong impact on children's long-term outcomes (NRC-IOM 2000; Sroufe et al. 2005).

Moreover, parental interaction with a child is only one factor influencing children's development. At least four other factors influence their development: the child's genetic make-up; the income, education, and family structure of the child's parent(s)[7]; the resources and opportunities provided to the child and parents by the state to enhance the child's health and education; and the child's interactions with other children, adults, and neighborhood environment. It is well established that there often is interaction among these factors and that parenting must be assessed in light of these interactions. While these factors may have their primary effects because they influence parenting, they also may have effects independent of this.

---

[7] I use the term parent to include other adults, such as grandparents, when they are the child's primary care taker.

In particular, there is a long-standing debate regarding the role of family income in determining outcomes for children, both as a factor in and of itself and as an influence on the quality of parenting (Drake and Jonson-Reid this volume, Chap. 7). Some commentators believe that raising family income is the best approach to improving children's outcomes and/or influencing parents' behaviors; many income transfer programs are supported primarily as a means of helping children. Others believe that the same parental characteristics that result in poor parenting often account for the parent's lack of economic success. The lack of clear evidence regarding causality poses a challenge in deciding whether to focus on parenting itself, poverty itself, or the combination of the two, as the primary means of helping children achieve particular outcomes (Drake and Jonson-Reid this volume, Chap. 7; Pianta et al. 1989; Thompson 1995; Mayer 1997; Duncan et al. 1998, 2010b; Ratcliffe and McKernan 2012).

It is clear, however, that parenting is greatly influenced by context (Cicchetti and Valentino 2006; Sroufe et al. 2005; Belsky 1990). Lack of resources makes it very hard to provide consistently adequate parenting. Raising the income of very poor families may not be a sufficient condition for achieving any of the desired outcomes, but it often will be a necessary one.

Finally, in choosing policies to help children, policy-makers need to recognize that changing parenting is very difficult, especially that of parents facing multiple problems. Given the limited knowledge about the effects of specific aspects of parenting on various outcomes of children, as well as the types of interventions that are effective in altering parenting, programs designed to directly alter parenting should focus on situations where such interventions are likely to be most necessary and useful. It also is necessary to realistically consider both the financial resources that are likely to be available to support various services and the capacity of organizations to provide high quality services; policies often are developed based on unrealistic assessments of these factors. Good programs may be expensive.

Based on these considerations, there is a very strong case for focusing on altering parenting primarily with respect to reaching the first two outcomes discussed above – protecting children's safety during childhood and helping children attain the skills needed to enable them to live at a **basic** economic level during adulthood. There is clear evidence that the nature of the parenting a child receives is strongly related to whether a child achieves these outcomes. In fact, it may be very difficult to help all children achieve these outcomes without a major focus on parenting, especially for children living in families suffering from multiple problems, including poor parental mental health, substance abuse, family violence, and deep poverty (Sroufe et al. 2005; Lansford et al. 2002). I am not suggesting that focusing directly on parenting itself is the only, or exclusive, way to help children attain these two basic outcomes; poverty, neighborhood conditions, and the quality of child care and schools are independently important for many children and also are factors strongly affecting parent–child interactions (Nikulina et al. 2011). These factors need to be addressed. However, it appears that for many children addressing these other factors alone will not be sufficient to ensure that they are safe and that they are able to acquire the skills needed for self-sufficiency. Helping these children requires altering parental behavior.

Protection From Harm. The need to focus on parenting itself is definitional with respect to achieving the outcome of protecting children from serious harm caused or threatened by the acts of parents, which is why there is a system devoted to trying to prevent the occurrence or reoccurrence of such behaviors. While, as discussed below, there is debate regarding the appropriate reach of the CPS system in addressing these behaviors, and the capacity of the system to help children who have experienced maltreatment, the types of parental behaviors that cause or threaten serious imminent harm are reasonably clear. They include directly inflicting physical injury on the child, consistently exposing children to conditions or situations that carry a substantial risk of causing physical injuries or threat to the child's health, engaging in sexual relations with the child or exposing a child to conditions or situations that carry a substantial risk of other adults engaging the child in sex, and failing to provide medical care to the child. Besides resulting in current harm, experiencing this type of parental conduct also impairs the future development of many children (Widom this volume, Chap. 12).

Basic Economic Sufficiency. There are also strong reasons to focus heavily on parenting itself in order to achieve this outcome. The great majority of children achieve basic self-sufficiency in adulthood if they have graduated from high school, have not given birth to a child before age 20, have not engaged in behaviors that led to incarceration in the juvenile or criminal justice system, and are not drug or alcohol dependent or suffering from substantial mental health problems (Sawhill et al. 2012; Wald and Martinez 2003). I estimate that at least 20 % of all children do not enter adulthood having met all these milestones (Wald and Martinez 2003). Multiple factors influence whether children attain these milestones as adults. There is, however, substantial evidence that the nature of the parenting a child receives is strongly associated with whether the child engages in these behaviors or suffers from serious mental health problems (Nikulina et al. 2011; Mersky and Topitzes 2010; NRC-IOM 2009a; Connell and Dishion 2008; Sroufe et al. 2005). Moreover, as discussed below, the types of parental behaviors that compromise a child's capacity to avoid dropping out of school etc. go beyond those that are considered maltreatment and dealt with by the CPS system. Therefore, there is a need to consider how best to help parents avoid the parenting behaviors that may undermine their children's capacity to become self-sufficient adults.

The case for focusing primarily on parenting is much weaker with respect to helping children achieve the other economic outcome identified above – earning a middle-class income. The same is true with respect to closing the achievement gap. At present, about 30 % of all children graduate from high school but do not attain a post-secondary degree or credential, which is a generally a prerequisite for earning higher incomes and social mobility.[8] Most of these children live in low-income households, where the parents generally have limited education themselves. There are strong reasons, however, to think that the quality of parenting in these households is not problematic in the same ways as the parenting in the households that produce the 20 % of children that dropout of school and/or engage in other behaviors that impair their **basic** futures. As described below, many of the parents of the children who fall within the latter group suffer from multiple problems that greatly impair their parenting ability. It will be hard to enable their children to succeed without directly addressing the parenting. Moreover, these parents often fail to take advantage of programs designed to help them or their children. And services for these parents often are in short supply. Therefore, a new, more proactive and systematic approach is needed to help these parents and children.

In contrast, the available evidence suggests that most of the parents of the children who graduate high school but do not go on to college provide basically adequate care of the children, although the levels of cognitive stimulation in their homes and the amount of some forms of positive nurturance may be relatively low (Kalil et al. 2012; Waldfogel and Washbrook 2011). Moreover, the evidence suggests that services focused solely on the children – in childcare, preschool, and school settings – are the most effective way of helping these children perform better in school (Barnett and Belfield 2006). While such efforts may be insufficient to close the achievement gap (Reardon 2011), high quality childcare, preschool, and K-12 schools can improve the likelihood that a child from a low-income family will not only graduate from high school, but will also obtain a post-secondary credential, even without involving parents. Most of these parents voluntarily take advantage of childcare, preschool, afterschool and other programs for their children. In addition, most of these parents are willing to participate when childcare settings, preschools, and schools offer to engage them in school activities and help them improve their parenting. It is not necessary to develop a new system that monitors these parents in order to help their children.

---

[8]Approximately half of children born in the US in 1985 received a BA or 2 year degree by age 25.

Adopting the goal of producing children who will live "happy…lives in caring relationships with others" (NRC-IOM 2009a, p 387) as a main outcome for parenting policies is problematic for several reasons. First, there is little understanding of the relationship of parenting, except at the extreme ends of the parenting continuum, to these outcomes and the extreme ends of parenting will be addressed through policies focused on the other goals. In addition, taken literally, achieving these outcomes seem overwhelming from a policy perspective. For example, studies find that as many as half of all adults in the U.S. experience a clinically diagnosable mental illness at some point during adulthood and that, in most instances, the onset of the problem occurred during childhood (NRC-IOM 2009a; Vericker et al. 2010). This led the members of the a National Academy of Sciences study committee to suggest that mental illness is "commonplace as a fractured limb" and that parenting programs should be made universal (NRC-IOM 2009a, p. 48). Yet, there is little, if any, evidence that universal parenting programs would produce more happy adults and caring relationships. Devoting resources to programs with these goals as the outcome is very likely to detract from the resources, thinking, and capacity building necessary to establish the type of system and programs for the families where the need is greatest.

Therefore, I focus here on assessing policies and systems that have the goals of (a) protecting children from parenting that has caused, or threatens to cause, physical injury or sexual abuse and (b) altering other types of parenting that threaten the ability of children to achieve "basic economic sufficiency," as defined above. I believe that these should be the prime outcomes for, and focus of, "parenting policy." If we develop policies that promote these outcomes, it is likely that the same policies also will enable most children to attain reasonable levels of mental and physical health during childhood and into adulthood.

Nature and Scope of the Problem

In order to target services and to design effective programs, it is necessary to determine the types of parental behaviors that significantly threaten children's current safety and/or are likely to impair a child's ability to develop the skills and behaviors needed to be able to reach basic self-sufficiency. It also is useful to have a reasonable idea of the scope of such parenting, in order to estimate the cost of any systemic approaches to address problematic parenting. In addition to affecting financial resources, the larger the number of parents who need services the more challenging it will be to develop high quality, intensive interventions, especially those requiring highly trained personnel. These are questions the field needs to examine in depth. I describe here some starting points for such a discussion.

Defining the type of parenting that requires active state involvement is reasonably clear when it comes to parental acts that endanger a child's safety and therefore require protective intervention. While there remains some debate over what parental actions justify CPS involvement, at a minimum they include acts by the parent that have caused or have a high potential of causing serious physical injuries that can impair bodily functioning, including the failure of the parent to provide supervision, food, or medical care, such that the child has suffered or has a high likelihood of suffering such injuries, and acts that constitute sexual abuse.[9] The seriousness of the harm, plus the possibility that the parental behavior may be repeated, makes the need for protective intervention essential. Moreover,

---

[9] In the 1970s, while serving as the reporter for American Bar Association's Juvenile Justice Standards Project, I proposed at set of harms that should be the focus of the CPS system. They included a limited definition of emotional injury, in addition to physical harms and sexual misuse of a child (Wald 1975). I still believe these are the harms that should be the focus of CPS.

the majority of the children who are subjected to any form of substantiated maltreatment cases evidence significant long-term developmental problems, problems that may have started years before CPS involvement (Widom this volume, Chap. 12; Barth et al. 2008). These children have very high rates of disruptive behavior at school, delinquent behavior, and mental health problems, as well as low rates of completing high school (Mersky and Topitzes 2010; Currie and Widom 2010; Lansford et al. 2002). Promoting the long-term development of these children is further reason for trying to prevent the parental behaviors that constitute maltreatment.

Identifying the parental behaviors that do not entail threats to the child's immediate safety but that might significantly impair children's future development is more difficult. Child development specialists identify a number of elements that are involved in parenting. These include nurturance, discipline, monitoring of the child's activities and needs, and intellectual stimulation (NRC-IOM 2000; Brooks-Gunn and Markham 2005). There may be added advantages when parents provide warmth in carrying out these activities. On all of these dimensions, however, there is a wide range of parenting behaviors that are likely to be generally adequate to help the child attain the basic outcomes I have identified. The issue for policy-makers is identifying the situations that require active efforts at intervention (or efforts aimed at prevention) because the parenting is likely to be associated with the onset of major developmental problems in childhood and/or failure to achieve basic self-sufficiency in adulthood.

Child development researchers posit several different mechanisms through which parental behaviors impair children's development (Aber et al. 1989). These include attachment theory, social-cognitive developmental theory, ecological theory, and more recently toxic stress (NRC-IOM 2000; Wulczyn et al. 2005). While these theories differ in many respects, they all agree that children are at substantial risk of experiencing very poor outcomes when their parents, regularly and over a period of time, interact with them in a manner that is highly chaotic or disorganized and/or non-responsive or emotionally hostile (Fiese and Winter 2010; Sroufe et al. 2005; Repetti et al. 2002; Hilyard and Wolfe 2002; NRC-IOM 2000). This type of parenting is especially detrimental when children are very young.

These deficiencies in parenting are of particular concern because they severely impair children's ability to develop self-regulation, which is a "cornerstone of early childhood development that cuts across all domains of behavior" (NRC-IOM 2000, p. 26). Children experiencing these types of parenting often suffer serious mental health problems. Moreover, this type of parenting can fundamentally impair a child's ability to adapt to, and utilize, the positive elements of other environments, including childcare settings and schools. For example, when parents are non-responsive or respond erratically, their children often learn to create crises to get attention, become demanding and or distrustful of people, and have difficulty processing cognitive information from their environments (Lieberman and Van Horn 2008). When parents fail to lay the developmental groundwork, it becomes much less likely that other programs focused solely on child will be able to compensate for the deficiencies (NRC-IOM 2009a, pp. 99–106; Repetti et al. 2002; Aber et al. 1989). Recent research indicates that all of this can play out biologically. Children may develop neural patterns that are hard to reverse (Proceedings NAS 2012; Center on the Developing Child 2012; Weithorn 2012).

To be sure, other factors, especially prolonged living in poverty, and in neighborhoods with high violence and poor schools, can lead to these outcomes, even when the child receives adequate parenting. Addressing these other factors will be necessary in order to totally eliminate bad outcomes. And there appear to be ways of reducing children's behaviors that lead to poor outcomes in adulthood (such as dropping out of school, delinquency, substance abuse, and teenage childbearing) that do not focus on altering parental behaviors. There have been substantial improvements with respect to each of these behaviors over the past 30 years, not all of which are likely associated with reductions in highly inadequate parenting. But if society is concerned with altering the life trajectories of children living in families facing multiple risks, this will require investments in efforts to alter problematic parenting, as well as on trying to prevent its emergence; other approaches alone will not be sufficient.

It is not possible to determine very precisely the percentage of children that will experience highly inadequate parenting over an extended period during their childhoods; no longitudinal studies track this. In fact, we even lack good evidence of how many children experience actual maltreatment by parents in a given year.[10] There are, however, several indicators that can be used to make estimates that are useful for policy purposes. Based on these indicators, I estimate that at least 15–20 % of all children will experience seriously deficient parenting at some point during their childhood and perhaps 10 % of children will experience such parenting for an extended period. This includes both parenting that falls within the definition of maltreatment and other forms of highly inadequate parenting.

The starting point for any estimate is the number of children that are considered maltreated. In recent years, approximately six million children have been reported each year to CPS, about 6–8 % of all children in the United States (these children lived in approximately 3.3 million households, since many reported households have more than one child).[11] About half of these reports were screened out without an investigation. CPS agencies investigated allegations involving approximately 3,000,000 children each year, nearly 4 % of all children. In 2011, approximately 700,000 children, about 1 % of all children, were found to have suffered from maltreatment, that is the allegations were substantiated (USDHHS 2011a). The allegations involving the other 2,300,000 were labeled unsubstantiated.

These are yearly numbers. A much higher percentage of all children born each year will be reported to a CPS agency at some point before they reach age 18 (Putnam-Hornstein et al. 2011; Bae et al. 2009). One recent study found that nearly 14 % of all children born in California between 1999 and 2002 were reported to CPS by age 5, two times the number reported in any given year. All but 9 % of these reported children ultimately received an investigation (although not always on the first report) and 5 % of all children in the birth cohort had a substantiated report by age 5 (Putnam-Hornstein et al. 2011). Many more of the children in this birth cohort will be the subjects of an investigated report between ages 6–18. In California, and across the United States, 40 % of all substantiated cases involve children five or younger; the rest involve older children (Child Trends 2011). If 5 % of children have a substantiated case by age 5, it is reasonable to project that approximately 8–10 % of all children of the children born in California will suffer from parental behaviors that are designated as actual maltreatment at some point during childhood.[12]

Confirmed cases of maltreatment are just the starting point in estimating the number of children who experience parenting that is likely to impair their safety or long-term basic development. As noted, CPS agencies in the U.S. investigate maltreatment allegations involving over three million children each year.[13] It is reasonable to assume that most substantiated cases involve parental conduct

---

[10] In the United States, issues related to child maltreatment are primarily within the purview of each state and often vary by county within states. Definitions of maltreatment vary, as do state policies regarding when to investigate and or substantiate an allegation of maltreatment. It is difficult to compare data across states because it often is unclear how a particular term is being used. All data should be approached with great caution.

[11] The number of households is key, since the needed resources will be determined by the number of parents that must be served. The number of children in the total population has been increasing over the past 20 years, while referrals have remained relatively constant, so the percentage of children reported varies over time.

[12] The 8–10 % estimate assumes that some of the children who have a substantiated case after they are five also will have had a previous substantiated case before age 5.

[13] There is out of six million reported children. There is little research indicating why reports are screened out. Some studies find that a high percentage of these cases get reported again, but anecdotal evidence indicates that many are situations that do not involve inadequate parenting. Given the absence of good data, I have not included these cases in my estimates.

that threatens the child's safety and development (USDHHS 2005).[14] The opposite conclusion is not appropriate with respect to unsubstantiated cases, however. A number of studies find that a high percentage of children in unsubstantiated cases evidence significant developmental problems (Cross and Casanueva 2009). In addition, several longitudinal studies have found that children reported to CPS agencies are considerably more likely to evidence serious behavioral problems over time, regardless of whether the report is substantiated, than are children from similar socio-economic households and neighborhoods who have not been reported to CPS (Hussey et al. 2005; Kohl et al. 2009; Mersky and Topitzes 2010). Thus, it seems reasonable to assume that most children in investigated cases, both substantiated and unsubstantiated, or 4 % of all children in any given year, have experienced highly inadequate parenting threatening their safety or basic long-term development.

Again, these are yearly figures; the California data indicate that over 12 % of children born between 1999 and 2002 had an investigated report by age 5 (Putnam-Hornstein et al. 2011). In addition, it appears that, throughout the United States, many children who are not reported to a CPS agency are living in households where the quality of parenting is similar to those that do come to the attention of CPS. There is great variation in the level of reports and substantiations among the states. For example, in 2009 the rate of substantiated maltreatment varied from 31.7 per 1,000 children in Massachusetts to 1.2 per 1,000 children in Pennsylvania (see Appendix).[15] Children are not 25 times more likely to be maltreated, or receive inadequate parenting, in Massachusetts as in Pennsylvania. There seems to be little correlation between the level of reporting or substantiation in a state and the known risk factors for maltreatment that are present in that state (such as poverty rate).[16] In addition, there is the data from the National Incidence Study (NIS), a Congressionally mandated study that has been conducted four times, with the goal of generating estimates of maltreatment based both on actual reports and information from community professionals across a broad spectrum of agencies regarding situations they believe constituted maltreatment but were not reported to CPS (Sedlak et al. 2010). Findings from the NIS indicate that many instances of "maltreatment" go unreported. The NIS estimates of maltreatment are about 50 % higher than reported rates (Sedlak et al. 2010). Most of the unreported cases involve emotional or educational neglect, not physical or sexual abuse.

Based on the California data, other studies (Sabol et al. 2004), and the NIS estimates, it appears that at least 15 % of children will experience some form of parental behavior that constitutes legally defined maltreatment at some point during childhood. Young children are at greatest risk (Child Trends 2011; Wulzcyn 2009). Unfortunately, for children from poor families that number goes up dramatically; as many as 35–40 %of white and African-American children living in low income families may be reported to CPS at some point before turning 18 (Putnam-Hornstein et al. in press; Sabol et al. 2004; IOM-NRC 2012). The same does not appear true with respect to low-income Latino families, especially if the parents are non-native (Dettlaff this volume, Chap. 8; Putnam-Hornstein et al. in press).

In estimating the need for programs to support parenting, it seems likely that there are additional children living in homes where their basic development is threatened by highly inadequate parenting that does not constitute maltreatment under various states' definitions. Since there are no studies that attempt to quantify the number of children living in households where the parenting is highly inadequate from a developmental perspective, it is necessary to estimate the percentage by looking at factors that are highly correlated with parenting. One indicator is the number of children living with

---

[14] Not all these cases involve safety, however. Some are situations of educational neglect and many cases involving teens are situations of high family conflict. In addition, not all of these cases involved maltreatment by parents. Some physical and sexual abuse cases involve actions by other caretakers or people not in the parent's household.

[15] The rate in Pennsylvania reflects the fact that its reporting law includes only abuse. However, under a separate law state agencies do deal with thousands of cases of "general neglect."

[16] If anything, those states with the highest percentage of poor, young, low-educated parents generally have lower reporting rates.

parents who are suffering from alcohol or substance addiction or severe mental health problems, since these conditions often affect parenting (NRC-IOM 2009b). According to various sources, 20 % of all children live with an adult who had a major depression in the past year (NRC-IOM 2009b) and nearly 12 % of children live with an alcoholic parent or a parent abusing drugs (Strengthening Families 2012). Many of these families are reported to CPS. We do not know what proportion of the others is providing highly inadequate; certainly not all, perhaps not most. But some are.

Another factor is the percentage of children who live in poverty, especially deep and prolonged poverty. According to a recent study, based on data from the Panel Study on Income Dynamics longitudinal study of families, over a third of children live in poverty at some point during their childhood (Ratcliffe and McKernan 2012). Over the past four decades, an average of 16 % of children were born to poor parents each year. Ten percent of all children were poor for 4–8 years and another 10 % were persistently poor – that is poor for 9 or more years during their childhood. Close to half of these children lived in deep poverty, less than half of the poverty level. Almost 5 % of white children and 37 % of all African American children were persistently poor. A significant proportion of the children raised in persistently poor families do not enter adulthood prepared for basic economic success. Nearly 30 % of persistently poor children do not complete high school, compared to 3 % of never-poor children. Twenty-two percent of persistently poor girls have a teenage premarital birth, compared with 2 % of never-poor girls (Ratcliffe and McKernan 2012).[17]

As noted above, there is mixed evidence regarding why living in poverty affects children's outcomes, especially the relationship of poverty and parenting behaviors. Certainly many parents who are poor provide adequate emotional care for their children, but cannot fully help their children overcome the effects of living in very poor neighborhoods, with bad schools, inadequate childcare, health hazards, etc. Some research finds that most poor parents do not exhibit different parenting practices than higher income parents (Hanson et al. 1997), although they may be less able to provide cognitive stimulation (Kalil et al. 2012). But there also is reason to believe that a proportion of parents who experience chronic poverty do not provide adequate parenting. There is a clear relationship between parental income and confirmed cases of physical abuse and neglect (Drake and Jonson-Reid this volume, Chap. 7; Putnam-Hornstein et al. 2011). Most of these parents have less than a high school education and low education is associated with poorer parenting.

There clearly is overlap in the various numbers, given the high correlation between poverty, these other factors, and being reported to CPS. But the correlation is not 100 %. It is reasonable to assume, based on the above numbers, that in addition to the 15 % of children experiencing parenting that legally constitutes maltreatment, an additional 5 % of children live with parents whose parenting is severely affected by poverty and/or mental health/substance use so that their children's basic development is compromised (SAMSHA 2009). Thus, I estimate that approximately 20 % of children experiencing highly inadequate parenting at some point during childhood.

On the positive side, after rising steadily and dramatically for 30 years, reports and substantiations of physical and sexual abuse have declined dramatically since 1994, as have estimates of these occurrences in the NIS (IOM-NRC 2012; Finkelhor and Jones 2006; Sedlak et al. 2010). Other indicators of factors associated with poor parenting, including domestic violence, births to young mothers, substance abuse by parents, and low parent education have also declined. The only factor that has not declined is neglect reports, which is puzzling given the other changes.

The rate of bad outcomes for children also is going down, which may reflect decline in very poor parenting, as well as the impact of various social programs (Wald 2012a). Births to teenaged mothers have fallen by more than 25 % since 1980, to a 40-year low. The drop in births has been driven by a decline in teen pregnancies; there has not been an increase in the abortion rate for young women. Youth-crime rates also are dramatically lower, particularly the violent crime rate, which has fallen

---

[17] These figures are only for children in persistently poor families; not ever-poor families (Duncan et al. 2010b).

more than 50 % from its peak in the mid-1990s. It is now lower than in 1980. Likewise, the percentage of youth who report engaging in either binge drinking or any drug use other than marijuana, the behaviors most predictive of later problems, have declined substantially. Binge drinking declined by almost 50 % and drug use by one-third between 1980 and 2010.

Even with these declines, the magnitude of the number of parents needing help and support in order to provide adequate parenting poses significant challenges for designing and funding any system to work with these families and in recruiting the large number of trained personnel needed to make services effective. At present, only a small percentage of these families come under the formal supervision of the CPS system; there is no other *system* dedicated to helping parents. It is critical that a system of parenting programs and services be available to all parents who need them. While such a system would not have the coercive powers of the CPS system, it should include active outreach and some monitoring of parental conduct, not just a variety of services for parents who actively seek help.

Towards a New System of Support for (and Regulation of?) Parenting

I turn now to examining the issues regarding the development and design of systems that have the goal of protecting children from harmful parenting and supporting parents experiencing significant difficulties in interacting with their children. I first look at situations where the parenting requires involvement of the CPS system. I then examine possible approaches to addressing parenting that should not be considered maltreatment, but that needs a more focused approach than is currently available. My goal is to identify a number of the key issues that need to be resolved in developing effective approaches to helping children attain the proposed outcomes. I do not try to resolve these issues. I believe that these need to be debated by the field and then there should be efforts that entail major legislative changes. Many of the other chapters in this volume focus on one or more of the issues I identify.

Protection from Imminent Serious Harm

The task of providing services for children who need protection from serious physical harm or sexual abuse is now assigned to specialized child protective agencies or departments. I concur with this allocation of responsibility (cf. Bergman 2010). These situations need to be the responsibility of a specialized government agency because protecting these children may require actions against the parent's will, including removal of the child from the home and even termination of parental rights (Wald 1976). In addition, child protection agencies must perform a variety of functions, including investigation and working with courts; these activities require an organization with very different structures, personnel, and resources from those that are likely to be best for working with parents through voluntary services.

While a CPS system is necessary, there has been considerable debate over the past 50 years with respect to both the proper scope of CPS jurisdiction and the goals of state involvement. The core question is what types of harms to children justify coercive intervention through CPS (Wald 1975). There has been concern that the CPS system is both over- and under- inclusive in terms of interventions with families (Waldfogel 1998). There also is debate regarding what outcomes for children the system should try to attain for those children appropriately in the system – should the goal of intervention be solely protecting the child from maltreatment or should it attempt to more generally enhance the well-being of children brought under CPS supervision (Wulczyn et al. 2005). Finally, there is a great deal of concern that the current system is not delivering services effectively. All of these issues are interrelated.

With respect to the scope of CPS jurisdiction, the basic issue is whether harms other than the threat of physical injuries and sexual abuse justify CPS intervention (cf. Wald 1975; Waldfogel 1998; Lindsey 2004; Bartholet 1999, 2012; Weaver 2011; Dwyer 2008). I estimate that no more than 20 % of the three million children whose situations are investigated by CPS have true safety needs, from physical abuse, sexual abuse, or severe neglect. Less than 10 % of investigated cases, involving about 250,000 children, lead to removal of the child. There are significant variations with respect to the potential for serious harm by the age of the child; young children appear to be at greater risk of physical harm, while teens suffer the most sexual abuse.

The remaining cases that come to the attention of CPS involve parenting that threatens children's emotional, social, and academic development, not physical safety. Should situations where the risk to the child is primarily with respect to emotional injuries and/or poor academic, social, or emotional developmental be handled in the CPS system? Under current procedures in most states, there is limited focus on emotional injuries and virtually none where the only problem is developmental delays, unless there also is a threat of physical injury or sexual abuse. Probably, most of these situations are referred to CPS as neglect allegations. The vast majority of cases that are investigated by CPS agencies, especially neglect cases, do not result in formal supervision of the family, even where there is some evidence of harmful parenting. Given that many of the children in cases that are not substantiated show long-term developmental problems and that many children at risk of poor development due to poor parenting are not being reported to CPS, some commentators argue for more CPS involvement and want legislatures to provide more resources to enable CPS agencies to work with these families (Bartholet 1999; Dwyer 2008). Several commentators call for more extensive changes, involving the greater use of termination of parental rights and placing children more quickly for adoption (Bartholet 2012; Dwyer 2008). Many other commentators have argued against this view; they would like to see different approaches to working with these families (Bergman 2010; US Advisory Board 1991). Some argue that mandatory reporting should be eliminated in order to reduce the reliance on the CPS system (Worley and Melton 2012; Melton 2005; cf. Drake and Jonson-Reid 2007).

I have recently written about why states should reduce, not expand, the role of CPS (Wald 2009, 2012b), with the concentration being on situations that raise major safety concerns. I will just briefly summarize my major reasons here.[18] First, given the coercive nature of the CPS system, it is necessary to have clear definitions of the conduct that justifies applying the full power of the state. This is very difficult to do with respect to parenting that does not involve the threat of physical injury or sexual relations with the child, such as emotional harm or general neglect (Wald 1991).[19] In addition, not enough is known about the relationship of parenting to specific *developmental* outcomes, or the impact of interventions as a means of achieving these outcomes, to justify *coercive* interventions in situations that do not pose the threat of imminent harm. Finally, the best evidence indicates the CPS system is not effectively dealing with cases of inadequate parenting that are currently in the system (IOM-NRC 2012).

Since the passage of the Adoption and Safe Family Act of 1997 (ASFA 1997), which added promotion of children's well-being to the list of desired outcomes for children under CPS supervision, CPS systems must do more than provide children under supervision with safety and with permanence, the two outcomes that had driven the system since the 1970s. There remains, however, considerably controversy over what well-being means and whether CPS can promote broader outcomes (Wulczyn et al. 2005). There is relatively little research on the impact of CPS intervention on the development

---

[18] Bartholet and Dwyer, as well as some other commentators, argue that the child protection system is based on a presumption for parental autonomy and undervalues children's rights and interests. I believe that the recommendations I am making here flow from a children's interest perspective. However, it is beyond the scope of this chapter to address fully the parental autonomy-child's rights debate.

[19] There also is reasonable clarity in situations involving refusal to provide critical medical treatment and active failure to send children to school.

of children who are not placed into foster care; most research has focused on whether services prevent the recurrence of the reported maltreatment. The limited evidence available indicates that becoming known to the CPS system does not lead to improved well-being for most of children (Wulczyn et al. 2005); in fact, some studies find that as many as half of all reported families get re-reported within 5 years (Thompson and Wiley 2009; cf. Fluke et al. 2008). This is not surprising since families referred to CPS receive "minimal services unless the situation is so severe that the child is removed from the home" (Schene 2005, p. 5; USDHHS 2003).

Some experts believe that a variety of new programs have been shown to work successfully with maltreating parents to meet their children's developmental needs (Chaffin et al. 2012; IOM-NRC 2012). New interventions targeted directly to children also are promising (IOM-NRC 2012; Casanueva et al. 2008). However, the capacity of CPS systems to implement these programs on a widespread basis has been questioned (IOM-NRC 2012, pp. 70, 73–74) and many (but not all) of the new interventions require intensive, costly services. If new resources become available, they should be used by CPS to meet the major needs of children who have been physical or sexually harmed, including their mental health and academic needs, as well as to provide them with safety and stability. To have the capacity and resources to do this, it is necessary to limit the scope of the CPS system. I believe that CPS is not likely to ever get the additional resources that would be needed to work effectively with the 75 % of families in investigated cases that now do not receive supervision or services from CPS, let alone with new cases that would come in under an expanded definition of maltreatment (Wald 2009). In an era of limited budgets, CPS must compete with schools, childcare, and health coverage for funds. Each of these systems has politically powerful advocates. It is highly unlikely that most political leaders will support the level of resources needed to develop high-quality programs targeted at responding to "neglect." If there is to be support for services to these children, it is much more likely to come through the health or education systems.

Promoting Attainment of Basic Outcomes in Adulthood: Choosing a Delivery System

If policy-makers want to help all children reach adulthood adequately ready, in terms of skills and behaviors, to be able to earn a basic living, and to have basic mental health, it will be necessary to do more than just expand the CPS system, even if that were a good idea.[20] The CPS system does not have jurisdiction to serve the millions of children in unsubstantiated cases, misses too many children, does not have a preventive component, and does not have the type of community support and confidence needed to effectively work with large numbers of parents. Alternative approaches are needed.

The challenges in designing a voluntary system targeting families exhibiting, or at risk of engaging in, highly inadequate parenting have been recognized for many years (Polansky et al. 1972; Kaplan et al. 2009). Many of these parents suffer from multiple problems and, while they are not intentionally doing things that hurt their children, it often is difficult to engage them in services and sustain their participation. Moreover, these parents are concentrated geographically in parts of cities and in rural areas where there often are few organizations capable of providing high quality services, the children often go to the worst schools, and may have limited access to health care.

In addition, the knowledge base for designing services is limited, although a number of successful programs have been identified in recent years (NRC-IOM 2000, pp. 378–380). It is clear that services must go beyond the types of parent education that have too long been a staple in child protection

---

[20] My discussion focuses largely on services for younger children, primarily birth to five and to a lesser extent 6–12 year olds. Many of the issues regarding teens are different and have received little attention, except for teens in foster care.

system; "evaluations of many forms of parenting education programs support the conclusion that (while) most programs for parents of young children can result in modest improvements in some aspects of parenting…such modest changes yield few and usually insignificant changes in children's developmental outcomes." (Duncan et al. 2010a, p. 39: McGroder and Hyra 2009). To be effective, programs must teach and model skills, not just provide information. There are debates about the level of needed services. Some experts stress the need for very intensive, high-quality services, delivered over a lengthy period by well-trained professionals, while others believe that shorter, less intensive interventions are possible, even desirable (cf. IOM-NRC 2012; Lieberman and Van Horn 2008; Bakermans-Kranenburg et al. 2003; Bernard et al. 2012). There is agreement, however, that in order to engage parents, programs must be positive, strength-based, and flexible in providing services to meet individual families needs. The limited success of prior efforts requires new thinking about designing policies to address these families.

In designing a system to work with parents, three major questions must be addressed; first, what are the necessary services; second, how are they best delivered; and third, is it best to build on what we have now or is a new system needed? I focus here primarily on issues related to delivery, although the type of services and mode of delivery are related. In the following discussion, I describe three major approaches currently being used to deliver services-one that focuses primarily on children, the other two on parents. I then identify some of the questions that must be resolved in choosing among alternatives. My goal is to frame the discussion that is necessary, not to propose a particular approach.

(a) Differential Response

While most people argue for a contraction, not expansion, of CPS involvement, there is a second debate regarding the reach of the CPS system. In recent years, many states have limited the types of cases that come under direct CPS supervision but have tried to use a maltreatment report as an occasion for connecting some of the families reported to CPS to alternative treatments; this is generally referred to as differential response (Fuller this volume, Chap. 24; Waldfogel 2008, 2009a). Under differential response, reported cases that involve less risky situations are not just closed. Instead, these families are referred for "voluntary" services. Differential response is generally used in situations where the threat is to a child's long-term development, not safety. The vast majority of cases involve families where it has been determined that the child is not a victim of maltreatment (USDHHS 2010, p. 13; Waldfogel 2009a, b)

A differential response "system" is one possible way of addressing the needs of some of the children and parents I am discussing. While the services are provided by community agencies, starting with reports to the child protection system can serve as means of identifying families needing services, providing limited case management, and for keeping a history of reports. There is some indication that programs in several jurisdictions have had some positive long-term effects on family functioning (see Fuller this volume, Chap. 24; Loman and Siegel 2004a, b). Until other systems are set-up to help these families, differential response may be the best possible approach and needed to protect some children. In addition, if the family is part of the CPS system some of the services might be funded under Title IVE of the Social Security Act, an entitlement program and therefore a potential source of open-ended funds.

While it is too early to assess these efforts fully, there are many questions about relying on a system that begins with a report to CPS, and has close connections to the CPS system, as a means of responding to highly inadequate parenting (Brown et al. 2012). First, it would be available only to families who have been reported; there are no outreach components or prevention efforts.[21] Moreover, differential response still often requires an investigation process that consumes critical CPS resources. If the situations being chosen for differential response do not generally raise con-

---

[21] Minnesota is developing outreach to screened-out cases. See Minnesota PSOP program. http://www.dhs.state.mn.us/main/idcplg?IdcService=GET_DYNAMIC_CONVERSION&dID=143876

cerns regarding child safety, which appears to be the case, funding investigations for these situations is an inefficient use of resources.

More critically, from my perspective, differential response does not create a **system** for helping these families, that is a programmatic response with a dedicated funding stream, clear mandates regarding outcomes, and clear criteria for who is served. "Differential Response is not a program intervention or even a model of practice, but rather an "approach" to organizing child protective service" (Daro and Benedetti this volume, Chap. 14; Hughes et al. 2013). It generally consists of CPS agencies referring some families to a range of local social service programs that vary greatly in quality, approach, and effectiveness. An effective system for working with multi-problem families requires performance standards, accountability measures, regular monitoring, and consistent data collection and evaluation (Reynolds 1998). These are not likely to be developed in an approach that consists largely of CPS personnel making referrals in a non-systematic manner to a disparate group of local agencies. Moreover, it is unrealistic to assume that most CPS agencies, which are routinely challenged in providing adequate services to the children under supervision, will have the capacity to effectively organize and monitor an effective set of community services. In addition, most differential response programs have limited funding and are not designed to provide intensive, long-term services to the families. Perhaps such services are not necessary in many situations, but this is an issue that must be examined closely.

In order to fully assess the desirability of relying on differential response, it is necessary to examine the alternatives. I discuss in section (c) below a different approach to organizing a set of services that I believe are needed in order to help parents provide the types of care necessary to meet children basic developmental needs. In the proposed approach, families experiencing difficulties in providing adequate care would be connected directly to a variety of supportive services by health professionals, childcare personnel, teachers, and even through family members. There would be far fewer reports to CPS and changes in mandatory reporting laws. While it may be very difficult to engender the political will needed to expand other funding streams for the alternative approaches I describe below, I am concerned that the existence of differential response systems may deter legislators from examining and funding a more comprehensive approach to the needs of these parents and children. I look next at various other possible approaches.

(b) Increase Funding and Scope of Child-Focused Programs

A second way of trying to improve outcomes for children is by expanding and improving programs that primarily work with children themselves. The main systems are childcare, pre-school and, to a lesser degree, after-school programs and school-based programs for older youth, such as school health clinics. These programs are now offered in most communities. Some of these programs work with parents, but not generally in a systematic or intensive manner.

For the most part, these programs seek to improve the child's cognitive skills, and to some degree self-regulation and social skills, in order to improve school performance and to reduce the achievement gap of children from low-income families. There is substantial evidence that high-quality childcare and preschool can improve children's academic performance and general development, thereby closing the achievement gap and increasing the likelihood of social mobility (Barnett and Belfield 2006; Magnuson and Waldfogel 2005). While preschool alone is not likely to be sufficient in achieving these goals, it should be a central part of a comprehensive strategy aimed at reaching these outcomes (Kirp 2011; Ludwig and Sawhill 2007).

It is questionable, however, whether programs that focus primarily on working with the child can have a significant impact for many of the children living in very poor, highly disorganized families (Duncan and Magnuson 2004; NRC-IOM 2000). The impact of these programs may be greatest for children where the parenting is basically adequate, except for the lack of intellectual stimulation and academic support (Kalil et al. 2012; Brooks-Gunn and Markham 2005). In these situations, a great deal can be accomplished in settings outside the home, especially if accompanied by efforts to help the parents provide more support for their children's cognitive development. This may be particularly true with respect to low-income, low-education immigrant parents.

But there are several factors cutting against relying too heavily on regular early childhood education (ECE) programs as the central venue for reaching and working with multi-problem families. Most critically, for many children the impact of highly disorganized/hostile/detached parenting on their academic and social development may be too great to be compensated for by programs focused primarily on the children themselves, especially programs focused on improving cognitive abilities (Duncan and Magnuson 2004; NRC-IOM 2000). To help these children, it is critical to engage the parents more extensively, which often requires working in the home as well as in other settings (Lieberman and Van Horn 2008; NRC-IOM 2000). As one of the leading researchers on the impact of early childhood has stated "(t)he simple provision of rich, center-based learning experiences for young children is not in itself sufficient for preventing developmental lags if their brain circuits are burdened by anxieties and fears that result from adverse life circumstances. These disruptive experiences must be addressed directly" (Shonkoff et al. 2011, p. 14).

In addition, most ECE programs are not likely to have the incentives or capacity to carry out the needed activities. ECE is increasingly being assessed in terms of the proportion of children helped to become academically ready for kindergarten. Even with additional resources, many ECE programs may not want to work with the highest-risk families, since the success rate in terms of achieving school readiness may be low and the resources required extensive. Moreover, many of these parents do not enroll their children in childcare or preschool.

Still, it is worth exploring enhancement of ECE programs to address parenting. They are becoming universal in the U.S. for low-income families, which may make them an attractive, non-stigmatizing setting for all parents. It may be desirable to have children from highly inadequate families socializing with children from other families and the parents as part of support groups in these settings. Education is a large funding stream that will not disappear, although there are many demands for the funds. In a number of places, ECE programs are receiving consultations from mental health providers on how to work with children experiencing significant behavioral problems.

However, given the push to have most early childhood programs focus on cognitive development, it may be preferable to develop special programs, like Early Head Start, that are designed to work with intensively with both parents and children and that will deliver services in the home as well and in childcare settings. In any case, working with parents through ECE systems must be supplemented by programs that reach families with children under 2 and over 5, since most ECE programs focus only on children in this age range. The most likely role for early childhood and other school based programs is as a component in system that begins with strong parenting program for new parents (at least those who are at statistical risk of not providing adequate parenting) and specialized services for other parents who face special challenges in childrearing. I look now at the possible elements of such a system.

(c) Community-Based Programs Focused on Higher-Risk Parents and Children

In most communities, there are multiple health and social service programs that are designed to help to prevent the emergence of harmful parental behaviors, to promote positive parent–child interactions, and to help parents who are experiencing difficulties with parenting. Many of these are described throughout the chapters in this volume (see the chapters by Daro and Benedetti, Chap. 14, Molnar and Beardslee, Chap. 15, and Hashima, Chap. 16). These programs may be provided by government agencies, non-profit community organizations, and in some cases by profit-making entities.

There are three main programmatic approaches currently being employed to support and enhance parenting. One, the federal Women, Infants, and Children Program (WIC), focuses primarily on pregnant mothers. WIC provides nutritional and counseling services to low-income, nutritionally at risk pregnant women and mothers of young children. WIC serves 53 % of all infants born in the United

States (WIC at a Glance http://www.fns.usda.gov/fns). While WIC employs activities designed to encourage pregnant women to adopt healthful behaviors, including eating well and refraining from smoking, drinking, and using drugs during pregnancy, the major focus is on providing access to medical care and nutrition. It does not focus on parenting skills outside of this domain.

The second, home visiting, focuses more directly on improving parenting, through home based parenting support and education, usually offered at the time a woman becomes pregnant or gives birth (see Daro and Benedetti this volume, Chap. 14). These programs now reach 500,000 children (Ammerman et al. 2010). Services are offered for differing periods of time, in some cases as long as 3 years (Paulsell et al. 2010). The mostly widely known program model is the Nurse Family Partnership (NFP) model, developed by David Olds over a number of years (Olds 2010). It currently provides services primarily to first time, young mothers; this is the group for whom the program has demonstrated the most effectiveness. There also are a number of other home visiting models that have been implemented in different jurisdictions. Although home visiting has been tried at the local level for over 40 years, it is just now is receiving major federal support, through a large-scale experimental initiative to test the effectiveness of various models (USDHHS 2011b).

The third approach seeks to improve children's cognitive and social development, while also improving parenting skills, through center-based education and support services that involve extensive focus on the parent as well as the child (distinguishing these programs from the types of preschool efforts discussed above). This approach includes Early Head Start and various preschool programs that include heavy parental involvement, such as the Chicago Parent Child Centers and some Head Start programs. Preschool programs that actively engage parents have been shown to have an impact on children's long-term behaviors, perhaps even to a greater degree than on their cognitive development (Schweinhart et al. 2005). There are several efforts underway to expand the capacity of childcare centers and preschools to work with multi-problem families. One major effort is Educare, a network of programs that provides at-risk children and their parents with center-based childcare, preschool, and social work support from birth to age 5 (Kirp 2011).[22]

In most communities, there also are various structured programs that provide skills training and advice to parents experiencing difficulties in childrearing. These generally are available to all parents on a voluntary basis, although they usually serve families with children ages 2 and older. Three such programs use well-developed and replicable models: the Triple P-Positive Parenting Program (Triple P) (Sanders et al. 2003; Prinz et al. 2009), Incredible Years (IY) (Webster-Stratton 2005), and the Strengthening Families Program (SFP) (Strengthening Families 2012). All three employ relatively short interventions, from 1 to 20 sessions (Barth 2009). In addition, some communities have available more intensive clinical services for parents experiencing significant problems in interacting with their children. These families may self-refer or be referred by organizations working with the child or parent. Two highly regarded programs are intensive parent child therapy (Lieberman and Van Horn 2008), which works with parents experiencing a variety of parenting problems and Multi-Systemic Therapy (Henggeller 1999), which focuses on families whose children are committing delinquent acts. These programs are distinguished by their intensity, the need for highly trained personnel, and expense. Most of the specific programs just described are considered evidence-based in that there is research indicating that the model of program delivery has proven more effective for participants than doing nothing or than being in a comparison programs.

---

[22] The program resembles the Abecedarian Project, conducted in the 1970s. In Abecedarian, a group of "high-risk" new parents were provided home-based parenting support; their children also received very high quality childcare and preschool from infancy until kindergarten. A long-term follow-up of the participants indicates that the program led to better long-term outcomes for many of the children. However, even with a program of this intensity and quality, 28 % of the children did not graduate high school and there was no apparent impact on the level of criminal convictions or substance abuse (Campbell et al. 2012). Interestingly, Abecedarian had stronger impact on college going and social mobility than on helping the bottom group, indicating that it might be best for poor, but reasonably functioning, parents.

In addition to such "evidence-based" programs, virtually all communities support a number of local programs that provide various services to parents experiencing difficulties with a child, such as family resources centers and community mental health centers (Hashima this volume, Chap. 16). While there are indications that some of these programs are highly effective, most have not been evaluated in a reasonably scientific manner. There is virtually no evidence about how small, good programs can be scaled to reach large numbers of families.

There clearly is clinical knowledge about how to work with these families (Lieberman and Van Horn 2008), and a number of individual programs in local jurisdictions offer high-quality services to multi-problem families. However, while a small a number of programs show positive results, the impacts generally are modest in size. In fact, even in programs considered as proven to be effective, a significant portion of the children have still experienced substantial problems upon follow-up, and the success may have involved children living with better functioning parents. Often it is not clear whether the programs are reaching the most highly disorganized, multi-problem families or having results with such families. This is true with respect to home visiting, Early Head Start, and parenting programs like Triple P and the Incredible Years. For example, in a recent report Olivia Golden and other researchers concluded that most home visiting programs were not reaching, or serving effectively, mothers suffering from depression (Golden and Fortuny 2011). Daro and Benedetti conclude that "the current prevention service network and system has failed to reach deep into the at-risk population and has not created the contextual and normative change necessary to maximize the safety and healthy development of the nation's children" (this volume, Chap. 14, p. 296; Walker et al. 2012). In reaching this conclusion, Daro is speaking about programs where reducing maltreatment is the goal. It may actually be the case that current programs are better able to reduce maltreatment than alter parenting that impairs children's longer-term development, which would make their conclusion even more sobering.

Most importantly, no state or community provides these types of services in a systematic manner that integrates the various approaches, connects families to on-going support as children age, and that examines community needs and makes funding priorities based on needs.[23] They largely work independently of each other, have different funding streams, and may serve different target populations. They often focus on a single problem, such as substance use, mental health, or domestic violence. Most of the programs do not have resources to reach even the full target population. Unlike school systems, that now are being held accountable for producing educational outcomes, no agency or program is accountable for producing any outcomes for the children.

Developing a Coordinated System

Given the depth of the barriers facing many multi-problem parents, it may not be adequate to just improve existing programs and make them available to all parents who seek them out. To really help children, a much more coordinated set of services, starting during pregnancy and available for as long as needed, is likely to be necessary.

Figure 13.1 shows what such a system might look like for parents with infants and young children. It would include several core programs, such as WIC and home-visiting, that would be provided to parents on a universal or targeted basis. There would then be three possible tracks of services for parents and children. One track would be for children in homes where there was no need for special parenting services; this track would focus on the child and include high-quality child care and pre-school designed to help prepare children for academic success in K-12. A second track would offer

---

[23] There are a few such efforts being tried on an experimental basis, such as the Durham Initiative (Dodge et al. 2004; Daro 2009) and the well-known Harlem Children's Zone. Community-wide initiatives are difficult to implement and sustain; a number have failed (Daro et al. 2009a, b; Walker et al. 2012).

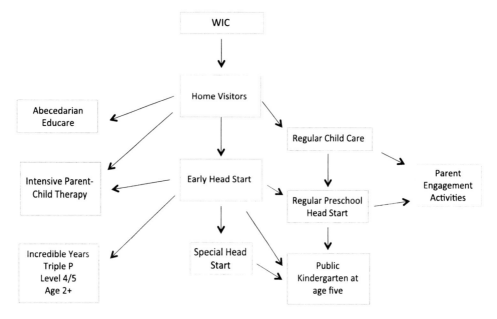

Fig. 13.1 Support system flowchart

services, such as Early Head Start and special preschool, for families that needed more focus on parenting; these programs would work with both the parents and the children. Finally, some children and parents with special needs would receive intensive services, such as Educare, intensive parent–child therapy, and Triple P. WIC personnel, home visitors, pediatricians, childcare and preschool personnel, and teachers might be both direct service providers and charged with referring families that need additional services to the appropriate resource, based on their knowledge of the family. As discussed below, this approach might include incentives to parents for participation, contingent upon their active participation; it would not just make services available and hope that all parents will voluntarily participate. Certain elements, such as home visits, might be made mandatory as a condition for receiving some forms of income support or job training.

The particular programs identified below are current programs that have a significant evidence base; they are examples of possible elements, not necessarily the recommended set of programs. One model for the creation of such a system might be Project LAUNCH, a system of coordinated services currently being tested in 35 communities throughout the United States, funded by the federal Department of Health and Human Services (http://projectlaunch.promoteprevent.org).

Moving Forward-Five Core Issues

There are a number of issues that must be resolved in designing a system that responds to parents' needs and is likely to improve the chances that children will have successful outcomes. Given the limited success of past efforts to help parents and alter problematic behaviors, there needs to be careful thought not only about the theory behind each program but also about the challenges of implementation.[24] It is rare that legislation establishing and funding programs addresses issues of

---

[24] Designing a system, or even individual programs, that can provide quality services may be especially hard in rural areas, as well as in cities with high levels of poverty. Yet, a large percentage of the target parents and children live in these areas. Policy proposals, and legislation, often ignore the special challenges created by geography.

implementation. It may be better to try to do a small number of things well than to continue to experiment with the wide range of approaches currently being tried.

1. Multiple Programs v. Small Number

   At present, a wide-range of program models are being utilized in different jurisdictions, even where there is an attempt to use evidence-based practices. Different jurisdictions employ various home visitor models, parent–child behavior modification models, etc. One key issue is whether to continue to support the use of multiple programs models or to concentrate funding on a small number of models and establish procedures to continuously improve these programs' through research and evaluation. As Daro and Benedetti discuss in their chapter, there are arguments for each approach.

   A number of factors support encouraging and funding local variation. Most communities have a variety of services in place that are not easy to alter. Building a more uniform approach around a small number of program models would require getting Congress and state legislatures to alter funding streams, which also is not easy to do. Given the absence of a single approach that has been clearly shown to be superior, many commentators suggest continued experimentation, encouraging states and localities to use a variety of both evidenced-based programs and local models in order to see which are most successful and for what populations. Allowing each community to select a program that best fits its capacities and integrates with local resources also may lead to better implementation. This is the approach ultimately adopted by the federal government to test home visitor programs and underlies the recommendations made by several committees of the National Academy of Sciences (NRC-IOM 2009a, b; IOM-NRC 2012).

   There is a strong argument, however, for adopting a very small number of programs and trying to build their capacity overtime. In families facing multiple problems, parenting is very difficult to change. In general, successful programs have a clear theory of how to influence both parent and child development (Reynolds 1998). It may be easier to improve the quality of available services if there are just a few models in operation. Rather than try to evaluate a large number of different approaches, which often leads to little really usable information, it may be preferable to implement the programs with the best available current theory and evidence and to create a capacity building entity to work with local units, engaging them in continuous improvement (Ammerman et al. 2010). Moreover, this approach may be superior from a research and evaluation perspective. Evaluation of a single program model may yield more useable information than the current scattered research approach, which often involves a small-scale evaluation of a particular program with no on-going research that builds knowledge. It also is possible to customize a program to meet the need for local variation.

   As a practical matter, moving to a very small number of models for any of the various approaches may not be politically feasible, as was evidenced by the reaction to the original intention of the federal Department of Health and Human Services to fund just one model in the home visiting experiment. This met widespread resistance by the field. Many programs have constituencies that can strongly influence funding. The research community always is calling for more research on a variety of approaches, without really addressing whether such research is likely to produce useable knowledge. But, I believe that the desire to do everything needs to be reexamined, particularly in an era of limited budgets. A more focused research agenda examining a small number of policy-relevant issues and designed to help existing programs improve, rather than create new models, should be discussed.

2. Expand Individual Programs or Build a System

   Whether it is decided to invest in multiple programs or a few models, there also is the issue of whether the various types of services should, and can, be integrated into a single systemic approach tying together the various services, as outlined above. Many people at the ground and policy levels push for an integrated, systemic approach. However, getting the funding and administrative structure for a coordinated system is very difficult; proponents of more coordination have been trying unsuccessfully for many years to change the behavior of federal, state, and local governments.

Funding, at both the federal and state levels is heavily siloed into different problem areas (mental health, domestic violence, substance abuse, etc.), with different agencies having oversight of different programs, making development of a fully coordinated system very difficult. The silo problem influences advocacy and research as well.

Given the politics, it may be best to continue funding a small number of specific programs at the federal and state levels and encourage local jurisdictions to develop coordinating mechanisms. The program(s) should be embedded in health and education systems, since these are the only systems with sufficient financial resources necessary to have a system of high quality programs. Clearly WIC should be supported, since parental participation in WIC reduces the likelihood of premature and low-birth weight infants, a group that is at high risk of developmental problems[25] (Almond and Currie 2010). For children 0–2, a high quality home health visitor program, such as the Olds model, could be adapted to work with a target population that exhibits multiple-risk (Boris et al. 2006). This would require connecting the HHV component into a system that provides treatment for mental health, substance abuse, and family violence. For somewhat older children, a substantial expansion of Early Head Start (EHS), which already is focused on working with higher-risk parents and children (Schumacher et al. 2006; Child Trends 2010; Ayoub et al. 2011), might be the best approach. These might be supplemented by one or several parent–child programs that have been tested and appear to work for fairly severe kinds of problems, such as Triple P and IY. Each of these approaches does have systemic qualities, although they are not coordinated with each other. They have program models and technical assistance capacity, although most operate more like a franchise without strong central control. Since most of these approaches are heavily dependent on federal support, it is possible to develop regulations or even new legislation that would focus on improving implementation, including perhaps giving less discretion to localities with respect to implementation issues.

3. Targeting and Identification

The debate over whether programs should be available universally or only supported for use with targeted populations is a continuing conundrum. Daro and Benedetti (this volume, Chap. 14) review some of the arguments that relate to prevention of maltreatment.

The main argument for universality generally is that only universal programs generate high levels of support. Targeted programs for higher risk families are seen as both stigmatizing and unable to generate a large enough constituency to influence government funding. It seems questionable, however, whether a set of adequate services can be put in place without some targeting, at least for some of the programs, like WIC, home visiting, and Early Head Start. Only a portion of all parents require relatively intensive services in order to be able to provide their children with protection and the type of supportive parenting necessary for them to attain basic economic well-being as adults. However, helping these families requires far more resources than is currently being invested; for example, Early Head Start is available to only 3 % of the eligible population and this is an income-tested program (which may of course reflect the problem of generating support). While a substantial portion of the population might benefit from some parenting support, especially at the time of a first baby, it seems highly unlikely that legislatures will provide funds to serve the entire population – and this may not be a good use of limited resources.

There are several possible ways of targeting, including means testing, placing services in areas with high levels of likely need, or by using some form of risk assessment tool to identify and reach out to high need families. Over the past 20 years there have been significant advances in the use of risk assessment tools in the juvenile justice and child welfare systems to determine the level of supervision and services that should be offered to people whose behavior requires intervention.

---

[25] This is primarily true for premature or low birth weight children who live with low-income parents.

These apply to people who have already engaged in problematic behaviors and the issue is what type of actions to take. However, several recent studies have identified factors that help predict which parents will place their children at high risk of very poor developmental outcomes. While the studies are not consistent with respect to specific factors, they all find that it is the presence of multiple factors, not any single factor, which is predictive of future problems (Dishion et al. 2008; Felitti et al. 1998; Putnam-Hornstein and Needell 2011). Resources also should be focused on families where a child already is exhibiting behaviors that are predictive of poor long-term outcomes, for example children with high levels of school absences, substantial developmental delays, or significant problem behaviors at school or preschool.

In addition, even within the target population, different families may require different levels of intensity of services. A number of studies have reported good outcomes for children through the provision of what seem to be relatively limited services to parents. These include Family Check-Up (Dishion et al. 2008), Parent–child Interaction Therapy (Thomas and Zimmer-Gembeck 2011), and various other programs (Bakermans-Kranenburg et al. 2003; Bernard et al. 2012). However, other parents may need more long-term, intensive services (Henggeller 1999; Lieberman and Van Horn 2008; DePanfilis et al. 2008). More thinking is needed regarding how to decide who needs what level and type of services.

4. Incentives and Monitoring
A core issue that has received little attention is how to get parents to engage in needed services. Many of the target parents either do not seek out services or do not complete participate fully after entering services. At present, this is not an issue that receives much attention, in part because for most programs there are not enough resources to serve all who volunteer, so there is no need to force or try to induce other parents to participate. However, if a system is developed and sufficiently funded so that it reaches all target families, it may be necessary to do more than just offer parents services and hope that they will utilize them.

There are several different possible approaches.[26] One is to offer various "hard" services to parents in connection with parenting training. For example, there are efforts to provide job training programs and education programs for mothers in coordination with childcare centers (Golden and Fortuny 2011). This is being tried in connection with both Early Head Start and Head Start (King et al. 2009). Such services may be able to attract parents who might not otherwise participate in parent–child programs and sustain their engagement. A second approach is to offer financial incentives to parents who participate in parenting programs, such as childcare subsidies, housing subsidies, or some type of children's allowance. A critical issue is whether allowing the parent to participate in training programs or receive various financial rewards should be made contingent on participation in a parenting program and evidence of improved parenting, as Mexico is doing through the Progresa program and as some states have done in connection with the TANF program; given low engagement and high attrition rates in various programs, making benefits contingent seems like an important element (Aber and Rawlings 2011). The potential monitoring role of support personnel, like home visitors, also needs to be explored.

5. Economic Support
As noted above, poverty is a central factor in the lives of many parents who struggle to provide adequate parenting to their children. While the causal issues are still unresolved by researchers (Duncan et al. 2010b; Mayer 2010; Costello et al. 2003; Drake and Jonson-Reid this volume, Chap. 7), it seems clear that reducing poverty, especially deep and persistent poverty, is a necessary element of any approach to helping children achieve the four outcomes I have been discussing. Since the passage of "welfare reform" in 1996 (PRWORA 1996), poverty policy in the United States revolves

---

[26] One possibility that has been proposed is to license parents (Westman 1994). There are a number of reasons this is problematic (Wald and Sandmire 1990).

largely around connecting all parents with jobs. This approach has had successes, but many parents still live in deep and persistent poverty. Little attention is being paid to their plight and the plight of their children. It is unrealistic to expect that parents facing major problems just surviving economically can or will participate fully in programs designed to help them parent better. Parenting programs must be connected to income-support and job training.

There are some current experiments with "two-generational" approaches that seek to support the academic and social development of young children while working with their parents on education and job skills (Aspen Institute 2012). It is too early to assess the impact of these efforts. But any new discussion of approaches to improving parenting must be accompanied by a new discussion of approaches to helping parents acquire the education and work skills needed to enable them to parent well (Sabol and Chase-Lansdale 2012; Blank 2007; Halpern 1999).

Conclusion

In the United States, there is a major focus on improving educational institutions in order to enable more children to perform at higher academic levels in K-12 schools, to graduate from college, and to close the achievement gap. Under current public policy, educational institutions are increasingly being held accountable for specific outcomes, through the use of rewards and sanctions tied to these outcomes. There is now a great deal of attention being paid by policy-makers, child care and school personnel, advocates, and researchers to the educational policies and programs that might be useful in helping children better succeed in school.

In contrast, there is far less discussion and public debate about how to improve policies and programs designed to help children by improving parenting in homes where the parenting is highly inadequate. Rather, the main policy movement has been to extend education into early childhood, with a focus on the child not the parent. This is part of the historic pattern in the United States to try to improve children's lives primarily through education. This tendency is reflected even in the most significant scientific effort to address public policy for children, **Neurons to Neighborhoods**, the report of the NRC-IOM Committee on Integrating the Science of Early Childhood Development. While this group recognized the critical importance of adequate parental care, it's recommendations focused largely on improving child care, not on ways of improving parenting (NRC-IOM 2000, pp. 392–393). At the same time, there has been a tendency among advocates, practitioners, and academics concerned with social services to propose exceptionally broad and ambitious social policy and research agendas that have little chance of being funded or effectively implemented.

A new discussion is needed, one that begins by specifying the outcomes society wants for children. It must be recognized that priorities among these outcomes need to be established because different policies and investments are associated with each outcome. The policies and programs that are most effective at increasing college enrollment and completion, or closing the achievement gap, may be quite different from those that try to help children attain more basic outcomes. It is likely to take far more resources and more controversial policies in order to help the children who are at greatest risk with respect to the outcomes of safety and basic economic well-being. Focusing on these children and parents is perhaps the most challenging task, in terms of the value choices, generating political will, and implementing effective approaches. I believe that there is a moral imperative to work with the most disadvantaged (Wald and Martinez 2003). Hopefully, more policy-makers will come to this conclusion.

Acknowledgments I wish to thank David Chambers, Brett Drake, Emily Putnam-Hornstein, David Kirp, and Dee Wilson for their very helpful comments on earlier drafts and Nisha Kishyap for her research assistance.

Appendix

Child maltreatment victims aged 0–5 per 1,000 population in FFY 2009, by state.

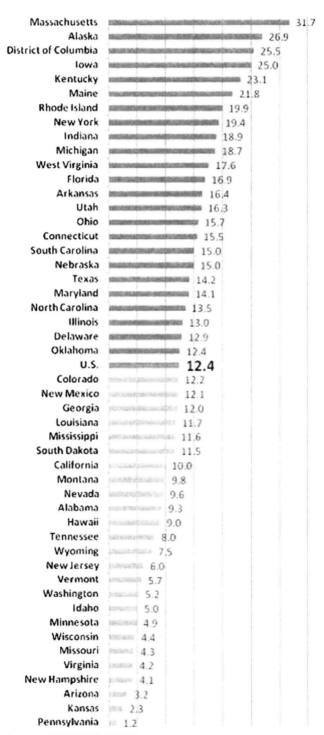

Massachusetts	31.7
Alaska	26.9
District of Columbia	25.5
Iowa	25.0
Kentucky	23.1
Maine	21.8
Rhode Island	19.9
New York	19.4
Indiana	18.9
Michigan	18.7
West Virginia	17.6
Florida	16.9
Arkansas	16.4
Utah	16.3
Ohio	15.7
Connecticut	15.5
South Carolina	15.0
Nebraska	15.0
Texas	14.2
Maryland	14.1
North Carolina	13.5
Illinois	13.0
Delaware	12.9
Oklahoma	12.4
U.S.	**12.4**
Colorado	12.2
New Mexico	12.1
Georgia	12.0
Louisiana	11.7
Mississippi	11.6
South Dakota	11.5
California	10.0
Montana	9.8
Nevada	9.6
Alabama	9.3
Hawaii	9.0
Tennessee	8.0
Wyoming	7.5
New Jersey	6.0
Vermont	5.7
Washington	5.2
Idaho	5.0
Minnesota	4.9
Wisconsin	4.4
Missouri	4.3
Virginia	4.2
New Hampshire	4.1
Arizona	3.2
Kansas	2.3
Pennsylvania	1.2

Source: USDHHS (2010)

References

Aber, L., & Rawlings, L. (2011). *North-South knowledge sharing on incentive based conditional cash transfer programs* (SP Discussion Paper NO. 1101). Washington, DC: The World Bank.

Aber, L., Allen, J., Carlson, V., & Cicchetti, D. (1989). The effects of maltreatment on development during early childhood: Recent studies and their theoretical, clinical, and policy implication. In D. Cicchetti & V. Carlson (Eds.), *Child maltreatment*. Cambridge, UK: Cambridge University Press.

Adoption and Safe Families Act of 1997. (1997). Public Law 105–189.

Almond, D., & Currie, J. (2010). *Human capital development before age five* (Handbook of labor economics, Vol. 4b). London: Elsevier.

Ammerman, T., Putnam, F., Bosse, N., Teeters, A., & Van Ginkel, J. (2010). Maternal depression in home visitation: A systematic review. *Aggression and Violent Behavior, 15*, 191–200.

Aspen Institute. (2012). *Two generations, one future: Moving parents and children beyond poverty together*. http://ascend.aspeninstitute.org/resources/two-generations-onefuture

Ayoub, C., Vallotton, C., & Mastergeorge, A. (2011). Developmental pathways to integrated social skills: The roles of parenting and early intervention. *Child Development, 82*(2), 583–600.

Bae, H., Solomon, P. L., & Gelles, R. J. (2009). Multiple child maltreatment recurrence relative to single recurrence and no recurrence. *Children and Youth Services Review, 31*, 617–624.

Bakermans-Kranenburg, M. J., Van IJzendoorn, M. H., & Juffer, F. (2003). Less is more: Meta-analysis of sensitivity and attachment interventions in early childhood. *Psychological Bulletin, 129*, 195–215.

Barnett, S., & Belfield, C. (2006). Early childhood development and social mobility. *The Future of Children, 16*(2), 73–98.

Barth, R. P. (2009). Preventing child abuse and neglect with parent training: Evidence and opportunities. *The Future of Children, 19*(2), 95–118.

Barth, R., Lloyd, E., Casanueva, C., Scarborough, A., Losby, J., & Mann, T. (2008). *Developmental Status and Early Intervention Needs of Maltreated Children*. Washington, DC: U.S. Department of Health and Human Services, Administration for Children, Youth, and Families.

Bartholet, E. (1999). *Nobody's children: Abuse and neglect, foster drift, and the adoption alternative*. Boston: Beacon.

Bartholet, E. (2012). Creating a child-friendly child welfare system: Effective early intervention to prevent maltreatment and protect victimized children. *Buffalo Law Review, 60*, 1315–1365.

Belsky, J. (1990). Child maltreatment: An ecological integration. *American Psychologist, 35*(4), 320–355.

Bergman, A. (2010). Child protective services has outlived its usefulness. *Archives of Pediatrics & Adolescent Medicine, 16*(10), 978–979.

Bernard, K., Dozier, M., Bick, J., Lewis-Morrarty, E., Lindhiem, O., & Carlson, E. (2012). Enhancing attachment organization among maltreated children: Results of a randomized clinical trial. *Child Development, 83*(2), 623–636.

Blank, R. (2007). Improving the safety net for single mothers who face serious barriers to work. *The Future of Children, 17*(2), 183–197.

Boris, N. W., Larrieu, J. A., Zeanah, P. D., Nagle, G. A., Steier, A., & McNeill, P. (2006). The process and promise of mental health augmentation of nurse home visiting programs: Data from the Louisiana Nurse family partnership. *Infant Mental Health Journal, 27*, 26–40.

Brooks-Gunn, J., & Markham, L. (2005). The contribution of parenting to racial and ethnic gaps in school readiness. *The Future of Children, 15*(1), 139–168.

Brown, B., Merkel-Holguin, L., & Hahn, A. (2012). *Differential response: Early implementation and fidelity*. Englewood: National Quality Improvement Center on Differential Response in Child Protective Services.

Campbell, et al. (2012). Adult outcomes as a function of an early childhood educational program: An Abecedarian project follow-up. *Developmental Psychology* online publication Jan. 16, 2012.

Casanueva, C. E., Cross, T. P., & Ringeisen, H. (2008). Developmental needs and individualized family service plans among infants and toddlers in the child welfare system. *Child Maltreatment, 13*(3), 245–258.

Center on the Developing Child. (2012). *Toxic shock: The facts*. Retrieved from http://developingchild.harvard.edu/topics/science_of_early_childhood/toxic_stress_response/

Chaffin, M., Hecht, D., Bard, D., Silovsky, J. F., & Beasley, W. H. (2012). A statewide trial of the safecare home-based services model with parents in child protective services. *Pediatrics, 129*(3), 509–515.

Child Trends. (2010). Early head start: Research findings. *Child Trends: Early Childhood Highlights, 1*(2), 1–3.

Child Trends. (2011). Young and vulnerable: Children five and under experience high maltreatment rates. *Child Trends: Early Childhood Highlights, 2*(2), 1–20.

Cicchetti, D., & Valentino, K. (2006). An ecological transactional perspective on child maltreatment: Failure of the average expectable environment and its influence upon child development. In D. Cicchetti & D. J. Cohen (Eds.), *Developmental psychopathology* (Risk, disorder, and adaptation 2nd ed., Vol. 3, pp. 129–201). New York: Wiley.

Connell, A., & Dishion, T. J. (2008). Reducing depression among at-risk early adolescents: Three year effects of a family-centered intervention embedded within schools. *Journal of Family Psychology, 22*, 574–585.

Costello, E. J., Compton, S., Keeler, G., & Angold, A. (2003). Relationships between poverty and psychopatholgy. *Journal of the American Medical Association, 290*(15), 2023–2029.

Cross, T., & Casanueva, C. (2009). Caseworker judgments and substantiation. *Child Maltreatment, 14*(1), 38–52.

Currie, J., & Widom, C. S. (2010). Long-term consequences of child abuse and neglect on adult economic well-being. *Child Maltreatment, 15*(2), 111–120.

Daro, D. (2009). Science and child abuse prevention: A reciprocal relationship. In K. Dodge & D. Coleman (Eds.), *Preventing child maltreatment: Community approaches*. New York: The Guilford Press.

Daro, D., Huang, L. A., & English, B. (2009a). *The Duke Endowment Child Abuse Prevention Initiative: Durham family initiative implementation report*. Chapin Hall: University of Chicago.

Daro, D., Huang, L. A., & English, B. (2009b). *The Duke Endowment Child Abuse Prevention Initiative: Strong communities implementation report*. Chapin Hall: University of Chicago.

DePanfilis, D., Dubowitz, H., & Kunz, J. (2008). Assessing the cost-effectiveness of family connections. *Child Abuse & Neglect, 32*, 335–351.

Dishion, T. J., Shaw, D., Connell, A., Gardner, F., Weaver, C., & Wilson, M. (2008). The family check-up with high-risk indigent families: Preventing problem behavior by increasing parents' positive behavior support in early childhood. *Child Development, 79*(5), 1395–1414.

Dodge, K. A., Berlin, L. J., Epstein, M., Spitz-Roth, A., O'Donnell, K., & Kaufman, M. (2004). The Durham family initiative: A preventive system of care. *Child Welfare, 83*, 109–128.

Drake, B., & Jonson-Reid, M. (2007). A response to Melton based on the best available data. *Child Abuse & Neglect, 31*, 343–360.

Duncan, G., & Magnuson, K. (2004). Individual and parent-based strategies for promoting human capital and positive behavior. In P. L. Chase-Lansdale, K. Kiernan, & R. Friedman (Eds.), *Human development across lives and generations: The potential for change*. Cambridge, UK: Cambridge University Press.

Duncan, G., & Murname, R. (2011). *Whither opportunity*. New York: Russell Sage.

Duncan, G., Brooks-Gunn, J., Yeung, W. J., & Smith, J. (1998). How much does childhood poverty affect the life chances of children? *American Sociological Review, 63*(3), 406–423.

Duncan, G., Ludwig, J., & Magnuson, K. (2010a). Child development. In P. Levine & D. Zimmerman (Eds.), *Targeting investments in children: Fighting poverty when resources are limited*. Chicago: University of Chicago Press.

Duncan, G., Ziol-Guest, K., & Kalil, A. (2010b). Early-childhood poverty and adult attainment, behavior, and health. *Child Development, 81*(1), 306–325.

Dwyer, J. (2008). The child protection pretense: States' continued consignment of newborn babies to unfit parents. *Minnesota Law Review, 93*, 407–492.

Felitti, V. J., Anda, R. F., Nordenberg, D., et al. (1998). Relationship of childhood abuse and household dysfunction to many of the leading causes of death in adults: the adverse childhood experiences (ACE) study. *American Journal of Preventive Medicine, 14*(4), 245–258.

Fiese, B., & Winter, W. (2010). The dynamics of family chaos and its relation to children's socio-emotional well-being. In G. Evans & T. Wachs (Eds.), *Chaos and its influence on children's development*. Washington, DC: American Psychological Association.

Finkelhor, D., & Jones, L. (2006). Why have child maltreatment and child victimization declined? *Journal of Social Issues, 62*(4), 685–716.

Fluke, J., Shusterman, G., Hollinshead, D., & Yuan, Y. (2008). Longitudinal analysis of repeated child abuse reporting and victimization: Multistate analysis of associated factors. *Child Maltreatment, 13*, 76–88.

Future of Children. (2006). Opportunity in America *16*(2).

Garbarino, J. (1977). The price of privacy in the social dynamics of child abuse. *Child Welfare, 56*(9), 565–575.

Golden, O., & Fortuny, K. (2011). *Improving the lives of young children: Two-generational services and interventions*. Washington, DC: The Urban Institute.

Goldstein, J., Freud, A., & Solnit, A. (1979). *Before the best interests of the child*. New York: Free Press.

Halpern, R. (1999). *Fragile families, fragile solutions*. New York: Columbia University Press.

Hanson, T., McLanahan, S., & Thomson, E. (1997). Economic resources, parental practices, and children's well-being. In G. Duncan & J. Brooks-Gunn (Eds.), *Consequences of growing up poor*. New York: Russell Sage.

Henggeller, S. (1999). Multisystemic therapy: An overview of clinical procedures, outcomes, and policy implications. *Child and Adolescent Mental Health, 4*(1), 2–10.

Hilyard, K., & Wolfe, D. (2002). Child neglect: developmental issues and outcomes. *Child Abuse & Neglect, 26*, 679–695.

Hughes, R., Rycus, J., Saunders-Adams, S., Hughes, L., & Hughes, K. (2013). Issues in differential response. *Research on Social Welfare Practice*. Published online 9 January 2013, 1–28.

Hussey, J., Chang, J., & Kotch, J. (2005). Child maltreatment in the United States: Prevalence, risk factors, and adolescent health consequences. *Pediatrics, 118*, 933–942.

Institute of Medicine & National Research Council. (2012). *Child maltreatment research, policy, and practice for the next decade*. Washington, DC: National Academies Press.

Kalil, A., Ryan, R., & Corey, M. (2012). Diverging destinies: Maternal education and the developmental gradient in time with children. *Demography*. Published online: 11 Aug 2012

Kaplan, C., Schene, P., DePanfilis, D., & Gilmore, D. (2009). Introduction: Shining light on child neglect. *Protecting Children, 24*, 2–8.

King, C. T., Glover, R. W., Smith, T. C., Coffey, R., Levy, B., Yoshikawa, H., Beardslee, W., & Kordsmeier, M. (2009). *The career/advance/pilot project: Recommended jobs strategy for families served by the community action project of Tulsa county.* Austin: Ray Marshall Center for the Study of Human Resources, Lyndon B. Johnson School of Public Affairs, The University of Texas at Austin.

Kirp, D. (2011). *Kids first.* New York: Public Affairs.

Kohl, P., Jonson-Reid, M., & Drake, B. (2009). Time to leave substantiation behind. *Child Maltreatment, 14*(1), 17–26.

Lansford, J., Dodge, K., Pettit, G., Bates, J., Crozier, J., & Kaplow, J. (2002). A 12-year prospective study of the long-term effects of early child physical maltreatment on psychological, behavioral, and academic problems in adolescence. *Archives of Pediatric and Adolescent Medicine, 156*, 824–830.

Levine, P., & Zimmerman, D. (2010). *Targeting investments in children: Fighting poverty when resources are limited.* Chicago: University of Chicago Press.

Lieberman, A., & Van Horn, P. (2008). *Psychotherapy with infants and young children.* New York: Guilford Press.

Lindsey, D. (2004). *The welfare of children.* New York: Oxford University Press.

Loman, L. A., & Siegel, G. L. (2004a). *Differential response in Missouri after five years: Final report.* St. Louis: Institute of Applied Research.

Loman, L. A., & Siegel, G. L. (2004b). *Minnesota alternative response evaluation: Final report.* St. Louis: Institute of Applied Research.

Lonne, B., Parton, N., Thompson, J., & Harries, M. (2009). *Reforming child protection.* London: Routledge.

Ludwig, J., & Sawhill, I. (2007). *Success by ten* (Policy Brief No. 2007-02). The Brookings Institution.

Magnuson, K., & Waldfogel, J. (2005). Early childhood care and education: effects on ethnic and racial gaps in school readiness. *The Future of Children, 15*(1), 169–196.

Mayer, S. (1997). *What money can't buy: Family income and children's life chances.* Cambridge, MA: Harvard University Press.

Mayer, S. (2010). Revisiting an old question: How much does parental income affect child outcomes? *Focus, 27*(2), 21–26.

McGroder, S., & Hyra, A. (2009). *Developmental and economic effects of parenting programs for expectant parents and parents of preschool-age children.* Philadelphia, PA: Pew Foundation Partnership for America's Economic Success.

Melton, G. (2005). Mandated reporting: A policy without reason. *Child Abuse & Neglect, 29*(1), 9–18.

Mersky, J., & Topitzes, J. (2010). Comparing early adult outcomes of maltreated and non-maltreated children: A prospective longitudinal investigation. *Children and Youth Services Review, 32*, 1086–1096.

National Research Council & Institute of Medicine. (2000). In J. Shonkoff & D. Phillips (Eds.), *From neurons to neighborhoods.* Washington, DC: National Academy Press.

National Research Council & Institute of Medicine, Committee on Depression, Parenting Practices, and the Healthy Development of Children, Board on Children, Youth, and Families, & Division on Behavioral and Social Sciences and Education. (2009a). *Preventing mental, emotional, and behavioral disorders among young people.* Washington, DC: National Academies Press.

National Research Council & Institute of Medicine, Committee on Depression, Parenting Practices, and the Healthy Development of Children, Board on Children, Youth, and Families, & Division on Behavioral and Social Sciences and Education. (2009b). *Depression in parents, parenting, and children: Opportunities to improve identification, treatment, and prevention.* Washington, DC: National Academies Press.

Nikulina, V., Widom, C., & Czaja, S. (2011). The role of childhood neglect and childhood poverty in predicting mental health, academic achievement and crime in adulthood. *American Journal of Community Psychology, 48*, 309–321.

Olds, D. (2010). The Nurse family partnership. In R. Haskins & W. Barnett (Eds.), *New directions for America's preschool policies.* Washington, DC: NIERR and Brookings.

Paulsell, D., Avellar, S., Martin, E., & Del Grosso, P. (2010). *Home visiting evidence of effectiveness review: Executive summary.* Washington, DC: U.S. Department of Health and Human Services, Administration for Children and Families, Office of Planning, Research and Evaluation.

Personal Responsibility and Work Opportunity Reconciliation Act of 1996. (1996). *Public Law* 104–193.

Pianta, R., Egeland, B., & Erickson, M. (1989). The antecedents of maltreatment: results of the mother-child interaction project. In D. Cicchetti & V. Carlson (Eds.), *Child maltreatment.* Cambridge, UK: Cambridge University Press.

Polansky, N., Borgman, R., & DeSaix, C. (1972). *The roots of futility.* San Francisco: Jossey Bass.

Prinz, R., Sanders, M., Shapiro, C., Whitaker, D., & Lutzger, J. (2009). Population-based prevention of child maltreatment: The U.S. Triple P System Population Trial. *Prevention Science.* Published online Jan. 22, 2009.

Proceedings of the National Academy of Sciences. (2012). Biological embedding of early Social adversity: From fruit flies to kindergartners. *9*(2), 17143–17308. 16, Oct. 2012.

Putnam-Hornstein, E., & Needell, B. (2011). Predictors of child protective service contact between birth and age five: An examination of California's 2002 birth cohort. *Children and Youth Services Review, 33*(11), 2400–2407.

Putnam-Hornstein, E., Webster, D., Needell, B., & Magruder, J. (2011). A public health approach to child maltreatment surveillance. *Child Abuse Review, 20,* 256–273.

Putnam-Hornstein, E., Needell, B., King, B., & Johnson-Motoyama, M. (in press). Race, poverty, and maternal nativity: an examination of risk and protective factors for involvement with child protective services. *Child Abuse & Neglect.*

Ratcliffe, C., & McKernan, S. M. (2012). *Child poverty and its lasting consequence.* Urban Institute Low-Income Working Families Paper 21

Reardon, S. (2011). The widening academic achievement gap between the rich and the poor: New evidence and possible explanations. In T. Smeeding, R. Erikson, & M. Jantii (Eds.), *Persistence, privilege, and parenting: The comparative study of intergenerational mobility.* New York: Russell Sage.

Repetti, R., Taylor, S., & Seeman, T. (2002). Risky families: Family social environments and the mental and physical health of offspring. *Psychological Bulletin, 128*(2), 330–336.

Reynolds, A. (1998). Developing early childhood programs for children and families at risk: Research-based principles to promote long-term effectiveness. *Children and Youth Services Review, 20*(6), 503–523.

Sabol, T., & Chase-Lansdale, P. L. (2012). *The influence of low-income children's participation in head start on parents' educational attainment.* Presentation at the annual conference of the Association of Public Policy Analysis and Management, Baltimore.

Sabol, W., Colton, C., & Polousky, E. (2004). Measuring child maltreatment risk in communities: a life table approach. *Child Abuse & Neglect, 28,* 967–983.

Sanders, M. R., Markie-Dadds, C., & Turner, K. M. T. (2003). *Theoretical, scientific and clinical foundations of the Triple P-Positive Parenting Program: A population approach to the promotion of parenting competence.* Queensland: The Parenting and Family Support Centre, The University of Queensland.

Sawhill, I., Winship, S., & Grannis, K. (2012). *Pathways to the middle class: Balancing personal and public responsibilities.* Washington, DC: Brookings Institution.

Schene, P. (2005). The emergence of differential response. *Protecting Children, 20*(2&3), 4–7.

Schumacher, R., Hamm, K., & Goldstein, A. (2006). *Starting off right: Promoting child development from birth in state early care and education initiatives.* Washington, DC: Center on Law and Social Policy.

Schweinhart, L., Montie, J., Xiang, Z., Barnett, W. S., Belfield, C., & Nores, M. (2005). *The high/scope Perry Preschool study through age 40-summary, conclusions, and frequently asked questions.* Ypisilanti: High Scope Press.

Sedlak, A., Mettenburg, J., Basena, M., Petta, I., McPherson, K., Greene, A., & Li, S. (2010). *Fourth national incidence of child abuse and neglect (NIS-4): Report to Congress.* Washington, DC: U.S. Department of Health and Human Services, Administration for Children and Families.

Shonkoff, J. P., Garner, A. S., The Committee on Psychosocial Aspects of Child and Family Health, Committee on Early Childhood, Adoption, and Dependent Care, & Section on Developmental and Behavioral Pediatrics. (2011). The lifelong effects of early childhood adversity and toxic stress. *Pediatrics, 129*(1), e232–e246.

Sroufe, A., Egeland, B., Carlson, E., & Collins, W. (2005). *The development of the person.* New York: The Guilford Press.

Strengthening Families Program. (2012). http://www.strengtheningfamilies.org/. Accessed 30 Nov 2012.

Substance Abuse and Mental Health Services Administration. (2009). *Children living with substance-dependent or substance-abusing parents: 2002–2007.* Available from http://oas.samhsa.gov.

Thomas, R., & Zimmer-Gembeck, M. (2011). Accumulating evidence for parent–child interaction therapy in the prevention of maltreatment. *Child Development, 82*(1), 177–192.

Thompson, R. (1995). *Preventing child maltreatment through social support.* Thousand Oaks: Sage.

Thompson, R., & Wiley, T. R. (2009). Predictors of re-referral to child protective services: A longitudinal follow-up of an urban cohort maltreated as infants. *Child Maltreatment, 14*(1), 89–99.

U. S. Department of Health and Human Services, Administration on Children, Youth, and Families. (2010). *Child maltreatment 2009.* Washington, DC: U.S. Government Printing Office.

U.S. Advisory Board on Child Abuse and Neglect. (1991). *Creating caring communities: Blueprint for an effective federal policy on child abuse and neglect.* Washington, DC: U.S. Government Printing Office.

U.S. Department of Health and Human Services. (2005). *National survey of child and adolescent well – Being, Wave 1 data analysis report.* Washington, DC: U.S. Department of Health and Human Services.

U.S. Department of Health and Human Services. (2011b). HHS announces $224 million to support evidence-based home visiting programs to help parents and children. *News Release.*

U.S. Department of Health and Human Services, Administration for Children and Families/Children's Bureau and Office of the Assistant for Planning and Evaluation. (2003). *National study of child protective services systems and reform efforts: Review of state CPS policies.* Washington, DC: U.S. Government Printing Office.

U.S. Department of Health and Human Services, Administration on Children, Youth, and Families (2011a). *Child maltreatment 2010.* Available from http://www.acf.hhs.gov/programs/cb/stats_research/index.htm#can

Vericker, T., Macomber, J., & Golden, O. (2010). *Infants of depressed mothers living in poverty: Opportunities to identify and serve.* Washington, DC: The Urban Institute.

Wald, M. (1975). State intervention on behalf of neglected children: A search for realistic standards. *Stanford Law Review, 27*, 985–1040.

Wald, M. (1976). State intervention on behalf of neglected children: Standards for removal of children from their homes, monitoring the status of children in foster care, and termination of parental rights. *Stanford Law Review, 28*, 623–706.

Wald, M. (1991). Defining psychological maltreatment: The relationship between questions and answers. *Development and Psychopathology, 3*, 111–131.

Wald, M. S. (2009). Preventing maltreatment or promoting positive development – where should a community focus its resources? In K. A. Dodge & D. L. Coleman (Eds.), *Preventing child maltreatment: Community approaches*. New York: The Guilford Press.

Wald, M. (2012a). Big government, better-off kids-the case for spending a lot of money on programs that help children. *Slate*. 14 May 2012.

Wald, M. S. (2012b). Taking the wrong message: The legacy of the identification of the battered-child syndrome. In J. Korbin & R. Krugman (Eds.), *C. Henry Kempe: A 50 year legacy to the field of child abuse and neglect*. Dordrecht: Springer.

Wald, M., & Martinez, T. (2003). *Connected by 25: Improving the life chances of the country's most vulnerable 14–25 year olds*. William and Flora Hewlett Foundation Working Papers.

Wald, M., & Sandmire, M. (1990). Licensing parents – A response. *Family Law Quarterly, 24*, 53–75.

Waldfogel, J. (1998). *The future of child protection*. Cambridge, MA: Harvard University Press.

Waldfogel, J. (2008). The future of child protection revisited. In D. Lindsey & A. Shlonsky (Eds.), *Child welfare research*. New York: Oxford University Press.

Waldfogel, J. (2009a). Prevention and the child protection system. *The Future of Children, 19*(2), 195–210.

Waldfogel, J. (2009b). Differential response. In K. Dodge & D. Coleman (Eds.), *Preventing child maltreatment community approaches*. New York: The Guilford Press.

Waldfogel, J., & Washbrook, E. (2011). Early years policy. *Child Development Research, 2011*, 1–12.

Walker, K., Arbreton, A., Pepper, S., & Farley, C. (2012). *Encouraging positive parenting in early childhood lessons from a community change initiative*. Philadelphia: Public Private Ventures.

Weaver, J. D. (2011). The principle of subsidiarity applied: Reforming the legal framework to capture the psychological abuse of children. *Virginia Journal of Social Policy and Law, 18*, 1–72.

Webster-Stratton, C. (2005). *The Incredible Years: A training series for the prevention and treatment of conduct problems in young children*. Seattle: The Incredible Years.

Weithorn, L. (2012). Developmental neuroscience, children's relationships with primary caregivers, and child protection policy reform. *Hastings Law Review, 63*, 1487–1554.

Westman, J. (1994). *Licensing parents*. New York: Insight Books.

Worley, N., & Melton, G. (2012). Mandated reporting laws and child maltreatment: The evolution of a flawed policy response. In K. A. Dodge & D. L. Coleman (Eds.), *Preventing child maltreatment: Community approaches*. New York: The Guilford Press.

Wulczyn, F., Barth, R., Yuan, Y., Jones Harden, B., & Landsverk, J. (2005). *Beyond common sense: Child welfare, child well-being, and the evidence for policy reform*. New Brunswick: Aldine Transaction.

Wulzcyn, F. (2009). Epidemiological perspectives on maltreatment prevention. *The Future of Children, 19*(2), 39–66.

Chapter 14
Sustaining Progress in Preventing Child Maltreatment: A Transformative Challenge

Deborah Daro and Genevieve Benedetti

Introduction

Developing an effective prevention response to maltreatment has long been stymied by the sheer breadth of behaviors and social conditions associated with the terms child abuse and neglect (Daro 1988; Helfer 1982; Daro and McCurdy 2007). Parental behaviors considered as abusive or neglectful include, among others, the willful or intentional physical beating of a child; the failure to provide for a child's basic emotional and physical needs; overt emotional abuse of a child through continuous belittling, inappropriate control or extreme inconsistency; and the sexual mistreatment of a child or use of a child for sexual pleasure (Myers 2006). Social norms and public policies that condone and, sometimes, promote corporal punishment or high levels of violence and sexually explicit language in the media as well as child poverty, inadequate housing, failing educational systems and limited access to preventive health care also represent, in the eyes of some, society's collective maltreatment of its children (Garbarino 1995; Straus 2000). Given this diversity in perspectives, it is understandable that the field has struggled with defining the problem's scope, consequences, and appropriate interventions to both remediate its effects and prevent its occurrence.

Setting aside the issue of social conditions and inadequate welfare and support systems, the number of children directly abused or neglected is substantial. One of the earliest and most rigorous studies on the annual incidence of maltreatment estimated that in 1968 between two and four million families either failed to act or used physical force with the intent of hurting, injuring or killing their children (Gil 1970). Since that time, repeated household surveys and national incidence studies consistently document a problem of notable proportion and one that affects children of all ages and socio-economic groups (Finkelhor et al. 2005; Gelles and Straus 1988; Sedlak and Broadhurst 1996; Sedlak et al. 2010).

More recently, child abuse reporting statistics as well as federally funded national incidence studies have observed a notable decline in certain types of maltreatment offering some evidence that investments in treatment and prevention strategies are yielding results (Finkelhor 2008). For example, the Fourth Federal National Incidence Study on Child Maltreatment (NIS-4) completed in 2010, reported a 19 % reduction in the overall rate of child maltreatment since the 1993 incidence study (Sedlak et al. 2010). The most recent study found significant drops in the rates of sexual abuse, physical abuse, and emotional abuse, changes that have been mirrored for several years in the administrative data maintained by state child welfare agencies (U.S. Department of Health and Human Services 2011a).

D. Daro (✉) • G. Benedetti
Chapin Hall, University of Chicago, Chicago, USA
e-mail: ddaro@chapinhall.org; gbenedetti@chapinhall.org

J.E. Korbin and R.D. Krugman (eds.), *Handbook of Child Maltreatment*, Child Maltreatment 2, DOI 10.1007/978-94-007-7208-3_14, © Springer Science+Business Media Dordrecht 2014

Unfortunately, these reductions are not consistent across populations or communities. For example, only minimal changes have been observed in reported rates for child neglect among the nation's poorest children and the number of child abuse fatalities, the vast majority of which involve children under the age of five, have increased in recent years (U.S. Department of Health and Human Services 2011a). And while declining, the absolute number of children confirmed as victims of maltreatment remains high. Indeed, state and local child protective services (CPS) agencies received an estimated 3.3 million referrals alleging child abuse or neglect in 2010. These referrals included more than 5.9 million children and, of those, approximately 695,000, or 9.2 per 1,000, were determined to be victims of maltreatment (U.S. Department of Health and Human Services 2011a).

Although reductions in the documented cases of maltreatment are uneven and many children continue to be victimized, the overall trend suggests that comprehensive prevention strategies, high-quality clinical interventions for victims and perpetrators, and policies and laws that hold those who harm children accountable for their actions all have the capacity to keep children safe (Finkelhor 2008; Daro 2010a). The critical question moving forward, however, is how to effectively extend and deepen this capacity.

Today, the United States and many world economies are facing significant challenges. Public safety nets as well as social and health service systems are operating with restricted budgets even as an increasing number of children are reared in households with fewer financial and human resources (Addy and Wight 2012). High unemployment rates among those just entering the work force, the absence of middle income jobs for those lacking advanced education and training, and the growing number of children being raised in households with a single caretaker create environments that can elevate parental stress and potentially create a higher risk for maltreatment (McLanahan et al. 2010). In order to address this increased need with diminishing public resources, the next generation of prevention strategies will need to be more effective and more efficient.

The purpose of this chapter is to take stock of where the prevention field is at and to identify those areas that offer the richest opportunities for doing better. The chapter is not simply a review of exemplary prevention programs but rather an overview of how the field has evolved and the core issues and challenges it faces moving forward. Beginning with a prevention history, the chapter examines the various stages through which the field has evolved, briefly summarizing the major gains observed during these stages. The chapter then summarizes the research emerging from four "pillars of prevention planning" which currently frame the field and generate the greatest interest among policy makers, practitioners, and researchers. These include a primary focus on strategies that target a child's first few years of life and strengthening early parent–child relationships; public policy initiatives making investments in a growing number of evidence-based program models with demonstrated success in achieving targeted outcomes; the emphasis on implementation research to insure program replication occurs with consistent fidelity and quality; and the importance of creating effective service delivery systems capable of sustaining and extending the reach of promising interventions. The chapter concludes with a discussion of the challenges facing the field and outlines a set of promising pathways available for improving prevention's reach and effectiveness.

What Has Been Accomplished

Several policy and contextual factors have influenced the general structure and focus of the prevention field over the past 40 years. At the most general level, efforts to prevent child maltreatment have moved through multiple stages – public recognition of the problem, experimentation with a wide range of prevention programs addressing one or more factors believed to increase a child's risk for maltreatment, an intentional focus on services targeting pregnant women and new parents, and the evolution of broadly defined preventive systems of care and service integration across diverse domains

(Daro and Cohn-Donnelly 2002; Daro 2009). At each stage, public policy and interventions have been shaped by research and practice lessons from the previous stage.

As initial awareness and understanding of the issue grew in the late 1970's, the field moved into the development and replication of a diverse set of interventions designed to both remediate the negative impacts of abuse and prevent its reincidence and initial occurrence (Cohn 1983). These programmatic investments followed two distinct paths – interventions targeting reductions in physical abuse and neglect (including emotional neglect and attachment disorders) and interventions targeting reductions in child sexual abuse (Daro 1988, 2010b). Programs in the first group emanated from a research base that suggested physical abuse and neglect resulted from a parent's lack of knowledge, resources and emotional capacity. These prevention strategies included, among others, services to new parents, general parenting education classes, parent support groups, family resource centers, and crisis intervention services such as hotlines and crisis nurseries (Cohn 1987). In contrast, the primary target population for sexual abuse prevention has been potential victims, not potential perpetrators. Strategies within this framework included a number of educational-based efforts, provided on a universal basis, to children on the distinction between good, bad and questionable touching and the concept of body ownership or the rights of children to control who touches their bodies and where they are touched (Wurtele and Miller-Perrin 1992). These educational programs also encouraged children and youth who had been victimized to report these incidences and seek services.

While this broad array of interventions most certainly assisted many families and addressed several of the most egregious problems and lack of options identified in early clinical studies, not all families were well served by this system. This prevention "continuum", while logical, missed an important aspect underlying ecological theories of maltreatment: the additive and interdependent impacts of multiple factors on a parent's ability to care for her child (Daro 1993). Further, program evaluations and basic research on the profound impacts of abuse and neglect on a young child's developmental trajectory and her capacity to form stable relationships as an adult, resulted in the prevention field placing primary emphasis on investments in services for new parents, particularly home based interventions (Carnegie Task Force 1994; Shonkoff and Phillips 2000).

With these lessons in mind, the field is now focusing on ways to better coordinate and integrate services provided through multiple domains and alter the context in which parents rear their children (Daro and Dodge 2009). The goal is shifting from individual level change to achieving population level change by creating safe and nurturing environments for all children, communities in which parents are supported through both formal services and normative values that foster mutual reciprocity. Strategies for creating these types of safe and nurturing environments are far from self-evident. As Melton, Thompson, and Small have noted, achieving child protection becomes a shared, moral responsibility "not merely to prevent wrongdoing, but to achieve positive obligations as well" (2002, p. 11). Although such systems are not fully operational in any community, the goal of altering both the individual and the context in which she lives potentially provides a more potent programmatic and policy response (Daro et al. 2009).

Moving forward, child abuse prevention efforts will continue to evolve in response to at least four trends framing the current research and policy landscape. First, a broad range of research and practice experiences suggest directing prevention resources to pregnant women and new parents is the most promising approach for achieving a meaningful reduction in population level maltreatment rates. Second, public and private programmatic investments are being directed to an increasing number of programs with evidence of effectiveness, as determined through rigorous research. Third, more focused attention is being paid to how programs are being implemented, documenting the degree to which program standards are being systematically followed over time. Finally, growing attention is being paid to how individual services are linked within a coordinated system of care and the attributes required for sustaining such systems over time. These characteristics are not unique to child abuse prevention efforts nor do they account for all of the investments currently being made in reducing the likelihood for maltreatment across diverse populations and circumstances. However, they are dimensions that are framing an increasing proportion of the field's research, practice and policy agendas. The following sections summarize key research in each of these areas.

Early Childhood Matters

While initiating prevention services at the time a child is born has long been a core component of child abuse prevention efforts, new advances in neuroscience have given rise to stronger empirical evidence supporting this approach. Such research has highlighted in very dramatic and visual ways the negative impacts that poor parenting and stress can have on a child's developing brain and the longer term implications of this damage into adulthood. During early childhood, neural connections in the brain are being formed, and "serve and return" activities – when an adult responds to an infant's coos and other verbalizations in a controlled manner – are instrumental to the healthy development of motor skills, language, memory, emotion, and behavioral control. Attentive care giving from adults is absolutely essential during formative years when the brain is most sensitive to external forces (Center on the Developing Child 2012).

In 2011, a collection of medical bodies published several academic journal articles and disseminated a press release calling attention to child maltreatment and other forms of toxic stress in the lives of children (Committee on Psychosocial Aspects of Child and Family Health et al. 2011; Shonkoff et al. 2011). Each publication identifies the field of human development as multidisciplinary, and emphasizes the importance of collaborative efforts and information exchange between the fields of neuroscience, molecular biology, genomics, developmental psychology, epidemiology, sociology, and economics. They link the effects of toxic stress to the failure to develop coping skills and adaptive capabilities and "unhealthy lifestyles" (e.g. substance abuse, poor diet, lack of exercise) that can lead to fragmented social networks and financial hardship in adulthood. Additionally, they reiterate the need for adult caregivers to buffer children to keep stress levels within a healthy range (Committee on Psychosocial Aspects of Child and Family Health et al. 2011). In an eco-bio-developmental (EBD) framework that describes the "inextricable interaction between biology (as defined by genetic predispositions) and ecology (as defined by the social and physical environment)", nature and nurture are highlighted as critical and intertwining components of human development (Shonkoff et al. 2011, p. 234).

Technological and methodological advances have played a large part in our rapid understanding of cognitive development. New MRI and fMRI capabilities and human and animal studies have led to a better understanding of both functional and structural changes in the developing brain (Blakemore 2011), and early life stress can now be connected to cognitive impairments in adolescence (Mueller et al. 2010). A number of studies have tested the neuroendocrine system that helps the body to maintain balance when experiencing child maltreatment and other stressful situations through the regulation of cortisol levels. Findings have shown atypical cortisol levels associated with abuse or neglect (Oosterman et al. 2011), a caregiver experiencing high stress (Fisher and Stoolmiller 2008), exposure to prenatal substance abuse (Fisher et al. 2011a), and time in the foster care system (Fisher et al. 2011b, c; Pears et al. 2011). These findings lead researchers and policymakers to raise questions about the types of interventions that will most effectively ensure healthy brain development, but also about whether it is possible for interventions to change neural processes in brains that have already undergone damage due to trauma. Some researchers suggest that the most recent findings on neural plasticity provide evidence that it may be possible to design interventions to reverse negative effects on brain development caused by environmental trauma in childhood, particularly in regard to executive function development (IOM and NRC 2012; Bryck and Fisher 2011).

Indeed, many interventions have proven effective in alternating the negative impacts of early trauma (Barnett et al. 2008; Bernard et al. 2012; Dozier et al. 2009) and improving the development of executive function (National Scientific Council on the Developing Child 2011). However, the prevention field has continued to place emphasis on expanding research and investments in programs targeting new parents. As discussed in the subsequent section, the provision of home based interventions offered at the time a woman becomes pregnant or gives birth are among the most widely disseminated child maltreatment prevention strategies (Daro 2010b). Although findings remain inconsistent across program models, target populations, and outcome domains, the approach continues to demonstrate impacts on child maltreatment frequency and harsh punishment (Chaffin et al. 2012; DuMont et al. 2010; Lowell et al. 2011; Olds 2010; Silovsky et al. 2011), parental capacity and positive parenting practices (Connell et al. 2008; Dishion et al. 2008; DuMont et al. 2010; LeCroy and Krysik 2011; Nievar et al. 2011; Roggman et al. 2009; Zigler et al. 2008) and healthy child development (DuMont et al. 2010; Shaw et al. 2009; Lowell et al. 2011; Olds et al. 2007). In addition, repeated follow-ups on families enrolled in Nurse Family Partnership's randomized clinical trials support the long-term efficacy of early intervention on parents (Eckenrode et al. 2010) and children (Kitzman et al. 2010; Olds 2010). Given the empirical strength of these findings and the strong support home visiting has from policymakers, we anticipate that the prevention field will continue to focus on extending the availability of such early intervention efforts for new parents.

Although home-based interventions have the most robust data base, a number of parenting education and group-based interventions also have achieved improvements in parental capacity, particularly in cases where they have targeted risk factors associated with child abuse and neglect such as substance abuse, mental illness, domestic violence, and child conduct problems (Barth 2009). A 2011 review of 46 randomized control trial evaluations of parenting programs focuses on long term outcomes across multiple developmental periods and finds that existing programs show a variety of positive effects up to 20 years after the intervention occurred (Sandler et al. 2011). Specific parenting program evaluations were conducted on The Incredible Years, an evidence-based parenting program that treats child conduct problems (Letarte et al. 2010; Marcynyszyn et al. 2011; Webster-Stratton et al. 2011), and Parents Anonymous, a mutual self-help group (Polinsky et al. 2010).

In addition to offering direct services to new parents, greater consideration is being given on how best to use existing service delivery systems that regularly interact with families to address the potential for maltreatment. For example, the medical field has long sought ways to better address healthy child development and child maltreatment within clinical settings. Historically, the traditional checkup appointment has been plagued by barriers preventing health professionals from taking up this responsibility. Doctors are oftentimes uncomfortable discussing sensitive issues, and they lack the training to instigate such conversations and the ability to recognize key warning signs. Additionally, adequate and comprehensive screening tools have not been made available to all primary care providers (Dubowitz et al. 2009). The Healthy Steps program, an evidence-based model which places child development specialists within selected pediatric practices, was initially created in the 1980s to address this issue. Today, Healthy Steps is available in 17 states, and has demonstrated consistent impacts on child health, child development and school readiness, and positive parenting practices (Caughy et al. 2003; Minkovitz et al. 2001, 2007).

More recently, the Safe Environment for Every Kid (SEEK) was created to help health professionals address risk factors for maltreatment through a training course, the introduction of a Parent Screening Questionnaire, and the addition of an in-house social worker team to work with families. Two studies were recently conducted to test existing SEEK programs: one to determine outcomes for children and families and one to measure effects on the health professionals participating in the intervention (Dubowitz et al. 2009). The first was a randomized trial conducted between 2002 and 2005 in resident clinics in Baltimore, Maryland. Those families enrolled in the SEEK treatment group showed significantly lower rates of maltreatment across all measures (Dubowitz et al. 2009). Two years later, a second study was conducted to determine if the program changed doctor attitudes, behaviors, and competence in addressing child maltreatment in their patients (Dubowitz et al. 2011). Eighteen private practice primary care clinics participated in a cluster randomized control trial. The pediatricians from the SEEK group significantly improved in their abilities to address substance use, intimate partner violence, depression, and stress, and they reported higher levels of comfort and perceived competence (Dubowitz et al. 2011).

Continued advancements in neuroscience, medicine, psychiatry and psychology increase our understanding of child development, and in turn, improve the scientific foundation of successful interventions to support healthy families. While the link between early experiences and optimal child development is becoming clearer, how to systematically intervene in this period remains a challenge. The period from birth until about 5 years of age is a period where families are not universally anchored to formal supports. From a policy standpoint, once children enter school, it is much easier to determine children's needs, monitor their progress, their challenges, and engage with families. Before kindergarten, it is much harder to establish systematic connections with the children and families that would benefit the most from programs designed to optimize developmental outcomes, teach good parenting techniques, and develop protective factors. Parenting needs vary widely based on factors like culture and income level, and thusly, successful techniques for engaging parents in different communities and across different populations vary. These differences are difficult to measure, and generally, parents improvise with what is available to them. Despite the challenges of early intervention, the quality of programs being developed and the diversity of strategies being employed are demonstrating that measurable and meaningful improvements can be achieved early in a child's life in a number of core outcome domains, including child maltreatment.

Investing in Evidence-Based Programs

In the current economic and political climate, public policy increasingly supports the implementation of evidence-based, tested programming. President Obama's administration has worked with the Office of Management and Budget (OMB) to roll out a series of "evidence-based initiatives" with the main goals of expanding effective social programs, eliminating ineffective programs, advancing evidence-based programming, and creating the opportunity for high quality research and evaluation (Haskins and Baron 2011, p. 6). This emphasis on selecting and replicating evidence-based programs have fostered several large scale federal initiatives that either directly, or indirectly, expand prevention services that reach families at risk of maltreatment.

Most notable has been the passage of the Maternal, Infant, and Early Childhood Home Visiting program (MIECHV), which was authorized as a part of the Affordable Care Act of 2010 (U.S. Department of Health and Human Services 2011b). Over 5 years, this program will allocate $1.5 billion worth of grants to states to implement evidence-based home visiting programs. The program is administered through the Health Resources and Services Administration (HRSA) and the Administration for Children and Families (ACF). The initial grant required that all state applications include a comprehensive needs assessment to identify the communities most at-risk for poor maternal and child health. In the assessment, states took stock of the communities' greatest deficiencies, assets, and resources, and they created a plan to address the unique needs of that community.

Federal regulations required that 75 % of state funding be invested in evidence-based program models approved by HRSA. In 2009, the federal government funded Home Visiting Evidence of Effectiveness (HomVEE) to conduct a systematic review of the research available on 22 home visiting programs. Of the original 22, nine programs met the evidence threshold and were subsequently approved by HRSA for state implementation.[1] Through implementation of these programs and the development of coordinated early intervention systems, states are required to set and achieve benchmarks in three of six core domains: maternal and child health, childhood injury prevention, school readiness and achievement, crime or domestic violence, economic self-sufficiency, and efforts to coordinate with existing community resources.

Following a similar process of interagency collaboration and investment in evidence-based programs, the U.S. Department of Health and Human Services in partnership with the U.S. Department of Education established a $500 million competitive grant competition to improve access to high quality early education programs. Specifically, the Race for the Top – Early Learning Challenge (RTT-ELC) assists states in achieving three goals: (1) increase the number of low-income and disadvantaged infants, toddlers, and preschoolers who are enrolled in a high quality education program; (2) create an integrated system of programs and services; and (3) require that assessments conform with the standards of the National Research Council in the area of early childhood education. In October of 2011, 35 states, Puerto Rico, and Washington DC applied for grants of $50–$100 million. The amount awarded was determined by the relative population of low-income children served by the state. The states recommended for funding were California, Delaware, Maryland, Massachusetts, Minnesota, North Carolina, Ohio, Rhode Island, and Washington.[2]

This emphasis on supporting evidence-based interventions also is reflected in current support for teen parents. Encouraged by a growing evidence base surrounding teen pregnancy prevention programming, the Obama Administration commissioned a literature review on existing research to inform a decision to launch a federal initiative in this area. In the review, program models were identified that were associated with high quality research, two of which showed sustained reductions in teen pregnancy in randomized control trials (Haskins and Baron 2011).[3] In 2010, under the Teen Pregnancy Prevention Initiative (TPPI), the Office of Adolescent Health (OAH) awarded $75 million to programs that had high quality research supporting their effectiveness. Seventy-five programs were chosen from 32 states.[4] Another $15 million was awarded to support promising strategies to second tier "demonstration programs" that have the potential to contribute new innovative approaches to addressing teen pregnancy.[5] Lastly, OAH partnered with the Centers for Disease Control (CDC) to support community-wide models in eight locations.[6]

Finally, the strategy has led to additional services on programming designed to improve father engagement in caring for young children. The Department of Health and Human Services (HHS)[7] has established a $150 million initiative to promote "healthy marriage promotion and responsible fatherhood." Under this initiative, the Administration for Children and Families (ACF) provides a resource

---

[1] The nine evidence-based programs chosen as "national models" and green-lighted for implementation as part of the MIECH-V program are: (1) Child FIRST, (2) Early Head Start-Home Visiting, (3) Early Intervention Program for Adolescent Mothers (EIP), (4) Family Check-Up, (5) Healthy Families America (HFA), (6) Healthy Steps, (7) Home Instruction for Parents of Preschool Youngsters (HIPPY), (8) Nurse Family Partnership (NFP), and (9) Parents as Teachers (PAT). For more information on the home visiting models assessed for effectiveness, visit the U.S. Department of Health and Human Services Home Visiting Evidence of Effectiveness website: http://homvee.acf.hhs.gov/Default.aspx.

[2] Department of Education website: http://www2.ed.gov/programs/racetothetop-earlylearningchallenge/awards.html.

[3] More information about evidence-based programs identified by the review can be found at the Office of Adolescent Health website here: http://www.hhs.gov/ash/oah/oah-initiatives/tpp/programs.html.

[4] More information about individual projects is available from the Office of Adolescent Health here: http://www.hhs.gov/ash/oah/oah-initiatives/tpp/grantees/tpp-tier1.pdf

[5] Demonstration programs funded by OAH: http://www.hhs.gov/ash/oah/oah-initiatives/tpp/grantees/tpp-tier2.pdf

[6] Information on community-based teen pregnancy prevention efforts can be found at the CDC site here: http://www.cdc.gov/TeenPregnancy/State-Community-Orgs.htm.

[7] HHS Promoting Responsible Fatherhood website: http://fatherhood.hhs.gov/2010Initiative/index.shtml.

called the National Responsible Fatherhood Clearinghouse (NRFC). NRFC is a media campaign disseminating information about responsible fatherhood and healthy marriage with the help of a website featuring aggregate resources available to individuals and families.[8] Additional monies fund activities like counseling, mentoring, marriage and relationship education, and the Strengthening Families Evidence Review, a database of research on fatherhood programming.[9] Increasing the accessibility to information and services for the public could contribute to the reduction of child maltreatment rates by preventing damaging parenting practices from ever occurring.

Obama's evidence-based initiatives to support healthy families and positive parenting are based on a blueprint that identifies the target social problem, chooses model programs that are proven to work through rigorous and high quality research, funds the large-scale implementation of model programming, and requires continued evaluation of ongoing interventions (Haskins and Baron 2011). While these methods are logical, responsible, and could lead to a reduction in programming costs in the future, the current economic crisis has created a political climate where sound research is not a sufficient reason for expanding investments (Haskins and Baron 2011). The need for greater fiscal austerity presents a danger to all of the current evidence-based initiatives and may lead to an overall downsizing of social spending in the United States over the next several years, a move that not only dampens enthusiasm for investing in quality research but also may well reduce the availability of services to families at risk for maltreatment.

Understanding Program Implementation

With a growing policy focus on the implementation of evidence-based models in large scale initiatives, it becomes necessary for research to test and examine how best to introduce these models into a diverse array of community settings. Implementation responsibilities include staff training and credentialing, fidelity to protocol, engagement of community members, connection of participants to other existing services and programs, continued evaluation of program components, attrition rates, and mostly importantly, positive outcomes for parents and children. There is common consensus that preventive strategies should be assessed in terms of their capacity to achieve both immediate and distal outcomes for children, parents and families. That being said, there is less understanding about which aspects of our service delivery system support these outcomes, even after rigorous evaluations prove a model's overall effectiveness. We have a propagating list of models proven to elicit positive outcomes, but far fewer evaluations have been done that test the actual process of implementation and dissemination (Mildon and Shlonsky 2011).

There is an existing body of literature on the subject of program implementation (Durlak and DuPre 2008), and in 2005 the National Implementation Research Network published a valuable stepwise process for program implementation (Fixsen et al. 2005). For any organization thinking about bringing their program model to scale, it is important to first clarify exact goals. There are three different ways of "going to scale" identified in the literature: expansion, which increases the scope of operation; replication, which involves getting others to import the model; and collaboration, which is forming partnerships to divide the responsibility of going to scale (Cooley and Kohl 2005). Before initiating any of these types of scaling up, it is recommended that an organization, after clarifying what is being brought to scale, test and refine the model, conduct a needs assessment and allot enough time for the site to develop readiness and capacity. Site readiness is essential to implementation success and most replication failures can be linked to inadequate site preparation or readiness (Elliot

---

[8] ACF maintains the NRFC website to provide up to date information to families: http://fatherhood.gov/home.

[9] ACF OPRE resources on fatherhood programming research: http://www.acf.hhs.gov/programs/opre/strengthen/proven_promising/index.html.

and Mihalic 2004). Additionally, a third party assessment of the implementation often provides other critical elements to the process of scaling up and helps accurately determine the impacts (Cooley and Kohl 2005). The main lesson the literature conveys is that for effective replication, it is essential for a site to develop a clear plan and allow enough time for readiness so as not to rush to implementation.

Program fidelity is another critical issue to consider when bringing a model to scale. Today, few evaluations have identified the specific components that can be used to determine program fidelity, but a history of research on the subject sheds some light on current efforts (Gearing et al. 2011). In 2009, the National Evidence-Based Practices (EBPs) Project published findings on a study in which interventions were evaluated for their use of a new implementation model that utilized fidelity feedback reports. Among the critical factors they identified: strong on-site leadership committed to high fidelity outcomes; effective educational trainings and materials provided to a skilled and competent workforce; ongoing technical assistance; and routine feedback to providers on the clinical aspects of their work (Bond et al. 2009). Unique challenges exist in measuring fidelity in child welfare systems, and while some measures of fidelity (e.g. frequency and dosage) are easily quantified, others are more subjective and rely on the practitioner's professional judgment (Kaye and Osteen 2011).

In a study of the implementation of one child safety program, model developers and local practitioners worked together to establish both fidelity instruments and measurement instruments. The observed model was successful in part because it was inclusive and built capacity amongst stakeholders, and it could be replicated in other sites in the future (Kaye and Osteen 2011). "Safeguarding fidelity" in one's interventions requires high quality training programs, an evidence base that is easily understood by practitioners and includes outcomes for interventions with diverse participants, and staff that are experienced in a number of different protocols. Additionally, clear and comprehensive program materials are essential, clinical outcome data should be collected, and staff should be both evaluated and supported at all steps of the process (Mazzucchelli and Sanders 2010).

In some cases the program model needs to be adapted to fit a specific population. Ensuring that the adaptation does not compromise the fidelity of the model is important to sustaining impacts. How do we effectively implement evidence-based programs with high fidelity, but also with adaptability to cultural, socioeconomic, and demographic difference? Those involved in the successful implementation of the universal, community-based Positive Parenting Program (Triple P) in different settings have offered findings from evaluations of such efforts. They conclude that strict adherence to manualized treatment does not necessarily lead to the best outcomes and believe it is possible to train practitioners to adapt to the circumstances of their work without moving outside the evidence-base (Mazzucchelli and Sanders 2010).

Taking a program to scale often raises questions about the sustainability of the program or initiative. Common sustainability challenges for prevention programs include: securing funding that supports services and system functions without compromising quality or the program model's design; demonstrating efficacy of the model and ensuring replication with quality; and maintaining the program characteristics that made the program successful in the past (Elliot and Mihalic 2004). When planning strategic implementation of an initiative, it is important to incorporate institutionalization of the program, to build community ownership from the start, and to secure long-term sustainable funding opportunities (Chavis and Trent 2009).

Building Service Delivery Systems

Maximizing prevention efforts at the population level requires new understanding of how to construct and sustain effective state systems, local community collaboratives, and robust community-based organizations. All stakeholders in the child welfare system, from the perspective of prevention to deep-end service provision, agree that greater focus must be paid to building human service delivery systems that facilitate pragmatic collaboration. In the current economic climate, pressure mounts to provide effective and efficient systems of care. Up until now, previous research efforts in the area of agency-collaboration have been predominantly descriptive, and for the most part they provide a summary and history of relevant research on the topic (Tseng et al. 2011). When considering changes to systems of care to increase the potential for agency collaboration, it is beneficial to first establish a framework to guide efforts. In the conception of this foundation certain questions should be asked, i.e. are these changes structural or operational and do they attempt to achieve long term or short term impacts? What is the collaborative's current "developmental" stage? (Tseng et al. 2011). The developmental stage of the system is important because different factors are crucial to the success of a collaborative at different times throughout the process. For example, in the formation stage, communication between member parties is essential as roles and responsibilities are assigned, and an overall system of operation is established. In the stage of conceptualization, the identity of the group takes precedence as a mission statement is created, goals and strategies are set, and so on (Tseng et al. 2011). Through the collection and categorization of data collected from successful collaborative systems, researchers will be able to determine which aspects of the process are necessary to achieve positive outcomes, and thusly, will have the basic tools with which to improve social service systems overall.

System building efforts require a firm and well-researched framework, but they also require attention to both individual organizations and the people they employ. Current work in organizational theory can provide useful guidance for establishing an organizational environment that is not only open to change, but one that fosters innovation. A review of relevant literature suggests that individuals are more likely to go along with change within their organization if (1) they have been trained in the new procedures and policies in advance of implementation; and (2) when they feel they are working in an environment with a "learning culture" (Choi and Ruona 2011). First, employees must be made to feel that the impending change is not only necessary, but likely to be successful. Therefore, investing in informing and training the entire organization about new upcoming initiatives is essential to the process (Choi and Ruona 2011, pp. 47–49). Second, contextual factors like environment and leadership are highly influential. As a result, a culture of learning must be established early, so that all members of an organization buy in to the idea that learning is a perpetual process and the best organizations are able to adapt easily to new improvements (Choi and Ruona 2011, p. 60).

In a study to determine if organization type (public vs. private) or organizational support influence the attitudes of providers towards the use of evidence-based programs, results indicate that providers working within private, for-profit organizations have more positive attitudes toward innovations like evidence-based programming and are more open to implementing evidence-based interventions (Aarons et al. 2009). Currently, a movement is underway to make government organizations and agencies more efficient by becoming more responsive to the needs of their client and changes in the environment (Daniels and Sandler 2008). The findings of Aarons and colleagues (2009) suggest that while a movement to redesign government with private business models in mind exists, there is still a long way to go before public agencies are as deft and open to the implementation of cutting edge programming. In the meantime, additional resources and attention should be paid to public institutions implementing new evidence-based programming.

Data-sharing is another important issue facing agencies that work together to benefit children and families. A 2011 study on data-sharing in a hospital setting for the purpose of quality improvement showed findings similar to those indicated as important to overall system-building efforts. In order for a hospital to excel in data-sharing efforts it should have strong organizational leadership, organizational reverence for the data, a strong vision for organizational goal attainment, data to track service quality and program outcomes, and staff who share an understanding of the importance of the collaborative effort (Korst et al. 2011). Results intended to increase data-sharing in hospitals can be extrapolated to agency collaboration efforts because in each instance separate and somewhat autonomous departments/agencies must work to meet goals designed to improve overall efficiency and effectiveness, thusly affecting outcome measures for clients.

These findings can be easily applied to data-sharing to promote child maltreatment prevention. In fact, a 2011 Government Accountability Office (GAO) report found that strengthening the national data on child fatalities could aid future prevention efforts (Brown 2011). The federal National Child Abuse and Neglect Data System (NCANDS) does not require inclusion of all available information regarding the circumstances of child deaths, and it is likely that a number of child deaths are not counted in NCANDS at all (Brown 2011). Challenges in data collection at the local level are caused by inconsistent interpretations by law enforcement, medical examiners, and child welfare workers. At the state level, coordination efforts across jurisdictions and state agencies can fail due to confidentiality issues (Brown 2011). The GAO recommends that the HHS invest in strengthening data quality, expanding available fatality information, and improving information-sharing (Brown 2011). Researchers call attention to the potential of new technologies in developing much needed longitudinal, multi-sector, multi-dimensional administrative data bases (Duncan et al. 2008; Jonson-Reid and Drake 2008). Better data on child maltreatment occurrence will lead to research that can shed light on how to build better prevention interventions and program components. With regard to the overall quality and efficiency of service delivery systems, future improvements will be dependent on successful collaborative initiatives, organizational and community buy-in, a fostered organizational "learning culture," and the smart collection, analysis, and sharing of data.

Current Debates Facing the Field

Ecological theory has been used for several decades to frame the child abuse prevention paradigm, recognizing that most maltreatment stems from a complex web of factors within a person's personality, family history and community context (Belsky 1980; Bronfenbrenner 1979; Garbarino 1977; Cicchetti and Rizley 1981). In addition to articulating a nested set of domains governing human behaviors, ecological theory identifies a set of risk factors as well as protective factors. As such, the theory underscores the importance of crafting prevention strategies that seek to reduce the interpersonal and environmental challenges families face and to build a network of protective or supportive factors that can help families cope with risks that are not easily eliminated or modified.

Although the theory has strong heuristic capabilities and has been useful in outlining the array of factors that contribute to abusive and neglectful behavior, it has demonstrated more limited utility as a policy and practice framework for several reasons. First, ecological theory, by definition, suggests prevention efforts are needed at multiple levels of the social ecology. Unfortunately, the more successful interventions, as noted earlier, are well-focused and build their strategies around a limited number of causal pathways. Indeed, multifaceted initiatives that attempt to alter an array of variables at multiple ecological levels frequently struggle with implementation issues and a sense of mission drift as they attempt to address myriad reasons parents may struggle to care for their children (Daro and Dodge 2009). Second, responsibility for health, education, economic well-being, housing, and child protection is distributed across many federal and state agencies, each of which define core outcomes and standards of best practice within their own disciplines and sphere of influence. Developing, managing and sustaining programs that cut across these defined areas in the manner suggested by an ecological framework is, at best, challenging. Finally, measuring outcomes and success is easier at the participant level than at a population level. As such, the prevention response has been more focused on creating a series of interventions that target distinct populations rather than efforts to alter community context or normative values.

In short, we have a theoretical framework that many in the field embrace at direct odds with the prevention field's current programmatic initiatives. Although there have been notable gains in both the field's awareness and understanding of maltreatment, the current prevention service network and system has failed to reach deep into the at-risk population and has not created the contextual and normative change necessary to maximize the safety and healthy development of the nation's children. Crafting a prevention framework that better aligns our programmatic efforts with our theoretical explanation for maltreatment requires policy, practice and research communities to address how resources are allocated along at least three continua:

• Universal versus targeted approaches to service delivery
• Evidence-based programs versus innovation
• Direct services versus infrastructure

None of these debates have an absolute answer nor can they fully be resolved through the empirical process. However, creative problem solving is best served when diverse opinions are recognized and openly debated. Effective policy directions are often those that capture the most promising elements of both ends of a continuum rather than limiting the choice to one end or the other. Within the child abuse prevention field, we believe these three dimensions represent this type of fertile opportunity for new learning.

Universal Versus Targeted Prevention Efforts

Much of the prevailing research on the effectiveness of various prevention programs argue for investing resources in targeted as opposed to universal services (Karoly et al. 1998; Heckman 2011). Targeted programs generally produce stronger outcomes with their participants, in part, because such participants have a higher likelihood to experience difficulties in the absence of intervention and, therefore, have more to gain if interventions are successful. As such, it is not surprising that the effect sizes in randomized trials of targeted programs exceed the effect sizes of programs that engage a broader spectrum of participants (Horowitz and Garber 2006). Although those engaging in high quality prevention services do indeed benefit from early intervention, it is equally true that many of the most difficult and challenged families fail to fully engage in these services (Daro et al. 2003; Guterman 2001; Navaie-Waliser et al. 2000). And once enrolled, they fail to stay enrolled for sufficient time to achieve targeted program objectives (Duggan et al. 2000; McCurdy and Daro 2001).

Further, the high cost of these interventions suggest care is needed if they are to be targeted solely on the basis of various demographic indicators of risk such as young maternal age, poverty, or single parent status. While low-income parents, those raising children on their own, and those birthing children before their own developmental trajectory has been stabilized face significant challenges, not all poor parents, teen parents or single parents require intensive, long term interventions to avoid abusive or neglectful behaviors.

Beyond these logistical challenges, targeted prevention programs suggest that struggles with parenting are limited to only certain segments of the population and that most parents have no need for additional assistance to avoid acts of abuse or neglect. This strategy does little to create a collective commitment to child well-being or to draw the public together in a shared obligation to insure the optimal health and development of all children. Targeted prevention efforts reinforce a stark line between parents that can meet their obligations and those that cannot, contributing to society's "coming apart" which as long troubled many social policy scholars (Bellah 1985; Murray 2012; Wuthnow 1991).

Moving forward, it seems prudent for prevention advocates to invest some resources in strategies that provide universal offers of assistance to parents at critical inflection points in the parenting process where the demands of caregiving are high. Possible timing for such universal assistance might be at the time a child is born, the transition to toddlerhood, and the onset of puberty. Limited evidence exists regarding the capacity of such interventions to have meaningful impacts on child maltreatment rates. However, initial findings regarding the benefits of universal assessments and offer of assistance at birth are promising (Alonso-Marsden et al. 2011; Dodge et al. 2012; Daro et al. 2005; Fischer et al. 2008) as are findings on the impacts of multi-tiered prevention strategies (Prinz et al. 2009; Sanders et al. 2003). The eventual impacts of this type of embedded system on child development outcomes and parental behaviors are not yet known because studies are now in progress. And, as with all interventions, ultimate impacts will be a function of implementation quality, the universal outreach system's ability to identify accurately the level of support parents require, and the capacity of local formal and informal resources to meet identified demands.

Evidence-Based Interventions Versus Innovations

As discussed earlier, public investments are increasingly being directed to program models identified as being "evidence-based" and ongoing assessment or monitoring of program effects are being built into service operations (Haskins and Baron 2011). This new clarion call for evidence-based decision-making is re-framing the process through which prevention strategies are selected for replication. When faced with the need to select a given strategy or define a specific service delivery process, policy makers, agency directors and direct service staff are asked to view those decisions through an "evidence-based" lens. Competing alternatives are weighted in relation to their ability to demonstrate significant and meaningful impacts on their target population. The evaluative findings included in such assessments generally reflect findings from clinical randomized trials or, in some instances, carefully crafted quasi-experimental designs (Tseng 2012). The logic behind this decision-making framework is that such standards increase the likelihood that programs and policies will reflect rigorous thinking and will, therefore, increase the odds that public and private resources will be invested in strategies most likely to achieve policy or programmatic objectives.

Although no one can seriously disagree with the importance of reviewing empirical findings before allocating public funds, the ability of existing evidence-based approaches to realize desired objectives is neither absolute nor sustainable. The strategy insures that one is implementing programs that have demonstrated effects. It cannot, however, insure that such effects will continue to occur indefinitely, particularly when the underlying characteristics of the population shift or the service and policy context is altered. Even if the population and context remains stable, research has repeatedly demonstrated that attempts to replicate strong programs often fail to adhere to program standards in such critical dimensions as dosage and duration or capture the original intent or manner in how such services should be delivered (Durlak and DuPre 2008).

This lack of certainty in replication and potential decline in relevance underscores the importance of also investing in innovations or alternative service delivery methods, which while untested, may provide important insights into extending the effectiveness of prevention services. Maximizing the benefits and minimizing the limitation of "rational decision-making" requires a more nuanced application of the concept. A rigid adoption of a decision-making process that would suggest you design a program, test it, determine that it works, and then market it without a clear pathway for learning how to do better will not create an informed program planning process. The policy target or message should not be simply a mandate to adopt empirically-based practice, but rather to establishing an implementation and decision-making process that will insure continuous program improvement.

Direct Service Investments Versus Infrastructure

As we have noted, many barriers exist in replicating programs with quality and extending the availability of services to those families facing the most difficult circumstances. While some of these barriers lie within the programs themselves, attention has shifted to consider the elements of context that support or complicate the initial implementation and sustainability of the most promising interventions (Tibbits et al. 2010; Wandersman et al. 2008). Just as any physical structure requires strong infrastructure, social service programs benefit from an array of elements that strengthen their capacity to deliver services at high quality and with consistency over time. Some have conceptually organized these elements into three groups – foundational infrastructure (planning and collaboration); implementation infrastructure (operations and workforce development); and sustaining infrastructure (fiscal capacity, community and political support, communications and evaluation) (Paulsell et al. 2012).

Investing all prevention dollars into program replication is insufficient for creating the type of prevention system needed to both strengthen programs and sustain them over time. Comprehensive planning efforts, establishing, staffing and sustaining robust collaborative networks, and staffing prevention programs with a diverse and well-trained work force will require substantial public investment. Just as one would not build a subdivision without adequate investments in streets, public utilities or police and fire services, continuous replication in individual interventions without a comparable investment in the efforts need to sustain them over time is unlikely to achieve desired outcomes.

Prevention Strategies for the Twenty-First Century

Moving forward, child abuse and neglect prevention planners will face many external challenges. However, they also will have a vast body of existing knowledge and many bright spots of innovation. Technological advancements in social media and improved access to the internet present exciting new opportunities to engage parents, to provide information while maintaining privacy, and to increase contact (Benedetti 2012). And, as we have indicated, much can be learned from successes and failures in other fields. All of these events will continue to inform the work of maltreatment prevention just as they have throughout history.

There are no guarantees of success. However, several promising pathways exist that, if pursued, can enhance our learning and potentially improve our capacity to prevent maltreatment. These strategies include the following.

End our singular focus on child abuse prevention and embrace the need to promote healthy child development: Preventing child abuse may best be served by shifting our focus from a singular emphasis on reducing negative behaviors to a more aggressive emphasis on promoting child well-being. Such change in focus, in addition to capturing the full spectrum of behaviors and outcomes parents' desire for their children, offers the possibility of engaging a broader array of scholars studying individual and systemic pathways that support positive child development and health promotion.

Extend the promise of equal opportunity to all children by offering support at the time a child is born: A core value in the United States is a commitment to equal opportunity, to offering all citizens the chance to advance their economic and social standing. Historically, this concept has been best exemplified by our commitment to universal public education and to creating a pathway to literacy and economic success. By initiating offers of support to all children at the time of birth, we have the capacity to establish this value at the earliest point in a child's life and reinforce the shared need for support all parents face.

Offer families choice in how they secure the help they need by engaging a range of stakeholders and drawing together both formal and informal sources of support: The public health perspective is grounded in the belief that collective goals are best realized when individuals act in ways supportive of their own health and the health of their children (Wallack and Lawrence 2005). Reduction in the rate of smoking, fatalities due to drunk driving and the increased use of safety devices such as car seats have, at their core, a set of specific behaviors around which individual citizens feel empowered to take personal action to insure collective outcomes. Community child abuse prevention will become a reality when a comparable set of behaviors are in place that will facilitate the ability of parents to provide nurturing and supportive environments for their children and to help others in their community achieve these same outcomes.

Continue to rigorously evaluate all of our assumptions – do not assume all ideas are worth replicating and once we do replicate, check to be sure we are replicating with quality and fidelity to the concept: Assessing the impacts of our efforts is an ongoing challenge. Achieving meaningful change in our capacity to prevent child abuse will not rest in the simple replication of what we know works but rather in the commitment to continuous program improvement and learning.

Build collaboratively not just at the institutional level but among the professions leading the field – make interdisciplinary thought and practice a reality in workforce development: An early feature of the child abuse prevention response included a focus on multidisciplinary teams in which a diverse array of professionals shared their unique perspectives on the factors contributing the abusive and neglectful behaviors and how best to remediate its effects (Schmitt 1978). Despite this commitment to multidisciplinary learning and case planning, relatively little progress has been made in breaking down walls across various disciplines. Correcting this shortcoming is a critical feature for enriching our interventions as well as building a stronger systemic response.

Conclusion

Child maltreatment policy and practice innovations have a long history of responding to new learning generated by careful research. Most recently, this reliance on doing what the research suggests may be promising has resulted in a particular concentration on supporting programs that engage pregnant women and new parents. Focusing on a child's first years of life provide a promising foundation on which to build the institutional infrastructure needed to produce sustained reductions in all forms of maltreatment. In maximizing the benefits of targeting prevention services to this population, public policy is directing its investments to evidence-based interventions which have been subject to rigorous evaluation and found to produce positive effects. Moving forward, it will be increasingly important to track program implementation to assure that services are delivered in the manner intended and with the recommended dosage and duration. When high quality services are diluted or implemented with staff poorly trained or inadequately supervised, positive outcomes and effect sizes suffer. Investing in evidence-based programs will not advance the prevention mission unless comparable and consistent attention is paid to how these programs are replicated.

Finally, the future of prevention lies only in part on the replication of promising program models. Perhaps more important will be insuring that such programs are effectively linked together into a coordinated system of care. As suggested by ecological theories of human development, combating child abuse as well as other threats to child well-being requires myriad efforts that address the quality of the parent–child interaction as well as the quality of the context in which parent rear their children. Simultaneously addressing these multiple threats to child well-being will require a network of interventions, greater collaboration, and outcome alignment among those agencies that direct their resources to families and young children and help to shape the communities in which children live.

References

Aarons, G., Sommerfeld, D., & Walrath-Greene, C. (2009). Evidence-based practice implementation: The impact of public versus private sector organization type on organizational support, provider attitudes, and adoption of evidence-based practice. *Implementation Science, 4*(1), 83.

Addy, S., & Wight, V. (2012). *Basic facts about low-income children, 2010: Children under age 6*. New York: National Center for Children in Poverty.

Alonso-Marsden, S., Dodge, K., O'Donnell, K., Murphy, R., Sato, J., & Christopoulos, C. (2011, April). *Predictors of family participation in a universal nurse home visiting program to prevent child maltreatment*. Paper presented at the Biennial Meeting of the Society of Research in Child Development, Montreal.

Barnett, W. S., Jung, K., Yarosz, D. J., Thomas, J., Hornbeck, A., Stechuk, R., & Burns, S. (2008). Educational effects of the tools of the mind curriculum: A randomized trial. *Early Childhood Research Quarterly, 23*(3), 299–313.

Barth, R. P. (2009). Preventing child abuse and neglect with parent training: Evidence and opportunities. *The Future of Children, 19*(2), 95–118.

Bellah, R. (1985). *Habits of the heart: Individualism and commitment to American life*. Berkeley: University of California Press.

Belsky, J. (1980). Child maltreatment: An ecological integration. *American Psychologist, 35*, 320–335.

Benedetti, G. (2012). *Innovations in the field of child abuse and neglect: A review of the literature*. Chicago: Chapin Hall at the University of Chicago.

Bernard, K., Dozier, M., Bick, J., Lewis-Morrarty, E., Lindhiem, O., & Carlson, E. (2012). Enhancing attachment organization among maltreated children: Results of a randomized clinical trial. *Child Development, 83*(2), 623–636.

Blakemore, S.-J. (2011). Imaging brain development: The adolescent brain. *NeuroImage, 61*(2), 397–406.

Bond, G. R., Drake, R. E., McHugo, G. J., Rapp, C. A., & Whitley, R. (2009). Strategies for improving fidelity in the national evidence-based practices project. *Research on Social Work Practice, 19*(5), 569–581.

Bronfenbrenner, U. (1979). *The ecology of human development: Experiments by nature and design*. Cambridge, MA: Harvard University Press.

Brown, K. E. (2011). *Strengthening national data on child fatalities could aid in prevention* (GAO Report GAO-11-599). Washington, DC: U.S. Government Accountability Office.

Bryck, R. L., & Fisher, P. A. (2011). Training the brain: Practical applications of neural plasticity from the intersection of cognitive neuroscience, developmental psychology, and prevention science. *American Psychologist, 67*(2), 87–100.

Carnegie Task Force on Meeting the Needs of Young Children. (1994). *Starting points: Meeting the needs of our youngest children*. New York: Carnegie Corporation of New York.

Caughy, M., Miller, T., Genevro, J., Huang, Y., & Nautiyal, C. (2003). The effects of healthy steps on discipline strategies of parents of young children. *Journal of Applied Developmental Psychology, 24*(5), 517–534.

Center on the Developing Child. (2012). *Toxic shock: The facts*. Retrieved from http://developingchild.harvard.edu/topics/science_of_early_childhood/toxic_stress_response/

Chaffin, M., Hecht, D., Bard, D., Silovsky, J. F., & Beasley, W. H. (2012). A statewide trial of the safecare home-based services model with parents in child protective services. *Pediatrics, 129*(3), 509–515.

Chavis, D. M., & Trent, T. R. (2009). Scope, scale, and sustainability: What it takes to create lasting community change. *The Foundation Review, 1*(1), 96–114.

Choi, M., & Ruona, W. E. A. (2011). Individual readiness for organizational change and its implications for human resource and organization development. *Human Resource Development Review, 10*(1), 46–73.

Cicchetti, D., & Rizley, R. (1981). Developmental perspectives on the etiology, intergenerational transmission, and sequelae of child maltreatment. *New Directions for Child Development, 11*, 31–55.

Cohn, A. (1983). *An approach to preventing child abuse*. Chicago: National Committee to Prevent Child Abuse.

Cohn, A. (1987). Our national priorities for prevention. In R. Helfer & C. H. Kempe (Eds.), *The battered child* (4th ed., pp. 444–445). Chicago: The University of Chicago Press.

Committee on Psychosocial Aspects of Child and Family Health, Committee on Early Childhood, Adoption, and Dependent Care, Section on Developmental and Behavioral Pediatrics, Garner, A. S., Shonkoff, J. P., Siegel, B. S., Dobbins, M. I., . . . Wood, D. L. (2011). Early childhood adversity, toxic stress, and the role of the pediatrician: Translating developmental science into lifelong health. *Pediatrics, 129*(1), e224–e231.

Connell, A., Bullock, B. M., Dishion, T. J., Shaw, D., Wilson, M., & Gardner, F. (2008). Family intervention effects on co-occurring early childhood behavioral and emotional problems: A latent transition analysis approach. *Journal of Abnormal Child Psychology, 36*(8), 1211–1225.

Cooley, L., & Kohl, R. (2005). *Scaling up – From vision to large-scale change: A management framework for practitioners*. Washington, DC: Management Systems International.

Daniels, V.-S., & Sandler, I. (2008). Use of quality management methods in the transition from efficacious prevention programs to effective prevention services. *American Journal of Community Psychology, 41*(3/4), 250–261.

Daro, D. (1988). *Confronting child abuse: Research for effective program design.* New York: The Free Press.

Daro, D. (1993). Child maltreatment research: Implications for program design. In D. Cicchetti & S. Toth (Eds.), *Child abuse, child development, and social policy* (pp. 331–367). Norwood: Ablex Publishing Corporation.

Daro, D. (2009). Science and child abuse prevention: A reciprocal relationship. In K. Dodge & D. Coleman (Eds.), *Preventing child maltreatment: Community approaches* (pp. 9–28). New York: Guilford Press.

Daro, D. (2010a). *Child abuse prevention: A job half done.* Chicago: Chapin Hall at the University of Chicago.

Daro, D. (2010b). Preventing child abuse and neglect. In J. Myers (Ed.), *APSAC handbook on child maltreatment* (3rd ed., pp. 17–38). Beverly Hills: Sage.

Daro, D., & Cohn-Donnelly, A. (2002). Charting the waves of prevention: Two steps forward, one step back. *Child Abuse & Neglect, 26,* 731–742.

Daro, D., & Dodge, K. A. (2009). Creating community responsibility for child protection: Possibilities and challenges. *The Future of Children, 19*(2), 67–94.

Daro, D., & McCurdy, K. (2007). Interventions to prevent child maltreatment. In L. Doll, J. Mercy, R. Hammond, D. Slett, & S. Bonzo (Eds.), *Handbook on injury and violence prevention intervention* (pp. 137–156). New York: Springer.

Daro, D., McCurdy, K., Falconnier, L., & Stojanovic, D. (2003). Sustaining new parents in home visitation services: Key participant and program factors. *Child Abuse & Neglect, 27,* 1101–1125.

Daro, D., Howard, E., Tobin, J., & Harden, A. (2005). *Welcome home and early start: An assessment of program quality and outcome.* Chicago: Chapin Hall at the University of Chicago.

Daro, D., Barringer, E., & English, B. (2009). *Key trends in prevention: Report for the National Quality Improvement Center on Early Childhood Education (QIC-EC).* Washington, DC: Children's Bureau, Administration for Children and Families, U.S. Department of Health and Human Services. Available from Chapin Hall at the University of Chicago.

Dishion, T. J., Shaw, D., Connell, A., Gardner, F., Weaver, C., & Wilson, M. (2008). The family check-up with high-risk indigent families: Preventing problem behavior by increasing parents' positive behavior support in early childhood. *Child Development, 79*(5), 1395–1414.

Dodge, K., Goodman, W. B., Murphy, R., O'Donnell, K., Sata, J., & Guptill, S. (2012, May). *The Durham Connects program: Proposing a population approach to preventing child maltreatment and promoting healthy development.* Presentation at the Second Annual Frontiers of Innovation Workshop, Cambridge, MA.

Dozier, M., Lindhiem, O., Lewis, E., Bick, J., Bernard, K., & Peloso, E. (2009). Effects of a foster parent training program on young children's attachment behaviors: Preliminary evidence from a randomized clinical trial. *Child and Adolescent Social Work Journal, 26*(4), 321–332.

Dubowitz, H., Feigelman, S., Lane, W., & Kim, J. (2009). Pediatric primary care to help prevent child maltreatment: The Safe Environment for Every Kid (SEEK) model. *Pediatrics, 123*(3), 858–864.

Dubowitz, H., Lane, W. G., Semiatin, J. N., Magder, L. S., Venepally, M., & Jans, M. (2011). The Safe Environment for Every Kid model: Impact on pediatric primary care professionals. *Pediatrics, 127*(4), e962–e970.

Duggan, A., Windham, A. M. E., Fuddy, L., Rohde, C., Buchbinder, S., & Sia, C. (2000). Hawaii's Healthy Start program of home visiting for at-risk families: Evaluation of family identification, family engagement, and service delivery. *Pediatrics, 105*(1), 250–260.

DuMont, K., Kirkland, K., Mitchell-Herzfeld, S., Ehrhard-Dietzel, S., Rodriguez, M. L., Lee, E., . . . Greene, R. (2010). *A randomized trial of Healthy Families New York (HFNY): Does home visiting prevent child maltreatment?* Albany: New York State Office of Children and Family Services.

Duncan, D. F., Kum, H.-C., Caplick Weigensberg, E., Flair, K. A., & Stewart, C. J. (2008). Informing child welfare policy and practice. *Child Maltreatment, 13*(4), 383–391.

Durlak, J., & DuPre, E. (2008). Implementation matters: A review of research on the influence of implementation on program outcomes and the factors affecting implementation. *American Journal of Community Psychology, 41*(3), 327–350.

Eckenrode, J., Campa, M., Luckey, D. W., Henderson, C. R., Jr., Cole, R., Kitzman, H., . . . Olds, D. (2010). Long-term effects of prenatal and infancy nurse home visitation on the life course of youths: 19-year follow-up of a randomized trial. *Archives of Pediatrics and Adolescent Medicine, 164*(1), 9–15.

Elliot, D., & Mihalic, S. (2004). Issues in disseminating and replicating effective prevention programs. *Prevention Science, 5*(1), 47–53.

Finkelhor, D. (2008). *Childhood victimization: Violence, crime, and abuse in the lives of young people.* New York: Oxford University Press.

Finkelhor, D., Ormrod, R., Turner, H., & Hamby, S. (2005). The victimization of children and youth: A comprehensive, national survey. *Child Maltreatment, 10*(1), 5–25.

Fischer, R., Lalich, N., & Coulton, C. (2008). Taking it to scale: Evaluating the scope and reach of a community-wide initiative on early childhood. *Evaluation and Program Planning, 31,* 199–208.

Fisher, P. A., & Stoolmiller, M. (2008). Intervention effects on foster parent stress: Associations with child cortisol levels. *Development and Psychopathology, 20*(3), 1003–1021.

Fisher, P. A., Kim, H. K., Bruce, J., & Pears, K. C. (2011a). Cumulative effects of prenatal substance exposure and early adversity on foster children's HPA-axis reactivity during a psychosocial stressor. *International Journal of Behavioral Development, 36*(1), 29–35.

Fisher, P. A., Stoolmiller, M., Mannering, A. M., Takahashi, A., & Chamberlain, P. (2011b). Foster placement disruptions associated with problem behavior: Mitigating a threshold effect. *Journal of Consulting and Clinical Psychology, 79*(4), 481–487.

Fisher, P. A., Van Ryzin, M. J., & Gunnar, M. R. (2011c). Mitigating HPA axis dysregulation associated with placement changes in foster care. *Psychoneuroendocrinology, 36*, 531–539.

Fixsen, D. L., Naoon, S. F., Blase, K. A., Friedman, R. M., & Wallace, F. (2005). *Implementation research: A synthesis of the literature*. Tampa: University of South Florida, Louis de la Parte Florida Mental Health Institute, the National Implementation Research Network.

Garbarino, J. (1977). The human ecology of child maltreatment: A conceptual model for research. *Journal of Marriage and the Family, 39*, 721–735.

Garbarino, J. (1995). *Raising children in a socially toxic environment*. San Francisco: Jossey-Bass.

Gearing, R. E., El-Bassel, N., Ghesquiere, A., Baldwin, S., Gillies, J., & Ngeow, E. (2011). Major ingredients of fidelity: A review and scientific guide to improving quality of intervention research implementation. *Clinical Psychology Review, 31*(1), 79–88.

Gelles, R., & Straus, M. (1988). *Intimate violence: The causes and consequences of abuse in the American family*. New York: Simon and Schuster.

Gil, D. (1970). *Violence against children: Physical child abuse in the United States*. Cambridge, MA: Harvard University Press.

Guterman, N. (2001). *Stopping child maltreatment before it starts: Emerging horizons in early home visitation services*. Thousand Oaks: Sage.

Haskins, R., & Baron, J. (2011). *Building the connection between policy and evidence the Obama evidence-based initiatives*. Retrieved from http://www.brookings.edu/%7E/media/Files/rc/reports/2011/0907%5Fevidence%5Fbased %5Fpolicy%5Fhaskins/0907%5Fevidence%5Fbased%5Fpolicy%5Fhaskins.pdf

Heckman, J. (2011). The economics of inequality: The value of early childhood education. *American Educator, 35*(1), 31–35. 47.

Helfer, R. (1982). A review of the literature on preventing child abuse and neglect. *Child Abuse & Neglect, 6*, 251–261.

Horowitz, J., & Garber, J. (2006). The prevention of depressive symptoms in children and adolescents: A meta-analytic review. *Journal of Consulting and Clinical Psychology, 74*(3), 401–415.

IOM (Institute of Medicine), & NRC (National Research Council). (2012). *Child maltreatment research, policy, and practice for the next decade: Workshop summary*. Washington, DC: The National Academies Press.

Jonson-Reid, M., & Drake, B. (2008). Multisector longitudinal administrative databases. *Child Maltreatment, 13*(4), 392–399.

Karoly, L., Greenwood, P., Everingham, S., Hoube, J., Kilburn, M. R., Rydell, C. P., . . . Chiesa, J. (1998). *Investing in our children: What we know and don't know about the costs and benefits of early childhood interventions*. Santa Monica: RAND Corporation.

Kaye, S., & Osteen, P. J. (2011). Developing and validating measures for child welfare agencies to self-monitor fidelity to a child safety intervention. *Children and Youth Services Review, 33*(11), 2146–2151.

Kitzman, H. J., Olds, D. L., Cole, R. E., Hanks, C. A., Anson, E. A., Arcoleo, K. J., . . . Holmberg, J. R. (2010). Enduring effects of prenatal and infancy home visiting by nurses on children: Follow-up of a randomized trial among children at age 12 years. *Archives of Pediatrics and Adolescent Medicine, 164*(5), 412–418

Korst, L. M., Aydin, C. E., Signer, J. M., & Fink, A. (2011). Hospital readiness for health information exchange: Development of metrics associated with successful collaboration for quality improvement. *International Journal of Medical Informatics, 80*, e178–e188.

LeCroy, C. W., & Krysik, J. (2011). Randomized trial of the Healthy Families Arizona home visiting program. *Children and Youth Services Review, 33*(10), 1761–1766.

Letarte, M.-J., Normandeau, S., & Allard, J. (2010). Effectiveness of a parent training program "Incredible Years" in a child protection service. *Child Abuse & Neglect, 34*, 253–261.

Lowell, D. I., Carter, A. S., Godoy, L., Paulicin, B., & Briggs-Gowan, M. J. (2011). A randomized controlled trial of child first: A comprehensive home-based intervention translating research into early childhood practice. *Child Development, 82*(1), 193–208.

Marcynyszyn, L. A., Maher, E. J., & Corwin, T. W. (2011). Getting with the (evidence-based) program: An evaluation of the Incredible Years parenting training program in child welfare. *Children and Youth Services Review, 33*(5), 747–757.

Mazzucchelli, T. G., & Sanders, M. R. (2010). Facilitating practitioner flexibility within an empirically supported intervention: Lessons from a system of parenting support. *Clinical Psychology: Science and Practice, 17*(3), 238–252.

McCurdy, K., & Daro, D. (2001). Parent involvement in family support programs: An integrated theory. *Family Relations, 50*(2), 113–121.

McLanahan, S., Garfinkel, I., Mincy, R., & Donahue, E. (2010). Introduction to issue on fragile families. *The Future of Children, 20*(2), 3–16.

Melton, G., Thompson, R., & Small, M. (Eds.). (2002). *Toward a child-centered, neighborhood-based child protection system*. Westport: Praeger.

Mildon, R., & Shlonsky, A. (2011). Bridge over troubled water: Using implementation science to facilitate effective services in child welfare. *Child Abuse & Neglect, 35*(9), 753–756.

Minkovitz, C., Strobino, D., Hughart, N., Scharfstein, D., Guyer, B., & The Healthy Steps Evaluation Team. (2001). Early effects of the Healthy Steps for Young Children program. *Archives of Pediatrics & Adolescent Medicine, 155*(4), 470–479.

Minkovitz, C. S., Strobino, B. A., Mistry, K. B., Scharfstein, D., Grason, H., Hou, W., . . . Guyer, B. (2007). Healthy Steps for Young Children: Sustained results at 5.5 years. *Pediatrics, 120*(3), 658–668.

Mueller, S. C., Maheu, F. S., Dozier, M., Peloso, E., Mandell, D., Leibenluft, E., . . . Ernst, M. (2010). Early-life stress is associated with impairment in cognitive control in adolescence: An fMRI study. *Neuropsychologia, 48*, 3037–3044.

Murray, C. (2012). *Coming apart: The state of white America, 1960–2010*. New York: Random House.

Myers, J. (2006). *Child protection in America: Past, present and future*. New York: Oxford University Press.

National Scientific Council on the Developing Child. (2011). *Building the brain's "air traffic control" system: How early experiences shape the development of executive function. Working Paper 11*. Cambridge, MA: National Scientific Council on the Developing Child

Navaie-Waliser, M., Martin, S., Campbell, M., Tessaro, I., Kotelchuck, M., & Cross, A. (2000). Factors predicting completion of a home visitation program by high-risk pregnant women: The North Carolina maternal outreach worker program. *American Journal of Public Health, 90*(1), 121–124.

Nievar, M. A., Arminta, J., Qi, C., Ursula, J., & Shannon, D. (2011). Impact of HIPPY on home learning environments of Latino families. *Early Childhood Research Quarterly, 26*, 268–277.

Olds, D. (2010). The nurse family partnership. In R. Haskins & W. Barnett (Eds.), *New directions for America's preschool policies* (pp. 69–78). Washington, DC: NIERR and Brookings.

Olds, D., Sadler, L., & Kitzman, H. (2007). Programs for parents of infants and toddlers: Recent evidence from randomized trials. *Journal of Child Psychology and Psychiatry, 48*(3&4), 355–391.

Oosterman, M., De Schipper, J. C., Fisher, P., Dozier, M., & Schuengel, C. (2011). Autonomic reactivity in relation to attachment and early adversity among foster children. *Development and Psychopathology, 22*(1), 109–118.

Paulsell, D., Hargreaves, M., Coffee-Borden, B., & Boller, K. (2012). *Evidence-based home visiting systems evaluation update: 2011 draft report*. Princeton: Mathematica Policy Research.

Pears, K. C., Heywood, C. V., Kim, H. K., & Fisher, P. A. (2011). Prereading deficits in children in foster care. *School Psychology Review, 40*(1), 140–148.

Polinsky, M. L., Pion-Berlin, L., Williams, S., Long, T., & Wolf, A. M. (2010). Preventing child abuse and neglect: A national evaluation of Parents Anonymous groups. *Child Welfare, 89*(6), 43–62.

Prinz, R. J., Sanders, M. R., Shapiro, C. J., Whitaker, D. J., & Lutzker, J. R. (2009). Population-based prevention of child maltreatment: The U.S. Triple P system population trial. *Prevention Science, 10*(1), 1–12.

Roggman, L. A., Boyce, L. K., & Cook, G. A. (2009). Keeping kids on track: Impacts of a parenting-focused Early Head Start program on attachment security and cognitive development. *Early Education & Development, 20*(6), 920–941.

Sanders, M. R., Markie-Dadds, C., & Turner, K. M. T. (2003). *Theoretical, scientific and clinical foundations of the Triple P-Positive Parenting Program: A population approach to the promotion of parenting competence*. Queensland: The Parenting and Family Support Centre, The University of Queensland.

Sandler, I. N., Schoenfelder, E. N., Wolchik, S. A., & MacKinnon, D. P. (2011). Long-term impact of prevention programs to promote effective parenting: Lasting effects but uncertain processes. *Annual Review of Psychology, 62*(1), 299–329.

Schmitt, B. (Ed.). (1978). *The child protection team handbook*. New York: Garland.

Sedlak, A., & Broadhurst, D. (1996). *Third national incidence study of child abuse and neglect (NIS-3): Executive summary*. Washington, DC: U.S. Department of Health and Human Services, National Center on Child Abuse and Neglect.

Sedlak, A., Mettenburg, J., Basena, M., Petta, I., McPherson, K., Greene, A., & Li, S. (2010). *Fourth national incidence study of child abuse and neglect (NIS-4): Report to Congress, executive summary*. Washington, DC: U.S. Department of Health and Human Services, Administration for Children and Families.

Shaw, D. S., Connell, A., Dishion, T. J., Wilson, M. N., & Gardner, F. (2009). Improvements in maternal depression as a mediator of intervention effects on early childhood problem behavior. *Development and Psychopathology, 21*(2), 417–439.

Shonkoff, J. P., & Phillips, D. (2000). *From neurons to neighborhoods: The science of early childhood development*. Washington, DC: National Academy Press.

Shonkoff, J. P., Garner, A. S., & The Committee on Psychosocial Aspects of Child and Family Health, Committee on Early Childhood, Adoption, and Dependent Care, and Section on Developmental and Behavioral Pediatrics. (2011). The lifelong effects of early childhood adversity and toxic stress. *Pediatrics, 129*(1), e232–e246.

Silovsky, J. F., Bard, D., Chaffin, M., Hecht, D., Burris, L., Owora, A., Beasley, L. . . . Lutzker, J. (2011). Prevention of child maltreatment in high-risk rural families: A randomized clinical trial with child welfare outcomes. *Children and Youth Services Review, 33*(8), 1435–1444.

Straus, M. (2000). Corporal punishment and primary prevention of physical abuse. *Child Abuse & Neglect, 24,* 1109–1114.

Tibbits, M., Bumbarger, B., Kyler, S., & Perkins, D. (2010). Sustaining evidence-based interventions under real-world conditions: Results from a large-scale diffusion project. *Prevention Science, 11,* 252–262.

Tseng, V. (2012). The uses of research in policy and practice. *Social Policy Report, 26*(2), 1–16.

Tseng, S. H., Liu, K., & Wang, W.-L. (2011). Moving toward being analytical: A framework to evaluate the impact of influential factors on interagency collaboration. *Children and Youth Services Review, 33,* 798–803.

U.S. Department of Health and Human Services. (2011a). *Child Maltreatment 2010.* Available from http://www.acf.hhs.gov/programs/cb/stats_research/index.htm#can

U.S. Department of Health and Human Services. (2011b). *HHS announces $224 million to support evidence-based home visiting programs to help parents and children.* News Release.

Wallack, L., & Lawrence, R. (2005). Talking about public health: Developing America's "second language". *American Journal of Public Health, 95*(4), 567–570.

Wandersman, A., Duffy, J., Flaspohler, P., Noonan, R., Lubell, K., Stillman, L., Blachman, M., . . . Saul, J. (2008). Bridging the gap between prevention research and practice: The interactive systems framework for dissemination and implementation. *American Journal of Community Psychology, 41,* 171–181.

Webster-Stratton, C., Rinaldi, J., & Reid, J. M. (2011). Long-term outcomes of incredible years parenting program: Predictors of adolescent adjustment. *Child & Adolescent Mental Health, 16*(1), 38–46.

Wurtele, S., & Miller-Perrin, C. (1992). *Preventing child sexual abuse: Sharing the responsibility.* Lincoln: University of Nebraska Press.

Wuthnow, R. (1991). *Acts of compassion: Caring for others and helping ourselves.* Princeton: Princeton University Press.

Zigler, E., Pfannenstiel, J., & Seitz, V. (2008). The parents as teachers program and school success: A replication and extension. *Journal of Primary Prevention, 29*(2), 103–120.

Chapter 15
Community-Level Prevention of Child Maltreatment

Beth E. Molnar and William R. Beardslee

As described elsewhere in this volume, evidence-based interventions to prevent child maltreatment by instructing and assisting parents in high-risk families (e.g. teen parents, single parents, families living in poverty), are being implemented throughout the U.S. This chapter describes a much newer, and, to date, largely overlooked area of inquiry: community-level approaches to child maltreatment prevention and the ways that they may augment existing individual and family-focused efforts. Informed by emerging research on neighborhood structural factors and potentially modifiable social processes such as collective efficacy – both of which are associated with fluctuations in maltreatment rates in expected directions – community-level interventions focus on changing environments to improve population rates of maltreatment (Coulton et al. 2007; Freisthler et al. 2006).

This chapter begins by describing the theoretical foundation of community-level prevention programs and reviewing empirical research on the utility of the community-level approach. Next, we outline how experts define community-level programs for child maltreatment prevention and describe the various types of existing programs. After detailing the strategies programs use to build relationships and work with culturally diverse communities, we identify existing barriers to implementation and discuss how these programs become sustainable. The chapter ends with recommendations for moving community-level child maltreatment prevention programs forward and increasing their efficacy and longevity.

Theoretical Foundation

Over the past 30 years, a multitude of research has identified and analyzed the ways in which neighborhoods influence child health (Leventhal and Brooks-Gunn 2000; Sellstrom and Bremberg 2006). From this vital body of work comes Bronfenbrenner's Bioecological Theory of Human Development – one of the most valuable lenses through which to examine the relationship between social context and individual behavior. According to Brofenbrenner (2005), all individuals negotiate relationships with their social environments through a process of reciprocity; changes in an

B.E. Molnar, ScD (✉)
Bouvé College of Health Sciences, Northeastern University, Boston, USA
e-mail: b.molnar@neu.edu

W.R. Beardslee, M.D.
Department of Psychiatry, Harvard Medical School, Boston Children's Hospital, Boston, USA
e-mail: william.beardslee@childrens.harvard.edu

J.E. Korbin and R.D. Krugman (eds.), *Handbook of Child Maltreatment*, Child Maltreatment 2,
DOI 10.1007/978-94-007-7208-3_15, © Springer Science+Business Media Dordrecht 2014

individual affect that individual's environment, and concomitantly, changes in an individual's environment affect that individual.

This theory informs understandings of child maltreatment prevention in that it posits that a variety of social contexts – and the relationships that exist within them – influence families and behaviors. Families lacking positive community-level resources are at higher risk for a myriad of poor outcomes (e.g. mental illness, substance abuse, homelessness, criminal activity, violence victimization and perpetration) – all of which are significant risk factors for maltreatment of children within and around those families. Thus, social contexts provide important opportunities for intervention (e.g. improving parenting, strengthening community resources, providing support to families) that can be used to prevent child maltreatment.

Social disorganization is another important piece of the maltreatment puzzle. Theories of social disorganization, which originated in sociology and social work traditions, address the ways that neighborhood conditions contribute to higher or lower stress levels and affect parents and children. Studies have identified numerous examples of child maltreatment as concentrated in neighborhoods characterized by stress-inducing structural factors such as concentrated poverty, residential instability, abundance of alcohol outlets, and disorder (Coulton 1995; Freisthler 2004; Freisthler and Holmes 2012; Freisthler et al. 2006; Garbarino 1981; Garbarino and Sherman 1980; Korbin et al. 1998; Zuravin 1989; Zuravin and Taylor 1987). Such conditions increase family stress, and, as the research on the etiology of child maltreatment demonstrates, families under tremendous stress have an increased risk of child abuse and neglect (Garbarino and Sherman 1980). Indeed, Guterman and colleagues' 2009 study of 20 U.S. cities found that perceived negative social processes affect parenting stress, which, in turn, affects the risk of neglect and physical abuse.

Relatedly, a more recent line of inquiry identifies that positive neighborhood social processes are predictive of lower rates of child maltreatment. Also guided by social disorganization theories, these studies have found that perceived support buffers family stress among those families living in neighborhoods in which residents work together for a common good. At the heart of this relationship is *collective efficacy*, a construct derived from Albert Bandura's work on self-efficacy, which he defines as "the belief in one's capabilities to organize and execute the courses of action required to manage prospective situations" (Bandura 1995, p. 2). Extending this understanding to the community level, Bandura (1995) postulated communities are strengthened by members' belief that working together will enable them to solve collective problems.

There is strong empirical evidence for neighborhood-level collective efficacy's influence on individual behaviors. For example researchers have found higher levels of neighborhood collective efficacy to be associated with lower rates of violent behavior (Morenoff and Sampson 1997; Sampson et al. 1997), firearm carrying by youth (Molnar et al. 2004), youth aggression and delinquency (Molnar et al. 2008), intimate partner violence (Browning and Cagney 2002), and dating violence perpetration (Jain et al. 2010; Rothman et al. 2011). Moreover, a number of studies have found an association between collective efficacy and several other advantageous outcomes, such as improved mental health (Xue et al. 2005), delayed onset of adolescent sexual initiation (Browning et al. 2004), improved educational and substance use outcomes (Coley et al. 2004), and higher standardized math test scores (Emory et al. 2008).

Researchers have also identified several other positive neighborhood social processes that contribute to lower levels of child maltreatment. For example, in a multi-level study that controlled for individual-level support (and thus represented a social process above the presence of individual support), researchers found lower rates of parent-to-child physical aggression (a measure combining physical abuse and physical punishment) in Chicago neighborhoods in which individuals reported having larger social networks of family and friends (Molnar et al. 2003). The finding was true only for Hispanic families, suggesting that culture played a role as well (Molnar et al. 2003).

Similarly, an ethnographic study of residents in poor neighborhoods with disparate rates of maltreatment found neighbors who were supportive of each others' parenting to be a potential mechanism of lower child maltreatment rates, even in the presence of poverty (Korbin et al. 1998). Zolotor and Runyan's 2006 study which employed a measure of social capital that combined collective efficacy, social cohesion, and a psychological sense of community into a 22-item instrument, predicted a 30 % reduction in the odds of neglect and psychologically harsh (but not physically harsh) parenting. Combining the structural and social characteristics of neighborhoods, Garbarino and Barry (1997) postulated that the *social impoverishment of neighborhoods* affects child maltreatment by producing: (1) high levels of need among residents that inhibits sharing; (2) a lack of positive role models that reinforces inappropriate and inadequate parenting behavior; and (3) a lack of intimate and confident interactions that inhibit both nurturance and feedback.

Community-Level Programs to Prevent Child Maltreatment

The following description of model community-level child maltreatment programs and the elements that have made them successful draws from published research, field work, and a series of in-depth interviews with 33 representatives from programs in the United States, Canada, and Australia. Using purposive sampling, we chose to interview those with experience in community programs, including community-based agency directors, academic researchers, community-involved government and law enforcement officials, program staff, and program evaluators. Respondents represented a diversity of programs with a variety of goals, including those that sought to unify community sectors, those working on efforts to build community-level infrastructure to coordinate services and prevention efforts, experts seeking to locate and expand the reach of family-focused programs, and those working to change norms of collective responsibility for child safety and healthy development, increase collective efficacy and build social fabric, and utilize resources that already existed in their communities.

Examples of Community-Level Programs

Evaluation studies have identified several promising community-level maltreatment prevention efforts (Daro and Dodge 2009; Dodge and Coleman 2009). One such effort is the *Triple-P* program, a tiered parenting intervention developed in Australia by Matthew Sanders and colleagues (2003). Utilizing a U.S.-based randomized trial of 18 counties in South Carolina to evaluate population-wide implementation of the program, researchers identified significant county-level intervention effects: counties with the *Triple-P* program had lower rates of out-of-home placements, child injuries related to maltreatment, and lower rates of reported child maltreatment than did counties without the program (Prinz et al. 2009). In addition, the *Triple-P* program's approach of providing different intensities of services depending on the different needs of families were both successful and cost effective (Prinz et al. 2009).

Another promising program, the *Durham Family Initiative*, utilizes the concepts developed in System of Care (Tolan and Dodge 2005), or "wraparound" services increasingly used in children's mental health services in recent decades. Researchers expanded this model to develop and evaluate what they call a Preventive System of Care (Dodge et al. 2004). This approach focuses on (1) using home visiting to connect families with needed prevention services and (2) enhancing the availability of evidence-based services in communities. The program has yielded promising evidence of efficacy, as substantiated rates of child maltreatment in Durham County decreased 49 % (more than twice the 22 % decrease experienced in five comparison communities over the initial evaluation period) (Daro and Dodge 2009; Dodge and Coleman 2009).

Strong Communities (described elsewhere in this volume) is a program that sought to increase collective efficacy for parents and children across an entire community in northwestern South Carolina.

Using outreach workers to build and promote norms of neighbors helping families keep their children safe, this community-wide initiative focused on primary prevention of child abuse and neglect. *Strong Communities* emphasizes the philosophy that "families should be able to get help where they are, when they need it, in a form that they can use it, with ease and without stigma," or, as they shortened it – "people shouldn't have to ask" (Melton 2009, 2010). The program successfully recruited over 5,000 volunteers who spent more than 60,000 hours welcoming and supporting families (Haski-Leventhal et al. 2008). Compared with matched communities, the areas with *Strong Communities* experienced significant benefits that speak to program success: Child maltreatment reports fell, and, parents involved in the program 5 years after it began reported experiencing a number of improved outcomes, including greater social support, more help from others, and a greater sense of community (Melton 2010).

There are also several community-level programs specifically focused on preventing child sexual abuse. On such program, *Stop It Now*, is a nationally available hotline where callers can anonymously find help if they suspect a child is at risk or being harmed but are not quite ready to make a report to authorities, if they are worried about possibly harming a child themselves, or if they have already sexually abused a child and want help in stopping the behavior. Evaluation of the impact of the *Stop It Now!* Georgia site from 2002 to 2007 found drops in state reports of child sexual abuse in 4 of the 5 years off the study period, with an overall drop from 99 to 56 cases per 100,000 children during this time. The helpline at the site fielded over 1,200 calls and trained 7,700 community members and professionals (Schober et al. 2012a). The *Enough Abuse* campaign, another effort targeting child sexual abuse, is a program that focuses on educating, communicating, and advocating for prevention of child sexual abuse using community and social change strategies. Although an outcome evaluation of this program, which was initially piloted in four sites in Massachusetts, has yet to be done, a process evaluation found that it met its goals and received high ratings from participants (Schober et al. 2012b).

In addition, a number of programs focus on community-level prevention of infant head trauma stemming from caregivers' shaking of an infant to a point where severe head trauma occurs. Although it has a relatively low incidence rate, this trauma, sometimes called Shaken Baby Syndrome is extremely damaging and often fatal. Recent research points to unsoothable crying, a developmentally normal infant-caregiver interaction, as a trigger for caregivers' shaking behavior (Barr 2012). The *Period of Purple Crying* program (PURPLE is an acronym representing the signs of unsoothable crying) targets this form of maltreatment. The program was created by a team in western New York who found that having parents sign a commitment not to shake their babies, watch an educational DVD, and read a related booklet resulted in a 50 % reduction of the infant head trauma incidence rate after 6 years (Dias et al. 2005). Expanded by the National Center on Shaken Baby Syndrome (www.dontshake.org) to include reinforcement by public health and physician practices, and a public health and media campaign for the general public, the program's effectiveness has been established through a number of studies, including randomized controlled trials in Seattle and Vancouver, B.C., (Barr et al. 2009a, b) and a trial in all 91 of North Carolina's hospitals. A recent randomized controlled trial in Japan also found the program to be effective in changing knowledge and walk away behavior during episodes of unsoothable crying (Fujiwara et al. 2012).

Defining a Community-Level Approach

Given that the focus on community-level strategies is relatively new in this field, we asked each of the experts we interviewed to share their definition of "community-level prevention of child abuse and neglect." We also asked them to discuss the elements they believe are necessary for program success. Despite variation, respondents' definitions of community-level interventions to reduce child maltreatment cohered around four themes:

First, community-level intervention programs are those that *work across sectors* of a community. Many of those interviewed noted that it is important that "everybody feels involved," and "all the players develop a shared vision of what the community should look like, then work together toward that vision." They also discussed efforts to build infrastructure that effectively coordinates services and prevention efforts. For example, one program evaluator described these programs as providing a "web of support," or a "group hug." Those interviewed agreed that the connectedness, monitoring, and opportunities for children were increased only through the creation and strengthening of the social fabric of a community. A stronger social fabric reduces stress and links families with needed resources, which, in turn, improves family interaction and child health.

A second emergent theme was the goal of *locating programs for families in community settings*. Those we talked with mentioned that programs should be available community-wide and should actively monitor the needs of the community in which they are set. Several of those interviewed described this method as taking a "systems approach." Their discussions centered around themes such as engaging members, assessing needs, increasing resources, fostering collaboration, and reassessing/retooling.

The next emergent theme emphasized *changing community conditions regarding safety for children*. For example, an interview participant from a community-level program that sought to increase collective efficacy discussed their efforts as creating norms of collective responsibility for child welfare and healthy child development. He noted, "(our) mantra has, in its various incarnations, been that…that families ought to be able to get help where they are, when they need it, in a form they can use it, with ease, and without stigma." Others described similar efforts, such as building dependable social networks for parents, providing interventions to change community/societal norms of parenting behaviors, and changing policies to support new behaviors.

The fourth and final theme to emerge from these definitional discussions was a broadly shared acknowledgement that community-level programs must *focus on changing population-level rates of child maltreatment*. This goal was mentioned by many of the respondents, even those who had found the changing of rates to be very difficult to demonstrate.

Challenge: Building Relationships with Communities

In addition to exploring how programs define their organizations and goals, we also sought to identify the ways that community-level programs gain entry, plan, and implement child maltreatment interventions in a variety of community settings. We asked interview participants to discuss the strategies they used to gain community access and build community trust. There was unanimous agreement on the absolute importance of doing careful work in order to gain the trust of communities, assess their needs and strengths, and gain buy-in for the goals and objectives of new initiatives. In analyzing participants' discussions of their approaches, we identified eight common strategies for successful community engagement.

To begin, many program experts discussed a strategy of *identifying or utilizing catalysts for action*. Several participants noted that a single case of child maltreatment in the media or the identification of a perpetrator within a community was a catalyst for action that led to the development of a community-level program. For example, one participant described how a high-profile child death was a catalyst that led to four countywide pilot studies of the effectiveness of evidence-based child maltreatment programs, which were then followed by statewide implementation within 6 months.

A second identified strategy was that of going through a process of *assessing readiness for change* in a community. Multiple interview participants described using a process for assessing whether a community had enough resources for a community-level intervention to succeed. Typically, they would present community agencies or leaders with a list of what a community needs to get started during early negotiations and would only move forward if and when they deemed a community ready. Related to this was a third emergent theme – *utilizing or enhancing existing infrastructure*. According to those interviewed, investing the initial time to conduct comprehensive needs assessments and assess organizational readiness enabled programs to identify those individuals and agencies already working on prevention.

Identifying key leaders was another important strategy identified by program representatives. Most participants described the identification of key leaders in a community as a vital step towards successful community engagement. One program worker explained, "finding that mover and shaker in the community who is going to be legitimate and is going to be able to provide energy. And I think we're always looking as we go out to the communities, either for a leader like that, or an organization that kind of has those…those qualities embedded in it."

Several community-based agency directors recalled quickly learning the strategic necessity of *promoting programs as those other than "child abuse prevention."* Recognizing the possibility of alienating clients or participants, several respondents noted that they made the strategic choices *not* to explicitly identify as focused on "child maltreatment prevention." However, whether or not they were always publicly explicit about program goals of lowering community rates of child abuse and neglect, the majority of respondents agreed that this was a consistent internal goal. An executive director of a community-based agency observed that this is particularly true for programs that target child sexual abuse, noting, "If child abuse is hard, child sexual abuse is harder, it has the tremendous yuck factor …. You know, nobody wants to think about this issue."

Finally, all program representatives recognized the strategy of *coalition building* to be an important part of community engagement. This essential strategy is well-illustrated by the following description of building relationships between churches, schools and individuals within communities:"Well, you rebuild the village. You create social fabric….we developed [an] interfaith partnership where we would go around in poor Black communities, find large Black churches within a half a mile of these schools, and tell the Black churches to go to the schools and link with schools so that the children could have mentors, connectedness, social fabric, monitoring, things to do to create social self esteem, build social skills. Give people some safety."

Challenge: Working with Culturally Diverse Communities

Diversity in the United States is continuously rising: Between 2000 and 2010, the U.S. minority population rose from 86.9 to 111.9 million – an increase of 29 % (Humes et al. 2011). It is unsurprising, then, that program success and sustainability require effective management of *cultural sensitivity, cultural humility, and cultural competence*. As Betancourt and Cervantes (2009) assert, "The foundation of cross-cultural care and communication is based on the attitudes central to professionalism: humility, empathy, curiosity, respect, sensitivity, and awareness of all outside influences on the patient" (472). Cultural competence must be a "commitment and active engagement… that requires humility as individuals continually engage in self-reflection and self-critique" (Tervalon and Murray-Garcia 1998, p. 118). Moreover, Teravalon and Murray-Garcia (1998), continues, (cultural) humility is required to check power imbalances, and to maintain respectful partnerships with communities. To successfully meet the challenge of working effectively both within and across community cultures, it is necessary to conceptualize opportunities and challenges – a process that requires recognition of the multiple levels (each with a unique set of challenges) involved in such work.

The first level entails delivering interventions to individuals or families in a specific program, in a specific geographic locale. Sensitivity to culture, language and family traditions are essential to effective delivery of services. To meet this challenge, some programs choose to pay higher salaries to staff members who can speak the language and know the culture from the inside. Program location is also key to delivery: It is important to choose locations where community members are most comfortable, be it a school, community center, or other arena.

Several of the experts we interviewed mentioned the importance of knowing – but not judging – the history of a particular people. For example, one interview subject described the challenges of helping their local Haitian community "envision a different way of modeling behavior" around severe physical punishment of children, paying close attention to historical context, noting: "the parents would say, you know, if you lived in Haiti under Papa Doc Duvalier, any misstep on the part of your kid could mean your kid was dead. And so harsh physical punishment to make them pay attention was certainly less serious than the kind of punishment you would get from soldiers." Another interview participant discussed the importance of analyzing larger, long-term patterns, explaining it is necessary to understand "why some communities … have less social capital, cultural capital, access to resources…to me, underlying the whole thing is racial segregation and discrimination…fifty percent of [African American children] will be investigated for child abuse and neglect … before their tenth birthday."

The second level of program implementation entails delivering interventions to groups of people from either similar or different cultural backgrounds. At this level, sensitivity to the settings in which interactions occur is absolutely crucial. One strategy employed by programs at this level is bringing community members from diverse backgrounds together in order to have them learn from each other and find common ground. As one expert described, "This area probably sets the record for people, the number of parents born in other countries … We do the best that we can to have people on the team who can connect to those cultures and languages but there is just such diversity in the city. There are just too many times you can't speak the language so we get creative… giving all of those parents from whatever cultures they come from, [the opportunity to] share … the ways they are different but ultimately come to the place of where they're the same, which is their children."

Many of those we talked with also emphasized the importance of advisory boards. They noted that, because advisory boards can be seen as representing diverse constituencies and cultures in a community, they often help with the processes of understanding cultural sensitivity and bringing different groups from different cultures together.

The third level of program implementation involves coordinating programs across a variety of different centers, each with their own organizational culture. At this level, it is important to demonstrate sensitivity and awareness to organizational diversity. Our own experiences with programs such as *Head Start* (www.nhsa.org) illuminated the ways in which various centers can be quite different from one another for multiple reasons. They may serve different cultural groups, have unique organizational histories, or have specific and unique connections to a community – all producing differing organizational cultures. In addition, organizational cultures are also heavily determined by the particular purpose of an organization (e.g. a traditional human services agency vs. a grassroots organization that has grown up around a particular issue).

For leaders, then, it is necessary to be sensitive to the various structures and cultures of diverse organizations and to devise strategies that will allow for coordination and effective program delivery. This necessity is well-illustrated by one respondent's description of working with a Native American community. Doing so often meant working with a variety of tribes and their diverse histories, different religions, and differing governmental structures – all of which had profound impact on how child abuse prevention could be organized: "the tribes have their own histories with each other over the years – sometimes good, sometimes not so good. And the cultures and the languages and things like that are to some extent distinct. And, you know, people naturally don't like being lumped in with everybody else. And so you have to go with a certain respect for even the differences between tribe-to-tribe, differences in the culture.

The fourth level entails working in multiple diverse settings with large programs in quite different geographic areas. At this level, it is important to devote attention to geographic differences as well as to differences in the structure of health care, education and social welfare. This work requires cultural sensitivity and attention to quality control and infrastructure across many different sites – tasks that present challenges significantly different than the ones involved in working in a single defined site or geographic area. When working in multiple diverse settings, it is necessary to balance the degree of need in each community with differing capacities to organize and deliver programs. Recognizing and meeting needs requires continuous listening and modification as needs evolve over time. Experts from our study gave several examples of how important it was to get practical help for a community. One respondent discussed an experience trying to balance their need to recognize the necessity of a community dental clinic with the need to help their community raise money to assist a family who had experienced a tragedy.

According to many, addressing pressing needs early on was an important part of cultural sensitivity. Respondents emphasized that listening and responding, in part, by tailoring programs to meet community needs, was essential. One said, "I think the guiding principle in all of this work is to listen and to pay respect, and to not assume that this organization has the answer [in this case, referring to a nurse-family program] and to really work with community stakeholders to first of all gain some understanding of the degree to which this program really is a good fit … listening and being respectful are fundamental to any kind of cultural or population level adaptation that may be appropriate."

Some of those we talked with emphasized that there were some important fundamental principles that worked across all cultures, no matter how different they may be. One respondent makes this very point, noting that most important for all communities are "a safe engaging environment for children, a positive learning environment, consistent, assertive discipline … reasonable expectations … and taking care of yourself [as a parent]. There is no culture anywhere, I believe, where those principles would not be helpful to children."

Challenge: Barriers

Barriers present another significant challenge that those doing community-level work must overcome. According to the experts we talked with, this work commonly entails overcoming multiple types of barriers, including those within agencies or programs themselves, those between agencies or programs and the barriers presented by community dynamics.

Within agencies or programs, financial challenges are a constant and significant barrier. Whether trying to stretch tight budgets or competing with other programs for limited available funds, financial challenges constrain the scope and duration of community programs. The challenges of managing organizational dynamics present another intra-organizational barrier. From working with differing organizational cultures and bridging divergent priorities to coordinating multiple partnered agencies and struggling for resources in a field full of others doing the same, the struggle to bridge differences is a significant obstacle to program implementation.

In our interviews with experts, several respondents also noted that time – or the lack thereof – is yet another significant barrier. They reported that this is exacerbated by a climate of scarce funding and noted feeling that they often didn't have enough time to implement community programs in the best possible way. One government official recalled, "We also had another problem in that, because we were having to do this so quickly, and we weren't really planning it. It was just kind of being pushed on us … there was just no forethought. It was just kind of go out and do, in mass chaos." The difficulty of training and coordinating personnel, and keeping them on board, is another logistical challenge to overcome.

In addition to the barriers within agencies, there are also multiple barriers constituted by gulfs and competition between agencies. The organizational field within which intervention programs operate is, by no means, sparsely populated. Often, community agencies feel threatened by something new coming into their community and fear that a new program will disrupt or replace work they are already doing. Many of those with experience in the child maltreatment field remarked that they regularly competed with other agencies and programs for resources (including funding, recognition, message resonance, and community perceptions of legitimacy and value). A government official recalling her experiences in grappling with this obstacle described the confusion and difficulty inherent in such competition: "We caused a lot of competition between the [new programs] here and the already existing programs that were trying to do good work.... At that time, we had…literally had programs standing on a front door of a family fighting over, "Will you enroll in our program?" "Well, no, enroll in our program," you know. Because everyone was targeting the same people."

When agencies partnered together, they also faced the difficulty of communicating and coordinating with multiple organizations/agencies (each with its own organizational culture). This presented a barrier to their efforts to construct, implement, and maintain consistent and effective intervention programs. The divergent organizational cultures within partnered agencies often made it very difficult for new ideas, practices, and programs to gain traction in a community. According to our sample of experts, open communication with existing programs is an important strategy for overcoming this barrier.

Both the characteristics of communities themselves and the specific dynamics of the organization-community interaction also constitute hurdles to be overcome. Some of these challenges include reaching communities, transforming community norms, and constructing and maintaining trusting, respectful, and inclusive relationships between the community and the organizations responsible for program implementation.

Stratification is one community characteristic that presented a barrier to effective program implementation. Many respondents reported that existing divisions within communities were a frequent source of tension and challenge. For some, these barriers were constituted by racial segregation and inequality. Others pointed to local cultures of isolation and alienation that created problematic environments that discouraged community member interaction and mutual assistance.

Similarly, established norms and traditions (e.g. physical forms of discipline, taboos surrounding discussions of sexuality, confrontational forms of communication) constituted another community characteristic that acted as an impediment to successful and effective community intervention programs. The information and practices taught by programs are often somewhat novel and counter the normative behaviors and beliefs predominant in many communities. As a result, workers routinely face extreme resistance to change, profound skepticism, and a powerful desire to adhere to the status quo – all stumbling blocks that have to be overcome for effective community intervention programs. One expert explaining why traditions and programs often clashed noted, "…it's a very tough situation… you know, the way you raise your child is probably one of the most personally deeply held things you will do in your entire life…" Another illustrated this point: "…I have families that, you know, when I talk about not spanking their kids as their pediatrician, they look at me like I'm from another planet…There are some big cultural differences." And another said that programs often raised "…in adults all these taboos…about their own prejudices (regarding) sexual abuse….because it's such an uncomfortable topic for adults to think that adults can engage in this with children." Issues that touch close to moral standards and religious beliefs can be particularly problematic.

Connecting with communities is another a basic requirement for program implementation that can run into barriers. In many instances, this requirement is not always an easy task, as simply reaching communities frequently involves obstacles to physical access as well as difficult interactional norms that act as barriers to effective education and communication. One primary impediment to physical access is community violence, which makes staffing programs and serving communities difficult.

Another impediment is working against pre-judgments, stereotypes, distrust, and skepticism that are prevalent in some areas. Specific to child maltreatment prevention, widespread fears that program workers are threats to their family unit and associated with punitive measures that will cause them to lose their children or their resources are common in many communities. The experts we interviewed told us that workers in these programs regularly had to grapple with skepticism and disdain that community members have for organizations and programs like theirs. An executive director of a community-based agency observed that many doubts and attitudes were often the result of community members' negative experiences with other similar organizations, which they felt were exploitative, ineffective, harmful, and insensitive. Building trust between all members of a community could be very challenging, as illustrated by this quote, "Who are you guys, coming again to my community, and what are you going to do for me? You're going to be here, and then you're going to be gone."

Another challenging component of fostering community involves bridging the gap between academic scholarship and approaches, and local experience and expertise. Many program experts were acutely aware of existing gaps between academic/scientific/state methods and understandings and the approaches used in community members' daily lives. One noted that programs that do not account for existing realities and norms were unlikely to become integrated into community life in any stable or long-term way, and explained, "…a big challenge, is how to co-develop a program with the community so that we bring positive principles of both university-based rigor…and fidelity of implementation and rigor of evaluation, from the university side. [While] on the other side, being community friendly, and sustainable, and fitting into ongoing community structures."

Community members' awareness of the divide between locals and experts may lead them to feel as if their knowledge and experiences are devalued and/or disrespected by experts. As such, our experts reported that community members were sometimes skeptical and fearful of program offerings, as they felt that they would be ineffective, harmful, or irrelevant to their own lived experiences. One expert emphasized the absolute necessity of bridging the expert/community divide: "making community-level change, it requires initiative, and commitment, and appreciation of the goal from both the top-down and the bottom-up…we can't impose a certain kind of reform or change in a community if it's not what the families themselves are engaged in and want." Thus, the gap between expert and community approaches may constitute a major barrier that threatens the ability to foster the open and respectful community so crucial for effective intervention programs if not addressed.

Challenge: Sustainability

Sustainability is an essential piece of the work of designing and implementing successful community intervention programs. Sustainable programs are those that continue to operate in communities long after their initial introduction and implementation. Sustaining community buy-in is one part of the challenge; finding ongoing resources to continue funding a program is another. According to many of those with experience in these efforts, it is essential that the introduction and implementation of intervention programs focus on community ownership and making long-term organizational dependence entirely unnecessary.

One common strategy to increase sustainability is to provide initial training and leadership and then quickly identify leaders within existing community organizations who can take over the program. This process was described by one of our experts this way: "In these communities, we see our role initially as the kind of like instigator if you will … very quickly we try to transfer leadership and, you know, to other entities in the community, so that we become more of the staff, if you will, to the project than the chairpeople, or the leaders…provide leadership without being arrogant … And so once we do that kind of motivational piece … It's… basically helping people become effective advocates, helping them see a vision that they believe they can achieve."

According the experts interviewed, community investment is the vital foundation that makes sustainability possible. One expert reflected on the inherent complexity of creating sustainable community-owned programs: "The challenge that comes with this goal of developing a program is that at the outset [it] has a goal of being owned and implemented by the community, and sustained by the community. That's a real challenge because it means collaborating, negotiating, giving up on certain ideas, and adhering to other ideals as you go along." After initial implementation, sustainability requires communities to assume ownership of intervention programs and become responsible for keeping them running over the long term. Those involved in these efforts agreed that their work is meant to act as a catalyst for long-term efforts. One expert described the experience as follows: "we were in there for 5 years, and it wasn't until the project really, really ended, and I remember … there was a big celebration. And I sat there and I thought, this isn't ours any more at all. It really is the community's." Discussions of program sustainability cohered around the importance of following four steps that would lead to program longevity and support.

First, experts noted that it is essential to *establish frameworks:* Sustainability begins with sharing program basics and training community members to implement the programs. This initial implementation involves tailoring programs to specific community needs and realities, finding the right people to fulfill organizational roles, training staff, and empowering professionals and community organizations. Helping organizations formulate a community action plan is one commonly used and effective strategy to establish frameworks.

Next, program sustainability requires that programs *build coalitions*, as mentioned earlier in our discussions of community engagement. Strong coalitions provide a broad foundation for programs and serve as a bridge to communities. Coalition building entails bringing together a variety of community groups and parties that are active on a local level and committed to a unified vision. Over time, networks between these groups strengthen and their commitment to program sustainability and growth becomes a foundational piece of community intervention programs. Strong coalitions act as the cement that binds programs and communities together.

Third, it is essential to *build capacities*. As one expert explained,"…we are also there to build capacity of staff…and so, every year, we do support for them, but less and less. I mean, they've taken on more and more … we'll do whatever the community piece that we need to do next, to just help build capacity in whatever way we can. Because we're promoting independence." Noting that building capacities involves equipping community members with the skills they need to maintain and expand programs, he went on to say, "Our commitment is to go wherever anybody wants to partner with us to start a new program. At least the first time they do it. And it very much is… building capacity in them so that after we assure they know what they're doing, and they have got this, and they're doing it in the best way for their community, we can move on and move to another community." By building capacities, organizations further the goal of program sustainability by equipping community members with training and skills they need to maintain and expand programs, secure financial support, and do what is necessary to ensure that programs continue into the future.

Organizations worked to build capacities by teaching community members how to reach out to philanthropic organizations and private businesses for funding, equipping them with the skills they need to teach locals to apply for federal and grassroots grants, encouraging creativity in seeking peer-to-peer support, and exploring other revenue ideas (e.g. matching initiatives, federal program reimbursements, selling training packs).

The final step on the path to program sustainability is to *diversify funding sources*: According to many, relying on multiple sources for funding and support increases sustainability because it ensures that the fate of a community program is not wholly tied to the fate of a single group or organization. Having a variety of funding streams enables program independence and allows programs to carry on even if one source of support runs out/disappears. For example, agencies build capacities by enabling community programs to develop new revenue streams and teaching them to find and apply for grants. Others develop dissemination systems that are capable of taking the program to scale with fidelity across communities, states, and nations.

Conclusion and Recommendations

Because research and experience have demonstrated that lowering rates of child maltreatment is possible, it is important that we use effective and innovative methods. As we have discussed, one promising category of prevention is the use of community-level programming. We described a range of programs that brought community residents and sectors together to strengthen social fabric and increase collective efficacy, that built community-level infrastructure to coordinate services, those that expanded the reach and resources available to family-focused programs, and those that sought to change norms of collective responsibility for children's safety and well-being. We discussed a number of issues that came up in interviews with experts doing all of the above, such as working with culturally diverse populations, overcoming barriers, and creating sustainable programming.

Drawn from existing research as well as the experience of multiple experts who work to prevent child maltreatment through community-level programming, the following recommendations are useful for planning, implementing, and sustaining effective and successful community-level programs to prevent child maltreatment.

1. **Understand Communities and Their Needs**: To effectively implement a community-level child maltreatment program, it is absolutely essential to engage in thorough, formative research that identifies the groups, structures, characteristics, and potential challenges to program goals and practices that exist within the community of interest. Such research entails an embedded, on-the-ground approach that seeks reflexive, accurate understanding of the life of a community. Doing this formative research first will enable programs to be tailored to address the needs, challenges, and resources unique to a community.
2. **Work for Holistic Community Change**: While tested, effective programs are essential, to successfully prevent child maltreatment, culture and behaviors must be transformed. In order to achieve fundamental cultural transformation, programs must identify community social norms, address their origin and their possible negative consequences, and provide reasonable and implementable alternatives to existing beliefs and practices.
3. **Make Community Members Stakeholders**: Community-level programs cannot succeed without the work, belief, and commitment of community members. It is important that community members feel that their input is essential, respected, and valued. To foster this understanding, work with locals from the very beginning by asking for their input, advice, and service. It is especially useful to strategically engage with community members in ways that may activate their resources (influence, financial benefits, formal support, large social networks) to benefit program operations.
4. **Plan for Sustainability from the Beginning**: Sustainability should be a consideration before program implementation. Because introducing a valuable but unsustainable program could undermine community faith and resources, it is essential that the design of the community-level program include plans for long-term operation and funding resources. Planning for and making sustainability a permanent priority are the best means to ensure that community-level programs will be enabled to reduce child maltreatment far into the future.

References

Bandura, A. (1995). Exercise of personal and collective efficacy in changing societies. In A. Bandura (Ed.), *Self-efficacy in changing societies* (pp. 1–45). Cambridge, UK: Cambridge University Press.

Barr, R. G. (2012). Preventing abusive head trauma resulting from a failure of normal interaction between infants and their caregivers. *Proceedings of the National Academy of Sciences, 109*(Supp 2), 17294–17301. doi:10.1073/pnas.1121267109.

Barr, R. G., Rivara, F. P., Barr, M., Cummings, P., Taylor, J., Lengua, L. J., & Meredith-Benitz, E. (2009a). Effectiveness of educational materials designed to change knowledge and behaviors regarding crying and shaken-baby syndrome in mothers of newborns: A randomized, controlled trial. *Pediatrics, 123*(3), 972–980. doi:10.1542/peds.2008-0908.

Barr, R. G., Barr, M., Fujiwara, T., Conway, J., Catherine, N., & Brant, R. (2009b). Do educational materials change knowledge and behaviour about crying and shaken baby syndrome? A randomized controlled trial. *Cmaj, 180*(7), 727–733. doi:10.1503/cmaj.081419.

Betancourt, J. R., & Cervantes, M. C. (2009). Cross-cultural medical education in the United States: Key principles and experiences. *The Kaohsiung Journal of Medical Sciences, 25*(9), 471–478. doi:10.1016/S1607-551X(09)70553-4.

Bronfenbrenner, U. (2005). *Making human beings human: Bioecological perspectives on human development.* Thousand Oaks: Sage.

Browning, C. R., & Cagney, K. A. (2002). Neighborhood structural disadvantage, collective efficacy, and self-rated physical health in an urban setting. *Journal of Health and Social Behavior, 43*(4), 383–399.

Browning, C. R., Leventhal, T., & Brooks-Gunn, J. (2004). Neighborhood context and racial differences in early adolescent sexual activity. *Demography, 41*(4), 697–720.

Coley, R. L., Morris, J. E., & Hernandez, D. (2004). Out-of-school care and problem behavior trajectories among low-income adolescents: individual, family, and neighborhood characteristics as added risks. *Child Development, 75*(3), 948–965.

Coulton, C. J. (1995). Using community-level indicators of children's well-being in comprehensive community initiatives. In J. P. Connell, A. C. Kubisch, L. B. Schorr, & C. H. Weiss (Eds.), *New approaches to evaluating community initiatives: Concepts, methods, and contexts.* Washington, DC: The Aspen Institute.

Coulton, C. J., Crampton, D. S., Irwin, M., Spilsbury, J. C., & Korbin, J. E. (2007). How neighborhoods influence child maltreatment: A review of the literature and alternative pathways. *Child Abuse & Neglect, 31*(11–12), 1117–1142. doi:10.1016/j.chiabu.2007.03.023.

Daro, D., & Dodge, K. A. (2009). Creating community responsibility for child protection: Possibilities and challenges. *The Future of Children, 19*(2), 67–93.

Dias, M. S., Smith, K., deGuehery, K., Mazur, P., Li, V., & Shaffer, M. L. (2005). Preventing abusive head trauma among infants and young children: A hospital-based, parent education program. *Pediatrics, 115*(4), e470–e477. doi:10.1542/peds.2004-1896.

Dodge, K. A., & Coleman, D. L. (Eds.). (2009). *Preventing child maltreatment: Community approaches. Duke series in child development and public policy.* New York: The Guildford Press.

Dodge, K. A., Berlin, L. J., Epstein, M., Spitz-Roth, A., O'Donnell, K., Kaufman, M., Amaya-Jackson, L., Rosch, J., & Christopoulos, C. (2004). The Durham Family Initiative: A preventive system of care. *Child Welfare, 83*(2), 109–128.

Emory, R., Caughy, M., Harris, I. R., & Franzini, L. (2008). Neighborhood social processes and academic achievement in elementary school. *Journal of Community Psychology, 36*(7), 885–898.

Freisthler, B. (2004). A spatial analysis of social disorganization, alcohol access, and rates of child maltreatment in neighborhoods. *Child and Youth Services Review, 26*(9), 803–819. http://dx.doi.org/10.1016/j.childyouth.2004.02.022.

Freisthler, B., & Holmes, M. R. (2012). Explicating the social mechanisms linking alcohol use behaviors and ecology to child maltreatment. *Journal of Sociology & Social Welfare, 39*(4), 25–48.

Freisthler, B., Merritt, D. H., & LaScala, E. A. (2006). Understanding the ecology of child maltreatment: A review of the literature and directions for future research. *Child Maltreatment, 11*(3), 263–280. doi:10.1177/1077559506289524.

Fujiwara, T., Yamada, F., Okuyama, M., Kamimaki, I., Shikoro, N., & Barr, R. G. (2012). Effectiveness of educational materials designed to change knowledge and behavior about crying and shaken baby syndrome: A replication of a randomized controlled trial in Japan. *Child Abuse and Neglect, 36*(9), 613–620. http://dx.doi.org/10.1016/j.chiabu.2012.07.003.

Garbarino, J. (1981). An ecological approach to child maltreatment. In L. H. Pelton (Ed.), *The social context of child abuse and neglect* (pp. 228–267). New York: Human Sciences Press.

Garbarino, J., & Barry, F. (1997). The community context of child abuse and neglect. In J. Garbarino & J. Eckenrode (Eds.), *Understanding abusive families: An ecological approach to theory and practice* (pp. 56–85). San Francisco: Jossey-Bass.

Garbarino, J., & Sherman, D. (1980). High-risk neighborhoods and high-risk families: The human ecology of child maltreatment. *Child Development, 51*(1), 188–198.

Guterman, N. B., Lee, S. J., Taylor, C. A., & Rathouz, P. J. (2009). Parental perceptions of neighborhood processes, stress, personal control, and risk for physical child abuse and neglect. *Child Abuse & Neglect, 33*(12), 897–906. doi:10.1016/j.chiabu.2009.09.008.

Haski-Leventhal, D., Ben-Arieh, A., & Melton, G. B. (2008). Between neighborliness and volunteerism: Participants in the strong communities initiative. *Family & Community Health, 31*(2), 150–161. doi:10.1097/01. FCH.0000314575.58905.a1.

Humes, K., Jones, N., & Ramirez, R. (2011). *Overview of race and hispanic origin: 2010.* Washington, DC: U.S. Department of Commerce Economics and Statistics Administration.

Jain, S., Buka, S. L., Subramanian, S. V., & Molnar, B. E. (2010). Neighborhood predictors of dating violence victimization and perpetration in young adulthood: A multilevel study. *American Journal of Public Health, 100*(9), 1737–1744. doi:10.2105/AJPH.2009.169730.

Korbin, J. E., Coulton, C. J., Chard, S., Platt-Houston, C., & Su, M. (1998). Impoverishment and child maltreatment in African American and European American neighborhoods. *Development and Psychopathology, 10*(2), 215–233.

Leventhal, T., & Brooks-Gunn, J. (2000). The neighborhoods they live in: The effects of neighborhood residence on child and adolescent outcomes. *Psychological Bulletin, 126*(2), 309–337.

Melton, G. B. (2009). How strong communities restored my faith in humanity: Children can live in safety. In K. A. Dodge & D. L. Coleman (Eds.), *Preventing child maltreatment: Community approaches* (Vol. Duke series in child development and public policy, pp. 82–101). New York: The Guildford Press.

Melton, G. B. (2010). Angels (and neighbors) watching over us: child safety and family support in an age of alienation. *The American Journal of Orthopsychiatry, 80*(1), 89–95. doi:10.1111/j.1939-0025.2010.01010.x.

Molnar, B. E., Buka, S. L., Brennan, R. T., Holton, J. K., & Earls, F. (2003). A multilevel study of neighborhoods and parent-to-child physical aggression: Results from the Project on Human Development in Chicago Neighborhoods. *Child Maltreatment, 8*(2), 84–97.

Molnar, B. E., Miller, M. J., Azrael, D., & Buka, S. L. (2004). Neighborhood predictors of concealed firearm carrying among children and adolescents. *Archives of Pediatrics & Adolescent Medicine, 158*, 657–664.

Molnar, B. E., Cerda, M., Roberts, A. L., & Buka, S. L. (2008). Effects of neighborhood resources on aggressive and delinquent behaviors among urban youths. *American Journal of Public Health, 98*(6), 1086–1093. AJPH.2006.098913 [pii] 10.2105/AJPH.2006.098913.

Morenoff, J., & Sampson, R. J. (1997). Violent crime and spatial dynamics of neighborhood transition: Chicago, 1970–1990. *Social Forces, 76*, 31–64.

Prinz, R. J., Sanders, M. R., Shapiro, C. J., Whitaker, D. J., & Lutzker, J. R. (2009). Population-based prevention of child maltreatment: The U.S. Triple P system population trial. *Prevention Science, 10*(1), 1–12. doi:10.1007/s11121-009-0123-3.

Rothman, E. F., Johnson, R. M., Young, R., Weinberg, J., Azrael, D., & Molnar, B. E. (2011). Neighborhood-level factors associated with physical dating violence perpetration: Results of a representative survey conducted in Boston, MA. *Journal of Urban Health, 88*(2), 201–213. doi:10.1007/s11524-011-9543-z.

Sampson, R. J., Raudenbush, S. W., & Earls, F. (1997). Neighborhoods and violent crime: A multilevel study of collective efficacy. *Science, 277*, 918–924.

Sanders, M. R., Cann, W., & Markie-Dadds, C. (2003). The Triple P-Positive Parenting Programme: A universal population-level approach to the prevention of child abuse. *Child Abuse Review, 12*(3), 155–171.

Schober, D. J., Fawcett, S. B., & Bernier, J. (2012a). The Enough Abuse campaign: Building the movement to prevent child sexual abuse in Massachusetts. *Journal of Child Sexual Abuse, 21*(4), 456–469.

Schober, D. J., Fawcett, S. B., Thigpen, S., Curtis, A., & Wright, R. (2012b). An empirical case study of a child sexual abuse prevention initiative in Georgia. *Health Education Journal, 71*(3), 291–298. doi:10.1177/0017896911430546.

Sellstrom, E., & Bremberg, S. (2006). The significance of neighbourhood context to child and adolescent health and well-being: A systematic review of multilevel studies. *Scandinavian Journal of Public Health, 34*(5), 544–554. doi:10.1080/14034940600551251.

Tervalon, M., & Murray-Garcia, J. (1998). Cultural humility versus cultural competence: A critical distinction in defining physician training outcomes in multicultural education. *Journal of Health Care for the Poor and Underserved, 9*(2), 117–125.

Tolan, P. H., & Dodge, K. A. (2005). Children's mental health as a primary care and concern: A system for comprehensive support and service. *The American Psychologist, 60*(6), 601–614. doi:10.1037/0003-066X.60.6.601.

Xue, Y., Leventhal, T., Brooks-Gunn, J., & Earls, F. J. (2005). Neighborhood residence and mental health problems of 5- to 11-year-olds. *Archives of General Psychiatry, 62*(5), 554–563.

Zolotor, A. J., & Runyan, D. K. (2006). Social capital, family violence, and neglect. *Pediatrics, 117*(6), e1124–e1131. doi:10.1542/peds.2005-1913.

Zuravin, S. J. (1989). The ecology of child abuse and neglect: Review of the literature and presentation of data. *Violence and Victims, 4*(2), 101–120.

Zuravin, S. J., & Taylor, R. (1987). The ecology of child maltreatment: Identifying and characterizing high-risk neighborhoods. *Child Welfare, 66*(6), 497–506.

Chapter 16
The Public Health Approach to the Prevention of Child Maltreatment

Patricia Y. Hashima

Introduction

More than two decades ago when the U.S. Advisory Board on Child Abuse and Neglect (1990) declared child maltreatment as a national emergency, it emphasized that the immense problems in the child protection system were not simply the product of insufficient resources or failures in child welfare agencies alone. Rather, the Board concluded that:

> [t]he most serious shortcoming of the nation's system of intervention on behalf of children is that it depends upon a reporting and response system that has punitive connotations and requires massive resources dedicated to the investigation of allegations. (U.S. Advisory Board 1990, p. 80)

The emphasis on reporting and investigation was due to an underestimate of the magnitude of the problem of child maltreatment (U.S. Advisory Board 1990). When it was believed to be a rare problem, action to investigate a few cases was indeed a reasonable strategy. Unfortunately, child maltreatment is not a rare problem anymore and in such a context, the problems of the child protection system are understandable.

The child protection system does serve an important role in intervening in situations where child maltreatment is already suspected. However, no one system or discipline has the capacity to address the issue of child maltreatment. If the nation ultimately wants to reduce the rates of child maltreatment, public health can and should intensify its efforts in the prevention of child maltreatment. This chapter discusses the reason why child maltreatment is a public health issue, the current state of child maltreatment work in the field of public health, and recommendations for future directions for the field in the prevention of child maltreatment.

Why Is Child Maltreatment a Public Health Problem?

In 1990 "violent and abusive behavior" was one of 22 public health priority areas in Healthy People 2000 (http://www.healthypeople.gov/2020/about/history.aspx), the national disease-prevention and health-promotion strategy. It continues to be one of the objectives ("injury and violence prevention") for Healthy People 2020 (http://www.healthypeople.gov/2020/default.aspx). Specifically, child

P.Y. Hashima (✉)
e-mail: phashima@gmail.com

J.E. Korbin and R.D. Krugman (eds.), *Handbook of Child Maltreatment*, Child Maltreatment 2,
DOI 10.1007/978-94-007-7208-3_16, © Springer Science+Business Media Dordrecht 2014

maltreatment is a major public health problem because children who experience maltreatment encounter increased risks for illness, injury, and death (for review, see Section IV of the handbook and Hashima et al. 2014). Children who are maltreated often suffer from injuries which may result in permanent physical disabilities and even death. Additionally, child maltreatment may alter healthy brain development leading to developmental delays, cognitive impairments, and risk behaviors over the life course (Carrion et al. 2007; Nelson and McCleery 2008; Shonkoff et al. 2009). Furthermore, studies have revealed that child maltreatment has been shown to have lifelong adverse health consequences on some of the nation's worst health problems, such as cancer (Felitti et al. 1998; Fuller-Thomson and Brennenstuhl 2009), heart disease (Dong et al. 2004), diabetes (Kendall-Tackett and Marshall 1999), and depression (Chapman et al. 2004; Fergusson et al. 2008). The association between child maltreatment and health (both short and long term) clearly makes a case that child maltreatment is a serious but preventable public health problem (Hashima et al. 2014; Mercy and Saul 2009; Office of the Surgeon General 2005).

Public Health Burden: Costs of Child Maltreatment

In addition to the tremendous human cost, the financial costs of child maltreatment are substantial also. Several studies have produced estimates of the national economic burden of child maltreatment (Bonomi et al. 2008; Conrad 2006; Currie and Widom 2010; Daro 1988; Fang et al. 2012; Florence et al. 2012; Fromm 2001; Miller et al. 1996; Wang and Holton 2007). Almost two decades ago, for instance, Miller and colleagues (1996) estimated the economic effects of child maltreatment to be approximately $56 billion per year (in which $3.6 billion was for medical and mental health care spending). The latest estimates of average lifetime cost per victim of nonfatal child maltreatment calculated by Fang and colleagues (2012) is $210,012 in 2010 dollars and the estimated average lifetime cost per death (as a result of child maltreatment) is $1,272,900. The estimate of nonfatal case of child maltreatment includes $32,648 in childhood health care costs; $10,530 in adult medical costs; $144,360 in productivity losses; $7,728 in child welfare costs; $6,747 in criminal justice costs; and $7,999 in special education costs. Fang and colleagues' (2012) estimate of fatal case of child maltreatment includes $14,100 in medical costs and $1,258,800 in productivity losses. Combined, the total lifetime economic burden resulting from new cases of fatal and nonfatal child maltreatment in the U.S. in 2008 was as large as $124 billion (in 2010 dollars) (Fang et al. 2012). In 2010, health expenditures in the United States neared $2.6 trillion and by 2020, it is projected to reach approximately $4.6 trillion (Centers for Medicare and Medicaid Services, n.d.). In order to reduce the health expenditures in the United States, preventing child maltreatment is a major public health policy priority.

The Role of Public Health in the Child Maltreatment Work

The mission of public health is "the fulfillment of society's interest in assuring the conditions in which people can be healthy" (Institute of Medicine 1988, p. 40) and its focus is to *prevent* disease, injury, and disability, and to *promote* physical and mental health (Winslow 1923 reprinted 1984). Within the formal structure of government, the federal government leads and supports state and local health departments but protection of public health is primarily a responsibility of the states (Turnock 2012; Wilson 2011) and the role of local health department is assigned by the state government (Turnock 2012; Wilson 2011).

The public health approach to child maltreatment work differs from the child welfare or criminal justice perspectives that have often dominated the efforts to address the problem of child maltreatment. Its approach is population-based and its three main functions are **assessment** (i.e., monitor health status, investigate health problems, evaluate health services), **development of policy** to reduce health problems (including developing research for innovative solutions to health problems), and **assurance** that needed action (i.e., provision of services, training competent public health staff, informing the public, mobilizing the community) occurs (Institute of Medicine 1988).

Public health has the potential to create broad population-level impact. It can and must play a critical role in addressing the issue of child maltreatment by: (1) advancing scientifically valid surveillance information on child maltreatment (assessment); (2) increasing the knowledge base of population-level approach to the prevention of child maltreatment (policy development); and (3) creating effective messages about the issues of child maltreatment to inform the public (assurance).

Assessment: Surveillance

Surveillance is the cornerstone of public health practice. As the former U.S. Surgeon General, David Satcher, commented, "In public health, we can't do anything without surveillance. That's where public health begins" (cited by Thacker et al. 2012, p. 3). To effectively respond to the problem of child maltreatment, policy and programmatic decision-makers at the national, state, and local levels need valid and reliable information on child maltreatment. State and local health departments currently rely on data from multiple data sources, most of which are collected for other purposes, for their child maltreatment data. According to the Centers for Disease Control and Prevention (CDC), the top five data sources used by state public health departments for their child maltreatment prevention planning and programming are Child Death Review data (86 % of state public health departments), Vital Statistics (78 %), child welfare and protection services data (73 %), Youth Risk Behavior Survey (67 %), and Pregnancy and Risk Assessment Monitoring System (63 %) (CDC 2011).

At the national level, child welfare and protection services data are mainly used to calculate estimates of child maltreatment. For example, the fourth and most recent congressionally mandated National Incidence Study (NIS-4), funded by the U.S. Department of Health and Human Services (DHHS), used a sentinel sample methodology which incorporates data of children who were investigated by the child protective service (CPS) agencies, those who were investigated by community professionals but were not reported to CPS, and those who were screened out by CPS without investigation (Sedlak et al. 2010). The NIS-4 revealed that the number of maltreated children under the study's "Harm Standard" (i.e., a standard requiring that demonstrable harm has occurred) was 1,256,600 with a prevalence rate of 17.1 per 1,000 children in the general population nationwide (Sedlak et al. 2010). In contrast, the 2005 and 2006 reports of the National Child Abuse and Neglect Data Systems (NCANDS), also funded by the U.S. DHHS, are based on CPS data only (U.S. DHHS 2006, 2007). The NCANDS reports revealed that an estimated 899,000 children were victims of child maltreatment in federal fiscal year 2005 (U.S. DHHS 2006) and 905,000 children in 2006 (U.S. DHHS 2007). For both years, the prevalence rate was 12.1 per 1,000 children in the general population nationwide (U.S. DHHS 2006, 2007).

A System of Linked Data. Indicators of child maltreatment are often embedded in various surveillance systems such as Vital Statistics and Child Death Review. Unfortunately, they do not necessarily communicate with one another. For a more accurate and richer epidemiologic data on child maltreatment, the collection and analysis of data on child maltreatment and data related to child maltreatment must be expanded. In order to do so, the linking of important data across various data sets must be improved. Public health should take a leadership role in developing a system of linked data sets from both public (e.g., Vital Statistics, Child Death Review reports, behavioral and school-based health assessments, program specific data such as the Women, Infants, and Children data, etc.) and private data (e.g., private health care providers' data systems). Furthermore, at the federal level, DHHS must support health departments seeking opportunities for active surveillance (e.g., adding questions on

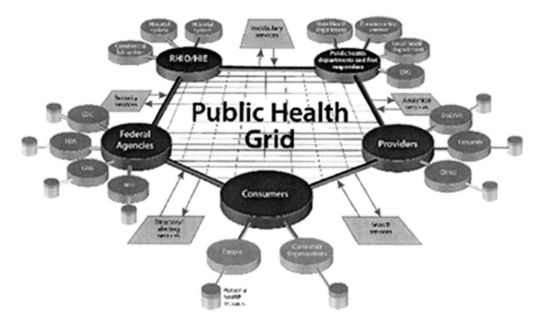

Fig. 16.1 National Public Health Grid (Thacker et al. 2012, p. 8). Abbreviations: *CMS* Centers for Medicare and Medicaid Services, *D0D/VA* U.S. Department of defense/Department of Veterans Affairs, *EMS* Emergency Medical Services, *FDA* Food and Drug Administration, *NIH* National Institutes of Health, *RHIO/HIE* Regional Health Information Organization/Health Information Exchange

modifiable risk and protective factors of child maltreatment to electronic health records). To facilitate data exchange within and outside the public health system, policies to enable partnering of state and local health departments as well as other federal agencies and private partners engaging in public health surveillance are also critically needed.

Furthermore, public health can and should provide a central setting to house comprehensive child maltreatment data which can be stored in a multi-dimensional matrix and secured in public cloud computing. In his 2009 keynote address for CDC's vision for public health surveillance in the twenty-first century, Thacker and colleagues (2012) cited Savel and colleagues' (2010) model of public health grid and speculated that the future surveillance system would be "an electronic health grid" (p. 7) that consolidates various health information for public health surveillance (Fig. 16.1).

Public health must take a leadership role in exploring various approaches, data sources, and capacities in order to develop such a system that can be supported and maintained. Of course, this is easier said than done. In 2009 when CDC surveyed 434 Division Directors of CDC and Agency for Toxic Substances and Disease Registry (ATSDR), members of the Surveillance Science Advisory Group (SurvSAG), and scientists on the CDC/ATSDR science distribution list, only 22 % of the respondents agreed that CDC surveillance systems work well in today's world of information technology (Thacker et al. 2012). The 2009 survey also revealed that the role of surveillance is "the most pressing issue that confronts the agency and its partners" (Thacker et al. 2012, p. 5). State and local health departments, their partners, and federal agencies must all commit to advancing the nation's child maltreatment surveillance data capacity. In addition to taking advantage of President Barack Obama's priority for an integrated health information system, the extraordinary advances in information technology does provide excellent opportunities for such a system. If a small start-up company can

scan up to 500 million e-mails, Facebook updates, and corporate documents to create a service that can outline the biography of a given person you meet, warn you to be home to receive a package or text a lunch guest that you are running late (Hardy 2012), surely linking and organizing child maltreatment data into a format that is accessible in a more timely manner and useful is possible. Naturally, for such a system to be possible, there is a critical need for workforce development at the national, state, and local levels as well. Only 28 % of the respondents of the 2009 survey conducted by the CDC agreed that "the agency maintains rigorous standards for the collection, maintenance, and analysis of data for CDC/ATSDR and its partners" (Thacker et al. 2012, p. 8). Thus, there is a critical need for the public health workforce to be trained in skills needed for effective and efficient public health surveillance of the twenty-first century.

Uniform Definition of Child Maltreatment. In order to accurately assess the magnitude, scope, characteristics, and consequences of child maltreatment, there are efforts by the federal government to consolidate the various definitions of child maltreatment. After a systematic review of child maltreatment definitions of NIS (including comparison against all state definitions as codified in the state statutes) by DHHS, the child maltreatment definitions were refined for NIS-4 and resulted in 60-form maltreatment typology (Sedlak et al. 2010). In addition to refinements of the maltreatment typology, coders of NIS-4 continued to evaluate each suspected child maltreatment case using two definitional standards or "countability criteria" (Sedlak et al. 2010, pp. 2–12): the Harm Standard and the Endangerment Standard. If a child experienced an observable harm, a case would be coded as child maltreatment under the Harm Standard. If "the source (CPS or sentinel) considered the perpetrator's actions or omissions to have placed the child at serious risk of harm" (Sedlak et al. 2010, pp. 2–12), a case would be coded as child maltreatment under the Endangerment Standard (Sedlak et al. 2010). Also, "the Endangerment Standard includes all Harm Standard countable children, but adds in other children as well" (Sedlak et al. 2010). The NIS-4 also specified elements (child's age, custody status, intention) that must be met for a case to be counted as a child maltreatment case (Sedlak et al. 2010). Furthermore, as the coders entered the data, a new Computer-Assisted Evaluative Decision System (CAEDS) was used to automatically remind the coders about the definitions and check for any coding error.

In 2008, the CDC published *Version 1.0 of Child Maltreatment Surveillance: Uniform Definitions and Recommended Data Elements* (Leeb et al. 2008). Designed "to promote and improve consistency of child maltreatment surveillance for public health practices" (Leeb et al. 2008, p. 5), *Version 1.0 of Child Maltreatment Surveillance* defined child maltreatment as "[a]ny act or series of acts of commission or omission by a parent or other caregiver that results in harm, potential for harm, or threat of harm to a child" (Leeb at al. 2008, p. 11). It also defined associated terms of child maltreatment (e.g., "harm," "caregiver," "acts of commission," "acts of omission"), and recommended data elements to include in a child maltreatment surveillance system (Leeb et al. 2008). Focusing on all types of child maltreatment, the document was intended to guide data collection for public health surveillance of child maltreatment. CDC's *Version 1.0 of Child Maltreatment Surveillance* is an important resource to assist states to improve the consistency and comparability of the child maltreatment data.

Unfortunately, a lack of uniform definitions for child maltreatment surveillance continues to be a major barrier in public health's child maltreatment work (CDC 2011). A survey funded by the Doris Duke Charitable Foundation revealed that less than half (47 %) of the state public health departments were aware of the CDC uniform definitions for child maltreatment surveillance, and only 14 % used the CDC uniform definitions for child maltreatment surveillance (CDC 2011). The reason was because each state has its own definition of child maltreatment (U.S. DHHS 2011). The Federal Child Abuse Prevention and Treatment Act (CAPTA) defined child maltreatment as:

> *at a minimum,* (italicized by author) [a]ny recent act or failure to act on the part of a parent or caretaker which results in death, serious physical or emotional harm, sexual abuse or exploitation; or an act or failure to act, which presents an imminent risk of serious harm (U.S. Department of Health and Human Services 2011, p. 19).

Obviously, when each state has its own definition of child maltreatment, data on child maltreatment are not captured in consistent ways. However, to effectively respond to the problem of child maltreatment, policy and programmatic decision-makers at the national, state, and local levels need valid and reliable information on child maltreatment. As surveillance being one of the essential public health services (IOM 2002), public health must take a lead in bolstering the surveillance system of child maltreatment in order to improve the consistency and comparability of child maltreatment data. Furthermore, every health department must agree on using a uniform definition of child maltreatment and its related terms (e.g., caretaker, harm), and develop ways to integrate them with their own definition of child maltreatment as required by their state statute so it can accurately estimate the public health burden, track trends, and evaluate prevention efforts of child maltreatment.

The strength of public health is its ability to integrate the efforts of diverse organizations, communities, and scientific disciplines. Thus, it can and must take a leadership role in garnering support for the use of a uniform definition of child maltreatment. State and local health departments, their partners, federal agencies, national organizations, philanthropic foundations, and academic institutions must all commit to providing, once and for all, a more scientifically valid and useful surveillance information on child maltreatment.

Policy Development: Research for New Insights and Innovative Solutions to Prevent Child Maltreatment

When state-level Maternal and Child Health (MCH) and Injury and Violence Prevention (IVP) program directors were surveyed in the country, only 21 % (a coordinated response of MCH and IVP program directors in 50 states and the District of Columbia) indicated that their agency was making progress in decreasing the rates of child maltreatment in their state/district (CDC 2011). In naming how state health departments were currently addressing the problem of child maltreatment, the five most common responses given by the MCH and IVP program directors were: (1) identifying and targeting at-risk populations (73 %); (2) making referrals to external child maltreatment resources (67 %); (3) communicating best practices, funding, and training for child maltreatment prevention (63 %); (4) convening child maltreatment prevention partners (55 %); and (5) building capacity for child maltreatment efforts within the state public health departments (CDC 2011). While they are all important roles for public health to play, one of the critical roles it can play is developing innovative solutions to prevent child maltreatment.

The child maltreatment field is beginning to address community-level risk factors which have long been shown to be important determinants of child maltreatment (Coulton et al. 1999; Deccio et al. 1994; Drake and Pandey 1996; Garbarino and Crouter 1978; Garbarino and Kostelny 1994; Garbarino and Sherman 1980; Korbin and Coulton 1996; Melton 1992; Melton and Barry 1994; Molnar et al. 2003; Runyan et al. 1998; Sampson et al. 1997; U.S. Advisory Board on Child Abuse and Neglect 1990, 1993; Vimpani 2000; Zuravin 1989). Unfortunately, it is still unclear what specific community factors are associated with child maltreatment (Daro and Dodge 2009; Hashima 2005). Thus, there are still only a handful of community-level interventions that have demonstrated positive impacts on risk factors of child maltreatment (Klevens and Whitaker 2007). Given the magnitude and seriousness of the problem of child maltreatment, there is an urgent need to advance the field's understanding of what works at the community-level to prevent child maltreatment. With a wealth of field experience in improving the health and well being of populations, public health can and must take a leadership role in creating innovative strategies to prevent child maltreatment at the community-level. Specifically, with infrastructure existing in every state and territory within the United States (ASTHO 2011), public health is well suited to gather information on prevention strategies that are "practical, affordable, suitable, evaluable, and helpful in the real-world" (Chen 2010, p. 207).

Public Health and Viable Validity. Regardless of its effectiveness, a prevention program has little chance of sustainability in a community unless it is relevant and useful to the community. Thus, the question, "Is it feasible?" is just as important as the question, "Does it work?" Warning that the

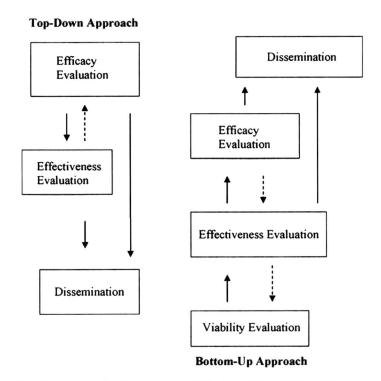

Fig. 16.2 Campbellian Model versus Chen's Integrative Validity Model (Chen 2010, p. 209)

evidence-based movement may mistakenly promote interventions that have little chance of real-world survival, Chen (2010) proposed an integrative validity model as an alternative to the Campbellian model (Campbell and Stanley 1963). In addition to internal validity (effectiveness) and external validity (generalizability), Chen's model (2010) addresses viable validity (viability in the real world). According to Chen (2010), viability evaluation assesses "practicality, affordability, suitability, evaluability, and helpfulness" (p. 207). Thus, in his model, which he refers to as "the bottom-up approach", the evaluation sequence begins with a viability study then goes through effectiveness study, efficacy study, and ends with dissemination (Chen 2010). In a Campbellian model, which Chen (2010) refers to as "the top-down approach," evaluation proceeds from efficacy study, to effectiveness study, then to dissemination (see Fig. 16.2).

It is imperative that public health recognize the role it can play in assessing the viability of existing or innovative solutions to the problem of child maltreatment and promoting a culture of innovation – a learning community – in which there is continuing attention to new knowledge created in the real world and continuous refinement of its prevention work. As Chen (2010) pointed out:

> Researchers should not be the only source of scientific knowledge. Rather, stakeholders' program efforts, knowledge, and experience in helping clients, as well as their evaluation priorities, should be recognized and included as an integral part of scientific knowledge (p. 213).

Assurance: Informing the Public and Changing Social Norms

Using public awareness campaigns to inform the public about health issues has long been regarded as a vital component of public health. For instance, as a result of anti-smoking campaigns, the public's perception of smoking, once socially an acceptable behavior, has gradually changed over time.

Growing awareness of the danger of smoking and changes in public policy (e.g., no advertisement on television, smoking not permitted in public areas, tax increase on cigarettes) resulted in the social norm change about smoking. Similar to a campaign against smoking, public health must develop a unified message that child maltreatment is a major, but preventable public health problem. Specifically, it must strive to create effective strategies to reach and inform the public (including policy-makers, health care professionals, *and* public health practitioners) about: (1) both the short and long-term health consequences of child maltreatment; (2) the associated financial costs of child maltreatment and how primary prevention of child maltreatment is critical in reducing health care costs; (3) the broader context in which child maltreatment occurs; (4) the unique role of public health in preventing child maltreatment. Such messaging also should reframe the prevention of child maltreatment as a promotion of healthy child development. As Wald (2009) recommended, "Preventing maltreatment must be a *desired outcome*, but *not the primary focus*, of public investments in children" (p. 183). Framing prevention of child maltreatment as promoting safety and well-being of children is more likely to strengthen social will and garner political support to protect children.

In the 2009 survey of state-level MCH and IVP program directors mentioned earlier, only 69 % of the respondents indicated that their agency considered child maltreatment a public health issue (CDC 2011). Furthermore, 45 % percent of the MCH and IPV programs directors responded that lack of "buy-in" from state level partners that child maltreatment is a public health issue as a major barrier limiting the health department efforts in child maltreatment prevention (CDC 2011). Without the understanding that child maltreatment is a public health issue, it is not surprising that only 37 % of the states/district reported that they had a statute, law, or executive order mandating that the health department participate in state child maltreatment prevention efforts and only 39 % had a designated child maltreatment staff person or program.

The Health Burden of Child Maltreatment. Public health must make a case that child maltreatment is a major but preventable public health problem. It must inform the public that children who experience maltreatment encounter increased risks for illness, injury, and death (Brown et al. 1997; Chapman et al. 2004; Dong et al. 2004; Felitti et al. 1998; Fergusson et al. 2008; Fuller-Thomson and Brennenstuhl 2009; Kendall-Tackett and Marshall 1999) in addition to altering brain development leading to developmental delays, cognitive impairments, and risk behaviors over the life course (Carrion et al. 2007; Nelson and McCleery 2008; Shonkoff et al. 2009). The public must be informed that preventing child maltreatment is strategic for achieving measurable and lasting impacts on the nation's health.

Additionally, it is critical to educate public health practitioners that many of the programs which may not specifically address child maltreatment but foster healthy child development are contributing to the child maltreatment prevention efforts. Every health department staff and leaders (not just those involved in MCH and IPV) must understand the relationship of their programs to child maltreatment prevention and the importance of incorporating child maltreatment prevention strategies into their services for children and adults. Such awareness and understanding will be an important step in facilitating the much needed alignment of health department programs and integration of services to create a comprehensive system of care for children and families.

The Economic Burden of Child Maltreatment. Public health also must inform the public about the financial cost of child maltreatment – that the total lifetime economic burden resulting from new cases of fatal and nonfatal child maltreatment in the U.S. in 2008 was as large as $124 billion (Centers for Medicare and Medicaid Services, n.d.; Fang et al. 2012). The message that preventing child maltreatment will reduce the health expenditures in the United States must especially reach business leaders and policy-makers. If health expenditure in 2020 is projected to reach approximately $4.6 trillion (Centers for Medicare and Medicaid Services, n.d.), the health burden of child maltreatment is a powerful message. Framing child maltreatment as nation's fiscal problem may serve as a final tipping point to create political commitment and push for effective action.

The Broader Context of Child Maltreatment. A telephone survey conducted in 1999 revealed that only 39 % of the 1,234 participants responded that environment plays an important role in causing child injuries (Hearne et al. 2000). Had the respondents been asked about how much impact environment has on child maltreatment, the answer would most likely be even lower. As the survey response reflects, the lay public is usually unaware of the environmental context in which child maltreatment occurs. In a culture where the notion of personal responsibility is highly valued, there also is resistance to acknowledge that child maltreatment is "inescapably a judgment about communities – communities that differ in the level of support and supervision they offer to individual parents" (Garbarino and Collins 1999, p. 5).

To prevent child maltreatment, public health must take a lead in educating the public that parenting behaviors (both positive and negative) are embedded in broader ecological (i.e., neighborhood, community, and cultural) contexts (Belsky 1980; Bronfenbrenner 1977; Cicchetti and Lynch 1993; Cicchetti and Rizley 1981; Garbarino 1977; Garbarino and Kostelny 1992; Hashima and Amato 1994). Because many are not aware that child maltreatment is usually more about parents being burdened and overwhelmed than being sadistic, public health must lead in creating well-formulated media campaigns to shift the current social norm which focuses solely on caretaker culpability. By changing social norms related to children's safety and well-being, it also will help strengthen the social will to take ownership of the problem of child maltreatment and galvanize communities toward the prevention of child maltreatment.

Conclusion

Solving the problem of child maltreatment requires a broad-sector coordination and public health is uniquely positioned to do so. Many complex issues seen as social and safety issues have achieved great progress from public health's contributions, such as vaccination, sanitation, and motor vehicle safety. As shown below (Fig. 16.3), such success is due to its practice of coordinating a collective action of a multidisciplinary team of professionals (e.g., public health officers, physicians, nurses, educators, social scientists, epidemiologists, statisticians, community development workers, communications officers, public health lawyers) and partners (both private and public) to carry out science-based approach into large-scale field settings.

Public health can build on its strength on child health and bring governments, nonprofit organizations, academic institutions, businesses, media, and public around a common agenda of child well-being and create collective impact on children's safety and health. Its collective approach can also

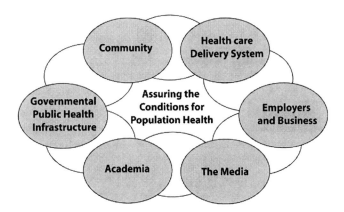

Fig. 16.3 The public health system: Government and some of its potential partners (IOM 2002)

push for a system-wide progress by aligning programs and integrating services (within departments and among partners) at the state and local levels. At the federal level, DHHS can establish a much needed agency-wide vision for child maltreatment prevention, and develop strategies to: (1) clarify the roles of the agency's operating divisions involved in the prevention of child maltreatment; (2) integrate its services for a more efficient use of resources; and (3) collaborate with other federal agencies (e.g., Department of Agriculture, Department of Housing and Urban Development) to better address the issue of child maltreatment. As a new system of health care delivery is being established, public health can and must seize the opportunity to lead the fight in promoting the safety and well-being of children.

References

ASTHO. (2011). *ASTHO Profile of State Public Health, Volume 2*. http://www.astho.org/uploadedFiles/_Publications/Files/Survey_Research/ASTHO_State_Profiles_Single[1]%20lo%20res.pdf). Accessed Dec 2011.

Belsky, J. (1980). Child maltreatment: An ecological integration. *American Psychologist, 35*, 320–355.

Bonomi, A. E., Anderson, M. L., Rivara, F. P., Cannon, E. A., Fishman, P. A., Carrell, D., Reid, R. J., & Thmpson, R. S. (2008). Health care utilization and costs associated with childhood abuse. *Journal of General Internal Medicine, 23*, 294–299.

Bronfenbrenner, U. (1977). Toward an experimental ecology of human development. *American Psychologist, 32*, 513–531.

Brown, L., Kessel, S., Lourie, K., Ford, H., & Lipsitt, L. (1997). Influence of sexual abuse on HIV-related attitudes and behaviors in adolescent psychiatric inpatients. *Journal of the American Academy of Child and Adolescent Psychiatry, 36*, 316–322.

Campbell, D. T., & Stanley, J. (1963). *Experimental and quasi-experimental designs for research*. Chicago: Rand McNally.

Carrion, V., Weems, C., & Reiss, A. (2007). Stress predicts brain changes in children: A pilot longitudinal study on youth stress, posttraumatic stress disorder, and the hippocampus. *Pediatrics, 119*, 509–516.

Centers for Disease Control and Prevention. (2011). *Findings from 2009 child maltreatment prevention environmental scan of state public health agencies*. http://www.cdc.gov/violenceprevention/pdf/PHLI_CM_environmental_scan-a.pdf

Centers for Medicare and Medicaid Services. (n.d.). *National health expenditure projections 2010–2020*. https://www.cms.gov/Research-Statistics-Data-and-Systems/Statistics-Trends-and-Reports/NationalHealthExpendData/downloads/proj2010.pdf. Accessed June 2012.

Chapman, D. P., Whitfield, C. L., Felitti, V. J., Dube, S. R., Edwards, V. J., & Anda, R. F. (2004). Adverse childhood experiences and the risk of depressive disorders in adulthood. *Journal of Affective Disorders, 82*, 217–225.

Chen, H. T. (2010). The bottom-up approach to integrative validity: A new perspective for program evaluation. *Evaluation and Program Planning, 33*, 205–214.

Cicchetti, D., & Lynch, M. (1993). Toward an ecological/transactional model of community violence and child maltreatment: Consequences for children's development. *Psychiatry, 53*, 96–118.

Cicchetti, D., & Rizley, R. (1981). Developmental perspectives on the etiology, intergenerational transmission, and sequelae of child maltreatment. In R. Rizley & D. Cicchetti (Eds.), *Developmental perspectives on child maltreatment: New directions for child development* (pp. 31–55). San Francisco: Jossey-Bass.

Conrad, C. (2006). Measuring costs of child abuse and neglect: A mathematic model of specific cost estimations. *Journal of Health and Human Services Administration, 29*, 103–123.

Coulton, C. J., Korbin, J. E., & Su, M. (1999). Neighborhoods and child maltreatment: A multi-level study. *Child Abuse & Neglect, 23*, 1019–1040.

Currie, J., & Widom, C. S. (2010). Long-term consequences of child abuse and neglect on adult economic well-being. *Child Maltreatment, 15*, 111–120.

Daro, D. (1988). *Confronting child abuse: Research for effective program design*. New York: Macmillan.

Daro, D., & Dodge, K. (2009). Creating community responsibility for child protection: Possibilities and challenges. *The Future of Children, 19*, 67–93.

Deccio, G., Horner, W. C., & Wilson, D. (1994). High-risk neighborhoods and high-risk families: Replication research related to the human ecology of child maltreatment. *Journal of Social Service Research, 18*, 123–137.

Dong, M., Giles, W. H., Felitti, V. J., Dube, S. R., Williams, J. E., Chapman, D. P., & Anda, R. F. (2004). Insights into causal pathways for ischemic heart disease: Adverse childhood experiences study. *Circulation, 110*, 1761–1766.

Drake, B., & Pandey, S. (1996). Understanding the relationship between neighborhood poverty and specific types of child maltreatment. *Child Abuse & Neglect, 20*, 1003–1018.

Fang, X., Brown, D. S., Florence, C. S., & Mercy, J. A. (2012). The economic burden of child maltreatment in the United States and implications for prevention. *Child Abuse & Neglect, 36*, 156–165.

Felitti, V. J., Anda, R. F., Nordenberg, D., Williamson, D. F., Spitz, A. M., Edwards, V., Koss, M. P., & Marks, J. S. (1998). Relationship of childhood abuse and household dysfunction to many of the leading casues of death in adults. The Adverse Childhood Experience (ACE) study. *American Journal of Preventive Medicine, 14*, 245–258.

Fergusson, D., Boden, J., & Horwood, L. (2008). Exposure to child sexual and physical abuse and adjustment in early adulthood. *Child Abuse & Neglect, 32*, 607–619.

Florence, S., Brown, D.S., Fang, X., & Thompson, H.F. (2012). *The health care costs associated with child maltreatment: Implications for Medicaid.* Manuscript submitted for publication.

Fromm, S. (2001). *Total estimated cost of child abuse and neglect in the United States; Statistical evidence.* Chicago: Prevent Child Abuse America. http://www.familyimpactseminars.org/s_nmfis02c02.pdf. Accessed June 2012.

Fuller-Thomson, E., & Brennenstuhl, S. (2009). Making a link between childhood physical abuse and cancer: Results from a regional representative survey. *Cancer, 115*, 3341–3350.

Garbarino, J. (1977). The human ecology of child maltreatment: A conceptual model for research. *Journal of Marriage and the Family, 39*, 721–735.

Garbarino, J., & Collins, C. C. (1999). Child neglect: The family with a hole in the middle. In H. Dubowitz (Ed.), *Neglected children: Research, practice, and policy* (pp. 1–23). Thousand Oaks: Sage.

Garbarino, J., & Crouter, A. (1978). Defining the community context of parent–child relations: The correlates of child maltreatment. *Child Development, 49*, 604–616.

Garbarino, J., & Kostelny, K. (1992). Child maltreatment as a community problem. *Child Abuse & Neglect, 16*, 455–464.

Garbarino, J., & Kostelny, K. (1994). Neighborhood-based programs. In G. B. Melton & F. D. Barry (Eds.), *Protecting children from abuse and neglect: Foundations for a new national strategy* (pp. 304–352). New York: Guilford Press.

Garbarino, J., & Sherman, D. (1980). High-risk neighborhoods and high-risk families: The human ecology of child maltreatment. *Child Development, 51*, 188–198.

Hardy, Q. (2012). Active in cloud, Amazon reshapes computing. *The New York Times.* http/:www.nytimes.com:2012:-08:28:technology:active-in-cloud-amazon-reshapes-computing.html%3F_r=1&src=me&ref=general.   Accessed 29 Aug 2012.

Hashima, P. Y. (2005). Prevention of child neglect: Toward a community-level approach. In K. A. Kendall-Tackett & S. M. Giacomoni (Eds.), *Child victimization* (pp. 17–20). New York: Civic Research Institute.

Hashima, P. Y., & Amato, P. R. (1994). Poverty, social support, and parental behavior. *Child Development, 65*, 394–403.

Hashima, P. Y., Wilkins, N. J., Mercy, J., & Graffunder, C. (2014). Promoting the health and well-being of children: The role of the Centers for Disease Control and Prevention in preventing child maltreatment. In S. Alexander, R. Alexander, & N. Guterman (Eds.), *Prevention of child maltreatment.* St. Louis MO: STM Learning, Inc.

Hearne, S. A., Locke, P. A., Mellman, M., Loeb, P., Dropkin, L., Bolger, G., Fink, N., & Byrnes, M. (2000). Public opinion about public health – United States, 1999. *Morbidity and Mortality Weekly Report, 49*, 258–260.

Institute of Medicine. (1988). *The future of public health.* Washington, DC: National Academy Press. http://iom.edu/Reports/1988/The-Future-of-Public-Health.aspx. Accessed June 2012.

Institute of Medicine. (2002). *Shaping the future for health: The future of the public's health in the 21st century.* Washington, DC: National Academy Press. http://www.iom.edu/~/media/Files/Report%20Files/2002/The-Future-of-the-Publics-Health-in-the-21st-Century/Future%20of%20Publics%20Health%202002%20Report%20Brief.pdf. Accessed June 2012.

Kendall-Tackett, K. A., & Marshall, R. (1999). Victimization and diabetes: An exploratory study. *Child Abuse & Neglect, 23*, 593–596.

Klevens, J., & Whitaker, D. J. (2007). Primary prevention of child physical abuse and neglect: Gaps and promising directions. *Child Maltreatment, 12*, 364–377.

Korbin, J. E., & Coulton, C. J. (1996). The role of neighbors and the government in neighborhood-based child protection. *Journal of Social Issues, 52*, 163–176.

Leeb, R. T., Paulozzi, L., Melanson, C., Simon, T., & Arias, I. (2008). *Child maltreatment surveillance: Uniform definitions for public health and recommended data elements, version 1.0.* Atlanta: Centers for Disease Control and Prevention, National Center for Injury Prevention and Control. http://www.cdc.gov/ViolencePrevention/pub/CMP-Surveillance.html.

Melton, G. B. (1992). It's time for neighborhood research and action. *Child Abuse & Neglect, 16*, 909–913.

Melton, G. B., & Barry, F. D. (1994). Neighbors helping neighbors: The vision of the U.S. Advisory Board on Child Abuse and Neglect. In G. B. Melton & F. D. Barry (Eds.), *Neighbors helping neighbors: The vision of the U.S. Advisory Board on Child Abuse and Neglect* (pp. 1–13). New York: Guilford Press.

Mercy, J. A., & Saul, J. (2009). Creating a healthier future through early interventions for children. *Journal of the American Medical Association, 301*, 2262–2264.

Miller, T. R., Cohen, M. A., & Wiersema, B. (1996). *Victim costs and consequences: A new look*. Washington, DC: U.S. Department of Justice, Office of Justice Programs, National Institute of Justice.

Molnar, B. E., Buka, S. L., Brennan, R. T., Holton, J. K., & Earls, F. (2003). A multi-level study of parent-to-child physical aggression: Results from the Project on Human Development in Chicago Neighborhoods. *Child Maltreatment, 8*, 84–97.

Nelson, C., & McCleery, J. (2008). Use of event-related potentials in the study of typical and atypical development. *Journal of the American Academy of Child and Adolescent Psychiatry, 47*, 1252–1261.

Office of the Surgeon General. (2005). Surgeon General's workshop on making prevention of child maltreatment a national priority: Implementing innovations of a public health approach: Lister Hill Auditorium, National Institutes of Health, Bethesda, Maryland, Mar 30–31, 2005. Rockville: Office of the Surgeon General (US). http://www.ncbi.nlm.nih.gov/books/NBK47486/

Runyan, D. K., Hunter, W. M., Socolar, R. R. S., Amaya-Jackson, L., English, D., Landsverk, J., Dubowitz, H., Browne, D. H., Bangdiwala, S. I., & Mathew, R. M. (1998). Children who prosper in unfavorable environments: The relationship to social capital. *Pediatrics, 101*, 12–18.

Sampson, R. J., Raudenbush, S. W., & Earls, F. (1997). Neighborhoods and violent crime: A multilevel study of collective efficacy. *Science, 277*, 918–924.

Savel, T. G., Hall, K. E., Lee, B., McMullin, V., Stinn, J., White, P., Washington, D., Boyd, T., & Lenert, L. (2010). A public health grid (PHGrid): Architecture and value proposition for 21st century public health. *International Journal of Medical Information, 79*, 523–529.

Sedlak, A. J., Mettenburg, J., Basena, M., Petta, I., McPherson, K., Greene, A., & Li, S. (2010). *Fourth national incidence study of child abuse and neglect (NIS–4): Report to Congress*. Washington, DC: U.S. Department of Health and Human Services, Administration for Children and Families. http://www.acf.hhs.gov/programs/opre/abuse_neglect/natl_incid/reports/natl_incid/nis4_report_congress_full_pdf_jan2010.pdf.

Shonkoff, J., Boyce, W. T., & McEwen, B. (2009). Neuroscience, molecular biology, and the childhood roots of health disparities: Building a new framework for health promotion and disease prevention. *Journal of the American Medical Association, 301*, 2252–2259.

Thacker, S. B., Qualters, J. R., & Lee, L. M. (2012). Public health surveillance in the United States: Evolution and challenges. *MMWR, 61*, 1–9.

Turnock, B. J. (2012). *Public health: What it is and how it works* (5th ed.). Burlington: Jones & Bartlett Learning.

U.S. Advisory Board on Child Abuse and Neglect. (1990). *Child abuse and neglect: Critical first steps in response to a national emergency*. Washington, DC: Government Printing Office.

U.S. Advisory Board on Child Abuse and Neglect. (1993). *Neighbors helping neighbors: A new national strategy for the protection of children*. Washington, DC: U.S. Government Printing Office.

U.S. Department of Health and Human Services, Administration on Children, Youth and Families. (2006). *Child maltreatment 2005*. Washington, DC: U.S. Government Printing Office. http://www.acf.hhs.gov/programs/cb/pubs/cm07/index.htm.

U.S. Department of Health and Human Services, Administration on Children, Youth and Families. (2007). *Child maltreatment 2006*. Washington, DC: U.S. Government Printing Office. http://www.acf.hhs.gov/programs/cb/pubs/cm08/index.htm.

U.S. Department of Health and Human Services, Administration for Children and Families, Administration on Children, Youth and Families, Children's Bureau. (2011). *Child maltreatment 2010*. Washington, DC: U.S. Government Printing Office.

Vimpani, G. (2000). Child development and civil society: Does social capital matter? *Developmental and Behavioral Pediatrics, 21*, 44–47.

Wald, M. S. (2009). Preventing maltreatment or promoting positive development – where should a community focus its resources?: A policy perspective, pp. 182–195. In K. A. Dodge & D. L. Coleman (Eds.), *Preventing child maltreatment: Community approaches*. New York: The Guilford Press.

Wang, C. T., & Holton, J. (2007). *Total estimated cost of child abuse and neglect in the United States*. Chicago: Prevent Child Abuse America. http://member.preventchildabuse.org/site/DocServer/cost_analysis.pdf?docID=144. Accessed June 2012.

Wilson, R. W. (2011). *Practice of public health 1: Definitions and structures of public health*. Washington, DC: CDC University lecture on public health concepts and competencies.

Winslow, C.E. (1923) *The evolution and significance of the modern public health campaign* (New Haven: Yale University Press; reprinted by the *Journal of Public Health Policy, 1*, 1984.)

Zuravin, S. J. (1989). The ecology of child abuse and neglect: Review of the literature and presentation of data. *Violence and Victims, 4*, 101–120.

Chapter 17
Strong Communities for Children: A Community-Wide Approach to Prevention of Child Maltreatment

Gary B. Melton

Making headlines in most major American news media with the release of its first report in 1990, the U.S. Advisory Board on Child Abuse and Neglect (U.S. ABCAN) declared a national emergency. The blue-ribbon panel based its conclusion on three findings: (a) the epidemic scope of the problem; (b) "chronic and critical multiple organ failure" (U.S. ABCAN 1990, p. 2); (c) the annual multi-billion-dollar cost of dealing with these failures.

The members of the Board also made clear, however, that the moral challenge that they – and indeed all American adults – confronted was found in the fact of child maltreatment itself, not its consequences. *"Even when* [*child maltreatment*] *causes no demonstrable harm to children,"* the Board lamented, *"it is shameful"* (U.S. ABCAN 1990, p. 6, emphasis in the original):

> Child abuse is wrong. Not only is child abuse wrong, but the nation's lack of an effective response to it is also wrong. Neither can be tolerated. Together they constitute a moral disaster....
>
> Beating children, chronically berating them, using them for sexual gratification, or depriving them of the basic necessities of life are repellent acts and cannot be permitted in a civilized society. Tolerating child abuse denies the worth of children as human beings and makes a mockery of the American principle of respect for the rights and needs of each individual.

The author served as vice-chair of the U.S. Advisory Board on Child Abuse and Neglect, co-chair (with Frank Barry) of its Committee on the National Strategy, and principal investigator of Strong Communities for Children.

Special thanks are due colleagues who were leaders in the Strong Communities research program (Asher Ben-Arieh, James McDonell, Jill McLeigh, John Berman, and Virginia Murphy-Berman), community outreach and volunteer services (Robin Kimbrough-Melton, Linda Smith, Dottie Campbell, Jill McLeigh, and Patricia Motes), and financing (The Duke Endowment). The extraordinary efforts of dedicated outreach staff, volunteers, and graduate assistants were also critical to the initiative. The Strong Communities initiative was thoughtfully advised by a distinguished external panel (Richard Krugman, chair; Andrew Billingsley, Scott Henggeler, Jill Korbin, and David Wolfe) and by The Duke Endowment staff and consultants.

The Strong Communities survey instrument was designed in tandem with other grantees (Kenneth Dodge, Desmond Runyan, and their colleagues), other Strong Communities staff (James McDonell and Patricia Hashima), and the principal program officer (Rhett Mabry) and consultant (Deborah Daro) of The Duke Endowment. James McDonell supervised the sample selection and data analyses in the community survey, and the data were collected and recorded by staff of Westat.

In relation to both the U.S. Advisory Board and Strong Communities, the diligent and creative work of colleagues is gratefully acknowledged. However, the opinions expressed in this chapter are the author's own and are not necessarily those of particular colleagues or their institutions.

More detailed descriptions of the Strong Communities initiative and its evaluation can be found in a special issue of *Family and Community Health* (Melton and Holaday 2008), a forthcoming special section of *Child Abuse and Neglect* (Melton in prep.-a), and a forthcoming edited volume (Melton in prep.-b).

G.B. Melton (✉)
University of Colorado School of Medicine, Denver, CO, USA
e-mail: Gary.Melton@ucdenver.edu

Child neglect is also wrong.... When those who have assumed responsibility for providing the necessary resources for children (usually parents) fail to do so, it is wrong. When parents and other caretakers have the psychological capacity to care for their children adequately but lack the economic resources to do so, *society itself is derelict* when it fails to provide assistance....

It is bad enough – simply immoral – that the nation permits assaults on the integrity of children as persons. To make matters worse, such negligence also threatens the integrity of a nation that shares a sense of community..., regards individuals as worthy of respect..., reveres family life, and...is competent in economic competition. (U.S. ABCAN 1990, pp. 3–4)

The Board further concluded that the nation's failure to meet its obligation to ensure the safety of its youngest citizens was the product of an ill-designed system:

The most serious shortcoming of the nation's system of intervention on behalf of children is that it depends upon a reporting and response process that has punitive connotations, and requires massive resources dedicated to the investigation of allegations. State and County child welfare programs have *not* been designed to get immediate help to families based on voluntary requests for assistance. As a result it has become far easier to pick up the telephone to report one's neighbor for child abuse than it is for that neighbor to pick up the telephone to request and receive help before the abuse happens. (U.S. ABCAN 1990, p. 80)

Consequently, the Board promised to devote its efforts to "the long-term development of a new, carefully planned, coherent approach for assuring the safety of children" (U.S. ABCAN 1990, p. 8). The Board asserted that the answer was "the development of plans for the coordinated, comprehensive, community-based prevention, identification, and treatment of abuse and neglect" (U.S. ABCAN 1990, p. 94). Toward that end, the Board articulated two "fundamental principles" for child protection: (a) the involvement of the entire community (not just the specialty child welfare system) and (b) a focus on children's individual needs. Subsequently, in a report focused on the federal role in child protection, the Board (U.S. ABCAN 1991) further asserted that "the principal goal of governmental involvement in child protection should be to facilitate comprehensive community efforts to ensure the safe and healthy development of children" (p. 46).

The U.S. Advisory Board's Proposed National Strategy

The Rationale

Keeping its promise and adhering to its principles, the Board undertook an ambitious initiative to discover and apply international norms of human rights and empirical knowledge about the social underpinnings of child maltreatment to the design of a comprehensive community strategy for protection of children. [Papers that were commissioned to inform the Board's discussions can be found in two edited volumes (Melton and Barry 1994a; Melton et al. 2002).] At the culmination of this process in 1993, the Board proposed the development of a national child-centered, neighborhood-based child protection system. The Board imagined a "neighborly" society in which "all American adults... resolve to be good neighbors – to know, watch, and support their neighbors' children and to offer help when needed to their neighbors' families" (U.S. ABCAN 1993, p. 82). The Board articulated a five-pronged strategy for fulfillment of this vision: (a) strengthening neighborhoods as environments for child development and family life; (b) reorienting human services to emphasize prevention of child maltreatment and promotion of family well-being; (c) improving government's involvement in child protection (e.g., developing comprehensive plans for child protection; reforming the financing of human services to facilitate integrated services); (d) re-shaping societal values that may contribute to child maltreatment [e.g., ratifying the Convention on the Rights of the Child; taking steps to "reduce the acceptance of violence as a means of resolving conflict, change attitudes that may contribute to the exploitation and sexualization of children, and promote appreciation of cultural differences as a source of strength in our society" (Melton and Barry 1994b, p. 9); and (e) generating knowledge useful in comprehensive community efforts to prevent child maltreatment.

The Board's proposal drew on research showing that poor neighborhood quality (*social poverty*, controlled for social class) and sustained *economic poverty* are strong factors in the etiology of child maltreatment (see generally Garbarino and Kostelny 1994; Melton 1992; Pelton 1994; Thompson 1994), although the mechanisms for such effects were and are less well known (Coulton et al. 2007). Since the time of the Board's report, research evidence has increased that neighborhood quality – especially concentration of economic poverty and instability of residence – is critical in the safety and well-being of children (see, e.g., Drake and Pandey 1996; Ernst 2001; Freisthier et al. 2006, 2007a; Korbin et al. 1998).

Such studies show in part that neighborhood quality is important in ensuring children's safety, because that task becomes much more difficult when social and economic resources important in care for children are absent or limited and when families are confronted with exceptional stressors. For example, a study in Chicago of families with children aged 3–15 showed decreased risk of child maltreatment as family support increased (Martin et al. 2012). Neighborhood rates of maltreatment of young children in an urban county were inversely related to (a) the proportion of 3- and 4-year-olds attending preschools and (b) the ratio of licensed child care spaces to the number of young children with working parents (Klein 2011). In the same study, risk was highest in high-poverty neighborhoods with ethnic heterogeneity and inadequate resources for informal child supervision. Risk also escalates when poverty is accompanied by easy access to alcohol and drugs (Freisthier 2004; Freisthier et al. 2005, 2007b) – in effect, offering the opportunity to cope by avoidance of severe challenges of daily life, in the context of a dearth of legitimate pathways to economic security.

Neighborhood physical characteristics are also important elements in children's safety. It is simply more difficult to keep a child safe in an unsafe environment. Moreover, physical markers (e.g., the presence of fences around residential yards; the availability of signs communicating the neighborhood identity) are powerful indicators of residents' collective concern for the neighborhood and their motivation and competence to maintain it. Such social variables in turn might reasonably be inferred to reflect neighbors' watchfulness, exercise of informal control, and engagement with one another (see Zolotor and Runyan 2006, on the relation between social capital and neglectful and harsh parenting). Presumably reflecting such processes, the neighborhood attributes that can be observed on a drive-through (see McDonell and Waters 2011), even after statistical controls for demographic variables (e.g., family income; residential stability), account for almost one-fourth of the variance in parents' perceptions of their children's safety in their homes (McDonell 2007). Among 168 neighborhoods studied in South Carolina, observed physical and social conditions accounted for 27.4 % of the variance in rates of physical abuse, 17.5 % of the variance in rates of sexual abuse, and 6.7 % of the variance in rates of neglect, as classified according to ICD-9 categories and as applied to all hospital inpatient and emergency-room care (McDonell and Skosireva 2009). Overall, physical and social conditions accounted for 28.3 % of the variance in rates of child maltreatment.

Not only do neighborhood factors influence risk of maltreatment, but they also mediate its long-term effects. Individual strengths are important predictors of resiliency after child maltreatment only when family and neighborhood stress is low (Jaffee et al. 2007). Chauhan and Widom (2012) found that a history of child maltreatment predisposes residential choices in adulthood (toward neighborhoods with weaker social cohesion and greater disadvantage) in a manner that increases risk of illicit drug use at least until middle adulthood. Similarly, in a study of a largely African American population in Detroit, a history of child maltreatment and current residence in a disorderly neighborhood interacted to predict the incidence of adult binge drinking (Keyes et al. 2012). Research also has shown that neighborhood-level sense of collective efficacy moderates the effect of a history of neglect on aggression by 12-year-olds (Yonas et al. 2010). More generally, the severity of neighborhood disadvantage and instability moderates the effect of early child maltreatment on adolescent and adult lawbreaking (Schuck and Widom 2005). In another long-term follow-up study, although neighborhood advantage did not directly affect resilience among adolescents and young adults who had experienced physical or sexual abuse as children, it did moderate the relationship between household stability and resilience in adolescence and between cognitive ability and resilience in young adulthood (DuMont et al. 2007).

The relatively few personal (psychological) factors that are known to be important in the etiology of child maltreatment (e.g., parental depression; perceived efficacy of parents as individuals, family members, and community members) are closely related to these social and economic variables (Pelton 1994). For example, family support in moderate- to high-violence neighborhoods has been shown to reduce the risk of child maltreatment by decreasing parents' vulnerability to depression (Martin et al. 2012).

Principles for Action

Apart from basic research on the relation of neighborhood factors to the prevalence of child maltreatment and the well-being of families, research also had suggested that programs within and of the community have the greatest effectiveness in helping children and families. Reviewing 21 contemporary programs generated in the family support movement and identified by national experts as exemplary, Wilson and Melton (2002) noted 12 commonalities:

- Focus on both prevention and treatment;
- Strengthen family and community supports and connections;
- Treat parents as vital contributors to child growth and development;
- Create opportunities for parents to feel empowered to act on their own behalf;
- Respect the integrity of the family unit and serve it holistically;
- Enhance parents' capacities to foster the optimal development of their children and themselves;
- Show sensitivity to the cultural, ethnic, religious, social, and economic characteristics of the community;
- Establish linkages with community support systems;
- Provide settings where parents and children can gather, interact, support each other, and learn from each other;
- Enhance coordination and integration of services needed by families;
- Enhance community awareness of the importance of healthy parenting practices;
- Provide 24-h emergency support when parents and children need help. (pp. 199–200)

Although some of these characteristics do not inherently require a community or neighborhood base, it is difficult to imagine a more distal base if these characteristics are taken as an integrated whole. In fact, the model programs generally grew from grassroots concerns and local needs. Programs commonly had non-professional origins in civic clubs, neighborhood associations, or ethnic associations, and they continued to operate with largely volunteer staffing. Moreover, the centers that were created went well beyond "one-stop shopping" for professional services to centers of community for creative integration of tailored programs and, like the settlement houses established about a century ago, for conversation, recreation, practical assistance (e.g., education in home repairs), and sharing of resources.

Indeed, the contemporary model family support programs created in part with goals of preventing and treating child abuse and neglect are strikingly similar to the settlement houses of the early-twentieth-century and the community action agencies in the War on Poverty in the 1960s. Note the descriptions in Levine and Levine's social history (2002):

> The settlement houses emphasized educational, recreational, and social purpose. Even though they dealt with children and families from different neighborhoods who had many problems associated with poverty, settlement workers emphasized uplift, development, and growth. They provided the opportunity for individuals to develop

themselves in ways those individuals thought desirable. They provided a place for children to do homework, for children and adults to learn to play music, participate in plays or athletics, and...develop organizational skills by providing positions of leadership in clubs. There were no eligibility requirements, no intake, no forms to fill out unless one signed up for a club or a service or became a member of the settlement. People came to the settlements for activities that they wanted and enjoyed and that helped them to participate successfully in the larger society. The settlement workers were there to assist others to develop, not to cure them....

Similarly, in the 1960s...people came to the [neighborhood service] centers for job leads, employment counseling, and training opportunities that often provided stipends.... The centers were located in neighborhoods and operated informally (one could drop in without an appointment).

Neighborhood center workers felt free to make informal home visits, to advise people of opportunities, or simply to stay in touch with problem families. Because of the frequent, informal contacts, neighborhood workers learned about problems that individuals and families were having, and they could attempt to intervene by offering services. These services were often concrete and immediate; they ranged from advocacy efforts to such mundane matters as providing transportation to make a service available. Neighborhood workers greeted clients and former clients on the streets and inquired about them, exchanged Christmas cards, and responded when people asked for assistance not directly related to employment. (pp. 94–95)

The U.S. Advisory Board was impressed by these historical examples and the research and theory on which they were based. On logical grounds, the Board theorized that, to be effective, the child protection system must be a part of everyday life. It should be embedded in the settings where families live, work, study, worship, and play. Such settings have the capacity to strengthen parents' sense that they can make a difference in regard to the well-being of their own and their neighbors' children in their community. Such settings also provide opportunities to notice the needs of young families and to respond immediately, reciprocally, and usefully. Moreover, infusion of reciprocal help into the settings of everyday life "normalizes" assistance and thereby both minimizes stigma and maximizes its utility and generalizability (see Limber and Hashima 2002 and Thompson 1994 for reviews of the nature and potency of informal social support; see also Murphy-Berman and Melton 2002 on mutual assistance, including "self-help" groups).

By contrast, the U.S.-style child protection system that has dominated child welfare around the world in the past 50 years is based on allegations, not needs for help (see Melton 2005; Worley and Melton 2012). By emphasizing the central importance of state social workers' investigations, the system has inadvertently diminished community residents' sense of personal responsibility to assist neighbors in need. Ironically and tragically, the child protection system had been designed in a manner that had implicitly (but inadvertently) absolved citizens of any responsibility other than "telling" that they suspected child maltreatment and that had transformed helping professionals into detectives. In effect, the system had undermined the assistance that neighbors can give each other, both in ordinary daily life and times of crisis. Ironically and tragically, it had diverted the resources designated for child protection to a law enforcement function, so that little help was available to families who ultimately go all the way through an inherently unfriendly system.

For a neighborhood-based system to work, the Board recognized, it must be universal. Exclusion of affluent families with relatively few unmet needs diminishes the resources available in a system of reciprocity. Moreover, as families become more and more isolated (an endemic process in 21st-century industrialized societies), even those families with the greatest resources may find themselves alone at times of crisis (e.g., parental illness).

The system must also be inclusive of those families whom communities might otherwise exclude. Although the removal of adult offenders from communities may be justified by the offenders' conduct, de facto punishment should not extend to their children. Those who do or will care for children during and after their parents' incarceration should be held within the community safety net. So too should new immigrants and ethnic minorities who otherwise might not be fully integrated into communities.

The ideas presented by the U.S. Advisory Board were given broad public attention but with mixed impact (Melton 2002). By the mid-1990s, the Board's arguments pushed the (U.S.) National Child Abuse Coalition to broaden its federal advocacy beyond programs in the specialty child welfare sector. The Board's work also was catalytic in expansion of infant home visitation, especially in the non-profit sector in the United States. Developments in public discourse and professional aspirations are not trivial accomplishments, especially amid the continuing clash of interest groups and the resulting iterative, relatively slow-paced change that typically results in the American political process. However, these developments fell far short of the level of change that the Board envisioned in the federal sector alone – reforms that would have required action by scores of congressional committees and subcommittees (U.S. ABCAN 1991).

The Board had recognized that fulfillment of its vision would not be easy:

> It will require reversal of powerful social trends, within neighborhoods at highest risk (those that have been "drained") and the nation as a whole. The problem of child maltreatment is so complex – increasingly so – that the strategy necessarily includes many elements, and the science and technology of neighborhood development are only minimally developed…. Moreover, a focus on the social conditions that undermine the safety of children means that the responsibility for change must be shared not only by the individual families involved but also by service providers, the community, and all levels of government – in fact, by society itself…. Although the Board's strategy builds on such historic values of our society, it does so with recognition of the need to accommodate to trends in the post-industrial age that have weakened the expectation of voluntary help by neighbors for each other and that have reshaped not only neighborhoods but also the families within them. (U.S. ABCAN 1993, p. 81)

Accordingly, the Board's number one recommendation when it released its report on the neighborhood-based strategy was in effect a request for tryouts of the approach. Specifically, the Board recommended the creation of Prevention Zones – model neighborhoods in which intensive efforts would be made to promote economic and social development designed to facilitate the implementation of a neighbors-helping-neighbors strategy for prevention of child maltreatment.

Although support for such Prevention Zones was conceived as primarily a federal responsibility, action occurred in the philanthropic sector. Specifically, The Duke Endowment made a generous multi-year (2002 to approximately 2008) grant to the Clemson University Research Foundation to undertake such an initiative through the CU Institute on Family and Neighborhood Life (then under the author's leadership) in a portion of metropolitan Greenville, South Carolina. That initiative, known as Strong Communities for Children and based at the Center for Community Services in Simpsonville, remains to my knowledge the only comprehensive attempt to apply the U.S. Advisory Board's strategy at scale.

(A still larger-scale outgrowth of the Board's recommendations was Healthy Families America, a national initiative for infant home visitation sponsored by Prevent Child Abuse America and also originally supported in the philanthropic sector. However, the scope of services in Healthy Families is substantially more limited than was envisioned in Strong Communities, which was intended to engage all sectors of the community in prevention of child maltreatment and to enable support for all families, not just those at high risk.)

Strong Communities for Children

The Approach

Greenville is a widely dispersed metropolitan area. The service area included the southern third of Greenville County and the northeastern section of Anderson County – an area that at the time had about 125,000 people. It is ethnically and economically diverse, with an urban area, suburban areas, small towns, and rural areas.

In consonance with the analysis in the preceding section, Strong Communities was designed to change the *norms* of the participating communities and to enable easy implementation of those norms, in both cases by mobilizing communities through primary institutions (e.g., schools; businesses; churches; family health clinics; public safety agencies). In particular, efforts were made to create or enhance a sense of community (norms of caring [e.g., attentiveness; neighborliness] and inclusion) and a sense of efficacy (optimism [e.g., the belief that action on behalf of families will be effective because the community is welcoming and supportive] and action [e.g., the belief that practical activity could and should be directed toward family support]). Taken together, *the goal was to ensure that every child and every parent would know that if they had reason to celebrate, worry, or grieve, someone would notice, and someone would care.*

The key actors in the initiative were community outreach workers (roughly 1 to a community), who strove to organize community action in keeping with a set of 10 core principles (e.g., "Strong Communities is directed toward the establishment or enhancement of *relationships* among families or between families and community institutions"). In the early phases of the initiative, the outreach workers focused on spreading the word, first to community leaders and then with the leaders' help to the community as a whole. Campaigns (e.g., pledges to learn the names of the children in the 10 closest homes) and special events (e.g., community festivals; special religious observances) were tools in these efforts.

Thereafter, the outreach workers engaged in grassroots mobilization to enhance both social and material resources for families within community settings. E.g., firefighters in one community knocked on doors to bring residents to community meetings, mentored children everyday, distributed bicycle helmets, and built a front porch for the fire station.

The outreach staff also sought to institutionalize neighborly activity that would enhance the resources available to families of young children and that would maximize their chance of being noticed at critical times. Generally using existing human resources (unpaid volunteer service and donated professional time) in existing community facilities (e.g., churches; fire stations; parks; schools), outreach workers collaborated with key volunteers to create numerous family activity centers. Among the services that the centers offered were play groups (a chance for parents to make connections with other parents of young children), parents' nights out, and chats with family advocates.

The Results

The conservative nature of the findings. Strong Communities was extensively evaluated. The outcome evaluations yielded conservative results because the baseline was 2 years after the initiative started. The statistical power was lower than anticipated and the level of institutionalization of reforms was also less extensive than planned, because the grant supporting the initiative ended approximately 3 years earlier than was originally contemplated. Given these deviations from the original plan and the inherent difficulty in measuring some of the variables of most interest, the results of Strong Communities lends credibility and support to this community-based approach (McDonell et al. 2013).

The engagement of the communities. Despite the fact that activities associated with Strong Communities were often not recorded, the records of activities in the presence of an outreach worker or with her or his direct knowledge are by themselves impressive (see Haski-Leventhal et al. 2008, for an overview of the strategy and process of volunteer engagement in Strong Communities). In less than 5 years, more than 5,000 people volunteered their time (more than 60,000 h) in an area with about 90,000 adults. Both the number of volunteers and the amount of time that they contributed grew steadily throughout the initiative – remarkable achievements in an era of ever-increasing alienation and isolation.

Analogously, the number of organizations involved in the initiative and the number and diversity of activities in which they were engaged during that period grew steadily to impressive levels (e.g., 188 businesses; 213 religious organizations; 85 voluntary organizations). The most vigorous involvement originated in organizations (e.g., fire departments; churches) that typically have little, if any, engagement in primary prevention of child maltreatment.

The volunteers were remarkably representative of the communities in which they live. About 40 % of the volunteers were male – unusual for a children's initiative. The proportion of volunteers who were ethnic-minority or who were resident in high-need communities was higher than in the population as a whole.

There is evidence that Strong Communities was transformative, not just in its effects on children and families in the participating communities, but also in its effects on the volunteers themselves. Such effects were particularly notable among approximately 50 individuals who were "key volunteers" and who thus were *leaders* in the literal sense – i.e., residents who *initiated* numerous projects in the context of the Strong Communities initiative (Hashima and Melton 2008). Importantly, these leaders were not elected officials; they were not major corporate CEOs. Indeed, they were not people whose names often, if ever, appeared in the local newspaper. In terms of demographics, the key volunteers were similar to the "regular" volunteers – just a little older. However, they were distinguished by lifelong commitment to service and unusually heavy involvement in their churches. These individuals achieved a new level of self-confidence and new commitment to community service because they found in Strong Communities that they could work at scale (not "just" with individuals) to improve the well-being of the community. Notwithstanding their lifelong expressions of altruism, many truly became "new people" in the magnitude of their aspirations and the depth of their commitment to their neighbors.

Although with less intensity, the volunteers in general shared that perspective. They were serving in Strong Communities to do good for the community, not to make social or business connections, learn job skills, or build a résumé for their own betterment (Haski-Leventhal et al. 2008).

The safety of children. Many would argue that the level of community engagement by itself justified the investment in Strong Communities. Certainly, many foundations and government agencies have invested substantial sums of money in order to promote such a goal, but often with little success.

There is strong evidence, however, that Strong Communities not only changed the communities per se, but that by doing so, they also made children safer. The linchpin of the studies of the latter outcome was a random survey (conducted in waves 3 years apart) of parents of young children in the Strong Communities service area and in matched block groups (neighborhoods) in other parts of South Carolina. Across time and relative to the comparison communities, parents in the Strong Communities area reported extraordinary change: less parental stress; greater social support; more frequent help from others; greater sense of community and personal efficacy; more frequent positive parental behavior; more frequent use of household safety devices (e.g., baby gates); less frequent disengaged (inattentive) parenting; less frequent neglect.

These self- and community perceptions were reflected in actual changes in relevant outcomes in institutions charged with protecting children's safety. For example, marked positive changes were seen in founded referrals of young children to Child Protective Services as a result of suspected child maltreatment. Again in comparison of the service area with matched block groups across time, officially substantiated cases of maltreatment among children aged 2 and under declined by 11 % in the service area but increased by 85 % in the comparison area. For children aged 4 and under, founded maltreatment decreased by 41 % in the service area but increased by 49 % in the comparison area. For children aged 9 and under, founded maltreatment decreased by 8 % in the service area but increased by 30 % in the comparison area.

Strong Communities focused on families of young children (roughly, birth through first grade). The CPS data, which are echoed in other service systems, show remarkable effects on the safety of young children, but they also show some spillover to other elementary-school-age children. The latter finding is unsurprising for two reasons:

1. Many families of young children include children in the upper elementary grades.
2. Changes in the school climate for families in kindergarten and first-grade classes (and other primary grades) often involve whole schools.

The CPS data were complemented by the findings drawn from examination of records in emergency rooms and pediatric inpatient units. Emergency room visits and inpatient stays attributable to neglect declined by 68 % among children of all ages in the service area but by only 19 % in the comparison area. All admissions for injuries resulting from maltreatment of children aged 2 and under declined by 23 % in the service area but only 6 % in the comparison area. All admissions for injuries resulting from maltreatment of children aged 4 and under declined by 38 % in the service area but only 13 % in the comparison area.

Perhaps showing the spillover effect, secondary analyses of state-collected surveys of teachers, parents, and children in the service area showed significant increases in the beliefs of the adults, but even more so the children, that pupils are safe at and in transit to and from school. Respondents in the service area also were more likely over time to report that parents were taken seriously by school personnel. However, such beliefs about child safety and school acceptance of parents became less common in families of children in matched comparison schools.

Conclusions

The results of the evaluation studies of Strong Communities show unequivocally that one person can make a difference. Following principles derived from knowledge about the causes and correlates of child maltreatment, a small group of outreach workers (about one per community; optimally, about one per 10,000 people) created a social movement inclusive of people of diverse age, ethnicity, class, politics, and theology. Remarkably, there were *never* conflicts among volunteers, groups, and organizations of different backgrounds. Participants were united in the goal to *Keep Kids Safe* by changing social norms so that children and parents are *noticed* and *cared for*, by their peers and by others in the community.

Strong Communities demonstrated that a universal approach to primary prevention that relies on principles to achieve changes in norms can result in a translation of those norms into practice. Applying resources generated as a result of such community engagement to meet families' material needs, to provide volunteer overnight care, and to deliver mentoring and other support for families of prisoners, we also have shown that Strong Communities can be constructed in a way that it serves as a safety net even for those families already involved in formal child protection and justice systems. The result is that children are safer; they are safer even without their families having to ask for help or to be labeled as clients or patients. With implications for other social problems and indeed, stated positively, the quality of life in general (especially for young families at times of great need), Strong Communities also provided compelling evidence of the potential for broad-based community engagement in a way that crosses all of the usual social boundaries.

The communities in which Strong Communities was based were sufficiently diverse that they offer strong evidence for the effectiveness of such an approach in various neighborhoods and probably various cultures. The grassroots organizing approach had its greatest effect in mobilization of the communities of highest need, although it took about 2 years before the new community structures and civic engagement began to be fully manifest. By contrast, in affluent suburban communities, the same ultimate effects on children's safety were demonstrated, even though some of the intermediate changes in community process that had been observed in less advantaged communities did not appear.

It is now important to see if others can apply the principles of Strong Communities and achieve results of such impressive magnitude, whether in terms of community-building per se or of the safety and well-being of children. We are convinced in that regard that a substantial economy of scale is possible. A unit consisting of planners, supervisors, and evaluators probably can support outreach workers across multiple metropolitan areas and/or rural regions.

The promise of Strong Communities is broad. In that regard, staff and visitors in Strong Communities came from widely disparate societies. Without exception (see Melton et al. in prep.), they were impressed by the apparent applicability of the initiative in diverse cultures, whether in industrialized or developing societies. In particular, implementation appears to be feasible in diverse societies because of the reliance on community volunteers and the attention given to neighborhoods' particular assets, norms, and needs.

References

Chauhan, P., & Widom, C. S. (2012). Childhood maltreatment and illicit drug use in middle adulthood: The role of neighborhood characteristics. *Development and Psychopathology, 24*, 723–738.

Coulton, C. J., Crampton, D. S., Irwin, M., Spilsbury, J. C., & Korbin, J. E. (2007). How neighborhoods influence child maltreatment: A review of the literature and alternative pathways. *Child Abuse & Neglect, 31*, 1117–1142.

Drake, B., & Pandey, S. (1996). Understanding the relationship between neighborhood poverty and specific types of child maltreatment. *Child Abuse & Neglect, 20*, 1003–1018.

DuMont, K. A., Widom, C. S., & Czaja, S. J. (2007). Predictors of resilience in abused and neglected children grown-up: The role of individual and neighborhood characteristics. *Child Abuse & Neglect, 31*, 255–274.

Ernst, J. S. (2001). Community-level factors and child maltreatment in a suburban community. *Social Work Research, 25*, 133–142.

Freisthier, B. (2004). A spatial analysis of social disorganization, alcohol access, and rates of child maltreatment in neighborhoods. *Children and Youth Services Review, 26*, 803–819.

Freisthier, B., Needell, B., & Gruenewald, P. J. (2005). Is the physical availability of alcohol and illicit drugs related to neighborhood rates of child maltreatment? *Child Abuse & Neglect, 29*, 1049–1060.

Freisthier, B., Merritt, D. H., & LaScala, E. A. (2006). Understanding the ecology of child maltreatment: A review of the literature and directions for future research. *Child Maltreatment, 11*, 263–280.

Freisthier, B., Bruce, E., & Needell, B. (2007a). Understanding the geospatial relationship of neighborhood characteristics and rates of maltreatment for Black, Hispanic, and White children. *Social Work, 52*, 7–16.

Freisthier, B., Gruenewald, P. J., Remer, L. G., Lery, B., & Needell, B. (2007b). Exploring the spatial dynamics of alcohol outlets and child protective services referrals, substantiations, and foster care entries. *Child Maltreatment, 12*, 114–124.

Garbarino, J., & Kostelny, K. (1994). Neighborhood-based programs. In G. B. Melton & F. D. Barry (Eds.), *Protecting children from abuse and neglect: Foundations for a new national strategy* (pp. 304–352). New York: Guilford.

Hashima, P. Y., & Melton, G. B. (2008). "I can conquer a mountain": Ordinary people who provide extraordinary community service. *Family & Community Health, 31*, 162–172.

Haski-Leventhal, D., Ben-Arieh, A., & Melton, G. B. (2008). Between neighborliness and volunteerism: Participants in the strong communities initiative. *Family & Community Health, 31*, 150–161.

Jaffee, S. R., Caspi, A., Moffitt, T. E., Polo-Tomás, M., & Taylor, A. (2007). Individual, family, and neighborhood factors distinguish resilient from non-resilient maltreated children: A cumulative stressors model. *Child Abuse & Neglect, 31*, 231–253.

Keyes, K. M., McLaughlin, K. A., Koenen, K. C., Goodman, E., Uddin, M., & Galea, S. (2012). Child maltreatment increases sensitivity to adverse social contexts: Neighborhood physical disorder and incident binge drinking in Detroit. *Drug and Alcohol Dependence, 122*, 77–85.

Klein, S. (2011). The availability of neighborhood early care and education resources and the maltreatment of young children. *Child Maltreatment, 16*, 300–311.

Korbin, J. E., Coulton, C. J., Chard, S., Platt-Houston, C., & Su, M. (1998). Impoverishment and child maltreatment in African American and European American neighborhoods. *Development and Psychopathology, 10*, 215–233.

Levine, M., & Levine, A. (2002). Neighborhood-based services: Lessons from the settlement house movement and the War on Poverty. In G. B. Melton, R. A. Thompson, & M. A. Small (Eds.), *Toward a child-centered, neighborhood-based child protection system: A report of the Consortium on Children, Families, and the Law* (pp. 91–103). Westport, CT: Praeger.

Limber, S. P., & Hashima, P. Y. (2002). The social context: What comes naturally in child protection. In G. B. Melton, R. A. Thompson, & M. A. Small (Eds.), *Toward a child-centered, neighborhood-based child protection system: A report of the Consortium on Children, Families, and the Law* (pp. 41–66). Westport, CT: Praeger.

Martin, A., Gardner, M., & Brooks-Gunn, J. (2012). The mediated and moderated effects of family support on child maltreatment. *Journal of Family Issues, 33*, 920–941.

McDonell, J. R. (2007). Neighborhood characteristics, parenting, and children's safety. *Social Indicators Research, 83*, 177–199.

McDonell, J. R., Ben-Arieh, A., & Melton, G. B. (2013). Strong Communities for Children: Results of a multi-year community-based initiative to protect children from harm. Manuscript submitted for publication.

McDonell, J. R., & Skosireva, A. (2009). Neighborhood characteristics, child maltreatment, and child injuries. *Child Indicators Research, 2,* 133–153.

McDonell, J. R., & Waters, T. J. (2011). Construction and validation of an observational scale of neighborhood characteristics. *Social Indicators Research, 104,* 439–457.

Melton, G. B. (1992). It's time for neighborhood research and action. *Child Abuse & Neglect, 16,* 909–913.

Melton, G. B. (2005). Mandated reporting: A policy without reason. *Child Abuse & Neglect, 29,* 9–18.

Melton, G. B. (Ed.). (in prep.-a). *Good neighbors: Safe and humane communities for children and families.* Dordrecht: Springer.

Melton, G. B. (Ed.). (in prep.-b). Strong communities for children [Special section]. *Child Abuse and Neglect.*

Melton, G. B., Agani, F., Fernandez, N., Hassall, I., Lavenda, O., Moore de Peralta, A., Sianko, N., Skosireva, A., & Ben-Arieh, A (in prep.). The international application of Strong Communities for Children. *Child Abuse and Neglect.*

Melton, G. B., & Barry, F. D. (Eds.). (1994a). *Protecting children from abuse and neglect: Foundations for a new national strategy.* New York: Guilford.

Melton, G. B., & Barry, F. D. (1994b). Neighbors helping neighbors: The vision of the U.S. Advisory Board on Child Abuse and Neglect. In G. B. Melton & F. D. Barry (Eds.), *Protecting children from abuse and neglect: Foundations for a new national strategy* (pp. 1–13). New York: Guilford.

Melton, G. B., & Holaday, B. J. (Eds.). (2008). Strong communities as safe havens for children [Special issue]. *Family and Community Health, 31*(2), 100–112.

Melton, G. B., Thompson, R. A., & Small, M. A. (Eds.). (2002). *Toward a child-centered, neighborhood-based child protection system: A report of the Consortium on Children, Families, and the Law.* Westport, CT: Praeger.

Murphy-Berman, V., & Melton, G. B. (2002). The self-help movement and neighborhood support for troubled families. In G. B. Melton, R. A. Thompson, & M. A. Small (Eds.), *Toward a child-centered, neighborhood-based child protection system: A report of the Consortium on Children, Families, and the Law* (pp. 233–244). Westport, CT: Praeger.

Pelton, L. H. (1994). The role of material factors in child abuse and neglect. In G. B. Melton & F. D. Barry (Eds.), *Protecting children from abuse and neglect: Foundations for a new national strategy* (pp. 131–181). New York: Guilford.

Schuck, A. M., & Widom, C. S. (2005). Understanding the role of neighborhood context in the long-term criminal consequences of child maltreatment. *American Journal of Community Psychology, 36,* 207–222.

Thompson, R. A. (1994). Social support and the prevention of child maltreatment. In G. B. Melton & F. D. Barry (Eds.), *Protecting children from abuse and neglect: Foundations for a new national strategy* (pp. 40–130). New York: Guilford.

U.S. Advisory Board on Child Abuse and Neglect. (1990). *Child abuse and neglect: Critical first steps in response to a national emergency.* Washington, DC: U.S. Government Printing Office.

U.S. Advisory Board on Child Abuse and Neglect. (1991). *Creating caring communities: Blueprint for an effective federal policy on child abuse and neglect.* Washington, DC: U.S. Government Printing Office.

U.S. Advisory Board on Child Abuse and Neglect. (1993). *Neighbors helping neighbors: A new national strategy for the protection of children.* Washington, DC: U.S. Government Printing Office.

Wilson, K. K., & Melton, G. B. (2002). Exemplary neighborhood-based programs for child protection. In G. B. Melton, R. A. Thompson, & M. A. Small (Eds.), *Toward a child-centered, neighborhood-based child protection system: A report of the Consortium on Children, Families, and the Law* (pp. 197–213). Westport, CT: Praeger.

Worley, N. K., & Melton, G. B. (2012). Mandated reporting laws and child maltreatment: The evolution of a flawed policy response. In R. D. Krugman & J. E. Korbin (Eds.), *C. Henry Kempe: A 50 year legacy to the field of child abuse and neglect* (pp. 103–118). Dordrecht: Springer.

Yonas, M. A., Lewis, T., Hussey, J. M., Thompson, R., Newton, R., English, D., & Dubowitz, H. (2010). Perceptions of neighborhood collective efficacy moderate the impact of maltreatment on aggression. *Child Maltreatment, 15,* 37–47.

Zolotor, A. J., & Runyan, D. K. (2006). Social capital, family violence, and neglect. *Pediatrics, 117,* e1124–e1131.

Chapter 18
Child Maltreatment Prevention: The Problem of Resource Allocation

Fred H. Wulczyn, Sara Feldman, Sarah McCue Horwitz, and Lily Alpert

Introduction

Although the emphasis on evidence-based interventions is a major step toward improving child protection systems, there are other equally important decisions to be made if we expect to use prevention as a way to reduce exposure to and the consequences of child maltreatment. Among them, allocating preventive service capacity is perhaps the most important. It is surprising therefore to learn just how little attention is devoted to understanding whether service allocations are at all related to need or outcomes when both are measured at a public health level.

In this paper, we address three empirical questions. First, we examine the extent to which social disadvantage is related to basic indicators of contact with the child welfare system. Contact with the child welfare system is measured as maltreatment investigations, reports of abuse and neglect, substantiated reports, preventive case openings, and foster care placements, all of which are rates per 1,000 children. We next examine the allocation of preventive services relative to need and contact with the child welfare system. Preventive services allocation is defined as the number of preventive service slots available in a community. Service slots are similar to foster care beds in the sense that they represent a basic measure of service supply. If slots are open, services are available, and referrals are a measure of utilization. Finally, we examine the relationship between placements, the number of service slots per maltreatment victim, and socio-structural characteristics of the neighborhoods where children live.

Findings suggest that the allocation of preventive services follows need, but that within the cluster of high-need communities, allocations vary considerably, with some high-need communities receiving smaller prevention investments. To close the paper, we argue that closer attention to hotspots where need, resources, and outcomes are misaligned represent fundamentally different resource allocation problems.

F.H. Wulczyn (✉) • S. Feldman • L. Alpert
Center for State Child Welfare Data, Chapin Hall, University of Chicago,
1313 E. 60th St., Chicago, IL, USA
e-mail: fwulczyn@chapinhall.org

S.M. Horwitz
Department of Child and Adolescent Psychiatry, New York University,
1 Park Ave., New York NY, USA

J.E. Korbin and R.D. Krugman (eds.), *Handbook of Child Maltreatment*, Child Maltreatment 2,
DOI 10.1007/978-94-007-7208-3_18, © Springer Science+Business Media Dordrecht 2014

Placement Prevention and Service Allocation

As a response to maltreatment, placement prevention has been a key policy and practice priority since at least 1980 when the federal government required states to use diligent efforts to keep children out of foster care. As a service goal, placement prevention has both a legal and clinical rationale. From a legal perspective, the government is reluctant to interfere with a parent's right to raise his/her children. The concept of diligent efforts to prevent placement – a legal requirement – affirms the belief that a parent's right to raise his/her children is at the forefront of child welfare policy in the U.S.

The clinical rationale for preventing placement is the flip side of the legal rationale. Though placement into foster care – the act of removing children from risks faced at home – may prevent further harm from maltreatment, the iatrogenic effects of placement are thought to be both common and clinically significant. For example, group and other forms of congregate care have been linked to negative developmental sequelae (Barth 2005; Berger et al. 2009), yet 22 % of all children and 48 % of all teenagers are placed in some type of group facility at admission. Caregiver changes, which are also associated with negative developmental sequelae (Aarons et al. 2010; Barth et al. 2007; Newton et al. 2000), affect more than half of all children who are placed, with roughly 30 % of foster children experiencing three or more placements. There is, as well, significant variation between and within states with respect to how long children remain in foster care. The median length of stay ranges from 5 to 24 months at the state level and 2 to 35 months at the county level. Finally, about one in five children will return to care within 2 years of exit and for some child populations, the reentry rate is as high as 35 % (Wulczyn et al. 2007, 2011).

Although placement prevention is at the forefront of policy and practice concerns, the available fiscal evidence suggests that prevention receives smaller investments than placement. Federal funding for child welfare services comes from a variety of sources, but core federal support for child protection is lodged within Title IV of the Social Security Act. According to the latest figures, from 2010, aggregate federal spending for foster care maintenance payments was approximately $1.5 billion, compared to $614 million spent from the Title IV-B program (DeVooght et al. 2012). In part, the discrepancy in spending is a function of the fact that foster care maintenance payments are part of an entitlement program whereas federal investments in prevention are discretionary. The imbalance is emblematic of how spending is perceived: services for maltreatment prevention are underfunded.

The chronic shortage of funds for prevention services has tended to produce policy reforms focused on increasing revenue for preventive services, either by expanding the type of covered services or expanding the population of covered individuals (children or families). Research has followed the same pattern and largely addresses the need to know more about what to do (i.e. the efficacy of covered services) and for whom (i.e. the covered populations). Missing almost entirely from the dialogue between advocates, policy-makers, and researchers is any real focus on where existing resources are being spent and whether those investments pay off, for example, in the form of lower placement rates.

Analytically, the challenge is identifying patterns in the allocation of prevention services relative to need and outcomes. Unfortunately, within the literature, there is virtually no research that discusses the allocation of child maltreatment prevention services relative to need. To the extent research has looked at the issue of capacity, which is different than the allocation of resources, the focus has been on readiness, community coalitions, fit, fidelity, adequate resources, dissemination, and implementation (Saul et al. 2008; Stith et al. 2006), but not on the number of service slots, which is a simple measure of supply. Service accessibility – program availability in relation to need – has been examined (Stanley and Kovacs 2003), but results reported were impressions gathered through a survey rather than an assessment of prevalence relative to the measured supply of services. Faver and colleagues (1999) reviewed the literature on services for child maltreatment and attributed the dearth of services to policy, a focus on the most urgent cases, and a poor match between needs and services. They also discussed help-seeking processes and barriers to utilization, but they did not specifically mention the need to study the quantity of services in relationship to need. Similarly, Whitaker and colleagues

(2005), writing about the child maltreatment prevention priorities at the Centers for Disease Control and Prevention, emphasized the public health approach to prevention and the need to implement empirically supported practices, but again they did not address the match between service availability and need as a research priority and practice for which empirical support was needed.

The Study

It is easy to understand why increased investment in preventive services sounds like good policy. What is less clear is how any new spending should be allocated. The tacit assumption is that more spending is uniformly useful, with level benefits across service contexts. In reality, different returns on new spending should be expected in part because current spending is already differentially effective and some of the decisions yet to be made will work well and others will not. Some neighborhoods already have a below average placement rate, given social conditions on the ground, so the type of preventive service purchased in those areas may well be different than the services purchased by communities where placement rates are at the other end of the adjusted scale. If nothing else one should expect different effects from the next preventive dollar spent if the resources target areas where placement rates vary. Among the nuances, if placements rates exceed an adjusted average placement rate, after controlling for the supply of preventive services, the underlying problem may have more to do with the use of different services (i.e., an evidence-based intervention) rather than simply more services. The reverse may also be true. In places where there is a serious shortage of services, prevention may be as much about quantity as it is about quality. These are important questions to ask and answer if new spending on preventing maltreatment is to be optimized.

Toward this end, we examined preventive service capacity in a large urban child welfare system. We looked at service capacity in relation to need, preventive service capacity, and foster care placement rates. We approach the problem by answering three questions. First we wanted to understand the level of contact with the child welfare system at the community area level. A child welfare agency can be present in a community area in various ways. For the *CPS system* in each community area, we have a count of all CPS investigations, a count of reports by type of allegation, and a count of victims. For the placement system, we have a count of children placed for the first time and for those children we have a count of exits to family within 1 year (reunification), exits to permanency within 1 year, and reentry to placement following an exit to permanency. For the preventive services system, we know how many preventive services cases were opened and we have a count of preventive service slots. As noted, preventive slots are analogous to foster care beds. Without a foster home a child cannot be placed; without a preventive service slot a child (or a family) cannot receive a preventive service, although there are some exceptions to this principle. Together they represent the capacity of the system in its fundamental form.

Measured in any one of the ways described, the child welfare system has a presence in every part of every city. The presence is, however, larger in some community areas than others. Thus, our second question addresses if and how the size of the presence is associated with what can be called the social ecological character of the community area. We specifically expect the presence to be greater in the areas with the higher levels of social disadvantage. The measures of social disadvantage we used are described below.[1]

Finally, we want to understand the distribution of service slots across community areas differentiated by the level of social disadvantage. We are also interested in whether placement rates vary with respect to the overall quantity of preventive services. Thus, we would expect that if there are two communities

---

[1] We use the terms social need and social disadvantage interchangeably. As attributes of populations as opposed to individuals, use of the terms is tied to their ecological meaning.

with identical social-ecological profiles but a widely disparate resource base (i.e., some services versus no services), the community with more services will have lower placement rate assuming there is a even only a modest impact associated with the quantity of services available.

Social Ecological Character: Independent Variables

To assess need, we follow a basic epidemiological or ecological approach (Regier 1984; Durbin et al. 2001; Spearly and Lauderdale 1983). We used 12 census-based measures that are associated with the incidence of maltreatment. The indicators capture social disadvantage (Coulton et al. 1995, 1999; Lery 2009; Wulczyn et al. 2013) and are predictive of both higher incidence of maltreatment and foster care placement.

The community-level measures, which are 2006 estimates, include:

- Female headed households (%)
- Married couple households (%)
- Family poverty rate (%)
- Poverty rate female headed families (%)
- Adults with less than a high school education (%)
- Unemployment rate (%)
- Owner occupied housing (%)
- Renter occupied housing units (%)
- Male/female ratio
- Child/adult ratio
- Persons living in group quarters (%)
- Proportion of the population that is elderly

In addition to the social indicators, we have for each community area a count of the number of children living in that area to compute incidence rates.[2] All of the indicators are estimates based on the year 2006.

Each indicator was converted into a 0/1 value based on whether, for a given community area, the observed proportion was above or below the unweighted citywide average. Because the indicators have different valences with respect to whether more is advantageous, each indicator was assigned 1 if the valence was positive. For example, lower poverty rates are generally more desirable socially, so community areas with below average poverty rates were assigned a 1. For owner-occupied housing, more is better, so above average community areas were assigned a 1. Constructed in this way, the index ranges from 0 to 12, with 12 indicating that across all individual indicators, the community area rated a positive valence in relation to the citywide average. The index is used to determine whether, for example, the number of maltreatment reports is correlated with the summary index. Because social disadvantage is associated with a lower index value, we expect the correlation to be negative.

Child Welfare Activity

Child welfare activity was measured as follows:

- Number of maltreatment investigations
- Number of neglect reports

---

[2] The calculation of incidence rates is managed through the Poisson count models using variable exposure (Raudenbush and Bryk 2001; Sampson et al. 1997).

- Number of physical abuse reports
- Number of preventive services cases opened
- Number of placements
- Number of preventive service cases opened per 100 victims
- Number of preventive service slots per 100 victims.

Statistical Methods

To establish the link between need measured at the community-level and child welfare activity, we used a multilevel, random effects Poisson event count model. Because Poisson event count models are well established in biostatistics (Hedeker and Gibbons 2006), criminology (Osgood 2000), and sociology (Raudenbush and Bryk 2001), we do not undertake a detailed description of the model and its advantages in this context. The basic count model is of the following form. If Y_j is the number of events in county j and m_j is the number of children living in the county (i.e., exposure), then the expected number of events is:

$$E\left(Y_j \mid \lambda_j\right) = m_j \lambda_j.$$

The log link $\eta_j = \log\left(\lambda_j\right)$ provides a fixed effect model for estimating the number of events:

$$\eta_j = \beta_{0j}.$$

The unconditional level-two model, with a random effect, is:

$$\beta_{0j} = \gamma_{00} + \mu_{0j}.$$

The mixed model is:

$$\eta_{ij} = \gamma_{00} + \mu_{0j}.$$

The random effect model adjusts for the fact that small community areas with small event counts provide less reliable estimates of the true event rate (Osgood 2000).

Without the random effect, the expected number of events is simply:

$$\eta_{ij} = \gamma_{00}.$$

With respect to the counts of events, the unconditional fixed effect estimate of n_{ij} is equivalent to the empirically observed weighted event rate.

For the study we estimate a number of different event rates. The investigation rate, maltreatment rate, and the placement rate all use the number of children living in the community area as the measure of exposure. For placements per maltreatment victim, slots per victim, and preventive openings per victim, the event rates are based on the number of maltreatment victims.

Finally, the key model result of interest is the empirical Bayes residual (μ_{0j}). The EB residual is an estimate of the deviation of β_{0j} from its predicted value based on the level two model (Gibbons et al. 2007; Hedeker and Gibbons 2006; Raudenbush and Bryk 2001). In essence, the multi-level model generates a predicted event rate (e.g. maltreatment reports per 1,000 children) for each level-2 unit, given the model predictors. The residual indicates how far above or below the expected rate the observed rate is. Large residuals indicate that the observed event rate for the given unit (i.e., community area)

Table 18.1 Child welfare activity and social disadvantage

Fixed effect		Coefficient	Event rate ratio	Confidence interval
Investigations per 1,000				
Intercept	γ_{00}	3.224224	25.134067	(22.940,27.539)
Social disadvantage	γ_{01}	−0.096329[a]	0.908165	(0.891,0.925)
Neglect reports per 1,000				
Intercept	γ_{00}	3.072240	21.590217	(19.701,23.661)
Social disadvantage	γ_{01}	−0.094608[a]	0.909730	(0.893,0.927)
Physical abuse per 1,000				
Intercept	γ_{00}	1.851334	6.368307	(5.832,6.954)
Social disadvantage	γ_{01}	−0.078135[a]	0.924840	(0.909,0.941)
Victims per 1,000				
Intercept	γ_{00}	2.279041	9.767312	(8.814,10.824)
Social disadvantage	γ_{01}	−0.119602[a]	0.887274	(0.868,0.907)
Preventive openings per 1,000				
Intercept	γ_{00}	1.377019	3.963068	(3.512,4.473)
Social disadvantage	γ_{01}	−0.133498[a]	0.875030	(0.852,0.898)
Placements per 1,000				
Intercept	γ_{00}	0.596604	1.815941	(1.565,2.107)
Social disadvantage	γ_{01}	−0.157367[a]	0.854391	(0.830,0.880)

[a]Indicates a significant finding

differs from ecologically similar units. Multiplying the square root of the variance by 1.96 and then adding the result to the residual tests the significance of the residual. If zero falls within the resulting range, then the residual varies by chance. Otherwise, the magnitude of the residual is suggestive of a significant departure from the model, in which case the associated community area is regarded as an outlier (Marshall and Spiegelhalter 2007; Racz and Sedransk 2010).

Practically speaking, in this study we are interested in whether, after controlling for the social-ecological character of the community area, the rate of maltreatment is higher (or lower) than predicted. If higher, the results suggest that the rate of maltreatment is elevated relative to other community areas with the same social-ecological make up; if lower, it suggests that the rate of maltreatment is lower than expected, given the variability in the underlying data. With regard to preventive service slots, we are interested in whether there are community areas that have relatively more (or fewer) slots than community areas with the same level of assessed need and whether the placement rates in those community areas with relatively fewer slots are also elevated.

Findings

The analysis begins with an assessment of whether the number of investigations, neglect reports, physical abuse reports, and foster care admissions (all of which are rates per 1,000) vary with respect to the social ecology of the community area. The results, which are reported in Table 18.1, indicate that significantly lower levels of child welfare activity are reported in areas with less social disadvantage. Specifically, the expected investigation rate in a community area with an average level of social disadvantage (γ_{00}) was 25.1 per 1,000 children.[3] In community areas with lower levels of disadvantage, the expected number of investigations drops by about 10 % (γ_{01}) with each change in the level of disadvantage along the scale of 0–12. Community areas with higher levels of disadvantage have higher per capita rates of investigation.

---

[3]All of the models run use grand mean centering.

Table 18.2 Preventive services and placements

Fixed effect		Coefficient	Event rate ratio	Confidence interval
Slots per victim				
Intercept	γ_{00}	−0.995939	0.369376	(0.3334,0.408)
Social disadvantage	γ_{01}	−0.008625	0.991769	(0.966,1.018)
Preventive cases per victim				
Intercept	γ_{00}	−0.895513	0.408398	(0.378,0.441)
Social disadvantage	γ_{01}	−0.012927	0.987156	(0.972,1.002)

Note: Coefficients associated with γ_{01} are not statistically significant

Findings for neglect reports, physical abuse reports, victims, preventive case openings, placement follow the same pattern (see Table 18.1). Social disadvantage is associated with higher rates of contact with the child welfare system.

As expected, contact with the child welfare system is greater in community areas where ecologically defined levels of need are greater. Our question now turns to if and how the supply of services is correlated with social disadvantage. In contrast to our hypothesis regarding contact and social disadvantage, we expect to find no association between service allocations and need because although there may be more contact in some community areas than others, service availability will be proportionate with social disadvantage as measured.

To test this assertion, we use two measures of preventive service availability. The first is simply the number of preventive slots available in each community area; the second is the number of preventive case openings. Slots are a measure of capacity whereas preventive case openings are a measure of utilization. Because we want to adjust both measures for need, we adjust the number of slots and case openings for the number of victims (the exposure) and the level of social disadvantage.

Presented in Table 18.2, these data suggest that preventive services are reasonably well distributed. Specifically, there are about 37 preventive service slots per 100 victims and there is no relationship between social disadvantage and the number of slots. That is, the number of preventive slots varies by community area but when the number of victims and social disadvantage are taken into account, the adjusted supply of slots is consistent across community areas. From the perspective of supply, this is positive. The utilization data (second panel of Table 18.2) are similar. As a fraction of all victims, the rate of case opening per 100 victims is comparable across the community areas.

Overall, social disadvantage and system contact are correlated in the expected direction and service supply is equitably distributed on average between community areas organized into clusters based on their level of need. What the results also suggest is that among community areas that have the same social ecological makeup, the within cluster variation is nevertheless significant. To illustrate this point, we turn now to the issue of the residuals – the difference between the expected and observed event rates.

The data in Table 18.3 show slot/victim ratios for a selected group of community areas. The first group consists of five community areas where the level of social disadvantage is the highest; the second group consists of six community areas where the level of social disadvantage is the lowest. Also displayed are the model-derived expected number of preventive service slots, the observed number of slots, the residual (observed minus the expected) and a summary indicator with values −1, 0, and 1 that indicate whether the observed placement rate for the given community area was significantly different from the predicted placement rate given the level of social disadvantage. The placement rate residual is meant to convey whether, given the availability of preventive services, the allocation of slots has an impact on placement at a population level.

The evidence in Table 18.3 suggests the following. First, the expected number of slots in high need communities is only slightly higher than in low need communities, which is consistent with the early findings. The residual data indicate that the within cluster variation is nevertheless considerable. In high need community area 1, there were 26 slots per 100 victims, which is about 11 slots per 100

Table 18.3 Expected and observed slots per victim, slots per victim residual and placement rate residual

Community area need-based cluster	Slots per 100 victims		Residual	Placement rate residual
	Expected	Observed		
High need 1	37	26	−11.000	−1
High need 2	37	32	−5.000	0
High need 3	37	35	−2.000	0
High need 4	37	38	1.000	−1
High need 5	37	41	4.000	0
Low need 1	33	2	−32.000	0
Low need 2	33	30	−3.000	0
Low need 3	33	28	−6.000	0
Low need 4	33	38	4.000	0
Low need 5	33	39	5.000	−1
Low need 6	33	57	24.000	1

victims fewer than the average for the high need communities. At the other end of the continuum, high need community area 5 had 4 slots per 100 victims more than the cluster average. We also observed within cluster variation within the low need community areas. For example, low need area 1 had 31 slots per 100 victims fewer slots than expected whereas low need area 6 had 24 more slots than the cluster average.

When the observed/expected slot residual is compared to the placement rate residual we get an indication that the allocation of slots may have an impact on placement rates at least in some communities. For example, in the high need community with the greatest difference between the observed and expected slot allocation (high need community area 1) we do in fact see a higher than expected need adjusted placement rate. We also find that in the low need community with the greatest positive observed/expected slot differential there is a much lower adjusted rate of placement. These data suggest that a preventive service shortfall may have an impact on the placement into out-of-home care. Likewise, a surplus of services, as in low need community 6, may help keep the utilization of placement to level below what might otherwise be expected.

Summary

There is little doubt that more resources are needed to help families avoid child maltreatment. It is also clear that new investments in prevention should rely more heavily on evidence-based interventions. But, it is equally clear that more and better services are not the only policy and practice questions facing the child welfare system. The federal government, along with state and county governments, spends a considerable sum of money on prevention services each year, yet the field knows very little about how those expenditures align with opportunity.

From a return on investment perspective, there are two allocation questions of central importance. First, does the current preventive service allocation achieve discernable results at a public health level? Second, if there is no discernable impact, the impact is mixed, or the effect is considerable, what does that say about how new resources should be used?

To answer these questions, we studied need-adjusted placement rates at the community area level in a large city. The need-adjusted analysis was used to identify community areas where the placement rate was much higher than expected, given the underlying levels of social disadvantage. These data were then compared with the supply of preventive services as a test of the idea that communities with lower than expected service slots might have higher than expected rates of entry into foster care.

The results suggest the following:

- Resource allocation in this city appeared to be equitable *on average*.
- Within community areas clustered together on the basis of their ecological similarity, we found considerable within cluster variation in the slot/victim ratio. Some areas have many more slots than expected; others have far fewer slots.
- There are community areas where the undersupply of preventive service slots coincides with an above average placement rate even after controlling for social need.

With respect to the undersupply of preventive services in relationship to placement prevention, the findings are not conclusive. There are unmeasured attributes of the community areas that could account for a measured undersupply of preventive services; communities may make up for what they lack in preventive services with other assets. Nevertheless, the data do demonstrate the ways in which communities differ and how those differences might be used to target prevention services more effectively.

Perhaps the most important observation is that otherwise similar community areas differ with respect to the allocated preventive service capacity. Importantly, there is evidence that the relative oversupply of preventive services sometimes coincides with a weak public-health level effect on placement rates. That is to say that despite a relative abundance of preventive services, the rate of placement is higher than expected. Arguably the policy and fiscal response in communities with this profile involves reallocation of service types (i.e., quality) as opposed to simply adding more capacity. Put another way, more inert service capacity should not be expected to generate a significant return on investment. One might achieve as much by converting the services to evidence-based interventions while bringing the supply more in line with observed levels of need (Donaldson and Mooney 1991).

It is also the case that some community areas are characterized by an undersupply of services and an above average placement rate. Where that is the case, the policy response should focus on quantity and quality. While not a reason to ignore the value of evidence-based interventions, the situation does raise a question about where the marginal rate of return is the greatest. It could be that in the near term, investments in general support services will deliver as much benefit as higher-end, evidence-based interventions, particularly in resource starved communities where the capacity to deliver services with fidelity has been shaped by a chronic undersupply.

Cautious policy makers are often concerned about expanding prevention services because the public health return on taxpayer investments is difficult to demonstrate. It is, however, an example of fixed effects thinking in a variable effects world. At the community-level, the child welfare system is a mixture of needs, resources, and results. If the alignment of needs and resources varies, one should not expect a fixed rate of return tied to preventive service investments because baseline conditions differ.

References

Aarons, G., James, S., Monn, A., Raghavan, R., Wells, R., & Leslie, L. (2010). Behavior problems and placement change in a national child welfare sample: A prospective study. *Journal of the American Academy of Child & Adolescent Psychiatry, 49*(1), 70–80.

Barth, R. (2005). Foster home care is more cost-effective than shelter care: Serious questions continue to be raised about the utility of group care in child welfare services. *Child Abuse & Neglect, 29*(6), 623–625.

Barth, R., Lloyd, E., Green, R., James, S., Leslie, L., & Landsverk, J. (2007). Predictors of placement moves among children with and without emotional and behavioral disorders. *Journal of Emotional and Behavioral Disorders, 15*(1), 46–55.

Berger, L., Bruch, S., Johnson, E., James, S., & Rubin, D. (2009). Estimating the "impact" of out-of-home placement on child well-being: Approaching the problem of selection bias. *Child Development, 80*(6), 1856–1876.

Coulton, C. J., Korbin, J. E., Su, M., & Chow, J. (1995). Community level factors and child maltreatment rates. *Child Development, 66*(5), 1262–1276. doi:10.1111/j.1467-8624.1995.tb00934.x.

Coulton, C., Korbin, J., & Su, M. (1999). Neighborhoods and child maltreatment: A multi-level study. *Child Abuse & Neglect, 23*(11), 1019–1040.

DeVooght, K., Fletcher, M., Vaughn, B., & Cooper, H. (2012). *Federal, state, and local spending to address child abuse and neglect in SFYs 2008 and 2010* (pp. 1–68). Washington, DC: Child Trends.

Donaldson, C., & Mooney, G. (1991). Needs assessment, priority setting, and contracts for health care: An economic view. *BMJ: British Medical Journal, 303*(6816), 1529.

Durbin, J., Cochrane, J., Goering, P., & Macfarlane, D. (2001). Needs-based planning: Evaluation of a level-of-care planning model. *The Journal of Behavioral Health Services and Research, 28*(1), 67–80. doi:10.1007/BF02287235.

Faver, C. A., Crawford, S. L., & Combs-Orme, T. (1999). Services for child maltreatment: Challenges for research and practice. *Children and Youth Services Review, 21*(2), 89–109.

Gibbons, R. D., Hur, K., Bhaumik, D., & Bell, C. (2007). Profiling of county-level foster care placements using random-effects Poisson regression models. *Health Services and Outcomes Research Methodology, 7*(3), 97–108.

Hedeker, D., & Gibbons, R. D. (2006). *Longitudinal data analysis* (p. 1). New York: Wiley.

Lery, B. (2009). Neighborhood structure and foster care entry risk: The role of spatial scale in defining neighborhoods. *Children and Youth Services Review, 31*(3), 331–337.

Marshall, E., & Spiegelhalter, D. (2007). Identifying outliers in Bayesian hierarchical models: A simulation-based approach. *Bayesian Analysis, 2*(2), 409–444.

Newton, R., Litrownik, A., & Landsverk, J. (2000). Children and youth in foster care: Disentangling the relationship between problem behaviors and number of placements. *Child Abuse & Neglect, 24*(10), 1363–1374.

Osgood, D. (2000). Poisson-based regression analysis of aggregate crime rates. *Journal of Quantitative Criminology, 16*, 21–43.

Racz, M. J., & Sedransk, J. (2010). Bayesian and frequentist methods for provider profiling using risk-adjusted assessments of medical outcomes. *Journal of the American Statistical Association, 105*(489), 48–58.

Raudenbush, S., & Bryk, A. (2001). *Hierarchical linear models: Applications and data analysis methods* (2nd ed.). Newbury Park: Sage.

Regier, D. A., Shapiro, S., Kessler, L. G., & Taube, C. A. (1984). Epidemiology and health service resource allocation policy for alcohol, drug abuse, and mental disorders. *Public Health Reports, 99*(5), 483.

Sampson, R., Raudenbush, S., & Earls, F. (1997). Neighborhoods and violent crime: A multilevel study of collective efficacy. *Science, 277*(5328), 918–924.

Saul, J., Duffy, J., Noonan, R., Lubell, K., Wandersman, A., Flaspohler, P., et al. (2008). Bridging science and practice in violence prevention: Addressing ten key challenges. *American Journal of Community Psychology, 41*(3–4), 197–205.

Spearly, J. L., & Lauderdale, M. (1983). Community characteristics and ethnicity in the prediction of child maltreatment rates. *Child Abuse & Neglect, 7*(1), 91–105.

Stanley, J., & Kovacs, K. (2003). *Accessibility issues in child abuse prevention services*. Melbourne: Australian Institute of Family Studies.

Stith, S., Pruitt, I., Dees, J., Fronce, M., Green, N., Som, A., & Linkh, D. (2006). Implementing community-based prevention programming: A review of the literature. *The Journal of Primary Prevention, 27*(6), 599–617.

Whitaker, D. J., Lutzker, J. R., & Shelley, G. A. (2005). Child maltreatment prevention priorities at the Centers for Disease Control and Prevention. *Child Maltreatment, 10*(3), 245–259.

Wulczyn, F., Chen, L., & Hislop, K. B. (2007). *Foster care dynamics, 2000–2005: A report from the multistate foster care data archive*. Chicago: Chapin Hall Center for Children.

Wulczyn, F., Chen, L., Collins, L., & Ernst, M. (2011). Babies in foster care: The numbers call for attention. *Zero to Three, 22*(4), 14–15.

Wulczyn, F., Gibbons, R., Snowden, L., & Lery, B. (2013). Poverty, social disadvantage, and the black/white placement gap. *Children and Youth Services Review, 35*(1), 1–10.

Chapter 19
Empirically Based Treatments for Maltreated Children: A Developmental Perspective

Susan G. Timmer and Anthony J. Urquiza

The 2010 review of child maltreatment in the United States showed that among children 18 years of age and younger, children under 7 years of age have a rate of maltreatment of 57.4 per 1,000 children (USDHHS 2011), with the greater share being that of children under 3 years of age (34.0 %; USDHHS 2011). In a large scale, longitudinal study of low-income children from a large Midwestern city, researchers found a strong relationship between the number of maltreatment reports and negative outcomes during childhood (Jonson-Reid et al. 2012). Jonson-Reid and colleagues (2012) found that the more maltreatment reports children had, the more likely they were to report adverse outcomes during childhood, such as a mental health diagnosis, emergency department treatment for suicide attempt, health care for head injury, or a delinquency petition for either violence or substance abuse as children. Most concerning was that more maltreatment reports in childhood significantly increased the chances their perpetrating child maltreatment as adults (Jonson-Reid et al. 2012), confirming the existence of an intergenerational cycle of maltreatment. When the number of adverse outcomes these children reported was taken into account, their likelihood of perpetrating maltreatment increased significantly (Jonson-Reid et al. 2012). These findings suggest that when maltreatment is unchecked and untreated (or ineffectively treated), the next generation of children is likely to suffer the same consequences. The burden is upon us, as mental health scholars and practitioners, to try to understand what maltreatment is doing to children and how we can effectively intervene.

Effects of Maltreatment on Children

Research on the outcomes of abuse and neglect for children has repeatedly affirmed its long-lasting, multi-level negative effects. Research has documented neurological effects (Heim et al. 2008; Nemeroff 2004), hormonal effects related to physiological arousal (Cicchetti et al. 2010) and emotional regulation (Maughan and Cicchetti 2002), cognitive effects related to attention deficits and hyperarousal (Pollak et al. 2000). Maltreated children also have high rates of physical, aggression, noncompliance, and antisocial behaviors (Cicchetti and Toth 2000; Mersky and Reynolds 2007). What we are just beginning to investigate is whether there is a difference in the severity of effects of maltreatment

S.G. Timmer (✉) • A.J. Urquiza
CAARE Diagnostic and Treatment Center, Department of Pediatrics, University of California at Davis Children's Hospital, 3300 Stockton Blvd, Sacramento, CA 95825, USA
e-mail: susan.timmer@ucdmc.ucdavis.edu

J.E. Korbin and R.D. Krugman (eds.), *Handbook of Child Maltreatment*, Child Maltreatment 2, DOI 10.1007/978-94-007-7208-3_19, © Springer Science+Business Media Dordrecht 2014

depending upon when it occurs. Additionally, and to the point of this chapter, there is an accompanying awareness that the interventions we use might need to be differently focused with different aged children in order to most effectively treat them.

Theoretical Context: The Ecological – Transactional Model of Development

More than 20 years ago, Cicchetti and Lynch (1993) developed a theory to explain how child maltreatment could have such a potent effect on children's development: the ecological-transactional model of development. Ecological-transactional theory is founded on an understanding that different qualities of children's environments – their cultural environments, social resources, family environments, and individual differences all combine to shape the way children respond to the surrounding world. They proposed that characteristics of these environmental systems influence the way children negotiate different developmental tasks, providing foundations of structures at one point in time that influence later development. These environmental systems were seen as having "potentiating factors," or conditions that increase the likelihood that either maltreatment might occur or negatively affect the child, and "compensatory factors," that reduce the likelihood of maltreatment and violence, and their accompanying negative effects.

So far this model seems simple – the ratio of positives to negatives from different parts of the child's environment should indicate the likelihood of maladaptation. However, it is important to point out that the same negative event occurring at two different points in children's development can have different outcomes for children's mental health because of differences in their abilities to understand the event (i.e., differences in cognitive ability), the meaning the event has at the particular point in development that it occurred, and the meaning the event has for the child's ongoing ability to adapt positively, "collecting" protective and buffering factors.

While the development of mental health problems seems inevitable when considering the trauma of witnessing violence or experiencing abuse, there is always the mystery of the resilience inherent in child's physiological, neurological, and cognitive makeup and how they work together in the developing child. From an ecological-transactional perspective, the best that we can say is that the development of psychopathology is probabilistic – not certain. Furthermore, this theory views development as "a series of qualitative reorganizations among and within biological and psychological systems" as children mature (Cicchetti and Toth 2000, p. 94). In other words, as children mature cognitively they perceive the world around them qualitatively differently. This maturation is thought to drive reorganization of previous experiences, prompting children to adopt a more complex understanding of their environment and life history.

While cognitive maturation limits or shapes children's understanding of their worlds, it is also believed that each developmental stage contains different "tasks" considered central to children's ability to successfully negotiate that stage. How well these tasks are resolved determines the quality of the organization and integration of different systems (e.g., neurological, cognitive, social, emotional) in that stage. The network of integrated systems is believed to provide a groundwork upon which developmental structures are built. In this way, different developmental tasks always retain significance over time, even when current tasks are more salient. In other words, if a developmental task in one system is negotiated poorly or incompletely – this affects not only the quality of that system, but of the whole – as the weakness of one system can limit the strength of other integrated systems, both at that developmental stage and at hierarchically more advanced developmental stages.

However, in spite of the gloomy prognosis one might have for a child exposed to violence or maltreatment at an early age, not all of these children end up with problems (Cicchetti and Rogosch 1997; Masten 2001; Werner 1989). Hence, we say that negative outcomes are not inevitable, but probabilistic. There is always room to build resilience and improve functioning. The assumption that the development of psychopathology is probabilistic, and that these probabilities are constantly being shaped and reshaped by experience is the most important assumption of this theory for people interested in prevention and intervention for traumatized children. What this means is that changing the trajectory of development is always possible when there is new experience, particularly when the new experience forces a reorganization of old experiences and thought patterns through the lens of new experience. In other words, effective mental health interventions should be able to help modify the negative effects of early trauma on future functioning – because irrespective of past difficulties with adaptation, there is always a path to a new, more positive way of functioning.

While we understand that theoretically there should be a path to more positive functioning for maltreated children, finding that path is not always simple. What determines the most effective intervention for different children? We believe that to make a proper judgment about which intervention to use, it is important to understand what is happening to children neurologically, physiologically, cognitively, emotionally, and behaviorally.

Maltreatment and Development

Ecological-transactional theory (Cicchetti and Lynch 1993) would suggest that the younger a child is when he or she experiences an adverse event – such as maltreatment – the more far-reaching its effects would be, since these same systems affected by the stress of maltreatment rapidly develop in the early years of life. While this makes logical sense, we look at infants, knowing that they will not remember their preverbal experience, and think that they are probably safe from the most devastating effects of maltreatment. These adverse events do not generate memories and learning in the way it might in a 5-year old. And yet, accumulating evidence from research on animals and humans suggests that chronic exposure to fear and anxiety, and abusive caregiving leaves a neurological footprint (e.g., Cicchetti et al. 2010; Sanchez et al. 2010) that is part of the building blocks of attachment to their caregivers (Cicchetti et al. 2010), determine which events in their environment are perceived and how they are interpreted (Pollak et al. 2000), and which events are remembered (Goodman et al. 1997).

Chronic or acute stress, such as that resulting from maltreatment or other adverse early life experiences, can cause different types of neurological responses in infants: (1) through the sympathetic adrenomedullary system, causing a release of norepinephrine and epinephrine (flight or fright response); (2) through the locus coeruleus, which increases neural activity in the amygdala (Ellis et al. 2006) causing corticotropin-releasing hormone (CRH) production, with the potential of increasing hypothalamic-pituitary axis (HPA) activity (Herman et al. 2003); and (3) through hypothalamic activation, which can directly excite the HPA axis, causing the release of cortisol, which activates or inhibits other physiological systems involved in promoting survival in response to acute stress. When infants are chronically exposed to stress hormones, the body's feedback systems for managing and regulating stress hormone production can become dysregulated, showing a hyperresponse to stressors, followed by a period of hyporesponsiveness (Heim et al. 2000) Animal studies have shown that high levels of cortisol in the system has been found to have harmful, even toxic effects on neural tissue (Zhang et al. 2002) and regulating gene transcription (McEwen 2000), thus influencing the way the infant perceives and interprets environmental threat and the quality of the response to that threat (Tarullo and Gunnar 2006). HPA-axis dysregulation resulting from early adverse care or maltreatment has the potential for disrupting healthy development, because it increases allostatic load – the physiological vulnerability from chronic exposure to stressful adverse experiences and their accompanying neuroendocrine responses (McEwen and Stellar 1993). Increased allostatic load may cause dysregulation in the physiological stress management system (e.g., Juster et al. 2009) and challenges with emotional, cognitive, and physical health (Felitti et al. 1998). The take-away message of this research is that early trauma affects the way children respond to future stressful events;

and the way they respond makes them vulnerable to difficulties and delays that create other problems later in development.

While any infant's first experience with an extreme threat is likely to result in the "high-cost" endocrine response described above (e.g., Lupien et al. 2006), subsequent encounters (or anticipated encounters) with the threat should result in the infant seeking out their primary caregivers for help in modulating their anxiety and fear (Heim et al. 2008). Infants are dependent on their caregivers for help in soothing, and their soothing helps regulate the infant's stress response system. These social and behavioral solutions have been termed "low-cost" solutions for the infant because of the relatively low expenditure of neurobiological resources needed to accomplish system regulation (Lupien et al. 2006). As an example, maternal separation can cause considerable anxiety for infants once they reach about 8 months of age. When an infant cries inconsolably upon separation from the mother, the baby's HPA axis kicks into gear and sends cortisol into the blood stream. However, one study found that cortisol levels did not increase in 1-year olds who interacted with their babysitters when faced with a separation from their mothers, although it did increase in infants who withdrew and in those who fell asleep (Gunnar et al. 1992). In other words, receiving caregiving helped regulate these children's stress response system. It is also important to note that even when the child reacted in a way that would seem benign to an observer – falling asleep or withdrawing – there were still signs of increased stress.

Related to the research establishing the connection between social-behavioral solutions for coping with stress and cortisol levels in infancy, other investigations show the power of sensitive and responsive caregiving in promoting children's emotion regulation, stress responsivity, and healthy development (e.g., Sroufe 2005; Bugental et al. 2003). In fact, the quality of the parent-child relationship, which includes both the child's attachment strategy and parenting quality have been shown to play important roles in determining the effect of children's early experience of maltreatment on later development of psychopathology.

Attachment

John Bowlby, who first wrote on attachment, observed that infants appeared driven to form attachment relationships, but that the quality of these relationships might vary considerably (Bowlby 1982). He believed that the quality of infants' attachment provided a foundation for later personality development, in particular the growth of qualities such as self-reliance and emotional regulation (Bowlby 1973). For example, Bowlby believed that when caregivers successfully helped regulate infants' emotions, infants would discover through experience that they could regulate their own emotions, growing increasingly more confident in this ability.

Later research found that infants displayed one of three different consistent, organized strategies to get a particular parent's help when they were anxious or perceived a threat (Ainsworth et al. 1978). Some infants showed a secure attachment-an easy ability to use their caregivers for help in regulating distress. Some showed anxious-avoidant strategies, where they behave as though they do not need help, and some showed an anxious-ambivalent strategy where they were difficult to soothe and often seeking help. Later research showed that not all infants showed organized attachment (Main and Solomon 1986). When infants did not have an organized strategy for obtaining help, they are labeled disorganized.

Unlike the organized insecure and secure attachment strategies, children with disorganized attachment show a variety of behaviors. For example, an infant that approaches the caregiver when agitated and then turns away or freezes might be classified as disorganized. Main and Hesse (1990) proposed that when caregivers were a source of fear and anxiety in addition to being a protective source, this created a psychological contradiction for the infant and would increase the likelihood of developing insecure or disorganized attachment. In fact, Carlson and colleagues (1989) noted a higher incidence of disorganized attachment among maltreated than non-maltreated children.

Alan Sroufe and his colleagues at the University of Minnesota began exploring the role of attachment in child development in a longitudinal study in 1975, testing this hypothesis. In a 2005 article, Sroufe describing the results of many different studies, confirmed Bowlby's hypotheses that attachment is linked with critical development pathways like arousal modulation and emotional regulation, but also describes considerable complexity in the attachment system over the course of development. Outcomes were probabilistic, not definite, and subject to the influences of a changing environment. Secure infant attachment, occurring when the caregivers were a source of comfort and emotional regulation, "promoted" the likelihood of future adaptive responses (Sroufe 2005). Luijk and her colleagues (2010) tied attachment quality together with variations in stress response in a study of 369 infants and their mothers. They found that infants with insecure- anxious strategies showed increasing stress in an assessment exposing them to multiple separations from their caregivers (i.e., Strange Situation Procedure) and a flattened, shut down response to the same assessment among infants with a disorganized attachment (Luijk et al. 2010). Trying to discover what disorganized attachment meant for ongoing development, Lyons-Ruth, Alpern, and Repacholi (1993) found that 71 % of preschoolers who showed high levels of hostile behavior toward classroom peers had been classified as having disorganized attachment at 18 months. Even more convincingly, Sroufe (2005) reported that disorganized attachment was a strong predictor of later disturbance: the degree of disorganization in infancy correlated strongly ($r = .40$) with the number and severity of psychiatric symptoms at age 17.5 years.

Taken together, the evidence suggests a strong connection between early attachment and stress response systems, particularly those of emotional regulation during infancy. In general, researchers have found considerable flexibility in the degree to which attachment predicted outcomes as infants matured, confirming the idea that many environmental and family factors play a part in ongoing personality development. However, researchers have found that disorganized attachment seems to be accompanied by greater ongoing vulnerability.

Maltreated children's vulnerability to disorganized attachment, and the subsequent negative outcomes (including accompanying risks), suggest that the ingredients of attachment – the infant-caregiver relationship and particularly caregiver responsiveness and warmth – would be excellent targets for early intervention.

Parenting

In addition to the clear effects of violence and trauma on children, results of numerous studies have also illustrated different effects of harsh and coercive parenting both on children's stress response system (Blair et al. 2008; Bugental et al. 2003; Hill-Soderlund et al. 2008), as well as the subsequent likelihood of observing aggression (e.g., Denham et al. 2000; Gershoff 2002), anxiety (McLeod et al. 2007a), and depression (McLeod et al. 2007b), withdrawn behavior (e.g., Booth-LaForce and Oxford 2008) and other mental health problems (e.g., Cicchetti and Toth 2000; Patterson 1982; Schechter and Willheim 2009). Why does harsh parenting have such a toxic effect on young children? Evolutionary psychologists might argue that infants are attuned to threatening tones of voices and behaviors, and react as they would to any other high stress situation, usually with distress (e.g., screaming, crying, and other dysregulated behavior). Over time, they may learn other ways of managing their emotional dysregulation through social learning (e.g., externalizing, internalizing behaviors). In this way their aversive behavior can be thought of as a way that infants and young children have adapted to a frightening, threatening environment (Ellis et al. 2011). However, if these behaviors are adaptive responses within their family system, they are not functional outside the system and may be reasons for a mental health referral.

Parenting does not have to be harsh or coercive to cause problems in the parent-child relationship or to be associated with problem behaviors in children. Children of depressed mothers are reported to have more behavior problems (e.g., Gartstein et al. 2009) and a higher risk of later psychopathology (e.g., Downey and Coyne 1990; Goodman and Gotlib 1999). Some of the most dramatic findings illustrating the importance of sensitive parenting for children's healthy development has been conducted with children who experienced neglect or inconsistent caregiving. In 1951, John Bowlby first reported to the World Health Organization that even when all their physical needs were met, children still showed serious negative effects from institutional care, which he attributed to their inability to form stable, continuous attachment relationships with a primary caregiver (Bowlby 1951). Recent studies have also documented effects of inadequate caregiving on attachment security, finding even higher rates of disorganized attachment strategies than among maltreated children (Cyr et al. 2010). Since this time, researchers have explored the effects of institutional care on children and have found that children who spent their first few years in institutions showed retarded physical (Van Ijzendoorn et al. 2007) and cognitive growth (e.g., Zeanah et al. 2005). Atypical diurnal cortisol patterns have also been noted in these children (Carlson and Earls 1997), similar to the pattern found in children in foster care (Fisher et al. 2000). In sum, studies of children who spend their early years in institutions show disruptions in most areas of development, suggesting that neglectful caregiving also undermines the foundations of healthy physical, neurological, and psychological development.

Taken all together, research suggests that in the early years, emotional dysregulation resulting from attempts to manage the anxiety of perceived threats is at the root of many mental health problems in young children. Furthermore, parenting seems to directly influence the stress response system and are key to children's developing capacity for emotional regulation. When parenting is sensitive, it appears to buffer the effects of stress on children (Dozier et al. 2009). When parenting is ineffective and non-optimal, it magnifies the stressfulness of early traumatic experiences, possibly by increasing their perceived threat (Martorell and Bugental 2006).

Adolescence

While trauma continues to have the same biological effect on the stress response system in older children as it does for younger children, there is clear evidence that certain individual factors mediate the effects of trauma on older children's mental health (Heim et al. 2008). These include early maltreatment (Cicchetti et al. 2010), early attachment relationships, social support, attributional styles, self-esteem, developing cognitions about self and others, and social competence (Cicchetti and Valentino 2006).

For example, one of the most widely documented effects of child maltreatment is an increased risk of internalizing behaviors in childhood (Keiley et al. 2001; Kim and Cicchetti 2006) and depression/suicidal ideation in adolescence (Dube et al. 2001). Dube and colleagues (2001) found that among a cohort of more than 17,000 primary care clinic patients, having a history of adverse experiences in childhood such as abuse, neglect, domestic violence, and parents' substance abuse doubled to quintupled the likelihood of attempted suicide in adolescence. This raises the question, 'What is the mechanism that links maltreatment with depression in adolescence?'

Children's social environments expand throughout the childhood era – from child-primary caregiver relationships (e.g., child-mother), to family relationships (e.g., child-family), to early peer relationships (e.g., child-playmates, chums), to more intimate inter- and intrapersonal relationships (child-best friend, boyfriend/girlfriend). Concurrently, the contexts in which these relationships are managed also expands – from the family circle to peer groups, schools and classrooms, and communities. There are more opportunities to succeed and try out adaptive behaviors and more opportunities to solidify maladaptive ones. When children are young, their caregivers and the caregiving environment give meaning to experience (Sameroff and Chandler 1975). When children mature, their memories and cognitions link these experiences together through a continual re-evaluative process (Harter 2001). Apart from the physical growth and maturity that takes place from childhood to adolescence, one of the most notable changes occurs in the way they think and interpret events in the world around them. An increasing number of studies connect maltreatment experiences with differences in cognitions and perceptions, including the perception of emotion in others (Pollak et al. 2009), in their perceptions of the cause of emotional states (Perlman et al. 2008), in attributions they make about their responsibility for traumatic events (Deblinger and Runyon 2005), social information processing (Chen et al. 2012), and perceptions of internal vs. external control over events (Bolger and Patterson 2001). These findings combine to suggest that cognition begins to play a significant role in adolescent mental health, in a way that does not seem to exist among younger children.

Sensitive Periods

There is thought that some of these early negative effects may have long-lasting consequences for children, possibly because these experiences make them more sensitive to later stressors because the early experience occurred at a *sensitive period* of development (Knudsen 2004), where many changes occur at many levels of development, thus the early maltreatment might have a particularly strong effect, affecting many aspects of the child's development. Alternately, early maltreatment could be particularly devastating for children because there may be *critical periods*, where certain positive experiences are necessary for optimal, healthy development to occur (Knudsen 2004), so that when children experience maltreatment, their developmental trajectories are irrevocably altered. There is no doubt that when maltreatment occurs early, children's likelihood of later exposure to risk is also heightened (Appleyard et al. 2005), which naturally increases the likelihood of seeing long-term negative outcomes for these children. But does early maltreatment that results in dysregulation of the stress response system doom the child to a future of psychological problems?

Results of studies comparing children adopted out of Eastern European orphanages at different ages give some evidence for sensitive periods. These studies typically compare the cognitive functioning and attachment quality of children who have spent varying amounts of time in environments of neglect with non-institutionalized children, allowing the investigator to test the notion that if social deprivation occurs before a certain age, it is less likely to cause permanent psychological damage. Several studies' findings suggest that in fact, if children are adopted out of the institution within the first 6 months of their lives, they are indistinguishable from non-institutionalized infants and fare better than their later-adopted counterparts across a range of developmental outcomes (e.g., Fisher et al. 1997; Beckett et al. 2006;). A meta-analysis of adoption studies conducted by Bakermans-Kranenburg, van IJzendoorn, and Juffer (2008) reported no significant differences in the probability of secure attachment of children adopted before they reached 1 year of age compared to non-adopted children.

In addition to studies of institutionally raised children, recently, scholars investigating the effects of maltreatment on neural circuitry have described results that support the notion of critical periods or sensitive periods, in which early maltreatment (before 5 years of age) appeared to be associated with more negative outcomes than maltreatment that occurred later in childhood (Cicchetti et al. 2010).

In spite of these convincing findings supporting the existence of sensitive periods, it is important to remember the principle of *multifinality*, one of the guiding theories of developmental psychopathology. This principle asserts that given a similar history, many outcomes are possible, since many environmental events and internal psychophysiological strengths and challenges work together to forge a particular outcome. Furthermore, accepting that a complex array of behaviors such as the behaviors associated with attachment could be subject to a sensitive period is difficult. According to Knudsen (2004), sensitive periods are properties of neural circuits even though they tend to be defined in terms of behavior and in a way, dependent upon experience. When a circuit is repeatedly and intensely activated during a sensitive period, the synapses associated with the neural circuit consolidate, and the architecture of the circuit stabilizes a "preferred" pattern of connectivity (Knudsen 2004). Afterwards, the circuits retain some plasticity, but Knudsen (2004) asserts that the plasticity is limited by the architecture established during the sensitive period. At the same time, it is also important to remember that the brain is organized so that higher order circuits can compensate for maladaptive neural circuits at lower levels.

Interventions

The first part of this chapter described the early effects of maltreatment on the developing child and the role of parenting in exacerbating or buffering these effects. We spent time describing these effects to emphasize for the reader the unseen foundational ways that maltreatment harms children, believing that understanding the nature of the effects will help us understand why certain interventions are effective for maltreated children.

There is a strong body of research supporting the value of early positive and responsive caregiving for infants and toddlers, and the value of emotional regulation for development. We present two interventions that focus specifically on these target areas, but for two different populations and with slightly different focuses. For pre-school and early school-aged children, the parent-child relationship has been shown to be a lynchpin in efforts to improve mental health. We present four interventions that focus on improving caregiving and the caregiver-child relationship as a way to improve emotional regulation and reduce children's behavior problems. These interventions use different modes of delivery, showing the wide range of methods that can be used to achieve similar treatment goals. In middle childhood, cognitions emerge as important mediators of mental health. We present two different types cognitive-behavioral therapies, showing the flexibility of these treatment systems. Finally, we examine two very different multi-modal intervention approaches for difficult-to-treat adolescents that similarly combine cognitive-behavioral strategies, family support, case management to reduce their clients' risk of self-destructive behavior.

Interventions for Infants

We describe two interventions appropriate for infants with strong body of research supporting them: Attachment and Biobehavioral Catch-up (ABC; Bernard et al. 2012) and Child-Parent Psychotherapy (CPP; Lieberman and van Horn 2005). A randomized controlled trial (RCT) supports the efficacy of ABC in improving infants responsiveness to their foster caregivers (Dozier et al. 2009) and another RCT showing lower rates of disorganized and higher rates of secure attachment in a group of children at high risk for maltreatment. CPP's effectiveness in treating traumatized children is also supported by several RCTs (Cicchetti et al. 2006; Lieberman et al. 2005, 2006; Toth et al. 2006).

Attachment and Biobehavioral Catch-up (ABC)

Guiding Principles

This intervention is based on the theory that the foundation of children's mental health rests upon the responsiveness and predictability of their caregiving environment. The pillars of this foundation are infants' attachment quality and their emotional, behavioral, and biobehavioral regulation. The attachment strategies are viewed as a response to both their biological and foster parents' attachment-driven behaviors.

Goals of Treatment

Three primary goals or components are identified. Component A is to insure that biological or foster parents understand the meaning of their infants' rejecting cues. The caregivers learn nurturing skills even if the children fail to ask for comfort or reject their attempts to provide comfort. Component B is to insure that caregivers who do not respond in nurturing ways need to learn new strategies for reacting to their children's distress. Adapted from Child Parent Psychotherapy (CPP; Lieberman et al. 1991), therapists intervene to help caregivers recognize their own attachment-related issues that interfere with their ability to nurture their children, helping them to become more responsive. Component C is to reduce behavioral and biobehavioral dysregulation. Foster and biological caregivers are taught to create a caregiving environment that is predictable, responsive, and child-centered to decrease dysregulation in their stress response system, similar to an intervention developed for regulating the stress response system in premature infants developed by Barnard (1999).

Strategies for Achieving Goals/Procedures

The intervention is designed for the parents of children between 10 and 24 months of age, but can be modified for parents of younger children. Treatment is conducted over ten sessions, each lasting about an hour, in the home. Therapists use a daily diary to find out about the child's behavior, and the parent's and child's contingent behavior; they use video to record the parent and child interacting, for review and to illustrate for the caregiver the progress made in treatment.

The caregiver learns to interact with the child during the ten sessions. First, the therapist teaches the caregiver the basic concepts of the intervention; then follows with a collaborative process of analyzing the child's attachment cues and reframing them. In the subsequent two sessions, therapists explore attachment issues that may interfere with the parent's ability to respond positively to the infant. Once the attachment-related reactions have been discussed, the therapists discuss and practice the importance of positive physical touch for the infant. Then the parents are taught to be able to let the child take the lead in play and to attend to the child's signals. Therapists focus on teaching caregivers to read and respond effectively to children's emotional cues in the ninth session, and wrap-up in the tenth.

Child-Parent Psychotherapy (CPP)

Guiding Principles

CPP is based on the belief that a warm, safe, and supportive parent-infant relationship sets a foundation for mental health in infancy and early childhood, creating working models (i.e., psychological structures) of intimate relationships that set a model for later interactions with intimate others. CPP is grounded in Fraiberg's Infant-Parent Psychotherapy (Fraiberg et al. 1975) but extends beyond it by incorporating other theoretical perspectives in a treatment plan incorporating children up to 5 years of age. Believing that "development occurs through relationships," (Lieberman and Van Horn 2008), CPP uses attachment theory as a way of defining the standards for ideal relationships and the framework for identifying its deficits. However, the structure and goals of CPP are most strongly influenced by Fraiberg's notion of "ghosts in the nursery," or parents' experience of trauma that continues to influence the way the parent responds and interacts with the infant (Fraiberg et al. 1975). However, instead of focusing on this unresolved pain that Fraiberg believed interfered with adaptive development, Lieberman and Van Horn (2005) focus on "angels in the nursery" or creating positive shared experiences and interpretations of behavior that support its strengthening.

Goals of Treatment

The primary goals of CPP treatment are to promote healthy development in the child and parent, with simultaneous attention to both the child's and parent's experiences in order to support their relationship. CPP draws from an understanding of the normative developmental anxieties first identified by

Freud (1959) of fear of separation and loss, fear of losing parents' love, fear of bodily damage, and fear of not living up to the relevant social group, believing that children manifest these anxieties in difficult behaviors like temper tantrums, aggression, withdrawal, defiance, etc. However, instead of analysis and reflection, CPP uses children's free play and spontaneous parent-child interaction as raw material for teaching parents about themselves and their children. Therapists' primary aim is to help parents and children put feeling into words, play together, and use positive physical contact as a way to build trust and empathy in the relationship.

Strategies for Achieving Goals/Procedures

Treatment is targeted for 0–5 year olds and their primary caregivers, and averages approximately 50 sessions. The course of treatment is not scripted, but uses different intervention modalities depending on the specific needs of the client. Furthermore, the format of the individual treatment sessions are not scripted; the strategies used depend on the available "Ports of Entry," or elements in the parent-child relationship that need the most attention at the moment and which are avenues (or ports) for entering into deeper issues in the relationship. CPP typically consists of joint parent-child sessions during which the therapist "translates" the developmental and emotional meaning of children's affect and behavior for the parent. The therapists target children's and caregivers' intrapersonal conflicts that interfere with their developing a sensitive and reciprocal relationship using insight-oriented interpretation. They engage the parent-child dyad in activities that foster mutual pleasure, interpersonal trust, and understanding.

Interventions for Young Children

We describe four different evidence–based treatments designed specifically for young children in approximately the 2–8 year age range and their parents: The Incredible Years (IY; Webster-Stratton 2012a), Triple-P (PPP; Sanders 1999), Parent-Child Interaction Therapy (PCIT; Eyberg and Robinson 1982), and Multidimensional Treatment Foster Care for Preschoolers (MTFC-P; Fisher and Kim 2007). The interventions use different methods of delivery and may target different populations (e.g., MTFC), but their purposes are similar. For the most part, these treatments are parenting-oriented, teaching parents skills and discussing strategies for managing their children's difficult behaviors.

Incredible Years (IY)

Guiding Principles

A basic premise of the model, common to the other parenting-oriented interventions, is that the parent-child dyad must have the foundation of a positive relationship foundation before the parent can be successful at implementing discipline strategies; and that parents should attend to their children's positive behaviors far more than their negative behaviors. Without the foundation of a positive relationship, long lasting change is unlikely to occur.

Goals of Treatment

At its core, the primary focus of IY has been to nurture positive parenting tools to strengthen parent-child attachment and empathy through child-directed play, social and emotional coaching methods, sensitivity to children's cues, praise and warmth. Once the parent-child relationship is strengthened, IY encourages implementing predictable rules and routines, clear limit settings and non-intrusive behavior management strategies such as ignoring, distracting, and redirecting. Time Out and loss of privileges are taught as behavior management tools, as well as teaching children self-regulation and problem-solving skills.

Strategies for Achieving Goals/Procedures

The current version of Incredible Years (IY) is a multiple-component system of care designed as an intervention for children with disruptive behavior problems. Originally conceptualized as a 12-week parenting group intervention for parents with difficult-to-manage children from toddler-age through middle childhood, it now consists of a basic parenting program, with options of an "advanced" parenting module for parents with their own mental health problems, a child group program that runs concurrently with the parent group, a school-based group program, and a home-visiting program to help parents generalize the principles learned in group sessions to the home environment. In addition, there is a strong case management component: group leaders contact parents between group sessions to discuss achievements and challenges.

The "Basic" IY model has been heavily researched, with multiple randomized trials, in high-risk populations and parents of children with a diagnosis of Oppositional Defiant Disorder (see Webster-Stratton 2012a, b, for a review of this research). Most of the newer components also have empirical support based on randomized control trials (Webster-Stratton 2012a). The effectiveness of IY in child welfare populations is just now in the process of being confirmed. Hurlburt and colleagues (under review) re-analyzed data from an earlier RCT looking at the efficacy of IY in a Head Start population to determine if subset of parents with child welfare system involvement responded differently to the IY program than those whose parents had no prior involvement. Results showed similar significant improvement in both groups.

Parent-Child Interaction Therapy (PCIT)

Guiding Principles

Like IY, PCIT is founded on the belief that the parent's attention must be a source of reward for the child before behavior management strategies can be effective. Also like IY, PCIT works toward increasing the degree to which parents attend to their children's positive behaviors. However, unlike IY, PCIT emphasizes the power of changing the behavioral mechanics of the interaction as a way to change its emotional quality – changing the numbers of parents' specific positive verbal behaviors when playing with the child.

Goals of Treatment

While the child is the client in treatment, and reducing the intensity of disruptive behavior problems is the putative goal of treatment, parents' behaviors are the real target of PCIT so that by their positive parenting and consistent and predictable behavior management, they become the agent of change in reducing their child's behavior problems.

Strategies for Achieving Goals/Procedures

PCIT incorporates both parent and child (aged 2–7 years old) in the treatment sessions and uses live, individualized therapist 'coaching' for an idiographic (i.e., individualized) approach to changing the dysfunctional parent-child relationship. Treatment is conducted in two phases over 14–20 weeks.

Both phases of treatment begin with an hour of didactic training, when parents are taught and practice specific skills of communication and behavior management with their children. Teaching sessions are followed by sessions in which the therapist coaches the parent during play with the child. From an observation room behind a two-way mirror, via an FM receiver, the therapist provides the parent with feedback on parents' use of the skills. In the first phase (Child Directed Interaction; CDI), the therapist focuses on enhancing the parent-child relationship and decreasing negative behavior by both the parent and child. By the end of CDI, parents generally have shifted from rarely noticing their children's positive behavior to more consistently attending to, praising, and reinforcing appropriate behavior. In the second phase of treatment, therapists (Parent-Directed Interaction; PDI) focus on improving the child's compliance with the behavioral limits and expectations established by the parent. Therapists train parents to give only essential directions and commands, to make them clear and direct, maximizing chances for compliance by the child. Parents participating in PCIT traditionally learn a specific method of using time-out for dealing with noncompliance. These strategies are designed to provide caregivers tools for managing their children's behavior while helping them to avoid using physical power and to focus instead on using positive incentives and promoting children's emotional regulation. In addition to practicing these skills during clinic sessions, parents are asked to practice with their children at home for 5 min every day.

There have been numerous studies demonstrating the efficacy of PCIT in reducing child behavior problems (e.g., Eyberg and Robinson 1982) and maintaining these effects up to 6 years post-treatment (Hood and Eyberg 2003). Recent research has supported similar benefits with high-risk families, including maltreating parents (Chaffin et al. 2004; Timmer et al. 2005), and families involved in domestic violence (Timmer et al. 2010).

The Triple P-Positive Parenting Program (Triple-P)

Guiding Principles

The Triple P-Positive Parenting Program (Sanders 1999), like the other behaviorally-oriented parenting programs, is based on the premise that for children to be well-adjusted and families to be harmonious, parents should build positive relationships with their children, encourage the behaviors they like, deal positively, consistently, and decisively with misbehavior, and take care of themselves as parents.

Goals of Treatment

The emphasis of Triple-P is on teaching parents on how to apply positive parenting and child management skills to different behavioral, emotional and developmental issues in children to reduce child behavior problems and parental stress. Triple-P teaches 35 specific strategies and parenting skills that cluster into several major categories: (a) parent–child relationship enhancement, (b) encouraging desirable behavior, (c) teaching new skills and behaviors, (d) managing misbehaviors, (e) preventing problems in high-risk situations, (f) self-regulation skills, (g) parental mood management and coping skills, and (h) partner support and communication skills.

Strategies for Achieving Goals/Procedures

One of the unique characteristics of Triple-P is that it provides a public health-approach to address problems in parenting difficult children (Sanders 1999). It has five types of programs, varying in the intensity of intervention needed to insure positive change. Programs are designed for families having at least one child in the birth to 16-year-old range. We describe here the two levels of intervention in which maltreated children often participate: Standard and Group Triple-P (Level 4), and Enhanced Triple-P (Level 5).

The *Standard and Group Triple P* (*Level 4*) program benefits populations of children who have clearly identifiable problems but may not yet meet diagnostic criteria for a behavioral disorder, and/or parents who are struggling with parenting challenges. Parents learn a variety of child management skills and how to apply these skills at home and in community locations (e.g., grocery store, shopping). This program combines psychoeducation, teaching, and active skills training and support. Therapists help parents to apply and practice their new skills to a broad range of target behaviors in both home and community settings with the target child (client) and siblings.

The *Enhanced Triple-P*, *Pathways Triple-P* (*Level 5*) programs are two modules that can be added to the Standard Triple-P program when parents have problems that interfere with their ability to make progress in treatment. Both are intensive individually tailored programs that involve face-to-face clinician contact or group sessions to enhance parenting skills, mood management strategies and stress coping skills, and partner support skills. Enhanced Triple-P is designed for families with dysfunction resulting from parent mental health problems, stress, or marital conflict. Pathways Triple-P is helpful for parents with problems often found associated with child physical abuse, involving attribution retraining and anger management.

The evidence base supporting the effectiveness of Triple-P is extensive, consisting of more than 43 clinical trials (e.g., Morawska and Sanders 2006; Plant and Sanders 2007; Sanders 1999). Research also supported the use of Triple-P to reduce coercive parenting practices (Sanders et al. 2008). In the United States, Prinz and colleagues (2009) conducted a large-scale 18 county investigation in a southeastern state and found that counties using Triple-P had fewer substantiated child maltreatment referrals, out of home (foster) placements, and child maltreatment injuries.

Multidimensional Treatment Foster Care for Preschoolers (MTFC-P)

Guiding Principles

MTFC-P is guided by the belief that if children must be in foster care because of often traumatic, negative parental behavior or family circumstances, that a stable, supportive, positive environment can build children's resilience and improve their prognosis for ongoing mental health. Built on Masten and Coatsworth's (1998) resiliency framework, MTFC strives to change the ordinary processes in children's lives that have been found to build resilience: individual characteristics (e.g., cognitive functioning, sociability, self-efficacy), family characteristics (e.g., close relationships with caring adults, authoritative parenting), and extrafamilial characteristics (e.g., social support, effective schooling) (Leve et al. 2009).

Goals of Treatment

MTFC is a multilevel intervention that targets children's foster parent and peer interaction processes with the aim of preventing negative interactions and enhancing positive interactions between caregivers and children. Using case management and foster parent support services, MTFC improves caregiver monitoring and supervision skills, to improve children's positive and prosocial behavior at home and at school. Using individual therapy when needed and social skills training, other mental health and adaptive functioning issues are addressed.

Strategies for Achieving Goals/Procedures

In MTFC, children are placed with foster parents who have been intensively trained. Placements typically last 6–9 months and involve a coordinated array of services, including interventions in the home, with peers, at school, and with the child's birth parents or adoptive family, depending on their long-term plans. Specific services vary depending on the child's age and developmental level, but often include family and individual therapy, social skills training, academic support, and case management by a program supervisor to direct and coordinate the services. Additionally, children receive consistent behavior management in the foster home and at school that emphasizes reinforcement for positive and appropriate behavior and strengths via small tangible rewards or behavior charts. Similarly, children will lose points or privileges for engaging in negative behavior. Foster parents are encourage to avoid arguing with children and to try to follow a "four-to-one" rule, where any criticism is accompanied by at least four positive statements. Foster parents also receive ongoing support while an MTFC client is in their home. Foster parents meet together for 90 min a week with an MTFC program supervisor. They receive support and instruction during this time and are encouraged to share their successful parenting strategies with each other. A program supervisor leads each child's treatment team, providing support and consultation to the foster parents. There is a family therapist, an individual therapist, a child skills trainer, and a daily telephone contact person to obtain information about the child's behavior. The team meets weekly to review progress on each case.

The Basic MTFC model is supported by several RCTs (e.g., Chamberlain and Reid 1998) and the downward extension of this model for preschoolers (MTFC-P) has also been proven effective in a randomized trial (Fisher and Kim 2007).

Interventions for Middle Childhood

We present two interventions commonly used with maltreated and traumatized children in middle childhood and older, Trauma-Focused Cognitive Behavioral Therapy (TF-CBT; Cohen et al. 2006) and Alternatives for Families: A Cognitive Behavioral Therapy (AF-CBT; Kolko and Swenson 2002). TF-CBT, a rigorously researched intervention (e.g., Cohen and Mannarino 1996, 1998; Cohen et al. 2004), has received the highest ratings for its effectiveness. It was originally designed to treat victims of sexual abuse, but has been adapted to treat victims of multiple maltreatment and domestic violence. AF-CBT, supported by an RCT (Kolko 1996), was designed to help families coping with the consequences of physical abuse, violence, harsh or coercive parenting.

Trauma-Focused Cognitive Behavioral Therapy (TF-CBT)

Guiding Principles

TF-CBT is based on the idea that a combination of processing and reframing thoughts about trauma and the implementation of active behavioral strategies to avoid or minimize physiological responses to stressors increases positive functioning and reduces trauma symptoms.

Goals of Treatment

TF- CBT specifically aims to reduce trauma-related symptoms including PTSD, depression, anxiety, trauma-related shame, and trauma-related cognitions such as self-blame in children and adolescents. TF-CBT also includes a component for non-offending (nonsexually abusive or nonperpetrator) parents to enhance their support of the traumatized child, decrease their own emotional distress, and enhance positive parenting practices.

Strategies for Achieving Goals/Procedures

As Cohen and colleagues (2006) describe, the strategies TF-CBT uses to achieve its treatment goals can be summarized by the acronym PRACTICE: Parenting Skills, Psychoeducation, Relaxation Skills, Affective Modulation Skills, Cognitive Processing, Trauma Narration, In Vivo Desensitization, Conjoint Child–Parent Sessions, and Enhancing Safety and Future Development. Parenting skills consist of enhancing parents' abilities to use praise, selective attention, time-out, and contingency reinforcement programs. Psychoeducation involves giving parents and children information about the type of trauma the child has experienced, validating their reactions to their trauma. The relaxation component includes teaching parents and children focused breathing, progressive muscle relaxation, and other personalized interventions, helping to control their physiological hyperarousal. With affective modulation, children identify feelings, practice expression and thought interruption skills, which enhance their ability to use positive self-talk, to problem-solving and social skills. Cognitive processing consists of guiding children and parents through a process of recognizing the connection among thoughts, feelings, and behaviors, and changing thoughts to be more accurate and helpful. By developing a narrative of the child's trauma experience, a detailed description of what occurred during the child's maltreatment or violence exposure experiences is documented, revealing cognitive distortions about these experiences. Using in vivo desensitization therapists help children overcome generalized avoidance of trauma reminders. Conjoint sessions occur between children and parents after the above components have been successfully completed. Last, by enhancing safety, therapists address present and future safety issues for the child and parent. Accomplishing the PRACTICE usually takes approximately 12–16 sessions lasting 60–90 min.

Alternatives for Families: A Cognitive Behavioral Therapy (AF-CBT)

Guiding Principles

AF-CBT promotes the idea that by adjusting thoughts, identifying feelings, and controlling physiological stress levels, it is possible to reduce the risk of physical abuse and violence. This intervention focuses on intrapersonal and interpersonal skills training for improving self-control, promoting positive family relations, and reducing violent behavior.

Goals of Treatment

Goals of AF-CBT are two-pronged. First, the intervention aims to improve parents' parenting skills or practices, including increasing adherence to positive child management practices and decreasing harsh and coercive discipline. At the same time, AF-CBT aims to reduce physically abused children's externalizing behavioral problems, increase their positive social behaviors, and improve the quality of their peer interactions.

Strategies for Achieving Goals/Procedures

To accomplish treatment goals, AF-CBT is organized into three phases: (1) Psychoeducation and Engagement; (2) Individual and Family Skills Training, and (3) Family Applications Treatment. The primary techniques used in the last two phases include affect regulation, behavior management, social skills training, cognitive restructuring/problem-solving, and communication. Children and parents have separate goals and procedures. In specific components for children, therapists conduct an exercise in which the child describes the exposure to family hostility and violence; cognitive processing of the circumstances and outcomes of the violent incident(s) that produced the mental health referral as a way to modify distortions, and aggression supporting beliefs; teaching about child abuse laws, child safety, and common child abuse reactions. They also learn to regulate their negative affect by identifying abuse-specific triggers, stress management, and anger control. Therapists describe and practice healthy coping skills, discussing how using them can help the children address everyday problems. They also work with the children to develop social support plans and skills to enhance social competence. Components specific to parents' needs include the following: socialization to models of stress and CBT, and a discussion about factors that contribute to violent or coercive behaviors. Therapists discuss with the parent their view on hostility and violence, including child-related developmental expectation and general attributions that may promote coercive interactions to get a better understanding of the parents perspective. They work on affect management with parents, identification and management of abuse-specific triggers, heightened anger or anxiety and depression, so that the parents may have more control over their emotions and behavior. Parents also receive training in alternative disciplinary strategies that minimize the use of physical force through instruction in behavioral management principles and techniques. Families generally need 12–24 h of service over a period of 12–24 weeks to complete treatment.

Interventions for Adolescents

We describe two interventions often used with maltreated and high-risk adolescents, Dialectical Behavior Therapy (Linehan 1993) and Multisystemic Therapy – for Child Abuse and Neglect (Swenson et al. 2010). Although both interventions have a strong empirical research foundation, both are also interventions that have been adapted for treating adolescent clients with severe, unremitting, and complex mental health symptoms associated with child maltreatment. Dialectical Behavior Therapy (DBT), originally shown effective in the treatment of clients with borderline personality disorder (Linehan et al. 1993), has been shown to be effective in the treatment of mood disorders that often included suicidal behavior and self-harm (Kliem et al. 2010; Rathus and Miller 2002) and with victims of sexual abuse (Decker and Naugle 2008). Multisystemic Therapy for Child Abuse and Neglect (MST-CAN; Swenson et al. 2010) is an evidence-based treatment for families with serious clinical needs who come to the attention of Child Protective Services because of abuse or neglect referrals. Importantly, MST-CAN addresses the referral behaviors plus key risk factors that keep families coming through the revolving door of child protection.

Dialectical Behavior Therapy (DBT)

Guiding Principles

Fundamentally, DBT (Linehan 1993) is based on the premise that once a successful therapeutic alliance has been established as unconditionally though neutrally accepting, that acceptance and change occurs through a dialectical process, in which the thesis (i.e., clients' original beliefs) plus antithesis (adaptive alternatives) equal change. This dialectical change is enabled by clients increased ability to tolerate distress, regulate emotions, improve interpersonal functioning, and increase their mindfulness of themselves in their environment.

Goals of Treatment

The overall goal of DBT is helping clients create "lives worth living," which involves achieving four distinct primary treatment objectives: (1) Increased control over behavior (e.g., eliminating life-threatening behaviors and behaviors that interfere with treatment; decreasing behaviors that destroy the quality of life; increase attention; increased distress tolerance); (2) Improve emotional expression (e.g., reduce dissociation, reduce symptoms of PTSD); (3) Improve problem-solving skills (e.g., solve ordinary problems like marital or partner conflict, job dissatisfaction); (4) Increase interpersonal connectedness (e.g., support with 'existential' problems, connect with churches, synagogues, or temples).

Strategies for Achieving Goals/Procedures

DBT combines behavioral techniques (e.g., affective skills training, exposure) together with cognitive restructuring, and it introduces the importance of mindfulness practice, validation, and principles of dialectical philosophy. The primary clinical tools used in DBT are diary cards, on which the client records self-injurious and therapy interfering behaviors throughout the week, and chain analysis, a functional analysis of sequences behaviors, aimed at increasing mindfulness. Clients have weekly individual and group treatment sessions. In individual sessions, the therapist and client discuss issues written on the diary cards that arose that week, following a treatment target hierarchy. Self-injurious and suicidal behaviors take first priority. Second in priority are behaviors that interfere with the course of treatment, followed by issues related to the client's quality of life. During the individual therapy, the therapist and patient work towards improving skill use. Groups typically meet once weekly, during which clients learn to use mindfulness skills, assertiveness skills for increasing interpersonal effectiveness, emotion regulation, and distress tolerance skills. Individual sessions are considered necessary to keep suicidal urges or uncontrolled emotional issues from disrupting group sessions, while the group sessions teach the skills unique to DBT, and also provide practice with regulating emotions and behavior in a social context. Clients have telephone access to therapists 24 h a day to acquire additional assistance in managing new skills and urgent problems. Finally, it is a requirement that therapists participate in ongoing consultation team meetings to maintain or improve their own motivation. It takes approximately 1 year to master the skills required by a typical course of treatment in DBT.

Multisystemic Therapy for Child Abuse and Neglect (MST-CAN)

Guiding Principles

MST-CAN is a networked system of interventions based on a social-ecological model (Bronfenbrenner 1979), which asserts that children are parts of various systems or "ecologies" (e.g., school, family, parents) that they influence and that influence them. MST-CAN is guided by the belief that treatment must attend to the children's functioning in all of their social systems in order to be successful.

Goals of Treatment

The overarching goals for MST-CAN are to keep families together safely by preventing placement out of the home, eliminating further incidents of maltreatment, and altering key factors that heighten maltreatment risk. As a strengths-based model MST-CAN, first targets protective factors in children's social systems, particularly social support, and designs strategies to build upon them and use them as leverage for change. Likewise, in cases where maltreatment has occurred, the MST team assesses risk factors and functioning across these systems and develops strategies to reduce risk (e.g., parent mental health problems, housing and employment problems) and improve child functioning (e.g., aggressive behavior, depressive symptoms).

Strategies for Achieving Goals/Procedures

The families referred to MST-CAN are those with multiple, serious clinical problems who have a child in the family who is between 6 and 17 years of age with a documented history of physically abuse or neglect within the last 180 days.

A full-time supervisor oversees the work of three to four masters-level therapists and a bachelor-level case manager. Approximately 20 % psychiatrist protected time is reserved for youth and parents in the project. Because families are referred to MST-CAN because of parents' maltreating behavior, the focus of treatment is with the adults in the family. On average, five people per family are treated. For example, the parent may be treated for substance abuse, the grandmother for depression, and the child for behavioral problems at school. The team works a flexible schedule seeing families at times that are convenient for them. Sessions may be during traditional work hours, at night or on the weekend. The team operates a 24-h per day, 7 days per week, on call rotation service to help families manage crises.

The majority of the research-supported treatments used in MST-CAN are behavioral or cognitive behavioral. When family members exhibit difficulty in managing anger, therapists use cognitive behavioral treatments for anger management (e.g., Feindler et al. 1986). When families have difficulty with communication and problem solving, therapists use a behavioral family treatment (Robin et al. 1994). When family members are experiencing PTSD symptoms, therapists use Stress Inoculation Training (SIT: Kilpatrick et al. 1982) and Prolonged Exposure therapies (Foa and Rothbaum 1998). Finally, for treatment of substance misuse, Reinforcement-Based Treatment (RBT; Tuten et al. 2012) is provided.

MST-CAN is an evidence-based treatment model with 15 years of clinical and research piloting, efficacy and effectiveness studies, and transportability piloting to its history. Two randomized clinical trials (RCT) form the current evidence base supporting MST-CAN (Brunk et al. 1987; Swenson et al. 2010).

Policy Considerations

There are many children and families adversely affected by child maltreatment: thousands of children experiencing child sexual abuse, child physical abuse, and neglect every day. Much of this chapter has detailed the impact of maltreatment on the developing child, followed by multiple interventions that have strong empirical support in alleviating child mental health symptoms, improving parent-child relationships, and improving the overall health of the child. We have also described the developmental context of maltreatment, the core components of change, and how different empirically based interventions for maltreated children affect that change. We have not discussed how we can insure that mental health providers perform these interventions with fidelity to all maltreated children in need. This discussion leads us in a direction away from developmental psychopathology and towards "implementation science" and public policy. It is the burden of those advocating the use of empirically based treatments to also find a way reliably implement them and continue to support these interventions so that they are proven effective not just in university laboratories, but in the community mental health programs throughout our country (Steinfeld et al. 2009; Weisz et al. 2012).

There has been remarkable movement during the last two decades in the development and refinement of empirically based treatments (Aarons et al. 2009). Additionally, several organizations have detailed descriptions of promising and well-researched interventions specifically for maltreated children and their families (e.g., California Evidence-based Clearinghouse for Child Welfare, n.d.; Center for the Study and Prevention of Violence, n.d.; Substance Abuse and Mental Health Services Administration [SAMHSA]). Policymakers and legislators understandably have been persuaded by the research supporting evidence-based practices, wanting to take action that could show results either in preventing or disrupting the negative effects of maltreatment. However, there has been a lag between the development of empirically tested interventions and the implementation of these interventions in various community mental health programs (Aarons and Palinkas 2007; Proctor et al. 2009; Aarons et al. 2011). While it may be reasonably argued that development of effective interventions is difficult, it appears that development of effective methods to disseminate these interventions is much more complex.

The large body of research documenting efforts to implement effective home-visiting programs illustrates some of the reasons for the lag between treatment development and dissemination. Early efforts at large-scale implementation focused on replicating the program content, not considering the fact that whether people actually providing services knew how to reliably and effectively produce the same content in varied situations might make a differences in the quality of outcomes. Using "agents of change" with little training or insufficient supervision instead of registered nurses explained the reduced effectiveness of a evidence-base home visiting program taken to scale on a state level (e.g., Duggan et al. 2004). Michalopoulos and colleagues (2011) noted that evaluations rarely collect detailed information on the services actually delivered when evidence based practices are taken to scale, which makes it possible that weak effects in evaluation studies could result from problems with dissemination and reflect very little about the effectiveness of the program model. They observed that nurses and paraprofessionals using the same home-visiting protocol, provided very different services to their clients: nurses targeted issues relating to physical health and infant behavior, while paraprofessionals worked on connecting their clients to community services, addressing more practical, logistical problems (Korfmacher et al. 1999). These findings underscore the importance of training providers to effectively deliver particular content to insure the fidelity of evidence-based interventions. Research has long shown that fidelity is related to effectiveness and that decreases in fidelity is likely to decrease program effectiveness (e.g., Battistich et al. 1996; Blakely et al. 1987; Kam et al. 2003). We argue that inadequate training and implementation also can compromise the effectiveness of these interventions.

Simpson (2002) points out that the process of disseminating evidence based treatments, or translating "science to service," traditionally has been a passive process that involves scientists communicating information to leaders who then put the proven treatments into practice. This process serves as the foundation for most U.S. federal and state policies related to making use of evidenced-based programs and other human service innovations (Fixsen et al. 2009). Those who train front-line practitioners quickly realized the limitations of this strategy, since trainees are not equipped to practice a new treatment using only a manual or a didactic-style, workshop training (Herschell et al. 2009). Fixsen and colleagues (2009) describe a more active style of implementing empirically based interventions with fidelity, defining seven core implementation components which combine to help change individuals' practice and organizational culture. These components are (1) selecting appropriate staff; (2) pre-service and in-service training, (3) ongoing coaching and consultation, (4) staff evaluation, (5) decision support data systems, (6) administrative support, and (7) systems interventions. The selection of this combination of individual level and organizational level factors, the combination of action and evaluation, creating multiple supports for individuals and programs, demonstrates the multidimensional character of disseminating evidence-based practices. Evidence-based practices involve more than understanding the principles behind an intervention and an understanding of the processes. Evidence-based practices require a commitment to a system of practice, a willingness to be held accountable for what you do and how you conduct therapy – if you claim to be providing an evidence-based treatment. It is impossible for therapists to make this commitment to provide evidence-based therapies with quality and fidelity if they are not supported by their home agencies, and their county and state systems of care (who control reimbursement for these services). There is a natural tension between the budget requirements of evidence-based practices – the time required for assessment, special requirements of documentation for these services, and their intensity and comprehensiveness – and states' and counties' desires to get the greatest amount of mental health services for their dollars. Many counties see reductions in child mal-treatment allegations and prolonged needs for services, and are willing to make this commitment. Others, facing difficult budgetary decisions, may need persuasive data showing them the many advantages of demanding that providers maintain quality and fidelity, even if supporting evidence-treatments means more complex and costly support mechanism. It is the responsibility of developers and trainers to con-duct the research, and provide information to child advocates and treatment providers to make it easier to make the argument for quality in mental health treatment.

Conclusions

In this chapter, we described the broad and long-lasting effects of maltreatment on children via the neurobiological stress-response system. We also described the connection between attachment and the stress-response system, and the ways in which parenting and the context of the family continues to play a part in the way children respond to stress in their environment. The observable effects of maltreatment have been described: externalizing, disruptive behaviors in early years, social problems, school difficulties, and depression and other problems as children grew older, to name a few. The ten different evidence-based treatments that we described are based on a variety of premises, designed to treat children of different ages using different treatment modalities, with different treatment goals, and different strategies for achieving those treatment goals. Interestingly, they all incorporated some strat-egy for increasing emotional regulation, and often targeted parenting strategies or family systems as mechanisms of change or methods for sustaining change in maltreated children.

We argue that the increasingly sophisticated literature describing the neurobiological underpin-nings of maltreatment effects suggest that HPA-axis dysfunction may continue to play a part in under-mining mental health throughout childhood and adolescence, and that the most effective treatments will include a component to help clients use active and cognitive strategies for controlling their responses to stress. Furthermore, early caregiving quality, inexorably linked to the stress-response system, also appears to set the stage for later interpersonal functioning, and continues to be supported by risk and resilience inherent in the family system. We argue that the most effective treatments for young children will consider the parent-child relationship as integral to treatment success. Consideration of the health and support of the family system in middle childhood and adolescence may also prove key to treatment success.

In spite of our trying to take a more "meta" view of empirically based treatments for maltreated children and trying to choose different types and modalities of treatment delivery as representative interventions, we acknowledge that we have missed some important contributors to the evidence base. We hope that others will continue the work of examining mechanisms of effectiveness of evidence-based treatments for maltreated children and continue to document the core components of effective mental health treatments.

References

Aarons, G., & Palinkas, L. A. (2007). Implementation of evidence-based practice in child welfare: Service provider perspectives. *Administration and Policy in Mental Health and Mental Health Services Research, 34*, 411–419.

Aarons, G., Wells, R. S., Zagursky, K., Fettes, D. L., & Palinkas, L. A. (2009). Implementing evidence-based practice in community mental health agencies: A stakeholder analysis. *American Journal of Public Health, 99*(11), 2087–2095.

Aarons, G. A., Hurlburt, M., & Horowitz, S. M. (2011). Advancing a conceptual model of evidence-based practice implementation in public service sectors. *Administration and Policy in Mental Health and Mental Health Services Research, 38*, 4–23.

Ainsworth, M. D. S., Blehar, M. C., Waters, E., & Wall, S. (1978). *Patterns of attachment: A psychological study of the strange situation.* Hillsdale: Erlbaum.

Appleyard, K., Egeland, B., van Dulmen, M. H., & Sroufe, L. A. (2005). When more is not better: The role of cumulative risk in child behavior outcomes. *Journal of Child Psychology and Psychiatry, 46*(3), 235–245.

Bakermans-Kranenburg, M., van IJzendoorn, M., & Juffer, F. (2008). Earlier is better: A meta-analysis of 70 years of intervention improving cognitive development in institutionalized children. *Monographs of the Society for Research in Child Development, 73*(3), 279–293.

Barnard, K. E. (1999). *Beginning rhythms: The emerging process of sleep-wake behaviors and self regulation.* Seattle: NCAST, University of Washington.

Battistich, V., Schaps, E., Watson, M., Solomon, D., & Lewis, C. (1996). Prevention effects of the child development project: Early findings from an ongoing multisite demonstration trial. *Journal of Adolescent Research, 11*, 12–35.

Beckett, C., Maughan, B., Rutter, M., Castle, J., Colvert, E., et al. (2006). Do the effects of early severe deprivation on cognition persist into early adolescence? Findings from the English and Romanian adoptees study. *Child Development, 77*(3), 696–711.

Bernard, K., Dozier, M., Carlson, E., Bick, J., Lewis-Morrarty, E., & Lindhiem, O. (2012). Enhancing attachment organization among maltreated children: Results of a randomized clinical trial. *Child Development, 83*(2), 623–636.

Blair, C., Granger, D. A., Kivlighan, K. T., Mills-Koonce, R., Willoughby, M., Greenberg, M. T., & Fortunato, C. K. (2008). Maternal and child contributions to cortisol response to emotional arousal in young children from low-income, rural communities. *Developmental Psychology, 44*, 1095–1109. doi:10.1037/0012-1649.44.4.1095.

Blakely, C., Mayer, J., Gottschalk, R., Schmitt, N., Davidson, W., Roitman, D., & Emshoff, J. (1987). The fidelity-adaptation debate: Implications for the implementation of public sector social programs. *American Journal of Community Psychology, 15*, 253–268.

Bolger, K., & Patterson, C. (2001). Pathways from child maltreatment to internalizing problems: Perceptions of control as mediators and moderators. *Development and Psychopathology, 13*(4), 913–940.

Booth-LaForce, C., & Oxford, M. (2008). Trajectories of social withdrawal from grades 1 to 6: Prediction from early parenting, attachment, and temperament. *Developmental Psychology, 44*(5), 1298–1313.

Bowlby, J. (1951). *Maternal care and mental health.* World Health Organization (WHO) Monograph, Serial No. 2. Geneva: WHO.

Bowlby, J. (1973). *Attachment and loss* (Separation: Anxiety and anger, Vol. 2). New York: Basic Books.

Bowlby, J. (1982). *Attachment and loss* (Attachment 2nd ed., Vol. 1). New York: Basic Books. Original work published 1969.

Bronfenbrenner, U. (1979). *The ecology of human development: Experiments by design and nature.* Cambridge: Harvard University Press.

Brunk, M., Henggeler, S. W., & Whelan, J. P. (1987). Comparison of multisystemic therapy and parent training in the brief treatment of child abuse and neglect. *Journal of Consulting and Clinical Psychology, 55*, 171–178. doi:10.1037/0022-006X.55.2.171.

Bugental, D. B., Martorell, G. A., & Barraza, V. (2003). The hormonal costs of subtle forms of infant maltreatment. *Hormones and Behavior, 43*, 237–244. doi:10.1016/S0018-506X(02)00008-9.

California evidence-based clearinghouse for child welfare: information and resources for child welfare professionals. Website: http://wwwcebc4cw.org

Carlson, M., & Earls, F. (1997). Psychological and neuroendocrinological sequelae of early social deprivation in institutionalized children in Romania. In M. Carlson & F. Earls (Eds.), *In the integrative neurobiology of affiliation* (pp. 419–428). New York: New York Academy of Sciences.

Carlson, V., Cicchetti, D., Barnett, D., & Braunwald, K. (1989). Disorganized/disoriented attachment relationships in maltreated infants. *Developmental Psychology, 25*(4), 525–531.

Center for the Study and Prevention of Violence, Blueprints Program; Institute of Behavioral Science, University of Colorado, Boulder. http://www.blueprintsprograms.com/

Chaffin, M., Silovsky, J., Funderburk, B., Valle, L., Brestan, E., Balachova, T., Jackson, S., & Bonner, B. L. (2004). Parent–child interaction therapy with physically abusive parents. Efficacy for reducing future abuse reports. *Journal of Consulting and Clinical Psychology, 72*, 491–499.

Chamberlain, P., & Reid, J. (1998). Comparison of two community alternatives to incarceration for chronic juvenile offenders. *Journal of Consulting and Clinical Psychology, 6*, 624–633.

Chen, P., Coccaro, E. F., Lee, R., & Jacobson, K. C. (2012). Moderating effects of childhood maltreatment on associations between social information processing and adult aggression. *Psychological Medicine, 4*(6), 1293–1304.

Cicchetti, D., & Lynch, M. (1993). Toward an ecological/transactional model of community violence and child maltreatment: Consequences for children's development. *Psychiatry, 56*, 96–118.

Cicchetti, D., & Rogosch, F. A. (1997). The role of self-organization in the promotion of resilience in maltreated children. *Development and Psychopathology, 9,* 799–817.

Cicchetti, D., & Toth, S. L. (2000). Developmental processes in maltreated children. In D. Hansen (Ed.), *Nebraska symposium on motivation* (Motivation and maltreatment, Vol. 46, pp. 85–160). Lincoln: University of Nebraska Press.

Cicchetti, D., & Valentino, K. (2006). An ecological transactional perspective on child maltreatment: Failure of the average expectable environment and its influence upon child development. In D. Cicchetti & D. J. Cohen (Eds.), *Developmental psychopathology* (2nd ed., Vol. 3, pp. 129–201). New York: Wiley.

Cicchetti, D., Rogosch, F. A., & Toth, S. L. (2006). Fostering secure attachment in infants in maltreating families through preventive interventions. *Development and Psychopathology, 18,* 623–650.

Cicchetti, D., Rogosch, F. A., Gunnar, M. R., & Toth, S. L. (2010). The differential impacts of early physical and sexual abuse and internalizing problems on daytime cortisol rhythm in school-aged children. *Child Development, 81*(1), 252–269. doi:10.1111/j.1467-8624.2009.01393.

Cohen, J. A., & Mannarino, A. P. (1996). A treatment study for sexually abused preschool children: Initial findings. *Journal of the American Academy of Child and Adolescent Psychiatry, 35,* 42–50.

Cohen, J. A., & Mannarino, A. P. (1998). Interventions for sexually abused children: Initial treatment findings. *Child Maltreatment, 3,* 17–26.

Cohen, J. A., Deblinger, E., Mannarino, A. P., & Steer, R. (2004). A multisite randomized controlled trial for multiply traumatized children with sexual abuse-related PTSD. *Journal of the American Academy of Child and Adolescent Psychiatry, 43*(4), 393–402.

Cohen, J. A., Mannarino, A. P., & Deblinger, E. (2006). *Treating trauma and traumatic grief in children and adolescents.* New York: The Guilford Press.

Cyr, C. A., Euser, E. M., Bakermans-Kranenburg, M. J., & Van Ijzendoorn, M. H. (2010). Attachment insecurity and disorganization in maltreating and high-risk families: A series of meta-analyses. *Development and Psychopathology, 22,* 87–108.

Deblinger, E., & Runyon, M. K. (2005). Understanding and treating feelings of shame in children who have experienced maltreatment. *Child Maltreatment, 10,* 364–376.

Decker, S. E., & Naugle, A. E. (2008). DBT for sexual abuse survivors: Current status and future directions. *Journal of Behavior Analysis of Offender and Victim: Treatment and Prevention, 1*(4), 52–69.

Denham, S. A., Workman, E., Cole, P. M., Weissbrod, C., Kendziora, K. T., & Zahn-Waxler, C. (2000). Prediction of externalizing behavior problems from early to middle childhood: The role of parental socialization and emotional expression. *Development and Psychopathology, 12,* 23–45. doi:10.1017/S0954579400001024.

Downey, G., & Coyne, J. C. (1990). Children of depressed parents: An integrative review. *Psychological Bulletin, 108,* 50–76.

Dozier, M., Lindhiem, O., Lewis, E., Bick, J., & Bernard, K. (2009). Effects of a foster parent training program on young children's attachment behaviors: Preliminary evidence from a randomized clinical trial. *Child and Adolescent Social Work Journal, 26*(4), 321–332.

Dube, S. R., Anda, R. F., Felitti, V. J., Chapman, D. P., Williamson, D. F., & Giles, W. H. (2001). Childhood abuse, household dysfunction, and the risk of attempted suicide throughout the life span: Findings from the adverse childhood experiences study. *Journal of the American Medical Association, 286,* 3089–3096.

Duggan, A., McFarlane, E., Fuddy, L., Burrell, L., Higman, S., Windham, A., & Sia, C. (2004). Randomized trial of a statewide home visiting program to prevent child abuse: Impact in reducing parental risk factors. *Child Abuse & Neglect, 28*(6), 596–622.

Ellis, B., Jackson, J., & Boyce, W. T. (2006). The stress response system: Universality and adaptive individual differences. *Developmental Review, 26*(2), 175–212.

Ellis, B. J., Boyce, W. T., Belsky, J., Bakermans-Kranenburg, M. J., & Van Ijzendoorn, M. H. (2011). Differential susceptibility to the environment: An evolutionary neurodevelopmental theory. *Development and Psychopathology, 23,* 7–28. doi:10.1017/S0954579410000611.

Eyberg, S., & Robinson, E. A. (1982). Parent-child interaction training: Effects on family functioning. *Journal of Clinical Child Psychology, 11*(2), 130–137.

Feindler, E. L., Ecton, R. B., Kingsley, D., & Dubey, D. R. (1986). Group anger-control training for institutionalized psychiatric male adolescents. *Behavior Therapy, 17,* 109–123. doi:10.1016/S0005-7894(86)80079-X.

Felitti, V. J., Anda, R. F., Nordenberg, D., Williamson, D. F., Spitz, A. M., Edwards, V., Koss, M. P., & Marks, J. S. (1998). Relationship of childhood abuse and household dysfunction to many of the leading causes of death in adults: The Adverse Childhood Experiences (ACE) study. *American Journal of Preventive Medicine, 14,* 245–258.

Fisher, P. A., & Kim, H. K. (2007). Intervention effects on foster preschoolers' attachment-related behaviors from a randomized trial. *Prevention Science, 8,* 161–170.

Fisher, L., Ames, E., Chisholm, K., & Savoie, L. (1997). Problems reported by parents of Romanian orphans adopted to British Columbia. *International Journal of Behavioral Development, 20*(1), 67–82.

Fisher, P. A., Gunnar, M. R., Chamberlain, P., & Reid, J. B. (2000). Preventive intervention for maltreated preschoolers: Impact on children's behavior, neuroendocrine activity, and foster parent functioning. *Journal of the American Academy of Child and Adolescent Psychiatry, 39*, 1356–1364.

Fixsen, D., Blasé, K., Naoom, S., & Wallace, F. (2009). Core implementation components. *Research on Social Work Practice, 19*(5), 531–540.

Foa, E. B., & Rothbaum, B. O. (1998). *Treating the trauma of rape: Cognitive behavioral therapy for PTSD*. New York: Guilford Press.

Fraiberg, S., Adelson, E., & Shapiro, V. (1975). Ghosts in the nursery: A psychoanalytic approach to the problems of impaired infant-mother relationships. *Journal of the American Academy of Child Psychiatry, 14*, 387–402.

Freud, S. (1959). *Collected papers*. Oxford: Basic Books.

Gartstein, M., Bridgett, D., Dishion, T., & Kaufman, N. (2009). Depressed mood and maternal report of child behavior problems: Another look at the depression-distortion hypothesis. *Developmental Psychology, 30*(2), 149–160.

Gershoff, E. T. (2002). Corporal punishment by parents and associated child behaviors and experiences: A meta-analytic and theoretical review. *Psychological Bulletin, 128*, 539–579. doi:10.1037/0033- 2909.128.4.539.

Goodman, S., & Gotlib, I. (1999). Risk for psychopathology in the children of depressed mothers: A developmental model for understanding mechanisms of transmission. *Psychological Review, 106*(3), 458–490.

Goodman, G. S., Quas, J. A., Batterman-Faunce, J. M., Riddlesberger, M. M., & Kuhn, J. (1997). Children's reactions to and memory for a stressful event: Influences of age, anatomical dolls, knowledge, and parental attachment. *Applied Developmental Science, 1–2*, 54–75.

Gunnar, M., Larson, M., Hertsgaard, L., & Harris, M. (1992). The stressfulness of separation among nine-month-old infants: Effects of social context variables and infant temperament. *Child Development, 63*(2), 290–303.

Harter, S. (2001). *The construction of the self: A developmental perspective*. New York: Guilford.

Heim, C., Ehlert, U., & Hellhammer, D. H. (2000). The potential role of hypocortisolism in the pathophysiology of stress-related bodily disorders. *Psychoneuroendocrinology, 25*, 1–35.

Heim, C., Newport, D. J., Mletzko, T., Miller, A. H., & Nemeroff, C. B. (2008). The link between childhood trauma and depression: Insights from HPA axis studies in humans. *Psycho-neuroendocrinology, 33*, 693–710.

Herman, J. P., Figueiredo, H., Mueller, N. K., Ulrich-Lai, Y., Ostrander, M., Choi, D., & Cullinan, W. (2003). Central mechanisms of stress integration: Hierarchical circuitry controlling hypothalamo-pituitary-adrenocortical responsiveness. *Frontiers in Neuroendocrinology, 24*, 151–180.

Herschell, A., McNeil, C., Urquiza, A., McGrath, J., Zebell, N., Timmer, S., & Porter, A. (2009). Evaluation of a treatment manual and workshops for disseminating, parent–child interaction therapy. *Administration and Policy in Mental Health and Mental Health Services Research, 36*(1), 63–81.

Hill-Soderlund, A. L., Mills-Koonce, W. R., Propper, C., Calkins, S., Granger, D. A., Moore, G. A., & Cox, M. J. (2008). Parasympathetic and sympathetic responses to the strange situation in infants and mothers from avoidant and securely attached dyads. *Developmental Psychobiology, 50*, 361–376. doi:10.1002/dev.20302.

Hood, K., & Eyberg, S. (2003). Outcomes of parent–child interaction therapy: Mothers' reports of maintenance three to six years after treatment. *Journal of Clinical Child and Adolescent Psychology, 32*, 412–429.

Hurlburt, M. S., Nguyen, K., Reid, M. J., Webster-Stratton, C., & Zhang, J. (under review). Efficacy of Incredible Years group parent program with families in Head Start with a child maltreatment history. Child Abuse and Neglect.

Jonson-Reid, M., Kohl, P., & Drake, B. (2012). Child and adult outcomes of chronic child maltreatment. *Pediatrics, 129*(5), 839–845.

Juster, R.-P., McEwen, B. S., & Lupien, S. J. (2009). Allostatic load biomarkers of chronic stress and impact on health and cognition. *Neuroscience and Biobehavioral Reviews, 35*, 2–16.

Kam, C., Greenberg, M., & Walls, C. (2003). Examining the role of implementation quality in school-based prevention using the PATHS curriculum. *Prevention Science, 4*, 55–63.

Keiley, M. K., Howe, T. R., Dodge, K. A., Bates, J. E., & Pettit, G. S. (2001). The timing of child physical mal- treatment: A cross-domain growth analysis of impact on adolescent externalizing and internalizing problems. *Development and Psychopathology, 13*, 891–912.

Kilpatrick, D. G., Veronen, L. J., & Resick, P. A. (1982). Psychological sequelae to rape: Assessment and treatment strategies. In D. M. L. Dolays & R. L. Meredith (Eds.), *Behavioral medicine: Assessment and treatment strategies* (pp. 473–497). New York: Plenum Press.

Kim, J., & Cicchetti, D. (2006). Longitudinal trajectories of self-system processes and depressive symptoms among maltreated and nonmaltreated children. *Child Development, 77*, 624–639.

Kliem, S., Kröger, C., & Kossfelder, J. (2010). Dialectical behavior therapy for borderline personality disorder: A meta-analysis using mixed-effects modeling. *Journal of Consulting and Clinical Psychology, 78*, 936–951.

Knudsen, E. I. (2004). Sensitive periods in the development of brain and behavior. *Journal of Cognitive Neuroscience, 16*, 1412–1425.

Kolko, D. J. (1996). Individual cognitive-behavioral treatment and family therapy for physically abused children and their offending parents: A comparison of clinical outcomes. *Child Maltreatment, 1*, 322–342.

Kolko, D. J., & Swenson, C. C. (2002). *Assessing and treating physically abused children and their families: A cognitive behavioral approach*. Thousand Oaks: Sage.

Korfmacher, J., O'Brien, R., Hiatt, S., & Olds, D. (1999). Differences in program implementation between nurses and paraprofessionals providing home visits during pregnancy and infancy: A randomized trial. *American Journal of Public Health, 89*(12), 1847–1851.

Leve, L., Fisher, P., & Chamberlain, P. (2009). Multidimensional treatment foster care as a preventive intervention to promote resiliency among youth in the child welfare system. *Journal of Personality, 77*(6).

Lieberman, A. F., & Van Horn, P. (2005). *Don't hit my mommy!: A manual for child-parent psychotherapy with young witnesses of family violence*. Washington, DC: Zero to Three Press.

Lieberman, A. F., & Van Horn, P. (2008). *Psychotherapy with infants and young children*. New York: Guilford Press.

Lieberman, A. F., Weston, D., & Pawl, J. (1991). Preventive intervention and outcome with anxiously attached dyads. *Child Development, 62*, 199–209.

Lieberman, A. F., Van Horn, P., & Ghosh Ippen, C. (2005). Toward evidence-based treatment: Child-parent psychotherapy with preschoolers exposed to marital violence. *Journal of the American Academy of Child and Adolescent Psychiatry, 44*(12), 1241–1248.

Lieberman, A. F., Ghosh Ippen, C., & Van Horn, P. (2006). Child-parent psychotherapy: 6-month follow-up of a randomized controlled trial. *Journal of the American Academy of Child and Adolescent Psychiatry, 45*(8), 913–918.

Linehan, M. M. (1993). *Skills training manual for treating borderline personality disorder*. New York: Guilford Press.

Linehan, M. M., Heard, H. L., & Armstrong, H. E. (1993). Naturalistic follow-up of a behavioural treatment of chronically parasuicidal borderline patients. *Archives of General Psychiatry, 50*(12), 971–974.

Luijk, M. P. C. M., Saridjan, N., Tharner, A., van IJzendoorn, M. H., Bakermans-Kranenburg, M. J., Jaddoe, V. W. V., et al. (2010). Attachment, depression, and cortisol: Deviant patterns of insecure-resistant and disorganized infants. *Developmental Psychobiology, 52*, 441–452. doi:10.1002/dev.20446.

Lupien, S., Oueliet-Morin, I., Hupbach, A., Tu, M., Buss, C., et al. (2006). Beyond the stress concept: Allostatic load – a developmental biological and cognitive perspective. In S. Lupien, I. Oueliet-Morin, A. Hupbach, M. Tu, C. Buss, D. Walker, J. Pruessner, & B. McEwen (Eds.), *Developmental psychopathology* (Developmental neuroscience 2nd ed., Vol. 2, pp. 578–628). Hoboken: Wiley.

Lyons-Ruth, K., Alpern, L., & Repacholi, B. (1993). Disorganized infant attachment classification and maternal psychosocial problems as predictors of hostile-aggressive behavior in preschool children. *Child Development, 64*, 572–585.

Main, M., & Hesse, E. (1990). Parents' unresolved traumatic experiences are related to infant disorganized attachment status: Is frightened and/or frightening parental behavior the linking mechanism? In M. T. Greenberg, D. Cicchetti, & E. M. Cummings (Eds.), *Attachment in the preschool years: Theory, research, and intervention* (pp. 161–182). Chicago: University of Chicago Press.

Main, M., & Solomon, J. (1986). Discovery of an insecure-disorganized/disoriented attachment pattern. In M. Main & J. Solomon (Eds.), *Affective development in infancy* (pp. 95–124). Westport: Ablex Publishing.

Martorell, G. A., & Bugental, D. B. (2006). Maternal variations in stress reactivity: Implications for harsh parenting practices with very young children. *Journal of Family Psychology, 20–4*, 641–647.

Masten, A. S. (2001). Ordinary magic: Resilience processes in development. *The American Psychologist, 56*(3), 227–238. doi:10.1037/0003-066X.56.3.227.

Masten, A. S., & Coatsworth, J. D. (1998). The development of competence in favorable and unfavorable environments: Lessons from research on successful children. *The American Psychologist, 53*, 205–220.

Maughan, A., & Cicchetti, D. (2002). Impact of child maltreatment and interadult violence on children's emotion regulation abilities and socioemotional adjustment. *Child Development, 73*(5), 1525–1542. doi:10.1111/1467-8624.00488.

McEwen, B. (2000). Allostasis and allostatic load: Implications for neuro-psychopharmacology. *Neuropsychopharmacology, 22*, 108–124.

McEwen, B., & Stellar, E. (1993). Stress and the individual mechanisms leading to disease. *Journal of the American Medical Association, Archives of Internal Medicine, 153*, 2093–2101.

McLeod, B. D., Wood, J. J., & Weisz, J. R. (2007a). Examining the association between parenting and childhood anxiety: A meta-analysis. *Clinical Psychology Review, 27*, 155–172. doi:10.1016/j.cpr.2006.09.002.

McLeod, B. D., Weisz, J. R., & Wood, J. J. (2007b). Examining the association between parenting and childhood depression: A meta-analysis. *Clinical Psychology Review, 27*, 986–1003. doi:10.1016/j.cpr.2007.03.001.

Mersky, J. P., & Reynolds, A. J. (2007). Child maltreatment and violent delinquency: Disentangling main effects and subgroup effects. *Child Maltreatment, 12*(3), 246–258.

Michalopoulos, C., Duggan, A., Knox, V., Filene, J., Lundquist, E., Snell, E., et al. (2011). ACF- OPRE report 2011-16. *Design options for the home visiting evaluation: Draft final report*. Washington, DC: U.S. Department of Health and Human Services.

Morawska, A., & Sanders, M. R. (2006). Self-administered behavioral family intervention for parents of toddlers: Part I – efficacy. *Journal of Clinical and Consulting Psychology, 74*, 10–19. doi:10.1037/0022-006X.74.1.10.

Nemeroff, C. (2004). Neurobiological consequences of childhood trauma. *The Journal of Clinical Psychiatry, 65*, 18–28.

Patterson, G. R. (1982). *Coercive family process*. Eugene: Castilia.

Perlman, S. B., Kalish, C. W., & Pollak, S. D. (2008). The role of maltreatment experience in children's understanding of the antecedents of emotion. *Cognition and Emotion, 22*(4), 651–670. doi:10.1080/02699930701461154.

Plant, K. M., & Sanders, M. R. (2007). Reducing problem behavior during care-giving in families of preschool-aged children with developmental disabilities. *Research in Developmental Disabilities, 28*, 362–385. doi:10.1016/j.ridd.2006.02.009.

Pollak, S., Cicchetti, D., Hornung, K., & Reed, A. (2000). Recognizing emotion in faces: The developmental effects of child abuse and neglect. *Developmental Psychology, 36*, 679–688.

Pollak, S., Messner, M., Kistler, D., & Cohn, J. (2009). Development of perceptual expertise in emotion recognition. *Cognition, 110*, 242–247.

Prinz, R. J., Sanders, M. R., Shapiro, C. J., Whitaker, D. J., & Lutzker, J. R. (2009). Population-based prevention of child maltreatment: The U.S. Triple P System population trial. *Prevention Science, 10*(1), 1–12. doi:10.1007/s11121-009-0123-3.

Proctor, E. K., Landsverk, J., Aarons, G., Chambers, D., Glisson, C., & Mittman, B. (2009). Implementation research in mental health services: An emerging science with conceptual, methodological, and training challenges. *Administration and Policy in Mental Health and Mental Health Services Research, 36*, 24–34.

Rathus, J. H., & Miller, A. L. (2002). Dialectial behavior therapy adapted for suicidal adolescents. *Suicide & Life-Threatening Behavior, 32*(2), 146–157.

Robin, A. L., Bedway, M., & Gilroy, M. (1994). Problem solving communication training. In C. W. LeCroy (Ed.), *Handbook of child and adolescent treatment manuals* (pp. 92–125). New York: Lexington Books.

Sameroff, A. J., & Chandler, M. J. (1975). Reproductive risk and the continuum of caretaking casualty. In F. D. Horowitz, M. Hetherington, S. Scarr-Salapatek, & G. Siegal (Eds.), *Review of child development research* (Vol. 4, p. 1870244). Chicago: University of Chicago Press.

Sanchez, M. M., McCormack, K., Grand, A. P., Fulks, R., Graff, A., & Maestripieri, D. (2010). Effects of sex and early maternal abuse on adrenocorticotropin hormone and cortisol responses to the corticotrophin-releasing hormone challenge during the first 3 years of life in group-living rhesus monkeys. *Development and Psychopathology, 22*, 45–53.

Sanders, M. R. (1999). Triple P-positive parenting program: Towards an empirically validated multilevel parenting and family support strategy for the prevention of behavior and emotional problems in children. *Clinical Child and Family Psychology Review, 2*(2), 71–90. doi:10.1023/A:1021843613840.

Sanders, M. R., Ralph, A., Sofronoff, K., Gardiner, P., Thompson, R., Dwyer, S., et al. (2008). Every family: A population approach to reducing behavioral and emotional problems in children making the transition to school. *Journal of Primary Prevention, 29*(3), 197–222. doi:10.1007/s10935-008-0139-7.

Schechter, W., & Willheim, E. (2009). Disturbances of attachment and parental psychopathology in early childhood. *Child and Adolescent Psychiatric Clinics of North America, 18*(3), 665–686.

Simpson, D. D. (2002). A conceptual framework for transferring research to practice. *Journal of Substance Abuse Treatment, 22*, 171–182.

Sroufe, L. A. (2005). Attachment and development: A prospective study from birth to adulthood. *Attachment & Human Development, 7*(4), 349–367.

Steinfeld, B. I., Coffman, S. J., & Keyes, J. A. (2009). Implementation of an evidence-based practice in a clinical setting: What happens when you get there? *Professional Psychology: Research and Practice, 40*(4), 410–416.

Substance Abuse and Mental Health Services Administration [SAMHSA]. (2010). SAMHSA's national registry of evidence-based programs and practices. Website: http://www.nrepp.samhsa.gov/

Swenson, C. C., Schaeffer, C. M., Henggeler, S. W., Faldowski, R., & Mayhew, A. (2010). Multisystemic therapy for child abuse and neglect: A randomized effectiveness trial. *Journal of Family Psychology, 24*, 497–507.

Tarullo, A., & Gunnar, M. (2006). Child maltreatment and the developing HPA axis. *Hormones and Behavior, 50*(4), 632–639.

Timmer, S., Urquiza, A. J., Zebell, N., & McGrath, J. (2005). Parent-child interaction therapy: Application to physically abusive and high-risk parent-child dyads. *Child Abuse & Neglect, 29*(7), 825–842.

Timmer, S. G., Ware, L., & Urquiza, A. (2010). The effectiveness of parent–child interaction therapy for victims of interparental violence. *Violence Against Women, 25*(4), 486–503.

Toth, S. L., Rogosch, F. A., Manly, J. T., & Cicchetti, D. (2006). The efficacy of toddler-parent psychotherapy to reorganize attachment in the young offspring of mothers with major depressive disorder: A randomized preventive trial. *Journal of Consulting and Clinical Psychology, 74*(6), 1006–1016.

Tuten, M., Jones, H. E., Schaeffer, C. M., Wong, C. J., & Stitzer, M. L. (2012). *Reinforcement-based treatment (RBT): A practical guide for the behavioral treatment of drug addiction*. Washington, DC: American Psychological Association.

U. S. Department of Health & Human Services (USDHHS), Administration for Children, Youth and Families, Children's Bureau. (2011). Child maltreatment 2010. Available from http://www.acf.hhs.gov/programs/cb/stats_research/index.htm#can

Van Ijzendoorn, M., Bakermans-Kranenburg, M., & Juffer, F. (2007). Plasticity of growth in height, weight, and head circumference: Meta-analytic evidence of massive catch-up after international adoption. *Journal of Developmental and Behavioral Pediatrics, 28*(4), 334–343.

Webster-Stratton, C. (2012a). *The Incredible Years parents, teachers, and children's training series: Program content, methods, research and dissemination 1980–2011*. Seattle: Incredible Years.

Webster-Stratton, C. (2012b). *Blueprints for violence prevention* (Book Eleven: The incredible years – Parent, teacher, and child training series). Seattle: Incredible Years.

Weisz, J., Miranda, J., Hoagwood, K., Schoenwald, S., Chorpita, B., & Glisson, C. (2012). From lab to clinic: Expanding evidence-based practice in child mental health. http://www.macfound.org/press/info-sheets/network-youth-mental-health-care-information-sheet/

Werner, E. E. (1989). High-risk children in young adulthood: A longitudinal study from birth to 32 years. *The American Journal of Orthopsychiatry, 59*(1), 72–81.

Zeanah, C., Smyke, A., Koga, S., & Carlson, E. (2005). Attachment in institutionalized and community children in Romania. *Child Development, 76*(5), 1015–1028.

Zhang, L. X., Levine, S., Dent, G., Zhan, Y., Xing, G., Okimoto, D., et al. (2002). Maternal deprivation increases cell death in the infant rat brain. *Brain Research: Developmental Brain Research, 133*, 1–111.

Chapter 20
Psychosocial Consequences and Treatments for Maltreated Children

Monica M. Fitzgerald and Lucy Berliner

Introduction

It is encouraging that child abuse rates are gradually declining in the U.S., but a staggering number of youth are still maltreated each year and experience traumatic events in their childhood (Finkelhor and Jones 2004; Finkelhor et al. 2009). In 2011, an estimated 3.4 million child abuse referrals were received by child protective services (CPS) agencies concerning 6.2 million children, and an estimate of 681,000 cases of child abuse and neglect were substantiated and/or indicated in 50 states (National Child Abuse and Neglect Data System [NCANDS] 2011; U.S. Department of Health and Human Services 2010). Similar to prior years, the greatest percentage of children (78 %) suffered from neglect, 18 % suffered physical abuse, and 9 % suffered sexual abuse, with many of these children experiencing multiple forms of maltreatment (NCANDS 2011). Epidemiological and clinical research also confirms the high prevalence of trauma and abuse experiences occurring in childhood in the general population. For example, in a large national survey by Copeland and colleagues (2007), over 65 % of American children reported experiencing at least one potentially traumatic event before adulthood including child abuse, family violence, assault, accidents, robbery, or sudden death of a loved one (Copeland et al. 2007; McLaughlin et al. 2012). Trauma and abuse experiences are even more common in clinical samples, and children involved with the child welfare system are a particularly vulnerable population with many mental health needs (Finkelhor et al. 2009; Casanueva et al. 2012; Leslie et al. 2004).

It is well known that child abuse and neglect (CAN) and trauma exposure typically occurs within a child's immediate environment (i.e., home, neighborhood, or school) and childhood interpersonal trauma is most often perpetrated by acquaintances and family members (Hamby et al. 2005; Kilpatrick et al. 2003; U.S. Department of Health and Human Services 2010). Youth typically experience more than one type of victimization and/or traumatic experiences that occur on multiple occasions, rather than a single episode (Copeland et al. 2007; Hamby et al. 2005; Stevens et al. 2005; Finkelhor et al.

M.M. Fitzgerald, Ph.D. (✉)
Kempe Center for the Prevention and Treatment of Child Abuse and Neglect, University of Colorado, School of Medicine, Anschutz Medical Campus, 13123 E. 16th Ave B390, Aurora, CO 80045, USA

Department of Pediatrics, SOM, The Gary Pavilion, The Children's Hospital, Anschutz Medical Campus, 13123 E. 16th Ave B390, Aurora, CO 80045, USA
e-mail: monica.fitzgerald@ucdenver.edu

L. Berliner
Harborview Center for Sexual Assault & Traumatic Stress, University of Washington, 401 Broadway, Suite 2075, 325 Ninth Avenue, MS 359947, Seattle, WA 98104, USA
e-mail: lucyb@u.washington.edu

J.E. Korbin and R.D. Krugman (eds.), *Handbook of Child Maltreatment*, Child Maltreatment 2, DOI 10.1007/978-94-007-7208-3_20, © Springer Science+Business Media Dordrecht 2014

2009; NCANDS 2011; Turner 2010). While we have important prevalence estimates, it is hard to gain an accurate scope of impact of abuse and trauma, given that we also know that many youth delay in disclosing or never disclose victimizations and abuse experiences after they occur (Ruggiero et al. 2004). This is understandable given that children's disclosures are influenced by threats or fear of retribution by the perpetrator, being blamed or punished, fear of consequences to the family, psychological distress about the event(s), sense of stigma or shame, lack of encouragement to disclose or speak honestly, and history of negative outcomes from prior disclosures.

The Impact of Abuse and Trauma in Childhood and Adulthood

Decades of research shows that child abuse and early trauma can result in significant developmental disruptions, short-term and long-term mental and physical health problems (Felitti et al. 1998; Pynoos et al. 2006), and increased involvement in child welfare and juvenile justice systems (Ford et al. 2007). A significant proportion of children who experience abuse or other trauma develop posttraumatic stress disorder (PTSD) and also experience co-morbid problems such as depression, anxiety disorders, substance use, and externalizing behavior problems (Copeland et al. 2007). Further, children affected by child abuse and trauma tend to have more cognitive deficits and academic challenges including learning and attention problems, decreased IQ and reading ability, lower grade point average, higher absenteeism, and decreased high school graduation rates (Beers and De Bellis 2002; Delany-Black et al. 2002; Hurt et al. 2001; Grogger 1997).

The specific condition associated with trauma exposure is Post-Traumatic Stress Disorder (PTSD), characterized by symptoms of *re-experiencing*, *avoidance*, and *hyper-arousal* (American Psychiatric Association [APA] 2000). PTSD *re-experiencing symptoms* include frightening or otherwise distressing memories, including thoughts or dreams of the traumatic event as well as frightening thoughts or dreams that may seem unrelated to the specific event. Children may also exhibit behaviors that suggest traumatic re-experiencing or "re-enactment." For example, a child who was sexually abused may exhibit sexually inappropriate behaviors, or a child who experiences physical abuse or bullying may become aggressive towards others. These memories and fears may interfere with the child's focus on schoolwork, social interactions, or home life. At other times, the child may seem perfectly normal. PTSD *avoidance symptoms* are characterized by attempts to avoid memories, images, thoughts, discussions, people, places, or things that remind him/her of their traumatic experience(s). Avoidance can also be manifested by emotional numbing, social withdrawal, and not wanting to engage in usual activities such as school, sports, or being with friends. PTSD *hyperarousal* symptoms include sleep difficulties, increased anger, physical symptoms, and increased jumpiness. Youth may have new fears, show more difficulty with anger, be more irritable, moody, bored, inattentive, or seem to 'go from 0 to 60' in terms of escalating emotional and behavioral outbursts. With emotional or behavioral dysregulation, or maladaptive cognitions, the child may have trouble modulating thoughts, feelings, and/or behaviors, especially when reminded of the trauma.

It is important to remember that manifestation of trauma symptoms is idiosyncratic to the individual child and situation; the manner in which children show their distress can vary by age and developmental level. The type and severity of problems varies greatly among abused children. The nature of the abuse experiences, prior psychological and abuse history, and family characteristics and functioning contribute to child outcomes (Kearney et al. 2010). For example, there are some group differences in the types of emotional or behavioral problems with sexually abused children having higher rates of posttraumatic stress and depression, and physically abused children being more likely to exhibit disruptive behavior and social competence problems (Burns et al. 2004).

The effects of childhood trauma can continue into adulthood. Child abuse is a risk factor for psychiatric disorders, antisocial behavior, health problems, relationship impairments, and reduced economic success (Currie and Widom 2010). Wegman and Stetler's (2009) meta-analysis found that childhood abuse is associated with increased risk of a wide range of medical problems, and Chen and colleagues' (2010) meta-analysis of the effects of sexual abuse across 37 longitudinal observational studies, with more than three million participants, found that sexual abuse increased the odds of being diagnosed with mental health problems such as anxiety, depression, and PTSD, as well eating disorders, sleep disorders, and suicide attempts by double, triple, or sometimes more. Weich and colleagues (2009) conducted a systematic review of prospective studies that measured aspects of family relationships in childhood and then followed the participants and evaluated psychiatric disorders in adulthood; childhood abuse was consistently related to adult psychiatric issues such as PTSD and depression. Hovens and colleagues (2010) also found that childhood trauma increases adults' risk of depression and anxiety.

Children in the Child Welfare System

Numerous studies have documented that children involved in the child welfare system have significant rates of mental health and behavioral problems (Leslie et al. 2005). Horwitz and colleagues (2012) report an average of one fourth of children 2–18 years old have clinical levels of emotional and behavioral problems, with older children having higher rates. Almost one third had moderate to severe problems in daily living skills, with close to half having poor socialization skills. The presence of emotional and behavioral problems has consequences for the course of the child welfare cases. Children with behavior problems are more likely to have placement disruptions and less likely to be successfully reunified (James et al. 2004; Landsverk et al. 1996).

Children in the child welfare system (CWS) have some advantages in accessing services compared to other children in need. First, they are usually eligible to for Medicaid supported mental health services; all foster children are automatically and immediately eligible. Medicaid provides relatively generous coverage, often without the limits on visits or inpatient days that are common in commercial insurance. Another is that professionals are involved in their family life and are in a position to identify unmet behavioral health need and facilitate connection to services. In addition to safety and permanency, a goal of the CWS is to promote child wellbeing by insuring that they receive the needed services for recovery for the effects of child maltreatment.

Although children in the child welfare system are more likely to access services compared to children in the general population, there is still a significant gap between need and services receipt. Less than half of younger children and only about 70 % of older children with need received services. Children in foster care are the most likely to be served (Landsverk et al. 2009; Horwitz et al. 2012). In addition, when services are provided to CW-involved youth, the majority of children do not receive high-quality, effective mental health treatment that is matched to their specific needs (Landsverk et al. 2009; Chadwick Center for Children and Families 2004; Stahmer et al. 2005).

It is important to be aware that not all children who have been exposed to trauma and abuse develop persisting mental health problems that require formal treatment (Bonanno 2004; Bonanno et al. 2010, 2011; Copeland et al. 2007; Masten 2001). However, involvement in the child welfare system creates the opportunity for systematically identifying those children who have need and facilitating access to mental health or other needed services.

Intervention Approaches for Children and Families Affected by Child Maltreatment and Trauma

Fortunately, highly effective services do exist for children and adolescents who have experienced abuse and trauma and many of the mental health interventions have been found to be relevant and helpful for children with complex abuse histories and trauma and children in the child welfare system. It is important to recognize that formal mental health therapy is only one of the services that may be necessary for abused children; they may need medical evaluation and assistance to address children's immediate physical well-being, advocacy and legal services to help families navigate the overwhelming and complicated legal process, psychological evaluation and mental health treatment, and educational interventions. Children's Advocacy centers (National Alliance) are intended to serve this broader array of service need.

This chapter first briefly describes the importance of evidence-based psychosocial assessment to guide treatment selection and monitor treatment progress, and then describes the primary psychosocial treatment approaches that are effective for main problems of maltreated children and their families. Therapy does not treat abuse per se, but rather addresses the consequences of abuse in a particular child and family. Since the impact may vary among children and families, determining the specific impacts is a necessary first step to deciding on the proper treatment regimen. There are well-established interventions for the primary target problems that abused children have, and treatments have been found to work with children in the child welfare system even though they often have complex histories and compromised psychosocial circumstances.

There are web-based resources for learning about effective interventions and detailed descriptions of each treatment's research outcomes and readiness for dissemination. The most well known include the *California Evidence-Based Clearinghouse for Child Welfare* (CEBC, www.cebc4cw.org) and the *National Registry of Evidenced-Based Programs and Practices* (NREPP, http://nrepp.samhsa.gov). In particular, the CEBC website provides child welfare professionals a forum where information and research data regarding EBPs relevant to child welfare is available. The National Child Traumatic Stress Network (NCTSN, http://www.nctsn.org/) is a specific resource for trauma-focused interventions.

Responding to the Impact of Child Maltreatment and Trauma

The clinical conditions presented by children affected by child maltreatment and trauma generally fall into two categories: internalizing problems (e.g., anxiety, posttraumatic stress, depression) and externalizing problems (e.g., disobedience, defiance, aggression, rule breaking). Although many children have both internalizing and externalizing conditions, the overall treatment approaches have important differences that are relevant for service planning. For internalizing problems, effective treatments focus on teaching the children to recognize and manage or overcome intense negative feelings, learn and use behavioral skills, and assist caregivers to support the children in using coping strategies. Effective treatments for externalizing problems primarily focus on caregivers to help them enhance positive relationships with their children and change the environmental contingencies to reward and maintain positive behaviors. When caregiver responses to children change, behavior problems are reduced. With younger children, often only caregivers need to be involved in therapy, whereas for older children it is often helpful that they participate in the therapy and learn new skills as well. Because co-morbidity is not uncommon, there are interventions that teach children skills to manage negative feelings and achieve personal or social goals, as well as teach caregivers how to promote positive behaviors and manage negative behaviors.

Treatments for the Impacts of Child Maltreatment

An "Evidence-Based" Era. One of the major movements that has taken place with regard to mental health treatments in the past two decades is the advent of evidence-based treatments (EBT) as the recommended standard of care. EBTs are intervention programs that have been shown to have overall better results compared to non-specific or alternative interventions. Interventions may have varying levels of evidence and it may be useful to consider "evidence-based" from a dimensional continuum versus a categorical perspective (see Weisz and Kazdin 2010). The broader term "evidence-based practice (EBP)" is often used in the field and can be defined as treatment interventions, services, and supports that have consistently shown positive outcomes for children and families through research studies. The Institute of Medicine's (2001) definition of EBP follows: "Evidence-based practice is the integration of best research evidence with clinical expertise and patient values". Taken together, EBP represents both a set of principles that are applied to interventions and specific individual interventions, both of which are important in effectively addressing emotional and behavioral problems. EBP characteristics are structured, focused, and goal-oriented; skill teaching oriented; and, incorporate measurement to monitor treatment progress.

The proven interventions for the most common clinical problems among child abuse victims share common characteristics. They are brief, highly structured, and focus primarily on teaching children and/or parents skills to help them think, feel, and behave in more constructive ways, especially when experiencing stressful circumstances. Although the specific content found in a given treatment guide may vary, the clinician generally models and rehearses the new skills with children and parents in session, and gives homework to practice the new skills in real life.

Routine Screening and Assessment. As described, children who experience maltreatment and traumatic events, often, but not always, have clinically significant emotional or behavioral problems that would benefit from evidence-based treatment. One key method for insuring that children with need are connected to services is routine screening and/or assessment of children the child welfare system. There are a variety of standardized measures that are free, reliable and valid, and brief that could be used to identify children in need (e.g., Pediatric Symptom Checklist 17 [PSC-17]) (Gardner et al. 2007). For example, Washington State has implemented routine screening for all children in foster care more than 30 days with a requirement that children who score positive must be referred for mental health services (Dorsey et al. 2012). Almost all children in care receive this screening, the results of which are made available to the caseworker. Many states have versions of routine screening and assessment with in child welfare.

Screening can provide important information for selection of the right evidence-based treatment and create a baseline for assessing achievement of service plan objectives. EBPs are specific in the clinical target for which they have been shown to work; different kinds of problems respond to different approaches. A standardized measure or an assessment process can inform the referral process. Dorsey and colleagues (2012) trained caseworkers in the basic principles of EBP and provided telephone case consultation. They learn the key differences between treatments for internalizing versus externalizing problems and the critical importance of caregiver involvement for externalizing behaviors. Results found that therapists improved in their knowledge of EBPs; there was a trend for an increase in referrals for EBPs. Enhancing caseworker knowledge and skills to broker more effectively for EBPs using the results of standardized screening methods may increase access to services. Currently, there is a pilot project currently underway in Colorado that is implementing and evaluating this caseworker training and consultation model with an added trauma-focused component with caseworkers in child welfare agencies in Colorado (personal correspondence, Fitzgerald 2013).

Once children enter a mental health system, standardized assessment can add to the usual clinical assessment process. Standardized measurement is especially important in evidence-abased practice because EBPs treat to the clinical target (Van Eys and Truss 2011). Evidence-based trauma screening and assessment is essential for quality case formulation and targeted treatment planning for abuse and trauma exposed children and a core component of best practice (Saunders 2011). The results inform the type of treatment program that is matched to the identified clinical need. Effective assessment is not limited to a one-time event, but instead it is an on-going process used to understand and prioritize children's mental health needs, select appropriate evidence-based treatment, and assess clients' treatment progress. There are numerous standardized measures available for the full array of emotional and behavioral problems that children may have. Many are proprietary and must be purchased, but there are a number that are reliable and valid and free. For example, the Strengths and Difficulties Questionnaire (SDQ) is available in many languages and includes youth self-report, parent report and teacher report versions (Goodman 1997). There are measures for PTSD (CPSS; Foa et al. 2001), depression (MFQ, Angold et al. 1995; PHQ; Kroenke and Spitzer 2002), anxiety (SCARED; Birmaher et al. 1997) and overall behavior problems (PSC-17; Gardner et al. 2007); these conditions encompass about 80 % of children in public mental health settings). Administering measures and discussing results with children and families enhances engagement and focus in the therapy process.

The other value of standardized assessment is to track progress over time in therapy. Brief and free measures can be administered at very regular intervals with very low burden to providers and clients. Bickman and colleagues (2011) found that when clients completed a standardized assessment of symptoms and functioning every other week and the results were reported back to the clinicians, they improved faster than clients whose providers did not receive routine feedback. In addition, the effects of the feedback were greater when clinicians had more frequent feedback.

Standardized assessment of children in the child welfare system has many advantages. It identifies children with clinical need. It provides caseworkers with key information about the type of emotional and behavioral problems, which enhances the ability of caseworkers to be effective brokers. Standardized assessment at the mental health setting identifies the clinical target so the treatment can be matched to the problem and establishes the baseline level of the emotional or behavioral problems. Repeated assessment with a standardized measure with feedback to the clinician increases the efficiency of treatment. Feedback can also assist therapists in paying closer attention to cases where children are not improving and seeking consultation on adjusting or changing the treatment plan.

Evidence-Based Mental Health Interventions. Mental health interventions for the primary targets of externalizing and internalizing problems will be described: treatments for (1) *Child Behavior Problems* (e.g., child oppositionality, defiance, aggression) *Parenting Behaviors* (e.g., emotionally and physically harsh, coercive, abusive, and/or neglectful), and (2) *Child Psychological Distress* (i.e., posttraumatic stress, anxiety and depression). In some cases all of these targeted may be addressed by a single intervention, whereas in other cases separate interventions may be necessary. Determining the priority target and intervention approach is based on a systematic abuse focused assessment process described above.

Treating Child Behavior Problems and Parenting Behaviors. Many effective interventions exist for externalizing child behavior problems. All of these interventions are versions of behavioral parent training (BPT) or parent management training (PMT), terms that are used indistinguishably. Patterson (1973), an early developer of a behavioral theory on the causes of behavior problems, proposed that they develop in the context of a coercive family process where parents are harsh and/or inconsistent. Negative behaviors arise because they serve a function for the child and they persist because the behaviors are reinforced, even if negatively. Contemporary theories recognize that child behaviors also contribute to parenting responses. Some children have more difficult temperaments that are more challenging for parents to manage; this can result in ineffective parenting that tends to inadvertently reinforce negative behaviors (Snyder et al. 2005). Once a pattern of negative, coercive interactions exists, behavior becomes increasingly unpleasant which in turn leads to fewer positive and more negative or unhelpful parental responses, and these coercive parent-child reciprocities contribute to difficulties with emotion regulation (Scaramella and Level 2004). The most well established interventions for child behavior problems focus on these negative interactional patterns by teaching parents more effective and positive ways to respond to their children (Eyberg et al. 2008).

It is not surprising that many maltreated children have significant behavior problems. Child maltreatment at its core is a parenting problem. Parents have departed from the accepted standards of parenting by acts of omission such as failing to ensure that basic needs are met, protecting children from known harm, and providing proper supervision and acts of commission including emotionally, sexually or physically abusing them. The specific parenting problems frequently found in cases of child maltreatment are inconsistent, harsh, or physically abusive parenting and a lack of positive interactions. In addition, in many child abuse cases there is insecure attachment in the child, which is the result of inconsistent, unresponsive, emotionally coercive or abusive, or dangerous parental responses during very early childhood (Kolko and Swanson 2002).

Persistence of behavior problems in childhood, especially in the context of a severely compromised parent-child relationship or child maltreatment, has very serious implications. Children with behavior problems are at risk for impaired functioning at school and with peers and beginning a trajectory towards antisocial behavior. In the child maltreatment context the risk includes subsequent abuse, placement out of the home, delay in reunification, and failed adoption (Kolko et al. 2010). Therefore, effective parent-child interventions that target parenting and the parent-child relationship are central to child abuse interventions.

PMTs are all built on the same basic principles and contain similar components (Brestan and Eyberg 1998; Kaminski et al. 2008). Caregivers are actively involved in the treatment process; with younger children, only the parent may need to participate directly in the treatment. Treatment programs help parents increase positive parent-child experiences; use selective attention to reward positive behavior with praise or acknowledgement, while ignoring minor negative behaviors; and, learn skills to respond to misbehavior by managing contingencies in the environment. Typical strategies are time-out, rewards and consequence plans. The therapies are behaviorally focused and emphasize acquisition and application of new skills through practice in session and between sessions.

There are many brand name versions of these interventions. Among the best known and most well researched include Kazdin Parent Management Training (Kazdin 1997), Parenting Management Training-Oregon (Forgatch et al. 2005), Parent-Child Interaction Therapy (PCIT, http://pcit.phhp.ufl.edu/), Incredible Years (Webster-Stratton 1992), Helping the Non Complaint Child (McMahon and Forehand 2005), and Triple P (Sanders 2008). The programs are time-limited, usually involving 14–18 sessions. They can be delivered in the clinic, the home, at schools, or other community settings and are often available in individual and group versions.

While not originally developed for behavior problems in maltreated children, a number of these parenting interventions have been specifically shown to be effective with the population. One of the earliest studies was conducted by Wolfe and colleagues (1988). In a randomized trial, maltreating parents who received a behavioral parent-training program compared to an educational intervention had lower maltreatment risk and child behavior problems improved. Urquiza and McNeil (1996) published an article in *Child Maltreatment* making the case for PCIT as a child maltreatment intervention and PMTs in child maltreatment began to spread. Although parenting classes had long been a staple of child maltreatment service plans, these classes were primarily didactic and did not involve teaching skills and were not conceptualized as an intervention for child behavior problems. What was appealing about PCIT as a maltreatment intervention was that in addition to addressing behavior problems in the children, it focused on enhancing the warmth and closeness in the parent-child relationship as a means of reducing future risk. PCIT is now a well- established intervention that has been used extensively in child maltreatment situations (Timmer et al. 2005; Chaffin et al. 2011) and has specific evidence for its effectiveness in reducing subsequent child maltreatment reports (Chaffin et al. 2004, 2011). PCIT has a unique delivery vehicle in that parents receive live coaching via a bug in the ear to practice their new skills. It is designed for younger children, although it is effective in reducing future child abuse reports for children up to 12 who do not have serious behavior problems.

It has now been shown that a variety of PMTs can be effective for behavior problems in maltreated children with their biological parents and foster parents including PCIT (Timmer et al. 2005, 2006), The Incredible Years (www.incredibleyears.com), and Parent Management Training-Oregon Model (PMTO, http://www.isii.net/index.html). PMTs not only address the children's behavior problems, but they are also effective for many of the other common concerns in child welfare situations including insecure attachment in children, parenting deficits, impaired parent-child bond, parenting stress, and anger toward the child (Horwitz et al. 2010).

Finally, these evidence-based programs also improve child welfare outcomes by reducing reabuse, rereferral and placement disruption. KEEP (Price et al. 2009), a group based PMT for foster parents and kinship caregivers, is more effective in reducing placement disruption as well as child behavior problems compared to usual foster care training. PCIT, a fully parent-mediated intervention for younger children reduces the risk of future child abuse when combined with a motivational enhancement component (Chaffin et al. 2004, 2011).

Some parent management interventions include parent, child, and parent-child components to address both individual skills deficits and relationship or interactional problems (Kolko et al. 2010). *Alternatives for Families Cognitive Behavioral Therapy* (AF-CBT, www.afcbt.org) is an intervention for physically abusive parents and children ages 5–15 years. Because there has been violence in the relationship, safety planning and routine assessment of the use of force, hostility and coercion are incorporated. It includes the standard CBT components of psychoeducation including information about violence, teaching both children and parents skills for emotional regulation especially anger, teaching positive parenting, and teaching both parents and children useful skills such as problem solving and communication. A unique component is the clarification process in which the parents explicitly take responsibility for the abuse and make amends to the child for the abuse. AF-CBT has shown to improve family functioning and reduce child-to-parent aggression, child behavior problems, parental abuse risk, and re-abuse among physically abusive parents (see Kolko 1996a, b; Kolko et al. 2011). A group version called *Combined Parent-Child Cognitive Behavioral Therapy* (CPC-CBT, http://www.caresinstitute.org/services_parent-child.php) has also been tested for physically abusive parents and at-risk parents (Runyon et al. 2010). In this model, the children and parents meet in separate groups initially and then later conjointly. This intervention also includes the children doing a trauma narrative as part of the clarification process. It has been shown to decrease posttraumatic stress as well improve behavior problems and reduce later violence and physical abuse (Runyon et al. 2010).

There are several effective child type interventions for youth with very serious behavior problems. Multisystemic Therapy for Childhood Abuse and Neglect (MST-CAN), multi-component intervention for physically abusive families addresses parenting, child skills, and environmental changes (Swenson et al. 2010). It is a structured package of specific strategies based on a functional analysis of the child abuse behavior. Some of the intervention strategies involve environmental interventions (e.g., school, separation from deviant peers), whereas others are based on CBT and parent management training principles. It has been found to maintain the youth in the community, improve their functioning and decrease rereferral to the child welfare system. MST-CAN has been shown to be effective in reducing behavior problems, improving child functioning and reducing future child abuse reports (http://www.mstcan.com/).

Multidimensional Treatment Foster Care-Adolescent. (MTFC-A; www.mtfc.com) and the young child version *Multidimensional Treatment Foster Care-Preschool* (MTFC-P) are intensive parent management interventions for severely disturbed children and adolescents who require out of home placement due to behavior problems and/or severe delinquency (Fisher et al. 2009). The foster parent serves as the therapeutic agent and is supported by a consultant who helps develop the behavior management plan and provides support and consultation carrying out the plan as well as additional therapies that may be needed. This intervention has been proven effective reducing outcomes such as runaways, criminal referrals, self-reported criminal acts, and fewer days in locked settings and associations with delinquent peers. Youth that would have ordinarily been sent to residential treatment are typically able to step down to regular foster care within 4–6 months.

There are three tested interventions for young children that are primarily based on attachment theory and use a more reflective and interpretive approach than parent management training. *Child Parent Psychotherapy* (CPP) was developed for situations in which young children (ages 0–5) were exposed to domestic violence (Lieberman et al. 2005). CPP emphasizes the importance of treating mental health problems within the context of the parent-child relationship to enhance parental responsiveness, attunement and consistency to their children. The trauma experience is directly addressed and processed jointly. *Attachment and Bio-behavioral Catch-up* (ABC) takes a similar approach to promoting secure attachment and nurturance via increasing parental or caregiver responsiveness in physically neglectful families with young children (ages 0–5), and also has a component increasing children's regulatory capabilities (Bernard et al. 2012; Dozier et al. 2005). *Promoting First Relationships* is another infant mental health intervention that focuses on enhancing parental attunement and responsiveness that has been specifically tested with child welfare sample (Spieker et al. 2012). All have growing evidence supporting their effectiveness.

Sexual behavior problems are a particularly troubling type of misbehavior in abused children. Although the risk for sexual behavior problems is increased in sexually abused, children, most sexually abused children do not develop sexual behavior problems. Regardless of the cause, sexual behaviors in children produce strong reaction that are often unhelpful, counterproductive and actually harmful to the children (Chaffin et al. 2008). In the child welfare system, the presence of sexual behavior problems can make it difficult to place children and lead to unnecessary placement in residential settings. This is in contrast to the evidence showing that a brief CBT intervention is highly successful in addressing the behaviors (Carpentier et al. 2006). A 10 year follow up showed that the children receiving CBT had a 2 % recidivism rate which compared favorably to children seen for nonsexual behavior problems.

In sum, a single behavioral parent management intervention or parent-child cognitive behavioral intervention can not only improve child behavior problems that are the result of child maltreatment, but as well can address a myriad of other child maltreatment concerns including parent deficits, disrupted bonding, placement disruption, reabuse and rereferral. These interventions go to the heart of the matter for child maltreatment which is parenting and the parent-child relationship. In a majority of cases, an evidence-based parenting program should be the primary service intervention; in some cases it may be the only one that is necessary.

Child Psychological Distress: Posttraumatic Stress, Anxiety, and Depression

Posttraumatic-Stress or PTSD. The most specific psychological impact of sexual or physical abuse is clinical posttraumatic stress (PTS) or PTSD. As previously described, PTSD is persistent high levels of distress connected to memories or reminders of the abuse experiences accompanied by actively avoiding reminders or shutting down emotionally, and excessive arousal related reactions. These symptoms include jumpiness, irritability, and concentration and sleep problems. In addition, children who have PTSD typically have maladaptive beliefs about the trauma, why it happened, why it happened to them and what it means about them. Children may blame themselves, have shame, and see the world as very dangerous and other people as untrustworthy (Kolko et al. 2002).

Trauma-focused Cognitive Behavioral Therapy (TF-CBT) (Cohen 2006a, b) and other trauma-focused CBTs have been found to be very effective and cost beneficial (Cisler et al. 2012; Washington State Institute for Public Policy [WSIPP] 2012). When children are co-morbid for depression, anxiety or moderate behavior problems, these conditions improve as well with TF-CBT. TF-CBT is a short-term (12–16 sessions) cognitive-behavioral intervention used to treat children and adolescents ages 3–18 years who are impacted by childhood PTSD and co-occurring mental health and behavioral problems resulting from trauma exposure. TF-CBT was originally developed and tested with sexually abused children, but has now been demonstrated to work with children affected by the full range of trauma experiences, including child abuse, witnessing domestic violence or community violence, rape and crime, natural disasters, and accidents. Cohen and colleagues (2011) showed that TF-CBT was more effective in reducing PTS in children exposed to DV, most of whom still had contact with or lived with the offender, compared with the usual care domestic violence program therapy program. It also works for children from preschool to adulthood, from a variety of backgrounds and ethnicities, for children in foster care, and for what is called "complex trauma." A preschool version in which the parents are involved in all aspects of the treatment is demonstrated to be effective (Scheeringa and Haslett 2010).

As a CBT intervention, TF-CBT involves psychoeducation about trauma and its impact and how the therapy works; teaching a variety of skills to identify and cope with negative emotions; exposure and cognitive processing of the trauma experiences which is called the Trauma Narrative, sharing the Trauma Narrative with a caregiver, and learning new skills (Cohen et al. 2006a). The evidence shows that TF-CBT has sustained effects over time (Mannarino et al. 2012). The developers have published articles and books describing how TF-CBT can be adjusted for various situations including children living in situations of ongoing traumas (Cohen et al. 2011), children who have experienced complex traumas (Cohen et al. 2012) and children in foster care (Dorsey and Deblinger 2012).

TF-CBT as originally developed and tested is a child and parent intervention. About half the therapy time is spent with the children and half with the caregiver. During some stages of therapy the sessions involve both parents and children. An important component of TF-CBT is a parent management training component to teach parents skills to address trauma related behavior problems. While not intended for situations where child behavior problems are the primary presenting treatment concern, modifications to the delivery method can be made when parent or caregivers are very concerned about trauma-related disruptive behavior (Cohen et al. 2010).

Anxiety and Depression. Not all children develop clinically significant PTS, but they may have anxiety and depression as a consequence of child maltreatment. CBT is the first line treatment for anxiety in children and is one of the two main treatments for depression in youth (Labellarte et al. 1999; Weersing and Brent 2006). These CBT are brief, structured and focused like TF-CBT and address contain the same basic components: psychoeducation about depression or anxiety and the treatment model, skills to manage difficult emotions, cognitive therapy to change unhelpful thoughts, and exposure for anxiety and activation for depression. While no studies have specially tested CBT for maltreated children with anxiety or depression, there is no reason to believe they would not be effective. It is also possible that the youth would benefit by the TF-CBT component of developing a helpful narrative for their maltreatment experiences even though they may not need exposure to the trauma memories per se.

In sum, when children have internalizing psychological consequences to child maltreatment experiences, TF-CBT or CBT for depression or anxiety are the preferred treatment approaches. Although only TF-CBT has been widely tested with abused children, it seems likely as in the case of proven PMTs extending the proven treatments for the psychological condition to maltreated children will be effective. The advantage is that these treatments are brief and skill-oriented and should produce results in relatively short periods of time. There is no empirical support for the idea that children with PTSD, anxiety or depression require long-term therapy for these conditions.

Mobilizing Brokers of Services for Children Affected by Child Maltreatment: Evidence-Based Service Planning

Child welfare researchers and policy makers have called for increased access to EBPs for CW-involved youth and families (Chaffin and Friedrich 2004; Kerker and Dore 2006). Professionals in child-service settings such as caseworkers, advocates, and guardian ad litems in the Child Welfare System (CWS) are often familiar with the array of social support services available within their communities and facilitate access to the services for which families are eligible. Thus these professionals play a critical role as "brokers" or "gateway providers" and are well positioned to link youth and their families with services (Stiffman et al. 2004). Just as clinicians have a responsibility to be reasonably familiar, knowledgeable, and skilled in delivering EBTs to children and families who need them, service "brokers" such as caseworkers in the CWS have the responsibility to (a) identify emotional and behavioral problems, including trauma-related mental health difficulties that require intervention (i.e., identify youth in need of mental health services), (b) be knowledgeable about EBTs for mental health problems common among CW-involved youth and families, (c) know how to access EBTs in their communities and ask questions to assess provider appropriateness for the mental health need, (d) refer and engage youth and families to appropriate EBPs targeted to their specific mental health needs, and finally, (e) monitor treatment outcome. However, within child welfare and among other potential brokers, research has demonstrated low recognition of mental health needs, few targeted referrals, and limited monitoring of treatment outcomes for youth in the child welfare system (Burns et al. 1995). This is, in large part, due to the recent advancement in EBTs appropriate for children in the child welfare system and to a lack of training provided to caseworkers in skills critical to making effective linkages between CW-involved youth and EBTs. Unfortunately, these skills are rarely taught to caseworkers during their graduate school or professional training (Dorsey et al. 2012; Kerns et al. 2010; Rakovshik and McManus 2010; Rubin 2011; Thyer and Myers 2011), despite their incredible capacity to ensure that youth and families receive EBTs targeted to their specific mental health needs.

Connecting families with relevant services, and tracking their response and outcomes, is facilitated by taking an "evidence-based service planning" (EBSP) approach with families to optimally prescribe a service or set of services designed to benefit children and families (Chaffin et al. n.d.). EBSP service recommendations favor interventions proven effective for clinical problems or needs associated with the causes or consequences of CAN, and are constructed and carried out in a respectful and collaborative way with families. EBSP considers the evidence supporting individual interventions, as well as the number, focus, and intensity of the interventions selected, and reduces the conventional service planning approach which often requires "boiler plate" sets of services, versus individually tailored services to meet the case needs. EBPs and EBIs are an essential part of public child welfare's mission to work to keep families safe (and when possible intact) and enhancing permanence and family and child "well being" (Adoption and Safe Families Act of 1997 [Public Law 105–89]). Some progress is being made towards this objective (Kolko et al. 2010). Evidence-based service brokering is a model that shows great promise for increasing abused children's access to care that is matched to their problems and needs and more likely to be effective. Kerns and colleagues (2010) demonstrated that child welfare caseworkers responded favorably to training and case consultation on the basic principles of EBTs and particular packaged models that work for abused children.

Mental health problems may be only one element of a service plan, but, if done with principles of EBSP, will increase the likelihood of successful outcome across the three CWS goals. Evidence-Based Service Planning (EBSP) includes a few key elements. First, EBSP involves selecting interventions/services from the available scientific research literature that have the strongest evidence for *effectively and efficiently* achieving a specific desired goal – choosing services that are proven to work and produce change in the shortest time period possible. Second, EBSP involves *focus and parsimony* of services to reduce unnecessary burden and respect family autonomy. Finally, EBSP recommends *triaging and sequencing* services when necessary so that services with the highest priority and direct relationship to CAN are emphasized first and the plan begins with the least intensive service level necessary with evidence of achieving the desired goal.

EBSP approach provides a framework for conceptualizing service planning in light of emerging knowledge about the principles for effective service planning and the selection of evidence based services matched to particular case needs. In addition to improving outcomes, this framework addresses several key problems facing the CWS including costs, length of stay, placement disruption and delays in achieving permanency.

Conclusion

EBTs are interventions that have the demonstrated scientific and clinical support for their effectiveness. Effective treatments exist for abused children that address both the consequences of abuse and the causes of abuse and neglect. These EBTS can work for children and families of all backgrounds and with the full range of types of experiences. A single evidence-based intervention may be sufficient in many cases, not only to ameliorate the emotional and behavioral consequences of abuse, but also to reduce future abuse risk. Greater attention should be paid to increasing the availability of these interventions within the child welfare system and to proactive brokering for access to these interventions when they are available in a community.

References

Adoption and Safe Families Act (ASFA) of 1997 (PL 105-89, Nov. 19, 1997). (1997). United States Statutes at Large 105.

American Psychiatric Association. (2000). *Diagnostic and statistical manual of mental disorders* (Revised 4th ed.). Washington, DC: Author.

Angold, A., Prendergast, M., Cox, A., Harrington, R., Simonoff, E., & Rutter, M. (1995). The child and adolescent psychiatric assessment (CAPA). *Psychological Medicine, 25*, 739–753.

Beers, S. R., & De Bellis, M. D. (2002). Neuropsychological function in children with maltreatment-related posttraumatic stress disorder. *The American Journal of Psychiatry, 159*, 483–486.

Bernard, K., Dozier, M., Bick, J., Lewis-Morrarty, E., Lindheim, O., & Carlson, E. (2012). Enhancing attachment organization among maltreated children: Results of a randomized clinical trial. *Child Development, 83*(2), 623–636.

Bickman, L., Kelley, S. D., Breda, C., Regina de Andrade, A., & Riemer, M. (2011). Effects of routine feedback to clinicians on mental health outcomes of youths: Results of a randomized trial. *Psychiatric Services, 62*(12), 1423–1429.

Birmaher, B., Khetarpal, S., Brent, D., Cully, M., Balach, L., Kaufman, J., & Neer, S. M. (1997). The screen for child anxiety related emotional disorders (SCARED): Scale construction and psychometric characteristics. *Journal of the American Academy of Child and Adolescent Psychiatry, 36*(4), 545–553.

Bonanno, G. A. (2004). Loss, trauma, and human resilience: Have we underestimated the human capacity to thrive after extremely aversive events? *American Psychologist, 59*, 20–28.

Bonanno, G. A., Brewin, C. R., Kaniasty, K., & La Greca, A. M. (2010). Weighing the costs of disaster: Consequences, risks, and resilience in individuals, families, and communities. *Psychological Science in the Public Interest, 11*(1), 1–49.

Bonanno, G. A., Westphal, M., & Mancini, A. D. (2011). Resilience to loss and potential trauma. *Annual Review of Clinical Psychology, 7*, 511–535.

Brestan, E. V., & Eyberg, S. M. (1998). Effective psychosocial treatments of conduct-disordered children and adolescents: 29 years, 82 studies, and 5,272 kids. *Journal of Clinical Child Psychology, 27*(2), 180–189.

Burns, B. J., Costello, E. J., Angold, A., Tweed, D., Stangl, D., Farmer, E. M., & Erkanli, A. (1995). Children's mental health service use across service sectors. *Health Affairs, 14*(3), 147–159.

Burns, B. J., Phillips, S. D., Wagner, H. R., Barth, R. P., Kolko, D. J., Campbell, Y., & Landsverk, J. (2004). Mental health need and access to mental health services by youths involved with child welfare: A national survey. *Journal of the American Academy of Child and Adolescent Psychiatry, 43*(8), 960–970.

Carpentier, M. Y., Silovsky, J. F., & Chaffin, M. (2006). Randomized trial of treatment for children with sexual behavior problems: Ten-year follow-up. *Journal of Consulting and Clinical Psychology, 74*(3), 482.

Casanueva, C., Smith, K., Dolan, M., Tueller, S., & Lloyd, S. (2012). *NSCAW II wave 2 report: Child safety* (OPRE Rep. #2013–07). Washington, DC: Office of Planning, Research and Evaluation, Administration for Children and Families, U.S. Department of Health and Human Services.

Chadwick Center for Children and Families. (2004). *Closing the quality chasm in child abuse treatment: Identifying and disseminating best practices. The findings of the Kauffman Best Practices Project to help children heal from child abuse.* San Diego: Children's Hospital–San Diego.

Chaffin, M., Berliner, L., Block, R., Johnson, T. C., Friedrich, W. N., Louis, D. G., & Madden, C. (2008). Report of the ATSA task force on children with sexual behavior problems. *Child Maltreatment, 13*(2), 199.

Chaffin, M., & Friedrich, B. (2004). Evidence-based treatments in child abuse and neglect. *Children and Youth Services Review, 26*(11), 1097–1113.

Chaffin, M., Funderburk, B., Bard, D., Valle, L. A., & Gurwitch, R. (2011). A combined motivation and parent–child interaction therapy package reduces child welfare recidivism in a randomized dismantling field trial. *Journal of Consulting and Clinical Psychology, 79*(1), 84.

Chaffin, M., Silovsky, J. F., Funderburk, B., Valle, L. A., Brestan, E. V., Balachova, T., Jackson, S., Lensgraf, J., & Bonner, B. L. (2004). Parent-child interaction therapy with physically abusive parents: Efficacy for reducing future abuse reports. *Journal of Consulting and Clinical Psychology, 72*(3), 500–510.

Chen, L. P., Murad, M. H., Paras, M. L., Colbenson, K. M., Sattler, A. L., Goranson, E. N., Elamin, M. B., Seime, R. J., Shinozaki, G., Prokop, L. J., & Zirakzadeh, A. (2010). Sexual abuse and lifetime diagnosis of psychiatric disorders: Systematic review and meta-analysis. *Mayo Clinic Proceedings, 85*(7), 618–629.

Cisler, J. M., Begle, A. M., Amstadter, A. B., Resnick, H. S., Kmett Danielson, C., Saunders, B. E., & Kilpatrick, D. G. (2012). Exposure to interpersonal violence and risk for PTSD, depression, delinquency, and binge drinking among adolescents: Data from NSA-R. *Journal of Traumatic Stress, 25*, 33–40.

Cohen, J. A., Berliner, L., & Mannarino, A. (2010). Trauma focused CBT for children with co-occurring trauma and behavior problems. *Child Abuse & Neglect, 34*(4), 215–224.

Cohen, J. A., Mannarino, A. P., & Deblinger, E. (2006a). *Treating trauma and traumatic grief in children and adolescents.* New York: Guilford Press.

Cohen, J. A., Mannarino, A., Murray, L. K., & Igelman, R. (2006b). Psychosocial interventions for maltreated and violence-exposed children. *Journal of Social Issues, 62*(4), 737–766.

Cohen, J. A., Mannarino, A. P., & Iyengar, S. (2011). Community treatment of post traumatic stress disorder for children exposed to intimate partner violence: A randomized controlled trial. *Archives of Pediatrics & Adolescent Medicine, 165*(1), 16–21.

Cohen, J. A., Mannarino, A. P., Kliethermes, M., & Murray, L. A. (2012). Trauma-focused CBT for youth with complex trauma. *Child Abuse & Neglect, 36*(6), 528–541.

Copeland, W. E., Keeler, G., Angold, A., & Costello, E. J. (2007). Traumatic events and posttraumatic stress in childhood. *Archives of General Psychiatry, 64*(5), 577–584.

Currie, J., & Widom, C. S. (2010). Long-term consequences of child abuse and neglect on adult economic well-being. *Child Maltreatment, 15*(2), 111–120.

Delany-Black, V., Covington, C., Ondersma, S., Nordstrom-Klee, B., Templin, T., Ager, J., Janisse, J., & Sokol, R. J. (2002). Violence exposure, trauma, and IQ and/or reading deficits among urban children. *Archives of Pediatrics & Adolescents Medicine, 156*(3), 280–285.

Dorsey, S., & Deblinger, E. (2012). *Children in foster care. Trauma-focused CBT for children and adolescents: Treatment applications* (pp. 49–72). New York: Guilford Press.

Dorsey, S., Kerns, S. E., Trupin, E. W., Conover, K. L., & Berliner, L. (2012). Child welfare caseworkers as service brokers for youth in foster care findings from project focus. *Child Maltreatment, 17*(1), 22–31.

Dozier, M., Lindhiem, O., & Ackerman, J. P. (2005). Attachment and Biobehavioral Catch-Up: An intervention targeting empirically identified needs of foster infants. In L. J. Berlin, Y. Ziv, L. Amaya-Jackson, & M. T. Greenberg (Eds.), *Attachment and Biobehavioral Catch-Up: An intervention targeting empirically identified needs of foster infants.* New York, NY: Guilford Press.

Eyberg, S. M., Nelson, M. M., & Boggs, S. R. (2008). Evidence-based psychosocial treatments for children and adolescents with disruptive behavior. *Journal of Clinical Child and Adolescent Psychology, 37*(1), 215–237.

Felitti, V. J., Anda, R. F., Nordenberg, D., Williamson, D. F., Spitz, A. M., Edwards, V., Koss, M. P., & Marks, J. S. (1998). Relationship of childhood abuse and household dysfunction to many of the leading causes of death in adults. *American Journal of Preventive Medicine, 14*(4), 245–258.

Finkelhor, D., Hamby, S. L., Ormrod, R. K., & Turner, H. A. (2009). Violence, abuse, & crime exposure in a national sample of children & youth. *Pediatrics, 24*(5), 1–14.

Finkelhor, D., & Jones, L. M. (2004). *Explanations for the decline in child sexual abuse cases* (Juvenile Justice Bulletin No. NC199298). Washington, DC: Office of Juvenile Justice and Delinquency Prevention.

Fisher, P. A., Kim, H. K., & Pears, K. C. (2009). Effects of Multidimensional Treatment Foster Care for Preschoolers (MTFC-P) on reducing permanent placement failures among children with placement instability. *Children and Youth Services Review, 31*(5), 541–546.

Foa, E. B., Johnson, K., Feeny, N. C., & Treadwell, K. R. T. (2001). The child PTSD symptom scale (CPSS): Preliminary psychometrics of a measure for children with PTSD. *Journal of Clinical Child Psychology, 30*, 376–384.

Ford, J. D., Chapman, J. F., Hawke, J., & Albert, D. (2007). *Trauma among youth in the juvenile justice system: Critical issues and new directions* (p. 8). New York: National Center for Mental Health and Juvenile Justice.

Forgatch, M. S., Patterson, G. R., & DeGarmo, D. S. (2005). Evaluating fidelity: Predictive validity for a measure of competent adherence to the Oregon model of parent management training. *Behavior Therapy, 36*(1), 3–13.

Gardner, W., Lucas, A., Kolko, D., & Campo, J. (2007). Comparison of the PSC-17 and alternative mental health screens in an at-risk primary care sample. *Journal of the American Academy of Child and Adolescent Psychiatry, 46*(5), 611–618.

Goodman, R. (1997). The strengths and difficulties questionnaire: A research note. *Journal of Child Psychology and Psychiatry, 38*, 581–586.

Grogger, J. (1997). Local violence and educational attainment. *Journal of Human Resources, 32*, 659–682.

Hamby, S. L., Finkelhor, D., Ormrod, R., & Turner, H. (2005). The juvenile victimization questionnaire: Reliability, validity, and national norms. *Child Abuse & Neglect, 29*, 383–412.

Horwitz, S. C., Chamberlain, P., Landsverk, J., & Mullican, C. (2010). Improving the mental health of children in child welfare through the implementation of evidence-based parenting interventions. *Administration and Policy in Mental Health and Mental Health Services Research, 37*(1–2), 27–39.

Horwitz, S. M., Hurlburt, M. S., Goldhaber-Fiebert, J. D., Heneghan, A. M., Zhang, J., Rolls-Reutz, J., Fisher, E., Landsverk, J., & Stein, R. E. (2012). Mental health services use by children investigated by child welfare agencies. *Pediatrics, 130*(5), 861–869.

Hovens, J. G. F. M., Wiersma, J. E., Giltay, E. J., Van Oppen, P., Spinhoven, P., Penninx, B. W. J. H., & Zitman, F. G. (2010). Childhood life events and childhood trauma in adult patients with depressive, anxiety and comorbid disorders vs. controls. *Acta Psychiatrica Scandinavica, 122*(1), 66–74.

Hurt, H., Malmud, E., Brodsky, N. L., & Giannetta, J. (2001). Exposure to violence: Psychological and academic correlates in child witnesses. *Archives of Pediatric Adolescent Medicine, 155*(12), 1351–1356.

Institute of Medicine. (2001). *Crossing the quality chasm: A new health system for the 21st century*. Washington, DC: National Academy Press.

James, S., Landsverk, J., & Slymen, D. J. (2004). Placement movement in out-of-home care: Patterns and predictors. *Children and Youth Services Review, 26*(2), 185–206.

Kaminski, J. W., Valle, L. A., Filene, J. H., & Boyle, C. L. (2008). A meta-analytic review of components associated with parent training program effectiveness. *Journal of Abnormal Child Psychology, 36*, 567–589.

Kazdin, A. E. (1997). Parent management training: Evidence, outcomes, and issues. *Journal of the American Academy of Child and Adolescent Psychiatry, 36*(10), 1349–1366.

Kearney, C. A., Wechsler, A., Kaur, H., & Lemos-Miller, A. (2010). Posttraumatic stress disorder in maltreated youth: A review of contemporary research and thought. *Clinical Child and Family Psychology Review, 13*(1), 46–76.

Kerker, B. D., & Dore, M. M. (2006). Mental health needs and treatment of foster youth: Barriers and opportunities. *The American Journal of Orthopsychiatry, 76*(1), 138–147.

Kerns, S. E. U., Dorsey, S., Trupin, E. W., & Berliner, L. (2010). Project focus: Promoting emotional health and wellbeing for youth in foster care through connections to evidence-based practices. *Report on Emotional and Behavioral Disorders in Youth, 10*, 30–38.

Kilpatrick, D. G., Saunders, B. E., & Smith, D. W. (2003). *Youth victimization: Prevalence and implications*. Retrieved from the U.S. Department of Justice National Institute of Justice website: https://www.ncjrs.gov/pdffiles1/nij/194972.pdf

Kolko, D. J. (1996a). Individual cognitive behavioral treatment and family therapy for physically abused children and their offending parents: A comparison of clinical outcomes. *Child Maltreatment, 1*(4), 322–342.

Kolko, D. J. (1996b). Clinical monitoring of treatment course in child physical abuse: Psychometric characteristics and treatment comparisons. *Child Abuse & Neglect, 20*(1), 23–43.

Kolko, D., & Swanson, C. C. (2002). *Assessing and treating physically abused children and their families: A cognitive-behavioral approach*. Thousand Oaks, CA: Sage.

Kolko, D. J., Brown, E. J., & Berliner, L. (2002). Children's perceptions of their abusive experience: Measurement and preliminary findings. *Child Maltreatment, 7*, 41–53.

Kolko, D. J., Hoagwood, K. E., Springgate, B. (2010). Treatment research for children and youth exposed to traumatic events: Moving beyond efficacy to amp up public health impact. *General Hospital Psychiatry, 32*(5), 465–476.

Kolko, D. J., Iselin, A. M. R., & Gully, K. J. (2011). Evaluation of the sustainability and clinical outcome of alternatives for families: A Cognitive-Behavioral Therapy (AF-CBT) in a child protection center. *Child Abuse & Neglect, 35*(2), 105–116.

Kroenke, K., & Spitzer, R. L. (2002). The PHQ-9: A new depression diagnostic and severity measure. *Psychiatric Annals, 32*(9), 509–515.

Labellarte, M. J., Ginsburg, G. S., Walkup, J. T., & Riddle, M. A. (1999). The treatment of anxiety disorders in children and adolescents. *Biological Psychiatry, 46*(11), 1567–1578.

Landsverk, J. A., Burns, B. J., Stambaugh, L. F., & Rolls Reutz, J. A. (2009). Psychosocial interventions for children and adolescents in foster care: Review of research literature. *Child Welfare, 88*(1), 49–69.

Landsverk, J., Davis, I., Ganger, W., Newton, R., & Johnson, I. (1996). Impact of child psychosocial functioning on reunification from out-of-home placement. *Children and Youth Services Review, 18*(4), 447–462.

Leslie, L. K., Hulburt, M. S., Landsverk, J., Barth, R., & Slymen, D. J. (2004). Outpatient mental health services for children in foster care: A national perspective. *Child Abuse & Neglect, 28,* 697–712.

Leslie, L. K., Hurlburt, M. S., James, S., Landsverk, J., Slymen, D. J., & Zhang, J. (2005). Relationship between entry into child welfare and mental health service use. *Psychiatric Services, 56*(8), 981–987.

Lieberman, A. F., Van Horn, P., & Ippen, C. G. (2005). Toward evidence-based treatment: Child-parent psychotherapy with preschoolers exposed to marital violence. *Journal of the American Academy of Child and Adolescent Psychiatry, 44*(12), 1241–1248.

Mannarino, A. P., Cohen, J. A., Deblinger, E., Runyon, M. K., & Steer, R. A. (2012). Trauma-Focused Cognitive-Behavioral Therapy (TF-CBT) for children sustained impact of treatment 6 and 12 months later. *Child Maltreatment, 17*(3), 231–241.

Masten, A. S. (2001). Ordinary magic: Resilience processes in development. *American Psychologist, 56,* 227–238.

McLaughlin, K. A., Green, J. G., Gruber, M. J., Sampson, N. A., Zaslavsky, A. M., & Kessler, R. C. (2012). Childhood adversities and first onset of psychiatric disorders in a national sample of U.S. adolescents. *Archives of General Psychiatry, 69*(11), 1151–1161.

McMahon, R. J., & Forehand, R. L. (2005). *Helping the noncompliant child: Family-based treatment for oppositional behavior.* New York: Guilford Press.

National Child Abuse and Neglect Data System (NCANDS). U.S. Department of Health and Human Services. (2011). *Child maltreatment 2011.* Retrieved from Children's Bureau website: http://www.acf.hhs.gov/sites/default/files/cb/cm11.pdf

Patterson, G. R. (1973). *Changes in status of family members as controlling stimuli: A basis for describing treatment process* (4th ed., Vol. 12). Eugene, OR: Oregon Research Institute.

Price, J. M., Chamberlain, P., Landsverk, J., & Reid, J. (2009). KEEP foster-parent training intervention: Model description and effectiveness. *Child & Family Social Work, 14*(2), 233–242.

Pynoos, R. S., Steinberg, A. M., Schreiber, M. D., & Brymer, M. J. (2006). *Children and families: A new framework for preparedness and response to danger, terrorism, and trauma. Psychological effects of catastrophic disasters: Group approaches to treatment* (pp. 83–112). Binghamton: Hawthorn Press.

Rakovshik, S. G., & McManus, F. (2010). Establishing evidence-based training in cognitive behavioral therapy: A review of current empirical findings and theoretical guidance. *Clinical Psychology Review, 30*(5), 496–516.

Rubin, A. (2011). Teaching EBP in social work: Retrospective and prospective. *Journal of Social Work, 11*(1), 64–79.

Ruggiero, K. J., Smith, D. W., Hanson, R. F., Resnick, H. S., Saunders, B. E., Kilpatrick, D. G., & Best, C. L. (2004). Is disclosure of childhood rape associated with mental health outcome? Results from the National Women's Study. *Child Maltreatment, 9*(1), 62–77.

Runyon, M. K., Deblinger, D., & Steer, R. (2010). Comparison of combined parent-child and parent-only cognitive-behavioral treatments for offending parents and children in cases of child physical abuse. *Child & Family Behavior Therapy, 32,* 196–218.

Sanders, M. R. (2008). Triple P-Positive Parenting Program as a public health approach to strengthening parenting. *Journal of Family Psychology, 22*(4), 506–517.

Saunders, B. E. (2011). Determining best practice for treating sexually victimized children. In P. Goodyear-Brown (Ed.), *Handbook of child sexual abuse: Identification, assessment, and treatment* (pp. 171–197). Hoboken: Wiley.

Scaramella, L. V., & Leve, L. D. (2004). Clarifying parent-child reciprocities during early childhood: The Early Childhood Coercion model. *Clinical Child and Family Psychology Review, 7*(2), 89–107.

Scheeringa, M. S., & Haslett, N. (2010). The reliability and criterion validity of the diagnostic infant and preschool assessment: A new diagnostic instrument for young children. *Child Psychiatry and Human Development, 41*(3), 299–312.

Snyder, J., Cramer, A., Afrank, J., & Patterson, G. R. (2005). The contributions of ineffective discipline and parental hostile attributions of child misbehavior to the development of conduct problems at home and school. *Developmental Psychology, 41*(1), 30–41.

Spieker, S. J., Oxford, M. L., Kelly, J. F., Nelson, E. M., & Fleming, C. B. (2012). Promoting first relationships: Randomized trial of a relationship-based intervention for toddlers in child welfare. *Sage Journals, 17,* 271–286.

Stahmer, A. C., Leslie, L. K., Hurlburt, M., Barth, R. P., Webb, M. B., Landsverk, J., & Zhang, J. (2005). Developmental and behavioral needs and service use for young children in child welfare. *Pediatrics, 116*(4), 891–900.

Stevens, T., Ruggiero, K., Kilpatrick, D., Resnick, H., & Saunders, B. (2005). Variables differentiating singly and multiply victimized youth: Results from the national survey of adolescents and implications for secondary prevention. *Child Maltreatment, 10*, 211–223.

Stiffman, A. R., Pescosolido, B., & Cabassa, L. J. (2004). Building a model to understand youth service access: The Gateway Provider model. *Mental Health Services Research, 6*(4), 189–198.

Swenson, C. C., Schaeffer, C. M., Henggeler, S. W., Faldowski, R., & Mayhew, A. M. (2010). Multisystemic therapy for child abuse and neglect: A randomized effectiveness trial. *Journal of Family Psychology, 24*(4), 497–507.

Thyer, B. A., & Myers, L. L. (2011). The quest for evidence-based practice: A view from the United States. *Journal of Social Work, 11*(1), 8–25.

Timmer, S. G., Urquiza, A. J., Herschell, A. D., McGrath, J. M., & Zebell, N. M. (2006). Parent-child interaction therapy: Application of an empirically supported treatment to maltreated children in foster care. *Journal of Policy, Practice and Program, 85*(6), 919–939.

Timmer, S. G., Urquiza, A. J., Zebell, N. M., & McGrath, J. M. (2005). Parent-child interaction therapy: Application to maltreating parent-child dyads. *Child Abuse & Neglect, 29*(7), 825–842.

Turner, H. A., Finkelhor, D., & Ormrod, R. (2010). Poly-victimization in a national sample of children and youth. *American Journal of Preventive Medicine, 38*(3), 323–330.

U.S. Department of Health and Human Services, Administration for Children and Families, Administration on Children, Youth and Families, Children's Bureau. (2010). *Child maltreatment.* Retrieved from http://www.acf.hhs.gov/programs/cb/stats_research/index.htm#can

Urquiza, A. J., & McNeil, C. B. (1996). Parent-child interaction therapy: An intensive dyadic intervention for physically abusive families. *Child Maltreatment, 1*(2), 134–144.

Van Eys, P., & Truss, A. (2011). Comprehensive and therapeutic assessment of child sexual abuse: A bridge to treatment. In P. Goodyear-Brown (Ed.), *Handbook of child sexual abuse* (1st ed., pp. 2011–2143). Hoboken: Wiley.

Washington State Institute for Public Policy (WSIPP). (2012). Inventory of evidence-based, research-based, and promising practices. Retrieved from Washington State Institute for Public Policy and University of Washington Evidence-based Practice Institute website: www.wsipp.wa.gov

Webster-Stratton, C. (1992). The incredible years. Seattle [citerad dec. 2007]. http://www.incredibleyears.com

Weersing, V. R., & Brent, D. A. (2006). Cognitive behavioral therapy for depression in youth. *Child and Adolescent Psychiatric Clinics of North America, 15*(4), 939–957.

Wegman, H. L., & Stetler, C. (2009). A meta-analytic review of the effects of childhood abuse on medical outcomes in adulthood. *Psychosomatic Medicine, 71*(8), 805–812.

Weich, S., Patterson, J., Shaw, R., & Stewart-Brown, S. (2009). Family relationships in childhood and common psychiatric disorders in later life: Systematic review of prospective studies. *The British Journal of Psychiatry, 194*(5), 392–398.

Weisz, J. R., & Kazdin, A. E. (2010). *Evidence-based psychotherapies for children and adolescents.* New York: Guilford Press.

Wolfe, D. A., Edwards, B., Manion, I., & Koverola, C. (1988). Early intervention for parents at risk of child abuse and neglect: A preliminary investigation. *Journal of Consulting and Clinical Psychology, 56*(1), 40–47.

Chapter 21
Foster Care and Child Well-Being: A Promise Whose Time Has Come

Heather N. Taussig and Tali Raviv

The subject of the most recent (April, 2012) Information Memorandum (ACYF-CB-IM-12-04) issued by the United States Department of Health and Human Services, Administration on Children, Youth and Families Administration is "Promoting Social and Emotional Well-Being for Children and Youth Receiving Child Welfare Services." The IM reads:

> The Administration on Children, Youth and Families (ACYF) is focused on promoting the social and emotional well-being of children and youth who have experienced maltreatment and are receiving child welfare services. To focus on social and emotional well-being is to attend to children's behavioral, emotional and social functioning – those skills, capacities, and characteristics that enable young people to understand and navigate their world in healthy, positive ways. (ACYF 2012, p. 1)

The promotion of well-being among children, adolescents, and emerging adults who are in foster care or have a history of out-of-home placement is not a novel idea, yet the emergence of "evidence-based" treatments, the burgeoning of implementation science, and the understanding that safety and permanency (two longstanding central tenets of child welfare practice) are not sufficient for child well-being have renewed child welfare's focus in this area. This chapter aims to: (1) briefly review the history of foster care in the US, (2) review the efficacy of programs designed to promote well-being for youth in foster care, (3) discuss the challenges of adapting existing evidence-based programs for this population and review some adaptations, and (4) conclude with suggestions for the field.

Foster Care and Child Welfare Legislation in the United States: A Brief History

The origins of modern day foster care began in colonial America, when children were indentured into others' homes in order to be trained in a trade. Orphans and other poor children were primarily indentured, although families of children from other socioeconomic strata also took advantage of the

H.N. Taussig, Ph.D. (✉)
Kempe Center for the Prevention and Treatment of Child Abuse and Neglect, University of Colorado School of Medicine, The Gary Pavilion at Children's Hospital Colorado, Anschutz Medical Campus, 13123 East 16th Avenue, Box 390, Aurora, CO 80045, USA
e-mail: heather.taussig@childrenscolorado.org

T. Raviv, Ph.D.
Department of Child and Adolescent Psychiatry, Ann and Robert H. Lurie Children's Hospital of Chicago, Northwestern University, Feinberg School of Medicine, 225 East Chicago Avenue, Box 10, Chicago, IL 60611-2605, USA
e-mail: traviv@luriechildrens.org

J.E. Korbin and R.D. Krugman (eds.), *Handbook of Child Maltreatment*, Child Maltreatment 2, DOI 10.1007/978-94-007-7208-3_21, © Springer Science+Business Media Dordrecht 2014

opportunity to have their children learn a trade. In the first half of the nineteenth century, orphan asylums became the more predominant way of caring for poor and dependent children until Charles Loring Brace established the system of "placing out" children through the New York Children's Aid Society in 1853. Brace was less concerned about the well-being of children; rather, he sought to protect society from the ills of problem children. Children from urban areas were sent westward to rural communities, where there was little oversight of their treatment by their new families. Children's ties with their biological parents were typically severed.

In 1886, however, the Boston Children's Aid Society, under the guidance of Charles Birtwell, developed a new philosophy of "placing children" that included both prevention efforts and the goal of reuniting children with their families after being placed in foster care. This coincided with changing conceptualizations of childhood at the turn of the century; society shifted from viewing children as "little adults" to an understanding that children needed support and guidance throughout their development (Hacsi 1995; McDonald et al. 1996). This, in addition to the growth of social work as a profession, may have sown the seeds for an increasing focus on child well-being throughout the twentieth century.

A grassroots approach to addressing child well-being, spearheaded by Lillian Wald and Florence Kelly, got the attention of President Roosevelt, who convened The First White House Conference on the Care of Dependent Children in 1909. This was followed by the creation of the Children's Bureau in 1912, which was charged to "investigate and report…upon all matters pertaining to the welfare of children and child life among all classes of our people" (US DHHS 2012). This anti-institutionalization movement led to greater governmental oversight of child welfare, and "boarding out" or "foster care" became the predominant practice as the use of asylums for children declined. In 1935, the creation of Aid to Dependent Children as Title IV of the Social Security Act enabled federal funds to be used to support impoverished families to keep children at home. In the 1950s, the number of children in foster care outnumbered children in institutions, and by the 1960s and 1970s there was an even greater increase in the number of children in foster care, attributed both to the increase in availability of funding for such placements and the significantly heightened awareness of child abuse following the publication of "Battered Child Syndrome" in 1962 by Henry Kempe and colleagues (Kempe et al. 1962). In 1974, The Child Abuse Prevention and Treatment Act required states to enact child abuse reporting and investigative procedures; this also led to an increase in the number of children placed in foster care.

The rise in the number of children placed in foster care, however, was followed by a concern about "foster care drift" – children languishing in foster care and not returning to their biological families – which was believed to lead to more negative outcomes. As a result of this ideological shift, the Indian Child Welfare Act (ICWA) of 1978 and the Adoption Assistance and Child Welfare Act of 1980 (PL 96-272) were passed. ICWA granted more authority to tribal courts for the placement of their tribe members into foster care. PL 96-272 funded services aimed at preventing removal of children from their homes, leading to the development of "family preservation" and reunification programs. A hierarchy of preferential outcomes for children in foster care was set by this legislation: long-term foster care was the least desirable outcome, followed by guardianship and adoption. Reunification was the most preferred. This focus on the importance of the biological family led to the increase of formal kinship foster care, which gained popularity in the 1990s and is still the preferred placement option in many jurisdictions today (Hacsi 1995; McDonald et al. 1996; Murray and Gesiriech 2004).

The focus on "preserving" the family and increasing permanency was reflected in legislation passed and programs authorized between 1986 and 1996, including: (1) the Family Preservation and Family Support Services Program of 1993 – providing flexible funding to prevent child abuse and neglect and foster care placement; (2) the Court Improvement Program of 1993 – enabling the testing of new court approaches for juvenile and family cases; (3) Child Welfare Waivers in 1994 – enabling states to test innovative methods for delivering and financing child welfare services as long as they were cost neutral; and (4) the Multi-ethnic Placement Act of 1994 and the Interethnic Placement Provisions of 1996 – prohibiting states from denying adoption and foster care on the basis of race/ethnicity (Hacsi 1995; McDonald et al. 1996; Murray and Gesiriech 2004).

In 1997, the Adoption and Safe Families Act (ASFA; PL 105-89), laid the groundwork for the current system under which child welfare practice currently operates. The legislation was passed out of concern that children were spending too long in foster care, that adoption was not receiving enough emphasis in permanency decisions, and most importantly, that the system was biased toward family preservation at the expense of children's safety and well-being. The focus on child safety and permanency was not new, but the focus on child well-being represented a shift in the ideology about what was important. Never before had there been an explicit emphasis on *child well-being*, separate from safety and permanency (which were often equated with well-being).

Legislation subsequent to ASFA also reflected this new focus on child well-being. For example: (1) the John H. Chafee Foster Care Independence Program of 1999 increased funding and allowed for the provision of services and Medicaid coverage for former foster youth up the age of 21; (2) the Promoting Safe and Stable Families Amendments of 2001 focused on providing education and vocational training for youth emancipating from foster care (through the Foster Care Independence Program) and prioritized post-adoption services and substance abuse treatment; (3) the Fostering Connections to Success and Increasing Adoptions Act of 2008 focused on the coordination of health care services, supporting kinship caregivers, and improving outcomes for youth in foster care; and (4) the Child and Family Services Improvement and Innovation Act of 2011 had many provisions focusing on child well-being, including targeted services to enhance children's development and to address emotional trauma suffered by children in foster care, the appropriate use of psychotropic medications for these youth, supporting educational stability, monitoring identity theft for teenagers in foster care, and increasing the rate of monthly caseworker visits to children (Child Welfare Information Gateway 2012; Murray and Gesiriech 2004).

As is evident from this brief review of foster care in the United States, an explicit emphasis on child well-being is relatively new although its origins can be traced to Lillian Wald and Florence Kelly at the beginning of the twentieth century. The 2012 ACYF Information Memorandum has now made it a "priority to promote social and emotional well-being for children and youth receiving child welfare services, and to encourage child welfare agencies to focus on improving the behavioral and social-emotional outcomes for children who have experienced abuse and/or neglect."

Who Are the Children in Foster Care?

The number of children in foster care has been steadily declining over the past decade, with 523,000 youth in care on September 30, 2002 and 401,000 on that same date in 2011. Similarly, the number of children served by the public foster care system declined dramatically, from 800,000 in 2002 to 646,000 in 2011. Despite the decline, there continues to be significant overrepresentation of racial and ethnic minority youth in the system. In 2010 (the year for which there are the most recent statistics), over half (58 %) the youth in foster care belonged to a racial or ethnic minority group. On the other hand, there was fairly equal distribution of boys (52 %) and girls in foster care. About a third of the youth were younger than 5, a third were between the ages of 5 and 12, and about a third were teenagers. Almost half of the children (48 %) were living in non-relative foster care, a quarter (26 %) were living with relatives, 15 % were in group homes or institutions, and the remainder were in pre-adoptive homes (4 %), on trial home visits (4 %), in supervised independent living (1 %), or had run away (2 %). Children had been in care for an average of 25.3 months (median = 14.0 months) on September 30, 2010 (US DHHS 2012).

The National Survey of Child and Adolescent Well-Being (NSCAW) is a nationally representative longitudinal study of over 6,200 children who had contact with the child welfare system. Of those who had been in foster care for a year ($N = 727$), neglect was the primary cause for placement for 60 % of the youth, physical abuse was the primary reason for 10 % of youth, and sexual abuse precipitated placement for 8 % of youth. Of note is that 41 % of youth in foster care experienced more than one type of maltreatment (US DHHS 2012).

While the decline in the number of youth in foster care has been hailed as a success, these numbers do not necessarily reflect better well-being among these young people in our nation. Indeed, as the current (2012) Commissioner of the Administration on Children, Youth and Families, Bryan Samuels, has stated, "Safety and permanency are necessary but not sufficient to ensure well-being" (Samuels 2012).

A Framework for Child and Youth Well-Being

As described above, the recent Information Memorandum from the Administration on Children Youth and Families (ACYF) calls for increased focus on child well-being in child welfare policy and practice. Shifting away from the status quo in child welfare (i.e., focusing primarily on safety and permanency outcomes) towards increased attention to child well-being requires comprehensive screening and functional assessment of indicators of child well-being as well as the adoption of effective, evidence-based interventions aimed at enhancing those elements of child well-being that require bolstering based on the results of such assessments.

As the understanding of the pervasive negative effects conferred by trauma exposure has grown, researchers, policymakers, and clinicians are increasingly adopting a "trauma lens;" that is, conceptualizing many of the developmental challenges observed in maltreated children as a direct result of their exposure to trauma. Since the 1998 publication of the landmark Adverse Childhood Experiences (ACE) study which demonstrated the devastating effects that adverse childhood experiences (including maltreatment) exert on physical and mental health outcomes in adulthood (Felitti et al. 1998), increasing attention has been paid to articulating the mechanisms through which these risks are conferred and to intervening to ameliorate these risks. Accumulating evidence supports the initial theoretical model proposed by the authors of the ACE study, which proposes that exposure to ACEs negatively affects social, emotional, and cognitive development, which in turn increases the risk for the adoption of high-risk behaviors which ultimately lead to disease, disability, and early death (Felitti et al. 1998).

Consistent with this view, the ACYF has adopted a framework by Lou and colleagues (2008) which defines child well-being according to four core areas: cognitive functioning, physical health and development, behavioral/emotional functioning, and social functioning. This framework includes not only indicators that are internal to the child, but also takes into account the ecological environment that encompasses the child. This framework emerges from a developmental perspective, with the specific indicators of well-being varying according to the developmental level of the child.

Despite the breadth of this definition, the ACYF has made a strong case for honing in more intensively on the social, emotional, and behavioral arenas of child well-being. This emphasis is consistent with strong empirical evidence that has established, (a) the critical role that social, emotional, and behavioral functioning play in the prediction of life-course outcomes, and (b) the severity of the disruption to these aspects of development caused by maltreatment. Common indicators of social, emotional, and behavioral functioning include internalizing symptoms (such as sadness and anxiety), externalizing symptoms (such as disruptive behavior), the ability to regulate emotions and behavior, attachment to caregivers, social competence, self-concept and identity development, coping skills, peer relationships, and self-esteem.

Well-Being Outcomes, Service Utilization, and Associated Costs for Youth in Foster Care

Several other chapters in this handbook delineate the adverse consequences of child maltreatment, and therefore we will not review them in detail here. Because children are not randomly assigned to foster care following maltreatment, it is impossible to tease apart the impact of placement in foster care independent of the consequences of maltreatment. What we do know is that children in foster care, and those who have emancipated from care, experience high rates of cognitive, academic, physical, social, emotional and behavior problems and are more likely to experience negative outcomes (Clausen et al. 1998; dosReis et al. 2001; Garland et al. 2001; Harman et al. 2000; Landsverk and Garland 1998; NSCAW, (n.d.); Stewart et al. 2002; Stouthamer-Loeber et al. 2001; Taussig and Culhane 2005; Thornberry et al. 2004; US DHHS 2012; Wiebush et al. 2001; Widom and Maxfield 1996).

Outcomes for young adults who have recently emancipated from foster care suggest that they are at continued risk for problems of significant public health concern as demonstrated by findings from *The Midwest Evaluation of the Adult Functioning of Former Foster Youth* study. The Midwest study is a longitudinal study following 732 youth as they emancipate from foster care. It consists of interviews with participants at ages just prior to emancipation, and at several timepoints post-emancipation. At all timepoints, the study documented high rates of substance use; early and multiple pregnancies; sexually transmitted diseases and other significant physical health problems; mental health problems; criminal behavior and criminal justice involvement; victimization; sporadic employment and low earnings; economic hardship and receipt of government assistance; homelessness; and barriers to service receipt. In most domains and at most timepoints, the rates of problems in the Midwest sample were significantly higher than those reported for same-age peers in the National Longitudinal Study of Adolescent Health (Ahrens et al. 2010; Courtney and Barth 1996; Courtney and Dworsky 2005, 2006; Courtney et al. 2001, 2004, 2007, 2009; Courtney and Heuring 2005).

The costs of providing foster care are, not surprisingly, substantial. The Urban Institute estimated that during Fiscal Year 2000, states spent more than nine billion dollars in federal, state, and local funds on providing support services and room and board to youth placed in foster care (Bess et al. 2002). This estimate does not include long-term costs associated foster youths' over-representation in multiple service systems including juvenile justice, special education, and mental health, which generate substantial additional costs (Blumberg et al. 1996; Halfon et al. 1992; Widom 1991). For example, children in foster care use 15–20 times more mental health services than other low income children covered by Medicaid (dosReis et al. 2001; Halfon et al. 1992, 2002).

Despite these high rates, not all children in foster care who demonstrate need for services receive them. The NSCAW study found that for all youth referred to child protective services (not just those in foster care), 48 % had clinically significant mental health or behavior problems, yet only 25 % of them had received mental health services in the prior year (Burns et al. 2004). Similarly, among a subsample of youth in foster care, caseworkers reported that over half the youth were in need of mental health services, yet only 26 % were receiving services (Bellamy et al. 2010). Another study using NSCAW data found that foster children who received traditional mental health services did not evidence better outcomes; in fact, they scored worse on mental health problems than children who did not receive such services (McCrae et al. 2010). Another study examining the effectiveness of treatments for children in long-term foster care also found no benefit and concluded that youth were receiving "untested treatments with questionable effectiveness" (Bellamy et al. 2010, p. 474).

In this era when evidence-based mental health treatment is the zeitgeist, why aren't children in foster care benefitting? To begin to address this very question, we review the evidence base for interventions designed specifically for youth in foster care as well as barriers to designing and adapting evidence-based interventions for this population.

Evidence-Based Interventions Designed Specifically for Youth in Foster Care

Identifying interventions that can ameliorate the pervasive deleterious effects of maltreatment, childhood trauma, and foster care placement is no simple undertaking. Successful interventions must be grounded in theory and research, have good track records for recruiting and retaining children and families, and be contextually sensitive. It is no longer sufficient to refer a child for generic mental health services and hope that the clinician will identify and implement services that effectively meet the child's needs, as concerning evidence has emerged of the ineffectiveness of mental health services "as usual" for children involved with the child welfare system (McCra et al. 2010) and within foster care samples (Bellamy et al. 2010). Growing recognition of the importance of ensuring that services are supported by empirical evidence has increased the demand for evidence-informed mental health resources. But what constitutes evidence?

Although we cannot assume that evidence-based interventions for the general population work for children in foster care, there have been several programs that have been specifically designed for, and tested via randomized controlled trials, with youth in foster care. Below, we briefly review interventions for foster youth that aim to improve: (1) social, emotional and behavioral outcomes, (2) educational outcomes, and (3) the transition to independence for emancipating youth. This is not meant to be an exhaustive list, and our focus is on programs that have been tested in randomized controlled trials.

Social, Emotional, and Behavioral Interventions for Foster Youth

Attachment and Biobehavioral Catch-Up. Attachment and Biobehavioral Catch-up (ABC) is a ten-session, manualized in-home intervention designed to help foster caregivers provide sensitive care to maltreated infants and toddlers (aged 0–3) in order to promote children's attachment and self-regulation skills. The intervention focuses on helping caregivers provide nurturing care (even when the baby or toddler may act in ways that push the caregiver away), learn to follow the child's lead, appreciate the value of affectionate touch, and create conditions that encourage emotional expression and teach emotion recognition to their children. Results of two randomized controlled trials demonstrated significant improvements in children's cortisol regulation, indicating lower levels of this stress hormone (Dozier et al. 2006, 2008). One of these trials also yielded positive results regarding the caregiver-child attachment relationships, such that children of caregivers who had received the intervention showed significantly less avoidant attachment behavior than children in the control group (although there were no between-group differences in secure attachment behaviors; Dozier et al. 2009). ABC has also been tested by researchers other than the developers (Sprang 2009) in a sample of maltreated children (aged 0–6) in foster care whose biological parents' rights had been terminated. This randomized controlled trial found significant improvements in child internalizing and externalizing problems, greater decreases in negative parenting attitudes, and greater decreases in parenting stress in the intervention group as compared to the wait-list control group. One study that followed children who had received the intervention over time found that these children demonstrated more cognitive flexibility and theory of mind skills (skills related to self-regulation and cognitive development) relative to foster children who had received the control intervention approximately 2 years post-intervention (Lewis-Morrarty et al. 2012).

Bucharest Early Intervention Project. The Bucharest Early Intervention Project (BEIP) is a program implemented in Romania, designed to evaluate whether foster care placement can enhance developmental outcomes for children exposed to early environmental deprivation due to institutionalization. Children between the ages of 6 and 30 months who had been abandoned early in their lives and placed in institutional care were randomly assigned to remain in institutional care or be placed with foster caregivers and receive the BEIP intervention. Foster families in the BEIP receive services delivered by trained social workers that include in-home observation of child adjustment, education to foster parents about developmental stimulation and positive behavior management for young children, referral to outside services, and foster parent support groups. As compared to children who remained in institutional care, children in the intervention group demonstrated better attention levels at 42 months of age, more positive affect at both 30 and 42 months, and were less likely to experience internalizing disorders, including anxiety disorders, at 54 months (Ghera et al. 2009; Zeanah et al. 2009). Another study with this population found more positive change in attachment status at 42 months among children in the intervention group (Smyke et al. 2010). The intervention group showed improved cognitive development as measured both by standardized cognitive assessments at 42 and 54 months (Nelson et al. 2007) and improved EEG power and coherence at 42 months (Marshall et al. 2012). The results of these studies demonstrate that foster care placement for young children is superior to institutional care, particularly as it is provided in Romania. The BEIP thus provides critical, potentially policy-altering evidence for countries in which institutional care is a placement option. However, the implications for countries such as the U.S. may be more limited. Since all foster caregivers in this sample were recipients of the enhanced foster care intervention, it is unclear to what extent the positive outcomes were due to the enhanced foster care support services families received versus simple removal from the institutional setting.

Fostering Healthy Futures (FHF). Fostering Healthy Futures is a preventive intervention for maltreated youth, ages 9–11, who entered foster care over the prior year. The intervention is primarily child-focused, providing one-on-one mentoring and skills groups to children over a 30-week period. The one-on-one mentoring is provided by graduate students in social work and psychology, who spend 3–4 h per week with each child, advocate for services to ameliorate challenges, and connect them with resources and activities to build on their strengths. Children attend a 1.5-h manualized weekly skills group that consists of units including basic social skills, healthy coping strategies, and resisting peer pressure for risky behaviors. Mentors work with children to generalize these skills in real-world settings. A randomized controlled trial has demonstrated positive outcomes, including: (1) an improvement in quality of life immediately post-intervention, (2) a reduction in mental health symptoms (including trauma symptoms) according to youth, their caregivers and teachers, and a reduction in mental health service utilization 6-months post-intervention, and (3) fewer placement changes, less placement in residential treatment centers, and greater permanency 1-year post-intervention (Taussig and Culhane 2010; Taussig et al. 2012, 2007).

Fostering Individualized Assistance Program. The Fostering Individualized Assistance Program is an intervention designed to improve permanency, placement stability, and behavioral and emotional adjustment of 7–15-year-old children in foster care. The intervention included four components: (1) a comprehensive strengths-based assessment conducted by a family specialist who reviewed case records and interviewed multiple relevant adults as well as observing the child; (2) life-domain planning conducted by a team of adults in the child's life who met regularly to create and evaluate plans to address the child's needs; (3) clinical case management that included short-term home-based counseling and advocacy; and (4) linkage to follow-along supports and services. Results of a randomized controlled trial demonstrated improvements in caregiver-reported behavior problems, attention problems, and symptoms of withdrawal in the short term, and improvements in externalizing and delinquent behaviors for males, less runaway behavior and fewer days on the run or incarcerated for older youth, as well as greater permanency, an average of 3.5 years post-study entry (Clark et al. 1994, 1998).

Multidimensional Treatment Foster Care and Associated Interventions. Researchers at the Oregon Social Learning Center and Center for Research to Practice have developed and tested a number of interventions for children in foster care. Most are modifications of the Multidimensional Treatment Foster Care for Adolescents (MTFC-A) program initially designed for youth with chronic delinquency who were referred for out-of-home placements due to their behavioral difficulties. Although eligibility did not depend on whether or not the adolescents had a history of maltreatment or child welfare involvement, many of them did have such histories. Core components of the intervention include placing children in specialized foster homes with caregivers who are trained to provide intense supervision and monitoring, as well as consistent limit setting within a well-defined a behavior management program. Caregivers also receive daily phone calls that provide supervision and support and also allow for ongoing data collection (Chamberlain and Reid 1998; Leve et al. 2005).

Maltreated children who had been placed in foster care were participants in several related interventions. These include the **Multidimensional Treatment Foster Care for Preschoolers** (MTFC-P) program which incorporates several components of MTFC-A, including the parent training and support components, but adds a weekly playgroup session for the children. MTFC-P has demonstrated better attachment and placement outcomes and has improved children's ability to respond to stress (as measured by diurnal cortisol) (Fisher et al. 2005, 2007; Fisher and Kim 2007). **Keeping Foster Parents Trained and Supported** (KEEP) was a randomized controlled trial of an intervention for foster caregivers who were having a new child placed in their care through the child welfare system. Again, similar to MTFC-A, the chief components of the intervention include parent training in behavior management and ongoing parent support. The intervention demonstrated a reduction in child behavior problems as well as improvements in placement stability (Chamberlain et al. 2008; Price et al. 2008). The most recent adaptation of MTFC-A for children in foster care due to maltreatment is **Middle School Success** (MSS) for girls entering 6th grade. Similar to KEEP, parents receive group-based training in behavior management techniques, but unlike KEEP, youth participate in group sessions prior to the start of middle school and then individual coaching sessions throughout the school year. Intervention participants evidenced fewer mental health and behavior problems, less substance use, and greater prosocial behaviors up to 3 years post-baseline (Kim and Leve 2011; Smith et al. 2011).

Educational Interventions

Although mental health is the domain most frequently discussed and researched within the realm of child well-being for youth in foster care, educational interventions are also sorely needed. Children in foster care have high rates of academic failure, grade retention and dropout. Between 30 % and 50 % of children in foster care are placed in special education due to academic and/or behavioral/emotional difficulties (Zetlin et al. 2004). Despite the staggering need for intervention, no known randomized controlled trials of educational interventions have been conducted. One quasi-experimental study that employed an educational liaison for advocacy was conducted, but the results were equivocal (Zetlin et al. 2004).

Independent Living Programs

As reviewed above, young adults who emancipate from foster care evidence high rates of poor outcomes in multiple domains. Recent legislation has been passed in an attempt to improve these outcomes. Independent living programs, which are nearly universal in the US, aim to teach life skills and provide vocational and education support to emerging adults. But do these widespread programs work? There have been some rigorous trials of programs for non-foster youth transitioning to adulthood that have demonstrated positive educational and career outcomes (Hadley et al. 2010). None of these programs, however, has been tested with foster care populations. Indeed, the Campbell Systematic Review of independent living programs for foster youth concluded, "After an exhaustive search, no study was found that met our criteria" (Donkoh et al. 2006, p. 2).

Summary of Interventions for Foster Youth. While the programs described above have been tested in randomized controlled trials with positive child well-being outcomes, there are still significant holes when examining the cumulative state of the evidence for interventions to promote well-being among youth in foster care. First, trials of interventions to promote positive educational and emancipation outcomes are non-existent. Although there are a few interventions to promote, social, emotional and/or behavioral well-being that have been rigorously tested and demonstrated efficacy, when taken in sum total, they do not represent a menu of options for child welfare workers that would be near comprehensive enough to cover the great demand for evidence-based programming for their heterogeneous clients. While MTFC provides an excellent model for taking an efficacious program and making sensitive adaptations based on different developmental stages (Leve et al. 2009), most other interventions reviewed target only a narrow age range, and their efficacy for other ages is unknown. A few of the studies have examined multiple outcomes but the range of outcomes in most studies is typically limited. The measurement strategies have also been limited, with many studies using only parent and/or youth reports; findings would be strengthened by greater inclusion of teacher reports and record reviews. A notable exception is the collection of neurobiological data in several of the studies (i.e., ABC, BEIP, and MTFC-P) to assess the impact of the intervention on the stress response system and neurocognitive development. Finally, the studies' findings would be strengthened if they demonstrated outcomes several years post-intervention.

Strengths of most of the studies reviewed include: (1) few exclusion criteria, increasing their generalizability to the population studied; (2) working along the prevention/intervention continuum, as most studies recruited children in foster care before the onset of problems or diagnoses and most did not use referrals to recruit; and (3) high rates of recruitment and retention which suggests that they are contextually sensitive. Unfortunately, most of these trials had a small number of participants and few have undergone independent evaluation. Thus, although the ACYF IM has called for the "scaling up" of effective practices, the array of existing evidence-based programs that have been developed specifically for children in foster care will not meet the need.

Challenges to Adapting Existing Evidence-Based Programs for Youth in Foster Care

Because of the dearth of programs designed for, and tested with, foster care populations, the call has been made to use existing evidence-based programs with children in foster care and their families. Why, then, hasn't this happened? There are a number of challenges to both testing and implementing these programs in a foster care population.

Screening and Diagnostic Challenges. There has been an increased emphasis on screening and diagnosis to better understand the needs and strengths of children in foster care. This, coupled with the existence of symptom- or diagnosis-specific interventions, particularly for children exposed to trauma, can provide a promising point of departure to fulfill the call articulated by the ACYF IM to, "…identify effective and promising interventions that meet the needs of the specific population to be served; *making needed adaptations* to bring the interventions to scale within the child welfare system" (ACYF 2012, p. 10, italics added). Yet there are challenges in both screening and diagnosing.

First, there is the question of when to assess children in foster care for services. Should this be done soon after a child enters foster care? A month later? After each placement change? Then, there is the question of who should conduct the assessments. Should they be screened by caseworkers? Mental health workers? Finally, there is the question of who should be screened. All youth, ages 0–18, entering foster care? Only those displaying emotional or behavioral problems? In addition to determining when, how, and who to screen, we need to better understand when different interventions are appropriate. Before problems start, or only if the screen indicates a need? As a component of our program, Fostering Healthy Futures, described above, we conducted mental health, cognitive, and academic screenings with 9–11 year olds in foster care at the baseline interview. One recruitment period, we found that 10 % of the youth we screened were actively suicidal and in most cases, their caregivers and caseworkers were unaware. This suggests that we may not be able to wait until problems come to the attention of adults before we screen youth.

There are also diagnostic challenges for children in foster care. Questions have been raised regarding the validity of standard diagnoses as outlined by the Diagnostic and Statistical Manual of Mental Disorders, Fourth Edition Text Revision (DSM-IV-TR; American Psychiatric Association 2000) for children in foster care. In addition, diagnostic co-morbidity is more common among these children (Tarren-Sweeney 2010). Children in foster care have often experienced early and chronic interpersonal trauma such as domestic violence exposure, neglect, and physical or sexual abuse by a primary caregiver. This type of maltreatment history is likely to disrupt primary attachments and increases the risk that the child will develop a profile characterized by a constellation of difficulties including significant problems in the formation and maintenance of attachments and relationships with adults and peers, dysregulation of emotions and behaviors, poor self-concept, and cognitive difficulties, often called "complex trauma" (Cook et al. 2005). In the absence of a diagnosis that encompasses these areas of impairment, children often receive multiple other diagnoses (e.g., Attention Deficit Hyperactivity Disorder, Oppositional Defiant Disorder, Depression, Generalized Anxiety Disorder, Reactive Attachment Disorder). Psychological treatments are intended to modify those factors that have been shown through research to affect the etiology and maintenance of specific disorders and symptoms. To the extent that the factors that affect the etiology and maintenance of presenting problems differ among maltreated children in foster care, alternative, complementary, or more intense treatment approaches may be warranted. In addition, complex attachment and trauma-related clinical issues are likely to require longer-term intervention which may be at odds with the movement towards time-limited clinical services that conform to current managed-care-standards of mental health care funding. These issues complicate the adaptation of evidence-based interventions for youth in foster care.

Screening, diagnostic and treatment issues for foster youth are also complicated by the fact that screening, assessment, and treatment services are typically provided in the context of an open child welfare case in which permanency determinations and other legal issues are still being decided. This means that these services are not provided after a trauma has come to its natural conclusion. As one clinician put it, "we are trying to diagnose and treat Post-Traumatic Stress Disorder when 'post' hasn't happened yet!" In our own clinical experience, youth in foster care are often hesitant to participate in screening assessments or therapy and disclose the traumatic experiences to which they were exposed while living with their biological families because of their sometimes valid concerns that this information may impact the courts decisions about visitation and reunification with biological parents. Similarly, foster families are continuously monitored by child welfare, which could limit their willingness to frankly acknowledge challenges in their parenting or their relationship with the foster children in their care due to concerns about the repercussions. Finally, because most children are involved in multiple systems (e.g., child welfare, legal, educational, mental health and/or juvenile justice), the coordination of screening, diagnostic and treatment services among providers who have different, and sometimes competing, priorities can challenge the implementation of evidence-based practices.

Placement Challenges. Some years ago, the first author of this chapter was at a National Institute of Mental Health conference on evidence-based treatments and the developers of the most well-known and tested treatment models were on a panel answering questions. An audience member asked, "Have any of these interventions been tested for use with children in foster care?" One by one, the developers articulated why it would be infeasible to use their models with a foster care population. Primarily, they discussed the changing of placements as a major barrier to the testing and implementation of their programs with fidelity. Children in foster care can move homes or reunify without much advance warning, which makes continuity of care difficult. Changes in placement are often accompanied by changes in legal guardianship, further challenging sustained intervention or treatment. The researchers asked: How could they work with parent-child dyads if the dyads changed? How would they engage biological parents who may or may not have their children returned to their care? How could they even begin to think about testing whether or not their intervention was efficacious with this population when consent for these children's participation in research studies was so difficult? How would they conduct follow-up studies if children moved or had a change in legal guardianship?

Indeed, the BEIP study described above highlights some of the research challenges presented by children changing placements. In the BEIP study, of the 68 participants randomized to continue "care as usual" (that is, to remain in institutional care), 27 (40 %) of them were not in the institution at the 42-month follow-up, as they had reunified, been placed in foster care, etc.(Smyke et al. 2010). Although the authors utilized intent-to-treat methods in their analyses, which likely resulted in an underestimate of the true treatment effects, this study highlights the complexity of testing rigorous randomized controlled trials with children in foster care. Such challenges are commonplace for clinical researchers who work with children in foster care, but are much more difficult to accommodate in adaptations of existing evidence-based programs. In addition to the challenges accompanying placement changes, different types of placement settings pose challenges for the testing and use of evidence-based programs. School-age children in foster care may be placed in congregate care settings, psychiatric hospitals and detention facilities, which present their own set of challenges for testing and delivering evidence-based interventions. Finally, many evidence-based programs focus on caregivers' parenting abilities; placement changes and placement in congregate care can be particularly difficult to accommodate in the context of parenting interventions.

Substitute Caregiver Challenges. The demands on substitute caregivers (i.e., foster parents and kinship providers) are often great, as they typically care for multiple children and are responsible for transporting them to visitation with their biological parents as well as to services to address any physical, mental health, and/or educational needs. We often hear from foster parents that they do not want to participate in therapy with their child and certainly do not need to attend more "parenting classes." Adoptive families often voice their desire to have their child "put it all behind them" and share concerns about "bringing up the past." Biological parents who have reunified with their children express that they would like "to be done with the system," and for them, "the system" often encompasses mental health treatment. In addition, transportation, child care, and the costs of services are challenges for many families. For those interventions with a primary parenting component, it is particularly important to establish the ability to positively affect child well-being, even in the context of caregiver resistance and child placement transitions, adoption, and/or reunification.

Cultural and Maltreatment Issues. The lack of cultural sensitivity in the service settings may pose an additional barrier, especially in regards to engagement (McKay et al. 2004). Like many high-risk populations, referral and receipt of mental health services for children in foster care (after controlling for need for services) differ by sociodemographic, maltreatment, and placement factors. Studies have found that ethnic minority children in foster care are less likely to receive services, as are children in kinship care and those who have reunified with their biological parents. Some studies have shown that sexually and physically abused youth are more likely to receive services than children who have experienced neglect but not abuse (Burns et al. 2004; Garland et al. 1996, 2001; Leslie et al. 2000, 2004; McMillen et al. 2004). In addition, no known randomized controlled studies with foster youth have examined whether their interventions are equally effective across different types of maltreatment and/or different racial/ethnic groups. Indeed, this is difficult to test, as many children have experienced multiple types of maltreatment and self-identify as belonging to multiple racial/ethnic groups. Despite the challenges, one non-experimental study of adaptations of evidence-based programs for youth in foster care did examine their retention and outcome data by race, and found no differences between minority and non-minority youth on these indices (Weiner et al. 2009).

Summary of Challenges. We know from other studies of high-risk youth, that rates of engagement in treatment are poor, as are rates of treatment completion (Koverola et al. 2007). If we are to adapt existing evidenced-based services for children in foster care they *must* be contextually sensitive, or they will not demonstrate positive outcomes (Leathers et al. 2009; Maher et al. 2009). As Maher and colleagues conclude, "Policymakers and other funders need to recognize that providing needed services and documenting their effectiveness can be challenging, time-consuming, and expensive, but the payoff in improving the well-being of these youth makes overcoming these challenges a matter of necessity" (2009, p. 561).

Examples of Adaptations of Evidence-Based Programs for Use with Children in Foster Care

Despite the challenges in testing and implementing evidence-based programs for children in foster care, there have been, or are currently, a few adaptations of evidence-based interventions for this population. One good example is the Incredible Years (IY) program, a parent training intervention that was originally designed for non-maltreated samples to prevent and treat children's behavior problems. IY has demonstrated positive impacts on strengthening parental behavior management skills and reducing children's behavior problems in non-maltreated youth (Webster-Stratton 1984) and has also shown positive results when implemented with maltreating parents whose children were not placed in foster care (Letarte et al. 2010). An adaptation of the IY intervention was conducted to better match the needs of a foster care population (Linares et al. 2006). This study targeted foster parents and biological parents working towards the goal of reunification with their child. The intervention included two components. First, foster parents and biological parents pairs participated together in a group formed of 4–7 such pairs. The second component was a newly-created co-parenting curriculum aimed at individual families comprised of the child, foster parent, and biological parent. The randomized trial of the IY adaptation provides both hopeful and cautionary evidence for this type of adaptation: findings indicated improved positive parenting practices and collaborative co-parenting among foster and biological parents in the intervention group. However, only 16 % of families completed the co-parenting component, indicating that this component was not acceptable and/or feasible with the target population. Finally, although IY has well-documented effects on children's behavioral problems, this trial did not demonstrate statistically significant differences in child internalizing or externalizing behavior problems.

Another group of researchers in Wales implemented the IY program without significant modification in a small study (N = 36) to determine the feasibility of providing this intervention to foster caregivers without the involvement of biological parents (Bywater et al. 2010). This small scale study (employing a wait-list control design) showed promise in reducing children's problem behaviors. Unexpectedly, a significant difference in positive parenting strategies favored the control group rather than the intervention group, indicating the need for additional research. Qualitative analysis of feedback from the foster care providers indicated that the program was generally acceptable and perceived as helpful; however, there were also indications that some adaptations for the target population would be desirable. For example, both foster caregivers and intervention facilitators suggested that because of the unique challenges and skills deficits demonstrated by some children in foster care, the program should be extended to permit additional focus on topics of play and problem-solving. In addition, it was suggested that the intervention facilitators would benefit from additional training on the complex issues and legislation governing the care of children in foster care. Specifically, foster caregivers stated that these factors impacted the implementation of the program with regard to the creation of a rewards system for the child (a core IY intervention strategy), as using hugs or financial incentives as rewards was potentially inappropriate for some children.

Another evidence-based parent-child intervention, Parent-Child Interaction Therapy (PCIT) developed for children ages 2–7 with externalizing behavior problems, has also undergone testing with foster families. What is striking about this adaptation is that it followed a thoughtful and logical progression – first, adaptation for use with maltreating parents (Chaffin et al. 2004; Timmer et al. 2005), followed by a case study demonstrating its viability for use with a foster parent-child dyad (Timmer et al. 2006a), and finally a more rigorous study with 75 foster parent-child dyads (Timmer et al. 2006b). Although the latter study was not a randomized controlled trial, it compared the effectiveness of PCIT for foster families to that of non-foster families, using a pre/post measurement strategy. Encouragingly, the study found that PCIT improved child behavior problems and reduced foster parent distress, although the results were not quite as strong for the foster families as compared to the non-foster families. Importantly, the study was very transparent about the rates of recruitment and attrition, and actually modeled predictors of attrition. The findings highlight the challenges of intervening with this high risk population (both maltreating families and foster families): 691 dyads were referred to the clinic but 124 did not return after the initial clinical interview, 74 dyads had missing data and had to be excluded from analyses, and only 50 % of the remaining eligible dyads completed treatment. Interestingly, foster parents who were highly distressed at the baseline interview were less likely to drop out of the intervention, whereas the more distressed biological parents were most likely to attrit. Foster parents who reported a higher severity of behavior problems in their foster children, however, were more likely to drop out (Timmer et al. 2006a). This study highlights a critical issue for adaptations of existing evidence-based programs – even though adaptations can result in positive outcomes for families that engage, high rates of engagement and retention (even with planful, contextually-sensitive adaptations), are incredibly difficult to attain. This was also true for an additional adaptation of PCIT for foster families in which a group format was used to deliver the intervention. Only 27 % of families in this study participated in the follow-up interview, conducted 5 months post-intervention (McNeil et al. 2005).

Finally, there was a non-experimental study (Weiner et al. 2009) of three evidence-based programs (EBPs) for children in foster care: (1) Trauma-Focused Cognitive Behavioral Therapy (TF-CBT; Cohen et al. 2006), (2) Child-Parent Psychotherapy (CPP; Lieberman et al. 2005) and (3) Structured Psychotherapy for Adolescents Responding to Chronic Stress (SPARCS; DeRosa et al. 2006). Although the study was primarily designed to examine whether these programs operated differentially for different racial/ethnic groups and was not a randomized controlled trial, the results are illuminating for several reasons. First, they enrolled only children who had experienced moderate or severe trauma and who had adjustment issues as a result. Of the 2,434 youth who were potentially eligible for the services, only 216 were enrolled in one of the three EBPs. It is unclear as to whether that was because so few met criteria or due to a poor recruitment rate. Unfortunately, only 133 of the 216 had multiple assessments and could be included in statistical analyses. Furthermore, of the 133, 24 (or 18 %) dropped out of treatment. The authors reported positive outcomes across the racial/ethnic groups and attributed this, in part, to several flexible adaptations that were made. For example, research has shown that intervention effects of TF-CBT are maximized with the involvement of a caregiver (Deblinger et al. 1996), which can be a challenge for the foster care population. In this study, they included both foster parents and biological parents in treatment in cases where reunification was the goal. Other adaptations included providing treatment at off-site locations (including in the home) to reduce barriers to participation, providing transportation, and utilizing alternatives to traditional narration of the trauma narrative in TF-CBT (e.g., using dance/movement). While initial results of this study were promising, randomized controlled trials with higher rates of recruitment, engagement, and retention are necessary before drawing firm conclusions.

The need for testing evidence-based interventions with youth in foster care is further highlighted by a study that compared the efficacy of individual psychotherapy versus group psychotherapy for sexually abused girls. This study utilized a sample that included sexually abused girls living in foster care at the time of the intervention and sexually abused girls who were living with their families of origin at the time of the intervention. Results indicated that there were differential effects of the intervention for those living with their family of origin versus those in foster care; participants living at home demonstrated significantly better scores on a global assessment of functioning 1-year post intervention than participants in foster care (Trowell et al. 2002).

To summarize, although there are some exciting adaptations and testing of existing evidence-based programs for children in foster care, there are not enough of them currently available that have demonstrated efficacy through rigorous research in this population. The barriers identified above are salient impediments to more widespread testing of these adaptations. Even if the availability of such programming is increased, we need to use the burgeoning field of implementation science to study how we screen, refer, and retain youth and families in these services, as the recruitment and retention rates demonstrated thus far are quite concerning.

Conclusion

As the history of foster care in the United States demonstrates, there has been a gradual shift towards an emphasis on child well-being. The current administration at ACYF has clearly prioritized this aspect of child welfare practice and has charged the field to respond with evidence-based programming. But, as our review clearly demonstrates, we have a long way to go. While there have been some programs that have demonstrated efficacy in improving social, emotional, and behavioral well-being in maltreated children and adolescents in foster care, there are not nearly enough evidence-based interventions to meet the needs of these youth and their families. A review of the 255 programs on the California Evidence-Based Clearinghouse for Child Welfare (CEBC 2012) finds only two with the highest scientific rating that also have high child welfare relevance. In fact, among the 109 programs rated high in child welfare relevance, only a third ($N=32$) were even able to be rated for scientific merit.

We must also caution that our review is biased towards programs with efficacy, as many programs that demonstrate no findings or poor findings are never published. One important exception in a related literature highlights the caution by which we must proceed in adapting programs for new populations. Home visitation by public health nurses has been shown to prevent child maltreatment, yet a rigorous study of the adaptation of the model to reduce maltreatment recidivism did not demonstrate efficacy. The authors concluded that, "Successful remediation with families in which child maltreatment has already occurred might need very different services from those offered in early prevention programs" (MacMillan et al. 2005, p. 1792). Indeed, we cannot simply take programs that have been designated "evidence-based" and begin to use them with children and families in the foster care system. We cannot assume they will be effective. The field needs to conduct more rigorous trials to ensure that these existing interventions can be implemented with fidelity with children in foster care and that they produce the intended outcomes.

As reviewed above, there are also programs, albeit fewer, that have been specifically designed for youth in foster care and have demonstrated efficacy. The segment of the foster care population targeted, however, is narrow in most cases, and it would be difficult to serve the entire foster care population with the existing programs that have demonstrated positive outcomes. Clearly, more work is needed. We need more innovative and contextually-sensitive programs. We need replication trials of programs that have been tested in limited geographical areas or with small numbers of participants. We need an array of programs spanning the prevention-intervention spectrum as well as programs that span the age spectrum. We need programs that work for youth in kinship care, for youth in non-relative foster care, for those in congregate care, and for those who have reunified. We need programs that work when children bounce between these placement types and have multiple "primary" caregivers. We need programs that have enduring effects beyond the post-test assessments. We need programs that focus on well-being in multiple realms and aim to promote positive youth development and not just ameliorate problems. We need rigorously trained clinician-scientists to conduct this work, and they need time and money to move the field forward. Children in foster care deserve to have a fair shot at positive well-being – it's a promise whose time has come.

References

Administration on Children, Youth and Families, Administration for Children, Youth and Families, U.S. Department of Health and Human Services (ACYF). (2012). Information memorandum: Promoting social and emotional well-being for children and youth receiving child welfare services (ACYF-CB-IM-12-04). Washington, DC.

Ahrens, K. R., Richardson, L. P., Courtney, M. E., McCarty, C., Simoni, J., & Katon, W. (2010). Laboratory-diagnosed sexually transmitted infections in former foster youth compared with peers. *Pediatrics, 126*(1), e97–e103.

American Psychiatric Association. (2000). *Diagnostic and statistical manual of mental disorders (text rev)* (4th ed., text rev.). Washington, DC: Author.

Bellamy, J. L., Gopalan, G., & Traube, D. E. (2010). A national study of the impact of outpatient mental health services for children in long-term foster care. *Clinical Child Psychology and Psychiatry, 15*(4), 467–479.

Bess, R., Andrews, C., Jantz, A., Russell, V., & Geen, R. (2002). *The cost of protecting vulnerable children III: What factors affect states' decisions (No. 61)*. Washington, DC: Urban Institute.

Blumberg, E., Landsverk, J., Ellis-MacLeod, E., Ganger, W., & Culver, S. (1996). Use of the public mental health system by children in foster care: Client characteristics and service use patterns. *The Journal of Behavioral Health Services & Research, 23*(4), 389–405.

Burns, B. J., Phillips, S. D., Wagner, H. R., Barth, R. P., Kolko, D. J., Campbell, Y., & Landsverk, J. (2004). Mental health need and access to mental health services by youth involved with child welfare: A national survey. *Journal of the American Academy of Child and Adolescent Psychiatry, 43*(8), 960–970.

Bywater, T., Hutchings, J., Linck, P., Whitaker, C., Daley, D., Yeo, S. T., & Edwards, R. T. (2010). Incredible years parent training support for foster carers in Wales: A multi-centre feasibility study. *Child: Care, Health and Development, 37*(2), 233–243.

California Evidence-Based Clearinghouse. (2012). Retrieved from www.cebc4cw.org

Chaffin, J., Silovsky, J., Funderburk, B., Valle, L., Brestan, E., Balachova, T., Jackson, S., et al. (2004). Parent-child interaction therapy with physically abusive parents. Efficacy for reducing future abuse reports. *Journal of Consulting and Clinical Psychology, 72*, 491–499.

Chamberlain, P., & Reid, J. (1998). Comparison of two community alternatives to incarceration for chronic juvenile offenders. *Journal of Consulting and Clinical Psychology, 66*(4), 624–633.

Chamberlain, P., Price, J., Leve, L. D., Laurent, H., Landsverk, J., & Reid, J. B. (2008). Prevention of behavior problems for children in foster care: Outcomes and mediation effects. *Prevention Science, 9*(1), 17–27.

Child Welfare Information Gateway, Children's Bureau/Administration for Children, Youth and Families. (2012). *Major federal legislation concerned with child protection, child welfare and adoption* [Fact sheet]. Washington, DC.

Clark, H. B., Prange, M. E., Lee, B., Boyd, L. A., McDonald, B. A., & Stewart, E. S. (1994). Improving adjustment outcomes for foster children with emotional and behavioral disorders: Early findings from a controlled study on individual services. *Journal of Emotional and Behavioral Disorders, 2*(4), 207–218.

Clark, H. B., Prange, M. E., Lee, B., Stewart, E. S., McDonald, B. B., & Boyd, L. A. (1998). An individualized wrap-around process for children in foster with emotional/behavioral disturbances: Follow-up findings and implications from a controlled study. In M. H. Epstein, K. Kutash, & A. Duchnowski (Eds.), *Outcomes for children and youth with emotional and behavioral disorders and their families: Program and evaluation best practices* (pp. 513–542). Austin: Pro Ed.

Clausen, J. M., Landsverk, J., Ganger, W., Chadwick, D., & Litrownik, A. (1998). Mental health problems of children in foster care. *Journal of Child and Family Studies, 7*(3), 283–296.

Cohen, J. A., Mannarino, A. P., & Deblinger, E. (2006). *Treating trauma and traumatic grief in children and adolescents*. New York: Guilford Press.

Cook, A., Spinazzola, J., Ford, J., Lanktree, C., Blaustein, M., Cloitre, M., DeRosa, R., et al. (2005). Complex trauma in children and adolescents. *Psychiatric Annals, 35*, 390–398.

Courtney, M. E., & Barth, R. P. (1996). Pathways of older adolescents out of foster care: Implications for independent living services. *Social Work, 41*(1), 75–83.

Courtney, M. E., & Dworsky, A. (2005). *Midwest evaluation of the adult functioning of former foster youth: Outcomes at age 19*. Chicago: Chapin Hall Center for Children at the University of Chicago.

Courtney, M. E., & Dworsky, A. (2006). Early outcomes for young adults transitioning from out-of-home care in the U.S.A. *Child and Family Social Work, 11*, 209–219.

Courtney, M. E., & Heuring, D. H. (2005). The transition to adulthood for youth "aging out" of the foster care system. In D. W. Osgood, E. M. Foster, C. Flanagan, & G. R. Ruth (Eds.), *On your own without a net: The transition to adulthood for vulnerable populations*. Chicago: University of Chicago Press.

Courtney, M., Piliavin, I., Grogan-Kaylor, A., & Nesmith, A. (2001). Foster youth in transitions to adulthood: A longitudinal view of youth leaving care. *Child Welfare, 80*(6), 685–717.

Courtney, M. E., Terao, S., & Bost, N. (2004). *Midwest evaluation of the adult functioning of former foster youth: Conditions of youth preparing to leave state care*. Chicago: Chapin Hall Center for Children at the University of Chicago.

Courtney, M. E., Dworsky, A., Cusick, G., Havlicek, J., Perez, A., & Keller, T. (2007). *Midwest evaluation of the adult functioning of former foster youth: Outcomes at age 21*. Chicago: Chapin Hall Center for Children at the University of Chicago.

Courtney, M. E., Dworsky, A., Lee, J., & Raap, M. (2009). *Midwest evaluation of the adult functioning of former foster youth: Outcomes at age 23 and 24*. Chicago: Chapin Hall at the University of Chicago.

Deblinger, E., Lippman, J., & Steer, R. (1996). Sexually abused children suffering posttraumatic stress symptoms: Initial treatment outcome findings. *Child Maltreatment, 1*(4), 310–321.

DeRosa, R., Habib, M., Pelcovitz, D., Rathus, J., Sonnenklar, J., Ford, J., Sunday, S., et al. (2006). Structured psychotherapy for adolescents responding to stress [Brochure]. Manhasset.

Donkoh, C., Underhill, K., & Montgomery, P. (2006). Independent living programmes for improving outcomes for young people leaving the care system. *Children and Youth Services Review, 28*(12), 1435–1448.

dosReis, S., Zito, J. M., Safer, D. J., & Soeken, K. L. (2001). Mental health services for foster care and disabled youth. *American Journal of Public Health, 91*(7), 1094–1099.

Dozier, M., Peloso, E., Lindhiem, O., Gordon, M. K., Manni, M., Sepulveda, S., Ackerman, J., et al. (2006). Developing evidence-based interventions for foster children: An example of a randomized clinical trial with infants and toddlers. *Journal of Social Issues, 62*(4), 767–785.

Dozier, M., Peloso, E., Lewis, E., Laurenceau, J. P., & Levine, S. (2008). Effects of an attachment-based intervention on the cortisol production of infants and toddlers in foster care. *Development and Psychopathology, 20*(3), 845–859.

Dozier, M., Lindhiem, O., Lewis, E., Bick, J., Bernard, K., & Peloso, E. (2009). Effects of a foster parent training program on young children's attachment behaviors: Preliminary evidence from a randomized clinical trial. *Child and Adolescent Social Work Journal, 26*(4), 321–332.

Felitti, V. J., Anda, R. F., Nordenberg, D., Williamson, D. F., Spitz, A. M., Edwards, V., et al. (1998). Relationship of childhood abuse and household dysfunction to many of the leading causes of death in adults: The Adverse Childhood Experiences (ACE) study. *American Journal of Preventive Medicine, 14*(4), 245–258.

Fisher, P. A., & Kim, H. K. (2007). Intervention effects on foster preschoolers' attachment-related behaviors from a randomized trial. *Prevention Science, 8*(2), 161–170.

Fisher, P. A., Burraston, B., & Pears, K. C. (2005). The early intervention foster care program: Permanent placement outcomes from a randomized trial. *Child Maltreatment, 10*(1), 61–71.

Fisher, P. A., Stoolmiller, M., Gunnar, M. R., & Burraston, B. (2007). Effects of a therapeutic intervention for foster preschoolers on diurnal cortisol activity. *Psychoneuroendocrinology, 32*(8–10), 892–905.

Garland, A. F., Landsverk, J. L., Hough, R. L., & Ellis-MacLeod, E. (1996). Type of maltreatment as a predictor of mental health service use for children in foster care. *Child Abuse & Neglect, 20*, 675–688.

Garland, A. F., Hough, R. L., McCabe, K. M., Yeh, M. Y., Wood, P. A., & Aarons, G. A. (2001). Prevalence of psychiatric disorders in youths across five sectors of care. *Journal of the American Academy of Child and Adolescent Psychiatry, 40*(4), 409–418.

Ghera, M. M., Marshall, P. J., Fox, N. A., Zeanah, C. H., Nelson, C. A., Smyke, A. T., & Guthrie, D. (2009). The effects of foster care intervention on socially deprived institutionalized children's attention and positive affect: Results from the BEIP study. *Journal of Child Psychology and Psychiatry, 50*(3), 246–253.

Hacsi, T. (1995). From indenture to family foster care: A brief history of child placing. *Child Welfare, 74*(1), 162–180.

Hadley, A. M., Mbwana, K., & Hair, E. C. (2010). *What works for older youth during transition to adulthood: Lessons from experimental evaluations of programs and interventions* (Report No. 2010-05). Washington, DC: Child Trends.

Halfon, N., Berkowitz, G., & Klee, L. (1992). Mental health service utilization by children in foster care in California. *Pediatrics, 89*(6), 1238–1244.

Halfon, N., Zepeda, A., & Inkelas, M. (2002). Mental health services for children in foster care. *UCLA Center for Healthier Children, Families and Communities, 4*(9), 1–13.

Harman, J. S., Childs, G. D., & Kelleher, K. J. (2000). Mental health care utilization and expenditures by children in foster care. *Archives of Pediatrics & Adolescent Medicine, 154*(11), 1114–1117.

Kempe, C. H., Silverman, F. N., Steele, B. F., Droegemueller, W., & Silver, H. K. (1962). The battered-child syndrome. *Journal of the American Medical Association, 181*(1), 17–24.

Kim, H. K., & Leve, L. D. (2011). Substance use and delinquency among middle school girls in foster care: A three-year-follow-up of a randomized controlled trial. *Journal of Consulting and Clinical Psychology, 79*(6), 740–750.

Koverola, C., Murtaugh, C. A., Connors, K. M., Reeves, G., & Papas, M. A. (2007). Children exposed to intra-familial violence. *Journal of Maltreatment and Trauma, 14*(4), 19–42.

Landsverk, J., & Garland, A. (1998). Foster care and pathways to mental health services. In P. A. Curtis, G. Dale Jr., & J. C. Kendall (Eds.), *The foster care crisis: Translating research into practice and policy* (pp. 193–210). Nebraska: The University of Nebraska Press.

Leathers, S. J., Atkins, M. S., Spielfogel, J. E., McMeel, L. S., Wesley, J. M., & Davis, R. (2009). Context-specific mental health services for children in foster care. *Children and Youth Services Review, 31*, 1289–1297.

Leslie, L. K., Landsverk, J., Ezzet-Lofstrom, R., Tschann, J. M., Slymen, D., & Garland, A. F. (2000). Children in foster care: Factors influencing outpatient mental health service use. *Child Abuse & Neglect, 24*(4), 465–276.

Leslie, L. K., Hurlburt, M. S., Landsverk, J., Barth, R., & Slymen, D. J. (2004). Outpatient mental health services for children in foster care: A national perspective. *Child Abuse & Neglect, 28*(6), 697–712.

Letarte, M., Normandeau, S., & Allard, J. (2010). Effectiveness of a parent training program "Incredible Years" in a child protection service. *Child Abuse & Neglect, 34*, 253–261.

Leve, L. D., Chamberlain, P., & Reid, J. B. (2005). Intervention outcomes for girls referred from juvenile justice: Effects on delinquency. *Journal of Consulting and Clinical Psychology, 73*(6), 1181–1185.

Leve, L. D., Fisher, P. A., & Chamberlain, P. (2009). Multidimensional treatment foster care as a preventive intervention to promote resilience among youth in the child welfare system. *Journal of Personality, 77*(6), 1869–1902.

Lewis-Morrarty, E., Dozier, M., Bernard, K., Terracciano, S. M., & Moore, S. V. (2012). Cognitive flexibility and theory of mind outcomes among foster children: Preschool follow-up results of a randomized clinical trial. *The Journal of Adolescent Health, 51*(2), S17–S22.

Lieberman, A. F., Van Horn, P., & Ippen, C. G. (2005). Toward evidence-based treatment: child-parent psychotherapy with preschoolers exposed to marital violence. *Journal of American Academy of Child and Adolescent Psychiatry, 44*(12), 1241–1248.

Linares, L. O., Montalto, D., Li, M., & Oza, V. S. (2006). A promising parenting intervention in foster care. *Journal of Consulting and Clinical Psychology, 74*(1), 32–41.

Lou, C., Anthony, E. K., Stone, S., Vu, C. M., & Austin, M. J. (2008). Assessing child and youth well-being: Implications for child welfare practice. *Journal of Evidence-Based Social Work, 5*(1–2), 91–133.

MacMillan, H. L., Thomas, B. H., Jamieson, E., Walsh, C. A., Boyle, M. H., Shannon, H. S., & Gafni, A. G. (2005). Effectiveness of home visitation by public-health nurses in prevention of the recurrence of child physical abuse and neglect: A randomised controlled trial. *The Lancet, 365*(9473), 1786–1793.

Maher, E. J., Jackson, L. V., Pecora, P. J., Schultz, D. J., Chandra, A., & Barnes-Proby, D. S. (2009). Overcoming challenges to implementing and evaluating evidence-based interventions in child welfare: A matter of necessity. *Children and Youth Services Review, 31*, 555–562.

Marshall, P. J., Reeb, B. C., Fox, N. A., Nelson, C. A., & Zeanah, C. H. (2012). Effects of early intervention on EEG power and coherence in previously institutionalized children in Romania. *Development and Psychopathology, 20*(3), 861–880.

McCrae, J. S., Barth, R. P., & Guo, S. (2010). Changes in maltreated children's emotional-behavioral problems following typically provided mental health services. *The American Journal of Orthopsychiatry, 80*(3), 350–361.

McDonald, T. P., Allen, R. I., Westerfelt, A., & Piliavin, I. (1996). *Assessing the long-term effects of foster care: A research synthesis*. Washington, DC: CWLA Press.

McKay, M. M., Hibbert, R., Hoagwood, K., Rodriguez, J., Murray, L., Legerski, J., & Fernandez, D. (2004). Integrating evidence-based engagement interventions into "real world" child mental health settings. *Brief Treatment and Crisis Intervention, 4*(2), 177–186.

McMillen, J. C., Scott, L. D., Zima, B. T., Ollie, M. T., Munson, M. R., & Spitznagel, E. (2004). Use of mental health services among older youths in foster care. *Psychiatric Services, 55*(7), 811–817.

McNeil, C. B., Herschell, A. D., Gurwitch, R. H., & Clemens-Mowrer, L. (2005). Training foster parents in parent-child interaction therapy. *Education and Treatment of Children, 28*(2), 182–196.

Murray, K. O., & Gesiriech, S. (2004). *A brief legislative history of the child welfare system*. Washington, DC: Pew Charitable Trust.

National Survey of Child and Adolescent Well-Being. (n.d.). *Who are the children in foster care? Research brief, findings from the NSCAW study* (NSCAW No. 1). Retrieved from http://www.acf.hhs.gov/programs/opre/abuse_neglect/nscaw/reports/children_fostercare/childrefostercare.html

Nelson, C. A., Zeanah, C. H., Fox, N. A., Marshall, P. J., Smyke, A. T., & Guthrie, D. (2007). Cognitive recovery in socially deprived young children: The Bucharest Early Intervention Project. *Science, 318*(5858), 1937–1940.

Price, J. M., Chamberlain, P., Landsverk, J., Reid, J. B., Leve, L. D., & Laurent, H. (2008). Effects of a foster parent training intervention on placement changes of children in foster care. *Child Maltreatment, 13*(1), 64–75.

Samuels, B. (2012). Looking to the future: An agenda for the Children's Bureau's next 100 years. 18th *National conference on child abuse and neglect*. Conference conducted at the Washington Hilton Hotel of Washington, DC.

Smith, D. K., Leve, L. D., & Chamberlain, P. (2011). Preventing internalizing and externalizing problems in girls in foster care as they enter middle school: Impact of an intervention. *Prevention Science, 12*(3), 269–277.

Smyke, A. T., Zeanah, C. H., Fox, N. A., Nelson, C. A., & Guthrie, D. (2010). Placement in foster care enhances quality of attachment among young institutionalized children. *Child Development, 81*(1), 212–223.

Sprang, G. (2009). The efficacy of a relational treatment of maltreated children and their families. *Child and Adolescent Mental Health, 14*(2), 81–88.

Stewart, A., Dennison, S., & Waterson, E. (2002). Pathways from child maltreatment to juvenile offending. Trends and issues in crimes and criminal justice, *241*. Australian Institute of Criminology.

Stouthamer-Loeber, M., Loeber, R., Homish, D. L., & Wei, E. (2001). Maltreatment of boys and the development of disruptive and delinquent behavior. *Development and Psychopathology, 13*(4), 941–944.

Tarren-Sweeney, M. (2010). It's time to re-think mental health services for children in care, and those adopted from care. *Clinical Child Psychology and Psychiatry, 15*(4), 613–626.

Taussig, H. N., & Culhane, S. E. (2005). Foster care as an intervention for abused and neglected children. In K. A. Kendall-Tackett & S. M. Giacomoni (Eds.), *Child victimization: Maltreatment, bullying and dating violence, prevention and intervention* (pp. 20:1–20:25). Kingston: Civic Research Institute.

Taussig, H. N., & Culhane, S. E. (2010). Impact of a mentoring and skills group program on mental health outcomes for maltreated children in foster care. *Archives of Pediatrics & Adolescent Medicine, 164*(8), 739–746.

Taussig, H. T., Culhane, S. E., & Hettleman, D. H. (2007). Fostering healthy futures: An innovative preventive intervention for preadolescent youth in out-of-home care. *Child Welfare, 86*(5), 113–131.

Taussig, H. T., Culhane, S. E., Garrido, E., & Knudtson, M. D. (2012). RCT of a mentoring and skills group program: Placement and permanency outcomes for foster youth. *Pediatrics, 130*(1), e33–e39.

Thornberry, T. P., Huizinga, D., & Loeber, R. (2004). The causes and correlates studies: Findings and policy implications. *Journal of the Office of Juvenile Justice and Delinquency Prevention, 9*, 3–19. Reprinted in T. J. Bernard (ed.). (2006). *Serious delinquency: An anthology* (pp. 39–52). Los Angeles: Roxbury.

Timmer, S. G., Urquiza, A. J., Zebell, N. M., & McGrath, J. M. (2005). Parent-child interaction therapy: Application to maltreating parent-child dyads. *Child Abuse & Neglect, 29*, 825–842.

Timmer, S. G., Urquiza, A. J., Herschell, A. D., McGrath, J. M., Zebell, N. M., Porter, A. L., & Vargas, E. C. (2006a). Parent-child interaction therapy: An application of empirically supported treatment to maltreated children in foster care. *Child Welfare League of America, 85*(6), 919–939.

Timmer, S. G., Urquiza, A. J., & Zebell, N. M. (2006b). Challenging foster caregiver-maltreated child relationships: The effectiveness of parent-child interaction therapy. *Children and Youth Services Review, 28*, 1–19.

Trowell, J., Kolvin, I., Weeramanthri, T., Sadowski, H., Berelowitz, M., Glasser, D., & Leitch, I. (2002). Psychotherapy for sexually abused girls: Psychopathological outcome findings and patterns of change. *The British Journal of Psychiatry, 180*, 234–247.

United States Department of Health and Human Services, Administration for Children and Families, Administration for Children, Youth, and Families. (2012). *AFCARS data: Trends in foster care and adoption – FY 2002-FY 2011*. www.acf.hhs.gov/programs/cb

Webster-Stratton, C. (1984). Randomized trial of two parent-training programs for families with conduct-disordered children. *Journal of Consulting and Clinical Psychology, 52*(4), 666–678.

Weiner, D. A., Schneider, A., & Lyons, J. S. (2009). Evidence-based treatments for trauma among culturally-diverse foster care youth: Treatment retention and outcomes. *Children and Youth Services Review, 31*(11), 1199–1205.

Widom, C. S. (1991). The role of placement experiences in mediating the criminal consequences of early childhood victimization. *The American Journal of Orthopsychiatry, 6*(2), 195–209.

Widom, C. S., & Maxfield, M. G. (1996). A prospective examination of risk for violence among abused and neglected children. *Annals of the New York Academy of Sciences, 794*, 224–237.

Wiebush, R., Frietag, R., & Baird, C. (2001). *Preventing delinquency through improved child protection services*. OJJDP Bulletin. Available at: http://www.ojjdp.gov/publications/PubAbstract.asp?pubi=187759

Zeanah, C. H., Egger, H. L., Smyke, A. T., Nelson, C. A., Fox, C. A., Marshall, P. J., & Guthrie, D. (2009). Institutional rearing and psychiatric disorders in Romanian preschool children. *Journal of American Psychiatry, 166*, 777–785.

Zetlin, A., Weinberg, L., & Kimm, C. (2004). Improving education outcomes for children in foster care: Intervention by an education liaison. *Journal of Education for Students Placed at Risk, 9*(4), 421–429.

Chapter 22
Addressing Child Maltreatment Through Mutual Support and Self-Help Among Parents

Arlene Bowers Andrews

Introduction

To begin with the obvious: humans develop slowly, over long periods of time. Thus parents must be prepared for the ebbs and flows of change as they and their children mature and their social networks evolve. This essential fact poses a problem for many programs that aim to prevent or remediate child maltreatment.

Much of the research about effective methods of child maltreatment prevention and treatment focuses on formal programs, those that involve trained professionals and paraprofessionals delivering services through carefully developed protocols. Most formal programs touch the lives of families for relatively brief periods, entering for support of highly focused goals, most often related to parental education, skills training, or therapy. The program personnel or family members terminate services after a couple of years, a few months, days, or even hours. Even when formal programs are routinely available, as at health care centers, schools, or through home visits, they offer only passing periods of support relative to the steady momentum of family life. When program involvement ceases, family life moves on and child and parental development continues for better or for worse. The natural social environment of the family may change little, if at all, after the program is gone.

Ask any parents how they cope with the constant ups and downs of childrearing and they are most likely to say: "My mom...," "My wife (husband)," "My best friend...," "My co-workers," or "My faith community." They might say, "My parents' group," "my home visitor," "my therapist," or perhaps even, "my caseworker." Parents value receiving social and emotional support. They also benefit from the opportunity to *give* mutual aid in reciprocal, informal relationships. Giving to another parent can affirm the dignity and worth of the contributing parent. And parents who support one another as they lead and influence how formal family supports are provided, rather than engaging in programs as humble recipients, report enhanced sense of competence as parents.

Multiple studies about risk and protective factors associated with child maltreatment have concluded that the provision of social support through mutual aid among parents is an important component of child maltreatment prevention and treatment programs (see, e.g., Appleyard et al. 2007; Constantino et al. 2001; Frame et al. 2006; Green et al. 2007; Li et al. 2011; Lyons et al. 2005; Thomlison 2003). Parents show stronger and more persistent improvement if they participate in mutual support (Moran et al. 2004). Their children show longer-lasting benefits of participation in therapeutic programs (Appleyard et al. 2007; Layzer et al. 2001). Though parental mutual support and

A.B. Andrews, Ph.D., LISW (✉)
College of Social Work, University of South Carolina, Columbia, SC 29208, USA
e-mail: Arlene.andrews@sc.edu

J.E. Korbin and R.D. Krugman (eds.), *Handbook of Child Maltreatment*, Child Maltreatment 2,
DOI 10.1007/978-94-007-7208-3_22, © Springer Science+Business Media Dordrecht 2014

self-help are valued in the professional literature, remarkably few research studies with rigorous designs have examined effective practices for such processes among parents, particularly those at risk of child maltreatment (Barth and Haskins 2009; Kang 2012; Lyons et al. 2005). While these processes sound naturalistic, they may not occur spontaneously. Efforts to prevent and treat child maltreatment could benefit from more systematic research about mutual support and self-help.

In some ways, mutual support and self-help are the core of any family care system. Families have persistent, intense emotional and pragmatic needs that can be met only through natural helping networks. Formal family services may help parents cope, learn, heal, nurture, and manage in many ways; providing services in a way that strengthens mutual support among parents and self-help by parents can enhance service effectiveness, as noted above. But when formal parenting programs are done and gone, parental mutual support and self-help are all there is. And in many cases, parents may prefer not to engage in services, or services may be nonexistent or poorly matched to the family's unique needs.

A core concept here requires emphasis: Mutual support occurs among parents in natural networks. Social support may be provided to parents through other people, such as informally or formally designated parents or professionals who are not part of the support recipient's natural system. The focus in this article is on mutual support, not general parental social support. The reason for this emphasis is that readers who are trained in professions are likely to see parent support through their own lens, with a frame that says, "I can support you." The focus of that lens is on "I," the professional. Or it might be "we," the formal family support system. The implication is that parents primarily have deficits that need remediation through professional and other formal supports.

The goal here is to promote research through a lens that examines parents' support systems and the role of professionals relative to parents in a way that shifts focus to "you," the parent, with questions such as, "Will you help me understand how you and your friends and family support one another? How may I partner with you to strengthen your support?" This approach is certainly not new but it has yet to become common in research about service delivery for family systems at high risk of child maltreatment. Conducting research through the lens of the parent engaged in mutual support and self-help, i.e., practice-informed research, may increase the relevance of research evidence to inform practice for strengthening natural helping systems.

This chapter offers a foundation for further research about parental mutual support and self-help. The first section defines parental mutual support and self-help and summarizes the theoretical rationale for why they are vital components of any community system of family care. The subsequent discussion focuses on the current research evidence about interventions designed to strengthen parental mutual support and self-help, including challenges and opportunities in translating current research knowledge to practice within communities.

Why Parental Mutual Support and Self-Help Matter

To say that all parents need support at times is tautological. The challenge is to discover effective ways to operationalize "support" and actualize capacity to deliver support and strengthen naturalistic support for any parent with regard to culture, socioeconomic status, gender, place, and other critical factors. Universal safe, stable, and nurturing environments for children will not magically happen but must be intentionally developed, with parental support as an essential component of the environment.

The terms "parental mutual support and self-help" are derived from research and practice literature that uses multiple related terms, so this discussion begins with a clarification of terms as used here. Next is a synopsis of theories that support the value of parental mutual support and self-help in the context of child maltreatment risk reduction.

Definitions of Terms in This Chapter

Parenting persists throughout the lifespan but the focus here is on parents with dependent-age children. Often the term "caregiver" refers to the person who cares for a child; here "parent" will be used. A parent may be a biological or adoptive parent, stepparent, grandparent, kinship care provider, foster parent, noncustodial parent, or anyone in a primary familial role that involves nurturing children from birth through age 17.

For ease of reading, "at risk" will refer to "at risk of committing child maltreatment."

"Self-help" refers to the capacity to autonomously seek assistance to solve one's own problems (Reissman and Carroll 1995). A related construct is self-efficacy, or the belief in one's competence and ability to influence decisions that affect one's own well-being (Bandura 1997). Parental self-efficacy is a parent's belief in her or his ability to perform parenting skills; higher levels of parental self-efficacy are associated with lower levels of child maltreatment and higher levels of parenting competence (Coleman and Karraker 1997; Jones and Prinz 2005). Parental self-help may be associated with greater parental self-efficacy and competence. A vast industry exists to facilitate independent self-help (e.g., websites, books, media programs), but in this chapter, the focus is on mutual aid as a means to self-help.

Self-help and "mutual support" are terms that often co-occur as individuals engage in self-help together (Lee and Swenson 1994). Mutual support, also called "mutual aid," is reciprocal "social support." Social support may take several forms, such as concrete aid (e.g. food, transportation), information (e.g. advice or facts), and emotion (e.g. affirmation, empathy, affection) (Haines et al. 2002). A person's social support can be described in terms of how the person perceives the support (i.e., belief that it is available), the enactment of the support, and the degree to which the person feel integrated into a social support system (Barrera 1986; Uchino 2009). Enhancing social support and maximizing its positive effects can be complicated. While the literature about benefits of social support is extensive, empirical research about mutual support (reciprocal support) is limited, and is particularly sparse with regard to parents at risk.

A parent's "social network" is the number and type of people with whom the parent interacts. People in the network may be supportive or not; in fact, in families at risk of child maltreatment, much of the stress comes from relationships in the social network (e.g. history of harsh or abusive relationships in childhood or adulthood, instability, or unreliable capacity for support) (Easterbrooks et al. 2011; Lyons et al. 2005). In one study of young mothers who reported negative childhood family contexts, greater resilience in parenting was associated with less caregiving and emotional support from their mothers (Easterbrooks et al. 2011). Some parents have large networks, but if the support capacity is minimal, the parent may feel alone or challenged. A well-established practice when trying to help people change harmful behavior (e.g. drinking, drug use, crime) is to help people replace former, negative social networks with more positive networks. Generally, people who have positive, supportive networks of adequate size have better well-being (Coyne and Downey 1991).

A "support group" is a small network of people who meet regularly or socially interact in other ways (e.g. in-person, by telephone, on websites, or social media). Parent mutual support is often assumed to be in the form of groups that meet, but mutual aid can take several forms, including dyadic relationships, neighborly interactions, and a variety of shared social situations.

As used here, "traditional family services" refers to interventions and supports for families that are developed and delivered primarily by professionals (e.g., teachers, nurses, social workers, physicians, mental health practitioners, public health workers) or paraprofessionals under professional supervision (e.g. home visitors or parent aides). The notion of a "service" is that someone (the service provider) delivers something to (perhaps with) another (the parent).

Parental mutual support does not include programs that rely on trained parents as paraprofessionals in a nonreciprocal, traditional model (e.g. home visitor, parent aide, or consumer advocate or providers within a traditional family service program).

The focus here also is not on parent education or training. Colloquially, when family service providers refer to parent support, they often mean some form of intervention to promote parenting skills or knowledge development. Such education may occur in a variety of ways, ranging from sharing information by phone or email to one-on-one in-person coaching sessions to large classes, with good effects in many cases (Lundahl et al. 2006). A recent Rand Corporation survey regarding preferred child abuse prevention modes found parent education to be most favored among respondents, who were primarily professionals in child and family services (Shaw and Kilburn 2009). Parent education and support are complementary processes. While parental mutual support sometimes has an educational aspect, its goals are more complex.

In this chapter, the terms "parental mutual support and self-help" refer to voluntary activities among parents in different families coping with similar situations. The activities may be facilitated by workers in traditional programs, but the primary activities are among the parents and are not led by professionals. And the focus here is on support across families, i.e., nonfamilial support, not support that is primarily within family systems.

Theoretical Foundation for Parental Mutual Support and Self-Help

Parental mutual support and self-help are the core processes in the proverbial village that raises the child. They are the crux of what has been called "natural helping networks" for families with children (Watson and Collins 1982). In theory, parental mutual support and self-help will benefit parents, their children, and their communities in ways that are effective and sustainable. The benefits derive from the processes of receiving and giving to build family assets and meet family needs. As parents support one another, they tend to influence the transformation of traditional family services into parent-informed and parent-led resources. The theories and constructs that support this claim to benefits include social ecology and systems theory, cultural sensitivity, family strengthening, self-determination and empowerment, and reciprocity and collective efficacy.

Social Ecology and Systems Theory. Parenting behavior is complex and can exert harmful, helpful, neutral, or mixed effects on child development. A systems framework helps to explain how people develop parenting behaviors and how they can change (Belsky 1993; Bronfenbrenner 1979, 2005; Germain 1991; Shulman and Gitterman 1994; Swenson and Chaffin 2006).

At the heart of the system are the individual child and individual parent. They are nested in a family system that involves interactions among parent and child, multiple adults in parenting roles (e.g. fathers, mothers, grandparents), multiple children, and others in the family. Family members tend to live in multiple households in developed countries. Individuals and the family are influenced by relationships in their social networks, such as peers, mentors, neighbors, and co-workers (Cochran and Walker 2005). These groups are affected by organizational dynamics, neighborhood norms, and community characteristics. For example, research has long substantiated that neighborhood characteristics are associated with parenting practices: disadvantaged neighborhoods have more parents at high risk and, conversely, advantaged neighborhoods include parents who engage in positive parenting practices (Barrera et al. 2002; Cantillon 2006; Coulton et al. 1995; Garbarino and Kostelny 1992; Leventhal and Brooks-Gunn 2000). One study found that neighborhood collective efficacy particularly predicts parents' perception of support from friends (Tendulkar et al. 2012). How neighborhoods affect parents seems to involve complex processes that require further study, which should include a search for how mutual relationships among neighbors influence parenting behavior.

Parents' social networks are influenced by societal characteristics, public policies, media messages, and cultural norms. All these elements of the social environment exchange such resources as information, material goods, and social and emotional support and also create challenges such as conflict and deprivation. Much of the resource exchange occurs through natural (informal) relationships, though some is grounded in traditional services. What looks like a simple parent-child relationship in a family is actually a complex social system.

Time is also a factor in systems. Known as the parents' chronosystem, factors in the parents' social history and life events (past, current, and anticipated) influence how the parent interacts with and makes decisions within the family's social system. People learn to be parents through the influences of their social systems, starting in their own childhoods. When they become parents themselves, how they behave depends in part on what they have learned in terms of beliefs, knowledge, communication skills, emotional expression, and other behavior. Responsible parents are mindful that how they interact with their child today will affect how the child interacts with others into the future. How parents actually relate to a child also depends on their unique relationship with the child, perceptions of social support, and the specific situations they encounter over time.

Parents may benefit from help through mutual support or formal services as they assess the needs and strengths of their unique social systems. As change in the parent and family's life evolves, spontaneously or by intention, the entire system will change – for better or for worse. Theoretically, strengthening the assets of people who naturally interact in the system by increasing their capacity for mutual support will promote positive adaptation by the parents and the people in the support network. With appropriate competence and prosocial interactions, members of the system can generate the necessary resources for parental support, and the supportive system will sustain itself over long periods of time. Mutual support and self-help can address the professional's dilemma of how to sustain family support in ways that adapt to changing needs and resources over time.

Building on Karoly's (1993) self-regulation theory, Sanders (2008) emphasizes the importance of parental self-regulation as a unifying concept in family systems; it is at the core of programs such as the Triple-P parenting program (Prinz et al. 2009; Sanders et al. 2003; Sanders and Prinz 2008). Five aspects of parental self-regulation include parental self-sufficiency (resilience, personal resources, knowledge, and skills), self-efficacy (belief in own capacity to solve problems), self-management (setting one's own goals and standards as a parent and monitoring performance), personal agency (awareness of one's own capacity to create change rather than attribute change to factors outside self) and active problem solving. Sanders notes that self-regulating parents can do so with "minimal or no additional support" (2008 p. 507), but the implication that parents function independently has not been empirically examined. Mutual support may be a key to effective parental self-regulation.

Parental mutual support and self-help are environmentally adaptable. They can occur any time and in places that are most comfortable for parents. Even parents in involuntary situations – such as prison or homeless – can benefit from mutual support. The core process are voluntary, so cost is minimal, though resources are needed to assure training and technical assistance for parents who need help strengthening their mutual support networks. For example, given that many high-risk parents are survivors of trauma and coercive control and have safety concerns, when they are in help seeking mode they often feel vulnerable if in a place associated with power, such as a school or health or human services agency. They may feel reluctant or unable to voluntarily participate in traditional services. How to engage and retain parents in programs are constant concerns and the foci of considerable research. McCurdy and Daro (2001) found that family and neighborhood factors influence parental participation, suggesting peers and neighbors are important motivators. Mutual aid reduces access barriers and can facilitate parental connections to necessary traditional services.

Cultural Sensitivity. Systems theory predicts that support delivered in culturally sensitive ways is most likely to produce benefits. Culture, the systematic organization of social behavior through customs, beliefs, and values, pervades all life and powerfully affects parenting behavior (Santisteban 2002). Each parent affiliates with several cultures (e.g. racial-ethnic identity, gender, religion, or socioeconomic class). Within their communities, parents learn cultural expectations. Parental self-efficacy develops through messages about parenting values and childrearing techniques communicated through media, education, community-based experiences and, most powerfully, the people in the parents' family and social networks (Coleman and Karraker 1997; Falconer 2005–2006). People from populations that have suffered oppression are particularly likely to engage in mutual aid (Shulman and Gitterman 1994).

Parents from nonwhite racial, ethnic, and cultural groups that have experienced historical oppression are disproportionately in need of support. African Americans, American Indians, and other minority groups are disproportionately represented in the child welfare system; yet research about effective practice rarely attends to the cultural context of the interventions (Wells et al. 2009). Recently Ayón (2011) found that Latino parents required to become involved in the child welfare system relied heavily on their social networks for emotional support, advice, information, and advocacy; more knowledge is needed to identify ways to involve and strengthen such network involvement. Until recently some groups, such as noncustodial fathers and grandparents, were often excluded from traditional parenting support programs. Programs are becoming more inclusive, but much more work is needed to determine effective practices (Gerberding et al. 2008). For example, Dumas and colleagues (2008) found that matching parents and group leaders by socioeconomic status mattered more than ethnicity in increasing parents' attendance, retention, and active participation in parenting support groups.

By examining the complexity of any family's social ecology and how resources are generated and sustained across components of the system, the value of mutual support becomes clear.

Family Strengthening. Families at risk are known to have fragile or conflicted social networks. Their positive supports may be eroded by exceptional stressors such as challenges that are personal (e.g. mental health or physical health conditions, addiction, cognitive impairment), social (e.g., intimate partner violence, child with a behavioral or emotional problem, family isolation), economic (e.g. poverty, housing, employment problems), or legal (e.g., civil or criminal problems, immigration). Such factors are well established correlates of risk for child maltreatment (CDC 2007; Cicchetti and Lynch 1993; Daro and McCurdy 1994; Dukewich et al. 1996; English 1998; Fagan and Browne 1994; Horton 2003; Kotch et al. 1995; Mash et al. 1983; Marcenko et al. 2011; Reid et al. 1987; Rinehart et al. 2005; Rosenberg 1987; Zuravin 1988).

A major factor predicting risk is the parents' exposure to stressors and capacity for managing stress. Because of multiple adverse life events, at-risk parents may cope with childrearing through a lens of complex stress and trauma effects. But their coping resources may be limited. For example, Horton's (2003) review of risk factors found that poor, dangerous neighborhoods characterized by low levels of social trust and cohesion produce high degrees of familial isolation and stress.

Parents at low risk of child maltreatment are likely to believe they can access support when needed and they demonstrate resilience in coping with stress, accurate information about child development and effective parenting skills, belief in their own competence as parents, attachment to their children, comfort with help seeking, and a positive regard for their children's abilities (Belsky 1993; CDC 2007, FRIENDS National Resource Center n.d.). Higher levels of parental social support are associated with lower levels of parental stress, ineffective parenting, and child difficulties, even in the context of financial hardship, a prevalent factor in at-risk families (McConnell et al. 2011). The physiological and psychological buffering effects of perceived social support on the association of caregiving stress and adverse health effects is well established (see e.g. Lovell et al. 2012). Social connection is one of the core protective factors in the widely acclaimed "Strengthening Families" approach promulgated by the Center for the Study of Social Policy (CSSP) (2011). The CSSP approach's four other protective factors – parental resilience, knowledge of parenting and child development, concrete support in times of need, and social and emotional competence of children – are also embedded in strong social support and environments.

The benefits of parental social support are well established. Informal social support can reduce parental stress and isolation and promote positive identity and well-being (Cameron et al. 1997; Cameron 2002; Kurtz 1990; Lin et al. 2009). Self-help and mutual aid participants increase knowledge and skills, contribute to their communities, and rely less on formal systems (Borkman 1999; Kyrouz et al. 2002; Toseland 1990). Parents develop resilience in part through sustained, trusting relationships and learning from successful help seeking experiences (Easterbrooks et al. 2011; Walsh 1998). Although most professionals are now trained in the strengths perspective (see e.g. Saleeby 1992); Steinberg (2010) observed that many still practice in ways that suggest they lack faith in the capacity of high-risk parents to help themselves and others. More research is needed to find effective methods to build confidence and skills among professionals so they might enable mutual support and self-help among at-risk parents. They would need to focus on enhancing family and parental resilience and other assets, thus enriching the protective potential of the family.

Self-Determination and Empowerment. Client empowerment and self-determination have long been the ideological norm in human services and a nurturing worker-client relationship has been the standard in direct child and family services (Maluccio 1981; Neff 2000). Yet parents still report, in practice, they are often excluded or treated as objects in need of correction. In traditional services parents report that while they are struggling to promote holistic development of their children, families, and selves, staff often see the parents' and children's lives in fragments based on particular issues (like recovery or learning needs) or specific services (like parenting skills class or after school program). This breach between the ideology of family support and practice needs to be closed (Langford and Wolf 2001).

Mutual support among parents mutes the potential imbalance of power that is implicit in professional-participant role (Dunst and Dempsey 2007). The relationship is a safe place to share pain or distress without fear of sanctions and to find hope, acceptance, and belonging (Davidson et al. 1999; Hogan et al. 2002). For at-risk parents, peer support is de-stigmatizing and helps overcome the sense of shame or self-blame.

The core elements of parent empowerment are personal mastery, self-determination, and collective empowerment (Boehm and Staples 2004). Social learning theory predicts – and research confirms – people learn from one another and become open to new ideas (Dunst et al. 1994). By relating to someone in similar straits, a parent is more likely to feel efficacious about trying new skills. Parent outcomes are enhanced when services meet the unique needs of the parent, particularly when the parent has multiple challenges, such as risk of child maltreatment and substance abuse (Choi and Staudt 2011). When parents collectively support one another on their paths to self-help and self-determination regarding their unique needs, empowerment is likely to emerge.

Reciprocity and Collective Efficacy. Steinberg (1997, 2010) summarized the qualities of the mutual aid practitioner as: joy in sharing, faith in strengths, courage to accept and stay in the mess and chaos of mutual aid, and curiosity to seek and understand diverse views and feelings. People learn empathy by being in caring relationships such as those formed in mutual support networks (Egeland et al. 2002; Horton 2003). Parents who support one another on their self-help journeys reap the benefits of giving, which may include enhanced sense of competence, moral satisfaction, and feelings of social usefulness (Halabi and Nadler 2010; Luks 2001; Staub and Vollhardt 2008). Giving support is associated with receiving support (Plickert et al. 2007).

Social support is often not reciprocal but is a charitable act, a generous gesture by someone who has resources toward someone who is relatively dependent. People may need to be dependent from time to time, particularly in periods of crisis. But dependency over the long term is associated with negative mental and emotional health. Beeman (1997) conducted a study that demonstrated mothers who were found to neglect their children were likely to be dependent, lack mutuality, and have conflict and distrust in their social networks. By comparison, non-neglecting mothers balanced independence and reciprocity in their relationships and expressed more trust and flexibility.

Peer support among parents often leads to personal transformation and development of advocacy and empowerment skills. Parents reinforce one another as confidence and assertion grow and collective efficacy can emerge. Together parents engaged in mutual support are more likely to assert collective action and parent leadership for the development of more effective family supports in community systems (Kurtz 1990).

Parental empowerment can even lead to parent-led organizations. Client-run self-help organizations create opportunities for clients to meaningfully participate in decisions about their care and the care of others in the organizations. They are increasingly common in the mental health recovery field. Research suggests clients who participate are more likely to engage with the services, express satisfaction, increase their social functioning, and report personal empowerment (Segal and Silverman 2002).

Practice-Informed Theory and Research. Professionals and lay people who have facilitated or participated in mutual aid identify several processes that seem to contribute to the effects of mutual support: sharing information (especially about helpful solutions and resources), engaging in dialectical processes (e.g., discussing different approaches to a parenting problem), discussing taboo topics with trust (sharing unspeakable topics), finding comfort with people who are "in the same boat," exchanging various forms of support, perceiving mutual demand (willingness to confront one another to promote change), perceiving that personal problems are getting solved, and feeling "strength in numbers" (Shulman and Gitterman 1994, pp. 14–18). Berry and colleagues (2007) studied an intensive family reunification program that included twice-weekly meetings of parents and staff as well as time for parent-child interactions. The program had reunification rates that were double those of parents treated with routine services. Parents who participated particularly valued the fellowship of the peer support; they reported their peers normalized their hurt, anger, and problems as well as providing friendships and concrete help and information. They reported learning to respect differences and being more accepting of ideas that came from peers than their caseworkers. One parent put it this way: "I don't get judged here… I don't need therapy, I just need someone to hear me out…" and another said, "These are friends that don't diss you, don't judge you, don't hold things against you" (Berry et al. 2007, pp. 488–489).

Conceptually, a rather overwhelming argument exists for the value of mutual support and self-help among parents. Principles to guide practice emerge from social ecology and systems theory and values pertaining to cultural sensitivity, family strengths and parental assets, self-determination and empowerment, and reciprocity and collective efficacy. These principles suggest that a community or society that supports parental self-help and mutual support is also likely to sustain more relevant and effective services for families at risk of child maltreatment.

Why, then, have intervention researchers in the field of child maltreatment prevention so rarely studied methods to intentionally strengthen mutual support and self-help? While this question has no empirical answer at this point, the discussion below will argue for increased research. First, a brief overview of what is available.

Research Evidence About the Effects of Promoting Parental Self-Help and Mutual Support

Since the reinvigorated child abuse prevention movement began 50 years ago, some communities have worked to build systems that intentionally facilitate and sustain mutual support and self-help among at-risk parents. These efforts are often regarded as incidental or secondary to more traditional forms of support, particularly parent education. This section reviews the limited available research about effective methods of promoting mutual support and self-help and summarizes emerging evidence-based practices. Most of the studies are program evaluations with non-randomized rigorous designs. The findings are summarized in Table 22.1 to illustrate the promising effects of such interventions.

The interventions have tended to focus on these general methods: parent leadership, parent-to-parent mentoring, and mutual support groups. Typically the interventions are adjunct to other services (e.g., mutual support and self-help programs supplement parent education, home visiting, parent-child

Table 22.1 Examples of emerging program evaluation evidence about methods to promote mutual support and self-help among parents at-risk for child maltreatment

Source	Focus	Key findings/implications for practice
Casey Family Programs (Annie E. Casey Fdtn, n.d.; Casey family programs 2007; Fiester 2008; Jemmot-Rollins Group 2006)	**Parent leadership**: trained parents in self-help, mutual support, and leadership skills as they navigated family services systems; family members (constituents) moved from isolation to direct services to policy process participation	*Process*: major change was required by staff; the organizational culture had to shift to overcome factors that exclude constituents, such as jargon, accessibility; constituents are best able to contribute after their crises have resolved
Child welfare fund (Pelton 2011)	**Parent leadership**: organized to help parents in the child welfare system know their rights, build skills, and help child welfare staff and policymakers understand parent perspectives	*Outcomes*: establishment of a parent's advisory board for the child welfare agency; employment of parent advocates in the foster care system; *Rise Magazine*, a print and web-based peer support resource, by and for parents
Parents Anonymous® shared leadership in action (Parents Anonymous® 2005; Polinsky 2007)	**Parent leadership**: systematic shared leadership skills development program, including training and mentoring, for parents and staff together	*Outcomes*: steady increases in parent leadership activities; child welfare agency staff attitudes toward parent leaders became increasingly open to parent participation in agency programs and policies
Parent mentors (National Coalition for Parent Advocacy in Child Protective Services 2011; Parent Partner 2011)	**Parent-to-parent partners/mentors**: mentors reunified with their children after removal provide support, mentoring, and navigation to parents in the child welfare system	*Outcomes*: *California parent partner*s: 60 % of children whose parents had a partner reunified within 12 months of removal, compared to 26 % of children whose parents were not served. Parents valued credibility, trust, encouragement, and hope based in their shared experience with mentor, flexible communication, support for emotions, material needs, self-reliance, and substance abuse recovery (Anthony et al. 2009)
Parent-to-parent (P2P) (Robbins et al. 2008)	**Parent-to-parent partners/mentors**: experienced parents of children with disabilities matched with parents whose children are newly diagnosed	*Process*: parents were most satisfied with their mentor if they were similar in these ways: personality characteristics; philosophy about parenting; communication style; attitudes about health and mental health, type disability, and expectations for their children (Santelli 2006; Santelli et al. 1997; Singer et al. 1999)
Parents Anonymous® (2001)	**Mutual support groups**: weekly meeting co-facilitated by professional and parent leader. Strengths-based model incorporates four basic principles: *mutual support*, *shared leadership*, *parent leadership*, and *personal growth*	*Outcomes*: participation in support groups reduced child abuse potential, life stress, drug and alcohol abuse, and intimate partner violence; parents with highest levels of risk showed greatest gains (Nelson et al. 2001, Polinsky et al. 2010). *Process*: groups can be sustained, e.g., as long as 25 continuous years (Liles and Wahlquist 2006)
Circle of Parents® (Falconer et al. 2008)	**Mutual support groups**: weekly meeting co-facilitated by professional and parent leader	*Outcomes*: Circle of Parents® participation contributes to gains in parenting knowledge, system awareness, family management, peer relationships, and social support (Falconer et al. 2008)

(continued)

Table 22.1 (continued)

Source	Focus	Key findings/implications for practice
Parent Mutual Aid Organizations (PMAO) (Cameron and Birnie-Lefcovitch 2000)	**Informal mutual support groups**: child welfare agency created opportunities for parents in the child welfare system to meet informally	*Outcomes*: compared to parents who did not participate, PMAO parents showed greater gains in: reduced out-of-home child placement, independence from formal service providers, integration in the community, levels of perceived social support, self-esteem, perceived stress, and parental attitudes; the program also realized cost savings (Cameron 2002; Cameron and Birnie-Lefcovitch 2000)
Family reunification peer support (Frame et al. 2006)	**Formal support groups** facilitated by child welfare agency staff for parents whose children were involuntarily removed	*Process*: support took the form of expressing interest and concern about one another, offering emotional support inside and outside the group, offering concrete help (e.g. furniture), offering prayer, giving practical advice (such as how to handle social workers), helping to solve problems, and sharing experiences
Home visiting parent group (Constantino et al. 2001)	**Group for parents in home visiting program**: Ten sessions followed a curriculum and promoted free and active exchanges among the participants	*Outcomes*: compared with no-group controls, group participants were more likely to stay engaged with the home visiting program and showed greater ability to respond to their infants' emotional cues
Special Social Support Training model (SSST) (Lovell and Richey 1997)	**Social skills group**: for families involuntarily in the child welfare system, 12-week SSST program focused on relationships skills with friends, neighbors, and family. An informal parent discussion group was comparison	*Outcomes*: the informal discussion group among parents had similar effects as SSST participation: increased social networks and quality of contacts, increased social support satisfaction, and increased contacts with friends, neighbors, and professionals
Children's Family Centres (CFCs) (Fernandez 2004)	**Holistic, multi-service community centers**: provide a range of services that include parent groups, home visiting, child care, respite care, counseling, and short-term residential family care (in Australia)	*Process*: participants reported making friends and creating support networks, their children's increased sense of security, and concrete aid such as housing. Relative benefits of the parent groups have not been differentiated
Chicago (preschool) Child-Parent Centers (CPCs) (Mersky et al. 2011)	**Parent support at preschool**: CPCs emphasize parental involvement in the preschool for at least a half-day a week and focus on parent-child interactions, parent and child attachment to the school, and mutual support among parents	*Outcomes*: CPC participation led to reduced rates of child maltreatment and neglect; family support processes had a substantial mediating effect on the reduction
New Zealand Early Childhood Education (ECE) programs (Duncan et al. 2006)	**Parent support at preschool**: the ECE program staff focused on informal relationships with parents and creating opportunities for sharing	*Process*: parents reported the informal focus put less pressure on them and showed more respect for their rights and choices than more organized meetings

interaction training, child welfare services, psychotherapy, alcohol and drug abuse recovery, or grief support). The programs are often co-located with other parent resources (e.g. at a child development program, school, or family shelter).

Formal programs to support parental self-help and mutual support vary in many ways (Budde 2003; Carter and Harvey 1996; Ireys et al. 2001; Falconer 2005–2006; Moran et al. 2004). The focus parent population may have a common identity, such as residence in a particular neighborhood, ethnicity, single parenthood, or incarcerated child. The purpose may be open and flexible or intentionally focused on such topics as life skills, stress management, or system awareness and use. Most aim to help parents overcome isolation and feel cohesion with a community of parents who are learning from one another. They vary in terms of frequency of contact among parents, duration of parent-to-parent relationships, and intensity of communication and focus (Hoagwood et al. 2010; Horton 2003).

Although parental self-help and mutual support are regarded as "informal" services, formal mechanisms may be required to fuel maintenance of the services. What each program has in common is that the parent-to-parent relationship is reciprocal – everyone is seeking help and everyone gives help. The parent-to-parent relationship may start as one person seeking help from another, but the help seeking parent is encouraged to engage in mutually supportive relationships with other parents.

Leadership: **Peer Parent Leaders**. Some studies have examined how family service systems can become more effective through leadership by parents. Across health and human services systems, involvement by program participants in system governance can lead to enhanced client commitment, program relevance, and positive child and family outcomes (Andrews et al. 2003; Buck et al. 2004; Cunningham et al. 1999; McAllister and Walsh 2004; Taub et al. 2001; Resendez et al. 2000). In health and mental health care, the push toward evidence-based practice has led to enhanced recognition of the role that patient preferences play in clinical decisions, calling for new models of shared and integrated patient-professional decision making (Borkman 1999; Edwards et al. 2003; Kurtz 1997; Trevena and Barrett 2003). This body of research suggests formal parenting programs are likely to achieve more potent effects if parents have influenced their development and delivery. Parents are in the best position to identify effective ways for people in communities to help families meet concrete needs like food, housing, school supplies, clothing, and health care. As consumers and peer advocates, they may identify more effective responses to intimate partner violence, mental illness, substance abuse, and family crisis. They can tailor respite and other supports for parents who are caregivers for family members with special needs,

The federal government and many state governments recognize the value of parent leadership by requiring parent participation in policy processes concerning development of family support programs (e.g., Child Abuse Prevention and Treatment Act (CAPTA) Reauthorization Act of 2010, P.L. 111–320) (Child Welfare Info Gateway 2011). The federal Community-Based Child Abuse Prevention (CBCAP) program provides grants to support a variety of prevention efforts including comprehensive support for parents, parenting skills development, family access to informal as well as formal resources, and promotion of parent leadership (FRIENDS 2011).

Formal parent leader *training*, which can be found in many communities through schools and advocacy organizations, is necessary but rarely sufficient to produce effective parent leaders. Trained parent leaders who sustain their leadership are likely to have engaged, mutually supportive relationships with one another (Polinsky 2007). And a key to effective parent leadership is that personnel (administrators and staff) at child and family services organizations are supportive of parent leaders and competent in parent relations (Hardina 2011). Programs that train and mentor parent leaders must also train and mentor staff to work in partnership with parents.

Given the challenges of at-risk parents, including stigma and other factors that may inhibit parent participation in leadership roles, shared leadership models have emerged that train parent leaders and match professional facilitators with parent leaders. Achieving stature and skills can be an uphill battle because, as Leroy Pelton observed, "There is hardly any class of people whose voice has been more discredited than parents, especially mothers, known to the child welfare system" (2011, p. 484). Their voices are discredited among parents as well as professionals, and yet they have more influence over their children than anyone else ever can. Building alliances among diverse parents – those at highest risk as well as those at low risk – with each other and with professionals as partners lays a foundation for system transformation.

This author recently surveyed 28 parents and 31 staff members at child welfare agencies about perceived barriers to parent leadership. The perceptions of parents and staff were similar. The primary barriers that originated with parents were social (feeling like they did not fit in as a leader) and logistical (such as lost income, transportation, child care, time, and access to a computer). Barriers that originated in the agency included limited resources to support parents or leadership activities and staff resentment, negative attitudes, and limited time.

The limited evaluation information thus far suggests that the core principles of shared leadership, i.e., democratic participation by parent leaders as equal partners in services systems, are easy to promote but the practices of shared leadership, i.e., parents and staff working together as they learn leadership skills and plan, enact, and evaluate systems change, require more extraordinary effort.

Parent-to-Parent Support. Parent-to-parent support typically involves parent mentors who have managed serious challenges reaching out to parents who are in the midst of challenges. Of course parents' situations change continually, so programs that start with mentoring relationships may evolve to a peer relationship, with the mentor receiving reciprocal help from the mentee. The idea of mutual support is that each parent has assets that can be shared. Matching parents one-on-one is particularly useful for reaching parents who are isolated, coping with exceptional stressors, or otherwise in need of unique support.

Evaluations suggest that parent-to-parent mentoring for parents in the child welfare system promotes child stability and family reunification while promoting positive parental attitudes and feelings (Anthony et al. 2009). Chaffin and colleagues (2001) found parent mentoring had stronger effects than any other nonmaterial family support programs aimed at child maltreatment prevention. Several studies have shown that peer mentoring or support can enhance the effectiveness of formal family services (Cohen and Canan 2006; Constantino et al. 2001; Layzer et al. 2001; Moran et al. 2004; Santelli et al. 1997; Singer et al. 1999; Thomlison 2003).

Mutual Support and Self-Help Groups. Parental mutual support groups (distinct from professionally-led parent support groups or training) can reduce child maltreatment and juvenile delinquency (Polinsky et al. 2010; Nelson et al. 2001) and, for parents in the child welfare system, promote self-esteem, confidence, less reliance on services, fewer child placements, and agency savings (Budde and Schene 2004; Cameron 2002; Cameron and Birnie-Lefcovitch 2000; Thompson 1995).

Given the widespread use of peer support groups to help people recover from mental illness or alcohol and drug abuse, known correlates of child maltreatment, some parents are familiar with a group model and easily engage in a group that focuses on their roles as parents. Studies of mutual support groups among people with mental illness suggest that participation leads to improved symptoms, larger social networks, enhanced quality of life, and improved access to care (Davidson et al. 1999) and that the outcomes are equivalent to those of more costly professional interventions (Pistrang et al. 2008).

Developing and sustaining mutual support groups requires careful attention to member engagement and participation processes (Liles and Wahlquist 2006). Given high rates of depression and social withdrawal among parents at-risk of child maltreatment, special processes may be needed to engage some parents in mutual support groups. Studies show that once involved, informal social support can reduce parental stress and isolation and promote positive identity and well-being (Cameron et al. 1997; Cameron 2002; Zlotnik et al. 2000). Self-help and mutual aid participants increase knowledge and skills, contribute to their communities, and rely less on formal systems (Borkman 1999; Kyrouz et al. 2002; Toseland 1990).

Carter and Harvey (1996) concluded that parenting group success is related to the quality of interpersonal relationships and processes, voluntary participation, a minimum duration of 6–8 weekly meetings, a flexible agenda that responds to participants' interests and needs, and well-trained, regularly supervised facilitators. They found the substantive focus of the meetings is less important than these participation qualities. Thus parents engaged in mutual support through groups need assistance, through training or professional partners, to manage these critical group processes.

Bit-by-bit, research evidence is growing to support the value of programs that effectively recognize and strengthen the natural helping potential of parental mutual support and self-help.

Advancing Research About Parental Self-Help and Mutual Support

Although professionals are currently working with relatively little research evidence about parental mutual support and self-help, a body of documented practice wisdom is emerging, as the review here demonstrates. The practice wisdom, ideological norms, and a solid theoretical foundation predict that parental self-efficacy, natural helping, and reciprocal support among parents will contribute to reduced risk of child maltreatment and positive parent, child, and family outcomes.

In an ideal world, parents would naturally know how to help themselves and support one another. In the real world, many parents need help to do this. More and better research can inform community systems and public policy development so that resources to enable parental mutual support and self-help can emerge. A clear foundation exists for more substantive, rigorous research. A sample of questions that emerge from the discussions in this chapter include:

- Does mutual support among parents reduce the risk of child maltreatment? In the published literature, no randomized, controlled study has yet addressed this question.
- What factors and processes characterize the reciprocal nature of mutual support? How can these be assessed and monitored in research studies?
- What is nature of the relationship between parental mutual support and self-help? Parental capacity for self-regulation seems to affect positive family outcomes; how does this relate to self-help, and to what extent does mutual support affect self-regulation?
- What are the relative contributions of mutual support and other family services (e.g. parent education, formal parent support, therapy, or other formal services) to parent, child, or family outcomes?
- By what mechanisms do mutual support processes lead to changes in parental behavior? How can these be enhanced?
- What are the relative benefits of various forms of mutual support (e.g. group, one-on-one, social media, other)?
- Does parent leadership in child and family services lead to better outcomes?
- What factors influence staff attitudes and behaviors toward parental mutual support and/or parent leadership?
- What effects do ambiguous mutual relationships, i.e., those that generate support and conflict, have on parenting behavior?
- How does mutual support vary among cultures and by gender, age, or other parental characteristics?
- How does mutual support in parents' social networks change over time?

Many other questions have been raised by the emerging program evaluations that revealed the influence of mutual support. As noted early in this chapter, ideologically and theoretically, studies to answer the questions will benefit from a research lens that acknowledges the parental perspective and builds on parental assets (Coghlan et al. 2003) Researchers in this field cannot presume to know how at-risk families and their friends support one another or how to strengthen their mutual support. They need partnerships to frame the questions and gather the data.

But normative barriers inhibit the development of such research. Inventories of child abuse prevention programs are weighted heavily toward parent education, home visitors, and therapies – activities that require professionals and trained paraprofessionals. Many of the available programs target one parent, not the parent's social network. Many books and articles about child maltreatment prevention do not even mention mutual support and self-help. While these resources are clearly valuable and many have demonstrable results, the relative neglect of self-help and mutual support among at-risk families signifies lost opportunities for effective change.

Intervention research seems to reflect state-of-the-art in family and child welfare services, which emphasizes the role of professional expertise. A review of literature and websites quickly reveals family services providers seem to be primarily concerned about how to engage families in the family support efforts offered by professionals, rather than how to engage professionals in the family support efforts offered by parents to one another. Of course, engaging parents in programs that have known effects is important, but such program involvement is likely to be insufficient in meeting the holistic needs of the family over time. Professionals have much to offer, particularly with regard to helping parents discover ways to manage relatively discrete challenges, such as child misbehavior or their own frustration. But for day-in, day-out management of the continuous context and potential chaos of family life, parents are still on their own, with whatever natural resources are at hand.

Investments in parental mutual support and self-help research are clearly needed. While community, state, and federal investments in child abuse prevention and recovery have come a long way in the last 50 years, and programs to reinforce parental self-help and mutual support have been a part of those efforts, investments in research, evaluation, training, and program development to discover and disseminate effective natural parental support and parent leadership have been minimal. Perhaps people believe that because natural helping is free then investments are unnecessary. Although parent mutual support and self-help are naturalistic, they may not be spontaneous, particularly for at-risk parents. The success of sustained parent support depends on training, mentoring, trained co-facilitation or consultation, and concrete supports (e.g., child care, transportation, food, or occasional curriculum materials or speakers).

Theory and existing research, though limited, point to an aspirant scenario where community norms and policy support parental mutual support and self-help. In this scenario, managers of effective comprehensive systems of care for the prevention and treatment of child maltreatment acknowledge the need to strengthen the family's social environment for the long term. They strive to build community systems grounded in solid theories of change that reflect the dynamic nature of social systems and honor values of cultural sensitivity, family strengths, self-determination, empowerment, and reciprocity. They recognize that families have persistent, intense, evolving emotional and pragmatic needs that can be met only through natural helping networks. They realize that staff often sees family needs based on here and now, whereas parents are dealing with now and forever. They acknowledge that professional and formal services can help strengthen families, but they cannot provide what self-help and mutual support offer, which is support that is available where and when the parent needs it, in forms that naturally fit with the parent's family and social environment. And professionals cannot lead or develop services systems with the insight and wisdom of parent leaders from at-risk families. A profound system change is required if transformation such as the aspirant scenario is to be realized.

References

Andrews, A. B., Guadalupe, J. L., & Bolden, E. (2003). Faith, hope and mutual support: Paths to empowerment as perceived by women in poverty. *Journal of Social Work Research and Evaluation: An International Journal, 4*(1), 5–14.

Annie, E., Casey Foundation. (n.d.). Family to family tools for rebuilding foster care: Walking our talk in the neighborhoods – partnerships between professionals and natural helpers. http://www.aecf.org/upload/PublicationFiles/walking%20 our%20talk.pdf. Retrieved 24 July 2012.

Anthony, E. K., Berrick, J. D., Cohen, E., & Wilder, E. (2009). *Partnering with parents: Promising approaches to improve reunification outcomes for children in foster care.* Berkeley, CA. Retrieved from https://www.strengthening-families. org/cpec/docs/Final_Report_UC_Berkeley_2009_Evaluation_of_Contra_Costa_Parent_Parners.pdf

Appleyard, K., Egeland, B., & Sroufe, L. A. (2007). Direct social support for young high risk children: Relations with behavioral and emotional outcomes across time. *Journal of Abnormal Child Psychology, 35*, 443–457.

Ayón, C. (2011). Latino families and the public child welfare system: Examining the role of social networks. *Children and Youth Services Review, 33*(10), 2061–2066.

Bandura, A. (1997). *Self-efficacy: The exercise of control*. New York: Freeman.

Barrera, M. (1986). Distinctions between social support concepts, measures, and models. *American Journal of Community Psychology, 14*, 413–445.

Barrera, M. J., Prelow, H. M., Dumka, L. E., Gonzales, N. A., Knight, G. P., Michaels, M. L., et al. (2002). Pathways from family economic conditions to adolescents' distress: Supportive parenting, stressors outside the family, and deviant peers. *Journal of Community Psychology, 30*(2), 135–152.

Barth, R. P., & Haskins, R. (2009). Will parent training reduce abuse, enhance development, and save money? Let's find out. *The Future of Children Policy Brief*, pp. 1–7.

Beeman, S. K. (1997). Reconceptualizing social support and its relationship to child neglect. *Social Service Review* (Sept. 1997), pp. 421–440.

Belsky, J. (1993). Etiology of child maltreatment: A developmental-ecological analysis. *Psychological Bulletin, 114*(3), 413–434.

Berry, M., McCauley, K., & Lansing, T. (2007). Permanency through group work: A pilot intensive reunification program. *Child and Adolescent Social Work Journal, 24*, 477–493.

Boehm, A., & Staples, L. H. (2004). Empowerment the point of view of consumers. *Families in Society – The Journal of Contemporary Social Services, 85*(2), 270–280.

Borkman, T. J. (1999). *Understanding self-help/mutual aid: Experiential learning in the commons*. New Brunswick: Rutgers University Press.

Bronfenbrenner, U. (1979). *The ecology of human development: Experiments by nature and design*. Cambridge: Harvard University Press.

Bronfenbrenner, U. (2005). Ecological systems theory (1992). In U. Bronfenbrenner (Ed.), *Making human beings human: Bioecological perspectives on human development* (pp. 106–173). Thousand Oaks: Sage.

Buck, D. S., Rochon, D., Davidson, H., McCurdy, S., & CHANGE Committee. (2004). Involving homeless persons in the leadership of a health care organization. *Qualitative Health Research, 14*(4), 513–525.

Budde, S. (2003). The indicators study: A cross-site implementation evaluation of the community partnerships for protecting children in America. In I. Katz & J. Pinkerton (Eds.), *Evaluating family support: Thinking internationally, thinking critically* (pp. 227–251). England: Wiley.

Budde, S., & Schene, P. (2004). Informal social support interventions and their role in violence prevention: An agenda for future evaluation. *Journal of Interpersonal Violence, 19*(3), 341–355.

Cameron, G. (2002). Motivation to join and benefits from participation in parent mutual aid organizations. *Child Welfare Journal, 81*(1), 33–57.

Cameron, G., & Birnie-Lefcovitch, S. (2000). Parent mutual aid organizations in a child welfare demonstration project: A report of outcomes. *Children and Youth Services Review, 22*(6), 421–440.

Cameron, G., Vanderwoerd, J., & Peirson, L. (1997). *Protecting children and supporting families: Promising programs and organizational realities*. New York: Aldine de Gruyter.

Cantillon, D. (2006). Community social organization, parents, and peers as mediators of perceived neighborhood block characteristics on delinquent and prosocial activities. *American Journal of Community Psychology, 37*, 111–127.

Carter, N., & Cathie, H. (1996). Gaining perspective on parenting groups. *Zero to Three, 16*(6), 1–8. June–July 1996.

Casey Family Programs (CFP). (2007). Breakthrough services collaborative: Supporting kinship care – promising practices and lessons learned. http://www.casey.org/Resources/Publications/pdf/BreakthroughSeries_Kinship.pdf. Retrieved 9 Nov. 2011.

Center for the Study of Social Policy (CSSP). (2011). Strengthening families: A protective factors framework. http://www.cssp.org/reform/strengthening-families. Retrieved 29 Sept. 2011.

Centers for Disease Control and Prevention (CDC). (2007). *Child maltreatment prevention*. U.S. Department of Health and Human Services. Retrieved from http://www.cdc.gov/ncipc/dvp/CMP/default.htm

Chaffin, M., Bonner, B., & Hill, R. (2001). Family preservation and family support programs: Child maltreatment outcomes across client risk levels and program types. *Child Abuse & Neglect, 25*, 1269–1289.

Child Welfare Information Gateway. (2011). *About CAPTA: A legislative history*. Washington, DC: Department of Health and Human Services, Children's Bureau.

Choi, S., & Staudt, M. (2011). Service use by parents in child welfare: Current knowledge and future needs. *APSAC Adviser, 25*(1&2), 20–23.

Cicchetti, D., & Lynch, M. (1993). Toward an ecological/transactional model of community violence and child maltreatment: Consequences for children's development. *Psychiatry, 53*, 96–118.

Cochran, M., & Walker, S. K. (2005). Parenting and personal social networks. In T. Luster & L. Okagaki (Eds.), *Parenting: An ecological perspective* (2nd ed., pp. 235–273). Mahwah: Lawrence Erlbaum.

Coghlan, A. T., Preskill, H., & Catsambas, T. T. (2003). An overview of appreciative inquiry. *New Directions for Evaluation, 100*, 5–22.

Cohen, E., & Canan, L. (2006). Closer to home: Parent mentors in child welfare. *Child Welfare, 85*(5), 867–884.

Coleman, P. K., & Karraker, K. H. (1997). Self-efficacy and parenting quality: Findings and future applications. *Developmental Review, 18*, 47–85.

Constantino, J. N., Hashemi, N., Solis, E., Alon, T., Haley, S., McClure, S., Nordlicht, N., Constantino, M. A., Elmen, J., & Carlson, V. K. (2001). Supplementation of urban home visitation with a series of group meetings for parents and infants: Results of a "real world" randomized, controlled trial. *Child Abuse & Neglect, 25*(12), 1571–1581.

Coulton, C. J., Korbin, J. E., Su, M., & Chow, J. (1995). Community level factors and child maltreatment rates. *Child Development, 66*, 1262–1276.

Coyne, J. C., & Downey, G. (1991). Social factors and psychopathology: Stress, social support, and coping processes. *Annual Review of Psychology, 42*, 401–425.

Cunningham, P. B., Henggeler, S. W., Brondino, M. J., & Pickrel, S. G. (1999). Testing underlying assumptions of the family empowerment perspective. *Journal of Child and Family Studies, 8*(4), 437–449.

Daro, D., & McCurdy, K. (1994). Preventing child abuse and neglect: Programmatic interventions. *Child Welfare, 73*, 405–430.

Davidson, L., Chinman, M., Kloos, B., Weingarten, R., Stayner, D., & Tebes, J. K. (1999). Peer support among individuals with severe mental illness: A review of the evidence. *Clinical Psychology: Science and Practice, 6*(2), 165–187.

Dukewich, T. L., Borkowski, J. G., & Whitman, T. L. (1996). Predicting adolescent child abuse potential in adolescent mothers. *Child Abuse & Neglect, 20*, 1031–1047.

Dumas, J. E., Moreland, A. D., Gitter, A. H., Pearl, A. M., & Nordstrom, A. H. (2008). Engaging parents in preventive parenting groups: Do ethnic, socioeconomic, and belief match between parents and group leaders matter? *Health Education & Behavior, 35*(5), 619–633.

Duncan, J., Bowden, C., & Smith, A. B. (2006). A gossip or a good yack? Reconceptualizing parent support in New Zealand early childhood centre based programmes. *International Journal of Early Years Education, 14*(1), 1–13.

Dunst, C., & Dempsey, I. (2007). Family-professional partnerships and parenting competence, confidence, and enjoyment. *International Journal of Disability, Development and Education, 54*(3), 305–318.

Dunst, C. J., Trivette, C. M., & Deal, A. G. (1994). *Supporting and strengthening families: Methods, strategies, and practices* (Vol. 1). Cambridge: Brookline.

Easterbrooks, M. A., Chaudhuri, J. H., Bartlett, J. D., & Copeman, A. (2011). Resilience in parenting among young mothers: Family and ecological risks and opportunities. *Children and Youth Services Review, 33*, 42–50.

Edwards, E., Evans, R., & Elwyn, G. (2003). Manufactured but not imported: New directions for research in shared decision making. *Patient Education and Counseling, 50*, 33–38.

Egeland, B., Bosquet, M., & Levy, A. C. (2002). Continuities and discontinuities in the intergenerational transmission of child maltreatment: Implications for breaking the cycle of abuse. In K. Browne, H. Hanks, P. Stratton, & C. Hamilton (Eds.), *Early prediction and prevention of child abuse: A handbook (Chap. 13*. West Sussex: Wiley.

English, D. J. (1998). The extent and consequences of child maltreatment. *The Future of Children, 8*(1), 39–53.

Fagan, J., & Browne, A. (1994). Violence between spouses and intimates: Physical aggression between women and men in intimate relationships. In A. J. Reiss & J. S. Roth (Eds.), *Understanding and preventing violence: Social influences* (Vol. 3, pp. 115–292). Washington, DC: National Academy Press.

Falconer, M. K. (2005–2006). *Mutual self-help parent support groups in the prevention of child abuse and neglect, Ounce of Prevention Fund of Florida*. Retrieved from http://www.ounce.org/pdfs/mutual_self-help_parent_support_groups_2005-2006.pdf

Falconer, M. K., Haskett, M. E., McDaniels, L., Dirkes, T., & Siegel, E. C. (2008). Evaluation of support groups for child abuse prevention: Outcomes of four state evaluations. *Social Work with Groups, 31*(2), 162–182.

Fernandez, E. (2004). Effective interventions to promote child and family wellness: A study of outcomes of intervention through Children's Family Centres. *Child and Family Social Work, 9*, 91–104.

Fiester, L. (2008). The story of Family to Family – an initiative to improve child welfare systems: The early years 1992–2006. The Annie E. Casey Foundation. http://www.aecf.org/~/media/PublicationFiles/F2F%20Book%20layout%20DRAFT%209%2012.pdf. Retrieved 24 July 2012.

Frame, L., Conley, A., & Berrick, J. D. (2006). The real work is what they do together: Peer support and birth parent change. *Families in Society: The Journal of Contemporary Social Services, 87*(4), 509–520.

FRIENDS – Family Resource Information, Education and Network Development Services the National Resource Center for Community-Based Child Abuse Prevention. http://www.friendsnrc.org/

FRIENDS. (2011). *Community-based child abuse prevention: Accomplishments and new directions*. Retrieved from http://friendsnrc.org/

Garbarino, J., & Kostelny, K. (1992). Child maltreatment as a community problem. *Child Abuse & Neglect, 16*, 455–464.

Gerberding, J. L., Falk, H., Arias, L., & Hammond, W. R. (2008). *Promoting healthy parenting practices across cultural groups: A CDC research brief*. Atlanta: Centers for Disease Control and Prevention. http://www.cdc.gov/ncipc/images/DVP/Healthy_Parenting_RIB_a.pdf. Retrieved 24 July 2012.

Germain, C. B. (1991). *Human behavior in the social environment: An ecological view*. New York: Columbia University Press.

Green, B. L., Furrer, C., & McAllister, C. (2007). How do relationships support parenting? Effects of attachment style and social support on parenting behavior in an at-risk population. *American Journal of Community Psychology, 40*, 96–108.

Haines, V. A., Beggs, J. J., & Hurlbert, J. S. (2002). Exploring the structural contexts of the support process: Social networks, social statuses, social support, and psychological distress. *Social Networks and Health, 8*, 269–292.

Halabi, S., & Nadler, A. (2010). Receiving help: Consequences for the recipient. In S. Stürmer & M. Snyder (Eds.), *The psychology of prosocial behavior: Group processes, intergroup relations, and helping* (pp. 121–138). Hoboken: Wiley-Blackwell.

Hardina, D. (2011). Are social service managers encouraging consumer participation in decision making in organizations? *Administration in Social Work, 35*, 117–137.

Hoagwood, K. E., Cavaleri, M. A., Olin, S. S., Burns, B. J., Slaton, E., Gruttadaro, D., & Hughes, R. (2010). Family support in children's mental health: A review and synthesis. *Clinical Child and Family Psychology Review, 13*, 1–45.

Hogan, B. E., Linden, W., & Najarian, B. (2002). Social support interventions: Do they work? *Clinical Psychology Review, 22*, 381–440.

Horton, C. (2003). Protective factors literature review: Early care and education programs and the prevention of child abuse and neglect. www.cssp.org. Retrieved 19 Sept 2011.

Ireys, H. T., Chernoff, R., Stein, R. E. K., DeVet, K. A., & Silver, E. J. (2001). Outcomes of community-based family-to-family support: Lessons learned from a decade of randomized trials. *Children's Services: Social Policy, Research, and Practice, 4*(4), 203–216.

Jemmot-Rollins Group. (2006). *Powerful families: Advocacy in action – Toolkit*. Seattle: Casey Family Programs.

Jones, T. L., & Prinz, R. J. (2005). Potential roles of parental self-efficacy in parent and child adjustment: A review. *Clinical Psychology Review, 25*, 341–363.

Kang, J. (2012). Pathways from social support to service use among caregivers at risk of child maltreatment. *Children and Youth Services Review, 34*, 933–939.

Karoly, P. (1993). Mechanisms of self-regulation: A systems view. *Annual Review of Psychology, 44*, 23–52.

Kotch, J. B., Browne, D. C., Ringwalt, C. L., & Stewart, P. W. (1995). Risk of child abuse or neglect in a cohort of low income children. *Child Abuse & Neglect, 19*(9), 1115–1130.

Kurtz, L. F. (1990). The self-help movement review of the past decade of research. *Social Work with Groups, 13*(3), 101–115.

Kurtz, L. F. (1997). *Self-help and support groups: A handbook for practitioners*. Thousand Oaks: Sage.

Kyrouz, E. M., Humphreys, K., & Loomis, C. (2002). A review of research on the effectiveness of self-help mutual aid groups. In B. J. White & E. J. Madara (Eds.), *American self-help clearinghouse self-help group sourcebook* (7th ed., pp. 1–16). Denville, NJ: American Self-Help Clearinghouse.

Langford, J., & Wolf, K. G. (2001). *Guidelines for family support practice* (2nd ed.). Chicago: Family Resource Coalition.

Layzer, J. I., Goodson, B. D., Bernstein, L., & Price, C. (2001). National evaluation of family support programs: Volume A: The meta-analysis – final report. Cambridge, MA: Abt Assoc. Retrieved from http://www.acf.hhs.gov/programs/opre/abuse_neglect/fam_sup/reports/famsup/fam_sup_vol_a.pdf

Lee, J. A. B., & Swenson, C. (1994). The concept of mutual aid. In A. Gitterman & L. Shulman (Eds.), *Mutual aid groups, vulnerable populations, and the life cycle* (pp. 413–429). New York: Columbia University Press.

Leventhal, T., & Brooks-Gunn, J. (2000). The neighborhoods they live in: The effects of neighborhood residence on child and adolescent outcomes. *Psychological Bulletin, 126*(2), 309–337.

Li, F., Godinet, M. T., & Arnsberger, P. (2011). Protective factors among families with children at risk of maltreatment: Follow up to early school years. *Children and Youth Services Review, 33*, 139–148.

Liles, R. E., & Wahlquist, L. (2006). Twenty-five years in Parents Anonymous. *Groupwork, 16*(3), 26–45.

Lin, J., Thompson, M. P., & Kaslow, N. J. (2009). The mediating role of social support in the community environment: Psychological distress link among low-income African American women. *Journal of Community Psychology, 37*, 459–470.

Lovell, M. L., & Richey, C. A. (1997). The impact of social support skill training on daily interactions among parents at risk of child maltreatment. *Children and Youth Services Review, 19*(4), 221–251.

Lovell, B., Moss, M., & Wetherell, M. A. (2012). With a little help from my friends: Psychological, endocrine, and health corollaries of social support in parental caregivers of children with autism or ADHD. *Research in Developmental Disabilities, 33*(2), 682–687.

Luks, A. (2001). *The healing power of doing good: The health and spiritual benefits of helping others*. New York: Universe.

Lundahl, B., Nimer, J., & Parsons, B. (2006). Preventing child abuse: A meta-analysis of parent training programs. *Research on Social Work Practice, 16*, 251–262.

Lyons, S. J., Henly, J. R., & Schuerman, J. R. (2005). Informal support in maltreating families: Its effect on parenting practices. *Children and Youth Services Review, 27*, 21–38.

Maluccio, A. N. (1981). Casework with parents of children in foster care. In P. A. Sinanoglu & A. N. Maluccio (Eds.), *Parents of children in placement: Perspectives and programs* (pp. 15–25). New York: Child Welfare League of America.

Marcenko, M. O., Lyons, S. J., & Courtney, M. (2011). Mothers' experiences, resources, and needs: The context for reunification. *Children and Youth Services Review, 33*, 431–438.

Mash, E. J., Johnston, C., & Kovitz, K. (1983). A comparison of the mother-child interactions of physically abused and non-abused children during play and task situations. *Journal of Clinical Child Psychology, 12*, 337–346.

McAllister, M., & Walsh, K. (2004). Different voices: Reviewing and revising the politics of working with consumers in mental health. *International Journal of Mental Health Nursing, 13*, 22–32.

McConnell, D. D., Breitkreuz, R. R., & Savage, A. A. (2011). From financial hardship to child difficulties: Main and moderating effects of perceived social support. *Child: Care, Health and Development, 37*(5), 679–691.

McCurdy, K., & Daro, D. (2001). Parent involvement in family support programs: An integrated theory. *Family Relations, 50*, 113–121.

Mersky, J. P., Topitzes, J. D., & Reynolds, A. J. (2011). Maltreatment prevention through early childhood intervention: A confirmatory evaluation of Chicago child-parent center preschool program. *Children and Youth Services Review, 33*, 1454–1463.

Moran, P., Ghate, D., & van der Merwe, A. (2004). What works in parenting support: A review of international evidence. Research report no. 574, Dept. for Education and Skills. Retrieved from http://www.dcsf.gov.uk/research/programmeofresearch/projectinformation. cfm?projectid=14408&resultspage=1

National Coalition for Parent Advocacy in Child Protective Services. http://parentadvocacy.org

National Parent Helpline®. http://www.nationalparenthelpline.org/what-we-do/

Neff, M. A. (2000). *Best practices of empowerment-oriented permanency planning: Facilitating change and self-development in parents and families : A handbook for caseworkers* (4th ed.). New York: Council of Family and Child Caring.

Nelson, G., Laurendeau, M., Chamberland, C., & Peirson, L. (2001). A review and analysis of programs to promote family wellness and prevent the maltreatment of preschool and elementary-school-aged children. In I. Prilleltensky, G. Nelson, & L. Peirson (Eds.), *Promoting family wellness and preventing child maltreatment* (pp. 220–272). Toronto: University of Toronto Press.

Parent Partner Program, Iowa Department of Human Services. http://www.dhs.state.ia.us/cppc/networking/Parent%20 Partners.html. Retrieved 10 Nov. 2011.

Parents Anonymous®. (2001). *Best practices of Parents Anonymous® group facilitators*. Claremont: Parents Anonymous®.

Parents Anonymous®. (2005). *Pathways to meaningful shared leadership*. Claremont: Parents Anonymous®.

Pelton, L. H. (2011). Concluding commentary: Varied perspectives on child welfare. *Children and Youth Services Review, 33*, 481–485.

Pistrang, N., Barker, C., & Humphreys, K. (2008). Mutual help groups for mental health problems: A review of effectiveness studies. *American Journal of Community Psychology, 42*, 110–121.

Plickert, G., Côté, R. R., & Wellman, B. (2007). It's not who you know, it's how you know them: Who exchanges what with whom? *Social Networks, 29*(3), 405–429.

Polinsky, M. L. (2007). *Strengthening the child welfare system through parent leadership: Final report on evaluation findings, 2002–2004*. Claremont: Parents Anonymous®.

Polinsky, M. L., Pion-Berlin, L., Williams, S., Long, T., & Wolf, A. M. (2010). Preventing child abuse and neglect: A national evaluation of Parents Anonymous® groups. *Child Welfare, 89*(6), 43–62.

Prinz, R. J., Sanders, M. R., Shapiro, C. J., Whitaker, D. J., & Lutzker, J. R. (2009). Population-based prevention of child maltreatment: The U.S. Triple P system population trial. *Prevention Science, 10*(1), 1–12.

Reid, J. B., Kavanagh, K., & Baldwin, D. V. (1987). Abusive parent's perceptions of child problem behaviors: An example of parental bias. *Journal of Abnormal Child Psychology, 15*, 457–466.

Reissman, F., & Carroll, D. (1995). *Redefining self-help: Policy and practice*. San Francisco: Jossey-Bass.

Resendez, M. G., Quist, R. M., & Matshazi, D. G. M. (2000). A longitudinal analysis of family empowerment and client outcomes. *Journal of Child and Family Studies, 9*(4), 449–460.

Rinehart, K., Becker, M. A., Buckley, P. R., Dailey, K., Reichardt, C. S., Graeber, C., et al. (2005). The relationship between mothers' child abuse potential and current mental health symptoms: Implications for screening and referrals. *Journal of Behavioral Health Services and Research, 32*, 155–166.

Rise Magazine. http://www.risemagazine.org/pages/about.html

Robbins, V., Johnston, J., Barnett, H., Hobstetter, W., Kutash, K., Duchnowski, A. J., & Annis, S. (2008). *Parent to parent: A synthesis of the emerging literature*. Tampa: University of South Florida, The Louis de la Parte Florida Mental Health Institute, Department of Child & Family Studies.

Rosenberg, M. S. (1987). New directions for research on the psychological maltreatment of children. *American Psychologist, 42*, 166–171.

Saleeby, D. (1992). *The strengths perspective in social work practice*. New York: Longman.

Sanders, M. (2008). Triple P – Positive Parenting Program as a public health approach to strengthening parenting. *Journal of Family Psychology, 22*(3), 506–517.

Sanders, M. R., & Prinz, R. J. (2008). Using the mass media as a population level strategy to strengthen parenting skills. *Journal of Clinical Child and Adolescent Psychology, 37*(3), 609–621.

Sanders, M. R., Markie-Dadds, C., & Turner, K. J. T. (2003). Theoretical, scientific and clinical foundations of the Triple P-Positive Parenting Program: A population approach to the promotion of parenting competence. *Parenting Research and Practice Monograph No.1*. Retrieved from http://www.gov.mb.ca/triplep/pdf/monograph1.pdf

Santelli, B. (2006). Evidence based practices for parent to parent support. Retrieved at www.P2PUSA.org

Santelli, B., Turnbull, A., Marquis, J., & Lerner, E. (1997). Parent-to-parent programs: A resource for parents and professionals. *Journal of Early Intervention, 21*(1), 73–83.

Santisteban, D. A. (2002). Integrating the study of ethnic culture and family psychology intervention science. In H. A. Little, D. A. Santisteban, R. F. Levant, & J. H. Bray (Eds.), *Family psychology: Science-based interventions* (pp. 331–351). Washington, DC: American Psychological Association.

Segal, S. P., & Silverman, C. (2002). Determinants of client outcomes in self-help agencies. *Psychiatric Services, 53*(3), 304–309.

Shaw, R., & Kilburn, M. R. (2009). WR-632. Child abuse and neglect prevention: Reports from the field and ideas for the future. RAND Corporation. http://www.rand.org/pubs/working_papers/WR632.html. Retrieved 25 July 2011.

Shulman, L., & Gitterman, A. (1994). The life model: Mutual aid, oppression, and the mediating function. In A. Gitterman & L. Shulman (Eds.), *Mutual aid groups, vulnerable populations, and the life cycle* (pp. 3–28). New York: Columbia University Press.

Singer, G. H. S., Marquis, J., Powers, L. K., Blanchard, L., DiVenere, N., & Santelli, B. (1999). A multi-site evaluation of parent to parent programs for parents of children with disabilities. *Journal of Early Intervention, 22*(3), 217–229.

Staub, E., & Vollhardt, J. (2008). Altruism born of suffering: The roots of caring and helping after victimization and other trauma. *The American Journal of Orthopsychiatry, 78*(3), 267–280.

Steinberg, D. M. (1997). *The mutual-aid approach to working with groups: Helping people help each other*. London: Jason Aronson.

Steinberg, D. M. (2010). Mutual aid: A contribution to best-practice social work. *Social Work with Groups, 33*(1), 53–68.

Swenson, C. C., & Chaffin, M. (2006). Beyond psychotherapy: Treating abused children by changing their social ecology. *Aggression and Violent Behavior, 1*, 120–137.

Taub, J., Tighe, T. A., & Burchard, J. (2001). The effects of parent empowerment on adjustment for children receiving comprehensive mental health services. *Children's Services: Social Policy, Research, and Practice, 4*(3), 103–122.

Tendulkar, S. A., Koenen, K. C., Dunn, E. C., Buka, S., & Subramanian, S. V. (2012). Neighborhood influences on perceived social support among parents: Findings from the project on human development in Chicago neighborhoods. *PLoS ONE, 7*(4), e34235. doi:10.1371/journal.pone.0034235.

Thomlison, B. (2003). Characteristics of evidence-based child maltreatment interventions. *Child Welfare, 82*(5), 541–569.

Thompson, R. A. (1995). *Preventing child maltreatment through social support*. Thousand Oaks: Sage.

Toseland, R. W. (1990). Long-term effectiveness of peer-led and professionally led support groups for caregivers. *Social Service Review, 64*(2), 301–327.

Trevena, L., & Barratt, A. (2003). Integrated decision making: Definitions for a new discipline. *Patient Education and Counseling, 50*, 265–268.

Uchino, B. N. (2009). Understanding the links between social support and physical health: A life-span perspective with emphasis on the separability of perceived and received support. *Perspectives on Psychological Science, 4*, 236–255.

Walsh, F. (1998). *Strengthening family resilience*. New York: Guilford.

Watson, E. L., & Collins, A. H. (1982). Natural helping networks in alleviating family stress. *The Annals of the American Academy of Political and Social Science, 461*(1), 102–112.

Wells, S. J., Merritt, L. M., & Briggs, H. E. (2009). Bias, racism, and evidence-based practice: The case for more focused development of the child welfare evidence base. *Children and Youth Services Review, 31*, 1160–1171.

Zlotnick, C., Wright, M. A., Cox, K., Te'o, I., & Stewart-Felix, P. (2000). The family empowerment club: Parent support and education for related caregivers. *Child and Youth Care Forum, 29*(2), 97–112.

Zuravin, S. J. (1988). Child maltreatment and teenage first births: A relationship mediated by chronic sociodemographic stress? *American Journal of Orthopsychiatry, 58*(1), 91–103.

Chapter 23
Nonoffending Mothers of Sexually Abused Children

Viola Vaughan-Eden

Child sexual abuse is a complex, multidimensional problem of epidemic proportions in the United States (Russell and Bolen 2000). During the 1980s, there were increasing numbers of active cases being reported, and more adults than ever before disclosing they had been abused as children (Finkelhor 1994; Wolfe 1999). It is suspected that due to an overall increase in education, public awareness, media attention, and legal advocacy, there was more of a willingness on the part of children to disclose, parents to seek help, and adults to report childhood experiences (Fergusson and Mullen 1999). Although in recent years, the incidence of child sexual abuse has leveled off and started to decline in comparison to other forms of maltreatment (Finkelhor and Jones 2006; Sedlak et al. 2010), the rate of child sexual abuse remains problematic.

Children who experience sexual abuse often subsequently experience a great deal of biopsychosocial trauma (Berliner and Elliott 1996; Browne and Finkelhor 1986; Cole and Putnam 1992; Corcoran and Vijavan 2008; Hall and Lloyd 1993; Jenny 1996; Kendall-Tackett et al. 1993; Tavkar and Hansen 2011; Wells et al. 1995). Without proper intervention, they often suffer long-term negative consequences that impede their physical and mental well-being including their health, education, relationships, sexuality, and a multitude of other life factors, any of which may impact their ability to become healthy functioning members of their communities and the larger society (Faust et al. 1995; Kirschner et al. 1993; Sawyer et al. 2006; Smith and Kelly 2008; Wyatt et al. 1992). Many mediating factors may influence coping abilities (Berliner and Elliott 1996; Friedrich 1990), but it is argued that how well individual children cope with sexual abuse is largely dependent on how well their caregivers, particularly mothers are able to provide support and obtain professional assistance for their children (Corcoran 2004; Everson et al. 1989; Faller 2007; Famularo et al. 1989; Sirles and Franke 1989).

But, who are these caregivers? By definition, nonoffending caregivers have not sexually abused or directly participated in the sexual abuse of their children. They are the primary guardians of children including blood relatives and foster parents. They come from all socioeconomic statuses, races and ethnicities, as well as from all educational and employment backgrounds. Essentially, they are everyday people – family, friends, neighbors, and colleagues. However, since the majority of sexual abuse is perpetrated by men, many caregivers are women – mothers – therefore, the focus of this discussion.

Working with nonoffending caregivers has taken a more prominent role upon the realization that they are the gateway to effective investigations and child victims receiving treatment services. One major factor that seemingly decreases the severity of symptoms some children experience is maternal

V. Vaughan-Eden (✉)
Child and Family Resources, Newport News, Virginia, USA
e-mail: info@violavaughaneden.com

J.E. Korbin and R.D. Krugman (eds.), *Handbook of Child Maltreatment*, Child Maltreatment 2, DOI 10.1007/978-94-007-7208-3_23, © Springer Science+Business Media Dordrecht 2014

support at time of disclosure. A mother's ability to believe and support her child following disclosure has a positive influence on the child's future psychosocial functioning. Additionally, children who receive an evaluation and/or treatment intervention as soon after their disclosure as possible fare better. Yet, professionals who work with nonoffending caregivers continue to voice frustration that mothers are not more protective of their children and more cooperative with investigators.

Mothers often experience close scrutiny and unrealistic expectations from the professionals working with their children. Mothers of victims voice feeling shame related to their children's sexual abuse. And some agree, arguing that nonoffending mothers are as much the victims as their children (Coohey and O'Leary 2008; Deblinger et al. 1993; Faller 2007; Gavey et al. 1990; Schonberg 1992), while others question if they may have contributed to situations which led to the abuse (Faust et al. 1995; Friedrich 1991; Shadoin and Carnes 2006; Wilson 1995).

However, there are limited studies on mothers parenting their sexually abused children. Prior to 1975, the pediatric research literature on child sexual abuse was riddled with misconceptions, including that mothers were somehow culpable for the abuse of their children (Myers et al. 1999). And, more recent literature emphasized the importance of mothers believing and supporting their children following the disclosure of sexual abuse (Bolen and Lamb 2007; Coohey and O'Leary 2008). Additionally, some literature addressed the impact of childhood sexual abuse on mothers' parenting attitudes and practices (Banyard 1997; Benedict 1998; Hernandez et al. 2009; Parr 2010). Of note, nonoffending mothers who have a history of childhood sexual trauma make up the vast majority of women who have child victims of sexual abuse (Deblinger et al. 1993; Friedrich 1991; Hebert et al. 2007). Therefore, all three issues – culpability, support, and childhood sexual abuse – will be discussed as it relates to understanding nonoffending mothers.

Mothers' Culpability

Again, by definition nonoffending mothers have no history of sexually abusing their children. However, they often withstand close scrutiny including parenting capacity evaluations, loss of custody, and character assassination. Although some researchers insist that nonoffending mothers are also victims of their children's abuse (Deblinger et al. 1993; Faller 2007; Gavey et al. 1990; Newberger et al. 1993), others query if they may unconsciously contribute to conditions that increase the likelihood of their children being abused (Faust et al. 1995; Friedrich 1991; Muram et al. 1994; Wilson 1995).

As Myers and colleagues (1999) found in their review of the medical, psychological and sociological literature from 1900 to 1975, mothers of sexually abused children were often seen as responsible for their children's victimization. This culpability took the form of criticism for lack of supervision or inappropriate supervision by males, inadequate or neglectful parenting, blindly entering into relationships with or failure to protect their children from unfamiliar men, neglecting their sexual partners, and a multitude of other unproven circumstances attributed to incidents of child sexual abuse.

Yet, somewhat overlooked in the research literature is the extent to which the nonoffending mothers' own history of sexual abuse influences their ability to protect their children from potential abuse and respond constructively to the sexual abuse situations of their children (Ellenson 1986; Kim et al. 2007; Leifer et al. 1993; Parr 2010). Mothers without a reported history of childhood sexual abuse were more than three times more amenable to believing and protecting their sexually abused children than mothers with reported histories (Pintello and Zuravin 2001).

One dynamic among mothers with unresolved histories of childhood sexual trauma is they often suffer psychological difficulties that may impair their judgment related to protecting their children from similar abuse experiences. As opposed to consciously allowing their children to be abused, they lack the necessary insight to prevent their children's sexual abuse. They themselves become victims of male perpetrators who seek women that may not be as perceptive or emotionally strong enough to protect themselves or their children from a variety of abuses. Moreover, these mothers are frequently victims of domestic violence (Coohey and O'Leary 2008; Deblinger et al. 1993).

On average, when nonoffending mothers with a history of child sexual abuse are compared to those without, they are younger, of lower socioeconomic status, have greater family stress (Famularo et al. 1989; Faust et al. 1995), experience spousal abuse (Deblinger et al. 1993), suffer with lower psychosocial functioning, and have personalities that may unconsciously put their children at risk for more severe and long lasting sexual abuse (Friedrich 1991).

Support/Belief of Child

Beyond culpability, there is the notion that nonoffending mothers do not believe, support, protect, or obtain help for their sexually abused children (Coohey and O'Leary 2008; Elliott and Carnes 2001; Shadoin and Carnes 2006; Walters 2002). When assessing maternal support, four areas have been identified for consideration: (a) the mother's belief in the child's allegations of abuse, (b) the mother's level of emotional support of the child, (c) the mother's actions toward the perpetrator following the disclosure, and (d) the mother's use of professional services (Everson et al. 1989).

Overall, mothers do support and believe their children when sexual abuse is disclosed (Berliner 2011; Runyan et al. 1992). However, when they do not, it is problematic for a number of reasons. First of all, if the nonoffending parent acts unsupportive or doubtful about the allegations, children are less likely to disclose (Faller 2007) and second, they are more likely to recant (Malloy et al. 2007). Third, children have a harder time coping with and recovering from their abuse. Fourth, it is harder to protect the child from future victimization. Fifth, when social service agencies and the courts determine that a mother has indeed failed to protect or that the perpetrator continues to live in the home, they often recommend alternative placement for the child. Sixth, mothers with a history of intrafamilial abuse are more likely to have dysfunctional families of origin and therefore, may be less likely to have the emotional resources available to support the child through the process (Deblinger et al. 1994).

Bolen and Lamb (2004, 2007) explained that mothers can be both ambivalent and supportive, and viewed this perceived lack of support as mothers' vacillating ambivalence in an attempt to cope with the stress of disclosure as well as the magnitude of the disclosure on their daily lives. It is likely the stress, anxiety, and feelings of aloneness are often misinterpreted by professionals as a failure to protect and cooperate. Malloy and Lyon (2006) expound by asserting that maternal support is not a fixed measurement but fluid and likely can improved with intervention.

Although the majority of mothers believe their children, they were more likely to believe if the perpetrator was an extended family member than a partner (Sirles and Franke 1989) or if they were divorced or no longer living with the perpetrator (Faller 1988). Further, Faller (1988) found that nonoffending mothers had warmer relationships with their abused children when they did not live with or were married to the perpetrator, or when the perpetrator was the biological father. Yet, when perpetrator fathers acknowledged their abuse of the children, mothers were more inclined to provide immediate support (Lipovsky et al. 1992). But, even when mothers held the perpetrators responsible for the abuse, due to their own stress they had difficulty providing emotional support and professional services to their children (Deblinger and Heflin 1996). Additionally, mothers with childhood sexual abuse and substance abuse histories were less supportive of their children's disclosures of sexual abuse (Leifer et al. 1993; Pareses et al. 2001).

A lack of maternal support increases the likelihood of a child's placement into foster care (Leifer et al. 1993). Social services and courts often place children in foster care to give parents an opportunity to demonstrate their willingness to protect their children from future trauma. However, the threat of a child's removal is often not enough to compel parents to adequately respond to their children's needs or comply with court ordered assessments (Butler et al. 1994; Famularo et al. 1989; Tingus et al. 1996).

A mother's belief that her child's abuse has occurred, her child needs counseling, and she needs to separate her child from the offender, were not significant factors in determining whether or not the mother kept the child's first counseling appointment (Haskett et al. 1991). More specifically, in cases with greater incidence of intrafamilial perpetrators and higher frequency of abuse, if both social services and law enforcement were involved, children were more likely to have therapy (Tingus et al. 1996).

Some biopsychosocial issues faced by nonoffending mothers appear to be unrelated to the current abuse of their child but more likely related to their own history of abuse (Ovaris 1991). When mothers appear less supportive, research indicates they are often victims themselves who did not receive treatment or feel supported during their own abuse (Howard 1993). They may minimize the impact of their child's trauma if they used minimization to cope with their own abuse, believing that they turned out 'OK' and their children will, too. However, researchers found the quality of care given by these mothers and their ability to positively engage with child protective agencies were significant predictors of their children being re-molested in the future (McDonald and Johnson 1993).

One can attribute some of these difficulties to life situations such as having a child victimized, that then triggers memories or a re-experiencing of the abuse (Goldstein 1995) as well as the powerlessness experienced in her own abuse (Friedrich 1990; New et al. 1999; Sgroi 1982). Yet, regardless of a history of abuse, mothers of sexually abused children experience less distress when they have support from family and friends, and when they use active behavioral and/or cognitive strategies instead of avoidance (Hiebert-Murphy 1998).

Parenting Attitudes and Practices

Another dynamic requiring additional study is the impact of child sexual abuse on parenting attitudes and practices. Multiple predictors can account for parenting difficulties but child sexual abuse researchers (Benedict 1998; Cole and Woolger 1989; Faller 2007; Hiebert-Murphy 2000) found one long-term negative consequence is on the later parenting abilities of survivors. Although the definition of parenting can take on a wide variety of issues related to child rearing, for the purpose of this discussion, effective parenting is defined by a mother's ability to (a) demonstrate developmentally appropriate parenting attitudes and expectations, and (b) appropriately respond to her sexually abused child by demonstrating adequate maternal support in response to the abuse situation.

Ultimately, there are three questions for consideration. First, do mothers in general parent differently when they find out that their child has been sexually abused? Second, do mothers with a history of childhood sexual abuse parent differently than those without such a history, and third, is this affected by whether their child was sexually abused?

Referring agencies often make an initial appraisal of mothers' parenting attitudes. If they have concerns, agency workers may require an objective assessment of the mothers' potential to adequately parent and protect their children from future harm. Additionally, such an assessment can aid in determining if children should remain in the home or be returned from foster care.

However, it is argued that one cannot formulate a reliable or valid profile of the mothers or their children based solely on assessments because the examination is being made when they are likely experiencing severe distress from the allegations or findings of abuse (Bandcroft et al. 2011; Ovaris 1991). Even high functioning mothers can become overwhelmed and incapacitated upon learning her child may have been sexually abused. Furthermore, the mothers are aware that their performance on the evaluation could determine the fate of their children going to or remaining in foster care, and in some cases, having parental rights terminated. For those invested in their children remaining or returning home, they may believe it important to present themselves in a positive light even if it means denying their own abuse or denying common everyday parenting problems.

In situations of child sexual abuse, the literature indicates that many mothers often feel devastated and tend to assume that somehow they should have known or protected their child from the abuse (Banyard et al. 2001; Hooper 1992; Ovaris 1991). This guilt can be pervasive and often inhibit their responsiveness to their children's behavior at a time when their children generally need more structure to enhance their feelings of security. Frequently, this leads to mothers attempting to nurture their abused child by being too lenient, which often has the opposite effect and can actually increase behavioral difficulties. Further, this has the potential to exacerbate confusion in children, whose mothers may have previously been structured and consistent, but because of the abuse situation may behave in less organized and dependable ways.

In contrast to mothers without a history of childhood sexual trauma, mothers who were abused as children, and whose children may or may not have been abused, have significantly more dysfunctional parenting attitudes and behaviors (Ruscio 2001). They may find it difficult to feel confident, organized, and in control, and may have always had inappropriate expectations or given mixed messages to their children, and exhibited inconsistent parenting styles (Cohen 1995; Cole and Woolger 1989). They likely had difficulty providing adequate parental supervision and raised their children in a less protected environment (Friedrich 1991).

However, similar to the dynamics of sexual abuse, parenting practices are too complex and multifaceted to limit the explanation to just one variable: mother's history of abuse. Complicating our understanding of this issue, it's been found that children whose mothers are experiencing psychosocial stressors such as depression and substance abuse are more likely to have problems parenting regardless of their child being sexually abused (Leifer et al. 1993; Pareses et al. 2001). Substance abuse as an intervening variable between mothers' history of sexual abuse and maternal supportiveness can interfere with mothers' ability to help their children cope with their sexual abuse experiences (Pareses et al. 2001).

Additionally, studies on parenting attitudes and practices have found significant differences in styles of parenting as well as ability to establish positive relationships among mothers with a history of incest compared to nonabused mothers (Cole et al. 1992). Particularly, mothers with a history of childhood sexual abuse endorsed more parenting practices that were considered weaker, abusive, punishing, and neglectful as well as messages that belittle and devalue children than mothers who had not experienced sexual abuse (Banyard 1997; Burkett 1991; Cohen 1995; Cole et al. 1992; Thompson et al. 1999). Also, the literature described these mothers as tending to have more negative views of themselves as parents (Banyard 1997) and were more permissive (Ruscio 2001), including being less confident, consistent, and emotionally controlled (Cole et al. 1992). They often place the needs of their partners before the needs of their child and are more self-focused than child-focused, frequently resulting in issues of parent-child role reversal (Parr 2010). An overall issue found in research literature was they expected their children to be more self-sufficient (Cole et al. 1992) and relied on their children for emotional support, viewing them more as caretakers, companions, or friends (Burkett 1991).

Contextual Basis

It is suggested that mothers' own unresolved trauma affects their personality, perception, and decision making (Ellenson 1986; Friedrich 1991; Parr 2010) and thereby influences (a) their ability to obtain help for their children, (b) their responsiveness to their children's physical and emotional needs, and (c) their overall parenting practices. As such, it is believed that adult survivors of sexual abuse are less likely to respond or are slower to constructively respond to situations of their child's abuse (Courtois 1988; Hernandez et al. 2009; Howard 1993; Ovaris 1991).

This impaired psychosocial functioning has been known to result in sexually abused mothers having significantly less empathy and awareness than nonabused mothers (Cohen 1995). Cohen speculated that mothers who experienced incest may live with the fear and anxiety of being unable to protect their own children from similar abuse, and therefore respond poorly when their child's abuse is revealed. Additionally, Hiebert-Murphy (1998) postulates that mothers with childhood sexual abuse histories experience greater emotional distress following their children's disclosure of sexual abuse and lack the social support to adequately cope with their children's disclosure.

In clinical practice, mothers who have experienced childhood sexual abuse often report a great deal of self-doubt with their own life skills and abilities (Parr 2010). Additionally, many reported anxiety in parenting their children through developmental phases that they had difficulty mastering due to their own abuse. When faced with parenting a sexually abused child, they reported feeling angry that they were unable to protect their children from harm and that their child's abuse triggered their own unresolved history.

Conclusion

Nonoffending mothers are often scrutinized by social service agencies and the judicial system for contributing to the abuse of their children or for failing to protect their children from harm. Social service agencies often identify mothers as having questionable parenting practices and therefore, ask the mother to participate in or the court to mandate parenting capacity assessments. As part of the evaluation process of the mother and/or their child victim, social histories may reveal mother's history of childhood sexual abuse. Although there are many mediating factors in childhood sexual abuse situations, the current discussion supports the notion that mothers with histories of childhood sexual trauma – in general – face more challenges in accurately perceiving and responding to their children's needs and gaining the necessary assistance for their children than their nonabused counterparts.

Additionally, mothers report a broad range of maternal support in response to their children's disclosure of sexual abuse. Their response can fall anywhere on the continuum from supportive to disbelief to rejection. And, as a consequence for mothers who react in non-supportive ways, some children are placed in foster care.

Oftentimes mothers who have unresolved histories of childhood abuse lack the necessary internal resources and coping skills to adequately manage life stressors, especially parenting a sexually abused child. Of the mothers who deny abuse histories, it is unclear how many fail to disclose for fear they would be further scrutinized. Yet, nonoffending mothers may have experienced numerous other life stressors including childhood maltreatment, domestic violence, employment losses, substance abuse, and prior criminal charges that confound their ability to cope with their child's abuse. Research in the area of nonoffending mothers' parenting their sexually abused children is limited, but suggests that mothers' own histories of childhood abuse may adversely impact their ability to appropriately parent and support their abused children regardless of other adverse experiences (Banyard 1997; Ruscio 2001).

Theoretical Implications

Childhood sexual trauma can alter the course of normal development and often occurs in conjunction with other forms of maltreatment or stressful life events (Finkelhor 2008). Therefore, a comprehensive or holistic approach is essential. Similar to an ecological systems model, methods that address the biopsychosocial and cultural needs of victims and their families are imperative to understanding nonoffending caregivers parenting their sexually abused (Zielinski and Bradshaw 2006). Child sexual abuse and parenting are by definition complex, multidimensional issues that cannot be fully appreciated using singular theoretical models. Employing a multi-theoretical perspective that considers the long-term developmental consequences of traumatic experiences can offer better awareness in understanding this population and hopefully, create a paradigm shift to a more holistic approach.

Research Implications

Child sexual abuse is an ever evolving field. Active and ongoing research on parenting sexually abused children benefits children, families, and communities by providing direction for intervention and prevention services. Research-informed practice can be used to identify needs and establish intervention services for this population. However, victims and their nonoffending caregivers are under enormous psychosocial stress and not likely the best candidates for psychological testing or other measurable strategies. Caution must be used in interpreting results because trauma often impedes accurate and generalizable assessment.

Even though some mothers do not have a history childhood sexual abuse, their parenting may be drastically impacted by the sexual abuse of their children. Additionally, there may be numerous other family dynamics that may or may not be related to having a sexually abused child. Therefore, when parenting capacity assessments or other instruments are used to determine whether or not children should remain in the care of or be returned to their families, research-informed interventions such as forensic interviewing (American Professional Society on the Abuse of Children [APSAC] 2012) can only support efforts concerning the best interest of mothers, children, and families. Evidence-based research is necessary to knowing what services would likely be helpful to mothers and professionals meeting the needs of child victims and their families. A number of mental health treatment approaches are used, but trauma-focused cognitive behavioral therapy is most promising because of the extensive research that supports it efficacy (Pollio et al. 2010).

Practice Implications

The discussion on nonoffending mothers emphasizes the need for frontline workers and multidisciplinary team participants to be more unified in their response to victims of childhood sexual abuse. As stated above, treatment interventions should be research-informed. A consistent and organized way of gathering information from referring agencies, parents, and children is needed. Further, a consistent measure regularly used to assess their overall parental functioning is important in formulating long-term recommendations. Although open-ended questions can be vital to building rapport, inconsistencies in styles can led to gaps in information and incomplete services. Likewise, families in need of services may be missed because their issues are not severe enough to warrant this level of assessment.

Child advocacy center-based treatment programs have the greatest potential for meeting the needs of victims and their families (Tavkar and Hansen 2011). They provide an opportunity for the entire team of professionals working with the family to coordinate from the beginning of the investigative and legal procedures all the way through the treatment process (Bonach et al. 2010). Families often complain about the lack of continuity with intervention services and child advocacy centers are posed to provide both child- and family-focused programs (Hernandez et al. 2009).

A goal of practice should be to provide education, advocacy, and counseling for caregivers whose children are suspected of being abused and especially for those who disclose childhood abuse issues or difficulties coping with their children's disclosure. Treatment of sexual trauma is a specialty area that the average frontline practitioner is not trained to handle. Sexual abuse intervention services must emphasize and provide direction for ongoing services to ensure clients' needs are being met. Ongoing training in child sexual abuse for frontline investigators and treatment providers is vital to good quality practice with this population.

Additionally, providing supportive services to caregivers and their families prior to children being placed in foster care is essential in facilitating nonoffending mothers supporting their sexually abused children. Many mothers have more than one child abused. Low functioning mothers may benefit from earlier detection services, including screening services at the time children are born into high-risk families.

Ideally, a center that evaluates, treats, and supervises the ongoing needs of victims of sexual abuse and their families is necessary. A child advocacy center could offer a comprehensive assessment of all family members and guide intervention services as needed. In addition, it could serve as a resource to identify community-based support services including education, financial assistance, job skills training, and the like, which are often more beneficial when done in collaboration with treatment providers. The goal of the services would be to empower and restore a healthy sense of self for all family members and re-establish them the community.

Policy Implications

Protecting children and preventing child sexual abuse must be a higher priority for policymakers if we have any hope of breaking the intergenerational cycle of abuse. One major obstacle for both prevention and intervention programs is funding. Until policymakers and society as a whole recognize child sexual abuse as a health crisis, policy and funding resources will not rise to the level of the problem. Health insurance offers limited financial support and managed care has restricted services, further complicating caregivers ability to obtain the professional assistance their children require.

Educating policymakers, courts, social services and law enforcement in understanding the long-term consequences of child sexual abuse becomes imperative when considering the future biopsychosocial impact on individuals and society. The difficulties created by denying the gravity of the problem only exacerbate healthcare and judicial management expenditures.

The greater societal benefits in prevention and early intervention programs call for policymakers to be held accountable. Interdisciplinary collaboration among community leaders, agencies, and service providers is required for directing policymakers in the establishment of programs that empower caregivers and families, as well as laws that support prevention and intervention.

Summary

Discussions such as this are needed to clarify generalizations made about how mothers respond to the abuse of their children. An effort to understand the aspects of how sexual abuse impacts children, families, and society is a must if we are ever to break the intergenerational cycle of abuse. First of all, such information can provide greater theoretical insight into the psychosocial factors influencing the behavior of nonoffending mothers when their own children are subsequently abused. Secondly, understanding how nonoffending mothers are affected by childhood sexual abuse can help inform the intervention and prevention needs of this population as well as child victims. Thirdly, it is important to educate the judiciary regarding the needs of victims, their families, and decisions as they relate to case management and custody. Finally, studies that address the prevalence and impact of child sexual abuse on society are needed to guide policymakers as they struggle to establish prevention laws and policies. In our quest to end child sexual abuse, we must acknowledge and include on the team those who serve as primary nonoffending caregivers.

References

American Professional Society on the Abuse of Children. (2012). *Practice guidelines: Forensic interviewing in cases of suspected child abuse.* Chicago: APSAC.

Bandcroft, L., Silverman, J., & Ritchie, D. (2011). *The batterer as parent: Addressing the impact of domestic violence on family dynamics* (2nd ed.). Thousand Oaks: Sage.

Banyard, V. L. (1997). The impact of childhood sexual abuse and family functioning on four dimensions of women's later parenting. *Child Abuse and Neglect, 21*(11), 1095–1107.

Banyard, V. L., Englund, D. W., & Rozelle, D. (2001). Parenting the traumatized child: Attending to the needs of nonoffending caregivers of traumatized children. *Psychotherapy, 38*(1), 74–87.

Benedict, M. I. (1998). *Parenting among women sexually abused in childhood.* Report for Office of Child Abuse and Neglect, Children's Bureau, U. S. Department of Health and Human Services (Contract No. 90-CA-1544). Washington, DC.

Berliner, L. (2011). Child sexual abuse: Definitions, prevalence, and consequences. In J. E. B. Myers (Ed.), *The APSAC handbook on child maltreatment* (3rd ed., pp. 215–232). Thousand Oaks: Sage.

Berliner, L., & Elliott, D. M. (1996). Sexual abuse on children. In J. Briere, L. Berliner, J. A. Bulkley, C. Jenny, & T. Reid (Eds.), *The APSAC handbook on child maltreatment* (pp. 51–71). Thousand Oaks: Sage.

Bolen, R. M., & Lamb, J. L. (2004). Ambivalence of nonoffending guardians after child abuse disclosure. *Journal of Interpersonal Violence, 19*(2), 185–211.

Bolen, R. M., & Lamb, J. L. (2007). Can nonoffending mothers of sexually abused children be both ambivalent and supportive? *Child Maltreatment, 12*(2), 191–97.

Bonach, K., Mabry, J. B., & Potss-Henry, C. (2010). Exploring nonoffending caregiver satisfaction with a Children's Advocacy Center. *Journal of Child Sexual Abuse, 19*(6), 687–708.

Browne, A., & Finkelhor, D. (1986). Initial and long-term effects: A review of the research. In D. Finkelhor (Ed.), *A source book on child sexual abuse* (pp. 143–179). Newbury Park: Sage.

Burkett, L. P. (1991). Parenting behaviors of women who were sexually abused as children in their families or origin. *Family Process, 30*, 421–434.

Butler, S. M., Radia, N., & Magnatta, M. (1994). Maternal compliance to court-ordered assessment in cases of child maltreatment. *Child Abuse and Neglect, 18*(2), 203–211.

Cohen, T. (1995). Motherhood among incest survivors. *Child Abuse and Neglect, 19*(12), 1423–1429.

Cole, P. M., & Putnam, F. W. (1992). Effect of incest on self and social functioning: A development psychopathology perspective. *Journal of Consulting and Clinical Psychology, 60*, 174–184.

Cole, P. M., & Woolger, C. (1989). Incest survivors: The relation of their perceptions of their parents and their own parenting attitudes. *Child Abuse and Neglect, 13*, 409–416.

Cole, P. M., Woolger, C., Power, T. G., & Smith, K. D. (1992). Parenting difficulties among adult survivors of father-daughter incest. *Child Abuse and Neglect, 16*, 239–249.

Coohey, C., & O'Leary, P. (2008). Mothers' protection of their children after discovering they have been sexually abused: An information-processing perspective. *Child Abuse and Neglect, 32*(2), 245–259.

Corcoran, J. (2004). Treatment outcome research with the nonoffending parents of sexually abused children: A critical review. *Journal of Child Sexual Abuse, 13*(2), 59–84.

Corcoran, J., & Vijavan, P. (2008). A meta-analysis of parent-involved treatment for child sexual abuse. *Research on Social Work Practice, 18*(5), 453–464.

Courtois, C. A. (1988). *Healing the incest wound: Adult survivors in therapy.* New York: W. W. Norton.

Deblinger, E., & Heflin, A. H. (1996). *Treating sexually abused children and their nonoffending parents: A cognitive behavioral approach.* Thousand Oaks: Sage.

Deblinger, E., Hathaway, C. R., Lippmann, J., & Steer, R. (1993). Psychosocial characteristics and correlates of symptom distress in nonoffending mothers of sexually abused children. *Journal of Interpersonal Violence, 8*, 155–168.

Deblinger, E., Stauffer, L., & Landsberg, C. (1994). The impact of a history of child sexual abuse on maternal response to allegations of sexual abuse concerning her child. *Journal of Child Sexual Abuse, 3*(3), 67–75.

Ellenson, G. S. (1986). Disturbances of perception in adult female incest survivors. *Social Casework: The Journal of Contemporary Social Work (March), 67*(3), 149–159.

Elliott, A. N., & Carnes, C. N. (2001). Reactions of nonoffending parents to the sexual abuse of their child: A review of the literature. *Child Maltreatment, 6*(4), 314–331.

Everson, M. D., Hunter, W. M., Runyon, D. K., Edelsohn, G. A., & Coulter, M. L. (1989). Maternal support following disclosure of incest. *American Journal of Orthopsychiatry, 59*(2), 197–196.

Faller, K. C. (1988). The myth of the collusive mother: Variability in the functioning of intrafamilial sexual abuse. *Journal of Interpersonal Violence, 3*(2), 190–196.

Faller, K. C. (2007). *Interviewing children about sexual abuse: Controversies and best practices.* New York: Oxford University Press.

Famularo, R., Kinscherff, R., Bunshaft, D., Spivak, G., & Fenton, T. (1989). Parental compliance to court-ordered treatment interventions in cases of child maltreatment. *Child Abuse and Neglect, 13*, 507–514.

Faust, J., Runyon, M. K., & Kenny, M. C. (1995). Family variables associated with the onset and impact of intrafamilial childhood sexual abuse. *Clinical Psychology Review, 15*, 443–456.

Fergusson, D. M., & Mullen, P. E. (1999). *Childhood sexual abuse*. Thousand Oaks: Sage.

Finkelhor, D. (1994). Current information the scope and nature of child sexual abuse. *The Future of Children: Sexual Abuse of Children, 4*(2), 31–53.

Finkelhor, D. (2008). *Childhood victimization: Violence, crime, and abuse in the lives of young people*. New York: Oxford University Press.

Finkelhor, D., & Jones, L. M. (2006). Why have child maltreatment and child victimization declined? *Journal of Social Issues, 62*(4), 685–716.

Friedrich, W. N. (1990). *Psychotherapy of sexually abused children and their families*. New York: Norton.

Friedrich, W. N. (1991). Mothers of sexually abused children: An MMPI study. *Journal of Clinical Psychology, 47*, 778–783.

Gavey, N., Florence, J., Pazaro, S., & Tan, J. (1990). Mother-blaming, the perfect alibi: Family therapy and the mothers of incest survivors. *Journal of Feminist Family Therapy, 2*(1), 1–25.

Goldstein, E. G. (1995). *Ego psychology and social work practice*. New York: The Free Press.

Hall, L., & Lloyd, S. (1993). *Surviving child sexual abuse: A handbook for helping women challenge their past*. Washington, DC: The Farmer Press.

Haskett, M. E., Nowlan, N. P., Hutcheson, J. S., & Whitworth, J. M. (1991). Factors associated with the successful entry into therapy in child sexual abuse cases. *Child Abuse and Neglect, 15*, 467–476.

Hebert, M., Daigneault, I., Collin-Vezina, D., & Cyr, M. (2007). Factors linked to distress in mothers of children disclosing sexual abuse. *Journal of Nervous and Mental Disease, 195*(10), 805–811.

Hernandez, A., Ruble, C., Rockmore, L., McKay, M., Messam, T., Harris, M., & Hope, S. (2009). An integrated approach to treating non-offending parents affected by sexual abuse. *Social Work in Mental Health, 7*(6), 533–555.

Hiebert-Murphy, D. (1998). Emotional distress among mothers whose children have been sexually abused: The role of a history of child sexual abuse, social support, and coping. *Child Abuse and Neglect, 22*(5), 423–435.

Hiebert-Murphy, D. (2000). Factors related to mothers' perceptions of parenting following their children's disclosure of sexual abuse. *Child Maltreatment, 5*(3), 251–260.

Hooper, C. A. (1992). *Mothers surviving child sexual abuse*. New York: Routledge, Chapman and Hall.

Howard, C. A. (1993). Factors influencing a mother's response to her child's disclosure of incest. *Professional Psychology: Research and Practice, 24*(2), 176–181.

Jenny, C. (1996). Medical issues in sexual abuse. In J. Briere, L. Berliner, J. A. Bulkley, C. Jenny, & T. Reid (Eds.), *The APSAC handbook on child maltreatment* (pp. 195–205). Thousand Oaks: Sage.

Kendall-Tackett, K. A., Williams, L. M., & Finkelhor, D. (1993). Impact of sexual abuse on children: A review and synthesis of recent empirical studies. *Psychological Bulletin, 113*(1), 164–180.

Kim, K., Noll, J. G., Putnam, F. W., & Trickett, P. K. (2007). Psychosocial characteristics of nonoffending mothers of sexually abused girls: Findings from a prospective, multigenerational study. *Child Maltreatment, 12*(4), 338–351.

Kirschner, S., Kirschner, D. A., & Rappaport, R. L. (1993). *Working with adult incest survivors: The healing journey*. New York: Brunner/Mazel.

Leifer, M., Shapiro, J. P., & Kassem, L. (1993). The impact of maternal history and behavior upon foster placement and adjustment in sexually abused girls. *Child Abuse and Neglect, 17*, 755–766.

Lipovsky, J. A., Saunders, B. E., & Hanson, R. F. (1992). Parent-child relationships of victims and siblings in incest families. *Journal of Child Sexual Abuse, 1*(4), 35–49.

Malloy, L. C., & Lyon, T. D. (2006). Caregiver support and child sexual abuse: Why does it matter? *Journal of Child Sexual Abuse, 15*(4), 97–103.

Malloy, L. C., Lyon, T. D., & Quas, J. A. (2007). Filial dependency and recantation of child sexual abuse allegations. *Journal of the American Academy of Child and Adolescent Psychiatry, 46*(2), 162–170.

McDonald, T. P., & Johnson, W. (1993). Tracking reported sexual abuse cases. *Journal of Child Sexual Abuse, 2*(2), 1–11.

Muram, D., Rosenthal, T. L., & Beck, K. W. (1994). Personality profiles of mothers of sexual abuse victims and their daughters. *Child Abuse and Neglect, 18*(5), 419–423.

Myers, J. E. B., Diedrich, S., Lee, D., Fincher, K. M., & Stern, R. (1999). Professional writing on child sexual abuse from 1900 to 1975: Dominant themes and impact on prosecution. *Child Maltreatment, 4*(3), 201–216.

New, M. J. C., Stevenson, J., & Skuse, D. (1999). Characteristics of mothers of boys who sexually abuse. *Child Maltreatment, 4*(1), 21–31.

Newberger, C. M., Gremy, I. M., Waternaux, C. M., & Newberger, E. H. (1993). Mothers of sexually abused children: Trauma and repair in longitudinal perspective. *American Journal of Orthopsychiatry, 63*(1), 92–102.

Ovaris, W. (1991). *After the nightmare*. Holmes Beach: Learning Publications.

Pareses, M., Leifer, M., & Kilbane, T. (2001). Maternal variables related to sexually abused children's functioning. *Child Abuse and Neglect, 25*(9), 1159–1176.

Parr, D. O. (2010). *Molested mommies: When incest survivors become parents.* Bloomington: Xlibris Corporation.

Pintello, D., & Zuravin, S. (2001). Intrafamilial child sexual abuse: Predictors of post disclosure maternal belief and protective action. *Child Maltreatment, 6*(4), 344–352.

Pollio, E., Deblinger, E., & Runyon, M. (2010). Mental health treatment for the effects of child sexual abuse. In J. E. B. Myers (Ed.), *The APSAC handbook on child maltreatment* (3rd ed., pp. 215–232). Thousand Oaks, CA: Sage Publications.

Runyan, D., Hunter, W. M., Everson, M. D., DeVos, E. D., Cross, T., Peeler, N., & Whitcomb, D. (1992). *Maternal support for child victims of sexual abuse: Determinants and implications.* Report for the National Center on Child Abuse and Neglect (Grant No. 90CA-1368). Washington, DC.

Ruscio, A. M. (2001). Predicting the child-rearing practices of mothers sexually abused in childhood. *Child Abuse and Neglect, 25*(3), 133–146.

Russell, D. E. H., & Bolen, R. M. (2000). *The epidemic of rape and child sexual abuse in the United States.* Thousand Oaks: Sage.

Sawyer, G., Tsao, E., Hansen, D., & Flood, M. (2006). Weekly problems scales: Instruments for sexually abused youth and their nonoffending parents in treatment. *Child Maltreatment, 11*(1), 34–48.

Schonberg, I. J. (1992). The distortion of the role of mother in child sexual abuse. *Journal of Child Sexual Abuse, 1*(3), 47–61.

Sedlak, A. J., Mettenburg, J., Basena, M., Petta, I., McPherson, K., Greene, A., & Li, S. (2010). *Fourth national incidence study of child abuse and neglect (NIS–4): Report to Congress, executive summary.* Washington, DC: U.S. Department of Health and Human Services, Administration for Children and Families.

Sgroi, S. M. (1982). Family treatment. In S. M. Sgroi (Ed.), *Handbook of clinical intervention in child sexual abuse* (pp. 241–268). Lexington: Lexington Books.

Shadoin, A. L., & Carnes, C. N. (2006). Comments on how child protective services investigators decide to substantiate mothers for failure-to-protect in sexual abuse cases. *Journal of Child Sexual Abuse, 15*(4), 97–103.

Sirles, E. A., & Franke, P. J. (1989). Factors influencing mothers' reactions to intrafamily sexual abuse. *Child Abuse and Neglect, 13*, 131–139.

Smith, A. P., & Kelly, A. B. (2008). An exploratory study of group therapy for sexually abused adolescents and nonoffending guardians. *Journal of Child Sexual Abuse, 17*(2), 101–116.

Tavkar, P., & Hansen, D. J. (2011). Interventions for families victimized by child sexual abuse: Clinical issues and approaches for child advocacy center-based services. *Aggression and Violent Behavior, 16*(3), 188–199.

Thompson, R. A., Christiansen, E. H., Jackson, S., Wyatt, J. M., Colman, R. A., Peterson, R. L., Wilcox, B. L., & Buckendahl, C. W. (1999). Parent attitudes and discipline practices: Profiles and correlates in a nationally representative sample. *Child Maltreatment, 4*(4), 316–330.

Tingus, K. D., Heger, A. H., Foy, D. W., & Leskin, G. A. (1996). Factors associated with entry into therapy in children evaluated for sexual abuse. *Child Abuse and Neglect, 20*(1), 63–68.

Walters, S. (2002). Working with the nonoffending caregiver. *Sex Offender Law Report, 4*(3), 35–38.

Wells, R. D., McCann, J., Adams, J., Voris, J., & Ensign, J. (1995). Emotional, behavioral, and physical symptoms reported by parents of sexually abused, nonabused, and allegedly abused prepubescent females. *Child Abuse and Neglect, 19*(2), 155–163.

Wilson, M. K. (1995). A preliminary report on ego development in nonoffending mothers of sexually abused children. *Child Abuse and Neglect, 19*(4), 511–518.

Wolfe, D. A. (1999). *Child abuse: Implications for child development and psychopathology.* Thousand Oaks: Sage.

Wyatt, G. E., Guthrie, D., & Notgrass, C. M. (1992). Differential effects of women's child sexual abuse and subsequent sexual revictimization. *Journal of Consulting and Clinical Psychology, 60*, 167–173.

Zielinski, D. S., & Bradshaw, C. P. (2006). Ecological influences on the sequelae of child maltreatment: A review of the literature. *Child Maltreatment, 11*(1), 49–62.

Chapter 24
Beyond Investigations: Differential Response in Child Protective Services

Tamara Fuller

Until relatively recently, the only way that most Child Protective Services (CPS) systems could respond to allegations of child abuse and neglect was through an investigation. Concerns with certain elements of this forensic approach to child protection led to the development of a CPS reform known as Differential Response.[1] This chapter will describe the key elements of a Differential Response approach to child protective services and highlight how it differs from a traditional investigative approach. Although a core set of practice elements have been defined that characterize Differential Response systems, wide variations in practice exist between systems, several of which will be described. As with most child welfare interventions, rigorous research on the effectiveness of Differential Response systems is limited, but quickly growing. A summary and critical review of the current evidence is provided, as well as suggestions for next steps.

Development and Evolution of Differential Response in Child Protective Services

Traditional Child Protective Service Systems

Although some variations in practice exist, all child protection systems are designed to respond to child maltreatment through several key functions: (1) maintaining a hotline that receives referrals of alleged child maltreatment, (2) screening these referrals to determine CPS response, and (3) investigating the screened-in reports to determine (a) whether child maltreatment has occurred or the risk of future maltreatment is high and (b) what actions, if any, are needed to ensure the child's safety (U.S. Department of Health and Human Services [DHHS] 2003). Figure 24.1 shows a typical case flow in a traditional, single-track CPS system. Families become involved with the child protection system following a referral call of suspected child abuse or neglect made to a hotline by either a mandated reporter or by a family member, friend, or other concerned citizen. Trained CPS intake workers gather

---

[1] Differential Response is sometimes referred to as Alternative Response, Multiple Response, or Family Assessment Response.

T. Fuller (✉)
Children and Family Research Center School of Social Work,
University of Illinois at Urbana-Champaign, Champaign, IL, USA
e-mail: t-fuller@illinois.edu

J.E. Korbin and R.D. Krugman (eds.), *Handbook of Child Maltreatment*, Child Maltreatment 2,   443
DOI 10.1007/978-94-007-7208-3_24, © Springer Science+Business Media Dordrecht 2014

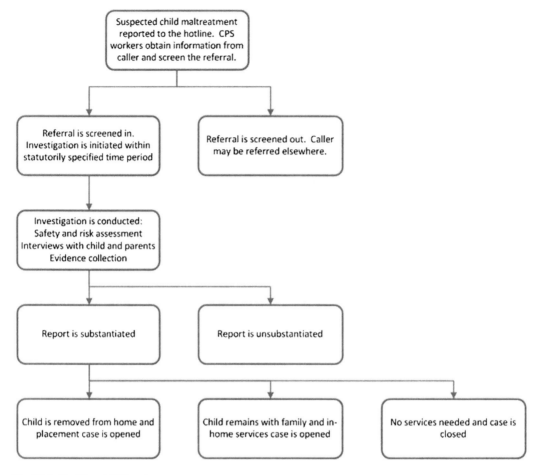

Fig. 24.1 Traditional CPS system

information from the reporter about the alleged incident and make a decision to either screen the referral call into the system or reject the call and screen it out of the system.

Referrals may be screened out if there is not enough information to investigate or if the reported circumstances do not meet the state's statutory definition of child abuse or neglect. Some states provide services or community referrals to screened-out calls, but many do not. In FFY 2010, there were an estimated 3.3 million referrals involving 5.9 million children made to child protective services in the United States (DHHS 2011). Of these referrals, 60.7 % were screened in and 39.3 % were screened out.

Once a referral is screened in, the child protection system must respond to the allegations of child maltreatment. In a traditional CPS system, this response consists of an investigation, which is initiated within a particular time period from a few hours to several days, depending on the type of maltreatment alleged, the potential severity of the situation, and state statutes (Child Welfare Information Gateway 2012). Investigators contact the family, typically through an unannounced home visit, to gather information from the child, parents, and other relevant informants regarding the alleged maltreatment incident. Most CPS agencies have implemented the use of structured safety or risk assessment instruments to guide investigators' decision-making regarding the child's immediate or long-term risk of moderate to severe harm. Investigators may gather additional evidence through interviews with collateral contacts or screening protocols for specific risks such as domestic violence or parental substance abuse. An investigator's primary purpose is to determine whether the child is safe in the home, whether abuse or neglect occurred, and whether there is a high risk of additional maltreatment. Once sufficient evidence is collected, the investigator makes a determination about whether maltreatment occurred; the maltreatment allegations are either substantiated or unsubstantiated. In FFY 2010, 24.3 % of the reports that received an investigation were substantiated and 70.4 % were unsubstantiated (DHHS 2011).[2]

A number of additional actions may occur when a report is substantiated, although their likelihood of occurrence varies significantly among CPS agencies (DHHS 2003, 2011). In nearly all states, the names of the maltreatment perpetrators are entered into a central registry so that reports can be tracked over time and used for background checks. Some families receive post-investigation services; decisions about services depend on a number of factors, including state policy; results of safety, risk, and needs assessments; and local service availability. If there is little to no risk of future maltreatment or few family needs, the case may be closed without services or the family may be provided with referrals to community-based services. If there is moderate to high risk of future maltreatment or many family needs, post-investigation child welfare services may be provided to the family. Voluntary services may be provided to the family while the children remain at home, or, if the family refuses to participate, a court petition may be obtained to mandate participation with in-home services. If the child has been seriously harmed or is considered at risk of serious harm, the court may order the child's removal from the home and mandate the family's participation in services. Post-investigation services may be provided to families with unsubstantiated maltreatment reports as well, although this occurs less frequently than among families with substantiated reports. In FFY 2010, 61.1 % of the children in substantiated reports received post-investigation services, compared to 24.0 % of children in unsubstantiated reports (DHHS 2011).

Development of Differential Response in Child Protective Services

Soon after its inception, pressures began to mount in the child protection system as the number of annual reports made to hotlines increased from fewer than 10,000 in 1967 to more than 2.6 million in 2010 (DHHS 2011). By 1990 a U.S. Advisory Board on Child Abuse and Neglect concluded that child maltreatment was a "national emergency" and that "the system the nation has devised to respond to child abuse and neglect is failing. It is not a question of acute failure of a single element of the system; there is chronic and critical multiple organ failure" (U.S. Advisory Board on Child Abuse and Neglect 1990, p. 2, as cited in Siegel 2012). Blue ribbons panels of child welfare experts were convened and tasked with pinpointing problems and developing solutions. One such task force, the Harvard Executive Session, brought together child welfare administrators, practitioners, policy-makers and experts between 1994 and 1997; this group identified five major concerns of the CPS system: over-inclusion, system capacity, under-inclusion, service orientation, and service delivery (Waldfogel 1998). As a wider range of child welfare concerns were included in state definitions of child maltreatment, "reports concerning relatively low-risk families unnecessarily add to the volume of cases flooding the CPS system" (Waldfogel 1998, p. 107); inappropriately referred cases were problematic not only because many families were being investigated that did not need to be, but they also impeded the ability of the system to respond effectively to other, higher-risk cases. The type of over-inclusion identified by the Harvard

---

[2] An additional 1.4 % were indicated (an infrequently used category meaning that the report could not be substantiated but there was reason to suspect that the child was maltreated) and minor numbers were closed without a determination or had another disposition, so percentages do not add to 100 %.

Executive Session remains true today: the vast majority of CPS investigations involve allegations of neglect (78.3 %) and less than 20 % require court action (DHHS 2011).

In addition, in order to gather the evidence needed to make a determination of maltreatment, CPS investigators tend to approach families in an adversarial manner, by arriving unannounced and interviewing children and collateral contact to corroborate evidence about the facts of the case. Receiving such a visit from child protective services usually elicits feelings of fear, anger, shame, or humiliation from parents (Buckley et al. 2011; Gallagher et al. 2011; Harris 2012; Platt 2001). Many parents find the investigation process coercive and intrusive, and respond by overtly resisting the intervention, hiding important information or concerns, or feigning cooperation out of fear of being negatively perceived by the worker and agency (Forrester et al. 2012; Harris 2012; Thoburn et al. 1995). Research indicates the importance of parent engagement with child welfare services in achieving better outcomes for families, yet the adversarial nature of traditional CPS investigations inhibits engagement and makes parents less likely to accept services and less motivated to change their behavior (Schene 2005).

Although many parents who are investigated by CPS report feeling coerced into accepting services, most are not offered services at all. The vast majority of reports made to CPS are unsubstantiated, and rates of service provision even among substantiated cases are very low in many states (DHHS 2011). This does not mean that investigated families have no service needs; many have underlying problems such as unstable housing, severe poverty, chronic physical and mental health conditions, and issues with substance abuse (Ringeisen et al. 2011). Yet, contact with the traditional child protection system does little to alleviate these problems (Campbell et al. 2010). As a result, many families come into repeated contacts with the child protection system while their needs and problems go unresolved.

Combined, these criticisms led one noted child welfare researcher to describe the traditional CPS response to maltreatment as "an adversarial investigation, leading to minimal services unless the situation is so severe that the child is removed from the home" (Schene 2005, p. 5). It was these perceived limitations that led child welfare administrators and policy-makers in several states to develop and implement practices and policies designed to increase parent engagement, individualize services to match identified family needs, and improve long-term family well-being, all without sacrificing the focus on child safety that was the hallmark of traditional child protective services. Several reform efforts grew from the dissatisfaction with the child protection system of the early 1990s (Waldfogel 1998), and one eventually took shape into what is now known as Differential Response. Loosely defined, Differential Response allows child protection systems the option of responding to screened-in reports of child abuse and neglect in more than one way. Differential Response systems recognize that while some maltreatment reports require court involvement and are best approached through a traditional investigation, many do not and would be better served through an alternative approach that emphasized family-involvement and needs-driven service provision.

Differential Response reforms were piloted in several states during the 1990s, including Florida, Missouri, Oklahoma, Virginia, Washington, and Texas (National Quality Improvement Center on Differential Response [QIC-DR] 2011). Several of these pilot projects, including those in Florida and Texas, were discontinued due to funding and service capacity issues, or because child welfare administrators or legislators shifted reform efforts to other programs. Reforms in other states flourished, however, and the Missouri Differential Response system served as a model for reform in several other states, including Minnesota (Siegel 2012). In the 2000s, interest in Differential Response continued to climb, and reached a tipping point around the middle of the decade. In 2005, the American Humane Association "launched a national initiative on Differential Response" with the release of a double issue of their *Protecting Children* journal, addressing the use of Differential Response with varying case characteristics, county and state-specific lessons surrounding implementation, early evaluation findings, and discussions of the policy, practice, and data implications moving forward (Marley and Kaplan 2011, p. 3). American Humane Association also convened the first National Conference on Differential Response in San Diego in 2006, which drew together national and state experts in an effort to share information. Another indication of the growing interest in Differential Response was a national study that was jointly conducted by the American Humane Association and the Child Welfare League of America (Merkel-Holguin et al. 2006). The results of this study were instrumental in refining the field's understanding of the various ways in which states were implementing Differential Response and developing a more precise definition of the approach.

Another key event in the history of Differential Response occurred in 2008, when the Children's Bureau awarded a 5 year cooperative agreement to the American Humane Association and its partners, Walter R. McDonald & Associates Inc. and the Institute of Applied Research, to operate the National Quality Improvement Center on Differential Response in Child Protective Services (QIC-DR) (Nolan et al. 2012). One of the foremost goals of the QIC-DR is to "build cutting-edge, innovative, and replicable knowledge about differential response, including guidance on best practice" (Marley and Kaplan 2011, p. 3). Phase 1 of the project focused on the identification of knowledge gaps, service gaps, and research priorities. Phase 2 involves generating and disseminating new knowledge and robust evidence by funding three research and demonstration sites in Colorado, Illinois, and Ohio to pilot and evaluate Differential Response reforms using the most rigorous methods and measures (Nolan et al. 2012). The results of these evaluations will be available in 2013 and will be disseminated widely.

In December 2010, the Child Abuse Prevention and Treatment Act (CAPTA) Reauthorization Act of 2010 was passed. It contained a "thematic emphasis on differential response, States' use of this approach, and reporting on these efforts" (Nolan et al. 2012, p. 4). Although Differential Response is not explicitly defined in CAPTA, allowing states to define it in a manner that is consistent with state law, they are now required to "describe their actions and submit additional data in the annual State data reports, including the number of families that receive differential response as a preventive service" (Nolan et al. 2012, p. 3). Though counting the number of states and tribes that have implemented Differential Response is a bit like hitting a moving target, the most recent estimates suggest that 20 states or tribes have Differential Response systems as of September 2012, and another seven are contemplating its adoption.

Core Elements of Differential Response Child Protection Systems

One of the primary purposes of the 2006 national study on Differential Response was to identify which states had implemented Differential Response and describe practice in each state. Although there was a great deal of variation among the state and county Differential Response practice, the authors identified a core set of elements that characterized most Differential Response systems in an effort to "achieve definitional clarity and distinguish among the multitude of child protection reforms" (Merkel-Holguin et al. 2006, p. 10):

1. The use of two or more discrete response pathways are used for screened-in reports, including an investigation response and a family assessment response;
2. The establishment of discrete response pathways is formalized in statute, CPS policy, or CPS protocols;
3. Initial response pathway assignment depends on a variety of factors, such as the presence of imminent danger, level of risk, number of previous reports, source of the reporter, presenting case characteristics such as type of alleged maltreatment and age of the alleged victim. Typically, low-to-moderate risk reports are assigned to the family assessment pathway;
4. Initial pathway assignment can change based on new information obtained by the agency that alters the risk level or safety concerns;
5. Services are voluntary in the family assessment pathway, that is, families can accept or refuse the offered services if there are no safety concerns;

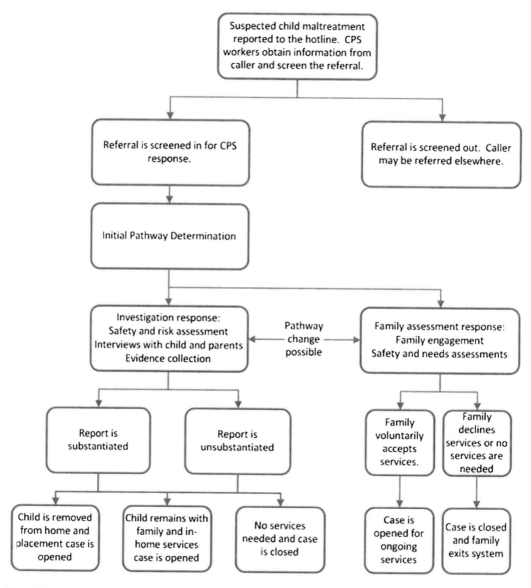

Fig. 24.2 Differential response CPS system

6. Families in the assessment pathway are served without a formal determination of child maltreatment (i.e., substantiation); and
7. Family members in the assessment pathway are not entered into a central registry as maltreatment perpetrators.

Figure 24.2 shows a typical case flow in a child protection system that has implemented Differential Response. A comparison of the flow charts for a traditional and Differential Response CPS highlights the ways in which they are similar and distinct, and Table 24.1 summarizes the major distinctions between the two approaches. In a Differential Response system, referrals come into the system through a hotline and are screened to determine if a CPS response is warranted in the same manner as a traditional CPS. However, a second screening occurs to determine the initial pathway assignment.

Table 24.1 Comparison of investigation and assessment approaches to child protection

	Investigation	Family assessment
Focus	To understand what happened to the child in the reported incident, who was responsible, and steps to ensure child safety in immediate future	To understand underlying conditions and factors that jeopardize child safety as well as areas of family functioning that can be strengthened
Goal	Determination of findings related to maltreatment allegations, identify maltreatment perpetrators and victims	Engage parents, extended family, and community partners in identifying problems and participating in services and supports that address family needs
Disposition	Substantiation of maltreatment allegations	No substantiation decision is made; families identified as "in need of services or supports" or "services recommended"
Central Registry	Perpetrators' names are entered into a central registry in accordance with state statutes and policies	No names are entered into the central registry
Services	If case is opened, service plan is written by the worker and services are provided; families can be ordered by the court to participate in services	Voluntary services are offered; if family declines and there are no safety concerns, the case is closed; if safety concerns exist, case can be reassigned to investigation

Adapted from Schene (2005) and Child Welfare Information Gateway (2008)

Moderate- to high-risk cases are typically assigned to a traditional investigation pathway; these cases then proceed through the child protection system in the same manner as those described in Fig. 24.1. Low- to moderate-risk cases, defined in a variety of ways, can be assigned to a family assessment pathway. Once assigned to this pathway, the worker meets with the family and engages them as active partners in the assessment process, which includes not only safety assessment but strengths and needs assessments as well. Extended family members, friends, and community professionals may be included in this process, but as sources of support rather than as collateral contacts. Parents are treated as the experts on their family's needs and strengths rather than as alleged perpetrators of maltreatment. If the initial assessments change the worker's view of the level of risk present in the family, cases can be re-assigned from the family assessment pathway to an investigation pathway. If the risk level remains low to moderate and the family has identified needs that would benefit from supportive services, services can be offered to the family following the assessment. Families may choose to accept these services, at which point an ongoing service case is opened. Alternatively, no service needs may be identified by the family or they may choose not to accept the offered services, and the case would be closed.

The core elements described above form the most commonly-accepted definition of Differential Response systems. This definition excludes certain child protection system reforms that include some, but not all, of the core elements. For example, California's CPS reform, which is also called "Differential Response," focuses on family engagement, strengths-based assessments, and enhanced service delivery provided through one of "three distinct paths for ensuring child safety" (Merkel-Holguin et al. 2006, p. 83). However, *both* of the pathway responses available to families with screened-in reports – even the "community response" pathway designed for low to moderate risk reports – end with a determination of substantiated, inconclusive, or unfounded maltreatment. Since the lack of a maltreatment determination in the assessment pathway is a core element of the Differential Response approach, the California CPS approach does not meet this definition (QIC-DR 2011). In addition, California, like several other states, has a formal pathway designed to provide services to families with screened-out reports of child maltreatment (see Marley and Kaplan 2011, for results of a recent national survey of state efforts in this arena). Although formal CPS responses to screened-out reports of alleged maltreatment are often confused with Differential Response, perhaps because many states implement them in conjunction with Differential Response reforms, these responses are not considered to be Differential Response under the current conceptualization (Marley and Kaplan 2011). Likewise, the numerous interventions developed in recent years to engage vulnerable families at risk of maltreatment in supportive services do not fall under the general rubric of Differential Response, because these programs typically are not targeted at families with screened-in reports of maltreatment.

Variations in Differential Response Child Protection Systems

The flowchart presented in Fig. 24.2 describes a typical Differential Response system. Despite sharing basic characteristics, there is a great deal of variability in the Differential Response systems that have been implemented to date. States and counties have adapted the basic principles of Differential Response to meet local needs and resources in a variety of ways, and differences in practice occur at each point in the case flowchart.

Initial Pathway Determinations. All child protection systems have policies in place to screen incoming referrals of alleged maltreatment to determine whether or not to respond. Differential Response systems require a second level of decision-making to determine which of the available pathway responses is most appropriate for screened-in reports. Systems differ widely on who makes the decision, when it is made, how it is made, and the criteria that are considered. In many systems, the same state or county CPS intake worker that screens the initial referrals into the system also makes the initial pathway determination. Oftentimes supervisory review and approval of this decision is required. To improve the consistency with which the pathway determinations are made, Olmsted County in Minnesota implemented a group decision-making process known as the RED team (Review, Evaluate, and Direct) (Sawyer and Lohrbach 2005a). This approach has also been adopted by the Colorado Differential Response system (Winokur et al. 2012). RED team membership includes wide representation of social workers from various units including intake, assessment, investigation, and ongoing services. New social workers also regularly observe RED team meetings as part of their orientation to child protective services. Meetings are held every morning and chaired by a child protection supervisor who is responsible for facilitating the presentation of information and for ensuring a decision is reached. A consultation framework is used to organize the presenting information into several categories for discussion: danger/harm, complicating factors, strengths/protective factors, safety, risk statements, gray area, and next steps. In the rare event that the RED team is unable to make a decision, the supervisor may ask the intake worker to gather more specific information and return to a subsequent RED meeting (Sawyer and Lohrback 2005a).

The criteria used by workers or teams to determine initial pathway assignments are typically defined in either department policy or enabling legislation (QIC-DR 2011). There are numerous variations among states in the types of cases that are allowed to receive an assessment response, as well as in the amount of discretion given to workers in making these determinations. Almost all states require an investigation of reports that involve sexual abuse, fatalities or other types of serious or egregious harms, or other types of reports that could result in criminal court proceedings (QIC-DR 2011). In addition, several states require an investigation for any report involving young children, who are perceived as being more vulnerable than older children. Others add additional restrictions that limit the assessment pathway from families with numerous or recent prior reports with the child protection system (Kearney et al. 2012; Merkel-Holguin et al. 2006). Beyond these mandatory exclusion criteria, however, agencies have developed highly distinct criteria for determining which families are eligible to receive a family assessment response. In some states or counties, the majority of families are eligible to receive a family assessment, while in others, assessments are limited to a small minority of families.

For example, in the ten Ohio Differential Response pilot counties, the working assumption used by intake workers when making the initial pathway determination is that families will be provided with a family assessment response unless there are reasons why a traditional investigation has to be pursued (Loman et al. 2010). Reports that must be investigated include those that allege sexual abuse or serious harm to a child, those involving suspicious child fatality or homicide, and those involving persons acting in place of parents (e.g., day care providers or foster parents), or child welfare workers. In addition to these mandatory investigation criteria, several items allow intake workers to use their discretion in deciding whether a report is appropriate for the family assessment response: currently open investigation; frequency, similarity or recentness of past reports; long-term court-ordered placement will be needed; legal intervention due to violent activities in household; parent has declined services in past or is unable/unwilling to achieve child safety; past maltreatment concerns unresolved at previous closing; or previous child harm offenses charged against alleged perpetrator. Using these criteria, about 52 % of screened-in reports were determined to be appropriate for a family assessment response (Loman et al. 2010). Some systems limit the family assessment response to reports with specific types of allegations or those assigned the lowest "priority" response level. For instance, in Illinois, the assessment pathway is limited to families with no previous reports of maltreatment who are reported for inadequate food, shelter, or clothing, environmental neglect, mental injury, medical neglect, and inadequate supervision of children 8 years or older (Kearney et al. 2012). In Nevada, only those reports classified as Priority 3 are eligible to receive a family assessment response; Priority 3 reports involve allegations such as educational neglect, environmental neglect, medical neglect, improper supervision or inappropriate discipline with non-severe physical harm. In addition, Nevada statute requires that any report in which a child five or younger is identified as a possible victim receives an investigation. Because of these fairly restrictive criteria, the percentage of reports in Nevada that have been referred to the family assessment pathway since 2009 averages 9 % across counties (Siegel et al. 2010). Three of the six New York counties that implemented Differential Response in the first round pilot limited the family assessment response to reports of educational neglect (Ruppel et al. 2011), which equaled about 4–7 % of screened in reports. State child welfare administrators discovered, however, that allowing county Differential Response programs to limit their criteria to just educational neglect made the programs so small that there was little impact on the overall CPS culture. Later Differential Response applicant counties were required to commit to assigning a significant percentage of their screened-in reports to the family assessment pathway (30–40 %) to receive approval (Ruppel et al. 2011).

Number of Response Pathways. Not including pathways designed to respond to families with screened-out reports of maltreatment, the vast majority of Differential Response systems have two pathways: a traditional investigation pathway and a family assessment pathway. A few places have developed a third pathway for screened-in reports of maltreatment. For instance, Olmsted County in Minnesota has a three pathway Differential Responses system: a traditional child protection response that is statutorily required for reports of child sexual abuse, licensed facility reports, and egregious and serious harm to a child; and two alternative response pathways that provide a family assessment and voluntary service provision without a formal finding of child maltreatment. One alternative pathway is for families with a screened-in report of child exposure to domestic violence and the other is for all other screened-in reports that fall outside the narrowly defined reports that require a traditional investigation (Sawyer and Lohrback 2005a, b).

Staffing. A variety of staffing configurations have been developed to accommodate Differential Response systems. Most states utilize existing county or state public child welfare workers to provide assessments and services in the family assessment pathway, although a few contract with private agencies to perform these duties. The Illinois Differential Response system selected a "paired team" approach to service provision in the family assessment pathway. A public agency worker and private agency worker made a joint first visit to families, with the public agency worker taking primary responsibility for completing a safety assessment to determine the present or emerging harm in the household and the private agency worker engaging the family in an assessment of their current needs and strengths (Kearney et al. 2012). Another staffing consideration is whether workers carry "mixed" caseloads consisting of both investigations and family assessments, or whether they work a single type of case only. Justifications for both staffing structures have been made: some states believe that carrying a mixed caseload is too confusing and that workers had a difficult time switching back and forth (Ruppel et al. 2011), while some counties are too small to maintain specialized staff.

Assessment and Service Provision. As with CPS investigations, child safety is a paramount concern in the family assessment pathway, and most states require some form of formal safety or risk assessment during the initial contacts. Equally important is the assessment of family strengths and needs, and states have developed a wide variety of assessment instruments to guide worker conversations with families into the development of a voluntary service plan. Service provision in the family assessment pathway tends to be brief (usually between 30 and 90 days) but intense, with caseworker visits typically occurring once a week or more frequently (Brown et al. 2012; Merkel-Holguin et al. 2006). Beyond these commonalities, however, the actual services provided to families in the assessment pathway can differ significantly from one county or state to the next. This is partially dependent on both the types of reports that are eligible to receive services and local service availability. Consistent with the focus on low-to-moderate risk reports, programs focus on the provision of concrete assistance, sometimes through the use of flexible funds offered to families (Kearney et al. 2012). Other Differential Response programs have no extra funds available for services or cash assistance and must rely entirely on community referrals and informal supports (Seigel 2012). Some CPS agencies have combined Differential Response with other family-oriented approaches such as solution-based casework or family group decision making.

Summary

As this brief overview illustrates, there is no single "model of practice" called Differential Response, but many. A handful of Differential Response programs grew from the "parent" model in Minnesota and share many of the same features, but differences exist even among these "siblings." Other Differential Response systems, such as the one in Illinois, have little in common with the Minnesota model other than two response pathways, one of which ends with substantiation and the other of which does not. One could argue that Differential Response is not a program intervention or even a model of practice, but rather an "approach" to organizing child protective services. This distinction is not purely semantic, but raises important questions about model fidelity and best practice. How does one measure fidelity to an approach, as opposed to a manualized intervention? How can best practice be developed, when there is no one standardized practice model? Evaluations of Differential Response have just begun to tease apart the practice elements that are associated with positive outcomes for families, although some practical lessons have already been learned from the states that were early implementers of Differential Response (Seigel 2012).

Evaluation of Differential Response Systems

Several outcome evaluations of Differential Response have been completed to date, and a handful used experimental or quasi-experimental designs that allow comparisons to be made between families that were "treated" through the assessment pathway and those that received "treatment as usual," through an investigation. In addition, in 2009 the National Quality Improvement Center on Differential Response initiated a coordinated, multi-site evaluation by awarding competitive grants to three sites that were required to implement randomized control trials: a consortium of five counties in Colorado, another consortium of six counties in Ohio, and a statewide effort in Illinois (Brown 2012). Although the results of these three RCT evaluations are not yet available, there is enough accumulated evidence to date to begin to answer the primary questions about the effectiveness of Differential Response in comparison to traditional child protective services.

Most logic models for Differential Response, including that put forth by the QIC-DR, suggest that there are two essential elements that differentiate the family assessment approach and the traditional investigation approach (QIC-DR 2009; Seigel 2012). The first is the manner in which the families are approached in the assessment pathway "from the start as a unit and in a respectful, supportive, friendly and non-forensic manner consistent with sound family-centered practice, focusing broadly on strengths and needs, and involving family members in decisions about what to do" (Seigel 2012, p. 18). Approaching families in this manner is thought to increase their *engagement* with both the worker and the service provision process. The second element is the provision of "services and assistance, often of a basic kind, that fit the needs and circumstances of the family, utilizing the family's strengths and natural support network and linking the family to community resources when these are available and helpful" (Seigel 2012, p. 19). Providing these services after engaging the family in the assessment process is hypothesized to lead to a decrease in family *needs*. These two initial outcomes, increased engagement and decreased needs, are then thought to improve intermediate and long-term outcomes that are of interest to the child protection system: *child safety* and *child and family well-being*. The following sections review the evidence that has been collected from experimental or quasi-experimental studies that compare these outcomes among similar families that receive either an investigation or a family assessment.

Family Engagement

Engaging families in child protection services, which are often viewed by parents as intrusive and unwanted, can be difficult. The majority of families who are contacted by CPS did not initiate the contact of their own accord, and interviews with parents who have experienced CPS intervention describe the initial visit as frightening and intimidating (Dumbrill 2006). Child protection workers are faced with the daunting task of overcoming parent anger and anxiety and forming a working relationship in which information is openly shared and decisions are made. Despite its central importance in many child welfare reforms, there is little consensus about the proper way to define or measure parent engagement. Although a measure of parent engagement in child protective services exists (Yatchmenoff 2005) it has not been incorporated into evaluations of Differential Response. Instead, studies have relied on one or two item measures of parent satisfaction with services or checklists of parental emotional responses following the first visit from CPS workers, neither of which are conceptually the same as engagement. Many Differential Response evaluations also attempt to measure parent engagement by asking CPS workers questions about parent "cooperation." Although it is common practice, there is little to suggest that worker ratings of parent cooperation have anything to do with engagement in services. It could even be argued that parents might be more likely to "cooperate" with workers using a traditional CPS approach, as the threat of child removal is more likely to be viewed as a motivator for parental cooperation.

Differential Response evaluations that collect information from parents typically utilize paper and pencil surveys distributed at case closure. Although not all evaluations report the response rates for the family surveys, those that do describe response rates in the 20–30 % range. These low response rates speak to the difficulty of gaining adequate research participation from families involved with child protective services, especially through methods with typically low response rates such as mail surveys. In the QIC-DR multisite evaluation, a variety of methods were used in an attempt to increase the family survey response rate above 30 % – such as providing pre-incentives or larger incentives and conducting follow-up phone calls – but none of them increased the response rate to any significant degree. The low response rates suggest the possibility that the results obtained from the family surveys are not representative of the entire group of families that were included in the evaluation, as perhaps only those parents that were highly engaged took the time to complete and return the survey.

Despite these methodological and conceptual concerns, it is informative to compare the survey responses of parents who received a traditional investigation response with those that received a family assessment response. The family survey used in several of the evaluations contained a question that asked parents to retrospectively describe their emotional response after the first visit from the worker by checking as many emotions as applied and was distributed to parents in both pathways so that responses could be compared (Loman et al. 2010; Loman and Siegel 2004a; Ruppel et al. 2011). In general, the positive emotions were checked by a higher percentage of parents who received a family assessment than parents who received an investigation, and the reverse was true of the negative emotions. For example, in the Ohio evaluation, significantly more families who received an assessment reported that following the first visit, they felt encouraged, positive, grateful, reassured, comforted, thankful, pleased, helped, hopeful, and relieved; and significantly fewer reported that they felt tense, worried, irritated, stressed, and angry (Loman et al. 2010). In Onondaga County, New York, significantly more parents in the family assessment pathway reported feeling comforted, and significantly fewer parents reported feeling annoyed, stressed, irritated, angry and worried (Ruppel et al. 2011). Similarly, in the Minnesota evaluation, significantly more parents in the assessment pathway reported feeling relieved, hopeful, helped, pleased, reassured, and encouraged; and significantly fewer felt angry, afraid, irritated, dissatisfied, worried, negative, pessimistic, and discouraged (Loman and Siegel 2004a).

The family survey also asked parents a series of questions about their worker and the extent to which the worker listened to what they had to say, understood their families' needs, treated them in a respectful manner, and involved them in decisions about their family. For the most part, parents that received a family assessment were more likely to answer these questions affirmatively than were parents who received an investigation. However, the differences between the two groups, although often significant, were not large; and also indicated a fairly high level of satisfaction among the parents who received an investigation. For example, in the Ohio evaluation, 78 % of parents who received an assessment felt that their worker listened "very carefully" to what they had to say, compared to 72 % of parents who received an investigation, a non-significant difference (Loman et al. 2010). In the New York evaluation, these percentages were 87 % in the assessment group and 75 % in the investigation group, a significant difference (Ruppel et al. 2011). Similarly, 58 % of the families in Ohio that received an assessment were "very satisfied" with the way their worker treated them, compared to 50 % of parents who received an investigation (Loman et al. 2010), and the percentages reported in the Minnesota evaluation were also significantly different (58 % vs. 45 %, respectively) (Loman and Siegel 2004a). In the New York evaluation, 58 % of parents who received an assessment reported that they felt "very positively" about their experience compared to 41 % of those who received an investigation, a significant difference (Ruppel et al. 2011).

Family Needs and Services

Information about service provision collected from families has given us a good indication of the types of services families receive in the assessment pathway and how they differ from those received in an investigation. In the Minnesota, Ohio, and New York evaluations, families who were randomly assigned to the assessment pathway and the investigation pathway identified each service they received from a checklist of services. Families in Minnesota who were assigned to the assessment pathway were significantly more likely than those assigned to an investigation to report that their worker had helped them obtain *any* service (54 % vs. 36 %), and they were significantly more likely to receive specific services: food or clothing (11 % vs. 3 %); help paying utilities (11 % vs. 3 %); other financial help (9 % vs. 4 %); counseling for their child (8 % vs. 5 %); home repair, appliances, or furniture (5 % vs. 2 %); respite care (5 % vs. 2 %); and help looking for employment or changing jobs (4 % vs. 1 %) (Loman and Siegel 2004a). There were no differences in the two groups related to service provision of other types of services, such as help getting mental health services, medical or dental care, parenting classes, child care or daycare, marital or family counseling, housing, alcohol or drug treatment, or job training. Reports from workers confirmed that assessment caseworkers provided a higher number of services per family as well as a broader range of services and referrals to families than investigators (Loman and Siegel 2004a).

Findings from the other two experimental studies regarding service provision did not reveal as many differences as the Minnesota evaluation, but confirmed that families in the assessment pathway were more likely to get certain types of services to address basic needs. In Onondaga County, New York, parents in the assessment group were significantly more likely than those in the investigation group to report that they received some type of help (70 % vs. 56 %) and more likely to receive certain specific services: basic things for their child like diapers, formula, food or clothes (18 % vs. 7 %), help dealing with a difficult relationship with their partner or ex-partner (11 % vs. 5 %), and help getting public assistance (10 % vs. 3 %) (Ruppel et al. 2011). In the Ohio evaluation (Loman et al. 2010), families who received an assessment were significantly more likely than those who received an investigation to report that they were offered at least one service, and were offered certain types of services more often: food or clothing; help paying utilities; other financial help; car repair or transportation; money for rent; and counseling. Medical and dental services, however, were reported more often by parents in the investigation pathway.

Service provision in and of itself does not mean that families received the type of services they needed, or that the amount of services they received was enough to adequately address their needs. Although family surveys are limited in the amount of information that can be gathered about family needs, several questions have been included that address service adequacy and family needs following their CPS intervention. Families in Minnesota who received an assessment response were significantly less likely than those that received an investigation to report that there was any help they wanted or needed and did not receive (18 % vs. 23 %) (Loman and Siegel 2004a). Among the families that received services, families in the assessment pathway were much more likely to report that the services they received were the kind they needed and were enough to really help their family (Loman and Siegel 2004a). There were no differences between the two groups' responses to these questions in the Ohio evaluation, however (Loman et al. 2010).

Child Safety

The primary goal of child protective services is to keep children safe from child maltreatment. States that have implemented Differential Response often experience a certain amount of resistance to the approach, based on the assumption that a family assessment absent "fact finding" about the circumstances of the maltreatment will not protect children and keep them safe as well as a traditional investigation (Hughes et al. in press). This assumes, of course, that fact-finding is an essential element associated with child safety, which is an untested assumption. Nevertheless, child safety is typically the outcome that child welfare administrators and other stakeholders are most concerned about, and therefore almost all evaluations of Differential Response include outcome measures that examine child safety.

The measure most often used to assess child safety outcomes in child protective services is maltreatment recurrence, typically defined as the occurrence of a second accepted report of abuse or neglect within a specified time following an initial accepted report. Some measures of recurrence include only subsequent reports that are substantiated by child protection workers, while others include all subsequent screened-in reports regardless of their eventual disposition. Although a sizeable percentage of families experiences more than one re-report to CPS (Bae et al. 2009; Loman 2006), most measures only capture the first recurrence. Most of the evaluations of Differential Response have measured child safety as a subsequent screened-in report that occurs after the initial report date; some include only re-reports that occur after initial case closure (Loman and Siegel 2004a, 2012), while others include all re-reports following the initial case opening (Loman et al. 2010; Ruppel et al. 2011). In some evaluations, the length of the recurrence follow-up time period was limited to 6 months (Ruppel et al. 2011), while in others families were followed for 2 years or longer (Loman and Siegel 2004a, 2012; Siegel and Loman 2006).

Of the three studies that used an experimental design (Ohio, Minnesota, and Onondaga County, New York): one (Minnesota) found that a significantly smaller percentage of families randomly assigned to the assessment response experienced a re-report to CPS when compared to families assigned to the investigation response (Loman and Siegel 2004a; Siegel and Loman 2006); one (Onondaga County, New York) found no differences in re-report rates in the two groups (Ruppel et al. 2011), and one (Ohio) found a small but statistically significant difference between the two groups when re-reports were measured from the initial report date but no difference when re-reports were measured after the initial case had closed (Loman and Siegel 2012). Results have also been mixed in studies that have utilized various types of quasi-experimental designs. In Missouri, when re-report rates were compared for families in the 14 demonstration counties and 14 comparison counties that were similar to the demonstration counties in population and caseload characteristics, a significantly smaller percentage of families in the demonstration group experienced a re-report following case closure (Loman and Siegel 2004b). Evaluators in Tompkins County, New York used propensity score matching to closely match families who received an assessment to those who received an investigation, and found no differences in the percentages of families who experienced a subsequent report to CPS (Ruppel et al. 2011). Evaluators in North Carolina compared rates of "re-assessment of children who had previously been assessed" in the nine counties that implemented their Multiple Response System (MRS) and nine matched control group counties and found that "both MRS and control counties showed a lower re-assessment rate after the implementation of MRS" although the change could not be attributed to MRS (Center for Child and Family Policy 2006). Later analysis of North Carolina data using more sophisticated interrupted time series analyses concluded that although rates of repeat assessments fell in both the treatment and control group counties after MRS implementation, repeat assessment rates fell more steeply in MRS counties than did those in control counties (Lawrence et al. 2011).

In addition to individual state evaluation, one study used case-level data from the National Child Abuse and Neglect Data System (NCANDS) to compare outcomes for 313,838 children across six states (Kentucky, Minnesota, Missouri, New Jersey, Oklahoma, and Wyoming) that offered both Differential Response and traditional investigation response (Shusterman et al. 2005). Contrary to state-level findings, the multistate analysis found that rates of recurrence within 6 months of the initial report did not differ between children who received an assessment response and those that received an investigation, except in Oklahoma, where the risk of recurrence was lower for children who received an assessment. The authors conclude that in general, children that receive an assessment are not at any greater risk of subsequent reports than those that receive an investigation.

Child and Family Well-Being

While safety is the primary concern of child protection services agencies and workers, there is also recognition that long-term safety of children is closely tied to their families' well-being. By focusing less on fact-finding and substantiation and more on underlying conditions and needs, a family assessment approach to CPS is thought to improve long-term child and family well-being. Unfortunately, few studies have collected data on indicators of child or family well-being beyond a couple of single item questions included on the family survey that is completed at the time of case closure. The only information about longer-term child and family well-being following Differential Response comes from an extended follow-up study of the families in the original Minnesota evaluation (Siegel and Loman 2006). Random samples of families were contacted at 9 months, 18 months, and 2.5 years following case closure and asked questions about various child well-being indicators (serious illness, delinquent behaviors, learning difficulties, truancy, depression and anxiety), specific life stressors (money, job, adult relationships, relationships with child, living arrangements) and how they have changed in the past year, and social support. At the first follow-up, parents who received an assessment were significantly more likely to report that their family was better off because of their CPS experience, they reported less stress about their relationships, and were less likely to report family problems related to domestic violence or drug abuse (Loman and Siegel 2004a). At the second follow-up, parents who received a family assessment were still more likely to report that their family was better off because of their initial CPS involvement, and also reported significantly higher household income than parents who received an investigation. At the third follow-up, parents in the assessment group reported less stress about adult relationships and less stress in general, and also continued to report higher household income levels than parents in the investigation group.

Worker and System Impacts

In addition to family-level impacts, the conversion of a traditional, single-pathway child protection system to a Differential Response child protection system may have an impact on other aspects of the system, such as worker satisfaction, organizational culture, and public perception of the system. Longitudinal studies of worker satisfaction following the implementation of Differential Response practices have indicated that while overall worker satisfaction with their jobs stays about the same, satisfaction with workload and duties decreased slightly among workers providing family assessments and services (Loman and Siegel 2004a; Ruppel et al. 2011; Siegel et al. 2010), with about half of the workers reporting an increase in their workload and the amount of paperwork required (Loman and Siegel 2004a). Although most workers who switched from other child protection jobs to provide assessments and services through a non-investigation pathway felt that they were more effective working with families using assessments, investigators felt that their practice was equally effective and often better at keeping children safe.

One impact that is of particular concern to administrators and policy-makers is that of costs to the system – both in terms of initial start-up costs and average costs per case. No study has examined the costs associated with implementing Differential Response, although the three QIC-DR research and demonstration sites are collecting this information as a component of their cost evaluations. Two evaluations have attempted to calculate both the short-term and long-terms costs per case of providing child protective services through an investigation or a family assessment (Loman and Siegel 2004a; Loman et al. 2010). Costs for the initial case, starting from the first contact through the end of the CPS intervention, were estimated by calculating the costs for worker time and direct services. Follow-up costs, which began the day after the initial case ended through end of the follow-up period, consisted of costs associated with any subsequent investigation, assessment, or services provided to the family once the original case was closed.

The Minnesota cost evaluation calculated the costs associated with a random sample of about 300 cases assigned to either the assessment or investigation response pathway and followed for 39–56 months after case closure. Results indicated that initial costs were significantly higher for cases served through a family assessment compared to an investigation, primarily due to the higher costs of service provision among assessment cases, although costs associated with worker time were higher in assessment cases as well. However, because assessment cases were less likely to experience a re-report during the follow-up period and the associated costs of additional investigations, assessments, or services; the costs during the follow-up period were significantly smaller for assessment cases than investigations. Over the entire period (initial case plus follow-up period), costs for the assessment cases were significantly lower than those for the investigations (Siegel and Loman 2006). The Ohio cost evaluation, which was hampered by data collection problems and a much shorter observation period of 10–15 months from intake (Loman et al. 2010), found that total costs (initial case plus follow-up period) were higher for assessment cases compared to investigations. Although it is possible that additional cost savings for the assessment response versus the investigation response would be realized if the follow-up period were longer, the results of the Ohio cost evaluation illustrate an important point. Because more services are provided to families in the assessment response, initial case costs will be higher when compared to a traditional investigation. Costs during the follow-up period (however long it may be) are entirely dependent on whether the family is re-reported to child protective services. Therefore, costs associated with serving families through a family assessment pathway will not be lower than those associated with investigations, unless there are fairly significant differences in the rates at which these two groups of families return to the child protection system. Results from the outcome evaluations summarized earlier suggest that this occurs in some, but not all systems that have implemented Differential Response. Thus, it is not a given that there will be cost savings associated with the implementation of Differential Response, especially once the potentially large start-up costs associated with implementation, such as worker training and modifications to data systems, are taken into account.

Summary

Early implementers of Differential Response were faced with concerns that a de-emphasis on forensic fact-finding and substantiation of maltreatment allegations would lead to decreases in child safety. To quell these concerns, many early evaluations of Differential Response examined the child safety outcomes associated with receiving a family assessment response, and some compared the safety outcomes of children in families that received an assessment response versus an investigation. The results to date clearly refute the notion that children that receive a CPS response that does not include substantiation are less safe than those do – not a single study has found higher rates of maltreatment recurrence among families that receive an assessment compared to similar families that receive an investigation. While a few studies have found small differences in maltreatment recurrence that favor the assessment approach, others have not, which suggests that differences in outcomes between studies may have more to do with differences in the programs themselves.

As described earlier, wide variations exist in practice from program to program. Evaluations have revealed that families that are offered CPS services through an assessment approach describe their experiences in more positive terms and are provided with a wider variety of services, especially poverty-related services, than families that are investigated. Beyond these very basic conclusions, however, little is known about which aspects of practice in the assessment response are most effective with which families: Do certain strategies for engagement produce better outcomes than others? Which service array produces the best results? Are both engagement and services necessary for improved outcomes or is one more critical than the other? Which families are most likely to benefit from receiving child protective services through an assessment response as opposed to an investigation? Although the emphasis on documenting the differences in outcomes between investigations and assessment approaches should not be abandoned, the next phase of Differential Response evaluation should also focus on the identification of the core components of successful interventions.

Policy-makers and practitioners in related fields have faced similar obstacles to the development of knowledge about best practice. For instance, states have struggled for years to implement the most effective programs to reduce juvenile offender recidivism rates. Juvenile justice programs vary considerably, similar to Differential Response programs, and research has shown some programs to be effective and others less so. A meta-analysis of 548 programs aimed at reducing recidivism among delinquent youth attempted to identify program attributes that could account for the most successful programs' effectiveness (Lipsey et al. 2010). Their results indicated that much of the programs' effectiveness could be boiled down to a small number of factors, and that programs implemented with these factors stood a high chance of achieving positive outcomes. While the research on Differential Response may not be advanced enough to allow this type of large-scale meta-analysis, the accumulated knowledge to date plus the additional knowledge that will be contributed through the three evaluations funded through the QIC-DR should allow the search for such "common factors" in effective practice to begin.

Conclusions

In the early 1990s, concerns about the traditional child welfare system led to discussions in several states and among national experts that culminated in the development of Differential Response. It has been over 20 years since the first state passed legislation that allowed its child protection agency to reorganize into a "dual response" system; in the ensuing years over 20 states have implemented Differential Response and many more are currently considering or planning implementation (QIC-DR 2011). Interest in Differential Response shows no sign of waning, and additional incentive for implementation was provided in the recent authorization of CAPTA, which encourages states to consider family engagement approaches such as Differential Response. Critics of the approach worried that serving children through a less authoritative approach would lower their safety, but mounting evidence from rigorous evaluations suggest that this is not the case, and that low-risk families can be effectively engaged and served without the threat of authoritative action.

There are challenges to child protective service in implementing this approach. States that have attempted to implement Differential Response without additional funding for services or with a very limited service array have seen limited impact on family outcomes, as have those that have restricted the assessment approach to a small minority of families (Seigel 2012). Much more remains to be learned about the critical elements of best practice in Differential Response, as it is currently unclear what differentiates successful programs from unsuccessful ones. Current evaluation efforts coordinated through the National Quality Improvement Center on Differential Response should add to our understanding.

Concerns about the best way to respond to child maltreatment stimulated a national discussion about child protective services in the early 1990s. Regardless of the its eventual life span as a CPS reform, discussions about Differential Response have reinvigorated the national discussion about the mandates of public child protective services and the means through which services to families get allocated: "Having raised such questions, Differential Response[3] may have identified a more fundamental issue. Perhaps the future of Differential Response is not solely a different response to the investigation of allegations of abuse and but rather an alternative way to understanding the needs of families in contemporary society and the interaction of public and private responses to those needs. Differential Response, therefore, is an example of a current child welfare reform effort that may thrive and grow, or be replaced by the next reform effort, depending on how much child welfare and other human

---

[3] The original quotation labeled the intervention as "AR" for Alternative Response, which is merely another term that is used interchangeably for Differential Response.

service professionals engage in debates on the broader social policies related to improving the lives of children and their families" (Yuan 2005, p. 31).

References

Bae, H., Solomon, P. L., & Gelles, R. J. (2009). Multiple child maltreatment recurrence relative to single recurrence and no recurrence. *Children and Youth Services Review, 31*, 617–624.

Brown, B. (2012). Building a multi-site evaluation of differential response. *Protecting Children, 26*, 60–68.

Brown, B., Merkel-Holguin, L., & Hahn, A. (2012). *Differential response: Early implementation and fidelity. Cross-site report of the national quality improvement center on differential response in child protective services.* Englewood: National Quality Improvement Center on Differential Response in Child Protective Services.

Buckley, H., Carr, N., & Whelan, S. (2011). 'Like walking on eggshells': Service user views and expectations of the child protection system. *Child and Family Social Work, 16*, 101–110.

Campbell, K. A., Cook, L. J., LaFluer, B. J., & Keenan, H. T. (2010). Household, family, and child risk factors after an investigation for suspected child maltreatment. *Archives of Pediatric and Adolescent Medicine, 164*, 943–949.

Center for Child and Family Policy. (2006). *Multiple Response System (MRS) evaluation report to the North Carolina Division of Social Services (NCDSS)*. Raleigh: Terry Sanford Institute of Public Policy, Duke University.

Child Welfare Information Gateway. (2008). *Differential response to reports of child abuse and neglect*. Washington, DC: U.S. Department of Health and Human Services.

Child Welfare Information Gateway. (2012). *How the child welfare system works*. Washington, DC: U.S. Department of Health and Human Services.

Dumbrill, G. C. (2006). Parental experience of child protection intervention: A qualitative study. *Child Abuse & Neglect, 30*, 27–37.

Forrester, D., Westlake, D., & Glynn, G. (2012). Parental resistance and social worker skills: Towards a theory of motivational social work. *Child and Family Social Work, 17*, 118–129.

Gallagher, M., Smith, M., Wosu, H., Stewart, J., Hunter, S., Cree, V. E., et al. (2011). Engaging with families in child protection: Lessons from practitioner research in Scotland. *Child Welfare, 90*, 117–134.

Harris, N. (2012). Assessment: When does it help and when does it hinder? Parents' experiences of the assessment process. *Child & Family Social Work, 17*, 180–191.

Hughes, R.C., Rycus, J.S., Saunders-Adams, S.M., Hughes, L.K., & Hughes, K.N. (in press). Issues in differential response. *Research on Social Work Practice*.

Kearney, K. A., Fuller, T. L., Jones, W., & McEwen, E. (2012). Putting it all together: Lessons learned from the planning and development phases of implementing differential response in Illinois. *Protecting Children, 26*, 8–20.

Lawrence, C. N., Rosanbalm, K. D., & Dodge, K. A. (2011). Multiple response system: Evaluation of policy change in North Carolina's child welfare system. *Children and Youth Services Review, 33*, 2355–2365.

Lipsey, M., Howell, J., Kelly, M., Chapman, G., & Carver, D. (2010). *Improving the effectiveness of juvenile justice programs: A new perspective on evidence-based practice*. Washington, DC: Georgetown University Center for Juvenile Justice Reform.

Loman, L. A. (2006). *Families frequently encountered by child protective services: A report on chronic child abuse and neglect*. St. Louis: Institute of Applied Research.

Loman, L. A., & Siegel, G. L. (2004a). *Minnesota alternative response evaluation: Final report*. St. Louis: Institute of Applied Research.

Loman, L. A., & Siegel, G. L. (2004b). *Differential response in Missouri after five years: Final report*. St. Louis: Institute of Applied Research.

Loman, L. A., & Siegel, G. L. (2012). *Ohio alternative response evaluation extension interim report*. St. Louis: Institute of Applied Research.

Loman, L. A., Filonow, C. S., & Siegel, G. (2010). *Ohio alternative response evaluation: Final report*. St. Louis: Institute of Applied Research.

Marley, L., & Kaplan, C. (2011). *Formal public child welfare responses to screened-out reports of alleged maltreatment*. Englewood: National Quality Improvement Center on Differential Response in Child Protective Services.

Merkel-Holguin, L., Kaplan, C., & Kwak, A. (2006). *National study on differential response in child welfare*. Englewood: American Humane Association and Child Welfare League of America.

National Quality Improvement Center on Differential Response in Child Protective Services (QIC-DR). (2009). *Request for applications for research and demonstration*. Englewood: Author.

National Quality Improvement Center on Differential Response in Child Protective Services (QIC-DR). (2011). *Differential response in child protective services: A literature review (Version 2)*. Englewood: Author.

Nolan, C., Blankenship, J., & Sneddon, D. (2012). Research and practice advancements in differential response. *Protecting Children, 26*, 4–6.

Platt, D. (2001). Refocusing children's services: Evaluation of an initial assessment process. *Child and Family Social Work, 6*, 139–148.

Ringeisen, H., Casanueva, C., Smith, K., & Dolan, M. (2011). *NSCAW II baseline report: Caregiver health and services*. Washington, DC: Office of Planning, Research and Evaluation, Administration for Children and Families, U.S. Department of Health and Human Services.

Ruppel, J., Huang, Y., & Haulenbeek, G. (2011). *Differential response in child protective services in New York State: Implementation, initial outcomes and impacts of pilot project*. Albany: New York State Office of Children and Family Services.

Sawyer, R., & Lohrback, S. (2005a). Differential response in child protection: Selecting a pathway. *Protecting Children, 20*, 44–53.

Sawyer, R., & Lohrback, S. (2005b). Integrating domestic violence intervention into child welfare practice. *Protecting Children, 20*, 62–77.

Schene, P. (2005). The emergence of differential response. *Protecting Children, 20*, 4–7.

Seigel, G. L. (2012). *Lessons from the beginning of differential response: Why is works and when it doesn't*. St. Louis: Institute of Applied Research.

Shusterman, G. P., Hollinshead, D., Fluke, J. D., & Yuan, Y. (2005). Alternative responses to child maltreatment: Findings from NCANDS. Washington, DC: U.S. Department of Health and Human Services, Office of the Assistant Secretary for Planning and Evaluation. Retrieved August 20, 2012 from http://aspe.hhs.gov/hsp/05/child-maltreat-resp/report.pdf

Siegel, G. L., & Loman, L. A. (2006). *Extended follow-up study of Minnesota's family assessment response: Final report*. St. Louis: Institute of Applied Research.

Siegel, G. L., Filonow, C. S., & Loman, L. A. (2010). *Differential response in Nevada final evaluation report*. St. Louis: Institute of Applied Research.

Thoburn, J., Lewis, A., & Shemmings, D. (1995). Family participation in child protection. *Child Abuse Review, 4*, 161–171.

U.S. Advisory Board on Child Abuse and Neglect. (1990). *Child abuse and neglect: Critical first steps in response to a national emergency*. Washington, DC: Government Printing Office.

U.S. Department of Health and Human Services [DHHS], Administration for Children and Families/Children's Bureau and Office of the Assistant for Planning and Evaluation. (2003). *National study of child protective services systems and reform efforts: Review of state CPS policies*. Washington, DC: U.S. Government Printing Office.

U.S. Department of Health and Human Services [DHHS], Administration for Children and Families, Administration on Children, Youth, and Families, Children's Bureau. (2011). Child maltreatment 2010. Retrieved from http://www.acf.hhs.gov/programs/cb/pubs/cm10/cm10.pdf

Waldfogel, J. (1998). Rethinking the paradigm for child protection. *The Future of Children, 8*, 104–119.

Winokur, M., Drury, I., Batchelder, K., & Mackert, M. (2012). Decision point: Screening practice as the foundation for differential response. *Protecting Children, 26*, 32–49.

Yatchmenoff, D. K. (2005). Measuring client engagement from the client's perspective in nonvoluntary child protective services. *Research on Social Work Practice, 15*, 84–96.

Yuan, Y. T. (2005). Potential policy implications of alternative response. *Protecting Children, 20*, 22–31.

Chapter 25
Decisions to Protect Children: A Decision Making Ecology

John D. Fluke, Donald J. Baumann, Len I. Dalgleish, and Homer D. Kern

Introduction

This chapter traces individual decision-making frameworks through the decision sciences and child welfare, arriving at a new empirically based theoretical framework called the Decision Making Ecology. An understanding of statistical decision-making errors is viewed through this lens, providing a context and a process for understanding child protection decision-making. The lynch pin is the idea of thresholds for taking action. We argue that the theory makes important contributions to child welfare because it enhances both prediction and understanding. The chapter concludes with several applications. We begin with a brief history.

Though rational thought has been championed for several centuries, beginning with the writings of Freud and others in the late nineteenth and early twentieth centuries and up through the present, the landscape has changed. Herbert Simon (e.g., 1956, 1972), who later received a Nobel Prize for his efforts, was demonstrating in the last half of the twentieth century that reason had its limits, proposing a new "Bounded Rationality" model of decision-making. Amos Tversky and Daniel Kahneman (1974), the latter of whom also received the Nobel Prize for their efforts (see Kahneman 2002), were suggesting that reasoning is even more limited than we had thought. They provided us with ample demonstrations of errors in decision-making, suggesting that humans applied a number of heuristics (mental shortcuts) under conditions of uncertainty and these often led to errors. Even the unconscious was making a comeback, stripped of its psychoanalytic trappings (Bowers 1984). By the later part of the twentieth century and the early part of the twenty-first century the idea of the

J.D. Fluke (✉)
Department of Pediatrics, Kempe Center for the Prevention of Child Abuse and Neglect,
University of Colorado School of Medicine, The Gary Pavilion at Children's Hospital Colorado,
Anschutz Medical Campus, 13123 East 16th Avenue, Box 390, Aurora, CO 80045, USA
e-mail: john.fluke@ucdenver.edu

D.J. Baumann
Saint Edwards University, 3001 South Congress Avenue, Austin, Texas 78704, USA
e-mail: donaldb@stedwards.edu

L.I. Dalgleish
University of Sterling, Scotland, UK

H.D. Kern
Independent Child Welfare Consultant, China Springs, TX, USA
e-mail: hdkbesk@msn.com

J.E. Korbin and R.D. Krugman (eds.), *Handbook of Child Maltreatment*, Child Maltreatment 2,
DOI 10.1007/978-94-007-7208-3_25, © Springer Science+Business Media Dordrecht 2014

rational decision-maker had given way to a less rational one, though whether the use of heuristics were as error prone as had been previously thought was debatable (see Gigerenzer 1991, 1993, 1994, 1996, 2005; Kahneman and Tversky 1996 for that debate).

Kahneman and Tversky (1979) achieved a breakthrough and solidified the underpinnings of non-rational decision in their formulation of prospect theory and cumulative prospect theory (Tversky and Kahneman 1992). While more complex than can be presented in this introduction, a simplified presentation of the principles are that (1) when faced with a choice involving a tangible value such as money, individuals make these choices based on a personal reference point, (2) presented with a certain loss individuals will take the risker option if the resulting loss might be lower even though it is unlikely, and that individuals will take sure gains even if a risk might improve the value of the gain, (3) given an equal choice of a larger gain and smaller loss individuals don't choose either, and (4) individuals tend to make choices based on unlikely events as if they were likely.

The text box below provides an example of a set of loss and gain choices pertinent to child welfare permanency and safety outcomes where the value of time is substituted for money. In informal anonymous tests of these choices in educational settings involving around 80 participants the author's found that over 80 % of naïve respondents tend to favor A over B for the first choice (a loss), and choose B for the second choice (a gain). This result is entirely consistent with prospect theory, the potential for a smaller loss is much more important than the potential for a gain, and the sure gain is favored. This is an illustration of non-rational thinking in as much as the likely outcomes are the same for both choices, and thus we would expect results that are consistently about even.

There have been a number of other important theoretical and empirical decision-making frameworks advanced in the sciences. Other founders of the field of judgment and decision making were Ken Hammond (1955) and Ward Edwards (1954, 1961). This field has had both application to and input from many diverse fields such as economics (e.g., Simon 1959), artificial intelligence (e.g., Weiss et al. 1978), psychology (e.g., Tversky and Kahneman 1974) engineering (e.g., Triantaphyllou and Mann 1995), Medicine (e.g., Hunink et al. 2003) and even meteorology (e.g., Monahan and Steadman 1996; National Research Council 1989). These contributions can provide insight and understanding about child welfare protective services decisions. Yet, the child welfare field has struggled to take advantage of the knowledge gains and progress regarding decision-making research, focusing on correcting errors through building risk and safety instruments, rather than understanding the source of the errors.

How did this come to pass? Several decades ago, when what we now know as risk or safety assessment was in the distant future, when the spotlight had not fully shown on abuse and neglect,

To illustrate a principle of prospect theory related to the second principle concerning gains and losses consider the child welfare scenario below:

Choice 1 – Choose either A or B:
    A Child has
        A. 25 % chance of being reunified in 6 months, or has a 75 % chance of being in placement after 12 months.
        or,
        B. No chance of reunification in 12 months

Choice 2 – Choose either A or B:
    A Child has
        A. 50 % chance of being remaltreated in 10 months
        or,
        B. No chance of being remaltreated in 4 months

assessment was less an empirical undertaking and more a way to understand the characteristics of people and situations that might produce harm to a child. Academic institutions and training organizations taught what is referred to as "good social work practice" with an eye toward protection of children and service to families. Concepts were developed in social work departments and borrowed from other fields. Most were reasonable ideas resulting in "best practices" guidelines that enabled caseworkers with few empirically sound instruments to both assess and treat families. Against a backdrop of criticism for not having a rational basis for decision-making, little growth in resources in the face of increasing caseloads and a concern over the effectiveness of interventions, child welfare in the 1980s came to believe that risk and safety assessment could be used to screen reports and prioritize cases for ongoing child welfare involvement. The idea was to try to move risk and safety assessment and the concepts that surrounded it onto more solidly defensible ground. Several consensus based risk and safety assessment models were thus born (e.g., Washington State's 1986 WRAM, and Holder and Corry's 1989 CARF models).

Accountability pressures continued to grow in the 1990s. Now, in addition to other public pressures, individuals with strong academic credentials weighed in with critiques of these "home grown" and consensus-based risk assessment models. An early critique of clinical judgment itself had come from psychologists and others working the field of decision-making. Beginning as early as 1956 (Meehl 1956a, b, c), researchers noted that clinical judgment did not seem superior to decision-making that had an empirical basis, and often seemed inferior to it. Bolstered by this critique, later criticisms came more broadly from the social sciences, and in particular social work. These researchers additionally began to criticize the empirical standards upon which many of the consensus-based models used in decision making rested. Further, many early models were lengthy and difficult to use, and although the workers may have appreciated the concepts built into them, they often felt that the scaled scoring system fragmented their judgment (Sheets 1991). In an attempt to produce more efficient risk and empirical assessment models the number of items measuring important concepts were empirically reduced (usually from four or more to one) and many concepts that were difficult to measure with a one-dimensional single item were eliminated all-together.

As we now enter the new millennium, the mounting pressures have produced what has become a familiar pattern of responses in the U.S. and abroad when abuse and neglect are under public scrutiny. We engage in crisis driven reform (Mansell et al. 2011), and attempt to standardize our practices through the increased use of protocols and monitoring (Munro 2005). Risk and safety assessments are usually targeted to both understand why children are so unsafe and to minimize future errors. The problem is that most of our focus on risk and safety does not really promote understanding as it would have had we spent more of our time during the last several decades focusing on understanding decision-making.

There is a distinction we will make shortly between an assessment (of risk and otherwise) and taking action. Understanding, through the use of an assessment instrument, can be improved as in the case of Concept Guided Risk Assessment (Baumann et al. 2011a), but even knowing this perfectly does not help us fully understand the process and context of decision-making errors. Moreover, "black box" actuarial models such as those that provide check boxes for risk factors can have the unintended consequence of lulling us into a false sense of security. They make us believe we have corrected the source of the errors (the caseworker, of course) when we have not. This is true on several counts. First, we are relying on models that predict only a small amount of variance (Baumann et al. 2005) and as a result leave a great deal unexplained. Second, there are still factors that cause (or force) decision-makers to take action (e.g., fear of public scrutiny) that differ from those mandated by actuarial feedback. Thus far, our actuarial models cannot account for or help us resolve what those factors are so we remain largely in the dark.

There are three child welfare decision-making models in the literature that are noteworthy, however. The first is an early decision-making model by Stein and Rzepnicki (1983). This model outlined the systematic goals of child welfare (e.g., safety and family preservation), pointing out some key process that included decision-making along with important domains of information (e.g., family others, agency, courts, law, etc.). The model broadly sketched the landscape but got little traction empirically. The second is a systems approach by Eileen Munro (2005) that takes human error as the starting point for understanding decision-making. It takes into account individual factors (e.g., skills, knowledge), resources and constraints (e.g., analytic vs. intuitive judgment), as well as the organizational context in which decisions are made (e.g., changes in thresholds). This model too has gotten little empirical traction, but has been a major source of policy analysis and dialogue in the field (Munro 2011).

A third model that has been formulated by Benbenishty and Davidson-Arad (2012, personal communication) to explain placement decisions is called the Judgments and Decisions Processes in Context (JUDPIC). This model is focused on multi-level decision making factors and particularly risk factors at the case level, and worker attitudes toward placements. The model has been empirically tested with child protection caseworkers who responded to case scenario data. It makes a strong case for the role of worker attitudes concerning placement as a moderating influence on the assessment of risk and which have a direct relationship statistically to the likelihood of placement (Davidson-Arad and Benbenishty 2010; Shapira and Benbenishty 1993).

The Munro and Davidson-Arad and Benbenishty models share considerable compatibility with the one we present here. Like the Munro model, it takes human error as the starting point for understanding decision-making and like both models suggests that decisions need to be understood within their context. However, it departs from both in that it describes a psychological decision making mechanism and enables testable predictions about *both* the process and outcomes of decision-making. In the discussion that follows we first present the Decision Making Ecology framework that contains a description of the Decision Making Continuum and the psychological process of decision-making. We follow that with a discussion of how the model has evolved from a conceptual and theoretical standpoint. We then conclude with illustrative applications of the concepts.

The Decision Making Ecology was conceived in the mid 1990s (Baumann et al. 1997a). In what follows below we first present the Decision Making Ecology Framework, followed by a description of the Decision-Making Continuum, the General Assessment and Decision-Making Model (GADM) that explains the psychological process of decision-making, why we believe the model is evidenced based and we conclude with some applications of the concepts.

Decision Making Ecology Framework

> There is nothing so useful as a good theory. – Kurt Lewin

The Decision Making Ecology represents an effort to advance the field of child welfare decision-making using the knowledge gained from the decision sciences. It is a theoretical framework for organizing decision-making research in child welfare and places the topic squarely in the context of actual protective-service operations in this field. It is intended to provide an understanding of both the context and process of decision-making, the goal of which is to predict "behavioral thresholds for action". This is done because decisions take place within an agency culture where a systemic context combines with the case decisions made by the management and staff of the agency.

The model has been successfully applied to the problem of disproportionality (Baumann et al. 2010; Fluke et al. 2010; Rivaux et al. 2008.) the substantiation decision (Fluke et al. 2001), the decision to place children into care (Graham et al. 2013; Fluke et al. 2010), burnout and turnover (Baumann et al. 1997b) and the decision to reunify children with their families (Wittenstrom et al. 2013).

As shown in Fig. 25.1, the systemic context for decision-making includes a set of decision-making influences displayed as ovals. They cover the range of case, external, organizational, and individual

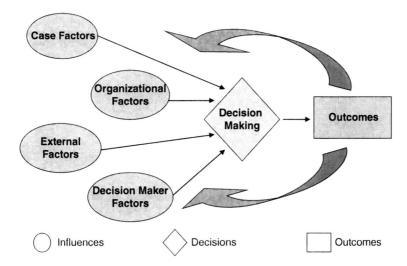

Fig. 25.1 Decision making ecology (Baumann et al. 2011b)

factors that combine in various ways to influence decisions and outcomes. These influences can be divided into dimensions that represent their important features, and decisions can be understood as a part of this entire context.

For example, *case* information regarding an incident of maltreatment is necessary for a caseworker to make informed assessments and decisions, yet some of the assessments and decisions depend on *external* factors, such as law translated into policies that govern what constitutes an appropriate response. Furthermore, the translation of such standards by *organizational* management, and their use by staff, will vary as a function of *individual decision-maker* factors, such as knowledge and skill, as well as the actual and perceived costs and benefits (*outcomes*) of the decision to the decision maker, the client and/or the agency.

Consider first some evidence on case factors. In two studies (Rivaux et al. 2008; Dettlaff et al. 2011) researchers were able to show that both the substantiation decision and placement decision were affected by race, risk and poverty in predictable ways. Now consider individual factors. Findings here (Baumann et al. 2010) indicated that disparate placement decisions can be ameliorated by caseworkers having higher case skills, especially those involving cultural awareness. Consider too organizational factors. Having a higher proportion of African Americans or Hispanics on one's caseload (exposure) also ameliorates disparate placement decisions for African Americans or Hispanics, respectively. Finally, consider external factors. Fluke and his colleagues (2010), using the Canadian incidence data, provide some evidence that the lack of community resources was one of the sources of placement disparity among Aboriginal children. What these findings illustrate is that sources of decision-making errors can be empirically understood and their remediation made possible within the Decision Making Ecology.

The diamond in Fig. 25.1 represents caseworker decision-making. The three key features of decision-making in child welfare are: (1) the *range of decisions* made by the caseworker, referred to as a *Decision Making Continuum*, (2) the psychological *process* of decision-making and (3) the outcomes, or consequences, of the decision. This is represented by the rectangle on the right side of Fig. 25.1 with arrows indicating that decision-making has consequences for children (e.g., recurrence), the workers themselves (e.g., distress) and the agency (e.g., public scrutiny).

The key feature of the Decision Making Continuum shown in Fig. 25.2 (Baumann et al. 2011b) is that *it runs through the episodes, or stages of service*, involved in cases processed by child welfare. In fact, one way to think about caseworkers' jobs is that they are coordinators of a Decision Making Continuum.

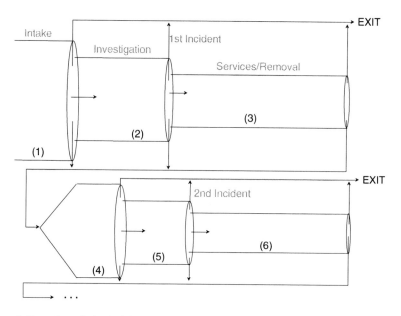

Fig. 25.2 Flow of clients through the decision making continuum

This continuum starts at intake ("Do I initiate an investigation or not?") and ends at case closure when all children in a family are deemed to be safe from maltreatment in the foreseeable future. It is not uncommon for a very large number of minor decisions to be made leading to each of the major or key decisions which taken together provide situational context for the key decisions.

The relative size of the cylinders in Fig. 25.2 can be viewed as representing case volume and the length of the cylinders duration. The episodes are shown at the top of the continuum, and cover case-worker decisions that range from intake (1) through investigation (2) and service provision and removal (3) for the first incident and labelled as 4, 5 and 6 for the second incident.

The Psychological Process of Decision-Making: The General Assessment and Decision-Making Model (GADM)

There are three important features to the psychological process of decision-making. First, it is useful to make a distinction between a judgement and a decision. As shown in Fig. 25.3, a judgment is an assessment of a situation given the current information. This judgment may be about the amount of risk or the strength of evidence, or overall level of concern. Each of these can be an estimate along a dimension going from low to high. A decision is about whether to take a course of action or not. So the GADM's alternative title could be "a general model for assessing the situation and deciding what to do about it". In the model we assume there is a threshold for action that turns an assessment of a situation into a decision about action using a decision rule.

A second important feature of the psychological process of decision-making is a decision threshold. A decision threshold refers to the point at which the assessment of the case information (e.g., amount and weight of evidence) is of sufficient intensity for a decision to be made about taking action. This decision threshold is a personal 'line in the sand'. It is influenced by the experiences and history of the decision maker. These are both their actual or vicarious experience and their interpretation of external factors, like policy. The theoretical base for the threshold concept is Signal Detection Theory (Swets

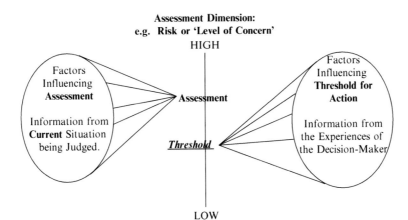

Fig. 25.3 A general model for assessing the situation and deciding what to do about it (Baumann et al. 2011b)

et al. 1955) and more recently Dalgleish (1988, 2003) who, in the child welfare field, proposed the GADM that makes the important distinction between judgment and action.

A third component in the process of decision-making is a shift in this threshold. A shift in threshold refers to a change in the amount of evidence deemed to be sufficient; that is, a change in threshold. A threshold shift would be involved if various features of the Decision Making Ecology changed the basis for the decisions that fall along the decision making continuum. One organizational influence that would alter the decision would be a policy dictating which cases would be accepted or should be attended to immediately (e.g., age and injury requirements for cases accepted and prioritized). An individual factor influencing a threshold shift might be experience: a new worker might have a tendency to render more affirmative decisions to be on the "the safe side." Or an 'old hand' may know of the consequences for children once in the fostering and adoption system. Both of these types of factors would change the thresholds of the individuals and also impact the volume of cases moving through the Decision-Making Continuum.

Decision Making Practice

Good practice has as its basis both sound theory and solid evidence for it (Shlonscky and Benbenishty 2013). Furthermore, it must overcome the criticism that evidence based approaches rely too heavily on "ideological assumptions and subjective views about decision-making" (McDonald 1994) and begin to rely more heavily on models that recognize both the context in which decisions are made and the limited rationality by which they are made (Webb 2001). The Decision Making Ecology just described contains a theoretical linkage between its features that allow for a better understanding of this context with a focus on these limits, and thus the causes and errors. In fact, causes in the model are often tested through the use of structural equation modeling (e.g., Graham et al. 2013) which is used for theory testing and development (Bentler 1983). Its confirmatory methods[1] and goodness of

---

[1] Some believe that tests should seek to disconfirm the theory at hand (e.g., the logical positivists). However, such refutations of theory rarely happen and, instead, theory testing involves ruling out alternative explanations, multiple observations, and more (Shadish et al. 2001). The tests conducted on the Decision-Making Ecology are more in line with the latter view.

fit tests have been used to test and reduce unnecessary variables and constructs in three studies thus far (Baumann et al. 1997b, 2010; Graham et al. 2013), and in several tests have been able to rely on observed decision-making behavior as an outcome. For example, the formation of an individual's disparity index which measures a caseworker's behavioral propensity to make decisions over time that over or under-represent Hispanics or African Americans, relative to Anglos. Predictions of decision threshold behavior (increases and decreases) in that index were then modeled based on case, individual, and organizational factors (Baumann et al. 2010).

Understanding and Prediction

A key role of the Decision Making Ecology is to produce understanding. It provides a theoretical and testable basis for understanding the context, process and outcomes or consequences of child welfare decision-making. It allows for an understanding of how thresholds and threshold shifts operate when changes occur in the context of decision-making.

A second feature is that the Decision Making Ecology makes predictions. Thus far, factors in the ecology have resulted in predictions of threshold mediators. For example, perceptions about community resources and actual caseloads are associated with changes in the thresholds for action (e.g., child placements into care; Baumann et al. 2010). So too does the stage of the Decision-Making Continuum where threshold differences influence decisions at intake, removal and reunification (see the applications section below).

New predictions are also possible. Psychologists have been informing us for a number of years that situational forces exert a great deal of influence on our behavior (often unnoticed). Evidence from child welfare suggests that when situational forces are pitted against individual ones, the power of the situation seems to be stronger than that of the individual decision makers (e.g., Graham et al. 2013; Rossi et al. 1999; Schwab et al. 1997). These findings would indicate that there may be a hierarchy to the factors in the Decision Making Ecology: the stronger the situational factors in the Decision Making Ecology, the more impact they have on changing the individual's threshold. We would expect case factors to have the greatest strength (data from Schwab et al. 1997 and Rossi et al. 1999 suggest this) because of their immediacy and consequences to the child. Somewhat less immediate and consequential are organizational factors. External forces would be likely to have the least impact (highly publicized fatalities notwithstanding).

The model also predicts a pattern of behavioral differences for individual threshold level and variability across the Decision-Making Continuum. At early stages in the continuum (e.g., intake) thresholds are lower and a relatively high number of cases are investigated whereas in later stages (e.g., removal) a comparatively low number of children are placed into care. From the GADM this would be a function of random and fixed variability in the underlying Decision Making Ecology. For example, in situations when the perceived level of concern is moderate, the greatest threshold variability would be anticipated; whereas high or low levels of concern have less individual threshold variability. To elaborate, at intake individual thresholds for action are likely to be both low and consistent across individuals (small variability). Hypothetically, this is due to, (1) the limited nature of the assessment data, and (2) the relatively small concern with consequences. Interestingly, this decision is apparently susceptible to organizational and external factors (see Mansell et al. 2011). Moving further along the continuum, in considering the decision to remove a child, threshold behavior for moderate risk are likely to be higher on average, but also more variable across decision makers (Rossi et al. 1999). Hypothetical considerations here are much more complex and include (1) more data for assessment, (2) situational factors such as the supply of placements, (3) the individual's attitude (Davidson-Arad and Benbenishty 2010) and values (Dalgleish 2003), and (4) the experience of the decision maker regarding the consequences (Dalgleish 2003).

One important question is whether individual thresholds for action change permanently as a function of situational forces or whether they reflect a temporary shift. The evidence cited earlier suggests the strength of the situation is the most important determinant, however. For example, as discussed at the outset of this chapter, research does suggest that worker attitudes predict placement decisions (Benbenishty and Davidson-Arad, 2012, personal communication). Thus, particularly strong emotions, motivations, attitudes, or values may produce more resistance to situational forces resulting in less mutable threshold behavior. More weakly held individual attributes would coincide with more individual variability in response to pressures from situational features in the Decision Making Ecology. Ultimately, these hypothesized relationships are testable, and if shown to be operating have important implications for such issues as staff recruitment and retention.

To some extent the relationships between the elements of the Decision Making Ecology and the related insights and predictions are illustrated through the applications that follow. However, these illustrations merely touch the surface of what could be learned to aid our understanding of child welfare decision-making.

Applications: The DME and Thresholds Along the Continuum

The model can be applied at each of the key decision points of the Decision-Making Continuum, i.e. intake (Dalgleish 2003), removal (Dalgleish 1988) and reunification (Dalgleish and Newton 1996). Consider the intake and the removal decisions. The threshold for each requires adequate information to make an assessment. The threshold may be higher for removal, compared to that required at intake, and this is reflected in the size of the cylinders in Fig. 25.2 which indicate that as one moves further along the continuum there are fewer children in the system. Furthermore, at the right end of the Decision-Making Continuum one might not only expect a higher level of risk (or concern or evidence) needed to reach threshold, but different types of information as well. For example, an intake worker may primarily consider information about the *allegation* whereas an investigator making a removal decision may additionally consider the amenability of the situation to intervention. For reunification, Dalgleish and Newton (1996) found that information about the 'sustainability of change in the family' was a factor influencing the assessment of risk. Aside from different case information needed to make a decision at different stages along the Decision-Making Continuum, other influences in the Decision Making Ecology can alter decisions as well. For example, lowered appropriations or the passage of legislation limiting the length of time a child may remain in foster care (environmental influences) might cause the agency to alter its policy (an organizational influence) on the permanency planning for children in care.

Applications: The DME and Outcomes

Earlier we indicated that in the Decision Making Ecology outcomes are viewed from three perspectives: consequences to the decision maker, the client, and the agency. The more familiar perspectives involve outcomes to the client and/or the agency. In the present framework, a distinction is made between these outcomes and those *to the* decision maker. Thus, the immediate utility of a decision is to the decision maker, whereas a second type of utility is related to outcomes to the client and/or the agency.[2] The large reversed arrows in Fig. 25.1 indicate the assumption that, to the degree that the

---

[2]These outcomes are all related in the sense that they can operate simultaneously. For example, a serious recurrence of maltreatment impacts the caseworker that may have closed the case, the family, and the agency. All could be held accountable in one sense or the other and would experience the event itself in a negative way.

Table 25.1 Outcomes for decisions to take action or not: the four-fold table

	Should have taken action	Should NOT have taken action
Decision: **YES** – remove	**Hit** Correct outcome	**False alarm** Error Damned if you do False positive
Decision: **NO** – not remove	**Miss** Error Damned if you don't False negative	**Correct no** Correct outcome

consequences of decisions can be presumed or known, thresholds may shift through the four influences of the Decision Making Ecology.

Because these decisions are fraught with uncertainty, the decision-maker can't avoid the possibility of an error. According to signal detection theory, there are two types of mistakes that can be made: If action is taken, the decision-maker might be wrong and if action is not taken they might be wrong as well – She can be "damned if she does" and "damned if she doesn't". Hammond (1996) calls it the "duality of error." A point that can be made that the 'feared outcomes' may not be equally bad and that people may value those outcomes differently.

Table 25.1 shows the four possible outcomes for the decision to remove the children from their home and place them in care (McMahon 1998). As shown in the table, there are two types of correct outcomes in addition to the two mistakes we have described. The first is correctly deciding to remove the child from the home (upper left corner). The second is to not remove the child (lower right corner). And again, the problem is that errors resulting in false positives (upper right corner) can result in an unwarranted placement in care because the child was safe, or the lack of action (lower left corner) resulting in the child being harmed.

Applications: Training in Threshold Placement and Threshold Differences

Different caseworkers will value these consequences differently. A way to demonstrate this and roughly identify threshold placement is for a decision maker to answer this question: Given that you can't avoid the possibility of error, which one do you want to avoid the most? At one level it is nearly as simple as that. However, it might be difficult to articulate why you have a preference to avoid one error and not the other. One reason for this is that there are a number of stakeholders involved in the decision. In child protection these include: the child, the family, the caseworker themselves, their work unit, their supervisor, their agency, other professionals, the courts, and society in general. There are sets of consequences for each of these stakeholders for each outcome. Do people working in child protection differ in the values they place on consequences? A memorable example came to one of the authors (Dalgleish) during a workshop on thresholds for people working in multidisciplinary child protection teams. After doing the exercise of making the consequences explicit for different stakeholders, a family physician said that he wanted to avoid 'False Alarms' because of the harm to families falsely accused of child abuse. This was vehemently challenged by a social worker from a public children's hospital who wanted to avoid 'Misses' because she had seen many dead and injured children.

In terms of the GADM model, the physician's threshold was high and he would need a lot of concern in a case before he took action. The social worker's threshold was low and would need little concern before taking action. Let us assume that they are both told about a case and given the case information. Assume also that they have been well trained in an assessment tool and have jointly assessed the case to have a moderate degree of concern.

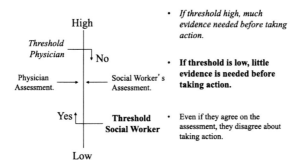

Fig. 25.4 Application of the threshold concept – decisional conflict (Baumann et al. 2011b)

Figure 25.4 indicates why the physician would not want to take action and the social worker would. They don't differ in their assessment of the case but they do in their decision to take action or not. In the GADM model we call this 'decisional conflict'. Alternatively, but though less commonly, (Rossi et al. 1999), it could be that two people might have the same threshold for action but differ in their assessment of the case factors and the integration of the case factor information into a summary assessment like risk. In the GADM we call this 'judgmental conflict'. Judgmental conflict is easier to resolve since it involves both people reviewing the case factors and agreeing on what ones to include in their assessment and the relative importance of the case factors. Decisional conflict is much more difficult to resolve since it depends on the relative value people place on the consequences of the possible outcomes (see Table 25.1).

Summary and Conclusions

Presented in this brief chapter is a case for the usefulness of the Decision Making Ecology combined with the General Assessment and Decision-Making Model (GADM). Beginning by making the point that the field of child welfare has been slow to take advantage of decision-making frameworks that has impeded efforts at understanding errors in decision-making and their context. The importance of this is that if it is not possible to learn something from the errors, the options available to address these errors in the future are more limited.

From this beginning we presented what we have learned thus far using this framework. For instance, the DME can be applied to a number of contexts, including the substantiation, removal and reunification decisions; all key decision-making points along the Decision-Making Continuum. It is also applicable to the context of social problems such as disproportionality, where disparate decisions at key decision points can increase overall disproportionality. Indeed, key factors in the DME, such as case, individual, organizational and external factors, are found to increase or decrease disparities and allow for a better understanding of sources of disparities.

The DME also contains the General Assessment and Decision-Making Model (GADM) which helps to more fully explain the psychological process of decision-making. Three psychological processes were described. The first was the distinction between the psychological process of assessment and that of deciding to take a course of action. The point being that although the assessment (e.g., of case factors) might be the same, individuals may differ in what action they might decide to take. This second process is known as a decision threshold that we again note varies for individuals based upon various experiences in the DME. The final important psychological process is that this threshold can shift. A good example of such a shift is provided by Mansell (2011) who describes threshold changes in the New Zealand child welfare system as a function of the degree to which family preservation or child protection is emphasized by policy makers over time, as a function of outcome concerns related to child safety in dynamic balance with the costs of services.

The Decision Making Ecology was applied to three situations as further demonstrations of its usefulness. In the first decisions along the Decision-Making Continuum were used as an example of decision-makers having different thresholds for different decisions. The intake decision was used as example of a low threshold, relative to the removal decision where higher thresholds for taking action are more likely. A related application that helps explain this difference is the outcomes, or consequences, to the decision-maker. In this application the idea was introduced of two types of errors that decision-makers try to avoid; false positives and negatives. Depending on the value of avoiding either type of error, thresholds may differ. Finally, a last application to training was introduced involving an exercise where different outcomes carried different consequences for participants and one error was more likely to be avoided over another, depending on the consequences to the decision-maker.

All of this has strong implications for policy and practice. From a policy perspective, knowing the source and magnitude of errors and what factors in the DME may mitigate these errors allows clearer and more precise policy to be written, and resources to be better targeted. If, for example it is known that the amount and mixture of cases on a workers caseload affects decisions, explicitly designed experiences with different caseload mixes can be structured as part of an on the job training. Practice can also be affected more directly by training programs that target specific errors and how they are mitigated. For example, one source of error uncovered by Detlaff and his colleagues (2011) and by Rivaux and her colleagues (2008) is the fundamental attribution error. This error appears to lie behind disparate decisions to substantiate and to place children in care. It seems that workers may attribute poverty to the person, rather than the situation and are thus more likely have a lower threshold for decision-making for African Americans than Anglos. Importantly, exposure to African American clients (Baumann et al. 2010) mitigates these decisions implying that such exposure should be a part of training.

In closing, it is noted that in the decade or so since starting to work within the Decision Making Ecology framework it appears to be a productive way of organizing hypotheses and studies as indicated in this chapter. Most important, however, is the critical need for improvement of decision-making in the field of child welfare. This will require on-going efforts to develop the evidence required to understand the context of decisions, the psychological process of decision making, and the sources of decision-making errors.

References

Baumann, D. J., Kern, H., & Fluke, J. D. (1997a). Foundations of the Decision Making Ecology and overview. In H. D. Kern, Baumann, D. J., & Fluke, J. D. (Eds.), *Worker Improvements to the Decision and Outcome Model (WISDOM): The child welfare decision enhancement project.* Washington, DC: The Children's Bureau.

Baumann, D. J., Kern, H. D., McFadden, T., & Law, J. R. (1997b). Individual and organizational factors in burnout and turnover: A Decision Making Ecology approach. In H. D. Kern, D. J. Baumann, & J. D. Fluke (Eds.), *Worker Improvements to the Decision and Outcome Model (WISDOM): The child welfare decision enhancement project.* Washington, DC: The Children's Bureau.

Baumann, D. J., Law, R., Sheets, J. H., Reid, G., & Graham, J. C. (2005). Evaluating the effectiveness of actuarial risk assessment models. *Children and Youth Services Review, 27,* 465–490.

Baumann, D. J., Fluke, J., Graham, J. C., Wittenstrom, K., Hedderson, J., Riveau, S., Detlaff, A., Rycraft, J., Ortiz, M. J., James, J., Kromrei, L., Craig, S., Capouch, Sheets, J., Ward, D., Breidenbach, R., Hardaway, A., Boudreau, B., & Brown, N. (2010, March). *Disproportionality in child protective services: The preliminary results of Statewide reform efforts.* Austin, Texas: Texas Department of Family and Protective Services.

Baumann, D. J., Grigsby, C., Sheets, J., Reid, G., Graham, J. C., Robinson, D., Holoubek, J., Farris, J., & Jeffries, V. (2011a). Concept guided risk assessment: Promoting prediction and understanding. *Children and Youth Services Review, 33,* 1648–1657.

Baumann, D. J., Dalgleish, L., Fluke, J. D., & Kern, H. D. (2011b). *The Decision Making Ecology.* Denver: American Humane Association.

Bentler, P. M. (1983). Some contributions to efficient statistics in structural models: Specification and estimation of moment structures. *Psychometrika, 48,* 493–517.

Bowers, K. S. (1984). On being unconsciously influenced and informed. In K. S. Bowers & D. Meichenbaum (Eds.), *The unconscious reconsidered* (pp. 227–272). New York: Wiley.

Dalgleish, L. I. (1988). Decision making in child abuse cases: Applications of social judgment theory and signal detection theory. In B. Brehmer & C. R. B. Joyce (Eds.), *Human judgment: The SJT view*. North Holland: Elsevier.

Dalgleish, L. I. (2003). Risk, needs and consequences. In M. C. Calder (Ed.), *Assessments in child care: A comprehensive guide to frameworks and their use* (pp. 86–99). Dorset: Russell House Publishing.

Dalgleish, L. I., & Newton, D. (1996). *Reunification: Risk assessment and decision making*. Presented at the 11th International Congress on Child Abuse and Neglect, Dublin, August.

Davidson-Arad, B., & Benbenishty, R. (2010). Contribution of child protection workers' attitudes to their risk assessments and intervention recommendations: A study in Israel. *Health & Social Care in the Community, 18*(1), 1365–2524.

Dettlaff, A., Rivaux, S., Baumann, D. J., Fluke, J. D., & Rycraft, J. R. (2011). Disentangling substantiation: The influence of race, income, and risk on the substantiation decision in child welfare. *Children and Youth Services Review, 33*(9), 1630–1637.

Edwards, W. (1954). The theory of decision making. *Psychological Bulletin, 41*, 380–417.

Edwards, W. (1961). Behavioral decision theory. *Annual Review of Psychology, 12*, 473–498.

Fluke, J. D., Parry, C., Shapiro, P., Hollinshead, D., Bollenbacher, V., Baumann, D., & Davis-Brown, K. (2001). *The dynamics of unsubstantiated reports: A multi-state study – Final report*. Denver: American Humane Association.

Fluke, J. D., Chabot, M., Fallon, B., MacLaurin, B., & Blackstock, C. (2010). Placement decisions and disparities among aboriginal groups: An application of the decision-making ecology through multi-level analysis. *Child Abuse & Neglect, 34*, 57–69.

Gigerenzer, G. (1991). How to make cognitive illusions disappear: Beyond "heuristics and biases". In W. Stroebe & M. Hewstone (Eds.), *European review of social psychology* (Vol. 2, pp. 83–115). Chichester: Wiley.

Gigerenzer, G. (1993). The bounded rationality of probabilistic mental models. In K. Manktelow & D. E. Over (Eds.), *Rationality* (pp. 284–313). London: Routledge.

Gigerenzer, G. (1994). Why the distinction between single-event probabilities and frequencies is relevant for psychology and vice versa. In G. Wright & P. Avion (Eds.), *Subjective probability* (pp. 129–162). New York: Wiley.

Gigerenzer, G. (1996). On narrow norms and vague heuristics: A reply to Kahneman and Tversky. *Psychology Review, 103*(3), 592–596.

Gigerenzer, G. (2005). I think, therefore I err. *Social Research, 72*, 1–24.

Graham, J. C., Fluke, J. D., Baumann D. J., & Detlaff, A. (2013). The Decision-Making Ecology of placing children in foster care: A structural equation model (in preparation).

Hammond, K. R. (1955). Probabilistic functioning and the clinical method. *Psychology Review, 62*, 255–262.

Hammond, K. (1996). *Human judgment and social policy*. New York: Oxford University Press.

Holder, W., & Corry, M. (1989). *The child at risk field system: A family preservation approach to decision-making in child protective services*. Charlotte: ACTION for Child Protection.

Hunink, M. G., Glasziou, P., Siegel, J., Weeks, J., Pliskin, J., Elstein, A., & Weinstein, M. (2003). *Decision making in health and medicine: Integrating evidence and values*. Cambridge: University of Cambridge/Cambridge University Press.

Kahneman, D. (2002). Maps of bounded rationality: A perspective on intuitive judgment and choice. Nobel Prize Lecture. http://www.nobelprize.org/nobel_prizes/economic-sciences/laureates/2002/kahneman-lecture.html. Accessed 8 Dec 2002.

Kahneman, D., & Tversky, A. (1979). Prospect theory: An analysis of decision under risk. *Econometrica, 47*(2), 263–291.

Kahneman, D., & Tversky, A. (1996). On the reality of cognitive illusions: A reply to Gigerenzer's critique. *Psychology Review, 103*, 582–591.

Mansell, J., Ota, R., Erasmus, R., & Marks, K. (2011). Reframing child protection: A response to a constant crisis of confidence in child protection. *Children and Youth Services Review, 33*(11), 2076–2086. doi:10.1016/j.childyouth.2011.04.019.

McDonald, G. (1994). Developing empirically-based practice in probation. *British Journal of Social Work, 24*, 405–427.

McMahon, A. (1998). *Damned if you do, damned if you don't – Working in child welfare*. Aldershot: Ashgate.

Meehl, P. E. (1956a). *Clinical versus actuarial prediction*. In Proceedings of the 1955 Invitational Conference on Testing Problems (pp. 136–141). Princeton: Educational Testing Service.

Meehl, P. E. (1956b). Symposium on clinical and statistical prediction (with C. C. McArthur & D. V. Tiedeman). *Journal of Counseling Psychology, 3*, 163–173.

Meehl, P. E. (1956c). Wanted — A good cookbook. *American Psychologist, 11*, 263–272.

Monahan, J., & Steadman, H. J. (1996). Violent storms and violent people: How meteorology can inform risk communication in mental health law. *American Psychologist, 51*(9), 931–938.

Munro, E. (2005). Improving practice: Child protection as a systems problem. *Children and Youth Services Review, 27*, 375–391.

Munro, E. (2011). *The Munro review of child protection: Final report, a child centred system.* Presented to Parliament by The Secretary of State for Education by Command of Her Majesty. May.

National Research Council. (1989). *Improving risk communication.* Washington, DC: National Academy Press.

Rivaux, S. L., James, J., Wittenstrom, K., Baumann, D. J., Sheets, J., Henry, J., & Jeffries, V. (2008). The intersection of race, poverty and risk: Understanding the decision to provide services to clients and to remove children. *Child Welfare: Special Issue, Racial Disproportionality in Child Welfare, 87*(2), 151–168.

Rossi, P. H., Schuerman, J., & Budde, S. (1999). Understanding decisions about child maltreatment. *Evaluation Review, 23*(6), 599–619.

Schwab, J., Baumann, D. J., & Gober, K. (1997). Patterns of decision-making. In D. J. Baumann, H. Kern, & J. Fluke (Eds.), *Worker Improvements to the Decision and Outcome Model (WISDOM): The child welfare decision enhancement project.* Washington, DC: The Children's Bureau.

Shadish, W. B., Cook, T. D., & Campbell, D. T. (2001). *Experimental and quasi-experimental designs for generalized causal inference.* Boston: Houghton Mifflin.

Shapira, M., & Benbenishty, R. (1993). Modeling judgments and decisions in cases of alleged child abuse and neglect. *Social Work Research & Abstracts, 29*(2), 14–20.

Sheets, D. (1991). *The Texas CARF evaluation.* Austin: The Texas Department of Human Services.

Shlonsky, A., & Benbenishty, R. (2013). From evidence to outcomes in child welfare: An international reader. Edited volume in preparation.

Simon, H. (1956). Rational choice and the structure of the environment, 1956. *Psychology Review, 29*(2), 129–138.

Simon, H. (1959). Theories of decision-making in economics and behavioral sciences. *The American Economic Review, XLIX*(3), 253–283.

Simon, H. (1972). Theories of bounded rationality. In C. B. McGuire & R. Radner (Eds.), *Decision and organization* (pp. 161–176). North Holland: North Holland Publishing Company.

Stein, T., & Rzepnicki, T. L. (1983). *Decision-making in child welfare intake: A handbook for practitioners.* New York: Child Welfare League of America.

Swets, J. A., Tanner, W. P., Jr., & Birdsall, T. G. (1955). Decision processes in perception. *Psychology Review, 68,* 301–340.

Triantaphyllou, E., & Mann, S. H. (1995). Using the analytic hierarchy process for decision making in engineering applications: Some challenges. *International Journal of Industrial Engineering: Applications and Practice, 2*(1), 35–44.

Tversky, A., & Kahneman, D. (1974). Judgment under uncertainty: Heuristics and biases. *Science, 185,* 1124–1131.

Tversky, A., & Kahneman, D. (1992). Advances in prospect theory: Cumulative representation of uncertainty. *Journal of Risk and Uncertainty, 5*(4), 297–323.

Washington State Department of Social and Health Services. (1986). *Washington Risk Assessment Matrix (WRAM).* Olympia: WADSHS.

Webb, S. A. (2001). Some considerations on the validity of evidence based practice in social work. *British Journal of Social Work, 31,* 57–79.

Weiss, S. M., Kulikowski, C. A., Amarel, S., & Safir, A. (1978). A model-based method for computer-aided medical decision-making. *Artificial Intelligence, 11*(1–2), 145–172.

Wittenstrom, K., Baumann, D. J., Fluke, J. D., Graham, J. C., & James, J. (2013). *The impact of drugs, infants, single mothers, and relatives on reunification: A Decision-Making Ecology approach* (in preparation).

Chapter 26
Using Law to Identify and Manage Child Maltreatment

Ben Mathews and Donald C. Bross

Introduction

There are many legal traditions and cultures, historical practices and degrees of awareness related to child 'maltreatment' in today's world. Fully analyzing the many ways in which law can help to identify and manage maltreatment, given the range of possible approaches and diversity of human cultures, cannot be achieved in a single chapter. However, identifying and outlining some of the ways in which law acts as both an immediate regulator of conduct and an influence on a society's cultural development forms a necessary background to any consideration of key options for responding to child maltreatment. While the authors' predominant experience is in the common law tradition prevailing in nations like the UK, the USA, Canada, Australia and other Western nations that adopted the common law heritage of the UK, there are a number of different legal systems in the world, including Napoleonic Code, Islamic Code, and the law of Communist countries. Rather than analyzing all these traditions, our intention is to provide examples of legal mechanisms from common law systems that might inform consideration of sociolegal strategies to identify and manage child maltreatment in many different political, economic and legal systems, including those in common law jurisdictions. Where possible, both positive and negative aspects of these mechanisms will be noted, especially when made obvious by specific experience, empirical data, or cross-cultural considerations.

These different legal scaffolds contain an extensive repertoire of remedies and preventive mechanisms for societies and professionals working with child protection, health care, behavioral health, justice, policy, and the public they serve. These legal scaffolds and the tools within them shape policy and practice in maltreatment prevention and response, both at individual, family and community levels.

There are many controversies that can be associated with law and child maltreatment, including why the problem was not addressed systematically for so many centuries, why so many individuals continue to deny that the problem exists, and why some societies find child maltreatment so difficult

B. Mathews (✉)
School of Law, Faculty of Law, Queensland University of Technology, Brisbane, Australia
e-mail: b.mathews@qut.edu.au

D.C. Bross, J.D., Ph.D.
University of Colorado School of Medicine, The Kempe Center for the Prevention and Treatment of Child Abuse and Neglect, The Gary Pavilion at Children's Hospital Colorado, Anschutz Medical Campus, Denver, USA
e-mail: donald.bross@ucdenver.edu; donald.bross@childrenscolorado.org

J.E. Korbin and R.D. Krugman (eds.), *Handbook of Child Maltreatment*, Child Maltreatment 2,
DOI 10.1007/978-94-007-7208-3_26, © Springer Science+Business Media Dordrecht 2014

to address while others have begun to do so with substantial success. Controversies arise as to what kinds of laws are best in preventing and responding to child maltreatment, and even, more fundamentally, whether there is a role for law in protecting children. Illuminating and providing possible solutions to all of these controversies is beyond the scope of this chapter, for several reasons: further work is needed to demonstrate when law can be and is most helpful in the effort to protect children from different kinds of maltreatment, and when law is producing adverse results or mostly unjustifiable interference; and research is also required to establish what types of societies are most reluctant to address the various manifestations of child abuse and neglect and why. Rather, this chapter will offer evidence that a variety of legal tools can be employed to address child abuse and neglect, for any cultural setting in which there is willingness to act to prevent and treat its various forms.

For our purposes, despite the difficulties inherent in defining the different kinds of child abuse and neglect, we will use the following definitions, drawing on definitions which are both proposed by eminent scholars and which are consistent with typical legal rights and obligations in criminal law, civil law and child protection law:

- *Physical abuse* includes acts of physical assault by parents or caregivers which result in death or serious physical harm or present an imminent risk of doing so[1];
- *Sexual abuse* includes acts not only of penetrative abuse, but also acts of masturbation, oral sex, fondling, voyeurism, exposure to sexual acts, exposure to or involvement in pornography and other forms of commercial sexual exploitation, all of which are acts done to sexually gratify the abuser; it is usually inflicted by an adult, but is often and can be inflicted by another, usually older child, where the victim is not developmentally capable of understanding the acts (World Health Organisation 2006);
- *Psychological or emotional abuse* exists when the relationship between the parent or caregiver and the child is characterized by pervasive or persistent acts or omissions which result in serious emotional harm or present an imminent risk of doing so (APSAC 1995; Glaser 2002, 2011);[2]
- *Neglect* is constituted by omissions by parents or caregivers to provide the basic necessities of life such as food, shelter, clothing, supervision and medical care, which result in serious harm or present an imminent risk of doing so (Dubowitz 2000).[3]

A Preliminary Note: The United Nations Convention on the Rights of the Child, Other International Human Rights Instruments, and Domestic Law

Since this book is one in a series looking at the international scope of child maltreatment, one controversy that should first be noted is the degree to which either or both international and domestic law are most likely to lead to children's protection. On one view, dating from the late twentieth century,

---

[1] Consistent with criminal laws, acts creating rights to civil damages in actions such as battery and negligence, and child protection laws such as the US federal Child Abuse Prevention and Treatment Act s 5106 g(2), which defines 'child abuse and neglect' as 'at a minimum, any recent act or failure to act on the part of a parent or caretaker, which results in death, serious physical or emotional harm, sexual abuse or exploitation, or an act or failure to act which presents an imminent risk of serious harm'. A clear challenge is presented by the question of whether and when corporal punishment is 'physical abuse'; this point will be returned to later.

[2] According to Glaser's (2011) typology, there are five categories of such harmful acts and omissions: first: emotional unavailability, unresponsiveness and neglect; second: interacting with the child with hostility, blame, denigration, rejection or scapegoating; third: developmentally inappropriate or inconsistent interactions with the child; fourth: failure to recognize or acknowledge the child's individuality and the psychological boundary between the parent and the child, and fifth: failure to promote the child's socialization within the child's context, by either active mis-socialization or corruption; isolating the child; or by failing to provide adequate stimulation and opportunities for learning.

[3] Consistent with criminal laws regarding neglect, civil laws concerning a parent's duty of care, and child protection laws.

the international community's commitment to child wellbeing appears to have never been greater, as demonstrated most clearly by the near universal ratification of the United Nations Convention on the Rights of the Child (UNCRC), which entered into force in 1990. The almost universal affirmation of the UNCRC indicates at least a rhetorical commitment to protecting children from maltreatment, since article 19(1) requires States parties to take all appropriate legislative, administrative, social and educational measures to protect the child from all forms of maltreatment while in the care of parents or guardians. The UNCRC is an aspirational document which is intended to guide the substance of law, policy and practice regarding children's rights, as well as being intended to facilitate cultural changes which will promote children's rights in lived experience. However, achieving domestic cultural change remains crucial if contemporary international efforts are to have enduring power; this is so because of the varying effects of ratification of the UNCRC in nations' domestic law, and because it is simply not realistic to expect all children to have legally enforceable rights to all of the aspirations in the UNCRC.

The domestic legal effect of ratifying the UNCRC varies by country. In some nations, such as the USA, ratification of a Convention can have a 'self-executing' effect, which automatically translates the adopted articles of that Convention into domestic law. This would prove problematic because since aspirations are distinct from realistic expectations, no nation can currently enforce a requirement that children will have these rights in lived experience. Laws which are created, but are largely unenforceable, undermine key tenets of the rule of law (Bingham 2007) by neutralizing their efficacy and creating a civic attitude that these laws can be ignored. Unenforceable laws also undermine the legitimacy of parliament and destroy the beneficial potential of the law's objectives. A key reason why the USA has not ratified the UNCRC is that many provisions are currently unenforceable or conflict with other US human rights laws. Recognition that some clauses of the UNCRC cannot be enforced in a given country explains why many nations have recorded 'reservations' concerning some articles of the UNCRC, meaning that while nations generally ratify the UNCRC, they exclude many articles from its endorsement. In other nations, such as Australia, courts have established clearly that ratification of a Convention by the executive arm of government does not give it domestic legal force; only implementation of a Convention into legislation by Parliament can translate it into law: *Mabo v Queensland* (1992). However, ratification can still have 'soft' legal effects such as influencing the nature of new legislation concerning children, and creating a right of procedural fairness regarding decisions made by Commonwealth administrative decision makers involving children.[4]

Despite the legal and practical limitations of nations' ratification of the UNCRC (and of other instruments regarding children's rights, such as those regarding child prostitution, and genital mutilation: Mathews 2011a), its capacity to change attitudes and culture, and through these changes, to enhance children's lived experience, arguably remains. It is not prudent to be unrealistically naïve about its effect, yet nor should its power as an aspirational document be cynically derided and dismissed. While it is difficult to measure tangible outcomes from the widespread ratification of the UNCRC, it is still reasonable to assume that it plays a real role in promoting children's rights and lived experience. This may occur through various mechanisms, such as the creation or encouragement of new beneficial attitudes and cultural norms of conduct regarding child welfare. Attitudes towards a phenomenon can be a powerful influence on actual behavior (Ajzen 2005; Ajzen and Fishbein 2005). Runyan and colleagues (2010) recently stated in the context of harsh parental discipline that "culture helps form parental attitudes about how children should be disciplined" (708). Adults' attitudes towards children's place in society and their rights are inextricably related with a society's culture, including how it perceives and treats children. As well, the role played by the UNCRC and similar

---

[4] *Minister for Immigration and Ethnic Affairs v Teoh* (1995) 183 CLR 273. Ratification of the UNCRC creates a legitimate expectation that an executive or administrative decision would be made in conformity with its principles. The legitimate expectation does not amount to a rule of law, and so does not compel a decision-maker to make a particular decision. However, if the decision-maker proposes to settle the issue inconsistently with the legitimate expectation, the decision-maker must give persons affected by the proposed decision an opportunity to present their case against it.

instruments in promoting children's safety and flourishing may occur by influencing developments in law, policy and practice, and facilitating the creation and continuance of governmental and nongovernmental support agencies which exist to help maltreated children and work towards reducing maltreatment.

International Variation in the Enactment and Enforcement of Law to Respond to Child Maltreatment

Notwithstanding changes in attention to child maltreatment and children's rights in many places, it is undeniable that awareness of and commitment to various dimensions of child wellbeing still varies greatly both across the globe and within nations. For social, economic, historical, religious and cultural reasons, societies vary in both their *enactment* of and *commitment* to laws regarding child maltreatment. As with all laws, those regarding child maltreatment should possess "legitimacy" (sufficient societal acceptance) and be supported by appropriate enforcement. As used here, the concept of "legitimacy" is related to political power being used in a largely consensual, or at least widely endorsed, fashion to resolve conflicts, protect rights, and enable commerce and communication. For example, the more force that is required for laws to be obeyed, the less cohesiveness and agreement that generally exists between citizens. Some societies appear to rely more on law as the ultimate arbiter of conflict than other societies. When societies are very homogenous, there are many non-legal methods for resolving conflict. When societies are extremely diverse, as in the U.S. and increasingly in Europe and other parts of the world, homogeneity is increasingly rare, due to the effects of immigration, proliferating variations of religious and political institutions, and the creation of new interests and interest groups. Again, especially in societies where law is a crucial final arbiter of conflict, if a society passes laws that cannot be enforced, the legitimacy of the legal system as an effective means of conflict resolution can be weakened.[5] Laws which lack legitimacy then become denuded of real substance and resulting benefit; this applies to any laws, including those related to child maltreatment.

Some societies enact few or no laws concerning the identification and management of child maltreatment. Some child protection laws that are enacted without necessary enabling responses may accomplish little other than a pretence. However, as already noted, societies may pass laws that are not likely to be enforced immediately, but have the goal of proclaiming a societal aspiration for better practices and behavior which it is hoped will crystallize over longer periods of time, accompanied by other supportive mechanisms. Many examples might be provided of different approaches in legal cultures, which have profound effects on not only how children are treated, but how children are perceived: for example, laws relating to education, marriage, sexual assault, human trafficking, child labor, adoption, involvement of children in warfare, and the punishment of those who offend against children. The way a society treats its children through its legal systems embodies its understanding of the respective roles and rights of the individual, the child, the family, and society. In addition, there

---

[5] One example of a national law that overreached the public's endorsement and hence compliance was the 18th Amendment to the U.S. Constitution, referred to the States for ratification by the U.S. Congress in 1917, prohibiting the sale or consumption of alcohol. After being ratified by 36 of the then existing 48 States, Congress passed enabling legislation in 1919 (The National Prohibition Act, also known as the "Volstead Act"), and the amendment and enabling legislation commenced in early 1920. Supporters strongly opposed the consumption of alcohol on moral and religious grounds. Subsequent to the enactment of the national law, flagrant disobedience by consumers as well as an eruption of criminal activity involving the importation and black market manufacture of alcohol caused public dismay at the unintended consequences of Prohibition. Within very few years, the dismay resulted in the repeal of Prohibition in 1933, via the 21st Amendment to the U.S. Constitution. This remains the only time in American history that a Constitutional Amendment has been repealed.

can be different treatment of children according to gender, exemplified by socio-legal approaches to inheritance, child marriage (Deb and Mathews 2012), and female genital mutilation (Rasheed et al 2011; Rajabi-Ardeshiri 2009; Mathews 2011a). All of these issues are in play along with other contextual factors such as race, ethnicity, and religion. Law embeds a society's fundamental values and preferences and helps those values to endure or develop. This can happen in both positive and negative ways, and this can be seen starkly in the field of child maltreatment. Law can play a crucial catalytic role in changing attitudes and behavior, or can be prominent in its absence and allow the perpetuation of injustice and suffering.[6]

Our task here is to provide a broad yet succinct summary of key mechanisms from common law systems for identifying and managing child maltreatment, and to highlight issues presented by these mechanisms to help inform progress within and beyond these jurisdictions. Before discussing ways in which law can manage child maltreatment, we will first consider the precondition to any meaningful societal response to child maltreatment: its recognition as a phenomenon, and mechanisms through which it can be identified.

Identification of Child Maltreatment: The First Step

Historical Background

In Roman law, which influenced the development of English law, the concept of *patria potestas* gave a father almost total dominion over his children including the powers of life and death, punishment, and sale (Borkowski 1986; Gardner 1986). Consequently, the Dark Ages and Middle Ages were times when children had few if any rights, and the treatment of children was extremely harsh, with infanticide and abandonment being common, even up until the 1800s (Ten Bensel et al. 1997; Eisenberg 1981). Children were generally seen as a father's chattels and as units of labor (Eisenberg 1981).

Substantial change in society's perception and treatment of children crystallized after the possibility of education emerged and English legislation in 1880 made schooling compulsory. These social and legal changes were driven by a new understanding and acceptance that a child was different from, and hence had qualitatively different needs than, an adult. The possibility and desirability of literacy – enabling a child to develop into a citizen capable of contributing to society in ways exceeding basic labor – and its enforcement through legislative machinery was the basic impetus behind this change. Maltreatment of children would still continue, and the various forms of maltreatment now identified would not yet be conceptualized. The first English laws regarding maltreatment, such as the Poor Law 1868, were aimed at intervening in cases of severe neglect but were poorly implemented. Prosecutions for severe maltreatment were rare (McGillivray 2011).

In the UK, despite these early changes, there were no laws about the identification of severe cases of maltreatment. There was no general public awareness of maltreatment in the senses we possess today, and much conduct constituting maltreatment was normalized. Some forms of abuse, such as sexual abuse, were generally ignored, even by professionals such as medical practitioners. There were several reasons for the general lack of recognition of maltreatment, but perhaps most prominent among them is that most severe maltreatment occurs in the privacy of parents' homes and is inflicted by parents. In a sociopolitical atmosphere that endorses individual rights, it is usually agreed that

---

[6]The essence of the 'rule of law' – the concept underpinning common law jurisdictions–is 'that all persons and authorities within the state, whether public or private, should be bound by and entitled to the benefit of laws publicly and prospectively promulgated and publicly administered in the courts' (Bingham 2007). Adjudicative procedures should be fair, means must be provided to resolve disputes, and the law must adequately protect fundamental human rights. These are fundamental and indispensable elements of a just society.

adults' private sphere should remain free from interference by the State, that parents have the right to treat and discipline their children as they see fit, and that neither children nor society are entitled to any other mechanism that alters this state of affairs. Having grown from and still drawing immense power from centuries-old doctrines, these sociolegal assumptions are embedded within many western nations and are common in social and political cultures across the globe. Few voices were raised against these ideas of parental privacy, despite luminaries such as Locke and Mill being among them (Mathews and Bross 2008), hence leaving undisturbed the wide and deep power of these forces.

Situating this discussion in a historical social and legal context helps to appreciate how it may be necessary to counterbalance and reverse the social power of an undesirable practice with responses that might include the persuasive or compelling force of a therapeutic legal intervention. Throughout most of human history there has been scant meaningful recognition of child abuse and neglect, and children have been left largely unprotected from maltreatment (de Mause 1974; Pinker 2011). Social customs and obliviousness to children's suffering and children's vulnerability have impeded the development of helpful social and legal influences. The absence of legal interventions to recognize, identify and respond to child maltreatment may be the most important influence in the historical pattern of child maltreatment. The absence of legal regulation of a context is just as powerful an influence as its presence. Without legal prohibition of maltreatment, it is permitted and even endorsed. Similarly, without legal approaches requiring certain people to report known severe maltreatment, a society makes a statement about what it deems acceptable, and about what it prioritizes. The presence or absence of legal mechanisms creates a culture which promotes or denigrates children's rights to personal safety and liberty.

The Landmark Changes: Recognition of Severe Physical Abuse, and Legislation Requiring Reports of Suspected Serious Child Maltreatment

Arguably, the landmark legal change in identifying severe maltreatment occurred in the USA in the 1960s. The catalyst for this legal change was a groundbreaking 1962 publication by C. Henry Kempe, a Colorado pediatrician, and his medical colleagues in which severe physical abuse of children, especially those aged under 3, was identified and conceptualized as the 'battered-child syndrome' (1962). Importantly, the emphasis was on *severe* injury – often involving fractures to the skull and or subdural haematoma – not *any* injury. As well as identifying the intentional infliction by parents of severe physical injury, the authors effectively declared that such treatment could no longer be ignored or tolerated and recommended that medical practitioners report this condition to agencies which could intervene to protect the child (Bross and Mathews 2012). Kempe and his colleagues recognized the fact that severe maltreatment occurs in private, inflicted by parents, most frequently and seriously against very young children, and the likely lack of disclosure of severe maltreatment by parents produces the need for a person outside the family to facilitate the identification of maltreatment where neither the child nor the child's parents would. After sustained lobbying and advocacy, by 1967 laws were passed in each American state requiring medical practitioners to report reasonable suspicions of severe child physical abuse. Importantly, these laws provided those who made reports in good faith with confidentiality and immunity from various kinds of legal and disciplinary action if the case turned out not to involve maltreatment (Mathews and Kenny 2008).[7]

---

[7] Note also that law can provide other protections in this context, for example by allowing physicians to take photos, x-rays and conduct other tests without fear of suit for acting without permission as long as the tests are required for the diagnostic procedure of estimating the likelihood of intentionally inflicted trauma.

The scale, impact and revolutionary character of this change cannot be underestimated. Recently, in a book published to mark 50 years since the publication of 'The Battered-Child Syndrome', the work published by Kempe and his colleagues (1962) was described as the force behind 'a massive tectonic plate shift [which] was occurring that would eventually have an impact in all corners of the world and on the lives of billions of children' (Runyan 2012, p. v). In ensuing years, the new legal obligation to report reasonable suspicions of severe child physical abuse was extended to other groups of professionals whose work involved frequent contact with children, such as teachers and police. Later, with new evidence emerging of other forms of maltreatment, reporting obligations were extended to other types of maltreatment: sexual abuse, emotional or psychological abuse, and neglect. More recently, some states have even extended the duty to report suspected exposure to domestic violence and exposure to drug-related activity (Mathews and Kenny 2008).

Many other countries would enact similar laws in ensuing decades. All these legal developments about the reporting of suspected serious child abuse and neglect were accompanied by other legally-sanctioned infrastructure and mechanisms. Such legislation for child protection and child welfare both confers and limits the authority possessed by state child protection agencies and children's courts to respond to cases in various ways. In addition to authorizing evaluation or treatment services for maltreated children, legislation can also provide fiscal appropriations and incentives for appropriate responses to child abuse.

A review of the nature and scope of these laws about the reporting of cases of suspected serious child abuse and neglect demonstrates not only their expansion beyond the original laws motivated by the work of Kempe and colleagues, but the legal differences that now exist between states even in the same country (Mathews and Kenny 2008). Yet, the enduring principle motivating all these laws was the need for persons outside the family to identify cases of severe child maltreatment which would otherwise likely remain hidden, to enable the protection of children from severe harm, and to facilitate the provision of appropriate assistance to children and families. Law hence becomes a powerful means for institutionalizing child protection.

Legislative Duties Versus Policy-Based Duties

The introduction in the USA of mandatory reporting laws and their associated child protection systems influenced similar developments in dozens of other countries. For example, all jurisdictions within Canada and Australia have enacted legislation, albeit sometimes differing in nature and scope (Mathews and Kenny 2008). In contrast, demonstrating ideological and political differences, and different practical imperatives which relate to decisions about enacting such duties, other nations including the United Kingdom and New Zealand have chosen not to enact mandatory reporting laws. However, in many of these jurisdictions, policy-based duties to report child maltreatment have been created by peak industry groups such as medical and educational professions (Mathews 2012). There are complex questions about whether policy duties (and associated systems) are as effective as legislative duties in creating a harmonized and well-informed professional culture best able to identify cases of severe child abuse. While rigorous research into this question is required, there is some evidence that policy-based duties are not as effective as legislative duties. Doctors in the UK, for example, have a policy-based reporting duty that does not provide the normal protections given to reporters by legislative duties regarding confidentiality and immunity from proceedings. This less robust and coherent approach has not only exposed doctors making good faith reports to harassment by parents and to professional disciplinary proceedings; there has been a consequential reduction in doctors' willingness to make child protection reports and to occupy child protection roles (Mathews et al. 2009a). As well, policy duties do not possess the imprimatur of Parliament, are decentralized and fragmented (and hence prone to error), and inhibit best practice in the development and administration of training for reporters. There is also some evidence that legislative duties, together with systematic training and support, can also affect the actual identification by reporters of cases of serious abuse. A comparative study of the reporting by teachers of sexual abuse found that teachers in a state without legislative reporting obligations reported three times fewer cases of substantiated sexual abuse than teachers in two other states with more robust legislative duties (Mathews et al. 2009b). An earlier study found that introduction of a legislative duty for teachers to report sexual abuse resulted, at least in the short term, of three times the number of both substantiated and unsubstantiated reports (Lamond 1989). We will discuss the issue of 'unsubstantiated' reports shortly.

Reporting Practices and Outcomes

Data Collection and Monitoring

People often ask whether laws about the reporting of suspected severe child maltreatment are 'effective'. There are many ways in which one could seek to answer this question. Certainly, for the most part, from the perspective of a seriously maltreated child who has benefitted from a report (and hopefully, from successful intervention), then such reports would be seen as being more than simply 'effective', and rather as facilitating a major change in the child's life chances. At one end of the spectrum, there is strong evidence that the incidence of fatalities has plummeted since the introduction of reporting laws and their associated support mechanisms (Besharov 2005).

As well as declines in fatalities, the success of reporting laws can be seen in evidence collated regarding the number of referrals made by mandated reporters, the proportion of substantiated cases identified as a result of these referrals, *and* the numbers of cases referred by these reporters which may not have been officially substantiated after investigation but which still resulted in the provision of helpful services to the child and her or his family.

The most detailed evidence is collated in the USA in its annual reports by the US Department of Health and Human Services, which has published detailed reports every year since 1990. The collection of detailed data about child maltreatment, ideally with as much information standardized across regions or jurisdictions within a nation, is an essential element of a well-functioning system. This monitoring is an essential feature of a public health approach to child maltreatment, enabling understandings of the features of maltreatment (state by state data about numbers and characteristics of child victims, perpetrators, who makes referrals, outcomes of referrals, and more). This also enables tracking of trends over time, and assessments of the impact of policy approaches. If the data is sufficiently detailed, it enables more precise identification of the nature and extent of failures and successes, within and across systems, jurisdictions, reporter groups and maltreatment subtypes.

Law plays an important role here also, because the regular conduct and publication of such studies is not guaranteed to occur without adequate policy, financial and structural support. In 1988, the US Child Abuse Prevention and Treatment Act required the establishment of a system of national data collection and analysis, involving the collation of state data about the reporting of maltreatment. The DHSS has published annual reports of such data since 1992. Similarly, other federal legislation establishes a requirement for population-based incidence studies, which are more accurate measurements of maltreatment incidence. All four *National Incidence Study* projects (Sedlak et al. 2008) have been required by the Keeping Children and Families Safe Act 2003 (PL 108-36). In contrast, nations without such detailed data and studies lack a rigorous evidence base, and so are unable to evaluate progress, to identify specific problems, and to plan strategically for the future.

Reports by Mandated Reporters Identify the Majority of Maltreatment Cases

As a result of its legislative frameworks surrounding data collection, the most detailed data on reporting is published in the USA, although data about precise topics is not always reported annually. Annual records consistently indicate that mandated reporters make approximately 55–60 % of all reports (US Department of Health and Human Services 2010b, p. 6, Fig. 2.1). Reports made by mandated reporters result in the identification of approximately 70 % of all proven cases (US Department of Health and Human Services 2010b, p. 9, Fig. 2.3). Detailed data reported in 2009 by subtype and profession indicates that an even higher proportion of substantiated cases of physical abuse (78.1 %) and sexual abuse (74.0 %) are identified after reports by mandated reporters (US Department of Health and Human Services 2009, p. 45, Table 3.9). A similar overall pattern was found in Canada, where reports by mandated reporters disclosed 75 % of all cases of substantiated severe maltreatment (Trocme et al. 2005, p. 86, Table 8.1). The USA data also show a general developmental vulnerability from infancy for all types of maltreatment except sexual abuse (Mathews 2012; US Department of Health and Human Services 2009, p. 47, Table 3.12).

Evidence Suggests Mandatory Reporting and Its Associated Response Mechanisms Have Contributed to Significant Declines in Physical and Sexual Abuse

Several sources of data in the USA indicate very substantial declines in both physical abuse and sexual abuse since the early 1990s (Finkelhor et al. 2011). The declines are supported by two major sources of data (Finkelhor 2008): annual official government investigations into reports of suspected maltreatment (US Department of Health and Human Services 2011, 2007), and the National Crime Victimization Survey. They gain further support from two other different kinds of repeated national population studies (Sedlak et al. 2008; Finkelhor et al. 2010), and victim self-report surveys (Finkelhor and Jones 2012a). The declines are sufficiently substantial, and have occurred over a sufficiently long period, that Finkelhor and Jones (2006, p. 700) stated:

> We believe the evidence for the existence of a decline in youth victimization is extremely strong. It is a reality deserving of much more attention and discussion. Something positive is going on in the social environment.

In 2012, after an updated review of seven different data sources consistently a range of declines the same authors concluded that 'Our judgment is that the decline in sexual abuse is about as well established as crime trends can be in contemporary social science' (Finkelhor and Jones 2012a).

Finkelhor and Jones (2006) note several factors potentially influencing these declines. They discuss the contributions possibly made by economic prosperity, changing social norms and practices, dissipation of the side-effects of the 1960s cultural revolution, and the introduction of psychiatric medication. Two other major factors they discuss are "incarceration and incapacitation", and "agents of social intervention, police and others". Reporting laws and their associated response mechanisms – increased numbers of police, social workers, child protection workers and other personnel engaged in child safety and child abuse prevention activities – are among the important "agents of social intervention" noted by Finkelhor and Jones as contributing to the declines in physical and sexual abuse in the USA. Others include a range of different public education, response and prevention efforts, some systematic, others more localized.

Debates continue about the decline (Gilbert et al. 2012a, b; Finkelhor and Jones 2012b; Radford et al. 2012). However, if these data are accurate, or are even close to a real indication of a significant reduction in child physical and sexual abuse, these declines represent a remarkable development in child welfare and social progress. Given the generally accepted view that such maltreatment has been more frequent in societies over many centuries, there is much to be learnt from these significant and recent developments.

Purpose of Legislative Reporting Duties: Reporting Also Facilitates Provision of Assistance to Children and Families

Reports of suspected maltreatment enable the provision of assistance not only in cases that are substantiated after investigation, but also in those that are not. In the USA, substantiated victims are proportionally more likely to receive post-response services, but almost twice the actual number of children (and families) in 'unsubstantiated' cases receive 'post-response services' than those who are in substantiated cases (US Department of Health and Human Services 2010a, p. 84, p. 89). This further demonstrates the utility of referrals, and the inappropriateness of labeling only those referrals that are 'substantiated' as 'good' referrals. There are many reasons why a report may be treated as 'unsubstantiated', including the decision not to investigate at all, but this does not mean the case does not involve maltreatment (Drake and Jonson-Reid 2007; Kohl et al. 2009; Mathews 2012). The making of a referral and the provision of helpful support can itself act as a preventive mechanism, stopping maltreatment from happening or preventing it from getting worse. The law can also play a role in requiring and creating financial capacity for the provision of preventive services. Several USA statutes confer funds to establish preventive intervention (US Department of Health and Human Services 2010a, p. 89).

The making of reports also facilitates the utility of a 'differential response' approach to child and family welfare after receiving a report of maltreatment. Differential response approaches emphasize assessing the family's needs and delivering helpful services, rather than initiating investigation to determine whether maltreatment has occurred. They are particularly appropriate for low-risk and moderate-risk cases, especially for cases involving neglect. There is an increasing emphasis on enabling these quicker, sensitive responses to identify the child's and family's needs and to provide services which meet those needs, with over 20 states now implementing these systems (Conley and Berrick 2010). In the US, CAPTA and other laws have influenced the development and delivery of differential response and US federal legislation establishes funding systems for its provision. Jurisdictions in other countries including Australia – such as via Victoria's Children, Youth and Families Act 2005 – have also adopted these methods, both as a method of delivering the most appropriate response in a given case, and as a complementary pathway of making reports in the first instance about cases which do not involve serious harm but which are excellent candidates for helpful and preventative interventions (Government of Victoria 2006).

Overreporting

There is evidence indicating that legislative reporting duties will, at least in the short term, produce an increase in the number of reports which when investigated result in a finding of being 'unsubstantiated' (Lamond 1989; Mathews 2012). Overall, many reports are 'screened out' at intake, many more are referred directly to assisting agencies, and hence a relatively low percentage of all reports result in both an investigation and a substantiation of that investigation. Some have labeled all such reports as problematic, and have argued that this so-called 'overreporting' and its effects on scarcely-resourced child protection systems are a reason for not adopting the legislative model (Melton 2005).

However, others have responded to these claims, arguing that it is not sound to simply rely on the number or proportion of 'unsubstantiated' cases to draw global conclusions about the success or failure of reporting laws and practices, and that it is not appropriate to use 'substantiated' cases as a proxy for a justified report (Drake and Jonson-Reid 2007; Finkelhor 1990, 2005; Kohl et al. 2009; Mathews 2012). Several of the important facts to engage with in this regard are:

- Many, and often a majority, of reports (and unsubstantiated reports) are made by members of the public, not by mandated reporters; this applies especially to neglect and emotional abuse, which are responsible for a very large proportion of reports;

- Reporting patterns by discrete mandated reporter groups can vary dramatically; for example, reports by one reporter group of even one type of maltreatment can account for a substantial proportion of all reports: Mathews (2012) showed this occurred in New South Wales, with police reports of exposure to domestic violence);
- Reports of different subtypes of maltreatment can differ enormously; reports of physical and sexual abuse combined represent only a small proportion of all reports (Mathews 2012);
- Often, more than one report is made about a child (both in quick succession by an individual or multiple reporters, or through the year), so that a very large proportion of all reports are being made about a relatively small number of children, as has been found in some jurisdictions in Australia (Mathews 2012);
- The maltreatment subtypes themselves are discrete and reports are only one feature of a child protection and child welfare system (for example, many reports of neglect and domestic violence are best responded to by differential response either in the first instance, or by prompt referral by CPS intake).

All these facts mean it is problematic to make global descriptive or normative statements about 'all reporting' and hence about the reporting laws. Extremely precise questions need to be asked of data about reporting to ascertain the nature of trends in reporting practice by discrete reporter groups, for each maltreatment subtype, and the outcomes of these subsets of reports, to relate them to law, policy and practice, and to make informed judgments about matters of concern or which may need attention. Quantitative and qualitative data may indeed disclose undesirable or 'hypersensitive' reporting practices which may be influenced by the legislation and or inadequate policy and reporter training, but such evidence needs to be identified with precision and rigor (Mathews 2012). In Australia, recent government inquiries into child protection systems have considered the operation of mandatory reporting laws, including the phenomenon of 'overreporting'. Both identified aspects of reporting that could be improved, but concluded that as a policy it remains a beneficial part of a child protection system (Wood 2008; Cummins et al. 2012).

Difficulties for Reporters

Several difficulties are posed for legislatively mandated reporters, caused by this multifaceted and complex context. Some of these are caused by conceptual ambiguities and similar difficulties within the reporting laws. For example, the laws generally use the terms 'reasonable suspicion' or 'reasonable belief' to activate the reporting duty, and the concept of 'significant harm' (or a synonymous concept) to limit the reporting duty to sufficiently serious cases; both concepts can produce confusion and undesirable levels of disagreement about practical application (Levi and Crowell 2011; Levi and Portwood 2011; Levi and Loeben 2004). Other studies show reporters may fail to report because while they have a suspicion that the injury has been caused by maltreatment, they are not certain, or are not sufficiently sure (Feng and Levine 2005; Kalichman and Brosig 1993; Mathews et al. 2009b; Zellman 1990). Reporters need to be reassured that the legislative duty requires only a reasonable suspicion (or a reasonable belief, depending on the jurisdiction) and that this does not require certainty; nor is their role an investigative one. However, they also need to know that the terms of the legislation require (generally) the reporting only of *significant* harm (or some synonymous version of this), not of *any* degree of harm (Mathews et al. 2008). Reporters' lack of awareness of this is known to produce undesirable consequences. It is also often overlooked by opponents of the laws, which clearly weakens their arguments.

Other difficulties are caused by the nature of maltreatment. Many cases will not be reported because maltreatment is frequently not readily apparent and reporters may simply not be able to detect it.

Reporters are not expected to be perfect detectors of maltreatment. Even severe maltreatment can be difficult to detect, even for medical practitioners who are able to conduct physical examinations. Indicators of maltreatment can be consistent with innocent explanations, or other medical conditions (Besharov 1990). Serious intentional head injuries are often misdiagnosed (Jenny et al. 1999). Even penetrative sexual abuse frequently leaves no physical signs in female genitalia (Anderst et al. 2009).

Yet, there is evidence of failure to report despite having suspicions of abuse. Studies of actual past reporting behavior have found medical practitioners' failure to report suspicions of severe physical abuse (Flaherty et al. 2006, 2008a) and failure to report by other reporter groups such as teachers (Mathews et al. 2009b) and nurses (Mathews et al. 2008). There are varied reasons why reporters sometimes fail to report, which can differ according to the type of maltreatment involved. In addition to the lack of sufficient certainty referred to above, prominent among these is the belief that child protection agencies will not respond effectively even when a report is made (Jones et al. 2008). Sufficiently resourced child protection agencies need to establish excellent working relationships with the professional groups who are required to report suspected maltreatment, and each of these parties must understand the difficulties and constraints experienced by the other (McCarthy 2008). Importantly, reporters should be made aware that not all reports will be investigated (and the reasons why); that even when investigated there can be many reasons for a finding of unsubstantiated (but that this does not mean the report was not worthwhile or that services were not provided or the child not protected); and reporters should be told by the child protection agency of the outcome of their report, and why. Other mechanisms may also assist reporters, such as the availability of child abuse experts with whom the reporter can consult (Flaherty et al. 2008b; Berkowitz 2008).

Issues Faced by Legislatures and Policymakers

The role of legislation in helping to identify cases of severe maltreatment presents challenges for legislators, policymakers, reporters, and CPS workers. In some jurisdictions, reporting laws have been expanded far beyond the initial duties catalyzed by Kempe and colleagues' recommendations about doctors reporting severe physical abuse. The fact that different jurisdictions enact laws of varying breadth – differing particularly in which subtypes of maltreatment must be reported, and by which groups of reporters – demonstrates that for ideological, political, economic and practical reasons, the decision to enact a reporting law is not straightforward.

A legislature intending to create its first reporting laws, and any legislature continually monitoring its existing legislative approach, will benefit from careful consideration of several questions. Regarding the nature and scope of the laws, such questions include (Mathews and Kenny 2008): (i) What types of maltreatment are required to be reported? (ii) Which occupations are to be mandated reporters? (iii) What state of mind is required to activate the reporting duty? (iv) What extent of harm, if any, is required to be reported; is this harm qualification the same for each subtype; and how is this to be expressed? (v) Are reports required only of past or present abuse, or are reports also required of suspected risk of future abuse (and if so, how is this to be expressed)?

Legislatures and policymakers also will need to consider how reporters are to be trained, since it is well established that legislative reporting duties alone are insufficient. Studies have repeatedly found that mandated reporters often have not had the training required to equip them to fulfill their role, which can produce failure to report, and clearly unnecessary reporting (Abrahams et al. 1992; Christian 2008; Reiniger et al. 1995; Hawkins and McCallum 2001; Kenny 2004; Mathews et al. 2009b; Mathews 2011b; Starling et al. 2009; Walsh et al. 2008). Those persons who are required by such laws to report suspected maltreatment require excellent, and repeated, training to ensure they have a sound knowledge of the indicators of various types of maltreatment, what types of maltreatment they are required to report, the state of mind required which activates their reporting duty (which is not certainty, or even a state of mind near this; reporters are not expected to be perfect), the protections provided to them upon making a report, and how to make a report. Some jurisdictions, such as South Australia, have enacted legislation requiring the training of mandated reporters; this approach helps to facilitate high quality and coherent training approaches.

Whatever form of legal reporting obligation is created, in addition to excellent training methods, a government must ensure that there is a sufficiently well-resourced child protection system to receive, act on and respond to reports, and that there are agencies to provide services to children and families in need (Mathews 2012). Where used, these laws must be framed so that their content fits the realistic ambition of the jurisdiction's overall child protection and family welfare plan. Whatever the scope of such a plan, it should be considered, coherent and adequately resourced. The relationship of reporting laws with differential response and investigative responses must be soundly designed, both these response methods should be implemented appropriately, and reporting behavior should be monitored quantitatively and qualitatively so that problems can be identified and resolved. Ideally, as part of a public health approach, the laws should be seen as but one essential element, and the incidence of maltreatment monitored by repeated rigorous studies. The content of a jurisdiction's law therefore must be sensitive and adapted to its entire child protection apparatus.

Management: Law Can and Should Provide Many Tools: Criminal and Non-Criminal Law

The authors share the view that debates over whether child maltreatment should always or never become a matter of punishment, involuntary evaluation and treatment, or entirely voluntary choices by a child's caregivers, are rarely helpful. This is so because the discussion is then presented primarily as a dichotomy which is often a false choice between only one legal approach or none. What is far more productive is a nuanced approach that asks under what circumstances various legally based interventions are helpful. Even more helpful would be direct evidence from research or successful models of law-authorized practices that produce a reduction in the advent of, or improvements in the response to, child abuse or neglect. Considerations of the negative effects of even successful legally-required interventions should be part of such research. Law may have its own universe of legal philosophy and practice, but it is unlikely to survive a societal belief that it is not supporting conflict resolution.

Once a report of child maltreatment is made and confirmed, what role can law play? For a percentage of cases, voluntary intervention will be sufficient (Tjaden and Thoennes 1992).[8] This can stem from a conclusion that abuse or neglect occurred but no further intervention is necessary because the harm was minimal or unlikely to be repeated. It is also possible that the child, parents, or both require mental health or other types of evaluation and treatment to prevent recurrence of the maltreatment, and that because the parents refuse treatment or because the need for subsequent treatment is essential for the child's safety, a legal proceeding is necessary. Because so many factors can contribute to a lack of safety or adequate nurturance of a child's development, any legal responses should be as fair, non-traumatic, nuanced and individualized as possible.

Two broad and yet distinct categories of law can be identified as operating within all major legal cultures: criminal law and non-criminal law. Once criminal and noncriminal laws are defined and being applied, law-based attempts to remedy child maltreatment under these two distinct subcultures of law can be explored. As succinctly as possible, we will here view legal doctrines and systems as

---

[8] An analysis of child protection agency and criminal court records from California, Delaware and Colorado (N = 833 substantiated cases) found that a voluntary approach was used in different types of cases as follows: physical child abuse (76 %), sexual child abuse (51 %), child neglect (71 %), abandonment (32 %), emotional child abuse (93 %).

providing a powerful source for enabling and perhaps even institutionalizing a large number of ways to prevent and treat child abuse and neglect. There is no one law, nor is there even one kind of law, that can alone adequately support the efforts of a human society committed to reducing child abuse and neglect. But without laws to 'mark out' enforceable standards of conduct towards children, it is not realistic to expect that child maltreatment will diminish.

Criminal Law Applied to Child Maltreatment

Criminal laws exist to punish human conduct viewed by the prevailing culture as harmful to other members of the society, with the related purpose of deterrence. Deterrence is the concept that by causing pain (punishment) to an individual who has offended, he or she will be less likely to reoffend. Deterrence also assumes that knowledge of prohibition and punishment will persuade those who are considering criminal behavior to desist in the first place. A further policy objective of many legal traditions' criminal law is rehabilitation. This assumes that unless law also supports convicted individuals, for example through treatment for substance abuse (Burrus et al. 2011; Worcel et al. 2008) or providing occupational and life skills that provide a basis for non-criminal self-sufficiency, efforts to prevent criminal recidivism will be less successful. Another objective of criminal laws is to incapacitate extremely dangerous offenders to protect the public. Finally, criminal laws also exist to set community standards of conduct and denounce behavior which contravenes those standards.

At the same time, while having these goals centered on justice for victims and the community, laws in common law jurisdictions also usually contain protective measures aimed at ensuring fairness and due process to accused persons.[9] As well, in a more general sense, legal measures can be taken to prevent unjust application of laws against child maltreatment. Law can attempt to circumscribe what is and is not considered to be child abuse. Laws can lower the level of criminal intent required to prosecute a child abuse fatality, reflecting the vulnerability of infants; felony child abuse statutes hold a caregiver responsible not only for deliberately causing death, but also for recklessly allowing a child to die.

Crime can occur within or outside of the family, and criminal laws have been enacted to address child maltreatment in many different settings. For maltreatment in the family, "unreasonable corporal punishment", sexual abuse, and reckless negligence or abandonment of children have all been subjected to legal punishment in some societies (Howell 1980; Cross et al. 1994). At least in the U.S., child sexual abuse and fatal child abuse are the forms of child maltreatment most prosecuted when the problem occurs within families (Tjaden and Thoennes 1992), even though general neglect, emotional abuse and physical abuse are far more common problems (US Department of Health and Human Services 2011). Still, while the frequency of prosecution is seldom researched, one such study of cases confirmed by child protection agencies found that only 4 % were prosecuted (Tjaden and Thoennes 1992), and this trend can be seen elsewhere (Cossins 2010). As explored below in the section on non-criminal law, there are a number of reasons why child maltreatment within families, at least in the common law countries, is only rarely addressed through criminal proceedings.

When other familiar caregivers of children, such as teachers, religious counselors, and sports coaches are included, it is again child sexual abuse and, in the example of baby-sitters, fatal child abuse, that are more likely to be prosecuted. Perhaps the single group most clearly to have become a

---

[9] One issue alone has consumed thousands of pages of research and legal precedent in common law countries is the issue of which statements and testimony of children are admissible to prove sexual abuse: with respect to U.S. law, see Myers (2005). Due process cannot occur unless there are societal commitments and investments to train law enforcement, prosecution and judicial officials, uphold standards of proof, guarantee both the rights of victims and the rights of defendants to respectful investigations and trials, and to provide sufficient resources for these standards to be upheld.

focus of criminal prosecution consists of persons who prey on children sexually by using the internet, trafficking, or any other means. Separate websites, NGOs, and, in some nations, funded governmental enforcement agencies address 'third party sexual exploitation' of children.[10] When the family has not caused or permitted the abuse, obstacles to the use of criminal law to address intrafamilial child maltreatment are removed. The criminal law is one of the few ways in which societies can try to protect children from sexual abuse and exploitation by persons outside the family.

With time, but only with time, there will be more scientific investigation of the uses of law as a deliberated instrument of child protection policy. As just one important question: Which maltreatment cases are prosecuted and why? As already noted, fewer than 5 % of confirmed cases appear to be prosecuted. Other research indicates factors influencing the decision to prosecute sexual abuse: victim age, presence of oral-genital abuse, use or threat of force, duration of abuse, presence of physical or eyewitness evidence, and the presence of maternal support (Cross et al. 1994).

In addition to instances where a child is seriously victimized by nonfamilial perpetrators, criminal law has a role to play in family situations that are simply not treatable by other means, where it is necessary to keep children safe from individuals with a persistent record of violence or sexual predation who do not respond to treatment. Another example would be specific, particularly heinous acts of torture or sadism, or unacceptable recklessness with respect to a vulnerable infant or child. Such situations are generally investigated for potential prosecution. The cost and difficulties of gathering evidence for a trial that will succeed in the courts of countries with high standards of proof, along with the many other due process protections afforded criminal defendants in societies where individual rights are cherished, are among the reasons why criminal prosecutions do not always occur even when prosecution appears merited. Additionally, in many places in the world, prosecuting crimes against children committed either within or outside of the family are not priorities, often because there is no adult economic, religious, or political interest group or institution organized to support prosecution of crimes against children. In addition, the laws of evidence and procedure are often inappropriate for vulnerable children generally, and in particular for sexual offenses, where the child has often been extremely traumatised and can be further psychologically harmed by the rigours of appearing in court, testifying, enduring cross-examination and facing the offender. Some countries have made progress in amending these laws to better enable processes, which recognize the child's developmental vulnerability, but there clearly remains much to be done (Cossins 2010). Related to this general lack of commitment is probably a lack of understanding of the extraordinary costs to the hopes of the society as a whole for a prosperous nation-state if the well-being of the country's children is not secured.

Among other reasons for not responding to child maltreatment within families through the criminal system is the general concern that, except for the most unforgivable offenses, the criminal system does more harm than good to the survivors in the family. If an abusive parent who earns the family's income is convicted and imprisoned and not allowed to work, then the family will suffer further harm from economic deprivation. However, there is at least one reportedly successful approach to incest that combined criminal accountability with continued work to support the family through court-ordered therapy (Giarretto 1976). Perhaps most generally, the concern is that to treat the intimate problems of private family life, no punitive system is sufficiently well-designed, even though modifications are possible, and adapted systems are claimed to offer potential solutions in some cases (Cossins 2010; Daly 2008; Daly and Proietti-Scifoni 2011). Yet this question remains open to empirical examination that will confirm or disconfirm through careful scientific research when criminal law can and cannot usefully address problems of child sexual abuse, serious physical abuse and emotional abuse, and serious neglect. In the following section, the use of non-criminal law to enable or even require treatment for major problems within the family is reviewed.

---

[10] For example, see the website of the U.S. National Center for Missing and Exploited Children: http://www.missingkids.com/missingkids/servlet/PublicHomeServlet?LanguageCountry = en_US, (Verified April 19, 2012).

Non-Criminal Law Applied to Child Maltreatment: Law Conceptualized as Supportive of Health, Prevention, and Melioration

It is difficult to know if criminal law or non-criminal law is the most common international form of official law applied in cases of child maltreatment. *World Perspectives on Child Abuse*, a biennial publication of the International Society for the Prevention of Child Abuse and Neglect, provides the most detailed periodic assessment of world-wide child protection developments. Prepared and published with the support of governments and NGOs, the specific focus of the *World Perspectives* report varies every 2 years. What is clear, however, is that countries striving to be "nations of law" are at varied stages of development with respect to child maltreatment. A useful example is the reported experience of Croatia over the last decade, which documents many new or additional protections for children in Family Law (2003, 2004), Law on Protection of Violence in the Family (2003), Law on Criminal Proceedings (2003) and Law on Children's Ombudsman (2003) (Gray 2010, p. 14). A detailed world survey would reveal great variation in the type and degree of effort devoted to non-criminal child protection law. Given the limited understanding of child protection laws world-wide, it is still possible and perhaps useful to define and describe possible non-criminal legal responses to the need to protect children.

A broad term of art that encompasses non-criminal legal processes in common law nations is *civil law*. Used here, civil law is a short hand term for non-criminal law. Within the large category of non-criminal kinds of law, there are both public and private legal proceedings. Private law proceedings are covered at the end of this section. Most citizens encounter civil law sanctions imposed by government through social governance systems including taxation, zoning, business regulation, and licensing. Of special interest for our purposes are the many possible governmental actions involving public health, mental health, drug dependence, and child welfare authority. Each of these authorized governmental responses addresses a particular danger or challenge for society as a whole due to the behavior of one or many individuals.

The term 'public health', as a concept and an operational guide, was originally directed at community-wide health concerns such as clean water, clean food, and sewage systems (Turnock 2009; Gostin 2008). It is now often the concept stated as the optimal approach underpinning governments' child maltreatment prevention and intervention services (Krugman 2009; O'Donnell et al. 2008; Scott 2006). As discussed above, laws about the reporting of suspected abuse and neglect, and differential response systems, are widely seen as elements of a public health approach. According to the classical tenets of 'public health' systems, for optimal effectiveness, such systems must contain elements of primary prevention (aimed at the whole population); secondary prevention (aimed at individuals and groups who are particularly vulnerable to the phenomenon) and tertiary prevention (aimed at those who have suffered the phenomenon). There seems little reason to doubt that this conceptualization is appropriate, especially for neglect, and probably also for emotional abuse and much physical abuse. Yet, for sexual abuse, given its manifest differences in aetiology, there may be more debate about whether 'public health' is an appropriate framework, especially regarding primary prevention; nevertheless, some have called for prevention of sexual abuse to be seen as a challenge for public health (Mercy 1999).

Mental health law historically has been less preventive than public health, and normally is used to respond to individual behaviors that appear to be caused by mental illness. The efficacy of ordering persons with mental illness to have medical treatment could be more extensively researched but some studies have been published (Patel et al. 2001). When problems such as post-partum depression are recognized for their potential to create child neglect or abuse, the importance of mental health law becomes relevant to the general discussion of child protection law.

Drug courts, as noted already, and court-ordered substance abuse treatment as part of criminal sentencing (Ditton 1999) are also relevant to child protection because the overlap between substance abuse disorder and child maltreatment is well known (Smarsh et al. 2006). While the fields of public health, mental health and substance abuse research the effects of mandated therapies, professionals in child welfare and protection have been quite slow to address law as an intervention variable (Bross 2009). However, there are a few published studies and these suggest that involuntary services can provide better results than voluntary services for some families (Wolfe et al. 1980). For those who wish to have no role for law, it is worth noting that most published research on effective treatment of abused children and maltreating parents has occurred within populations that faced involuntary governmental involvement, either directly due to court orders, or indirectly with the prospect of court involvement if parents refused treatment.

One of the problems of determining which cases should include a court response (or other type of response) is that there is no perfect science of triage in child protection services. There are many possible interventions for assuring child safety and well-being. Evaluations and treatment services for children and their caregivers, foster or kinship care, or even systems for adoption, can be done on a voluntary basis, or by court orders. Triage – deciding which situations must be attended to immediately to prevent further harm (and by which means), which situations will be likely to resolve themselves without external intervention, and which situations are not an emergency but must be attended to soon to avoid further harm – involves the central problem of prediction in a context in which financial and human resources will never be so plentiful as to allow 'perfect' responses to every case. Systematic and principled methods of the optimal and most appropriate allocation of scarce resources and responses, such as by providing for a statutory child protection response in some cases, and for differential response in others, are becoming more widely adopted, but are yet to be extensively and objectively evaluated. Over time, careful research should reveal when different options are most likely to produce the best outcome for a particular child.

Private Legal Remedies for Child Maltreatment

In a few countries, there are robust traditions for litigating private law suits in which individuals go to court to recover money for injuries caused by various private activities (Hoyano and Keenan 2007). To a limited degree, some of the same countries permit enforcement of private claims by individuals against local and even national governments. An early although unusual example of possible personal responsibility for harm to an abused child arose in Landeros v Flood (1976), a leading American case on failure to report suspected child abuse. Dr. Flood, a physician, was sued for negligence in failing to diagnose and report suspected child abuse.

Far more frequently, private litigation occurs in the numerous cases brought against those who have inflicted serious abuse on children, whether by citizens, clerics (Berry 1992, 2011) and volunteers or employees who sexually abused children in institutions such as churches, and other bodies like the Boy Scouts of America (Boyle 1994). These cases can be seen in nations including the UK, the USA, Canada, Australia, among many others (Hoyano and Keenan 2007). In the US, there have been literally thousands of lawsuits brought in situations of clerical abuse. Even where private law suits are possible, it can still be a government itself that takes on the role of 'private attorney general' and seeks compensation for wrongs against children perpetrated by non-governmental agencies. The capacity of a child survivor of serious abuse to bring a civil action for compensation for injuries suffered, whether as a child through a 'next friend', or as an adult, is a critical aspect of a functional legal system. The essence of the 'rule of law' – the concept underpinning common law jurisdictions – is 'that all persons and authorities within the state, whether public or private, should be bound by and entitled to the benefit of laws publicly and prospectively promulgated and publicly administered in the courts' (Bingham 2007). Adjudicative procedures should be fair, means must be provided to resolve disputes, and the law must adequately protect fundamental human rights. These are fundamental and indispensable elements of a just society. Laws enabling such lawsuits not only allow a management response to individual cases, but can have a preventative effect, especially in cases involving maltreatment in institutions.

Where severe abuse has been inflicted on numerous children within State and or religious institutions – unfortunately, a pattern that can be seen in many nations – governments can implement redress schemes to compensate these large groups of survivors and can join with responsible religious institutions in doing so. An example can be seen in the case of institutional abuse of children in Ireland in State orphanages, industrial schools and other institutions. A major Irish compensation scheme was established by legislation. The *Residential Institutions Redress Act 2002* was passed on 10 April 2002, establishing the Residential Institutions Redress Board, conferring on it functions and powers, and establishing associated bodies. The Residential Institutions Redress Board scheme, funded by government with contributions from responsible religious authorities, was launched on 2 December 2002.[11]

The Law Commission of Canada (2000) undertook a comprehensive review of State responses to institutional abuse. It concluded that the most effective response in meeting the needs of survivors is the use of redress programs, which should be designed with survivors, and which include responses to all their needs. Such programs are more flexible, less costly, less time-consuming, less psychologically traumatic and less confrontational than conventional legal proceedings. In Canada, provincial governments established compensation schemes in situations where children were abused and neglected in State-funded and State-operated institutions. These include the British Columbia Jericho Individual Compensation Program 1995; the New Brunswick Compensation Program; the Nova Scotia Compensation Program 1996; the Ontario Grandview Agreement Compensation Scheme 1994; and the Ontario St John's and St Joseph's Helpline Agreement 1993. The Law Commission of Canada also recommended that ex gratia payments should be offered in cases where an otherwise meritorious and provable claim cannot be pursued because it falls outside a statutory limitation period.

Prevention and the Role of Legislation

Changes in public understanding and awareness, as in the example of the hygienist movement of the early nineteenth century, can have a great positive effect on the health and welfare of the entire population (Faria 2002). In the twentieth century, some of the largest scale implementations of prevention programs have occurred through legislation and governmental appropriations. Spending authorization is frequently the law's most crucial activity in addressing significant health problems, codifying the political commitment of tax revenues and budgets to the cause of child protection. The first Child Abuse and Neglect Prevention and Treatment Act (U.S. Public Law 93–247) led in the ensuing 35 years to more than $70 million spent on public awareness and professional training. Riders to Titles XX and IVe of the Social Security Act have yielded more treatment dollars for services to children and families. Another major policy contributing to child well-being is the practice of legally authorized and paid maternity and paternity leave during the time immediately after a baby's birth. Many nations in the world not only provide tax deductions for each child, but in some nations cash payments are made to parents to assist them in meeting the costs of child-care. Tax deductions are given for donations to charities whose mission and work is intended to prevent cruelty to children. Pediatrician Ray Helfer developed the concept of Children's Trust Funds that would enable all

---

[11] See generally the website of the RIRB at (http://www.rirb.ie/). The contribution required by the Church is now so large that its capacity to pay is under threat: http://www.irishcentral.com/news/news_from_ireland/Irish-Catholic-Church-unable-to-foot-19-billion-abuse-bill-146552675.html (checked 23 August 2012). See also Mathews 2004.

individuals to make a contribution to child abuse prevention in lieu of all of the taxes owed to the government by the citizens living in a specific American state, instead of the taxes owed all going to general tax fund accounts. These funding mechanisms exist in many of the American states, and a private coordinating and lobbying organization called the National Alliance of Children's Trust and Prevention Funds has been established to support the Children's Trust Fund movement.

Care for newborns and their parents is a major prevention initiative which requires not only rigorous, tested programs, but massive financial support. In 1976, C. Henry Kempe called for a universal system of lay health visitors' support for children and parents, especially in the first four years, and for more specialized intensive interventions and preventative efforts for high-risk families (Kempe 1976). These ideas would later motivate the development of various home-visiting programs in different parts of the world, some of which have been shown to deliver more positive effects than others after being rigorously tested (Olds 2012; Dalziel and Segal 2012). Here again, legislation can play a crucial role in providing the political and economic impetus for the promotion of social policy, and can do so in a way which is far more powerful, widespread, secure and durable than localised, ad hoc handouts. As Olds points out (2012, p. 169), recent federal U.S. legislation (the Affordable Care Act 2010) secured $1.5 billion in funding to proven programs over a 5 year term.

A specific program, the Nurse Family Partnership, has now been extended to over one in ten of the over 3,400 American counties. Great Britain, Germany and Japan are adopting the Nurse Family Partnership model because of its very favorable outcomes for mothers and their children. In the U.S. perhaps 20–25 % of eligible first time mothers refuse the service. However, in other societies more receptive to preventive public health nursing services, as in the United Kingdom and the Plunkett nurses in New Zealand, these support services are considered an entitlement which is the nature of a right, obviating the need for involuntary intervention in a great many situations.

Among other ways that laws can assist in the prevention of child maltreatment are by enacting financial support for trauma informed cognitive behavioral therapy and similar evidence-based practices (Shipman and Taussig 2009), legally requiring private insurance to pay for behavioral health therapy for victims of child maltreatment, and victim's assistance including victim's advocates and therapy for child victims of crimes including child abuse.[12] In addition, there are examples of government legislative interventions in cases of extreme community dysfunction. In Australia, some indigenous communities have been made subject to legislation banning or restricting the sale of alcohol through 'alcohol management plans'. This measure, adopted through liquor legislation, has been taken to respond to endemic alcoholism and resultant violence, child maltreatment and general social dysfunction, including child truancy from school and lack of adequate supervision. Such measures have been vigorously attacked by some, who claim they unjustly infringe the rights of people to consume liquor (and the rights of others to sell it). Others defend the plans, based on what they assert are the superior rights of women and children to safety. There is powerful evidence of the positive effect of the bans and limits on reducing child maltreatment, with recent data indicating dramatic declines in violence and equally dramatic increases in school attendance in one prominent community (Walker 2012). Yet, the politics of such policies can threaten their existence; in Queensland, the conservative government has foreshadowed possible changes to the existing policy, and recently the High Court of Australia granted special leave to a plaintiff arguing that the laws are unconstitutional (*Maloney v The Queen* [2012] HCA Trans 243).

It is worth noting another means by which legislation can enact a political and fiscal commitment to improved practice in child maltreatment responses. The U.S. Children's Justice Act (CJA) provides grants to states to improve the investigation, prosecution and judicial handling of cases of child abuse

---

[12] See, for example, United Nations Office on Drugs and Crime (2009) *Justice in Matters involving Child Victims and Witnesses of Crime: Model Law and Related Commentary*. New York, United Nations. http://www.unodc.org/documents/justice-and-prison-reform/Justice_in_matters...pdf (checked 10 September 2012).

and neglect, particularly child sexual abuse and exploitation, in a manner that limits additional trauma to the child victim. This also includes the handling of child fatality cases in which child abuse or neglect is suspected and some cases of children with disabilities and serious health problems who also are victims of abuse and neglect. Since 2000, $17 million in funds have been made available annually for distribution to the 50 states, and U.S. districts and principalities. States must apply for the funds and meet certain eligibility requirements, including receipt of the CAPTA State Grant and establishment of a CJA Task Force as outlined in the legislation. Funds are allocated in the amount of $50,000 per state, plus an additional amount based on the population of children under 18 years of age in the applicant's jurisdiction. Funding comes from the Crime Victims' Fund, which collects fines and fees charged to persons convicted of Federal crimes. The Fund is administered by the U.S. Department of Justice, Office of Victims of Crime (OVC) and the grants are awarded by the Administration on Children, Youth and Families, U.S. Department of Health and Human Services, as outlined in Section 107 of the Child Abuse Prevention and Treatment Act (CAPTA), as amended, by the Keeping Children and Families Safe Act of 2003.

Future Questions and Possibilities

Flowing from these numerous examples, we can identify salient questions for cultures in the process of developing legal response systems to promote child protection, and for those which have already made substantial progress. Perhaps the most challenging question for an emerging economy is whether and how to choose to focus on addressing some forms of maltreatment more than others, perhaps in a context of scarce resources and widespread poverty, a nascent or developing culture of children's rights, and low political will to change the status quo. It is beyond doubt that in general, parents and caregivers are the greatest threat to children for most forms of abuse and neglect, and that the younger the child, the more vulnerable they generally are. Yet, persons outside the family can also offend. In the case of sexual abuse, offenders include other relatives and acquaintances, teachers, and religious figures. With other types of maltreatment, different classes of persons can be the offenders, and this can also be influenced by, and can in fact reflect the implementation of, entire social norms. Where child marriage is the norm, girls may be commonly betrothed against their will at very young ages and subjected to frequent sexual, physical and emotional abuse. Where child labor is common, employers can impose brutal and unsafe conditions on very young children. While a country should work to reduce severe child maltreatment within the family, it is also possible that phenomena like sex trafficking, sex tourism, on-line exploitation, the use of children in war, child marriage, and extreme physical labor may perhaps more readily receive public and philanthropic concern and support. Aspects of child maltreatment involving 'other' people, and customs whose durability is wavering, may be particularly promising targets for priority intervention. India is an example of a nation which has recently introduced legislation aimed at responding to and reducing various forms of these kinds of child maltreatment, including trafficking, harsh labor, marriage (Deb and Mathews 2012; Ghosh 2009).

Areas that deserve further attention by all nations with respect to law as an intervention variable are numerous. The extent to which laws created to address conflicts between adults are inadequate, misapplied or even harmful when applied to childhood is insufficiently explored. The effects of different legal processes on individual children and parents are rarely examined. Exceptions include a study of the possible effects of court participation on child witnesses (Runyan et al. 1994), a survey of the views of parents when involuntarily enrolled in child protection services (Fryer et al. 1990), and a comparison of treatment completion and success for families enrolled in voluntary versus court-ordered services (Wolfe et al. 1980). The possibility that there are legal and policy measures that are underused or overused is rarely considered, and thus the question of how we can know what policy to follow with any confidence remains unanswered.

On a broader scale, other questions exist. What differentiates countries which more energetically comply with the UNCRC from those that ratify the UNCRC but ignore it in practice? What explains the anomaly of the U.S., which has not ratified but has enforced many elements of the UNCRC, while ignoring other elements of the CRC? Similar questions can be applied to other international rights instruments which embed human rights which are seen as so fundamental to human flourishing that they have been recognized as universal norms. Why are some nations more active than others in supporting such rights and implementing them in the lived experience of their citizens? What conditions and attitudes are required in a society so that it is most likely to recognize and promote these rights?

Even more broadly yet, and taking a longer term view, how might law and society develop to manage and prevent child maltreatment in light of the best knowledge about attachment, child development and trauma, and about the circumstances which are more likely to prevent and produce severe maltreatment? Is it possible that law can further develop to minimize some forms of child maltreatment, such as by prohibiting corporal punishment? Corporal punishment is still seen by many as a natural incident of physical discipline possessed by parents, and in some cultures by other adults. Yet, despite it being a customary practice for thousands of years, in recent decades dozens of countries have prohibited it, influenced by evidence of its detrimental effects on physical and mental health (Gershoff 2002; Gershoff and Bitensky 2007; Landsford et al. 2002; Springer et al. 2007), its association with more severe abuse (Zolotor et al. 2008) and the impact of recognizing children's rights to personal inviolability. By 2011, 29 nations had prohibited corporal punishment in all forms, and many more had prohibited it within defined contexts such as schools and institutions (Durrant and Smith 2011). An update in October 2012 shows that 33 nations now prohibit corporal punishment (Global Initiative to End All Corporal Punishment of Children 2012). While some commentators still appear unconvinced, many have concluded that such prohibitions, with supportive educational measures, have influenced positive changes in attitudes and behavior (Naylor and Saunders 2012; Janson et al. 2011; Bussman 2011).

Further, is it possible that law can be one supportive factor in establishing social, educational and public health systems which promote prevention of child maltreatment? Much physical and emotional maltreatment might be minimized by greater efforts in educating children (and adults) in psychosocial skills, the possession of which are protective factors against maltreating offspring. Skill development in empathy and impulse control could occur in schools, as well as through the types of home visit programmes already seen as beneficial. School education could also build in exposure to parenting education and birth control. Law could entrench beneficial approaches to parental leave for both mothers and fathers. Greater public health initiatives to respond to alcohol and drug dependence, and to mental illness, offers the prospect of reduction in maltreatment and exposure of children to domestic violence. Legal measures to respond to gender inequalities also offer the intriguing prospect of reducing gender-specific maltreatment, usually afflicting girls. Laws aimed at reducing poverty-related neglect can target the adequate provision of nutrition and education (Deb and Mathews 2012).

Summary

Many different legal scaffolds can combine to offer an extensive repertoire of remedies and preventive mechanisms for societies and professionals working with child protection, health care, behavioral health, justice, policy, and the public they serve. These legal tools can be designed to facilitate maltreatment prevention and response. In order to apply these legal tools appropriately, law must be employed whenever possible informed by scientific studies of law as an "intervention variable". Rigorous studies can explore and trace the potential and limits of law within various traditions and legal systems. The actual workings and effects of laws and associated policies and systems must be understood, so that better laws and policies can be designed and applied in an effective and appropriate manner.

One of the most important controversies, and one that is unlikely to be settled completely during the lifetime of contemporary readers, is the problem of why addressing child abuse and neglect has historically taken so long, and why nations remain so varied today in their capacity and willingness to address the problem. Law reflects and enforces societal norms, but laws do not change easily in the face of denial and gaze aversion, and of embedded cultural norms that are antithetical to children's safety and flourishing. Rejecting any form of enforceable child protection is a convenient but transparent way of ignoring the problem. In this chapter, a case has been made that changes in law have helped respond to and reduce child abuse and neglect, with consequent improvements for the lives of everyone in society affected by child maltreatment.

An overview of human history reveals that many societies world-wide have achieved remarkable advances in child welfare in the last 50 years, with new socio-legal responses to identifying and managing child maltreatment that for many centuries would have been inconceivable. Examples include the US response to child maltreatment generally, laws in India prohibiting child marriage (Deb and Mathews 2012), and the enactment in 19 African nations of laws prohibiting female genital mutilation, supported by international instruments including the Protocol to the African Charter on Human and Peoples' Rights on the Rights of Women in Africa (the Maputo Protocol) (Mathews 2011a, 2013). Recent advances, exemplified by the US, have shown that it is possible for such measures to dramatically minimize severe child maltreatment. A cautiously optimistic yet realistic approach gives reason to think that further advances are within reach, so that in another 50 years, the situation for children generally will be even better than it is today.

As is to be expected given nations' different economic, historical, religious and cultural positions and priorities, such improvements will occur in ways that are informed by each society's context. In societies with higher economic capacity, a longer tradition of individual rights to safety and equality, and a strong political and cultural commitment to child welfare, advances may be more widespread in the sense of applying to all four 'classical' forms of maltreatment. In societies with different contexts and with different levels of capacity and or inclination to commit to broader change in these four contexts, advances may in one sense be more narrowly circumscribed in that they may not focus on all four types of maltreatment. Yet, progress regarding selected immediate priorities may be extremely significant, such as efforts to eradicate trafficking and female genital mutilation. Moreover, other priorities may offer even broader gains related to child welfare and indirect reduction of child maltreatment, such as prohibiting child marriage and harsh labor, and embedding universal education. Progress in responding to and reducing child maltreatment is possible in various contexts. Societies that do not make meaningful attempts to create law, policy and cultural change leading to prevention and treatment of child abuse and neglect are effectively choosing not to address a fundamental obstacle to individual flourishing and social progress.

References

Abrahams, N., Casey, K., & Daro, D. (1992). Teachers' knowledge, attitudes and beliefs about child abuse and its prevention. *Child Abuse & Neglect, 16*, 229–238.

Ajzen, I. (2005). *Attitudes, personality and behavior* (2nd ed.). Maidenhead: Open University Press.

Ajzen, I., & Fishbein, M. (2005). The influence of attitudes on behaviour. In D. Albarracin, B. Johnson, & M. Zanna (Eds.), *The handbook of attitudes* (pp. 173–221). Mahwah: Lawrence Erlbaum Associates Publishers.

Anderst, J., Kellogg, N., & Jung, I. (2009). Reports of repetitive penile-genital penetration often have no definitive evidence of penetration. *Pediatrics, 124*(3), e403.

APSAC. (1995). *Psychosocial evaluation of suspected psychological maltreatment in children and adolescents: Practice guidelines*. American Professional Society on the Abuse of Children. Elmhurst: IL.

Berkowitz, C. (2008). Child abuse recognition and reporting: Supports and resources for changing the paradigm. *Pediatrics, 122*, S10–S12.

Berry, J. (1992). *Lead us not into temptation: Catholic priests and the sexual abuse of children*. New York: Doubleday.

Berry, J. (2011). *Render unto Rome: The secret life of money in the Catholic Church*. New York: Crown.

Besharov, D. (1990). *Recognizing child abuse*. New York: Free Press.

Besharov, D. (2005). Overreporting and underreporting of child abuse and neglect are twin problems. In D. Loseke, R. Gelles, & M. Cavanaugh (Eds.), *Current controversies on family violence* (2nd ed., pp. 285–298). Thousand Oaks: Sage.

Bingham, L. T. (2007). The rule of law. *Cambridge Law Journal, 66*(1), 67–85.

Borkowski, A. (1986). *Textbook on Roman law*. London: Blackstone Press.

Boyle, P. (1994). *Scouts honor: Sexual abuse in America's most trusted institution*. Rocklin: Prima Publishing.

Bross, D. (2009). Involuntary therapy: A good idea? In A. Kellogg (Ed.), *Standing at the forefront: Effective advocacy in today's world* (pp. 229–250). Denver: National Association of Counsel for Children.

Bross, D., & Mathews, B. (2012). The battered child syndrome: Changes in the law and child advocacy. In R. Krugman & J. Korbin (Eds.), *C. Henry Kempe: A 50 year legacy to the field of child abuse and neglect* (pp. 39–50). Springer Scientific. Dordrecht, Netherlands.

Burrus, S., Mackin, J., & Finigan, M. (2011). Show me the money: Child welfare cost savings of a family drug court. *Juvenile and Family Court Journal, 62*(3), 1–14.

Bussman, K. (2011). Background and legal consequences of the right to be raised without violence. In J. Durrant & A. Smith (Eds.), *Global pathways to abolishing physical punishment: Realizing children's rights* (pp. 134–145). New York: Routledge.

Christian, C. (2008). Professional education in child abuse and neglect. *Pediatrics, 122*(1), S13–S17.

Conley, A., & Berrick, J. (2010). Community-based child abuse prevention: Outcomes associated with a differential response program in california. *Child Maltreatment, 15*, 282–292.

Cossins, A. (2010). *Alternative models for prosecuting child sex offences in Australia*. Sydney: National Child Sexual Assault Reform Committee, University of New South Wales.

Cross, T., De Vos, E., & Whitcomb, D. (1994). Prosecution of child sexual abuse: Which cases are accepted? *Child Abuse & Neglect, 18*(8), 663–677.

Cummins, P., Scott, D., & Scales, B. (2012). *Report of the protecting Victoria's vulnerable children inquiry*. Melbourne: State of Victoria Department of Premier and Cabinet.

Daly, K. (2008). Setting the record straight and a call for radical change: A reply to Annie Cossins on 'Restorative justice and child sex offences'. *British Journal of Criminology, 48*(4), 557–566.

Daly, K., & Proietti-Scifoni, G. (2011). Reparation and restoration. In M. Tonry (Ed.), *Oxford handbook of crime and criminal justice* (pp. 207–253). Oxford: Oxford University Press.

Dalziel, K., & Segal, L. (2012). Home visiting programmes for the prevention of child maltreatment: Cost-effectiveness of 33 programmes. *Archives of Disease in Childhood, 97*, 787–798.

de Mause, L. (Ed.). (1974). *The history of childhood*. New York: Psychohistory Press.

Deb, S., & Mathews, B. (2012). Children's rights in India: Parents' and teachers' attitudes, knowledge and perceptions. *The International Journal of Children's Rights, 20*, 1–24.

Ditton, P. (1999). *Mental health treatment of inmates and probationers*. Washington, DC: U.S. Department of Justice, Office of Justice Programs, Bureau of Justice Statistics.

Drake, B., & Jonson-Reid, M. (2007). A response to Melton based on the best available data. *Child Abuse & Neglect, 31*, 343–360.

Dubowitz, H. (2000). What is child neglect? In H. Dubowitz & D. DePanfilis (Eds.), *The handbook for child protection*. Thousand Oaks: Sage.

Durrant, J., & Smith, A. (Eds.). (2011). *Global pathways to abolishing physical punishment: Realizing children's rights*. New York: Routledge.

Eisenberg, L. (1981). Cross-cultural and historical perspectives on child abuse and neglect. *Child Abuse & Neglect, 5*, 299–308.

Faria, M. (2002). Medical history: Hygiene and sanitation. *Medical Sentinel, 7*(4), 122–123.

Feng, J.-Y., & Levine, M. (2005). Factors associated with nurses' intention to report child abuse: A national survey of Taiwanese nurses. *Child Abuse & Neglect, 29*(7), 783–795.

Finkelhor, D. (1990). Is child abuse overreported? The data rebut arguments for less intervention. *Public Welfare, 48*(1), 23.

Finkelhor, D. (2005). The main problem is underreporting child abuse and neglect. In D. Loseke, R. Gelles, & M. Cavanaugh (Eds.), *Current controversies on family violence* (2nd ed., pp. 299–310). Thousand Oaks: Sage.

Finkelhor, D. (2008). *Childhood victimization*. Oxford: Oxford University Press.

Finkelhor, D., & Jones, L. (2006). Why have child maltreatment and child victimization declined? *Journal of Social Issues, 62*(4), 685–716.

Finkelhor, D., & Jones, L. (2012a). *Have sexual abuse and physical abuse declined since the 1990s?* Durham: Crimes Against Children Research Center, University of New Hampshire. http://www.unh.edu/ccrc/pdf/CV267_Have%20SA%20%20PA%20Decline_FACT%20SHEET_11-7-12.pdf.

Finkelhor, D., & Jones, L. (2012b). Trends in child maltreatment. *The Lancet, 379*, 2048–2049.

Finkelhor, D., Jones, L., & Shattuck, A. (2011). *Updated trends in child maltreatment, 2010.* Durham: Crimes Against Children Research Center, University of New Hampshire. http://www.unh.edu/ccrc/pdf/CV203_Updated%20 trends%202010%20FINAL_12-19-11.pdf.

Finkelhor, D., Turner, H., Ormrod, R., & Hamby, S. (2010). Trends in childhood violence and abuse exposure: Evidence from 2 national surveys. *Archives of Pediatrics & Adolescent Medicine, 164*(3), 238–242.

Flaherty, E., Sege, R., Price, L., et al. (2006). Pediatrician characteristics associated with child abuse identification and reporting: Results from a national survey of pediatricians. *Child Maltreatment, 11*(4), 361–369.

Flaherty, E., Sege, R., Griffith, J., et al. (2008a). From suspicion of physical child abuse to reporting: Primary care clinician decision-making. *Pediatrics, 122*(3), 611–619.

Flaherty, E., Sege, R., & Hurley, T. (2008b). Translating child abuse research into action. *Pediatrics, 122*, S1–S5.

Fryer, G., Bross, D., Krugman, R., et al. (1990). Good news for CPS workers: An Iowa survey shows parents value services. *Public Welfare, 48*(1), 38–41.

Gardner, J. (1986). *Women in Roman law and society.* London: Routledge.

Gershoff, E. (2002). Corporal punishment by parents and associated child behaviors and experiences: A meta-analytic and theoretical review. *Psychological Bulletin, 128*, 539.

Gershoff, E., & Bitensky, S. (2007). The case against corporal punishment of children. *Psychology, Public Policy, and Law, 13*(4), 231–272.

Ghosh, B. (2009). Trafficking in women and children in India: Nature, dimensions and strategies for prevention. *International Journal of Children's Rights, 13*(5), 716–738.

Giarretto, H. (1976). Humanistic treatment of father-daughter incest. In R. Helfer & C. H. Kempe (Eds.), *Child abuse and neglect, the family and the community* (pp. 143–158). Cambridge: Ballinger Publishing.

Gilbert, R., Fluke, J., O'Donnell, M., et al. (2012a). Child maltreatment: Variation in trends and policies in six developed countries. *The Lancet, 379*, 758–772.

Gilbert, R., Fluke, J., O'Donnell, M., et al. (2012b). Authors' reply. *The Lancet, 379*, 2049.

Glaser, D. (2002). Emotional abuse and neglect (psychological maltreatment): A conceptual framework. *Child Abuse & Neglect, 26*, 697–714.

Glaser, D. (2011). How to deal with emotional abuse and neglect—Further development of a conceptual framework (FRAMEA). *Child Abuse & Neglect, 35*, 866–875.

Global Initiative to End All Corporal Punishment of Children. (2012). Prohibiting all corporal punishment of children: progress and delay. http://www.crin.org/docs/Progress%20and%20delay%20leaflet%20October%202012%20 EN%20singles.pdf

Gostin, L. (2008). *Public health law: Power, duty, restraint* (2nd ed.). Berkeley: University of California Press.

Government of Victoria. (2006). *The Children, Youth and Families Act 2005 and The Child Wellbeing and Safety Act 2005: A framework to promote children's safety, wellbeing and development.* Melbourne: Government of Victoria. http://www.cyf.vic.gov.au/__data/assets/pdf_file/0004/41728/ecec_fact2_april_2006.pdf.

Gray, J. (Ed.). (2010). *World perspectives on child abuse* (9th ed.). Aurora: International Society for the Prevention of Child Abuse and Neglect.

Hawkins, R., & McCallum, C. (2001). Mandatory notification training for suspected child abuse and neglect in South Australian schools. *Child Abuse & Neglect, 25*, 1603–1625.

Howell, J. (1980). The role of law enforcement in the prevention, investigation, and treatment of child abuse. In C. H. Kempe & R. Helfer (Eds.), *The battered child* (3rd ed., pp. 306–329). Chicago: University of Chicago Press.

Hoyano, L., & Keenan, C. (2007). *Child abuse: Law and policy across boundaries.* Oxford: Oxford University Press.

Janson, S., Langberg, B., & Svensson, B. (2011). A 30-year ban on physical punishment. In J. Durrant & A. Smith (Eds.), *Global pathways to abolishing physical punishment: Realizing children's rights* (pp. 241–255). New York: Routledge.

Jenny, C., Hymel, K., Ritzen, A., et al. (1999). Analysis of missed cases of abusive head trauma. *Journal of the American Medical Association, 282*(7), 621–626.

Jones, R., Flaherty, E., Binns, H., et al. (2008). Clinicians' descriptions of factors influencing their reporting of suspected child abuse: Report of the child abuse reporting experience study research group. *Pediatrics, 122*(2), 259–266.

Kalichman, S., & Brosig, C. (1993). Practicing psychologists' interpretations of and compliance with child abuse reporting laws. *Law and Human Behavior, 17*(1), 83–93.

Kempe, C. H. (1976). Approaches to preventing child abuse. The health visitors' concept. *American Journal of Diseases of Children, 130*, 941–947.

Kempe, C. H., Silverman, F., Steele, B., Droegemueller, W., & Silver, H. (1962). The battered-child syndrome. *Journal of the American Medical Association, 181*, 17–24.

Kenny, M. (2004). Teachers' attitudes toward and knowledge of child maltreatment. *Child Abuse & Neglect, 28*, 1311–1319.

Kohl, P., Jonson-Reid, M., & Drake, B. (2009). Time to leave substantiation behind: Findings from a national probability study. *Child Maltreatment, 14*(1), 17.

Krugman, R. (2009). Time to medicalise child maltreatment. *The Lancet, 373*, 19.

Lamond, D. (1989). The impact of mandatory reporting legislation on reporting behaviour. *Child Abuse & Neglect, 13*, 471.

Landeros v Flood. (1976). 551 P.2 d. 389.

Landsford, J., Dodge, K., Pettit, G., et al. (2002). A 12 year prospective study of the long-term effects of early child physical maltreatment on psychological, behavioural, and academic problems in adolescence. *Archives of Pediatric and Adolescent Medicine, 156*, 824.

Law Commission of Canada. (2000). Restoring dignity: Responding to child abuse in Canadian institutions, executive summary. http://www.lcc.gc.ca/en/themes/mr/ica/2000/pdf/execsum.pdf

Levi, B., & Crowell, K. (2011). Child experts disagree about the threshold for mandated reporting. *Clinical Pediatrics, 50*(4), 321–329.

Levi, B., & Loeben, G. (2004). Index of suspicion: Feeling not believing. *Theoretical Medicine, 25*, 277–310.

Levi, B., & Portwood, S. (2011). Reasonable suspicion of child abuse: Finding a common language. *Journal of Law, Medicine & Ethics, 39*, 62–69.

Mabo v Queensland [*No 2*]. (1992). 175 CLR 1.

Mathews, B. (2004). Queensland government actions to compensate survivors of institutional abuse: A critical and comparative evaluation. *Queensland University of Technology Law & Justice Journal, 4*(1), 23–45.

Mathews, B. (2011a). Female genital mutilation: Australian law, policy and practical challenges for doctors. *Medical Journal of Australia, 194*(3), 139–141.

Mathews, B. (2011b). Teacher education to meet the challenges of child sexual abuse. *Australian Journal of Teacher Education, 36*(11), 13–32.

Mathews, B. (2012). Exploring the contested role of mandatory reporting laws in the identification of severe child abuse and neglect. In M. Freeman (Ed.), *Current legal issues volume 14: Law and childhood studies* (pp. 302–338). Oxford: Oxford University Press.

Mathews, B. (2013). Legal, cultural and practical developments in responding to female genital mutilation: Can an absolute human right emerge? In C. Sampford, R. Maguire, & B. Lewis (Eds.), *Human rights and shifting global powers*. London: Routledge.

Mathews, B., & Bross, D. (2008). Mandated reporting is still a policy with reason: Empirical evidence and philosophical grounds. *Child Abuse & Neglect, 32*(5), 511–516.

Mathews, B., & Kenny, M. (2008). Mandatory reporting legislation in the USA, Canada and Australia: A cross-jurisdictional review of key features, differences and issues. *Child Maltreatment, 13*, 50–63.

Mathews, B., Fraser, J., Walsh, K., Dunne, M., et al. (2008). Queensland nurses' attitudes towards and knowledge of the legislative duty to report child abuse and neglect: Results of a state-wide survey. *Journal of Law and Medicine, 16*(2), 288–304.

Mathews, B., Payne, H., Bonnet, C., & Chadwick, D. (2009a). A way to restore British paediatricians' engagement with child protection. *Archives of Disease in Childhood, 94*(5), 329–332.

Mathews, B., Walsh, K., Rassafiani, M., et al. (2009b). Teachers reporting suspected child sexual abuse: Results of a three-state study. *University of New South Wales Law Journal, 32*(3), 772–813.

McCarthy, C. (2008). Doing the right thing: A primary care pediatrician's perspective on child abuse reporting. *Pediatrics, 122*, S22.

McGillivray, A. (2011). Children's rights, paternal power and fiduciary duty: From Roman law to the supreme court of Canada. *International Journal of Children's Rights, 19*, 21–54.

Melton, G. (2005). Mandated reporting: A policy without reason. *Child Abuse & Neglect, 29*, 9–18.

Mercy, J. (1999). Having new eyes: Viewing child sexual abuse as a public health problem. *Sexual Abuse: A Journal of Research and Treatment, 11*(4), 317–321.

Minister for Immigration and Ethnic Affairs v Teoh. (1995). 183 CLR 273.

Myers, J. (2005). *Myers on evidence in child abuse, domestic violence and elder abuse cases*. New York: Aspen Publishers.

Naylor, B., & Saunders, B. (2012). Parental discipline, criminal laws, and responsive regulation. In M. Freeman (Ed.), *Current legal issues volume 14: Law and childhood studies* (pp. 506–529). Oxford: Oxford University Press.

O'Donnell, M., Scott, D., & Stanley, F. (2008). Child abuse and neglect – Is it time for a public health approach? *Australian and New Zealand Journal of Public Health, 32*(4), 325.

Olds, D. (2012). Moving towards evidence-based preventive interventions for children and families. In R. Krugman & J. Korbin (Eds.), *C. Henry Kempe: A 50 year legacy to the field of child abuse and neglect* (pp. 165–173). Dordrecht: Springer.

Patel, M., & Hardy, D. (2001). Encouraging pursuit of court-ordered treatment in a state hospital. *Psychiatric Service, 52*, 1656–1657.

Pinker, S. (2011). *The better angels of our nature*. New York: Viking.

Radford, L., Corral, S., Bradley, C., & Fisher, H. (2012). Trends in child maltreatment. *The Lancet, 379*, 2048.

Rajabi-Ardeshiri, M. (2009). The rights of the child in the Islamic context: The challenges of the local and the global. *International Journal of Children's Rights, 17*, 475–489.

Rasheed, S., Abd-Ellah, A., & Yousef, F. (2011). Female genital mutilation in Upper Egypt in the new millennium. *International Journal of Gynecology & Obstetrics, 114*, 47–50.

Reiniger, A., Robison, E., & McHugh, M. (1995). Mandated training of professionals: A means for improving reporting of suspected child abuse. *Child Abuse & Neglect, 19*, 63–69.

Runyan, D. (2012). Foreword. In R. Krugman & J. Korbin (Eds.), *C. Henry Kempe: A 50 year legacy to the field of child abuse and neglect* (p. v). Dordrecht: Springer.

Runyan, D., Hunter, W., Everson, M., et al. (1994). The intervention stressors inventory: A measure of the stress of intervention for sexually abused children. *Child Abuse & Neglect, 19*(4), 319–329.

Runyan, D., et al. (2010). International variations in harsh child discipline. *Pediatrics, 126*(3), e701–e711.

Scott, D. (2006). Towards a public health model of child protection in Australia. *Communities, Families and Children Australia, 1*(1), 9.

Sedlak, A., Gragg, F., Mettenburg, J., et al. (2008). *Fourth national incidence study of child abuse and neglect (NIS-4) design and methods summary*. Rockville: Westat.

Shipman, K., & Taussig, H. (2009). Mental health treatment of child abuse and neglect: The promise of evidence-based practices. *Pediatric Clinics of North America, 56*, 417–428.

Smarsh, T., Myers, B., & Elswick, R. (2006). Child abuse potential among mothers of substance-exposed and nonexposed infants and toddlers. *Child Abuse & Neglect, 30*(2), 145–156.

Springer, K., Sheridan, J., Kuo, D., et al. (2007). Long-term physical and mental health consequences of childhood physical abuse: Results from a large population-based sample of men and women. *Child Abuse & Neglect, 31*, 517.

Starling, S., Heisler, K., Paulson, J., et al. (2009). Child abuse training and knowledge: A national survey of emergency medicine, family medicine, and pediatric residents and program directors. *Pediatrics, 123*(4), e595–e602.

Ten Bensel, R., Rheinberger, M., & Radbill, S. (1997). Children in a world of violence: The roots of child maltreatment. In M. Helfer, R. Kempe, & R. Krugman (Eds.), *The battered child* (5th ed., pp. 3–28). Chicago: University of Chicago Press.

Tjaden, P., & Thoennes, N. (1992). Legal intervention in child maltreatment cases. *Child Abuse & Neglect, 16*, 807–821.

Trocme, N., Fallon, B., MacLaurin, B., et al. (2005). *Canadian incidence study of reported child abuse and neglect—2003: Major findings*. Ottawa: Minister of Public Works and Government Services.

Turnock, B. (2009). *Public health: What it is and how it works* (4th ed.). Sudbury: Jones and Bartlett.

US Department of Health and Human Services. (2007). *Child maltreatment 1990–2005: Reports from the states to the national child abuse and neglect data system*. Washington, DC: US Government Printing Office.

US Department of Health and Human Services. (2009). *Child maltreatment 2007*. Washington, DC: US Government Printing Office.

US Department of Health and Human Services. (2010a). *Child maltreatment 2009*. Washington, DC: US Government Printing Office.

US Department of Health and Human Services. (2010b). *Child maltreatment 2008*. Washington, DC: US Government Printing Office.

US Department of Health and Human Services. (2011). *Child maltreatment 2010*. Washington, DC: US Government Printing Office.

Walker, J. (2012). Bad old days surface as through a boozy haze. *The Weekend Australian*, 13-14 October 2012, p. 21.

Walsh, K., Bridgstock, R., Farrell, A., et al. (2008). Case, teacher and school characteristics influencing teachers' detection and reporting of child physical abuse and neglect: Results from an Australian survey. *Child Abuse & Neglect, 32*(10), 983–993.

Wolfe, D., Aragona, K., & Kaufman, J. (1980). The importance of adjudication in the treatment of abusive and neglectful parents. *Child Abuse & Neglect, 4*(2), 127–135.

Wood, J. (2008). *Report of the special committee of inquiry into child protection services in New South Wales*. Accessible at http://www.lawlink.nsw.gov.au/cpsinquiry.

Worcel, S., Furrer, C., Green, B., et al. (2008). Effects of family treatment drug courts on substance abuse and child welfare outcomes. *Child Abuse Review, 17*(6), 427–443.

World Health Organisation. (2006). *Preventing child maltreatment: A guide to taking action and generating evidence*. Geneva: World Health Organisation and International Society for Prevention of Child Abuse and Neglect.

Zellman, G. (1990). Child abuse reporting and failure to report among mandated reporters. *Journal of Interpersonal Violence, 5*(1), 3–22.

Zolotor, A., Theodore, A., Chang, J., et al. (2008). Speak softly – and forget the stick: Corporal punishment and child physical abuse. *American Journal of Preventive Medicine, 35*(4), 364–369.

Chapter 27
Judicial Issues in Child Maltreatment

Jesse R. Russell, Nancy Miller, and Michael Nash

Judicial Issues in Child Maltreatment

Taking a broad historical perspective is often an efficient strategy for gauging the current state of a policy or practice area. Judicial involvement in child maltreatment, though, has not had a long history. It has only been since the passage of the Foster Care and Adoption Assistance Act in 1980 that oversight of child maltreatment cases became a priority for the courts. Since that time, court involvement has increased, judicial leadership has grown, and a research platform around the effects of judicial action has begun.

In 1995, the National Council of Juvenile and Family Court Judges in its *Resource Guidelines* expressed:

> Juvenile and family court judges are the gatekeepers of our nation's foster care system. They must ultimately decide whether a family in crisis will be broken apart and children placed in foster care or whether placement can be safely prevented through the reasonable efforts of our social service system (p. 10).

Since that time, many juvenile dependency courts and judges have taken on the mantle of that mandate – to be the gatekeepers and ultimate arbiters of the nation's child welfare system. The expansion of the role of the court led to the development of national efforts to improve court performance. Over time, the leadership role of the judge became better defined and stakeholders began to expect and appreciate leadership from judges both on and off the bench, leading to stronger collaboration in system reform efforts. Alongside these efforts, a greater capacity has been established for performance measurement, program evaluation, and a research program focused on the effect of juvenile dependency judges and courts on outcomes for children and families.

J.R. Russell (✉)
National Council on Crime and Delinquency, Madison, Wisconsin, USA

National Council of Juvenile and Family Court Judges, Reno, Nevada, USA
e-mail: JRussell@nccdglobal.org

N. Miller
National Council of Juvenile and Family Court Judges, Reno, Nevada, USA

M. Nash
Edmund D. Edelman Children's Court, Los Angeles Superior Court, and National Council
of Juvenile and Family Court Judges, Los Angeles, California, USA

J.E. Korbin and R.D. Krugman (eds.), *Handbook of Child Maltreatment*, Child Maltreatment 2,   503
DOI 10.1007/978-94-007-7208-3_27, © Springer Science+Business Media Dordrecht 2014

This chapter outlines the expectations, legal constraints, and obligations of juvenile dependency courts; considers the role of the juvenile court judge; discusses judicial leadership and broad system improvement efforts; reviews the current status of research and evaluation in juvenile dependency judicial practice; highlights several current controversial and contested issues for juvenile dependency courts; and offers some concluding remarks.

Laws, Constraints, and Obligations on Juvenile Dependency Courts

The United States court system is made up of both federal and "state" courts. Court systems on the state and county level are locally defined and operated. Unified state court systems exist in many states and both federal and state law drive their decision-making; others operate their court system from a county level, in which local ordinances may also affect judicial decision-making. Two levels of appellate courts, the Court of Appeals and the Supreme Court, hear appeals in most states, but in a few, the first and only level of appeal is to a single appellate court.

There is no national "standard" for juvenile court operation that has been adopted by all state and local courts. Complicating the matter further, judges are not chosen in a similar fashion across all the states. In some states, judges are elected for specific terms, in others they stand for retention in a popular election, and yet in others, they are appointed and retained, either by the executive or legislative branch. Judges are elected or assigned to a position on the juvenile court bench. They may be elected to a specific seat to serve only in the juvenile and/or family court or they may be elected or appointed to a general jurisdiction bench, then assigned to the juvenile court bench by a presiding or administrative judge. Assignments can be voluntary or mandated by the presiding or administrative judge. Assignments to the juvenile court can also vary in duration. In some courts, judges are permanently assigned to juvenile court work. In others, judges rotate on and off the juvenile bench at periodic intervals that differ by state and local practice.

While both federal and state statutes set the framework for court oversight, given the many different types of court structures and judicial selection processes described above, local practice and local judges often determine how thorough and effective that oversight may be. In the field of child welfare law, both federal and state laws provide judges in the U.S. with broad discretion to decide issues of jurisdiction, disposition, and ongoing review in child welfare matters. The knowledge and commitment of an individual judge coupled with the local mores and beliefs in a community all affect the operation of the juvenile courts across the U.S.

Child welfare was first addressed in federal law in 1935 with the passage of the Social Security Act, but it was not until 1961 that state agencies were required to report to the court system when children were at risk of removal from their homes. Courts became involved in the child welfare system at that time, but carried little authority in directing service delivery from the system (Portune et al. 2009).

In 1974, the Child Abuse Prevention and Treatment Act (CAPTA) was passed, becoming the first piece of major federal legislation specifically addressing child abuse and neglect cases. Through CAPTA, federal funding was attached to child abuse prevention and treatment and all states were required to create child abuse reporting procedures and investigation systems. State implementation of mandatory reporting laws resulted in a rapid increase in the number of children who were removed from their homes and placed in foster care. It also resulted in increased caseloads for juvenile and family court judges.

Also in 1974, Congress held hearings to focus on the treatment of Native American children who had been removed from their homes. In 1978, the Indian Child Welfare Act (ICWA) was enacted into law, establishing requirements for child welfare agencies and a rigorous oversight role of the court when Indian children were at risk of foster care placement. Under ICWA, in order to place an

Indian child, dependency courts must find, by clear and convincing evidence, based on the testimony of a qualified expert witness, that the Indian child is at imminent risk of serious emotional or physical damage if they remain in the care of their parent or Indian custodian. Courts must also find that child welfare agencies made active efforts to prevent the removal of the child from the home. This placement standard is higher than the standard for non-Indian children.

Court oversight of child welfare case management increased significantly in 1980 when Congress enacted the Foster Care and Adoption Assistance Act. Leading up to the enactment of the Act, Congress held a series of hearings with a range of child welfare professionals and experts. According to the House Ways and Means Committee Green Book (1990), by 1980 Congress had concluded that there were several problems with the child welfare system at the state level. These problems included: (1) placement in foster care without the provision of alternative services that might help the child remain at home; (2) foster care placements that were too restrictive (institutional settings) and too far from home; (3) a lack of written case plans; (4) a lack of periodic reviews of cases; (5) parents not being apprised of their child's situation; (6) a failure to provide reunification services; (7) the creation of unnecessary barriers to adoption for children who could not be reunited with their families; and (8) a lack of information on the children in the system (Child Welfare League of America 2012). Because of these concerns, Congress vested the juvenile dependency court with significant oversight responsibilities of the foster care system. A number of new requirements and protections were added to the law, including a requirement that states must make "reasonable efforts" to prevent placement in foster care and to reunify children and their parents in cases where they were removed (Child Welfare League of America 2012).

Prior to the passage of the Foster Care and Adoption Assistance Act, child abuse and neglect cases were not a high priority on state court dockets. Hearings were cursory at best. Even after the passage of the Foster Care and Adoption Assistance Act, court hearings did not change significantly. Even though Congress intended that reasonable efforts findings would help ensure foster care was utilized only as a last resort, early implementation of the Foster Care and Adoption Assistance Act focused more on "checking the box on the court order" and ensuring state receipt of federal funds. Few dependency judges embraced their expanded role under the federal statute to truly make inquiry about the efforts that were made to prevent removal and to safely return children home. As dependency judges did begin to embrace this new role, tension arose in the relationships between courts and child welfare agencies. Child welfare had historically had relatively unfettered decision making authority and as some of this authority transferred to the courts, perceptions about roles and authority created conflicts, most markedly in those courts where the judges truly embraced their new roles.

The expansion of the role of the court led to the development of national efforts to improve court performance spearheaded by the National Council of Juvenile and Family Court Judges (NCJFCJ), the American Bar Association Center on Children and the Law (ABA), and the National Center for State Courts (NCSC). Court reforms, led by dependency judges who embraced their oversight role, began in several jurisdictions across the country.

In the 1993 Budget Reconciliation Act, Congress created the Court Improvement Program (CIP), requiring state courts to assess their practices in child abuse and neglect cases and to develop strategic plans for system improvement based on those assessments. An era of strong focus on child welfare court improvement began. Prior to the advent of the Court Improvement Program, in the vast majority of states, state and local funding was, and is not currently, provided to the courts for specific case types. Funding is provided to manage the court system in its entirety. Judges and court administrators must balance the effective administration of justice in many case types, criminal, civil, family, and juvenile, thereby creating almost a competition for funding among case type advocates both inside and outside the court. Unfortunately, for many years, juvenile courts did not enjoy a priority status. Almost from its inception, the Court Improvement Program changed that in many states, because courts, for the first time, had dedicated resources to assess court performance, create action plans for improvement, and actually see those improvements through.

In 1995, the NCJFCJ published the *Resource Guidelines: Improving Court Practice in Child Abuse and Neglect Cases*, the first comprehensive publication to guide court improvement efforts. The *Resource Guidelines* were utilized across the country in the first-ever assessments of court performance in child abuse and neglect cases. Initial court improvement assessments found that hearings were not timely, continuances were common, and that the dependency court was not a sought-after assignment by judges. The juvenile dependency bench is generally viewed as less important and as having less status than other bench assignments (Edwards 1992, 1997). For this reason, it is difficult to attract experienced and/or interested judges. This often results in new judges being assigned to the dependency bench and then rotating out or burning out after several years (Edwards 1992; Hardin and Koenig 2008).

As a result of the CIP assessments and the availability of federal funding, specialized, intensive training was developed for juvenile dependency judges to help them understand their oversight role. Juvenile dependency court "champions" emerged and led efforts to realize the intent of Congress to ensure the court was actively overseeing foster care cases. Hearings began to be more substantive, findings more thoroughly explored, and system improvement efforts more pervasive across the country (Dobbin et al. 2003).

The court role expanded further in 1997 when, informed by the *Resource Guidelines*, Congress passed the Adoption and Safe Families Act (ASFA). ASFA contained several provisions focused on moving children more expeditiously to permanency. The law specified that the health and safety of children was the paramount concern, leading to a favoring of children's rights over those of their parents. Timelines for parents to complete services were created, and timelines for court oversight were tightened. Congress also outlined circumstances under which parents' rights could be terminated without service delivery by the child welfare agencies. Many courts, who now had available training dollars as a result of the Court Improvement Programs, conducted rigorous training on the role of the dependency judge.

States passed conforming legislation for ASFA implementation. In many states, the ASFA implementation legislation provided an opportunity for clarification of the courts' role. Requirements for court hearings became much more stringent in terms of timing and required findings to be made by the courts. In Oregon, for example, state law clarified that courts bore the responsibility to determine the permanency plan for children, whether there were compelling reasons not to file termination of parental rights petitions once a child was in care for 15 of 22 months, and when and how children would leave care. While the court continued to rely on expert testimony (including caseworker recommendations) for actual case planning, including treatment needs of the children and families, the ultimate permanency plan determination was transferred to the court in several states.

The ensuing years saw the dependency courts take a much more active role in child welfare oversight both on and off the bench. Dependency judges also began to take a more active leadership role in system reform efforts.

Role of the Juvenile Court Judge

When it comes to the handling of child maltreatment cases, the juvenile dependency court and the juvenile dependency judge play a critical role. That role is comprised of both traditional and non-traditional elements.

Traditionally, judges are the triers of facts. That is, they establish and/or enforce the rules that are designed so that the different sides in a court case can present their cases in a fair and impartial manner. Judges, among other things, decide what evidence is admissible, and the order in which each side presents its evidence.

Judges are also finders of fact. They decide what facts are true depending on the standards of proof established by law, such as preponderance of the evidence or beyond a reasonable doubt. These facts may be preliminary, which may be necessary for other facts to be admitted into evidence, or they may be ultimate facts or findings such as guilty or not guilty. Juvenile dependency judges are triers of fact and finders of fact and more.

The non-traditional aspects of juvenile dependency judges were best described by Judge Leonard Edwards. Among other things, Judge Leonard Edwards (2005) stated:

> Judges in the juvenile court are charged with keeping children safe, restoring families, finding permanency for children, and holding youth, families, and service providers accountable. Every day, hundreds of judges make thousands of decisions regarding children in crisis. We decide whether a child should be removed from parental care, whether a child has committed a delinquent act, whether a child should be committed to the state for corrections, whether parental rights shall be terminated and similar issues. When parenting fails, when informal community responses are inadequate, our juvenile and family courts provide the state's official intervention in the most serious cases involving children and families. We are the legal equivalent to an emergency room in the medical profession. We intervene in crisis and figure out the best response on a case-by-case, individualized basis. In addition, we have to get off the bench and work in the community. We have to convene child and family-serving agencies, schools, and the community around the problems facing our most vulnerable and troubled children. We have to ask these agencies and the community to work together to support our efforts so that the orders we make on the bench can be fulfilled. We have to be the champions of collaboration (p. 8).

Much of this role can be traced to the oversight responsibility placed on the juvenile dependency court by the Adoption Assistance and Child Welfare Act of 1980, which was enacted by Congress. This landmark legislation requires that, among other things: (1) the state provides services to prevent removal of children from their homes in order to be eligible for federal funds; (2) the juvenile dependency court makes reasonable efforts findings that the state has provided services to keep children at home before they are placed in foster care; (3) the juvenile dependency court finds that the state has made reasonable efforts to reunite foster children with their parents; (4) the juvenile dependency court determines there is a case plan to ensure placement in family-like settings, close to the parents' home and consistent with the best interests and needs of the child; and (5) the juvenile dependency court regularly reviews the status of every foster child so that a child receives timely permanence, either by going home or through adoption.

Generally speaking, the juvenile dependency court must determine whether abuse or neglect has occurred; whether a child should be removed from home; whether there are services to prevent removal; where and with whom a child should be placed upon removal; which services are necessary for the parents to reunite with the child; what is the visitation plan; what services are necessary for the care of the child; whether the agency has provided a reasonable effort for the parents to have a meaningful opportunity to reunify with the child; whether permanency has been achieved for the child in a timely manner, and more.

In addition to these courtroom functions, the juvenile dependency judge has administrative, collaborative and advocacy obligations (Edwards 1992). For example, under California's Judicial Administration Standards, Standard 5.40, the administrative obligations of a presiding juvenile court judge are to motivate and educate other dependency judges about the significance of the dependency court; work to ensure there are adequate staff, facilities, and financial resources for the juvenile court to have adequate time to hear matters before it; provide training for attorneys in the juvenile court; *inter alia*. To fulfill their collaborative and advocacy obligations, juvenile dependency judges are encouraged to provide active leadership within the community. As a leader, judges should encourage attorneys to practice in juvenile court, establish minimum standards of practice, work directly with the community to assess the needs of, and develop resources and services for at-risk children (e.g., delinquents, dependents, and status offenders) and families. Further, dependency judges should investigate and determine the availability of specific prevention, intervention, and treatment services in the community for at-risk children and their families and exercise their authority by statute or rule to review, order, and enforce the delivery of specific services and treatment as needed for the children and families they serve. As a leader in the community, it is the responsibility of the juvenile dependency judge to educate the community and its institutions through every available means, including the media, concerning the role of the juvenile court in meeting the complex needs of at-risk children and their families. Collectively, these obligations highlight the importance and complexity of the juvenile court judge's position.

Judicial Leadership and Systems Improvement

Juvenile dependency judges are in a unique position to assume the mantle of leadership to effect system change and to bring dependency stakeholders to the table and to lead a change effort by nature of their positional power. When a judge calls a meeting, people come (Dobbin et al. 2004). Early collaborative system reform efforts began in "Model Court" sites supported by the NCJFCJ. These innovative courts and strong judicial leaders "model" an ongoing commitment to court and system reform.

Over time, the leadership role of the judge became better defined, stakeholders began to expect and appreciate leadership from judges both on and off the bench, leading to stronger collaboration in system reform efforts. During the late 1990s and early 2000s, these efforts focused mostly on output measures. Courts were improving the timeliness of their hearings, the thoroughness of their hearings, the number of parties attending, and other key components of the *Resource Guidelines*. As time passed, courts and their collaborative reform teams evolved to measuring actual child and family outcomes. For example, juvenile courts in New York, Los Angeles, and Chicago safely reduced their foster care populations by over 60,000 children, correlating with judicially-led collaborative reform efforts and changes in child welfare agency practice and attorney practice. Some assessments in response to these trends have concluded that the evidence demonstrates that children who have come into contact with the child welfare system have been overall as safe, and possibly safer, during this era of foster care reductions as when the number of children in foster care was at its peak (Casey Family Programs 2011a).

Just as leadership by individual judges can change one court in one county in one state, leadership by a group of Chief Justices, the highest judicial officers in the states, can change a country. In 2005, with funding from the Pew Charitable Trust, the first Chief Justices' Summit was convened in Minnesota. Supported by the National Center for State Courts, Chief Justices from across the country brought together system reform-minded teams to the first gathering of its kind focused on high judicial leadership. Almost all states were represented in the Chief Justices' Summit. Two subsequent summits were held in New York, New York, and Austin, Texas. As a result of the involvement of the Chief Justices, some states created Judicial Commissions to help lead reform efforts. These Commissions have been responsible for improving educational outcomes and improving services for children aging out of the system, among other topic areas.

While some questions remain about the role of the judge off the bench, leading system reform efforts have become widely accepted across the country. State Court Improvement Programs have helped to establish judicially-led statewide reform efforts with collaborative teams working on systems change goals ranging from process to outcome.

Research and Evaluation in Juvenile Dependency Judicial Practice

It is clear that juvenile dependency court cases require a high level of judicial oversight and decision-making. Juvenile dependency court cases tend to be lengthy – averaging nearly 2 years to resolve (U.S. Department of Health and Human Services 2008). Juvenile dependency judges make decisions regarding placement of a child, the service plans and safety assessments, and parenting time (visitation). Judges must decide if parents have made sufficient progress in resolving the issues that brought the child before the court so that the child can be returned home.

Historically, there has been a dearth of rigorous research on juvenile dependency court practices, judicial decision-making, or the impact of the court on children and families. Russell and Summers (2013) point out that, in particular, research on judicial decision-making in juvenile dependency cases is limited. A report by Summers and colleagues (2008) concluded that juvenile dependency judges need more and better research, especially research that ties findings to practical policy implications. Courtney and Hook (2012) echoed the scarcity of knowledge about the functioning of child welfare services and juvenile courts, noting a lack of research and evaluation on program impacts and practice evaluations. They too highlighted deficiencies in methodological rigor, research on outcomes of the juvenile dependency court process, and research on legal representation.

Aside from these limitations, there recently have been important contributions to the research literature on juvenile dependency courts and judicial practice in child welfare cases. Some of this recent literature focuses on new or emerging issues in child welfare and how the courts react or attend to these issues (e.g., Chuang et al. 2012; Coakley 2008; Han and Osterling 2012). Other contributions focus on empirical testing or examining the evidence for long-standing best practices, such as those outlined in the National Council of Juvenile and Family Court Judges' (1995) *Resource Guidelines* (Summers et al. 2011; Wood and Russell 2011).

Three areas of empirical research on court practice highlighted here are how courts respond to juvenile dependency cases involving the children of immigrants, family drug courts, and court programs to provide representation to parents and children. These three examples represent research on court practice that is still in its infancy. They do not, however, represent a comprehensive review of all research that has been, or that is currently being conducted on juvenile dependency courts. Research is emerging in other areas as well, including the efficacy of court mediation programs, the impacts of conducting thorough hearings, the constraints of judicial workloads, issues surrounding court compliance with the Indian Child Welfare Act (ICWA) compliance, the role of judicial leadership, the efficiency of one-family, one-judge programs, and court-led efforts to reduce disparities and disproportionality for children of color. Future work will have to continue to explore these topics as well as consider how changing child welfare practices might affect how courts respond to the child maltreatment cases that are brought before them.

Dettlaff (2012) examined the challenges juvenile dependency courts face when children of immigrants enter the child welfare system and how their experiences might affect their well-being. He found that courts need to collaborate more closely with child welfare agencies to facilitate positive outcomes for children in immigrant families. The experiences of immigrant families and children in the child welfare system have been examined broadly (see for example Han and Osterling 2012), but there has been little research on how court decision-making relates to outcomes for immigrant children and families.

Research on family drug courts has been solidifying. From their beginning 12 years ago, family drug courts today are commonplace, with more than 300 variations of the program throughout the United States (Huddleston and Marlowe 2011). In reviewing the extant literature on family drug courts, Marlowe and Carey (2012) highlighted the results of several evaluations they found methodologically sound. They concluded that family drug courts result in significantly better outcomes for dependency cases as compared to traditional family reunification services. In another review of drug court programs, Green and colleagues (2009) found that the programs were effective in supporting parents in substance abuse treatment so they could be reunited with their children, but evidence for better outcomes (i.e. time to permanency) was mixed. Another recent review of the research literature found that family drug courts are most effective at improving substance abuse treatment initiation and completion, but evidence for effectiveness in improving permanency timelines or increasing the likelihood of reunification was lacking (Oliveros and Kaufman 2011).

There has been interest from judges and other court stakeholders in a better understanding of the effects of appointing legal representation for parents and for children involved in juvenile dependency cases. Interest in the areas has focused on timeliness of appointment of representation as well as the quality of representation for both parents and children. Questions remain about how these factors may affect case timelines (i.e. time from petition filing to a permanency planning hearing) and case outcomes (i.e. the likelihood of reunification or of termination of parental rights). In a review of a pilot program to enhance the quality of parent representation Washington State, Courtney and Hook (2012) found that the program helped families achieve reunification about a month sooner, and children who could not be reunified achieved other permanency outcomes about a year sooner. Using data from four California counties and three Colorado counties, Wood and Russell (2011) found that the likelihood over time of returning children to the parents they were removed from was significantly higher when the mother and the mother's attorney were present at court hearings. Beyond these specific examples, there has been a clear impetus toward more research, program evaluation, and evidence based practices in juvenile dependency courts.

To engender a greater capacity for performance measurement, in 2008, the Department of Health and Human Services' Children's Bureau and the Department of Justice's Office of Juvenile Justice and Delinquency Prevention, in partnership with the NCJFCJ, the NCSC and the ABA, released *The Toolkit for Court Performance Measures in Child Abuse and Neglect Cases*. Through an extensive collaborative process, the *Toolkit* identifies 30 measures of court performance in juvenile dependency cases focusing on court practice in four areas: safety, permanency, due process, and timeliness (see Flango 2001, for the development of the measures). While the development of court performance measures was a necessary first step to bolstering program evaluation for courts, in the *Toolkit Users Guide*, Gatowski and Dobbin (2008), noted that "few courts currently have the capacity to effectively measure their performance in child abuse and neglect cases" (v).

In a corresponding effort, the Court Improvement Program (CIP) has been working with courts nationally to build capacity to measure court performance and currently expects states and courts to focus on continuous quality improvement (CQI). The 2012 CIP Program Instruction indicates that "state courts must focus on incorporating CQI into CIP activities for each grant by identifying: the outcomes they intend to achieve; measurable objectives to determine progress toward achieving outcomes; the data that will be necessary to monitor progress and measure success; and how those data will be measured and by whom" (U.S. Department of Health and Human Services, Administration for Children and Families 2012). This represents a significant and ongoing shift in focus for juvenile dependency courts.

The future of research on juvenile dependency court practice is likely to continue in this vein – a greater focus on outcomes, further evaluation of established best practices, continued assessment of how courts react to new social issues, and an increased focus on objective performance measurement. This progression is important; courts need to know what works well to improve the experiences of children and families with the juvenile dependency court system, what works well to improve outcomes, including well-being, for children and families, and what works well to operate an efficient and timely court system. In a world of scarce resources, courts cannot afford to ignore research, empirical evidence, and court performance statistics.

The progression will be challenging, however. As Gatowski and Dobbin (2008) stated, many courts do not currently have the capacity to measure their outcomes, to track performance measures, or to evaluate their programs and practices. However, many courts are on a learning track to better understand the role of evidence and evaluation, to build effective data tracking systems, and establish a culture of using evidence to improve practice to better serve children and families.

Current Controversial and Contested Issues

There are a number of controversial and contested issues within the juvenile dependency field – including the over-representation of African American and Native American children in foster care, an increased focus on the well-being of children who become involved with juvenile dependency courts, and the opening of courts to the press and the public – that are currently being addressed on the national, state, and local levels. These issues have become the subject of much debate and research in the field, as stakeholders are seeking answers to the important questions regarding how to respond.

Disproportionality, disparity, and courts catalyzing change. African American children are consistently overrepresented in foster care. The most recent data report, taken from the Adoption and Foster Care Reporting System in 2010, shows that African American youth are represented in foster care at a rate that is twice their rate in the general population nationally, with state variations ranging from no disproportionality to rates more than six times the population (Summers et al. 2012). This overrepresentation appears to begin with reporting of suspected abuse and increases as the case progresses through child welfare and into the court system, often resulting in longer stays in foster care for children of color (Hill 2007; Westat and Chapin Hall Center for Children 2001). Researchers in the field have debated the cause – and to some extent the existence – of disproportionality and disparities in child welfare, leading many court to engage in system change efforts to improve treatment and outcomes of minority families.

The Courts Catalyzing Change: Achieving Equity and Fairness in Foster Care (CCC) Initiative was developed by the NCJFCJ in pursuit of a national goal to reduce disproportionality and disparate treatment of minorities in the child welfare system. Funded by Casey Family Programs and the U.S. Department of Justice, Office of Juvenile Justice and Delinquency Prevention (OJJDP), the CCC Initiative builds on the successful work of the Casey Breakthrough Series Collaborative (e.g., Casey Family Programs 2011b). The mission of the CCC Initiative is to create and disseminate judicial tools, policy and practice guidelines, and associated action plans that court systems can implement to reduce disproportionality and disparities. The CCC Initiative, informed by existing and newly developed research, evaluates decision points in the dependency court system, re-evaluates federal, state, and local policy, makes recommendations for changes or improvements, and recommends strategies for court and child welfare systemic change.

One of the tools created by the CCC Initiative, meant to help transform judicial practice, was the CCC Preliminary Protective Hearing (PPH) Benchcard. The PPH Benchcard is a practical and concrete judicial tool for use at the first hearing in the dependency court process, developed by building on the *Resource Guidelines* and reflects aspirational "best practices" for the Preliminary Protective Hearing, one of the most critical stages in a child abuse and neglect case. The Benchcard is built around two types of inquiry: internal and external. The internal inquiry is set forth in a self-reflection section containing questions designed to help judges examine potential biases at play that may affect their decisions. The external inquiry is laid out in both the due process related questions as well as the actual judicial inquiry of the hearing participants related to key dependency topics and salient issues that should be determined at the PPH.

An evaluation study of the PPH Benchcard gathered data from case file information (both court and agency files) and from courtroom observations on more than 500 children in Los Angeles, California; Omaha, Nebraska; and Portland, Oregon. Data from a baseline sample were collected at each of the three sites, and judicial officers at each site were randomly assigned to either a Benchcard group or a control group. Benchcard implementation appears to be associated with substantially higher quantity and quality of discussion of key dependency topics during preliminary protective hearings and increased judicial inquiry and parent engagement (NCJFCJ 2011).

Well-being. With the passage of the ASFA in 1997, Congress declared that the health and safety of children at risk of entering or in the child welfare system must be "the paramount concern" (p. 1). ASFA also provided payment to states to increase the number of adoptions. Because federal law imposed new timelines on foster care placement episodes, court oversight of foster care placement, and incentives for completing adoptions, the ensuing years brought a strong child welfare focus on permanency and safety. The length of time children stayed in foster care and how they exited were strong areas of focus for courts and agencies. The issue of how the children were actually doing in terms of their well-being was an afterthought at best and something child welfare workers thought was "not their job" at worst. In recent years, courts have taken a more active role in ensuring the well-being of children in care by focusing on their physical health, dental health, educational success, and other measures of well-being. In the last year, the Commissioner of the Administration for Children, Youth, and Families, Bryan Samuels, has clearly articulated a vision that children should be "better off" when they leave the foster care system. The Commissioner is clear that he does not believe courts and agencies should lose their focus on permanency and safety, but he is very strongly suggesting that states will be measured in the future by not only the length of stay, permanency goals, and re-entries, but also by measures of their actual success in education, employment, and other measures of well-being.

Courts have a role in ensuring that child welfare agencies are providing services to enhance the well-being of the children in their care. They must also ensure that children do not remain in the foster care system when only issues of the child's well-being are left to address. This is a tight rope for courts to walk. Children belong at home as long as they can be safe. They do not belong in foster care because a foster parent will support their educational goals more aggressively than their parent might. A focus on well-being should not result in children staying in foster care longer. It should, however, result in courts ordering child welfare agencies to provide services to children, once they do return home, that are aimed at completing the work begun while the children were in care to improve their well-being outcomes.

Open courts. Beginning in 1980, the United States Supreme Court held in a series of cases that, with some minor exceptions, the public and the press have a First Amendment right to attend criminal trials (Richmond Newspaper, Inc v. Virginia 1980; Globe Newspaper Co. v. Superior Court 1982; Press-Enterprise Co. v. Superior Court of California 1984; Press-Enterprise Co. v. Superior Court 1986). The United States Supreme Court has not extended the right of public access to civil or juvenile cases. Consequently, states have been free to decide how to handle public and media access in these cases.

Historically, juvenile courts have been closed. They were originally intended to be informal, non-adversarial and private to further the goal of rehabilitation and eliminate the social stigma associated with the juvenile court involvement. However, it has been stated, "Although private hearings were and are intended to further the rehabilitative mission of the juvenile system, the system has not operated effectively in all cases and has been criticized for its failings" (San Bernardino County Department of Social Services v. Superior Court of San Bernardino County 1991, p. 7). This has led to an ongoing debate on whether the public and media should be allowed to attend dependency court hearings.

Opponents of opening dependency courts argue that children who have already been harmed will suffer additional harm by public exposure and that exposing family dysfunction will interfere with the goal of rehabilitation and reunification of families. There is also a general lack of trust that the media will accurately report on cases and will mostly report on sensational cases that will create a misleading perception in the minds of the public. Opponents also express concerns that courts will still be closed to protect "prominent" citizens which will cause further mistrust of the system. To date, there is no research that demonstrates significant improvements in the system in those states which have already opened their courts.

Those in favor of opening dependency courts argue that increased public visibility of the system will create greater accountability of judges, lawyers, social workers and others who work in the system. Proponents also believe that the increased visibility will educate the public and lead to reform and resources for a traditionally under-resourced system. The underlying assumption is that the public has the right to know about the details of such an important system that is supported by taxpayers' dollars.

While a number of states have opened dependency proceedings, generally through legislation or court rules that grant judicial discretion to close, the substantial majority of states still keep dependency courts closed with some giving judicial discretion to open. The debate on this issue is not likely to subside any time soon.

Child welfare finance reform and the courts. Title IV-E foster care funding is guaranteed funding for all eligible children in state foster care, paying the costs of keeping the child in foster care, the administrative costs associated with placement, and some related training costs. It does not provide for services to the child's family before or after the child is placed in foster care (NCJFCJ 2012). Broad based groups are currently engaged in developing recommendations for child welfare finance reform. The current federal funding structure incentivizes placement rather than keeping children out of the foster care system. Court functions, like the hearings required by law to ensure children are not placed in care unless there are no reasonable services that would keep them safe at home, are not allowable costs under Title IV-E.

Because court functions are not allowable costs under Title IV-E, state courts must rely on their state legislatures to adequately fund their oversight responsibilities. Beginning with the recession in 2003, and expanding through the country's current budget crisis, state court budgets have suffered. While budgets for juvenile court services have decreased, mandates by the federal government have increased. State courts find themselves in a unique position. In order for state and local child welfare agencies to receive federal matching funds for foster care services, state courts must be in compliance with the mandates of Title IV-E law and policy. However, many do not have adequate resources to meet the mandates for timely and thorough hearings.

In other efforts to keep children safely out of foster care whenever possible, many courts have instituted programs such as pre-petition mediation and pre-hearing conferences to ensure children are not placed needlessly in foster care or languish there too long if they are placed. Similar to the court functions mentioned above, because these front-loaded services are court-based, they are not currently allowable Title IV-E costs. Amending federal policy regarding federal funding for court functions would allow many more courts to create programming and implement hearing practice to ensure children do not enter care unless it is the last resort and that they leave care as soon as they can be safe at home or when that is not possible, safely placed with another permanent family.

Conclusion

The discussions highlighted in this chapter suggest that both the expectations and constraints of the juvenile dependency court have been increasing over recent years. The role of the juvenile court judge has become clearer and more codified, as well as substantially more expansive – both on and off the bench. The collaborative efforts led by juvenile dependency court judges have led to substantive system improvement in many areas, while other areas still face resistance. Research and evaluation on judicial and court practice has been gaining traction, but many performance measurement, program evaluation, and broad research efforts face continuing challenges.

Big questions remain about the direction of system change and the role of juvenile dependency courts. In part, the role of juvenile dependency courts, and its evolution across time, is defined by how varied the practice of the judiciary is across the United States. Increases in federal funding, along with shifts in the structure of that funding and mandates supported by that funding, have created both opportunities and commitments for system change efforts led by dependency court judges. The sustainability of those opportunities, commitments, and efforts could, of course, be challenged by future funding uncertainties. It remains to be seen how juvenile dependency courts might respond to future federal funding, national political, and broad societal value changes.

These shifts can be seen already in jurisdictions that have experimented with or embraced differential response programs. Significantly, differential response has the potential to reduce judicial oversight of the population of children involved with child protection agencies. Some judges are deeply troubled by the reduction in oversight, while others view the issue as a separation of powers between the judicial function of government and the executive function of government. The long-term impact on the role of the juvenile dependency court has yet to be fully understood.

The potential effect of research around best practice recommendations is developing. While organizations like the NCJFCJ, ABA, and NCSC have begun to differing degrees to promote and commit themselves to the testing of long-standing best practice recommendations, that work is still in its infancy. Presumptions about the appropriate role of juvenile court judges and the potential impact of judicial leadership may be confirmed or challenged as systematic research and evaluation efforts delve deeper.

Ultimately, it is clear that the expectations and constraints of the juvenile dependency court have changed substantially over time and have expanded over recent years. Federal involvement, through funding and mandates, has clearly established opportunities for system change efforts led by dependency court judges. Many judges and supporting organizations have committed themselves to these efforts. How durable those commitments are moving into the future in the face of financial, political, social changes at the level of policy, practice, and programs is yet to be determined.

References

Adoption and Safe Families Act of 1997. (1997). Pub. L. No. 105–89, 111 Stat. 2115.

Adoption Assistance and Child Welfare Act of 1980. (1980). Pub. L. No. 96–272, 94 Stat. 500.

Casey Family Programs. (2011). *Ensuring safe, nurturing and permanent families for children: Foster care reductions and child safety*. Seattle: Author. http://www.casey.org/Resources/Publications/pdf/FosterCareReductionsand ChildSafety.pdf

Casey Family Programs. (2011). *New England safety and risk assessments*. Seattle: Author. http://www.casey.org/resources/publications/pdf/BreakthroughSeries_NewEnglandSafetyRisk_FR.pdf

Child Abuse Prevention and Treatment Act of 1974, Pub. L. No. 93–247, 88 Stat. 4 (1974). Child Welfare League of America (2012).

Chuang, E., Moore, K., Barrett, B., & Young, M. S. (2012). Effect of an integrated family dependency treatment court on child welfare reunification, time to permanency and re-entry rates. *Children and Youth Services Review, 34*, 1896–1902.

Coakley, T. M. (2008). Examining African American fathers' involvement in permanency planning: An effort to reduce racial disproportionality in the child welfare system. *Children and Youth Services Review, 30*, 407–417.

Courtney, M. E., & Hook, J. L. (2012). Evaluation of the impact of enhanced parental legal representation on the timing of permanency outcomes for children in foster care. *Children and Youth Services Review, 34*(3), 1337–1343.

Dettlaff, A. J. (2012). Immigrant children and families and the public child welfare system: Considerations for legal systems. *Juvenile and Family Court Journal, 63*(1), 19–30.

Dobbin, S. A., Gatowski, S. I., Litchfield, M. M., Maxwell, D. M., & Oetgen, J. A. (2003). An evaluation of Utah Court Improvement Project reforms and best practices: Results and recommendations. *Technical Assistance Bulletin, 7*(1), 1–147. Reno: National Council of Juvenile and Family Court Judges.

Dobbin, S. A., Gatowski, S. I., & Maxwell, D. M. (2004). Building a better collaboration: Facilitating change in the court and child welfare system. *Technical Assistance Bulletin, 8*(2). Reno: National Council of Juvenile and Family Court Judges. Retrieved from http://ncjfcj.org/sites/default/files/Building%20a%20Better%20Collaboration.pdf

Edwards, L. (1992). The juvenile court and the role of the juvenile court judge. *Juvenile and Family Court Journal, 43*, 1–2.

Edwards, L. (2005). The role of the juvenile court judge revisited. *Juvenile and Family Court Journal, 56*, 33–51.

Flango, V. E. (2001). Measuring progress in improving court processing of child abuse and neglect cases. *Family Court Review, 39*, 158–169.

Gatowski, S., & Dobbin, S. (2008). *Court performance measures in child abuse and neglect cases: User's guide to nonautomated data collection*. Reno: National Council of Juvenile and Family Court Judges.

Globe Newspaper Co. v. Superior Court. (1982). 457 U.S. 596.

Green, B. L., Furrer, C. J., Worcel, S. D., Burrus, S. W. M., & Finigan, M. W. (2009). Building the evidence base for Family Drug Treatment Courts: Results from recent outcome studies. *Drug Court Review, 6*, 53–82.

Han, M., & Osterling, K. L. (2012). Characteristics and factors impacting reunification outcomes among Vietnamese immigrant families in the child welfare system. *Children and Youth Services Review, 34*(1), 103–111.

Hardin, M., & Koenig, S. (2008). *Court performance in child abuse and neglect cases: Technical guide.* Washington, DC: U.S. Department of Justice, Office of Justice Programs, Office of Juvenile Justice and Delinquency Prevention. Retrieved from https://www.ncjrs.gov/pdffiles1/ojjdp/223570.pdf.

Hill, R. B. (2007). *An analysis of racial/ethnic disproportionality and dispartiy at the national, state, and county levels.* Seattle: Casey Family Programs.

House Ways and Means Committee. (1990). *Green book.* Washington, DC: U.S. Government Printing Office.

Huddleston, W., & Marlowe, D. B. (2011). *Painting the current picture: A national report on drug courts and other problem-solving court programs in the United States.* Alexandria: National Drug Court Institute. Retrieved from http://www.ndci.org/sites/default/files/nadcp/PCP%20Report%20FINAL.PDF.

Marlowe, D. B., & Carey, S. M. (2012). *Research update on family drug courts.* Alexandria: National Association of Drug Court Professionals. http://www.nadcp.org/sites/default/files/nadcp/Reseach%20Update%20on%20Family%20Drug%20Courts%20-%20NADCP.pdf.

National Council of Juvenile and Family Court Judges. (1995). *Resource guidelines: Improving court practice in child abuse & neglect cases.* Reno: Author.

National Council of Juvenile and Family Court Judges. (2011). *Right from the start: The CCC preliminary protective hearing benchcard study report – testing a tool for judicial decision-making.* Reno: Author.

National Council of Juvenile and Family Court Judges. (2012). *Child welfare finance reform policy statement.* Reno: National Council of Juvenile and Family Court Judges.

Oliveros, A., & Kaufman, J. (2011). Addressing substance abuse treatment needs of parents involved with the child welfare system. *Child Welfare, 90,* 25–41.

Portune, L., Gatowski, S., & Dobbin, S. (2009). *RESOURCE GUIDELINES: Supporting best practices and building foundations for innovation in child abuse and neglect cases.* Reno: National Council of Juvenile and Family Court Judges. Retrieved from http://ncjfcj.org/sites/default/files/The%20RG%20Supporting%20Best%20Practices%20and%20Building%20Foundations%20for%20Innovation%20in%20CAN%20Cases.pdf.

Press-Enterprise Co. v. Superior Court. (1986). 478 U.S. 1.

Press-Enterprise Co. v. Superior Court of California. (1984). 464 U.S. 501.

Richmond Newspaper, Inc. v. Virginia. (1980). 448 U.S. 555.

Russell, J., & Summers, A. (2013). Reflective decision-making and foster care placements. *Psychology, Public Policy, and Law, 19*(2), 127.

San Bernardino County Department of Social Services v. Superior Court of San Bernardino County. (1991). 232 Cal. App. 3d 188, 201.

Summers, A., Dobbin, S. A., & Gatowski, S. I. (2008). *The state of juvenile dependency court research: Implications for practice and policy.* Reno: National Council of Juvenile and Family Court Judges.

Summers, A., Wood, S., & Russell, J. (2011). Assessing efficiency and workload implications of the King County mediation pilot. *Journal of Juvenile Justice, 1,* 48–59.

Summers, A., Wood, S., & Russell, J. (2012). *Disproportionality rates for children of color in foster care.* Reno: National Council of Juvenile and Family Court Judges.

U.S. Department of Health and Human Services. (2008). *Child maltreatment 2006.* Washington, DC: GPO. www.acf.hhs.gov/programs/cb/resource/child-maltreatment-2008.

U.S. Department of Health and Human Services, Administration for Children and Families. (2012). *Instructions for state courts applying for Court Improvement Program (CIP) funds for fiscal years (FYs) 2012–2016.* Washington, DC: Author. http://www.acf.hhs.gov/programs/cb/laws_policies/policy/pi/2012/pi1202.pdf

Westat & Chapin Hall Center for Children. (2001). *Assessing the context of permanency and reunification in the foster care system.* Washington, DC: Department of Health and Human Services.

Wood, S. M., & Russell, J. R. (2011). Effects of parental and attorney involvement on reunification in Juvenile dependency cases. *Children and Youth Services Review, 33,* 1730–1741.

Chapter 28
Law Enforcement's Evolving Mission to Protect Children

Stephanie C. Stronks Knapp

Our lives begin to end the day we begin to become silent about the things that matter.

Dr. Martin Luther King

Introduction

The mission of protecting children and adolescents from maltreatment and exploitation has seen many advances since the initial publication of C. Henry Kempe's landmark research and publication of the first edition of "The Battered Child Syndrome" (Kempe and Helfer 1968). Society as a whole was finally able to recognize child abuse and neglect as a predominantly social issue and establish a platform point from which to proceed with the identification, assessment, investigation, prosecution, treatment and the prevention of child maltreatment. Prior to this, child abuse was not identified or acknowledged as an issue requiring an external response outside one's immediate family.

As our fundamental understanding and knowledge of investigating child abuse and neglect cases and the development of improved investigative techniques have increased dramatically over the last 50 years, so too have the challenges associated with law enforcement's role in protecting children. This higher level of awareness by dedicated law enforcement professionals to provide their best efforts to successfully investigate cases has come with both the celebration of achievements coupled with lasting and impactful changes in the field, as well as the struggles inherent in redefining traditional investigative principles.

This chapter will address the current state of the law enforcement communities' efforts to combat child abuse. It will attempt to celebrate the highlights of the field, outline the current status of **best practice** in the field of child abuse investigations, and raise challenging issues which are currently encouraging the field to continue to move forward with the arrival of an always-growing awareness of best practices for law enforcement that continue to evolve. It will also attempt to address some of the controversial issues currently facing law enforcement in its efforts to continue to battle against those who prey on children.

S.C.S. Knapp, MSW, LCSW (✉)
Child/Adolescent Forensic Interviewer, FBI Office for Victim Assistance,
Denver Division, Loveland RA, Loveland, Colorado, USA
e-mail: stephanie.knapp@ic.fbi.gov

J.E. Korbin and R.D. Krugman (eds.), *Handbook of Child Maltreatment*, Child Maltreatment 2,
DOI 10.1007/978-94-007-7208-3_28, © Springer Science+Business Media Dordrecht 2014

Finally, it will address questions about the short and long term impact the direct work of investigating crimes against children has on law enforcement professionals. Generations of investigators have committed their lives to investigating horrible crimes of violence against children. As a result, they have become members of an exclusive group of professionals sharing experiences unique only to those who share their passion.

Best Practice

Each discipline responsible for providing safety and protection to child victims of violence has a vested interest in developing best practice methods for addressing child maltreatment in their field. The standardization of the investigative process must continue to be influenced and directed by the combination of evidence-based research and the collection of valid and reliable data, in conjunction with the practical real-life application of knowledge and experience from the field. Jones and her colleagues (2005) reviewed the research relevant to seven practices considered by many to be amongst the most progressive approaches to criminal child abuse investigations. Despite the popularity of these practices, little outcome research is currently available documenting their success.

The creation of specialized units, teams, and squads for investigating child abuse and neglect within agencies and departments prompted them to develop expertise in their specific field. The development of local, state, tribal, national and international partnerships established relationships critical to the growing need for law enforcement to continue to expand and increase their abilities and investigative efforts beyond individual agency jurisdictions, as well as perceived personal limitations.

The steady progression of collaborative efforts by law enforcement has led to the realization of the need for functioning and integrated partnerships in order to effectively investigative all types of crimes against children. Several national organizations have realized the importance of establishing "teams" capable of responding immediately to an alleged case of child abuse, abduction, homicide etc. by providing a surge of resources involving skilled and trained professionals and support staff to most effectively and expeditiously respond to a child in crisis.

The National Center for the Analysis of Violent Crime (NCAVC) is a component of the FBI's Critical Incident Response Group (CIRG), located at the FBI Academy in Quantico, Virginia. The primary mission of the NCVAC is to provide behaviorally-based operational support to federal, state, local, and international enforcement agencies involved in the investigation of unusual or repetitive violent crimes, communicated threats, terrorism, and other matters of interest to law enforcement (Federal Bureau of Investigation n.d.). Similar efforts are underway across the globe to pull together the resources of professionals and communities to best address the issue of violence against children.

The National Center for Missing and Exploited Children (NCMEC) is a private (501) (C) (3) non-profit organization which was created in 1984. The mission of the organization is to serve as the nation's largest resource on the issues of missing and sexually exploited children. The organization provides information and resources to law enforcement, parents, and children including child victims, as well as other professionals. Currently, the work of the organization includes 25 additional US Congressional mandates which demonstrate the efforts by policy makers to recognize the importance of developing and implementing policies applicable to assist those working to protect children (NCMEC 2013).

There are numerous other state, national, tribal and international groups designed to provide a multi-disciplinary approach to child abuse investigations.

The creation of Multi-Disciplinary Teams (MDT) as a fundamental expectation of how crimes against children investigations must proceed in order to produce successful outcomes is, in many ways, one of the largest successes of the progress made thus far (Bross 1988). An effective MDT is dependent on a shared understanding of its goals and mission, but also on shared knowledge of the general practices and procedures the team will follow in its efforts to investigate and prosecute child abuse cases as well as provide vital intervention services to child abuse victims and their families (Poole and Lamb 1998). The spirit of cooperation, the sharing of information, and case coordination are some of the benefits supported by a multi-disciplinary approach to investigating cases of child abuse and neglect.

Currently most states have passed legislation mandating the multidisciplinary team approach to child abuse (Jacobson 2001). There is also a statutorily-based mandate by the federal government for investigations of crimes against children to be conducted in a multi-disciplinary fashion (18 USC § 3509(g)):

- Medical diagnoses and evaluation of services
- Telephone consultation services in emergencies and other situations
- Psychological and psychiatric diagnoses and evaluation services for the child, parent, etc.
- Expert medical, psychological and related professional testimony
- Case service coordination
- Training services

This also includes requiring law enforcement and child protective services to respond to serious (criminal) allegations of child abuse within hours of the initial report being made. The challenge facing the early Child Advocacy Centers (CAC)/Multi-Disciplinary Teams (MDT) was convincing law enforcement and child protective systems to coordinate their investigations. Another challenge continues to be the difficulty of navigating the civil and criminal parallel processes which do not overlap legally, but can cause great controversy amongst the individuals responding to one or the other court. Instead of finding ways to assist one another, efforts tend to focus on isolating the processes. Failure to remove a child who remains in an unsafe or negatively influential environment is just one example. Children, who are not emotionally or psychologically supported by the caregivers in the home, may have safety and protection issues that should be addressed. This may also cause significant potential harm to criminal cases.

The MDT approach is integral to the success in the vast majority of child maltreatment investigations. "Children's Advocacy Centers stress coordination of investigation and intervention services by bringing together professionals and agencies as a multidisciplinary team to create a child-focused approach to child abuse cases" (Snell 2003).

The origin of the Child Advocacy Center came as the brainchild of Congressman Robert E. "Bud" Cramer (AL), who, as District Attorney in Huntsville, AL, noted that child sexual abuse victims were being bounced from agency to agency and interviewed multiple times by multiple professionals. It was his revelation that the very process that was set to protect children was traumatizing them and resulted in inconsistent statements, poor investigations, and uncooperative child victims and parent/guardians (NCA 2009). Congressman Cramer's goal to improve the criminal justice system's response to child abuse became a reality that has been replicated worldwide.

The research conducted by Kathleen Coulborn-Faller and James Henry in their case study on community collaboration in child sexual abuse cases suggests the focus of policy and practice in child sexual abuse investigations should be on professionals and system coordination. "Adults can and should bear primary responsibility for obtaining successful outcomes in child sexual abuse cases, not child witnesses" (Faller and Henry 2004). There is a responsibility to provide the best response possible to children, in the most effective, supportive and expedient manner. These multi-disciplinary best practice standards raise the bar to its highest level. They are achievable, and once in place, will make the admirable work of our colleagues much easier, and more importantly, will make the investigative process less traumatic for those involved.

Professionals in this field have a responsibility to implement best practices in conducting child abuse investigations. Investigative units, child protection systems and CACs need to be able to accommodate the needs of multi-disciplinary team members' investigative responsibilities when the child is in need of protection. When those resources are not made available at the time of outcry, then the systems which were designed to provide protection may only hinder individuals' ability to perform at the highest standard of protection and investigative practices for children.

Along with the growing movement of the multi-disciplinary approach to investigating child maltreatment, came the realization that MDT members required abuse-specific training in order to best execute child abuse investigations. Currently many states hold their own conferences on child maltreatment to bring together professionals dedicated to providing the best possible and most up-to-date training for members providing investigative services to their communities. Local jurisdictions also provide training on a smaller scale to those involved in the investigation of child abuse cases. Nationally, conferences aimed at providing state-of-the-art and up-to-date training on the best practice models for investigating cases are held annually: the Internet Crimes Against Children (ICAC) conference, Dallas Crimes Against Children conference, San Diego Child Maltreatment Conference, the Drug Endangered Children's Alliance, the National Advocacy Center's Symposium on Child Abuse, International Conference on Shaken Baby Syndrome/Abusive Head Trauma and the Indian Nations Conference are just a few examples of trainings held annually or bi-annually. These conferences provide a gathering place for experts and attendees to increase their knowledge of current best practice models for investigating child abuse, to learn practices supported by research, new trends in investigating cases, and to network with the larger community of law enforcement professionals in the field.

Although great efforts have been made to improve and standardize the training law enforcement receives in order to prepare new investigators for the field of child abuse and neglect investigations, one of the largest deficiencies that has been identified is a failure to provide adequate training **prior** to investigators entering the field. Investigators are often rotated in to and out of investigator positions, with very little knowledge and experience into the unique challenges of investigating various types of crimes against children. Often times, newly assigned investigators are given very little time to learn from experienced colleagues and are forced to conduct investigations with a limited or sometimes non-existent level of experience, placing them at a distinct disadvantage. Although basic investigatory skills can be applied, understanding the distinct differences between investigating various forms of abuse can mean the difference between a successful case outcome and a case being closed from the onset. Simply stated, investigators new to these violations "don't know what they don't know". This hinders investigators with their subjects and other multi-disciplinary team members and can result in growing frustration, incomplete investigations, and a building apathy towards the investigative process. Unlike most criminal investigations, often times the first step in determining involvement in a case is to determine whether or not a crime has actually been committed. Did the child die as a result of an accidental injury, natural causes, or did someone intentionally inflict the trauma or neglectfully behave resulting in a child's death? Is the abnormal medical finding to this young child's genital area a result of inflicted penetrating trauma (sexual abuse) or is it explained by some reasonable medical condition or accidental trauma? These dilemmas can be missed by an untrained investigator and cases that should have been pursued are not, and cases that should not be investigated are engaged in while resources and valuable time is expended unnecessarily.

If we are to see continued growth in the quality of child abuse investigations, we must advocate for a change in this practice. Investigators assigned to or even volunteering for positions in specialized units or specifically designated to investigate case of child abuse and neglect must receive training and support for expanding their knowledge base of these types of investigations, prior to receiving their first case. Each type of child abuse violation requires a very different and unique skill set to be investigated properly. Training that prepares individuals in these areas is imperative for maintaining high quality investigations and guaranteeing the best possible investigation by law enforcement members of the MDT. Additionally, it is equally important for child abuse investigators to be encouraged and supported, both financially and administratively, to participate in cross-discipline trainings that are conducted by experts within the MDT community. Gaining a baseline understanding of the elements of how a forensic pediatrician diagnoses an abusive head injury, or how a child protection worker must meet certain civil elements in order to mandate a family to treatment or ask for temporary placement of a child while an investigation is being conducted can be instrumental for the lead investigator if he or she understands how his/her efforts impact and affect the other team member's ability to be successful.

Law enforcement leadership needs to understand the importance of investigating child maltreatment from all disciplines' perspective. Mandating that investigators be trained "outside" of their stated expertise is a valuable investigative process. Often there is a lack of support and understanding for the importance of cross-training their crimes against children personnel. Simply having employees meet their departments' minimum-mandatory training requirements often becomes the highest priority for training. This developing trend will ultimately adversely affect the child abuse investigator's ability to most effectively conduct investigations that will result in best outcomes for the case and best outcomes for the children they work to protect.

Another essential element for law enforcement management to consider is their obligation to "put some real effort in screening and identifying the right investigators for child abuse and what a train wreck it is when you have apathetic or indifferent people assigned to this work," comments a veteran child abuse investigator. Vetting out the appropriate candidate for a position whose primary responsibility will be to investigate cases of child maltreatment, and requires the capacity for skillful decision making and relationship building should be a high priority. It should also be as important to assure that the candidate has the right temperament for this work. In failing to do so, we see a high turn-over rate of investigators which greatly impedes these investigations. By the time someone is trained and understands the intricate details and dynamics of these cases, they have been transferred, promoted, or removed and replaced with a novice investigator, compelling the process to start all over.

The ability of a child abuse investigator to connect and work collaboratively with a prosecutor responsible for the prosecution of child abuse cases is also an understated and underappreciated relationship. As noted above, working with other disciplines and understanding how they function within their discipline is critical to successful outcomes of cases. Arguably, the most important relationship the child abuse investigator has is with his/her prosecuting attorney. Trusting that the prosecutor assigned to your case will execute the same effort and dedication investigators demand of themselves can result in positive prosecutorial results.

This relationship is important for many reasons including the end result of holding someone accountable for their violent actions against children, stops the abuse from happening, prevents that individual from abusing additional children, and validates the child's involvement in the process. This encourages the MDT to continue their quest to address child abuse and neglect in their communities. If cases are not prosecuted, if efforts are not made to bring justice for victims through the criminal justice system, investigators begin to question the very time and effort they commit.

In the words of an investigator, "What does it matter if I do my job, when no one is going to take my work and do something with it? What's the point?" Sadly, this sentiment is shared across the world. Investigators and prosecutors must work cooperatively to ensure successful outcomes and avoid a breakdown of the system.

There are arguments on both sides of this issue. Prosecutors complain that cases aren't investigated to the level necessary for successful prosecution in the criminal justice system; Prosecutors are frustrated with shoddy investigations and incomplete case preparation. Investigators feel as if prosecutors want perfection, and are often unwilling to risk "losing" a case in court than taking a chance with a judge or a jury.

Sadly, at times, both disciplines are accurate in their assessments of other team members. Unless a case is investigated properly and with diligence, having covered as many potential defense issues they can anticipate, prosecutors are left with little options but to decline or are forced to refuse prosecution of the case. Conversely, prosecutors who are unwilling to work with investigators to provide guidance and support through the investigative process, such as failing to respond in a timely fashion to requests for search warrants or to address other legal issues that arise as a result of the investigation, can have detrimental effects on the investigators' work. When prosecutors fail to take cases, due to lack of experience or confidence in their abilities, or to prohibit judges and juries from evaluating cases because the prosecutors believe they already know what the outcome will be and want to determine the validity of cases without engaging the process, then the system fails the very children it is aiming to protect. Better efforts must be made to work together, communicate needs, and work in unison.

Investigative Window of Opportunity

> We must use time as a tool, not as a couch. –John F. Kennedy

The single most important advantage a multi-disciplinary team or lone investigator has in any type of child abuse investigation is the Investigative Window of Opportunity (IWOP) (for further information see Johnson 2009).

Simply defined, these are the precious minutes that occur either during or immediately after the initial outcry of a child victim of abuse or report of concern made to an appropriate person of authority. This is the optimum time to conduct investigative tasks for the purpose of gleaning the most detailed information. For every hour that goes by after the initial outcry without multi-disciplinary team investigative intervention, information critical to case evaluation is lost. As days pass, critical information may be lost forever.

Each child abuse case presents six "windows of opportunity:"

1. Forensic/Investigative Interview of Child Abuse Victims/Witnesses

The goal of a forensic interview is to obtain a statement from a child/adolescent, in a developmentally sensitive, unbiased and legally defensible manner, that will support accurate and fair decision making in the criminal justice and child welfare systems.

Information obtained from an investigative interview might be useful for making treatment decisions; although the interview is not part of the treatment process.

The two overriding features of a forensic interview (Poole and Lamb 1998):

1. Forensic interviews are **hypothesis testing** rather than **hypothesis confirming** (Ceci and Bruck 1995).
2. Forensic interviews should be **child-centered**.

Forensic interviews have emerged in the field as a vital step to the investigative process. It should be noted, that the "forensic" interview must emphasize the importance of "obtaining legally relevant information" (Connell 2012) – the details that assist investigator and child protection workers in corroborating statements by the interviewee. The crime of victimizing children most often happens within the secrecy and isolation of a perpetrators' control, and during any number of circumstances. Therefore, more often than not, a victim's statement about the alleged crime is a primary focus for developing corroborative evidence to support the allegations or to assist in determining that child abuse has not occurred.

Children outcry for a multitude of reasons, which can be characterized in two areas: the purposeful outcry and the accidental outcry. In discussing the "traumagenics" of child sexual abuse, David Finkelhor and Angela Brown (1985) write that in situations of accidental outcries of children, the forensic interview may create an "acute psychological episode that may lead to fragmented and unconvincing statements." In other words, unlike the purposeful outcry where the victim experiences "relief" at disclosing the abuse, the "accidental" child may still feel partnership in the abuse, thus disclosing the abuse is tantamount to a confession of guilt. The purposeful outcry usually occurs when the child intends to disclose to someone that the abuse is occurring. This outcry is frequently accompanied by a heightened emotional state in the child, who may state that she is "afraid" or "tired" of the abuse. Many of these children, due to their developmental age, have only recently become aware that the abuse is wrong. Conversely, the accidental outcry occurs when the child makes offhand statements, demonstrates behaviors or another person unintentionally discovers that abuse may be occurring. Although the child may not be prepared to make the outcry, the resulting crisis has the same accompanying heightened emotional state, which may allow investigators to obtain more detailed information (Finkelhor and Brown 1985). Yet, there is a critical distinction between children who have already disclosed to someone and children who have not. And, research supports that "most victims delay their disclosure" (Ceci et al. 2005).

In general, the window of opportunity for conducting these forensic interviews in child sexual abuse cases is immediately after the child makes the outcry. With each passing minute without intervention, several factors begin to occur, none of which are helpful to the investigation:

The Process of Multiple Interviews. The child may be spoken to by counselors, nurses or school personnel who may not be trained in forensic interviewing or are otherwise unaware of the importance of obtaining detailed, accurate information from the child. All of these "unofficial" interviews can cloud the pure information that should be obtained from the child during the forensic/investigative interview.

The Family's Access to the Child. Others may notify the child's caregivers – the non-offending caregiver and the potential perpetrator – who will then have access to the child. Additionally, siblings in the household have been known to be unsupportive of child abuse victims due to the emotional upheaval that the child's outcry causes in the home. Ultimately this may impact the nature, accuracy, and content of the child's statement. This phenomenon is known as taint and/or contamination and can have lasting detrimental effects on both the child and the case.

The Victim Feels Responsible for the Responses of Others. The child comes to understand very quickly that the outcry has caused a considerable amount of reaction from those around him/her (family, school, siblings, law enforcement, child protective services, etc.). This dynamic is a major causal factor for recantation. Although timely interviews of children and adolescents are critical, so too is the need to assess the child's ability to make a statement at any given time. Interviews of witnesses and victims, if not conducted immediately, may need to occur at a later time if it is determined that participating in the interview process may potentially have detrimental effects on the child's best interest. The MDT must discuss the prospective harms and risks associated with interviewing a child, who is not mentally or emotionally prepared or considered physically safe before the interview is conducted. This may also impact the child's ability to participate in the legal process in the future.

Many will agree that "the field of children's testimony is in turmoil, but a resolution to seemingly intractable debates now appears attainable… Although there has been consistent interest in children's suggestibility over the past century, the past 15 years have been the most active in terms of the number of published studies and novel theorizing about the causal mechanisms that underpin the observed findings (Ceci and Bruck 1993). Until or unless there is an alternative resolution to requiring children to provide testimony, investigators must seriously weigh the impact of how, when, where and by whom a statement is obtained by a child for investigative purposes.

Professionals in the field of maltreatment and in particular, subject matter experts for the field of forensic interviewing, would agree that any interview conducted of an alleged child or adolescent victim or witness of violence should be conducted in a forensically sound manner, by a specifically trained and experienced professional skilled in the art and science of interviewing. Conversely, there are a multitude of developing practices in the field that have generated growing controversy, and at times conflict amongst these same experts.

The increase of research addressing the issues associated with forensic interviews, how they are conducted, by whom they are conducted, where they occur, the efficacy of aspects of researched-based protocols, and how interviews are defended in court has impacted the role of law enforcement in conducting their own investigative interviews of children. It still remains that limiting the number of interviews of a child victim or witness through the investigative process is considered best practice. As stated in the American Prosecution Research Institute's *Investigation and Prosecution of Child Abuse* manual: "The number of investigative interviews should be limited to one whenever possible" (APRI 2004).

The growth of the CAC movement has created a dependency on CACs for forensic interviewing in some jurisdictions. When there is a delay in scheduling a forensic interview due to the lack of capacity to meet the need, this may interfere with the investigative process. There are also practices that have developed within the CAC movement that have shifted the focus of the investigative interview to one focused increasingly on treatment and assessment which can also impede the investigative process and result in additional interviews of victims/witnesses. Some of these practices have created conflict amongst the multi-disciplinary team members. More importantly, "information critical to case evaluation is lost" (Johnson 2009). Delaying quality investigative interviews from being conducted because of CAC or departmental policies and procedures can have detrimental effects. There is a chance the perpetrator will learn of the allegations and a multitude of problems can occur. He could contact and manipulate or pressure the victim, siblings and the non-offending caregiver, which can result in recantation or refusal to cooperate with authorities. The perpetrator might solidify his statement, create an alibi, destroy evidence, or seek defense counsel. Additional backlash from a delay in interviewing includes: multiple interviews by untrained, non-professionals; the child's inability to recall or unwillingness to disclose specific details of the event(s); and failure to support the child victim after outcry. The unintended consequence of this shift of the forensic interview being conducted at some CAC's has been a de-emphasis on the investigative detail-specific interview; one that must contain the necessary criminal elements required by law enforcement in order to substantiate charges and to further a complete investigation.

As a response to minimize the impact of delayed availability of having a forensic interview conducted, the concept of a minimal fact interview or "unofficial" interview was developed. "The purposes of a minimum facts interview are to allow the mandated reporter or the first responder to provide for the child's safety and to obtain the very basic facts concerning the child's maltreatment" (Children's Law Center n.d.).

In some jurisdictions law enforcement's reaction to this growing need for age-appropriate/victim sensitive interviews to be conducted in a timely manner, without interfering or jeopardizing the investigative process, has been the departure from a unilateral focus on forensic interviews being conducted at CAC's by non-law enforcement persons. If "the primary purpose of an interview of a child is to gain investigative information, law enforcement must be involved and …should never abdicate its control over the investigative interview" (Lanning 1996, p. 332). For this reason and others, investigators must be trained to conduct investigative interviews and be prepared to perform interviews with the victim during the investigative process. There has also been an increase in the creation of soft-interview rooms that are located within police departments and other law enforcement physical space. These interview rooms are minimally furnished and are meant to create an environment conducive to focusing on the victim. It is a victim-friendly environment that conveys the message of formality, yet comfort and support. Many of these rooms are used by law enforcement to conduct investigative interviews in an environment alternative to the CAC.

One of the reasons cited by law enforcement for this alteration, in addition to that noted previously, is a growing awareness of the changing face of victims. There has been a dramatic change in the manner of which children are being victimized. Victims and witnesses are increasingly different than the "traditional" sexualized victim. Compliant victims, travelers, sexually exploited victims (computer facilitated); victims of commercial sexual exploitation (human trafficking), abducted children, and other vulnerable populations are just some of the more common types of victims law enforcement is working to protect.

Additionally, victims who may also present as potential subjects of criminal behavior during their victim interview are a prevalent victim population with unique circumstance and considerations that must be addressed, prior to, during and after an investigative interview. Victims who have no conscious knowledge of their victimization, who are now adults and being confronted with the photo-evidence of their abuse may suffer significant psychological and emotionally charged responses to the investigative interview. Developmentally-challenged and severely traumatized victims, both juveniles and adults, require a skilled interviewer who is not only able to glean critical evidentiary statements for the purposes of the investigation, but also prioritize the mental and emotional needs of the victim in order to not further victimize or potentially cause unintended harm. A victim-centered approach to working with these victim populations has proven in the field to have the best outcomes for both the victims in these cases, as well as successful case outcomes.

The changing face of the victim or witness in contrast to the "traditional" victim of sexual violence has challenged the status quo of investigatory interviews. Investigators must now be familiar with and competent in addressing issues of compliance, human trafficking, cyber-related offenses, computer facilitated criminal behavior, presenting evidence in interviews, modification of a traditional "forensic" interview to accommodate a juvenile victim of prostitution whose own illegal activity often makes them less than a cooperative victim, and a host of other changes to the traditional investigative interview. One of the struggles for the field is that it lacks reliable research and data specific to the evolving practice for conducting forensic interviews of these evolving victim populations. It is unclear how the evolving change in practice of interviewing adolescents and victims of crimes previously mentioned will impact victims and their cases in the long run.

It is also unknown how the practice of conducting interviews of victims specific to the violations previously mentioned will impact the mental and emotional well-being of those engaging in the investigative process. Increasingly, law enforcement has had to address issues of mental health, substance abuse, suicide, self-harming behaviors and traumatic emotional responses to their efforts. They are often unprepared and untrained in assessing these issues. Law enforcement has been forced to engage in this process and had to develop programs and procedures for referring acutely traumatized victims to the appropriate services. The invention of police-based advocate programs has provided significant relief to investigators needing assistance with making sure victim needs are being met, while maintaining the integrity of their investigation.

Much more data and research is required for us to continue to develop best practices in terms of effectively managing these new victim populations and evolving practices. Investigators must work in coordination with the MDT to continue to improve services to victims that further the investigative process, but does not also cause unintended harm.

2. Interview of the Non-Offending Parent (NOP)

Interviews with the non-offending guardian or caregiver can yield incredible amounts of detailed information that can be corroborated by investigators. The investigative window for this interview begins with the first person who speaks with the non-offending caregiver about the abuse allegations. The professionals, who do this, typically from law enforcement and child protective services, are in a position to observe the non-offending caregiver's first reaction (including surprise or non-surprise) and make critical assessment decisions. Every day that goes by following an outcry increases the chance that the non-offending parent will be made aware of the allegations by someone other than law enforcement, thus depriving the investigator of the opportunity to be present during the caregiver's initial reaction.

The emotions of the non-offending parent during these early stages can be used to accomplish numerous investigative functions. Observing the response of the non-offending caregiver to the information about their child's trauma can provide valuable information to the investigator. It is during this time that the non-offending caregiver is often most cooperative, providing detailed information about the incident and surrounding circumstances or cooperating with consensual searches and search warrants. Investigators who miss this window of opportunity risk having the non-offending caregiver contacted by the perpetrator or defense counsel, both of whom will most-likely suggest non-cooperation with investigators.

The non-offending caregiver is often dealing with issues such as humiliation, anger, guilt, abandonment, mistrust, loss of affection, jealousy, past victimization, and questions about their care giving skills. He/she may be in need of job training, financial assistance, housing, emotional support, and protection. The role of the police-based victim advocate is to introduce or reiterate the importance of victim-based services that include services to non-offending family members. Despite these factors, services are typically directed towards the victim and leave the non-offending care-giver with no one to turn to accept the perpetrator, who may be actively trying to regain his/her loyalties. If he/she reunites with the perpetrator you have lost your victim, because the perpetrator will work to persuade the non-offending caregiver to be uncooperative and pressure the victim to recant. By strengthening the non-offending caregiver, it helps to ensure the child's needs are being met. Additionally, the integrity and progress of the investigative process remains intact.

3. Interview of Collateral Witnesses

As with the non-offending caregiver and the perpetrator, the investigators who ask the first questions of the collateral witnesses have the window of opportunity for the most detailed information. This is especially critical because the information provided by these witnesses can be tainted by the perpetrator, defense counsel, non-offending caregiver or others. The witnesses may align themselves with the non-offending caregiver, the perpetrator or the child, thereby making their information less objective and more subjective. Additionally, people who may generally carry strong opinions about being pro-child, will suddenly believe that their family member, friend, relative, coach or spiritual counselor is the exception, and couldn't possibly be guilty of the allegations being raised.

Investigators are continually challenged to identify and interview collateral witnesses. The nature of the crime makes it frequently difficult to locate collateral witness. This is one of the weakest areas in all child abuse investigations. Defense attorneys know this and frequently try to use it to their client's advantage by charging that the investigators were not acting as objective fact-finders but as subjective believers who spoke only with witnesses the investigators believed would complement the prosecution's case. It is extremely important for investigators to immediately find, interview and "nail-down" collateral witnesses' knowledge of the incident, prior to the collateral witnesses speaking with anyone else.

Any statements by potential witnesses, to either corroborate secondary information about the alleged crime and/or report that witness's firsthand knowledge of the victimization of a primary victim, become increasingly important in terms of providing additional supportive corroborative evidence to the investigation.

Character witnesses suggested to investigators by defense attorneys should be interviewed or at least an interview should be attempted, even when it appears futile. If investigators refuse to interview a character witness, defense counsel is in an excellent position to portray the investigative process as biased against his client. This area is referred to as "fertile ground" for impeaching the credibility of the investigator and the investigation.

4. Perpetrator/Subject

Investigators are seeing an evolving form of offenders in that they are no longer just the one-victim, one mode of abuse but are also victimizing a large number of victims, over a large geographic area in conjunction with other perpetrators, and in an increasing complex manner. Children/adolescents are being victimized in multiple ways through a variety of media. Computer facilitated crimes have sky-rocketed, with the advent of technology. So too has the number and manner in which children and young adults are being victimized. The goal of the 2009 Butner Study Redux was to determine whether the former group of offenders were "merely" collectors of child pornography at little risk of engaging in hands-on offenses, or if they were contact sex offenders whose criminal sexual behavior involving children, with the exception of internet crimes, went undetected. The findings showed "internet offenders were significantly more likely than not to have sexually abused a child via a hands-on act" (Bouke and Hernandez 2009). Additionally, the study indicated that the "offenders who abused children were likely to have offended against multiple victims, and that the incidence of "crossover" by gender is high" (Bourke and Hernandez 2009). Possessors of child pornography will tend to offend children they have access to, regardless of the child's gender.

The internet has enabled offenders to gain unlimited access to potential victims and to increase the number of victims they are able to engage unconstrained by the proximity of victims. Offenders from across the globe can assault and victimize multiple children at a time, and do so with very little fear of apprehension by authorities. Their crimes often go undetected and they often remain anonymous offenders of children.

As with the non-offending caregiver, investigators who first broach the subject of child abuse with the alleged perpetrator have a "distinct investigative advantage" in gaining incriminating statements (confessions). The ability to see and hear the perpetrator's initial reaction is invaluable to the investigator's interview. However, this raises an interesting dilemma for many investigators regarding when the interview should take place. Should a majority of information be gathered before approaching the perpetrator, or should the investigator interview him in the earliest stages? After the forensic interview of the child is completed and the non-offending caregiver and witnesses have been interviewed, it is commonly believed that the next most critical function is the interview with the perpetrator. Ideally, especially with cases involving in-home abuse, interviews should be initiated as soon as the investigator has obtained enough information to conduct an effective interview. Under ideal circumstances this should be accomplished after the forensic interview of the child and the interview of the non-offending caregiver. "Interview the (alleged) subject as soon as practical. Utterly ridiculous and absurd statements that are not plausible, while not as good as a confession, have investigative and prosecutorial value," suggests a veteran child abuse investigator.

Most perpetrators can be described as manipulative, controlling and narcissistic (Johnson 2009). A long delay in interviewing the perpetrator gives him time to prepare an alibi or an excuse as to why he could not have committed the offense. It also allows him a chance to access those involved in the outcry (including the victim, non-offending caregiver or other pertinent collateral witness) to determine the nature of the allegation. Alleged perpetrators then have time to destroy critical evidence that may have been maintained, had the subject not notified that law enforcement was aware of his/her alleged illegal activities with children. It is a common experience amongst investigators that perpetrators will only confess to what they think the investigators already know. In a related issue, child protective service (CPS) workers and law enforcement need to have a mutual agreement about what details of the allegation should and should not be discussed during interviews conducted with the alleged perpetrator by CPS workers.

Polygraph examinations are a tool that can be useful in a child maltreatment case. In its traditional role, it can be used to determine if a suspect is responsible for the crime. In cases which a victim can't articulate who hurt them, a polygraph can also be used on multiple subjects determine if the examinee committed the offense, knows who committed the offense, and how the offense was committed. For example, parents, child care givers, or any other person with access to a child can all be tested for complicity in or knowledge of the crime. It is paramount to use a competent polygraph examiner with up-to-date education and state licensing (where necessary).

Offenders who have been convicted of a sex offense regularly undergo Post-Conviction Sex Offender Testing (PSCOT) as part of their sentencing. This is important to remember in an investigation involving known offenders who may have experience with polygraphs. An offender will potentially realize that taking a polygraph exam, if guilty, will focus the investigation upon him and may therefore refuse to submit to the exam.

Finally, a delayed interview gives an offender time to contact an attorney. This lawyer will almost always advise the offender not to speak with an investigator and not to cooperate with the investigation. This curtails not only an opportunity to obtain a statement from the subject, but additionally, the investigator looses any chance of the potential for consensual searches of phones, social media sites, computers, cars, homes etc. The loss of an alleged offender's statement can potentially be devastating to a subsequent prosecution. Regardless of whether or not the subject makes a full or partial admission any statement can be helpful to a future prosecution. Being able to "lock" an offender into a statement early on in an investigation is likely to be helpful to the prosecution. As stated by Katie Kutz, Deputy District Attorney for the Jefferson County Crimes Against Children unit. "Often a non-admission statement doesn't make sense and doesn't match what the investigator finds during the course of the investigation." This inconsistency can be especially useful in a subsequent prosecution.

5. Forensic Medical Evaluation

The investigative window of opportunity for performing the forensic medical examination of a sexual assault victim is immediately after the perpetrator disengages from the assault of the child. There is a recognized 72-h rule (or window) for conducting this medical evaluation. This 72-h rule has been grossly misconstrued. The untrained investigator believes he or she has "up to 72 h" to have a medical exam of the child victim completed. This is far from correct. Keep in mind that we get a positive medical finding of sexual abuse in less than 15 % of our cases.[1] Delayed medical evaluations by untrained forensic medical professionals can shift this percentage to almost zero.

Investigators should remember that the IWOP starts when the perpetrator withdraws his penis, tongue, hand or object from the child's mouth, body or sexual organ. The initial hours after the assault provide the medical forensic evaluator the best opportunity for identifying marks, bruises or tears, which immediately begin to heal, as well as for collecting other biological evidence such as semen, saliva and lubricants, which immediately begin to be absorbed, wiped or transferred away, thereby eliminating the very evidence that is highly corroborative of abuse. Likewise, once an alleged offender has been "put on notice", the integrity of the crime scene(s) is in jeopardy. Clean up of the area in which a child was brutally assaulted, burned in the tub, thrown against a wall or slammed down causing abusive injuries can be compromised.

It is imperative that investigators have access to competent and specifically trained medical providers, preferably, forensically trained child abuse pediatricians to assist in the diagnosis and treatment of alleged abuse victims. The partnership between law enforcement and the medical community is a valuable tool. Investigators who work in coordination with their medical community have great access to information and medical opinions without having to jump through unnecessary hoops that non-experts may impose. These partnerships allow investigators and medical providers to exchange valuable information in a timely manner. This relationship can also avoid the misuse of the Health Information Privacy and Protection Act (HIPPA) by some which has impeded the expedient exchange of critical medical information and the collection of evidence between investigators and medical providers. HIPPA specifically identifies the investigation of possible child abuse as an exception to the Act.

6. Crime Scene Evaluation

The window of opportunity for conducting the investigative function of evaluating a crime scene is immediately after the assault, before the perpetrator or others have the opportunity to disturb it. This can include individuals unaware that a crime was committed. For every minute that goes by, the crime scene is altered. Whether investigators become involved in the case immediately after the incident or

---

[1] Heger and colleagues (2002) find that only 4 % of all children referred for medical evaluation of sexual abuse have abnormal examinations at the time of evaluation. Kellogg and colleagues (2009) note that only 2 of 36 pregnant adolescent girls presented for sexual abuse evaluations had "definitive findings of penetration."

several months later, every attempt should be made to use as many crime scene identification techniques as possible, especially photo documentation (Vieth 2009), and other evidence collection techniques.

Although the IWOP focuses on the immediate response by investigators to current allegations of abuse or neglect, the reality still remains that the vast majority of child sexual abuse cases are historical in nature, meaning, the child discloses a significant period of time after the abuse occurred. As stated previously, disclosure often occurs for a number of reasons, none the least of which is when the child is in a "safe place" or hits a developmental stage where they realize or understand they were subjected to abuse. This dramatically impacts the investigator's response, as well as the MDT's reaction to the recently made allegation. The response must be timely, but well thought out and reasoned. The scene in a historical case has often changed greatly and generally things are not the same as they were when the abuse occurred. The investigator's focus becomes corroborating the child's statement in as many ways as possible. Obtaining the most specific details of the abuse is critically important. Additionally, the elapsed time period often means the subject has "moved on," in most cases, this equates to additional victims. This is why it is critically important for investigators to perform an in-depth look or historical review of the subject to identify other potential victims. Usually, if you identify a similar circumstance in the subject's life, you may locate another victim. Most courts allow these victims' histories to be used as evidence, even if they cannot be charged in the current jurisdiction. "This type of evidence is as good as a confession, so it cannot be overlooked by the investigator", remarks a veteran Special Agent with the FBI working sexual assault cases in Indian Country.

In regards to technology based-offenses, law enforcement continues to develop techniques to monitor and identify users of internet networks and systems. These techniques assist law enforcement in identifying individuals and groups who may be involved in the exploitation of children.

Investigators and prosecutors must be keenly aware of the "CSI-effect" and the popularity this television show has had on American society (Shelton et al. 2006). This is the same American society that makes up our juries. The influence of "CSI" on the issue of crime scene evaluation and the entire investigative process cannot be understated. All investigators are challenged to discuss this issue with their prosecutors and, at a minimum, provide clear documentation on results of crime scene evaluations and techniques used.

Cultural Considerations

All people, whether identified by their culture, language, rituals or customs, are also identified by how it protects its most precious gift, its children.

The incidence of child maltreatment has been found to be at a higher rate for racial/ethnic minorities. Income or socio-economic status is the strongest predictor of maltreatment rates (Sedlak et al. 2010). Although there are a number of factors not inherently related to race that have a strong correlation with child abuse and neglect, the NIS-4 report to Congress indicated that the three predictive factors identified in the study were all present in at higher levels in many minority populations, including South Dakota's Native American population (Sedlak et al. 2010).

Poverty, historical trauma, institutionalization of racial and ethnic minorities, multi-cultural environments, the inherent lack of trust in law enforcement, a conscious or sub-conscious bias, and societal apathy towards racial/ethnic minorities are some of the contributing factors to the disproportional representation of minorities in the child welfare system, although it is not conclusive or "evidence of race-based discrimination" (Krause 2011). On a community level, jurisdictional issues, lack of resources, lack of investigative training, poor child abuse laws, and nepotism are all factors to be considered that contribute to the perpetuation of child maltreatment in these communities. Additionally within individual families, guilt, shame, hopelessness, lack of knowledge of the child victimization phenomena, generational victimization and frustration with an ineffective system all play a role. According to research, elevated chronic trauma exposure and high prevalence of DSM IV-TR disorders (including both mental health and substance abuse disorders) have been found among large samples of American Indian adults living on reservations (Beals et al. 2005). "The bottom line is that people's individual needs vary and no one should be pushed to discuss trauma if they do not wish to do so" (Perry 2007). As all of these layers intersect, focus should be placed primarily on the needs of each individual child victim or witness, even when those needs seemingly interfere or contradict the investigative process.

Historical trauma is defined as a cumulative emotional response and wounding across generations, including the lifespan, which emanates from massive group trauma (Brave Heart 1998, 2003). Brave Heart and colleagues (2011) refer to the "historical trauma response; it has been conceptualized as a constellation of features associated with a reaction to massive group trauma. Historical unresolved grief, a component of this response, is the profound unsettled bereavement resulting from cumulative devastating losses, compounded by the prohibition and interruption of indigenous burial practices and ceremonies".

As violence and suffering of children and adolescents continues across the lifespan, the opportunity for victimization of this vulnerable population amongst indigenous people increases at enormous rates. The risk for children and adolescents to become victims of abuse, sexual, physical, emotional and severe neglect is a sad reality. Many indigenous communities experience many traumatic deaths with great frequency due to elevated morbidity and mortality rates, lowered life expectancy, and high accidental death rates (Brave Heart et al. 2011). Traditional American Indian/Alaska Native mourning practices and cultural *protective factors* were impaired due to the federal prohibition around 1883 against practice of traditional ceremonies, which lasted until the 1978 American Indians Religious Freedom Act (Brave Heart et al. 2011). Congress passed ICWA in 1978 in response to the alarmingly high number of Indian children being removed from their homes by both public and private agencies. The intent of Congress under ICWA was to "protect the best interests of Indian children and to promote the stability and security of Indian tribes and families" (25 U.S.C. § 1902) (NICWA 2012). Additionally, the Indian Child Protection and Family Violence Act PL 101-630 (25 USC § 3203) was passed.

Although efforts have been made to reduce the higher rates of violence, child abuse and associated criminal behavior amongst certain populations, the prevalence of abuse occurring over multiple generations continues to be a great concern amongst the law enforcement community. Generations of families become known to investigators. Their role as a subject, victim, witness or some combination of all three is a discouraging reality for many investigators responsible for providing services to these communities. The Adverse Childhood Experiences (ACE) Study found a strong graded relationship between the breadth of exposure to abuse or household dysfunction during childhood and multiple risk factors for several of the leading causes of death in adults (Felitti et al. 1998). It is not enough to stop the abuse, hold the responsible party accountable for their behavior, and remove children who are at risk from dangerous environments. Efforts must be made to stop the cycle of abuse and violence against children if any sustainable and long-term change is to occur in our communities. Law enforcement must work with various other disciplines to implement effective prevention programs, and work with those entities to promote policy development so investigations can occur within the context of a comprehensive program of protection, prosecution, prevention and partnerships.

Gaining Better Access to the Investigative Windows of Opportunity

Recognizing windows of opportunity is a critical step, but it is useless if procedural and monetary/resource issues prevent investigators from accessing them. The chapter assumes there are ample resources available for law enforcement in these cases; sadly this is simply untrue in many jurisdictions. The small departments and lightly resourced agencies that form the majority of law enforcement resources in the fly-over states and rural communities often do not have the resources the chapter addresses. If they are available, they are not nearby. This does not mean effective alternatives cannot be developed. Individuals who truly understand child abuse and are committed to developing these systems are needed to advocate for change and resource allocation. This is a whole other challenge.

Some of the most common errors that violate the investigative window of opportunity occur at the earliest stages of outcry, typically at a school, medical facility, therapist's office, or by a relative to whom the victim initially disclosed, by officials who delay in recognizing the abuse and fail to report their suspicions to appropriate authorities. Instead, they elect to notify the non-offending caregiver and/or the perpetrator, even worse, ignore the issue all-together.

In the recent highly publicized trial of Jerry Sandusky, former defensive coordinator for Penn State's football team, questions about the University's "culture" of insularity were highlighted. After Sandusky was convicted of 45 counts of a variety of sexual misconduct charges, Louis Freeh, former Director of the FBI from 1993 to 2001, publicized his findings in his report to the investigative counsel regarding the Penn State sex abuse scandal stating, "Their failure to protect the …child victim, or make attempts to identify him, created a dangerous situation for other unknown, unsuspecting young boys who were lured to the Penn State campus and football games by Sandusky and victimized repeatedly by him" (Freeh et al. 2012).

Freeh's report is a "very strong reminder of the dangers inherent in the culture of insularity" remarks Terry Hartle, Sr. Vice President of the American Council on Education in his response to the Freeh report condemning the "pervasive and damaging culture at Penn State in which the levers of power were tightly controlled by four men….and their repeated failure to deal with troubling allegations….always seemed to be directed by one goal: to avoid the troubling consequences of bad publicity" (Johnson and Egan 2012).

There are numerous obstacles investigators must contend with during the course of their investigation, not the least of which is outside influence. Investigators have been pressured by those with political power and financial means, notoriety and fame. Some will use these resources and authority to encourage investigators or their administration to deviate from investigative procedures in order to manipulate an investigation. Though not always with harmful intentions, it may ultimately affect the outcome of an investigation into allegations of child maltreatment.

Therefore, it is crucial to establish appropriate procedures and protocols and ensure that the entities responsible for alerting law enforcement to suspicions of abuse or neglect understand their role and responsibilities for reporting and know the appropriate course of action at all times. In addition, law enforcement needs to ensure that a trained investigator is promptly notified about each call and that the investigator responds immediately.

All programs benefit from evaluating the work and efforts of its members. Child fatality review teams, governors' task forces and other similar groups have been established with the goal of evaluating the effectiveness of the work being conducted and to identify areas for improvement for those working to protect children. These groups have generated recommendations to the field which have resulted in changes to policy and procedures, both on local, state, tribal, and national levels. Progress, in terms of continuing to develop best practice that is based on research and academic advances must, be tempered with the reality of implementation of investigative practice and common sense.

Everyone involved in a case must review cases for delays prohibiting investigators from responding immediately. The suggested evaluation technique from an investigative perspective, for the quality of a case, is to review the following factors:

- The exact time the child made the outcry;
- Identifying who spoke with the child before CPS or law enforcement became involved;
- Determining when and how the alleged perpetrator was first notified;

- Establishing when the non-offending caregiver or potential conspirator was notified and noting their response to the allegations;
- Identification of collateral witnesses and how long it took before they were contacted;
- Determining the last occurrence of the offense;
- Establishing how long it took before the crime scene was evaluated; and
- Indentifying any impediments by systems that may have had a harmful impact on the outcome of the case and for the child.

Additionally, it would be wise to determine the manner in which the MDT worked well and identify areas of conflict, challenges to investigative cooperation and areas to improve the working relationship with MDT members. Most often, poor communication amongst team members, lack of understanding each other's roles and responsibilities and misinformation about a particular case result in conflict and negative attitudes towards other team members that impede productive progress and have a detrimental impact on collaborative efforts.

Coordinated Response of Law Enforcement and Child Protective Services

Reviewing these situations will better illuminate violations of the investigative windows of opportunity. It also begins the discussion for establishing procedures/protocols to place investigators in the best possible position to access the detailed facts and information needed for investigative corroboration to protect the children in our communities.

There is a need to have a cooperative response system for child protective services and law enforcement. Law enforcement operates on a "call for service system," which means if a 911 call is made, an officer will respond day or night. However, a child protective service operates on a "priority system," in which a caller contacts a hotline and the call-taker assesses the need for intervention. If it meets certain criteria, a priority is placed on the call and the information is subsequently sent to the local CPS jurisdiction for evaluation by a supervisor, who will assign a caseworker to investigate. These two systems are inherently incompatible. Both address their agencies' policies and procedures, but neither gives paramount attention to the needs of the child. Specific issues, such as risk assessment by child protective services, medical evaluation, crime scene evaluation, and interviews of important parties should take precedence. No system should violate the investigative windows of opportunity by forcing the investigators to delay their response, thus losing access to detailed information. The cases in which we have been most successful were identified and investigated within hours, from the initial outcry to the major parts of the investigative conclusion.

The Elephant in the Room

"One of the most critical and ignored areas in law enforcement is the emotional toll this stressful occupation takes on its own people" notes author Alexis Artwohl, Ph.D. (Gilmartin 2002). Add to this, a concept that is so complex to understand and emotionally charged, even for those of us caught in the middle of its reality: The act of committing various forms of violence, neglect, and abuse against a child. It is this collision between the duty as an officer and the responsibility of investigating crimes against children that can have devastating effects on investigators. It is a challenge to explain to an "outsider" how deeply one may be affected by the work we have committed our lives to pursuing.

Often times, investigators are not readily able to acknowledge the impact this work has on them personally and professionally. Administrators rarely acknowledge the toll the work takes on their staff. Doing so would make painfully clear the vulnerabilities that are acquired as a result of a career of working these violations. The ability to express the thoughts and feelings with the trauma associated with this work is difficult; mostly because so many of us are not able to comprehend what is happening, until the impact is so profoundly evident. Moreover, acknowledgment of this impact is often feared to be a sign of weakness or incompetence by the individual. However, our loved ones often times are able to recognize the changes developing within the investigator, even before we do. "Although officers are winning the battle of street survival, they appear to be fatally losing the battle of emotional survival" (Gilmartin 2002). According to the first full study of police suicides in all 50 states which was published in 2009 it was learned that the suicide rate for police officers was 17/100,000, approximately 141 confirmed police suicides for the year, which has its comparisons to the shorter tours of duty by the military in a war zone (O'Hara and Violanti 2009). Police appear to be at greater risk of posttraumatic stress reactions (resulting from higher exposure to trauma) and job burnout (resulting from the way in which police work is organized), both of which increases the risk of psychosocial problems and suicide (Stuart 2008). Regardless of our attempts to deny its impact, there is no escaping the inevitable changes that occur within each and every one of us before, during, and after a career in this field. "Suicide isn't the only form of self-destruction: Depression, social isolation, and chronic anger also lead to the destruction of many other aspects of officers' lives that are not readily visible. The journey through the police career clearly takes its toll. Suicides are just the extreme tip of the iceberg" (Gilmartin 2002).

Professionally, child abuse investigations are some of the most difficult cases an investigator will work in the course of his or her law enforcement career. There are complex emotional, psychological and intellectual dynamics at play. These cases are by far, the least desirable ones to be assigned when working investigations. Very few investigators are willing or able to commit their entire professional life to a career in child abuse investigations. "People need to believe they have a significant degree of control over their day-to-day existence, a sense of predictability to most major events affecting their lives" (Gilmartin 2002). Sadly, the reality of investigating crimes against children is neither predicable nor easily controlled. It is often perceived as a constant battle. At times it can feel as if everything is a struggle, from collecting evidence, to complying with procedural issues, to avoiding inter-agency conflict, to battling motivational factors with other colleagues, and even getting resolution to cases. Investigators are often left with feelings of failure and deep sadness knowing the chances are high that a child's abuse will continue, that timely resolution to cases is often out of their control, and that very little ever changes.

Investigating child abuse cases removes the innocence and optimism about society in general. If all you see through the course of your career is unimaginable terror through the eyes of a child, senseless acts of violence targeted at children, children learning that adults can't be trusted and that their caregivers, whose love and affection a child should never have to question are not protecting, but causing unimaginable pain and suffering, investigators are forced to see the world through tainted lenses. "Law enforcement personnel, like all other human beings, form their worldviews and predictions about life from the situations and events they see every day" (Gilmartin 2002).

The ultimate impact on professionals is that we can no longer look at a child and not see them as a potential victim. We are not ignorant of seemingly innocent actions by adults with children, often interpreting them as attempts at victimization. We temper our interactions with other children, cautious of how our interactions may be interpreted by others, as we so often do. As an example, if you work child abduction violations, it's difficult to see a child riding their bike, walking alone to school or from a friend's home without looking around to identify someone who may be waiting to cause that child harm.

Conversely, we cautiously allow our children to experience the world with limits and boundaries that may be considered extreme or over-protective and unwarranted. We struggle to find a balance between protecting our own children from the ugliness of the world we see daily and their need to experience and grow from their own unique interactions with the world we have come to mistrust. Working in this field, there is no such thing as an innocent mistake when it comes to the safety and well-being of a child. Our jaded and cautious outlook on humanity has made us a rare and complex group of individuals. Patrons quietly move further away from us at the local establishment we have gathered at to share some of our experiences from the day. No one really knows what we do, because at social events when we are asked, "So what do you do?" we simply can't respond honestly, so we gloss over the truth by stating, "Oh, I work with kids" or we skillfully avoid the topic by switching the focus back to the inquisitor. No one really wants to know that I spent my day processing a brutal crime scene where two children's lives were taken by their drunken father as he slashed their bodies until they bled to death. Nor do they want to hear about the hours of child pornography video I had to endure watching in order to review the evidence and locate a child at risk. These aren't socially acceptable dinner conversations, but they are the real-life circumstances crimes against children investigators endure every day.

Investigators can't or don't want to bring this trauma home to their families. It is difficult to burden our colleagues, or acknowledge the affect a certain case has had on one's own ability to cope, and so we live alone in our world, compartmentalizing experiences so we can manage to continue to make a difference in the life of a child.

However, when our loved ones are protected and isolated from our work, they often believe it's because we don't want to communicate with them. Instead, it is because we want so badly to protect them from the pain and suffering we endure vicariously every day. We want to shield them from the nightmares that come with the fear that we didn't or couldn't do enough. **Questioning, what could I have done differently to change the outcome for this child and the others that will follow**? "The case" too often becomes the focus of our emotional time and energy, and perspective is often lost. We are at risk for failing to survive emotionally in this work because we care and we make ourselves vulnerable to the atrocities committed against children, believing we are able to and desperately seek to absorb some of their trauma.

All professionals, working worldwide to combat the epidemic pattern of violence against children, are affected each and every day, by the stories they hear, the violence they see and the scenes they enter into. We must do a better job of recognizing the ramifications of this work on the emotional, psychological, and physical impact on these professionals. We must develop ways in which to better address the short and long term consequences of surviving a career in law enforcement dedicated to protecting children if we are to maintain an experienced group of investigators whose careers can survive and thrive. We must also learn to identify when it is time to leave the vocation, and pursue different work. Most importantly, recognize that this level of self-awareness is a sign of competence and strength, not one of failure.

Conclusion

Valiant efforts have been made worldwide to develop and standardize investigative efforts proven to be most successful in combating crimes against children. As the types of criminal activity and manner of victimization expands, so too must the response by law enforcement. Consideration must be given to the efforts that will result in best outcomes for children, as well, as best outcomes for cases. This balance of doing what is best for both does not come without struggle. Attempts to judge one's commitment to the cause of protecting children creates unnecessary division and conflict amongst professionals, ultimately distracting efforts away from the noble contributions being made by devoted individuals.

Although everyone may not completely agree with the statements and observations made in this chapter the purpose is to challenge investigators and multi-disciplinary team members to continually increase the quality of investigations in order to protect children. We must hold one another accountable regardless of the obstacles before us. We must acknowledge that practice in the field will change as we develop standards and best practice models based in combination on science and research, as well as experience from the field.

The protection of a child hinges on the intervener's ability to acknowledge that a child's need for protection manifest in a multitude of ways. Members of the multi-disciplinary team must be ready to mobilize on behalf of the child. Investigative windows of opportunity are not contingent upon caseloads, schedules, personality conflicts, or notification procedures. When a child is in need of protection, members of the law enforcement community must be ready to respond.

We must balance the desire to commit efforts to the work without letting it define who we are and how we view the world. We must maintain perspective so as to not lose sight of the children, spouses, family members and loved ones who have the potential to become casualties of our work. Sometimes we need to realize that we too may be the one to need each other's protection in order to keep this balance.

We need to police ourselves to insure we are holding each other accountable to our commitment and duties but also be respectful of our colleagues. Working collaboratively and collectively to realize our goal protects those who cannot protect themselves. Respectfully challenge one another, but **do not** personalize these as attacks. We should never allow interagency or personality-driven conflict to interfere with the end goal, protection of children.

Aiming for the same goal brings us together but our differences make us better. However, we need to understand and be willing to accept the fact that good intentions sometimes result in bad outcomes. We need to view these bad outcomes for what they are, opportunities for growth and improvement, not as an opportunity to demolish others. Most importantly, have a willingness to accept criticism and be open to change.

The next generation of investigators honored with the responsibility of dedicating themselves and their work to the cause must understand that this work be done with diligence and passion. In remembrance of C. Henry Kempe's own words spoken on April 26, 1978:

> It is just not possible to worry about all the needs of the children all the time…For each of us there must be only one patient at a time. Thus one keeps one's sanity and does the very best job. At the same time, all of us who are devoting our professional life to the cause of children must engage our minds and our hearts on their behalf, each of us, and wherever we can: by the quality of our work, by being the child's advocate in our towns, in our states and by influencing national policy to our best ability.
>
> Do so with passion.

Acknowledgement The author acknowledges that various titles exist when referring to those responsible for the investigation of any crime against a child, for the purposes of this chapter they will be referred to as an *investigator*.

While acknowledging that perpetrators can be both male and female, for the sake of continuity, the pronoun he will be used to designate the offender. This use is not meant to generalize or make assumptions.

The author wishes to acknowledge Retired Child Abuse Detective Michael V. Johnson of the Plano Police Department for his significant contribution to this chapter. His conception of the investigative philosophy, the "Investigative Window of Opportunity" (Johnson 2009) resonates with this author and is used as a framework in this chapter with Michael's support and blessing.

References

American Prosecutor's Research Institute. (2004). *Investigation and prosecution of child abuse 39* (3rd ed.). New York: Sage.

Beals, J., Novins, D. K., Whitesell, N. R., Spicer, P., Mitchell, C. M., Manson, S., & American Indian Service Utilization, Psychiatric Epidemiology, Risk, and Protective Factors Project Team. (2005). Prevalence of mental disorders and utilization of mental health services in two American Indian reservation populations: Mental health disparities in a national context. *American Journal of Psychiatry, 162*, 1723–1732.

Bourke, M. L., & Hernandez, A. E. (2009). Butner study redux: A report of the incidence of hands-on child victimization of child pornography offenders. *Journal of Family Violence, 24*, 183–191.

Brave Heart, M. Y. H. (1998). The return to the sacred path: Healing the historical trauma response among the Lakota. *Smith College Studies in Social Work, 68*(3), 287–305.

Brave Heart, M. Y. H. (2003). The historical response among natives and its relationship with substance abuse: A Lakota illustration. *Journal of Psychoactive Drugs, 35*(1), 7–13.

Bross, D. C. (1988). *The new child protection team handbook*. New York: Garland.

Ceci, S. J., & Bruck, M. (1993). Suggestibility of the child witness: A historical review and synthesis. *Psychological Bulletin, 113*(3), 403–439.

Ceci, S. J., & Bruck, M. (1995). *Jeopardy in the courtroom: A scientific analysis of children's testimony*. Washington, DC: American Psychological Association.

Ceci, S., et al. (2005). Disclosure of child sexual abuse. What does the research tell us about the ways that children tell? *Psychology, Public Policy, and Law, 11*(1), 194–226.

Children's Law Center. (n.d.) *Interviewing child victims of maltreatment including physical and sexual abuse*. Available at: http://childlaw.sc.edu/frmPublications/InterviewingChildVictimsofMaltreatment.pdf. Accessed 19 February 2013.

Connell (2012). *Child and adolescent forensic interviewing: Human trafficking and sexually exploited children*. Seattle FBI Field Office. Innocent Images National Initiative and Child Against Children Unit of the FBI. Seattle, Washington. August 8–9, 2012.

Faller, K. C., & Henry, J. (2004). Child sexual abuse: A case study in community collaboration. *Child Abuse and Neglect, 24*(9), 1215–1225.

Federal Bureau of Investigations. (n.d.). *Critical incidence response group*. Available at: http://www.fbi.gov/about-us/cirg/investigations-and-operations-support/investigations-operations-support#cirg_ncavc. Accessed 7 February 2013.

Felitti, V. J., Anda, R. F., Nordenberg, D., Williamson, D. F., Spitz, A. M., Edwards, V., Koss, M. P., & Marks, J. S. (1998). Relationship of childhood abuse and household dysfunction to many of the leading causes of death in adults: The Adverse Childhood Experiences (ACE) study. *American Journal of Preventive Medicine, 14*(4), 245–258.

Finkelhor, D., & Brown, A. (1985). The traumatic impact of child sexual abuse: A conceptualization. *American Journal of Orthopsychiatry, 55*(4), 530.

Freeh, Sporkin & Sullivan, LLP. (2012). *Report of the Investigative Counsel regarding the actions of the Pennsylvania State University related to the child sexual abuse committed by Gerald A. Sandusky*. Available at: http://progress.psu.edu/the-freeh-report

Gilmartin, K. M. (2002). *Emotional survival for law enforcement: A guide for officers and their families*. Tucson: E-S Press.

Heart, B., et al. (2011). Historical trauma amongst indigenous peoples of the Americas: Concepts, research, and clinical considerations. *Journal of Psychoactive Drugs, 43*(4), 282–290.

Heger, et al. (2002). Children referred for possible sexual abuse: Medical finding in 2384 children. *Child Abuse & Neglect, 26*, 645.

Jacobson, M. (2001). Child sexual abuse and the multidisciplinary team approach: Contradictions in practice. *Childhood, 8*(2), 231–250.

Johnson, M. V. (2009). Investigative windows of opportunity: The vital link to corroboration in child sexual abuse cases. *Center Piece, 1*(9), 1–4.

Johnson, K., & Egan, E. (2012). Freeh report blasts culture of Penn State. *USA Today*, July 13, p. 2A.

Jones, L., Cross, T., Walsh, W., & Simone, M. (2005). Criminal investigations of child abuse: The research behind "best practices". *Trauma, Violence, and Abuse, 6*, 254–268.

Kellogg, et al. (2009). Genital anatomy in pregnant adolescents: "Normal" does not mean "Nothing Happened". *Pediatrics, 113*(1), 67.

Kempe, C. H., & Helfer, R. E. (1968). *The battered child*. Chicago: University of Chicago Press.

Krause, K. (2011). *Disproportional representation of minorities in foster care – a closer look*. Retrieved from: http://www.dakotahillslaw.com/disproportional-representation-of-minorities-in-foster-care-a-closer-look/

Lanning, K. V. (1996). Criminal investigation of sexual victimization of children. In J. E. B. Myers, L. Berliner, J. Briere, C. T. Hendrix, C. Jenny, & T. A. Reid (Eds.), *The APSAC handbook on child maltreatment* (pp. 329–348). Thousand Oaks: Sage.

National Center for Missing & Exploited Children (NCMEC). (2013). *Mission and history*. Available at: http://www.ncmec.org/missingkids/servlet/PageServlet?LanguageCountry=en_US&PageId=4362. Accessed 7 February 2013.

National Children's Alliance (NCA). (2009). *History of national children's alliance*. Available at: http://www.nationalchildrensalliance.org/index.php?s=35 Accessed 7 February 2013.

National Indian Child Welfare Association. (2012). *Indian Child Welfare Act of 1978*. Available at: http://www.nicwa.org/Indian_Child_Welfare_Act/

O'Hara, A. F., & Violanti, J. M. (2009). Police suicide – a web surveillance of national data. *International Journal of Emergency Mental Health, 11*(1), 17–23.

Perry, B., & Szalavitz, M. (2007). *The boy who was raised as a dog: And other stories from a child psychiatrist notebook: What traumatized children can teach us about life, love, and healing*. New York: Basic Books.

Poole, D. A., & Lamb, M. E. (1998). *Investigative interviews of children: A guide for helping professionals.* Washington, DC: American Psychological Association.

Sedlak, A., McPhereson, K., & Das, B. (2010). *Fourth national incidence study of child abuse and neglect (NIS-4): Supplementary analyses of race difference in child maltreatment rates in the NIS-4.* Washington, DC: U.S. Department of Health and Human Services.

Shelton, D. E., Kim, Y. S., & Barak, G. (2006). A study of juror expectations and demands concerning scientific evidence: Does the '*CSI* Effect' exist? *Vanderbilt Journal of Entertainment and Technology Law, 9*(2), 331. E2 80 93368.

Snell, L. (2003). *Child advocacy center: One stop on the road to performance-based child protection.* The Reason Foundation. Available at: http://reason.org/news/show/child-advocacy-centers. Accessed 7 February 2013.

Stuart, H. (2008). Suicidality among police. *Current Opinion in Psychiatry, 21*(5), 505–509.

Vieth, V. (2009). Picture this: Photographing a child sexual abuse crime scene. *CenterPiece* 1(5). Retrieved from: http://www.ncptc.org/vertical/Sites/%7B8634A6E1-FAD2-4381-9C0D-5DC7E93C9410%7D/uploads/%7B997647FB-79F1-4C5F-BF8A-B3340672BEE9%7D.PDF

Part V
Child Maltreatment:
Is It the Same Everywhere?

Chapter 29
Child Maltreatment as a Problem in International Law

Robin Kimbrough-Melton

Child Maltreatment as a Problem in International Law

In Kempe's (1982) editorial in *Pediatrics*, he expressed optimism that the "shift in attitude" about children, as evidenced by the International Year of the Child (IYC), in 1979, would "rapidly lead to more understanding of how to prevent and treat child abuse and neglect" (p. 497). Kempe's optimism was not unfounded. The IYC marked the beginning of a decade-long process to draft a comprehensive, transformative international legal instrument – the Convention on the Rights of the Child (CRC 1989). By 1979, dramatic changes were occurring in the international arena so that children were no longer being perceived as the chattel of their parents. Children, too, have dignity and worth, and they are entitled to the same human rights and freedoms as any other human beings.

Based on the Universal Declaration of Human Rights (UDHR 1948), the CRC (1989) extends the principles of the UDHR to children. The UDHR was the first widely accepted statement of human rights and fundamental freedoms to which all peoples of the world are entitled. As a declaration, the UDHR is not legally binding on governments. However, the guarantees of the UDHR are enforceable through two subsequent documents – the International Covenants on Civil and Political Rights (1976) and Economic, Social and Cultural Rights (1976). Together, the three documents form the International Bill of Rights. Since adoption of the UDHR in 1948, it has inspired an array of subsequent international treaties, including the CRC, regional human rights instruments, national constitutions and laws. The CRC is groundbreaking in setting forth a comprehensive and coherent set of rights for children.

The impact of the CRC (1989)[1] on the protection of children has been substantial, especially in the developing world. An indicator of change is the extent to which governments that have ratified a treaty adopt national legislation to enable their implementation. Because a treaty may not be enforceable in domestic law without implementing legislation, such action signals a certain level of commitment on the part of the government. The adoption of national legislation also can raise awareness and provide a framework for changing normative behavior and stimulating improvements in services.

A recent survey by the International Society for Prevention of Child Abuse and Neglect (ISPCAN) indicates that legal reform to improve national policies and programs related to child protection is occurring. Ninety percent of the countries surveyed had implemented a national law or policy regarding child maltreatment, and 87 % had implemented a mechanism for responding to child maltreatment cases

---

[1] See Appendix for selected provisions of the key human rights documents discussed.

R. Kimbrough-Melton (✉)
University of Colorado School of Medicine, Kempe Center for the Prevention and Treatment of Child Abuse & Neglect, The Gary Pavilion at Children's Hospital Colorado, Anschultz Medical Campus, 13123 East 16th Avenue, Box 390, Aurora 80045, CO, USA
e-mail: Robin.Kimbrough-Melton@ucdenver.edu

J.E. Korbin and R.D. Krugman (eds.), *Handbook of Child Maltreatment*, Child Maltreatment 2, DOI 10.1007/978-94-007-7208-3_29, © Springer Science+Business Media Dordrecht 2014

(Dubowitz 2012), approximately 54 % of which have been implemented since 1990, the year that the CRC (1989) went into force. Mandated reporting by professionals (92 %) is the most common element of these national policies, followed by specific criminal penalties for abusing a child (90 %) and provisions for removing a child (87 %) from the child's parents or caregivers (Dubowitz 2012).

The CRC (1989) also requires governments to provide needed support for the child and the child's caregivers to prevent child maltreatment and to treat victims when child maltreatment does occur (Article 19(2)). Again, ISPCAN's survey shows improvement. Nearly three-quarters of respondents (72 %) indicated that their policies require the provision of some form of service or intervention to the victims; 63 % of these policies include provisions for the development and support of prevention services (Dubowitz 2012).

Since the approval of the CRC, there have been other indicators of international progress in preventing and reducing child maltreatment. In addition to legal reform and service improvements, adherence to the provisions of a treaty can be demonstrated by increased awareness of behaviors or practices that are unacceptable and in violation of a child's right to grow up in a safe and supportive environment. On a range of issues (e.g., child sexual abuse, child prostitution, corporal punishment), the voices of the NGO Group for the Convention on the Rights of the Child, a coalition of international nongovernmental organizations that work together to facilitate implementation of the CRC, and other national and international organizations, the Committee on the Rights of the Child, and children themselves have focused attention on the rudiments of dignity within the international community and the elements of a right to protection for all children. More than ever before, the international community is speaking out against practices, including traditional cultural practices, that are abusive to children and that strip them of their dignity.

Although these developments are significant, it is not enough. Even in the advanced democracies, children continue to experience unacceptably high levels of violence. As researchers, advocates and policy makers learn more about the causes and correlates of child abuse and neglect, it has become increasingly apparent that child maltreatment is complex and that the ordinary mechanisms and services for responding to and treating child abuse and neglect are not very effective in addressing the multiple determinants of child maltreatment.

Addressing child maltreatment in international law is difficult for a variety of reasons that will be discussed later in this article, but not impossible. The CRC and its related documents establish a framework for the protection of children, including the stimulation of more humane policies and practices and opportunities for engaging children as active members of the community. Unfortunately, the implementation of the CRC, in general, has been narrowly focused on helping children after they have been victimized rather than developing approaches to prevent child maltreatment. The approval of a new General Comment (GC13 2011), as discussed in depth later, may provide the impetus for fully realizing the potential of the CRC as it relates to child protection.

The International Framework for Protecting Children

The Convention on the Rights of the Child (CRC 1989) is the centerpiece of an array of international documents, including other treaties, declarations, General Comments, and advisory opinions, that define and interpret guidelines related to the status of children more generally and the protection of children more specifically in international law. Proposed by the Polish Government as a tangible outcome of the IYC, the CRC set the standard for subsequent treaties in its articulation of civil and political rights and economic, social and cultural rights in one document.

The IYC was designed to commemorate the 20th Anniversary of the Universal Declaration of the Rights of the Child (UNDRC) (1959) by drawing attention to the special status and needs of children worldwide. Children had been mentioned in the international arena as early as 1924 when the United

Nations approved the Geneva Declaration of the Rights of the Child. The Geneva Declaration (1924) recognized an obligation to ensure that children "be given the means requisite for…normal development," (Paragraph 1) and "be protected against every form of exploitation" (Paragraph 4). In contrast to the CRC (1989) or for that matter, the UNDRC (1959), the Geneva Declaration viewed children as belonging to their parents.

The foundation for recognizing children as rights-holders had its genesis in the Universal Declaration of Human Rights (UDHR) of 1948. In declaring that everyone (including children) is entitled to fundamental human rights emanating from the inherent dignity of the person (preamble 1948), Article 25 of the UDHR singled out children as being "entitled to special care and assistance," a phrase that was later defined in the International Covenant of Economic, Social and Cultural Rights (ICESCR 1976) as meaning "protection from economic and social exploitation" (Article 10(3)).

The UNDRC (1959) further explicated the essential rights and needs of children, including the right to be protected from "all forms of neglect, cruelty and exploitation" (Article 9). It also expanded upon Article 16 of the UDHR, which recognized the family as the "natural and fundamental group unit of society," in acknowledging the importance of the parent–child relationship to the "full and harmonious development" of the child's personality and the preference for children to grow up in the "care and under the responsibility of…parents" (Article 6). In international law, "the term 'personality' is synonymous with 'personhood' or the opportunity to develop fully as human beings" (Melton 2005, p. 922).

The framework established by the UDHR (1948) and the UNDRC (1959), however, left significant gaps with respect to the specific rights of children (Oberg 2012). Moreover, as declarations, the principles established in the two documents were not binding on any government that approved them. In contrast, governments that sign treaties, such as the CRC (1989), are held accountable for meeting its legal obligations.

The 42 substantive principles contained in the CRC (1989) are concerned with four "Ps": (a) *protection* of children from discrimination and all forms of neglect and exploitation; (b) *prevention* of harm to them by focusing on their best interests; (c) *provision* of assistance so that they survive and develop to their full potential; and (d) *participation* in decisions affecting them (Van Bueren 1995). When considered together, the CRC provides a roadmap for protecting and strengthening the well-being of children.

Article 19 of the CRC (1989) is the central provision outlining the basic protections from harm and exploitation that all children enjoy. Articles 32, 33, and 34 of the CRC expand on the protections of Article 19 by emphasizing the right to be protected from economic exploitation, illicit drugs, and sexual exploitation and sexual abuse, and Article 37 protects children from torture and cruel, inhuman or degrading treatment or punishment. In emphasizing freedom from all forms of violence--not just child maltreatment--the concept of protection in the CRC subsumes the right of children to "full respect for their dignity and physical and personal integrity" (Hodgkin and Newell 2000, p. 249). The right to protection is related to the right to life, survival and development (Article 6), the right to registration of a name (Article 7), the preservation of the child's identity (Article 8) and the right to a family environment (preamble 1989). Thus, governments that have signed the treaty are obligated to provide support and assistance to the child and the child's parents so that children have the opportunity to develop physically, mentally, morally, spiritually and socially (Article 27).

Since the adoption of the CRC in November 1989, more progress has been made on behalf of children worldwide than in any comparable period (United Nations 2007). The international community has started to tackle some of the more difficult issues involving the protection of children, including strengthening international standards for protecting children. For example, the principles of the CRC have been extended to address growing concerns about the vulnerability of female children to sexual exploitation (Optional Protocol to the Convention on the Rights of the Child on the Sale of Children, Child Prostitution and Child Pornography (A/RES/54/263 *entered into force* Jan. 18, 2002). A second Optional Protocol to the CRC addresses the use of children in armed conflict (A/RES/54/263 *entered into force* Feb. 12, 2002).

The Committee on the Rights of the Child has organized Days of General Discussion to examine specific provisions of the CRC related to the protection of children (e.g., Days of General Discussion in 2000 on "State violence against children" and in September 2001 on "Violence against children within the family, and in schools") (Hodkins and Newell 2000) and issued general comments (a statement by a treaty body providing guidance on the interpretation of the procedural and substantive content of the treaty) interpreting the content of specific provisions of the CRC related to the use of corporal punishment and to violence more generally. Other efforts have focused on populations of children that may be especially vulnerable to child maltreatment, including child refugees, unaccompanied children, children with disabilities, and child soldiers. Multiple summits and meetings (e.g., World Summit on Children in 1990; UN General Assembly Special Session on Children in 2002) have reaffirmed the commitment of governments and nongovernmental organizations to child protection (O'Donnell 2004). In 2006, the first *World Report on Violence Against Children* was completed by an independent expert representing the Secretary-General of the United Nations. The report was the "first comprehensive global attempt to describe the scale of all forms of violence against children and its impact" (Pinheiro 2006, p. xiii). More recently, the Committee on the Rights of the Child completed its General Comment No. 13 to the CRC (CRC/C/GC/13, 2011). GC13 attempts to address some of the more intransigent problems within international law in protecting children. Its major contribution, however, may be a reconceptualization of the rights to protection, which will be discussed in more detail later.

Challenges in Protecting Children Through International Law

Despite growing attention to the problem of child maltreatment, protecting children through international law generally and the CRC (1989) specifically has proven to be challenging. Governments that have attempted to implement the CRC have not been effective in preventing maltreatment of millions of children worldwide or in providing services to these children (Svevo-Cianci et al. 2011).

The difficulty in protecting children through international law is related to several issues that have undoubtedly hindered implementation, including the scope of the right to protection set forth in the CRC, the view of the family in international law, cultural beliefs and attitudes, and the focus of international law on governments rather than individuals.

The Scope of the Right to Protection

The right to protection in the CRC (1989) addresses a wide range of conditions (e.g., physical or mental violence, injury or abuse, neglect or negligent treatment, maltreatment or exploitation) that threaten the safety of children. One challenge in implementing the right is that it has not been clear, until recently, what specific acts constitute child maltreatment. For example, does corporal punishment constitute child abuse? Does early marriage of girls constitute abuse? The drafters of the CRC intentionally did not define the conditions enumerated in Article 19, because they wished to avoid the possibility that a definition of child abuse and neglect could unwittingly be based on arbitrary or ethnocentric assumptions (Van Bueren 1995). Although well intended, the lack of a common understanding of unacceptable behaviors has meant that some societies think differently about what will and will not be tolerated.

The Committee on the Rights of the Child has attempted to address this shortcoming in the CRC (1989) by more clearly articulating the acts that may constitute child maltreatment in General Comment No. 13 (2011 (GC13). GC13 begins by defining *violence*, in part because that term has increasingly been used in the international community as a catch-all for the various acts that might constitute child maltreatment. Violence is defined as referring to any of the conditions mentioned in Article 19 of the CRC. As used by the international community, *violence* does not mean only physical harm or intentional harm. GC13 clarifies that *violence* also includes non-physical and non-intentional forms of harm, such as psychological maltreatment and neglect (Hart et al. 2011).

In an effort to further clarify the types of conduct encompassed in Article 19 (CRC 1989), the Committee provides specific guidance as to the meaning of the various terms in Article 19. For example, neglect or negligent treatment is defined as the "failure to meet children's physical or psychological needs, protect them from danger, or obtain medical, birth registration or other services…." (GC13 Paragraph 20). Paragraph 20 of GC13 then proceeds to identify types of neglect and to define them.

But the Committee goes further. For the first time, it directs States Parties to establish national standards for "child well-being, health and development" and to develop "clear operational legal definitions," based on the guidance provided in GC13, for the different forms of violence outlined in Article 19 of the CRC.

Closely related to the definitional issue is the problem of who is covered by the provisions of the CRC (1989). The CRC guarantees rights to children up to 18 years of age. However, questions have arisen as to the treatment of children who are married before the age of 18, or who are married by their parents because of traditional practices. GC13 clearly states that these children should be protected under the CRC (Svevo-Cianci et al. 2011). Marriage and emancipation prior to the age of 18 are "merely social constructions which should not overshadow the child's need for protection" (Svevo-Cianci et al. 2011). Finally, in GC13 (Paragraph 29), the Committee specifically enumerates some of the more common traditional or harmful practices that will not be tolerated:

29. **Harmful practices**. These include, but are not limited to:

a) Corporal punishment and other cruel or degrading forms of punishment;
b) Female genital mutilation;
c) Amputations, binding, scarring, burning and branding;
d) Violent and degrading initiation rites; force-feeding of girls; fattening; virginity testing (inspecting girls' genitalia);
e) Forced marriage and early marriage;
f) "Honour" crimes; "retribution" acts of violence (where disputes between different groups are taken out on children of the parties involved); dowry-related death and violence;
g) Accusations of "witchcraft" and related harmful practices such as "exorcism";
h) Uvulectomy and teeth extraction.

A Reluctance to Intrude into the Family

The importance of the parent–child relationship to the healthy development of children is well-established in international law (e.g., UDHR, Article 16; International Covenant on Civil and Political Rights (ICCPR), Article 23; International Covenant on Economic, Social and Cultural Rights (ICESCR), Article 10; CRC, preamble). It is within the family where a child's rights are most likely to be secured so, within the international arena, families are to be given the "widest possible protection and assistance," (ICESCR Article 10 1976) including protection from "arbitrary interference" (UDHR, Article 12 1948). The goal of supporting families has created a reluctance to intrude into the private sphere of the family. As a result, international law has traditionally not concerned itself with the problem of abuse within the family (Van Bueren 1995).

Views concerning the privacy of the family also have made it difficult to detect child maltreatment, especially child neglect, early and if necessary, to respond to protect children when abuse does occur. Often it is difficult to assert with certainty that an injury to a child is the result of abuse or neglect as opposed to a fall or other mishap. This is especially true with psychological maltreatment where a pattern of conduct must be shown. Even in the area of sexual maltreatment, early efforts tended to focus on protecting children from prostitution and pornography (Levesque 1994) rather than from sexual abuse occurring within the family.

In short, balancing the rights of parents to raise their children as they see fit against the rights of the child to be free from violence has been a major challenge for states (Van Bueren 1995). It is only in recent years that the prevalence of violence against children by parents and other family members has begun to be acknowledged and documented (Pinheiro 2006). The fact that younger children are more vulnerable to violence in the home has undoubtedly contributed to an increased willingness to examine the parent–child relationship.

In GC13, the Committee on the Rights of the Child acknowledges the "primary position of families, including extended families, in child caregiving and protection and in the prevention of violence" (Paragraph 3(h)). The General Comment, however, also "recognizes that the majority of violence takes place in the context of families" (Paragraph 3(h)). Certainly, the remainder of the GC13 signals a willingness to intrude into the family if necessary. An example of this can be seen in the Committee's interpretation of Article 19 (CRC 1989) as it relates to corporal punishment. Even before GC13, the Committee had routinely challenged the legal and social acceptance of corporal punishment in examining States Parties' reports (Hodgkin and Newell 2000). Their concern about the widespread use of violence against children in the home led them to issue General Comment No. 8 in 2006 (CRC/C/GC/8). GC8 highlighted the obligation of all States Parties to move quickly to prohibit and eliminate all corporal punishment and all other cruel or degrading forms of punishment of children….in the family, schools and other settings. Paragraph 24 of GC13 reaffirms the Committee's position that corporal punishment is prohibited by Article 19 of the CRC (1989).

Although the use of corporal punishment is still legal in many states of the United States and in many countries, the attention of the Committee to the problem has raised awareness and change has started. As of July 2012, 33 countries had fully banned corporal punishment (Global Initiative to End All Corporal Punishment of Children 2012). More than 100 nations have banned corporal punishment in the schools. Even, in the United States, where support for corporal punishment has been strong, corporal punishment in the schools has now been banned in 31 states (Center for Effective Discipline 2012).

Conflicts with Culture

Some of the most intransigent issues related to child maltreatment are grounded in cultural beliefs. Traditional practices such as female genital mutilation, the sexual use of children in ritualistic initiation ceremonies, honor killings of adolescent girls who have breached moral codes, and early marriage of girls are culturally-based practices that are still prevalent in some countries.

Dealing with cultural attitudes and beliefs has been challenging in international law, in part because international law has had a goal of preserving the cultural rights of peoples (e.g. UDHR Article 27 1948) as indispensable to their dignity (Levesque 1994). Nonetheless, as indicated earlier, GC13 departs from the norm by specifically enumerating harmful practices that constitute child maltreatment and must be prohibited by governments (Paragraph 29).

GC13 (2011) also emphasizes the fact that children have rights; they are not simply the chattel of their parents. This perspective is important in addressing cultural norms where children often lack power within the family relationship or other adult relationships to fully exercise their rights and to object to maltreatment. GC13 reminds States Parties that protection is not provided as an act of adult benevolence but rather as an "entitlement of all children, without discrimination and on conditions that are beneficial to the child's well-being" (Bessell and Gal 2009).

International Law Applies to Governments, Not Individuals

Another challenge in preventing and reducing child maltreatment is that international law is directed at governments, not individuals. Treaties usually obligate governments to either do something for its citizens to protect their rights (positive rights) or to refrain from doing something (negative rights). In the case of child maltreatment, States parties are obligated to take "all appropriate legislative, administrative, social and educational measures to protect the child" (CRC Article 19 1989). As noted earlier, governments that have passed legislation or established processes to address child maltreatment are attempting to comply with this requirement. In GC13 (2011), the Committee notes that "legal frameworks in a majority of States still fail to prohibit all forms of violence against children, and where laws are in place, their enforcement is inadequate" (Paragraph 12). Where measures have been implemented, the impact is limited because governments tend to be reactive and, when they do respond, services are fragmented rather than integrated (GC13 Paragraph 12 2011). Finally, the Committee emphasizes that "legislative measures," not only refers to legislation, but it also refers to the implementation of budgetary measures (GC13 Paragraph 40 2011).

Beyond implementing legislative and administrative measures, Article 19 of the CRC (1989) also requires States Parties to "provide necessary support for the child and for those who have the care of the child, as well as for other forms of prevention and for identification, reporting, referral, investigation, treatment and follow-up of instances of child maltreatment." This has been much more challenging for governments than passing legislation. The increasing complexity of child maltreatment has literally overwhelmed governments. In the United States, for example, often the only service that is actually provided to families accused of maltreatment is the investigation (Melton 2004). Because the vast majority of referrals to the child protective service system involve allegations of neglect, governments are often ill equipped to respond effectively, much less to prevent problems. Moreover, the diverse needs of the child and family often are ill-matched to the available resources.

Sadly, in instances where there is a response by the social service system (i.e. the State), it may do more harm than good for the children. Service systems have inadequate resources, they are stigmatizing, and for many children, they are confusing. Little support is provided to children who often must navigate relationships, not only with their birth parents and families, but with caseworkers, foster parents, legal professionals and counselors (Bessell and Gal 2009).

A recent development that could strengthen the implementation of the CRC's provisions related to child maltreatment is the approval by the UN General Assembly in December 2011 of a Third Optional Protocol to the CRC that will provide a complaints mechanism. The Third Optional Protocol does not create any new rights. Rather, it provides a mechanism for addressing violations of rights under the CRC and the first two optional protocols. The new optional protocol was opened for signatures in February 2012.

Rethinking Child Protection

The challenges facing governments in protecting children through international law are due, in part, to implementation that has been narrowly focused on identifying cases of child maltreatment and, in some cases, providing treatment or, when necessary, removing children from their homes. Bessell and Gal (2009) note that "human rights can be understood at two levels: first, as the international system of treaties, visionary statements and commitments, and second as a conceptual framework that shapes action" (p. 286). The CRC (1989) is illustrative of the potential of international human rights law to guide policy in a manner that transforms life at the neighborhood level" (Melton 2005, p. 919). Unfortunately, very little attention has been given to developing the infrastructure at the community or neighborhood level that is essential to preventing child maltreatment and that could make a difference in the well-being of children. This lack of attention may be understandable for developing countries that are striving to create a legal framework for implementing the CRC. It is less understandable in the advanced democracies, especially in light of the ineffectiveness of current child protection efforts.

General Comment No. 13 (2011) is the Committee on the Rights of the Child's effort to address this problem. GC13 has the ambitious goal of trying to refocus the implementation of Article 19 of the CRC (1989) to be more closely aligned with the original intent of the Convention.

In explaining the rationale for a general comment on Article 19 (CRC 1989), the Committee on the Rights of the Child expressed alarm at the extent and intensity of violence against children. The Committee further stressed that "measures to end violence must be massively strengthened and expanded in order to effectively put an end to these practices which jeopardize children's development" (GC13 Paragraph 2 2011). To assist governments, the Committee provided very specific guidance as to how Article 19 (CRC 1989) and its related provisions should be implemented.

Positive Right to Protection

Fundamental to the CRC is the perspective that children have rights based in their dignity. The rights articulated in the CRC require more than simply preventing a child from being harmed. Rather, Article 19 (CRC, 1989) creates a positive right to protection (Ezer 2004). In addition to taking steps to protect the physical integrity of children, governments must also protect the psychological integrity of the child (GC13 Paragraph 13 2011; Ezer 2004). This means providing access to education and opportunities for children to be heard and to participate in decisions affecting them (CRC Article 12 1989). GC13 (2011) reminds States Parties that Article 19 (CRC 1989) must be implemented holistically based on the Convention's overall focus on "securing children's rights to survival, dignity, well-being, health, development, participation, and non-discrimination" (Paragraph 11(d)).

A Focus on Prevention

Central to GC13 is a focus on prevention, which is consistent with the Committee's emphasis on respecting and promoting the human dignity and the physical and psychological integrity of children as rights-bearing individuals (GC13 Paragraph 3 2011). The Committee expressed concern about the failure of governments to take seriously paragraph 2 of Article 19 (CRC 1989), which requires governments to establish measures to provide necessary support to children and their caregivers. In noting that prevention is *proactive* (GC13 Paragraph 46), the Committee stressed that child protection strategies must be holistic. Such strategies involve measures that promote public health and safety, reduce poverty, improve access to health, housing and other social services, and encourage the development of employment and educational opportunities (GC13 Paragraph 43 2011).

The Committee further directs governments to strengthen implementation, not only at the national level, but at regional and local levels. GC13 (2011) provides the beginnings of a roadmap for strengthening protection at the local level – in every community or neighborhood – with the goal of supporting children in their own environment (Svevo-Cianci et al. 2011). Such an approach is essential to fully implementing strategies that will enable children to participate as required by Article 12 of the CRC.

The Committee emphasized the importance of involving all sectors of society, including children, and provided specific guidance to stakeholders, children, families and communities, and professionals as to their role in preventing violence (GC13 Paragraph 47 2011). Further, the Committee noted that prevention measures include changing attitudes which perpetuate the tolerance and condoning of violence and disseminating information regarding the Convention's holistic and positive approach to child protection (GC13 Paragraph 47 2011).

Although implementing community-wide approaches to preventing child maltreatment is undoubtedly the most challenging aspect of GC13, models are beginning to emerge to guide such activities (see Chap. 17, of this volume). One such model, Strong Communities, is among those that would be consistent with a recent global survey on innovation in community-based child protection that was led by the Columbia University Care and Protection of Children Learning Network (Wessells 2009). Wessells identified seven factors that influence the effectiveness of a community-based child protection strategy: (a) community ownership; (b) building on existing community resources, (c) engaging local leaders, (d) engaging children, (e) inclusiveness and diversity of participants, (f) resources, and (g) linkages to both formal and informal networks.

Conclusion

Kempe's hope that the enthusiasm associated with the International Year of the Child would lead to a better understanding of how to prevent and treat child abuse and neglect has been realized to some extent. Our knowledge and understanding of the causes and correlates of child abuse and neglect is much better than in 1979. We also have a better appreciation of the complexity and magnitude of the problem and the limits of strategies that have thus far been implemented to address child maltreatment.

Although there are obvious limitations to international law in addressing child protection, the body of international documents that includes the Universal Declaration on Human Rights (1948) and the Convention on the Rights of the Child (1989) provides a framework for achieving Kempe's objective that all children will be safe. The CRC and General Comment 13, in particular, clearly articulate the elements for preventing child maltreatment, helping children when abuse or neglect does occur, and ultimately creating safer environments. Moreover, the adoption of General Comment 13 (2011) provides new opportunities to realize the full potential of the CRC in promoting a holistic approach, focused on prevention, and rooted at the community level where it can have the greatest impact on the well-being of children.

Appendix

Selected Provisions of Key Human Rights Documents

Document	Selected provisions
Universal Declaration of Human Rights, 1948	**Art. 25**
http://www.un.org/en/documents/udhr/ index.shtml	(2) Motherhood and childhood are entitled to special care and assistance. All children, whether born in or out of wedlock, shall enjoy the same social protection
International Covenant of Economic, Social and Cultural Rights, 1976	**Art. 10**
	The States Parties to the present Covenant recognize that:
http://www2.ohchr.org/english/law/cescr.htm	(3) Special measures of protection and assistance should be taken on behalf of all children and young persons without any discrimination for reasons of parentage or other conditions. Children and young persons should be protected from economic and social exploitation. Their employment in work harmful to their morals or health or dangerous to life or likely to hamper their normal development should be punishable by law. States should also set age limits below which the paid employment of child labour should be prohibited and punishable by law

(continued)

(continued)

Document	Selected provisions
United Nations Declaration on the Rights of the Child, 1959 http://www.un.org/cyberschoolbus/humanrights/resources/child.asp	**Art. 2** The child shall enjoy special protection, and shall be given opportunities and facilities, by law and by other means, to enable him to develop physically, mentally, morally, spiritually and socially in a healthy and normal manner and in conditions of freedom and dignity. In the enactment of laws for this purpose, the best interests of the child shall be the paramount consideration **Art. 9** The child shall be protected against all forms of neglect, cruelty and exploitation. He shall not be the subject of traffic, in any form The child shall not be admitted to employment before an appropriate minimum age; he shall in no case be caused or permitted to engage in any occupation or employment which would prejudice his health or education, or interfere with his physical, mental or moral development
Convention on the Rights of the Child, 1989 http://www2.ohchr.org/english/law/crc.htm	**Art. 19** (1) States Parties shall take all appropriate legislative, administrative, social and educational measures to protect the child from all forms of physical or mental violence, injury or abuse, neglect or negligent treatment, maltreatment or exploitation, including sexual abuse, while in the care of parent(s), legal guardian(s), or any other person who has the care of the child (2) Such protective measures should, as appropriate, include effective procedures for the establishment of social programmes to provide necessary support for the child and for those who have the care of the child, as well as for other forms of prevention and for identification, reporting, referral, investigation, treatment, and follow-up of instances of child maltreatment described heretofore, and as appropriate, for judicial involvement

References

Bessell, S., & Gal, T. (2009). Forming partnerships: The human rights of children in need of care and protection. *International Journal of Children's Rights, 17*, 283–298.

Center for Effective Discipline, http://www.stophitting.com/index.php?page=statesbanning. Accessed 26 Nov 2012.

Dubowitz, H. (Ed.). (2012). *World perspectives on child abuse* (10th ed.). Aurora: The International Society for Prevention of Child Abuse and Neglect.

Ezer, T. (2004). A positive right to protection for children. *Yale Human Rights & Development Journal, 7*, 1–50.

General Comment No. 13. (2011). *The right of the child to freedom from all forms of violence.* Committee on the Rights of the Child. http://www2.ohchr.org/english/bodies/CRC/docs/CRC.C.GC.13-en.pdf.

Global Initiative to End All Corporal Punishment of Children, http://www.endcorporalpunishment.org/pages/progress/prohib_states.html, Accessed 11/26/2012.

Hart, S. N., Lee, Y., & Wernham, M. (2011). A new age for child protection – General comment 13: Why it is important, how it was constructed, and what it intends? *Child Abuse & Neglect, 35*, 970–978.

Hodgkin, R., & Newell, P. (2000). *Implementation handbook for the convention on the rights of the child.* Geneva: UNICEF.

Kempe, C. H. (1982). Cross-cultural perspectives in child abuse. *Pediatrics, 69*(4), 497–498.

Levesque, R. J. R. (1994). Sexual use, abuse and exploitation of children: Challenges in implementing children's human rights. *Brooklyn Law Review, 60*, 959–998.

Melton, G. B. (2004). Mandated reporting: A policy without reason. *Child Abuse & Neglect, 29*, 9–18.

Melton, G. B. (2005). Building humane communities respectful of children: The significance of the convention on the rights of the child. *American Psychologist, 60*(8), 918–926.

O'Donnell, D. (2004). *Child protection: A handbook for parlimentarians.* Geneva: UNICEF.

Oberg, C. N. (2012). Embracing international children's rights: From principles to practice. *Clinical Pediatrics, 51*(7), 619–624.

Pinheiro, P. S. (2006). *World report on violence against children.* Geneva: United Nations.

Svevo-Cianci, K. A., Herczog, M., Krappmann, L., & Cook, P. (2011). The new UN CRC General Comment 13: "The right of the child to freedom from all forms of violence" – Changing how the world conceptualizes child protection. *Child Abuse & Neglect, 35,* 979–989.

United Nations. (2007). *The United Nations development agenda: Development for all.* New York: United Nations.

Van Bueren, G. (1995). *The international law on the rights of the child.* Dordrecht: Nijhoff.

Wessells, M. (2009). *What are we learning about protecting children in the community: An interagency review of evidence on community based child protection mechanisms.* London: Save the Children Fund.

Chapter 30
Child Maltreatment and Global Health: Biocultural Perspectives

Brandon A. Kohrt

Child maltreatment is a global problem. Of the greater than two billion children in the world, the majority lives in low- and middle-income countries. Half of these children grow up in poverty, two-thirds are affected by armed conflict, and a third is underweight or stunted (UNDP 2009; UNICEF 2009). Abuse and neglect are present throughout the world and there are tremendous gaps in availability of child protection services, training programs for persons working in prevention and treatment, and legal structures and policies to protect children from abuse and neglect (Engle et al. 2011; Walker et al. 2011). Low human development, measured by poor performance on education, economic, and equalities indices characteristic of low-income countries, is associated with more physical discipline and verbal abuse according to UNICEF cross-national data (Britto and Ulkuer 2012; Lansford and Deater-Deckard 2012).

In addition to universal problems of child physical, emotional, and sexual abuse and neglect, there are other risks overrepresented among children in low- and middle-income countries. These risks include child marriage, forced conscription into armed groups as child soldiers, child trafficking for labor and sexual exploitation, and ritual practices that may endanger physical and mental health. Child marriage affects 60 million girls worldwide (Raj 2010). Armed groups from 86 conflicts across the world have conscripted greater than 300,000 children as child soldiers (Coalition to Stop the Use of Child Soldiers 2004). Each year, 1.2 million children are trafficked for labor including commercial sex work (International Labour Organization 2002). Between 100 and 140 million girls and women have undergone female genital cutting, and three million girls are at risk every year (World Health Organization 2008). With the majority of the world's children living in these settings of social instability and political violence, it is concerning that less than 5 % of published child mental health research originates from work in low- and middle-income countries (Patel 2007; Patel et al. 2008).

Addressing the role of culture is vital to bridge the gaps in research, support services, and prevention related to child maltreatment. Too often cross-national comparisons become essentialized as cultural, biological, or structural differences. Cultural explanations focus on differences in parenting models such as the perceived acceptability of corporal punishment (Gershoff et al. 2010). Biological models often conflate genetic differences with racial and ethnic differences (Gravlee and Sweet 2008; Krieger 2005). This has been a problem less frequently in child maltreatment research. However, with increasing studies of gene-by-environment interactions there is the possibility that claims could be made regarding genetic group differences in maltreatment or sequelae of maltreatment due

B.A. Kohrt, MD, Ph.D. (✉)
Department of Psychiatry and Behavioral Sciences and Duke Global Health Institute,
Duke University, 213 Trent Hall, 310 Trent Drive, Duke Box #90519, Durham, NC 27708, USA
e-mail: brandon.kohrt@dm.duke.edu

J.E. Korbin and R.D. Krugman (eds.), *Handbook of Child Maltreatment*, Child Maltreatment 2,
DOI 10.1007/978-94-007-7208-3_30, © Springer Science+Business Media Dordrecht 2014

to differences in prevalence of risk and resilience genetic haplotypes. Structural arguments of differences in maltreatment have focused on associations of maltreatment with economic and educational conditions (Lansford and Deater-Deckard 2012). Neighborhood factors also are crucial to risk of child maltreatment (Coulton et al. 2007). Krieger and colleagues (2005) have demonstrated that structural factors such as census tract poverty significantly reduces health disparities attributed to racial and ethnic differences. However, lack of racial and ethnic differences does not equate with lack of cultural influences. When controlling for economic factors, symbolic issues related to culture may still make important contributions to child development (Panter-Brick et al. 2012). "...[N]eighborhood activities, city layout, or social hierarchy are themselves shaped by local norms, values, and behaviors," (Hruschka and Hadley 2008 p. 947). Ultimately, the field is challenged by a wide range of definitions of culture, which variably include both biological and structural factors. To prevent child abuse and support survivors of child abuse, models will be needed that incorporate facets of all of these domains.

In this chapter, the challenges of applying cultural, biological, and structural models to child maltreatment are discussed. Opportunities for using combined cultural, biological, and structural approaches are explored within a biocultural framework. While there is a history of cultural research on child maltreatment (Harkness and Super 1996; Korbin 1991, 2002), this chapter will focus on research at the intersection of biological and cultural factors, with an emphasis on conditions in low- and middle-income countries. As a prolegomenon toward more biocultural approaches of conceptualizing maltreatment in the field of global mental health, the relationship between culture and biology is explored from multiple vantages. First, culture moderates the relationship risk of maltreatment and biological factors such as sex, disabilities, and medical illness. Examples of cultural moderation include high rates of abuse of girls in South Asia and maltreatment related to seizure disorders in West Africa. Second, the evidence for biological sequelae of maltreatment is scarce from a cross-cultural perspective. Other than studies of Romanian orphans and a limited number of studies from East Asia, studies of biological sequelae outside high income countries are significantly lacking. Some forms of maltreatment are overrepresented in low- and middle-income countries such as female genital cutting, and forced conscription of child soldiers, leading to increased and diverse health consequences. Third, the cross-cultural evidence for gene-by-environment interactions is limited by variation in prevalence of alleles and exposures. Fourth, structural factors and macro-cultural processes underlie most biocultural interactions. In addition to an approach that is biocultural in nature, a dual approach to micro-cultural processes (mechanisms underlying specific encounters of maltreatment) and macro-cultural processes (factors shaping context) is needed. Macro-cultural process should be targets of intervention. Before reviewing these pathways of associations among culture, biology, and structural factors, it is important to examine how culture can be interpreted in variable ways influencing research and intervention implementation and design.

Cultural and Biocultural Approaches

Definitions of Culture

Definitions of culture and ways of measuring and analyzing the role of culture vary tremendously by discipline and theoretical approach (Hruschka 2009a; Hruschka and Hadley 2008). Studies of culture run the risk of doing harm by reinforcing racial stereotypes rather than unpacking fluctuating social groupings and associated behaviors. Ideally, studies of culture should help to identify sites and avenues to intervention rather than stigmatizing specific communities, ethnicities, or social classes. There is no consensus on the definition and operationalization of culture, nor how to best measure and analyze it.

For some researchers, culture is a substitute for race or ethnicity. For other individuals invetigators, culture refers to ecology. One individual's definition of culture may be closer to another individual's definition of social ecology than it is to another's definition of culture. In an attempt to document commonality, Hruschka and Hadley find that shared components of culture definitions are "values, beliefs, knowledge, norms, and practices and the notion that these are shared among a specific set of people" (2008, p. 947). Beliefs refer to conscious psychological processes. Norms are behaviors maintained by social sanctioning and affective responses. Values are valences placed on beliefs, knowledge, and norms that lead to engagement in or avoidance of behaviors.

Explanatory models are research categories used to group stimuli (such as disease symptoms), perceived etiology (such as causes of behavior or illness), and behavioral response (such as help-seeking for an illness) (Weiss et al. 1992). Explanatory models can be grouped into shared systems of behavior and beliefs known as ethnotheories. There is a detailed body of research on ethnotheories of parenting and child development (Harkness and Super 1996; Harkness et al. 2000). For example, middle-class European-American ethnotheories of parenting have been compared with French, Dutch, East African, and Chinese ethnotheories in areas such as sleep training, co-sleeping, napping, etc. (Harkness and Super 1994; Harkness et al. 2000).

However, beliefs alone only partially explain variance related to behavior. For example, most cross-cultural studies explore caregiver attitudes toward physical punishment in child rearing. However, when actual use of physical punishment is recorded, the rates are higher than the level of endorsement (Akmatov 2011; Casillas 2011), thus demonstrating a lack of one-to-one association between belief and behavior. This holds true for help-seeking behavior for an illness (Hruschka et al. 2008; Khoury et al. 2012). Often structural constraints such as distance and cost are more relevant than beliefs in determining healthcare behavior. In other situations, social association is one of the strongest predictors of health factors with limited additional variance explained by beliefs (Edmonds et al. 2012; Hruschka et al. 2011). Korbin (2002) describes the need to unpack cultural explanations related to child abuse because presumptive norms may reflect neither practices nor guarantee an association between belief and behavior. For example, child abuse reporting differences between Samoan-Americans and Japanese-Americans were attributed to Samoan values toward physical punishment and aggressiveness (Dubanoski and Snyder 1980), but multiple types of data were missing to make such a conclusion:

> Although it was assumed that the value on physical discipline was causally linked to actual physical discipline and abuse, there were no data on the distribution of the value on physical punishment within the Samoan (or Japanese) populations studied, and whether or not such values predict which Samoans (or Japanese) will be reported for abuse. (Korbin 2002, p. 640)

There is considerable debate regarding the relationship among belief, behavior, and health in studies of culture (Calvete 2007; Griffith et al. 1990; Hruschka 2009b; Paul 1989). Therefore, equating beliefs with behavior as the only avenue to study culture and maltreatment is incomplete. To examine how beliefs can be used, it is helpful to consider different relationships between beliefs and behavior. Framings of beliefs and behavior can be lumped grossly into three groups: causation, justification, and confabulation. Causation assumes that beliefs drive behavior. Causation leads to research models in which explanatory models are collected to identify motives for behaviors (Mshana et al. 2008; van de Weg et al. 1998). In child maltreatment research, a causation model would assume the "spare the rod, spoil the child" is the belief system that drives corporal punishment behavior.

Justification and confabulation models assume that relationships between stimuli and behavior are not always explicit. Implicit associations are characterized as preconscious reactions, as has been demonstrated in examination of gender, racial, and self-appraisal biases with neuropsychological implicit association tests or with effects of unconscious cuing on subsequent behaviors (Nock et al. 2010; Waters et al. 2010). While these approaches to unconscious connections between stimuli, behavior, and health are evaluated through neuropsychological and social neuroscience research

(Griffith 2010), historically, the precedent for acknowledging unconscious associations between stimuli and behavior was established through psychoanalytic theory (Butler and Binder 1987; Paul 1989). These implicit associations between stimuli and behavior have been considered justifications, especially in the area of discrimination and stigma research (Griffith 2010; Olafsdottir and Pescosolido 2011; Pescosolido et al. 2007; Rusch et al. 2009). Beliefs are offered to justify behaviors rather than the cause of them; in referring to the saying "spare the rod, spoil the child", Konner points out, "…many who have mutilated or killed a child cite discipline as justification" (2010, p. 551).

Confabulation, as a third type of association, is used in neuropsychological research where individuals are asked to explain motivation for behaviors. Frontal lobe damage and impairment of executive functioning, such as in dementia, clinically leads to confabulation that is more apparent than daily confabulation which is often taken for granted (Fotopoulou 2010; Lorente-Rovira et al. 2011). In research on culture, justification and confabulation are important when considering customs of a group. In Harkness and Super's model of the developmental niche to analyze child health, they refer to customs as "culturally prescribed sequences of behavior so commonly used by members of the community, and so thoroughly integrated into the larger culture, that they do not require individual rationalization and are not necessarily given conscious thought," (1994, p. 219). In the process of researching connections of belief and behavior, customs may be explained through justification or confabulation. However, the boundaries among causation, justification, and confabulation are fluid in cultural transmission. This is especially true for children who experience child maltreatment and try to make sense of the experience: causation, justification, and confabulation beliefs are continuously in flux. Moreover, what is a justification or confabulation for one individual or in one generation may lead to causation models in a larger group or in subsequent generations.

To further complicate the association of normative beliefs, behavior, and outcomes, questions arise if physical discipline in settings where it is normative has a weaker effect of child outcomes. In a study of children in China, India, Italy, Kenya, Philippines, and Thailand, there appears to be group differences in aggression and anxiety based on child ratings of normativeness of discipline types (Gershoff et al. 2010). In settings where children rate corporal punishment as normative (Kenya and Italy), there are few children who report low levels aggression compared to settings where corporal punishment is non-normative (East Asian countries: China, Thailand, and Philippines). Aggression levels are high among children who report no personal experience of corporal punishment, but who live in a society where it is perceived by children as normative. Conversely, in settings, where children identify parental expression of disappointment as normative (India, Italy, and Kenya), there are few children with low anxiety compared to settings where disappointment is non-normative (China). Children who themselves do not directly experience expressions of parental disappointment still report moderate levels of anxiety compared to child who experience no expressions of disappointment in societies where it is non-normative. Taken together, this suggests that children's perceptions of their cultural environment beyond their own individual experiences have an association with mental health and behavior. Pathways from cultural normative beliefs to behavioral practices to health outcomes are not sequential processes. Normative beliefs may be associated with health outcomes but only partially be explained by behavioral practices. Furthermore, this study showed that maternal expression of disappointment had a greater effect on child anxiety in settings where it was non-normative. Therefore, in settings where a behavior is considered normative, it may not have the same effect on child development.

The issue of causation, justification, and confabulation is an important consideration for cross-cultural research and intervention, including in the prevention of child abuse and treatment of survivors. Causation framing leads to public health campaigns and clinical interventions where dispensing of knowledge is assumed to produce changes in behavior (Panter-Brick et al. 2006). However, as discussed above, beliefs may not necessarily translate into behavior, and behaviors consistent with stated beliefs may have differential impact.

Justification and confabulation models suggest that changing knowledge alone is inadequate for behavior change. Increasingly, public health interventions are demonstrating that knowledge change alone is insufficient. For example, stigma against mental illness is more effectively reduced through exposure to individuals with mental illness and their family members than through education about biological rather than moral models of mental illness causation (Pescosolido et al. 2010). In fact, Pescosolido and colleagues found that education in genetic and neurobiological models of mental illness can increase stigma against mental illness. Thus, it is likely through changing implicit association through exposure to people with mental disorders that behaviors change – not necessarily through knowledge change alone. Similarly, in child abuse prevention, home visits by community health workers is more effective than campaigns only focused on messages to reduce corporal punishment (MacMillan et al. 2009). The limitations in proceeding from belief to behavior call for an anthropology that considers behavior to be an over determined phenomena with multiple motive and deterrent forces. One avenue to address this is through approaches that address interactions of culture and biology against the background of structural political-economic constraints.

Biocultural Approaches

Biocultural anthropology is a discipline that takes into account biological and structural factors as well as variable models of beliefs systems, both implicit and explicit (Armelagos et al. 1992; Hinton 1999; Lende 2005). This field relies upon mixed-methods research with an emphasis on the interaction of biology and culture (Hruschka et al. 2005a). Biocultural anthropology often is concerned with culture as moderator and biology as mediator. Practitioners also recognize complex interplays and argue that the separation of the two is artificial for heuristic and measurement purposes, while theories must combine them both (Worthman and Costello 2009). Biocultural anthropologists have examined how culture "gets under the skin" through connections among culture, biology, and behavior (Lende 2005; Worthman and Brown 2005). Biocultural topics include mechanisms of cultural transmission, life history, pathways to health outcomes and health disparities, and political and economic influences on culture and biology (Goodman and Leatherman 1998; Leatherman and Goodman 1997; Pike et al. 2010; Worthman and Kohrt 2005).

Biocultural approaches combining anthropology, epidemiology, and political economy are ideal to improve the study of the underlying pathways of racial and ethnic disparities in population health (Hahn 1995; McGarvey 2007), including maltreatment. Anthropologists' disciplinary orientation is towards examining, challenging, and deepening understanding of how culture bears relevance to biological and social processes (Worthman and Kohrt 2005). One aspect of biocultural anthropology is the attempt to account for both explicit and implicit associations by trying to study actual mechanisms – often with biomarker measurement – and by taking into account context that affects how stimuli is perceived and responded to (Worthman 2009; Worthman and Costello 2009). For example, political and economic constraints, the physical and symbolic environment, and especially the social environment frame what and how stimuli are perceived and the possible world of behavioral responses.

Biocultural approaches attempt to examine how ecological factors influence norms, values, and behaviors, and how norms, values, and behaviors shape ecological factors. One way to categorize these two approaches delineates *micro-cultural processes*, referring to practices that happen within specific ecological constraints, from *macro-cultural processes*, referring to how culture shapes ecological constraints through politics, economics, the physical built environment, and the symbolic environment through media, art, literature. Biocultural approaches examine risk factors in context of the political-economic, social, built, and symbolic environment to elucidate broader structural changes as targets for interventions.

Biological Factors in Culture and Child Maltreatment

Sex and Maltreatment

Biological factors including sex, medical illnesses, disabilities, and some behaviors have been documented to show greater risk for abuse in cross-cultural settings (Walker et al. 2007). Sex of a child is a salient biological marker that carries different degrees of risk across cultures and context (Harkness and Super 1994). Biological sex through cultural constructs of gender triggers expectations about appropriate and inappropriate behavior. Higher rates of malnutrition, reduced access to health care, and excess mortality rates for infant girls relative to boys have been documented in South Asia (D'Souza and Chen 1980; Das Gupta 1987; Super 1984). This is mediated by longer delays in seeking medical attention for girls compared to boys (Chen 1988; Simkhada et al. 2006; Singh et al. 2012). This has been tied to cultural models of gender related to economics (Raj 2010). In the 1980s, cultural preferences related to child gender became strikingly evident with the increased use of prenatal imaging to determine biological sex:

> In one of the first hospitals to offer low-cost tests, a study by a Bombay women's organization between 1979 and 1982 found that of 8,000 women who came from all over India, 7,999 wanted an abortion if the test revealed a female child. Many advertisements set the costs of the sex texts and abortions against the future costs of a daughter, including that of her dowry, with slogans such as "better 500 rupees now than 10,000 rupees later on." (Croll 2000, p. 95)

Health differences persist throughout life with female members of households having less access to protein and sources of micronutrients, thus being at greater risk for malnutrition and micronutrient deficiency (Kohrt et al. 2005a).

Disabilities, Epilepsy, and Neglect in Low-Income Countries

In low- and middle-income countries, 23 % of children have or are at risk for disabilities, and children with disabilities are at greater risk of maltreatment (Walker et al. 2011). Untreated or incompletely treated medical conditions can be perceived as life-long disabilities in some settings. In Turkey, medical neglect of children with diseases and disabilities has been attributed to "cultural fatalistic beliefs" about health outcomes and reasons for children's illness (Ertem et al. 2002). In many parts of the world, disabilities and serious illnesses among children are viewed as moral or religious violations by parents and other ancestors, especially infractions by mothers. In some parts of South Asia, this is encapsulated by beliefs of *karma* in which a child with a deformity or disability is due to the mother's lack of piety or bad deeds in this or prior lives (Bennett 1983; Kohrt and Hruschka 2010).

Epilepsy and other histories of seizures can be a major biological risk-factor for abuse. In India, having a child with epilepsy is associated with greater caregiver stress and depression, as well as reduced access to school and health services, partially due to restrictions parents placed on children with epilepsy for perceived protection (Pal et al. 2002). In low- and middle-income countries with limited medical care and child protection resources, seizure disorders can increase risk of gross prolonged deprivation. A case report from rural Thailand describes a 3½ year-old girl who was bitten by a puppy (Bartlet and Limsila 1992). The girl was caged because of fear that she had contracted rabies. There was a history of rabies with subsequent child deaths in other villages in the area. The child did not display signs of rabies, but after prolonged deprivation she did develop seizures, lost fine motor control, and was incontinent of urine and feces. She was kept continuously in a bamboo cage for 6 years. Eventually, a missionary nun brought her to a psychiatric facility in Bangkok where she was treated for 4 years. By the age of 13 years old she had the cognitive function of a 7 year old.

In rural Liberia, children with seizures may be locked in "stick-cuffs", a heavy tree branch that locks onto one foot to prevent ambulation. When asked why this behavior is used, family members explain that if children wandered they could have a "spell" (seizure) and fall into a fire or river and hurt themselves (Kohrt and Swaray 2011). Moreover, "spells" are considered to be contagious if one comes into contact with the saliva of a person having a seizure. Therefore, the stick-cuffs are seen as keeping children safe and protecting others from contagion. Many health professionals (e.g. 44 % of nurses) also endorse the potential for "spell" transmission from one person to another saliva (Medicins du Monde 2010). While contagion beliefs of the public and health workers could be dismissed as ignorance, Liberia also has had outbreaks of rabies resulting in fatalities (Monson 1985). Cultural knowledge related to rabies may have contributed to these beliefs of an association between seizures and saliva transmission. The practice of stick-cuffs raises risks of foot wounds including osteomyelitis, sepsis, and death. The stick-cuffs are only one form of maltreatment for children who suffer from seizures. They may also be prevented from visiting health facilities and excluded from schools. In a recent draft of the Liberia National Education Plan, proposed language stated that "children with epilepsy could be restricted from school for their own benefit," (Kohrt and Swaray 2011). Stick cuffs and other forms of maltreatment as behavioral control are not uncommon for mental retardation, other developmental disorders, and psychotic disorders for children and adolescents in low- and middle-income countries.

Child maltreatment due to biological stimuli, such as seizures, in cross-cultural context raises questions for the best approaches to preventing such forms of neglect and abuse. From a 'causation' belief-based model, public messaging that epilepsy is not contagious is one form knowledge change. One campaign used slogans such as, "Spell is not catching. It is a one-person sickness. Help people with epilepsy," (Kohrt and Swaray 2011). However, in an analysis after 6 months of such messaging, there appeared to be no changes in behavior among health professionals or the general public. Other avenues to consider from a biocultural perspective are reduction of biological cues, such as through treatment. Medication use can lead to models that seizure disorders can be treated. Moreover, medication use can lead to more independent activity to reduce the safety concerns. Ultimately, through increased exposure to children receiving treatment for epilepsy, ideas of contagion may also abate. Policy changes to make anti-epileptic medication available throughout the country may be more impactful than messaging alone with regards to reducing maltreatment of children with seizures.

HIV, Malnutrition, and Other Biological Risk Factors

Maltreatment is a concern for children with HIV in low- and middle- income countries. Stigma has a direct impact on how HIV-positive children are treated in developing countries. In research with institutional and community caregivers of orphans and abandoned children in Cambodia, Ethiopia, India, Kenya, and Tanzania, caregivers carried significant HIV-related stigma toward the children in their care (Messer et al. 2010). Qualitative data from Zambia suggests that HIV-affected children are at high risk of defilement and domestic violence (Murray et al. 2006). Medical neglect also has been documented in Burkina Faso: mothers with HIV-positive children felt they had to conceal the problem due to community stigma and were conflicted about seeking care (Hejoaka 2009). In rural Lesotho, HIV-positive mothers feared revelation of their status, thus hampering drug treatment through a community outreach program and raising the risk of passing HIV to their nursing infants (Towle and Lende 2008).

Malnutrition and micronutrient deficiencies are both a result of and trigger for maltreatment of children in low- and middle-income countries. In 2005, stunting (height for age less than two standard deviations below normative values) still affected 30 % of children, and wasting (weight for age < two standard deviations below median) affected 20 % (Worthman 2011). The majority of these deficiencies was in low- and middle-income countries. Malnutrition, iodine deficiency, as well as intrauterine health factors, all increase risk for developmental and cognitive deficiencies, which increase risk of maltreatment (Walker et al. 2011; Worthman and Brown 2005).

Another framework to consider is the impact of the developing child on the caregiver and his/her social environment (Bronfenbrenner 1979, 1994; Cicchetti and Lynch 1993; Cicchetti et al. 2000). Children with aggressive behavior are in transaction with their social world thus, in part, conditioning caregiver responses. In some settings, children with certain genetic or early-determined biological and behavioral profiles may elicit an array of possible responses, which could include negative or abusive interactions. While this in no way implies that children dictate caregiver behavior, a transactional approach to understanding interactions helps identify how certain child characteristics may place them at greater risk for abuse (Cicchetti et al. 2000). In Mongolia, boys with oppositional defiant disorder (ODD) were more likely to have caregivers who endorsed physical punishment (Kohrt et al. 2004). However, in the cross-sectional study it was not possible to differentiate between physical discipline being a risk factor for ODD, or if parents of boys with ODD were more likely to endorse physical punishment in reaction to the disruptive behavior.

One last area at the intersection of biological cues and child maltreatment comes from socio-biolology research, most notably the work of Daly and Wilson (1988). According to sociobiological perspectives, non-biological children are at greater risk of maltreatment than biological children. With demographic data from high-income countries, this is generally consistent with patterns of child maltreatment: non-biological children suffer greater rates of abuse (Daly and Wilson 1988).

Biological Sequelae of Child Maltreatment in Cross-Cultural Context

Child maltreatment contributes to a range of biological sequelae including alterations in hypothalamic pituitary adrenal (HPA) functioning, structural and functional neuroanatomic changes, and many physical and mental health disorders (Brown et al. 2006; Dong et al. 2004; McCrory et al. 2010). A review of high-income, predominantly English-speaking, countries finds prospective studies of survivors of child maltreatment show strong associations with obesity, and retrospective studies show moderate association with general adult health (Gilbert et al. 2012). Biological impacts of child maltreatment may also influence intergenerational transmission of child maltreatment (Caspi et al. 2002), as has been demonstrated in animal models (Barr et al. 2004; Boyce et al. 1995; Francis et al. 2002; Liu et al. 1997). To what do degree is this observed in other cultural settings, i.e. are there universal biological responses to child abuse? Understanding health sequelae and potential biological mediators are important to help design appropriate interventions for mental health physical health consequences.

Hypothalamic Pituitary Adrenal Activity

Alterations of the HPA axis commonly have been investigated as potential sequelae of child maltreatment and a mediator of other future physical, mental, and behavioral problems. Pathways from child maltreatment to adverse neurostructural and neurophysiological outcomes in children highlight the role of early exposure to glucocorticoids on brain development (Carrion et al. 2001, 2007; Resnick et al. 1995; Teicher 2002; Teicher et al. 2002, 2003; Watts-English et al. 2006). McGowan and colleagues (2009) have demonstrated how early abuse alters glucocorticoid receptor activity in adults. However, studies have demonstrated a varying and at times conflicting associations between cortisol and histories of maltreatment. Number of collections, type of collection, analytic strategy, and controlling for known covariates in HPA activity contribute to variation in outcomes between cortisol and behavioral and psychiatric phenotypes (Hruschka et al. 2005b; Sapolsky et al. 2000).

Studies have shown hypocortisolism related to childhood maltreatment (Gunnar and Donzella 2002; Gunnar and Vazquez 2001; Shea et al. 2007; Yehuda et al. 2001). Among 101 African American adolescents, higher exposure to peer violence was associated with lower basal cortisol, and witnessed violence associated with flatter awakening response (Kliewer 2006). Other studies identified similar inverse associations between violence exposure and cortisol levels (Cooley-Quille et al. 2001; Cooley-Quille and Lorion 1999). Children in foster care, a high-risk group, more frequently displayed hypocortisolism compared with children living with their biological family (Dozier et al. 2006). Neglect was associated with low cortisol among adult women (Power et al. 2012). However, other studies have found positive associations between cortisol levels and stress exposure (Schreier and Evans 2003). In one review, inverse findings were reported with elevated cortisol among abused children and low cortisol among adult survivors of child maltreatment (Tarullo and Gunnar 2006).

Studies of Romanian and Russian formerly institutionalized children have demonstrated major lifelong biological, psychiatric, and physical health sequelae (Fries et al. 2008; Rutter et al. 2010). In one study 22 % of Romanian orphans living in Canada six years after adoption exhibited cortisol levels averaged over the day that exceeded the means of early-adopted children and Canadian-born children (Gunnar et al. 2001). In a study of international adoptees who had experienced pre-adoption deprivation, the level of pre-adoption deprivation associated with higher morning cortisol levels and a larger diurnal cortisol decrease (Kertes et al. 2008).

There are also associations among maltreatment, cortisol levels, and psychiatric disorders. Among maltreated children low cortisol predicts depression (Rogosch et al. 2011). Low cortisol and low cortisol responses to stress among maltreated children associated with higher rates of aggressive and disruptive behaviors (Alink et al. 2012; Ouellet-Morin et al. 2011). Children with low cortisol and a history of maltreatment also demonstrate heightened false recognition memory on neuropsychological testing (Cicchetti et al. 2010).

Cross-cultural research on biological sequelae of child maltreatment is beneficial to uncover whether the consequences are universal, are modified by cultural context, or may be the result of other risk factors that often covary with child maltreatment. This will help elucidate keys to prevention of maltreatment, treatment of survivors, and interruption of violence cycles across cultural context. Cortisol differences may be related to social expectations that could differ among cultures. For example, verbalization of thoughts decreased the level of cortisol response among European Americans but not among East Asian Americans (Kim 2008). Unfortunately, there is a dearth of data from non-Western cultural groups and low and middle income countries.

On the Caribbean island of Dominica, child development research with longitudinal cortisol collection conducted over two decades by Flinn and colleagues is one of the few studies outside of high-income settings (Flinn 2009; Flinn and England 1997; Flinn et al. 2009). It also stands out because it pays attention to the "causal arrow from culture to biology" (Konner 2010, p. 542). By collecting daily saliva samples alongside household activities, Flinn demonstrated that family disruption such as marital conflict and separation was associated with aberrant cortisol levels. Furthermore, through long-term monitoring, he found that children with single mothers or stepparents experienced a greater burden of physiological stress, often displaying elevated cortisol levels.

Studies in Asia have examined differences by institutionalization status and mental health. In Mongolia, boys were compared across settings of institutional and home care, with the former representing potentially a greater history of early maltreatment (Kohrt et al. 2004). Group differences between institutionalized and non-institutionalized boys did not account for a significant amount of variation. However, caregiver's endorsement of physical punishment accounted for 9 % of between individual variation in cortisol levels not explained by other covariates, with boys of caregivers who endorsed physical punishment displaying hypocortisolism (Kohrt et al. 2005b). Oppositional defiant disorder (ODD) accounted for 17 % of between-individual variation in cortisol levels not explained by other covariates: boys with ODD displayed hypocortisolism. There was substantial covariance of parental attitudes toward physical punishment and ODD. The association of hypocortisolism with disruptive behavior also has been seen in East Asian populations (Kaneko et al. 1993; Yang et al. 2007). In Japan, the majority of children with attention deficit hyperactivity disorder (ADHD) displayed atypical diurnal rhythms (Kaneko et al. 1993).

In Nepal, researchers compared institutionalized boys with boys from middle- and upper-class families at boarding schools (Hruschka et al. 2005b; Kohrt, et al. 2005b). Maltreatment histories were not available; residing in the institution was considered a proxy for greater abuse or neglect history. Group differences between institutionalized and boarder boys accounted for 14 % of between-individual variation in cortisol levels, with institutionalized boys displaying hypocortisolism. Boys with oppositional defiant disorder displayed a non-significant trend toward hypocortisolism. Aggression accounted for 11 % of between individual variation in cortisol levels, with aggressive boys displaying hypocortisolism (Hruschka et al. 2005b).

Comparisons also have been made on the association of homelessness with HPA functioning. In Nepal boys were recruited from four settings: urban homeless, urban squatter, urban school-attending, and rural village (Worthman and Panter-Brick 2008). Village boys displayed the highest allostatic load and lowest residual cortisol. Given expected associations between hypocortisolism and high risk environment, the research showed unexpected findings with greater biological vulnerability among village boys living with their families compared to urban homeless and squatter boys. Stunting and pathogen burden also were greatest among village boys. In-depth ethnographic work showed that homelessness was best understood as a "career" move away from life in villages or squatter settlements to escape material poverty and the family stressors poverty engenders (Baker and Panter-Brick 2000). The study did not include information on history of maltreatment but raises questions about which risk factors translate into alterations in HPA axis and how one defines a "healthy" environment of child development.

Neuroimaging and Neuropsychological Functioning

Neuroimaging studies and neuropsychological testing have revealed associations with exposure to child maltreatment, such as structural differences in the corpus callosum and functioning differences in the prefrontal cortex (Gould et al. 2012; McCrory et al. 2010; Spann et al. 2012). Regarding cross-cultural replication, studies in high and middle income countries in East Asia also have found differences in survivors of maltreatment. In Japan, differences in structural ratios for the posterior midbody of the corpus callosum were found when comparing survivors of maltreatment with non-abused controls; however, all survivors of maltreatment were also diagnosed with PTSD (Kitayama et al. 2007). History of parental verbal abuse was associated with alterations in the left superior temporal gyrus in another Japanese study (Tomoda et al. 2011). In China, female victims of child abuse demonstrated decreased neuropeptide Y compared with non-abused controls (Huang et al. 2005). In this Chinese sample, survivors of child abuse also demonstrated impairments on multiple neuropsychological tests. In South Africa, when women with HIV were compared with women who survived child abuse, the child abuse survivors displayed verbal learning delays (Spies et al. 2012). In a neuroimaging study comparing 14 Romanian adoptee adolescents and 11 non-adopted British adolescents, the Romanian adoptees had significantly lower volumes of white and grey matter and greater amygdala volume, especially on the right (Mehta et al. 2009). The duration of time in institutions was correlated negatively with left amygdala volume among the Romanian adoptees. More research is needed to evaluate cross-cultural prevalence of neuroanatomical, neurofunctional, and neuropsychological deficits and the impact of cultural context.

Health Consequences of Other Cultural Practices

Child marriage, defined as marriage before the age of 18 years, is a major human rights issue. UNICEF and other groups have pursued campaigns for the eradication of child marriage. Campaigns against child marriage are grounded in moral models based on cultural definitions of childhood, transition to adulthood, and definitions of what is and who can provide consent. From a biocultural perspective, researchers have investigated if child marriage produces negative health consequences. Child marriage is associated with higher levels of infant mortality, maternal mortality, HIV and other STDs, and mental illness and suicidality (Raj 2010); compared to the children of women who marry at 20 years or older, the children of girls who marry below the age of 14 years have six times greater odds of neonatal mortality, five times greater odd of post-neonatal infant mortality, and 85 times greater odd of child mortality before the age of five. Girls who marry before 14 years of age also have five times greater risk of experiencing spousal violence and three time greater risk of a spouse being greater than 10 years older, compared with women who marry at 20 years of age or older. Moreover, girl marriage is also associated with daughters born of teenage girls at greater risk of harmful gender beliefs; for example, girls who marry before 14 years of age are three times more likely to display a preference for sons over daughters, compared to women who marry after 20 years of age. Thus, the cycle of maltreatment risk is perpetuated.

Another cross-cultural issue that raises concerns of child maltreatment is procedures referred to as female genital mutilation, female genital cutting, and female circumcision. In Egypt, women who underwent these genital procedures reported emotional trauma (94.9 %), hemorrhage (33.3 %), dysuria (7.7 %), and sexual problems (72.7 %) (Zayed and Ali 2012). There is less information on cross-cultural differences in male ritual practices and long-term health outcomes. Male initiation ceremonies in Papua New Guinea and other areas of Melanesia involve anal intercourse and felatio between adolescent boys and adult males in the community (Herdt 1984). Within this cultural context, there is a lack of evidence that this has the same health and psychological consequences as in cases of adolescent sexual abuse in Western cultural settings.

In addition to child marriage and female genital cutting, another form of child maltreatment is forced conscription into armed groups. There is a dearth of studies investigating biomarkers in former child soldiers. However, there is a growing body of literature on the mental health consequences of children associated with armed groups (Betancourt et al. 2013). Unfortunately, variations in prevalence rates of mental health problems are influenced by irregularity in methodology, sampling, and instrumentation. Even within similarly-designed studies there was notable heterogeneity in PTSD rates. For example, in studies of formerly abducted youth conducted in rehabilitation centers in northern Uganda, documented PTSD rates ranged from 97 % in a study of 301 youth that used a non-validated Western psychiatric scale (Amone-P'Olak 2005; Amone P'Olak et al. 2007; Derluyn et al. 2004) to 27 % in a study of 82 youth evaluated using a clinical interview (Okello et al. 2007). In three of five studies with comparison groups, PTSD prevalence was greater among former child soldiers compared with never-conscripted children (Kohrt et al. 2008; MacMullin and Loughry 2004; Okello et al. 2007). In Nepal, this distinction was maintained even after controlling for exposure to violence (Kohrt et al. 2008). By contrast, studies from northern Uganda (Blattman and Annan 2010) found little difference in psychosocial distress levels between former child soldiers and comparison groups.

Female gender was a predictor of poorer mental health in studies in Sierra Leone (Betancourt et al. 2011) and Nepal (Kohrt et al. 2008). In the Sierra Leone research, more females scored within the clinical range for anxiety (80 % of girls vs. 52 % of boys) as well as depression (72 % of girls vs. 55 % of boys). When controlling for war exposures, female gender was significantly associated with lower levels of confidence and prosocial behaviors over time (Betancourt et al. 2010, 2011). In the Nepal sample, there was a significant interaction between gender and child soldier status: girl soldiers had six times greater odds of having PTSD compared to never-conscripted girls, whereas boy soldiers had nearly three times greater odds of having PTSD compared with never-conscripted boys (Kohrt et al. 2008). Of note, only one study to date examined experiences of child abuse prior to conscription into an armed group (Kohrt et al. 2010a). In that study, childhood physical abuse had the strongest effect size for depression among former child soldiers. However, physical abuse was not associated with PTSD and function impairment, which were better explained by exposures such as torture and bombings.

Gene by Environment Interactions in Global Mental Health

Gene-by-environment (GxE) studies have received attention from the psychiatry community as a way to understand mental health risk factors. The growing literature on GxE in mental illness suggests that genetic polymorphisms may associate with greater vulnerability or resilience in the context of early childhood trauma (Binder et al. 2008; Bradley et al. 2008; Caspi et al. 2002; Weder et al. 2009). However, a meta-analysis failed to support these findings regarding stressful life events (Risch et al. 2009), and some studies of childhood trauma have yielded little or no genetic effects (Lasky-Su et al. 2005). The variation and lack of consistency among findings suggests possible variation in culture and context with regard to how "early stress" is defined and measures. Increasing studies in non-Western cultural settings will help to evaluate the role of maltreatment on genetic vulnerability for psychiatric disorders. Below the studies related to serotonin transporters and HPA-pathway receptors are discussed with a cross-cultural critique.

Serotonin Transporter Linked Polymorphic Region (5-HTTTLPR)

In the field of child maltreatment and mental health, there has been considerable interest in the serotonin transporter linked polymorphic region (5-HTTTLPR). Individuals with the low-expressing short (s) allele have shown greater risk for depression when exposed to stressors when compared with individuals expressing long (l) alleles who are exposed to stressors (Caspi et al. 2003). In a review by Caspi and colleagues (2010), 44 studies of GxE interaction for 5-HTTLRP were identified, nine of these studies examined the childhood maltreatment as the environmental stressor. One of the studies compared English and Romanian orphans to examine the effect of institutional deprivation (Kumsta et al. 2010). Carriers of short alleles who experienced severe institutional deprivation showed the highest emotional problem scores, while long allele homozygotes in the severe institutional deprivation group showed the lowest overall levels.

Of the 44 studies in the review, 89 % had been in conducted in high-income countries in Europe or English speaking high-income countries such as United States, Australia, and New Zealand. The only other countries including populations not of European descent were Japan (one study), Korea (two studies), China (one study), and Taiwan (one study). However, none of the studies of child maltreatment as the environmental stressor were conducted with populations of non-European descent. Of note, while the Asian studies in Caspi and colleagues review represented only 11 % of studies reviewed, they represented 33 % of associations in the opposite direction of the commonly reported pattern in the literature, i.e. the long allele posed greater risk than the short allele (Zhang et al. 2009). This raises questions about whether risk and resilience alleles may operate differently across cultural settings.

Kim and colleagues (2010) investigated a three-way interaction of culture (defined in this case as ethnicity), oxytocin polymorphisms, and emotional distress as predictors of support seeking. They found a genotype in a European American sample that predicted level of support seeking when experiencing distress. However, the same genotype was not associated with support seeking distress in the Korean sample. A sample of Korean Americans had an intermediate outcome with a trend toward support seeking associated with the investigated genotype. Kim and colleagues suggest that the oxytocin genotype reflects sensitivity to the environment such that those carrying the target genotype will be more likely to follow culturally normative behavior when exposed to distress. Of note, the allele frequency of the target oxytocin genotype was significantly different in Korean and European descent samples. The work of Kim and colleagues and the reverse finding by Zhang and colleagues related to 5-HTTPLR in China raise questions about potential cultural, biological, or structural difference that can influence gene by environment relationships.

Corticotrophin Releasing Hormone Receptor (CRHR1)

Allele frequency across populations, cultural context, methodological approach, and other factors contribute to differences in the effect of genetic polymorphisms on child maltreatment and risk for depression. Single nucleotide polymorphisms (SNPs) in corticotrophin releasing hormone receptor 1 (CRHR1), a gene related to the hypothalamic pituitary adrenal axis, influences depression risk in adults. In an early study of CRHR1 in a population of highly traumatized African Americans those with a protective version of an CRHR1 SNP and a history of childhood maltreatment showed less depression than participants with a risk version of the SNP and a history of maltreatment (Bradley et al. 2008). In a separate population, differences in cortisol levels based on CRHR1 suggested a mechanism for this association: early abuse and high internalizing symptoms interacted to predict atypical diurnal cortisol regulation (Cicchetti et al. 2011a).

The association between CRHR1, childhood maltreatment, and adult mental health problems, however, is not consistent across all populations studied. In the original study conducted in the United States, the population was predominantly African Americans and child maltreatment was assessed through subjective retrospective recall using the Childhood Trauma Questionnaire (CTQ) (Bradley et al. 2008). In a replication study conducted in the U.S., the interaction of CRHR1 polymorphisms, and child maltreatment was only significant for depression risk among female African Americans, but not among male African Americans or European Americans (Kranzler et al. 2011). Childhood maltreatment was measured in this population using the CTQ as well. In a British sample, CRHR1 risk polymorphisms were associated with depression using the CTQ to measure maltreatment (Polanczyk et al. 2009). A comparison sample in New Zealand in the same analysis did not demonstrate an association, and abuse was measured through court reports in that sample (Polanczyk et al. 2009). In Germany, the polymorphism showed an association with physical neglect on depression, but not on any other outcomes (Grabe et al. 2010). In Japan, the CRHR1 polymorphism showed a direct effect on depression (Ishitobi et al. 2012).

Taken together, the CRHR1 SNP of interest showed an interaction in both female African American populations studied. The SNP showed an association in two out of the four European descent groups. In the one Asian sample, it was a main effect, not an interaction. From a population standpoint, it is important to point out that the frequency of the CRHR1 polymorphism varied significantly among groups. In African American groups, the frequency was 8 % in two different populations. In European American groups, the frequency ranged from 18 % to 25 %. The British sample was 19 %. The German sample was 11 % and the New Zealand sample 18 %. In contrast, the Japanese sample was 84 %.

Exposure to childhood maltreatment in the CRHR1 studies also varied significantly among these groups ranging from 8 % in the British sample to 33–39 % in the African American samples. The frequency of exposure and frequency of polymorphisms has a large effect on statistical analyses of GxE interactions (Caspi et al. 2010). Thus, the manner in which maltreatment is measured needs to be comparable across cultures and needs to be salient to experiences within a cultural group, as with measures of psychopathology across cultural groups (Kohrt et al. 2011). As studies expand to include low- and middle-income countries, the validity of existing measures will need to be explored. For example, the Childhood Trauma Questionnaire (CTQ) used in three of CRHR1 studies has been used in Nepal. Prevalence of maltreatment as measured by the CTQ in Nepal was greater than 80 % (Kohrt 2009), more than double the highest rates observed in the United States. However, the neglect component was the major contributor to this difference. Neglect rates were higher in Nepal because of endemic poverty and widespread food insecurity. However, this does not necessarily represent parental pathology or mal-intent as it may in some settings. Physical neglect was the main predictor in the GxE interaction with CRHR1 in Germany, but would the same interaction be found in Nepal where neglect may have different meaning and impact on development. There is currently limited support for most GxE interactions related to child maltreatment and mental health outcomes from a cross-cultural perspective. More studies are needed to determine if similar patterns emerge.

Macro-Cultural Context

Micro-cultural context refer to specific inter-personal exchanges, but macro-cultural processes refer to how the environment is shaped and how the environment constrains the world of possible behavioral reactions. Micro-cultural models of parenting are driven by symbolic representations attached to the meaning of caregiver responsibilities and the social value of children (Panter-Brick et al. 2012). These intersect with macro-cultural social policies that institutionalize a narrow range of parenting norms and govern resource provision. This may lead to behaviors and actions that place children at greater risk. For example, gun ownership increases the risk of suicide and accidental and intentional homicide, including among of children (Dahlberg et al. 2004; Grossman et al. 1999; Kellermann et al. 1993). However, gun ownership may be valued for other symbolic reasons that pertain to group identity despite the risk placed on children. From a societal perspective, programs such as Head Start show long-term benefits for social capital including educational and economic outcomes (Beeber et al. 2007; Blair et al. 2005; Miller et al. 2006; Stormshak et al. 2002). However, policy makers may choose not to support programs because of conflicts with other belief or value systems. Panter-Brick and colleagues point this out in their discussion of conflicts between child health outcomes and *symbolic* health, represented by notions of cultural status and identity:

> There exist, throughout the world, striking examples of parental decision making that systematically place children in harm's way—due to poverty forcing the hand of parents, worldviews loading the dice of decision making, and social policies changing the landscape of reproductive opportunities. (Panter-Brick et al. 2012, p. 615)

Ultimately, macro-cultural processes lead to wide variation in investment in child welfare both within and between countries.

In low-income non-Western settings, families are forced to make decision in the context of pervasive food insecurity (Panter-Brick et al. 2012). In conditions of famine, households often prefer to preserve household wealth rather than "waste" money or food sources on further calories or nutrients (Baro and Deubel 2006). Household wealth may trump the health or nutrition of any one individual. Families are often willing to trade off physical health for the monetary health of a household. In Niger in the midst of a severe food crisis, the importance of household wealth can even trump cultural values of egalitarian support for children (Hampshire et al. 2009). In this case, benign neglect led to faltering in the growth and health of already vulnerable children. Pervasive poverty can overwhelm even cultural values of investment in children.

In this section, macro-cultural processes are explored as they shape biological risk factors for child maltreatment. Interventions can combat macro-cultural risk factors through both macro-cultural and micro-cultural changes. Macro-cultural changes are policy changes, increasing access to healthcare or increasing wealth and resources. Micro-cultural changes are typified by home-visitation programs to reduce child maltreatment. Such micro-cultural interventions mitigate the effects of macro-cultural systemic risks. Two examples are discussed from the perspective of macro-cultural to micro-cultural processes. First, the case of girls in South Asia is discussed in terms of risk factors for medical and health neglect, girl marriage, and recruitment as child soldiers. Then, the relationship among poverty and disruptive behavioral disorders is discussed.

Maltreatment of Girls in South Asia

As discussed above, biological sex influences type and frequency of abuse and neglect, with variability across cultures. In South Asia, girls suffer maltreatment including medical neglect, dietary deprivation resulting in malnutrition and micronutrient deficiency, forced marriage, trafficking for commercial sex work, and exploitation in armed groups as girl soldiers. Individual parental ethnotheories on the value of daughters versus sons influences these practices, with economic burden of girls cited as justification for gender discrimination. What are the macro-cultural processes that create and perpetuate the symbolic and structural devaluing of women?

In Raj's (2010) model of risk for girl child marriage in India, she highlights social vulnerabilities (rural poverty, low development, conflict, and low access to health care), gender inequities pre-marriage (lack of girl's education and job opportunity), dowry bride prices, and arranged marriage structure. Girls are seen as a greater financial burden because a girl leaves her parents home to join the husband's family at the time of marriage, and the bride's family must pay a dowry to the husband's family. Sons are perceived as more beneficial because they do not leave the household, and they bring in extra resources in terms of their bride's labor and dowry. This model highlights structural issues related to economics.

The dowry is just one of the gendered economic limitations. For example, only after the Maoist-led People's War in Nepal ended in 2006 were women able to inherit property. Previously, unmarried daughters had no right to their father's property and wealth. The perceived economic burden of girls engenders situations where fathers decide to sell their daughters to traffickers who sell girls into commercial sex institutions in India. Because of maltreatment in the home, many girls in Nepal perceived joining the Maoist Army as a better alternative to village life because of the perception of gender equality within the Maoists (Kohrt et al. 2010b).

What are macro-cultural interventions to reduce maltreatment risks to girls? Girls' education has been identified as a key component of improving health outcomes, lowering fertility rates, and postponing marriage until adulthood (Kamal 2012; Levine et al. 2001; Raj et al. 2009). Girls married before the age of 14 years old are 11 times more likely to have no formal education when compared with women who marry at 20 years of age or older (Raj 2010). The active ingredient of education for women on health and behavioral outcomes may be that schooling affects maternal outlooks and fosters skills such as mastery of communications skills needed for navigating health care systems, political processes, and other bureaucracies (Levine et al. 2001), and possibly communication with male partners. Mothers are able to independently bring a child for healthcare if they are literate (Levine et al. 2001). Therefore, from a macro-social perspective increasing opportunities for girls to go to school can reduce various forms of maltreatment. However, one challenge is gendered educational deprivation in which boys are preferentially sent to school. One avenue to counter this is paying families to send their daughters to school. Other approaches focus on attitudinal change and using examples of women who were educated and now have employment.

The importance of improving access to education in South Asia for girls at a macro-cultural and micro-cultural level also was demonstrated in the area of maltreatment through exploitation of girl soldiers. Lack of education was a risk factor for joining armed groups. In Nepal greater than half of girl soldiers reported joining the Maoist army voluntarily because their parents did not support them going to school. Maoists actively promoted a gender-equal "real-life" education as an alternative to gender-biased education in villages.

After the war, education was again a focus of former girl soldiers. Girl soldiers resisted participating in reintegration rituals, preferring instead to return to school. UNICEF and other organizations have advocated for the use of traditional rituals for reintegration of girl soldiers in Africa. In Sierra Leone and Uganda, traditional rituals have been documented as a pathway for former soldiers, especially girl soldiers, to reenter society. However, girl soldiers in Nepal refused to participate in rituals identified by the community as promoting acceptance (Kohrt in press). They explained that the ritual makes them more palatable to the community by placing them in a subservient position to men. They saw the ritual as symbolic submission to patriarchy (c.f. Bennett 1983; Denov 2007). The girls instead wanted to participate in school and secular activities such as clubs and drama teams. This demonstrates that while the community had identified pathways to reintegration that would reduce discrimination, for the girl soldiers this came at the cost of their identity as independent women. They stated that they would prefer to be mistreated as rebel girls than to be accepted as submissive women.

Increased access to education appears to be both an effective macro-cultural agent of improving women's lives as demonstrated by child marriage and reproductive health studies (Levine et al. 2001; Raj 2010) and a preferred route of social improvement as demonstrated by girl soldiers in Nepal (Kohrt et al. 2010b).

Global Poverty and Disruptive Behavioral Disorders

One of the most salient findings in child maltreatment relates to disruptive behavioral disorders (DBD) and poverty. Disruptive behavioral disorders (oppositional defiant disorder and conduct disorder) are strongly associated with experiences of maltreatment (Burke et al. 2002; Yeager and Lewis 2000). The causal pathway is challenging to unpack. DBDs may precipitate increased parental stress and risk for maltreatment. Conversely, maltreatment may generate DBDs.

Based on cross-national studies, there is an association between parental discipline norms and reports of aggression among children (Gershoff et al. 2010) and an association between human development index (HDI) and types of discipline (Britto and Ulkuer 2012; Lansford and Deater-Deckard 2012). In higher HDI settings, there are higher quality housing and material resources related to child development. However, structural versus cultural factors can be extremely difficult to parse. All low HDI countries were in West Africa and all high HDI countries were in Eastern Europe. In another analysis of the same data set, regional differences rather than development index were cited as associations with child maltreatment refering to the highest prevalences in African countries (Akmatov 2011). The covariance of region, education, literacy, poverty, and putative cultural groups makes it difficult to separate customs and belief systems from structural constraints. Interventions are key to see if changing factors such as education or income produces changes in behavior within a specific region, or within country studies about education and income in relation to child maltreatment.

From a natural experiment that grew out of a longitudinal study in the U.S., one aspect of the relationship among poverty, maltreatment, and DBDs can be addressed: if poverty is reduced does this change rates of disruptive behavioral disorders? Or, do customs and norms perpetuate risk factors for DBDs even in improved economic circumstances? In the natural experiment, the Great Smoky Mountain Study followed Cherokee Indian and European-American children from youth into adulthood. During the study, a casino opened on Cherokee reservation land. This led to income supplements for many Cherokee families. As a result of the income supplements, a number of families were no longer living below the poverty level. The income supplements were associated with reduced rates of DBDs (Costello et al. 2010). Family income supplements did not affect depression or anxiety in children.

The impact of income supplements on behavioral disorders appears to be mediated partially by increased time spent with children after the income supplements because parents did not need to pursue multiple jobs to financially support the family (Costello et al. 2010). Although data were not available on abuse, this also raises questions if there were less neglect or abuse exposures as a result of the income supplements given that abuse and neglect are associated strongly with behavioral disorders in children. Importantly, the change came about without a specific parenting intervention focusing on practices or beliefs: it was through increased opportunity for parent–child interactions. In combination, educating parents through micro-cultural interventions of in-home teaching of parenting strategies reduces abusive behavior at the household level (Daro and Harding 1999; Engle et al. 2011; MacMillan et al. 2009) while macro-cultural interventions to reduce poverty may strongly contribute to reducing DBDs at a population level (Britto and Ulkuer 2012; Casillas 2011).

A further question is whether a reduction in maltreatment is associated with reduced biological risk profiles for DBDs. Do macro-cultural or micro-cultural interventions affect biological mediators? One intervention study from the United States demonstrated that maltreated children participating in an intervention did not show lowering of cortisol over time whereas a comparison group of maltreated children showed a decline in cortisol over time (Cicchetti et al. 2011b). This intervention suggests that a change in environment can prevent the hypocortisolism associated with adult physical and mental health sequelae. The study raises questions about cross-cultural variation in HPA sequelae of child maltreatment. Because social ecology varies tremendously, one could imagine sociocultural context where resilience structures are in place to prevent hypocortisolism in the face of early maltreatment, while in other settings those structures are not naturally occurring and need to be developed in the form of culturally-compelling interventions.

Conclusion

Addressing child maltreatment globally is challenging because of the interwoven factors of culture, biology, and structural factors. These processes are not exclusive, but rather interact to produce patterns of risk and resilience. Biocultural approaches are one avenue to address how biological factors are moderated by culture, how cultural processes produce differential biological outcomes, and ultimately how culture determines biological niches and constrains behavioral potentials. Culture is best operationalized when both macro-cultural and micro-cultural processes are addressed, with the former referring to political, economic, and symbolic influences whereas micro-cultural processes refer to how norms, values, and preferences are translated into specific behaviors. Future research will require interdisciplinary methods that evaluate biomarkers, parental ethnotheories, and political-economic constraints on lived ecologies.

It is the responsibility of researchers, clinicians, policy makers, and funders of social programs to identify the key elements of protective environments of children. It is also crucial to observe how children and adolescents navigate their social ecologies and constraints. Throughout this chapter, child maltreatment has been described through the lens of researchers, interventionists, and policy makers. The voice of children and their preferences also need to be taken into account, even in a macro-cultural framework. Observations of how children and adolescents weigh risks and benefits on micro-cultural transactions may shed light on key elements for successful macro-cultural risk reduction. In Nepal, former girl soldiers prioritized internal models of gender equality over participating in community reintegration rituals, which were expected to reduce maltreatment but came at the cost of models of equality. Ultimately, girls in South Asia and children throughout the world should not need to choose between personal models of equality and reducing risk of community maltreatment. Biocultural models and keen attention to the lived experience of children are tools to build that world.

References

Akmatov, M. K. (2011). Child abuse in 28 developing and transitional countries–results from the multiple indicator cluster surveys. *International Journal of Epidemiology, 40*(1), 219–227.

Alink, L. R., Cicchetti, D., Kim, J., & Rogosch, F. A. (2012). Longitudinal associations among child maltreatment, social functioning, and cortisol regulation. *Developmental Psychology, 48*(1), 224–236.

Amone P'Olak, K., Garnefski, N., & Kraaij, V. (2007). The impact of war experiences and physical abuse on formerly abducted boys in Northern Uganda. *South African Psychiatry Review, 10*, 76–82.

Amone-P'Olak, K. (2005). Psychological impact of war and sexual abuse on adolescent girls in Northern Uganda. *Intervention: International Journal of Mental Health, Psychosocial Work & Counselling in Areas of Armed Conflict, 3*(1), 33–45.

Armelagos, G. J., Leatherman, T., Ryan, M., & Sibley, L. (1992). Biocultural synthesis in medical anthropology. *Medical Anthropology, 14*(1), 35–52.

Baker, R., & Panter-Brick, C. (2000). A comparative perspective on children's' career's and abandonment in Nepal. In C. Panter-Brick & M. T. Smith (Eds.), *Abandoned children* (pp. 161–181). New York: Cambridge University Press.

Baro, M., & Deubel, T. F. (2006). Persistent hunger: perspectives on vulnerability, famine, and food security in Sub-Saharan Africa. *Annual Review of Anthropology, 35*(1), 521–538.

Barr, C. S., Newman, T. K., Shannon, C., Parker, C., Dvoskin, R. L., Becker, M. L., et al. (2004). Rearing condition and rh5-HTTLPR interact to influence limbic-hypothalamic-pituitary-adrenal axis response to stress in infant macaques. *Biological Psychiatry, 55*(7), 733–738.

Bartlet, L. B., & Limsila, P. (1992). Severe deprivation in childhood: A case report from Thailand. *The British Journal of Psychiatry, 161*, 412–414.

Beeber, L. S., Chazan-Cohen, R., Squires, J., Harden, B. J., Boris, N. W., Heller, S. S., et al. (2007). The early promotion and intervention research consortium (E-PIRC): Five approaches to improving infant/toddler mental health in early head start. *Infant Mental Health Journal, 28*(2), 130–150.

Bennett, L. (1983). *Dangerous wives and sacred sisters: Social and symbolic roles of high-caste women in Nepal.* New York: Columbia University Press.

Betancourt, T. S., Borisova, I. I., Brennan, R. B., Williams, T. P., Whitfield, T. H., de la Soudiere, M., et al. (2010). Sierra Leone's former child soldiers: A follow-up study of psychosocial adjustment and community reintegration. *Child Development, 81*(4), 1077–1095.

Betancourt, T. S., Borisova, I., de la Soudière, M., & Williamson, J. (2011). Sierra Leone's child soldiers: War exposures and mental health problems by gender. *Journal of Adolescent Health, 49*(1), 21–28.

Betancourt, T. S., Borisova, I., Williams, T. P., Meyers-Ohki, S. E., Rubin-Smith, J. E., Annan, J., et al. (2013). Research review: Psychosocial adjustment and mental health in former child soldiers – a systematic review of the literature and recommendations for future research. *Journal of Child Psychology and Psychiatry, 54*(1), 17–36.

Binder, E. B., Bradley, R. G., Liu, W., Epstein, M. P., Deveau, T. C., Mercer, K. B., et al. (2008). Association of FKBP5 polymorphisms and childhood abuse with risk of posttraumatic stress disorder symptoms in adults. *JAMA: The Journal of the American Medical Association, 299*(11), 1291–1305.

Blair, C., Granger, D., & Peters Razza, R. (2005). Cortisol reactivity is positively related to executive function in preschool children attending head start. *Child Development, 76*(3), 554–567.

Blattman, C., & Annan, J. (2010). The consequences of child soldiering. *The Review of Economics and Statistics, 92*(4), 882–898.

Boyce, W. T., Champoux, M., Suomi, S. J., & Gunnar, M. R. (1995). Salivary cortisol in nursery-reared rhesus monkeys: Reactivity to peer interactions and altered circadian activity. *Developmental Psychobiology, 28*(5), 257–267.

Bradley, R. G., Binder, E. B., Epstein, M. P., Tang, Y., Nair, H. P., Liu, W., et al. (2008). Influence of child abuse on adult depression: Moderation by the corticotropin-releasing hormone receptor gene. *Archives of General Psychiatry, 65*(2), 190–200.

Britto, P. R., & Ulkuer, N. (2012). Child development in developing countries: Child rights and policy implications. *Child Development, 83*(1), 92–103.

Bronfenbrenner, U. (1979). *The ecology of human development: Experiments by nature and design.* Cambridge: Harvard University Press.

Bronfenbrenner, U. (1994). *Ecological models of human development international encyclopedia of education* (2nd ed., Vol. 3, pp. 37–43). Oxford: Elsevier.

Brown, D. W., Young, K. E., Anda, R. F., Felitti, V. J., & Giles, W. H. (2006). Re: Asthma and the risk of lung cancer. Findings from the adverse childhood experiences (ACE). *Cancer Causes & Control, 17*(3), 349–350.

Burke, J. D., Loeber, R., & Birmaher, B. (2002). Oppositional defiant disorder and conduct disorder: A review of the past 10 years, part II. *Journal of the American Academy of Child and Adolescent Psychiatry, 41*(11), 1275–1293.

Butler, S. F., & Binder, J. L. (1987). Cyclical psychodynamics and the triangle of insight: An integration. *Psychiatry, 50*(3), 218–231.

Calvete, E. (2007). Justification of violence beliefs and social problem-solving as mediators between maltreatment and behavior problems in adolescents. *Spanish Journal of Psychology, 10*(1), 131–140.

Carrion, V. G., Weems, C. F., Eliez, S., Patwardhan, A., Brown, W., Ray, R. D., et al. (2001). Attenuation of frontal asymmetry in pediatric posttraumatic stress disorder. *Biological Psychiatry, 50*(12), 943–951.

Carrion, V. G., Weems, C. F., & Reiss, A. L. (2007). Stress predicts brain changes in children: A pilot longitudinal study on youth stress, posttraumatic stress disorder, and the hippocampus. [see comment]. *Pediatrics, 119*(3), 509–516.

Casillas, K. L. (2011). Commentary: Violent child disciplinary practices in low- and middle-income households. *International Journal of Epidemiology, 40*(1), 227–229.

Caspi, A., McClay, J., Moffitt, T. E., Mill, J., Martin, J., Craig, I. W., et al. (2002). Role of genotype in the cycle of violence in maltreated children. [see comment]. *Science, 297*(5582), 851–854.

Caspi, A., Sugden, K., Moffitt, T. E., Taylor, A., Craig, I. W., Harrington, H., et al. (2003). Influence of life stress on depression: Moderation by a polymorphism in the 5-HTT gene. [see comment]. *Science, 301*(5631), 386–389.

Caspi, A., Hariri, A. R., Holmes, A., Uher, R., & Moffitt, T. E. (2010). Genetic sensitivity to the environment: The case of the serotonin transporter gene and its implications for studying complex diseases and traits. *The American Journal of Psychiatry, 167*(5), 509–527.

Chen, L. C. (1988). Micro-approaches to the study of child mortality in rural Bangladesh. In A. Hill (Ed.), *Micro-approaches to demongratic research*. London: Kegan Paul.

Cicchetti, D., & Lynch, M. (1993). Toward an ecological/transactional model of community violence and child maltreatment: Consequences for children's development. *Psychiatry, 56*, 96–118.

Cicchetti, D., Toth, S. L., & Maughan, A. (2000). An ecological-transactional model of child maltreatment. In A. J. Sameroff, M. Lewis, & S. M. Miller (Eds.), *Handbook of developmental psychopathology* (2nd ed., pp. 689–722). New York: Kluwer Academic/Plenum.

Cicchetti, D., Rogosch, F. A., Howe, M. L., & Toth, S. L. (2010). The effects of maltreatment and neuroendocrine regulation on memory performance. *Child Development, 81*(5), 1504–1519.

Cicchetti, D., Rogosch, F. A., & Oshri, A. (2011a). Interactive effects of corticotropin releasing hormone receptor 1, serotonin transporter linked polymorphic region, and child maltreatment on diurnal cortisol regulation and internalizing symptomatology. *Development and Psychopathology, 23*(4), 1125–1138.

Cicchetti, D., Rogosch, F. A., Toth, S. L., & Sturge-Apple, M. L. (2011b). Normalizing the development of cortisol regulation in maltreated infants through preventive interventions. *Development and Psychopathology, 23*(3), 789–800.

Coalition to Stop the Use of Child Soldiers. (2004). *Child soldiers: Global report 2004*. London: Coalition to Stop the Use of Child Soldiers.

Cooley-Quille, M., & Lorion, R. (1999). Adolescents' exposure to community violence: Sleep and psychophysiological functioning. *Journal of Community Psychology, 27*(4), 367–375.

Cooley-Quille, M., Boyd, R. C., Frantz, E., & Walsh, J. (2001). Emotional and behavioral impact of exposure to community violence in inner-city adolescents. *Journal of Clinical Child Psychology, 30*(2), 199–206.

Costello, E. J., Erkanli, A., Copeland, W. E., & Angold, A. (2010). Association of family income supplements in adolescence with development of psychiatric and substance use disorders in adulthood among an American Indian population. *JAMA: The Journal of the American Medical Association, 303*(19), 1954–1960.

Coulton, C. J., Crampton, D. S., Irwin, M., Spilsbury, J. C., & Korbin, J. E. (2007). How neighborhoods influence child maltreatment: A review of the literature and alternative pathways. *Child Abuse & Neglect, 31*(11–12), 1117–1142.

Croll, E. (2000). *Endangered daughters*. London: Routledge.

D'Souza, S., & Chen, L. C. (1980). Sex differentials in mortality in rural Bangladesh. *Population and Development Review, 6*(2), 257–270.

Dahlberg, L. L., Ikeda, R. M., & Kresnow, M. J. (2004). Guns in the home and risk of a violent death in the home: Findings from a national study. *American Journal of Epidemiology, 160*(10), 929–936.

Daly, M., & Wilson, M. (1988). *Homicide*. New Brunswick: Transaction Publishers.

Daro, D. A., & Harding, K. A. (1999). Healthy Families America: Using research to enhance practice. *The Future of Children, 9*(1), 152–176.

Das Gupta, M. (1987). Selective discrimination against female-children in rural Punjab, India. *Population and Development Review, 13*(1), 77–100.

Denov, M. (2007). Is culture always right? The dangers of reproducing gender stereotypes and inequalities in psychosocial interventions for war-affected children. In L. Dowdney (Ed.), *Psychosocial web page*. London: Coalition to Stop the Use of Child Soldiers.

Derluyn, I., Broekaert, E., Schuyten, G., & De Temmerman, E. (2004). Post-traumatic stress in former Ugandan child soldiers. *Lancet, 363*(9412), 861–863.

Dong, M., Giles, W. H., Felitti, V. J., Dube, S. R., Williams, J. E., Chapman, D. P., et al. (2004). Insights into causal pathways for ischemic heart disease: Adverse childhood experiences study. *Circulation, 110*(13), 1761–1766.

Dozier, M., Manni, M., Gordon, M. K., Peloso, E., Gunnar, M. R., Stovall-McClough, K. C., et al. (2006). Foster children's diurnal production of cortisol: An exploratory study. *Child Maltreatment, 11*(2), 189–197.

du Monde, M. (2010). *Mental health in-service training.* Liberia: Bong County.

Dubanoski, R., & Snyder, K. (1980). Patterns of child abuse and neglect in Japanese- and Samoan-Americans. *Child Abuse & Neglect, 4*, 217–225.

Edmonds, J. K., Hruschka, D., Bernard, H. R., & Sibley, L. (2012). Women's Social networks and birth attendant decisions: Application of the network-episode model. *Social Science & Medicine, 74*(3), 452–459.

Engle, P. L., Fernald, L. C. H., Alderman, H., Behrman, J., O'Gara, C., Yousafzai, A., et al. (2011). Child development 2 strategies for reducing inequalities and improving developmental outcomes for young children in low-income and middle-income countries. *Lancet, 378*(9799), 1339–1353.

Ertem, I. O., Bingoler, B. E., Ertem, M., Uysal, Z., & Gozdasoglu, S. (2002). Medical neglect of a child: Challenges for pediatricians in developing countries. *Child Abuse & Neglect, 26*(8), 751–761.

Flinn, M. V. (2009). Are cortisol profiles a stable trait during child development? *American Journal of Human Biology, 21*(6), 769–771.

Flinn, M. V., & England, B. G. (1997). Social economics of childhood glucocorticoid stress response and health. *American Journal of Physical Anthropology, 102*(1), 33–53.

Flinn, M. V., Muehlenbein, M. P., & Ponzi, D. (2009). Evolution of neuroendocrine mechanisms linking attachment and life history: The social neuroendocrinology of middle childhood. *The Behavioral and Brain Sciences, 32*(1), 27–28.

Fotopoulou, A. (2010). The affective neuropsychology of confabulation and delusion. *Cognitive Neuropsychiatry, 15*(1), 38–63.

Francis, D. D., Diorio, J., Plotsky, P. M., & Meaney, M. J. (2002). Environmental enrichment reverses the effects of maternal separation on stress reactivity. *Journal of Neuroscience, 22*(18), 7840–7843.

Fries, A. B. W., Shirtcliff, E. A., & Pollak, S. D. (2008). Neuroendocrine dysregulation following early social deprivation in children. *Developmental Psychobiology, 50*(6), 588–599.

Gershoff, E. T., Grogan-Kaylor, A., Lansford, J. E., Chang, L., Zelli, A., Deater-Deckard, K., et al. (2010). Parent discipline practices in an international sample: Associations with child behaviors and moderation by perceived normativeness. *Child Development, 81*(2), 487–502.

Gilbert, R., Fluke, J., O'Donnell, M., Gonzalez-Izquierdo, A., Brownell, M., Gulliver, P., et al. (2012). Child maltreatment: Variation in trends and policies in six developed countries. *Lancet, 379*(9817), 758–772.

Goodman, A. H., & Leatherman, T. L. (1998). *Building a new biocultural synthesis: Political-economic perspectives on human biology.* Ann Arbor: University of Michigan Press.

Gould, F., Clarke, J., Heim, C., Harvey, P. D., Majer, M., & Nemeroff, C. B. (2012). The effects of child abuse and neglect on cognitive functioning in adulthood. *Journal of Psychiatric Research, 46*(4), 500–506.

Grabe, H. J., Schwahn, C., Appel, K., Mahler, J., Schulz, A., Spitzer, C., et al. (2010). Childhood maltreatment, the corticotropin-releasing hormone receptor gene and adult depression in the general population. *American Journal of Medical Genetics. Part B, Neuropsychiatric Genetics, 153B*(8), 1483–1493.

Gravlee, C. C., & Sweet, E. (2008). Race, ethnicity, and racism in medical anthropology, 1977–2002. *Medical Anthropology Quarterly, 22*(1), 27–51.

Griffith, J. L. (2010). *Religion that heals, religion that harms: A guide for clinical practice.* New York: Guilford Press.

Griffith, J. L., Griffith, M. E., & Slovik, L. S. (1990). Mind-body problems in family therapy: Contrasting first- and second-order cybernetics approaches. *Family Process, 29*(1), 13–28.

Grossman, D. C., Reay, D. T., & Baker, S. A. (1999). Self-inflicted and unintentional firearm injuries among children and adolescents: The source of the firearm. *Archives of Pediatrics & Adolescent Medicine, 153*(8), 875–878.

Gunnar, M. R., & Donzella, B. (2002). Social regulation of the cortisol levels in early human development. *Psychoneuroendocrinology, 27*(1–2), 199–220.

Gunnar, M. R., & Vazquez, D. M. (2001). Low cortisol and a flattening of expected daytime rhythm: Potential indices of risk in human development. *Development and Psychopathology, 13*(3), 515–538.

Gunnar, M. R., Morison, S. J., Chisholm, K., & Schuder, M. (2001). Salivary cortisol levels in children adopted from Romanian orphanages. *Development and Psychopathology, 13*(3), 611–628.

Hahn, R. A. (1995). *Sickness and healing: An anthropological perspective.* New Haven: Yale University Press.

Hampshire, K., Casiday, R., Kilpatrick, K., & Panter-Brick, C. (2009). The social context of childcare practices and child malnutrition in Niger's recent food crisis. *Disasters, 33*(1), 132–151.

Harkness, S., & Super, C. M. (1994). The developmental niche: A theoretical framework for analyzing the household production of health. *Social Science & Medicine, 38*(2), 217–226.

Harkness, S., & Super, C. M. (1996). *Parents' cultural belief systems: Their origins, expressions, and consequences.* New York: Guilford Press.

Harkness, S., Super, C. M., & van Tijen, N. (2000). Individualism and the "western mind" reconsidered: American and Dutch parents' ethnotheories of the child. *New Directions for Child and Adolescent Development, 87*, 23–39.

Hejoaka, F. (2009). Care and secrecy: Being a mother of children living with HIV in Burkina Faso. *Social Science & Medicine, 69*(6), 869–876.

Herdt, G. H. (Ed.). (1984). *Ritualized homosexuality in Melanesia.* Berkeley: University of California Press.

Hinton, A. L. (1999). *Biocultural approaches to the emotions.* Cambridge, England: Cambridge University Press.

Hruschka, D. (2009a). Defining cultural competence in context: Dyadic norms of friendship among US high school students. *Ethos, 37*(2), 205–224.

Hruschka, D. J. (2009b). Culture as an explanation in population health. *Annals of Human Biology, 36*(3), 235–247.

Hruschka, D. J., & Hadley, C. (2008). A glossary of culture in epidemiology. *Journal of Epidemiology and Community Health, 62*(11), 947–951.

Hruschka, D. J., Lende, D. H., & Worthman, C. M. (2005a). Biocultural dialogues: Biology and culture in psychological anthropology. *Ethos, 33*(1), 1–19.

Hruschka, D. J., Kohrt, B. A., & Worthman, C. M. (2005b). Estimating between- and within-individual variation in cortisol levels using multilevel models. *Psychoneuroendocrinology, 30*(7), 698–714.

Hruschka, D. J., Sibley, L. M., Kalim, N., & Edmonds, J. K. (2008). When there is more than one answer key: Cultural theories of postpartum hemorrhage in Matlab, Bangladesh. *Field Methods, 20*(4), 315–337.

Hruschka, D. J., Brewis, A. A., Wutich, A., & Morin, B. (2011). Shared norms and their explanation for the social clustering of obesity. *American Journal of Public Health, 101*(Suppl 1), S295–S300.

Huang, G. P., Zhang, Y. L., Shen, J. J., Zou, S. H., Xiang, H., & Zhao, L. (2005). Cognitive function and posttraumatic stress symptoms among the victims of child sexual abuse in female inmates. *Chinese Mental Health Journal, 19,* 702–705.

International Labour Organization. (2002). *Every child counts: New global estimates on child labour.* Geneva: International Programme on the Elimination of Child Labour.

Ishitobi, Y., Nakayama, S., Yamaguchi, K., Kanehisa, M., Higuma, H., Maruyama, Y., et al. (2012). Association of CRHR1 and CRHR2 with major depressive disorder and panic disorder in a Japanese population. *American Journal of Medical Genetics. Part B, Neuropsychiatric Genetics, 159B*(4), 429–436.

Kamal, S. M. (2012). Decline in child marriage and changes in its effect on reproductive outcomes in Bangladesh. *Journal of Health, Population and Nutrition, 30*(3), 317–330.

Kaneko, M., Hoshino, Y., Hashimoto, S., Okano, T., & Kumashiro, H. (1993). Hypothalamic-pituitary-adrenal axis function in children with attention-deficit hyperactivity disorder. *Journal of Autism and Developmental Disorders, 23*(1), 59–65.

Kellermann, A. L., Rivara, F. P., Rushforth, N. B., Banton, J. G., Reay, D. T., Francisco, J. T., et al. (1993). Gun ownership as a risk factor for homicide in the home. [Erratum appears in N Engl J Med. 1998 Sep 24;339(13):928–9; PMID: 9750102]. *The New England Journal of Medicine, 329*(15), 1084–1091.

Kertes, D. A., Gunnar, M. R., Madsen, N. J., & Long, J. D. (2008). Early deprivation and home basal cortisol levels: A study of internationally adopted children. *Development and Psychopathology, 20*(2), 473–491.

Khoury, N. M., Kaiser, B. N., Keys, H. M., Brewster, A.-R. T., & Kohrt, B. A. (2012). Explanatory models and mental health treatment: Is vodou an obstacle to psychiatric treatment in rural Haiti? *Culture, Medicine and Psychiatry.* doi:10.1007/s11013-11012-19270-11012.

Kim, H. S. (2008). Culture and the cognitive and neuroendocrine responses to speech. *Journal of Personality and Social Psychology, 94*(1), 32–47.

Kim, H. S., Sherman, D. K., Sasaki, J. Y., Xu, J., Chu, T. Q., Ryu, C., et al. (2010). Culture, distress, and oxytocin receptor polymorphism (OXTR) interact to influence emotional support seeking. *Proceedings of the National Academy of Sciences of the United States of America, 107*(36), 15717–15721.

Kitayama, N., Brummer, M., Hertz, L., Quinn, S., Kim, Y., & Bremner, J. D. (2007). Morphologic alterations in the corpus callosum in abuse-related posttraumatic stress disorder: A preliminary study. *The Journal of Nervous and Mental Disease, 195*(12), 1027–1029.

Kliewer, W. (2006). Violence exposure and cortisol responses in urban youth. *International Journal of Behavioral Medicine, 13*(2), 109–120.

Kohrt, B. A. (2009). *Political violence and mental health in Nepal: War in context, structural violence, and the erasure of history.* Ph.D. Dissertation, Emory University, Atlanta.

Kohrt, B. A. (in press). The Role of Traditional Rituals for Reintegration and Psychosocial Wellbeing of Child Soldiers in Nepal. In A. L. Hinton & D. E. Hinton (Eds.), *Legacies of Mass Violence.* Durham, North Carolina: Duke University Press.

Kohrt, B. A., & Hruschka, D. J. (2010). Nepali concepts of psychological trauma: The role of idioms of distress, ethnopsychology and ethnophysiology in alleviating suffering and preventing stigma. *Culture, Medicine and Psychiatry, 34*(2), 322–352.

Kohrt, B. A., & Swaray, S. (2011). *Community-based mental health: Advocacy, family support, and stigma reduction* (p. 31). Monrovia: The Carter Center.

Kohrt, B. A., Kunz, R. D., Baldwin, J. L., Koirala, N. R., Sharma, V. D., & Nepal, M. K. (2005a). "Somatization" and "comorbidity": A study of jhum-jhum and depression in rural Nepal. *Ethos, 33*(1), 125–147.

Kohrt, B. A., Hruschka, D. J., Kunz, R. D., Kohrt, H. E., Carrion, V. G., & Worthman, C. M. (2005b). *Low cortisol levels and disruptive behaviors in Mongolian and Nepali boys.* Los Angeles: Foundation for Psychocultural Research, University of California.

Kohrt, B. A., Jordans, M. J., Tol, W. A., Speckman, R. A., Maharjan, S. M., Worthman, C. M., et al. (2008). Comparison of mental health between former child soldiers and children never conscripted by armed groups in Nepal. *JAMA: The Journal of the American Medical Association, 300*(6), 691–702.

Kohrt, B. A., Jordans, M. J. D., Tol, W. A., Perera, E., Karki, R., Koirala, S., et al. (2010a). Social ecology of child soldiers: Child, family, and community determinants of mental health, psychosocial well-being, and reintegration in Nepal. *Transcultural Psychiatry, 47*(5), 727–753.

Kohrt, B. A., Tol, W. A., Pettigrew, J., & Karki, R. (2010b). Children and revolution: The mental health and psychosocial wellbeing of child soldiers in Nepal's Maoist army. In M. Singer & G. D. Hodge (Eds.), *The War Machine and Global Health* (pp. 89–116). Lanham: Altamira Press: Rowan & Littlefield Publishers, Inc.

Kohrt, B. A., Jordans, M. J., Tol, W. A., Luitel, N. P., Maharjan, S. M., & Upadhaya, N. (2011). Validation of cross-cultural child mental health and psychosocial research instruments: Adapting the depression self-rating scale and child PTSD symptom scale in Nepal. *BMC Psychiatry, 11*(1), 127.

Kohrt, H. E., Kohrt, B. A., Waldman, I., Saltzman, K., & Carrion, V. G. (2004). An ecological-transactional model of significant risk factors for child psychopathology in outer Mongolia. *Child Psychiatry and Human Development, 35*(2), 163–181.

Konner, M. (2010). *The evolution of childhood: Relationships, emotion, mind.* Cambridge, MA: Belknap Press of Harvard University Press.

Korbin, J. E. (1991). Cross-cultural perspectives and research directions for the 21st-century. *Child Abuse & Neglect, 15*, 67–77.

Korbin, J. E. (2002). Culture and child maltreatment: Cultural competence and beyond. *Child Abuse & Neglect, 26*(6–7), 637–644.

Kranzler, H. R., Feinn, R., Nelson, E. C., Covault, J., Anton, R. F., Farrer, L., et al. (2011). A CRHR1 haplotype moderates the effect of adverse childhood experiences on lifetime risk of major depressive episode in African-American women. *American Journal of Medical Genetics. Part B, Neuropsychiatric Genetics: The Official Publication of the International Society of Psychiatric Genetics, 156B*(8), 960–968.

Krieger, N. (2005). Stormy weather: Race, gene expression, and the science of health disparities. *American Journal of Public Health, 95*(12), 2155–2160.

Krieger, N., Chen, J. T., Waterman, P. D., Rehkopf, D. H., & Subramanian, S. V. (2005). Painting a truer picture of US socioeconomic and racial/ethnic health inequalities: The public health disparities geocoding project. *American Journal of Public Health, 95*(2), 312–323.

Kumsta, R., Stevens, S., Brookes, K., Schlotz, W., Castle, J., Beckett, C., et al. (2010). 5HTT Genotype moderates the influence of early institutional deprivation on emotional problems in adolescence: Evidence from the English and Romanian adoptee (ERA) study. *Journal of Child Psychology and Psychiatry, and Allied Disciplines, 51*(7), 755–762.

Lansford, J. E., & Deater-Deckard, K. (2012). Childrearing discipline and violence in developing countries. *Child Development, 83*(1), 62–75.

Lasky-Su, J. A., Faraone, S. V., Glatt, S. J., & Tsuang, M. T. (2005). Meta-analysis of the association between two polymorphisms in the serotonin transporter gene and affective disorders. *American Journal of Medical Genetics, Part B, Neuropsychiatric Genetics: The Official Publication of the International Society of Psychiatric Genetics, 133B*(1), 110–115.

Leatherman, T. L., & Goodman, A. H. (1997). Expanding the biocultural synthesis toward a biology of poverty. *American Journal of Physical Anthropology, 102*(1), 1–3.

Lende, D. H. (2005). Wanting and drug use: A biocultural approach to the analysis of addiction. *Ethos, 33*(1), 100–124.

Levine, R. A., Levine, S. E., & Schnell, B. (2001). "Improve the women": Mass schooling, female literacy, and worldwide social change. *Harvard Educational Review, 71*(1), 1–50.

Liu, D., Diorio, J., Tannenbaum, B., Caldji, C., Francis, D., Freedman, A., et al. (1997). Maternal care, hippocampal glucocorticoid receptors, and hypothalamic-pituitary-adrenal responses to stress. [see comment]. *Science, 277*(5332), 1659–1662.

Lorente-Rovira, E., Berrios, G., McKenna, P., Moro-Ipola, M., & Villagran-Moreno, J. M. (2011). Confabulations (I): Concept, classification and neuropathology. *Actas Españolas de Psiquiatría, 39*(4), 251–259.

MacMillan, H. L., Wathen, C. N., Barlow, J., Fergusson, D. M., Leventhal, J. M., & Taussig, H. N. (2009). Child maltreatment 3 interventions to prevent child maltreatment and associated impairment. *Lancet, 373*(9659), 250–266.

MacMullin, C., & Loughry, M. (2004). Investigating psychosocial adjustment of former child soldiers in Sierra Leone and Uganda. *Journal of Refugee Studies, 17*(4), 460–472.

McCrory, E., De Brito, S. A., & Viding, E. (2010). Research review: The neurobiology and genetics of maltreatment and adversity. *Journal of Child Psychology and Psychiatry, and Allied Disciplines, 51*(10), 1079–1095.

McGarvey, S. T. (2007). Population health. *Annals of Human Biology, 34*(4), 393–396.

McGowan, P. O., Sasaki, A., D'Alessio, A. C., Dymov, S., Labonte, B., Szyf, M., et al. (2009). Epigenetic regulation of the glucocorticoid receptor in human brain associates with childhood abuse. [see comment]. *Nature Neuroscience, 12*(3), 342–348.

Mehta, M. A., Golembo, N. I., Nosarti, C., Colvert, E., Mota, A., Williams, S. C. R., et al. (2009). Amygdala, hippocampal and corpus callosum size following severe early institutional deprivation: The English and Romanian adoptees study pilot. *Journal of Child Psychology and Psychiatry, and Allied Disciplines, 50*(8), 943–951.

Messer, L., Pence, B., Whetten, K., Whetten, R., Thielman, N., O'Donnell, K., et al. (2010). Prevalence and predictors of HIV-related stigma among institutional- and community-based caregivers of orphans and vulnerable children living in five less-wealthy countries. *BMC Public Health, 10*(1), 504.

Miller, A. L., Seifer, R., Stroud, L., Sheinkopf, S. J., & Dickstein, S. (2006). Biobehavioral indices of emotion regulation relate to school attitudes, motivation, and behavior problems in a low-income preschool sample. *Annals of the New York Academy of Sciences, 1094*, 325–329.

Monson, M. H. (1985). Practical management of rabies and the 1982 outbreak in Zorzor District, Liberia. *Tropical Doctor, 15*(2), 50–54.

Mshana, G., Hampshire, K., Panter-Brick, C., & Walker, R. (2008). Urban-rural contrasts in explanatory models and treatment-seeking behaviours for stroke in Tanzania. *Journal of Biosocial Science, 40*(1), 35–52.

Murray, L. K., Haworth, A., Semrau, K., Singh, M., Aldrovandi, G. M., Sinkala, M., et al. (2006). Violence and abuse among HIV-infected women and their children in Zambia: A qualitative study. *The Journal of Nervous and Mental Disease, 194*(8), 610–615.

Nock, M. K., Park, J. M., Finn, C. T., Deliberto, T. L., Dour, H. J., & Banaji, M. R. (2010). Measuring the suicidal mind: Implicit cognition predicts suicidal behavior. *Psychological Science, 21*(4), 511–517.

Okello, J., Onen, T., & Musisi, S. (2007). Psychiatric disorders among war-abducted and non-abducted adolescents in Gulu district, Uganda: A comparative study. *African Journal of Psychiatry, 20*, 225–231.

Olafsdottir, S., & Pescosolido, B. A. (2011). Constructing illness: How the public in eight Western nations respond to a clinical description of "schizophrenia". *Social Science & Medicine, 73*(6), 929–938.

Ouellet-Morin, I., Odgers, C. L., Danese, A., Bowes, L., Shakoor, S., Papadopoulos, A. S., et al. (2011). Blunted cortisol responses to stress signal social and behavioral problems among maltreated/bullied 12-year-old children. *Biological Psychiatry, 70*(11), 1016–1023.

Pal, D. K., Chaudhury, G., Sengupta, S., & Das, T. (2002). Social integration of children with epilepsy in rural India. *Social Science & Medicine, 54*(12), 1867–1874.

Panter-Brick, C., Clarke, S. E., Lomas, H., Pinder, M., & Lindsay, S. W. (2006). Culturally compelling strategies for behaviour change: A social ecology model and case study in malaria prevention. *Social Science & Medicine, 62*(11), 2810–2825.

Panter-Brick, C., Lende, D. H., & Kohrt, B. A. (2012). Children in global adversity: Physical, mental, behavioral, and symbolic dimensions of health. In V. Maholmes & R. B. King (Eds.), *The Oxford handbook of poverty and child development* (pp. 603–621). New York: Oxford University Press.

Patel, V. (2007). Closing the 10/90 divide in global mental health research. *Acta Psychiatrica Scandinavica, 115*(4), 257–259.

Patel, V., Flisher, A. J., Nikapota, A., & Malhotra, S. (2008). Promoting child and adolescent mental health in low and middle income countries. *Journal of Child Psychology and Psychiatry, and Allied Disciplines, 49*(3), 313–334.

Paul, R. A. (1989). Psychoanalytic anthropology. *Annual Review of Anthropology, 18*, 177–202.

Pescosolido, B. A., Fettes, D. L., Martin, J. K., Monahan, J., & McLeod, J. D. (2007). Perceived dangerousness of children with mental health problems and support for coerced treatment. *Psychiatric Services, 58*(5), 619–625.

Pescosolido, B. A., Martin, J. K., Long, J. S., Medina, T. R., Phelan, J. C., & Link, B. G. (2010). "A disease like any other"? A decade of change in public reactions to schizophrenia, depression, and alcohol dependence. *The American Journal of Psychiatry, 167*(11), 1321–1330.

Pike, I. L., Straight, B. S., Hilton, C., & Oesterle, M. (2010). Embodying violence and the biocultural approach: How can we revise our models to better inform global health disparities? *American Journal of Human Biology, 22*(2), 268.

Polanczyk, G., Caspi, A., Williams, B., Price, T. S., Danese, A., Sugden, K., et al. (2009). Protective effect of CRHR1 gene variants on the development of adult depression following childhood maltreatment: Replication and extension. *Archives of General Psychiatry, 66*(9), 978–985.

Power, C., Thomas, C., Li, L., & Hertzman, C. (2012). Childhood psychosocial adversity and adult cortisol patterns. *The British Journal of Psychiatry, 201*(3), 199–206.

Raj, A. (2010). When the mother is a child: The impact of child marriage on the health and human rights of girls. *Archives of Disease in Childhood, 95*(11), 931–935.

Raj, A., Saggurti, N., Balaiah, D., & Silverman, J. G. (2009). Prevalence of child marriage and its effect on fertility and fertility-control outcomes of young women in India: A cross-sectional, observational study. *Lancet, 373*(9678), 1883–1889.

Resnick, H. S., Yehuda, R., Pitman, R. K., & Foy, D. W. (1995). Effect of previous trauma on acute plasma-cortisol level following rape. *The American Journal of Psychiatry, 152*(11), 1675–1677.

Risch, N., Herrell, R., Lehner, T., Liang, K.-Y., Eaves, L., Hoh, J., et al. (2009). Interaction between the serotonin transporter gene (5-HTTLPR), stressful life events, and risk of depression: A meta-analysis. *JAMA: The Journal of the American Medical Association, 301*(23), 2462–2471.

Rogosch, F. A., Dackis, M. N., & Cicchetti, D. (2011). Child maltreatment and allostatic load: Consequences for physical and mental health in children from low-income families. *Development and Psychopathology, 23*(4), 1107–1124.

Rusch, L. C., Kanter, J. W., & Brondino, M. J. (2009). A comparison of contextual and biomedical models of stigma reduction for depression with a nonclinical undergraduate sample. *The Journal of Nervous and Mental Disease, 197*(2), 104–110.

Rutter, M., Sonuga-Barke, E. J., & Castle, J. (2010). I. Investigating the impact of early institutional deprivation on development: Background and research strategy of the English and Romanian adoptees (ERA) study. *Monographs of the Society for Research in Child Development, 75*(1), 1–20.

Sapolsky, R. M., Romero, L. M., & Munck, A. U. (2000). How do glucocorticoids influence stress responses? Integrating permissive, suppressive, stimulatory, and preparative actions. *Endocrine Reviews, 21*(1), 55–89.

Schreier, A., & Evans, G. W. (2003). Adrenal cortical response of young children to modern and ancient stressors. *Current Anthropology, 44*(2), 306–309.

Shea, A. K., Streiner, D. L., Fleming, A., Kamath, M. V., Broad, K., & Steiner, M. (2007). The effect of depression, anxiety and early life trauma on the cortisol awakening response during pregnancy: Preliminary results. *Psychoneuroendocrinology, 32*(8–10), 1013–1020.

Simkhada, B., van Teijlingen, E., Porter, M., & Simkhada, P. (2006). Major problems and key issues in maternal heatlh in Nepal. *Kathmandu University Medical Journal, 4*(2), 258–263.

Singh, L., Rai, R. K., & Singh, P. K. (2012). Assessing the utilization of maternal and child health care among married adolescent women: Evidence from India. *Journal of Biosocial Science, 44*(01), 1–26.

Spann, M. N., Mayes, L. C., Kalmar, J. H., Guiney, J., Womer, F. Y., Pittman, B., et al. (2012). Childhood abuse and neglect and cognitive flexibility in adolescents. *Child Neuropsychology, 18*(2), 182–189.

Spies, G., Fennema-Notestine, C., Archibald, S. L., Cherner, M., & Seedat, S. (2012). Neurocognitive deficits in HIV-infected women and victims of childhood trauma. *AIDS Care, 24*(9), 1126–1135.

Stormshak, E. A., Kaminski, R. A., & Goodman, M. R. (2002). Enhancing the parenting skills of head start families during the transition to kindergarten. *Prevention Science, 3*(3), 223–234.

Super, C. M. (1984). Sex differences in infant care and vulnerability. *Medical Anthropology, 8*, 84–90.

Tarullo, A. R., & Gunnar, M. R. (2006). Child maltreatment and the developing HPA axis. *Hormones and Behavior, 50*(4), 632–639.

Teicher, M. H. (2002). Scars that won't heal: The neurobiology of child abuse. *Scientific American, 286*(3), 68–75.

Teicher, M. H., Andersen, S. L., Polcari, A., Anderson, C. M., & Navalta, C. P. (2002). Developmental neurobiology of childhood stress and trauma. *Psychiatric Clinics of North America, 25*(2), 397–426.

Teicher, M. H., Andersen, S. L., Polcari, A., Anderson, C. M., Navalta, C. P., & Kim, D. M. (2003). The neurobiological consequences of early stress and childhood maltreatment. *Neuroscience and Biobehavioral Reviews, 27*(1–2), 33–44.

Tomoda, A., Sheu, Y. S., Rabi, K., Suzuki, H., Navalta, C. P., Polcari, A., et al. (2011). Exposure to parental verbal abuse is associated with increased gray matter volume in superior temporal gyrus. *NeuroImage, 54*(Suppl 1), S280–S286.

Towle, M., & Lende, D. H. (2008). Community approaches to preventing mother-to-child HIV transmission: Perspectives from rural Lesotho. *Ajar-African Journal of Aids Research, 7*(2), 219–228.

UNDP. (2009). *Human development report 2009: Movement largely reflects people's need to improve their livelihoods, this movement is constrained by policy and economic barriers.* Geneva: United Nations Development Programme.

UNICEF. (2009). *State of the world's children 2009: Maternal and newborn health.* New York: UNICEF.

van de Weg, N., Post, E. B., Lucassen, R., de Jong, J. T., & Van Den, B. J. (1998). Explanatory models and help-seeking behaviour of leprosy patients in Adamawa state, Nigeria. *Leprosy Review, 69*(4), 382–389.

Walker, S. P., Wachs, T. D., Gardner, J. M., Lozoff, B., Wasserman, G. A., Pollitt, E., et al. (2007). Child development in developing countries 2 – child development: Risk factors for adverse outcomes in developing countries. *Lancet, 369*(9556), 145–157.

Walker, S. P., Wachs, T. D., Grantham-McGregor, S., Black, M. M., Nelson, C. A., Huffman, S. L., et al. (2011). Inequality in early childhood: Risk and protective factors for early child development. *Lancet, 378*(9799), 1325–1338.

Waters, A. J., Miller, E. K., & Li, Y. (2010). Administering the implicit association test in an ecological momentary assessment study. *Psychological Reports, 106*(1), 31–43.

Watts-English, T., Fortson, B. L., Gibler, N., Hooper, S. R., & DeBellis, M. D. (2006). The psychobiology of maltreatment in childhood. *Journal of Social Issues, 62*(4), 717–736.

Weder, N., Yang, B. Z., Douglas-Palumberi, H., Massey, J., Krystal, J. H., Gelernter, J., et al. (2009). MAOA genotype, maltreatment, and aggressive behavior: The changing impact of genotype at varying levels of trauma. *Biological Psychiatry, 65*(5), 417–424.

Weiss, M. G., Doongaji, D. R., Siddhartha, S., Wypij, D., Pathare, S., Bhatawdekar, M., et al. (1992). The Explanatory Model Interview Catalogue (EMIC). Contribution to cross-cultural research methods from a study of leprosy and mental health. *The British Journal of Psychiatry, 160*, 819–830.

World Health Organization. (2008). *Eliminating female genital mutilation: An interagency statement UNAIDS, UNDP, UNECA, UNESCO, UNFPA, UNHCHR, UNHCR, UNICEF, UNIFEM, WHO*. Geneva: World Health Organization.

Worthman, C. M. (2009). Habits of the heart: Life history and the developmental neuroendocrinology of emotion. *American Journal of Human Biology, 21*(6), 772–781.

Worthman, C. M. (2011). Inside-out and outside-in? Global development theory, policy, and youth. *Ethos, 39*(4), 432–451.

Worthman, C. M., & Brown, R. A. (2005). A biocultural life history approach to the developmental psychobiology of male aggression. In D. M. Stoff & E. J. Susman (Eds.), *Developmental psychobiology of aggression* (pp. 187–221). New York: Cambridge University Press.

Worthman, C. M., & Costello, E. J. (2009). Tracking biocultural pathways in population health: The value of biomarkers. *Annals of Human Biology, 36*(3), 281–297.

Worthman, C. M., & Kohrt, B. (2005). Receding horizons of health: Biocultural approaches to public health paradoxes. *Social Science & Medicine, 61*(4), 861–878.

Worthman, C. M., & Panter-Brick, C. (2008). Homeless street children in Nepal: Use of allostatic load to assess the burden of childhood adversity. *Development and Psychopathology, 20*(1), 233–255.

Yang, S.-J., Won Shin, D., Sun Noh, K., & Stein, M. A. (2007). Cortisol is inversely correlated with aggression for those boys with attention deficit hyperactivity disorder who retain their reactivity to stress. *Psychiatry Research, 153*(1), 55–60.

Yeager, C. A., & Lewis, D. O. (2000). Mental illness, neuropsychologic deficits, child abuse, and violence. *Child and Adolescent Psychiatric Clinics of North America, 9*(4), 793–813.

Yehuda, R., Hallig, S. L., & Grossman, R. (2001). Childhood trauma and risk for PTSD: Relationship to intergenerational effects of trauma, parental PTSD, and cortisol excretion. *Development and Psychopathology, 13*(3), 733–753.

Zayed, A. A., & Ali, A. A. (2012). Abusing female children by circumcision is continued in Egypt. *Journal of Forensic and Legal Medicine, 19*(4), 196–200.

Zhang, K., Xu, Q., Xu, Y., Yang, H., Luo, J., Sun, Y., et al. (2009). The combined effects of the 5-HTTLPR and 5-HTR1A genes modulates the relationship between negative life events and major depressive disorder in a chinese population. *Journal of Affective Disorders, 114*(1–3), 224–231.

Index

CPSIA information can be obtained at www.ICGtesting.com
Printed in the USA
LVOW11*1340060514

384639LV00009B/52/P